Lecture Notes in Computer Science 16271

The series Lecture Notes in Computer Science (LNCS), including its subseries Lecture Notes in Artificial Intelligence (LNAI) and Lecture Notes in Bioinformatics (LNBI), has established itself as a medium for the publication of new developments in computer science and information technology research, teaching, and education.

LNCS enjoys close cooperation with the computer science R & D community, the series counts many renowned academics among its volume editors and paper authors, and collaborates with prestigious societies. Its mission is to serve this international community by providing an invaluable service, mainly focused on the publication of conference and workshop proceedings and postproceedings. LNCS commenced publication in 1973.

Benny Applebaum · Huijia (Rachel) Lin
Editors

Theory of Cryptography

23rd International Conference, TCC 2025
Aarhus, Denmark, December 1–5, 2025
Proceedings, Part IV

Springer

Editors
Benny Applebaum
Tel Aviv University
Tel Aviv-Yafo, Israel

Huijia (Rachel) Lin
University of Washington
Seattle, WA, USA

ISSN 0302-9743 ISSN 1611-3349 (electronic)
Lecture Notes in Computer Science
ISBN 978-3-032-12289-6 ISBN 978-3-032-12290-2 (eBook)
https://doi.org/10.1007/978-3-032-12290-2

This Springer imprint is published by the registered company Springer Nature Switzerland AG
The registered company address is: Gewerbestrasse 11, 6330 Cham, Switzerland

Preface

The 23rd Theory of Cryptography Conference (TCC 2025) was held during December 1–5, 2025, at Aarhus University in Aarhus, Denmark. It was sponsored by the International Association for Cryptologic Research (IACR). The general chairs of the conference were Claudio Orlandi, Sophia Yakoubov, and Peter Scholl.

The conference received a record number of 242 submissions, of which the Program Committee (PC) selected 70 for presentation, resulting in an acceptance rate of 28.9%. Each submission was reviewed by at least three PC members in a single-blind process. The 41 PC members (including PC chairs), all top researchers in our field, were helped by 298 external reviewers, who were consulted as needed. These proceedings consist of the revised versions of the 70 accepted papers. The revisions were not reviewed, and the authors bear full responsibility for the content of their papers.

We are extremely grateful to Kevin McCurley for providing fast and reliable technical support for the HotCRP review software. We also thank Kay McKelly for her help with the conference website.

This was the eleventh year that TCC presented the Test of Time Award to an outstanding paper published at TCC at least eight years ago, recognizing a significant contribution to the theory of cryptography and its influence in related areas. This year, the Test of Time Award Committee selected the following paper, published at TCC 2017: "A modular analysis of the Fujisaki-Okamoto transformation," by Dennis Hofheinz, Kathrin Hövelmanns, and Eike Kiltz. The award committee recognized this paper "For modular designs of secure Key-Encapsulation Mechanisms with tight bounds in both classical and quantum settings, enabling the KEM constructions used in the NIST PQC standard." The authors were invited to deliver a talk at TCC 2025.

This year, TCC awarded the Luca Trevisan Young Researcher Award for the best paper authored solely by young researchers. The award was given to the paper "Special Genera of Hermitian Lattices and Applications to HAWK" by Guilhem Mureau. The committee also awarded, for the first time, Outstanding Paper Awards recognizing outstanding contributions. From among many excellent candidates, the committee selected the following three papers: "Separating Pseudorandom Codes from Local Oracles," by Nico Döttling, Anne Müller, and Mahesh Sreekumar Rajasree; "Optimal Bounds on the Existence of Pseudorandom Codes," by Sam Gunn, Sanjam Garg, and Mingyuan Wang; and "Generalized and Unified Equivalences between Hardness and Pseudoentropy," by Lunjia Hu and Salil P. Vadhan.

We are greatly indebted to the many people who contributed to making TCC 2025 a success. We thank all the authors who submitted papers, the Program Committee members for their hard work and diligence in reviewing and selecting papers, and the external reviewers for their generous contributions. Finally, we thank the general chairs,

Claudio Orlandi, Sophia Yakoubov, and Peter Scholl, and their team at Aarhus University, as well as the TCC Steering Committee.

October 2025

Benny Applebaum
Huijia (Rachel) Lin

Organization

General Chairs

Claudio Orlandi	Aarhus University, Denmark
Sophia Yakoubov	Aarhus University, Denmark
Peter Scholl	Aarhus University, Denmark

Program Committee Chairs

Benny Applebaum	Tel Aviv University, Israel
Huijia (Rachel) Lin	University of Washington, USA

Steering Committee

Jesper Buus Nielsen	Aarhus University, Denmark
Krzysztof Pietrzak	Institute of Science and Technology Austria, Austria
Huijia (Rachel) Lin	University of Washington, USA
Yuval Ishai	Technion, Israel
Tal Malkin	Columbia University, USA
Manoj M. Prabhakaran	IIT Bombay, India
Salil Vadhan	Harvard University, USA

Program Committee

Divesh Aggawal	National University of Singapore, Singapore
Prabhanjan Ananth	University of California, Santa Barbara, USA
Marshall Ball	New York University, USA
James Bartusek	New York University, USA
Andrej Bogdanov	University of Ottawa, Canada
Ran Canetti	Boston University, USA
Kai-Min Chung	Academia Sinica, Taiwan
Ivan Damgard	Aarhus University, Denmark
Nico Döttling	CISPA Helmholtz Center, Germany
Cody Freitag	Northeastern University, USA

Aarushi Goel	Purdue University, USA
Shai Halevi	Amazon Web Services, USA
Aayush Jain	Carnegie Mellon University, USA
Abhishek Jain	NTT Research and John Hopkins University, USA
Zhenzhong Jin	Northeastern University, USA
Daniel Jost	Blanqet, USA
Wei-kai Lin	University of Virginia, USA
Ji Luo	Boston University, USA
Hemanta Maji	Purdue University, USA
Peihan Miao	Brown University, USA
Tomoyuki Morimae	Kyoto University, Japan
Varun Narayanan	University of California, Los Angeles, USA
Ryo Nishimaki	NTT Social Informatics Laboratories, Japan
Eran Omri	Ariel University, Israel
Alexander Poremba	Boston University, USA
Leonid Reyzin	Boston University, USA
João Ribeiro	Instituto de Telecomunicações and Instituto Superior Técnico, Universidade de Lisboa, Portugal
Lior Rotem	Stanford University, USA
Guy Rothblum	Apple, USA
Luisa Siniscalchi	Technical University of Denmark, Denmark
Yifan Song	Tsinghua University and Shanghai Qi Zhi Institute, China
Katerina Sotiraki	Yale University, USA
Akshayaram Srinivasan	University of Toronto, Canada
Prashant Vasudevan	National University of Singapore, Singapore
Brent Waters	NTT Research and University of Texas at Austin, USA
Hoeteck Wee	NTT Research, USA
Shota Yamada	AIST, Japan
Takashi Yamakawa	NTT Social Informatics Laboratories and Kyoto University, Japan
Vassilis Zikas	Georgia Tech, USA

Additional Reviewers

Marius Aardal
Damiano Abram
Siddharth Agarwal
Bar Alon
Noga Amit
Harikrishnan P. Anilkumar
Diego Aranha
Gal Arnon

Gennaro Avitabile
Chen Bai
David Balbás
Laasya Bangalore
Rene Bardales
Mohammed Barhoush
Amit Behera
Zoë Bell
Tamar Ben David
Aner Ben-Efraim
Fabrice Benhamouda
Tan Hong Meng Benjamin
Divyanshu Bhardwaj
Archishna Bhattacharyya
Allison Bishop Lewko
Aniruddha Biswas
Alex Block
Erica Blum
John Bostanci
Vincenzo Botta
Pedro Branco
Davide Carnemolla
Joseph Carolan
Ignacio Cascudo
Champ Chairattana-Apirom
Jeffrey Champion
Anirudh Chandramouli
Rohit Chatterjee
Yanlin Chen
Jingwei Chen
Liyan Chen
Megan Chen
Binyi Chen
Yanbo Chen
Mingjie Chen
Nai-Hui Chia
Wonseok Choi
Arka Rai Choudhuri
Qiaohan Chu
Michele Ciampi
Valerio Cini
Quang Dao
Pranjal Datta
Pratish Datta
Alex Davidson
Lalita Devadas
Yuolong Ding
Leo Ducas
Jesko Dujmovic
Samed Düzlü
Saroja Erabelli
Reo Eriguchi
Islam Faisal
Giacomo Fenzi
Chase Fickes
Pouyan Forghani
Kyle Fridberg
Chaya Ganesh
Shang Gao
Radhika Garg
Rachit Garg
Gayathri Garimella
Robin Geelen
Fatemeh Ghasemi
Surendra Ghentiyala
Ashrujit Ghoshal
Emanuele Giunta
Eli Goldin
Junqing Gong
Tiantian Gong
Mayank Goswami
Scott Griffy
Jiaxin Guan
Ziyi Guan
Aditya Gulati
Sam Gunn
Rishav Gupta
Aparna Gupte
Mohit Gurumukhani
Julia Guskind
Iftach Haitner
Mohammad Hajiabadi
Peter Hall
Mathias Hall-Andersen
Shuai Han
Keisuke Hara
Franklin Harding
Ryuya Hayashi
Jinye He
Aditya Hegde

Julia Hesse
Minki Hhan
Shuichi Hirahara
Taiga Hiroka
Man Hou Hong
Akinori Hosoyamada
Yao Ching Hsieh
Miryam Huang
James Hulett
Jihun Hwang
Yuval Ishai
Xiaoyu Ji
Ziyang Jin
Haoxiang Jin
Giannis Kaklamanis
Fatih Kaleoglu
Chethan Kamath
Shuichi Katsumata
Victor Kemmoe
Hamidreza Khorasgani
Dakshita Khurana
Duhyeong Kim
Michael Kim
Fuyuki Kitagawa
Lisa Kohl
Sebastian Kolby
Dimitris Kolonelos
Ilan Komargodski
Chelsea Komlo
Venkata Koppula
Mikhail Kornilov
Haruhisa Kosuge
Rucha Kulkarni
Akshaya Kumar
Naman Kumar
Simran Kumari
Srijita Kundu
Daji Landis
Roman Langrehr
Oleksandra Lapiha
Arthur Lazzaretti
Seunghoon Lee
Tancrede Lepoint
Reynald Lercier
Jiatu Li
Yunqi Li
Xingjian Li
Junru Li
Minzhang Li
Hanjun Li
Shiyu Li
Xiao Liang
Daniel Liang
Enhui Lim
Yao-Ting Lin
Haoxing Lin
Cong Ling
Jiahui Liu
Feng-Hao Liu
Tianren Liu
Zeyu Liu
Xiangyu Liu
Jingbo Liu
Qipeng Liu
Paul Lou
Chuhan Lu
George Lu
Yiping Ma
Fermi Ma
Bernardo Magri
Christian Majenz
Nikos Makriyannis
Xinyu Mao
Varun Maram
Elisaweta Masserova
Surya Mathialagan
Takahiro Matsuda
Noam Mazor
Ian McQuoid
Ratnakar Medepalli
Pierre Meyer
Francesco Migliaro
Pratyush Mishra
Ankit Kumar Misra
Ethan Mook
Aditya Morolia
Tamer Mour
Ananta Mukherjee
Saswata Mukherjee
Marta Mularczyk

Saachi Mutreja
Anne Müller
Mridul Nandi
Shafik Nassar
Anand Natarajan
Sela Navot
Rohit Nema
Ky Nguyen
Hai Nguyen
Wilson Nguyen
Oded Nir
Chinmay Nirkhe
Olga Nissenbaum
Eileen Nolan
Claudio Orlandi
Connor Paddock
Aurel Page
Tapas Pal
Jai Hyun Park
Aditi Partap
Anat Paskin-Cherniavsky
Sikhar Patranabis
Robi Pedersen
Angelos Pelecanos
Spencer Peters
Phuoc Pham
Benny Pinkas
Guru Vamsi Policharla
Luowen Qian
Willy Quach
Rahul Rachori
Seyoon Ragavan
Justin Raizes
Mahesh Sreekumar Rajasree
Mayank Ratheee
Divya Ravi
Guilherme Rito
Bhaskar Roberts
Michael Rosenberg
Yannis Rouselakis
Luigi Russo
Yusuke Sakai
Giacomo Santato
Peter Scholl
Ignacio Sesar
Yannick Seurin
Yu Shen
Moshe Shenfled
Xinyi Shi
Kaiyan Shi
Jad Silbak
Mark Simkin
Satvinder Singh
Jaspal Singh
Fabrizio Sisinni
Eduardo Soria-Vazquez
Nick Spooner
Noah Stephens-Davidowitz
Kaoru Takemure
Ertem Nusret Tas
Stefano Tessaro
Sri AravindaKrishnan Thyagarajan
Kabir Tomer
Junichi Tomida
Toi Tomita
Max Tromanhauser
LaKyah Tyner
Dominique Unruh
Neekon Vafa
Fernando Virdia
Turan Vural
Hendrik Waldner
Yunhao Wang
Xiao Wang
Mingyuan Wang
Zhikun Wang
Jifeng Wang
William Wang
Yu Wei
Chenkai Weng
Bas Westerbaan
Daniel Wichs
David J. Wu
Keita Xagawa
Yu Xia
Zhiye Xie
Jiayu Xu
Anshu Yadav
Sophia Yakoubov
Shogo Yamada

Rupeng Yang
Yibin Yang
Mert Yassi
Xiuyu Ye
Xiaxi Ye
Albert Yu
Thomas Zacharias
Liav Zafar
Lydia Zakynthinou
Or Zamir
Riccardo Zanotto
Hadas Zeilberger
Runzhi Zeng
Mark Zhandry
Yiding Zhang
Fahong Zhang
Chenzhi Zhu
Anatoliy Zinovyev
Chiara-Marie Zok
Wessel van Woerden

Contents

Differential Privacy

Timed Cryptography and Verifiable Random Function

Secure Computation II

Proofs II

Plonk is Simulation Extractable in ROM Under Falsifiable Assumptions

Helger Lipmaa(✉)

University of Tartu, Tartu, Estonia
helger.lipmaa@gmail.com

Abstract. Solving a long-standing open problem, Faonio, Fiore, and Russo proved that the widely used Plonk zk-SNARK is simulation extractable. However, their proof assumes both the random oracle model (ROM) and the algebraic group model. We prove that the same holds in the ROM under falsifiable assumptions. We combine the template of Faust et al., who proved that simulation extractability follows from knowledge soundness, (weak) unique response, and trapdoorless zero-knowledge, with the recent result of Lipmaa, Parisella, and Siim (Crypto 2025), who proved that Plonk has knowledge soundness in the ROM under falsifiable assumptions. For this, we prove that Plonk satisfies new variants of the weak unique response and trapdoorless zero-knowledge properties. We prove that several commonly used gadgets, like the linearization trick, are not trapdoorless zero-knowledge when considered as independent commit-and-prove zk-SNARKs.

Keywords: Fiat-Shamir · Plonk · simulation extractability · trapdoorless zero-knowledge · unique response · zk-SNARK

1 Introduction

Zero-knowledge succinct non-interactive arguments of knowledge (zk-SNARKs, [10,25,37]) have revolutionized the verification of complex computations by enabling a prover to convince a verifier of a computation's correctness using extremely succinct arguments. A fundamental security property of zk-SNARKs is *knowledge soundness*—ensuring that any prover producing a valid proof must indeed *know* a corresponding witness. However, this guarantee is insufficient in many real-world applications: adversaries may exploit simulated proofs to construct valid-looking arguments for false statements.

These limitations motivate *simulation extractability* [8,26,39], which also implies non-malleability [11]. It ensures that even with access to simulated proofs, an adversary cannot forge a proof for a false statement without a valid witness. This guarantee is crucial in practice, where subtle malleability attacks could otherwise undermine security.

Among universal pairing-based zk-SNARKs, Plonk [20] stands out for its efficiency and flexibility. Plonk supports advanced features such as lookup arguments [4,12,19] and custom gates [18], which has led to its widespread adoption.

B. Applebaum and H. Lin (Eds.): TCC 2025, LNCS 16271, pp. 3–36, 2026.
https://doi.org/10.1007/978-3-032-12290-2_1

Plonk (and its extensions) is used in blockchain privacy solutions and zk-rollups with a considerable amount of money at stake. Given its broad use, it is imperative to establish the strongest possible security guarantees for Plonk under weakest possible assumptions. Due to this, ZKproof.org recently announced an initiative for formal verification of Plonk, [38], while the Ethereum foundation announced a verified verifier effort for formal verification of, in particular, Plonk.

Plonk's original knowledge soundness proof relies on both the ROM and the Algebraic Group Model (AGM [17]). Since both idealized models are separately known to be non-instantiable [5,9,28,41], proving security in the ROM under falsifiable assumptions is highly desirable.[1] In Crypto 2025, Lipmaa et al. [36] gave the first proof that Plonk is knowledge sound in the Random Oracle Model (ROM, [3]) under falsifiable assumptions.

Several works study simulation extractability for zk-SNARKs [13,21–23,29], including Plonk. Faonio, Fiore, and Russo [14] recently resolved a major open problem by proving simulation extractability for fully optimized Plonk [20]. Their proof, however, relies on both the ROM and the AGM. Whether Plonk is simulation extractable in the ROM under falsifiable assumptions remains unknown. The proof is also intricate.

Our Main Goal. *Can we prove that the fully optimized Plonk protocol has simulation extractability in the ROM under falsifiable assumptions?* Answering this question ensures that even when an adversary leverages simulation queries, it cannot produce a valid proof for an incorrect statement without knowing a witness. In doing so, we significantly strengthen Plonk's security against malleability attacks while avoiding reliance on idealized group models.

1.1 Our Contributions

We make the following key contributions:

1. **Tailored Security Definitions.** Building on the "TLZK+UR framework" [15,21,23], we refine trapdoorless zero-knowledge (TLZK) and weak unique response (WUR) for Plonk. We show that, together with knowledge soundness, these imply simulation extractability (Theorem 1).
2. **Plonk's Security Properties.** We prove that Plonk satisfies computational WUR (assuming KZG evaluation binding; see Theorem 6) and TLZK (see Theorem 5) in the ROM.
3. **Simulation Extractability of Plonk.** By integrating recent advances in proving interactive Plonk's computational special soundness under falsifiable assumptions [35,36], the TLZK+UR framework, and our new TLZK and WUR definitions, we prove that the fully optimized Plonk is simulation extractable in the ROM under falsifiable assumptions.

[1] Proving security under solely falsifiable assumptions is impossible [24]. The ROM is better understood than the AGM; moreover, no efficient universal zk-SNARKs are known whose security is not based on the ROM.

4. **Security of Gadgets.** We extend our analysis to commonly used gadgets, including a variant of KZG, batch opening (BatchKZG), the linearization trick (LinTrick), and the sanitized linearization trick (SanLinTrick). We prove that under standard assumptions, such commit-and-prove type gadgets are not TLZK, which means that the framework of [15] cannot be used to prove their simulation extractability.

By establishing simulation extractability for the fully optimized Plonk solely in the ROM under falsifiable assumptions, we provide a robust foundation for deploying secure, efficient zero-knowledge proofs in practical systems.

1.2 Related Work

Idealized Models. The simulation extractability proof of [14] relies on two idealized models, the ROM and the AGM. Since both are non-instantiable [5,9,28,41], their use can introduce unforeseen issues when transitioning from theory to real-world applications. Hence, if an ideal model must be employed, it is preferable to base the security proof on a single, well-understood model. We aim to minimize reliance on idealized group models in favor of the better understood ROM.

TLZK+UR Framework and Alternatives. Faust et al. [15] derive simulation extractability from knowledge soundness, trapdoorless zero-knowledge (TLZK), and unique response (UR) or weak unique response (WUR). A zk-SNARK is *TLZK* if a trapdoorless simulator $\tilde{\mathcal{S}}$ can only reprogram the random oracle. With such a simulator, it has *WUR* if forging a different accepting argument that shares a prefix with a simulated argument π^* is intractable. This approach is widely used [7,21,23,29]. We refine TLZK and WUR to match Plonk's structure and obtain simulation extractability in the ROM under falsifiable assumptions.

Kohlweiss et al. [13,29] take a different route by classifying properties for polynomial commitment schemes and polynomial IOPs needed to achieve simulation extractability after the standard compilation to an interactive protocol. Faonio, Fiore, and Russo [14] used this approach to prove that Plonk is (policy-based, see [14]) simulation extractable in the combined ROM-AGM.

Other Developments. Variants of simulation extractability have been proven for Groth16 [2,32], Bulletproofs [7,23], Spartan [7], and HyperPlonk [30]. These efforts underscore the broad interest in obtaining simulation extractability guarantees across modern zk-SNARKs.

1.3 Technical Overview

New Definitions and Analysis. Our proof strategy builds on the framework of [15,21,23]. To capture the nuances of Plonk, we introduce refined definitions (see Sect. 2.1): we define T-TLZK, where the simulator can reprogram the verifier's challenges only in rounds $k \in T$, and $\geq \varrho$-WUR, which requires the WUR property only from round ϱ onward. We prove (see Theorem 1) that for any set T and every round $\varrho = \min T$, these properties—combined with knowledge soundness—imply simulation extractability.

Gadgets. Plonk and other optimized KZG-based zk-SNARK rely on standard gadgets like the linearization trick. One possible way to prove Plonk's security properties is first to prove that gadgets satisfy the same properties and then use that modularly in Plonk's security proof. Unfortunately, we will prove that this cannot be done. In Sect. 4, we study non-interactive KZG (as an argument system, [35]) and non-interactive variants of KZG-based protocols like BatchKZG (batch-opening of several KZG commitments), LinTrick (linearization trick), and SanLinTrick (sanitized linearization trick), which were all studied in [36] in the context of knowledge soundness. We prove that if KZG is evaluation binding, then the gadgets *are not TLZK*. Intuitively, this holds since they are commit-and-prove zk-SNARKs with polynomial commitments as their inputs. One cannot simulate the arguments without knowing either the trapdoor or the corresponding witness (committed polynomials). Moreover, since WUR is only defined for TLZK zk-SNARKs, the gadgets do not have WUR. For completeness, we prove that, under a standard assumption, all gadgets have the last-round unique response property (defined formally in Sect. 2.1); however, we do not know how to use this property to prove simulation extractability. They are also trapdoor-based zero knowledge (we describe corresponding simulators).

Since the gadgets are not TLZK, the TLZK+UR framework cannot be used to establish that they have simulation extractability. This does not mean that the gadgets do not have simulation extractability. Rather, we establish a limitation of the TLZK+UR framework. Indeed, following a different framework, Faonio et al. [14] proved that the gadgets have simulation extractability in the combined AGM-ROM. We leave open the question of whether the gadgets have (even policy-based) simulation extractability in the ROM under falsifiable assumptions. Our results also do not stop us from proving that Plonk is TLZK.

Next, we will describe the gadgets and their security. For an interactive protocol Π, Π_{FS} is its non-interactive variant after applying Fiat-Shamir [16]. We use the standard additive bracket notation for groups (see Sect. 2).

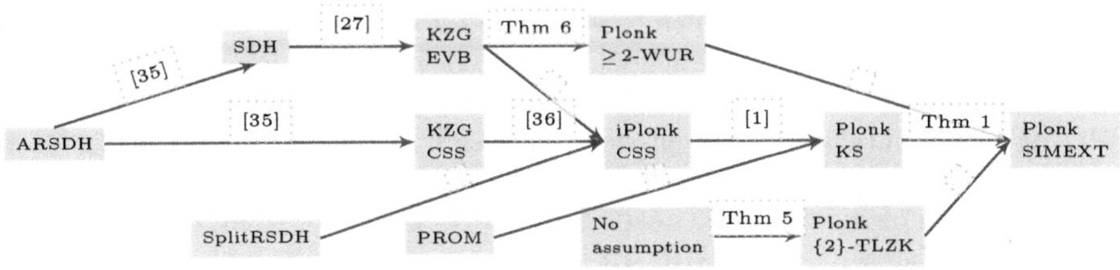

Fig. 1. Reductions leading to Plonk's simulation extractability. How evaluation binding (EVB), computational special soundness (CSS), and knowledge soundness (KS) of Plonk and interactive Plonk (iPlonk), when combined with TLZK and WUR properties, yield simulation extractability (SIMEXT) in the programmable ROM (PROM). Arrows ending up in the same node act as an AND: KZG EVB, KZG CSS, and SplitRSDH together imply iPlonk CSS, and iPlonk CSS implies Plonk KS in the PROM.

On $\mathrm{KZG}_{\mathsf{FS}}$. In the non-interactive zk-SNARK $\mathrm{KZG}_{\mathsf{FS}}$, a prover commits to a polynomial $\mathsf{f}(X)$ by computing the commitment $[f]_1 = [\mathsf{f}(x)]_1$, where x is a trapdoor. After the verifier issues a challenge $\mathfrak{z}$ via a random oracle, the prover reveals the evaluation $\bar{f} = \mathsf{f}(\mathfrak{z})$ and an evaluation proof $[h]_1 \leftarrow [(\mathsf{f}(x)-\bar{f})/(x-\mathfrak{z})]_1$. A trapdoorless simulator $\tilde{\mathcal{S}}$ of $\mathrm{KZG}_{\mathsf{FS}}$ would be able to, given any $[f]_1$, produce an accepting KZG transcript $([f]_1, \mathfrak{z}, \bar{f}, [h]_1)$. We show that this is intractable when KZG is evaluation binding. Assume that $\tilde{\mathcal{S}}$ succeeds for a random degree-1 polynomial $\mathsf{f}(X)$. Then, we can have two cases. First, if $\mathfrak{z} = x$, then one has recovered the KZG trapdoor and can break the evaluation binding. Second, if $\mathfrak{z} \neq x$, since the simulator only has information about f in one evaluation point, it cannot predict $\mathsf{f}(\mathfrak{z})$. Thus, one can break KZG's evaluation binding by outputting $([f]_1, \mathfrak{z}, \bar{f}, [h]_1, \mathsf{f}(\mathfrak{z}), [h']_1)$ for honestly computed $[h']_1 \leftarrow [(\mathsf{f}(x) - \bar{f})/(x - \mathfrak{z})]_1$. Thus, $\mathrm{KZG}_{\mathsf{FS}}$ is not $\{1\}$-TLZK. We prove that if one can break the last-round UR property, one can break KZG's evaluation binding. See Theorem 2.

On $\mathrm{BatchKZG}_{\mathsf{FS}}$. In the standard KZG batching protocol BatchKZG, the prover commits to m distinct polynomials and opens all of them at the same challenge $\mathfrak{z}$. Using a similar simulation strategy as for $\mathrm{KZG}_{\mathsf{FS}}$, we demonstrate that $\mathrm{BatchKZG}_{\mathsf{FS}}$ is not 1-TLZK under the assumption that KZG is evaluation binding. We show that if one can break the last-round UR property, one can compute the KZG trapdoor and thus break the standard $(n, 1)$-PDL assumption [31].

On $\mathrm{LinTrick}_{\mathsf{FS}}$ *and* $\mathrm{SanLinTrick}_{\mathsf{FS}}$. The linearization trick (LinTrick) is widely adopted in zk-SNARKs to prove quadratic relations. However, as proven in [36], LinTrick does not have computational special soundness (CSS) in the standard model. To address this, [36] proposed a sanitized variant, SanLinTrick, and proved its special soundness. In Theorem 4, we prove that $\mathrm{LinTrick}_{\mathsf{FS}}$ and $\mathrm{SanLinTrick}_{\mathsf{FS}}$ do not have TLZK, assuming that KZG is evaluation binding. We then show that if one can break the last-round UR property, one can compute the KZG trapdoor and thus break the standard $(n, 1)$-PDL assumption.

On Plonk. Our central challenge is proving simulation extractability of the fully optimized Plonk. In [21], a less optimized variant of Plonk was shown to be T-TLZK, for a set T that includes round 3, and ≥ 3-WUR; proving ≥ 3-WUR seems natural when the prover sends claimed evaluations (such as $\bar{a}$) in round 4. However, Plonk's trapdoor-based simulator [40] uses the trapdoor in round 2, which means that one needs to prove T-TLZK for a set T that includes round 2, together with $\geq$2-WUR. We develop a novel analysis that leverages an auxiliary polynomial $\mathsf{z}(X)$ transmitted in Plonk's second round to achieve this. The internal structure of Plonk enforces a linear system on the evaluations $\mathsf{z}(\omega^i)$ (with ω being a subgroup generator). Solving this system lets a trapdoorless simulator interpolate $\mathsf{z}(X)$. Hence Plonk is $\{2\}$-TLZK (see Theorem 5).

We prove Plonk has computational $\geq$2-WUR in the ROM (see Theorem 6), assuming that KZG is evaluation binding, i.e., under SDH. Proving WUR is most challenging when the adversarial argument differs from the round 3. In this case, we craft a reduction that exploits that the simulator's and adversary's challenges $\mathfrak{z}^*$ and $\mathfrak{z}$ (computed by the random oracle in the third round) differ with an overwhelming probability. Intuitively, while the simulator knows the actual value $\mathsf{z}(\mathfrak{z})$, an adversary's incorrect guess of $\mathsf{z}(\mathfrak{z})$ allows us to break the evaluation binding by exhibiting conflicting openings.

By combining the TLZK and WUR properties with interactive Plonk's computational special soundness [36] and the guarantees provided by the Fiat-Shamir transformation [1], we deduce that Plonk is simulation extractable in the ROM under falsifiable assumptions. Notably, while Plonk uses the linearization trick (that is not TLZK) as a gadget, Plonk itself is TLZK. Intuitively, this is possible since the gadgets are commit-and-prove zk-SNARK, where the prover has to open the committed polynomial (given as an input to the zk-SNARK) at a random evaluation point. However, Plonk uses the gadgets in a white-box manner, providing them with the committed polynomials as inputs.

See Fig. 1 for the landscape of the results we use to prove Plonk's simulation extractability. Note that some results like Theorem 6 rely on the ROM.

On Simplicity. Establishing Plonk's simulation extractability has been daunting, only recently culminating with Faonio et al. [14]'s proof in the combined AGM+ROM. Our proof is much simpler and shorter, making it more amenable to independent (possibly formal) verification. An important benefit of modularity is that one can separately (formally) verify the results of previous papers like [1,35,36] and the results of the current paper. Simplicity is a goal in itself.

Open Questions. We leave analyzing the simulation extractability of other pairing-based updatable zk-SNARKs in the ROM under falsifiable assumptions for future work. We did not generalize to other zk-SNARKs because Plonk is the only highly efficient KZG-based zk-SNARK that has been proven *knowledge sound* in the ROM under falsifiable assumptions. Proving knowledge soundness of other KZG-based zk-SNARK like Marlin [6] in the ROM under falsifiable assumptions requires a separate paper (if possible). Similarly, it is important to establish if KZG-based lookup arguments like cq [4,12] are simulation extractable in the ROM under falsifiable assumptions; however, it is not even known if they are knowledge sound in the ROM under falsifiable assumptions. Can one use a different framework to prove that the gadgets are (policy-based) simulation extractable in the ROM under falsifiable assumptions?

2 Preliminaries

Let $\varnothing$ denote the empty string. PPT stands for probabilistic polynomial time. For any set S, $\mathsf{Z}_S(X) := \prod_{t \in S}(X - t)$ is its vanishing polynomial. $\mathbb{F}$ is a finite field of prime order p. $\mathbb{F}[X]$ is the polynomial ring in variable X over the field $\mathbb{F}$ and $\mathbb{F}_{\leq n}[X] \subset \mathbb{F}[X]$ is the set of polynomials of degree at most n. Let λ denote the security parameter. $f(\lambda) \approx_\lambda 0$ means that f is a negligible function. $\mathcal{A}^{\mathcal{H}}$ denotes that an algorithm $\mathcal{A}$ has black-box access to the random oracle $\mathcal{H} : \{0,1\}^* \to \mathsf{Ch}$, where Ch is an exponentially big set (by default, $\mathsf{Ch} = \mathbb{F}$). Our notation is inspired by Plonk's original paper [20] (for example, we denote polynomials by using $\mathsf{SansSerif}$ and evaluation points by $\mathfrak{z}$).

A bilinear group generator $\mathsf{G}(1^\lambda)$ returns $\mathsf{p} = (p, \mathbb{G}_1, \mathbb{G}_2, \mathbb{G}_T, \hat{e}, [1]_1, [1]_2)$, where $\mathbb{G}_1$, $\mathbb{G}_2$, and $\mathbb{G}_T$ are additive[2] cyclic (thus, abelian) groups of prime order p, $\hat{e} : \mathbb{G}_1 \times \mathbb{G}_2 \to \mathbb{G}_T$ is a non-degenerate efficiently computable bilinear pairing, and $[1]_\iota$ is a fixed generator of $\mathbb{G}_\iota$. While $[1]_\iota$ is part of p, we often give it as an explicit input to different algorithms for clarity. The bilinear pairing is of Type-3, that is, there is no efficient isomorphism between $\mathbb{G}_1$ and $\mathbb{G}_2$. We use the standard bracket notation, that is, for $\iota \in \{1, 2, T\}$ and $a \in \mathbb{Z}_p$, we write $[a]_\iota$ to denote $a[1]_\iota$. We denote $\hat{e}([a]_1, [b]_2)$ by $[a]_1 \bullet [b]_2$ and assume $[1]_T = [1]_1 \bullet [1]_2$. Thus, $[a]_1 \bullet [b]_2 = [ab]_T$ for any $a, b \in \mathbb{F}$, where $\mathbb{F} = \mathbb{Z}_p$.

G is (n_1, n_2)-*PDL (Power Discrete Logarithm,* [31]*) secure* if for any PPT $\mathcal{A}$, $\mathsf{Adv}^{\mathrm{pdl}}_{n_1,n_2,\mathsf{G},\mathcal{A}}(\lambda) :=$

$$\Pr\left[\mathcal{A}(\mathsf{p}, [1, x, \ldots, x^{n_1}]_1, [1, x, \ldots, x^{n_2}]_2) = \mathsf{x} \mid \mathsf{p} \leftarrow \mathsf{G}(1^\lambda); x \leftarrow_{\$} \mathbb{F}\right] \approx_\lambda 0 \ .$$

Polynomial Commitment Schemes (PCSs). In a (univariate) PCS [27], the prover commits to a polynomial $\mathsf{f} \in \mathbb{F}_{\leq n}[X]$ and later opens it to $\mathsf{f}(\mathfrak{z})$ for $\mathfrak{z} \in \mathbb{F}$ chosen by the verifier. A *non-interactive* PCS consists of five algorithms. (1) $\mathsf{G}(1^\lambda)$ returns system parameters p. (2) Given p and an upperbound n on the polynomial degree, $\mathsf{K}(\mathsf{p}, n)$ returns $(\mathsf{ck}, \mathsf{tk})$, where ck is the commitment key and tk is the trapdoor. We assume ck implicitly contains p. (3) Given ck and a polynomial $\mathsf{f} \in \mathbb{F}_{\leq n}[X]$, deterministic $\mathsf{Com}(\mathsf{ck}, \mathsf{f})$ returns a commitment C to f. (4) Given ck, C, an evaluation point $\mathfrak{z} \in \mathbb{F}$, and $\mathsf{f} \in \mathbb{F}_{\leq n}[X]$, $\mathsf{Open}(\mathsf{ck}, C, \mathfrak{z}, \mathsf{f})$ returns $(\bar{f}, \pi)$, where $\bar{f} \leftarrow \mathsf{f}(\mathfrak{z})$ is an evaluation, and π is an evaluation proof. (5) Given ck, C, $\mathfrak{z}$, $\bar{f}$, and π, $\mathsf{Vf}(\mathsf{ck}, C, \mathfrak{z}, \bar{f}, \pi)$ returns 1 (accept) or 0 (reject).

[2] In the literature, $\mathbb{G}_T$ is often denoted as a multiplicative group, but we find the use of uniformly additive notation more convenient.

A non-interactive polynomial commitment scheme PC is *complete*, if for any λ, $\mathsf{p} \leftarrow \mathsf{G}(1^\lambda)$, $n \in \mathsf{poly}(\lambda)$, $\mathfrak{z} \in \mathbb{F}$, $\mathsf{f} \in \mathbb{F}_{\leq n}[X]$,

$$\Pr\left[\mathsf{Vf}(\mathsf{ck}, C, \mathfrak{z}, \bar{f}, \pi) = 1 \middle| \begin{array}{l}(\mathsf{ck}, \mathsf{tk}) \leftarrow \mathsf{K}(\mathsf{p}, n); C \leftarrow \mathsf{Com}(\mathsf{ck}, \mathsf{f});\\ (\bar{f}, \pi) \leftarrow \mathsf{Open}(\mathsf{ck}, C, \mathfrak{z}, \mathsf{f})\end{array}\right] = 1.$$

A non-interactive polynomial commitment scheme PC is *evaluation binding* for G, if for any $n \in \mathsf{poly}(\lambda)$, and PPT adversary $\mathcal{A}$, $\mathsf{Adv}^{\mathrm{evb}}_{\mathsf{G},\mathsf{PC},n,\mathcal{A}}(\lambda) :=$

$$\Pr\left[\begin{array}{l}\mathsf{Vf}(\mathsf{ck}, C, \mathfrak{z}, \bar{f}, \pi) = 1 \wedge \\ \mathsf{Vf}(\mathsf{ck}, C, \mathfrak{z}, \bar{f}', \pi') = 1 \wedge \bar{f} \neq \bar{f}'\end{array} \middle| \begin{array}{l}\mathsf{p} \leftarrow \mathsf{G}(1^\lambda); (\mathsf{ck}, \mathsf{tk}) \leftarrow \mathsf{K}(\mathsf{p}, n);\\ (C, \mathfrak{z}, \bar{f}, \pi, \bar{f}', \pi') \leftarrow \mathcal{A}(\mathsf{ck})\end{array}\right] \approx_\lambda 0 .$$

Following [35], $\mathsf{tr} = (C, \mathfrak{z}, \bar{f}, \pi)$ is a *transcript* of the PCS. Given a commitment key ck, a transcript tr is *accepting* when $\mathsf{Vf}(\mathsf{ck}, \mathsf{tr}) = 1$. We define the following relations for any $n \geq 1$ and any ck outputted by $\mathsf{K}(\mathsf{p}, n)$.

$$\begin{aligned}\mathsf{Rel}_{\mathsf{ck}} &:= \{(C, \mathsf{f}) : C = \mathsf{Com}(\mathsf{ck}, \mathsf{f}) \wedge \deg(\mathsf{f}) \leq n\} ,\\ \mathsf{Rel}_{\mathsf{ck},\mathbf{tr}} &:= \{(C, \mathsf{f}) : (C, \mathsf{f}) \in \mathsf{Rel}_{\mathsf{ck}} \wedge (\forall j \in [n+1])(\mathsf{f}(\mathfrak{z}_j) = \bar{f}_j)\} ,\end{aligned} \tag{1}$$

where $\mathbf{tr} = (\mathsf{tr}_1, \ldots, \mathsf{tr}_{n+1})$ contains $n+1$ accepting transcripts $\mathsf{tr}_j = (C, \mathfrak{z}_j, \bar{f}_j, \pi_j)$ s.t. C is the same in all transcripts, but $\mathfrak{z}_j$-s are pairwise distinct.

Let $n \in \mathsf{poly}(\lambda)$ with $n \geq 1$. A non-interactive PCS PC has *computational* $(n+1)$*-special soundness (CSS,* [35]*)* for G, if there exists a deterministic polynomial-time extractor $\mathcal{E}_{\mathsf{ss}}$, such that for any PPT adversary $\mathcal{A}_{\mathsf{ss}}$, $\mathsf{Adv}^{\mathrm{ss}}_{\mathsf{G},\mathsf{PC},\mathcal{E}_{\mathsf{ss}},n+1,\mathcal{A}_{\mathsf{ss}}}(\lambda) :=$

$$\Pr\left[\begin{array}{l}\mathbf{tr} = (\mathsf{tr}_j)_{j=1}^{n+1} \wedge \\ (\forall j \in [n+1])\begin{pmatrix}\mathsf{tr}_j = (C, \mathfrak{z}_j, \bar{f}_j, \pi_j)\\ \wedge \mathsf{Vf}(\mathsf{ck}, \mathsf{tr}_j) = 1\end{pmatrix} \\ \wedge ((\forall i \neq j)(\mathfrak{z}_i \neq \mathfrak{z}_j)) \wedge (C, \mathsf{f}) \notin \mathsf{Rel}_{\mathsf{ck},\mathbf{tr}}\end{array} \middle| \begin{array}{l}\mathsf{p} \leftarrow \mathsf{G}(1^\lambda);\\ (\mathsf{ck}, \mathsf{tk}) \leftarrow \mathsf{K}(\mathsf{p}, n);\\ \mathbf{tr} \leftarrow \mathcal{A}_{\mathsf{ss}}(\mathsf{ck});\\ \mathsf{f} \leftarrow \mathcal{E}_{\mathsf{ss}}(\mathsf{ck}, \mathbf{tr})\end{array}\right] \approx_\lambda 0 .$$

The non-interactive KZG [27] commitment scheme is defined as follows:

$\mathsf{G}(1^\lambda)$: return $\mathsf{p} \leftarrow \mathsf{G}(1^\lambda)$. ($\mathsf{G}$ from pairings).
$\mathsf{K}(\mathsf{p}, n)$: $\mathsf{tk} = x \leftarrow_\$ \mathbb{F}$; $\mathsf{ck} \leftarrow (\mathsf{p}, [1, x, \ldots, x^n]_1, [1, x]_2)$; return $(\mathsf{ck}, \mathsf{tk})$.
$\mathsf{Com}(\mathsf{ck}, \mathsf{f})$: return $C \leftarrow [\mathsf{f}(x)]_1 = \sum_{j=0}^{n} \mathsf{f}_j [x^j]_1$.
$\mathsf{Open}(\mathsf{ck}, C, \mathfrak{z}, \mathsf{f})$: $\bar{f} \leftarrow \mathsf{f}(\mathfrak{z})$; $\mathsf{h}(X) \leftarrow \frac{\mathsf{f}(X) - \bar{f}}{X - \mathfrak{z}}$; $\pi \leftarrow [\mathsf{h}(x)]_1$; return $(\bar{f}, \pi)$.
$\mathsf{Vf}(\mathsf{ck}, C, \mathfrak{z}, \bar{f}, \pi)$: Return 1 iff $(C - \bar{f}[1]_1) \bullet [1]_2 = \pi \bullet [x - \mathfrak{z}]_2$.

KZG is evaluation binding under the n-SDH assumption [27] and non-black-box extractable in the AGM [17] under the PDL assumption [6] and in the AGMOS (AGM with oblivious sampling, [34]) under the PDL and TOFR assumptions [35]. We note that ARSDH implies SDH [35]. Lipmaa, Parisella, and Siim [35] proved the following.

Fact 1. *Let $n \geq 1$. If n-ARSDH holds, then KZG for degree $\leq n$ polynomials has $(n+1)$-CSS: There exists a deterministic polynomial-time KZG computational special-soundness extractor $\mathcal{E}^{\mathrm{kzg}}_{\mathsf{ss}}$, such that for any PPT $\mathcal{A}_{\mathsf{ss}}$, there exists a PPT ARSDH adversary $\mathcal{B}$, such that* $\mathsf{Adv}^{\mathrm{ss}}_{\mathsf{G},\mathsf{PC},\mathcal{E}^{\mathrm{kzg}}_{\mathsf{ss}},n+1,\mathcal{A}_{\mathsf{ss}}}(\lambda) \leq \mathsf{Adv}^{\mathrm{arsdh}}_{\mathsf{G},n,\mathbb{G}_1,\mathcal{B}}(\lambda)$.

2.1 Security Properties of NARGs in ROM

We consider non-interactive argument systems (NARGs) obtained via the Fiat-Shamir transformation [16], which converts a public-coin interactive argument system into a non-interactive one in the random oracle model. Formally, given a $(2\mu+1)$-round interactive argument system $\Pi = (\mathsf{K}, \mathcal{P}, \mathcal{V})$, we define its Fiat-Shamir variant $\Pi_{\mathsf{FS}} = (\mathsf{K}_{\mathsf{FS}}, \mathcal{P}_{\mathsf{FS}}, \mathcal{V}_{\mathsf{FS}})$ as follows.

$\mathsf{K}_{\mathsf{FS}}(\mathsf{p})$: the setup algorithm runs $\mathsf{K}(\mathsf{p})$ to obtain a structured reference string and a trapdoor, $(\mathtt{srs}, \mathsf{td}) \leftarrow \mathsf{K}(\mathsf{p})$. In many applications, K also takes an additional parameter n (for example, the maximum circuit size).

$\mathcal{P}^{\mathcal{H}}_{\mathsf{FS}}(\mathtt{srs}, \mathbb{x}, \mathbb{w})$: For each round $i \in \{1, \dots, \mu+1\}$, the prover computes its message as follows. It runs the stateful next-message function of $\mathcal{P}(\mathtt{srs}, \mathbb{x}, \mathbb{w})$ using the previous challenge $\mathfrak{v}_{i-1}$ to obtain the message $\mathfrak{p}_i$. It computes the challenge for round i by setting $\mathfrak{v}_i \leftarrow \mathcal{H}(\mathtt{srs}, \mathbb{x}, (\mathfrak{p}_j)_{j=1}^{i})$.[3] The prover outputs an argument $\pi = (\mathfrak{p}_1, \mathfrak{v}_1, \dots, \mathfrak{p}_\mu, \mathfrak{v}_\mu, \mathfrak{p}_{\mu+1})$.[4]

$\mathcal{V}^{\mathcal{H}}_{\mathsf{FS}}(\mathtt{srs}, \mathbb{x}, \pi)$: The verifier accepts the proof ($b = 1$) if $\mathsf{Vf}(\mathtt{srs}, \mathbb{x}, \pi) = 1$ and $\mathfrak{v}_i = \mathcal{H}(\mathtt{srs}, \mathbb{x}, (\mathfrak{p}_j)_{j=1}^{i})$ for all $i \in [\mu]$.

In Plonk (see Sect. 5.1), one $\mathfrak{v}_i$ (namely, $\mathfrak{v}_1$) consists of two challenges $\mathfrak{v}_{i0}$ and $\mathfrak{v}_{i1}$, modeled in the ROM as $\mathfrak{v}_{ik} \leftarrow \mathcal{H}(\mathtt{srs}, \mathbb{x}, (\mathfrak{p}_j)_{j=1}^{i}, k)$. This is a standard modification of Fiat-Shamir.

Let $\pi := (\mathfrak{p}_1, \mathfrak{v}_1, \dots, \mathfrak{p}_\mu, \mathfrak{v}_\mu, \mathfrak{p}_{\mu+1})$ and $\mathfrak{p} = (\mathfrak{p}_1, \mathfrak{p}_2, \dots, \mathfrak{p}_\mu, \mathfrak{p}_{\mu+1})$. For $i \le \mu$ (resp., $i \le \mu + 1$), we define *the prefixes of* π *(resp.,* $\mathfrak{p}$*) up to round* i as

$$\pi|_i := (\mathfrak{p}_1, \mathfrak{v}_1, \mathfrak{p}_2, \dots, \mathfrak{p}_{i-1}, \mathfrak{v}_{i-1}, \mathfrak{p}_i, \mathfrak{v}_i) \ , \quad \mathfrak{p}|_i := (\mathfrak{p}_1, \mathfrak{p}_2, \dots, \mathfrak{p}_{i-1}, \mathfrak{p}_i) \ .$$

For completeness, set $\pi|_0 := \varnothing$ and $\mathfrak{p}|_0 := \varnothing$.

A NARG $\Pi_{\mathsf{FS}} = (\mathsf{K}_{\mathsf{FS}}, \mathcal{P}_{\mathsf{FS}}, \mathcal{V}_{\mathsf{FS}})$ for relation Rel has *perfect completeness* if for all λ and for all PPT adversaries $\mathcal{A}$,

$$\Pr\left[\begin{array}{c} \mathcal{V}^{\mathcal{H}}_{\mathsf{FS}}(\mathtt{srs}, \mathbb{x}, \pi) = 1 \\ \wedge\, (\mathbb{x}, \mathbb{w}) \in \mathsf{Rel} \end{array} \middle| \begin{array}{l} (\mathtt{srs}, \mathsf{td}) \leftarrow \mathsf{K}_{\mathsf{FS}}(1^\lambda); (\mathbb{x}, \mathbb{w}) \leftarrow \mathcal{A}^{\mathcal{H}}(\mathtt{srs}); \\ \pi \leftarrow \mathcal{P}^{\mathcal{H}}_{\mathsf{FS}}(\mathtt{srs}, \mathbb{x}, \mathbb{w}) \end{array}\right] = 1 \ .$$

We define zero knowledge for non-interactive arguments in the explicit (restricted) programmable random oracle model, in which the simulator can program the random oracle in specific rounds. The formalization below can be seen as that of [15] adapted to multi-round protocols.

We define a stateful NIZK simulator $\tilde{\mathcal{S}}$ that operates in two modes:

---

[3] This is how [20] uses Fiat-Shamir [16] (more precisely, $\mathfrak{v}_i$ is computed as the hash of the current transcript, which does not contain the verifier's messages), and we stick to this throughout the paper. An alternative (that we will not pursue) is to define $\mathfrak{v}_i \leftarrow \mathcal{H}(\mathfrak{v}_{i-1}, \mathfrak{p}_i)$ when $i > 1$.

[4] In this paper, we include $\mathfrak{v}_i$ to the argument π since this will make it easier to discuss various elements of the argument, for example, when defining prefixes of an argument. In an actual implementation, π would not include $\mathfrak{v}_i$.

1. *Random oracle simulation mode:* On input t, the simulator returns a response and an updated state via $(\mathfrak{v}_i, \mathsf{st}') \leftarrow \tilde{\mathcal{S}}(1, \mathsf{st}, t)$.
2. *Proof simulation mode:* On input $(\mathtt{srs}, \mathbb{x})$, the simulator outputs a simulated proof and an updated state via $(\pi^*, \mathsf{st}') \leftarrow \tilde{\mathcal{S}}(2, \mathsf{st}, (\mathtt{srs}, \boxed{\mathsf{td},} \mathbb{x}))$.

Figure 2 provides state-sharing wrapper oracles $\tilde{\mathcal{S}}_{\mathsf{ro}}(t)$, $\tilde{\mathcal{S}}_{\mathsf{true}.\pi}(\mathbb{x}, \mathbb{w})$, and $\tilde{\mathcal{S}}_{\mathsf{any}.\pi}(\mathbb{x})$. Since zero knowledge is only guaranteed for in-language statements, the NIZK definition uses $\tilde{\mathcal{S}}_{\mathsf{true}.\pi}$ as the proof simulation oracle. Simulation extractability uses $\tilde{\mathcal{S}}_{\mathsf{any}.\pi}$. Within its state st, the simulator maintains four lists. $\mathcal{Q}_{\mathsf{ro}}$ and $\mathcal{Q}_{\mathsf{sero}}$ record random oracle queries. $\mathcal{Q}_{\mathsf{ro}}$ captures direct queries to the random oracle, whereas $\mathcal{Q}_{\mathsf{sero}}$ additionally stores the values that the simulator programmed during simulation queries in the simulation extractability game. $\mathcal{Q}_{\mathsf{arg}}$ stores $(\mathbb{x}, \pi)$ pairs, where π are accepting simulated proofs.

$\tilde{\mathcal{S}}_{\mathsf{true}.\pi}(\mathbb{x}, \mathbb{w})$

if $(\mathbb{x}, \mathbb{w}) \notin \mathsf{Rel}$
  then return $\bot$;
$(\pi, \mathsf{st}) \leftarrow \tilde{\mathcal{S}}(2, \mathsf{st}, (\mathtt{srs}, \boxed{\mathsf{td},} \mathbb{x}))$;
$\mathcal{Q}_{\mathsf{arg}} \leftarrow \mathcal{Q}_{\mathsf{arg}} \cup \{(\mathbb{x}, \pi)\}$;
return π

$\tilde{\mathcal{S}}_{\mathsf{ro}}(t)$

$y \leftarrow \tilde{\mathcal{S}}(1, \mathsf{st}, t)$;
$\mathcal{Q}_{\mathsf{ro}}[t] \leftarrow y$;
return y;

$\tilde{\mathcal{S}}(1, \mathsf{st}, t)$

if $\mathcal{Q}_{\mathsf{sero}}[t] = \bot$
  then $\mathcal{Q}_{\mathsf{sero}}[t] \leftarrow_{\$} \mathsf{Ch}$;
return $\mathcal{Q}_{\mathsf{sero}}[t]$;

$\tilde{\mathcal{S}}_{\mathsf{any}.\pi}(\mathbb{x})$

$(\pi, \mathsf{st}) \leftarrow \tilde{\mathcal{S}}(2, \mathsf{st}, (\mathtt{srs}, \mathbb{x}))$; $\mathcal{Q}_{\mathsf{arg}} \leftarrow \mathcal{Q}_{\mathsf{arg}} \cup \{(\mathbb{x}, \pi)\}$;
return π

$\tilde{\mathcal{S}}(2, \mathsf{st}, (\mathtt{srs}, \boxed{\mathsf{td},} \mathbb{x}))$

$\mathsf{rst} \leftarrow \emptyset$; **for** $i \in T$ **do** $\mathfrak{v}_i \leftarrow_{\$} \mathsf{Ch}$;
for $i \in [\mu + 1]$ **do**
  if $i \in T$ **then**
    $(\mathfrak{p}_i, \mathsf{rst}_i) \leftarrow \tilde{\mathcal{S}}_i^{\mathsf{rnd}}(\mathtt{srs}, \boxed{\mathsf{td},} \mathbb{x}, \pi|_{i-1}, (\mathfrak{v}_j)_{j \in T}, \mathsf{rst})$;
  else
    $(\mathfrak{p}_i, \mathsf{rst}_i) \leftarrow \tilde{\mathcal{S}}_i^{\mathsf{rnd}}(\mathtt{srs}, \boxed{\mathsf{td},} \mathbb{x}, \pi|_{i-1}, \mathsf{rst})$;
    if $i < \mu + 1$ **then** $\mathfrak{v}_i \leftarrow_{\$} \mathsf{Ch}$;
  if $i < \mu + 1$ **then**
    $\mathsf{rst} \leftarrow \mathsf{rst} \| \mathsf{rst}_i$;
    if $\mathcal{Q}_{\mathsf{sero}}[\mathtt{srs}, \mathbb{x}, \mathfrak{p}|_i] \neq \bot$ **then return** $\bot$;
    else $\mathcal{Q}_{\mathsf{sero}}[\mathtt{srs}, \mathbb{x}, \mathfrak{p}|_i] \leftarrow \mathfrak{v}_i$;
$\pi \leftarrow (\mathfrak{p}_1, \mathfrak{v}_1, \dots, \mathfrak{v}_\mu, \mathfrak{p}_{\mu+1})$;
return (π, st);

Fig. 2. The oracles in the NIZK and simulation extractability games. td is not an oracle input in non-generalized canonical simulators (thus, we $\boxed{\text{highlight}}$ its uses).

To abstractly capture the typical behaviors of the TLZK simulator, we define the notion of canonical simulation. Here, T is the set of rounds where the simulator can program the random oracle.

Definition 1 (Generalized canonical simulator). *Fix a set* $T \subseteq \{1, \dots, \mu\}$. *A NIZK simulator* $\tilde{\mathcal{S}}$ *for* Π_{FS} *is* generalized T-canonical *if:*

1. *For mode 1,* $\tilde{\mathcal{S}}(1, \mathsf{st}, t)$ *answers random oracle queries as in Fig. 2.*

2. *For mode 2,* $\tilde{\mathcal{S}}(2, \mathsf{st}, (\mathtt{srs}, \boxed{\mathsf{td},} \mathbb{x}))$ *operates as in Fig. 2 using round functions* $\tilde{\mathcal{S}}_i^{\mathsf{rnd}}$*, with the following behavior:*
   (a) *For every* $i \in T$*, the simulator first samples a challenge* $\mathfrak{v}_i$*.*
   (b) *After that, for every round* $i \in [\mu + 1]$*, (i) If* $i \in T$*, it uses the set* $\{\mathfrak{v}_j\}_{j \in T}$ *to compute the message* $\mathfrak{p}_i$*, (ii) If* $i \notin T$*, the simulator computes* $\mathfrak{p}_i$ *(without using* $\{\mathfrak{v}_j\}_{j \in T}$*) and then samples a random challenge* $\mathfrak{v}_i$ *to serve as the hash value, (iii) It programs the random oracle so that its response on the corresponding query equals* $\mathfrak{v}_i$*.*

A non-generalized T*-canonical simulator is a* T-canonical simulator *when in none of the subroutines in Fig. 2 (*$\tilde{\mathcal{S}}(2, \ldots)$ *and* $\tilde{\mathcal{S}}_i^{\mathsf{rnd}}$*) receives* td *as an input.*

Generalized canonical simulators allow to capture trapdoor-based simulation scenarios, while canonical simulators must perform trapdoorless simulation.

We allow the round functions to be stateful. In our arguments, round functions that generate polynomial commitments output the committed polynomials as part of the state. Subsequent round functions can use these polynomials.

Let $\Pi_{\mathsf{FS}} = (\mathsf{K}_{\mathsf{FS}}, \mathcal{P}_{\mathsf{FS}}^{\mathcal{H}}, \mathcal{V}_{\mathsf{FS}}^{\mathcal{H}})$ be a non-interactive proof for relation Rel with a generalized canonical simulator $\tilde{\mathcal{S}}$. Π_{FS} is *non-interactive zero-knowledge (NIZK)* in the random oracle model if there exists a PPT simulator $\tilde{\mathcal{S}}$ with wrapper oracles $\tilde{\mathcal{S}}_{\mathsf{ro}}$ and $\tilde{\mathcal{S}}_{\mathsf{true}.\pi}$ (see Fig. 2), such that for all PPT distinguishers $\mathcal{D}$,

$$\mathsf{Adv}^{\mathrm{nizk}}_{\Pi_{\mathsf{FS}},\mathcal{D},\tilde{\mathcal{S}}}(\lambda) := \left| \begin{array}{l} \Pr[\mathcal{D}^{\mathcal{H},\mathcal{P}_{\mathsf{FS}}^{\mathcal{H}}}(\mathtt{srs}) = 1 \mid (\mathtt{srs}, \mathsf{td}) \leftarrow \mathsf{K}_{\mathsf{FS}}(1^\lambda)] - \\ \Pr[\mathcal{D}^{\tilde{\mathcal{S}}_{\mathsf{ro}},\tilde{\mathcal{S}}_{\mathsf{true}.\pi}}(\mathtt{srs}) = 1 \mid (\mathtt{srs}, \mathsf{td}) \leftarrow \mathsf{K}_{\mathsf{FS}}(1^\lambda)] \end{array} \right| \approx_\lambda 0 \ .$$

Definition 2 (T**-TLZK).** Π_{FS} *is* T-trapdoorless zero-knowledge (TLZK) *if it admits a (non-generalized)* T*-canonical simulator as defined in Definition 1, where* $\tilde{\mathcal{S}}(2, \ldots)$ *and* $\tilde{\mathcal{S}}_i^{\mathsf{rnd}}$ *do not know the trapdoor.*

Note that this means that Π_{FS} admits both $\tilde{\mathcal{S}}_{\mathsf{true}.\pi}$ and $\tilde{\mathcal{S}}_{\mathsf{any}.\pi}$ (see Fig. 2).

Next, we define two somewhat novel variants of the (weak) unique response property [7,15,21,23,29].

Definition 3 (ϱ**-UR).** *Consider a* $(2\mu + 1)$*-move public-coin interactive argument system* $\Pi = (\mathsf{K}, \mathcal{P}, \mathcal{V})$ *with* $\Pi_{\mathsf{FS}} = (\mathsf{K}_{\mathsf{FS}}, \mathcal{P}_{\mathsf{FS}}, \mathcal{V}_{\mathsf{FS}})$*. Let* $\varrho \in [\mu]$*.* Π_{FS} *has* computational ϱ-unique responses *(*ϱ*-UR) in the random oracle model if, for any stateful PPT adversary* $\mathcal{A}$*,* $\mathsf{Adv}^{\mathrm{ur}}_{\Pi_{\mathsf{FS}},\mathcal{A},\varrho}(\lambda) :=$

$$\Pr\left[\begin{array}{c} \pi = (\mathfrak{p}_1, \mathfrak{v}_1, \ldots, \mathfrak{p}_{\mu+1}) \wedge \\ \pi^* = (\mathfrak{p}_1^*, \mathfrak{v}_1^*, \ldots, \mathfrak{p}_{\mu+1}^*) \wedge \\ \mathcal{V}_{\mathsf{FS}}^{\mathcal{H}}(\mathtt{srs}, \mathbb{x}, \pi) = 1 \wedge \mathcal{V}_{\mathsf{FS}}^{\mathcal{H}}(\mathtt{srs}, \mathbb{x}, \pi^*) = 1 \wedge \\ \pi|_\varrho = \pi^*|_\varrho \wedge \mathfrak{p}_{\varrho+1} \neq \mathfrak{p}_{\varrho+1}^* \end{array} \middle| \begin{array}{l} (\mathtt{srs}, \mathsf{td}) \leftarrow \mathsf{K}_{\mathsf{FS}}(1^\lambda); \\ (\mathbb{x}, \pi, \pi^*) \leftarrow \mathcal{A}^{\mathcal{H}}(\mathtt{srs}) \end{array} \right] \approx_\lambda 0 \ .$$

Π_{FS} *has* last-round UR *if it has* μ*-UR.*

Definition 4 (ϱ-WUR). *Let $\Pi = (\mathsf{K}, \mathcal{P}, \mathcal{V})$ be a $(2\mu+1)$-move public-coin interactive argument system with $\Pi_{\mathsf{FS}} = (\mathsf{K}_{\mathsf{FS}}, \mathcal{P}_{\mathsf{FS}}, \mathcal{V}_{\mathsf{FS}})$. Let $\tilde{\mathcal{S}}$ be any non-generalized canonical simulator witnessing T-TLZK for Π_{FS} with wrapper oracles $(\tilde{\mathcal{S}}_{\mathsf{ro}}, \tilde{\mathcal{S}}_{\mathsf{any}.\pi})$. Let $\varrho \in [\mu]$. Π_{FS} has* computational ϱ-weak unique responses *(ϱ-WUR) with respect to $\tilde{\mathcal{S}}$ if, for any stateful PPT adversary $\mathcal{A}$,* $\mathsf{Adv}^{\mathrm{wur}}_{\Pi_{\mathsf{FS}},\mathcal{A},\tilde{\mathcal{S}},\varrho}(\lambda) :=$

$$\Pr\left[\begin{array}{c} \pi = (\mathfrak{p}_1, \mathfrak{v}_1, \dots, \mathfrak{p}_{\mu+1}) \wedge \\ \pi^* = (\mathfrak{p}^*_1, \mathfrak{v}^*_1, \dots, \mathfrak{p}^*_{\mu+1}) \wedge \\ \mathcal{V}^{\tilde{\mathcal{S}}_{\mathsf{ro}}}_{\mathsf{FS}}(\mathtt{srs}, \mathbb{x}, \pi) = 1 \wedge \\ \pi|_\varrho = \pi^*|_\varrho \wedge \mathfrak{p}_{\varrho+1} \neq \mathfrak{p}^*_{\varrho+1} \end{array} \middle| \begin{array}{l} (\mathtt{srs}, \mathsf{td}) \leftarrow \mathsf{K}_{\mathsf{FS}}(1^\lambda); \\ \mathbb{x} \leftarrow \mathcal{A}^{\tilde{\mathcal{S}}_{\mathsf{ro}}}(\mathtt{srs}); \\ \pi^* \leftarrow \tilde{\mathcal{S}}_{\mathsf{any}.\pi}(\mathbb{x}); \pi \leftarrow \mathcal{A}^{\tilde{\mathcal{S}}_{\mathsf{ro}}}(\pi^*) \end{array}\right] \approx_\lambda 0 \enspace .$$

We say Π_{FS} has $\geq \varrho$-WUR if it has k-WUR for $k \geq \varrho$. Thus, $\mathsf{Adv}^{\mathrm{wur}}_{\Pi_{\mathsf{FS}},\mathcal{A},\tilde{\mathcal{S}},\geq\varrho}(\lambda) :=$

$$\Pr\left[\begin{array}{c} \mathcal{V}^{\tilde{\mathcal{S}}_{\mathsf{ro}}}_{\mathsf{FS}}(\mathtt{srs}, \mathbb{x}, \pi) = 1 \wedge \\ \pi|_\varrho = \pi^*|_\varrho \wedge \pi \neq \pi^* \end{array} \middle| \begin{array}{l} (\mathtt{srs}, \mathsf{td}) \leftarrow \mathsf{K}_{\mathsf{FS}}(1^\lambda); \mathbb{x} \leftarrow \mathcal{A}^{\tilde{\mathcal{S}}_{\mathsf{ro}}}(\mathtt{srs}); \\ \pi^* \leftarrow \tilde{\mathcal{S}}_{\mathsf{any}.\pi}(\mathbb{x}); \pi \leftarrow \mathcal{A}^{\tilde{\mathcal{S}}_{\mathsf{ro}}}(\pi^*) \end{array}\right] \approx_\lambda 0 \enspace .$$

(No need to check $\mathcal{V}^{\tilde{\mathcal{S}}_{\mathsf{ro}}}_{\mathsf{FS}}(\mathtt{srs}, \mathbb{x}, \pi^*) = 1$ since $\tilde{\mathcal{S}}_{\mathsf{any}.\pi}$ outputs an acceptable argument π^*).

UR and WUR are incomparable: If Π is TLZK and thus has a (non-generalized) canonical simulator, then UR implies WUR. However, if Π is not TLZK, then WUR is not defined, but Π might still have UR.

Next, we define adaptive knowledge soundness and simulation extractability for Fiat-Shamir NIZK.

Definition 5 (Knowledge soundness). *Let $\Pi_{\mathsf{FS}} = (\mathsf{K}_{\mathsf{FS}}, \mathcal{P}_{\mathsf{FS}}, \mathcal{V}_{\mathsf{FS}})$ be a non-interactive argument system. Π_{FS} is* knowledge-sound *for a relation* Rel *in the random oracle model if there exists a PPT* universal *extractor $\mathcal{E}_{\mathsf{ks}}$, such that for any PPT $\mathcal{B}_{\mathsf{ks}}$,* $\mathsf{Adv}^{\mathrm{ks}}_{\Pi_{\mathsf{FS}},\mathcal{E}_{\mathsf{ks}},\mathcal{B}_{\mathsf{ks}}}(\lambda) =$

$$\Pr\left[\begin{array}{l} \mathcal{V}^{\tilde{\mathcal{S}}_{\mathsf{ro}}}_{\mathsf{FS}}(\mathtt{srs}, \mathbb{x}, \pi) = 1 \wedge \\ (\mathbb{x}, \mathbb{w}) \notin \mathsf{Rel} \end{array} \middle| \begin{array}{l} Q_{\mathsf{ro}} \leftarrow \emptyset; (\mathtt{srs}, \mathsf{td}) \leftarrow \mathsf{K}_{\mathsf{FS}}(1^\lambda); \\ (\mathbb{x}, \pi) \leftarrow \mathcal{B}^{\tilde{\mathcal{S}}_{\mathsf{ro}}}_{\mathsf{ks}}(\mathtt{srs}); \mathbb{w} \leftarrow \mathcal{E}_{\mathsf{ks}}(\mathtt{srs}, \mathbb{x}, \pi, Q_{\mathsf{ro}}) \end{array}\right] \approx_\lambda 0 \enspace .$$

Here, Q_{ro} is the set of query-response pairs corresponding to queries to the random oracle $\mathcal{H}$. (See Fig. 2).

Here $\tilde{\mathcal{S}}_{\mathsf{ro}}$ is a lazily sampled random function with the same distribution as $\mathcal{H}$; we use it only to record Q_{ro} consistently.

We assume the existence of a universal knowledge-soundness extractor that can see the communication between the adversary and the random oracle (that is, Q_{ro}) but does not depend on the adversary otherwise.

Definition 6 (Simulation extractability). *Let $\Pi_{\mathsf{FS}} = (\mathsf{K}_{\mathsf{FS}}, \mathcal{P}_{\mathsf{FS}}, \mathcal{V}_{\mathsf{FS}})$ be a non-interactive argument system with a simulator $\tilde{\mathcal{S}}$. Π_{FS} is* simulation extractable *with respect to $\tilde{\mathcal{S}}$ for a relation* Rel *in the random oracle* *model, if there exists a PPT extractor* $\mathcal{E}_{\mathsf{se}}$*, such that for any PPT* $\mathcal{A}_{\mathsf{se}}$, $\mathsf{Adv}^{\mathrm{se}}_{\Pi_{\mathsf{FS}},\mathcal{E}_{\mathsf{se}},\mathcal{A}_{\mathsf{se}},\tilde{\mathcal{S}}}(\lambda) :=$

$$\Pr\left[\begin{array}{c|l} \mathcal{V}_{\mathsf{FS}}^{\tilde{\mathcal{S}}_{\mathsf{ro}}}(\mathtt{srs},\mathbb{x},\pi)=1 & \mathcal{Q}_{\mathsf{ro}},\mathcal{Q}_{\mathsf{arg}},\mathcal{Q}_{\mathsf{sero}} \leftarrow \varnothing; (\mathtt{srs},\mathsf{td}) \leftarrow \mathsf{K}_{\mathsf{FS}}(1^\lambda); \\ \wedge (\mathbb{x},\pi)\notin \mathcal{Q}_{\mathsf{arg}} & (\mathbb{x},\pi) \leftarrow \mathcal{A}_{\mathsf{se}}^{\tilde{\mathcal{S}}_{\mathsf{ro}},\tilde{\mathcal{S}}_{\mathsf{any}.\pi}}(\mathtt{srs}); \\ \wedge (\mathbb{x},\mathbb{w})\notin \mathsf{Rel} & \mathbb{w} \leftarrow \mathcal{E}_{\mathsf{se}}(\mathtt{srs},\mathbb{x},\pi,\mathcal{Q}_{\mathsf{ro}},\mathcal{Q}_{\mathsf{sero}},\mathcal{Q}_{\mathsf{arg}}) \end{array}\right] \approx_\lambda 0 \ .$$

3 Composition Theorem

Next, we prove a variant of the composition theorem from [21,23]. More precisely, we prove that if a Fiat-Shamir NARG has knowledge soundness, T-TLZK, and $\geq \varrho$-WUR (for $\varrho = \min T$), then it is simulation extractable. Intuitively, we construct a prover $\mathcal{B}_{\mathsf{ks}}$ that outputs an argument in the knowledge-soundness game by invoking $\mathcal{A}_{\mathsf{se}}$ who is playing the simulation extractability game. $\mathcal{B}_{\mathsf{ks}}$ answers $\tilde{\mathcal{S}}_{\mathsf{any}.\pi}$ queries by running $\tilde{\mathcal{S}}$ and forwards $\tilde{\mathcal{S}}_{\mathsf{ro}}$ queries made by $\mathcal{A}_{\mathsf{se}}$ to the random oracle $\mathcal{H}$ except for the inputs already programmed by $\tilde{\mathcal{S}}$. The programmed RO entries introduce inconsistencies between the responses of $\tilde{\mathcal{S}}_{\mathsf{ro}}$ and $\mathcal{H}$. Thus, $\mathcal{B}_{\mathsf{ks}}$ aborts if $\mathcal{A}_{\mathsf{se}}$ outputs a transcript that shares a common prefix (to the point of the first programming) with any simulated transcripts. The probability that $\mathcal{B}_{\mathsf{ks}}$ aborts can be bounded by a negligible function, assuming the WUR property. If $\mathcal{B}_{\mathsf{ks}}$ does not abort, we run a knowledge-soundness extractor against $\mathcal{B}_{\mathsf{ks}}$ to obtain a valid witness.

Faust et al. [15,21,23,29] prove variants of this theorem using different notions of WUR or TLZK, or omitting the trusted setup. The following proof serves as a quick check that the same reduction can be used in our setting.

Theorem 1. *Let* Π_{FS} *be a Fiat-Shamir non-interactive argument system with a (non-generalized) canonical NIZK simulator* $\tilde{\mathcal{S}}$*, where the interactive variant has* $2\mu+1$ *moves. Let* $T \subseteq [\mu]$ *and* $\varrho = \min T$*. If* Π_{FS} *has* T*-TLZK, knowledge soundness, and* $\geq \varrho$*-WUR, then it is simulation extractable with respect to* $\tilde{\mathcal{S}}$*: For any PPT* $\mathcal{A}_{\mathsf{se}}$ *and* $\mathcal{E}_{\mathsf{ks}}$*, there exist PPT* $\mathcal{B}_{\mathsf{ks}}$*,* $\mathcal{E}_{\mathsf{se}}$*, and* $\mathcal{C}_{\mathsf{wur}}$*, such that*

$$\mathsf{Adv}^{\mathrm{se}}_{\Pi_{\mathsf{FS}},\mathcal{E}_{\mathsf{se}},\mathcal{A}_{\mathsf{se}},\tilde{\mathcal{S}}}(\lambda) \leq \mathsf{Adv}^{\mathrm{ks}}_{\Pi_{\mathsf{FS}},\mathcal{E}_{\mathsf{ks}},\mathcal{B}_{\mathsf{ks}}}(\lambda) + q_{\mathsf{arg}} \cdot \mathsf{Adv}^{\mathrm{wur}}_{\Pi_{\mathsf{FS}},\mathcal{C}_{\mathsf{wur}},\tilde{\mathcal{S}},>\varrho}(\lambda) \ ,$$

where q_{arg} *is the number of* $\mathcal{A}_{\mathsf{se}}$*'s queries to* $\tilde{\mathcal{S}}_{\mathsf{any}.\pi}$*.*

Proof. Assume Π_{FS} has knowledge soundness. Thus (see Definition 5), there exists a *universal* PPT knowledge-soundness extractor $\mathcal{E}_{\mathsf{ks}}$, such that for any PPT $\mathcal{B}_{\mathsf{ks}}$: when $\mathcal{B}_{\mathsf{ks}}(\mathtt{srs})$ returns an accepting $(\mathbb{x},\pi)$, then (with probability $1-\mathsf{negl}(\lambda)$) $\mathcal{E}_{\mathsf{ks}}(\mathtt{srs},\mathbb{x},\pi,\mathcal{Q}_{\mathsf{ro}})$ returns $\mathbb{w}$, such that $(\mathbb{x},\mathbb{w}) \in \mathsf{Rel}$.

Assume simulation extractability does not hold. Thus (see Definition 6), for every PPT $\mathcal{E}_{\mathsf{se}}$, there exists a PPT $\mathcal{A}_{\mathsf{se}}$, such that the probability $\mathsf{Adv}^{\mathrm{se}}_{\Pi_{\mathsf{FS}},\mathcal{E}_{\mathsf{se}},\mathcal{A}_{\mathsf{se}},\tilde{\mathcal{S}}}(\lambda)$ that, in the simulation extractability game, $\mathcal{A}_{\mathsf{se}}^{\tilde{\mathcal{S}}_{\mathsf{ro}},\tilde{\mathcal{S}}_{\mathsf{any}.\pi}}(\mathtt{srs})$ outputs $(\mathbb{x},\pi) \notin \mathcal{Q}_{\mathsf{arg}}$ and $\mathcal{E}_{\mathsf{se}}(\mathtt{srs},\mathbb{x},\pi,\mathcal{Q}_{\mathsf{ro}},\mathcal{Q}_{\mathsf{sero}},\mathcal{Q}_{\mathsf{arg}})$ does not output $\mathbb{w}$, satisfying $(\mathbb{x},\mathbb{w}) \in \mathsf{Rel}$, is non-negligible.

$\mathcal{B}_{\mathsf{ks}}^{\mathcal{H},\mathcal{A}_{\mathsf{se}}}(\mathtt{srs})$

1 : $\mathcal{Q}_{\mathsf{ro}}, \mathcal{Q}_{\mathsf{sero}}, \mathcal{Q}_{\mathsf{arg}} \leftarrow \emptyset$;
2 : $(\mathbb{x}, \pi) \leftarrow \mathcal{A}_{\mathsf{se}}^{\tilde{\mathcal{S}}'_{\mathsf{ro}}, \tilde{\mathcal{S}}'_{\mathsf{any}.\pi}}(\mathtt{srs})$;
3 : $b \leftarrow \mathcal{V}_{\mathsf{FS}}^{\tilde{\mathcal{S}}_{\mathsf{ro}}}(\mathtt{srs}, \mathbb{x}, \pi)$;
4 : **if** $b = 0 \vee (\mathbb{x}, \pi) \in \mathcal{Q}_{\mathsf{arg}}$ **then return** $\perp$;
5 : **if** $(\exists(\mathbb{x}, \pi^*) \in \mathcal{Q}_{\mathsf{arg}})(\pi|_\varrho = \pi^*|_\varrho \wedge \pi \neq \pi^*)$
6 : **then** $\mathsf{bad} \leftarrow \mathsf{true}$; **return** $\perp$;
7 : **return** $(\mathbb{x}, \pi)$;

$\tilde{\mathcal{S}}'_{\mathsf{ro}}(t)$

$y \leftarrow \mathcal{Q}_{\mathsf{sero}}[t]$;
if $y = \perp$
then $y \leftarrow_{\$} \mathsf{Ch}$; $\mathcal{Q}_{\mathsf{sero}}[t] \leftarrow y$; $\mathcal{Q}_{\mathsf{ro}}[t] \leftarrow y$;
return y;

$\mathcal{E}_{\mathsf{se}}(\mathtt{srs}, \mathbb{x}, \pi, \mathcal{Q}_{\mathsf{ro}}, \mathcal{Q}_{\mathsf{sero}}, \mathcal{Q}_{\mathsf{arg}})$

if $(\exists(\mathbb{x}, \pi^*) \in \mathcal{Q}_{\mathsf{arg}})$
$(\pi|_\varrho = \pi^*|_\varrho \wedge \pi \neq \pi^*)$
then $\mathsf{bad} \leftarrow \mathsf{true}$; **return** $\perp$;
$\mathbb{w} \leftarrow \mathcal{E}_{\mathsf{ks}}(\mathtt{srs}, \mathbb{x}, \pi, \mathcal{Q}_{\mathsf{ro}})$;
return $\mathbb{w}$;

$\tilde{\mathcal{S}}'_{\mathsf{any}.\pi}(\mathbb{x})$

$\pi \leftarrow$ $\tilde{\mathcal{S}}_{\mathsf{any}.\pi}(\mathbb{x})$ // Run internally
$(\pi, \mathsf{st}) \leftarrow \tilde{\mathcal{S}}(2, \mathsf{st}, (\mathbb{x}, \mathtt{srs}))$;
$\mathcal{Q}_{\mathsf{arg}} \leftarrow \mathcal{Q}_{\mathsf{arg}} \cup \{(\mathbb{x}, \pi)\}$;
return π;

Fig. 3. $\mathcal{B}_{\mathsf{ks}}^{\mathcal{H}}$, $\mathcal{E}_{\mathsf{se}}$, and the related oracles in Theorem 1. $\tilde{\mathcal{S}}$ is as in Fig. 2.

Next, we construct a knowledge-soundness adversary $\mathcal{B}_{\mathsf{ks}}$, a simulation extractability extractor $\mathcal{E}_{\mathsf{se}}$, a WUR adversary $\mathcal{C}_{\mathsf{wur}}$, and oracles used by them. (See Figs. 3 and 4). Both $\mathcal{B}_{\mathsf{ks}}$ and $\mathcal{E}_{\mathsf{se}}$ set $\mathsf{bad} \leftarrow \mathsf{true}$ and abort when the argument returned by $\mathcal{A}_{\mathsf{se}}$ has a long common prefix with some simulated argument that uses the same input. This influences the success probabilities of $\mathcal{B}_{\mathsf{ks}}$ and $\mathcal{E}_{\mathsf{se}}$.

Adversary $\mathcal{B}_{\mathsf{ks}}$. $\mathcal{B}_{\mathsf{ks}}^{\mathcal{H},\mathcal{A}_{\mathsf{se}}}(\mathtt{srs})$ calls $\mathcal{A}_{\mathsf{se}}^{\tilde{\mathcal{S}}'_{\mathsf{ro}}, \tilde{\mathcal{S}}'_{\mathsf{any}.\pi}}(\mathtt{srs})$, simulating its view of oracles. Here, $\tilde{\mathcal{S}}'_{\mathsf{any}.\pi}$ is the same as $\tilde{\mathcal{S}}_{\mathsf{any}.\pi}$ in Fig. 2 except that it runs $\tilde{\mathcal{S}}(2, \ldots)$ from Fig. 2 internally. When $\mathcal{A}_{\mathsf{se}}$ queries $\tilde{\mathcal{S}}'_{\mathsf{ro}}$ (see Fig. 2), $\mathcal{B}_{\mathsf{ks}}$ queries the random oracle $\mathcal{H}$ except when the corresponding entry was already defined by $\tilde{\mathcal{S}}(2, \ldots)$. Thus, the simulated random oracle responses in $\mathcal{Q}_{\mathsf{sero}}$ are identical to those of $\mathcal{H}$, except for the ones programmed by $\tilde{\mathcal{S}}(2, \ldots)$ inside $\tilde{\mathcal{S}}_{\mathsf{any}.\pi}$. The first such programming can occur in round ϱ; thus, we must avoid adversarial arguments that share the common prefix with π^* up to round ϱ but differ later. Thus, $\mathcal{B}_{\mathsf{ks}}$ sets $\mathsf{bad} \leftarrow \mathsf{true}$ and aborts if there exists $(\mathbb{x}, \pi^*) \in \mathcal{Q}_{\mathsf{arg}}$ such that $\pi|_\varrho = \pi^*|_\varrho$ and $\pi \neq \pi^*$ (some prefix is reused by $\mathcal{A}_{\mathsf{se}}$). Since the prefix check performed by $\mathcal{B}_{\mathsf{ks}}$ on line 5 of Fig. 3 rules out a forgery pair $(\mathbb{x}, \pi)$ involving simulated random oracle entries, $\mathcal{B}_{\mathsf{ks}}$ is guaranteed to output $(\mathbb{x}, \pi)$, s.t. $\mathcal{H}(\mathtt{srs}, \mathbb{x}, \pi|_{i-1}, \mathbb{p}_i) = \mathbb{v}_i$ for $i \in [\mu]$.

Extractor $\mathcal{E}_{\mathsf{se}}$. After $\mathcal{A}_{\mathsf{se}}$ outputs $(\mathbb{x}, \pi) \leftarrow \mathcal{A}_{\mathsf{se}}^{\tilde{\mathcal{S}}_{\mathsf{ro}}, \tilde{\mathcal{S}}_{\mathsf{any}.\pi}}(\mathtt{srs})$ (creating $\mathcal{Q}_{\mathsf{ro}}$, $\mathcal{Q}_{\mathsf{sero}}$, and $\mathcal{Q}_{\mathsf{arg}}$), $\mathcal{E}_{\mathsf{se}}$ obtains $(\mathtt{srs}, \mathbb{x}, \pi, \mathcal{Q}_{\mathsf{ro}}, \mathcal{Q}_{\mathsf{sero}}, \mathcal{Q}_{\mathsf{arg}})$ as input. If there exists $(\mathbb{x}, \pi^*) \in \mathcal{Q}_{\mathsf{arg}}$ such that $\pi|_\varrho = \pi^*|_\varrho$ and $\pi \neq \pi^*$, then $\mathcal{E}_{\mathsf{se}}$ sets $\mathsf{bad} \leftarrow \mathsf{true}$ and aborts. Otherwise, $\mathcal{E}_{\mathsf{se}}$ obtains $\mathbb{w} \leftarrow \mathcal{E}_{\mathsf{ks}}(\mathtt{srs}, \mathbb{x}, \pi, \mathcal{Q}_{\mathsf{ro}})$ and returns $\mathbb{w}$. Clearly, whenever $\mathcal{E}_{\mathsf{ks}}$ outputs a valid witness $\mathbb{w}$, $\mathcal{E}_{\mathsf{se}}$ succeeds.

$\mathcal{C}_{\mathsf{wur}}^{\tilde{\mathcal{S}}_{\mathsf{ro}},\mathcal{A}_{\mathsf{se}}}(\mathbf{srs})$

$k \leftarrow_{\$} [q_{\mathsf{arg}}]$; $q \leftarrow 1$;
$(\mathbb{x}, \pi) \leftarrow \mathcal{A}_{\mathsf{se}}^{\tilde{\mathcal{S}}^{\dagger}_{\mathsf{ro}},\tilde{\mathcal{S}}^{\dagger}_{\mathsf{any}.\pi}}(\mathbf{srs})$;
if $(\exists(\mathbb{x}, \pi^*) \in Q_{\mathsf{arg}})(\pi|_{\varrho} = \pi^*|_{\varrho} \wedge \pi \neq \pi^*)$
then $\mathsf{bad} \leftarrow \mathsf{true}$; **return** π;
else $\mathsf{bad} \leftarrow \mathsf{false}$; **return** $\perp$;

$\tilde{\mathcal{S}}^{\dagger}_{\mathsf{ro}}(t)$

return $\tilde{\mathcal{S}}_{\mathsf{ro}}(t)$;

$\tilde{\mathcal{S}}^{\dagger}_{\mathsf{any}.\pi}(\mathbb{x}_q)$ // qth query

if $q = k$ **then** $\pi^* \leftarrow \tilde{\mathcal{S}}_{\mathsf{any}.\pi}(\mathbb{x}_q)$;
else
$\pi^* \leftarrow$ $\tilde{\mathcal{S}}_{\mathsf{any}.\pi}(\mathbb{x}_q)$ // Run internally
  $(\pi^*_q, \mathsf{st}) \leftarrow \tilde{\mathcal{S}}(2, \mathsf{st}, (\mathbf{srs}, \mathbb{x}_q))$;
  $Q_{\mathsf{arg}} \leftarrow Q_{\mathsf{arg}} \cup \{(\mathbb{x}_q, \pi^*_q)\}$;
  return π^*_q;
$q \leftarrow q + 1$;
return π^*;

Fig. 4. Adversary $\mathcal{C}_{\mathsf{wur}}$ and two oracles in Theorem 1. $\tilde{\mathcal{S}}$, $\tilde{\mathcal{S}}_{\mathsf{ro}}$, $\tilde{\mathcal{S}}_{\mathsf{any}.\pi}$ are as in Fig. 2.

Adversary $\mathcal{C}_{\mathsf{wur}}$. In Fig. 4, we depict a $\geq \varrho$-WUR adversary $\mathcal{C}_{\mathsf{wur}}$ with respect to $\tilde{\mathcal{S}}$ succeeding with probability $1/q_{\mathsf{arg}}$ whenever bad is set. (We ignore the case $q_{\mathsf{arg}} = 0$ since then simulation extractability is equivalent to knowledge soundness). Recall that, by definition, in the $\geq \varrho$-WUR game with $\mathcal{C}_{\mathsf{wur}}$, (1) $\mathsf{K}_{\mathsf{FS}}(1^{\lambda})$ returns $(\mathbf{srs}, \mathsf{td})$, (2) $\mathcal{C}_{\mathsf{wur}}^{\tilde{\mathcal{S}}_{\mathsf{ro}}}(\mathbf{srs})$ returns $\mathbb{x}$, (3) $\tilde{\mathcal{S}}_{\mathsf{any}.\pi}(\mathbb{x})$ returns π^*, and (4) $\mathcal{C}_{\mathsf{wur}}^{\tilde{\mathcal{S}}_{\mathsf{ro}}}(\pi^*)$ returns π. $\mathcal{C}_{\mathsf{wur}}$ is successful when $\mathcal{V}_{\mathsf{FS}}^{\tilde{\mathcal{S}}_{\mathsf{ro}}}(\mathbf{srs}, \mathbb{x}, \pi) = 1$, $\pi|_{\varrho} = \pi^*|_{\varrho}$, and $\pi \neq \pi^*$.

$\mathcal{C}_{\mathsf{wur}}$ plays the WUR game using $\mathcal{A}_{\mathsf{se}}$ as a helper, while simulating $\mathcal{A}_{\mathsf{se}}$'s oracles $\tilde{\mathcal{S}}^{\dagger}_{\mathsf{ro}}$ and $\tilde{\mathcal{S}}^{\dagger}_{\mathsf{any}.\pi}$, described in Fig. 4. Since it is not known in advance which simulation query k to $\tilde{\mathcal{S}}^{\dagger}_{\mathsf{any}.\pi}$ will result in the common prefix, we use the strategy of [15,23,29] and guess k randomly.

More precisely, $\mathcal{C}_{\mathsf{wur}}$ first samples a query index $k \leftarrow_{\$} [q_{\mathsf{arg}}]$. Then, $\mathcal{C}_{\mathsf{wur}}$ invokes $\mathcal{A}_{\mathsf{se}}^{\tilde{\mathcal{S}}^{\dagger}_{\mathsf{ro}},\tilde{\mathcal{S}}^{\dagger}_{\mathsf{any}.\pi}}(\mathbf{srs})$, simulating $\mathcal{A}_{\mathsf{se}}$'s oracle queries as follows.

1. When $\mathcal{A}_{\mathsf{se}}$ queries $\tilde{\mathcal{S}}^{\dagger}_{\mathsf{any}.\pi}(\mathbb{x}_q)$: // qth query
   (a) If this is the kth simulation query ($q = k$), as part of the WUR game, $\mathcal{C}_{\mathsf{wur}}$ forwards $\mathbb{x}_k = \mathbb{x}_q$ to $\tilde{\mathcal{S}}_{\mathsf{any}.\pi}$ who returns π^*_k (see Fig. 2).
   (b) Otherwise ($q \neq k$), $\mathcal{C}_{\mathsf{wur}}$ executes $\tilde{\mathcal{S}}_{\mathsf{any}.\pi}(\mathbb{x}_q)$ internally (see Fig. 2).
2. When $\mathcal{A}_{\mathsf{se}}$ queries $\tilde{\mathcal{S}}^{\dagger}_{\mathsf{ro}}(t)$: $\mathcal{C}_{\mathsf{wur}}$ queries $\tilde{\mathcal{S}}_{\mathsf{ro}}(t)$ (given to $\mathcal{C}_{\mathsf{wur}}$ as an oracle in the WUR game) and returns the answer.

Finally, when $\mathcal{A}_{\mathsf{se}}$ outputs $(\mathbb{x}, \pi)$, $\mathcal{C}_{\mathsf{wur}}$ checks whether for some $(\mathbb{x}, \pi^*) \in Q_{\mathsf{arg}}$, $\pi|_{\varrho} = \pi^*|_{\varrho}$ and $\pi \neq \pi^*$. If so, $\mathcal{C}_{\mathsf{wur}}$ sets $\mathsf{bad} \leftarrow \mathsf{true}$ and returns π.

Clearly, $\mathcal{C}_{\mathsf{wur}}$ perfectly simulates $\mathcal{A}_{\mathsf{se}}$'s view. If $\mathbb{x} = \mathbb{x}_k$, $\pi \neq \pi^*_k$, and $\pi|_{\varrho} = \pi^*_k|_{\varrho}$, then π is a valid forgery in the WUR game and $\mathcal{C}_{\mathsf{wur}}$ breaks WUR with respect to $\tilde{\mathcal{S}}$. Conditioned on $\mathsf{bad} = \mathsf{true}$, the probability that $\mathcal{C}_{\mathsf{wur}}$ wins is at least $1/q_{\mathsf{arg}}$. Hence, $1/q_{\mathsf{arg}} \cdot \Pr[\mathsf{bad}] \leq \mathsf{Adv}^{\mathrm{wur}}_{\Pi_{\mathsf{FS}},\mathcal{C}_{\mathsf{wur}},\tilde{\mathcal{S}}}(\lambda)$.

Finally, let $\mathsf{Adv}^{\mathrm{se}}_{\Pi_{\mathsf{FS}},\mathcal{E}_{\mathsf{se}},\mathcal{A}_{\mathsf{se}},\tilde{\mathcal{S}}}(\lambda) = \Pr[\overline{\mathcal{E}_{\mathsf{se}}} \wedge \mathcal{A}_{\mathsf{se}}]$ be the probability $\mathcal{A}_{\mathsf{se}}$ succeeded but $\mathcal{E}_{\mathsf{se}}$ did not extract the witness, and similarly $\mathsf{Adv}^{\mathrm{ks}}_{\Pi_{\mathsf{FS}},\mathcal{E}_{\mathsf{ks}},\mathcal{B}_{\mathsf{ks}}}(\lambda) = \Pr[\overline{\mathcal{E}_{\mathsf{ks}}} \wedge \mathcal{B}_{\mathsf{ks}}]$

with $\mathcal{B}_{\mathsf{ks}}$ and $\mathcal{E}_{\mathsf{ks}}$. Considering everything we proved,

$$\begin{aligned}\mathsf{Adv}^{\mathrm{se}}_{\Pi_{\mathsf{FS}},\mathcal{E}_{\mathsf{se}},\mathcal{A}_{\mathsf{se}},\tilde{\mathcal{S}}}(\lambda) &= \Pr[\overline{\mathcal{E}_{\mathsf{se}}} \wedge \mathcal{A}_{\mathsf{se}}] \leq \Pr[\overline{\mathcal{E}_{\mathsf{se}}} \wedge \mathcal{A}_{\mathsf{se}} \mid \overline{\mathsf{bad}}] + \Pr[\mathsf{bad}] \\ &\leq \Pr[\overline{\mathcal{E}_{\mathsf{ks}}} \wedge \mathcal{B}_{\mathsf{ks}} \mid \overline{\mathsf{bad}}] + \Pr[\mathsf{bad}] \leq \Pr[\overline{\mathcal{E}_{\mathsf{ks}}} \wedge \mathcal{B}_{\mathsf{ks}}] + \Pr[\mathsf{bad}] \\ &= \mathsf{Adv}^{\mathrm{ks}}_{\Pi_{\mathsf{FS}},\mathcal{E}_{\mathsf{ks}},\mathcal{B}_{\mathsf{ks}}}(\lambda) + q_{\mathsf{arg}} \cdot \mathsf{Adv}^{\mathrm{wur}}_{\Pi_{\mathsf{FS}},\mathcal{C}_{\mathsf{wur}},\tilde{\mathcal{S}},\geq\varrho}(\lambda) \ .\end{aligned}$$

□

4 Security of Gadgets

Lipmaa, Parisella, and Siim [35] proved that KZG has CSS under the ARSDH assumption. In [36], they proved that if KZG has CSS, some gadgets (BatchKZG and SanLinTrick) have CSS. On the other hand, they proved that LinTrick does not have CSS. Faonio, Fiore, and Russo [14] proved that, after applying Fiat-Shamir, some gadgets are so-called "policy-based" simulation extractable assuming both the AGM and the ROM. Using Theorem 1, one could aim to prove that $\mathrm{KZG}_{\mathsf{FS}}$, $\mathrm{BatchKZG}_{\mathsf{FS}}$ and $\mathrm{SanLinTrick}_{\mathsf{FS}}$ are simulation extractable in the ROM under falsifiable assumptions. For this, one would need to prove that they are T-TLZK and $\geq\varrho$-WUR for some T and $\varrho = \min T$.[5]

We show that if KZG is evaluation binding, then $\mathrm{KZG}_{\mathsf{FS}}$ and other mentioned gadgets are *not* TLZK. This holds since such gadgets are commit-and-prove zk-SNARKs, with their inputs containing a polynomial commitment to an unknown polynomial that is opened within the gadget at an evaluation point defined by the random oracle. A trapdoorless simulator has only one extra power: reprogramming the random oracle. Reprogramming changes either the valuation point or the evaluation and opening produced by the simulator. This does not matter for the reduction from the security of evaluation binding since an evaluation-binding adversary is not required to be successful for a *given* evaluation point or opening value; instead, it can freely choose both.

Since the gadgets do not have a trapdoorless simulator, the notion of WUR is not defined for them. For completeness, we prove that all gadgets are last-round-UR under a standard assumption. However, we do not know how to use this result to prove simulation extractability.

The current section's results show the limitations of the approach of [15] and subsequent papers basing simulation extractability on (variants) of WUR and TLZK. Since these gadgets are not TLZK, one cannot use Theorem 1 to prove they are simulation extractable. However, by using a different framework, [14] proved their ("policy-based") simulation extractability in the joint AGM-ROM. We leave it as an open question whether their approach can be used to prove the simulation extractability of the gadgets in the ROM under falsifiable assumptions. The current section's impossibility results do not apply to Plonk since Plonk's prover produces all polynomial commitments.

[5] We note that [35,36] did not prove (even trapdoor-based) ZK for BatchKZG and SanLinTrick, but the corresponding proofs are not complicated. For completeness, we describe trapdoor-based simulators for all gadgets.

$\mathsf{K}(\mathsf{p}, n)$: $\mathsf{tk} = x \leftarrow_{\$} \mathbb{F}$; $\mathbf{srs} \leftarrow (\mathsf{p}, [1, x, \ldots, x^n]_1, [1, x]_2)$; return $(\mathbf{srs}, \mathsf{tk})$;

$\mathscr{P}_{\mathsf{FS}}(\mathbf{srs}, \mathbb{x} = [f]_1, \mathbb{w} = \mathsf{f})$: // $[f]_1 = [\mathsf{f}(x)]_1$
$\mathfrak{p}_1 \leftarrow \varnothing$; $\mathfrak{v}_1 \leftarrow \mathfrak{z} \leftarrow \mathcal{H}(\mathbf{srs}, \mathbb{x})$; // $\mathfrak{p}_1$ is an empty string

$\bar{f} \leftarrow \mathsf{f}(\mathfrak{z})$; $\mathsf{h}(X) \leftarrow (\mathsf{f}(X) - \bar{f})/(X - \mathfrak{z})$; $\mathfrak{p}_2 \leftarrow (\bar{f}, [h]_1 \leftarrow [\mathsf{h}(x)]_1)$;
return $\pi \leftarrow (\mathfrak{p}_1, \mathfrak{v}_1, \mathfrak{p}_2)$;

$\mathscr{V}_{\mathsf{FS}}(\mathbf{srs}, \mathbb{x} = [f]_1, \mathfrak{z}, \bar{f}, [h]_1)$: check $([f]_1 - \bar{f}[1]_1) \bullet [1]_2 = [h]_1 \bullet [x - \mathfrak{z}]_2$, $\mathfrak{z} = \mathcal{H}(\mathbf{srs}, \mathbb{x})$.

$\mathcal{S}(\mathbf{srs}, \mathsf{td} = x, \mathbb{x} = [f]_1, \bar{f})$: $\mathfrak{p}_1 \leftarrow \varnothing$; $\mathfrak{v}_1 \leftarrow \mathfrak{z} \leftarrow \mathcal{H}(\mathbf{srs}, \mathbb{x})$;

$\mathfrak{p}_2 \leftarrow \left(\bar{f}, [h]_1 \leftarrow \frac{1}{x - \mathfrak{z}}[f - \bar{f}]_1\right)$;
return $\pi \leftarrow (\mathfrak{p}_1, \mathfrak{v}_1, \mathfrak{p}_2)$;

Fig. 5. KZG$_{\mathsf{FS}}$ with the trapdoor-based simulator.

4.1 KZG$_{\mathsf{FS}}$

Consider KZG$_{\mathsf{FS}}$ (i.e., KZG, after applying Fiat-Shamir to compute the evaluation point; see Fig. 5). We state a corollary of known results that KZG$_{\mathsf{FS}}$ has knowledge soundness in the ROM under falsifiable assumptions. We prove that under standard assumptions, KZG$_{\mathsf{FS}}$ has computational 1-UR but is not $\{1\}$-TLZK. In what follows, we highlight the places that depend on the simulator's extra power (either knowing the trapdoor or reprogramming the random oracle).

Theorem 2 (Security of KZG$_{\mathsf{FS}}$**).** *(1) If n-ARSDH is intractable, then* KZG$_{\mathsf{FS}}$ *has knowledge soundness. (2) If KZG is evaluation binding, then* KZG$_{\mathsf{FS}}$ *has computational* 1*-UR. (3) If KZG is evaluation binding, then* KZG$_{\mathsf{FS}}$ *is not* $\{1\}$*-TLZK. More precisely, there does not exist a canonical* $\{1\}$*-trapdoorless simulator* $\tilde{\mathcal{S}}$ *succeeding with a non-negligible probability.*

Proof. Knowledge soundness (Item 1). Since KZG has $(n+1)$-CSS under n-ARSDH (see Fact 1), it follows from [1] that KZG$_{\mathsf{FS}}$ has knowledge soundness.

1-UR (Item 2). Assume that a UR adversary $\mathcal{A}$ outputs $\mathbb{x} = [f]_1$ and two accepting arguments $\pi = (\mathfrak{z}, \bar{f}, [h]_1)$ and $\pi^* = (\mathfrak{z}, \bar{f}^*, [h^*]_1)$, such that $(\bar{f}, [h]_1) \neq (\bar{f}^*, [h^*]_1)$. Since the arguments are accepting, $([f]_1 - \bar{f}[1]_1) \bullet [1]_2 = [h]_1 \bullet [x - \mathfrak{z}]_2$ and $([f]_1 - \bar{f}^*[1]_1) \bullet [1]_2 = [h^*]_1 \bullet [x - \mathfrak{z}]_2$. Subtracting, $(\bar{f}^*[1]_1 - \bar{f}[1]_1) \bullet [1]_2 = [h - h^*]_1 \bullet [x - \mathfrak{z}]_2$. If $\bar{f} \neq \bar{f}^*$, we have broken KZG's evaluation binding. If $\bar{f} = \bar{f}^*$, then $(\bar{f}, [h]_1) \neq (\bar{f}^*, [h^*]_1)$ implies $[h]_1 \neq [h^*]_1$. But then $[0]_1 \bullet [1]_2 = [\neq 0]_1 \bullet [x - \mathfrak{z}]_2$. By non-degeneracy, this implies $[x - \mathfrak{z}]_2 = [0]_2$ and thus $x = \mathfrak{z}$. Knowing the trapdoor $x = \mathfrak{z}$, we can break the evaluation binding by producing an alternative proof for $\mathfrak{z}' = \mathfrak{z} + 1$ (see Item 3). Hence, KZG$_{\mathsf{FS}}$ has computational 1-UR, assuming that KZG is evaluation binding.

Not $\{1\}$-TLZK (Item 3). Assume KZG$_{\mathsf{FS}}$ is $\{1\}$-TLZK. Then, there exists a canonical $\{1\}$-trapdoorless simulator $\tilde{\mathcal{S}}$ (see Definition 1 and 2), such that, given

$\mathscr{B}_{\mathsf{eb}}(\mathsf{ck})$

$\mathbb{w} = \mathsf{f} \leftarrow_{\$} \mathbb{F}_{\leq 1}[X]; \mathbb{x} = [f]_1 \leftarrow [\mathsf{f}(x)]_1;$
$\pi = (\mathfrak{z}, \bar{f}, [h]_1) \leftarrow \tilde{\mathscr{S}}_{\mathsf{true}.\pi}(\mathbb{x}, \mathbb{w});$
if $\mathrm{KZG.Vf}(\mathsf{ck}, [f]_1, \mathfrak{z}, \bar{f}, [h]_1) = 0 \vee \mathsf{f}(\mathfrak{z}) = \bar{f}$ **then return** $\perp$;
elseif $[x]_1 \neq \mathfrak{z}[1]_1$
  $[h']_1 \leftarrow \mathsf{Open}(\mathsf{ck}, [f]_1, \mathfrak{z}, \mathsf{f}) = [(\mathsf{f}(x) - \mathsf{f}(\mathfrak{z}))/(x - \mathfrak{z})]_1;$
  return $([f]_1, \mathfrak{z}, \bar{f}, [h]_1, \mathsf{f}(\mathfrak{z}), [h']_1);$
elseif // $\mathscr{B}_{\mathsf{eb}}$ knows $x = \mathfrak{z}$
  $\mathfrak{z}' \leftarrow \mathfrak{z} + 1; [h_0]_1 \leftarrow \frac{1}{x - \mathfrak{z}'}[\mathsf{f}(x)]_1; [h_1]_1 \leftarrow \frac{1}{x - \mathfrak{z}'}[\mathsf{f}(x) - 1]_1;$
  return $([f]_1, \mathfrak{z}', 0, [h_0]_1, 1, [h_1]_1);$

Fig. 6. KZG's evaluation-binding adversary $\mathscr{B}_{\mathsf{eb}}$ in the proof of Item 3.

as an input $\mathbb{x} = [f]_1 = [\mathsf{f}(x)]_1 \in \mathbb{G}_1$ and witness $\mathbb{w} = \mathsf{f}(X)$, $\tilde{\mathscr{S}}_{\mathsf{true}.\pi}(\mathbb{x}, \mathbb{w})$ outputs $\pi = (\mathfrak{z}, \bar{f}, [h]_1)$, such that the KZG$_{\mathsf{FS}}$ verifier accepts. Since one can build a distinguisher $\mathscr{D}$ that queries $\tilde{\mathscr{S}}$ on any input, the latter must happen for essentially any $\mathbb{x}$. $\tilde{\mathscr{S}}_{\mathsf{true}.\pi}$ uses $\mathbb{w}$ to check that $(\mathbb{x}, \mathbb{w}) \in \mathsf{Rel}$ but $\tilde{\mathscr{S}}(2, \ldots)$ does not use the knowledge of $\mathbb{w}$. In addition, $\tilde{\mathscr{S}}(1, \ldots)$ can ask random oracle queries.

In Fig. 6, we depict a evaluation-binding adversary $\mathscr{B}_{\mathsf{eb}}$. Given $\mathsf{ck} = \mathtt{srs}$, $\mathscr{B}_{\mathsf{eb}}(\mathsf{ck})$ samples $\mathbb{w} = \mathsf{f} \leftarrow_{\$} \mathbb{F}_{\leq 1}[X]$. $\mathscr{B}_{\mathsf{eb}}(\mathsf{ck})$ queries $\tilde{\mathscr{S}}_{\mathsf{true}.\pi}(\mathbb{x} = [f]_1, \mathbb{w} = \mathsf{f})$, where $[f]_1 \leftarrow [\mathsf{f}(x)]_1$. Assume $\tilde{\mathscr{S}}$ returns an accepting $\pi = (\mathfrak{z}, \bar{f}, [h]_1)$. If $x \neq \mathfrak{z}$ (event bad), $\mathscr{B}_{\mathsf{eb}}$ returns $([f]_1, \mathfrak{z}, \bar{f}, [h]_1, \mathsf{f}(\mathfrak{z}), [h']_1)$ for $[h']_1 \leftarrow [(\mathsf{f}(x) - \mathsf{f}(\mathfrak{z}))/(x - \mathfrak{z})]_1$. Otherwise, $\mathscr{B}_{\mathsf{eb}}$ has recovered the KZG trapdoor x, and can use it to (trapdoor-based) simulate a collision by computing (say) opening proofs corresponding to the evaluation point $\mathfrak{z}' = \mathfrak{z} + 1$ and opening values 0 and 1.

Now, $\mathscr{B}_{\mathsf{eb}}$ clearly succeeds when $\mathsf{f}(\mathfrak{z}) \neq \bar{f}$. Moreover, if $x \neq \mathfrak{z}$, then $\Pr[\mathsf{f}(\mathfrak{z}) = \bar{f}] \leq 1/|\mathbb{F}|$ since $\deg(\mathsf{f}) \geq 1$ and $\tilde{\mathscr{S}}(2, \ldots)$ only knows the value of $[\mathsf{f}(x)]_1$. Thus, $\Pr[\tilde{\mathscr{S}} \text{ succeeds}] \leq \Pr[\mathscr{B}_{\mathsf{eb}} \text{ succeeds}] + 1/|\mathbb{F}|$. Thus, the impossibility of TLZK follows from KZG having evaluation binding. □

4.2 BatchKZG$_{\mathsf{FS}}$

Consider the non-interactive BatchKZG$_{\mathsf{FS}}$ protocol in Fig. 7, where the prover commits to m polynomials and provides a single batch proof to open all m polynomials at point $\mathfrak{z}$. Here, $[f_s]_1$ are commitments to polynomials, $\mathfrak{z}$ is the common evaluation point, $\bar{f}_s$ are the evaluations of $[f_s]_1$ at $\mathfrak{z}$, and $[h]_1$ is the batched opening of all m commitments. The BatchKZG verifier checks that $(\sum_{s=1}^{m} v^{s-1}[f_s]_1, \mathfrak{z}, \sum_{s=1}^{m} v^{s-1}\bar{f}_s, [h]_1)$ is an accepting interactive KZG argument and that $\mathfrak{z}$ and v are correctly computed.

Next, we state a corollary that BatchKZG$_{\mathsf{FS}}$ has knowledge soundness in the ROM under falsifiable assumptions. We prove that under standard assumptions, BatchKZG$_{\mathsf{FS}}$ has computational 2-UR but is not $\{1, 2\}$-TLZK.

$\mathsf{K}(\mathsf{p}, n)$: $x \leftarrow_{\$} \mathbb{F}$; return $\mathbf{srs} \leftarrow (\mathsf{p}, [1, x, \ldots, x^n]_1, [1, x]_2)$ and $\mathsf{td} \leftarrow x$;

$\mathcal{P}_{\mathsf{FS}}(\mathbf{srs}, \mathbb{x} = [(f_s)_{s=1}^m]_1, \mathbb{w} = (\mathsf{f}_s(X))_{s=1}^m)$: // $[f_s]_1 \leftarrow [\mathsf{f}_s(x)]_1$

$\mathfrak{p}_1 \leftarrow \varnothing$; $\mathfrak{v}_1 \leftarrow \mathfrak{z} \leftarrow \mathcal{H}(\mathbf{srs}, \mathbb{x})$; // Evaluation point, $\mathfrak{p}_1$ is an empty string

For $s \in [m]$: $\bar{f}_s \leftarrow \mathsf{f}_s(\mathfrak{z})$;

$\mathfrak{p}_2 \leftarrow (\bar{f}_s)_{s=1}^m$; $\mathfrak{v}_2 \leftarrow v \leftarrow \mathcal{H}(\mathbf{srs}, \mathbb{x}, \mathfrak{p}_2)$; // Batch coefficient

$\mathsf{h}(X) \leftarrow \left(\sum_{s=1}^m v^{s-1}(\mathsf{f}_s(X) - \bar{f}_s)\right) / (X - \mathfrak{z})$; $\mathfrak{p}_3 \leftarrow [h]_1 \leftarrow [\mathsf{h}(x)]_1$;

return $\pi \leftarrow (\mathfrak{p}_1, \mathfrak{v}_1, \mathfrak{p}_2, \mathfrak{v}_2, \mathfrak{p}_3)$;

$\mathcal{V}_{\mathsf{FS}}(\mathbf{srs}, \mathbb{x} = [(f_s)_{s=1}^m]_1, \pi)$: check $[\sum_{s=1}^m v^{s-1}(f_s - \bar{f}_s)]_1 \bullet [1]_2 = [h]_1 \bullet [x - \mathfrak{z}]_2$, $\mathfrak{z} = \mathcal{H}(\mathbf{srs}, \mathbb{x})$, and $v = \mathcal{H}(\mathbf{srs}, \mathbb{x}, \mathfrak{p}_2)$;

$\mathcal{S}(\mathbf{srs}, \mathsf{td} = x, \mathbb{x} = [(f_s)_{s=1}^m]_1, (\bar{f}_s)_{s=1}^m)$: $\mathfrak{p}_1 \leftarrow \varnothing$; $\mathfrak{v}_1 \leftarrow \mathfrak{z} \leftarrow \mathcal{H}(\mathbf{srs}, \mathbb{x})$;

$\mathfrak{p}_2 \leftarrow (\bar{f}_s)_{s=1}^m$; $\mathfrak{v}_2 \leftarrow v \leftarrow \mathcal{H}(\mathbf{srs}, \mathbb{x}, \mathfrak{p}_2)$;

$\mathfrak{p}_3 \leftarrow [h]_1 \leftarrow \frac{1}{x - \mathfrak{z}} \cdot [\sum_{s=1}^m v^{s-1}(f_s - \bar{f}_s)]_1$;
return $\pi \leftarrow (\mathfrak{p}_1, \mathfrak{v}_1, \mathfrak{p}_2, \mathfrak{v}_2, \mathfrak{p}_3)$;

Fig. 7. BatchKZG$_{\mathsf{FS}}$ with a trapdoor-based simulator.

Theorem 3 (Security of BatchKZG$_{\mathsf{FS}}$**).** *(1) If KZG has $(n+1)$-CSS, then* BatchKZG$_{\mathsf{FS}}$ *has knowledge soundness. (2) If $(n, 1)$-PDL is hard, then* BatchKZG$_{\mathsf{FS}}$ *has computational 2-UR. (3) If KZG is evaluation binding, then there does not exist a canonical $\{1, 2\}$-trapdoorless simulator $\tilde{\mathcal{S}}$ with a non-negligible success probability. Thus,* BatchKZG$_{\mathsf{FS}}$ *is not $\{1, 2\}$-TLZK.*

Proof. Knowledge soundness (Item 1). Lipmaa, Parisella, and Siim [36] proved that if KZG has $(n+1)$-CSS, then interactive BatchKZG has $(n+1, m)$-CSS. This and [1] imply that BatchKZG$_{\mathsf{FS}}$ has knowledge soundness.

2-UR (Item 2). Assume that a UR adversary $\mathcal{A}$ outputs $\mathbb{x} = [(f_s)_{s=1}^m]_1$ and accepting arguments $\pi = (\mathfrak{z}, (\bar{f}_s)_{s=1}^m, v, [h]_1)$ and $\pi^* = (\mathfrak{z}, (\bar{f}_s)_{s=1}^m, v, [h^*]_1)$, s.t. $[h]_1 \neq [h^*]_1$. Since both arguments accept, subtracting the verification equations from each other, $[0]_T = [h^* - h]_1 \bullet [x - \mathfrak{z}]_2$. Since $h \neq h^*$, non-degeneracy implies $[x - \mathfrak{z}]_2 = [0]_2$ and thus $x = \mathfrak{z}$. The reduction uses the challenge $\mathbf{srs}$ as input, runs $\mathcal{A}$, and outputs $x \leftarrow \mathfrak{z}$ in the $(n, 1)$-PDL game. Thus, we break the PDL assumption with an adversary $\mathcal{B}$, with $\mathsf{Adv}^{\mathrm{ur}}_{\mathrm{BatchKZG}_{\mathsf{FS}}, \mathcal{C}_{\mathsf{wur}}, 2}(\lambda) \leq \mathsf{Adv}^{\mathrm{pdl}}_{n,1,\mathsf{G},\mathcal{B}}(\lambda)$.

Not TLZK (Item 3). Assume BatchKZG$_{\mathsf{FS}}$ is $\{1, 2\}$-TLZK. Then, there exists a canonical $\{1, 2\}$-TLZK simulator $\tilde{\mathcal{S}}$ (see Definition 1), such that, given as an input $\mathbb{x} = [(f_s = \mathsf{f}_s(x))_{s=1}^m]_1 \in \mathbb{G}_1^m$ and witness $(\mathsf{f}_s(X))_{s=1}^m$, $\tilde{\mathcal{S}}_{\mathsf{any}.\pi}(\mathbb{x}, \mathbb{w})$ outputs $\pi = (\mathfrak{z}, (\bar{f}_s)_{s=1}^m, v, [h]_1)$, such that the BatchKZG$_{\mathsf{FS}}$ verifier accepts. Since one can build a distinguisher $\mathcal{D}$ that queries $\tilde{\mathcal{S}}$ on any input, the latter must happen for essentially any $\mathbb{x}$. $\tilde{\mathcal{S}}_{\mathsf{true}.\pi}$ uses $\mathbb{w}$ to check that $(\mathbb{x}, \mathbb{w}) \in \mathsf{Rel}$ but $\tilde{\mathcal{S}}(2, \ldots)$ does not use the knowledge of $\mathbb{w}$. In addition, $\tilde{\mathcal{S}}(1, \ldots)$ can ask random oracle queries.

$\mathscr{B}_{\mathsf{eb}}(\mathsf{ck})$

for $s \in [m]$ **do** $\mathsf{f}_s \leftarrow_\$ \mathbb{F}_{\le 1}[X]$;
$\mathbb{x} \leftarrow [(f_s \leftarrow \mathsf{f}_s(x))_{s=1}^m]_1$; $\mathbb{w} \leftarrow (\mathsf{f}_s)_{s=1}^m$;
$\pi = (\mathfrak{z}, (\bar{f}_s)_{s=1}^m, v, [h]_1) \leftarrow \tilde{\mathscr{S}}_{\mathsf{true}.\pi}(\mathbb{x}, \mathbb{w})$;
$\bar{e} \leftarrow \sum_{s=1}^m v^{s-1} \bar{f}_s$; $\mathsf{e}(X) \leftarrow \sum_{s=1}^m v^{s-1} \mathsf{f}_s(X)$;
if $\mathrm{KZG}.\mathsf{Vf}(\mathsf{ck}, \mathbb{x}, \pi) = 0 \vee \mathsf{e}(\mathfrak{z}) = \bar{e}$ **then return** $\perp$;
elseif $[x]_1 \ne \mathfrak{z}[1]_1$
  $[h']_1 \leftarrow \mathsf{Open}(\mathsf{ck}, [\mathsf{e}(x)]_1, \mathfrak{z}, \mathsf{e}) = [(\mathsf{e}(x) - \mathsf{e}(\mathfrak{z})) / (x - \mathfrak{z})]_1$;
  return $([\mathsf{e}(x)]_1, \mathfrak{z}, \bar{e}, [h]_1, \mathsf{e}(\mathfrak{z}), [h']_1)$;
else // $\mathscr{B}_{\mathsf{eb}}$ knows $x = \mathfrak{z}$
  $\mathfrak{z}' \leftarrow \mathfrak{z} + 1$; $[h_0]_1 \leftarrow \frac{1}{x - \mathfrak{z}'}[\mathsf{e}(x)]_1$; $[h_1]_1 \leftarrow \frac{1}{x - \mathfrak{z}'}[\mathsf{e}(x) - 1]_1$;
  return $([\mathsf{e}(x)]_1, \mathfrak{z}', 0, [h_0]_1, 1, [h_1]_1)$;

Fig. 8. KZG's evaluation-binding adversary $\mathscr{B}_{\mathsf{eb}}$ in the proof of Item 3.

In Fig. 8, we depict a evaluation-binding adversary $\mathscr{B}_{\mathsf{eb}}$. Given $\mathsf{ck} = \mathtt{srs}$, $\mathscr{B}_{\mathsf{eb}}(\mathsf{ck})$ samples $\mathsf{f}_s \leftarrow_\$ \mathbb{F}_{\le 1}[X]$, $s \in [m]$. $\mathscr{B}_{\mathsf{eb}}$ sets $\mathbb{x} \leftarrow [(f_s)_{s=1}^m]_1$ and $\mathbb{w} \leftarrow (\mathsf{f}_s)_{s=1}^m$ for $[f_s]_1 \leftarrow [\mathsf{f}_s(x)]_1$. $\mathscr{B}_{\mathsf{eb}}(\mathsf{ck})$ queries $\tilde{\mathscr{S}}_{\mathsf{true}.\pi}(\mathbb{x}, \mathbb{w})$. Assume $\tilde{\mathscr{S}}$ returns an accepting $\pi = (\mathfrak{z}, (\bar{f}_s)_{s=1}^m, v, [h]_1)$. Let $\bar{e} \leftarrow \sum_{s=1}^m v^{s-1} \bar{f}_s$ and $\mathsf{e}(X) \leftarrow \sum_{s=1}^m v^{s-1} \mathsf{f}_s(X)$. If $x \ne \mathfrak{z}$ (event bad), $\mathscr{B}_{\mathsf{eb}}$ returns $(\sum_{s=1}^m v^{s-1}[f_s]_1, \mathfrak{z}, \bar{e}, [h]_1, \mathsf{e}(\mathfrak{z}), [h']_1)$ for $[h']_1 \leftarrow [(\mathsf{e}(x) - \mathsf{e}(\mathfrak{z}))/(x - \mathfrak{z})]_1$. Otherwise, $\mathscr{B}_{\mathsf{eb}}$ has recovered the KZG trapdoor x and can use it to (trapdoor-based) simulate a collision by computing (say) opening proofs corresponding to the evaluation point $\mathfrak{z}' = \mathfrak{z} + 1$ and opening values 0 and 1. We need to choose $\mathfrak{z}' \ne \mathfrak{z}$ since otherwise $[1/(x - \mathfrak{z}')]_1$ is not invertible.

Now, $\mathscr{B}_{\mathsf{eb}}$ clearly succeeds when $\mathsf{e}(\mathfrak{z}) \ne \bar{e}$. Moreover, if $x \ne \mathfrak{z}$, then $\Pr[\mathsf{e}(\mathfrak{z}) = \bar{e}] \le (m-1)/|\mathbb{F}|$ since $\deg(\mathsf{f}_s) \ge 1$ and, for each s, $\tilde{\mathscr{S}}(2, \dots)$ only knows the value of $[\mathsf{f}_s(x)]_1$. Thus, $\Pr[\tilde{\mathscr{S}} \text{ succeeds}] \le \Pr[\mathscr{B}_{\mathsf{eb}} \text{ succeeds}] + (m-1)/|\mathbb{F}|$. Thus, the impossibility of TLZK follows from KZG having evaluation binding. □

4.3 LinTrick and SanLinTrick

In many zk-SNARKs, a natural subtask[6] is to prove that $\sum_{t=1}^{n_b} \mathsf{g}_t(\mathbf{a}(X)) \mathsf{d}_t(X) = 0$, where $\mathbf{g}(X) = (\mathsf{g}_t(X))_{t=1}^{n_b}$ are published polynomials, $\mathbf{a}(X) = (\mathsf{a}_s(X))_{s=1}^{n_a}$, and $\mathsf{a}_s(X)$ (for $s \in [n_a]$) and $\mathsf{d}_t(X)$ (for $t \in [n_b]$) are committed polynomials. For example, in the R1CS quadratic check, $n_b = 2$, $n_a = 1$, $\mathsf{g}_1(\mathbf{a}(X)) = \mathsf{a}_1(X)$, and $\mathsf{g}_2(\mathbf{a}(X)) = -1$. One checks that $\mathsf{a}_1(X)\mathsf{d}_1(X) - \mathsf{d}_2(X) = 0$.

The most efficient known solution to this task is the linearization trick (LinTrick, [6,14,20]). Using LinTrick, one performs a single batch-opening at a random point $\mathfrak{z}$, opening (1) all $\mathsf{a}_s(X)$, $s \in [n_a]$, to $\bar{a}_s := \mathsf{a}_s(\mathfrak{z})$, and (2) the *linearization polynomial* $\Lambda(X) := \sum_{t=1}^{n_b} \mathsf{g}_t(\bar{\mathbf{a}}) \mathsf{d}_t(X)$ to 0. (See Fig. 9).

[6] Here, we follow the formalism of [14] closely. One can easily generalize this framework to allow for more general expressions.

$\mathsf{K}(\mathsf{p}, n)$: $x \leftarrow_\$ \mathbb{F}$; return $\mathbf{srs} \leftarrow (\mathsf{p}, [1, x, \ldots, x^n]_1, [1, x]_2)$ and $\mathsf{td} \leftarrow x$;

$\mathscr{P}_{\mathsf{FS}}(\mathbf{srs}, \mathbb{x} = [(a_s)_{s=1}^{n_a}, (d_t)_{t=1}^{n_b}]_1, \mathbb{w} = ((\mathsf{a}_s(X))_{s=1}^{n_a}, (\mathsf{d}_t(X))_{t=1}^{n_b}))$:

// $[a_s]_1 = [\mathsf{a}_s(x)]_1$, $[d_t]_1 = [\mathsf{d}_t(x)]_1$

$\mathfrak{p}_1 \leftarrow \varnothing$; $\mathfrak{v}_1 \leftarrow \mathfrak{z} \leftarrow \mathscr{H}(\mathbf{srs}, \mathbb{x})$; // $\mathfrak{p}_1$ is an empty string

For $s \in [n_a]$: $\bar{a}_s \leftarrow \mathsf{a}_s(\mathfrak{z})$;

$\mathfrak{p}_2 \leftarrow (\bar{a}_s)_{s=1}^{n_a}$; $\mathfrak{v}_2 \leftarrow \gamma \leftarrow \mathscr{H}(\mathbf{srs}, \mathbb{x}, \mathfrak{p}_2)$;

$\mathfrak{p}_3 \leftarrow \bar{d} \leftarrow \sum_{t=1}^{n_b} \gamma^{t-1} \mathsf{d}_t(\mathfrak{z})$; $\mathfrak{v}_3 \leftarrow \beta \leftarrow \mathscr{H}(\mathbf{srs}, \mathbb{x}, \mathfrak{p}_2, \mathfrak{p}_3)$;

$\mathsf{h}^*(X) \leftarrow \sum_{s=1}^{n_a} \beta^{s-1}(\mathsf{a}_s(X) - \bar{a}_s) + \beta^{n_a} \cdot \sum_{t=1}^{n_b} \mathsf{g}_t(\mathbf{a}(X))\mathsf{d}_t(X)$
$\quad + \beta^{n_a+1} \cdot \left(\sum_{t=1}^{n_b} \gamma^{t-1}\mathsf{d}_t(X) - \bar{d}\right)$;

$\mathsf{h}(X) \leftarrow \mathsf{h}^*(X)/(X - \mathfrak{z})$; $\mathfrak{p}_4 \leftarrow [h]_1 \leftarrow [\mathsf{h}(x)]_1$;

return $\pi \leftarrow (\mathfrak{p}_1, \mathfrak{v}_1, \mathfrak{p}_2, \mathfrak{v}_2, \mathfrak{p}_3, \mathfrak{v}_3, \mathfrak{p}_4)$;

$\mathscr{V}_{\mathsf{FS}}(\mathbf{srs}, \pi)$: Check $\mathfrak{z} = \mathscr{H}(\mathbf{srs}, \mathbb{x})$, $\gamma = \mathscr{H}(\mathbf{srs}, \mathbb{x}, \mathfrak{p}_2)$, $\beta = \mathscr{H}(\mathbf{srs}, \mathbb{x}, \mathfrak{p}_2, \mathfrak{p}_3)$, and
$\left[\sum_{s=1}^{n_a} \beta^{s-1}(a_s - \bar{a}_s) + \beta^{n_a} \sum_{t=1}^{n_b} \mathsf{g}_t(\bar{\mathbf{a}}) d_t + \beta^{n_a+1}\left(\sum_{t=1}^{n_b} \gamma^{t-1} d_t - \bar{d}\right)\right]_1 \bullet$
$[1]_2 = [h]_1 \bullet [x - \mathfrak{z}]_2$;

$\mathscr{S}(\mathbf{srs}, \mathsf{td} = x, \mathbb{x} = [(a_s)_{s=1}^{n_a}, (d_t)_{t=1}^{n_b}]_1, (\bar{a}_s)_{s=1}^{n_a}, \bar{d})$: $\mathfrak{p}_1 \leftarrow \varnothing$; $\mathfrak{v}_1 \leftarrow \mathfrak{z} \leftarrow \mathscr{H}(\mathbf{srs}, \mathbb{x})$;

$\mathfrak{p}_2 \leftarrow (\bar{a}_s)_{s=1}^{n_a}$; $\gamma \leftarrow \mathscr{H}(\mathbf{srs}, \mathbb{x}, \mathfrak{p}_2)$; $\mathfrak{v}_2 \leftarrow \gamma$;

$\mathfrak{p}_3 \leftarrow \bar{d}$; $\beta \leftarrow \mathscr{H}(\mathbf{srs}, \mathbb{x}, \mathfrak{p}_2, \mathfrak{p}_3)$; $\mathfrak{v}_3 \leftarrow \beta$;

$\mathfrak{p}_4 \leftarrow [h]_1 \leftarrow \frac{1}{x - \mathfrak{z}}[\sum_{s=1}^{n_a} \beta^{s-1}(a_s - \bar{a}_s) + \beta^{n_a} \sum_{t=1}^{n_b} \mathsf{g}_t(\bar{\mathbf{a}}) d_t$
$\quad + \beta^{n_a+1}\left(\sum_{t=1}^{n_b} \gamma^{t-1} d_t - \bar{d}\right)]_1$;

$\pi \leftarrow (\mathfrak{p}_1, \mathfrak{v}_1, \mathfrak{p}_2, \mathfrak{v}_2, \mathfrak{p}_3, \mathfrak{v}_3, \mathfrak{p}_4)$; return π;

Fig. 9. LinTrick$_{\mathsf{FS}}$ and SanLinTrick$_{\mathsf{FS}}$ (without and with highlighted parts, resp.) with a trapdoor-based simulator.

Since in the AGM, one can extract polynomials $\mathsf{a}_s(X)$ and $\mathsf{d}_t(X)$ from their commitments, LinTrick has knowledge soundness in the AGM [6]. Lipmaa, Parisella, and Siim [34] showed that, generally, LinTrick does not have knowledge soundness in the AGMOS. Faonio, Fiore, and Russo [14] proved that LinTrick has knowledge soundness in the AGMOS iff $\mathsf{g}_t(\mathbf{a}(X))$ are linearly independent. They showed that in Plonk, $\mathsf{g}_t(\mathbf{a}(X))$ are linearly independent, thus justifying the use of LinTrick. Unfortunately, [36] proved that if discrete logarithm is hard, LinTrick cannot have CSS in the standard model.

Lipmaa, Parisella, and Siim [36] constructed SanLinTrick (see Fig. 9), a sanitized variant of LinTrick.[7] In SanLinTrick, the prover batch-opens a random linear combination of $\mathsf{d}_t(X)$ (by using a batching variable γ), making the attack of [14,34] inapplicable. [36] proved SanLinTrick has CSS for any choice of $\mathsf{a}_s(X)$ and $\mathsf{d}_t(X)$. We highlight the parts that are only present in SanLinTrick. The

[7] SanLinTrick has one extra round compared to LinTrick. To make comparing two protocols easier, we assume that LinTrick misses the intermediate round (i.e., no $\mathfrak{v}_2$ or $\mathfrak{p}_3$ is sent).

$\mathsf{LinTrick}_{\mathsf{FS}}$ / $\mathsf{SanLinTrick}_{\mathsf{FS}}$ verifier essentially checks that

$$\left(\begin{array}{c}\sum_{s=1}^{n_a}\beta^{s-1}[a_s]_1+\beta^{n_a}\sum_{t=1}^{n_b}\mathsf{g}_t(\bar{\mathbf{a}})[d_t]_1+\beta^{n_a+1}\left(\sum_{t=1}^{n_b}\gamma^{t-1}d_t-\bar{d}\right),\\ \mathfrak{z},\sum_{s=1}^{n_a}\beta^{s-1}\bar{a}_s+\beta^{n_a}\sum_{t=1}^{n_b}\mathsf{g}_t(\bar{\mathbf{a}})d_t,[h]_1\end{array}\right)$$

is an accepting KZG transcript and that $\mathfrak{z}$, γ, and β are correctly computed.

Next, we state a corollary of known results that $\mathsf{SanLinTrick}_{\mathsf{FS}}$ has knowledge soundness in the ROM under falsifiable assumptions. We also prove that under standard assumptions, $\mathsf{LinTrick}_{\mathsf{FS}}$ (resp, $\mathsf{SanLinTrick}_{\mathsf{FS}}$) has 2-UR (resp., 3-UR) but is not $\{1,2\}$-TLZK (resp., $\{1,2,3\}$-TLZK).

Theorem 4 (Security of $\mathsf{LinTrick}_{\mathsf{FS}}$ / $\mathsf{SanLinTrick}_{\mathsf{FS}}$**).** *(1) If KZG has $(n+1)$-CSS, then* $\mathsf{SanLinTrick}_{\mathsf{FS}}$ *has knowledge soundness. (2) If $(n,1)$-PDL is hard, then* $\mathsf{LinTrick}_{\mathsf{FS}}$ *(resp.,* $\mathsf{SanLinTrick}_{\mathsf{FS}}$*) has computational 2-UR (resp., 3-UR). (3) If KZG is evaluation binding, then* $\mathsf{LinTrick}_{\mathsf{FS}}$ *(resp.,* $\mathsf{SanLinTrick}_{\mathsf{FS}}$*) is not $\{1,2\}$-TLZK (resp., $\{1,2,3\}$-TLZK). More precisely, there does not exist a canonical $\{1,2\}$ (resp., $\{1,2,3\}$) trapdoorless simulator $\tilde{\mathcal{S}}$ succeeding with a non-negligible probability.*

Proof. KS (Item 1). Lipmaa, Parisella, and Siim [36] proved that if KZG has $(n+1)$-CSS, then interactive $\mathsf{SanLinTrick}$ has $(\max(n_{\mathsf{g}},n)+1,n_b,n_a+2)$-CSS for $n_{\mathsf{g}}:=\max_t\deg(\mathsf{g}_t(\mathbf{a}(X)))$. This and [1] imply that non-interactive $\mathsf{SanLinTrick}_{\mathsf{FS}}$ has knowledge soundness.

UR (Item 2). Assume that a UR adversary $\mathcal{A}$ outputs $\mathbb{x}=[(a_s)_{s=1}^{n_a},(d_t)_{t=1}^{n_b}]_1$ and two accepting arguments $\pi=(\mathfrak{z},(\bar{a}_s)_{s=1}^{n_a},\gamma,\bar{d},\beta,[h]_1)$ and $\pi^*=(\mathfrak{z},(\bar{a}_s)_{s=1}^{n_a},\gamma,\bar{d},\beta,[h^*]_1)$, such that $[h]_1\neq[h^*]_1$. Since both arguments are accepting, subtracting the verification equations yields $[0]_T=[h^*-h]_1\bullet[x-\mathfrak{z}]_2$. Since $h\neq h^*$, non-degeneracy implies $[x-\mathfrak{z}]_2=[0]_2$ and thus $x=\mathfrak{z}$. The reduction uses the challenge $\mathtt{srs}$ as input, runs $\mathcal{A}$, and outputs $x\leftarrow\mathfrak{z}$ in the $(n,1)$-PDL game. Thus, we have broken the PDL assumption with an adversary $\mathcal{B}$, with $\mathsf{Adv}^{\mathrm{ur}}_{\Pi_{\mathsf{FS}},\mathcal{C}_{\mathsf{wur}},2}(\lambda)\leq\mathsf{Adv}^{\mathrm{pdl}}_{n,1,\mathsf{G},\mathcal{B}}(\lambda)$, $\Pi\in\{\mathsf{LinTrick},\mathsf{SanLinTrick}\}$.

Not TLZK (Item 3). We postpone the proof of this case to the final version [33]. □

5 Simulation Extractability of Plonk

Next, we prove that the fully optimized Plonk is $\{2\}$-TLZK and $\geq$2-WUR. Since it is also knowledge-sound, it is thus simulation extractable (in the ROM under falsifiable assumptions). While Plonk uses LinTrick internally, using Plonk's structure, we prove that Plonk is trapdoorless zero-knowledge. This is possible since Plonk's prover creates all polynomial commitments and then uses the gadgets in a white-box manner, with the gadget witnesses being known to the Plonk prover. On the other hand, the impossibility proofs of Sect. 4 were based on the fact that the prover does not know the witnesses.

5.1 Preliminaries: Plonk

In this subsection, we describe Plonk, following the notation of [20]. Assume $\mathbb{F}$ contains a primitive nth root of unity ω. Let $\mathbb{H}$ be a multiplicative subgroup of $\mathbb{F}$ generated by ω, $\mathbb{H} = \{1, \omega, \ldots, \omega^{n-1}\}$. Let $\mathsf{Z}_{\mathbb{H}}(X) := X^n - 1$ be the vanishing polynomial on $\mathbb{H}$. For $i \in [n]$, $\mathsf{L}_i(X)$ denotes the ith Lagrange polynomial on $\mathbb{H}$. Namely, $\mathsf{L}_i(X)$ is the unique polynomial of degree at most $n - 1$ such that $\mathsf{L}_i(\omega^i) = 1$ and $\mathsf{L}_i(\omega^j) = 0$ for all $j \in [n] \setminus \{i\}$. We assume that the number of constraints is upper bounded by n. Let k_1 and k_2 be such that $\mathbb{H}$, $k_1 \cdot \mathbb{H}$, and $k_2 \cdot \mathbb{H}$ are different cosets of $\mathbb{H}$. Let $\sigma : [3n] \to [3n]$ be a public permutation.

Polynomials That Define A Specific Circuit. The following polynomials and the integer n uniquely define the circuit. First, $\mathsf{q_M}(X)$, $\mathsf{q_L}(X)$, $\mathsf{q_R}(X)$, $\mathsf{q_O}(X)$, $\mathsf{q_C}(X)$ are selector polynomials that define the circuit's arithmetization. Second, $\mathsf{S}_{\sigma 1}(X)$, $\mathsf{S}_{\sigma 2}(X)$, and $\mathsf{S}_{\sigma 3}(X)$ are permutation polynomials that fix the wiring of the circuit. See [20] for more information.

The SNARK Relation. Denote $\mathsf{q_X}_i := \mathsf{q_X}(\omega^i)$ for the polynomials defined above. Define $\mathsf{plonkpar} = \{\mathsf{q_M}(X), \mathsf{q_L}(X), \mathsf{q_R}(X), \mathsf{q_O}(X), \mathsf{q_C}(X), \mathsf{S}_{\sigma 1}(X), \mathsf{S}_{\sigma 2}(X), \mathsf{S}_{\sigma 3}(X)\}$, where the polynomials satisfy the above conditions. Thus, the set of polynomials $\mathsf{plonkpar}$ defines the circuit. Given $\ell \leq n$ and $\mathsf{plonkpar}$, we wish to prove statements of knowledge for the relation $\mathsf{Rel}_{\mathsf{plonkpar}} \subset \mathbb{F}^{\ell} \times \mathbb{F}^{3n-\ell}$ containing all pairs $\mathbb{x} = (w_i)_{i=1}^{\ell}$, $\mathbb{w} = (w_i)_{i=\ell+1}^{3n}$ such that

1. For $i \in [\ell]$: $\mathsf{q_M}_i = \mathsf{q_R}_i = \mathsf{q_O}_i = \mathsf{q_C}_i = 0$ and $\mathsf{q_L}_i = -1$, which guarantees $\mathsf{q_M}_i w_i w_{n+i} + \mathsf{q_L}_i w_i + \mathsf{q_R}_i w_{n+i} + \mathsf{q_O}_i w_{2n+i} + \mathsf{q_C}_i = -w_i$. We see later that this is needed to force the prover to use the correct $\mathbb{x}$.
2. For all $i \in [\ell + 1, n]$: $\mathsf{q_M}_i w_i w_{n+i} + \mathsf{q_L}_i w_i + \mathsf{q_R}_i w_{n+i} + \mathsf{q_O}_i w_{2n+i} + \mathsf{q_C}_i = 0$.
3. For all $i \in [3n]$: $w_i = w_{\sigma(i)}$.

Plonk's Description

Common Preprocessed Input: n, $[1, x, \ldots, x^{n+5}]_1$, $\mathsf{q_M}(X)$, $\mathsf{q_L}(X)$, $\mathsf{q_R}(X)$, $\mathsf{q_O}(X)$, $\mathsf{q_C}(X)$, $\mathsf{S}_{\sigma 1}(X)$, $\mathsf{S}_{\sigma 2}(X)$, $\mathsf{S}_{\sigma 3}(X)$.[8]

Verifier preprocessed input: $[q_\mathsf{M}]_1 := [\mathsf{q_M}(x)]_1$, $[q_\mathsf{L}]_1 := [\mathsf{q_L}(x)]_1$, $[q_\mathsf{R}]_1 := [\mathsf{q_R}(x)]_1$, $[q_\mathsf{O}]_1 := [\mathsf{q_O}(x)]_1$, $[q_\mathsf{C}]_1 := [\mathsf{q_C}(x)]_1$, $[s_{\sigma 1}]_1 := [\mathsf{S}_{\sigma 1}(x)]_1$, $[s_{\sigma 2}]_1 := [\mathsf{S}_{\sigma 2}(x)]_1$, $[s_{\sigma 3}]_1 := [\mathsf{S}_{\sigma 3}(x)]_1$, $[1, x]_2$,

Public input: $(\ell, (w_i)_{i=1}^{\ell})$.

First round. $\mathcal{P}(\mathtt{srs}, (w_i)_{i=1}^{3n})$ does: $(b_1, \ldots, b_9) \leftarrow_{\$} \mathbb{F}$; $\mathsf{a}(X) \leftarrow \sum_{i=1}^{n} w_i \mathsf{L}_i(X) + (b_1 X + b_2)\mathsf{Z}_{\mathbb{H}}(X)$; $\mathsf{b}(X) \leftarrow \sum_{i=1}^{n} w_{n+i} \mathsf{L}_i(X) + (b_3 X + b_4)\mathsf{Z}_{\mathbb{H}}(X)$; $\mathsf{c}(X) \leftarrow \sum_{i=1}^{n} w_{2n+i} \mathsf{L}_i(X) + (b_5 X + b_6)\mathsf{Z}_{\mathbb{H}}(X)$; Set $\mathfrak{p}_1 \leftarrow [\mathsf{a}(x), \mathsf{b}(x), \mathsf{c}(x)]_1$ and $\mathfrak{v}_1 \leftarrow (\beta, \gamma)$ for $\beta \leftarrow \mathcal{H}(\mathtt{srs}, \mathbb{x}, \mathfrak{p}_1, 0)$ and $\gamma \leftarrow \mathcal{H}(\mathtt{srs}, \mathbb{x}, \mathfrak{p}_1, 1)$.

---

[8] Given point values $(q_{\mathsf{X}i})_{i=1}^{n}$ one reconstructs $\mathsf{q_X}(X)$ via $\mathsf{q_X}(X) = \sum_{i=1}^{n} q_{\mathsf{X}i} \mathsf{L}_i(X)$.

Second round. $\mathscr{P}$ computes $\mathsf{z}(X) \leftarrow \mathsf{L}_1(X) + \sum_{i=1}^{n-1} \left(\prod_{j=1}^{i} \frac{(w_j+\beta\omega^j+\gamma)(w_{n+j}+\beta k_1\omega^j+\gamma)(w_{2n+j}+\beta k_2\omega^j+\gamma)}{(w_j+\beta \mathsf{S}_{\sigma 1}(\omega^j)+\gamma)(w_{n+j}+\beta \mathsf{S}_{\sigma 2}(\omega^j)+\gamma)(w_{2n+j}+\beta \mathsf{S}_{\sigma 3}(\omega^j)+\gamma)} \right) \mathsf{L}_{i+1}(X) + (b_7X^2 + b_8X + b_9)\mathsf{Z}_{\mathbb{H}}(X)$; Set $\mathfrak{p}_2 \leftarrow [\mathsf{z}(x)]_1$ and $\mathfrak{v}_2 \leftarrow \alpha \leftarrow \mathscr{H}(\mathtt{srs}, \mathtt{x}, \mathfrak{p}|_2)$;

Third round. The prover does the following. Let $\mathsf{PI}(X) = \sum_{i=1}^{\ell} w_i \mathsf{L}_i(X)$ be the public input polynomial. Compute

$$
\begin{aligned}
\mathsf{F}_0(X) &:= \mathsf{a}(X)\mathsf{b}(X)\mathsf{q_M}(X) + \mathsf{a}(X)\mathsf{q_L}(X) + \mathsf{b}(X)\mathsf{q_R}(X) + \mathsf{c}(X)\mathsf{q_O}(X) + \mathsf{PI}(X) + \mathsf{q_C}(X)\\
\mathsf{F}_{10}(X) &:= (\mathsf{a}(X) + \beta X + \gamma)(\mathsf{b}(X) + \beta k_1 X + \gamma)(\mathsf{c}(X) + \beta k_2 X + \gamma)\\
\mathsf{F}_{11}(X) &:= (\mathsf{a}(X) + \beta \mathsf{S}_{\sigma 1}(X) + \gamma)(\mathsf{b}(X) + \beta \mathsf{S}_{\sigma 2}(X) + \gamma)(\mathsf{c}(X) + \beta \mathsf{S}_{\sigma 3}(X) + \gamma)\\
\mathsf{F}_1(X) &:= \mathsf{F}_{10}(X)\mathsf{z}(X) - \mathsf{F}_{11}(X)\mathsf{z}(X\omega) \ , \\
\mathsf{F}_2(X) &:= (\mathsf{z}(X) - 1)\mathsf{L}_1(X)\\
\mathsf{F}(X) &:= \mathsf{F}_0(X) + \alpha \mathsf{F}_1(X) + \alpha^2 \mathsf{F}_2(X) \ , \\
\mathsf{t}(X) &:= \tfrac{\mathsf{F}(X)}{\mathsf{Z}_{\mathbb{H}}(X)} \ .
\end{aligned}
\tag{2}
$$

Split $\mathsf{t}(X)$ into polynomials $\mathsf{t}'_{\mathsf{lo}}(X), \mathsf{t}'_{\mathsf{mid}}(X)$ (of degree $< n$) and $\mathsf{t}'_{\mathsf{hi}}(X)$ (of degree $\leq n + 5$), such that $\mathsf{t}(X) = \mathsf{t}'_{\mathsf{lo}}(X) + X^n \mathsf{t}'_{\mathsf{mid}}(X) + X^{2n} \mathsf{t}'_{\mathsf{hi}}(X)$; $b_{10}, b_{11} \leftarrow_{\$} \mathbb{F}$; $\mathsf{t}_{\mathsf{lo}}(X) \leftarrow \mathsf{t}'_{\mathsf{lo}}(X) + b_{10}X^n$, $\mathsf{t}_{\mathsf{mid}}(X) := \mathsf{t}'_{\mathsf{mid}}(X) - b_{10} + b_{11}X^n$; $\mathsf{t}_{\mathsf{hi}}(X) \leftarrow \mathsf{t}'_{\mathsf{hi}}(X) - b_{11}$. Clearly, $\mathsf{t}(X) = \mathsf{t}_{\mathsf{lo}}(X) + X^n \mathsf{t}_{\mathsf{mid}}(X) + X^{2n} \mathsf{t}_{\mathsf{hi}}(X)$. Set $\mathfrak{p}_3 \leftarrow [\mathsf{t}_{\mathsf{lo}}(x), \mathsf{t}_{\mathsf{mid}}(x), \mathsf{t}_{\mathsf{hi}}(x)]_1$ and $\mathfrak{v}_3 \leftarrow \mathfrak{z} \leftarrow \mathscr{H}(\mathtt{srs}, \mathtt{x}, \mathfrak{p}|_3)$.

Fourth round. $\mathscr{P}$ does: $\bar{a} \leftarrow \mathsf{a}(\mathfrak{z})$; $\bar{b} \leftarrow \mathsf{b}(\mathfrak{z})$; $\bar{c} \leftarrow \mathsf{c}(\mathfrak{z})$; $\bar{s}_{\sigma 1} \leftarrow \mathsf{S}_{\sigma 1}(\mathfrak{z})$; $\bar{s}_{\sigma 2} \leftarrow \mathsf{S}_{\sigma 2}(\mathfrak{z})$; $\bar{z}_\omega \leftarrow \mathsf{z}(\mathfrak{z}\omega)$; Set $\mathfrak{p}_4 \leftarrow (\bar{a}, \bar{b}, \bar{c}, \bar{s}_{\sigma 1}, \bar{s}_{\sigma 2}, \bar{z}_\omega)$. Set $\mathfrak{v}_4 \leftarrow v \leftarrow \mathscr{H}(\mathtt{srs}, \mathtt{x}, \mathfrak{p}|_4)$.

Fifth round. Prover does the following.

$$
\begin{aligned}
\Lambda_0(X) &\leftarrow \bar{a}\bar{b} \cdot \mathsf{q_M}(X) + \bar{a} \cdot \mathsf{q_L}(X) + \bar{b} \cdot \mathsf{q_R}(X) + \bar{c} \cdot \mathsf{q_O}(X) + \mathsf{PI}(\mathfrak{z}) + \mathsf{q_C}(X) \ , \\
\Lambda_{10} &\leftarrow (\bar{a} + \beta\mathfrak{z} + \gamma)(\bar{b} + \beta k_1 \mathfrak{z} + \gamma)(\bar{c} + \beta k_2 \mathfrak{z} + \gamma)\\
\Lambda_{11} &\leftarrow (\bar{a} + \beta \bar{s}_{\sigma 1} + \gamma)(\bar{b} + \beta \bar{s}_{\sigma 2} + \gamma)(\bar{c} + \beta \cdot \mathsf{S}_{\sigma 3}(X) + \gamma) \ , \\
\Lambda_1(X) &\leftarrow \Lambda_{10}\mathsf{z}(X) - \Lambda_{11}\bar{z}_\omega \ , \\
\Lambda_2(X) &\leftarrow (\mathsf{z}(X) - 1)\mathsf{L}_1(\mathfrak{z}) \ , \\
\mathsf{r}(X) &\leftarrow \Lambda_0(X) + \alpha\Lambda_1(X) + \alpha^2\Lambda_2(X)\\
&\quad - \mathsf{Z}_{\mathbb{H}}(\mathfrak{z}) \cdot (\mathsf{t}_{\mathsf{lo}}(X) + \mathfrak{z}^n \mathsf{t}_{\mathsf{mid}}(X) + \mathfrak{z}^{2n}\mathsf{t}_{\mathsf{hi}}(X)) \ .
\end{aligned}
\tag{3}
$$

Let $\mathsf{h}^*(X) \leftarrow \mathsf{r}(X) + v\mathsf{a}(X) + v^2\mathsf{b}(X) + v^3\mathsf{c}(X) + v^4\mathsf{S}_{\sigma 1}(X) + v^5\mathsf{S}_{\sigma 2}(X)$; $\bar{h} \leftarrow v\bar{a} + v^2\bar{b} + v^3\bar{c} + v^4\bar{s}_{\sigma 1} + v^5\bar{s}_{\sigma 2}$; $\mathsf{W}_{\mathfrak{z}}(X) \leftarrow (\mathsf{h}^*(X) - \bar{h})/(X - \mathfrak{z})$; $\mathsf{W}_{\mathfrak{z}\omega}(X) = (\mathsf{z}(X) - \bar{z}_\omega)/(X - \mathfrak{z}\omega)$; $[W_{\mathfrak{z}}]_1 \leftarrow [\mathsf{W}_{\mathfrak{z}}(x)]_1$; $[W_{\mathfrak{z}\omega}]_1 \leftarrow [\mathsf{W}_{\mathfrak{z}\omega}(x)]_1$; Set $\mathfrak{p}_5 \leftarrow [W_{\mathfrak{z}}, W_{\mathfrak{z}\omega}]_1$.

Send $\pi \leftarrow (\mathfrak{p}_1, \mathfrak{v}_1, \mathfrak{p}_2, \mathfrak{v}_2, \mathfrak{p}_3, \mathfrak{v}_3, \mathfrak{p}_4, \mathfrak{v}_4, \mathfrak{p}_5)$ to the verifier. Note that $\pi = ([a, b, c]_1; \beta, \gamma; [z]_1; \alpha; [t_{lo}, t_{mid}, t_{hi}]_1; \mathfrak{z}; \bar{a}, \bar{b}, \bar{c}, \bar{s}_{\sigma 1}, \bar{s}_{\sigma 2}, \bar{z}_\omega; v; [W_{\mathfrak{z}}, W_{\mathfrak{z}\omega}]_1)$.

Verification algorithm. We describe Plonk's verification algorithm in Fig. 10. For the sake of simplicity, we describe a more readable variant of the fully optimized Plonk from [20]. (It can be re-optimized to obtain [20]'s description).

Fact 2 (*[36]*). *Let* $n \in \mathsf{poly}(\lambda)$, $\kappa_{\text{kzg}} := n+5$, $\boldsymbol{\kappa}_{\text{Plonk}} = (\kappa_\beta = 3n+1, \kappa_\gamma = 3n+1, \kappa_\alpha = 3, \kappa_{\mathfrak{z}} = 4\kappa_{\text{kzg}} + 1, \kappa_v^{\text{Plonk}} = 6)$. *Let* $\mathsf{par}_n = (m, n_\psi, n_1, n_S, (\psi_k(X))_{k=1}^m)$,

$\mathcal{V}_{\mathsf{FS}}(\mathbf{srs}, \mathbb{x}, \pi)$:
1. $\mathsf{PI}(\mathfrak{z}) \leftarrow \sum_{i \in [\ell]} w_i \mathsf{L}_i(\mathfrak{z})$;
2. Check $\beta = \mathcal{H}(\mathbf{srs}, \mathbb{x}, \mathfrak{p}_1, 0)$, $\gamma = \mathcal{H}(\mathbf{srs}, \mathbb{x}, \mathfrak{p}_1, 1)$, $\alpha = \mathcal{H}(\mathbf{srs}, \mathbb{x}, \mathfrak{p}|_2)$, $\mathfrak{z} = \mathcal{H}(\mathbf{srs}, \mathbb{x}, \mathfrak{p}|_3)$, and $v = \mathcal{H}(\mathbf{srs}, \mathbb{x}, \mathfrak{p}|_4)$.
3. $u \leftarrow \mathcal{H}(\mathbf{srs}, \mathbb{x}, \mathfrak{p}|_5)$.
4. Compute $[\Lambda_i]_1$ according to Eq. (3).
$[r]_1 \leftarrow [\Lambda_0(x) + \alpha\Lambda_1(x) + \alpha^2\Lambda_2(x)]_1 - [\mathsf{Z}_{\mathbb{H}}(\mathfrak{z}) \cdot (t_{lo} + \mathfrak{z}^n t_{mid} + \mathfrak{z}^{2n} t_{hi})]_1$.
5. Check $\begin{pmatrix} [r + v(a - \bar{a}) + v^2(b - \bar{b})]_1 + \\ [v^3(c - \bar{c}) + v^4(s_{\sigma 1} - \bar{s}_{\sigma 1})]_1 + \\ [v^5(s_{\sigma 2} - \bar{s}_{\sigma 2}) + u(z - \bar{z}_\omega)]_1 \end{pmatrix} \bullet [1]_2 = \begin{pmatrix} [W_\mathfrak{z}]_1 \bullet [x - \mathfrak{z}]_2 - \\ u[W_{\mathfrak{z}\omega}]_1 \bullet [x - \mathfrak{z}\omega]_2 \end{pmatrix}$.

Fig. 10. Plonk's verification algorithm.

with $m = 3$, $n_\psi = 2n$, $n_1 = \kappa_{\mathsf{kzg}} = n + 5$, $n_S = \kappa_\mathfrak{z} = 4\kappa_{\mathsf{kzg}} + 1$, *and* $\psi_k(X) = X^{(k-1)n}$. *If KZG has* $(\kappa_{\mathsf{kzg}}+1)$*-CSS and evaluation binding, and* par_n*-SplitRSDH holds, then interactive Plonk has* $\boldsymbol{\kappa}_{\mathsf{Plonk}}$*-CSS.*

Applying the result of Attema, Fehr, and Klooß [1], one gets that $\mathsf{Plonk}_{\mathsf{FS}}$ has knowledge soundness in the ROM under the same assumptions.

ZK. In Fig. 11, we depict Plonk's trapdoor-based simulator, motivated by [40]. Since Fig. 11 also describes the new trapdoorless simulator (needed later in Sect. 5.2, and explained there), we use notation from Fig. 2, describing round functions for every round. We highlight the formulas used only by one of the two simulators. Given the verifier's random challenges, Plonk's trapdoor-based simulator works like an honest prover with three differences. First, it creates $\mathsf{a}(X)$, $\mathsf{b}(X)$, $\mathsf{c}(X)$, and $\mathsf{z}(X)$ by using zero witnesses. Second, since $\mathsf{t}(X)$ and $\mathsf{W}_\mathfrak{z}(X)$ are not polynomials, $\mathcal{S}$ computes $[\mathsf{t}(x)]_1$, $[\mathsf{W}_\mathfrak{z}(x)]_1$ using the trapdoor. Third, $\mathcal{S}$ computes $[t_{lo}, t_{mid}, t_{hi}]_1$ by sampling two of the values at random and setting the third one so that it agrees with the computed value of $[\mathsf{t}(x)]_1$.

5.2 Plonk Is {2}-TLZK

Next, we prove Plonk is TLZK. We modify the trapdoor-based $\mathcal{S}$ from Fig. 11 to eliminate the trapdoor. $\mathcal{S}$ uses the trapdoor x in three places. First, it computes $[\mathsf{t}(x)]_1 \leftarrow 1/\mathsf{Z}_{\mathbb{H}}(x) \cdot [\mathsf{F}(x)]_1$, where $\mathsf{F}(X)$ is as in Eq. (2). Second, it computes $1/(x - \mathfrak{z}) \cdot [\mathsf{r}(x)]_1$, where $\mathsf{r}(X)$ is as in Eq. (3). Third, when randomizing $[t_{lo}, t_{mid}, t_{hi}]_1$, it multiplies t_{hi} by $x^{2n}[1]_1$. Since the TLZK simulator $\tilde{\mathcal{S}}$ does not know x, it must compute these values differently. Our approach is to compute $\mathsf{F}(X)$ so that $\mathsf{Z}_{\mathbb{H}}(X) \mid \mathsf{F}(X)$, and $\mathsf{r}(X)$ so that $(X - \mathfrak{z}) \mid \mathsf{r}(X)$. For this, we sample α and $\mathfrak{z}$ beforehand, and thus the simulator reprograms the random oracle in rounds 2 and 3. In these reprogrammings, the simulator $\mathcal{S}$ chooses the polynomial $\mathsf{z}(X)$ by carefully computing the values $\mathsf{z}(\omega^i)$ for each i by using a linear-algebraic approach, interpreting the equation of $\mathsf{F}(X)$ from Eq. (2) coefficient-wise. This guarantees that $\mathsf{t}(X) = \mathsf{F}(X)/\mathsf{Z}_{\mathbb{H}}(X)$ is a polynomial. Surprisingly, an honestly

$\mathcal{S}(\mathtt{srs}, \mathsf{td}, \mathbb{x} = (w_i)_{i=1}^{\ell})$ $\tilde{\mathcal{S}}(2, \mathsf{st}, (\mathtt{srs}, \mathbb{x}_{\tilde{\mathcal{S}}} = \mathbb{x} = (w_i)_{i=1}^{\ell}))$: $\mathfrak{v}_2 \leftarrow \alpha \leftarrow_{\$} \mathbb{F}$;

$(\mathfrak{p}_1, \mathsf{rst}_1 = (\mathsf{a}(X), \mathsf{b}(X), \mathsf{c}(X))) \leftarrow \tilde{\mathcal{S}}_1^{\mathsf{rnd}}(\mathtt{srs}, \mathbb{x})$;
$\beta \leftarrow \mathcal{H}(\mathtt{srs}, \mathbb{x}, \mathfrak{p}_1, 0)$; $\gamma \leftarrow \mathcal{H}(\mathtt{srs}, \mathbb{x}, \mathfrak{p}_1, 1)$; $\mathfrak{v}_1 \leftarrow (\beta, \gamma)$;
if $Q_{\mathsf{sero}}[\mathtt{srs}, \mathbb{x}, \mathfrak{p}_1] \neq \bot$ then return $\bot$; else $Q_{\mathsf{sero}}[\mathtt{srs}, \mathbb{x}, \mathfrak{p}_1] \leftarrow \mathfrak{v}_1$;
$(\mathfrak{p}_2, \mathsf{rst}_2 = \mathsf{z}(X)) \leftarrow \tilde{\mathcal{S}}_2^{\mathsf{rnd}}(\mathtt{srs}, \mathbb{x}, \mathfrak{p}_1, \mathfrak{v}_1, (\mathfrak{v}_i)_{i \in T} = \alpha, \mathsf{rst}_1 = (\mathsf{a}(X), \mathsf{b}(X), \mathsf{c}(X)))$;
$\mathsf{rst} \leftarrow (\mathsf{rst}_1, \mathsf{rst}_2)$;
$\mathfrak{v}_2 \leftarrow \alpha \leftarrow \mathcal{H}(\mathtt{srs}, \mathbb{x}, \mathfrak{p}|_2)$; Reprogram (round 2): $\mathcal{H}(\mathtt{srs}, \mathbb{x}, \mathfrak{p}|_2) := \alpha$;
if $Q_{\mathsf{sero}}[\mathtt{srs}, \mathbb{x}, \mathfrak{p}|_2] \neq \bot$ then return $\bot$; else $Q_{\mathsf{sero}}[\mathtt{srs}, \mathbb{x}, \mathfrak{p}|_2] \leftarrow \mathfrak{v}_2$;
$\mathfrak{p}_3 \leftarrow \tilde{\mathcal{S}}_3^{\mathsf{rnd}}(\mathtt{srs}, \mathbb{x}, \mathfrak{p}_1, \mathfrak{v}_1, \mathfrak{p}_2, \mathfrak{v}_2, \mathsf{rst} = (\mathsf{a}(X), \mathsf{b}(X), \mathsf{c}(X), \mathsf{z}(X)))$;
$\mathfrak{v}_3 \leftarrow \mathfrak{z} \leftarrow \mathcal{H}(\mathtt{srs}, \mathbb{x}, \mathfrak{p}|_3)$; Abort if $[\mathfrak{z}]_1 = [x]_1$ or $[\mathfrak{z}\omega]_1 = [x]_1$;
if $Q_{\mathsf{sero}}[\mathtt{srs}, \mathbb{x}, \mathfrak{p}|_3] \neq \bot$ then return $\bot$; else $Q_{\mathsf{sero}}[\mathtt{srs}, \mathbb{x}, \mathfrak{p}|_3] \leftarrow \mathfrak{v}_3$;
$\mathfrak{p}_4 \leftarrow \tilde{\mathcal{S}}_4^{\mathsf{rnd}}(\mathtt{srs}, \mathbb{x}, \mathfrak{p}_1, \mathfrak{v}_1, \mathfrak{p}_2, \mathfrak{v}_2, \mathfrak{p}_3, \mathfrak{v}_3, \mathsf{rst} = (\mathsf{a}(X), \mathsf{b}(X), \mathsf{c}(X), \mathsf{z}(X)))$;
$\mathfrak{v}_4 \leftarrow v \leftarrow \mathcal{H}(\mathtt{srs}, \mathbb{x}, \mathfrak{p}|_4)$;
if $Q_{\mathsf{sero}}[\mathtt{srs}, \mathbb{x}, \mathfrak{p}|_4] \neq \bot$ then return $\bot$; else $Q_{\mathsf{sero}}[\mathtt{srs}, \mathbb{x}, \mathfrak{p}|_4] \leftarrow \mathfrak{v}_4$;
$\mathfrak{p}_5 \leftarrow \tilde{\mathcal{S}}_5^{\mathsf{rnd}}(\mathtt{srs}, \mathbb{x}, \mathfrak{p}_1, \mathfrak{v}_1, \mathfrak{p}_2, \mathfrak{v}_2, \mathfrak{p}_3, \mathfrak{v}_3, \mathfrak{p}_4, \mathfrak{v}_4, \mathsf{rst} = (\mathsf{a}(X), \mathsf{b}(X), \mathsf{c}(X), \mathsf{z}(X)))$;
return $\pi \leftarrow (\mathfrak{p}_1, \mathfrak{v}_1, \mathfrak{p}_2, \mathfrak{v}_2, \mathfrak{p}_3, \mathfrak{v}_3, \mathfrak{p}_4, \mathfrak{v}_4, \mathfrak{p}_5)$;

$\tilde{\mathcal{S}}_1^{\mathsf{rnd}}(\mathtt{srs}, \mathbb{x})$: $\mathsf{r}_a(X), \mathsf{r}_b(X), \mathsf{r}_c(X) \leftarrow_{\$} \mathbb{F}_{\leq 1}[X]$; $\mathsf{a}(X) \leftarrow \mathsf{r}_a(X)\mathsf{Z}_{\mathbb{H}}(X)$;
$\mathsf{b}(X) \leftarrow \mathsf{r}_b(X)\mathsf{Z}_{\mathbb{H}}(X)$; $\mathsf{c}(X) \leftarrow \mathsf{r}_c(X)\mathsf{Z}_{\mathbb{H}}(X)$; $[a, b, c]_1 \leftarrow [\mathsf{a}(x), \mathsf{b}(x), \mathsf{c}(x)]_1$;
return $(\mathfrak{p}_1 \leftarrow [a, b, c]_1, \mathsf{rst}_1 \leftarrow (\mathsf{a}(X), \mathsf{b}(X), \mathsf{c}(X)))$;

$\tilde{\mathcal{S}}_2^{\mathsf{rnd}}(\mathtt{srs}, \mathbb{x}, \mathfrak{p}_1, \mathfrak{v}_1, (\mathfrak{v}_i)_{i \in T} = \alpha, \mathsf{rst}_1 = (\mathsf{a}(X), \mathsf{b}(X), \mathsf{c}(X)))$: $\mathsf{r}_z(X) \leftarrow_{\$} \mathbb{F}_{\leq 2}[X]$;
Let $\mathsf{F}_0(X)$, $\mathsf{F}_1(X)$, $\mathsf{F}_2(X)$ be as in Eq. (2).
$\mathsf{z}(X) \leftarrow \mathsf{r}_z(X)\mathsf{Z}_{\mathbb{H}}(X)$;
Set $\boldsymbol{A}$ and $\boldsymbol{y}$ as in Eq. (5); $\boldsymbol{z} \leftarrow \boldsymbol{A}^{-1}\boldsymbol{y}$; $\mathsf{z}(X) \leftarrow \sum_{i=1}^{n} z_i \mathsf{L}_i(X) + \mathsf{r}_z(X)\mathsf{Z}_{\mathbb{H}}(X)$;
return $(\mathfrak{p}_2 \leftarrow [z]_1 \leftarrow [\mathsf{z}(x)]_1, \mathsf{rst}_2 \leftarrow \mathsf{z}(X))$;

$\tilde{\mathcal{S}}_3^{\mathsf{rnd}}(\mathtt{srs}, \mathbb{x}, \mathfrak{p}_1, \mathfrak{v}_1, \mathfrak{p}_2, \mathfrak{v}_2, \mathsf{rst} = (\mathsf{a}(X), \mathsf{b}(X), \mathsf{c}(X), \mathsf{z}(X)))$:
$[\mathsf{t}(x)]_1 \leftarrow [\mathsf{F}(x)]_1 / \mathsf{Z}_{\mathbb{H}}(x)$; $t_{hi}, t_{mid} \leftarrow_{\$} \mathbb{F}$; $[t_{lo}]_1 \leftarrow [\mathsf{t}(x)]_1 - t_{mid}[x^n]_1 - t_{hi} x^{2n}[1]_1$;
$\mathsf{t}(X) \leftarrow \mathsf{F}(X)/\mathsf{Z}_{\mathbb{H}}(X)$; Compute $[t_{lo}, t_{mid}, t_{hi}]_1$ from it as the honest prover does;
return $\mathfrak{p}_3 \leftarrow [t_{lo}, t_{mid}, t_{hi}]_1$;

$\tilde{\mathcal{S}}_4^{\mathsf{rnd}}(\mathtt{srs}, \mathbb{x}, \mathfrak{p}_1, \mathfrak{v}_1, \mathfrak{p}_2, \mathfrak{v}_2, \mathfrak{p}_3, \mathfrak{v}_3, \mathsf{rst} = (\mathsf{a}(X), \mathsf{b}(X), \mathsf{c}(X), \mathsf{z}(X)))$:
$\bar{a} \leftarrow \mathsf{a}(\mathfrak{z})$, $\bar{b} \leftarrow \mathsf{b}(\mathfrak{z})$, $\bar{c} \leftarrow \mathsf{c}(\mathfrak{z})$; $\bar{s}_{\sigma 1} \leftarrow \mathsf{S}_{\sigma 1}(\mathfrak{z})$; $\bar{s}_{\sigma 2} \leftarrow \mathsf{S}_{\sigma 2}(\mathfrak{z})$; $\bar{z}_{\omega} \leftarrow \mathsf{z}(\mathfrak{z}\omega)$;
return $\mathfrak{p}_4 \leftarrow (\bar{a}, \bar{b}, \bar{c}, \bar{s}_{\sigma 1}, \bar{s}_{\sigma 2}, \bar{z}_{\omega})$;

$\tilde{\mathcal{S}}_5^{\mathsf{rnd}}(\mathtt{srs}, \mathbb{x}, \mathfrak{p}_1, \mathfrak{v}_1, \mathfrak{p}_2, \mathfrak{v}_2, \mathfrak{p}_3, \mathfrak{v}_3, \mathfrak{p}_4, \mathfrak{v}_4, \mathsf{rst} = (\mathsf{a}(X), \mathsf{b}(X), \mathsf{c}(X), \mathsf{z}(X)))$:
Compute $\mathsf{r}(X)$ and $[r]_1 \leftarrow [\mathsf{r}(x)]_1$ as in Eq. (3);
$[r']_1 \leftarrow [\mathsf{r}(x)]_1 / (x - \mathfrak{z})$;
$[r']_1 \leftarrow [\mathsf{r}(x)/(x - \mathfrak{z})]_1$; // $(X - \mathfrak{z}) \mid \mathsf{r}(X)$ in the TLZK case
$[W_{\mathfrak{z}}]_1 \leftarrow [r']_1 + \left[\frac{[v(\mathsf{a}(x)-\bar{a})+v^2(\mathsf{b}(x)-\bar{b})+v^3(\mathsf{c}(x)-\bar{c})+v^4(\mathsf{S}_{\sigma 1}(x)-\bar{s}_{\sigma 1})+v^5(\mathsf{S}_{\sigma 2}(x)-\bar{s}_{\sigma 2})]_1}{x-\mathfrak{z}}\right]_1$;
$[W_{\mathfrak{z}\omega}]_1 \leftarrow [(\mathsf{z}(x) - \bar{z}_{\omega})/(x - \mathfrak{z}\omega)]_1$;
return $\mathfrak{p}_5 \leftarrow [W_{\mathfrak{z}}, W_{\mathfrak{z}\omega}]_1$;

Fig. 11. Plonk's trapdoor-based simulator $\mathcal{S}$ [40] and new trapdoorless simulator $\tilde{\mathcal{S}}$, with differences highlighted: trapdoor-based ZK and TLZK. We highlight the places where $\mathcal{S}$ uses their extra power (the trapdoor in ZK or reprogramming in TLZK).

computed $\mathsf{r}(X)$ is sufficient, and thus, there is no need to reprogram the random oracle in round 3. Hence, Plonk is $\{2\}$-TLZK.

Theorem 5. *Plonk is* $\{2\}$*-TLZK.*

Proof. In Fig. 11, we depict (a variant of) Sefranek's trapdoor-based $\mathcal{S}$ and the new trapdoorless simulator $\tilde{\mathcal{S}}$. Clearly, $\tilde{\mathcal{S}}$ does not use the trapdoor. Next, we explain the change we made to $\tilde{\mathcal{S}}$ in each round compared to $\mathcal{S}$.

Round 1. In round one, $\tilde{\mathcal{S}}$ works exactly like the trapdoor-based simulator. It lets $\mathsf{a}(X)$, $\mathsf{b}(X)$, and $\mathsf{c}(X)$ interpolate the zero vectors but masked with random $\mathsf{r}_a(X)$, $\mathsf{r}_b(X)$, and $\mathsf{r}_c(X)$. Sampling (say) $\mathsf{r}_a(X)$ from $\mathbb{F}_{\leq 1}[X]$ is sufficient since the polynomial commitment $[a]_1 \leftarrow [\mathsf{a}(x)]_1$ will only be opened at one location.

Round 2. To compute $[\mathsf{t}(x)]_1$ as in Eq. (2) but without knowing x (since we prove TLZK), we need to set $\mathsf{F}(X)$ so that $\mathsf{Z}_{\mathbb{H}}(X) \mid \mathsf{F}(X)$, that is, $\mathsf{F}(X)$ vanishes on the subgroup $\mathbb{H}$. For this, $\tilde{\mathcal{S}}$ chooses the values $\mathsf{z}(\omega^i)$ carefully and then interpolates to obtain $\mathsf{z}(X)$. By considering the evaluation of different polynomials at points ω^i, we get from Eq. (2) that, for every $i \in [n]$,

$$\mathsf{F}(\omega^i) = \mathsf{F}_0(\omega^i) + \alpha\left(\mathsf{F}_{10}(\omega^i)\mathsf{z}(\omega^i) - \mathsf{F}_{11}(\omega^i)\mathsf{z}(\omega^{i+1})\right) + \alpha^2(\mathsf{z}(\omega^i) - 1)\mathsf{L}_1(\omega^i) \ . \quad (4)$$

Since $\omega^{n+1} = \omega$, $\mathsf{z}(\omega^{n+1}) = \mathsf{z}(\omega)$. Moreover, $\mathsf{L}_1(\omega^i) = 1$ if $i = 1$ and 0, otherwise. To enforce that $\mathsf{F}(X)$ vanishes on $\mathbb{H}$, we assume $\mathsf{F}(\omega^i) = 0$ for $i \in [n]$ and then solve the equation system in Eq. (4) for the vector $\boldsymbol{z} = (\mathsf{z}(\omega^i))_{i=1}^n$. After simple algebraic manipulation, we get that $\boldsymbol{A}\boldsymbol{z} = \boldsymbol{y}$, where

$$\boldsymbol{A} \leftarrow \begin{pmatrix} \alpha(\mathsf{F}_{10}(\omega^1)+\alpha) & -\alpha\mathsf{F}_{11}(\omega^1) & 0 & \dots & 0 \\ 0 & \alpha\mathsf{F}_{10}(\omega^2) & -\alpha\mathsf{F}_{11}(\omega^2) & \dots & 0 \\ \dots & \dots & \dots & \dots & \dots \\ 0 & 0 & 0 & \dots & -\alpha\mathsf{F}_{11}(\omega^{n-1}) \\ -\alpha\mathsf{F}_{11}(\omega^n) & 0 & 0 & \dots & \alpha\mathsf{F}_{10}(\omega^n) \end{pmatrix}, \quad \boldsymbol{y} \leftarrow \begin{pmatrix} \alpha^2 - \mathsf{F}_0(\omega^1) \\ -\mathsf{F}_0(\omega^2) \\ \dots \\ -\mathsf{F}_0(\omega^n) \end{pmatrix} . \quad (5)$$

If $n > 1$, $\det \boldsymbol{A} = \alpha^n \cdot ((\alpha + \mathsf{F}_{10}(\omega^1)) \cdot \prod_{i=2}^n \mathsf{F}_{10}(\omega^i) - \prod_{i=1}^n \mathsf{F}_{11}(\omega^i))$ while if $n = 1$, $\det \boldsymbol{A} = \alpha \cdot (\mathsf{F}_{10}(\omega^1) + \alpha)$. Noting that say

$$\mathsf{F}_{10}(\omega^i) = (a_i + \beta\omega^i + \gamma)(b_i + \beta k_1\omega^i + \gamma)(c_i + \beta k_2\omega^i + \gamma) \ ,$$

$\det \boldsymbol{A}$ is non-zero with a high probability over the random choice of α, β, and γ. Thus, w.h.p., $\boldsymbol{z} = \boldsymbol{A}^{-1}\boldsymbol{y}$. The simulator interpolates, getting $\mathsf{z}(X) = \sum_{i=1}^n \mathsf{z}(\omega^i)\mathsf{L}_i(X) + \mathsf{r}_z(X)\mathsf{Z}_{\mathbb{H}}(X)$. This guarantees $\mathsf{Z}_{\mathbb{H}}(X) \mid \mathsf{F}(X)$.

Round 3. We cannot choose $[t_{lo}, t_{hi}, t_{mid}]_1$ as in Sefranek's simulator since, for this, we would have to compute $[x^{2n}]_1$. However, since $\mathsf{t}(X)$ is a polynomial, $\tilde{\mathcal{S}}$ can implement the honest Plonk's prover. Namely, given $\mathsf{t}(X) = \mathsf{F}(X)/\mathsf{Z}_{\mathbb{H}}(X) \in \mathbb{F}_{\leq 3n+20}[X]$, $\tilde{\mathcal{S}}$ computes $\mathsf{t}_{\mathsf{lo}}(X)$, $\mathsf{t}_{\mathsf{mid}}(X)$, and $\mathsf{t}_{\mathsf{hi}}(X)$ exactly like in the paragraph after Eq. (2) and set $[t_{lo}, t_{mid}, t_{hi}]_1 \leftarrow [\mathsf{t}_{\mathsf{lo}}(x), t_{mid}(x), t_{hi}(x)]_1$. Note that the prover aborts if $[\mathfrak{z}]_1 = [x]_1$ or $[\mathfrak{z}\omega]_1 = [x]_1$. This is permitted since we only require statistical zero-knowledge (see Definition 2).

Round 4. In round 4, $\tilde{\mathcal{S}}$ behaves like the honest prover and the trapdoor-based simulator by opening some polynomial commitments at requested locations.

Round 5. Since $\mathsf{t}_{\mathsf{lo}}(X) + X^n\mathsf{t}_{\mathsf{mid}}(X) + X^{2n}\mathsf{t}(X) = \mathsf{F}(X)/\mathsf{Z}_{\mathbb{H}}(X)$, we have $\mathsf{t}_{\mathsf{lo}}(\mathfrak{z}) + \mathfrak{z}^n\mathsf{t}_{\mathsf{mid}}(\mathfrak{z}) + \mathfrak{z}^{2n}\mathsf{t}(\mathfrak{z}) = (\Lambda_0(\mathfrak{z}) + \alpha\Lambda_1(\mathfrak{z}) + \alpha^2\Lambda_2(\mathfrak{z}))/\mathsf{Z}_{\mathbb{H}}(\mathfrak{z})$. (Here, we use that $\Lambda_i(\mathfrak{z}) = \mathsf{F}_i(\mathfrak{z})$). But then, $\mathsf{r}(\mathfrak{z}) = 0$ and thus, $\tilde{\mathcal{S}}$ can efficiently compute $[r/(x - \mathfrak{z})]_1$.

The simulated transcript comes from the same distribution as an honestly generated transcript. The polynomial commitments $[a, b, c, z]_1$ are masked with sufficient randomness (and thus the choice of interpolating $\mathbf{0}$ does not change the distribution), $[t_{lo}, t_{mid}, t_{hi}, \mathsf{W}_{\mathfrak{z}}]_1$ are computed as in the honest case (but without requiring a trapdoor), and other elements are computed exactly as in the honest case. This proves the claim. □

5.3 Plonk Has ≥ 2-WUR

Next, we prove that if KZG is evaluation binding, i.e., SDH holds, Plonk has ≥ 2-WUR. We point out that this result is not straightforward. Creating two accepting arguments π^* and π, that first differ in prover's third message, is trivial: the WUR adversary uses a different randomization of $[t_{lo}]_1$, that is, different b_{10} and b_{11}. Thus, Plonk does not have 2-UR. However, since we are proving 2-WUR instead, π^* is created by the simulator, who has created all polynomial commitments and knows the corresponding polynomials. The evaluation points $\mathfrak{z}$ and $\mathfrak{z}^*$ are different (with an overwhelming probability) in the two transcripts since they are outputs of the random oracle at different inputs. Since the WUR adversary does not know $\mathsf{z}(X)$, it cannot predict the correct value of $\mathsf{z}(\mathfrak{z}\omega)$. Thus, with an overwhelming probability, $\mathsf{z}(\mathfrak{z}\omega) \neq \bar{z}_\omega$. Since the simulator knows $\mathsf{z}(X)$, the reduction can construct an evaluation proof for $\mathsf{z}(\mathfrak{z}\omega)$, and thus we can again break the evaluation binding. (In the UR proof, the reduction does not know $\mathsf{z}(X)$ and thus will not be able to succeed).

The proofs of 3-WUR and 4-WUR are similar in vein. The proof of 4-WUR relies on the fact that the random oracle chooses the batching factor u.

Theorem 6 (Plonk has ≥2-WUR). *(1) If KZG is evaluation binding, then Plonk has computational* 2-*WUR in the ROM. (2) If KZG is evaluation binding, then Plonk has computational* 3-*WUR in the ROM. (3) If* $(n, 1)$-*PDL is hard, then Plonk has computational* 4-*WUR in the ROM.*

Proof. Plonk has computational 2-WUR (Item 1). Let $\mathcal{C}_{\mathsf{wur}}$ be a 2-WUR adversary succeeding with the probability $\mathsf{Adv}^{\mathrm{wur}}_{\mathrm{Plonk},\mathcal{C}_{\mathsf{wur}},\tilde{\mathcal{S}},2}(\lambda)$, where $\tilde{\mathcal{S}}$ is as in Fig. 11. In Fig. 12, we depict a KZG evaluation-binding adversary $\mathcal{D}_{\mathsf{evb}}$. $\mathcal{D}_{\mathsf{evb}}(\mathtt{srs})$ obtains input $\mathbb{x}$ from $\mathcal{C}^{\tilde{\mathcal{S}}_{\mathsf{ro}}}_{\mathsf{wur}}(\mathtt{srs})$, and then executes $\tilde{\mathcal{S}}^*_{\mathsf{any}.\pi}(\mathbb{x})$ internally, obtaining an argument π^*. $\mathcal{D}_{\mathsf{evb}}$ stores $([z]_1, \mathsf{z}(X))$ (a part of $\tilde{\mathcal{S}}_{\mathsf{any}.\pi}$'s state), where $[z]_1 = [\mathsf{z}(x)]_1$. $\mathcal{D}_{\mathsf{evb}}$ then forwards π^* to $\mathcal{C}^{\tilde{\mathcal{S}}_{\mathsf{ro}}}_{\mathsf{wur}}$.

Assume that with probability $\mathsf{Adv}^{\mathrm{wur}}_{\mathrm{Plonk},\mathcal{C}_{\mathsf{wur}},\tilde{\mathcal{S}},2}(\lambda)$, $\mathcal{C}_{\mathsf{wur}}$ constructs an accepting argument π. Both π^* and π are depicted in Fig. 12. Thus, $[t_{lo}, t_{mid}, t_{hi}]_1 \neq [t^*_{lo}, t^*_{mid}, t^*_{hi}]_1$. With the probability $1 - 1/|\mathbb{F}|$ over the choice of a random u, defined by the random oracle, π is accepting iff

$$[z - \bar{z}_\omega]_1 \bullet [1]_2 = [W_{\mathfrak{z}\omega}]_1 \bullet [x - \mathfrak{z}\omega]_2 \tag{6}$$

$\mathscr{D}_{\mathsf{evb}}(\mathtt{srs})$
$\mathbb{x} \leftarrow \mathscr{C}_{\mathsf{wur}}^{\tilde{\mathscr{S}}_{\mathsf{ro}}}(\mathtt{srs})$;
$\pi^* := ([a,b,c]_1, \beta, \gamma, [z]_1, \alpha, [t_{lo}^*, t_{mid}^*, t_{hi}^*]_1, \mathfrak{z}^*, \bar{a}^*, \bar{b}^*, \bar{c}^*, \bar{s}_{\sigma 1}^*, \bar{s}_{\sigma 2}^*, \bar{z}_\omega^*, v^*, [W_\mathfrak{z}^*, W_{\mathfrak{z}\omega}^*]_1) \leftarrow \tilde{\mathscr{S}}_{\mathsf{any}.\pi}^*(\mathbb{x})$;
Store $\tilde{\mathscr{S}}_{\mathsf{any}.\pi}(\mathbb{x})$'s state;
$\pi := ([a,b,c]_1, \beta, \gamma, [z]_1, \alpha, [t_{lo}, t_{mid}, t_{hi}]_1, \mathfrak{z}, \bar{a}, \bar{b}, \bar{c}, \bar{s}_{\sigma 1}, \bar{s}_{\sigma 2}, \bar{z}_\omega, v, [W_\mathfrak{z}, W_{\mathfrak{z}\omega}]_1) \leftarrow \mathscr{C}_{\mathsf{wur}}^{\tilde{\mathscr{S}}_{\mathsf{ro}}}(\pi^*)$;
$[\widehat{W}_{\mathfrak{z}\omega}]_1 \leftarrow [(\mathsf{z}(x) - \mathsf{z}(\mathfrak{z}\omega))/(x - \mathfrak{z}\omega)]_1$;
if $\mathsf{z}(\mathfrak{z}\omega) = \bar{z}_\omega$ **then return** $\bot$; **else return** $([z]_1, \mathfrak{z}\omega, \bar{z}_\omega, [W_{\mathfrak{z}\omega}]_1, \mathsf{z}(\mathfrak{z}\omega), [\widehat{W}_{\mathfrak{z}\omega}]_1)$;

Fig. 12. Plonk's 2-WUR adversary $\mathscr{D}_{\mathsf{evb}}$ in the proof of Theorem 6.

and

$$\begin{pmatrix} [r]_1 + v[a - \bar{a}]_1 + v^2[b - \bar{b}]_1 + \\ v^3[c - \bar{c}]_1 + v^4[s_{\sigma 1}^* - \bar{s}_{\sigma 1}]_1 + v^5[s_{\sigma 2}^* - \bar{s}_{\sigma 2}]_1 \end{pmatrix} \bullet [1]_2 = [W_\mathfrak{z}]_1 \bullet [x - \mathfrak{z}]_2 \ . \quad (7)$$

It suffices to consider only one of those equations. Since Eq. (7) is batched and Eq. (6) is not, we chose to consider Eq. (6). Now, Eq. (6) states that $([z]_1, \mathfrak{z}\omega, \bar{z}_\omega, [W_{\mathfrak{z}\omega}]_1)$ is an accepting KZG argument. If $\mathsf{z}(\mathfrak{z}\omega) \neq \bar{z}_\omega$, then $\mathscr{D}_{\mathsf{evb}}$ (who knows $\mathsf{z}(X)$) can break KZG's evaluation binding by returning $([z]_1, \mathfrak{z}\omega, \bar{z}_\omega, [W_{\mathfrak{z}\omega}]_1, \mathsf{z}(\mathfrak{z}\omega), [\widehat{W}_{\mathfrak{z}\omega}]_1)$. (Note that $\mathscr{D}_{\mathsf{evb}}$ does not use the fact that π^* verifies! $\mathscr{D}_{\mathsf{evb}}$ can ignore π^* since π^* is honestly created by $\tilde{\mathscr{S}}_{\mathsf{any}.\pi}^*$ and thus π^* being accepting is a tautology. Instead, $\mathscr{D}_{\mathsf{evb}}$ uses the knowledge of $\mathsf{z}(X)$).

We argue that $\mathscr{D}_{\mathsf{evb}}$ succeeds with a non-negligible probability. Since $\mathscr{H}$ is a random oracle and $[t_{lo}^*, t_{mid}^*, t_{hi}^*]_1 \neq [t_{lo}, t_{mid}, t_{hi}]_1$, $\mathfrak{z}$ and $\mathfrak{z}^*$ are random oracle outputs (even if reprogrammed) on different inputs and thus independent random elements of $\mathbb{F}$. Thus, $\Pr[\mathfrak{z} = \mathfrak{z}^*] = 1/|\mathbb{F}|$. Even an unbounded $\mathscr{D}_{\mathsf{evb}}$ only has information about two evaluations of $\mathsf{z}(X)$: $\mathsf{z}(x)$ and $\bar{z}_\omega^* = \mathsf{z}(\mathfrak{z}^*\omega)$. Since $\mathsf{r}_z(X)$ is a pairwise independent hash function[9], if $\mathfrak{z} \neq \mathfrak{z}^*$, $\mathscr{D}_{\mathsf{evb}}$ can guess the correct value $\mathsf{z}(\mathfrak{z}\omega) = \bar{z}_\omega$ with probability $\leq \deg(\mathsf{r}_z(X)\mathsf{Z}_\mathbb{H}(X))/|\mathbb{F}| = (n+2)/|\mathbb{F}|$. Thus,

$$\mathsf{Adv}^{\mathrm{wur}}_{\mathrm{Plonk},\mathscr{C}_{\mathsf{wur}},\tilde{\mathscr{S}},2}(\lambda) \leq \mathsf{Adv}^{\mathrm{evb}}_{\mathsf{G},\mathrm{KZG},n,\mathscr{D}_{\mathsf{evb}}}(\lambda) + \frac{n+3}{|\mathbb{F}|} \ .$$

<u>Plonk has computational 3-WUR (Item 2).</u> Let $\mathscr{C}_{\mathsf{wur}}$ be a 3-WUR adversary succeeding with the probability $\mathsf{Adv}^{\mathrm{wur}}_{\mathrm{Plonk},\mathscr{C}_{\mathsf{wur}},\tilde{\mathscr{S}},3}(\lambda)$, where $\tilde{\mathscr{S}}$ is as in Fig. 11. In Fig. 13, we depict a KZG evaluation-binding adversary $\mathscr{D}_{\mathsf{evb}}$. $\mathscr{D}_{\mathsf{evb}}(\mathtt{srs})$ obtains input $\mathbb{x}$ from $\mathscr{C}_{\mathsf{wur}}^{\tilde{\mathscr{S}}_{\mathsf{ro}}}(\mathtt{srs})$, and then executes $\tilde{\mathscr{S}}_{\mathsf{any}.\pi}^*(\mathbb{x})$ internally, obtaining an argument π^*. $\mathscr{D}_{\mathsf{evb}}$ stores $([a,b,c,z]_1, \mathsf{a}(X), \mathsf{b}(X), \mathsf{c}(X), \mathsf{z}(X))$ (a part of $\tilde{\mathscr{S}}_{\mathsf{any}.\pi}$'s state), where, say, $[z]_1 = [\mathsf{z}(x)]_1$. $\mathscr{D}_{\mathsf{evb}}$ then forwards π^* to $\mathscr{C}_{\mathsf{wur}}^{\tilde{\mathscr{S}}_{\mathsf{ro}}}$.

Assume that with probability $\mathsf{Adv}^{\mathrm{wur}}_{\mathrm{Plonk},\mathscr{C}_{\mathsf{wur}},\tilde{\mathscr{S}},3}(\lambda)$, $\mathscr{C}_{\mathsf{wur}}$ constructs an accepting argument π. Both π^* and π are depicted in Fig. 13. Thus, $(\bar{a}, \bar{b}, \bar{c}, \bar{s}_{\sigma 1}, \bar{s}_{\sigma 2}, \bar{z}_\omega)$

[9] We need this property since $\mathscr{C}_{\mathsf{wur}}$ creates $\mathfrak{z}^*$ a round after the branching point.

$\mathscr{D}_{\mathsf{evb}}(\mathbf{srs})$
$\mathbb{x} \leftarrow \mathscr{C}_{\mathsf{wur}}^{\tilde{\mathscr{S}}_{\mathsf{ro}}}(\mathbf{srs})$;
$\pi^* := ([a, b, c]_1, \beta, \gamma, [z]_1, \alpha, [t_{lo}, t_{mid}, t_{hi}]_1, \mathfrak{z}, \bar{a}^*, \bar{b}^*, \bar{c}^*, \bar{s}^*_{\sigma 1}, \bar{s}^*_{\sigma 2}, \bar{z}^*_\omega, v^*, [W^*_{\mathfrak{z}}, W^*_{\mathfrak{z}\omega}]_1) \leftarrow \tilde{\mathscr{S}}_{\mathsf{any}.\pi}(\mathbb{x})$;
Store $\tilde{\mathscr{S}}_{\mathsf{any}.\pi}(\mathbb{x})$'s state;
$\pi := ([a, b, c]_1, \beta, \gamma, [z]_1, \alpha, [t_{lo}, t_{mid}, t_{hi}]_1, \mathfrak{z}, \bar{a}, \bar{b}, \bar{c}, \bar{s}_{\sigma 1}, \bar{s}_{\sigma 2}, \bar{z}_\omega, v, [W_{\mathfrak{z}}, W_{\mathfrak{z}\omega}]_1) \leftarrow \mathscr{C}_{\mathsf{wur}}^{\tilde{\mathscr{S}}_{\mathsf{ro}}}(\pi^*)$;
Compute $\mathsf{r}(X)$ as in Eq. (3); // Branch 1
$\mathsf{e}(X) \leftarrow \mathsf{r}(X) + v\mathsf{a}(X) + v^2\mathsf{b}(X) + v^3\mathsf{c}(X) + v^4\mathsf{S}_{\sigma 1}(X) + v^5\mathsf{S}_{\sigma 2}(X)$;
$[e^*]_1 \leftarrow [\mathsf{e}(x)]_1; \bar{e} \leftarrow 0 + v\bar{a} + v^2\bar{b} + v^3\bar{c} + v^4\bar{s}_{\sigma 1} + v^5\bar{s}_{\sigma 2}$;
$[\widehat{h}_1]_1 \leftarrow [(\mathsf{e}(x) - \mathsf{e}(\mathfrak{z}))/(x - \mathfrak{z})]_1$;
$[\widehat{h}_2]_1 \leftarrow [(\mathsf{z}(x) - \mathsf{z}(\mathfrak{z}\omega))/(x - \mathfrak{z}\omega)]_1$; // Branch 2
// Choose one branch
if $\mathsf{e}(\mathfrak{z}) \neq \bar{e}$ **then return** $([e^*]_1, \mathfrak{z}, \bar{e}, [h]_1, \mathsf{e}(\mathfrak{z}), [\widehat{h}_1]_1)$;
else if $\mathsf{z}(\mathfrak{z}\omega) \neq \bar{z}_\omega$ **then return** $([z]_1, \mathfrak{z}\omega, \bar{z}_\omega, [h]_1, \mathsf{z}(\mathfrak{z}\omega), [\widehat{h}_2]_1)$;
else return $\bot$;

Fig. 13. Plonk's 3-WUR adversary $\mathscr{D}_{\mathsf{evb}}$ in the proof of Theorem 6.

$\neq (\bar{a}^*, \bar{b}^*, \bar{c}^*, \bar{s}^*_{\sigma 1}, \bar{s}^*_{\sigma 2}, \bar{z}^*_\omega)$. Plonk's verifier batch-verifies in two batches: first, all openings at $\mathfrak{z}$, and second, all openings at $\mathfrak{z}\omega$. $\mathscr{D}_{\mathsf{evb}}$ first establishes which batch contains evaluations that differ between the simulated and adversarial views. For this, $\mathscr{D}_{\mathsf{evb}}$ computes the batched polynomial $\mathsf{e}(X)$ (see Fig. 13) and its claimed evaluation $\bar{e}$. If $\mathsf{e}(\mathfrak{z}) \neq \bar{e}$, the difference was in the first branch; otherwise, it was in the second. After that, $\mathscr{D}_{\mathsf{evb}}$ uses the knowledge of $\tilde{\mathscr{S}}_{\mathsf{any}.\pi}$'s state to compute the actual opening of $\mathsf{e}(X)$ or $\mathsf{z}(X)$, respectively, together with the corresponding opening proof. In both cases, $\mathscr{D}_{\mathsf{evb}}$ returns a collision.

We are left to compute the probability that $\mathsf{e}(\mathfrak{z}) \neq \bar{e}$ and $\mathsf{z}(\mathfrak{z}) \neq \bar{z}$, i.e., that $\mathscr{D}_{\mathsf{evb}}$ succeeds in computing a collision. Crucially, the WUR adversary does not know polynomials like $\mathsf{a}(X)$ and thus does not know $\mathsf{e}(X)$. Indeed, it can only compute a single evaluation $[e^*]_1 \leftarrow [\mathsf{e}(x)]_1$ of $\mathsf{e}(X)$. Based on this information, it has no information about the value $\mathsf{e}(\mathfrak{z})$ of $\mathsf{e}(X)$ at a random location $\mathfrak{z}$, chosen by the random oracle. Thus, the probability that $\mathsf{e}(\mathfrak{z}) = \bar{e}$ (resp., $\mathsf{z}(\mathfrak{z}) = \bar{z}$) is at most $\deg(\mathsf{e})/\mathbb{F} \leq (n+5)/|\mathbb{F}|$ (resp., $\deg(\mathsf{z})/\mathbb{F} \leq (n+5)/|\mathbb{F}|$). Thus,

$$\mathsf{Adv}^{\mathrm{wur}}_{\mathrm{Plonk}_{\mathsf{FS}}, \mathscr{C}_{\mathsf{wur}}, \tilde{\mathscr{S}}, 3}(\lambda) \leq \mathsf{Adv}^{\mathrm{evb}}_{\mathrm{G,KZG},n,\mathscr{D}_{\mathsf{evb}}}(\lambda) + (n+5)/|\mathbb{F}| \ .$$

<u>Plonk has computational 4-WUR (Item 3).</u> Assume the trapdoorless simulator returns $\pi^* = (\ldots, [W^*_{\mathfrak{z}}, \mathrm{W}^*_{\mathfrak{z}\omega}]_1)$ and the WUR adversary $\mathscr{C}_{\mathsf{wur}}$ outputs a transcript $\pi = (\ldots, [W_{\mathfrak{z}}, W_{\mathfrak{z}\omega}]_1)$. Thus, $[W_{\mathfrak{z}}, W_{\mathfrak{z}\omega}]_1 \neq [W^*_{\mathfrak{z}}, W^*_{\mathfrak{z}\omega}]_1$. Since both transcripts are accepting, we get from Fig. 10 that $[W_{\mathfrak{z}}]_1 \bullet [x - \mathfrak{z}]_2 - u[W_{\mathfrak{z}\omega}]_1 \bullet [x - \mathfrak{z}\omega]_2 - [u(z - \bar{z}_\omega)]_1 \bullet [1]_2 = [W^*_{\mathfrak{z}}]_1 \bullet [x - \mathfrak{z}]_2 - u^*[W^*_{\mathfrak{z}\omega}]_1 \bullet [x - \mathfrak{z}\omega]_2 - [u^*(z - \bar{z}_\omega)]_1 \bullet [1]_2$ or

$$u \cdot [A]_T - u^* \cdot [B]_T = [C]_T \tag{8}$$

for $[A]_T = [W_{\mathfrak{z}\omega}]_1 \bullet [x - \mathfrak{z}\omega]_2 + [z - \bar{z}_\omega]_1 \bullet [1]_2$, $[B]_T = [W^*_{\mathfrak{z}\omega}]_1 \bullet [x - \mathfrak{z}\omega]_2 + [z - \bar{z}_\omega]_1 \bullet [1]_2$, and $[C]_T = [W_\mathfrak{z} - W^*_\mathfrak{z}]_1 \bullet [x - \mathfrak{z}]_2$.

Since u and u^*, as outputs of the random oracle on different inputs, are independent uniformly distributed random variables, we can now apply Schwartz-Zippel. If either $[A]_T$, $[B]_T$, or $[C]_T$ is non-zero, Eq. (8) happens with probability $1/|\mathbb{F}|$ over the choice of u and u^*. Now, assume all $[A]_1$, $[B]_T$, and $[C]_T$ are zero. From $[C]_T = [0]_T$, we get that either $\mathsf{W}_\mathfrak{z} = \mathsf{W}^*_\mathfrak{z}$ (impossible, since the WUR adversary succeeded) or $x = \mathfrak{z}$ and we can break the PDL assumption. Thus, we have broken the PDL assumption with an obvious adversary $\mathcal{B}$ with

$$\mathsf{Adv}^{\mathrm{wur}}_{\mathsf{Plonk}_{\mathsf{FS}},\mathcal{C}_{\mathsf{wur}},\tilde{\mathcal{S}},4}(\lambda) \leq \mathsf{Adv}^{\mathrm{pdl}}_{n,1,\mathsf{G},\mathcal{B}}(\lambda) + 1/|\mathbb{F}| \ .$$

Since KZG's evaluation binding implies PDL, Plonk has 4-WUR under KZG's evaluation binding. □

5.4 Plonk is Simulation Extractable

Finally, we obtain the main result of the current paper. See Fig. 1 for a diagram of intermediate results.

Theorem 7. *Assume that Plonk is evaluation binding and knowledge sound, that is, ARSDH and* par_n*-SplitRSDH hold. Then Plonk is simulation extractable.*

Proof. According to Theorem 5, Plonk is {2}-TLZK. According to Theorem 6, Plonk has ≥ 2-WUR w.r.t. a canonical TLZK simulator under the evaluation binding of KZG, that is, if the SDH assumption holds. According to [35], SDH follows from ARSDH. Moreover, according to [35], Plonk has knowledge soundness, assuming that ARSDH and par_n-SplitRSDH hold. It follows from Theorem 1 that Plonk is simulation extractable with respect to $\mathcal{S}$. □

Acknowledgments. We thank Antonio Faonio for useful discussions about [14]. The author was co-funded by the European Union and Estonian Research Council via projects TEM-TA119 and PRG2531.

References

1. Attema, T., Fehr, S., Klooß, M.: Fiat-Shamir transformation of multi-round interactive proofs. In: Kiltz, E., Vaikuntanathan, V. (eds.) TCC 2022, Part I. LNCS, vol. 13747, pp. 113–142. Springer, Cham (2022). https://doi.org/10.1007/978-3-031-22318-1_5
2. Baghery, K., Kohlweiss, M., Siim, J., Volkhov, M.: Another look at extraction and randomization of Groth's zk-SNARK. In: Borisov, N., Diaz, C. (eds.) FC 2021, Part I. LNCS, vol. 12674, pp. 457–475. Springer, Heidelberg (2021). https://doi.org/10.1007/978-3-662-64322-8_22
3. Bellare, M., Rogaway, P.: Random oracles are practical: a paradigm for designing efficient protocols. In: Denning, D.E., Pyle, R., Ganesan, R., Sandhu, R.S., Ashby, V. (eds.) ACM CCS 1993, pp. 62–73. ACM Press (1993). https://doi.org/10.1145/168588.168596

4. Campanelli, M., Faonio, A., Fiore, D., Li, T., Lipmaa, H.: Lookup arguments: improvements, extensions and applications to zero-knowledge decision trees. In: Tang, Q., Teague, V. (eds.) PKC 2024, Part II. LNCS, vol. 14602, pp. 337–369. Springer, Cham (2024). https://doi.org/10.1007/978-3-031-57722-2_11
5. Canetti, R., Goldreich, O., Halevi, S.: The random oracle methodology, revisited (preliminary version). In: 30th ACM STOC, pp. 209–218. ACM Press (1998). https://doi.org/10.1145/276698.276741
6. Chiesa, A., Hu, Y., Maller, M., Mishra, P., Vesely, N., Ward, N.: Marlin: preprocessing zkSNARKs with universal and updatable SRS. In: Canteaut, A., Ishai, Y. (eds.) EUROCRYPT 2020, Part I. LNCS, vol. 12105, pp. 738–768. Springer, Cham (2020). https://doi.org/10.1007/978-3-030-45721-1_26
7. Dao, Q., Grubbs, P.: Spartan and bulletproofs are simulation-extractable (for free!). In: Hazay, C., Stam, M. (eds.) EUROCRYPT 2023, Part II. LNCS, vol. 14005, pp. 531–562. Springer, Cham (2023). https://doi.org/10.1007/978-3-031-30617-4_18
8. De Santis, A., Di Crescenzo, G., Ostrovsky, R., Persiano, G., Sahai, A.: Robust non-interactive zero knowledge. In: Kilian, J. (ed.) CRYPTO 2001. LNCS, vol. 2139, pp. 566–598. Springer, Heidelberg (2001). https://doi.org/10.1007/3-540-44647-8_33
9. Dent, A.W.: Adapting the weaknesses of the random oracle model to the generic group model. In: Zheng, Y. (ed.) ASIACRYPT 2002. LNCS, vol. 2501, pp. 100–109. Springer, Heidelberg (2002). https://doi.org/10.1007/3-540-36178-2_6
10. Di Crescenzo, G., Lipmaa, H.: Succinct NP proofs from an extractability assumption. In: Beckmann, A., Dimitracopoulos, C., Löwe, B. (eds.) CiE 2008. LNCS, vol. 5028, pp. 175–185. Springer, Heidelberg (2008). https://doi.org/10.1007/978-3-540-69407-6_21
11. Dolev, D., Dwork, C., Naor, M.: Non-malleable cryptography (extended abstract). In: 23rd ACM STOC, pp. 542–552. ACM Press (1991). https://doi.org/10.1145/103418.103474
12. Eagen, L., Fiore, D., Gabizon, A.: cq: Cached quotients for fast lookups. Cryptology ePrint Archive, Report 2022/1763 (2022). https://eprint.iacr.org/2022/1763
13. Faonio, A., Fiore, D., Kohlweiss, M., Russo, L., Zajac, M.: From polynomial IOP and commitments to non-malleable zkSNARKs. In: Rothblum, G.N., Wee, H. (eds.) TCC 2023, Part III. LNCS, vol. 14371, pp. 455–485. Springer, Cham (2023). https://doi.org/10.1007/978-3-031-48621-0_16
14. Faonio, A., Fiore, D., Russo, L.: Real-world universal zkSNARKs are non-malleable. In: Luo, B., Liao, X., Xu, J., Kirda, E., Lie, D. (eds.) ACM CCS 2024, pp. 3138–3151. ACM Press (2024). https://doi.org/10.1145/3658644.3690351
15. Faust, S., Kohlweiss, M., Marson, G.A., Venturi, D.: On the non-malleability of the Fiat-Shamir transform. In: Galbraith, S., Nandi, M. (eds.) INDOCRYPT 2012. LNCS, vol. 7668, pp. 60–79. Springer, Heidelberg (2012). https://doi.org/10.1007/978-3-642-34931-7_5
16. Fiat, A., Shamir, A.: How to prove yourself: practical solutions to identification and signature problems. In: Odlyzko, A.M. (ed.) CRYPTO 1986. LNCS, vol. 263, pp. 186–194. Springer, Heidelberg (1987). https://doi.org/10.1007/3-540-47721-7_12
17. Fuchsbauer, G., Kiltz, E., Loss, J.: The algebraic group model and its applications. In: Shacham, H., Boldyreva, A. (eds.) CRYPTO 2018, Part II. LNCS, vol. 10992, pp. 33–62. Springer, Cham (2018). https://doi.org/10.1007/978-3-319-96881-0_2
18. Gabizon, A., Williamson, Z.J.: The turbo-plonk program syntax for specifying snark programs (2019). https://docs.zkproof.org/pages/standards/accepted-workshop3/proposal-turbo_plonk.pdf

19. Gabizon, A., Williamson, Z.J.: plookup: a simplified polynomial protocol for lookup tables. Cryptology ePrint Archive, Report 2020/315 (2020). https://eprint.iacr.org/2020/315
20. Gabizon, A., Williamson, Z.J., Ciobotaru, O.: PLONK: permutations over Lagrange-bases for oecumenical noninteractive arguments of knowledge. Cryptology ePrint Archive, Report 2019/953 (2019). https://eprint.iacr.org/2019/953
21. Ganesh, C., Khoshakhlagh, H., Kohlweiss, M., Nitulescu, A., Zajac, M.: What makes Fiat-Shamir zkSNARKs (updatable SRS) simulation extractable? In: Galdi, C., Jarecki, S. (eds.) SCN 2022. LNCS, vol. 13409, pp. 735–760. Springer, Cham (2022). https://doi.org/10.1007/978-3-031-14791-3_32
22. Ganesh, C., Kondi, Y., Orlandi, C., Pancholi, M., Takahashi, A., Tschudi, D.: Witness-succinct universally-composable SNARKs. In: Hazay, C., Stam, M. (eds.) EUROCRYPT 2023, Part II. LNCS, vol. 14005, pp. 315–346. Springer, Cham (2023). https://doi.org/10.1007/978-3-031-30617-4_11
23. Ganesh, C., Orlandi, C., Pancholi, M., Takahashi, A., Tschudi, D.: Fiat-Shamir bulletproofs are non-malleable (in the algebraic group model). In: Dunkelman, O., Dziembowski, S. (eds.) EUROCRYPT 2022, Part II. LNCS, vol. 13276, pp. 397–426. Springer, Cham (2022). https://doi.org/10.1007/978-3-031-07085-3_14
24. Gentry, C., Wichs, D.: Separating succinct non-interactive arguments from all falsifiable assumptions. In: Fortnow, L., Vadhan, S.P. (eds.) 43rd ACM STOC, pp. 99–108. ACM Press (2011). https://doi.org/10.1145/1993636.1993651
25. Groth, J.: Short pairing-based non-interactive zero-knowledge arguments. In: Abe, M. (ed.) ASIACRYPT 2010. LNCS, vol. 6477, pp. 321–340. Springer, Heidelberg (2010). https://doi.org/10.1007/978-3-642-17373-8_19
26. Groth, J., Maller, M.: Snarky signatures: minimal signatures of knowledge from simulation-extractable SNARKs. In: Katz, J., Shacham, H. (eds.) CRYPTO 2017, Part II. LNCS, vol. 10402, pp. 581–612. Springer, Cham (2017). https://doi.org/10.1007/978-3-319-63715-0_20
27. Kate, A., Zaverucha, G.M., Goldberg, I.: Constant-size commitments to polynomials and their applications. In: Abe, M. (ed.) ASIACRYPT 2010. LNCS, vol. 6477, pp. 177–194. Springer, Heidelberg (2010). https://doi.org/10.1007/978-3-642-17373-8_11
28. Khovratovich, D., Rothblum, R.D., Soukhanov, L.: How to prove false statements: practical attacks on Fiat-Shamir. Cryptology ePrint Archive, Report 2025/118 (2025). https://eprint.iacr.org/2025/118
29. Kohlweiss, M., Pancholi, M., Takahashi, A.: How to compile polynomial IOP into simulation-extractable SNARKs: a modular approach. In: Rothblum, G.N., Wee, H. (eds.) TCC 2023, Part III. LNCS, vol. 14371, pp. 486–512. Springer, Cham (2023). https://doi.org/10.1007/978-3-031-48621-0_17
30. Libert, B.: Simulation-extractable KZG polynomial commitments and applications to HyperPlonk. In: Tang, Q., Teague, V. (eds.) PKC 2024, Part II. LNCS, vol. 14602, pp. 68–98. Springer, Cham (2024). https://doi.org/10.1007/978-3-031-57722-2_3
31. Lipmaa, H.: Progression-free sets and sublinear pairing-based non-interactive zero-knowledge arguments. In: Cramer, R. (ed.) TCC 2012. LNCS, vol. 7194, pp. 169–189. Springer, Heidelberg (2012). https://doi.org/10.1007/978-3-642-28914-9_10
32. Lipmaa, H.: A unified framework for non-universal SNARKs. In: Hanaoka, G., Shikata, J., Watanabe, Y. (eds.) PKC 2022, Part I. LNCS, vol. 13177, pp. 553–583. Springer, Cham (2022). https://doi.org/10.1007/978-3-030-97121-2_20
33. Lipmaa, H.: Plonk is simulation extractable in ROM under falsifiable assumptions. Technical report 2025/?, IACR (2025). https://eprint.iacr.org/2025/

34. Lipmaa, H., Parisella, R., Siim, J.: Algebraic group model with oblivious sampling. In: Rothblum, G.N., Wee, H. (eds.) TCC 2023, Part IV. LNCS, vol. 14372, pp. 363–392. Springer, Cham (2023). https://doi.org/10.1007/978-3-031-48624-1_14
35. Lipmaa, H., Parisella, R., Siim, J.: Constant-size zk-SNARKs in ROM from falsifiable assumptions. In: Joye, M., Leander, G. (eds.) EUROCRYPT 2024, Part VI. LNCS, vol. 14656, pp. 34–64. Springer, Cham (2024). https://doi.org/10.1007/978-3-031-58751-1_2
36. Lipmaa, H., Parisella, R., Siim, J.: On knowledge-soundness of plonk in ROM from falsifiable assumptions. In: Kalai, Y.T., Kamara, S.F. (eds.) CRYPTO 2025, Part VII. LNCS, vol. 16006, pp. 362–395. Springer, Cham (2025). https://doi.org/10.1007/978-3-032-01907-3_12
37. Micali, S.: CS proofs (extended abstracts). In: 35th FOCS, pp. 436–453. IEEE Computer Society Press (1994). https://doi.org/10.1109/SFCS.1994.365746
38. Rouach, J.: Choosing PLONK, the Verified Verifier (2025). https://www.youtube.com/watch?v=dNLa5B2ER74, presentation at ZKProof 7
39. Sahai, A.: Non-malleable non-interactive zero knowledge and adaptive chosen-ciphertext security. In: 40th FOCS, pp. 543–553. IEEE Computer Society Press (1999). https://doi.org/10.1109/SFFCS.1999.814628
40. Sefranek, M.: How (not) to simulate PLONK. In: Galdi, C., Phan, D.H. (eds.) SCN 24, Part I. LNCS, vol. 14973, pp. 96–117. Springer, Cham (2024). https://doi.org/10.1007/978-3-031-71070-4_5
41. Zhandry, M.: To label, or not to label (in generic groups). In: Dodis, Y., Shrimpton, T. (eds.) CRYPTO 2022, Part III. LNCS, vol. 13509, pp. 66–96. Springer, Cham (2022). https://doi.org/10.1007/978-3-031-15982-4_3

Time-Space Trade-Offs for Sumcheck

Anubhav Baweja[1(✉)], Alessandro Chiesa[2], Elisabetta Fedele[3], Giacomo Fenzi[2], Pratyush Mishra[1], Tushar Mopuri[1], and Andrew Zitek-Estrada[2]

[1] University of Pennsylvania, Philadelphia, USA
abaweja@upenn.edu
[2] École Polytechnique Fédérale de Lausanne (EPFL), Lausanne, Switzerland
[3] Eidgenössische Technische Hochschule (ETH) Zürich, Zürich, Switzerland

Abstract. The sumcheck protocol is a fundamental building block in the design of probabilistic proof systems, and has become a key component of recent work on efficient succinct arguments.

We study time-space trade-offs for the prover of the sumcheck protocol in the streaming model, and provide upper and lower bounds that tightly characterize the efficiency achievable by the prover.

- For sumcheck claims about a single multilinear polynomial we demonstrate an algorithm that runs in time $O(kN)$ and uses space $O(N^{1/k})$ for any $k \geq 1$. For non-adaptive provers (a class which contains all known sumcheck prover algorithms) we show this trade-off is optimal.
- For sumcheck claims about products of multilinear polynomials, we describe a prover algorithm that runs in time $O(N(\log\log N + k))$ and uses space $O(N^{1/k})$ for any $k \geq 1$. We show that, conditioned on the hardness of a natural problem about multiplication of multilinear polynomials, any "natural" prover algorithm that uses space $O(N^{1/2-\varepsilon})$ for some $\varepsilon > 0$ must run in time $\Omega(N(\log\log N + \log\varepsilon))$.

We implement and evaluate the prover algorithm for products of multilinear polynomials. We show that our algorithm consumes up to 120× less memory compare to the linear-time prover algorithm, while incurring a time overhead of less than 2×.

The foregoing algorithms and lower bounds apply in the interactive proof model. We show that in the polynomial interactive oracle proof model one can in fact design a new protocol that achieves a better time-space trade-off of $O(N^{1/k})$ space and $O(N(\log^* N + k))$ time for any $k \geq 1$.

Keywords: Sumcheck · Interactive proofs

1 Introduction

The sumcheck protocol [22] occupies a central role in the study of probabilistic proof systems. Its applications span a wide range of areas, from complexity theory [3,4,18,30] to the construction of concretely efficient succinct argument

B. Applebaum and H. Lin (Eds.): TCC 2025, LNCS 16271, pp. 37–70, 2026.
https://doi.org/10.1007/978-3-032-12290-2_2

systems [12,28,29]. Hence, it is of fundamental importance to understand the time and space efficiency of the prover in the sumcheck protocol, especially when considering the application to succinct arguments. Indeed, much effort has been devoted recently to construct succinct arguments [8–10,23,25,35] that reduce the prover's memory usage, and a key bottleneck in a number of these works [23,35] has been the prover's time and space complexity in the sumcheck protocol.

Existing State-of-the-Art. We focus on prover algorithms for sumcheck of products of n-variate multilinear polynomials where the prover has streaming access to evaluations of the multilinear polynomials over the boolean hypercube, as this is the setting that sumcheck-based succinct arguments typically operate in.In this setting, prior algorithms achieve either $O(N)$-time and $O(N)$-space complexity [16], or $O(N \log N)$-time and $O(\log N)$-space complexity [15].

1.1 Our Contributions

In this work, we study time-space trade-offs for the prover of the sumcheck protocol, and provide upper and lower bounds that tightly characterize the efficiency achievable by the prover in a wide range of settings. We prove the following theorems (over any field).

Theorem 1 (informal, see Theorem 3). *For any $k \geq 1$, we construct a sumcheck prover algorithm which performs $O(N(\log\log N + k))$ field operations and uses $O(N^{1/k})$ space.*

Note that for space $O(\log N)$, the algorithm runs in time $O\left(\frac{N \log N}{\log\log N}\right)$, which improves upon the $O(N \log N)$ time complexity of prior work [15].

We show that the algorithm in Theorem 2 achieves an essentially optimal time-space trade-off.

Theorem 2 (informal, see Theorem 5). *Assuming the worst-case hardness of a certain natural problem regarding polynomial multiplication, every "natural" prover algorithm for the sumcheck protocol that maintains an internal state of size $N^{1/2-\varepsilon}$ for some $\varepsilon \in (0, 1/2)$, must use $\Omega(N(\log\log N + \log\varepsilon))$ field operations.*

Unlike our upper bound, our lower bound applies to algorithms that have *random access* to the input polynomials. We note that our lower bounds apply to *non-adaptive* algorithms whose accesses to the input do not depend on the verifier challenges nor the input polynomials. All known provers for the sumcheck protocol satisfy this property [15,16,33], including the ones we study in this work.

Tight Bounds for Multilinear Polynomials. When the sumcheck claim is about a single multilinear polynomial, we improve these results and provide a tight characterization of the time-space trade-off for the prover of the sumcheck protocol: there exists a prover algorithm that uses $O(N^{1/k})$ space and runs in time $O(kN)$, and this is optimal. These results are of particular interest when the characteristic of the field is 2, where the techniques of [19] do not apply.

Concrete Efficiency. We show that our algorithm exhibit a time-space trade-off that is of practical interest. In particular, the algorithm underlying Theorem 1, when parameterized with $k = 2$ (i.e., to use $O(N^{1/2})$ space), is only 1.8-2× slower than the linear-space prover algorithm of [16], and is 5-6× faster than the log-space streaming prover of [15]. Our algorithm requires approximately 0.008× the memory required by the linear-time prover. A discussion of our implementation and experimental results can be found in the full version.[1]

Sumcheck Protocols in the PIOP Model. Our lower bounds apply to interactive *proofs.* To do better we design a family of protocols with better efficiency in the polynomial interactive oracle proof (PIOP) model [11,14] that bypass our lower bound and exhibit a better time-space trade-off:

Theorem 3 (informal, see full version for formal statement and proof). *For any $k \geq 1$ and FFT-friendly field $\mathbb{F}$, we construct a $O(\log^* N + k)$-round PIOP for sumcheck claims of product of polynomials over $\mathbb{F}$ such that the prover algorithm performs $O(N(\log^* N + k))$ field operations and uses $O(N^{1/k})$ space.*

Our protocol improves upon Sparrow [25], a recent work which introduced a new protocol for sumcheck claims about products of multilinear polynomials, and described a prover algorithm for this protocol that requires $O(N \log\log N)$ field operations and $O(N^{1/2})$ space. In the linear space regime, we present a protocol with a linear-time prover and $O(\log^* N)$ round complexity, proving a generalization of the sumcheck protocol of [2] to the large field setting[2].

Theorem 4 (informal, see full version for formal statement and proof). *For any FFT-friendly field $\mathbb{F}$, we construct a $O(\log^* N)$-round PIOP for sumcheck claims about sums of products of polynomials over $\mathbb{F}$ where the prover performs $O(N)$ field operations and uses $O(N)$ space.*

This algorithm achieves *linear prover time* with a round complexity of $O(\log^* N)$, as opposed to the $O(\log\log N)$ round complexity achieved by the linear-time sumcheck provers of [21,32].

1.2 Related Work

Existing Algorithms for the Sumcheck Protocol. As mentioned in Sect. 1, existing prover algorithms for the sumcheck protocol achieve various points in the time-space trade-off spectrum. Cormode, Mitzenmacher, and Thaler [15] give a prover algorithm that performs $O(N \log N)$ field operations and uses $O(\log N)$ space, while Cormode, Thaler, and Yi [16] give a prover algorithm that perform $O(N)$ field operations and uses $O(N)$ space.

---

[1] The full version of this paper is available at https://eprint.iacr.org/2025/1473.

[2] [2] constructed a linear-time sumcheck protocol with $O(\log^* N)$ round complexity over $\mathbb{F}_2$, and stated but did not prove a generalization to the large field setting.

A recent note by a subset of the authors [13] introduced the prover algorithm for multilinear polynomials; this work subsumes that note and complements it with a lower bound that shows that the time-space trade-off achieved by the algorithm is optimal. The full version of this paper describes this algorithm in detail in the appendix.

Setty, Thaler, and Wahby [29, Appendix G] propose a prover for the classical sumcheck protocol for products of multilinear polynomials where one of the polynomials is *sparse*. The techniques in their work are similar to those employed in [13] (where the dense polynomial is set to be identically one), but are not identical. In particular, space-efficiency was not a focus of their work, and an adaptation of the protocol must be performed to capture this feature. In concurrent work, Nair, Thaler, and Zhu [23, Appendix A] show how to perform this adaptation, and their technique generalizes the algorithm in [13].

Low-Memory Succinct Arguments from Space-Efficient Sumcheck. Recent works such as [23,35] have constructed succinct arguments with reduced memory requirements by using the space-efficient sumcheck prover of [15]. Using the prover algorithm of Theorem 1 in these arguments would directly reduce the time complexity of their prover algorithms, while maintaining the same space complexity.

Alternate Sumcheck Protocols and Their Provers. We survey some alternate approaches to proving sumcheck claims.

Aurora [7] proposes a *univariate* sumcheck protocol for checking the sum of a univariate polynomial over a multiplicative subgroup that run in $O(N \log N)$ field operations. Gemini [10] proposes a different sumcheck protocol for univariate polynomials with two different prover algorithms: a space-intensive algorithm that requires $O(N)$ time and $O(N)$ space, and a space-efficient algorithm that requires $O(N \log N)$ time and $O(\log N)$ space. It would be interesting to see if our techniques can be adapted to achieve a similar time-space trade-off for the Gemini protocol.

As noted previously, Sparrow [25] proposes a new PIOP for sumcheck of products of multilinear polynomials, and describes a prover algorithm for it that performs $O(N \log\log N)$ field operations and uses space $O(N^{1/2})$.

Two recent works [21,32] design PIOPs for sumcheck of products of multilinear polynomials that achieve lower round complexity of $O(\log\log N)$. They provide provers that perform $O(N)$ field operations and use space $O(N)$. Hobbit [24] also designs a PIOP for sumcheck of products of multilinear polynomial, achieving provers that performs $O(N)$ field operations and use space $O(N^{1/2})$, albeit at the cost of an increased round and verifier complexity of $O(N^{1/2})$.

Finally, Athamnah et al. [2] design a linear time sumcheck prover for sumcheck claims of products of multilinear polynomials with $O(\log^* N)$ round complexity over binary fields. We prove that their algorithm generalizes to the large field setting in Theorem 4 (as stated but not proven therein). We further provide in Theorem 3 a space-time trade-off for a similar family of protocols.

Alternate Memory Models. Scribe [5] proposes a *read-write* streaming computation model where, the prover has random-access to only a limited amount of memory, but additionally has *read-write* streaming access to a large amount of external memory. In this model, Scribe achieves a prover algorithm for the sumcheck protocol that performs $O(N)$ field operations while using $O(\log N)$ random-access space and $O(N)$ external memory. This reliance on $O(N)$ external memory means that Scribe's algorithm does not violate the lower bound of Theorem 2.

2 Technical Overview

2.1 Background and Notation

We use $\langle i \rangle_n$ to denote the n-bit binary representation of $i \in \mathbb{N}$ in the most-significant-bit order. Given a multilinear polynomial $p(\boldsymbol{X}) \in \mathbb{F}^{\leq 1}[X_1, \ldots, X_n]$, we use $\boldsymbol{p} := [p(\langle i \rangle)]_{i=0}^{2^n-1}$ to denote its evaluations over the n-dimensional boolean hypercube $\{0,1\}^n$. The *multilinear extension* of a vector $\boldsymbol{v} \in \mathbb{F}^{2^n}$ is the unique multilinear polynomial $\hat{v}(\boldsymbol{X}) \in \mathbb{F}^{\leq 1}[X_1, \ldots, X_n]$ such that $\hat{v}(\boldsymbol{i}) = \boldsymbol{v}[\mathsf{int}(\boldsymbol{i})]$ for all $\boldsymbol{i} \in \{0,1\}^n$. We always use N to denote 2^n. Given a finite set S, we use $x \xleftarrow{\$} S$ to denote that x is chosen uniformly at random from S.

Lagrange Basis Polynomials. The *Lagrange basis polynomial* with respect to $\boldsymbol{y} \in \{0,1\}^n$ is defined as $\chi_{\boldsymbol{y}}(\boldsymbol{X}) := \prod_{i=1}^{n}(y_i X_i + (1-y_i)(1-X_i))$. This is a multilinear polynomial which evaluates to 1 at $\boldsymbol{y}$ and 0 at all other points in $\{0,1\}^n$. Given a multilinear polynomial $p(\boldsymbol{X}) \in \mathbb{F}^{\leq 1}[X_1, \ldots, X_n]$ and an evaluation point $\boldsymbol{z} \in \mathbb{F}^n$, one can write

$$p(\boldsymbol{z}) = \sum_{\boldsymbol{x} \in \{0,1\}^n} \chi_{\boldsymbol{x}}(\boldsymbol{z}) \cdot p(\boldsymbol{x}) \ .$$

Streaming Oracles. Given a vector $\boldsymbol{v} \in \mathbb{F}^N$, $\mathcal{S}(\boldsymbol{v})$ is a streaming oracle to $\boldsymbol{v}$ that allows an algorithm $\mathcal{A}$ to access the elements of $\boldsymbol{v}$ in a sequential streaming manner. That is, $\mathcal{A}$ can only read elements of $\boldsymbol{v}$ from left to right, and reset to the beginning of the stream at any time. We use $\mathcal{S}(\boldsymbol{v}).\mathsf{next}$ to denote the operation of returning the element of $\boldsymbol{v}$ at the current position and increments the pointer, and $\mathcal{S}(\boldsymbol{v}).\mathsf{reset}$ to denote the operation of resetting the pointer to the beginning of the stream.

Access to Multilinear Polynomials. We consider three types of access that an algorithm $\mathcal{A}$ can have to a multilinear polynomial $p(\boldsymbol{X}) \in \mathbb{F}^{\leq 1}[X_1, \ldots, X_n]$:

- Oracle access: $\mathcal{A}$ has *oracle access* to $p(\boldsymbol{X})$ if it can query the value of $p(\boldsymbol{x})$ at any $\boldsymbol{x} \in \mathbb{F}^n$ in constant time. $[\![p]\!]$ denotes an oracle to the polynomial $p(\boldsymbol{X})$.
- Random access: $\mathcal{A}$ has *random access* to $p(\boldsymbol{X})$ if it can query the value of $p(\boldsymbol{x})$ at any $\boldsymbol{x} \in \{0,1\}^n$ in constant time.
- Streaming access: $\mathcal{A}$ has *streaming access* to $p(\boldsymbol{X})$ if it has access to a streaming oracle $\mathcal{S}(\boldsymbol{p})$ to the evaluations of p over the hypercube $\{0,1\}^n$.

Clearly, streaming access is a restriction of random access, which is a restriction of oracle access.

The Sumcheck Protocol. The sumcheck protocol for n-variate polynomials [22] is an n-round interactive protocol that allows a prover to convince a verifier that the sum of the evaluations of an n-variate polynomial $p(\boldsymbol{X})$ over the hypercube $\{0,1\}^n$ is equal to some claimed value σ.

Definition 1 (Sumcheck language). *Let $p_1(\boldsymbol{X}), \ldots, p_d(\boldsymbol{X})$ be n-variate multilinear polynomials over a finite field $\mathbb{F}$, and let $\sigma \in \mathbb{F}$. The* d-product-sumcheck language $\mathsf{SC}^{(\mathbb{F},n,d)}$ *consists of tuples of the form $(p_1(\boldsymbol{X}), \ldots, p_d(\boldsymbol{X}), \sigma)$ where $\sigma = \sum_{\boldsymbol{x} \in \{0,1\}^n} \prod_{j=1}^{d} p_j(\boldsymbol{x})$.*

Definition 2 (Classical sumcheck protocol [22]**).** *Let $p_1(\boldsymbol{X}), \ldots, p_d(\boldsymbol{X}) \in \mathbb{F}^{\leq 1}[X_1, \ldots, X_n]$ be n-variate multilinear polynomials, and let $\sigma \in \mathbb{F}$ be a claimed sum. The* classical sumcheck protocol *is an n-round interactive protocol for the d-product-sumcheck language between a prover $\mathcal{P}$ and a verifier $\mathcal{V}$ such that $\mathcal{P}$ has random/streaming access to the d polynomials, $\mathcal{V}$ has oracle access to the d polynomials, and both know σ. In each round $i \in [n]$, $\mathcal{P}$ sends to $\mathcal{V}$ a univariate "round" polynomial $t_i(X)$ of degree d, and $\mathcal{V}$ sends a random challenge $r_i \xleftarrow{\$} \mathbb{F}$ to $\mathcal{P}$. $\mathcal{V}$ checks that $t_i(0) + t_i(1) = \sigma_i$, where $\sigma_1 = \sigma$, and $\sigma_i = t_{i-1}(r_{i-1})$.*

If $\mathcal{P}$ is honest, then $t_i(X)$ is defined as follows:

$$t_i(X) := \sum_{\boldsymbol{b} \in \{0,1\}^{n-i}} \prod_{j=1}^{d} p_j(r_1, \ldots, r_{i-1}, X, \boldsymbol{b}) \ .$$

Finally, $\mathcal{V}$ accepts if and only if the checks in all n rounds pass and $t_n(r_n) = \prod_{j=1}^{d} p_j(\boldsymbol{r})$.

Lemma 1 (Completeness and soundness of sumcheck [22]**.** *The classical sumcheck protocol satisfies the following properties:*

- *If $(p_1(\boldsymbol{X}), p_2(\boldsymbol{X}), \ldots, p_d(\boldsymbol{X}), \sigma) \in \mathsf{SC}^{(\mathbb{F},n,d)}$, then $\mathcal{V}$ accepts with probability 1.*
- *If $(p_1(\boldsymbol{X}), p_2(\boldsymbol{X}), \ldots, p_d(\boldsymbol{X}), \sigma) \notin \mathsf{SC}^{(\mathbb{F},n,d)}$, then $\mathcal{V}$ accepts with probability at most $\frac{n \cdot d}{|\mathbb{F}|}$.*

We will use "classical prover for $\mathsf{SC}^{(\mathbb{F},n,d)}$" to refer to an honest prover that follows the classical sumcheck protocol and sends the correct round polynomial $t_i(X)$ in each round $i \in [n]$.

Remark 1. The provers presented in Sects. 2.2 and 2.3 will only require streaming access to their input polynomials, and we call such provers "streaming provers". The lower bounds in Sects. 2.4 and 2.5, however, apply to the more general case of provers with random access to their inputs.

2.2 Space-Efficient Multilinear-Sumcheck Prover

We present our space-efficient multilinear-sumcheck prover $\mathcal{P}$ that only requires streaming access to the input polynomial. Given an input polynomial

$p(X_1, \ldots, X_n) \in \mathbb{F}^{\leq 1}[X_1, \ldots, X_n]$, $\mathcal{P}$ makes only 2 passes over $\mathcal{S}(\boldsymbol{p})$, and runs in $O(N)$ time while using $O(\sqrt{N})$ space.[3]

Existing Ideas. For each $i \in [n]$, in the i-th round of the multilinear-sumcheck protocol, $\mathcal{P}$ must send the following polynomial to the verifier $\mathcal{V}$ (in order to satisfy completeness):

$$t_i(X) := \sum_{\boldsymbol{b} \in \{0,1\}^{n-i}} p(r_1, \ldots, r_{i-1}, X, \boldsymbol{b})$$

$$= \sum_{\boldsymbol{x} \in \{0,1\}^{i-1}} \chi_{\boldsymbol{x}}(r_1, \ldots, r_{i-1}) \cdot \left(\sum_{\boldsymbol{b} \in \{0,1\}^{n-i}} p(\boldsymbol{x}, X, \boldsymbol{b}) \right) ,$$

where for each $j \in [i-1]$, $r_j \in \mathbb{F}$ is the random challenge chosen by $\mathcal{V}$ in the j-th round. It suffices for $\mathcal{P}$ to compute and send $t_i(0)$ and $t_i(1)$, since for all $i \in [n]$, $t_i(X)$ is a degree-1 polynomial in X and can thus be uniquely described by its evaluations at 0 and 1.

If $\mathcal{P}$ was allowed to make a pass over the input stream in every round, then it could compute every t_i in $O(N)$ time and $O(\log N)$ space [15] since each value of $[\chi_{\boldsymbol{x}}(r_1, \ldots, r_{i-1})]_{\boldsymbol{x} \in \{0,1\}^{i-1}}$ can be computed in amortized constant time in a streaming manner using only $O(\log N)$ space (see Sect. 3.1 for details). Thus, $t_i(0)$ and $t_i(1)$ can be computed in $O(N)$ time using $O(\log N)$ space, yielding a streaming prover that runs in $O(N \log N)$ time and uses $O(\log N)$ space.

Using More Space. We now describe a $\mathcal{P}$ that uses $O(\sqrt{N})$ working space, but only needs to make a pass over $\mathcal{S}(\boldsymbol{p})$ in round 1 and another in round $m := \lceil n/2 \rceil$.

Round 1. In the first round, $\mathcal{P}$ stores the following table M, which is indexed by $\boldsymbol{x} \in \{0,1\}^m$:

$$M[\boldsymbol{x}] := \sum_{\boldsymbol{b} \in \{0,1\}^{n-m}} p(\boldsymbol{x}, \boldsymbol{b}) \ .$$

Clearly, this table of size $O(2^m) = O(\sqrt{N})$ can be computed in $O(N)$ time with a single pass over $\mathcal{S}(\boldsymbol{p})$.

Using M, for any $i \in [m-1]$, $\mathcal{P}$ can compute the round polynomial $t_i(X)$ in $O(\sqrt{N})$ time without accessing $\mathcal{S}(\boldsymbol{p})$. This follows from the following expression:

$$t_i(y) = \sum_{\boldsymbol{b} \in \{0,1\}^{n-i}} p(r_1, \ldots, r_{i-1}, y, \boldsymbol{b})$$

$$= \sum_{\boldsymbol{x} \in \{0,1\}^{i-1}} \chi_{\boldsymbol{x}}(r_1, \ldots, r_{i-1}) \cdot \left(\sum_{\boldsymbol{b} \in \{0,1\}^{n-m-i}} M[\boldsymbol{x} \parallel y \parallel \boldsymbol{b}] \right) ,$$

[3] In the appendix of the full version, we show how to generalize this to perform k passes over $\mathcal{S}(\boldsymbol{p})$ and run in $O(kN)$ time, but only use $O(N^{1/k})$ space, for any $1 \leq k \leq \log N$.

for any $i \in [m-1]$ and $y \in \{0,1\}$.

Round m. In round $m = \lceil n/2 \rceil$, once $\mathcal{P}$ knows the values of $r_1, \ldots, r_{m-1}$, it computes the following table M' indexed by $\boldsymbol{x} \in \{0,1\}^{n-m+1}$:

$$M'[\boldsymbol{x}] := p(r_1, \ldots, r_{m-1}, \boldsymbol{x}) = \sum_{\boldsymbol{b} \in \{0,1\}^{m-1}} \chi_{\boldsymbol{b}}(r_1, \ldots, r_{m-1}) \cdot p(\boldsymbol{b}, \boldsymbol{x}) \ .$$

This table of size $O(2^{n-m+1}) = O(\sqrt{N})$ can also be computed in $O(N)$ time with a single pass over $\mathcal{S}(\boldsymbol{p})$, since that the Lagrange polynomial evaluations can be computed in constant amortized time in a streaming manner (see Sect. 3.1 for details). Using M', for each $m \leq i \leq n$, $\mathcal{P}$ can compute the round polynomial $t_i(X)$ in time $O(\sqrt{N})$ with no further accesses to $\mathcal{S}(\boldsymbol{p})$. This step is akin to the "folding-style" linear-time, linear-space sumcheck of [16,33], but invoked on a multilinear polynomial of size $O(\sqrt{N})$, and follows from the following expression:

$$\begin{aligned} t_i(y) &= \sum_{\boldsymbol{b} \in \{0,1\}^{n-i}} p(r_1, \ldots, r_{m-1}, \ldots, r_{i-1}, y, \boldsymbol{b}) \\ &= \sum_{\boldsymbol{x} \in \{0,1\}^{i-m}} \chi_{\boldsymbol{x}}(r_m, \ldots, r_{i-1}) \cdot \left(\sum_{\boldsymbol{b} \in \{0,1\}^{n-i}} M'[\boldsymbol{x} \parallel y \parallel \boldsymbol{b}] \right) \ , \end{aligned}$$

for any $m \leq i \leq n$ and $y \in \{0,1\}$.

Putting it all Together. Clearly, $\mathcal{P}$ only uses $O(\sqrt{N})$ space, and makes two passes over $\mathcal{S}(\boldsymbol{p})$ in addition to taking $O(\sqrt{N})$ time in each of the $\log N$ rounds, thus requiring $O(N)$ time in total.

2.3 Space-Efficient Product-Sumcheck Prover

We now present the space-efficient product-sumcheck prover from Theorem 1. We present the case for $k = 2$, i.e. an algorithm that runs in $O(N \log\log N)$ time while using $O(\sqrt{N})$ space. $\mathcal{P}$ must send the following degree-2 round polynomial $t_i(X)$ to $\mathcal{V}$ in each round $i \in [n]$ of the product-sumcheck protocol:

$$t_i(X) := \sum_{\boldsymbol{b} \in \{0,1\}^{n-i}} p(r_1, \ldots, r_{i-1}, X, \boldsymbol{b}) \cdot q(r_1, \ldots, r_{i-1}, X, \boldsymbol{b}) \ .$$

Each t_i is uniquely defined by 3 evaluation points. For clarity of notation, we will abuse notation and say $\mathcal{P}$ computes $t_i(X)$, when we actually mean that $\mathcal{P}$ computes $t_i(0)$, $t_i(1)$ and $t_i(z)$, for some fixed $z \in \mathbb{F} \setminus \{0,1\}$.

Furthermore, since $g(z) = (1-z) \cdot g(0) + z \cdot g(1)$ for any degree-1 polynomial $g(X)$, it actually suffices for $\mathcal{P}$ to compute $p_i(0)$ and $p_i(1)$, since it can obtain $p_i(z)$ from these. Hence, in the rest of this discussion, we will focus on computing $p_i(0), p_i(1)$, and $q_i(0), q_i(1)$.

We begin by discussing the "easy" case of handling the last $\lceil n/2 \rceil$ rounds, and then discuss the more challenging case of handling the first $\lfloor n/2 \rfloor$ rounds.

The Last $\lceil n/2 \rceil$ Rounds. Define $m := \lceil n/2 \rceil$. For rounds $i \geq m$, $\mathcal{P}$ can compute each round polynomial $t_i(X)$ in $O(\sqrt{N})$ time as follows: $\mathcal{P}$ makes a single pass over $\mathcal{S}(\boldsymbol{p})$ and $\mathcal{S}(\boldsymbol{q})$ in round m and stores the following two tables:

$$M'_p[\boldsymbol{x}] := p(r_1, \ldots, r_{m-1}, \boldsymbol{x}) \ , \ M'_q[\boldsymbol{x}] := q(r_1, \ldots, r_{m-1}, \boldsymbol{x}), \ \forall \boldsymbol{x} \in \{0,1\}^{n-m+1} \ .$$

Using these tables, $\mathcal{P}$ can compute $t_i(X)$ for any given $i \geq m$ in $O(\sqrt{N})$ time using similar ideas to those in Sect. 2.2. In more detail, $\mathcal{P}$ uses M'_p and M'_q to compute

$$[p(r_1, \ldots, r_{i-1}, y, \boldsymbol{b})]_{y \in \{0,1\}, \boldsymbol{b} \in \{0,1\}^{n-i}} \ , \ [q(r_1, \ldots, r_{i-1}, y, \boldsymbol{b})]_{y \in \{0,1\}, \boldsymbol{b} \in \{0,1\}^{n-i}} \ .$$

This step takes $O(\sqrt{N})$ time, and using the trick above, $\mathcal{P}$ can then compute

$$[p(r_1, \ldots, r_{i-1}, z, \boldsymbol{b})]_{\boldsymbol{b} \in \{0,1\}^{n-i}} \ , \ [q(r_1, \ldots, r_{i-1}, z, \boldsymbol{b})]_{\boldsymbol{b} \in \{0,1\}^{n-i}} \ ,$$

and hence also $t_i(z)$, as required.

Bottleneck: Computing Cross Products in the First m Rounds. Computing $t_i(X)$ for rounds $i \in [m-1]$ is more challenging. Say $\mathcal{P}$ makes a pass over $\mathcal{S}(\boldsymbol{p})$ and $\mathcal{S}(\boldsymbol{q})$ in the first round, and wants to precompute some tables M_p and M_q that allow it to compute $t_i(X)$ for all rounds $i \in [m-1]$. In every round $i \in [m-1]$, given the challenges $\boldsymbol{r} = (r_1, \ldots, r_{i-1})$, it must be able to compute

$$\begin{aligned} t_i(X) &= \sum_{\boldsymbol{b} \in \{0,1\}^{n-i}} p(\boldsymbol{r}, X, \boldsymbol{b}) \cdot q(\boldsymbol{r}, X, \boldsymbol{b}) \\ &= \sum_{\boldsymbol{b} \in \{0,1\}^{n-i}} \left(\sum_{\boldsymbol{x} \in \{0,1\}^{i-1}} \chi_{\boldsymbol{x}}(\boldsymbol{r}) \, p(\boldsymbol{x}, X, \boldsymbol{b}) \right) \left(\sum_{\boldsymbol{x} \in \{0,1\}^{i-1}} \chi_{\boldsymbol{x}}(\boldsymbol{r}) \, q(\boldsymbol{x}, X, \boldsymbol{b}) \right) \\ &= \sum_{\boldsymbol{x}, \boldsymbol{x}' \in \{0,1\}^{i-1}} \chi_{\boldsymbol{x}}(\boldsymbol{r}) \, \chi_{\boldsymbol{x}'}(\boldsymbol{r}) \sum_{\boldsymbol{b} \in \{0,1\}^{n-i}} p(\boldsymbol{x}, X, \boldsymbol{b}) q(\boldsymbol{x}', X, \boldsymbol{b}) \ . \end{aligned}$$

In round 1, $\mathcal{P}$ does not know the values of $r_1, \ldots, r_{m-1}$, and therefore needs to store values such that the above expression can be computed regardless of the challenges picked by $\mathcal{V}$. However, it is not clear how $\mathcal{P}$ can compute the following "cross products" efficiently for all $i \in [m-1]$:

$$\left[\sum_{\boldsymbol{b} \in \{0,1\}^{n-i}} p(\boldsymbol{x}, \boldsymbol{b}) \cdot q(\boldsymbol{x}', \boldsymbol{b}) \right]_{\boldsymbol{x}, \boldsymbol{x}' \in \{0,1\}^{i-1}} \ . \tag{1}$$

Solution: Reduce the Number of Rounds Between Passes. We take a different approach: instead of allowing $\mathcal{P}$ to make only a single pass before round m, we now allow it to make passes over $\mathcal{S}(\boldsymbol{p})$ and $\mathcal{S}(\boldsymbol{q})$ in multiple intermediate rounds $1 \leq j < m$. Intuitively, this helps because when $\mathcal{P}$ no longer needs to precompute tables that suffice for all rounds $i \in [m-1]$, and instead only needs to store enough information for the next few rounds, until it makes its next pass. We show that it suffices for the prover to make $\log\log N = \log n$ passes.

In more detail, we have the prover perform a pass in every round $j \in [2^s]_{s=0}^{\log n-2}$, and we show that the tables stored in round $j = 2^s$ suffices to compute the round polynomial $t_i(X)$ for all rounds $i \in [2^s, 2^{s+1})$. To do this, we leverage the fact that when $\mathcal{P}$ makes a pass in some intermediate round $j = 2^s$, it already knows the challenges $\boldsymbol{r}_L = (r_1, \ldots, r_{j-1})$. Thus, for a round $i \in [2^s, 2^{s+1}]$, given the new challenges $\boldsymbol{r}_R = (r_j, r_{j+1}, \ldots, r_{i-1})$, $\mathcal{P}$ now only has to compute

$$t_i(X) = \sum_{\boldsymbol{b}\in\{0,1\}^{n-i}} p(\boldsymbol{r}_L, \boldsymbol{r}_R, X, \boldsymbol{b}) \cdot q(\boldsymbol{r}_L, \boldsymbol{r}_R, X, \boldsymbol{b}) \tag{2}$$

$$= \sum_{\boldsymbol{x},\boldsymbol{x}'\in\{0,1\}^{i-j}} \chi_{\boldsymbol{x}}(\boldsymbol{r}_R)\, \chi_{\boldsymbol{x}'}(\boldsymbol{r}_R) \sum_{\boldsymbol{b}\in\{0,1\}^{n-i}} p(\boldsymbol{r}_L, \boldsymbol{x}, X, \boldsymbol{b}) q(\boldsymbol{r}_L, \boldsymbol{x}', X, \boldsymbol{b}) \ . \tag{3}$$

Accordingly, in each intermediate round $j = 2^s$, we have $\mathcal{P}$ compute the following table M_s consisting of "cross products", which we index by $\boldsymbol{x}, \boldsymbol{x}' \in \{0,1\}^j$:

$$M_s[\boldsymbol{x}, \boldsymbol{x}'] := \sum_{\boldsymbol{b}\in\{0,1\}^{n-2j+1}} p(\boldsymbol{r}_L, \boldsymbol{x}, \boldsymbol{b}) \cdot q(\boldsymbol{r}_L, \boldsymbol{x}', \boldsymbol{b}) \ .$$

This is sufficient due to the following reasons:

1. This table is of size $2^j \cdot 2^j = 2^{(2^s)} \cdot 2^{(2^s)}$, which is $O(\sqrt{N})$ for all $s \in [0, 1, \ldots, \log n - 2]$, so $\mathcal{P}$ has sufficient space to store it.
2. Given M_s, $\mathcal{P}$ can compute $t_i(X)$ for any $i \in [2^s, 2^{s+1})$ in $O(\sqrt{N})$ time. This is because each $t_i(X)$ is a linear combination of some at-most-$\sqrt{N}$-sized subset of M_s with respect to the coefficients in Eq. (3). We refer the reader to Sect. 4 for the details.
3. Each M_s can be computed in $O(N)$ time with a single pass over each of $\mathcal{S}(\boldsymbol{p})$ and $\mathcal{S}(\boldsymbol{q})$. This can be seen as follows: if $\mathcal{P}$ had access to $[p(\boldsymbol{r}_L, \boldsymbol{y})]_{\boldsymbol{y}\in\{0,1\}^{n-j+1}}$ and $[q(\boldsymbol{r}_L, \boldsymbol{y})]_{\boldsymbol{y}\in\{0,1\}^{n-j+1}}$, then it could compute each $M_s[\boldsymbol{x}, \boldsymbol{x}']$ in $O(2^{n-2j+1})$ time, thus taking $O(2^{2j} \cdot 2^{n-2j+1}) = O(N)$ time to compute all 2^{2j} elements of M_s. We show in Sect. 4 that $\mathcal{P}$ can simulate streaming access to $[p(\boldsymbol{r}_L, \boldsymbol{y})]_{\boldsymbol{y}\in\{0,1\}^{n-j+1}}$ and $[q(\boldsymbol{r}_L, \boldsymbol{y})]_{\boldsymbol{y}\in\{0,1\}^{n-j+1}}$, using its knowledge of $\boldsymbol{r}_L$ and streaming access to $\mathcal{S}(\boldsymbol{p})$ and $\mathcal{S}(\boldsymbol{q})$, with essentially no overhead.

2.4 Lower Bound for Multilinear-Sumcheck Provers

We provide a brief overview of the time-space trade-off lower bound for the multilinear-sumcheck protocol. We informally state the theorem below, and note that when we say "non-adaptive prover", we mean a prover that is non-adaptive with respect to the polynomial it receives as input and the random challenges it receives from the verifier.

Theorem 1 (informal, see Theorem 4). *Let $\mathcal{P}$ be a non-adaptive prover for the n-variate multilinear-sumcheck protocol that has random-access to its input $\boldsymbol{p} \in \mathbb{F}^N$, and which runs in time T and uses S units of random-access space. Then $T \log S = \Omega(N \log N)$.*

As before, for all $i \in [n]$, we require that $\mathcal{P}$ must compute and send the evaluations of the round polynomial $t_i(X)$ at 0 and 1.[4]

First Round. Since $\mathcal{P}$ is complete, it must be compute the correct round polynomials for all input polynomials p. We start by showing that $\mathcal{P}$ must read every element of $\boldsymbol{p}$ to compute $t_1(X)$. Assume not, i.e. that there exists a point $\boldsymbol{x} \in \{0,1\}^n$ such that $\mathcal{P}$ does not read $p(\boldsymbol{x})$. Then there exists a different polynomial q whose evaluation at $\boldsymbol{x}$ differs from that of p. However, because $\mathcal{P}$ is non-adaptive, and because the locations it reads are the same for both p and q, it will produce the same round polynomial for both, which will be incorrect for at least one of the two.

Further Rounds. An optimal $\mathcal{P}$ would use these N reads to store a state st of size S, which it can use to compute $t_j(X)$ for further rounds $j > 1$. Say $\mathcal{P}$ makes no further accesses to $\boldsymbol{p}$ for the next few rounds after round 1. Then, in round $j = \log S + 1$, $\mathcal{P}$ must be able to use this state to compute $t_j(0) = \sum_{\boldsymbol{b} \in \{0,1\}^{n-j}} p(\boldsymbol{r}, 0, \boldsymbol{b})$ and $t_j(1) = \sum_{\boldsymbol{b} \in \{0,1\}^{n-j}} p(\boldsymbol{r}, 1, \boldsymbol{b})$, for all $\boldsymbol{r}$ in the restricted set of verifier challenges $\{0,1\}^{j-1} \subset \mathbb{F}^{j-1}$.[5] For every choice of $\boldsymbol{r}$ and $y \in \{0,1\}$, $t_j(y)$ corresponds to a sum of evaluations of $p(\boldsymbol{X})$ over distinct sub-cubes of $\{0,1\}^n$, each of which is an arbitrary element in $\mathbb{F}$ (independent of the other sums). There are 2^j such disjoint sub-cubes, and since $\mathcal{P}$ makes no further accesses to $\boldsymbol{p}$ and must be able to correctly compute all of these values, it must either:

- store a state of size at least $2^j = 2S$, which is a contradiction, or
- "compress" the $2S$ arbitrary field elements into fewer than S field elements, which can be shown to be impossible using a compression argument.

Thus, regardless of the st it stored, $\mathcal{P}$ must make further accesses to $\boldsymbol{p}$ in order to be able to send the correct polynomial in round $\log S + 1$. Since there are at least $2S - S = S$ sums whose (arbitrary) values $\mathcal{P}$ has not stored in st, and each of these is a sum over 2^{n-j} elements of $\boldsymbol{p}$, $\mathcal{P}$ must make at least $S \cdot 2^{n-j} \geq S \cdot 2^{n - \log S - 1} = N/2$ further accesses to $\boldsymbol{p}$ in order to compute the these sums correctly.

Other Access Strategies. The argument so far agrees with the construction in Sect. 2.2 with $S = \sqrt{N}$, where $\mathcal{P}$ makes a pass over $\mathcal{S}(\boldsymbol{p})$ in the first round, and then further accesses in round $m = \log S + 1 = \lceil n/2 \rceil$. In fact, the full proof

[4] This is without loss of generality as $\mathcal{P}$ can compute $t_i(0)$ and $t_i(1)$ in constant time given any unique representation of t_i.

[5] Restricting the verifier to pick random challenges in $\{0,1\}^j$ as opposed to $\mathbb{F}^j$ makes the $\mathcal{P}$'s job easier, but as we show, it suffices for obtaining the lower bound.

shows that the prover cannot do better, and gains no advantage by making accesses spread over multiple rounds between rounds 1 and $\log S + 1$.

We complete the proof of Theorem 1 by repeating (an analog of) the above argument to show that in every round of the form $1, 1 + \log S, 1 + 2\log S, \ldots$, $\mathcal{P}$ must make $O(N)$ accesses to $\boldsymbol{p}$. There are $\lfloor \log N / \log S \rfloor$ such rounds, and therefore $\mathcal{P}$ must make $\Omega(N \log N / \log S)$ accesses to $\boldsymbol{p}$ in total. We provide more details in Sect. 5.

2.5 Lower Bound for Product-Sumcheck Provers

The lower bound for multilinear-sumcheck provers also applies to product-sumcheck provers. In addition, we present a stronger lower bound for the product-sumcheck protocol which shows that the prover described in Sect. 2.3 is optimal within a class of "natural" classical sumcheck provers for $\mathsf{SC}^{(\mathbb{F},n,2)}$.

Need for Conjecture. If there exists a fast matrix multiplication algorithm for $A, B \in \mathbb{F}^{m\times m}$ that outputs $A{\cdot}B$ while only using $O(m^2)$ field operations, then the prover in Sect. 2.3 can be improved to require only $O(kN)$ field operations when using $O(N^{1/k})$ space, thus matching the multilinear-sumcheck prover in Sect. 2.2. At a high level, this would remove the bottleneck in the algorithm in Sect. 2.3 for computing the cross products, since any table M_s that will fit in memory can be computed in linear time, regardless of the value of s (see full version for details). Consequently, a stronger lower bound cannot be unconditional and requires us to introduce the following conjecture that is related to matrix multiplication.

Definition 3 (Batch-polynomial-multiplication problem). *$\mathcal{A}$ solves the (n,ℓ)-*batch-polynomial-multiplication *problem (denoted by $\mathsf{BPM}(n,\ell)$) if for all $p_1, \ldots, p_\ell, q_1, \ldots, q_\ell \in \mathbb{F}^{\leq 1}[X_1, \ldots, X_n]$, $\mathcal{A}$ outputs $f(\boldsymbol{X}) := \sum_{i=1}^{\ell} p_i(\boldsymbol{X}) \cdot q_i(\boldsymbol{X})$ assuming that $\mathcal{A}$ has random-access to the evaluations of the inputs polynomials over $\{0,1\}^n$.*

Conjecture 1. There exists a constant $\omega > 0$ such that any algorithm $\mathcal{A}$ that solves $\mathsf{BPM}(n,\ell)$ requires $\Omega(2^{(\omega+1)n} \cdot \ell)$ field operations for all $n, \ell \in \mathbb{N}$.

The output of $\mathsf{BPM}(n,\ell)$ consists of 3^n field elements, and therefore the conjecture is trivially true if $\ell = O((3/2 - \kappa)^n)$ for any constant $\kappa > 0$. However, the instances of interest for our proof are when $\ell = \Omega(2^n)$, where it is not evident if the conjecture holds. We note that the conjecture is false if $\ell = \Omega(2^n)$ and there exists a fast matrix multiplication algorithm, but as mentioned earlier, if there exists such an algorithm then our product-sumcheck prover can be improved to break this lower bound.

Theorem 2 (informal, see Theorem 5**).** *If Conjecture 1 holds, then an honest, non-adaptive, field-agnostic*[6] *prover $\mathcal{P}$ for the product-sumcheck protocol that has $O(N^{1/2-\varepsilon})$ space and random-access to p and q requires $\Omega(N(\log\log N +$*

[6] The specific technical condition we require is only being *extension-agnostic*, which is weaker than being field-agnostic.

$\log \varepsilon)/\log(1+1/\omega))$ time, where $\varepsilon > 0$ is a constant, assuming that $\mathcal{P}$ reads $O(N^{1-\varepsilon})$ values of $\boldsymbol{p}$ and $\boldsymbol{q}$ in any round where it performs $\leq N/4$ field operations.

Remark 2. The last assumption regarding the number of reads may seem contrived, but all known product-sumcheck provers satisfy it [15,16,33], including our algorithm in Sect. 2.3. This assumption can be removed if we assume a slightly stronger conjecture, see the full statement (Theorem 5) for details.

Proof Intuition. For simplicity, we assume that in any round where $\mathcal{P}$ accesses its input, it must access all N evaluations of p and q. This assumption is removed in the full proof in Sect. 6, but it is not crucial to the intuition we present here. The proof is structured in a similar manner to the multilinear-sumcheck lower bound, where we pick two rounds of the sumcheck protocol, $\mathsf{m}_{\mathcal{A}}$ and $\mathsf{m}_{\mathcal{B}}$ that are far apart, and we show that a time-optimal prover which read the input in round $\mathsf{m}_{\mathcal{A}}$, must read the input in or before round $\mathsf{m}_{\mathcal{B}}$ as well. Proving this statement for $O(\log\log N + \log \varepsilon)$ pairs of rounds $\mathsf{m}_{\mathcal{A}}$ and $\mathsf{m}_{\mathcal{B}}$ is sufficient to complete the proof.

We are motivated by the bottleneck in the product-sumcheck prover from Sect. 2.3 for computing the cross products. Recall that if $\mathcal{P}$ reads the entire input in a round $\mathsf{m}_{\mathcal{A}}$, then it can compute a state st in linear time that allows it to compute the round polynomial $t_i(X)$ for every round $i \in [\mathsf{m}_{\mathcal{A}}, 2\mathsf{m}_{\mathcal{A}}]$, without reading the input again. The restriction of $i \leq 2\mathsf{m}_{\mathcal{A}}$ ensures that the table computation requires linear time. Therefore, if we consider a round $\mathsf{m}_{\mathcal{B}}$ such that $\mathsf{m}_{\mathcal{B}} \geq c \cdot \mathsf{m}_{\mathcal{A}}$ for some constant $c > 2$, then there are two possible cases:

- $\mathcal{P}$ reads the entire input in or before round $\mathsf{m}_{\mathcal{B}}$ to compute $t_{\mathsf{m}_{\mathcal{B}}}(X)$, or
- $\mathcal{P}$ uses st alone to compute $t_{\mathsf{m}_{\mathcal{B}}}(X)$, without reading the input again after round $\mathsf{m}_{\mathcal{A}}$.

We show that if c is large enough and we are in the second case, $\mathcal{P}$ must have performed $\Omega(N \log^{\omega} N)$ field operations in round $\mathsf{m}_{\mathcal{A}}$ to compute st, where ω is the constant from Conjecture 1. We refer to this statement as the "main technical lemma", and we provide a proof sketch of it below. This lemma is the crux of the proof, and implies that if we are not in the first case above, we obtain the desired lower bound.

If we are in the first case, then we have shown that $\mathcal{P}$ reads the entire input again in or before round $\mathsf{m}_{\mathcal{B}}$, despite having read the input in round $\mathsf{m}_{\mathcal{A}}$. The main technical lemma only holds if $\mathsf{m}_{\mathcal{B}}$ is at most $\varepsilon \log N$, but there must still be $\Omega(\log_c(\varepsilon \log N)) = \Omega(\log\log N + \log \varepsilon)$ pairs of such rounds which adhere to this constraint, completing the proof.

Main Technical Lemma. In round $\mathsf{m}_{\mathcal{B}}$, $\mathcal{P}$ outputs $t_{\mathsf{m}_{\mathcal{B}}}(X)$ using the following two components: (i) st, the state computed by $\mathcal{P}$ in round $\mathsf{m}_{\mathcal{A}}$, and (ii) $\boldsymbol{r}$, the random challenges received by $\mathcal{P}$ between rounds $\mathsf{m}_{\mathcal{A}}$ and $\mathsf{m}_{\mathcal{B}}$. Define $\mathsf{m} := \mathsf{m}_{\mathcal{B}} - \mathsf{m}_{\mathcal{A}} + 1$. Note that because $\mathsf{m}_{\mathcal{B}} \leq \varepsilon \log N$, $\mathsf{m} < \log N/2$. The goal of this lemma is to show that if $\mathcal{P}$ can compute $t_{\mathsf{m}_{\mathcal{B}}}(X)$ efficiently using these two components, then we can use $\mathcal{P}$ to construct an algorithm $\mathcal{A}^*$ that solves an instance of $\mathsf{BPM}(\mathsf{m}, 2^{n-\mathsf{m}_\mathcal{B}})$ in time $O(T+N)$, where T is the total time taken by $\mathcal{P}$ to compute st. Because $2^{n-\mathsf{m}_\mathcal{B}} = \Omega(\sqrt{N})$, and because $2^\mathsf{m} = O(\sqrt{N})$, we can apply Conjecture 1 to $\mathcal{A}^*$ to obtain $T = \Omega(N \log^\omega N)$, where ω is the constant from the conjecture.

Before describing the construction of $\mathcal{A}^*$, we first note that computing $t_{\mathsf{m}_\mathcal{B}}(X)$ for 3^m different values of $\boldsymbol{r}$ is equivalent to computing the following polynomial $f : \mathbb{F}^\mathsf{m} \to \mathbb{F}$:

$$f(\boldsymbol{X}) := \sum_{\boldsymbol{b} \in \{0,1\}^{n-\mathsf{m}_\mathcal{B}}} p(\boldsymbol{t}, \boldsymbol{X}, \boldsymbol{b}) \cdot q(\boldsymbol{t}, \boldsymbol{X}, \boldsymbol{b}) \ , \tag{4}$$

where $\boldsymbol{t} \in \mathbb{F}^{\mathsf{m}_\mathcal{A}-1}$ is the vector of random challenges $\boldsymbol{r}$ received by $\mathcal{P}$ before round $\mathsf{m}_\mathcal{A}$. Clearly, computing this polynomial is equivalent to solving $\mathsf{BPM}(\mathsf{m}, 2^{n-\mathsf{m}_\mathcal{B}})$. This motivates the construction of $\mathcal{A}^*$ as follows: using the fact that $\mathcal{P}$ is field-agnostic and non-adaptive, we can model $\mathcal{P}$ as an arithmetic circuit $\mathcal{C}$ such that each gate of $\mathcal{C}$ outputs a *bilinear* polynomial in the inputs of the circuit: $\boldsymbol{p}$ and $\boldsymbol{q}$. Therefore, the output of $\mathcal{C}$ can be expressed as follows:

$$f(\boldsymbol{r}) = \sum_{i,j=0}^{|\mathsf{st}^*|} c_{i,j}(\boldsymbol{r}) \cdot \mathsf{st}^*_i \cdot \mathsf{st}^*_j \ , \tag{5}$$

If $|\mathsf{st}^*| = O(N^{1/2-\varepsilon})$, and $3^\mathsf{m} = O(N^{2\varepsilon})$ (which holds because we restricted $\mathsf{m}_\mathcal{B} \leq \varepsilon \log N$), then the number of coefficients $c_{i,j}(\cdot)$ is $O(N)$, and therefore all $f(\boldsymbol{r})$ can be computed in $O(N)$ time by solving the system of linear equations defined by Eq. (5).

Therefore, using st alone, $\mathcal{A}^*$ can compute $f(\boldsymbol{r})$ in $O(N)$ time for 3^m values of $\boldsymbol{r}$, which uniquely defines the polynomial $f(\boldsymbol{X})$, and therefore $\mathcal{A}^*$ can solve $\mathsf{BPM}(\mathsf{m}, 2^{n-\mathsf{m}_\mathcal{B}})$ in $O(T+N)$ time. Proving the fact that $\mathcal{P}$'s output must satisfy Eq. (5) requires a lot of care, and we refer the reader to Sect. 6 for the details.

2.6 New Product-Sumcheck PIOP for FFT-Friendly Fields

We provide a brief overview of a proof of Theorem 3 and Theorem 4. For Theorem 3, we describe the protocol informally for the case when $k = 1$, and refer the reader to the full version for the details.

Protocol Overview. Let $s = \log^*(n/2)$, and let $\mathbb{G}_1, \mathbb{G}_2, \ldots, \mathbb{G}_{s+1}$ be multiplicative subgroups of $\mathbb{F}$ such that

- For $j \in [s-1]$: $|\mathbb{G}_j| = T(j)$, where $T(j)$ is the j-th tower power of 2 ($T(1) = 2$, $T(2) = 2^2 = 4$, $T(3) = 2^4 = 16$, $T(4) = 2^{16}$ and so on).
- For $j = s$: $|\mathbb{G}_s| = \sqrt{N} / \left(\prod_{j=1}^{s-1} |\mathbb{G}_j|\right)$.
- For $j = s+1$: $|\mathbb{G}_{s+1}| = \sqrt{N}$.

These subgroups exist if $\mathbb{F}$ is FFT-friendly, i.e., $|\mathbb{F}|-1$ is product of several small primes (in this case, it divides a large power of 2). We define the *mixed polynomial*

$\tilde{p} : \mathbb{F}^{s+1} \to \mathbb{F}$ as the unique polynomial such that for all $(g_1, \ldots, g_{s+1}) \in (\mathbb{G}_1 \times \ldots \times \mathbb{G}_{s+1})$, we have

$$\tilde{p}(g_1, \ldots, g_{s+1}) = p(\phi_1(g_1), \ldots, \phi_{s+1}(g_{s+1})) \ ,$$

where $\phi_j(g)$ is the binary representation of i such that $g = g_j^i$ where g_j is a generator of $\mathbb{G}_j$, and $\tilde{p}$ has degree at most $|\mathbb{G}_j|-1$ in the j-th variable. $\tilde{q}$ is defined analogously. Instead of the verifier $\mathcal{V}$ having oracle access to the multilinear polynomials $p, q : \mathbb{F}^n \to \mathbb{F}$, we assume that $\mathcal{V}$ has oracle access to the mixed polynomials $\tilde{p}, \tilde{q} : \mathbb{F}^{s+1} \to \mathbb{F}$.

In the classical sumcheck protocol, $\mathcal{P}$ sends a degree-2 polynomial t_j to $\mathcal{V}$ in round j, and $\mathcal{V}$ sends back a random challenge $r_j \in \mathbb{F}$. Instead, in the j-th round of our protocol, $\mathcal{P}$ sends a *polynomial oracle* to a $(2|\mathbb{G}_j| - 2)$-degree univariate polynomial t_j to $\mathcal{V}$, and $\mathcal{V}$ sends back a challenge $r_j \xleftarrow{\$} \mathbb{F}$. This round polynomial t_j is defined as follows:

$$t_j(X) = \sum_{\substack{g_{j+1} \in \mathbb{G}_{j+1} \\ \vdots \\ g_{s+1} \in \mathbb{G}_{s+1}}} \tilde{p}(r_1, ..., r_{j-1}, X, g_{j+1}, ..., g_{s+1}) \tilde{q}(r_1, ..., r_{j-1}, X, g_{j+1}, ..., g_{s+1})$$

$\mathcal{V}$ then performs the following check:

$$\sum_{g \in \mathbb{G}_j} t_j(g) = t_{j-1}(r_{j-1}) \ . \tag{6}$$

If the check passes, $\mathcal{V}$ continues to the next round, and otherwise it rejects. $\mathcal{V}$ has polynomial oracle access to both t_j and t_{j-1}, and therefore can obtain $t_{j-1}(r_{j-1})$ in one oracle query. The check in Eq. (6) is therefore simply a *univariate sumcheck* over the subgroup $\mathbb{G}_j$. The univariate sumcheck protocol of Aurora [7] can be used to implement this check, and requires $O(|\mathbb{G}_j| \cdot \log |\mathbb{G}_j|)$ field operations for the prover with only 1 round of communication.

$\mathcal{P}$'s time bottleneck is computing the round polynomials t_i for all $i \in [s]$. This involves multiplying $N/(|\mathbb{G}_1| \cdots |\mathbb{G}_{i-1}|)$ many pairs of $(|\mathbb{G}_i| - 1)$-degree univariate polynomials, which requires $O(|\mathbb{G}_i| \cdot \log |\mathbb{G}_i| \cdot N/(|\mathbb{G}_1| \cdots |\mathbb{G}_i|))$ field operations using FFTs. By our construction, $\log |\mathbb{G}_i| \leq |\mathbb{G}_{i-1}|$, and therefore the above complexity is simply $O(N)$. Since $s = O(\log^* N)$, we obtain the desired time and round complexity.

$\mathcal{P}$'s space bottleneck is simply storing the round polynomials t_j. The degree of t_j is $2|\mathbb{G}_j| - 2$, and therefore $\mathcal{P}$ requires $O(|\mathbb{G}_j|)$ space to it. The largest value of $|\mathbb{G}_j|$ for any $j \in [s+1]$ is $\sqrt{N}$, and therefore $\mathcal{P}$ requires $O(\sqrt{N})$ space.

We emphasize that unlike the algorithm described in Sect. 2.3, this is not an interactive proof for the sumcheck language. Rather, it is a PIOP similar to Sparrow's protocol [25]. However, the polynomial oracles for t_j can be realized via a univariate polynomial commitment scheme [1,6,20] to obtain an *interactive argument* for the sumcheck language. This does not affect the time complexity of the prover since each univariate polynomial has degree at most $\sqrt{N}$, and these commitment schemes require $O(d \log d)$ prover time to commit and open a polynomial of degree d.

Linear-Time Prover. If one is willing to use a linear-space prover, then a similar round complexity can be achieved with a linear-time prover by adapting the folding-style sumcheck of [16,33] to the mixed polynomials. In particular, the algorithm described above requires $O(N)$ in each round to simply compute the round polynomial t_j. However, if we allow $\mathcal{P}$ to store the following *folded polynomials* $\tilde{p}_j, \tilde{q}_j$ in round j where

$$\forall \boldsymbol{g} \in \mathbb{G}_{j+1} \times \ldots \times \mathbb{G}_{s+1} : \tilde{p}_j(\boldsymbol{g}) = \sum_{g_j \in \mathbb{G}_j} \tilde{p}_{j-1}(g_j, \boldsymbol{g}) \cdot \mathsf{L}_{j,g_j}(r_j) \ ,$$

where $\mathsf{L}_{j,g_j}(r_j)$ is the univariate Lagrange polynomial evaluated at r_j for subgroup $\mathbb{G}_j$ that evaluates to 1 at g_j and 0 at all other points in $\mathbb{G}_j$. Using $\tilde{p}_{j-1}$ and $\tilde{q}_j$ as opposed to $\tilde{p}$ and $\tilde{q}$ to compute t_j allows $\mathcal{P}$ to do so in $O\left(\prod_{i=j-1}^{s+1} |\mathbb{G}_i|\right)$ time, as opposed to $O(N)$ time. Adding the cost over all rounds, the total number of field operations required by $\mathcal{P}$ is $O(N)$. We refer the reader to the full version for the details of this linear-time prover.

3 Preliminaries

3.1 Computation of Lagrange Basis Polynomial in a Streaming Manner

Given $\boldsymbol{r} \in \mathbb{F}^n$, we can compute $\{\chi_{\langle 0 \rangle}(\boldsymbol{r}), \chi_{\langle 1 \rangle}(\boldsymbol{r}), \ldots, \chi_{\langle 2^n-1 \rangle}(\boldsymbol{r})\}$ in a streaming manner as follows. We first compute the Lagrange basis polynomial $\chi_{\langle 0 \rangle}(\boldsymbol{r})$, which is equal to $\prod_{i=1}^{n}(1-r_i)$. For each $v \in [2^n-1]$, we compute $\chi_{\langle v \rangle}(\boldsymbol{r})$ using $\chi_{\langle v-1 \rangle}(\boldsymbol{r})$ as follows:

$$\chi_{\langle v \rangle}(\boldsymbol{r}) = \chi_{\langle v-1 \rangle}(\boldsymbol{r}) \cdot \frac{r_j}{1-r_j} \cdot \prod_{i=1}^{j-1} \frac{1-r_i}{r_i} \ ,$$

where j is the index of the least significant bit of $\langle v \rangle$ that is equal to 0. This computation clearly requires only $O(n)$ space. Furthermore, when computing $\chi_{\langle 0 \rangle}(\boldsymbol{r}), \chi_{\langle 1 \rangle}(\boldsymbol{r}), \ldots, \chi_{\langle 2^n-1 \rangle}(\boldsymbol{r})$, the above algorithm multiplies by $(1-r_i)/r_i$ or $r_i/(1-r_i)$ only 2^i times. Therefore, the total number of multiplications performed is $\sum_{i=1}^{n} 2^i = O(2^n)$, and the amortized cost of computing one Lagrange basis polynomial is $O(1)$. This algorithm is used in previous work [5,34], and follows a similar approach to an unpublished observation by Vu. Furthermore, a note by Rothblum [27] demonstrates how to compute these evaluations in the *gray code ordering* in a streaming manner with only $O(n)$ space.

3.2 Model of Computation

Throughout this paper, we assume the arithmetic model of computation for a given finite field $\mathbb{F}$. That is, addition and multiplication of field elements takes constant time, and one field element can be stored in a single unit of space. Furthermore, specifically for the purposes of our lower bounds in Sects. 5 and 6, we model algorithms as *arithmetic circuits.*

Definition 4 (Arithmetic circuit). *An* arithmetic circuit $\mathcal{C}$ *is a directed acyclic graph G such that*

- *All vertices are labelled as constant gates, input gates, addition gates, or multiplication gates.*
- *The in-degree of input gates and constant gates is 0, and the in-degree of addition gates and multiplication gates is 2.*
- *Additionally, some vertices are labeled as output gates.*

$\mathcal{C}$ *is* equipped *with field* $\mathbb{F}$ *if the constant gates are labelled with elements of* $\mathbb{F}$*, and the addition and multiplication gates output the sum and product of their input wires in* $\mathbb{F}$ *respectively. A* $\mathcal{C}$ *equipped with* $\mathbb{F}$ computes functions $f_1, f_2, \ldots, f_k : \mathbb{F}^n \to \mathbb{F}$ *if the i-th output gate of* $\mathcal{C}$ *outputs* $f_i(\boldsymbol{x})$ *for all* $\boldsymbol{x} \in \mathbb{F}^n$ *where* $\boldsymbol{x}$ *is the vector of field elements corresponding to the input gates of* $\mathcal{C}$.

Classical Prover as Set of Arithmetic Circuits. The classical prover for $\mathsf{SC}^{(\mathbb{F},n,d)}$ can be modelled as n-many arithmetic circuits $\mathcal{C}_1, \mathcal{C}_2, \ldots, \mathcal{C}_n$, one for each round of the protocol. Since we prove our lower bounds in the random-access model, each $\mathcal{C}_i$ receives as input $\boldsymbol{p}_1, \boldsymbol{p}_2, \ldots, \boldsymbol{p}_d \in \mathbb{F}^N$ as $(d \cdot N)$-many input gates. We refer to this set of values as $\mathcal{J} \in \mathbb{F}^{d \cdot N}$. $\mathcal{C}_1$ receives as input $\mathcal{J}$ and outputs $\mathcal{O}_1$, which consists of the *state* that is passed to $\mathcal{C}_2$. Subsequent circuits $\mathcal{C}_i$ receive as input $\mathcal{J}$, $\mathcal{O}_{i-1}$ and random challenges $(r_1, \ldots, r_{i-1})$, and output $\mathcal{O}_i$.

Non-adaptive Algorithms. Arithmetic circuits capture the *non-adaptivity* assumption we make about the prover for our lower bounds. That is, the field operations performed by the prover do not depend on the input values $\mathcal{J}$ and the random challenges $(r_1, \ldots, r_{i-1})$. In particular, the total number of field operations performed by $\mathcal{C}_i$ is the same regardless of the input. To the best of our knowledge, all known prover algorithms for $\mathsf{SC}^{(\mathbb{F},n,d)}$ are non-adaptive [15,16,33], including ours. Section 5.1 discusses non-adaptivity in more detail.

Time and Space Complexity. This model implies natural lower bounds on the time and space complexity of the prover:

- The time complexity of the prover is at least the total number of wires leaving the input gates $\mathcal{J}$ in $\mathcal{C}_1, \ldots, \mathcal{C}_n$. In other words, the total number of reads made by the prover across n rounds.
- The space complexity of the prover is at least $\max_{i \in [n]}\{|\mathcal{O}_i|\}$.

When discussing the algorithms in Sect. 4, we will argue the time and space complexity in terms of number of field operations performed and number of field elements stored by the prover respectively.

Definition 5 (**S-space bounded classical prover for $\mathsf{SC}^{(\mathbb{F},n,d)}$**). *A classical prover for $\mathsf{SC}^{(\mathbb{F},n,d)}$ is S-space bounded if $\max_{i\in[n]}\{|\mathcal{O}_i|\} \leq S$, where $\mathcal{O}_i$ is the output of the i-th round of the protocol. That is, the prover can pass on a state of size at most S to the next round.*

3.3 Compression Lemma

Lemma 2 (**[17], Fact 8.1**). *Suppose these is a randomized encoding procedure $\mathsf{Enc} : \{0,1\}^N \times \{0,1\}^r \to \{0,1\}^M$ and a decoding procedure $\mathsf{Dec} : \{0,1\}^M \times \{0,1\}^r \to \{0,1\}^N$ such that*

$$\Pr_{\boldsymbol{r} \xleftarrow{\$} \{0,1\}^r} [\mathsf{Dec}(\mathsf{Enc}(\boldsymbol{v},\boldsymbol{r}),\boldsymbol{r}) = \boldsymbol{v}] \geq \delta \ ,$$

for all $\boldsymbol{v} \in \{0,1\}^N$. Then $M \geq N - \log 1/\delta$.

Corollary 1. *Suppose these is a randomized encoding procedure $\mathsf{Enc} : \mathbb{F}^N \times \{0,1\}^r \to \mathbb{F}^M$ and a decoding procedure $\mathsf{Dec} : \mathbb{F}^M \times \{0,1\}^r \to \mathbb{F}^N$ such that*

$$\Pr_{\boldsymbol{r} \xleftarrow{\$} \{0,1\}^r} [\mathsf{Dec}(\mathsf{Enc}(\boldsymbol{v},\boldsymbol{r}),\boldsymbol{r}) = \boldsymbol{v}] \geq \delta \ ,$$

for all $\boldsymbol{v} \in \mathbb{F}^N$. Then $M \geq N - \log_{2|\mathbb{F}|} 1/\delta$.

The proof of Corollary 1 is deferred to the full version.

4 Space-Efficient Prover for the Classical Sumcheck Protocol

We present a space-efficient prover for the classical sumcheck protocol for products of two multilinear polynomials, and prove the following trade-off between time and space for the prover.

Theorem 3. *For any $k > 0$, there exists an honest prover $\mathcal{P}$ for $\mathsf{SC}^{(\mathbb{F},n,2)}$ which has streaming access to the evaluations of two multilinear polynomials, p, q, and requires $O(N(\log\log N + k))$ field operations and $O\left(N^{1/k}\right)$ space.*

Substituting $k = \log N / \log\log N$ in the above theorem, we get the following corollary.

Corollary 2. *There exists an honest prover* $\mathcal{P}$ *for* $\mathsf{SC}^{(\mathbb{F},n,2)}$ *which has streaming access to the evaluations of two multilinear polynomials,* p, q*, and requires* $O(N \log N / \log\log N)$ *field operations and* $O(\log N)$ *space.*

In the full version, we present an overview of the prover algorithm which provides additional intuition for it. Here, we only present the detailed pseudocode and analysis.

4.1 Product-Sumcheck Prover Implementation

(See Fig. 1).

$\mathsf{ProductSC}_k^{p,q}$:

1. Define $\ell := \lfloor n/2k \rfloor$.
2. For every round $j \in [n]$:
   (a) Initialize $P \leftarrow 0$.
   (b) Define $s := \lfloor \log_2 j \rfloor$.
   (c) If $j \leq \ell - 1$: ▷ time-constrained phase
      i. If $2^s = j$: Set $P \leftarrow 1$.
      ii. Define $j' := 2^s$.
      iii. Define $w(j') := \min(2^s, n - j' + 1)$.
   (d) Else: ▷ space-constrained phase
      i. If $\ell \mid j$: Set $P \leftarrow 1$.
      ii. Define $j' := \ell \cdot \lfloor j/\ell \rfloor$.
      iii. Define $w(j') := \min(\ell, n - j' + 1)$.
   (e) If $P = 1$ (we must have $j = j'$): Let the challenges received so far be $\boldsymbol{r} \in \mathbb{F}^{j'-1}$. For all $\boldsymbol{\beta}_1, \boldsymbol{\beta}_2 \in \{0,1\}^{w(j')}$, compute and store

$$M_{j'}[\boldsymbol{\beta}_1, \boldsymbol{\beta}_2] := \sum_{\boldsymbol{b} \in \{0,1\}^{n-j'-w(j')+1}} p(\boldsymbol{r}_{:j'}, \boldsymbol{\beta}_1, \boldsymbol{b}) \cdot q(\boldsymbol{r}_{:j'}, \boldsymbol{\beta}_2, \boldsymbol{b})$$

   This table is computed as follows:
      i. For each $\boldsymbol{b} \in \{0,1\}^{n-j'-w(j')+1}$:
      ii. For each $\boldsymbol{\beta} \in \{0,1\}^{w(j')}$:

Fig. 1. Prover algorithm using $O(N(\log\log N + k))$ time and $O(N^{1/k})$ space for the classical sumcheck protocol for products of multilinear polynomials.

iii. Compute and store

$$X[\boldsymbol{\beta}] := p(\boldsymbol{r}, \boldsymbol{\beta}, \boldsymbol{b}) = \sum_{\boldsymbol{x} \in \{0,1\}^{j'-1}} \chi_{\boldsymbol{x}}(\boldsymbol{r})\, p(\boldsymbol{x}, \boldsymbol{\beta}, \boldsymbol{b})$$

iv. For each $\boldsymbol{\beta} \in \{0,1\}^{w(j')}$:

v. Compute and store

$$Y[\boldsymbol{\beta}] := q(\boldsymbol{r}, \boldsymbol{\beta}, \boldsymbol{b}) = \sum_{\boldsymbol{x} \in \{0,1\}^{j'-1}} \chi_{\boldsymbol{x}}(\boldsymbol{r})\, q(\boldsymbol{x}, \boldsymbol{\beta}, \boldsymbol{b})$$

vi. For each $\boldsymbol{\beta}_1, \boldsymbol{\beta}_2 \in \{0,1\}^{w(j')}$:

vii. Update $M_{j'}[\boldsymbol{\beta}_1, \boldsymbol{\beta}_2] \leftarrow M_{j'}[\boldsymbol{\beta}_1, \boldsymbol{\beta}_2] + X[\boldsymbol{\beta}_1] \cdot Y[\boldsymbol{\beta}_2]$

(f) Let the received challenges so far be $\boldsymbol{r}_{:j} = (\boldsymbol{r}_{:j'}, \boldsymbol{r}') \in \mathbb{F}^{j'-1} \times \mathbb{F}^{j-j'}$.

(g) Compute round polynomial evaluations:

$$f_j(0) = \sum_{\substack{\boldsymbol{b}_1, \boldsymbol{b}_2 \in \\ \{0,1\}^{j-j'}}} \chi_{\boldsymbol{b}_1}(\boldsymbol{r}')\, \chi_{\boldsymbol{b}_2}(\boldsymbol{r}') \sum_{\boldsymbol{b} \in \{0,1\}^t} M_{j'}[\boldsymbol{b}_{1,0}, \boldsymbol{b}_{2,0}] \tag{7}$$

$$f_j(1) = \sum_{\substack{\boldsymbol{b}_1, \boldsymbol{b}_2 \in \\ \{0,1\}^{j-j'}}} \chi_{\boldsymbol{b}_1}(\boldsymbol{r}')\, \chi_{\boldsymbol{b}_2}(\boldsymbol{r}') \sum_{\boldsymbol{b} \in \{0,1\}^t} M_{j'}[\boldsymbol{b}_{1,1}, \boldsymbol{b}_{2,1}] \tag{8}$$

$$f_j(z) = \sum_{\substack{\boldsymbol{b}_1, \boldsymbol{b}_2 \in \\ \{0,1\}^{j-j'}}} \chi_{\boldsymbol{b}_1}(\boldsymbol{r}')\, \chi_{\boldsymbol{b}_2}(\boldsymbol{r}') \sum_{\boldsymbol{b} \in \{0,1\}^t} \begin{pmatrix} (1-z)^2 M_{j'}[\boldsymbol{b}_{1,0}, \boldsymbol{b}_{2,0}] \\ + z(1-z) M_{j'}[\boldsymbol{b}_{1,0}, \boldsymbol{b}_{2,1}] \\ + z(1-z) M_{j'}[\boldsymbol{b}_{1,1}, \boldsymbol{b}_{2,0}] \\ + z^2 M_{j'}[\boldsymbol{b}_{1,1}, \boldsymbol{b}_{2,1}] \end{pmatrix} \tag{9}$$

where $t := w(j') - j + j' - 1$, and $\boldsymbol{b}_{1,0} := (\boldsymbol{b}_1 \| 0 \| \boldsymbol{b})$, $\boldsymbol{b}_{1,1} := (\boldsymbol{b}_1 \| 1 \| \boldsymbol{b})$, $\boldsymbol{b}_{2,0} := (\boldsymbol{b}_2 \| 0 \| \boldsymbol{b})$ and $\boldsymbol{b}_{2,1} := (\boldsymbol{b}_2 \| 1 \| \boldsymbol{b})$.

(h) Send $f_j(0), f_j(1), f_j(z)$ to $\mathcal{V}$.

(i) Receive r_j from $\mathcal{V}$.

Fig. 1. *(continued)*

Completeness. Completeness for rounds $j \in [n]$ such that $j = j' + w(j') - 1$ follows from the definition of $M_{j'}$. We now show completeness for the remaining rounds. In round j, $\mathcal{P}$ outputs

$$f_j(0) = \sum_{\boldsymbol{b}_1, \boldsymbol{b}_2 \in \{0,1\}^{j-j'}} \chi_{\boldsymbol{b}_1}(\boldsymbol{r}')\, \chi_{\boldsymbol{b}_2}(\boldsymbol{r}') \sum_{\boldsymbol{v} \in \{0,1\}^{w(j')-j+j'-1}} M_{j'}[(\boldsymbol{b}_1, 0, \boldsymbol{v}), (\boldsymbol{b}_2, 0, \boldsymbol{v})]$$

$$= \sum_{\boldsymbol{b}\in\{0,1\}^{n-j}} p(\boldsymbol{r}_{:j'},\boldsymbol{r}',0,\boldsymbol{b})\cdot q(\boldsymbol{r}_{:j'},\boldsymbol{r}',0,\boldsymbol{b}) \ ,$$

which is the correct value for $f_j(0)$. Similarly, it can be seen that $\mathcal{P}$ outputs the correct values for $f_j(1)$ and $f_j(z)$ as well.

Efficiency

$\mathcal{P}$'s work can be divided into two parts: computing the tables $M_{j'}$ and computing the round polynomial evaluations in every round j (given the corresponding $M_{j'}$). We will analyze the time and space complexity of each of these parts separately.

Computing the Tables. The computation of each table $M_{j'}$, requires $O(N)$ time. Consider an execution of Item 2e : for some fixed values of $\boldsymbol{r}\in\mathbb{F}^{j'-1}$, $\boldsymbol{\beta}_1\in\{0,1\}^{w(j')}$, $\boldsymbol{b}\in\{0,1\}^{n-j'-w(j')+1}$, $\mathcal{P}$ computes

$$p(\boldsymbol{r},\boldsymbol{\beta}_1,\boldsymbol{b}) = \sum_{\boldsymbol{x}\in\{0,1\}^{j'-1}} \chi_{\boldsymbol{x}}(\boldsymbol{r})\, p(\boldsymbol{x},\boldsymbol{\beta}_1,\boldsymbol{b})$$

The first $\chi_{\boldsymbol{x}}(\boldsymbol{r})$ takes $O(j')$ time to compute, but every subsequent value can be computed in amortized $O(1)$ time. Therefore each $p(\boldsymbol{r},\boldsymbol{\beta}_1,\boldsymbol{b})$ can be computed in $O(2^j)$ time and $O(1)$ space. The same can be said of each $q(\boldsymbol{r},\boldsymbol{\beta}_2,\boldsymbol{b})$. Thus computing and storing $p(\boldsymbol{r},\boldsymbol{\beta}_1,\boldsymbol{b})$ and $q(\boldsymbol{r},\boldsymbol{\beta}_2,\boldsymbol{b})$ for all $\boldsymbol{\beta}_1,\boldsymbol{\beta}_2\in\{0,1\}^{w(j')}$ would take $O(2^{w(j')}\cdot 2^{j'})$ time and $O(2^{w(j')})$ space.

Given these values, for fixed $\boldsymbol{r}$ and $\boldsymbol{b}$, the algorithm can update and store $M_{j'}[\boldsymbol{\beta}_1,\boldsymbol{\beta}_2]\leftarrow p(\boldsymbol{r},\boldsymbol{\beta}_1,\boldsymbol{b})\cdot q(\boldsymbol{r},\boldsymbol{\beta}_2,\boldsymbol{b})$ for all $\boldsymbol{\beta}_1,\boldsymbol{\beta}_2\in\{0,1\}^t$ in $O(2^{2t})$ time while using $O(2^{2w(j')})$ space.

Iterating over all possible values of $\boldsymbol{b}\in\{0,1\}^{n-j'-w(j')+1}$, the computation of the table $M_{j'}$ takes

$$O\left(2^{n-j'-w(j')+1}\cdot(2^{w(j')}\cdot 2^{j'}+2^{2w(j')})\right) = O(2^{n-j'}\cdot(2^{j'}+2^{w(j')}))$$

time and $O(2^{2w(j')})$ space. Since we ensure that $w(j')\le j'$ for each j', computing $M_{j'}$ takes $O(2^n)=O(N)$ time.

Since $\mathcal{P}$ makes $\lceil\log_2\ell\rceil - O(\log\log N)$ passes in phase 1 and $\lceil n/\ell\rceil - O(k)$ passes in phase 2, the total number of rounds j' where $\mathcal{P}$ computes $M_{j'}$ is $O(\log\log N + k)$. Thus the total time taken to compute the tables is $O(N(\log\log N + k))$. The space required to compute and store the tables can be reused between rounds, and is $O(2^{2w(j')}) = O(N^{1/k})$ since we ensure that $w(j')\le n/2k$ for all j'.

Computing the Round Polynomial Evaluations. In each round $j\in[n]$, $\mathcal{P}$ needs to compute $f_j(0)$, $f_j(1)$ and $f_j(z)$. We will examine the efficiency of computing $f_j(0)$ (the same asymptotic upper bound applies for $f_j(1)$ and $f_j(z)$) as can be seen from Eqs. (8) and (9). Firstly, computing each value of $\chi_{\boldsymbol{b}_1}(\boldsymbol{r}')$ and $\chi_{\boldsymbol{b}_2}(\boldsymbol{r}')$ takes amortized $O(1)$ field operations (see Sect. 3.1). For each value of $\boldsymbol{b}_1,\boldsymbol{b}_2\in\{0,1\}^{j-j'}$, we take a linear combination of $2^{w(j')-j+j'-1}$ values of $M_{j'}$, which requires $O(2^{w(j')-j+j'})$ field operations. Doing this computation for all values of $\boldsymbol{b}_1, \boldsymbol{b}_2$ therefore requires $O(2^{w(j')+j-j'}) \le O(2^j)$ field operations (since $w(j') \le j'$). Adding over all rounds $j \in [n]$, the total number of field operations required to compute all round polynomials is $O(\sum_{j=1}^{n} 2^j) = O(2^n) = O(N)$. Note that only $O(1)$ extra random-access space is required to output these values for each round.

Overall Efficiency. $\mathcal{P}$ requires $O(N(k + \log\log N))$ field operations to compute the tables $M_{j'}$ and $O(N)$ field operations to compute the round polynomial evaluations, which gives us the desired upper bound.

Furthermore, the input streams are only accessed in Item 2(e)iii and Item 2(e)v. In the pseudocode, we omitted the details of how $\mathcal{P}$ accesses $\mathcal{S}(p)$ and $\mathcal{S}(q)$, but we can see that $\mathcal{P}$ only needs streaming access to the evaluations of p and q in the most-significant-bit lexicographic order:[7] in Item 2(e)iii and Item 2(e)v we call $\mathcal{S}(p).\mathsf{next}()$ and $\mathcal{S}(q).\mathsf{next}()$ respectively $2^{w(j')}$ times, and with one pass over the input streams, $\mathcal{P}$ can compute $M_{j'}$ with only $O(N^{1/k})$ space as desired.

Remark 3 (Additional material in full version). In the full version of this paper, we extend our protocol to handle products of d multilinear polynomials. We additionally show that if there exists a matrix multiplication algorithm that can multiply two $n \times n$ matrices in $O(n^2)$ field operations, then we can design a prover for $\mathsf{SC}^{(\mathbb{F},n,2)}$ that runs in $O(k \cdot N)$ time and $O(N^{1/k})$ space, which matches our lower bound for multilinear-sumcheck in Sect. 5. Thus, proving a stronger lower bound for product-sumcheck necessitates the use of a conjecture.

5 Lower Bound for Multilinear-Sumcheck

In Sect. 5.1, we describe the general behavior of an honest prover $\mathcal{P}$ of the classical sumcheck protocol for $\mathsf{SC}^{(\mathbb{F},n,1)}$, and introduce the relevant notation. In Sect. 5.2, we give a formal statement of the lower bound theorem, and then prove it using the description of the honest prover in Sect. 5.1.

5.1 Behavior of Space-Bounded Sumcheck Provers

Consider $(p(\boldsymbol{X}), \sigma)$, an instance of $\mathsf{SC}^{(\mathbb{F},n,1)}$, and consider an honest multilinear-sumcheck prover $\mathcal{P}$ with space bound $S = 2^s$. We assume that in round $i \in [n]$, $\mathcal{P}$ sends a degree-1 polynomial $t_i(X)$ in the form of $a_i := t_i(0)$ and $b_i := t_i(1)$ to $\mathcal{V}$. This is without loss of generality for the purposes of this lower bound, since both $\mathcal{P}$ and $\mathcal{V}$ can compute $t_i(0)$ and $t_i(1)$ in $O(1)$ time and space using any two values that uniquely determine t_i.

We discuss the computation that $\mathcal{P}$ performs in the following rounds:

$$\mathcal{I} := \{1, 1+s, 1+2s, \ldots, 1+(\lfloor n/s \rfloor - 1)\, s\} \ .$$

[7] For $n = 3$, this order of evaluations is $(0,0,0), (1,0,0), (0,1,0), (1,1,0), (0,0,1), (1,0,1), (0,1,1), (1,1,1)$.

We assume that $\mathcal{P}$ can correctly compute $t_i(X)$ for each $i \notin \mathcal{I}$ for free, and focus on its behavior in the remaining rounds $i \in \mathcal{I}$. Any operations that $\mathcal{P}$ would have performed in any round $j \notin \mathcal{I}$ are therefore delegated to a round $i \in \mathcal{I}$ that follows it. Since we focus only on the rounds in $\mathcal{I}$, we can reinterpret the classical sumcheck protocol as a $|\mathcal{I}|$-round interaction, such that in round $i \in \mathcal{I}$, $\mathcal{V}$ sends s random field elements $(r_i, r_{i+1}, \ldots, r_{i+s-1})$ to $\mathcal{P}$. We define $\mathsf{chall}_i := (r_1, \ldots, r_{i-1})$ as all the challenges received by $\mathcal{P}$ before the start of round i, with $\mathsf{chall}_1 := \bot$.

In a particular round $i \in \mathcal{I}$, $\mathcal{P}$ begins with the state $\mathsf{state}_i \in \mathbb{F}^S$ (we assume that $\mathsf{state}_1 = 0^S$) and performs the following steps:

1. *Perform reads.* It outputs an ordered sequence of indices of $\boldsymbol{p}$ to read, $\mathsf{indices}_i$, given random access to $p(\boldsymbol{X})$. This is captured by the $\mathsf{ComputeIndices}_i$ function:
$$\mathsf{indices}_i \leftarrow \mathsf{ComputeIndices}_i^{\boldsymbol{p}}(\mathsf{state}_i, \mathsf{chall}_i) \ .$$
This specifies $\mathsf{values}_i = \boldsymbol{p}|_{\mathsf{indices}_i}$, the values of $\boldsymbol{p}$ corresponding to the indices that are read by $\mathcal{P}$. For convenience, we define the set of indices read in the i-th round along with the corresponding values as $\mathsf{reads}_i := \{((\mathsf{indices}_i)_j, (\mathsf{values}_i)_j) : j \in [|\mathsf{indices}_i|]\}$.
2. *Compute responses.* Using state_i, reads_i, chall_i, $\mathcal{P}$ computes the two field elements it must send to $\mathcal{V}$. This is captured by the $\mathsf{ComputeResponse}_i$ function:
$$(a_i, b_i) \leftarrow \mathsf{ComputeResponse}_i(\mathsf{state}_i, \mathsf{reads}_i, \mathsf{chall}_i) \ .$$
3. *Compute new state.* Finally, $\mathcal{P}$ uses state_i, reads_i, chall_{i+s} (this step takes place after the challenges for round i are received) to compute state_{i+s}, which is passed to the next round. This is captured by the $\mathsf{ComputeState}_i$ function:
$$\mathsf{state}_{i+s} \leftarrow \mathsf{ComputeState}_i(\mathsf{state}_i, \mathsf{reads}_i, \mathsf{chall}_{i+s}) \ .$$
Our lower bound proof does not rely on the implementation of $\mathsf{ComputeState}_i$, and applies for any $\mathsf{state}_{i+s} \in \mathbb{F}^S$.

Definition 6 (Non-adaptive provers). *An honest sumcheck prover $\mathcal{P}$ for $\mathsf{SC}^{(\mathbb{F},n,1)}$ is said to be* non-adaptive *if for all $i \in \mathcal{I}$, $\mathsf{ComputeIndices}_i^{\boldsymbol{p}}$ is independent of $\boldsymbol{p}$, state_i and chall_i.*

Ideal Provers. For the purposes of this lower bound, we are concerned with honest provers for $\mathsf{SC}^{(\mathbb{F},n,1)}$ which are deterministic, non-adaptive, and have a space bound of $S := 2^s$. We denote this set of "ideal provers" as $\mathfrak{I}^{(\mathbb{F},n,s)}$.

5.2 Lower Bound Theorem and Proof

Theorem 4. *Consider a prover $\mathcal{P} \in \mathfrak{I}^{(\mathbb{F},n,s)}$, and define $T := \sum_{i\in\mathcal{I}} |\mathsf{reads}_i(\mathcal{P})|$, $N := 2^n$ and $S := 2^s$. Then, we have*
$$T \geq N + \frac{N}{2} \cdot \left(\left\lfloor \frac{n}{s} \right\rfloor - 1 \right) \tag{10}$$
In particular, $T \log S = \Omega(N \log N)$.

We fix a prover $\mathcal{P} \in \mathfrak{I}^{(\mathbb{F},n,s)}$ and a multilinear polynomial $p(\boldsymbol{X})$ for the purposes of this proof. We first show that $\mathcal{P}$ must read N indices of $\boldsymbol{p}$ in round 1 (Lemma 3), and then show that $\mathcal{P}$ read at least $N/2$ indices of $\boldsymbol{p}$ in each round $i \in \mathcal{I}\setminus\{1\}$. Proving these two lemmas clearly implies Theorem 4.

Lemma 3. $|\mathsf{reads}_1(\mathcal{P})| \geq N$.

Proof. Follows straightforwardly from a "fooling set" argument. See full version for details. □

Lemma 4. *For all* $t \in \{1,\ldots,\lfloor n/s \rfloor - 1\}$, *we have* $|\mathsf{reads}_{ts+1}(\mathcal{P})| \geq N/2$.

Proof. Assume for the sake of contradiction that $|\mathsf{reads}_{ts+1}(\mathcal{P})| < N/2$ for some $t \in \{1,\ldots,\lfloor n/s \rfloor - 1\}$. Since $\mathcal{P}$ is non-adaptive, $\mathsf{indices}_{ts+1}$ is independent of $\boldsymbol{p}$. Since $\mathcal{P}$ is also complete, it must be the case that for every sequence of challenges $\mathsf{chall}_{ts+1} = \boldsymbol{r} \in \mathbb{F}^{ts}$ that $\mathsf{ComputeResponse}_{ts+1}(\mathsf{state}_{ts+1}, \mathsf{reads}_{ts+1}, \mathsf{chall}_{ts+1})$ outputs $(p^{\boldsymbol{r}}_{ts+1}(0), p^{\boldsymbol{r}}_{ts+1}(1))$. We partition $\mathsf{chall}_{ts+1} = (\boldsymbol{r}_L, \boldsymbol{r}_R)$, such that $\boldsymbol{r}_R := (r_{(t-1)s+1},\ldots,r_{ts})$ are the random challenges received after the round $(t-1)s+1$, and $\boldsymbol{r}_L := (r_1,\ldots,r_{(t-1)s})$ are the random challenges received in previous rounds. For each $v \in \{0,1\}$, we can rewrite the evaluations $p^{\boldsymbol{r}}_{ts+1}(v)$ as follows:

$$p^{\boldsymbol{r}}_{ts+1}(v) = \sum_{\boldsymbol{x}\in\{0,1\}^{n-ts-1}} p(\boldsymbol{r}_L, \boldsymbol{r}_R, v, \boldsymbol{x}) = \sum_{\boldsymbol{b}\in\{0,1\}^s} \chi_{\boldsymbol{b}}(\boldsymbol{r}_R) \cdot \mathsf{S}_{t-1}(\boldsymbol{b}, v) \ ,$$

where we define $\mathsf{S}_{t-1}(\boldsymbol{b}, v) := \sum_{\boldsymbol{x}\in\{0,1\}^{n-ts-1}} p(\boldsymbol{r}_L, \boldsymbol{b}, v, \boldsymbol{x})$. Therefore, if $\boldsymbol{r}_R \in \{0,1\}^s$, then we have

$$p^{\boldsymbol{r}}_{s+1}(v) = \sum_{\boldsymbol{b}\in\{0,1\}^s} \chi_{\boldsymbol{b}}(\boldsymbol{r}_R) \cdot \mathsf{S}_{t-1}(\boldsymbol{b}, v) = \mathsf{S}_{t-1}(\boldsymbol{r}_R, v) \ ,$$

where the last equality holds because $\chi_{\boldsymbol{b}}(\boldsymbol{r}_R) = 1$ if $\boldsymbol{b} = \boldsymbol{r}_R$ and 0 otherwise. Therefore, we have $\mathsf{ComputeResponse}_{ts+1}(\mathsf{state}_{ts+1}, \mathsf{reads}_{ts+1}, (\boldsymbol{r}_L, \boldsymbol{r}_R)) = (\mathsf{S}_{t-1}(\boldsymbol{r}_R, 0), \mathsf{S}_{t-1}(\boldsymbol{r}_R, 1))$, for any $\boldsymbol{r}_R \in \{0,1\}^s$.

Sub-cubes of Evaluations. For each $\boldsymbol{\beta} \in \{0,1\}^{s+1}$, we define a *sub-cube* of the hypercube $\{0,1\}^n$ as follows:

$$C(\boldsymbol{\beta}) := \left\{(\boldsymbol{x}_L, \boldsymbol{\beta}, \boldsymbol{x}_R) \ : \ \boldsymbol{x}_L \in \{0,1\}^{ts-s}, \boldsymbol{x}_R \in \{0,1\}^{n-ts-1}\right\}$$

For each $\boldsymbol{r}_R \in \{0,1\}^s$ and $v \in \{0,1\}$, $\mathsf{S}_{t-1}(\boldsymbol{r}_R, v)$ is a linear combination of the evaluations of p over a sub-cube $C(\boldsymbol{\beta})$, where $\boldsymbol{\beta} = (\boldsymbol{r}_R, v)$:

$$\begin{aligned}\mathsf{S}_{t-1}(\boldsymbol{r}_R, v) &= \sum_{\boldsymbol{x}_R\in\{0,1\}^{n-ts-1}} p(\boldsymbol{r}_L, \boldsymbol{r}_R, v, \boldsymbol{x}_R) \\ &= \sum_{(\boldsymbol{x}_L,\boldsymbol{\beta},\boldsymbol{x}_R)\in C(\boldsymbol{\beta})} \chi_{\boldsymbol{x}_L}(\boldsymbol{r}_L) \cdot p(\boldsymbol{x}_L, \boldsymbol{\beta}, \boldsymbol{x}_R) \ .\end{aligned}$$

For each $\boldsymbol{\beta} \in \{0,1\}^{s+1}$, we partition the sub-cube $C(\boldsymbol{\beta})$ into two sub-cubes: the read sub-cube $R(\boldsymbol{\beta}) \subseteq C(\boldsymbol{\beta})$, containing indices that $\mathcal{P}$ has read in round $ts+1$, and the unread sub-cube $U(\boldsymbol{\beta}) \subseteq C(\boldsymbol{\beta})$, containing indices that $\mathcal{P}$ has not read in round $ts+1$. More precisely, $C(\boldsymbol{\beta}) = U(\boldsymbol{\beta}) \cup R(\boldsymbol{\beta})$, and $U(\boldsymbol{\beta}) \cap \mathsf{indices}_{ts+1} = \emptyset$, and $R(\boldsymbol{\beta}) \cap \mathsf{indices}_{ts+1} = R(\boldsymbol{\beta})$.

Additionally, for each $\boldsymbol{\beta} \in \{0,1\}^{s+1}$, we define weighted sums of the unread and read parts of $C(\boldsymbol{\beta})$ as follows:

$$\mathsf{US}_{t-1}(\boldsymbol{\beta}) := \sum_{(\boldsymbol{x}_L, \boldsymbol{\beta}, \boldsymbol{x}_R) \in U(\boldsymbol{\beta})} \chi_{\boldsymbol{x}_L}(\boldsymbol{r}_L) \cdot p(\boldsymbol{x}_L, \boldsymbol{\beta}, \boldsymbol{x}_R)$$

$$\mathsf{RS}_{t-1}(\boldsymbol{\beta}) := \sum_{(\boldsymbol{x}_L, \boldsymbol{\beta}, \boldsymbol{x}_R) \in R(\boldsymbol{\beta})} \chi_{\boldsymbol{x}_L}(\boldsymbol{r}_L) \cdot p(\boldsymbol{x}_L, \boldsymbol{\beta}, \boldsymbol{x}_R)$$

Clearly, $\mathsf{S}_{t-1}(\boldsymbol{\beta}) = \mathsf{US}_{t-1}(\boldsymbol{\beta}) + \mathsf{RS}_{t-1}(\boldsymbol{\beta})$ for all $\boldsymbol{\beta} \in \{0,1\}^{s+1}$.

Several Partially Unread Sub-cubes. Since we assume that $|\mathsf{reads}_{ts+1}(\mathcal{P})| < N/2$, there are at least $S+1$ sub-cubes that are partially unread, where a sub-cube $C(\boldsymbol{\beta})$ is said to be partially unread if $U(\boldsymbol{\beta}) \neq \emptyset$.

To see this, assume for the sake of contradiction that there are at most S sub-cubes that are partially unread by $\mathcal{P}$ in round $ts+1$. Therefore, there are at least $2^{s+1} - S = S$ sub-cubes that are completely read by $\mathcal{P}$ in round $ts+1$, let these sub-cubes be $\boldsymbol{\beta}_1, \ldots, \boldsymbol{\beta}_M$. That is, $R(\boldsymbol{\beta}_i) = C(\boldsymbol{\beta}_i)$ for all $i \in [S]$. By construction of the sub-cubes, they are all disjoint, and each of them has size $N/2S$. Therefore, $|\mathsf{reads}_{ts+1}(\mathcal{P})| \geq \sum_{i=1}^{S} |R(\boldsymbol{\beta}_i)| = S \cdot (N/2S) = N/2$, contradicting our assumption.

Rewinding Algorithm. Let $\mathcal{J}$ be the set of all $\boldsymbol{\beta} \in \{0,1\}^{s+1}$ such that the corresponding sub-cube $C(\boldsymbol{\beta})$ is partially unread by $\mathcal{P}$ in round $ts+1$. Consider the following "rewinding" algorithm $\mathcal{R}$ in Fig. 2: it receives as input state_{ts+1} and reads_{ts+1}, and invokes the $\mathsf{ComputeResponse}_{ts+1}$ method to output the weighted sum $\mathsf{US}_{t-1}(\boldsymbol{\beta})$ for each $\boldsymbol{\beta} \in \mathcal{J}$:

$\mathcal{R}(\mathsf{state}_{ts+1}, \mathsf{reads}_{ts+1}) \rightarrow [\mathsf{US}_{t-1}(\boldsymbol{\beta})]_{\boldsymbol{\beta} \in \mathcal{J}}$:
1. For each $\boldsymbol{b} \in \{0,1\}^s$:
2. $(\mathsf{S}_{t-1}(\boldsymbol{b}, 0), \mathsf{S}_{t-1}(\boldsymbol{b}, 1)) \leftarrow \mathsf{ComputeResponse}_{ts+1}(\mathsf{state}_{ts+1}, \mathsf{reads}_{ts+1}, \boldsymbol{b})$.
3. For each $\boldsymbol{\beta} \in \mathcal{J}$:
4. Compute $\mathsf{RS}_{t-1}(\boldsymbol{\beta})$ using reads_{ts+1}.
5. Pick $\mathsf{S}_{t-1}(\boldsymbol{\beta})$ from $[\mathsf{S}_{t-1}(\boldsymbol{b})]_{\boldsymbol{b} \in \{0,1\}^{s+1}}$.
6. Compute $\mathsf{US}_{t-1}(\boldsymbol{\beta}) \leftarrow \mathsf{S}_{t-1}(\boldsymbol{\beta}) - \mathsf{RS}_{t-1}(\boldsymbol{\beta})$.
7. Output $[\mathsf{US}_{t-1}(\boldsymbol{\beta})]_{\boldsymbol{\beta} \in \mathcal{J}}$.

Fig. 2. Rewinding algorithm to compute unread sums.

We will now show that this ability to output the weighted sums of all the unread sub-cubes corresponding to $\mathcal{J}$ allows us to solve the problem in Corollary 1.

Reduction from Corollary 1. Let $S' := |\mathcal{J}| > S$. We show how $\mathcal{A}$, upon receiving a vector $\boldsymbol{u} \xleftarrow{\$} \mathbb{F}^{S'}$ as input, can send a message Π with $|\Pi| = S$ to $\mathcal{B}$, using which $\mathcal{B}$ outputs $\boldsymbol{u}$ with probability 1.

Since $\mathcal{P} \in \mathfrak{I}^{(\mathbb{F},n,s)}$ is non-adaptive, $\mathcal{A}$ and $\mathcal{B}$ both have access to $\mathsf{indices}_{ts+1}$, and therefore know $R(\boldsymbol{b})$ and $U(\boldsymbol{b})$ for all $\boldsymbol{b} \in \{0,1\}^{s+1}$. Additionally, $\mathcal{A}$ and $\mathcal{B}$ also know the set $\mathcal{J}$. Thus they can fix an indexing function $I : \mathcal{J} \to [S']$ (consider the natural bijection obtained by lexicographically ordering $\mathcal{J}$ and mapping the i-th element to i).

Before receiving $\boldsymbol{u}$, $\mathcal{A}$ and $\mathcal{B}$ can both fix a value for the challenges $\boldsymbol{r}_L$ from the space $\mathbb{F}^{ts-s} \setminus \{0,1\}^{ts-s}$, and partially initialize the polynomial p such that $p(\boldsymbol{j}) = 0$, for every $\boldsymbol{j} \in \cup_{\boldsymbol{b} \in \{0,1\}^{s+1}} R(\boldsymbol{b})$.

Upon receiving $\boldsymbol{u}$, $\mathcal{A}$ initializes the rest of the polynomial p such that for each $\boldsymbol{b} \in \mathcal{J}$ we have

$$u_{I(\boldsymbol{b})} = \mathsf{US}_{t-1}(\boldsymbol{b}) = \sum_{(\boldsymbol{x}_L,\boldsymbol{b},\boldsymbol{x}_R) \in U(\boldsymbol{b})} \chi_{\boldsymbol{x}_L}(\boldsymbol{r}_L) \cdot p(\boldsymbol{x}_L, \boldsymbol{b}, \boldsymbol{x}_R) \ .$$

This is possible because $\boldsymbol{r}_L \in \mathbb{F}^{ts-s} \setminus \{0,1\}^{ts-s}$ implies that $\chi_{\boldsymbol{x}_L}(\boldsymbol{r}_L) \neq 0$ for all $\boldsymbol{x}_L \in \{0,1\}^{ts-s}$, and the fact that $U(\boldsymbol{b})$ are all disjoint, over all $\boldsymbol{b} \in \mathcal{J}$, means that the evaluations of p that $\mathcal{A}$ sets to satisfy one equation do not affect the validity of the other equations.

Finally, $\mathcal{A}$ and $\mathcal{B}$ engage in the following protocol:

1. $\mathcal{A}$ simulates the sumcheck prover $\mathcal{P}$ on the polynomial p until round $ts+1$ using the random challenges $\boldsymbol{r}_L$ and obtains state_{ts+1}.
2. $\mathcal{A}$ sends $\Pi := \mathsf{state}_{ts+1}$ to $\mathcal{B}$.
3. $\mathcal{B}$ parses Π as state_{ts+1}, obtains reads_{ts+1} from the initialized values : $p(\boldsymbol{j}) = 0$, for every $\boldsymbol{j} \in \cup_{\boldsymbol{b} \in \{0,1\}^{s+1}} R(\boldsymbol{b})$.
4. $\mathcal{B}$ runs rewinding algorithm $\mathcal{R}(\mathsf{state}_{ts+1}, \mathsf{reads}_{ts+1})$ to compute $[\mathsf{US}_{t-1}(\boldsymbol{b})]_{\boldsymbol{b} \in \mathcal{J}}$.
5. $\mathcal{B}$ defines $u_{I(\boldsymbol{b})} := \mathsf{US}_{t-1}(\boldsymbol{b})$ for all $\boldsymbol{b} \in \mathcal{J}$ and outputs $\boldsymbol{u}$.

Clearly, the amount of communication in the above protocol is $|\mathsf{state}_{ts+1}| \leq S$, and $\mathcal{B}$ is able to output $\boldsymbol{u} \in \mathbb{F}^{S'}$ with probability 1, which contradicts Corollary 1. Therefore, $|\mathsf{reads}_{ts+1}(\mathcal{P})| \geq N/2$ as desired. □

6 Lower Bound for Product-Sumcheck

In this section we show that the space-efficient product-sumcheck prover presented in Sect. 4 achieves the optimal time-space trade-off within a class of natural provers. In particular, we make the following assumptions about the prover algorithm $\mathcal{P}$:

- Similar to Sect. 5, $\mathcal{P}$ is *non-adaptive* with respect to the input polynomials and the random challenges received in the interactive phase.
- $\mathcal{P}$ is extension-agnostic: for a fixed field characteristic χ, $\mathcal{P}$ implements the same arithmetic circuits $\mathcal{C}_1, \ldots, \mathcal{C}_n$ for all finite fields with characteristic χ.

- We assume that in any round of the sumcheck protocol where $\mathcal{P}$ makes at most $N/4$ field operations, it reads at most $N^{1-\varepsilon}$ values of p and q for some constant $\varepsilon > 0$. This assumption is not needed for the reduction to Conjecture 2.

The prover algorithm in Sect. 4 adheres to these restrictions, and so do the prover algorithms of [15,16,33].

6.1 Background

Conjectures. Consider n-variate multilinear polynomials that evaluate to 0 over a 2^{n-1}-sized subset of the hypercube $\{0,1\}^n$. In addition to Conjecture 1, we also propose a slightly stronger conjecture about the complexity of computing the sum of products of such multilinear polynomials. Assuming this stronger conjecture helps us remove the third assumption above.

Definition 7. *$\mathcal{A}$ solves the* batch half-polynomial multiplication *problem with parameters n, ℓ (denoted by $\mathsf{BHPM}(n,\ell)$) if there exist sets $B_1,\ldots,B_\ell \subseteq \{0,1\}^n$ such that each $|B_i| = 2^{n-1}$ and for all $p_1,\ldots,p_\ell,q_1,\ldots,q_\ell \in \mathbb{F}^{\leq 1}[X_1,\ldots,X_n]$, $\mathcal{A}$ outputs $f(\boldsymbol{X}) := \sum_{i=1}^{\ell} p_i'(\boldsymbol{X})\cdot q_i'(\boldsymbol{X})$ where $p_i'(\boldsymbol{x}) = p_i(\boldsymbol{x})$ if $\boldsymbol{x} \in B_i$, and $p_i'(\boldsymbol{x}) = 0$ if $\boldsymbol{x} \notin B_i$, assuming that $\mathcal{A}$ has random-access to the input polynomials.*

Conjecture 2. There exists a constant $\omega > 0$ such that any algorithm $\mathcal{A}$ that solves $\mathsf{BHPM}(n,\ell)$ requires $\Omega(2^{(\omega+1)n}\cdot\ell)$ field operations for all $n,\ell \in \mathbb{N}$.

Extension-Agnostic Prover. The output of the prover of a product-sumcheck protocol is bilinear in the two input polynomials p and q. Previous works that study lower bounds for arithmetic circuits computing bilinear functions [26,31] use the following high-level idea. Given an arithmetic circuit $\mathcal{C}$ over a field $\mathbb{F}$ of characteristic 0 that outputs bilinear functions $f_1(\boldsymbol{X},\boldsymbol{Y}),\ldots,f_k(\boldsymbol{X},\boldsymbol{Y})$, there exists a slightly modified circuit $\mathcal{C}'$ of similar size and structure that also outputs $f_1(\boldsymbol{X},\boldsymbol{Y}),\ldots,f_k(\boldsymbol{X},\boldsymbol{Y})$, but additionally *every gate is bilinear* in $\boldsymbol{X}$ and $\boldsymbol{Y}$. That is, the inputs of multiplication gates are always of the form $L_i(\boldsymbol{X})$ and $L_j(\boldsymbol{Y})$ where L_i and L_j are linear polynomials in $\boldsymbol{X}$ and $\boldsymbol{Y}$ respectively. We cannot directly apply this result to our setting since we are working with finite fields, but we get a similar result by assuming that the algorithm is *extension-agnostic*, i.e., its structure is independent of the field's extension degree.

Definition 8 (Extension-agnostic product-sumcheck prover). *Fix an input size $n \in \mathbb{N}$. An extension-agnostic prover for $\mathsf{SC}^{(\mathbb{F},n,2)}$ is a function that takes as input a field characteristic $\chi \geq 2$, and outputs a set of arithmetic circuits $\mathcal{C} := (\mathcal{C}_1,\ldots,\mathcal{C}_n)$ such that $\mathcal{C}$ is a prover for the classical sumcheck protocol (see Definition 2) for all finite fields $\mathbb{F}$ of characteristic χ. That is, the prover algorithm can be non-uniform with respect to different input sizes and characteristic of the field, but must be uniform with respect to the extension degree of the field.*

Since we restrict the structure of the arithmetic circuits to be the same for all fields of characteristic χ, we make the following observation:

Lemma 5. *Consider an extension-agnostic product-sumcheck prover $\mathcal{P}$. For a characteristic $\chi \geq 2$, let C_i be the arithmetic circuit that computes the i-th round polynomial $t_i(\boldsymbol{X}, \boldsymbol{Y})$ over all finite fields of characteristic χ. Let T_i and S_i be the time and space required to evaluate C_i respectively. Then, there exists an arithmetic circuit C_i^* which output $t_i(\boldsymbol{X}, \boldsymbol{Y})$, such that every gate of C_i^* outputs a bilinear polynomial in $\boldsymbol{X}$ and $\boldsymbol{Y}$, and the outputs of C_i^* can be computed in $O(T_i)$ time and $O(S_i)$ space.*

The proof of Lemma 5 is deferred to the full version.

Using this background we can formally state the lower bound theorem.

Theorem 5. *Consider an honest, non-adaptive, extension-agnostic prover $\mathcal{P}$ of the classical sumcheck protocol for $\mathsf{SC}^{(\mathbb{F},n,2)}$, which has access to at most $O(N^{1/2-\varepsilon})$ space for some constant $\varepsilon > 0$. If either*

- *Conjecture 2 holds, or*
- *Conjecture 1 holds and $\mathcal{P}$ reads $O(N^{1-\varepsilon})$ values of p and q in any round where it performs $\leq N/4$ field operations,*

then $\mathcal{P}$ requires $\Omega(N(\log\log N + \log\varepsilon)/\log(1+1/\omega))$[8] *field operations in total.*

6.2 Proving Lower Bound for Two Rounds that are Far Apart

Lemma 6. *Consider an honest, non-adaptive, extension-agnostic prover of the product-sumcheck protocol over a domain of size $N := 2^n$, which has access to at most $O(N^{1/2-\varepsilon})$ space for some constant $\varepsilon > 0$. Let Alice be the prover of the product-sumcheck protocol in round $\mathsf{m}_\mathcal{A}$ such that $\log\log N \leq \mathsf{m}_\mathcal{A} \leq \varepsilon\omega \log N/2$, and let Bob be the prover in round $\mathsf{m}_\mathcal{B} := \lceil 2(\omega+1)\mathsf{m}_\mathcal{A}/\omega + 1\rceil$. Let the message sent by Alice to Bob be $\Pi_\mathcal{A}(p,q)$ and the set of indices read by Bob be $R_\mathcal{B}(p,q)$. Given inputs $\Pi_\mathcal{A}(p,q)$, $R_\mathcal{B}(p,q)$, and random challenges $r_1, \ldots, r_{\mathsf{m}_\mathcal{B}-1} \in \mathbb{F}^{\mathsf{m}_\mathcal{B}-1}$, Bob outputs the polynomial*

$$f(X) := \sum_{\boldsymbol{b}\in\{0,1\}^{n-\mathsf{m}_\mathcal{B}}} p(r_1, \ldots, r_{\mathsf{m}_\mathcal{B}-1}, X, \boldsymbol{b}) \cdot q(r_1, \ldots, r_{\mathsf{m}_\mathcal{B}-1}, X, \boldsymbol{b}) \ .$$

If Bob performs at most $N/4$ field operations, and additionally, (i) Conjecture 1 holds and Bob reads at most $N^{1-\varepsilon}/4$ values of p and q, or (ii) Conjecture 2 holds, then Alice requires $\Omega(N\log^{\omega/2} N)$ field operations to output $\Pi_\mathcal{A}(p,q)$.

This lemma is similar to Lemma 4 in the multilinear-sumcheck lower bound proof, since we consider two rounds of the protocol $\mathsf{m}_\mathcal{A}$ and $\mathsf{m}_\mathcal{B}$ that are far apart. The pairs of rounds that we consider, $(\mathsf{m}_\mathcal{A}, \mathsf{m}_\mathcal{B})$, grow geometrically since $\mathsf{m}_\mathcal{B} \approx (2(\omega+1)/\omega)\mathsf{m}_\mathcal{A}$, as opposed to the linear growth in Lemma 4. We restrict

[8] ω is the constant from Conjecture 1 or Conjecture 2.

the number of field operations that Bob performs to $N/4$ so that it cannot simply compute the round polynomial $f(X)$ without using $\Pi_{\mathcal{A}}(p,q)$ at all. This restriction allows us to prove that $\Pi_{\mathcal{A}}(p,q)$ on its own is sufficient to solve an instance of BHPM, and therefore Alice must have performed a large number of field operations to compute $\Pi_{\mathcal{A}}(p,q)$. If additionally Bob reads at most $N^{1-\varepsilon}/4$ values of p and q, then we can similarly argue that $\Pi_{\mathcal{A}}(p,q)$ is sufficient to solve an instance of BPM.

Consider a fixed random challenge vector $\boldsymbol{t} \in \{0,1,z\}^{\mathsf{m}_{\mathcal{A}}-1}$, which consists of the first $(\mathsf{m}_{\mathcal{A}}-1)$ random challenges of the sumcheck protocol. Define multilinear polynomials $p_{\boldsymbol{t}} : \{0,1\}^{n-\mathsf{m}_{\mathcal{A}}+1} \to \mathbb{F}$ and $q_{\boldsymbol{t}} : \{0,1\}^{n-\mathsf{m}_{\mathcal{A}}+1} \to \mathbb{F}$ as follows, where $\boldsymbol{t}$ fixes the first $\mathsf{m}_{\mathcal{A}}-1$ variables of p and q:

$$p_{\boldsymbol{t}}(\boldsymbol{x}) := \sum_{\boldsymbol{b}\in\{0,1\}^{\mathsf{m}_{\mathcal{A}}-1}} \chi_{\boldsymbol{b}}(\boldsymbol{t})\, p(\boldsymbol{b},\boldsymbol{x}) \;, \; q_{\boldsymbol{t}}(\boldsymbol{x}) := \sum_{\boldsymbol{b}\in\{0,1\}^{\mathsf{m}_{\mathcal{A}}-1}} \chi_{\boldsymbol{b}}(\boldsymbol{t})\, q(\boldsymbol{b},\boldsymbol{x})$$

Define $\mathsf{m} := \mathsf{m}_{\mathcal{B}} - \mathsf{m}_{\mathcal{A}}$. Consider a fixed vector $\boldsymbol{r} \in \{0,1,z\}^{\mathsf{m}+1}$, which includes the m random challenges that Bob knows but Alice did not have access to, and the variable in the $\mathsf{m}_{\mathcal{B}}$-th position.

Now, depending on the restriction on $|R_{\mathcal{B}}(p,q)|$, we can initialize two different pairs of polynomials derived from p and q that $R_{\mathcal{B}}(p,q)$ does not intersect with.

- **Restricted case:** $|R_{\mathcal{B}}(p,q)| \le N^{1-\varepsilon}/4$. Let $V_{\mathsf{res}} := \{(\boldsymbol{x},\boldsymbol{b})\}_{\boldsymbol{x}\in\{0,1\}^{\mathsf{m}_{\mathcal{B}}},\boldsymbol{b}\in W_{\mathsf{res}}}$ be the set of indices whose suffix lies in W_{res}. There exists a set of "suffixes" $W_{\mathsf{res}} \subseteq \{0,1\}^{n-\mathsf{m}_{\mathcal{B}}}$ such that $|W_{\mathsf{res}}| \ge 2^{n-\mathsf{m}_{\mathcal{B}}-1}$, and $|R_{\mathcal{B}}(p,q) \cap V_{\mathsf{res}}| = 0$ (there are no indices read by Bob whose suffix lies in W_{res}). This follows from $N^{1-\varepsilon}/4 = 2^{n-\mathsf{m}_{\mathcal{B}}-2} \cdot 2^{\mathsf{m}_{\mathcal{B}}} \cdot 2^{-\varepsilon \log N} \le 2^{n-\mathsf{m}_{\mathcal{B}}-2} \cdot 2^{\varepsilon \log N+1} \cdot 2^{-\varepsilon \log N} = 2^{n-\mathsf{m}_{\mathcal{B}}-1}$.
- **Unrestricted case:** $|R_{\mathcal{B}}(p,q)| \le N/4$. Let $V_{\mathsf{unres}} := \{(\boldsymbol{x},\boldsymbol{b})\}_{\boldsymbol{x}\in\{0,1\}^{\mathsf{m}_{\mathcal{B}}},\boldsymbol{b}\in W_{\mathsf{unres}}}$ be the set of indices whose suffix lies in W_{unres}. Now, there exists a set of suffixes $W_{\mathsf{unres}} \subseteq \{0,1\}^{n-\mathsf{m}_{\mathcal{B}}}$ such that $|W_{\mathsf{unres}}| \ge 2^{n-\mathsf{m}_{\mathcal{B}}-1}$, and $|R_{\mathcal{B}}(p,q) \cap V_{\mathsf{unres}}| \le 2^{\mathsf{m}_{\mathcal{B}}-1}$ (W_{unres} consists of suffixes for which at most half the entries are read).

Accordingly, for the restricted and unrestricted cases we define the specific BPM and BHPM problem instance that we will solve using $\mathcal{B}$.

- **Restricted case:** Compute $f_{\mathsf{res}}(\boldsymbol{r}) := \sum_{\boldsymbol{b}\in W_{\mathsf{res}}} p_{\boldsymbol{t}}(\boldsymbol{r},\boldsymbol{b}) \cdot q_{\boldsymbol{t}}(\boldsymbol{r},\boldsymbol{b})$ for all values of $\boldsymbol{r} \in \{0,1,z\}^{\mathsf{m}+1}$. This is an instance of $\mathsf{BPM}(\mathsf{m}+1, 2^{n-\mathsf{m}_{\mathcal{B}}-1})$ since $|W_{\mathsf{res}}| \ge 2^{n-\mathsf{m}_{\mathcal{B}}-1}$.
- **Unrestricted case:** Compute $f_{\mathsf{unres}}(\boldsymbol{r}) := \sum_{\boldsymbol{b}\in W_{\mathsf{unres}}} p_{\boldsymbol{t}}^{U}(\boldsymbol{r},\boldsymbol{b}) \cdot q_{\boldsymbol{t}}^{U}(\boldsymbol{r},\boldsymbol{b})$ for all $\boldsymbol{r} \in \{0,1,z\}^{\mathsf{m}+1}$ where for all $\boldsymbol{x} \in \{0,1\}^{\mathsf{m}+1}$ and $\boldsymbol{b} \in W_{\mathsf{unres}}$,

$$p_{\boldsymbol{t}}^{U}(\boldsymbol{x},\boldsymbol{b}) := \sum_{\boldsymbol{y}\in U(\boldsymbol{x},\boldsymbol{b})} \chi_{\boldsymbol{y}}(\boldsymbol{t})\, p(\boldsymbol{y},\boldsymbol{x},\boldsymbol{b}) \;, \; q_{\boldsymbol{t}}^{U}(\boldsymbol{x},\boldsymbol{b}) := \sum_{\boldsymbol{y}\in U(\boldsymbol{x},\boldsymbol{b})} \chi_{\boldsymbol{y}}(\boldsymbol{t})\, q(\boldsymbol{y},\boldsymbol{x},\boldsymbol{b})$$

  where $U(\boldsymbol{x},\boldsymbol{b}) \subseteq \{0,1\}^{\mathsf{m}_{\mathcal{A}}-1}$ is the set of "unread prefixes" for $(\boldsymbol{x},\boldsymbol{r})$. Since $|R_{\mathcal{B}}(p,q)| \le N/4$, $p_{\boldsymbol{t}}^{U}(\boldsymbol{x},\boldsymbol{b})$ and $q_{\boldsymbol{t}}^{U}(\boldsymbol{x},\boldsymbol{b})$ are 0 for at most 2^{m} values of $\boldsymbol{x}$ for each $\boldsymbol{b} \in W_{\mathsf{unres}}$ (and the remaining values are arbitrary field elements), and therefore this is an instance of $\mathsf{BHPM}(\mathsf{m}+1, 2^{n-\mathsf{m}_{\mathcal{B}}-1})$. Analogously, we also define $p_{\boldsymbol{t}}^{R}(\boldsymbol{x},\boldsymbol{b})$ and $q_{\boldsymbol{t}}^{R}(\boldsymbol{x},\boldsymbol{b})$ that correspond to the read values.

Proof Outline of Lemma 6. The proof proceeds in 3 steps:

1. We first prove that $f_{\mathsf{res}}(\boldsymbol{r})$ and $f_{\mathsf{unres}}(\boldsymbol{r})$ can be computed efficiently using $\Pi_{\mathcal{A}}(p,q)$, $R_{\mathcal{B}}(p,q)$ and $\boldsymbol{r}$, and an additional message from Alice $\Pi'_{\mathcal{A}}(p,q) \in \mathbb{F}^{3^{\mathsf{m}+1}}$ by rewinding $3^{\mathsf{m}+1}$ times (see Lemma 7 and Lemma 8).
2. We then prove that Bob can compute the same values efficiently using a single message $\Pi^*_{\mathcal{A}}(p,q) \in \mathbb{F}^{3^{\mathsf{m}+1}}$ and $\boldsymbol{r}$ without using $R_{\mathcal{B}}(p,q)$ at all (see Lemma 9).
3. Finally, we show that Alice can compute $f_{\mathsf{res}}(\boldsymbol{r})$ and $f_{\mathsf{unres}}(\boldsymbol{r})$ for all $\boldsymbol{r} \in \{0,1,z\}^{\mathsf{m}+1}$ efficiently (see Lemma 10).

Lemma 7. *Let $\boldsymbol{r} \in \{0,1,z\}^{\mathsf{m}+1}$. If $\mathcal{B}$ can compute $\sum_{\boldsymbol{b}\in\{0,1\}^{n-\mathsf{m}_{\mathcal{B}}}} p_{\boldsymbol{t}}(\boldsymbol{r},\boldsymbol{b})\cdot q_{\boldsymbol{t}}(\boldsymbol{r},\boldsymbol{b})$ in at most $N/4$ field operations using $\Pi_{\mathcal{A}}(p,q)$, $R_{\mathcal{B}}(p,q)$, then there exists an algorithm $\mathcal{B}'$ that can compute $f_{\mathsf{res}}(\boldsymbol{r})$ in at most $N/2$ field operations using $\Pi_{\mathcal{A}}(p,q)$, $R_{\mathcal{B}}(p,q)$, and an additional message $\Pi'_{\mathcal{A}}(p,q) \in \mathbb{F}^{3^{\mathsf{m}+1}}$ from Alice.*

Lemma 8. *Let $\boldsymbol{r} \in \{0,1,z\}^{\mathsf{m}+1}$. If $\mathcal{B}$ can compute $\sum_{\boldsymbol{b}\in\{0,1\}^{n-\mathsf{m}_{\mathcal{B}}}} p_{\boldsymbol{t}}(\boldsymbol{r},\boldsymbol{b})\cdot q_{\boldsymbol{t}}(\boldsymbol{r},\boldsymbol{b})$ in at most $N/4$ field operations using $\Pi_{\mathcal{A}}(p,q)$, $R_{\mathcal{B}}(p,q)$, then there exists an algorithm $\mathcal{B}'$ that can compute $f_{\mathsf{unres}}(\boldsymbol{r})$ in at most $N/2$ field operations using $\Pi_{\mathcal{A}}(p,q)$, $R_{\mathcal{B}}(p,q)$, and an additional message $\Pi'_{\mathcal{A}}(p,q) \in \mathbb{F}^{3^{\mathsf{m}+1}}$ from Alice.*

See the full version for the proofs of Lemma 7 and Lemma 8.

Using $\mathcal{B}'$ from Lemma 7 or Lemma 8, we now show that exists an efficient algorithm $\mathcal{B}^*$ that computes $f_{\mathsf{res}}(\boldsymbol{r})$ and $f_{\mathsf{unres}}(\boldsymbol{r})$ using a different message $\Pi^*_{\mathcal{A}}(p,q)$ and $\boldsymbol{r}$ (without using $R_{\mathcal{B}}(p,q)$ at all). We must prove the following two claims to show this:

- If Alice requires T field operations to compute $\Pi_{\mathcal{A}}(p,q)$, then there exists an algorithm $\mathcal{A}^*$ that can compute $\Pi^*_{\mathcal{A}}(p,q)$ in at most $O(T+N)$ field operations.
- There exists an algorithm $\mathcal{B}^*$ that can compute $f_{\mathsf{res}}(\boldsymbol{r})$ and $f_{\mathsf{unres}}(\boldsymbol{r})$ for any $\boldsymbol{r} \in \{0,1,z\}^{\mathsf{m}+1}$ in at most $N/2$ field operations using $\Pi^*_{\mathcal{A}}(p,q)$.

We prove these claims by constructing algorithms $\mathcal{A}^*$ and $\mathcal{B}^*$ from $\mathcal{A}$ and $\mathcal{B}'$ respectively:

Lemma 9. *Suppose Alice computes $\Pi_{\mathcal{A}}(p,q)$ in T field operations, and $\mathcal{B}'$ computes $f_{\mathsf{res}}(\boldsymbol{r})$ for any $\boldsymbol{r} \in \{0,1,z\}^{\mathsf{m}+1}$ using $\Pi_{\mathcal{A}}(p,q)$. Then there exist a message $\Pi^*_{\mathcal{A}}(p,q)$ such that $|\Pi^*_{\mathcal{A}}(p,q)| = |\Pi_{\mathcal{A}}(p,q)|$ that can be computed in T field operations, such that there exists an algorithm $\mathcal{B}^*$ that requires at most $N/2$ field operations to output $f_{\mathsf{res}}(\boldsymbol{r})$ using $\Pi^*_{\mathcal{A}}(p,q)$.*

The proof of Lemma 9 is deferred to the full version. A similar statement can be proven for the unrestricted case, where $\mathcal{B}^*$ computes $f_{\mathsf{unres}}(\boldsymbol{r})$ instead of $f_{\mathsf{res}}(\boldsymbol{r})$. Lemma 9 shows that $\mathcal{A}^*$ can be executed in T field operations, and therefore it can be simulated by Alice. Thus, without loss of generality, we can assume that Alice sends $\Pi^*_{\mathcal{A}}(p,q)$ to Bob.

Finally, we proceed to the final step of the proof outline of Lemma 6.

Lemma 10. *There exists an algorithm $\mathcal{A}_{\mathsf{final}}$ that can compute*

$$\boldsymbol{h}_{\mathsf{res}} := [f_{\mathsf{res}}(\boldsymbol{r})]_{\boldsymbol{r}\in\{0,1,z\}^{\mathsf{m}}}$$

with $O(T+N)$ field operations, where T is the number of field operations required to compute $\Pi_{\mathcal{A}}(p,q)$.

Proof. Using Lemma 5, we know that $\mathcal{B}$ outputs a quadratic function of $\Pi_{\mathcal{A}}(p,q)$. By definition of $\mathcal{B}^*$, it must also be quadratic in $\Pi^*_{\mathcal{A}}(p,q)$, and therefore we can rewrite the output as

$$\sum_{\boldsymbol{b}\in W_{\mathsf{res}}} p_t(\boldsymbol{r},\boldsymbol{b})\cdot q_t(\boldsymbol{r},\boldsymbol{b}) = \sum_{i=0,j=0}^{|\Pi^*_{\mathcal{A}}(p,q)|} c_{i,j}(\boldsymbol{r})\cdot \Pi^*_{\mathcal{A}}(p,q)_i \cdot \Pi^*_{\mathcal{A}}(p,q)_j$$

where $\Pi^*_{\mathcal{A}}(p,q)_0 = 1$, and $c_{i,j}(\cdot)$ are polynomials in $\boldsymbol{r}$. We define $\mathcal{A}_{\mathsf{final}}$ as follows:

1. Compute $\Pi^*_{\mathcal{A}}(p,q)$ with T field operations using Lemma 9.
2. All $c_{i,j}(\boldsymbol{r})$ are only a function of $\boldsymbol{r}$, and not of p or q. Therefore, for all $\boldsymbol{r}\in\{0,1,z\}^{\mathsf{m}+1}$, $c_{i,j}(\boldsymbol{r})$ are simply constants, and can be precomputed irrespective of the inputs, and stored in a matrix $M\in\mathbb{F}^{3^{\mathsf{m}+1}\times(|\Pi_{\mathcal{A}}(p,q)|+1)^2}$. Since $\mathsf{m}+1\le\left(\frac{2}{\omega}\right)\mathsf{m}_{\mathcal{A}}\le\varepsilon\log N$, we have $3^{\mathsf{m}+1}\le 3^{\varepsilon\log N}\le N^{2\varepsilon}$. Therefore there are at most $O(N^{1/2-\varepsilon}\cdot N^{1/2-\varepsilon}\cdot N^{2\varepsilon}) = O(N)$ elements in M.
3. Compute $\boldsymbol{h}_{\mathsf{res}} = M\times\Pi^*_{\mathcal{A}}(p,q)$ with $O(N)$ field operations.

□

A similar statement can be proven for the unrestricted case, where $\mathcal{A}_{\mathsf{final}}$ computes $\boldsymbol{h}_{\mathsf{unres}} := [f_{\mathsf{unres}}(\boldsymbol{r})]_{\boldsymbol{r}\in\{0,1,z\}^{\mathsf{m}+1}}$. This leads us to the proof of Lemma 6:

Proof of Lemma 6. Since $\mathcal{A}_{\mathsf{final}}$ only requires $O(T+N)$ field operations to compute $\boldsymbol{h}_{\mathsf{res}}$ (or $\boldsymbol{h}_{\mathsf{unres}}$) according to Lemma 10, and only requires access to p, q, we have shown that $\mathsf{BPM}(\mathsf{m}+1, 2^{n-\mathsf{m}_{\mathcal{B}}-1})$ (or $\mathsf{BHPM}(\mathsf{m}+1, 2^{n-\mathsf{m}_{\mathcal{B}}-1})$) can be solved in $O(T+N)$ field operations. By Conjecture 1 (or Conjecture 2), this requires $\Omega(2^{(\omega+1)\mathsf{m}}\cdot 2^{n-\mathsf{m}_{\mathcal{B}}}) = \Omega(N\cdot 2^{\omega\mathsf{m}_{\mathcal{B}}-(\omega+1)\mathsf{m}_{\mathcal{A}}}) \ge \Omega(N\cdot 2^{\omega\mathsf{m}_{\mathcal{B}}/2}) = \Omega(N\log^{\omega/2}N)$ field operations to compute, and therefore $T=\Omega(N\log^{\omega/2}N)$ as desired. □

6.3 Proof of Theorem 5

Proof. Define a function that maps integers to round numbers of the sumcheck protocol: $f(q) := \lceil 2(\omega+1)q/\omega+1\rceil$. Let $m_i := f^i(\log\log N)$ and k be the number of rounds for which we will apply Lemma 6. We use Lemma 6 for all values of $\mathsf{m}_{\mathcal{A}}\in\{m_0,\ldots,m_{\mathsf{k}-1}\}$. We have

$$m_{\mathsf{k}-1} = f^{\mathsf{k}-1}(\log\log N) \le (\log\log N+1)\cdot\left(\frac{2(\omega+1)}{\omega}\right)^{\mathsf{k}-1}.$$

We need $m_{\mathsf{k}-1}\le\varepsilon\omega\log N/2$ as stated in Lemma 6. If we set $\mathsf{k} = \lfloor(\log\varepsilon+\log\log N/2)/\log(2(\omega+1)/\omega)-1\rfloor$, then this condition is satisfied. If

$\mathcal{P}$ requires less than $N/4$ field operations in round m_i for any $i \in [\mathsf{k}]$ to output $f_i(X)$, then $\mathcal{P}$ must use $\Omega(N \log^{\omega/2} N)$ field operations in round m_{i-1} by Lemma 6, in which case we are done since $N \log^{\omega/2} N \geq N \log\log N$ for large enough values of N. Otherwise, $\mathcal{P}$ requires at least $N/4$ field operations in round m_i for all $i \in [\mathsf{k}]$, and therefore the total number of field operations performed by $\mathcal{P}$ across these rounds is at least $N/4 \cdot \mathsf{k} = \Omega(N(\log\log N + \log\varepsilon)/\log(1+1/\omega))$ as desired. □

Acknowledgments. We thank Justin Thaler for pointing the connection of this work to [29, Appendix G]. We thank Ron Rothblum for discussions related to [27] and [2]. Alessandro Chiesa, Giacomo Fenzi, and Pratyush Mishra are supported in part by the Ethereum Foundation and the Sui Foundation. Pratyush Mishra and Tushar Mopuri are supported in part by a Sony Academic Research Award.

Disclosure of Interests. The authors have no competing interests to declare that are relevant to the content of this article.

References

1. Arnon, G., Chiesa, A., Fenzi, G., Yogev, E.: STIR: Reed-Solomon proximity testing with fewer queries. In: Reyzin, L., Stebila, D. (eds.) CRYPTO 2024. LNCS, vol. 14929, pp. 380–413. Springer, Cham (2024). https://doi.org/10.1007/978-3-031-68403-6_12
2. Athamnah, N., Ron-Zewi, N., Rothblum, R.: Linear Prover IOPs in Log Star Rounds (2025). ECCC TR25-090
3. Babai, L., Fortnow, L., Levin, L.A., Szegedy, M.: Checking computations in polylogarithmic time. In: Proceedings of the 23rd Annual ACM Symposium on Theory of Computing, STOC 1991, pp. 21–32 (1991)
4. Babai, L., Fortnow, L., Lund, C.: Non-deterministic exponential time has two-prover interactive protocols. Comput. Complex. **1**, 3–40 (1991)
5. Baweja, A., Mishra, P., Mopuri, T., Newatia, K., Wang, S.: Scribe: low-memory SNARKs via read-write streaming. Cryptology ePrint Archive Report 2024/1970 (2024). https://eprint.iacr.org/2024/1970
6. Ben-Sasson, E., Bentov, I., Horesh, Y., Riabzev, M.: Fast Reed-Solomon interactive oracle proofs of proximity. In: Proceedings of the 45th International Colloquium on Automata, Languages, and Programming, ICALP 2018, pp. 14:1–14:17 (2018)
7. Ben-Sasson, E., Chiesa, A., Riabzev, M., Spooner, N., Virza, M., Ward, N.P.: Aurora: transparent succinct arguments for R1CS. In: Ishai, Y., Rijmen, V. (eds.) EUROCRYPT 2019. LNCS, vol. 11476, pp. 103–128. Springer, Cham (2019). https://doi.org/10.1007/978-3-030-17653-2_4
8. Block, A.R., Holmgren, J., Rosen, A., Rothblum, R.D., Soni, P.: Public-coin zero-knowledge arguments with (almost) minimal time and space overheads. In: Pass, R., Pietrzak, K. (eds.) TCC 2020. LNCS, vol. 12551, pp. 168–197. Springer, Cham (2020). https://doi.org/10.1007/978-3-030-64378-2_7
9. Block, A.R., Holmgren, J., Rosen, A., Rothblum, R.D., Soni, P.: Time- and space-efficient arguments from groups of unknown order. In: Malkin, T., Peikert, C. (eds.) CRYPTO 2021. LNCS, vol. 12828, pp. 123–152. Springer, Cham (2021). https://doi.org/10.1007/978-3-030-84259-8_5

10. Bootle, J., Chiesa, A., Hu, Y., Orrú, M.: Gemini: elastic SNARKs for diverse environments. In: Dunkelman, O., Dziembowski, S. (eds.) EUROCRYPT 2022. LNCS, vol. 13276, pp. 427–457. Springer, Cham (2022)
11. Bünz, B., Fisch, B., Szepieniec, A.: Transparent SNARKs from DARK compilers. In: Canteaut, A., Ishai, Y. (eds.) EUROCRYPT 2020. LNCS, vol. 12105, pp. 677–706. Springer, Cham (2020). https://doi.org/10.1007/978-3-030-45721-1_24
12. Chen, B., Bünz, B., Boneh, D., Zhang, Z.: HyperPlonk: plonk with linear-time prover and high-degree custom gates. In: Hazay, C., Stam, M. (eds.) EUROCRYPT 2023. LNCS, vol. 14005, pp. 499–530. Springer, Cham (2023). https://doi.org/10.1007/978-3-031-30617-4_17
13. Chiesa, A., Fedele, E., Fenzi, G., Zitek-Estrada, A.: A time-space tradeoff for the sumcheck prover. Cryptology ePrint Archive Paper 2024/524 (2024). https://eprint.iacr.org/2024/524
14. Chiesa, A., Hu, Y., Maller, M., Mishra, P., Vesely, N., Ward, N.: Marlin: preprocessing zkSNARKs with universal and updatable SRS. In: Canteaut, A., Ishai, Y. (eds.) EUROCRYPT 2020. LNCS, vol. 12105, pp. 738–768. Springer, Cham (2020). https://doi.org/10.1007/978-3-030-45721-1_26
15. Cormode, G., Mitzenmacher, M., Thaler, J.: Practical verified computation with streaming interactive proofs. In: Proceedings of the 4th Symposium on Innovations in Theoretical Computer Science, ITCS 2012, pp. 90–112 (2012)
16. Cormode, G., Thaler, J., Yi, K.: Verifying computations with streaming interactive proofs. Proc. VLDB Endow. **5**(1), 25–36 (2011)
17. De, A., Trevisan, L., Tulsiani, M.: Time space tradeoffs for attacks against one-way functions and PRGs. In: Rabin, T. (ed.) CRYPTO 2010. LNCS, vol. 6223, pp. 649–665. Springer, Heidelberg (2010). https://doi.org/10.1007/978-3-642-14623-7_35
18. Goldwasser, S., Kalai, Y.T., Rothblum, G.N.: Delegating computation: interactive proofs for muggles. J. ACM **62**(4), 27:1–27:64 (2015)
19. Juma, A., Kabanets, V., Rackoff, C., Shpilka, A.: The black-box query complexity of polynomial summation. Comput. Complex. **18**(1), 59–79 (2009)
20. Kate, A., Zaverucha, G.M., Goldberg, I.: Constant-size commitments to polynomials and their applications. In: Abe, M. (ed.) ASIACRYPT 2010. LNCS, vol. 6477, pp. 177–194. Springer, Heidelberg (2010). https://doi.org/10.1007/978-3-642-17373-8_11
21. Levrat, C., Medevielle, T., Nardi, J.: A divide-and-conquer sumcheck protocol. IACR Commun. Cryptol. **2**(1), 15 (2025)
22. Lund, C., Fortnow, L., Karloff, H.J., Nisan, N.: Algebraic methods for interactive proof systems. J. ACM **39**(4), 859–868 (1992)
23. Nair, V., Thaler, J., Zhu, M.: Proving CPU executions in small space. Cryptology ePrint Archive, Paper 2025/611 (2025). https://eprint.iacr.org/2025/611
24. Pappas, C., Papadopoulos, D.: Hobbit: space-efficient zkSNARK with optimal prover time. Cryptology ePrint Archive, Paper 2025/1214 (2025). https://eprint.iacr.org/2025/1214
25. Pappas, C., Papadopoulos, D.: Sparrow: space-efficient zkSNARK for data-parallel circuits and applications to zero-knowledge decision trees. In: Proceedings of the ACM Conference on Computer and Communications Security, CCS 2024, pp. 3110–3124 (2024)
26. Raz, R.: On the complexity of matrix product. In: Proceedings of the 34th Annual ACM Symposium on Theory of Computing, STOC 2002, pp. 144–151 (2002)
27. Rothblum, R.: A Note on Efficient Computation of the Multilinear Extension (2024). https://eprint.iacr.org/2024/1103

28. Setty, S.: Spartan: efficient and general-purpose zkSNARKs without trusted setup. In: Micciancio, D., Ristenpart, T. (eds.) CRYPTO 2020. LNCS, vol. 12172, pp. 704–737. Springer, Cham (2020). https://doi.org/10.1007/978-3-030-56877-1_25
29. Setty, S., Thaler, J., Wahby, R.: Unlocking the lookup singularity with lasso. In: Joye, M., Leander, G. (eds.) EUROCRYPT 2024. LNCS, vol. 14656, pp. 180–209. Springer, Cham (2024). https://doi.org/10.1007/978-3-031-58751-1_7
30. Shamir, A.: IP = PSPACE. J. ACM **39**(4), 869–77 (1992)
31. Shpilka, A., Yehudayoff, A.: Arithmetic circuits: a survey of recent results and open questions. Found. Trends Theor. Comput. Sci. **5**(3–4), 207–388 (2010)
32. Singh, N., Patranabis, S.: SubLogarithmic linear time SNARKs from compressed sum-check. Cryptology ePrint Archive, Paper 2025/908 (2025). https://eprint.iacr.org/2025/908
33. Thaler, J.: Time-optimal interactive proofs for circuit evaluation. In: Canetti, R., Garay, J.A. (eds.) CRYPTO 2013. LNCS, vol. 8043, pp. 71–89. Springer, Heidelberg (2013). https://doi.org/10.1007/978-3-642-40084-1_5
34. Vu, V., Setty, S., Blumberg, A.J., Walfish, M.: A hybrid architecture for interactive verifiable computation. In: Proceedings of the 34th IEEE Symposium on Security and Privacy, S&P 2013, pp. 223–237 (2013)
35. Zhang, S., Cai, D., Li, Y., Kan, H., Zhang, L.: Epistle: elastic succinct arguments for plonk constraint system. IACR ePrint Report 2024/872 (2024). https://eprint.iacr.org/2024/872

A Hidden-Bits Approach to Statistical ZAPs from LWE

Eli Bradley[1], George Lu[1], Shafik Nassar[1], Brent Waters[1,2], and David J. Wu[1](✉)

[1] UT Austin, Austin, TX, USA
dwu4@cs.utexas.edu
[2] NTT Research, Sunnyvale, CA, USA

Abstract. We give a new approach for constructing statistical ZAP arguments (a two-message public-coin statistically witness indistinguishable argument) from quasi-polynomial hardness of the learning with errors (LWE) assumption with a polynomial modulus-to-noise ratio. Previously, all ZAP arguments from lattice-based assumptions relied on correlation-intractable hash functions. In this work, we present the first construction of a ZAP from LWE via the classic hidden-bits paradigm. Our construction matches previous lattice-based schemes by being public-coin and satisfying statistical witness indistinguishability.

1 Introduction

Zero-knowledge proofs for NP [GMR85] allow a prover to convince a verifier that an NP statement is true without revealing anything more than the fact that the statement is true. However, achieving zero-knowledge requires either a trusted setup (i.e., a common reference string) or interaction. Many works have studied the round complexity of zero-knowledge proofs for NP in the plain model, and it is known, for instance, that two-round zero-knowledge proofs for NP are impossible in the plain model [GO94, BLV03] under standard worst-case complexity assumptions (e.g., that $\mathsf{NP} \not\subseteq \mathsf{BPP}$). One way to overcome the barrier of two-round zero-knowledge in the plain model is to relax zero-knowledge to witness indistinguishability [FS90], which asks that a proof constructed using an NP witness w_0 is indistinguishable from a proof constructed using a witness w_1.

ZAPs. Dwork and Naor [DN00] gave the first construction of a two-round public-coin witness-indistinguishable proof (i.e., "ZAPs") in the plain model, and moreover, showed how to construct it from any non-interactive zero-knowledge (NIZK) proof in the uniform random string model (e.g., [FLS90]). Critically, the [DN00] approach relied on both *statistical* soundness and that the common reference string is a *uniform* random string. In the context of the ZAP, the public-coin property means the verifier's first message is a uniform random string (i.e., the random coins of the verifier). As such, ZAPs are publicly-verifiable since anyone who sees the verifier's first message can run the verification algorithm. Following the work of Dwork and Naor, there have been

B. Applebaum and H. Lin (Eds.): TCC 2025, LNCS 16271, pp. 71–104, 2026.
https://doi.org/10.1007/978-3-032-12290-2_3

many constructions of ZAPs from pairing-based assumptions [GOS06a, CKSU21], lattice-based assumptions [LVW19, BFJ+20, GJJM20], group-based assumptions (without pairings) [JJ21, CKSU21], and from indistinguishability obfuscation (together with one-way functions) [BP15]. Several works also considered a relaxation to ZAPs with private randomness [KKS18, LVW20].

This Work: Statistical ZAP Arguments. In this work, we focus on *statistical ZAP arguments* where witness indistinguishability holds against computationally-unbounded adversaries (and soundness holds against computationally-bounded adversaries). Public-coin statistical ZAP arguments are currently known from the decisional Diffie-Hellman (DDH) assumption in a pairing-free group [JJ21] as well as from the plain learning with errors (LWE) assumptions [LVW19, BFJ+20, GJJM20]. Notably, *all* of these approaches start by constructing a correlation-intractable hash function and using it to instantiate the Fiat-Shamir transform [CCRR18, CCH+19]. In this work, we ask whether we can construct a ZAP from LWE *without* relying on correlation intractability. Specifically, motivated by the recent advances in realizing NIZKs from LWE via the classic hidden-bits paradigm due to Waters [Wat24] and recently improved upon by Waters, Wee, and Wu [WWW25], we ask whether there is a hidden-bits model approach for building ZAPs from LWE. Indeed, the very first ZAP by [DN00] showed how to leverage the hidden-bits model NIZK from [FLS90] to obtain a computational ZAP proof. Later, [CKSU21] showed how to leverage the pairing-based hidden-bits model NIZK from [LPWW20] to also obtain a public-coin statistical ZAP argument using bilinear maps. In this work, we show how to construct a statistical ZAP argument from LWE via the hidden-bits approach. Our main result can be stated as follows:

Theorem 1.1 (Informal). *Assuming quasi-polynomial hardness of* LWE *with a polynomial modulus-to-noise ratio, there exists a statistical ZAP argument for* NP *with non-adaptive soundness.*

If we are willing to assume sub-exponential hardness of LWE, then we obtain an adaptively-sound statistical ZAP for statements of a priori bounded length. We refer to Remark 3.3 for additional details.

Comparison and Discussion. Theorem 1.1 achieves the same properties as previous lattice-based ZAPs [LVW19, BFJ+20, GJJM20], which also relied on quasi-polynomial security of LWE (with polynomial modulus-to-noise ratio). The previous approaches all relied on correlation-intractable hash functions. Essentially, in these constructions, both the prover and the verifier need to homomorphically evaluate the decryption function for a public-key encryption scheme (in order to evaluate the correlation-intractable hash function). In this work, we seek a conceptually-different approach that does not rely on correlation intractability.

We believe there is value in exploring different approaches for realizing a single cryptographic goal. For instance, in the setting of NIZKs, there have been two general (and incomparable) paradigms: the hidden-bits paradigm [FLS90,BY92,CHK03,GR13,CL18,LPWW20,KMY23,CW23,Wat24, BWW24,WWW25] and the correlation-intractability paradigm [CCRR18, CCH+19,PS19,CKU20,BKM20,JJ21,CJJQ23,DJJ24] that have yielded constructions from a broad array of algebraic assumptions. There are also many approaches that do not fall into either paradigm [BFM88,GOS06b, SW14,BKP+24]. Here, similar algebraic assumptions can yield very different approaches for realizing the primitive, and this enriches our understanding of the particular primitive. Moreover, having a broad set of approaches and constructions can enable new trade-offs for concrete efficiency. We believe the same is true for ZAPs. Here again, there have been two broad categories of approaches for constructing ZAPs, based either on the hidden-bits model or on the correlation-intractability approach. While previous lattice-based ZAPs relied critically on correlation-intractable hash functions, our approach shows that a construction is also feasible via the earlier hidden-bits approach.

1.1 Technical Overview

Our starting point for constructing a statistical ZAP argument from LWE is the recent (dual-mode) NIZK in the hidden-bits model from the work of [Wat24] (and subsequently improved upon in the work of [WWW25]). Both constructions operate by constructing a (dual-mode) *hidden-bits generator* [FLS90, QRW19, LPWW20]. We start by recalling this notion.

Hidden-Bits Generators. Roughly speaking, a hidden-bits generator (HBG) [FLS90, QRW19] is a cryptographic primitive in the common reference string model that allows the prover to generate a random string, alongside a commitment to the string and a local opening to each bit. Moreover, the scheme should satisfy the following properties:

- **Hiding:** First, we require that the openings to a subset of the bits hide the unopened bits.
- **Binding:** Second, given the commitment (and the CRS), the prover can only open to one possible hidden-bits string.

A dual mode HBG can be instantiated in one of two computationally indistinguishable modes: statistically hiding or statistically binding.

Shifted Multi-preimage Sampling. To construct a hidden-bits generator from lattice assumptions, the work of [WWW25] explicitly defined the *shifted multi-preimage sampling problem*, which was implicitly considered in the previous work of [Wat24]. The problem is parameterized by a collection of matrices $\mathbf{A}_1, \ldots, \mathbf{A}_t \in \mathbb{Z}_q^{n \times t}$ and requires the following: given target vectors $\mathbf{t}_1, \ldots, \mathbf{t}_\ell \in \mathbb{Z}_q^n$, sample a random vector $\mathbf{c} \xleftarrow{\mathrm{R}} \mathbb{Z}_q^n$ with short discrete Gaussian preimages $\boldsymbol{\pi}_1, \ldots, \boldsymbol{\pi}_\ell \in \mathbb{Z}_q^t$ satisfying $\mathbf{A}_i \boldsymbol{\pi}_i = \mathbf{t}_i + \mathbf{c}$ for all $i \in [\ell]$. That is, $\boldsymbol{\pi}_i \leftarrow \mathbf{A}_i^{-1}(\mathbf{t}_i + \mathbf{c})$ for each $i \in [\ell]$, where $\mathbf{x} \leftarrow \mathbf{A}_i^{-1}(\mathbf{y})$ denotes the discrete Gaussian distribution conditioned on $\mathbf{A}_i \mathbf{x} = \mathbf{y}$. The goal is to publish a hint that allows one to efficiently sample $(\boldsymbol{\pi}_1, \ldots, \boldsymbol{\pi}_\ell, \mathbf{c})$, while ensuring that problems like LWE remain hard with respect to any individual matrix $\mathbf{A}_i$. In particular, this latter requirement rules out the possibility of giving a trapdoor for each individual $\mathbf{A}_i$ as the hint. The work of [WWW25] shows how to solve this problem for a specific distribution of *correlated* matrices $\mathbf{A}_1, \ldots, \mathbf{A}_t \in \mathbb{Z}_q^{n \times t}$. Moreover, although the matrices are correlated, the marginal distribution of each individual matrix is actually uniform over $\mathbb{Z}_q^{n \times t}$.

The [Wat24, WWW25] *Hidden-Bits Generator.* We can now describe the LWE-based hidden-bits generator from [Wat24, WWW25] through the lens of the shifted multi-preimage sampling problem from [WWW25]:

- The common reference string (for the hidden-bits generator) consists of the CRS for the shifted multi-preimage trapdoor sampler together with ℓ vectors $\mathbf{v}_1, \ldots, \mathbf{v}_\ell \in \mathbb{Z}_q^t$. The distribution of the vectors $\mathbf{v}_i$ varies depending on whether we want the hidden-bits generator to be statistically binding or statistically hiding. The CRS for the shifted multi-preimage trapdoor sampler defines a set of ℓ matrices $\mathbf{A}_1, \ldots, \mathbf{A}_\ell \in \mathbb{Z}_q^{n \times t}$ and a hint td for solving the shifted multi-preimage sampling problem with respect to matrices $\mathbf{A}_1, \ldots, \mathbf{A}_\ell$.
- To generate the hidden-bits string, the user samples $(\boldsymbol{\pi}_1, \ldots, \boldsymbol{\pi}_\ell, \mathbf{c})$ using the multi-preimage sampler with targets $\mathbf{t}_i = \mathbf{0}$ for all $i \in [\ell]$. This means $\mathbf{A}_i \boldsymbol{\pi}_i = \mathbf{c}$ for all $i \in [\ell]$. The commitment of the hidden-bits generator is the vector $\mathbf{c} \in \mathbb{Z}_q^n$. Each bit ρ_i is now defined as $\rho_i = \lfloor \mathbf{v}_i^\mathsf{T} \boldsymbol{\pi}_i \rceil \in \{0, 1\}$, where $\lfloor \cdot \rceil$ denotes a rounding operation. The hidden-bits string is defined as $\boldsymbol{\rho} = \rho_1 \cdots \rho_\ell$, and the openings are $\boldsymbol{\pi}_1, \ldots, \boldsymbol{\pi}_\ell$.
- In hiding mode, the vectors $\mathbf{v}_1, \ldots, \mathbf{v}_\ell$ in the CRS are uniform over $\mathbb{Z}_q^t$. The security proof of [WWW25] now relies on the min-entropy of the conditional discrete Gaussian distribution $\mathbf{A}_i^{-1}(\mathbf{c})$ (even given $\mathbf{c}$) and the randomness of $\mathbf{v}_i$ to argue that $\mathbf{v}_i^\mathsf{T} \boldsymbol{\pi}_i$ is statistically close to uniform over $\mathbb{Z}_q$ (even given $\mathbf{v}_i$, but not $\boldsymbol{\pi}_i$) using the leftover hash lemma [HILL99].
- In binding mode, the vectors $\mathbf{v}_1, \ldots, \mathbf{v}_\ell$ are LWE samples (i.e., $\mathbf{v}_i^\mathsf{T} = \mathbf{s}_i^\mathsf{T} \mathbf{A}_i + \mathbf{e}_i^\mathsf{T}$). In this case, the commitment $\mathbf{c}$ determines the bit. For simplicity, if we ignore the error $\mathbf{e}_i$ and just consider the inner product, we have $\mathbf{v}_i^\mathsf{T} \boldsymbol{\pi}_i = \mathbf{s}_i^\mathsf{T}(\mathbf{A}_i \boldsymbol{\pi}_i) = \mathbf{s}_i^\mathsf{T} \mathbf{c}$. Specifically, the LWE secret $\mathbf{s}_i$ and the commitment $\mathbf{c}$ completely determines the value of $\mathbf{v}_i^\mathsf{T} \boldsymbol{\pi}_i$, and correspondingly, the bit $\rho_i = \lfloor \mathbf{v}_i^\mathsf{T} \boldsymbol{\pi}_i \rceil = \lfloor \mathbf{s}_i^\mathsf{T} \mathbf{c} \rceil$.
- Finally, the CRS in hiding mode is computationally indistinguishable from the CRS in binding mode by the LWE assumption.

Problem: Lack of a Trusted Setup. While the hidden-bits generator immediately implies a NIZK for NP [FLS90, QRW19], the same is not true for ZAPs. This is because a hidden-bits generator requires a common reference string, and the assumption is that the CRS is sampled *honestly*. In a ZAP, we do not have any trusted setup, so it is not clear where this common reference string comes from. Certainly, neither the prover nor the verifier should unilaterally choose the CRS, as this would violate either soundness or witness indistinguishability, respectively.

Relying on Re-randomization. The work of Dwork and Naor [DN00] shows that NIZKs can nonetheless be used to obtain ZAPs by having the prover and the verifier *jointly* sample a CRS via the following general template (also used in many subsequent works [LVW19, BFJ+20, GJJM20, CKSU21]):

- The verifier picks an initial common reference string crs_V, but then the prover re-randomizes it by choosing a tweak crs_P.
- The prover cannot "completely" re-randomize the CRS, since this would give the prover the ability to choose the full CRS. Instead, there should be a small set S of "tweaks" that the prover can choose from.
- The prover communicates the tweak crs_P it used to the verifier. The proof is then constructed with respect to the CRS derived from $(\mathsf{crs}_V, \mathsf{crs}_P)$.

For example, suppose the verifier chooses crs_V as its initial CRS. Then the prover may choose a string $\mathsf{crs}_P \in S$ from the (small) set S, and re-randomize the CRS by computing $\mathsf{crs} = \mathsf{crs}_P \oplus \mathsf{crs}_V$. The prover then generates a proof using the re-randomized reference string crs.

Arguing Soundness via Complexity Leveraging. To prove soundness, we use a complexity-leveraging idea similar to that from [LVW19, BFJ+20, GJJM20, CKSU21] where the verifier "guesses" the re-randomization crs_P that the prover will use. Namely, the verifier first samples a common reference string $\mathsf{crs}_{\mathsf{bind}}$ for which the hidden-bits generator is binding, and then chooses $\mathsf{crs}_V = \mathsf{crs}_{\mathsf{bind}} \oplus \mathsf{crs}_P$ as its common reference string. If the verifier correctly guesses the prover's common reference string crs_P, then the prover will compute $\mathsf{crs} = \mathsf{crs}_V \oplus \mathsf{crs}_P = \mathsf{crs}_{\mathsf{bind}}$ and generate a proof with respect to $\mathsf{crs}_{\mathsf{bind}}$. Since the hidden-bits generator is binding with respect to $\mathsf{crs}_{\mathsf{bind}}$, this guarantees soundness for the overall ZAP. If there are $|S|$ possibilities for crs_P, then the verifier correctly guesses crs_P with probability $1/|S|$. To show this works, we require the two following properties hold:

- The reference string $\mathsf{crs}_{\mathsf{bind}}$ that the verifier samples should hide crs_P. This is necessary to ensure that the prover does not "avoid" choosing the tweak the verifier guessed. More precisely, an efficient prover should not be able to distinguish a reference string $\mathsf{crs}_V = \mathsf{crs}_{\mathsf{bind}} \oplus \mathsf{crs}_P$ from $\mathsf{crs}'_V = \mathsf{crs}_{\mathsf{bind}} \oplus \mathsf{crs}'_P$ for any (adversarially-chosen) pair of tweaks $\mathsf{crs}_P, \mathsf{crs}'_P$, with probability better than $\varepsilon_{\mathsf{dis}}$. In this case, if the original prover is able to break the binding property of the hidden bits generator with probability ε, then with probability $\varepsilon/|S| - \varepsilon_{\mathsf{dis}}$, the prover will choose crs_P as its tweak and break binding with respect to the tweaked CRS $\mathsf{crs}_V \oplus \mathsf{crs}_P = \mathsf{crs}_{\mathsf{bind}}$.
- Next, we require that the probability $\varepsilon_{\mathsf{bind}}$ that an adversary breaks binding with respect to a reference string $\mathsf{crs}_{\mathsf{bind}}$ sampled in binding mode to be small.

If both properties hold, then $\varepsilon/|S| - \varepsilon_{\mathsf{dis}} \leq \varepsilon_{\mathsf{bind}}$, or equivalently, $\varepsilon \leq |S| \cdot (\varepsilon_{\mathsf{dis}} + \varepsilon_{\mathsf{bind}})$. In the context of the [WWW25] construction, these two requirements are satisfied as follows:

- In [WWW25], the reference string $\mathsf{crs}_{\mathsf{bind}}$ in binding mode is pseudorandom under the LWE assumption. An adversary that can distinguish between $\mathsf{crs}_{\mathsf{bind}} \oplus \mathsf{crs}_P$ and $\mathsf{crs}_{\mathsf{bind}} \oplus \mathsf{crs}'_P$ with advantage $\varepsilon_{\mathsf{bind}}$ can break LWE with the same advantage $\varepsilon_{\mathsf{bind}}$.
- Next, when the common reference string $\mathsf{crs}_{\mathsf{bind}}$ is sampled in binding mode, the resulting construction is statistically binding (e.g., the advantage $\varepsilon_{\mathsf{bind}}$ is exponentially small).

The remaining question is how big the set S should be. In [WWW25], when the CRS is binding, there is a trapdoor that can be used to extract the actual hidden-bit string (which in turn would violate zero-knowledge or witness indistinguishability when used to construct a NIZK or a ZAP, respectively). Therefore, we cannot have $1/|S|$ be inverse polynomial, as this allows the verifier to break witness indistinguishability with inverse polynomial advantage (namely, the verifier would choose $\mathsf{crs}_{\mathsf{bind}}$ with knowledge of the associated trapdoor). Thus, to argue hiding, we take $|S|$ to be quasi-polynomial (i.e., $|S| = 2^{\mathsf{polylog}(\lambda)}$) and rely on quasi-polynomial hardness of LWE (i.e., the LWE distinguishing advantage of any efficient adversary is at most $\varepsilon_{\mathsf{dis}} = 1/2^{\mathsf{polylog}(\lambda)}$).

Specialized CRS Re-randomization for Statistical Hiding. Arguing hiding is more complex and the set of possible tweaks S must be carefully chosen based on the specific algebraic structure of the base scheme. Recall first that the CRS for the hidden-bits generator consists of a common reference string $\mathsf{crs}_{\mathsf{samp}}$ for the shifted multi-preimage trapdoor sampler and the vectors $\mathbf{v}_1, \ldots, \mathbf{v}_\ell \in \mathbb{Z}_q^t$. In our construction, the verifier first picks an initial $\mathsf{crs}_{\mathsf{samp}}$ for the shifted multi-preimage trapdoor sampler and a set of vectors $\tilde{\mathbf{v}}_1, \ldots, \tilde{\mathbf{v}}_\ell \in \mathbb{Z}_q^t$. The prover re-randomizes the set of vectors $\tilde{\mathbf{v}}_1, \ldots, \tilde{\mathbf{v}}_\ell$, but does *not* change $\mathsf{crs}_{\mathsf{samp}}$.

More concretely, let $\mathsf{crs}_V = (\mathsf{crs}_{\mathsf{samp}}, \tilde{\mathbf{v}}_1, \ldots, \tilde{\mathbf{v}}_\ell)$ be the reference string chosen by the verifier. In our approach, the prover chooses a small subset of indices $I \subseteq [t]$ of the vectors and *fully* re-randomizes the components of $\tilde{\mathbf{v}}_i$ at these indices. Specifically, the prover chooses a single random *sparse* vector $\boldsymbol{\delta} \in \mathbb{Z}_q^t$, and then shifts each of the vectors $\tilde{\mathbf{v}}_i$ by $\boldsymbol{\delta}$ by computing $\mathbf{v}_i = \tilde{\mathbf{v}}_i + \boldsymbol{\delta}$. The prover then uses $\mathsf{crs} = (\mathsf{crs}_{\mathsf{samp}}, \mathbf{v}_1, \ldots, \mathbf{v}_\ell)$ as the CRS for the hidden-bits generator. Observe that if $\boldsymbol{\delta}$ has $N = \mathsf{polylog}(\lambda)$ non-zero entries (where λ is a security parameter), and if $t, q = \mathsf{poly}(\lambda)$, then there are at most $t^N q^N = 2^{\mathsf{polylog}(\lambda)}$ options for $\boldsymbol{\delta}$, so the set of tweaks indeed has quasi-polynomial size.

Introducing Min-Entropy into Proof Generation. The hiding analysis of [WWW25] employs a min-entropy argument which relies on the *preimage distribution* property of the shifted multi-preimage trapdoor sampler. This property essentially asserts that when the CRS for the shifted multi-preimage trapdoor sampler is *honestly* generated, then the distribution of $(\boldsymbol{\pi}_1, \ldots, \boldsymbol{\pi}_\ell, \mathbf{c})$ output by the multi-preimage sampler is statistically close to the distribution where $\mathbf{c} \xleftarrow{R} \mathbb{Z}_q^n$ and $\boldsymbol{\pi}_i \leftarrow \mathbf{A}_i^{-1}(\mathbf{c})$. Then, by relying on min-entropy of the (conditional) discrete Gaussian distribution $\mathbf{A}_i^{-1}(\mathbf{c})$, they show how to extract a random bit (by computing $\rho_i = \lfloor \mathbf{v}_i^\intercal \boldsymbol{\pi}_i \rceil$ and appealing to the leftover hash lemma where $\mathbf{v}_i$ is the seed for the extractor).

This preimage distribution property for the shifted multi-preimage trapdoor sampler critically assumed that the CRS (and correspondingly, the matrices $\mathbf{A}_1, \ldots, \mathbf{A}_\ell$) are sampled honestly. In particular, the previous argument relies on the marginal distribution of $\mathbf{A}_i$ being uniform. Unfortunately, in our case, the CRS for the multi-preimage sampler is chosen *adversarially* by the verifier, so we can no longer rely on $\boldsymbol{\pi}_i$ being distributed according to a discrete Gaussian or even on it having high min-entropy. To overcome this problem, the prover needs to introduces additional min-entropy during proof generation via the following procedure:

- First, for each $i \in [\ell]$, the prover samples a uniform vector $\mathbf{w}_i \xleftarrow{R} \{0,1\}^t$.
- Instead of setting the shifted multi-preimage trapdoor sampler targets to be $\mathbf{t}_1 = \cdots = \mathbf{t}_\ell = \mathbf{0}$ as in [WWW25], the prover now defines the targets to be $\mathbf{t}_1 = \mathbf{A}_1\mathbf{w}_1, \ldots, \mathbf{t}_\ell = \mathbf{A}_\ell\mathbf{w}_\ell$. This yields $(\boldsymbol{\pi}'_1, \ldots, \boldsymbol{\pi}'_\ell, \mathbf{c})$ such that $\mathbf{A}_i\boldsymbol{\pi}'_i = \mathbf{t}_i + \mathbf{c} = \mathbf{A}_i\mathbf{w}_i + \mathbf{c}$ for each $i \in [\ell]$.
- The prover now defines the openings to be $\boldsymbol{\pi}_i = \boldsymbol{\pi}'_i - \mathbf{w}_i$. Observe that this still preserves the [WWW25] verification invariant: $\mathbf{A}_i\boldsymbol{\pi}_i = \mathbf{A}_i(\boldsymbol{\pi}'_i - \mathbf{w}_i) = \mathbf{t}_i + \mathbf{c} - \mathbf{t}_i = \mathbf{c}$.
- The key observation is that the additional vector $\mathbf{w}_i$ introduces additional min-entropy into $\boldsymbol{\pi}_i$. In particular, $\boldsymbol{\pi}_i$ has high min-entropy even given the commitment $\mathbf{c}$ and the other openings $\boldsymbol{\pi}_j$ for all $j \neq i$. The latter property holds because $(\boldsymbol{\pi}_1, \ldots, \boldsymbol{\pi}_\ell, \mathbf{c})$ are functions of $\mathbf{t}_1 = \mathbf{A}_1\mathbf{w}_1, \ldots, \mathbf{t}_\ell = \mathbf{A}_\ell\mathbf{w}_\ell$, and $\mathbf{A}_i$ is a *compressing* function. Namely, the value of $\mathbf{t}_i = \mathbf{A}_i\mathbf{w}_i$ can only leak a limited number of bits of information about $\mathbf{w}_i$.

Preserving Min-Entropy. Having established that the opening $\boldsymbol{\pi}_i$ has high min-entropy (even given $\mathbf{c}$ and $\boldsymbol{\pi}_j$ for $j \neq i$), it remains to argue that the bit $\rho_i = \lfloor \mathbf{v}_i^\mathsf{T}\boldsymbol{\pi}_i \rceil$ is statistically close to uniform. By definition, $\mathbf{v}_i = \tilde{\mathbf{v}}_i + \boldsymbol{\delta}$ so

$$\mathbf{v}_i^\mathsf{T}\boldsymbol{\pi}_i = \tilde{\mathbf{v}}_i^\mathsf{T}\boldsymbol{\pi}_i + \boldsymbol{\delta}^\mathsf{T}\boldsymbol{\pi}_i.$$

Our argument critically relies on the fact that the re-randomization term $\boldsymbol{\delta}^\mathsf{T}\boldsymbol{\pi}_i$ is statistically close to uniform over $\mathbb{Z}_q$. Recall that $\boldsymbol{\delta} \in \mathbb{Z}_q^t$ is a sparse vector with up to N non-zero entries (and where the non-zero entries are uniformly random). Let $J \subseteq [t]$ be the indices where $\boldsymbol{\delta}$ is non-zero. Then $\boldsymbol{\delta}^\mathsf{T}\boldsymbol{\pi}_i = \sum_{j \in J} \delta_j \pi_{i,j}$. If we can argue that the sub-vector $(\pi_{i,j})_{j \in J}$ has high min-entropy, then we can appeal to the leftover hash lemma (treating $\boldsymbol{\delta}$ as the seed for the extractor and $(\pi_{i,j})_{j \in J}$ as the min-entropy source) and conclude that $\boldsymbol{\delta}^\mathsf{T}\boldsymbol{\pi}_i$ is statistically close to uniform over $\mathbb{Z}_q$. To do so, we use a standard entropy preservation argument (c.f., [NZ96, Vad06, ADW09]) that says that if $\boldsymbol{\pi}_i \in \mathbb{Z}_q^t$ has high min-entropy, then projecting $\boldsymbol{\pi}_i$ onto a *random* set of coordinates $J \subseteq [t]$ still yields a string with high min-entropy. By our earlier argument, the openings $\boldsymbol{\pi}_i$ have high min-entropy so projecting $\boldsymbol{\pi}_i$ onto the random subset $J \subseteq [N]$ preserves the min-entropy. We can now appeal to the leftover hash lemma to conclude that $\boldsymbol{\delta}^\mathsf{T}\boldsymbol{\pi}_i$ is statistically close to uniform over $\mathbb{Z}_q$. Since $\mathbf{v}_i^\mathsf{T}\boldsymbol{\pi}_i = \tilde{\mathbf{v}}_i^\mathsf{T}\boldsymbol{\pi}_i + \boldsymbol{\delta}^\mathsf{T}\boldsymbol{\pi}_i$, this means that $\mathbf{v}_i^\mathsf{T}\boldsymbol{\pi}_i$ is statistically close to uniform, which completes the hiding analysis.

Interactive Hidden-Bits Generators. Rather than build a ZAP directly, the work of [CKSU21] introduces an intermediate abstraction called an *interactive hidden-bits generator*, which models the key ingredients we described above. The approach described above readily maps to this abstraction. Once we have constructed an interactive hidden-bits generator from quasi-polynomial hardness of LWE, we can directly invoke the [CKSU21] compiler to obtain a public-coin statistical ZAP argument for NP. We give the formal definition of an interactive hidden-bits generator in Sect. 3, and give our construction in Sect. 4.

The previous work of [CKSU21] describe a pairing-based construction of an interactive hidden-bits generator. In their approach, the prover re-randomizes a matrix encoded in the exponent by applying a perturbation to the diagonal entries. They show that with overwhelming probability, this yields a full-rank matrix in the exponent, which ensures hiding for the unopened bits of the hidden-bits string. The starting point of our approach is the hidden-bits generator from [Wat24, WWW25], which has a different and incomparable structure. Correspondingly, our lattice-based approach uses an entirely different re-randomization approach.

Concurrent Work. Very recently, a concurrent work by [BCD+25] also followed up on the work of [Wat24] and presents a NIZK from LWE with a polynomial modulus (similar to [WWW25]). Like [WWW25], they do not construct a ZAP, although we believe a variation of our techniques can also be applied to their scheme as well. However, such an adaptation would inherit properties that result in a less efficient scheme (e.g., the verifier message would be ℓ^2, where ℓ is the output length of the hidden-bits generator and the size of the openings would be linear in ℓ). Their work also introduces a new statistically-sound NIZK from DDH and LPN. It is an interesting open question whether our techniques can be helpful to obtain a ZAP from DDH and LPN.

2 Preliminaries

Throughout this work, we write λ to denote the security parameter. We write $\boldsymbol{\eta}_i$ to denote the ith standard basis vector (with dimension implicit from the context). We say that a function $\mu(\lambda)$ is negligible if $\mu(\lambda) = o(\lambda^{-c})$ for every constant $c > 0$. We denote this by writing $\mu(\lambda) = \mathsf{negl}(\lambda)$. We say that an event happens with overwhelming probability if its complement happens with negligible probability. For any positive integer $n \in \mathbb{N}$, we write $[n] := \{1, \ldots, n\}$. For any positive integer $q \in \mathbb{N}$, we write $\mathbb{Z}_q$ to denote the ring of integers modulo q. Throughout this work, we use bold uppercase letters (e.g., $\mathbf{A}, \mathbf{B}$) to denote matrices and bold lowercase letters (e.g., $\mathbf{u}, \mathbf{v}$) to denote vectors. For a vector $\mathbf{v} = (v_1, \ldots, v_n) \in \mathbb{Z}_q^n$, and any vector of indices $I = (i_1 \ldots, i_k) \in [n]^k$, we write $\mathbf{v}[I]$ to denote the projection of $\mathbf{v}$ on I, that is $\mathbf{v}[I] = (v_{i_1}, \ldots, v_{i_k})$. We say that an algorithm is efficient if it runs in probabilistic polynomial time in the length of its input. For two distribution ensembles $\mathcal{X} = \{\mathcal{X}_\lambda\}_{\lambda \in \mathbb{N}}$ and $\mathcal{Y} = \{\mathcal{Y}_\lambda\}_{\lambda \in \mathbb{N}}$ indexed by a security parameter λ, we say that $\mathcal{X}$ and $\mathcal{Y}$ are computationally (respectively, statistically) indistinguishable if for all efficient (respectively, unbounded) adversaries $\mathcal{A}$, there exists a negligible function $\mathsf{negl}(\lambda)$ such that for all $\lambda \in \mathbb{N}$:

$$\left|\Pr[\mathcal{A}(1^\lambda, x) = 1 : x \leftarrow \mathcal{X}_\lambda] - \Pr[\mathcal{A}(1^\lambda, y) = 1 : y \leftarrow \mathcal{Y}_\lambda]\right| = \mathsf{negl}(\lambda).$$

Average Min-Entropy. For random variables X and Y, the *average min-entropy* of X given Y [DORS08] is defined to be

$$\widetilde{\mathbf{H}}_\infty(X \mid Y) := -\log\left(\mathbb{E}_{y \leftarrow Y}\left[\max_x \Pr[X = x \mid Y = y]\right]\right).$$

We will use the following bound on the average min-entropy from [DORS08]:

Lemma 2.1 (Average Min-Entropy [DORS08, **Lemma 2.2**]**).** *Let X, Y be random variables and suppose there are at most 2^k elements in the support of Y. Then, $\widetilde{\mathbf{H}}_\infty(X \mid Y) \geq \mathbf{H}_\infty(X) - k$.*

Leftover Hash Lemma. We recall the (generalized) leftover hash lemma [HILL99, DORS08] that shows how to extract a uniform random value from any source with high average min-entropy. While the general form of the leftover hash lemma can be instantiated with any universal hash function, we describe a specialization that is convenient for our specific application:

Lemma 2.2 (Generalized Leftover Hash Lemma [DORS08, **Lemma 2.4, adapted**]**).** *Let λ be a security parameter. Let $t, q \in \mathbb{N}$ and $\mathcal{D}$ be any distribution that outputs $\mathbf{x} \in \{0,1\}^t$ and auxiliary information aux. Suppose $\widetilde{\mathbf{H}}_\infty(\mathbf{x} \mid \mathsf{aux}) \geq \omega(\log \lambda) + \log q$. Then, there exists a negligible function $\mathsf{negl}(\lambda)$ such that the statistical distance between the following distributions is at most $\mathsf{negl}(\lambda)$:*

$$\left\{(\mathbf{z}^\mathsf{T}\mathbf{x}, \mathbf{z}, \mathsf{aux}) : \begin{array}{c}(\mathbf{x}, \mathsf{aux}) \leftarrow \mathcal{D} \\ \mathbf{z} \xleftarrow{\text{R}} \mathbb{Z}_q^t\end{array}\right\} \quad \textit{and} \quad \left\{(u, \mathbf{z}, \mathsf{aux}) : \begin{array}{c}(\mathbf{x}, \mathsf{aux}) \leftarrow \mathcal{D} \\ \mathbf{z} \xleftarrow{\text{R}} \mathbb{Z}_q^t, u \xleftarrow{\text{R}} \mathbb{Z}_q\end{array}\right\}$$

Entropy Preservation. We will also use the fact that if $\mathbf{x} \in \{0,1\}^t$ is a bit-string with high min-entropy, then taking a random subset of the bits of $\mathbf{x}$ still yields a bit-string with high min-entropy of $\mathbf{x}$. We use the statement from [ADW09] (similar statements can also be found in earlier works on randomness extractors [NZ96, Vad06]):

Lemma 2.3 (Entropy Preservation [ADW09, **Lemma A.3, adapted**]**).** *Let $\mathbf{x} \in \{0,1\}^t$ be a random variable. Suppose we sample $I \xleftarrow{\text{R}} [t]^k$. Then for all random variables aux and all $c > 0$, if $\widetilde{\mathbf{H}}_\infty(\mathbf{x} \mid \mathsf{aux}) \geq \frac{2c}{k} t(1 + \log t) + 3c + 5$, then $\widetilde{\mathbf{H}}_\infty(\mathbf{x}[I] \mid (\mathsf{aux}, I)) \geq c$.*

ZAPs. We now recall the formal notion of a statistical ZAP argument [DN00]. We consider two notions of soundness: non-adaptive soundness where the statement is fixed in advance and adaptive soundness where the (malicious) prover can choose the statement *after* it sees the verifier's first message.

Definition 2.4 (Statistical ZAP Argument). *Let λ be a security parameter. Let $\mathcal{R}$ be an NP relation defined by a family of polynomial-size circuits $\mathcal{C} = \{\mathcal{C}_n : \{0,1\}^n \times \{0,1\}^h \to \{0,1\}\}_{n\in\mathbb{N}}$, where n is the instance length and $h = h(n)$ is a polynomial denoting the witness length. Let $\mathcal{L}$ be the associated* NP *language. A (public-coin) statistical ZAP argument for $\mathcal{R}$ with public-coin length $t = t(\lambda, n)$ and proof size $\ell = \ell(\lambda, n)$ is a pair of efficient algorithms* (Prove, Verify) *with the following syntax:*

- $\mathsf{Prove}(1^\lambda, r, x, w) \to \pi$*: On input a public random coin $r \in \{0,1\}^t$, a statement $x \in \{0,1\}^n$, and a witness $w \in \{0,1\}^h$, the prove algorithm outputs a proof $\pi \in \{0,1\}^\ell$.*
- $\mathsf{Verify}(1^\lambda, r, x, \pi) \to 0/1$*: On input a public random coin $r \in \{0,1\}^t$, a statement $x \in \{0,1\}^n$, and a proof $\pi \in \{0,1\}^\ell$, the verification algorithm outputs a bit.*

We require (Prove, Verify) *satisfy the following properties:*

- ***Completeness:*** *For all $\lambda, n \in \mathbb{N}$, and all $(x, w) \in \mathcal{R}$, it holds that*

$$\Pr\left[\mathsf{Verify}(1^\lambda, r, x, \pi) = 1 : r \xleftarrow{R} \{0,1\}^t, \pi \leftarrow \mathsf{Prove}(1^\lambda, r, x, w)\right] = 1.$$

- ***Efficiency:*** *There exists a polynomial* $\mathsf{poly}(\cdot,\cdot)$ *such that for all $\lambda, n \in \mathbb{N}$ it holds that $t(\lambda, n) \leq \mathsf{poly}(\lambda, n)$ and $\ell(\lambda, n) \leq \mathsf{poly}(\lambda, n)$.*
- ***Computational non-adaptive soundness:*** *For all polynomials $n = n(\lambda)$ and all efficient adversaries $\mathcal{A}$, there exists a negligible function* $\mathsf{negl}(\lambda)$ *such that for all $\lambda \in \mathbb{N}$ and all $x \notin \mathcal{L}$, the following holds:*

$$\Pr\left[\mathsf{Verify}(1^\lambda, r, x, \pi) = 1 : r \xleftarrow{R} \{0,1\}^t, \pi \leftarrow \mathcal{A}(1^\lambda, r, x)\right] = \mathsf{negl}(\lambda).$$

- ***Statistical witness-indistinguishability:*** *For all polynomials $n = n(\lambda)$, and every (possibly unbounded) adversary $\mathcal{A}$, there exists a negligible function* $\mathsf{negl}(\lambda)$ *such that $\mathcal{A}$ wins the following game with probability* $\mathsf{negl}(\lambda)$*:*
  1. *On input a security parameter 1^λ, the adversary $\mathcal{A}$ chooses $r \in \{0,1\}^t, x \in \{0,1\}^n, w_0, w_1 \in \{0,1\}^h$ to the challenger.*
  2. *The challenger samples $b \xleftarrow{R} \{0,1\}$, computes $\pi \leftarrow \mathsf{Prove}(1^\lambda, r, x, w_b)$, and sends π to the adversary.*
  3. *The adversary outputs a guess $b' \in \{0,1\}$ and wins the game if all of the following holds:*

$$b = b' \quad \text{and} \quad (x, w_0) \in \mathcal{R} \quad \text{and} \quad (x, w_1) \in \mathcal{R}.$$

Definition 2.5 (Computational Adaptive Soundness). *A public-coin statistical ZAP argument for an* NP *relation $\mathcal{R}$ satisfies computational adaptive soundness if for all polynomials $n = n(\lambda)$, and all efficient adversaries $\mathcal{A}$, there exists a negligible function* $\mathsf{negl}(\cdot)$ *such that for all $\lambda \in \mathbb{N}$,*

$$\Pr\left[x \notin \mathcal{L} \wedge \mathsf{Verify}(1^\lambda, r, x, \pi) = 1 : r \xleftarrow{R} \{0,1\}^t, (x, \pi) \leftarrow \mathcal{A}(1^\lambda, r)\right] = \mathsf{negl}(\lambda).$$

2.1 Lattice Preliminaries

We now recall some preliminaries on lattice-based cryptography. First, we write $D_{\mathbb{Z},s}$ to denote the discrete Gaussian distribution over $\mathbb{Z}$ with width parameter $s > 0$. We will use the following tail bound on discrete Gaussian random variables:

Lemma 2.6 (Gaussian Tail Bound [MP12, **Lemma 2.6, adapted**]**).** *For all* $\lambda \in \mathbb{N}$,

$$\Pr[|x| > \sqrt{\lambda}s : x \leftarrow D_{\mathbb{Z},s}] \leq 2^{-\lambda}.$$

Learning with Errors. Next, we recall the standard learning with errors (LWE) assumption [Reg05]:

Assumption 2.7 (Learning with Errors [Reg05]**).** Let λ be a security parameter and $n = n(\lambda)$, $m = m(\lambda)$, $q = q(\lambda)$, and $s = s(\lambda)$ be lattice parameters. We say that the $\mathsf{LWE}_{n,m,q,s}$ assumption holds if the following two distributions are computationally indistinguishable:

$$\left\{ (\mathbf{A}, \mathbf{s}^{\mathsf{T}}\mathbf{A} + \mathbf{e}^{\mathsf{T}}) : \begin{array}{c} \mathbf{A} \xleftarrow{\text{R}} \mathbb{Z}_q^{n \times m} \\ \mathbf{s} \xleftarrow{\text{R}} \mathbb{Z}_q^n, \mathbf{e} \leftarrow D_{\mathbb{Z},s}^m \end{array} \right\} \quad \text{and} \quad \left\{ (\mathbf{A}, \mathbf{u}^{\mathsf{T}}) : \begin{array}{c} \mathbf{A} \xleftarrow{\text{R}} \mathbb{Z}_q^{n \times m} \\ \mathbf{u} \xleftarrow{\text{R}} \mathbb{Z}_q^m \end{array} \right\}$$

Moreover, for a constant $c > 1$, we say that the c-quasi-polynomial $\mathsf{LWE}_{n,m,q,s}$ assumption holds if for all efficient adversaries $\mathcal{A}$, there exists a negligible function $\mathsf{negl}(\cdot)$ such that for all $\lambda \in \mathbb{N}$, the advantage in distinguishing the distributions is bounded by $2^{-\log^c(\lambda)} \cdot \mathsf{negl}(\lambda)$.

Shifted Multi-preimage Trapdoor Sampler. Next, we recall the notion of a shifted multi-preimage trapdoor sampler introduced in [WWW25]:

Definition 2.8 (Shifted Multi-Preimage Trapdoor Sampler [WWW25, **adapted**]**).** *Let* λ *be a security parameter and* ℓ *be a dimension. Let* $n = n(\lambda, \ell)$, $t = t(\lambda, \ell)$, $q = q(\lambda, \ell)$, *and* $s = s(\lambda, \ell)$ *be functions. An* (n, t, q, s)*-shifted multi-preimage trapdoor sampler is a pair of efficient algorithms* $(\mathsf{Gen}, \mathsf{Expand}, \mathsf{SampleMultPre})$ *with the following syntax:*

- $\mathsf{Gen}(1^\lambda, 1^\ell) \rightarrow \mathsf{crs}$*: On input the security parameter* λ *and the dimension* ℓ*, the generator algorithm outputs a common reference string* crs.
- $\mathsf{Expand}(1^\lambda, 1^\ell, \mathsf{crs}) \rightarrow (\mathbf{A}_1, \ldots, \mathbf{A}_\ell, \mathsf{td})$*: On input the security parameter* λ*, the dimension* ℓ*, and the common reference string* crs*, the expand algorithm outputs a collection of matrices* $\mathbf{A}_i \in \mathbb{Z}_q^{n \times t}$ *and a trapdoor* td*. This algorithm is* deterministic.
- $\mathsf{SampleMultPre}(\mathsf{td}, \mathbf{t}_1, \ldots, \mathbf{t}_\ell) \rightarrow (\boldsymbol{\pi}_1, \ldots, \boldsymbol{\pi}_\ell, \mathbf{c})$*: On input a trapdoor* td *and a collection of preimages* $\mathbf{t}_1, \ldots, \mathbf{t}_\ell$*, the shifted multi-preimage sampling algorithm outputs a shift* $\mathbf{c} \in \mathbb{Z}_q^n$ *together with preimages* $\boldsymbol{\pi}_1, \ldots, \boldsymbol{\pi}_\ell \in \mathbb{Z}_q^t$.

The structured trapdoor sampler should satisfy the following properties:

– ***Correctness:*** *For all* $\lambda, \ell \in \mathbb{N}$, *all* crs *in the support of* $\mathsf{Gen}(1^\lambda, 1^\ell)$, *all target vectors* $\mathbf{t}_1, \ldots, \mathbf{t}_\ell \in \mathbb{Z}_q^n$, *and setting* $(\mathbf{A}_1, \ldots, \mathbf{A}_\ell, \mathsf{td}) = \mathsf{Expand}(1^\lambda, 1^\ell, \mathsf{crs})$, *it holds that:*

$$\Pr[\forall i \in [\ell]\ \mathbf{A}_i \boldsymbol{\pi}_i = \mathbf{t}_i + \mathbf{c}] = 1,$$

where the probability is over $(\boldsymbol{\pi}_1, \ldots, \boldsymbol{\pi}_\ell, \mathbf{c}) \leftarrow \mathsf{SampleMultPre}(\mathsf{td}, \mathbf{t}_1, \ldots, \mathbf{t}_\ell)$.

– ***Preimage norm bound:*** *For all polynomials* $\ell = \ell(\lambda)$, *there exists a negligible function* $\mathsf{negl}(\cdot)$ *such that for all* crs *in the support of* $\mathsf{Gen}(1^\lambda, 1^\ell)$, *setting* $(\mathbf{A}_1, \ldots, \mathbf{A}_\ell, \mathsf{td}) = \mathsf{Expand}(1^\lambda, 1^\ell, \mathsf{crs})$, *and for all target vectors* $\mathbf{t}_1, \ldots, \mathbf{t}_\ell \in \mathbb{Z}_q^n$:

$$\Pr\left[\|\boldsymbol{\pi}_i\| \geq \sqrt{\ell t} s\right] = \mathsf{negl}(\lambda),$$

where $(\boldsymbol{\pi}_1, \ldots, \boldsymbol{\pi}_\ell, \mathbf{c}) \leftarrow \mathsf{SampleMultPre}(\mathsf{td}, \mathbf{t}_1, \ldots, \mathbf{t}_\ell)$.

– ***Somewhere programmable:*** *There exists an efficient algorithm* $\mathsf{GenProg}$ *such that for all polynomials* $\ell = \ell(\lambda)$, *the following holds:*

- *For all* $\lambda \in \mathbb{N}$, *all indices* $i \in [\ell]$, *and all matrices* $\mathbf{A}_i \in \mathbb{Z}_q^{n \times t}$, *it holds that*

$$\Pr\left[\mathbf{A}_i = \widetilde{\mathbf{A}}_i : \begin{array}{c} \widetilde{\mathsf{crs}} \leftarrow \mathsf{GenProg}(1^\lambda, 1^\ell, i, \mathbf{A}_i) \\ (\widetilde{\mathbf{A}}_1, \ldots, \widetilde{\mathbf{A}}_\ell, \widetilde{\mathbf{T}}) = \mathsf{Expand}(1^\lambda, 1^\ell, \widetilde{\mathsf{crs}}) \end{array}\right] = 1.$$

- *There exists a negligible function* $\mathsf{negl}(\cdot)$ *such that for all* $\lambda \in \mathbb{N}$ *and all* $i \in [\ell]$, *the statistical distance between the following distributions is* $\mathsf{negl}(\lambda)$:

$$\{\mathsf{crs} : \mathsf{crs} \leftarrow \mathsf{Gen}(1^\lambda, 1^\ell)\} \quad \text{and} \quad \left\{\widetilde{\mathsf{crs}} : \begin{array}{c} \mathbf{A}_i \xleftarrow{R} \mathbb{Z}_q^{n \times t} \\ \widetilde{\mathsf{crs}} \leftarrow \mathsf{GenProg}(1^\lambda, 1^\ell, i, \mathbf{A}_i) \end{array}\right\}.$$

  When these distributions are identical, we say the shifted multi-preimage trapdoor sampler satisfies perfect *somewhere programmability.*

– **Transparent setup:** *The common reference string* crs *output by* Gen *is exactly the random coins given to* Gen.

Remark 2.9 (Preimage Distribution Property). The shifted multi-preimage trapdoor sampler definition from [WWW25] states a different preimage property which they call *preimage distribution.* Their property asserts that the outputs $(\boldsymbol{\pi}_1, \ldots, \boldsymbol{\pi}_\ell, \mathbf{c}) \leftarrow \mathsf{SampleMultPre}(\mathsf{td}, \mathbf{t}_1, \ldots, \mathbf{t}_\ell)$ are statistically close to the distribution obtained by sampling $\mathbf{c} \xleftarrow{R} \mathbb{Z}_q^n$ and $\boldsymbol{\pi}_i \leftarrow (\mathbf{A}_i)_s^{-1}(\mathbf{t}_i + \mathbf{c})$. However, this property only holds with overwhelming probability over the choice of $\mathsf{crs} \leftarrow \mathsf{Gen}(1^\lambda, 1^\ell)$. In contrast, the property we state here holds for *all* common reference strings, which is crucial for our application since the CRS may be chosen adversarially. Finally, it is easy to see that the construction of [WWW25], satisfies the preimage bound property. Specifically, for *every* choice of CRS (which determines the matrices $\mathbf{A}_1, \ldots, \mathbf{A}_\ell$), the work of [WWW25, Construction 4.6] shows how to construct a trapdoor $\mathbf{T}$ where $\|\mathbf{T}\| = 1$ and

$$\underbrace{\left[\begin{array}{ccc|c} \mathbf{A}_1 & & & \mathbf{G} \\ & \ddots & & \vdots \\ & & \mathbf{A}_\ell & \mathbf{G} \end{array}\right]}_{\mathbf{D}} \cdot \mathbf{T} = \mathbf{I}_\ell \otimes \mathbf{G},$$

where $\mathbf{G} \in \mathbb{Z}_q^{n\times n\lceil \log q\rceil}$ is the gadget matrix [MP12]. The SampleMultPre algorithm uses $\mathbf{T}$ to sample a Gaussian-distributed preimage $\mathbf{D}_s^{-1}(\mathbf{t})$ where $\mathbf{t} \in \mathbb{Z}_q^{n\ell}$ is the vertical concatenation of $\mathbf{t}_1, \dots, \mathbf{t}_\ell \in \mathbb{Z}_q^n$. Since the matrix $\mathbf{D}$ has a "gadget trapdoor" $\mathbf{T}$ with norm 1 (irrespective of the choice of the CRS), we can appeal to a standard Gaussian tail bound (c.f., [MP12, Lemma 2.6]) to conclude that the norm of the preimage is bounded with overwhelming probability (for the parameter choices from [WWW25, Theorem 4.7]).

Theorem 2.10 (Shifted Multi-Preimage Trapdoor Sampler [WWW25, **Theorem 4.7]).** *Let $n = n(\lambda, \ell)$, $q = q(\lambda, \ell)$ be arbitrary non-negative functions where $n \geq \lambda$. Let $m = 3n\lceil \log q\rceil$ and $t = m(\lceil \log q\rceil + 1)$. Then for all $s \geq (\ell t + m)\log(\ell n)$, there exists an (n, q, t, s)-shifted multi-preimage trapdoor sampler* (Gen, Expand, SampleMultPre) *with perfect somewhere programmability and transparent setup. The size of the CRS output by* $\mathsf{Gen}(1^\lambda, 1^\ell)$ *is* $nt\log q$.

3 Interactive Hidden-Bits Generator

The work of [CKSU21] introduce the notion of an *interactive hidden bits generator* to construct (statistical) ZAPs from pairings groups. Interactive hidden-bits are a generalization of standard (non-interactive) dual-mode hidden-bits generators [QRW19,LPWW20].

At a high level, an interactive hidden-bits generator is a two-message protocol that allows a prover and a verifier to jointly sample a hidden-bits string. The verifier is public-coin and sends the first message, which is simply a uniform random string (i.e., its random coins). The prover responds with a message. At the conclusion of the protocol, the prover receives the hidden-bits string while the verifier receives a commitment to the hidden-bits string. The prover can then open a subset of the bits to the verifier. The main requirements are as follows:

- **Hiding:** First, the unopened bits should remain hidden (and statistically close to uniform) from the perspective of the verifier.
- **Binding:** Second, the prover should not be able to significantly bias the distribution of the hidden-bits string. To formally capture this, the work of [CKSU21] introduces a trapdoor algorithm TrapCoin that outputs a string r^* (which is computationally indistinguishable from the verifier's first message) together with a trapdoor td. The trapdoor td can be used to extract the hidden-bits string from the commitment. Of course, if TrapCoin always succeeds, or even succeeds with non-negligible probability, then it violates the hiding property. For this reason, we require it to succeed with a negligible, but not too small, probability μ and refer to this as a μ-extraction property.
- **Succinctness:** Finally, the succinctness property asserts that the size of the commitment should be much shorter than the length of the hidden-bits string.

Definition 3.1 (Interactive Hidden-Bits Generator [CKSU21]**).** *Let λ be a security parameter and ℓ be an output length parameter, i.e., the number of hidden bits. An interactive hidden-bits generator with public-coin length*

$\ell_{\mathsf{pub}} = \ell_{\mathsf{pub}}(\lambda, \ell)$ and commitment length $\ell_{\mathsf{com}} = \ell_{\mathsf{com}}(\lambda, \ell)$ is a tuple of efficient algorithms $\Pi_{\mathsf{IHBG}} = (\mathsf{GenBits}, \mathsf{Verify})$ with the following syntax:

- $\mathsf{GenBits}(1^\lambda, 1^\ell, r) \to (\mathsf{com}, \pi_1, \ldots, \pi_\ell, \boldsymbol{\rho})$: *On input a security parameter λ, a length parameter ℓ, and a public-coin $r \in \{0,1\}^{\ell_{\mathsf{pub}}}$, the bit-generation algorithm outputs a commitment $\mathsf{com} \in \{0,1\}^{\ell_{\mathsf{com}}}$, openings $\pi_1, \ldots, \pi_\ell$, and a hidden-bits string $\boldsymbol{\rho} \in \{0,1\}^\ell$.*
- $\mathsf{Verify}(r, \mathsf{com}, i, b, \pi_i) \to \beta$: *On input a public-coin $r \in \{0,1\}^{\ell_{\mathsf{pub}}}$, a commitment $\mathsf{com} \in \{0,1\}^{\ell_{\mathsf{com}}}$, an index $i \in [\ell]$, a bit $b \in \{0,1\}$ and an opening π, the verification algorithm outputs a bit $\beta \in \{0,1\}$.*

We require Π_{IHBG} to satisfy the following properties:

- ***Correctness:*** *For all $\lambda \in \mathbb{N}$, $\ell \in \mathbb{N}$, $i \in [\ell]$, and $r \in \{0,1\}^{\ell_{\mathsf{pub}}}$, the following holds:*
$$\Pr\left[\mathsf{Verify}(r, \mathsf{com}, i, \rho_i, \pi_i) = 1\right] = 1,$$
where $(\mathsf{com}, \pi_1, \ldots, \pi_\ell, \boldsymbol{\rho}) \leftarrow \mathsf{GenBits}(1^\lambda, 1^\ell, r)$.
- ***Succinctness:*** *There exists a fixed polynomial $\mathsf{poly}(\cdot,\cdot)$ such that commitment length $\ell_{\mathsf{com}}(\lambda, \ell) \le \mathsf{poly}(\lambda, \log \ell)$.*
- ***Single-bit hiding:*** *For an adversary $\mathcal{A}$, a security parameter λ, a length parameter ℓ and a bit $b \in \{0,1\}$, we define the single bit hiding game as follows:*
  1. *On input a security parameter 1^λ and a length parameter 1^ℓ, the adversary $\mathcal{A}$ chooses public-coin $r \in \{0,1\}^{\ell_{\mathsf{pub}}}$ and an index $i^* \in [\ell]$, and sends (r, i^*) to the challenger.*
  2. *The challenger samples $(\mathsf{com}, \pi_1, \ldots, \pi_\ell, \boldsymbol{\rho}) \leftarrow \mathsf{GenBits}(1^\lambda, 1^\ell, r)$.*
  3. *If $b = 0$, the challenger sets $\beta = \rho_{i^*}$. If $b = 1$, the challenger samples a bit $\beta \xleftarrow{\mathrm{R}} \{0,1\}$.*
  4. *The challenger sends $(\mathsf{com}, (\rho_i, \pi_i)_{i \ne i^*}, \beta)$ to $\mathcal{A}$.*
  5. *The adversary $\mathcal{A}$ outputs a guess $b' \in \{0,1\}$.*

  We say that Π_{IHBG} satisfies single-bit hiding if for all polynomials $\ell = \ell(\lambda)$ and all (possibly unbounded) adversaries $\mathcal{A}$, there exists a negligible function such that
$$\left|\Pr\left[b' = 0 : b = 0\right] - \Pr\left[b' = 0 : b = 1\right]\right| \le \mathsf{negl}(\lambda)$$
  in the single-bit hiding game.
- ***Extraction:*** *We additionally require the following efficient algorithms:*
  - $\mathsf{TrapCoin}(1^\lambda, 1^\ell) \to (r^*, \mathsf{td})$: *On input a security parameter λ and a length parameter ℓ, the trapdoor public-coin generation algorithm outputs a public-coin $r^* \in \{0,1\}^{\ell_{\mathsf{pub}}}$ and a trapdoor td.*
  - $\mathsf{Extract}(\mathsf{td}, \mathsf{com}) \to \boldsymbol{\rho}$: *On input a trapdoor td and a commitment $\mathsf{com} \in \{0,1\}^{\ell_{\mathsf{com}}}$, the extraction algorithm outputs a string $\boldsymbol{\rho} \in \{0,1\}^\ell$.*

  We require the following properties:
  - ***Mode indistinguishability:*** *For all efficient adversaries $\mathcal{A}$ and all polynomials $\ell = \ell(\lambda)$, there exists a negligible function $\mathsf{negl}(\cdot)$ such that*
$$\Big|\Pr\left[\mathcal{A}(1^\lambda, 1^\ell, r) = 1 : r \xleftarrow{\mathrm{R}} \{0,1\}^{\ell_{\mathsf{pub}}}\right] - \Pr\left[\mathcal{A}(1^\lambda, 1^\ell, r^*) = 1 : (r^*, \mathsf{td}) \leftarrow \mathsf{TrapCoin}(1^\lambda, 1^\ell)\right]\Big| = \mathsf{negl}(\lambda).$$

Moreover, for a constant $c > 1$, we say that Π_{IHBG} satisfies c-quasi-polynomial mode indistinguishability if for all efficient adversaries $\mathcal{A}$, there exists a negligible function $\mathsf{negl}(\cdot)$ such that for all $\lambda \in \mathbb{N}$, the above distinguishing advantage is bounded by $2^{-\log^c(\lambda)} \cdot \mathsf{negl}(\lambda)$.

- ***μ-Extraction:*** *For an adversary $\mathcal{A}$, a security parameter λ, and a length parameter ℓ, we define the extraction game as follows:*
  - *The challenger samples $(r^*, \mathsf{td}) \leftarrow \mathsf{TrapCoin}(1^\lambda, 1^\ell)$ sends r^* to the adversary.*
  - *The adversary $\mathcal{A}$ either aborts (with output $\perp$) or outputs a commitment com, a set of indices $S \subseteq [\ell]$, and a tuple of openings $(\pi_i)_{i \in S}$.*

  Define the following events:
  - *Let E_{lose} be the event that for all $i \in S$ it holds that*

$$\mathsf{Verify}(r^*, \mathsf{com}, i, 1 - \rho_i, \pi_i) = 0,$$

    where $\boldsymbol{\rho} \leftarrow \mathsf{Extract}(\mathsf{td}, \mathsf{com})$.
  - *Let $E_{\top}$ be the event that $\mathcal{A}$ does not abort.*

  Let $\mu(\lambda)$ be any positive function of λ. We say that Π_{IHBG} is μ-extractable if for all polynomials $\ell = \ell(\lambda)$ and all efficient algorithms $\mathcal{A}$, there exists a negligible function $\mathsf{negl}(\cdot)$ such that for all $\lambda \in \mathbb{N}$,

$$\Pr\left[E_{\top} \wedge E_{\mathsf{lose}}\right] \geq \mu(\lambda) \cdot \Big(\Pr\left[E_{\top}\right] - \mathsf{negl}(\lambda)\Big).$$

Theorem 3.2 (Statistical ZAP Arguments [CKSU21]**).** *Suppose there exists an interactive hidden-bits generator that satisfies correctness, succinctness, statistical hiding and μ-extraction for some negligible function $\mu(\lambda) = \mathsf{negl}(\lambda)$. Then there exists a (public-coin) statistical ZAP argument for* NP *with non-adaptive soundness.*

Remark 3.3 (Adaptive Security). If the interactive hidden-bits generator is sub-exponentially secure, then the ZAP from Theorem 3.2 is also sub-exponentially (non-adaptively) sound. Using standard complexity leveraging, we can get an adaptively-sound ZAP for bounded-length statements from a sub-exponentially sound ZAP in a black-box way. Looking ahead, this means that our result can be extended to getting a statistical ZAP argument for NP with adaptive soundness assuming sub-exponential hardness of LWE (with a polynomial modulus-to-noise ratio).

Remark 3.4 (Single-Bit Hiding Definition). The work of [CKSU21] defines a different hiding property. In the full version of this paper [BLN+24], we prove that our single-bit hiding property implies the hiding property from [CKSU21]. In this work, we present our property because it is simpler to prove.

4 Constructing an Interactive Hidden-Bits Generator from Lattices

We now show how to use a shifted multi-preimage trapdoor sampler (Definition 2.8) to construct an interactive hidden-bits generator (Definition 3.1).

Construction 4.1. Let λ be a security parameter and ℓ be a length parameter. We start by defining the following parameters:

- Let $\Pi_{\mathsf{samp}} = (\mathsf{Gen}, \mathsf{Expand}, \mathsf{SampleMultPre})$ be a (n, t, q, s)-shifted multi-preimage trapdoor sampler, where n, t, q, s are functions of λ and ℓ. We assume Π_{samp} has a transparent setup procedure, and moreover, that the length of the (public) randomness needed by Gen is $\ell_{\mathsf{samp}} = \ell_{\mathsf{samp}}(\lambda, \ell)$.
- Let $s_{\mathsf{LWE}} = s_{\mathsf{LWE}}(\lambda, \ell)$ be a Gaussian width parameter.
- Let $N = N(\lambda, q)$ be the number of indices used for prover re-randomization.
- Let $B_{\mathsf{max}} = B_{\mathsf{max}}(\lambda, \ell)$ be a norm bound and $B_{\mathsf{round}} = B_{\mathsf{round}}(\lambda, \ell)$ be a rounding boundary parameter.
- Let $\ell_{\mathsf{pub}} = \ell_{\mathsf{samp}} + \ell t(\lceil \log q \rceil + \lambda)$ be the public-coin length. For each $r \in \{0,1\}^{\ell_{\mathsf{pub}}}$, we derive an associated tuple $(\mathsf{crs}_{\mathsf{samp}}, \tilde{\mathbf{v}}_1, \ldots, \tilde{\mathbf{v}}_\ell)$ from r as follows:
  1. First, parse $r = r_{\mathsf{samp}} \| r_1 \| \cdots \| r_\ell$ where $r_{\mathsf{samp}} \in \{0,1\}^{\ell_{\mathsf{samp}}}$ and $r_i \in \{0,1\}^{t(\lceil \log q \rceil + \lambda)}$ for all $i \in [\ell]$.
  2. Let $\mathsf{crs}_{\mathsf{samp}} = \mathsf{Gen}(1^\lambda, 1^\ell; r_{\mathsf{samp}})$.
  3. For each $i \in [\ell]$, we further parse $r_i = r_{i,1} \| \cdots \| r_{i,t}$ where $r_{i,j} \in \{0,1\}^{\lceil \log q \rceil + \lambda}$. We now interpret $r_{i,j}$ as the binary representation of a $(\lceil \log q \rceil + \lambda)$-bit integer and define the vector $\tilde{\mathbf{v}}_i \in \mathbb{Z}_q^t$ where $\tilde{v}_{i,j} = r_{i,j} \bmod q$ for all $j \in [t]$.

We now construct a interactive hidden-bits generator $\Pi_{\mathsf{IHBG}} = (\mathsf{GenBits}, \mathsf{Verify})$ with public-coin length ℓ_{pub} as follows:

- $\mathsf{GenBits}(1^\lambda, 1^\ell, r)$: On input a security parameter λ, a length parameter ℓ, and a public coin $r \in \{0,1\}^{\ell_{\mathsf{pub}}}$, the bit-generation algorithm proceeds as follows:
  1. Let $(\mathsf{crs}_{\mathsf{samp}}, \tilde{\mathbf{v}}_1, \ldots, \tilde{\mathbf{v}}_\ell)$ be the tuple associated with the public coin r. Expand $\mathsf{crs}_{\mathsf{samp}}$ by computing $(\mathbf{A}_1, \ldots, \mathbf{A}_\ell, \mathsf{td}_{\mathsf{samp}}) = \mathsf{Expand}(1^\lambda, 1^\ell, \mathsf{crs}_{\mathsf{samp}})$.
  2. Sample indices $i_1, \ldots, i_N \xleftarrow{\text{R}} [t]$ and $z_1, \ldots, z_N \xleftarrow{\text{R}} \mathbb{Z}_q$. Compute $\mathbf{v}_i = \tilde{\mathbf{v}}_i + \sum_{j \in [N]} z_j \boldsymbol{\eta}_{i_j}$ for $i \in [\ell]$, where $\boldsymbol{\eta}_i \in \mathbb{Z}_q^t$ denotes the ith standard basis vector.
  3. Repeat the following procedure up to λ times:
     (a) Sample $\mathbf{w}_1, \ldots, \mathbf{w}_\ell \xleftarrow{\text{R}} \{0,1\}^t$.
     (b) Compute $(\boldsymbol{\pi}'_1, \ldots, \boldsymbol{\pi}'_\ell, \mathbf{c}) \leftarrow \mathsf{SampleMultPre}(\mathsf{td}_{\mathsf{samp}}, \mathbf{A}_1 \mathbf{w}_1, \ldots, \mathbf{A}_\ell \mathbf{w}_\ell)$.
     (c) For each $i \in [\ell]$, set $\boldsymbol{\pi}_i = \boldsymbol{\pi}'_i - \mathbf{w}_i$. If $\|\boldsymbol{\pi}_i\| > B_{\mathsf{max}}$ then set $\rho_i = \bot$. Otherwise, compute $u_i = \mathbf{v}_i^{\mathsf{T}} \boldsymbol{\pi}_i$ and set ρ_i as follows:

$$\rho_i = \begin{cases} 0 & u_i \in [-B_{\mathsf{round}}, B_{\mathsf{round}}] \\ 1 & u_i \in \big[\lfloor q/2 \rfloor - B_{\mathsf{round}}, \lfloor q/2 \rfloor + B_{\mathsf{round}}\big] \\ \bot & \text{otherwise} \end{cases}$$

(d) If $\rho_i = \perp$ for some $i \in [\ell]$, then repeat the procedure. Otherwise, declare the procedure successful and continue.

4. If the procedure does not succeed after λ iterations, it sets $\mathbf{c} = \perp$ and $\pi_i = \perp$ and $\rho_i = 0$ for all $i \in [\ell]$. Finally, the algorithm sets $\boldsymbol{\rho} = \rho_1 \cdots \rho_\ell \in \{0,1\}^\ell$ and outputs $\mathsf{com} = (i_1, \ldots, i_N, z_1, \ldots, z_N, \mathbf{c})$, the openings $\boldsymbol{\pi}_1, \ldots, \boldsymbol{\pi}_\ell$, and the string $\boldsymbol{\rho}$.

– $\mathsf{Verify}(r, \mathsf{com}, i, b, \boldsymbol{\pi}_i)$: On input a string $r \in \{0,1\}^{\ell_{\mathsf{pub}}}$, a commitment $\mathsf{com} = (i_1, \ldots, i_N, z_1, \ldots, z_N, \mathbf{c})$, an index $i \in [\ell]$, a bit $b \in \{0,1\}$ and an opening $\boldsymbol{\pi}_i \in \mathbb{Z}_q^t$, the verification algorithm proceeds as follows:
  1. Let $(\mathsf{crs}_{\mathsf{samp}}, \tilde{\mathbf{v}}_1, \ldots, \tilde{\mathbf{v}}_\ell)$ be the tuple associated with r. Then compute $\mathbf{v}_i = \tilde{\mathbf{v}}_i + \sum_{j \in [N]} z_j \boldsymbol{\eta}_{i_j}$.
  2. If $\mathbf{c} = \perp$, then output 1 if $b = 0$ and output 0 if $b = 1$.
  3. Otherwise, expand $(\mathbf{A}_1, \ldots, \mathbf{A}_\ell, \mathsf{td}_{\mathsf{samp}}) \leftarrow \mathsf{Expand}(1^\lambda, 1^\ell, \mathsf{crs}_{\mathsf{samp}})$.
  4. Output 1 if
$$\|\boldsymbol{\pi}_i\| \leq B_{\mathsf{max}} \text{ and } \mathbf{A}_i \boldsymbol{\pi}_i = \mathbf{c} \text{ and } \mathbf{v}_i^\mathsf{T} \boldsymbol{\pi}_i \in \left[\, \lfloor q/2 \rfloor \cdot b - B_{\mathsf{round}}, \lfloor q/2 \rfloor \cdot b + B_{\mathsf{round}} \right].$$
  Output 0 otherwise.

In addition, we define the $(\mathsf{TrapCoin}, \mathsf{Extract})$ algorithms for the μ-extraction property as follows:

– $\mathsf{TrapCoin}(1^\lambda, 1^\ell)$: On input a security parameter λ and a length parameter ℓ, the trapdoor public-coin generation algorithm proceeds as follows:
  1. Sample $r_{\mathsf{samp}} \xleftarrow{\mathrm{R}} \{0,1\}^{\ell_{\mathsf{samp}}}$ and let $\mathsf{crs}_{\mathsf{samp}} = \mathsf{Gen}(1^\lambda, 1^\ell; r_{\mathsf{samp}})$. Then expand $\mathsf{crs}_{\mathsf{samp}}$ by computing
$$(\mathbf{A}_1, \ldots, \mathbf{A}_\ell, \mathsf{td}_{\mathsf{samp}}) = \mathsf{Expand}(1^\lambda, 1^\ell, \mathsf{crs}_{\mathsf{samp}}).$$
  2. Sample $i'_1, \ldots, i'_N \xleftarrow{\mathrm{R}} [t]$ and $z'_1, \ldots, z'_N \xleftarrow{\mathrm{R}} \mathbb{Z}_q$.
  3. Sample $\mathbf{s}_1, \ldots, \mathbf{s}_\ell \xleftarrow{\mathrm{R}} \mathbb{Z}_q^n$, $\mathbf{e}_1, \ldots, \mathbf{e}_\ell \leftarrow D_{\mathbb{Z}, s_{\mathsf{LWE}}}^t$. Set $\mathbf{v}_i^\mathsf{T} = \mathbf{s}_i^\mathsf{T} \mathbf{A}_i + \mathbf{e}_i^\mathsf{T}$ for $i \in [\ell]$.
  4. Compute $\tilde{\mathbf{v}}_i = \mathbf{v}_i - \sum_{j \in [N]} z'_j \boldsymbol{\eta}_{i'_j}$ for $i \in [\ell]$. Write $\tilde{\mathbf{v}}_i = [\tilde{v}_{i,1}, \ldots, \tilde{v}_{i,t}]$.
  5. For $i \in [\ell]$ and $j \in [t]$, sample $\gamma_{i,j} \xleftarrow{\mathrm{R}} [0, \lfloor 2^{\lceil \log q \rceil + \lambda}/q \rfloor - 1]$, and set $r_{i,j} = q\gamma_{i,j} + \tilde{v}_{i,j}$, represented as a binary string in $\{0,1\}^{\lceil \log q \rceil + \lambda}$. Finally, let $r_i = r_{i,1} \| \cdots \| r_{i,t} \in \{0,1\}^{t(\lceil \log q \rceil + \lambda)}$.
  6. Output $r^* = r_{\mathsf{samp}} \| r_1 \| \cdots \| r_\ell$ and
$$\mathsf{td} = (r^*, i'_1, \ldots, i'_N, z'_1, \ldots, z'_N, \mathbf{s}_1, \ldots, \mathbf{s}_\ell).$$

– $\mathsf{Extract}(\mathsf{td}, \mathsf{com})$:
  On input a trapdoor $\mathsf{td} = (r^*, i'_1, \ldots, i'_N, z'_1, \ldots, z'_N, \mathbf{s}_1, \ldots, \mathbf{s}_\ell)$ and a commitment $\mathsf{com} = (i_1, \ldots, i_N, z_1, \ldots, z_N, \mathbf{c})$, the extraction algorithm does the following:
  1. If $i'_k \neq i_k$ or $z'_k \neq z_k$ for any $k \in [N]$, abort.
  2. Output $\boldsymbol{\rho}$ where $\rho_i \leftarrow \lfloor \mathbf{s}_i^\mathsf{T} \mathbf{c} \rceil$ for $i \in [\ell]$.

Theorem 4.2 (Correctness). *If Π_{samp} is correct, then Construction 4.1 satisfies correctness.*

Due to space constraints, we defer this proof to the full version of this paper [BLN+24].

Theorem 4.3 (Succinctness). *If there exists a polynomial* $\mathsf{poly}(\cdot,\cdot)$ *such that* $N, t, \log q \leq \mathsf{poly}(\lambda, \log \ell)$*, then Construction 4.1 is succinct.*

Proof. Take any $r \in \{0,1\}^{\ell_{\mathsf{pub}}}$ and any $(\mathsf{com}, \boldsymbol{\pi}_1, \ldots, \boldsymbol{\pi}_\ell, \boldsymbol{\rho})$ in the support of $\mathsf{GenBits}(1^\lambda, 1^\ell, r)$, where $\mathsf{com} = (i_1, \ldots, i_N, z_1, \ldots, z_N, \mathbf{c})$ for $i_j \in [t]$, $z_j \in \mathbb{Z}_q$, and $\mathbf{c} \in \mathbb{Z}_q^t$. Then, com can be represented in $N(\lceil \log t \rceil + \lceil \log q \rceil) + t \lceil \log q \rceil$ bits, as required.

4.1 Security Analysis of Construction 4.1

In this section, we give the security analysis for Construction 4.1. In the following section, we show how to instantiate the underlying lattice parameters to obtain our main result (Theorem 1.1).

4.1.1 Mode Indistinguishability In this section, we prove that Construction 4.1 satisfies mode indistinguishability (Definition 3.1). While Theorem 3.2 only requires normal mode indistinguishability, our proof of μ-extractability (see Theorem 4.9 in Sect. 4.1.2) requires quasi-polynomial mode indistinguishability. For this reason, we rely on quasi-polynomially-secure LWE.

Theorem 4.4 (Mode Indistinguishability). *Suppose c-quasi-polynomial* $\mathsf{LWE}_{n,t,q,s_{\mathsf{LWE}}}$ *holds with constant $c > 1$ and Π_{samp} has a transparent setup and is perfectly somewhere programmable. Then, Construction 4.1 satisfies c-quasi-polynomial mode indistinguishability.*

Proof. Let $\mathcal{A}$ be an efficient mode indistinguishability adversary. Next, Π_{samp} satisfies perfect somewhere programmability, so let $\mathsf{GenProg}$ be the associated algorithm. For each $k \in [\ell+1]$, we define a sequence of hybrid experiments between a challenger and $\mathcal{A}$ as follows:

- Hyb_0: This is the mode indistinguishability game where the challenger samples a uniform random public-coin. Namely, the experiment proceeds as follows:
  1. The challenger samples $r^* \xleftarrow{\mathrm{R}} \{0,1\}^{\ell_{\mathsf{pub}}}$.
  2. The challenger gives $(1^\lambda, 1^\ell, r^*)$ to $\mathcal{A}$. Algorithm $\mathcal{A}$ outputs a bit $b \in \{0,1\}$, which is the output of the experiment.
- $\mathsf{Hyb}_{k,1}$: This is the mode indistinguishability game, except the challenger samples the vectors $\tilde{\mathbf{v}}_1, \ldots, \tilde{\mathbf{v}}_{k-1}$ as LWE instances and then reverse samples the public-coin $r^* \in \{0,1\}^{\ell_{\mathsf{pub}}}$. Specifically, the experiment proceeds as follows:

1. The challenger starts by sampling $r^*_{\mathsf{samp}} \xleftarrow{R} \{0,1\}^{\ell_{\mathsf{samp}}}$ and sets $\mathsf{crs}_{\mathsf{samp}} \leftarrow \mathsf{Gen}(1^\lambda, 1^\ell; r^*_{\mathsf{samp}})$. Then it computes
$$(\mathbf{A}_1, \ldots, \mathbf{A}_\ell, \mathsf{td}_{\mathsf{samp}}) = \mathsf{Expand}(1^\lambda, 1^\ell, \mathsf{crs}_{\mathsf{samp}}).$$
2. Next, the challenger samples $i'_1, \ldots, i'_N \xleftarrow{R} [t]$ and $z'_1, \ldots, z'_N \xleftarrow{R} \mathbb{Z}_q$.
3. For each $i \in [\ell]$, the challenger proceeds as follows:
   - If $i < k$, the challenger samples $\mathbf{s}_i \xleftarrow{R} \mathbb{Z}_q^n$, $\mathbf{e}_i \leftarrow D^t_{\mathbb{Z}, s_{\mathsf{LWE}}}$ and sets $\mathbf{v}_i^\mathsf{T} = \mathbf{s}_i^\mathsf{T}\mathbf{A}_i + \mathbf{e}_i^\mathsf{T}$.
   - If $i \geq k$, sample $\mathbf{v}_i \xleftarrow{R} \mathbb{Z}_q^t$.

   For each $i \in [\ell]$, the challenger sets $\tilde{\mathbf{v}}_i = \mathbf{v}_i - \sum_{j \in [N]} z'_j \boldsymbol{\eta}_{i'_j}$.
4. For all $i \in [\ell]$ and $j \in [t]$:
   (a) The challenger samples $\gamma_{i,j} \xleftarrow{R} [0, \lfloor 2^{\lceil \log q \rceil + \lambda}/q \rfloor - 1]$.
   (b) The challenger sets $r^*_{i,j} = q\gamma_{i,j} + \tilde{v}_{i,j}$, represented as a binary string in $\{0,1\}^{\lceil \log q \rceil + \lambda}$.

   Finally, the challenger sets $r^*_i = r^*_{i,1} \| \cdots \| r^*_{i,t} \in \{0,1\}^{t(\lceil \log q \rceil + \lambda)}$.
5. The challenger sets $r^* = r^*_{\mathsf{samp}} \| r^*_1 \| \cdots \| r^*_\ell \in \{0,1\}^{\ell_{\mathsf{samp}} + \ell t(\lceil \log q \rceil + \lambda)}$ and gives $(1^\lambda, 1^\ell, r^*)$ to $\mathcal{A}$. Algorithm $\mathcal{A}$ outputs a bit $b \in \{0,1\}$, which is the output of the experiment.

- $\mathsf{Hyb}_{k,2}$: Same as $\mathsf{Hyb}_{k,1}$, except the challenger samples $\mathbf{A}'_k \xleftarrow{R} \mathbb{Z}_q^{n \times t}$ and $\mathsf{crs}_{\mathsf{samp}} \leftarrow \mathsf{GenProg}(1^\lambda, 1^\ell, k, \mathbf{A}'_k)$. Let $r^* = \mathsf{crs}_{\mathsf{samp}} \| r^*_1 \| \cdots \| r^*_\ell$.
- $\mathsf{Hyb}_{k,3}$: Same as $\mathsf{Hyb}_{k,2}$, except the challenger samples $\mathbf{s}_k \xleftarrow{R} \mathbb{Z}_q^n$, $\mathbf{e}_k \leftarrow D^t_{\mathbb{Z}, s_{\mathsf{LWE}}}$ and sets $\mathbf{v}_k^\mathsf{T} = \mathbf{s}_k^\mathsf{T}\mathbf{A}_k + \mathbf{e}_k^\mathsf{T}$.

For a hybrid experiment Hyb, we write $\mathsf{Hyb}(\mathcal{A})$ to denote the random variable corresponding to the output of an execution of Hyb with adversary $\mathcal{A}$.

Claim 4.5. *For every constant $c > 1$, there exists a negligible function* $\mathsf{negl}(\lambda)$ *such that for all $\lambda \in \mathbb{N}$,*
$$\left|\Pr[\mathsf{Hyb}_{1,1}(\mathcal{A}) = 1] - \Pr[\mathsf{Hyb}_0(\mathcal{A}) = 1]\right| \leq 2^{-\log^c(\lambda)} \cdot \mathsf{negl}(\lambda).$$

Proof. Consider the distribution of $r^* = r^*_{\mathsf{samp}} \| r^*_1 \| \cdots \| r^*_\ell$ in the two experiments. First, the distribution of r^*_{samp} in the two experiments is identical, so it suffices to consider the distribution of r^*_i for $i \in [\ell]$. In Hyb_0, each r^*_i is uniform over $\{0,1\}^{t(\lceil \log q \rceil + \lambda)}$. We consider the distribution in $\mathsf{Hyb}_{1,1}$:

- In $\mathsf{Hyb}_{1,1}$, the challenger samples $\mathbf{v}_i \xleftarrow{R} \mathbb{Z}_q^t$. Since $\mathbf{v}_i$ is independent of $z'_1, \ldots, z'_N$, this means $\tilde{\mathbf{v}}_i = \mathbf{v}_i - \sum_{j \in [N]} z'_j \boldsymbol{\eta}_{i'_j}$ remains uniform over $\mathbb{Z}_q^t$.
- We conclude that each value $r_{i,j} = q\gamma_{i,j} + \tilde{v}_{i,j}$ is uniform over the set $[0, \lfloor 2^{\lceil \log q \rceil + \lambda}/q \rfloor \cdot q - 1]$. The statistical distance between this distribution and the uniform distribution over $[0, 2^{\lceil \log q \rceil + \lambda}]$ is at most $q/2^{\lceil \log q \rceil + \lambda} \leq 2^{-\lambda}$.
- The statistical distance between the uniform distribution over $\{0,1\}^{t(\lceil \log q \rceil + \lambda)}$ and r^*_i is then at most $t \cdot 2^{-\lambda}$.

We conclude that the statistical distance between the distribution of r^* in $\mathsf{Hyb}_{1,1}$ and the uniform distribution over $\{0,1\}^{\ell_{\mathsf{pub}}}$ is at most $\ell t \cdot 2^{-\lambda}$. This expression can be rewritten as $2^{-\log^c(\lambda)} \cdot 2^{-(\lambda - \log^c(\lambda))} \cdot \ell t$, which is $2^{-\log^c(\lambda)} \cdot \mathsf{negl}(\lambda)$ since $t, \ell = \mathsf{poly}(\lambda)$ and $2^{-(\lambda - \log^c(\lambda))}$ is negligible.

Claim 4.6. *Suppose Π_{samp} has a transparent setup and is perfectly somewhere programmable. Then, for all $k \in [\ell]$,*

$$\Pr[\mathsf{Hyb}_{k,2}(\mathcal{A}) = 1] = \Pr[\mathsf{Hyb}_{k,1}(\mathcal{A}) = 1].$$

Proof. Note that in any execution of $\mathsf{Hyb}_{k,1}$, $r^*_{\mathsf{samp}} = \mathsf{crs}_{\mathsf{samp}}$ by transparent setup of Π_{samp}. Since Π_{samp} is perfectly somewhere programmable, the distributions

$$\left\{\mathsf{crs} : \mathsf{crs} \leftarrow \mathsf{Gen}(1^\lambda, 1^\ell)\right\} \quad \text{and} \quad \left\{\widetilde{\mathsf{crs}} : \begin{array}{c} \mathbf{A}_k \xleftarrow{\mathrm{R}} \mathbb{Z}_q^{n \times t} \\ \widetilde{\mathsf{crs}} \leftarrow \mathsf{GenProg}(1^\lambda, 1^\ell, k, \mathbf{A}_k) \end{array}\right\}$$

are identically distributed for all $k \in [\ell]$. Thus, $\mathsf{Hyb}_{k,1}$ and $\mathsf{Hyb}_{k,2}$ are identical distributions and the claim follows.

Claim 4.7. *Suppose quasi-polynomial $\mathsf{LWE}_{n,t,q,s_{\mathsf{LWE}}}$ holds with constant $c > 1$. Then, there exists a negligible function $\mathsf{negl}(\lambda)$ where for all $\lambda \in \mathbb{N}$,*

$$\sum_{k \in [\ell]} (\Pr[\mathsf{Hyb}_{k,3}(\mathcal{A}) = 1] - \Pr[\mathsf{Hyb}_{k,2}(\mathcal{A}) = 1]) = 2^{-\log^c(\lambda)} \cdot \mathsf{negl}(\lambda).$$

Proof. We define an efficient adversary $\mathcal{B}$ in the $\mathsf{LWE}_{n,t,q,s_{\mathsf{LWE}}}$ game.

1. At the beginning of the game, algorithm $\mathcal{B}$ receives the LWE challenge $(\mathbf{A}^*, \mathbf{v}^*)$ from the challenger.
2. Algorithm $\mathcal{B}$ samples an index $k^* \xleftarrow{\mathrm{R}} [\ell]$ and sets $\mathbf{A}_{k^*} = \mathbf{A}^*$. Then, it samples $\mathsf{crs}_{\mathsf{samp}} \leftarrow \mathsf{GenProg}(1^\lambda, 1^\ell, k^*, \mathbf{A}_{k^*})$ and expands $(\mathbf{A}_1, \ldots, \mathbf{A}_\ell, \mathsf{td}_{\mathsf{samp}}) = \mathsf{Expand}(1^\lambda, 1^\ell, \mathsf{crs}_{\mathsf{samp}})$.
3. Algorithm $\mathcal{B}$ samples $i'_1, \ldots, i'_N \xleftarrow{\mathrm{R}} [t]$ and $z'_1, \ldots, z'_N \xleftarrow{\mathrm{R}} \mathbb{Z}_q$. For each $i \in [\ell]$, algorithm $\mathcal{B}$ sets $\mathbf{v}_i$ as follows:
   - If $i < k$, algorithm $\mathcal{B}$ samples $\mathbf{s}_i \xleftarrow{\mathrm{R}} \mathbb{Z}_q^n$, $\mathbf{e}_i \leftarrow D^t_{\mathbb{Z}, s_{\mathsf{LWE}}}$ and sets $\mathbf{v}_i^{\mathsf{T}} = \mathbf{s}_i^{\mathsf{T}} \mathbf{A}_i + \mathbf{e}_i^{\mathsf{T}}$.
   - If $i = k^*$, algorithm $\mathcal{B}$ sets $\mathbf{v}_{k^*} = \mathbf{v}^*$.
   - If $i > k^*$, algorithm $\mathcal{B}$ samples $\mathbf{v}_i \xleftarrow{\mathrm{R}} \mathbb{Z}_q^t$.

   For each $i \in [\ell]$, algorithm $\mathcal{B}$ sets $\tilde{\mathbf{v}}_i = \mathbf{v}_i - \sum_{j \in [N]} z'_j \boldsymbol{\eta}_{i'_j}$.
4. For $i \in [\ell]$ and $j \in [t]$:
   (a) Algorithm $\mathcal{B}$ samples $\gamma_{i,j} \xleftarrow{\mathrm{R}} [0, \lfloor 2^{\lceil \log q \rceil + \lambda}/q \rfloor - 1]$.
   (b) Algorithm $\mathcal{B}$ sets $r_{i,j} = q\gamma_{i,j} + \tilde{\mathbf{v}}_i[j]$, represented as a binary string of length $\lceil \log q \rceil + \lambda$.

   Finally, algorithm $\mathcal{B}$ sets $r_i^* = r_{i,1}^* \| \cdots \| r_{i,t}^* \in \{0,1\}^{t(\lceil \log q \rceil + \lambda)}$.
5. Algorithm $\mathcal{B}$ sets $r^* = r^*_{\mathsf{samp}} \| r_1^* \| \cdots \| r_\ell^* \in \{0,1\}^{\ell_{\mathsf{samp}} + \ell t(\lceil \log q \rceil + \lambda)}$ and gives $(1^\lambda, 1^\ell, r^*)$ to $\mathcal{A}$. Finally, algorithm $\mathcal{B}$ outputs whatever $\mathcal{A}$ outputs.

Consider a run of $\mathcal{B}$ where $k^* = k$ for some fixed value $k \in [\ell]$. First, the LWE challenger always samples $\mathbf{A}^* \xleftarrow{\text{R}} \mathbb{Z}_q^{n \times m}$, so algorithm $\mathcal{B}$ correctly simulates the distribution of $\mathbf{A}_k$ according to the specification of Hyb_k or Hyb_{k+1}. Consider now the distribution of $\mathbf{v}^*$:

- Suppose $\mathbf{v}_k = \mathbf{v}^* \xleftarrow{\text{R}} \mathbb{Z}_q^t$. In this case, algorithm $\mathcal{B}$ perfectly simulates an execution of $\mathsf{Hyb}_{k,2}$ for $\mathcal{A}$, and outputs 1 with probability $\Pr[\mathsf{Hyb}_{k,2}(\mathcal{A}) = 1]$.
- Suppose $\mathbf{v}_k = \mathbf{v}^* = \mathbf{s}^\mathsf{T}\mathbf{A}^* + \mathbf{e}^\mathsf{T}$ where $\mathbf{s} \xleftarrow{\text{R}} \mathbb{Z}_q^n$ and $\mathbf{e} \leftarrow D_{\mathbb{Z},s_{\mathsf{LWE}}}^t$. Then, algorithm $\mathcal{B}$ perfectly simulates an execution of $\mathsf{Hyb}_{k,3}$ for $\mathcal{A}$ and outputs 1 with probability $\Pr[\mathsf{Hyb}_{k,3}(\mathcal{A}) = 1]$.

Finally, algorithm $\mathcal{B}$ samples $k^* \xleftarrow{\text{R}} [\ell]$, so its overall advantage is then

$$\frac{1}{\ell} \sum_{k \in [\ell]} (\Pr[\mathsf{Hyb}_{k,3}(\mathcal{A}) = 1] - \Pr[\mathsf{Hyb}_{k,2}(\mathcal{A}) = 1]).$$

By c-quasi-polynomial hardness of $\mathsf{LWE}_{n,t,q,s_{\mathsf{LWE}}}$, this quantity is at most $2^{-\log^c(\lambda)} \cdot \mathsf{negl}'(\lambda)$ for some negligible function $\mathsf{negl}'(\cdot)$. Then,

$$\sum_{k \in [\ell]} (\Pr[\mathsf{Hyb}_{k,3}(\mathcal{A}) = 1] - \Pr[\mathsf{Hyb}_{k,2}(\mathcal{A}) = 1]) \leq \ell \cdot 2^{-\log^c(\lambda)} \cdot \mathsf{negl}'(\lambda).$$

Since $\ell = \mathsf{poly}(\lambda)$, the claim holds.

Claim 4.8. *Suppose Π_{samp} has a transparent setup and is perfectly somewhere programmable. Then, for all $k \in [\ell]$,*

$$\Pr[\mathsf{Hyb}_{k+1,1}(\mathcal{A}) = 1] = \Pr[\mathsf{Hyb}_{k,3}(\mathcal{A}) = 1].$$

Proof. Follows by the same argument as the proof of Claim 4.6.

Returning now to the proof of Theorem 4.4, we have the following:

- Hyb_0 is exactly the first mode indistinguishability experiment for algorithm $\mathcal{A}$.
- In $\mathsf{Hyb}_{\ell+1,1}$, every value $\mathbf{v}_i$ is sampled exactly as in $\mathsf{TrapCoin}$. In this case, algorithm $\mathcal{B}$ perfectly simulates an execution of the second mode indistinguishability experiment for algorithm $\mathcal{A}$.

By Claims 4.6 to 4.8, we have

$$\begin{aligned}
&\left| \Pr[\mathsf{Hyb}_{\ell+1,1}(\mathcal{A}) = 1] - \Pr[\mathsf{Hyb}_{1,1}(\mathcal{A}) = 1] \right| \\
&\quad = \left| \sum_{k \in [\ell]} (\Pr[\mathsf{Hyb}_{k+1,1}(\mathcal{A}) = 1] - \Pr[\mathsf{Hyb}_{k,3}(\mathcal{A}) = 1]) \right. \\
&\qquad + \sum_{k \in [\ell]} (\Pr[\mathsf{Hyb}_{k,3}(\mathcal{A}) = 1] - \Pr[\mathsf{Hyb}_{k,2}(\mathcal{A}) = 1]) \\
&\qquad \left. + \sum_{k \in [\ell]} (\Pr[\mathsf{Hyb}_{k,2}(\mathcal{A}) = 1] - \Pr[\mathsf{Hyb}_{k,1}(\mathcal{A}) = 1]) \right| \\
&\quad = \left| \sum_{k \in [\ell]} (\Pr[\mathsf{Hyb}_{k,3}(\mathcal{A}) = 1] - \Pr[\mathsf{Hyb}_{k,2}(\mathcal{A}) = 1]) \right| \\
&\quad = 2^{-\log^c(\lambda)} \cdot \mathsf{negl}(\lambda)
\end{aligned}$$

for some negligible function $\mathsf{negl}(\cdot)$. By plugging in Claim 4.5, we get

$$\left|\Pr[\mathsf{Hyb}_{\ell+1,1}(\mathcal{A})=1]-\Pr[\mathsf{Hyb}_0(\mathcal{A})=1]\right| = 2^{-\log^c(\lambda)}\mathsf{negl}(\lambda)$$

and Theorem 4.4 holds.

4.1.2 Extraction In this section, we show that Construction 4.1 satisfies μ-extractability for an inverse quasi-polynomial $\mu = 2^{-\Omega(\log^c \lambda)}$.

Theorem 4.9 (Extraction). *Suppose c-quasi-polynomial* $\mathsf{LWE}_{n,t,q,s_{\mathsf{LWE}}}$ *holds with constant* $c > 4$ *and* Π_{samp} *is perfectly somewhere programmable. Suppose also* $B_{\mathsf{round}} + B_{\mathsf{max}}\sqrt{\log^c(\lambda)+\lambda}\cdot s_{\mathsf{LWE}} \leq q/4$, *and* $N = O(\log^3 \lambda)$. *Then, Construction 4.1 satisfies* μ*-extraction where* $\mu = 2^{-\Omega(\log^c \lambda)}$.

Proof. Let $\mathcal{A}$ be an efficient adversary for the μ-extraction game. We define a sequence of hybrid games between a challenger and $\mathcal{A}$ as follows:

- Hyb_1: This is the μ-extraction game where the output is 1 if event $E_\top$ occurs (i.e., the game where the adversary $\mathcal{A}$ does not abort). Specifically, the game proceeds as follows:
  1. The challenger starts by sampling $(r^*, \mathsf{td}) \leftarrow \mathsf{TrapCoin}(1^\lambda, 1^\ell)$. Namely, the challenger proceeds as follows:
     (a) Sample $r_{\mathsf{samp}} \xleftarrow{R} \{0,1\}^{\ell_{\mathsf{samp}}}$ and let $\mathsf{crs}_{\mathsf{samp}} = \mathsf{Gen}(1^\lambda, 1^\ell; r_{\mathsf{samp}})$. Then expand $\mathsf{crs}_{\mathsf{samp}}$ by computing $(\mathbf{A}_1,\ldots,\mathbf{A}_\ell,\mathsf{td}_{\mathsf{samp}}) = \mathsf{Expand}(1^\lambda, 1^\ell, \mathsf{crs}_{\mathsf{samp}})$.
     (b) Sample $i'_1,\ldots,i'_N \xleftarrow{R} [t]$ and $z'_1,\ldots,z'_N \xleftarrow{R} \mathbb{Z}_q$.
     (c) Sample $\mathbf{s}_1,\ldots,\mathbf{s}_\ell \xleftarrow{R} \mathbb{Z}_q^n$, $\mathbf{e}_1,\ldots,\mathbf{e}_\ell \leftarrow D^t_{\mathbb{Z},s_{\mathsf{LWE}}}$. Set $\mathbf{v}_i^\top = \mathbf{s}_i^\top\mathbf{A}_i + \mathbf{e}_i^\top$ for $i \in [\ell]$.
     (d) Compute $\tilde{\mathbf{v}}_i = \mathbf{v}_i - \sum_{j\in[N]} z'_j \boldsymbol{\eta}_{i'_j}$ for $i \in [\ell]$.
     (e) For $i \in [\ell]$ and $j \in [t]$, sample $\gamma_{i,j} \xleftarrow{R} [0, \lfloor 2^{\lceil \log q\rceil+\lambda}/q\rfloor - 1]$ and set $r_{i,j} = q\gamma_{i,j} + \tilde{v}_{i,j}$, represented as a binary string in $\{0,1\}^{\lceil \log q\rceil+\lambda}$. Finally, let $r_i = r_{i,1}\|\cdots\|r_{i,t} \in \{0,1\}^{t(\lceil \log q\rceil+\lambda)}$.
     (f) Let $r^* = r_{\mathsf{samp}}\|r_1\|\cdots\|r_\ell$, $\mathsf{td} = (r^*, i'_1,\ldots,i'_N, z'_1,\ldots,z'_N, \mathbf{s}_1,\ldots,\mathbf{s}_\ell)$.
     The challenger sends $(1^\lambda, 1^\ell, r^*)$ to the adversary.
  2. The adversary $\mathcal{A}$ now either aborts with $\perp$ or outputs a set of indices $S \subseteq [\ell]$, a commitment $\mathsf{com} = (i_1,\ldots,i_N,z_1,\ldots,z_N,\mathbf{c})$ and openings $(\pi_i)_{i\in S}$.
  3. The output of the experiment is 1 if $\mathcal{A}$ does not abort. Otherwise, the output is 0.
- Hyb_2: Same as Hyb_1, except the challenger samples $\mathbf{v}_i \xleftarrow{R} \mathbb{Z}_q^t$ for all $i \in [\ell]$.
- Hyb_3: Same as Hyb_2, except the challenger additionally checks that $i'_k = i_k$ and $z'_k = z_k$ for all $k \in [N]$. If this condition does not hold, the output of the experiment is 0.
- Hyb_4: Same as Hyb_3, except the challenger reverts to setting $\mathbf{v}_i = \mathbf{s}_i^\top\mathbf{A}_i + \mathbf{e}_i^\top$ for all $i \in [\ell]$.
- Hyb_5: Same as Hyb_4, except the challenger aborts with output 0 if $\|\mathbf{e}_i\| > \sqrt{\log^c(\lambda)+\lambda}\cdot s_{\mathsf{LWE}}$ for any $i \in [\ell]$.

- Hyb_6: Same as Hyb_5, except the challenger also aborts with output 0 if there exists an index $i \in S$ where $\mathsf{Verify}(r^*, \mathsf{com}, i, 1 - \rho_i, \pi_i) = 1$ and $\rho_i = \lfloor \mathbf{s}_i^\mathsf{T} \mathbf{c} \rceil$.
- Hyb_7: Same as Hyb_6, except the challenger no longer checks if there exists an $i \in [\ell]$ where $\|\mathbf{e}_i\| > \sqrt{\log^c(\lambda) + \lambda} \cdot s_{\mathsf{LWE}}$. This is the μ-extraction game where the challenger outputs 1 if event $E_\top \wedge E_{\mathsf{lose}}$ occurs.

Claim 4.10. *Suppose c-quasi-polynomial* $\mathsf{LWE}_{n,t,q,s_{\mathsf{LWE}}}$ *holds with constant* $c > 1$ *and* Π_{samp} *is perfectly somewhere programmable. Then, there exists a negligible function* $\mathsf{negl}(\lambda)$ *where*

$$|\Pr[\mathsf{Hyb}_2(\mathcal{A}) = 1] - \Pr[\mathsf{Hyb}_1(\mathcal{A}) = 1]| = 2^{-\log^c(\lambda)} \cdot \mathsf{negl}(\lambda).$$

Proof. By Theorem 4.4, under the given conditions, Construction 4.1 satisfies c-quasi-polynomial mode indistinguishability. We use algorithm $\mathcal{A}$ to construct an adversary $\mathcal{B}$ for the mode indistinguishability game:

1. Algorithm $\mathcal{B}$ receives $(1^\lambda, 1^\ell, r^*)$, and sends $(1^\lambda, 1^\ell, r^*)$ to the adversary $\mathcal{A}$.
2. Algorithm $\mathcal{A}$ either aborts or outputs a set of indices $S \subseteq [\ell]$, a commitment $\mathsf{com} = (i_1, \ldots, i_N, z_1, \ldots, z_N, \mathbf{c})$ and a tuple of openings $(\pi_i)_{i \in S}$.
3. Algorithm $\mathcal{B}$ outputs 1 if $\mathcal{A}$ does not abort. Otherwise, algorithm $\mathcal{B}$ outputs 0.

We consider the two cases depending on the behavior of the mode indistinguishability challenger:

- If the challenger samples $r^* \leftarrow \mathsf{TrapCoin}(1^\lambda, 1^\ell)$, algorithm $\mathcal{B}$ perfectly simulates an execution of Hyb_1 for $\mathcal{A}$, and outputs 1 with probability $\Pr[\mathsf{Hyb}_1(\mathcal{A}) = 1]$.
- If the challenger samples $r^* \xleftarrow{\mathrm{R}} \{0,1\}^{\ell_{\mathsf{pub}}}$, then algorithm $\mathcal{B}$ perfectly simulates an execution of Hyb_2 for $\mathcal{A}$, and outputs 1 with probability $\Pr[\mathsf{Hyb}_2(\mathcal{A}) = 1]$.

Thus, the advantage of $\mathcal{B}$ for the mode indistinguishability game is

$$|\Pr[\mathsf{Hyb}_2(\mathcal{A}) = 1] - \Pr[\mathsf{Hyb}_1(\mathcal{A}) = 1]|.$$

By Theorem 4.4, we can bound this quantity by $2^{-\log^c(\lambda)} \cdot \mathsf{negl}(\lambda)$ for some negligible function $\mathsf{negl}(\cdot)$, as required.

Claim 4.11. *It holds that* $\Pr[\mathsf{Hyb}_3(\mathcal{A}) = 1] = t^{-N} q^{-N} \cdot \Pr[\mathsf{Hyb}_2(\mathcal{A}) = 1]$.

Proof. In Hyb_2 and Hyb_3, the only quantities that depend on i'_k and z'_k are the values $\tilde{\mathbf{v}}_i$ for $i \in [\ell]$. The challenger sets $\tilde{\mathbf{v}}_i = \mathbf{v}_i - \sum_{j \in [N]} z'_j \boldsymbol{\eta}_{i'_j}$. Since each $\mathbf{v}_i$ is uniform random, the values of i'_k and z'_k are information-theoretically hidden from the adversary $\mathcal{A}$ for all $k \in [N]$. Thus, the values $i_1, \ldots, i_N$ and $z_1, \ldots, z_N$ chosen by the adversary are *independent* of the values of $i'_1, \ldots, i'_N$ and $z'_1, \ldots, z'_N$. Since the challenger samples $i'_j \xleftarrow{\mathrm{R}} [t]$ and $z'_j \xleftarrow{\mathrm{R}} \mathbb{Z}_q$ for all $j \in [N]$, we have that whenever $\mathcal{A}$ does not abort (i.e., event $E_\top$ occurs), the probability that $i'_k = i_k$ and $z'_k = z_k$ for all $k \in [N]$ is exactly $t^{-N} q^{-N}$.

Claim 4.12. *There exists a negligible function* $\mathsf{negl}(\lambda)$ *where*

$$|\Pr[\mathsf{Hyb}_4(\mathcal{A}) = 1] - \Pr[\mathsf{Hyb}_3(\mathcal{A}) = 1]| = 2^{-\log^c(\lambda)} \cdot \mathsf{negl}(\lambda).$$

Proof. Follows by the same argument as the proof of Claim 4.10.

Claim 4.13. *There exists a negligible function* $\mathsf{negl}(\lambda)$ *where*

$$|\Pr[\mathsf{Hyb}_5(\mathcal{A}) = 1] - \Pr[\mathsf{Hyb}_4(\mathcal{A}) = 1]| = 2^{-\log^c(\lambda)} \cdot \mathsf{negl}(\lambda).$$

Proof. The only difference between Hyb_5 and Hyb_4 is we require for all $i \in [\ell]$ that $\|\mathbf{e}_i\| \le \sqrt{\log^c(\lambda) + \lambda} \cdot s_{\mathsf{LWE}}$. By Lemma 2.6, for each $i \in [\ell]$, $\|\mathbf{e}_i\| \le \sqrt{\log^c(\lambda) + \lambda} \cdot s_{\mathsf{LWE}}$ with all but probability $2^{-\log^c(\lambda) - \lambda}$. By a union bound, this occurs for all $i \in [\ell]$ with all but probability $2^{-\log^c(\lambda)-\lambda} \cdot \ell = 2^{-\log^c(\lambda)}(2^{-\lambda}\ell)$. Since $\ell = \mathsf{poly}(\lambda)$, the claim holds.

Claim 4.14. *Suppose* $B_{\mathsf{round}} + B_{\mathsf{max}}\sqrt{\log^c(\lambda) + \lambda} \cdot s_{\mathsf{LWE}} \le q/4$. *Then*

$$\Pr[\mathsf{Hyb}_6(\mathcal{A}) = 1] = \Pr[\mathsf{Hyb}_5(\mathcal{A}) = 1].$$

Proof. Consider a run of $\mathsf{Hyb}_5(\mathcal{A})$ outputting 1. In particular, we know $i'_k = i_k$ and $z'_k = z_k$ for every $k \in [N]$. Consequently, for all $i \in [\ell]$, the value $\tilde{\mathbf{v}}_i - \sum_{j \in [N]} z'_j \boldsymbol{\eta}_{i'_j}$ computed by the Verify algorithm is indeed equal to $\mathbf{v}_i$ where $\mathbf{v}_i^{\mathsf{T}} = \mathbf{s}_i^{\mathsf{T}}\mathbf{A}_i + \mathbf{e}_i$. Suppose for some $i \in S$ and $b \in \{0,1\}$, $\|\mathbf{e}_i\| \le \sqrt{\log^c(\lambda) + \lambda} \cdot s_{\mathsf{LWE}}$ and $\mathsf{Verify}(r^*, \mathsf{com}, i, b, \boldsymbol{\pi}_i) = 1$. Then, the following conditions hold:

$$\|\boldsymbol{\pi}_i\| \le B_{\mathsf{max}} \quad \text{and} \quad \mathbf{A}_i\boldsymbol{\pi}_i = \mathbf{c} \quad \text{and} \quad \mathbf{v}_i^{\mathsf{T}}\boldsymbol{\pi}_i \in \left[\lfloor q/2 \rfloor b - B_{\mathsf{round}}, \lfloor q/2 \rfloor b + B_{\mathsf{round}}\right].$$

Notice $\mathbf{v}_i^{\mathsf{T}}\boldsymbol{\pi}_i = (\mathbf{s}_i^{\mathsf{T}}\mathbf{A}_i + \mathbf{e}_i^{\mathsf{T}})\boldsymbol{\pi}_i = \mathbf{s}_i^{\mathsf{T}}(\mathbf{A}_i\boldsymbol{\pi}_i) + \mathbf{e}_i^{\mathsf{T}}\boldsymbol{\pi}_i = \mathbf{s}_i^{\mathsf{T}}\mathbf{c} + \mathbf{e}_i^{\mathsf{T}}\boldsymbol{\pi}_i$. Since $\|\boldsymbol{\pi}_i\| \le B_{\mathsf{max}}$, then $|\mathbf{e}_i^{\mathsf{T}}\boldsymbol{\pi}_i| \le B_{\mathsf{max}}\sqrt{\log^c(\lambda) + \lambda} \cdot s_{\mathsf{LWE}} \le q/4 - B_{\mathsf{round}}$, so

$$\mathbf{s}_i^{\mathsf{T}}\mathbf{c} = \mathbf{v}_i^{\mathsf{T}}\boldsymbol{\pi}_i - \mathbf{e}_i^{\mathsf{T}}\boldsymbol{\pi}_i \in \left[\lfloor q/2 \rfloor b - q/4, \lfloor q/2 \rfloor b + q/4\right].$$

Consequently, $\rho_i = \lfloor \mathbf{s}_i^{\mathsf{T}}\mathbf{c} \rceil = b$, and the claim follows.

Claim 4.15. *There exists a negligible function* $\mathsf{negl}(\lambda)$ *where*

$$|\Pr[\mathsf{Hyb}_7(\mathcal{A}) = 1] - \Pr[\mathsf{Hyb}_6(\mathcal{A}) = 1]| \le 2^{-\log^c(\lambda)}\mathsf{negl}(\lambda).$$

Proof. Follows by the same argument as the proof of Claim 4.13.

Since t, q are polynomials in λ and $N = O(\log^3 \lambda)$, then, $t^{-N}q^{-N} = 2^{O(\log^4 \lambda)}$ and $t^N q^N \cdot 2^{-\log^c(\lambda)} \le 2^{-\Omega(\log^c \lambda)}$ for any $c > 4$. By Claims 4.10 to 4.15, we conclude $\Pr[\mathsf{Hyb}_7(\mathcal{A}) = 1] \ge 2^{-\Omega(\log^c \lambda)}(\Pr[\mathsf{Hyb}_1(\mathcal{A}) = 1] - \mathsf{negl}(\lambda))$ and the theorem follows.

4.1.3 Statistical Single-Bit Hiding In this section, we show that Construction 4.1 satisfies statistical single-bit hiding. To argue this, we first abstract out the main information-theoretic problem that we are interested in. Namely, we define a *substring min-entropy preservation* game which the adversary must win in order to break single-bit hiding. At a high level, the game states that if the challenger samples a uniform $\mathbf{w} \xleftarrow{R} \{0,1\}^t$, then a random substring of $\mathbf{w}$ also has high entropy even given some information about $\mathbf{w}$. We give the formal definition below:

Definition 4.16 (Substring Min-Entropy Preservation). *Let n, t, q be lattice parameters k be a number of samples. For a bit $b \in \{0,1\}$ and an adversary $\mathcal{A}$, we define the following experiment $\mathsf{Exp}_b^{\mathsf{SMEP}}$:*

- *On input the security parameter 1^λ, the adversary outputs a matrix $\mathbf{A} \in \mathbb{Z}_q^{n \times t}$ and a vector $\mathbf{v} \in \mathbb{Z}_q^t$.*
- *The challenger samples $\mathbf{w} \xleftarrow{R} \{0,1\}^t$ and a vector of indices $I \xleftarrow{R} [t]^k$ (with repetitions) where $I = (i_1, \ldots, i_k)$. The challenger samples $\mathbf{z} \xleftarrow{R} \mathbb{Z}_q^k$. If $b = 0$, the challenger computes $u_b = \mathbf{z}^\intercal \mathbf{w}[I]$. If $b = 1$, the challenger samples $u_b \xleftarrow{R} \mathbb{Z}_q$.*
- *The challenger gives the challenge $(\mathbf{A}\mathbf{w}, \mathbf{v}^\intercal \mathbf{w}, I, \mathbf{z}, u_b)$ to $\mathcal{A}$. Algorithm $\mathcal{A}$ outputs a bit $b' \in \{0,1\}$, which is the output of the experiment.*

For any adversary $\mathcal{A}$, the advantage in the substring min-entropy preservation game is defined as

$$\mathsf{Adv}_{n,q,t,k}^{\mathsf{SMEP}}(\mathcal{A}) = \left| \Pr\left[\mathsf{Exp}_0^{\mathsf{SMEP}}(\mathcal{A}) = 1\right] - \Pr\left[\mathsf{Exp}_1^{\mathsf{SMEP}}(\mathcal{A}) = 1\right] \right|.$$

Lemma 4.17 (Min-Entropy Preservation Advantage). *Let n, t, q be lattice parameters such that $t \geq (2n+8)\log q + 6\log^2 \lambda + 10$, where λ is the security parameter. Let $k \geq 8\log^2 \lambda \log t + 8 \log q \log t$ be the number of samples. Then, for all (possibly unbounded) adversaries $\mathcal{A}$, there exists a negligible function $\mathsf{negl}(\cdot)$ such that for all $\lambda \in \mathbb{N}$,*

$$\mathsf{Adv}_{n,q,t,k}^{\mathsf{SMEP}}(\mathcal{A}) = \mathsf{negl}(\lambda).$$

Proof. Fix an unbounded adversary $\mathcal{A}$. Without loss of generality, we can assume that $\mathcal{A}$ is deterministic. Define the auxiliary view of the adversary as the random variable $\mathsf{aux}_{\mathcal{A}} := (\mathbf{A}, \mathbf{v}, \mathbf{A}\mathbf{w}, \mathbf{v}^\intercal \mathbf{w})$. Note that $\mathbf{A}\mathbf{w} \in \mathbb{Z}_q^n$ and $\mathbf{v}^\intercal \mathbf{w} \in \mathbb{Z}_q$. Thus, the pair $(\mathbf{A}\mathbf{w}, \mathbf{v}^\intercal \mathbf{w})$ can be described by a bit-string of length $(n+1)\log q$. Additionally, observe that $\mathbf{A}, \mathbf{v}$ are chosen independent of $\mathbf{w}$. Since $\mathbf{w} \xleftarrow{R} \{0,1\}^t$, we know that $\mathbf{H}_\infty(\mathbf{w}) = t$. By Lemma 2.1 and using the fact that the pair $(\mathbf{A}, \mathbf{v})$ is independent of $\mathbf{w}$, we have that

$$\widetilde{\mathbf{H}}_\infty(\mathbf{w} \mid \mathsf{aux}_{\mathcal{A}}) = \widetilde{\mathbf{H}}_\infty(\mathbf{w} \mid (\mathbf{A}\mathbf{w}, \mathbf{v}^\intercal \mathbf{w})) \geq t - (n+1)\log q.$$

Now, we appeal to Lemma 2.3 with $c = \log^2 \lambda + \log q$. To do so, we need to show that the following inequality holds:

$$\begin{aligned} \widetilde{\mathbf{H}}_\infty(\mathbf{w} \mid \mathsf{aux}_{\mathcal{A}}) &\geq t - (n+1)\log q \\ &\geq 2\frac{\log^2 \lambda + \log q}{k} t(1 + \log t) + 3\log^2 \lambda + 3\log q + 5 \end{aligned}$$

We rewrite the last inequality as

$$t\left(1-\frac{2}{k}\left(\log^2\lambda+\log q+\log^2\lambda\log t+\log q\log t\right)\right)\geq(n+4)\log q+3\log^2\lambda+5$$

By taking $k \geq 8(\log^2\lambda\log t+\log q\log t)$, we guarantee that

$$1-\frac{2(\log^2\lambda+\log q)}{k}-\frac{2(\log^2\lambda\log t+\log q\log t)}{k}\geq\frac{1}{2}.$$

By taking $t \geq (2n+8)\log q+6\log^2\lambda+10$, we guarantee that

$$\frac{t}{2}\geq(n+4)\log q+3\log^2\lambda+5.$$

Thus, by Lemma 2.3, we get that $\widetilde{\mathbf{H}}_\infty(\mathbf{w}[I] \mid (\mathsf{aux}_\mathcal{A}, I)) \geq \log^2\lambda+\log q$. Finally, we can apply Lemma 2.2 to get that the statistical distance between the following distribution is $\mathsf{negl}(\lambda)$:

$$\left\{(\mathbf{z}^\mathsf{T}\mathbf{w}[I], \mathsf{aux}_\mathcal{A}, \mathbf{z}, I): \begin{array}{c}\mathbf{w}\xleftarrow{\mathrm{R}}\{0,1\}^t\\ I\xleftarrow{\mathrm{R}}[t]^k\\ \mathbf{z}\xleftarrow{\mathrm{R}}\mathbb{Z}_q^t\end{array}\right\} \quad\text{and}\quad \left\{(u, \mathsf{aux}_\mathcal{A}, \mathbf{z}, I): \begin{array}{c}\mathbf{w}\xleftarrow{\mathrm{R}}\{0,1\}^t\\ I\xleftarrow{\mathrm{R}}[t]^k\\ \mathbf{z}\xleftarrow{\mathrm{R}}\mathbb{Z}_q^t\\ u\xleftarrow{\mathrm{R}}\mathbb{Z}_q\end{array}\right\}.$$

These distributions correspond to the view of $\mathcal{A}$ in $\mathsf{Exp}_0^{\mathsf{SMEP}}$ and $\mathsf{Exp}_1^{\mathsf{SMEP}}$, so the advantage of $\mathcal{A}$ in the substring min-entropy preservation game is at most $\mathsf{negl}(\lambda)$ and the claim follows.

Theorem 4.18 (Statistical Single-Bit Hiding). *Suppose* $t \geq (2n+8)\log q + 6\log^2\lambda + 10$ *and* $k \geq 8\log^2\lambda\log t + 8\log q\log t$ *and that* ℓ *is some polynomial in* λ. *Suppose also that* $B_{\mathsf{round}} \geq q/4 - q/(42\ell)$ *and* $B_{\mathsf{max}} \geq \sqrt{t}\ell s_{\mathsf{LWE}}$. *Then Construction 4.1 satisfies statistical single-bit hiding.*

Proof. We begin by defining a series of hybrids in order to show that the advantage of any unbounded adversary in the single-bit hiding game is negligible. Fix an unbounded adversary $\mathcal{A}$, and assume that $\mathcal{A}$ is deterministic without loss of generality. For any $d' \in [\lambda]$, define the hybrid experiment $\mathsf{Hyb}_{d'}$ as follows:

1. On input $(1^\lambda, 1^\ell)$, the adversary $\mathcal{A}$ sends a public-coin $r \in \{0,1\}^{\ell_{\mathsf{pub}}}$ and an index $i^* \in [\ell]$ to the challenger.
2. The challenger then proceeds as follows:
   (a) Let $(\mathsf{crs}_{\mathsf{samp}}, \tilde{\mathbf{v}}_1, \ldots, \tilde{\mathbf{v}}_\ell)$ be the tuple associated with the public-coin r. Then, the challenger expands $(\mathbf{A}_1, \ldots, \mathbf{A}_\ell, \mathsf{td}_{\mathsf{samp}}) = \mathsf{Expand}(1^\lambda, 1^\ell, \mathsf{crs}_{\mathsf{samp}})$.
   (b) Sample $i_1, \ldots, i_N \xleftarrow{\mathrm{R}} [t]$ and $z_1, \ldots, z_N \xleftarrow{\mathrm{R}} \mathbb{Z}_q$, and compute $\mathbf{v}_i = \tilde{\mathbf{v}}_i + \sum_{j\in[N]} z_j \boldsymbol{\eta}_{i_j}$.
   (c) Next, for $d \in [\lambda]$, the challenger proceeds as follows:
      – Sample $\mathbf{w}_{d,i} \xleftarrow{\mathrm{R}} \{0,1\}^t$ and compute $\mathbf{y}_{d,i} = \mathbf{A}_i\mathbf{w}_{d,i}$ for all $i \in [\ell]$.

- Sample $(\boldsymbol{\pi}'_{d,1}, \ldots, \boldsymbol{\pi}'_{d,\ell}, \mathbf{c}_d) \leftarrow \mathsf{SampleMultPre}(\mathsf{td}_{\mathsf{samp}}, \mathbf{y}_{d,1}, \ldots, \mathbf{y}_{d,\ell})$.
- For each $i \in [\ell]$, set $\boldsymbol{\pi}_{d,i} = \boldsymbol{\pi}'_{d,i} + \mathbf{w}_{d,i}$
- For each $i \neq i^*$, set $u_{d,i} = \mathbf{v}_i^{\mathsf{T}} \boldsymbol{\pi}_{d,i}$.
- If $d > d'$, set $u_{d,i^*} = \mathbf{v}_{i^*}^{\mathsf{T}} \boldsymbol{\pi}_{d,i^*}$. Otherwise if $d \leq d'$ then sample $u_{d,i^*} \xleftarrow{\mathrm{R}} \mathbb{Z}_q$.
- For each $i \in [\ell]$, if $\|\boldsymbol{\pi}_{d,i}\| > B_{\mathsf{max}}$ then set $\rho_{d,i} = \perp$. Otherwise, set $\rho_{d,i}$ as follows:

$$\rho_{d,i} = \begin{cases} 0 & u_{d,i} \in [-B_{\mathsf{round}}, B_{\mathsf{round}}] \\ 1 & u_{d,i} \in \left[\lfloor q/2 \rfloor - B_{\mathsf{round}}, \lfloor q/2 \rfloor + B_{\mathsf{round}}\right] \\ \perp & \text{otherwise.} \end{cases} \tag{4.1}$$

(d) The challenger constructs the challenge as follows:
- If for all $d \in [\lambda]$, there exists an index $i \in [\ell]$ where $\rho_{d,i} = \perp$, then the challenger sets $\mathbf{c} = \perp$ and $\rho_i = 0$ and $\boldsymbol{\pi}_i = \perp$ for all $i \in [\ell]$.
- Otherwise, let $d^* \in [\lambda]$ be the first index where $\rho_{d^*,i} \in \{0, 1\}$ for all $i \in [\ell]$. Then the challenger sets $\mathbf{c} = \mathbf{c}_{d^*}$, and $\rho_i = \rho_{d^*,i}$ and $\boldsymbol{\pi}_i = \boldsymbol{\pi}_{d^*,i}$ for all $i \in [\ell]$.

(e) The challenger sends $\mathsf{com} = (i_1, \ldots, i_N, z_1, \ldots, z_N, \mathbf{c})$ and $(\boldsymbol{\pi}_i, \rho_i)_{i \neq i^*}$ as well as $\beta = \rho_{i^*}$ to the adversary.

3. The adversary outputs a bit b', which is the output of the experiment.

Observe that Hyb_0 is identical to the single-bit hiding game with $b = 0$. On the other hand, Hyb_λ is *almost* identical to the single-bit hiding game with $b = 1$, but not exactly. We address this issue in the following section. For now, we prove that the adversary has negligible probability of distinguishing any two consecutive hybrids:

Lemma 4.19. *Suppose* $t \geq (2n + 8) \log q + 6 \log^2 \lambda + 10$ *and* $k \geq 8 \log^2 \lambda \log t + 8 \log q \log t$. *For all polynomials* $\ell = \ell(\lambda)$, *and all (possibly unbounded) adversaries* $\mathcal{A}$, *there exists a negligible function* $\mathsf{negl}(\lambda)$ *such that for all* $d' \in [\lambda]$:

$$\left|\Pr[\mathsf{Hyb}_{d'}(\mathcal{A}) = 1] - \Pr[\mathsf{Hyb}_{d'-1}(\mathcal{A}) = 1]\right| \leq \mathsf{negl}(\lambda).$$

Proof. Let $\mathcal{A}$ be an unbounded adversary for the single-bit hiding game and let $\ell(\lambda)$ be a polynomial. We construct an algorithm $\mathcal{B}$ for the substring min-entropy preservation game in Definition 4.16 as follows:

1. On input a security parameter 1^λ, algorithm $\mathcal{B}$ starts by sampling $d^* \xleftarrow{\mathrm{R}} [\lambda]$ and runs $\mathcal{A}$ on $(1^\lambda, 1^\ell)$ to gets a public-coin $r \in \{0,1\}^{\ell_{\mathsf{pub}}}$ and an index $i^* \in [\ell]$.
2. Algorithm $\mathcal{B}$ computes the tuple $(\mathsf{crs}_{\mathsf{samp}}, \tilde{\mathbf{v}}_1, \ldots, \tilde{\mathbf{v}}_\ell)$ associated with the public-coin r. Then, it expands the matrices $(\mathbf{A}_1, \ldots, \mathbf{A}_\ell, \mathsf{td}_{\mathsf{samp}}) \leftarrow \mathsf{Expand}(1^\lambda, 1^\ell, \mathsf{crs}_{\mathsf{samp}})$, and submits $(\mathbf{A}_{i^*}, \tilde{\mathbf{v}}_{i^*})$ to the challenger.
3. The challenger responds with $\mathbf{y}_{d^*,i^*} \in \mathbb{Z}_q^n$, $\alpha \in \mathbb{Z}_q$, $I \in [t]^N$, $\mathbf{z} \in \mathbb{Z}_q^N$ and a scalar $u \in \mathbb{Z}_q$.
4. Algorithm $\mathcal{B}$ sets $\mathbf{v}_i = \tilde{\mathbf{v}}_i + \sum_{j \in [N]} z_j \boldsymbol{\eta}_{i_j}$, where $I = (i_1, \ldots, i_N)$.
5. For all $d \neq d^*$, algorithm $\mathcal{B}$ samples $\mathbf{c}_d$, $\rho_{d,1}, \ldots, \rho_{d,\ell}$ and $\boldsymbol{\pi}_{d,1}, \ldots, \boldsymbol{\pi}_{d,\ell}$ according to the specification of Hyb_{d^*}.

6. For $d = d^*$, algorithm $\mathcal{B}$ does the following:
   (a) For all $i \neq i^*$, it samples $\mathbf{w}_{d^*,i} \xleftarrow{R} \{0,1\}^t$ and computes $\mathbf{y}_{d^*,i} = \mathbf{A}_i \mathbf{w}_{d^*,i}$.
   (b) It samples $(\boldsymbol{\pi}'_{d^*,1}, \ldots, \boldsymbol{\pi}'_{d^*,\ell}, \mathbf{c}_{d^*}) \leftarrow \mathsf{SampleMultPre}(\mathsf{td}_{\mathsf{samp}}, \mathbf{y}_{d^*,1}, \ldots, \mathbf{y}_{d^*,\ell})$.
   (c) For each $i \neq i^*$, it sets $\boldsymbol{\pi}_{d^*,i} = \boldsymbol{\pi}'_{d^*,i} + \mathbf{w}_{d^*,i}$ and $u_{d^*,i} = \mathbf{v}_i^{\mathsf{T}} \boldsymbol{\pi}_{d^*,i}$.
   (d) it computes $u_{d^*,i^*} = \mathbf{v}_{i^*}^{\mathsf{T}} \boldsymbol{\pi}'_{d^*,i^*} + u + \alpha$.
   (e) Finally, for all $i \in [\ell]$, it computes $\rho_{d^*,i}$ from $u_{d^*,i}$ according to Eq. (4.1).

   Finally, algorithm $\mathcal{B}$ sets $\mathbf{c}, \boldsymbol{\pi}_1, \ldots, \boldsymbol{\pi}_\ell, \rho_1, \ldots, \rho_\ell$ using the same procedure as in $\mathsf{Hyb}_{d'}$, and sends the commitment $\mathsf{com} = (i_1, \ldots, i_N, z_1, \ldots, z_N, \mathbf{c})$, the openings $(\boldsymbol{\pi}_i, \rho_i)_{i \neq i^*}$, and the challenge bit ρ_{i^*} to the adversary.

Fix some $d' \in [\lambda]$ and let $\varepsilon = |\Pr[\mathsf{Hyb}_{d'}(\mathcal{A}) = 1] - \Pr[\mathsf{Hyb}_{d'-1}(\mathcal{A}) = 1]|$. Since d^* is sampled uniformly, then $d' = d^*$ with probability $1/\lambda$. Assume this event happens. Note that since $z_1, \ldots, z_N \xleftarrow{R} \mathbb{Z}_q$ and $i_1, \ldots, i_N \xleftarrow{R} [t]$, then for all $d \neq d'$, algorithm $\mathcal{B}$ simulates $\mathbf{c}_d$, $\rho_{d,1}, \ldots, \rho_{d,\ell}$ and $\boldsymbol{\pi}_{d,1}, \ldots, \boldsymbol{\pi}_{d,\ell}$ according to the specification of $\mathsf{Hyb}_{d'}$ and $\mathsf{Hyb}_{d'-1}$. Moreover, for all $i \neq i^*$, we have that $y_{d',i}$ are also simulated according to the specification of $\mathsf{Hyb}_{d'}$ and $\mathsf{Hyb}_{d'-1}$. In addition, the challenger of $\mathsf{Exp}_b^{\mathsf{SMEP}}$ (from Definition 4.16) samples $\mathbf{w}_{d',i^*} \xleftarrow{R} \{0,1\}^t$ and sets $\mathbf{y}_{d',i^*} = \mathbf{A}_{i^*} \mathbf{w}_{d',i^*}$. This implies that $(\boldsymbol{\pi}'_{d',1}, \ldots, \boldsymbol{\pi}'_{d',\ell}, \mathbf{c}_{d'})$ is also sampled according to the specification of $\mathsf{Hyb}_{d'}$ and $\mathsf{Hyb}_{d'-1}$. Now we do a case analysis on the bit b in the definition of the $\mathsf{Exp}_b^{\mathsf{SMEP}}$ experiment:

- If $b = 0$, then $u = \mathbf{z}^{\mathsf{T}} \mathbf{w}_{d',i^*}[I]$ (where $\mathbf{z} \xleftarrow{R} \mathbb{Z}_q^N$ is sampled by the challenger). Recall also that $\alpha = \tilde{\mathbf{v}}_{i^*}^{\mathsf{T}} \mathbf{w}_{d',i^*}$. Hence $u + \alpha = \mathbf{z}^{\mathsf{T}} \mathbf{w}_{d',i^*}[I] + \tilde{\mathbf{v}}_{i^*}^{\mathsf{T}} \mathbf{w}_{d',i^*} = \mathbf{v}_{i^*}^{\mathsf{T}} \mathbf{w}_{d',i^*}$, where the last equality follows from the fact that $\mathbf{v}_{i^*} = \tilde{\mathbf{v}}_{i^*} + \sum_{j \in [N]} z_j \boldsymbol{\eta}_{i_j}$. In total, $u_{d',i^*} = \mathbf{v}_{i^*}^{\mathsf{T}} \boldsymbol{\pi}'_{d',i^*} + u + \alpha = \mathbf{v}_{i^*}^{\mathsf{T}} (\boldsymbol{\pi}'_{i^*} + \mathbf{w}_{d',i^*})$. Therefore u_{d,i^*} in this case is sampled according to the specification of $\mathsf{Hyb}_{d'-1}$.
- If $b = 1$, then $u \xleftarrow{R} \mathbb{Z}_q$, then u_{d,i^*} is a uniform random variable over $\mathbb{Z}_q$ and is thus sampled according to the specification of $\mathsf{Hyb}_{d'}$.

From here, we conclude that the advantage of $\mathcal{B}$ in breaking the game from Definition 4.16 is at least ε/λ and therefore ε is negligible by Lemma 4.17.

Handling Rejection Sampling. We would like to say now that Hyb_λ is identical to the single-bit hiding game with $b = 1$. However, the rejection sampling introduces a bad case: if the rejection sampling procedure fails in Hyb_λ, then the challenger sets $\beta = 0$. Whereas if the rejection sampling fails in the single-bit hiding game with $b = 1$, then the challenger would still set $\beta \xleftarrow{R} \{0,1\}$. This is natural, as we cannot expect the construction to be hiding when the rejection sampling fails (causing $\mathsf{GenBits}$ to output $\boldsymbol{\rho} = \mathbf{0}$). To address this, we show that each iteration of the rejection sampling fails with constant probability (e.g., at most $1/5$). After λ independent attempts, the probability that *every* iteration fails is then negligible. This suffice to show that Hyb_λ is negligibly close to the single-bit hiding game with $b = 1$.

Lemma 4.20. *Fix any $d' \in [\lambda]$ and any $i' \in [\ell]$. Let $\boldsymbol{\pi}_{d',i'}$ be distributed as in* Hyb_λ. *If $B_{\mathsf{max}} \geq \sqrt{t\ell}s_{\mathsf{LWE}}$ and Π_{samp} satisfies the preimage norm bound property, then*

$$\Pr\left[\|\boldsymbol{\pi}_{d',i'}\| > B_{\mathsf{max}}\right] \leq \frac{1}{10\ell}.$$

Proof. This follows immediately from the preimage norm bound property (Definition 2.8) and the choice of B_{max}.

Lemma 4.21. *Suppose $t \geq (2n+8)\log q + 6\log^2\lambda + 10$ and $k \geq 8\log^2\lambda \log t + 8\log q \log t$. Fix any $d' \in [\lambda]$ and any $i' \in [\ell]$. Let $u_{d',i'}$ be distributed as in* Hyb_λ. *If $B_{\mathsf{round}} \geq q/4 - q/(42\ell)$ then*

$$\Pr\left[u_{d',i'} \notin [-B_{\mathsf{round}}, B_{\mathsf{round}}] \wedge u_{d',i'} \notin \left[\lfloor q/2\rfloor - B_{\mathsf{round}}, \lfloor q/2\rfloor + B_{\mathsf{round}}\right]\right] \leq \frac{1}{10\ell}. \tag{4.2}$$

Proof. Fix $d' \in [\lambda]$ and $i' \in [\ell]$. Let ε be the probability from Eq. (4.2). If $i' = i^*$ then u_{d,i^*} is sampled uniformly from $\mathbb{Z}_q$, so

$$\varepsilon = 1 - \frac{4B_{\mathsf{round}}}{q} \leq \frac{1}{10\ell}$$

for our choice of B_{round}. Now suppose $i' \neq i^*$. We construct an adversary $\mathcal{B}$ for the game from Definition 4.16 as follows:

1. On input a security parameter 1^λ, algorithm $\mathcal{B}$ runs $\mathcal{A}$ on $(1^\lambda, 1^\ell)$ and gets a public-coin $r \in \{0,1\}^{\ell_{\mathsf{pub}}}$ and an index $i^* \in [\ell]$.
2. Algorithm $\mathcal{B}$ computes the tuple $(\mathsf{crs}_{\mathsf{samp}}, \tilde{\mathbf{v}}_1, \ldots, \tilde{\mathbf{v}}_\ell)$ associated with the public-coin r. Then, it expands the matrices $(\mathbf{A}_1, \ldots, \mathbf{A}_\ell, \mathsf{td}_{\mathsf{samp}}) \leftarrow \mathsf{Expand}(1^\lambda, 1^\ell, \mathsf{crs}_{\mathsf{samp}})$ and submits $(\mathbf{A}_{i^*}, \tilde{\mathbf{v}}_{i^*})$ to the challenger.
3. The challenger responds with $y_{d',i'} \in \mathbb{Z}_q^n$, $\alpha \in \mathbb{Z}_q$, $I \in [t]^N$, $\mathbf{z} \in \mathbb{Z}_q^N$ and a scalar $u \in \mathbb{Z}_q$.
4. Algorithm $\mathcal{B}$ now simulates the challenger of Hyb_λ in order to compute $u_{d',i'}$:
   (a) For all $i \neq i'$, it samples $\mathbf{w}_{d',i} \xleftarrow{\text{R}} \{0,1\}^t$ and computes $\mathbf{y}_{d',i} = \mathbf{A}_i \mathbf{w}_{d',i}$.
   (b) It samples $(\boldsymbol{\pi}'_{d',1}, \ldots, \boldsymbol{\pi}'_{d',\ell}, \mathbf{c}_{d',i}) \leftarrow \mathsf{SampleMultPre}(\mathsf{td}_{\mathsf{samp}}, \mathbf{y}_{d',1}, \ldots, \mathbf{y}_{d',\ell})$.
   (c) It sets $u_{d',i'} = \mathbf{v}_{i'}^{\mathsf{T}} \boldsymbol{\pi}'_{d',i} + u + \alpha$.
5. It outputs 1 if $u_{d',i'} \notin [-B_{\mathsf{round}}, B_{\mathsf{round}}]$ or $u_{d',i'} \notin \left[\lfloor q/2\rfloor - B_{\mathsf{round}}, \lfloor q/2\rfloor + B_{\mathsf{round}}\right]$ and outputs 0 otherwise.

We analyze what happens for both values of the bit b in the experiment $\mathsf{Exp}_b^{\mathsf{SMEP}}$:

- If $b = 0$, then $u = \mathbf{z}^{\mathsf{T}} \mathbf{w}_{d',i'}[I]$ for some $\mathbf{w}_{d',i,} \xleftarrow{\text{R}} \{0,1\}^t$ and thus, $u_{d',i'}$ is sampled according to the specification of Hyb_λ (by the same argument in the proof of Lemma 4.19). In this case, algorithm $\mathcal{B}$ outputs 1 with probability ε.
- If $b = 1$, then $u \xleftarrow{\text{R}} \mathbb{Z}_q$ and thus, $u_{d',i'}$ is uniform in the view of $\mathcal{B}$. In this case, algorithm $\mathcal{B}$ outputs 1 with probability $1 - \frac{4B_{\mathsf{round}}}{q}$.

By Lemma 4.17, the probability that $\mathcal{B}$ outputs 1 is negligibly close. Thus,

$$\varepsilon \leq 1 - \frac{4B_{\mathsf{round}}}{q} + \mathsf{negl}(\lambda).$$

Since ℓ is a polynomial and by our choice of B_{round}, we have

$$\varepsilon \leq 1 - \frac{4B_{\mathsf{round}}}{q} + \mathsf{negl}(\lambda) \leq \frac{4}{42\ell} + \mathsf{negl}(\lambda) \leq \frac{1}{10\ell}$$

and the claim follows.

Corollary 4.22. *Suppose* $t \geq (2n+8)\log q + 6\log^2\lambda + 10$ *and* $k \geq 8\log^2\lambda\log t + 8\log q\log t$ *and that* ℓ *is some polynomial in* λ. *Suppose also that* $B_{\mathsf{round}} \geq q/4 - q/(42\ell)$ *and* $B_{\mathsf{max}} \geq \sqrt{t}\ell s_{\mathsf{LWE}}$. *Then the rejection sampling procedure used* Hyb_λ *succeeds with overwhelming probability.*

Proof. By Lemmas 4.20 and 4.21 and a union bound over all $i \in [\ell]$, each iteration in the rejection sampling fails with probability at most 1/5. Since we have λ independent iterations, with all but negligible probability, at least one iteration succeeds.

Proof of Theorem 4.18. Fix an unbounded adversary $\mathcal{A}$ for the single-bit hiding game. By Lemma 4.19 and a standard hybrid argument,

$$|\Pr[\mathsf{Hyb}_\lambda(\mathcal{A}) = 1] - \Pr[\mathsf{Hyb}_0(\mathcal{A}) = 1]| = \mathsf{negl}(\lambda).$$

As we observed before, Hyb_0 is just the single-bit hiding game with $b = 0$. On the other hand, conditioned on the rejection sampling procedure not failing, Hyb_λ is identical the single-bit hiding game with $b = 1$. By Corollary 4.22, we know that the rejection sampling fails with negligible probability, therefore Hyb_λ is statistically close to the single-bit hiding game with $b = 1$. In total, the adversary $\mathcal{A}$ has only a negligible advantage in the single-bit hiding game and the theorem follows.

4.2 Parameter Instantiation

Let λ be a security parameter and ℓ be a length parameter. We now provide one possible instantiation of the parameters in Construction 4.1 to satisfy the requirements of Theorems 4.2, 4.4, 4.9 and 4.18. In the following, we assume that ℓ is some polynomial in λ, so $\log\ell = O(\log\lambda)$.

- We set $s_{\mathsf{LWE}} = \lambda^\delta$ for some constant $\delta > 0$ (to be determined later).
- We instantiate Π_{samp} using Theorem 2.10 with parameters $n = \lambda$ and $q = \lambda^2 \cdot \ell^2 \cdot s_{\mathsf{LWE}}^2 = \lambda^{2+2\delta}\ell^2 = \mathsf{poly}(\lambda)$. With this setting of parameter, we have that $t = \lambda \cdot \mathsf{polylog}(\lambda)$.
- Next, we set $N = 8\log^2\lambda\log t + 8\log q\log t = O(\log^3\lambda)$.
- We set the bounds to be $B_{\mathsf{round}}(\lambda,\ell) = q/4 - q/(42\ell) = \lambda^{2+\delta}\ell^2/4 - \lambda^{2+\delta}\ell/42$ and $B_{\mathsf{max}}(\lambda,\ell) = \sqrt{t}\ell s_{\mathsf{LWE}} = \sqrt{\ell}\lambda^{1/2+\delta} \cdot \mathsf{polylog}(\lambda,\ell)$.

- Finally, we choose $\delta > 0$ (recall that $s_{\mathsf{LWE}} = \lambda^{\delta}$) so that the c-quasi-polynomial $\mathsf{LWE}_{n,m,q,s_{\mathsf{LWE}}}$ assumption holds for some constant $c > 4$.

We briefly verify that these parameters satisfy the necessary requirements. For Theorem 4.18:

- Note that the setting of t by Theorem 2.10 gives $t > 3\lambda \log q$ which satisfies the requirement. In addition, $N, B_{\mathsf{round}}, B_{\mathsf{max}}$ were set to satisfy Theorem 4.18.

We now consider the conditions for Theorem 4.9:

- We require $B_{\mathsf{round}} + B_{\mathsf{max}}\sqrt{\log^c(\lambda) + \lambda} \cdot s_{\mathsf{LWE}} \leq q/4$. That is, we want to show $B_{\mathsf{max}}\sqrt{\log^c(\lambda) + \lambda} \cdot s_{\mathsf{LWE}} \leq q/(42\ell) = \lambda^{2+2\delta} \cdot \ell/42$. This exactly follows since $B_{\mathsf{max}}(\lambda, \ell) = \sqrt{\ell}\lambda^{1/2+\delta} \cdot \mathsf{polylog}(\lambda, \ell)$.
- Additionally, we have $N = O(\log^3 \lambda)$.

This proves that Construction 4.1 satisfies Definition 3.1. Using Theorem 3.2, we obtain a ZAP for NP from quasi-polynomial hardness of LWE with a polynomial modulus-to-noise ratio. This yields Theorem 1.1

Acknowledgments. We would like to thank Elahe Sadeghi for useful discussions. Brent Waters is supported by NSF CNS-1908611, CNS-2318701, and a Simons Investigator award. David J. Wu is supported by NSF CNS-2140975, CNS-2318701, a Sloan Fellowship, a Microsoft Research Faculty Fellowship, a Google Research Scholar Award, and an Amazon Research Award.

References

[ADW09] Alwen, J., Dodis, Y., Wichs, D.: Leakage-resilient public-key cryptography in the bounded-retrieval model. In: Halevi, S. (ed.) CRYPTO 2009. LNCS, vol. 5677, pp. 36–54. Springer, Heidelberg (2009). https://doi.org/10.1007/978-3-642-03356-8_3

[BCD+25] Branco, P., Choudhuri, A. R., Döttling, N., Jain, A., Malavolta, G., Srinivasan, A.: Black-box non-interactive zero knowledge from vector trapdoor hash. In: EUROCRYPT (2025)

[BFJ+20] Badrinarayanan, S., Fernando, R., Jain, A., Khurana, D., Sahai, A.: Statistical ZAP arguments. In: Canteaut, A., Ishai, Y. (eds.) EUROCRYPT 2020. LNCS, vol. 12107, pp. 642–667. Springer, Cham (2020). https://doi.org/10.1007/978-3-030-45727-3_22

[BFM88] Blum, M., Feldman, P., Micali, S.: Non-interactive zero-knowledge and its applications (extended abstract). In: STOC (1988)

[BKM20] Brakerski, Z., Koppula, V., Mour, T.: NIZK from LPN and trapdoor hash via correlation intractability for approximable relations. In: Micciancio, D., Ristenpart, T. (eds.) CRYPTO 2020. LNCS, vol. 12172, pp. 738–767. Springer, Cham (2020). https://doi.org/10.1007/978-3-030-56877-1_26

[BKP+24] Bitansky, N., Kamath, C., Paneth, O., Rothblum, R.D., Vasudevan, P.N.: Batch proofs are statistically hiding. In: STOC (2024)

[BLN+24] Bradley, E., Lu, G., Nassar, S., Waters, B., Wu, D.J.: A hidden-bits approach to statistical ZAPs from LWE. IACR Cryptol. ePrint Arch. (2024). https://eprint.iacr.org/2024/1663.pdf

[BLV03] Barak, B., Lindell, Y., Vadhan, S.P.: Lower bounds for non-black-box zero knowledge. In: FOCS (2003)

[BP15] Bitansky, N., Paneth, O.: Zaps and non-interactive witness indistinguishability from indistinguishability obfuscation. In: TCC (2015)

[BWW24] Bradley, E., Waters, B., Wu, D.J.: Batch arguments to NIZKs from one-way functions. In: TCC (2024)

[BY92] Bellare, M., Yung, M.: Certifying cryptographic tools: the case of trapdoor permutations. In: Brickell, E.F. (ed.) CRYPTO 1992. LNCS, vol. 740, pp. 442–460. Springer, Heidelberg (1993). https://doi.org/10.1007/3-540-48071-4_31

[CCH+19] Canetti, R., et al.: Fiat-Shamir: from practice to theory. In: STOC (2019)

[CCRR18] Canetti, R., Chen, Y., Reyzin, L., Rothblum, R.D.: Fiat-Shamir and correlation intractability from strong KDM-secure encryption. In: Nielsen, J.B., Rijmen, V. (eds.) EUROCRYPT 2018. LNCS, vol. 10820, pp. 91–122. Springer, Cham (2018). https://doi.org/10.1007/978-3-319-78381-9_4

[CHK03] Canetti, R., Halevi, S., Katz, J.: A forward-secure public-key encryption scheme. In: Biham, E. (ed.) EUROCRYPT 2003. LNCS, vol. 2656, pp. 255–271. Springer, Heidelberg (2003). https://doi.org/10.1007/3-540-39200-9_16

[CJJQ23] Couteau, G., Jain, A., Jin, Z., Quach, W.: A note on non-interactive zero-knowledge from CDH. In: CRYPTO (2023)

[CKSU21] Couteau, G., Katsumata, S., Sadeghi, E., Ursu, B.: Statistical ZAPs from group-based assumptions. In: Nissim, K., Waters, B. (eds.) TCC 2021. LNCS, vol. 13042, pp. 466–498. Springer, Cham (2021). https://doi.org/10.1007/978-3-030-90459-3_16

[CKU20] Couteau, G., Katsumata, S., Ursu, B.: Non-interactive zero-knowledge in pairing-free groups from weaker assumptions. In: Canteaut, A., Ishai, Y. (eds.) EUROCRYPT 2020. LNCS, vol. 12107, pp. 442–471. Springer, Cham (2020). https://doi.org/10.1007/978-3-030-45727-3_15

[CL18] Canetti, R., Lichtenberg, A.: Certifying trapdoor permutations, revisited. In: Beimel, A., Dziembowski, S. (eds.) TCC 2018. LNCS, vol. 11239, pp. 476–506. Springer, Cham (2018). https://doi.org/10.1007/978-3-030-03807-6_18

[CW23] Champion, J., Wu, D.J.: Non-interactive zero-knowledge from non-interactive batch arguments. In: CRYPTO (2023)

[DJJ24] Dao, Q., Jain, A., Jin, Z.: Non-interactive zero-knowledge from LPN and MQ. In: CRYPTO (2024)

[DN00] Dwork, C., Naor, M.: Zaps and their applications. In: FOCS (2000)

[DORS08] Dodis, Y., Ostrovsky, R., Reyzin, L., Smith, A.D.: Fuzzy extractors: how to generate strong keys from biometrics and other noisy data. SIAM J. Comput. **38**(1) (2008)

[FLS90] Feige, U., Lapidot, D., Shamir, A.: Multiple non-interactive zero knowledge proofs based on a single random string (extended abstract). In: FOCS (1990)

[FS90] Feige, U., Shamir, A.: Witness indistinguishable and witness hiding protocols. In: STOC (1990)

[GJJM20] Goyal, V., Jain, A., Jin, Z., Malavolta, G.: Statistical zaps and new oblivious transfer protocols. In: Canteaut, A., Ishai, Y. (eds.) EUROCRYPT 2020. LNCS, vol. 12107, pp. 668–699. Springer, Cham (2020). https://doi.org/10.1007/978-3-030-45727-3_23

[GMR85] Goldwasser, S., Micali, S., Rackoff, C.: The knowledge complexity of interactive proof-systems (extended abstract). In: STOC (1985)

[GO94] Goldreich, O., Oren, Y.: Definitions and properties of zero-knowledge proof systems. J. Cryptol. **7**(1) (1994)

[GOS06a] Groth, J., Ostrovsky, R., Sahai, A.: Non-interactive zaps and new techniques for NIZK. In: Dwork, C. (ed.) CRYPTO 2006. LNCS, vol. 4117, pp. 97–111. Springer, Heidelberg (2006). https://doi.org/10.1007/11818175_6

[GOS06b] Groth, J., Ostrovsky, R., Sahai, A.: Perfect non-interactive zero knowledge for NP. In: Vaudenay, S. (ed.) EUROCRYPT 2006. LNCS, vol. 4004, pp. 339–358. Springer, Heidelberg (2006). https://doi.org/10.1007/11761679_21

[GR13] Goldreich, O., Rothblum, R.D.: Enhancements of trapdoor permutations. J. Cryptol. **26**(3) (2013)

[HILL99] Håstad, J., Impagliazzo, R., Levin, L.A., Luby, M.: A pseudorandom generator from any one-way function. SIAM J. Comput. **28**(4) (1999)

[JJ21] Jain, A., Jin, Z.: Non-interactive Zero Knowledge from Sub-exponential DDH. In: EUROCRYPT (2021)

[KKS18] Kalai, Y.T., Khurana, D., Sahai, A.: Statistical witness indistinguishability (and more) in two messages. In: Nielsen, J.B., Rijmen, V. (eds.) EUROCRYPT 2018. LNCS, vol. 10822, pp. 34–65. Springer, Cham (2018). https://doi.org/10.1007/978-3-319-78372-7_2

[KMY23] Kitagawa, F., Matsuda, T., Yamakawa, T.: NIZK from SNARGs. J. Cryptol. **36**(2) (2023)

[LPWW20] Libert, B., Passelègue, A., Wee, H., Wu, D.J.: New constructions of statistical NIZKs: dual-mode DV-NIZKs and more. In: Canteaut, A., Ishai, Y. (eds.) EUROCRYPT 2020. LNCS, vol. 12107, pp. 410–441. Springer, Cham (2020). https://doi.org/10.1007/978-3-030-45727-3_14

[LVW19] Lombardi, A., Vaikuntanathan, V., Wichs, D.: 2-message publicly verifiable WI from (subexponential) LWE. IACR Cryptol. ePrint Arch. (2019)

[LVW20] Lombardi, A., Vaikuntanathan, V., Wichs, D.: Statistical ZAPR arguments from bilinear maps. In: Canteaut, A., Ishai, Y. (eds.) EUROCRYPT 2020. LNCS, vol. 12107, pp. 620–641. Springer, Cham (2020). https://doi.org/10.1007/978-3-030-45727-3_21

[MP12] Micciancio, D., Peikert, C.: Trapdoors for lattices: simpler, tighter, faster, smaller. In: Pointcheval, D., Johansson, T. (eds.) EUROCRYPT 2012. LNCS, vol. 7237, pp. 700–718. Springer, Heidelberg (2012). https://doi.org/10.1007/978-3-642-29011-4_41

[NZ96] Nisan, N., Zuckerman, D.: Randomness is linear in space. J. Comput. Syst. Sci. **52**(1) (1996)

[PS19] Peikert, C., Shiehian, S.: Noninteractive zero knowledge for NP from (plain) learning with errors. In: Boldyreva, A., Micciancio, D. (eds.) CRYPTO 2019. LNCS, vol. 11692, pp. 89–114. Springer, Cham (2019). https://doi.org/10.1007/978-3-030-26948-7_4

[QRW19] Quach, W., Rothblum, R.D., Wichs, D.: Reusable designated-verifier NIZKs for all NP from CDH. In: Ishai, Y., Rijmen, V. (eds.) EUROCRYPT 2019. LNCS, vol. 11477, pp. 593–621. Springer, Cham (2019). https://doi.org/10.1007/978-3-030-17656-3_21

[Reg05] Regev, O.: On lattices, learning with errors, random linear codes, and cryptography. In: STOC (2005)

[SW14] Sahai, A., Waters, B.: How to use indistinguishability obfuscation: deniable encryption, and more. In: STOC (2014)

[Vad06] Vadhan, S.P.: An unconditional study of computational zero knowledge. SIAM J. Comput. **36**(4) (2006)

[Wat24] Waters, B.: A new approach for non-interactive zero-knowledge from learning with errors. In: STOC (2024)

[WWW25] Waters, B., Wee, H., Wu, D.J.: New techniques for preimage sampling: improved NIZKs and more from LWE. In: EUROCRYPT (2025)

Justvengers: Batched VOLE ZK Disjunctions in $\mathcal{O}(R+B+C)$ Communication

Yibin Yang(✉)

Georgia Institute of Technology and NTT Research, Atlanta, USA
yyang811@gatech.edu

Abstract. Recent progress on zero-knowledge proofs (ZKPs) based on vector oblivious linear evaluation (VOLE) offers a promising paradigm for scaling ZKPs over extremely large statements. In particular, VOLE-based ZK is currently the best choice in terms of end-to-end execution time. However, VOLE-based ZK incurs high communication overhead—it usually scales linearly with the circuit size.

To mitigate this, existing literature considers VOLE-based ZK over structured statements. In this work, we focus on the *batched disjunctive statement*—$\mathcal{P}$ and $\mathcal{V}$ agree on B fan-in 2 circuits $\mathcal{C}_1, \ldots, \mathcal{C}_B$ over a field $\mathbb{F}$; each circuit is of size C with n_{in} inputs. $\mathcal{P}$'s goal is to demonstrate the knowledge of R witnesses $(id_j \in [B], \boldsymbol{w}_j \in \mathbb{F}^{n_{in}})$ for each $j \in [R]$ s.t. $\forall j \in [R], \mathcal{C}_{id_j}(\boldsymbol{w}_j) = 0$ where neither $\boldsymbol{w}_j$ nor id_j is revealed. Batched disjunctive statements are effective, e.g., in emulating the CPU execution inside ZK. Note, the naïve solution results in a circuit of size $\mathcal{O}(RBC)$.

To prove such a statement using VOLE-based ZK, the prior state-of-the-art protocol Antman (Weng et al., CCS'22) incurred $\mathcal{O}(BC+R)$ communication by additionally relying on AHE, whereas Batchman (Yang et al., CCS'23) achieved $\mathcal{O}(RC+B)$ communication using only VOLE.

In this work, we combine these two protocols non-trivially and present a novel protocol Justvengers—targeting the batched disjunctive statement—that incurs only $\mathcal{O}(R+B+C)$ communication and $\mathcal{O}(BC+(B+C)R\log R)$ computation for prover, using AHE and VOLE. As in Antman, Justvengers requires an AHE scheme that achieves *linear targeted malleability*, which is a non-falsifiable assumption.

1 Introduction

Zero-knowledge proofs (ZKPs) [GMR85] allow a prover $\mathcal{P}$ to convince a verifier $\mathcal{V}$ of the truth of a statement without revealing any information beyond its validity. ZKPs enable many applications, including private blockchains [BCG+14], privacy-preserving program analysis [FDNZ21, LAH+22], private bug bounty systems [HYDK21, YHKD22], secure machine learning [LXZ21, WYX+21], and many more. The last decade has seen rapid advances in the design, implementation, and practical deployment of concretely efficient ZKP systems.

The full version [Yan25] is available online: https://eprint.iacr.org/2025/936.

B. Applebaum and H. Lin (Eds.): TCC 2025, LNCS 16271, pp. 105–137, 2026.
https://doi.org/10.1007/978-3-032-12290-2_4

VOLE-Based ZK. A recent and increasingly popular line of research constructs ZKP protocols using *vector linear oblivious evaluation* (VOLE), known as VOLE-based ZK; see, e.g., [BBMH+21, BBMHS22, BCC+24, BMRS21, DEGL+23, DIO21, DILO22, HY24, LHLA25, LXY24a, LXY24b, WYKW21, YSWW21]. This direction is enabled by the efficient generation of VOLE correlations—i.e., random VOLE instances—using the PCG paradigm (see, e.g., [BCGI18, BCG+19, SGRR19, YWL+20]). In VOLE-based ZK, once the cryptographic overhead of generating VOLE correlations is handled, the remaining protocol is typically simple, often relying on lightweight or even information-theoretic cryptography, and can be made extremely efficient in practice.

Consider a fan-in 2 circuit $\mathcal{C}$ over a finite field, with C denoting the total number of gates. VOLE-based ZK over $\mathcal{C}$ typically requires cost (i.e., communication and computation of each party) of a small constant factor over C in terms of (extension) field elements and operations. State-of-the-art VOLE-based ZK systems (e.g., QuickSilver [YSWW21]) can evaluate millions of multiplication gates per second on modest hardware and network settings. Because of its high scalability, VOLE-based ZK has been especially effective in applications involving large statements, including privacy-preserving machine learning [WYX+21], secure static analysis [LAH+22, LJA+22, LKA+24], private string matching [LWS+24], and privacy-preserving databases [LWX+23].

We focus on VOLE-based ZK since it offers the fastest end-to-end proof time among all known ZKP approaches (e.g., zkSNARKs, MPC-in-the-head), enabling the efficient handling of statements at unprecedented scale—such as those in the applications mentioned above. For further discussion, see Sect. 1.2.

Batched Disjunctive Statements. In this work, we are interested in designing VOLE-based ZK protocols targeting the *batched disjunctive statements*. Here, $\mathcal{P}$ and $\mathcal{V}$ agree on B fan-in 2 circuits $\mathcal{C}_1, \ldots, \mathcal{C}_B$ over a field $\mathbb{F}$; each circuit is of size C with n_{in} inputs. $\mathcal{P}$'s goal is to demonstrate the knowledge of R witnesses $(id_j \in [B], \boldsymbol{w}_j \in \mathbb{F}^{n_{in}})$ for each $j \in [R]$ s.t. $\forall j \in [R], \mathcal{C}_{id_j}(\boldsymbol{w}_j) = 0$ where neither $\boldsymbol{w}_j$ nor id_j is revealed. We refer to each of the B circuits as a *branch*, and the one for which $\mathcal{P}$ holds a valid witness as the *active branch*.

Batched disjunctions are, in fact, common in computation—e.g., a physical CPU repeatedly evaluates the same disjunction over its instruction set as it executes each step of a program. Efficiently supporting such batched disjunctions in ZK is therefore a natural and important building block toward concrete ZK proofs (or arguments) for RAM programs (see, e.g., [GHAK24, IOS23, IOS25, YHH+24]). Our work continues this direction.

The naïve way to proving a disjunctive statement is to evaluate all branches independently and then use a *multiplexer* to select the output of the active branch. Repeating this multiplexed structure R times yields a circuit of size $\mathcal{O}(RBC)$—inferring $\mathcal{O}(RBC)$ communication in linear-cost VOLE-based ZK.

Given the importance of batched disjunctive statements, prior work has explored ways to improve their efficiency in VOLE-based ZK. In particular, the Batchman protocol [YHH+23a] achieves $\mathcal{O}(RC + B)$ communication with (sublinear) computation costs of $\mathcal{O}(BC + RC)$ for both parties, relying solely on

VOLE. Also, the Antman protocol [WYY+22] targets improvements for SIMD circuits in VOLE-based ZK, which implicitly improves batched disjunctive statements where the common circuit has size $\mathcal{O}(BC)$. Applied in this setting, Antman achieves $\mathcal{O}(BC + R)$ communication, with $\mathcal{P}$ performing $\mathcal{O}(BCR \log R)$ and $\mathcal{V}$ performing $\mathcal{O}(BC + R \log R)$ computation, using VOLE and—additionally—AHE. While Batchman outperforms Antman in $\mathcal{P}$'s computation, these two approaches are ultimately incomparable in terms of communication complexity.

We review more on non-batched and batched ZK disjunctions in Sect. 1.2.

Cost Model and Field Setting. In this work, we present our construction using circuits defined over a sufficiently large field $\mathbb{F}$, where the field size $|\mathbb{F}|$ is super-polynomial (i.e., $|\mathbb{F}| = \lambda^{\omega(1)}$). Communication is measured in the number of field elements, and computation is measured in the number of field operations.

However, to the best of our knowledge, all VOLE-based ZK protocols—including ours—can also be instantiated over small fields, such as the Boolean field $\mathbb{F}_2$, by embedding them into a sufficiently large extension field.[1] For the sake of simplicity, we focus on the large-field setting throughout this work.

Our Focus. Given the current landscape of VOLE-based ZK over batched disjunctive statements, a natural interesting question arises:

Can we design a VOLE-based ZK protocol for batched disjunctive statements that improves on both Batchman *[YHH+23a] and* Antman *[WYY+22] in communication, using only VOLE and AHE?*

Table 1. The performance of our protocol Justvengers, compared with the prior VOLE-based ZK work in handling batched disjunctive statements. Here, R is the number of repetitions, B is the number of branches, and each branch is a circuit of size C. Communication is measured in field elements, while computation is measured in field operations. Note that the complexity of Batchman [YHH+23a] incorporates the ZK SET [YH24] optimization; see [YHH+23b] for details.

Protocol	Comm.	$\mathcal{P}$'s Comp.	$\mathcal{V}$'s Comp.	Needs AHE?
QuickSilver [YSWW21]	$\mathcal{O}(RBC)$	$\mathcal{O}(RBC)$	$\mathcal{O}(RBC)$	✗
Batchman [YHH+23a]	$\mathcal{O}(RC + B)$	$\mathcal{O}(BC + RC)$	$\mathcal{O}(BC + RC)$	✗
Antman [WYY+22]	$\mathcal{O}(BC + R)$	$\mathcal{O}(BCR \log R)$	$\mathcal{O}(BC + R \log R)$	✓
Justvengers ours	$\mathcal{O}(R + B + C)$	$\mathcal{O}(BC + (B + C)R \log R)$	$\mathcal{O}(BC + R \log R)$	✓

[1] This can be done even more efficiently using the *subfield* VOLE (e.g., [WYY+22]).

1.1 Our Result

We answer the above questions affirmatively. Specifically, we construct a novel VOLE-based ZK protocol Justvengers—for batched disjunctive statements—by combining the techniques from Antman and Batchman in a non-trivial way.[2]

Table 1 summarizes Justvengers, compared to prior work. We highlight:

- Justvengers achieves $\mathcal{O}(R + B + C)$ communication, improving over both Batchman and Antman.
- Justvengers relies solely on VOLE and AHE, aligning with the cryptographic assumptions of Antman. (A RO can be used for concrete optimizations.)
- $\mathcal{V}$'s computation in Justvengers matches that of Antman and is incomparable to that of Batchman.
- $\mathcal{P}$'s computation in Justvengers is better than in Antman but worse than in Batchman. Crucially, in most parameter regimes, the complexity—$\tilde{\mathcal{O}}(BC + RB + RC)$—is sublinear in the size of the "flattening" circuit representation.
- A batched disjunctive statement becomes uninformative if the witnesses across repetitions are uncorrelated, i.e., reusing the same witness across all R repetitions proves nothing. In Sect. 4.3, we show how Justvengers can enforce the correlation between witnesses at different repetitions.
- Justvengers, same as Antman, needs an AHE with *linear targeted malleability.*

Intuition: A Bird's Eye View. We offer a brief yet intuitive explanation of how Justvengers achieves this. For a concise technical overview, see Sect. 3.

We begin by briefly reviewing the six core steps of Batchman [YHH+23a]: (1) $\mathcal{P}$ commits to the extended witness for each repetition, (2) $\mathcal{P}$ proves the well-formedness of all multiplications in R committed extended witnesses, (3) parties compress each branch into a length-$\mathcal{O}(C)$ vector called a *topology vector*, (4) $\mathcal{P}$ commits to the active topology vector for each repetition, (5) $\mathcal{P}$ proves that the inner product between the committed witness and the corresponding committed topology vector is zero, and (6) $\mathcal{P}$ proves that each committed topology vector is one of the valid public vectors. See Sect. 2.5 and [Yan25] for full details.

Justvengers builds on a key observation: Steps (1), (2), (4), and (5) can be viewed as a SIMD-style circuit—the SI circuit performs $\mathcal{O}(C)$ multiplications and a length-$\mathcal{O}(C)$ inner product. Thus, we apply the Antman technique to replace individual commitments with polynomial ones, reducing communication.

However, using polynomial encodings (and commitments) introduces a new challenge in performing Step (6), which checks membership in the public topology vector set. We address this by applying a random linear combination of the encoded polynomials, enabling an efficient universal hashing-based check.

1.2 Related Work

[2] Bat[ch]man hails from the "DC universe," while Antman belongs to "Marvel"—together, they unite to form the "Justice Revengers.".

VOLE-Based ZK. With the seminal work of [BCGI18] enabling cheap generation of VOLE correlations, a rich line of work on VOLE-based ZKP protocols soon emerged [BBMH+21, BBMHS22, BCC+24, BMRS21, DEGL+23, DIO21, DILO22, HY24, LHLA25, LXY24a, LXY24b, WYKW21, YSWW21]. See [BDSW23] for a survey. VOLE-based ZK is simple, highly efficient, and (mostly) information-theoretic in the VOLE-hybrid model. Its favorable scalability makes it especially well-suited for applications involving large statements.

Consider a standard fan-in 2 circuit $\mathcal{C}$ over a field $\mathbb{F}$, consisting of C gates. State-of-the-art VOLE-based ZK protocols [DIO21, YSWW21], which are IT secure, incur only linear costs with small constant factors.

VOLE-based ZK proofs are not succinct for arbitrary circuits when relying solely on VOLE correlations. By incorporating AHE, recent works have achieved sublinear communication—$\mathcal{O}(C^{3/4})$ in [WYY+22] and $\mathcal{O}(C^{1/2})$ in [BCC+24].

Non-batched and Batched ZK Disjunctions. The study of ZKP protocols for disjunctive statements dates back to the 1990s, beginning with the work of Cramer et al. [CDS94]. This problem was later revisited and refined by Heath and Kolesnikov [HK20], who focused on optimizing ZKPs based on *garbled circuits* [JKO13, Yao86]. Their work introduced the idea of "stacking," a technique that reuses transmitted cryptographic material from the active branch to process (and privately discard) inactive branches. This reduces communication to that of the largest single branch but still requires evaluating all branches.

Following [HK20], a growing body of research [BMRS21, GGHAK22, GHAK24, GHAKS23, HHK+24, YHH+23a, YHH+24] explores stacking-style ZKPs across various ZK techniques. Among these, the work of [YHH+23a] is particularly relevant to ours, as it explicitly improves VOLE-based ZK for batched disjunctions.

We also highlight [WYY+22], which improves VOLE-based ZK for SIMD circuits. This implicitly improves ZK for batched disjunctions.

The core contribution of our work can be viewed as a synthesis of ideas from both [WYY+22] and [YHH+23a], combining their techniques to achieve more efficient VOLE-based ZK for batched disjunctive statements.

Other Related Work. ZKP is a vast and rapidly evolving research area. Here, we highlight a few relevant developments beyond our focus.

Recent work [BBD+23] introduced the *VOLE-in-the-head* cryptographic compiler, which enables any ZK protocol that relies solely on VOLE correlations—though not applicable to Justvengers and Antman –to be transformed into a non-interactive and publicly verifiable protocol.

Beyond VOLE-based ZK, there is considerable interest in succinct ZK proofs. These constructions can achieve polylogarithmic (or even sub-polylogarithmic) communication and verification complexity for *general circuits*. From a theoretical perspective, they offer asymptotically stronger succinctness guarantees, sometimes relying only on seemingly weaker assumptions. However, this comes at the cost of heavy computational burden on $\mathcal{P}$.

In contrast, VOLE-based ZK protocols—including Justvengers—prioritize concrete efficiency. They provide lightweight computation for $\mathcal{P}$, yielding the fastest known end-to-end proof times. Notably, Justvengers achieves (almost) sublinear prover computation with respect to the circuit size. To the best of our knowledge, such efficiency is not achievable in the current succinct ZK landscape. We note that the commit-and-prove structure of Justvengers may enable adaptations to succinct settings, which we leave to future work.

2 Preliminaries

Notation. λ denotes the security parameter (e.g., 128). The prover is denoted by $\mathcal{P}$ (referred to using she/her), and the verifier by $\mathcal{V}$ (referred to using he/him). $x := y$ denotes that y is *assigned* to x. Sets are denoted by uppercase letters, and $x \xleftarrow{\$} S$ indicates uniform sampling from a set S; $[m]$ denotes the set $\{1, \ldots, m\}$. We use $\mathbb{F}$ to represent a sufficiently large field, i.e., $|\mathbb{F}| = \lambda^{\omega(1)}$.[3] Vectors are denoted by bold lowercase letters (e.g., $\boldsymbol{a}$), with a_i or $a[i]$ representing the i-th component (1-based). For vectors $\boldsymbol{a}$ and $\boldsymbol{b}$ of equal length, $\langle \boldsymbol{a}, \boldsymbol{b} \rangle$ denotes the inner product and $\boldsymbol{a} \odot \boldsymbol{b}$ the element-wise product. For a matrix M, $M_{i,j}$ refers to the entry in the i-th column and j-th row, and M_j denotes its j-th column. We use i to index branches ($i \in [B]$), j for repetitions ($j \in [R]$), k for gates ($k \in [n_{in}$ or $n_\times]$), and $id_j \in [B]$ to denote the active index of the j-th repetition.

2.1 Definitions Related to Polynomials

Definition 1 (Interpolation). *Let $\alpha_1, \ldots, \alpha_d \in \mathbb{F}$ be fixed, distinct public points. We define the procedure $\mathsf{Inter}_{\alpha_1,\ldots,\alpha_d}(y_1, \ldots, y_d)$ to return the unique degree-$(d-1)$ (or a constant when $y_1 = \cdots = y_d$) polynomial $f(X) \in \mathbb{F}[X]$ such that $f(\alpha_i) = y_i$ for all $i \in [d]$. This corresponds to standard Lagrange interpolation. When $\boldsymbol{\alpha}$ is clear from context, we omit it for simplicity.*

Definition 2 (Vanishing). *Let $\alpha_1, \ldots, \alpha_d \in \mathbb{F}$ be fixed, distinct public points. A polynomial $f(X) \in \mathbb{F}[X]$ is said to* vanish *at $\alpha_1, \ldots, \alpha_d$ if and only if $f(\alpha_i) = 0$ for all $i \in [d]$. When $\boldsymbol{\alpha}$ is clear from context, we omit it for simplicity.*

The soundness of Justvengers relies on the standard *Schwartz-Zippel-DeMillo-Lipton* (SZDL) lemma [DL78,Sch80,Zip79], stated in Lemma 1.

Lemma 1 (Schwartz-Zippel-DeMillo-Lipton). *Let $\mathbb{F}$ be a field and $p \in \mathbb{F}[x_1, \ldots, x_n]$ be a (multivariate) polynomial of degree d. Suppose $|\mathbb{F}| > d$, then*

$$\Pr\left[p(\boldsymbol{v}) = 0 \mid \boldsymbol{v} \xleftarrow{\$} \mathbb{F}^n\right] \leq \frac{d}{|\mathbb{F}|}$$

[3] Our protocol Justvengers assumes that each branch is expressed as an arithmetic circuit over $\mathbb{F}$, though it also supports small fields via field extensions.

Functionality $\mathcal{F}_{\mathsf{ZK}}^{R,B}$

Upon receiving ($\texttt{prove}, \mathcal{C}_1, \ldots, \mathcal{C}_B, id_1, \boldsymbol{w}_1, \ldots, id_R, \boldsymbol{w}_R$) from $\mathcal{P}$ and ($\texttt{verify}, \mathcal{C}_1, \ldots, \mathcal{C}_B$) from $\mathcal{V}$ where (1) $\mathcal{C}_1, \ldots, \mathcal{C}_B$ are fan-in 2 circuits over $\mathbb{F}_p$ each with n_{in} inputs, (2) each $id_j \in [B]$, and (3) each $\boldsymbol{w}_j \in \mathbb{F}^{n_{in}}$:

- If $\forall j \in [R], \mathcal{C}_{id_j}(\boldsymbol{w}_j) = 0$, then output ($\texttt{true}$) to $\mathcal{V}$; else output ($\texttt{false}$) to $\mathcal{V}$.

Fig. 1. The batched disjunctive ZK functionality.

Functionality $\mathcal{F}_{\mathsf{Com}}$

This functionality initializes two empty set $S_\mathcal{P}, S_\mathcal{V}$ and runs with $\mathcal{P}$ and $\mathcal{V}$ as follows:

Commit. Upon receiving ($\texttt{commit}, m, \tau_m$) from $\mathcal{P}$ (resp. $\mathcal{V}$) where there is no tuple $(\cdot, \tau_m)$ in $S_\mathcal{P}$ (resp. $S_\mathcal{V}$), store (m, τ_m) in $S_\mathcal{P}$ (resp. $S_\mathcal{V}$) and send τ_m to $\mathcal{V}$ (resp. $\mathcal{P}$). Here, τ_m is a handle that identifies the message m.

Open. Upon receiving ($\texttt{open}, \tau_m$) from $\mathcal{P}$ (resp. $\mathcal{V}$) where there is a tuple (m, τ_m) in $S_\mathcal{P}$ (resp. $S_\mathcal{V}$), send (m, τ_m) to $\mathcal{V}$ (resp. $\mathcal{P}$).

Fig. 2. The standard two-party commitment functionality.

2.2 Security Model and Ideal Functionalities

We formalize our protocol within the UC framework [Can01], proving its security against a *malicious, static* adversary. For simplicity, we omit standard UC (sub-)session IDs. We also omit that each time a party sends a message to the functionality, it provides a receipt to the simulator, and that whenever the functionality needs to deliver an output to a party, it waits for the simulator's instruction to do so. Note, this includes the standard *security with abort*.

The ideal functionality achieved by Justvengers is defined in Fig. 1. A standard commitment functionality, used by Justvengers, is defined in Fig. 2.

2.3 IT-MAC and VOLE

IT-MAC. *Information-theoretic message authentication codes* (IT-MACs)—named by [BDOZ11, NNOB12]—are a form of distributed correlated randomness between two parties (in our case, $\mathcal{P}$ and $\mathcal{V}$) that can be used as commitments. In IT-MACs over $\mathbb{F}$, $\mathcal{V}$ holds a uniformly sampled *global* key $\Delta \xleftarrow{\$} \mathbb{F}$. To commit to a value $x \in \mathbb{F}$, $\mathcal{V}$ samples a uniform *local* key $k_x \xleftarrow{\$} \mathbb{F}$, and $\mathcal{P}$ receives the corresponding MAC, computed as $m_x := k_x + x\Delta$. We denote the IT-MAC correlation of a value x as $[x]_\Delta := \langle (x, m_x), k_x \rangle_\Delta$. When clear from context, we omit Δ for simplicity. Below, we summarize several useful properties of IT-MACs:

Functionality $\mathcal{F}_{\mathsf{VOLE}}$

$\mathcal{F}_{\mathsf{VOLE}}$, parameterized by a field $\mathbb{F}$, proceeds as follows, running with a prover $\mathcal{P}$, a verifier $\mathcal{V}$ and an adversary $\mathcal{S}$:

Initialize. Upon receiving (`init`) from $\mathcal{P}$ and $\mathcal{V}$, if $\mathcal{V}$ is honest, sample $\Delta \xleftarrow{\$} \mathbb{F}$, else receive Δ from $\mathcal{S}$. Store Δ and send it to $\mathcal{V}$. Ignore subsequent (`init`).

Extend. Upon receiving ($\texttt{extend}, n$) from $\mathcal{P}$ and $\mathcal{V}$:

- If $\mathcal{V}$ is honest, sample $\boldsymbol{k_u} \xleftarrow{\$} \mathbb{F}^n$, else receive $\boldsymbol{k_u} \in \mathbb{F}^n$ from $\mathcal{S}$.
- If $\mathcal{P}$ is honest, sample $\boldsymbol{u} \xleftarrow{\$} \mathbb{F}^n$ and compute $\boldsymbol{m_u} := \boldsymbol{k_u} + \boldsymbol{u} \cdot \Delta \in \mathbb{F}^n$, else receive $\boldsymbol{u} \in \mathbb{F}^n$ and $\boldsymbol{m_u} \in \mathbb{F}^n$ from $\mathcal{S}$ and compute $\boldsymbol{k_u} := \boldsymbol{m_u} - \boldsymbol{u} \cdot \Delta \in \mathbb{F}^n$.
- Send $(\boldsymbol{u}, \boldsymbol{m_u})$ to $\mathcal{P}$ and $\boldsymbol{k_u}$ to $\mathcal{V}$.

Fig. 3. The VOLE correlation functionality.

1. **Hiding:** k_x and Δ, held by $\mathcal{V}$, are independent of the committed value x.
2. **Binding:** To open $[x]$, $\mathcal{P}$ sends x and m_x, and $\mathcal{V}$ accepts if $m_x = k_x + x\Delta$. To maliciously open $[x]$ as a different value $x' \neq x$ (i.e., forge x), $\mathcal{P}$ would need to guess Δ, succeeding with probability at most $\frac{1}{|\mathbb{F}|}$.
3. **Linear Homomorphism:** IT-MACs support linear operations—such as addition, scalar multiplication, and constant addition—*without* any communication. Specifically, for any *public* constants $c_0, c_1, \ldots, c_n \in \mathbb{F}$, the parties can *locally* compute $[c_0 + c_1 x_1 + \cdots + c_n x_n]$ from $[x_1], \ldots, [x_n]$.[4] We denote $[c_0 + c_1 x_1 + \cdots + c_n x_n] = c_0 + c_1 \cdot [x_1] + \cdots + c_n \cdot [x_n]$. Note, this implies that an IT-MAC of a public constant can be generated *for free*.

VOLE. Random IT-MAC instances (over $\mathbb{F}$) can be viewed as the standard *vector oblivious linear evaluation* (VOLE) correlation functionality, defined as $\mathcal{F}_{\mathsf{VOLE}}$ in Fig. 3. This functionality has been extensively studied in prior work (e.g., [BCGI18,BCG+19,SGRR19,YWL+20]). It can be realized efficiently, achieving even sublinear communication in n (e.g., [BCGI18]) with the *learning parity with noise* (LPN) assumption [BFKL94].

Lemma 2 (Informal). *Assuming the hardness of LPN, there exists a protocol that UC-emulates $\mathcal{F}_{\mathsf{VOLE}}$ (Fig. 3) with $o(n)$ communication for each* `extend`.

It is standard [Bea95] to *consume* a random IT-MAC $[u]$ to generate an IT-MAC $[x]$ for a value x chosen by $\mathcal{P}$: (1) $\mathcal{P}$ sends $x - u$, and (2) parties *locally* compute $[x] := [u] + (x - u)$. Note that each random u can only be used once.

4 For example, if $m_x = k_x + x\Delta$ and $m_y = k_y + y\Delta$, then $(m_x + m_y) = (k_x + k_y) + (x + y)\Delta$. Moreover, for any constant $c \in \mathbb{F}$, $\mathcal{P}$ sets $m_c = 0$ whereas $\mathcal{V}$ sets $k_c = -c\Delta$.

2.4 IT-PAC

The core technique introduced by Antman [WYY+22] (the protocol is reviewed in Sect. 2.5) is a novel method for committing to polynomials using IT-MACs. Specifically, $\mathcal{V}$ additionally holds a *privately* sampled global evaluation point $\Lambda \xleftarrow{\$} \mathbb{F}$. To commit to a polynomial $f(\cdot) \in \mathbb{F}[X]$ held by $\mathcal{P}$, parties obtain $[f(\Lambda)]$, i.e., the IT-MAC for the value $f(\Lambda)$. Clearly, we have the following properties:

1. **Hiding:** $[f(\Lambda)]$ reveals no information about the polynomial $f(\cdot)$ to $\mathcal{V}$.
2. **Binding:** To open the committed $f(\cdot)$, $\mathcal{P}$ sends $f(\cdot)$ and $m_{f(\Lambda)}$, and $\mathcal{V}$ accepts if $m_{f(\Lambda)} = k_{f(\Lambda)} + f(\Lambda)\Delta$. To forge the commitment to a different polynomial $f'(\cdot)$, $\mathcal{P}$ must either (1) guess Δ, which succeeds with probability at most $\frac{1}{|\mathbb{F}|}$, or (2) ensure that $f(\Lambda) = f'(\Lambda)$, which succeeds with probability at most $\frac{d}{|\mathbb{F}|}$, where d is the maximum degree of $f(\cdot)$ and $f'(\cdot)$ by Lemma 1.
3. **Linear Homomorphism:** $[c_0 + c_1 f_1(\Lambda) + \cdots + c_n f_n(\Lambda)] = c_0 + c_1 \cdot [f_1(\Lambda)] + \cdots + c_n \cdot [f_n(\Lambda)]$ for any *public* constants $c_0, c_1, \ldots, c_n \in \mathbb{F}$.

In Antman [WYY+22], this form of correlation—commitments to polynomials—is referred to as the *information-theoretic polynomial authentication code* (IT-PAC). We make the following remarks regarding IT-PACs:

Remark 1. The binding property of an IT-PAC $[f(\Lambda)]$ relies on the fact that the prover $\mathcal{P}$ has *no knowledge* of Λ, including the value $f(\Lambda)$. This contrasts with our notation for commitments like $[x]$ as IT-MACs, where the committed value x is known to $\mathcal{P}$. To emphasize this distinction, we use the notation $[f(\cdot)]$ to represent the IT-PAC of the polynomial $f(\cdot)$.

Remark 2. Looking ahead, $\mathcal{V}$ would reveal Λ to $\mathcal{P}$ at some step in Justvengers (as in Antman; see Sect. 2.5). To preserve soundness, we require $\mathcal{P}$ to commit to any polynomial to be opened (e.g., $f(\cdot)$) using the standard commitment functionality $\mathcal{F}_{\mathsf{Com}}$ (Fig. 2), *before* learning Λ. Once $\mathcal{P}$ learns Λ, the IT-PAC $[f(\cdot)]$ becomes a standard IT-MAC $[f(\Lambda)]$. Crucially, it is insecure for $\mathcal{P}$ to open any committed polynomials *after* learning Λ.

Remark 3. IT-PACs are weaker than traditional polynomial commitment schemes commonly used in the SNARK literature, e.g., [KZG10]. Notably, IT-PACs do *not* support evaluating the committed polynomial at arbitrary points.

Generating IT-PACs from AHE. IT-PACs can be efficiently generated using *additively homomorphic encryption* (AHE) combined with VOLE correlations, as demonstrated in [WYY+22]. To support degree-$\leq d$ polynomials, $\mathcal{V}$ sends d encrypted powers of Λ to $\mathcal{P}$, i.e., $[\![\Lambda]\!], [\![\Lambda^2]\!], \ldots, [\![\Lambda^d]\!]$, where $[\![m]\!] = \mathsf{Enc}(\mathsf{sk}, m; r)$ denotes an AHE encryption of m. Given these ciphertexts, a randomly sampled IT-MAC $[u]$, and a degree-d polynomial $f(\cdot)$ of $\mathcal{P}$'s choice, $\mathcal{P}$ can use the additive homomorphism to compute $[\![f(\Lambda) - u]\!]$, which will be sent to $\mathcal{V}$. Upon decryption, $\mathcal{V}$ learns $f(\Lambda) - u$, which effectively acts as a one-time pad on $f(\Lambda)$.

Note that $[f(\Lambda) - u]$ can be locally generated with only $\mathcal{V}$'s knowing $f(\Lambda) - u$.[5] Thus, parties can obtain $[f(\Lambda)] := [u] + [f(\Lambda) - u]$.

As noted by [WYY+22], this requires an AHE scheme that satisfies the standard *chosen plaintext attack* (CPA) security, and achieves the *circuit privacy* [IP07] and *linear targeted malleability* [BCI+22]. In particular, this AHE can be instantiated by the standard BGV-AHE scheme [BGV12], as analyzed in [KPR18,WYY+22]. We defer further discussion in the full version. We note that the above method only ensures security against a semi-honest $\mathcal{V}$. However, it already suffices for Justvengers (and Antman [WYY+22]). Looking ahead, $\mathcal{P}$ will eventually learn Λ and can safely learn the randomness used in the AHE encryptions. Thus, $\mathcal{P}$ can commit to the messages she intends to send (e.g., $[\![f(\Lambda) - u]\!]$) and disclose them only after verifying the correctness of the encrypted values of Λ and its powers. This elegant approach, used by Antman [WYY+22], can be traced back to GC-ZK [JKO13].

Finally, note that the d AHE encryptions can be reused to generate IT-PACs for multiple degree-$\leq d$ polynomials. This leads to the following:

Lemma 3 (Informal). *If* AHE *is an AHE scheme that satisfies CPA security, circuit privacy, and linear targeted malleability, then there exists a protocol for generating n IT-PACs over polynomials of degree at most d, communicating only $\mathcal{O}(n + d)$ AHE ciphertexts in the $\mathcal{F}_{\mathsf{VOLE}}$-hybrid model (Fig. 3).*

2.5 VOLE-Based ZK

In this section, we briefly review several VOLE-based ZK protocols, focusing in particular on Antman [WYY+22] and Batchman [YHH+23a], which are crucial to understand our novel protocol Justvengers.

LPZK [DIO21,YSWW21]. VOLE-based ZK follows the typical "commit-and-prove" paradigm: $\mathcal{P}$ commits to her extended witness with IT-MACs, and later proves to $\mathcal{V}$ that committed values are consistent with the proof statement.

Given a circuit $\mathcal{C}$ (over $\mathbb{F}$), $\mathcal{P}$ commits to its inputs and the outputs of multiplication gates. Due to the linear homomorphism, parties can locally derive IT-MACs for all wires in $\mathcal{C}$. The remaining task is for $\mathcal{P}$ to prove:

1. **Satisfied Circuit:** The IT-MAC on the output wire of $\mathcal{C}$ commits to a zero. This can be proved by simply opening the IT-MAC.
2. **Correct Multiplication:** Each multiplication gate in $\mathcal{C}$ must be well-formed. For the k-th multiplication gate, parties hold three IT-MACs $[\ell_k], [r_k], [o_k]$ corresponding to the left input, right input, and output wires. $\mathcal{P}$ must prove in ZK that $\ell_k \cdot r_k = o_k$.
   The LPZK technique [DIO21,YSWW21] enables this proof to be performed over n such triples using only $\mathcal{O}(1)$ communication by using an extra VOLE correlation. We provide a consise review of LPZK in the full version.

[5] $\mathcal{P}$ sets $m_{f(\Lambda)-u} = 0$ whereas $\mathcal{V}$ sets $k_{f(\Lambda)-u} = -(f(\Lambda) - u)\Delta$. We slightly abuse the IT-MAC notation by allowing $\mathcal{P}$ to hold a committed value she does *not* know.

Although the LPZK technique achieves constant communication overhead for verifying multiple MULT triples, $\mathcal{P}$ still needs to commit to the (extended) witness, incurring communication that scales linearly with the size of the circuit.

Antman [WYY+22]**.** Prior work has shown that communication costs can be reduced for circuits with special structures. For instance, Antman [WYY+22] optimizes VOLE-based ZK protocols for *single instruction multiple data* (SIMD) circuits, where the same circuit is proven R times with potentially different inputs. This optimization is directly applicable to our setting involving batched disjunctive statements, where the "single instruction" (SI) corresponds to a multiplexer spanning all branches—resulting in an SI circuit of size $\mathcal{O}(BC)$.

The core insight of Antman is that $\mathcal{P}$ can encode values on the same wire across R repetitions as a single polynomial. Specifically, $\mathcal{P}$ and $\mathcal{V}$ agree on R fixed, distinct public points $\alpha_1, \ldots, \alpha_R \in \mathbb{F}$. For the k-th input wire, $\mathcal{P}$'s witness defines R values across the R repetitions, denoted $in_k^{(1)}, \ldots, in_k^{(R)}$. $\mathcal{P}$ constructs the degree-$(R-1)$ polynomial $in_k(X) := \mathsf{Inter}\left(in_k^{(1)}, \ldots, in_k^{(R)}\right) \in \mathbb{F}[X]$, and commits to it using an IT-PAC, denoted $[in_k(\cdot)]$. The same approach applies to the output of each multiplication gate, which is also encoded and committed as a degree-$(R-1)$ polynomial. This polynomial-based encoding allows $\mathcal{P}$ to commit across all repetitions using only $\mathcal{O}(BC+R)$ communication; see Lemma 3.

Due to the linear homomorphism, parties can locally derive IT-PACs for all wires in the SI circuit. The remaining task is for $\mathcal{P}$ to prove:

1. **Satisfied Circuit:** The IT-PAC on the output wire of the SI circuit commits to a vanishing polynomial at $\boldsymbol{\alpha}$. Note that since the polynomial is of degree $(R-1)$ and vanishes at R distinct points, it must be the zero polynomial—the IT-PAC reduces to an IT-MAC of zero, which $\mathcal{P}$ can simply open to $\mathcal{V}$.
2. **Correct Multiplication:** Each multiplication gate in the SI circuit must be well-formed. For the k-th multiplication gate, parties hold three IT-PACs $[\ell_k(\cdot)], [r_k(\cdot)], [o_k(\cdot)]$ corresponding to the left input, right input, and output wires. $\mathcal{P}$ must prove in ZK that $\forall j \in [R], \ell_k(\alpha_j) \cdot r_k(\alpha_j) = o_k(\alpha_j)$.
   This can be done as follows:
   (a) $\mathcal{P}$ computes the degree-$(2R-2)$ polynomial $\widetilde{o_k}(X) := \ell_k(X) \cdot r_k(X)$, and commits to it using an IT-PAC as $[\widetilde{o_k}(\cdot)]$.
   (b) Parties locally compute IT-PAC $[\widetilde{o_k}(\cdot) - o_k(\cdot)]$, which, by construction, must be a vanishing polynomial in a valid proof. To prove this in ZK, $\mathcal{P}$ commits to a uniformly random vanishing polynomial $r(X)$ of degree $(2R-2)$ as $[r(\cdot)]$, and then opens the IT-PAC $[\chi\widetilde{o_k}(\cdot) - \chi o_k(\cdot) + r(\cdot)]$, where $\chi \in \mathbb{F}$ is a random challenge selected and sent by $\mathcal{V}$. Finally, $\mathcal{V}$ checks whether the revealed polynomial is indeed vanishing.
   Here, $r(X)$ is a one-time polynomial pad to preserve ZK. This approach naturally generalizes: to prove that n IT-PACs $[f_1(\cdot)], \ldots, [f_n(\cdot)]$ are all vanishing, $\mathcal{P}$ opens a single IT-PAC of the form $\left[\sum_{i=1}^{n} \chi^i f_i(\cdot) + r(\cdot)\right]$, and $\mathcal{V}$ verifies that the resulting polynomial is vanishing.[6]

[6] We note that this generalized technique is crucial for efficiency. Opening a degree-$\mathcal{O}(R)$ polynomial requires transmitting $\mathcal{O}(R)$ coefficients; thus, naïvely opening n

(c) $\mathcal{V}$ reveals Λ to $\mathcal{P}$. At this point, for each k, IT-PACs $[\ell_k(\cdot)], [r_k(\cdot)], [\widetilde{o_k}(\cdot)]$ become IT-MACs $[\ell_k(\Lambda)], [r_k(\Lambda))], [\widetilde{o_k}(\Lambda)]$. Parties then invokes a standard LPZK protocol to prove that $\ell_k(\Lambda) \cdot r_k(\Lambda) = \widetilde{o_k}(\Lambda)$ for all k, ensuring that each $\widetilde{o_k}(\cdot)$ was correctly constructed and committed.
We emphasize that Λ must only be disclosed after $\mathcal{P}$ has fully opened all committed polynomials via IT-PACs. This is achievable as these messages sent by $\mathcal{P}$ are independent of Λ.

Batchman [YHH+23a]. In contrast to Antman, the VOLE-based ZK protocol Batchman [YHH+23a] is restricted to batched disjunctive statements and relies solely on IT-MACs. Recall that in a batched disjunctive statement, $\mathcal{P}$ and $\mathcal{V}$ agree on B fan-in 2 circuits $\mathcal{C}_1, \ldots, \mathcal{C}_B$ over $\mathbb{F}$. W.l.o.g., assume that each circuit is of size C with n_{in} inputs and $n_\times$ multiplications. $\mathcal{P}$'s goal is to demonstrate the knowledge of R witnesses $(id_j \in [B], \boldsymbol{w}_j \in \mathbb{F}^{n_{in}})$ for each $j \in [R]$ s.t. $\forall j \in [R], \mathcal{C}_{id_j}(\boldsymbol{w}_j) = 0$ where neither $\boldsymbol{w}_j$ nor id_j is revealed.

To illustrate the basic idea behind Batchman, consider the special case where $R = 1$ and $\mathcal{P}$ holds a valid witness $\boldsymbol{w}$ on $\mathcal{C}_{id}$. In Batchman, $\mathcal{P}$ commits to her extended witness *only* for the active (i.e., *id*-th) branch. Specifically, $\mathcal{P}$ commits to the n_{in} input wires, as well as the left and right inputs and the outputs of the $n_\times$ multiplication gates, defined by $\mathcal{C}_{id}(\boldsymbol{w})$. That is, parties obtain:

$$[\boldsymbol{w}_{ext}] := [in_1], \ldots, [in_{n_{in}}], [\ell_1], \ldots, [\ell_{n_\times}], [r_1], \ldots, [r_{n_\times}], [o_1], \ldots, [o_{n_\times}]$$

Parties then invoke LPZK to verify that $\boldsymbol{\ell} \odot \boldsymbol{r} = \boldsymbol{o}$, ensuring that all multiplication constraints are satisfied. Crucially, the total number of IT-MACs is $\mathcal{O}(C)$, and $\mathcal{V}$ cannot distinguish which branch $\mathcal{P}$ intends to prove. Intuitively, it now suffices for $\mathcal{P}$ to show that the committed extended witness satisfies a specific linear relation corresponding to one of the branches—without revealing which one.

This is accomplished using the concept called *topology vector*. Specifically, each branch circuit $\mathcal{C}_i$ induces a public (randomized) vector $\boldsymbol{tv}_i$ of length $n_{in} + 3n_\times + 1$. The i-th branch is the active one *if and only if* the inner product $\langle \boldsymbol{w}_{ext} \| 1, \boldsymbol{tv}_i \rangle = 0$.[7] Naïvely checking all topology vectors via inner products would still incur $\mathcal{O}(BC)$ overhead. Instead, $\mathcal{P}$ additionally commits to the topology vector $\boldsymbol{tv}_{id}$ corresponding to the active branch, maintaining overall communication of $\mathcal{O}(C)$. Finally, $\mathcal{P}$ must prove that the committed topology vector is indeed one of the B publicly known vectors. This membership check can be performed efficiently using standard universal hashing techniques.

Casting this to more repetitions, the key observation is that the same topology vectors can be reused across all repetitions. The overall Batchman protocol consists of the following six core steps:

1. $\mathcal{P}$ commits to the extended witness for each of the R repetitions.

---

such randomized polynomials would incur $\mathcal{O}(nR)$ communication. On the other hand, this technique reduces the total communication to just $\mathcal{O}(R)$.

[7] The appended 1 accounts for constant-related gates; see the full version for details.

2. $\mathcal{P}$ proves in ZK that all multiplications are formed correctly.
3. Parties get the (randomized) topology vectors corresponding to each branch.
4. $\mathcal{P}$ commits to the topology vector for each of the R repetitions.
5. $\mathcal{P}$ proves in ZK that the inner product between each committed extended witness and its corresponding committed topology vector equals zero.
6. $\mathcal{P}$ proves that each committed topology vector belongs to the set of B publicly known topology vectors.

Clearly, committing to the extended witness across R repetitions already incurs $\mathcal{O}(RC)$ communication. Looking ahead, Justvengers implements each of these steps using IT-PACs, reducing the communication overhead.

For simplicity, we omit some details (e.g., the topology vector) and defer a more comprehensive discussion of Batchman to the full version.

3 Technical Overview

In this section, we provide a technical overview of Justvengers to highlight our core contribution. We note that understanding how Antman [WYY+22] and Batchman [YHH+23a] work (see Sect. 2.5 for a concise review) would be very helpful to contextualize the components in this section. We refer the reader to Sect. 1.1 for a high-level intuition behind Justvengers.

3.1 Operations Enabled by IT-PACs

In this section, we abstract out several operations on (committed) polynomials enabled by IT-PACs (see Sects. 2.4 and 2.5). We remark that these operations are significantly more complex when formally implemented—for example, involving the "commit-disclose-open" technique (as in GC-ZK [JKO13]) and the use of AHE to instantiate IT-PACs. However, these underlying details can be omitted for understanding the construction of Justvengers.

Recall that IT-PACs require specifying an upper bound on the degree of polynomials that $\mathcal{P}$ may commit to. In our setting, we fix this maximum degree to be $2R-2$, where R is the number of repetitions. Additionally, $\mathcal{P}$ and $\mathcal{V}$ agree on R fixed, distinct public points $\alpha_1, \dots, \alpha_R \in \mathbb{F}$.[8]

IT-PACs support the following operations:

- **Commit a Polynomial:** After a one-time initialization in which $\mathcal{V}$ sends $\mathcal{O}(R)$ communication (i.e., $\mathcal{O}(R)$ AHE ciphertexts over Λ and its powers), $\mathcal{P}$ can commit to each polynomial of degree at most $2R-2$ at a cost of $\mathcal{O}(1)$ communication and a single VOLE correlations per commitment. In Sect. 3.3, we omit the $\mathcal{O}(R)$ initialization cost for simplicity, i.e., the overall communication cost implicitly includes an additive $\mathcal{O}(R)$ term.

[8] In particular, choosing NTT-friendly points can significantly accelerate computation.

- **Multiply Two Polynomials:** Given IT-PACs $[f(\cdot)]$ and $[g(\cdot)]$, the parties can compute the IT-PAC $[f(\cdot)g(\cdot)]$ at a cost of $\mathcal{O}(1)$ communication and $\mathcal{O}(1)$ VOLE correlations per multiplication. One constraint is that the resulting product must have degree at most $2R-2$.
- **Prove Vanishing Polynomials:** Given n IT-PACs $[f_1(\cdot)], \ldots, [f_n(\cdot)]$, $\mathcal{P}$ can prove in ZK that each committed polynomial vanishes at the points $\boldsymbol{\alpha}$ with $\mathcal{O}(R)$ communication and $\mathcal{O}(1)$ VOLE correlations.
  If an IT-PAC $[f(\cdot)]$ commits to a vanishing polynomial of degree $<R$, then $f(\cdot)$ must be a zero polynomial. In this case, $\mathcal{P}$ can simply open the IT-MAC corresponding to zero, incurring only $\mathcal{O}(1)$ communication per proof.[9]
  In Sect. 3.3, whenever we refer to proving that a committed polynomial is vanishing, we implicitly mean that all such proofs are aggregated into a single batched proof (which costs $\mathcal{O}(R)$ communication in total).

3.2 Polynomial Interpolation over Matrices

In this section, we extend the procedure Inter for generating polynomials row-by-row from a matrix. Given an $n \times R$ matrix M, the procedure $\mathsf{Inter}(M)$ produces n polynomials of degree at most $(R-1)$ by performing interpolation over each row, using a fixed set of evaluation points $\boldsymbol{\alpha}$. This procedure is depicted as follows:

$$M = \begin{pmatrix} M_{1,1} & M_{2,1} & \cdots & M_{R,1} \\ M_{1,2} & M_{2,2} & \cdots & M_{R,2} \\ \cdots & \cdots & \cdots & \cdots \\ M_{1,n} & M_{2,n} & \cdots & M_{R,n} \end{pmatrix} \overset{\mathsf{Inter}}{\Longrightarrow} \begin{matrix} M_1(\cdot) := \mathsf{Inter}_{\alpha_1,\ldots,\alpha_R}(M_{1,1},\ldots,M_{R,1}) \\ M_2(\cdot) := \mathsf{Inter}_{\alpha_1,\ldots,\alpha_R}(M_{1,2},\ldots,M_{R,2}) \\ \cdots \\ M_n(\cdot) := \mathsf{Inter}_{\alpha_1,\ldots,\alpha_R}(M_{1,n},\ldots,M_{R,n}) \end{matrix}$$

The Crucial Observation is: Committing to each entry of the matrix M individually using IT-MACs requires $\mathcal{O}(nR)$ communication and VOLE correlations. In contrast, committing to each row as a degree-$\leq(R-1)$ polynomial using IT-PACs reduces the cost to just $\mathcal{O}(n)$ communication and VOLE correlations (and a one-time initialization overhead of $\mathcal{O}(R)$ communication).

3.3 Justvengers: A Step-by-Step Overview

Recall that Justvengers is constructed by replacing each step of Batchman with IT-PAC-based constructions to reduce communication. In particular, these replacements leverage the operations introduced in Sect. 3.1.

In this section, we revisit the six core steps of Batchman outlined in Sect. 2.5 and show how each is adapted in Justvengers. Alongside each modification, we highlight the corresponding communication improvements achieved by transitioning from IT-MACs to IT-PACs.

Batched Disjunctive Statements. As a reminder, Justvengers is designed specifically for handling batched disjunctive statements. In such a statement,

[9] By using the random oracle, n such zero IT-MAC proofs can be compressed into $\mathcal{O}(\lambda)$ total communication in bits; see Sect. 4.2.

$\mathcal{P}$ and $\mathcal{V}$ agree on B fan-in 2 circuits $\mathcal{C}_1, \ldots, \mathcal{C}_B$ over $\mathbb{F}$. W.l.o.g., assume that each circuit is of size C with n_{in} inputs and $n_\times$ multiplications. $\mathcal{P}$'s goal is to demonstrate the knowledge of R witnesses $(id_j \in [B], \boldsymbol{w}_j \in \mathbb{F}^{n_{in}})$ for each $j \in [R]$ s.t. $\forall j \in [R], \mathcal{C}_{id_j}(\boldsymbol{w}_j) = 0$ where neither $\boldsymbol{w}_j$ nor id_j is revealed.

Step 1: $\mathcal{P}$ commits to inputs and multiplication triples. Recall that in Batchman, for the j-th repetition, $\mathcal{P}$ commits—using IT-MACs—to the inputs and multiplication triples of the active branch, denoted as the extended witness. These committed values can be organized into a $(n_{in}+3n_\times)\times R$ matrix W, where the j-th column corresponds to the j-th extended witness.

In Justvengers, $\mathcal{P}$ applies the Inter procedure to W (see Sect. 3.2)—interpolating each row into a degree-$<R$ polynomial—and then commits to $\mathcal{O}(C)$ resulting polynomials using IT-PACs. This process is depicted as follows:

$$W = \begin{pmatrix} in_1^{(1)} & in_1^{(2)} & \cdots & in_1^{(R)} \\ \cdots & \cdots & \cdots & \cdots \\ in_{n_{in}}^{(1)} & in_{n_{in}}^{(2)} & \cdots & in_{n_{in}}^{(R)} \\ \ell_1^{(1)} & \ell_1^{(2)} & \cdots & \ell_1^{(R)} \\ \cdots & \cdots & \cdots & \cdots \\ \ell_{n_\times}^{(1)} & \ell_{n_\times}^{(2)} & \cdots & \ell_{n_\times}^{(R)} \\ r_1^{(1)} & r_1^{(2)} & \cdots & r_1^{(R)} \\ \cdots & \cdots & \cdots & \cdots \\ r_{n_\times}^{(1)} & r_{n_\times}^{(2)} & \cdots & r_{n_\times}^{(R)} \\ o_1^{(1)} & o_1^{(2)} & \cdots & o_1^{(R)} \\ \cdots & \cdots & \cdots & \cdots \\ o_{n_\times}^{(1)} & o_{n_\times}^{(2)} & \cdots & o_{n_\times}^{(R)} \end{pmatrix} \overset{\mathsf{Inter}}{\Longrightarrow} \begin{matrix} IN_1(\cdot) \\ \cdots \\ IN_{n_{in}}(\cdot) \\ L_1(\cdot) \\ \cdots \\ L_{n_\times}(\cdot) \\ R_1(\cdot) \\ \cdots \\ R_{n_\times}(\cdot) \\ O_1(\cdot) \\ \cdots \\ O_{n_\times}(\cdot) \end{matrix} \overset{\mathsf{Commit}}{\Longrightarrow} \begin{matrix} [IN_1(\cdot)] \\ \cdots \\ [IN_{n_{in}}(\cdot)] \\ [L_1(\cdot)] \\ \cdots \\ [L_{n_\times}(\cdot)] \\ [R_1(\cdot)] \\ \cdots \\ [R_{n_\times}(\cdot)] \\ [O_1(\cdot)] \\ \cdots \\ [O_{n_\times}(\cdot)] \end{matrix}$$

Here, $in_k^{(j)}$ denotes the k-th input in the j-th repetition for $j \in [R]$ and $k \in [n_{in}]$. The notation is analogous for $\ell_k^{(j)}$, $r_k^{(j)}$, and $o_k^{(j)}$ for $k \in [n_\times]$, representing the corresponding multiplication gate wires. On the other hand, $IN_k(\cdot)$ denotes the polynomial obtained by interpolating the k-th input values across the R repetitions, for $k \in [n_{in}]$. Namely, $IN_k(\alpha_j) = in_k^{(j)}$ for all $j \in [R]$. The same notation applies to $L_k(\cdot)$, $R_k(\cdot)$, and $O_k(\cdot)$ for $k \in [n_\times]$, representing the interpolated polynomials corresponding to the multiplication gate wires.

Cost: This step in Justvengers requires $\mathcal{O}(C)$ communication and $\mathcal{O}(C)$ VOLE correlations, improving over the corresponding step in Batchman, which incurs $\mathcal{O}(RC)$ communication and VOLE correlations.

Step 2: $\mathcal{P}$ proves well-formed multiplications. At this stage, $\mathcal{P}$ has encoded her extended witness using $\mathcal{O}(C)$ polynomials and committed to them via IT-PACs. To ensure correctness, the parties must verify that the multiplication gates are properly encoded within these polynomials. Formally, $\mathcal{P}$ must prove in ZK that:

$$\forall k \in [n_\times], \forall j \in [R], L_k(\alpha_j) \cdot R_k(\alpha_j) = O_k(\alpha_j)$$

Recall that Antman includes a sub-protocol designed explicitly for this purpose, which we directly incorporate into Justvengers. For each $k \in [n_\times]$, the parties (1) generate the IT-PAC $[L_k(\cdot)R_k(\cdot)]$ from the existing IT-PACs $[L_k(\cdot)]$ and $[R_k(\cdot)]$; and (2) prove that the IT-PAC $[L_k(\cdot)R_k(\cdot) - O_k(\cdot)]$ commits a vanishing polynomial. (Note that the subtraction is a free linear operation.)

Cost: This step in Justvengers requires $\mathcal{O}(C)$ communication (plus a one-time $\mathcal{O}(R)$ cost for batching the vanishing polynomial proofs) and $\mathcal{O}(C)$ VOLE correlations. While the corresponding step in Batchman incurs only $\mathcal{O}(1)$ communication, this additional overhead does *not* affect the overall asymptotic.

Step 3: Parties generate topology vectors for each branch. This step in Justvengers matches that of Batchman (see the full version) and requires only $\mathcal{O}(1)$ communication. We denote these B length-$\mathcal{O}(C)$ vectors as $\boldsymbol{tv}^{(1)}, \ldots, \boldsymbol{tv}^{(B)}$.

Step 4: $\mathcal{P}$ commits to active topology vectors. $\mathcal{P}$ must convince $\mathcal{V}$ that each column of W corresponds to a valid branch—that is, there exists a topology vector (among the B candidates) whose inner product with the column yields 0.

In Batchman, this is accomplished by having $\mathcal{P}$ commit—using IT-MACs—to the active topology vector used in each repetition. Similar to Step 1, Justvengers arranges the R active topology vectors column-wise—one per repetition—into a $(n_{in}+3n_\times+1)\times R$ matrix, denoted TV. $\mathcal{P}$ then applies interpolation row-by-row and commits to the resulting polynomials using IT-PACs.

For each repetition $j \in [R]$, let $id_j \in [B]$ denote the index of the active branch. This process is depicted as follows:

$$TV = \left(\boldsymbol{tv}^{(id_1)} \cdots \boldsymbol{tv}^{(id_R)}\right) \overset{\mathsf{Inter}}{\Longrightarrow} \begin{matrix} TV_1(\cdot) \\ \cdots \\ TV_{n_{in}+3n_\times+1}(\cdot) \end{matrix} \overset{\mathsf{Commit}}{\Longrightarrow} \begin{matrix} [TV_1(\cdot)] \\ \cdots \\ [TV_{n_{in}+3n_\times+1}(\cdot)] \end{matrix}$$

Here, for each $k \in [n_{in} + 3n_\times + 1]$, the polynomial $TV_k(\cdot)$ encodes the k-th entry of the active topology vector across all R repetitions.

Cost: This step in Justvengers requires $\mathcal{O}(C)$ communication and $\mathcal{O}(C)$ VOLE correlations, improving over the corresponding step in Batchman, which incurs $\mathcal{O}(RC)$ communication and VOLE correlations.

Step 5: $\mathcal{P}$ proves zero inner products. $\mathcal{P}$ must prove in ZK that the inner product between each committed extended witness and its corresponding committed topology vector equals zero. That is, for each $j \in [R]$, $\mathcal{P}$ must show that the inner product of W_j and TV_j is zero. Formally, this means: $\forall j \in [R]$,

$$\langle(\{IN_k(\alpha_j)\}_{k\in[n_{in}]}, \{L_k(\alpha_j)\}_{k\in[n_\times]}, \{R_k(\alpha_j)\}_{k\in[n_{in}]}, \{O_k(\alpha_j)\}_{k\in[n_{in}]}, 1),$$
$$(\{TV_k(\alpha_j)\}_{k\in[n_{in}+3n_\times+1]})\rangle = 0$$

Here, the constant term "1" is appended to account for constant-related gates.[10] Let $UNIT(\cdot) = 1$ denote the constant polynomial that evaluates to 1 everywhere. Note that the IT-PAC for $UNIT(\cdot)$ can be generated *for free*, as $[UNIT(\cdot)] = [1]$.

To finish this step, the core observation made by Justvengers is that parties can generate the following IT-PAC, denoted $[IP(\cdot)]$:

$$[\sum_{k=1}^{n_{in}} IN_k(\cdot)TV_k(\cdot) + \sum_{k=1}^{n_\times} L_k(\cdot)TV_{n_{in}+k}(\cdot) + \sum_{k=1}^{n_\times} R_k(\cdot)TV_{n_{in}+n_\times+k}(\cdot) \\ + \sum_{k=1}^{n_\times} O_k(\cdot)TV_{n_{in}+2n_\times+k}(\cdot) + UNIT(\cdot)TV_{n_{in}+3n_\times+1}(\cdot)]$$

Specifically, this polynomial can be constructed by multiplying $\mathcal{O}(C)$ pairs of IT-PACs. By construction, for each $j \in [R]$, the evaluation $IP(\alpha_j)$ corresponds to the inner product for the j-th repetition. Thus, it suffices for $\mathcal{P}$ to prove that the committed polynomial $IP(\cdot)$ is vanishing.

Cost: This step in Justvengers requires $\mathcal{O}(C)$ communication (plus a one-time $\mathcal{O}(R)$ cost for batching the vanishing polynomial proofs) and $\mathcal{O}(C)$ VOLE correlations. While the corresponding step in Batchman incurs only $\mathcal{O}(1)$ communication, this additional overhead does *not* affect the overall asymptotic.

Step 6: $\mathcal{P}$ proves membership of committed topology vectors. $\mathcal{P}$ must prove that each committed active topology vector—encoded within polynomials—is indeed one of the B publicly known topology vectors. To illustrate how this is achieved in Justvengers, we first recall how membership checks over committed vectors can be performed efficiently, as done in Batchman.

The core idea relies on universal hashing. Suppose $\mathcal{P}$ holds a committed vector $[\boldsymbol{v}]$ (using IT-MACs) and needs to prove that $\boldsymbol{v}$ is contained in the public set of topology vectors. It suffices for $\mathcal{V}$ to sample a random challenge $\gamma \xleftarrow{\$} \mathbb{F}$, and for $\mathcal{P}$ to prove the following relation holds:

$$\langle(1, \gamma, \gamma^2, \ldots), \boldsymbol{v}\rangle \in \left\{\left\langle(1, \gamma, \gamma^2, \ldots), \boldsymbol{tv}^{(i)}\right\rangle\right\}_{i \in [B]}$$

This method is highly efficient in the IT-MAC setting, as all linear operations can be performed locally without additional communication. Essentially, the parties compute the hash of the committed vector using the universal hashing approach, and $\mathcal{P}$ proves that this hash matches one of the B publicly known hash values corresponding to the topology vectors.

Similarly, IT-PACs enjoy free linear operations. Once $\mathcal{V}$ samples and sends the challenge γ, the parties can linearly combine the committed polynomials induced by active topology vectors (from Step 4). Crucially, for each $j \in [R]$, evaluating the aggregated polynomial at α_j yields the hash of the committed active topology vector for the j-th repetition!

[10] For example, the circuit may contain a MULT gate with a public constant as one of its inputs; the "1" is necessary to support such gates —see the full version.

However, this alone is insufficient, as we still need a mechanism to verify *in ZK* that the resulting hash (at each $\boldsymbol{\alpha}$) belongs to the public set of (topology) hashes. To address this, the key observation leveraged by Justvengers is that $\mathcal{P}$ can efficiently commit to this information using polynomials.

In particular, $\mathcal{P}$ can construct a $B \times R$ matrix MK as follows:

$$\forall i \in [B], j \in [R], MK_{i,j} = \begin{cases} 1, & \text{if the } i\text{-th branch is active in the } j\text{-th repetition} \\ 0, & \text{otherwise} \end{cases}$$

Namely, the matrix MK marks which branch is active in each repetition. $\mathcal{P}$ then applies interpolation row-by-row on MK and commits to the resulting polynomials using IT-PACs, *before γ is issued*, depicted as follows:

$$MK \overset{\text{Inter}}{\Longrightarrow} \begin{matrix} MK_1(\cdot) \\ \cdots \\ MK_B(\cdot) \end{matrix} \overset{\text{Commit}}{\Longrightarrow} \begin{matrix} [MK_1(\cdot)] \\ \cdots \\ [MK_B(\cdot)] \end{matrix}$$

Once $\mathcal{V}$ samples and sends γ, the parties compute B *public* hash values over the topology vectors as $h_{i \in [B]} := \langle (1, \gamma, \gamma^2, \ldots), \boldsymbol{tv}^{(i)} \rangle$. It then suffices for $\mathcal{P}$ to prove that the following polynomial is vanishing:[11]

$$\sum_{k=1}^{n_{in}+3n_{\times}+1} \gamma^{k-1} \cdot TV_k(\cdot) - \sum_{i=1}^{B} h_i \cdot MK_i(\cdot)$$

Thanks to the linear homomorphism of IT-PACs, the commitment to this polynomial can be computed locally. (Note, since its degree is strictly less than R, the polynomial must be identically zero if it vanishes at all $\alpha_{j \in [R]}$.)

Finally, $\mathcal{P}$ must prove that each entry in the matrix MK is either 0 or 1. This can be done straightforwardly: for each $i \in [B]$, the parties generate the IT-PAC for the polynomial $[MK_i(\cdot)(MK_i(\cdot) - 1)]$ and prove that it is vanishing. Moreover, parties need to verify that each column of MK contains exactly a single one, ensuring a valid branch selection per repetition. This could be efficiently checked by proving that $\sum_{i \in [B]} MK_i(\cdot)$ is the unit polynomial.

Cost: This step in Justvengers requires $\mathcal{O}(B)$ communication (plus a one-time $\mathcal{O}(R)$ cost for batching the vanishing polynomial proofs) and $\mathcal{O}(B)$ VOLE correlations. This matches that of Batchman.

Conclusion. In summary, Justvengers achieves $\mathcal{O}(R + B + C)$ communication and consumes $\mathcal{O}(R+B+C)$ VOLE correlations. Applying Lemma 2, the overall communication cost remains $\mathcal{O}(R+B+C)$ in the plain model (assuming LPN).

Important Note. For simplicity, several low-level but critical details have been omitted in this section. A full formalization with them is presented in Sect. 4. Here, we briefly highlight a few key aspects as a preview:

[11] Essentially, we compute the same hash in two different ways.

- The batched disjunctive setting is only meaningful when the witness can be "soldered" across repetitions, as supported by Justvengers; see Sect. 4.3.
- Generating IT-PACs requires the use of AHE. Justvengers relies solely on an AHE scheme without *verifiability*, made possible by the "commit-disclose-open" technique [JKO13, WYY+22]; see Sect. 4.1.
- Multiplication of two IT-PACs depends on the fact that Λ can be safely disclosed at some stage; see Sect. 4.1.
- We omit the computational complexity analysis in this section. As in Antman, the main bottleneck in Justvengers is NTT-based polynomial interpolation, and it requires $\mathcal{O}((B+C)R\log R)$ field operations; see Sect. 4.2.
- The protocol described in this section does not provide a proof of knowledge, i.e., the simulator *cannot* extract the inputs used by $\mathcal{P}$ in each repetition as they were committed inside polynomials. To address this, we follow the approach of Antman, where each input-related polynomial coefficient is additionally committed as an IT-MAC; see Sect. 4.1. Crucially, this modification does *not* affect overall communication asymptotic efficiency, since it adds only $\mathcal{O}(Rn_{in})$ overhead.

4 Formalization

4.1 UC Description of Justvengers

We formalize our protocol Justvengers as $\Pi_{\mathsf{Justvengers}}$ in Figs. 4 to 9. See Sect. 3 for a concise technical overview.

The formal definition of Justvengers consists of five major phases:

1. **Initialization** (Sect. 4): In this phase, parties set up the protocol by generating (1) AHE ciphertexts over Λ and its powers, and (2) a pool of VOLE correlations to be used in subsequent phases. Notably, in Step 2, $\mathcal{V}$ commits to the seed used for generating AHE randomness. This commitment is critical for security, as a malicious $\mathcal{V}$ could otherwise send ill-formed AHE ciphertexts. Later in the protocol, $\mathcal{V}$ is required to reveal this seed, allowing $\mathcal{P}$ to verify the correctness of the ciphertexts.
2. **Commitment** (Figs. 5 and 6): In this phase, $\mathcal{P}$ commits to the computed AHE ciphertexts (used to generate IT-PACs) via $\mathcal{F}_{\mathsf{Com}}$. This step is necessary because $\mathcal{P}$ has not yet verified the well-formedness of the ciphertexts from $\mathcal{V}$, and revealing them prematurely could compromise ZK.
Note, in Step 9, $\mathcal{P}$ additionally commits—using IT-MACs—to the coefficients of the input polynomials $IN_{k\in[n_{in}]}(\cdot)$. This is required for simulation, as the witness must be extractable, which is not possible from unopened polynomials alone. These extra commitments do not affect asymptotic efficiency, as it applies only to the input layer. Moreover, these IT-MACs are unrelated to the AHE ciphertexts and thus do not require the usage of $\mathcal{F}_{\mathsf{Com}}$.
During execution, $\mathcal{P}$ also maintains an ordered queue Q_{vanish} (initially empty) to track vanishing polynomials that need to be proved.
Finally, we note that the six steps in this phase correspond directly to those described in Sect. 3.3.

3. **Disclosure** (Fig. 7): In this phase, $\mathcal{P}$ proves in ZK that all polynomials in Q_{vanish} are vanishing. To do so, in Step 11, $\mathcal{P}$ samples a random vanishing polynomial $PAD(\cdot)$ and commits to it using IT-PAC (again, this goes to $\mathcal{F}_{\mathsf{Com}}$). In Step 12, $\mathcal{V}$ sends a random challenge ζ, which is used to linearly combine all vanishing polynomials. The resulting aggregated polynomial is one-time padded with $PAD(\cdot)$, forming $VP(\cdot)$, which $\mathcal{P}$ reveals to $\mathcal{V}$.
   Crucially, since $VP(\cdot)$ is independent of AHE, it does not require a commit-then-reveal strategy. However, it must be sent before $\mathcal{P}$ learns Λ—otherwise, a malicious $\mathcal{P}$ can always construct a vanishing polynomial $\widetilde{VP}(\cdot)$ that evaluates to an arbitrary value at Λ, violating soundness.
   In the final Step 13 of this phase, $\mathcal{V}$ reveals the committed seed and the value of Λ used to generate the corresponding AHE ciphertexts. This allows $\mathcal{P}$ to verify their correctness. If the ciphertexts are ill-formed, $\mathcal{P}$ aborts. Note that up to this point, $\mathcal{V}$ has learned only uniformly random values besides some handles from $\mathcal{F}_{\mathsf{Com}}$, so this abort preserves ZK. If the ciphertexts are well-formed, then other AHE ciphertexts generated by $\mathcal{P}$ are simply encryptions of one-time-padded values, which can now be safely revealed to $\mathcal{V}$.
4. **Open** (Fig. 8): In this phase, $\mathcal{P}$ reveals all previously committed AHE ciphertexts (in $\mathcal{F}_{\mathsf{Com}}$) to $\mathcal{V}$. Since $\mathcal{P}$ now knows Λ, all IT-PACs become IT-MACs.[12] That is, $\mathcal{P}$ can evaluate each committed polynomial at Λ. Crucially, knowing Λ does *not* enable $\mathcal{P}$ to forge any committed values within the IT-MACs, as the global key Δ still retains full entropy.
5. **Verification** (Fig. 9): In this phase, parties perform several remaining consistency checks. Step 20 verifies that the revealed (random-looking) vanishing polynomial is the correct one intended to be opened. This is done by checking whether $VP(\Lambda)$ matches the value committed in the corresponding IT-MAC. The check is sound as $\mathcal{P}$ opens the polynomial before learning Λ—any deviation would match at Λ with probability $\mathcal{O}\left(\frac{R}{|\mathbb{F}|}\right)$ by Lemma 1.
   Step 21 ensures that the committed polynomial correctly represents the product of two input polynomials. This follows the same technique used in Antman [WYY+22].
   Step 22 verifies that the IT-MACs of the committed coefficients match those used in the corresponding interpolated polynomials. This step ensures that the extracted witness aligns with what $\mathcal{P}$ actually uses in the proof (encoded inside committed polynomial IT-PACs).

[12] To some extent, IT-PACs are used purely as a conceptual tool in the formalization.

Protocol $\Pi_{\mathsf{Justvengers}}$, Part I

Let AHE = (Setup, KeyGen, Enc, Dec) be an additively homomorphic encryption scheme (defined in the full versioni). Let $G : \{0,1\}^\lambda \mapsto \{0,1\}^*$ be a PRG.

Inputs. $\mathcal{P}$ and $\mathcal{V}$ hold B circuits $\mathcal{C}_1, \ldots, \mathcal{C}_B$ over field $\mathbb{F}$, where each circuit has n_{in} inputs, $n_\times$ multiplications and 1 output. $\mathcal{P}$ also holds R witness $\boldsymbol{w}_j \in \mathbb{F}^{n_{in}}$ and R integers $id_j \in [B]$ for each $j \in [R]$ such that $\forall j \in [R], \mathcal{C}_{id_j}(\boldsymbol{w}_j) = 0$. Suppose that $\mathcal{P}$ and $\mathcal{V}$ have already agreed on (1) a set of public parameters $\mathsf{par} = \mathsf{Setup}(1^\lambda)$ for AHE and (2) R distinct fixed points $\alpha_1, \ldots, \alpha_R \in \mathbb{F}$.

Initialization.

1. $\mathcal{P}$ and $\mathcal{V}$ send (`init`) to $\mathcal{F}_{\mathsf{VOLE}}$, which returns a uniform $\Delta \xleftarrow{\$} \mathbb{F}$ to $\mathcal{V}$.
2. $\mathcal{V}$ samples a uniform $\mathsf{seed} \xleftarrow{\$} \{0,1\}^\lambda$, and sends $(\texttt{commit}, \mathsf{seed}, \tau_{\mathsf{seed}})$ to $\mathcal{F}_{\mathsf{Com}}$, which returns the handle τ_{seed} to $\mathcal{P}$. $\mathcal{P}$ aborts if she does not receive it.
3. $\mathcal{V}$ samples a uniform $\Lambda \xleftarrow{\$} \mathbb{F}$ and expands the PRG $G(\mathsf{seed})$ into a bit string $(r_0, r_1, \ldots, r_{2R-2})$, where r_0 is used for KeyGen and each r_j (for $j \in [2R-2]$) is used for Enc. $\mathcal{V}$ then computes the secret key $\mathsf{sk} := \mathsf{KeyGen}(\mathsf{par}; r_0)$ and encrypts Λ^j as $[\![\Lambda^j]\!] := \mathsf{Enc}(\mathsf{sk}, \Lambda^j; r_j)$ for each $j \in [2R-2]$. Finally, $\mathcal{V}$ sends $[\![\Lambda]\!], \ldots, [\![\Lambda^{2R-2}]\!]$ to $\mathcal{P}$.
4. $\mathcal{P}$ and $\mathcal{V}$ send $(\texttt{extend}, m)$ to $\mathcal{F}_{\mathsf{VOLE}}$, which returns a pool of m VOLE correlations (i.e., random IT-MACs), where $m = Rn_{in} + 2B + 3n_{in} + 10n_\times + 3 \in \mathcal{O}(R+B+C)$. Throughout the remainder of the protocol, any reference to a random IT-MAC or a single VOLE correlation refers to retrieving a new entry from this pre-allocated pool.[a]

[a] We assume that $\mathcal{P}$ and $\mathcal{V}$ retrieve them in a consistent, predetermined order.

Fig. 4. Justvengers (Part I): ZKP protocol for the batched disjunctive statement over $\mathbb{F}$ in the $\{\mathcal{F}_{\mathsf{Com}}, \mathcal{F}_{\mathsf{VOLE}}\}$-hybrid (Figs. 2 and 3) model.

Protocol $\Pi_{\mathsf{Justvengers}}$, Part II

Commitment.

5. For the j-th repetition ($j \in [R]$), $\mathcal{P}$ evaluates $\mathcal{C}_{id_j}(\boldsymbol{w}_j)$ and records corresponding extended witness including $in^{(j)}_{k\in[n_{in}]}$ for circuit inputs, $\ell^{(j)}_{k\in[n_\times]}$ (resp. $r^{(j)}_{k\in[n_\times]}$ and $o^{(j)}_{k\in[n_\times]}$) for left inputs (resp. right inputs and outputs) of MULT gates. Then, for each $k \in [n_{in}]$, $\mathcal{P}$ applies the interpolation procedure to obtain the polynomial $IN_k(\cdot) := \mathsf{Inter}(in^{(1)}_k, \dots, in^{(R)}_k)$; and $\mathcal{P}$ computes $\left[\!\left[IN_k(\Lambda) - s^{(in)}_k\right]\!\right]$ by using additive homomorphism based on $[\![\Lambda]\!], \dots, [\![\Lambda^{R-1}]\!]$ and a VOLE correlation $\left[s^{(in)}_k\right]$. The same applies to $L_k(\cdot)$, $R_k(\cdot)$, $O_k(\cdot)$ and corresponding $\left[\!\left[L_k(\Lambda) - s^{(\ell)}_k\right]\!\right], \left[\!\left[R_k(\Lambda) - s^{(r)}_k\right]\!\right], \left[\!\left[O_k(\Lambda) - s^{(o)}_k\right]\!\right]$ for each $k \in [n_\times]$. $\mathcal{P}$ commits to the above $n_{in}+3n_\times$ AHE ciphertexts via $\mathcal{F}_{\mathsf{Com}}$ using the handle τ_{wit}, which is then sent to $\mathcal{V}$. $\mathcal{V}$ aborts if he does not receive a handle. Finally, for each $k \in [n_{in}]$, let R coefficients on $IN_k(\cdot)$ be $c^{(in)}_{k,0}, \dots, c^{(in)}_{k,R-1}$: $\mathcal{P}$ and $\mathcal{V}$ generate R IT-MACs $\left[c^{(in)}_{k,0}\right], \dots, \left[c^{(in)}_{k,R-1}\right]$ from R VOLE correlations. $\mathcal{V}$ aborts if he fails to build these IT-MACs.
6. For each $k \in [n_\times]$, $\mathcal{P}$ computes $L_k(\cdot)R_k(\cdot)$ and $\left[\!\left[L_k(\Lambda)R_k(\Lambda) - s^{(\ell r)}_k\right]\!\right]$ by using additive homomorphism based on $[\![\Lambda]\!], \dots, [\![\Lambda^{2R-2}]\!]$ and a VOLE correlation $\left[s^{(\ell r)}_k\right]$; and $\mathcal{P}$ appends the polynomial $L_k(\cdot)R_k(\cdot) - O_k(\cdot)$ into the queue Q_{vanish}. $\mathcal{P}$ commits to the above $n_\times$ AHE ciphertexts via $\mathcal{F}_{\mathsf{Com}}$ using the handle τ_{mul}, which is then sent to $\mathcal{V}$. $\mathcal{V}$ aborts if he does not receive a handle.
7. $\mathcal{V}$ issues a random challenge χ. Parties compute the length-$(n_{in}+3n_\times+1)$ topology vector $\boldsymbol{tv}^{(i)}$ for each $\mathcal{C}_{i\in[B]}$; see [YHH+23a, Section 4].
8. $\mathcal{P}$ constructs the $(n_{in}+3n_\times+1)\times R$ matrix $TV := (\boldsymbol{tv}^{(id_1)}, \dots, \boldsymbol{tv}^{(id_R)})$. Then $\mathcal{P}$ applies the interpolation procedure over TV (see Sect. 3.2) to get polynomials $TV_1(\cdot), \dots, TV_{n_{in}+3n_\times+1}(\cdot)$. For each $k \in [n_{in}+3n_\times+1]$, $\mathcal{P}$ computes $\left[\!\left[TV_k(\Lambda) - s^{(tv)}_k\right]\!\right]$ by using additive homomorphism based on $[\![\Lambda]\!], \dots, [\![\Lambda^{R-1}]\!]$ and a VOLE correlation $\left[s^{(tv)}_k\right]$ $\mathcal{P}$ commits to the above $n_{in}+3n_\times+1$ AHE ciphertexts via $\mathcal{F}_{\mathsf{Com}}$ using the handle τ_{tv}, which is then sent to $\mathcal{V}$. $\mathcal{V}$ aborts if he does not receive a handle.

Fig. 5. Justvengers (Part II): ZKP protocol for the batched disjunctive statement over $\mathbb{F}$ in the $\{\mathcal{F}_{\mathsf{Com}}, \mathcal{F}_{\mathsf{VOLE}}\}$-hybrid (Figs. 2 and 3) model.

Protocol $\Pi_{\mathsf{Justvengers}}$, Part III

Commitment.

9. $\mathcal{P}$ computes the following:
   (a) For each $k \in [n_{in}]$: $IN_k(\cdot)TV_k(\cdot)$ and $\left[\!\left[IN_k(\Lambda)TV_k(\Lambda) - s_k^{(intv)} \right]\!\right]$ by using additive homomorphism and a VOLE correlation $\left[s_k^{(intv)} \right]$.
   (b) For each $k \in [n_\times]$: $L_k(\cdot)TV_{n_{in}+k}(\cdot)$ and $\left[\!\left[L_k(\Lambda)TV_{n_{in}+k}(\Lambda) - s_k^{(ltv)} \right]\!\right]$ by using additive homomorphism and a VOLE correlation $\left[s_k^{(ltv)} \right]$. $R_k(\cdot)TV_{n_{in}+n_\times+k}(\cdot)$ and $\left[\!\left[R_k(\Lambda)TV_{n_{in}+n_\times+k}(\Lambda) - s_k^{(rtv)} \right]\!\right]$ by using additive homomorphism and a VOLE correlation $\left[s_k^{(rtv)} \right]$. $O_k(\cdot)TV_{n_{in}+2n_\times+k}(\cdot)$ and $\left[\!\left[O_k(\Lambda)TV_{n_{in}+2n_\times+k}(\Lambda) - s_k^{(otv)} \right]\!\right]$ by using additive homomorphism and a VOLE correlation $\left[s_k^{(otv)} \right]$.
   (c) The polynomial $IP(\cdot) =$

$$\sum_{k=1}^{n_{in}} IN_k(\cdot)TV_k(\cdot) + \sum_{k=1}^{n_\times} L_k(\cdot)TV_{n_{in}+k}(\cdot) + \sum_{k=1}^{n_\times} R_k(\cdot)TV_{n_{in}+n_\times+k}(\cdot)$$
$$+ \sum_{k=1}^{n_\times} O_k(\cdot)TV_{n_{in}+2n_\times+k}(\cdot) + TV_{n_{in}+3n_\times+1}(\cdot)$$

   $\mathcal{P}$ commits to the above $n_{in}+3n_\times$ AHE ciphertexts via $\mathcal{F}_{\mathsf{Com}}$ using the handle τ_{ip}, which is then sent to $\mathcal{V}$. $\mathcal{V}$ aborts if he does not receive a handle. $\mathcal{P}$ appends $IP(\cdot)$ into the queue Q_{vanish}.
10. $\mathcal{P}$ constructs a $B\times R$ matrix MK such that for all $i \in [B]$ and $j \in [R]$, $MK_{i,j} = 1$ if $i = id_j$, and 0 otherwise. $\mathcal{P}$ applies the interpolation procedure over MK (see Sect. 3.2) to get polynomials $MK_1(\cdot), \dots, MK_B(\cdot)$. For each $i \in [B]$, $\mathcal{P}$ computes $\left[\!\left[MK_i(\Lambda) - s_i^{(mk)} \right]\!\right]$ by using AH and a VOLE correlation $\left[s_i^{(mk)} \right]$. $\mathcal{P}$ computes $MK_i(\cdot)(MK_i(\cdot)-1)$ and $\left[\!\left[MK_i(\Lambda)(MK_i(\Lambda)-1) - s_i^{(one)} \right]\!\right]$, for each $i \in [B]$, by using additive homomorphism and a VOLE correlation $\left[s_i^{(one)} \right]$; and $\mathcal{P}$ appends the polynomial $MK_i(\cdot)(MK_i(\cdot)-1)$ into the queue Q_{vanish}. $\mathcal{P}$ commits to the above $2B$ AHE ciphertexts via $\mathcal{F}_{\mathsf{Com}}$ using the handle τ_{mk}, which is then sent to $\mathcal{V}$. $\mathcal{V}$ aborts if he does not receive a handle. $\mathcal{V}$ issues a random challenge $\gamma \xleftarrow{\$} \mathbb{F}$, and $\mathcal{P}$ appends the following two polynomials into the queue Q_{vanish}: (1) $\sum_{i=1}^{B} MK_i(\cdot) - 1$ and (2) $\sum_{k=1}^{n_{in}+3n_\times+1} \gamma^{k-1} \cdot TV_k(\cdot) - \sum_{i=1}^{B} h_i \cdot MK_i(\cdot)$ where $h_{i\in[B]} := \left\langle (1,\gamma,\gamma^2,\dots), \boldsymbol{tv}^{(i)} \right\rangle$.

Fig. 6. Justvengers (Part III): ZKP protocol for the batched disjunctive statement over $\mathbb{F}$ in the $\{\mathcal{F}_{\mathsf{Com}}, \mathcal{F}_{\mathsf{VOLE}}\}$-hybrid (Figs. 2 and 3) model.

Protocol $\Pi_{\mathsf{Justvengers}}$, Part IV

Disclosure.

11. $\mathcal{P}$ samples a random vanishing polynomial $PAD(\cdot)$ of degree $2R-2$. Then $\mathcal{P}$ computes $\left[\!\left[PAD(\Lambda) - s^{(pad)}\right]\!\right]$ by using additive homomorphism based on $[\![\Lambda]\!], \ldots, [\![\Lambda^{2R-2}]\!]$ and a VOLE correlation $\left[s^{(pad)}\right]$. $\mathcal{P}$ commits to the above AHE ciphertext via $\mathcal{F}_{\mathsf{Com}}$ using the handle τ_{pad}, which is then sent to $\mathcal{V}$. $\mathcal{V}$ aborts if he does not receive a handle.
12. $\mathcal{V}$ samples a random element $\zeta \xleftarrow{\$} \mathbb{F}$ and sends it to $\mathcal{P}$. Then $\mathcal{P}$ computes and sends the following vanishing polynomial (i.e., its coefficients):
$$VP(\cdot) := PAD(\cdot) + \sum_{f_i(\cdot) \in Q_{\mathsf{vanish}} \text{ in order}} \zeta^i f_i(\cdot)$$
Upon receiving $VP(\cdot)$, $\mathcal{V}$ checks if it is vanishing; if not, he aborts.
13. $\mathcal{V}$ sends $(\mathsf{open}, \tau_{\mathsf{seed}})$ to $\mathcal{F}_{\mathsf{Com}}$, which returns $(\mathsf{seed}, \tau_{\mathsf{seed}})$ to $\mathcal{P}$. In parallel, $\mathcal{V}$ sends Λ to $\mathcal{P}$. If $\mathcal{P}$ does not receive them, she aborts; otherwise, $\mathcal{P}$ expands the PRG $G(\mathsf{seed})$ into a bit string $(r_0, r_1, \ldots, r_{2R-2})$, where r_0 is used for KeyGen and each r_j (for $j \in [2R-2]$) is used for Enc. $\mathcal{P}$ then computes the secret key $\mathsf{sk} := \mathsf{KeyGen}(\mathsf{par}; r_0)$ and checks whether $\forall j \in [2R-2]$, $[\![\Lambda^j]\!] \stackrel{?}{=} \mathsf{Enc}(\mathsf{sk}, \Lambda^j; r_j)$ (i.e., those AHE ciphertexts sent by $\mathcal{V}$ in Step 3); if not, she aborts.

Fig. 7. Justvengers (Part IV): ZKP protocol for the batched disjunctive statement over $\mathbb{F}$ in the $\{\mathcal{F}_{\mathsf{Com}}, \mathcal{F}_{\mathsf{VOLE}}\}$-hybrid (Figs. 2 and 3) model.

Protocol $\Pi_{\mathsf{Justvengers}}$, Part V

Open.

14. $\mathcal{P}$ sends $(\mathsf{open}, \tau_{\mathsf{wit}})$ to $\mathcal{F}_{\mathsf{Com}}$, which returns the $n_{in}+3n_\times$ AHE ciphertexts $\mathcal{P}$ committed to in Step 5. If $\mathcal{V}$ does not receive them, he aborts. Then $\mathcal{V}$ decrypts these ciphertexts. Since $\mathcal{P}$ knows Λ, parties can obtain the following IT-MACs:
$$[IN_1(\Lambda)], \dots, [IN_{n_{in}}(\Lambda)],$$
$$[L_1(\Lambda)], \dots, [L_{n_\times}(\Lambda)], [R_1(\Lambda)], \dots, [R_{n_\times}(\Lambda)], [O_1(\Lambda)], \dots, [O_{n_\times}(\Lambda)]$$
15. $\mathcal{P}$ sends $(\mathsf{open}, \tau_{\mathsf{mul}})$ to $\mathcal{F}_{\mathsf{Com}}$, which returns the $n_\times$ AHE ciphertexts $\mathcal{P}$ committed to in Step 6. If $\mathcal{V}$ does not receive them, he aborts. Then $\mathcal{V}$ decrypts these ciphertexts. Since $\mathcal{P}$ knows Λ, parties can obtain the following IT-MACs:
$$[L_1(\Lambda)R_1(\Lambda)], \dots, [L_{n_\times}(\Lambda)R_{n_\times}(\Lambda)]$$
16. $\mathcal{P}$ sends $(\mathsf{open}, \tau_{\mathsf{tv}})$ to $\mathcal{F}_{\mathsf{Com}}$, which returns the $n_{in}+3n_\times+1$ AHE ciphertexts $\mathcal{P}$ committed to in Step 8. If $\mathcal{V}$ does not receive them, he aborts. Then $\mathcal{V}$ decrypts these ciphertexts. Since $\mathcal{P}$ knows Λ, parties can obtain the following IT-MACs:
$$[TV_1(\Lambda)], \dots, [TV_{n_{in}+3n_\times+1}(\Lambda)]$$
17. $\mathcal{P}$ sends $(\mathsf{open}, \tau_{\mathsf{ip}})$ to $\mathcal{F}_{\mathsf{Com}}$, which returns the $n_{in}+3n_\times$ AHE ciphertexts $\mathcal{P}$ committed to in Step 9. If $\mathcal{V}$ does not receive them, he aborts. Then $\mathcal{V}$ decrypts these ciphertexts. Since $\mathcal{P}$ knows Λ, parties can obtain the following IT-MACs:
$$[IN_1(\Lambda)TV_1(\Lambda)], \dots, [IN_{n_{in}}(\Lambda)TV_{n_{in}}(\Lambda)]$$
$$[L_1(\Lambda)TV_{n_{in}+1}(\Lambda)], \dots, [L_{n_\times}(\Lambda)TV_{n_{in}+n_\times}(\Lambda)]$$
$$[R_1(\Lambda)TV_{n_{in}+n_\times+1}(\Lambda)], \dots, [R_{n_\times}(\Lambda)TV_{n_{in}+2n_\times}(\Lambda)]$$
$$[O_1(\Lambda)TV_{n_{in}+2n_\times+1}(\Lambda)], \dots, [O_{n_\times}(\Lambda)TV_{n_{in}+3n_\times}(\Lambda)]$$
18. $\mathcal{P}$ sends $(\mathsf{open}, \tau_{\mathsf{mk}})$ to $\mathcal{F}_{\mathsf{Com}}$, which returns the $2B$ AHE ciphertexts $\mathcal{P}$ committed to in Step 10. If $\mathcal{V}$ does not receive them, he aborts. Then $\mathcal{V}$ decrypts these ciphertexts. Since $\mathcal{P}$ knows Λ, parties can obtain the following IT-MACs:
$$[MK_1(\Lambda)], \dots, [MK_B(\Lambda)], [MK_1(\Lambda)(MK_1(\Lambda)-1)], \dots, [MK_B(\Lambda)(MK_B(\Lambda)-1)]$$
19. $\mathcal{P}$ sends $(\mathsf{open}, \tau_{\mathsf{pad}})$ to $\mathcal{F}_{\mathsf{Com}}$, which returns one AHE ciphertext $\mathcal{P}$ committed to in Step 11. If $\mathcal{V}$ does not receive them, he aborts. Then $\mathcal{V}$ decrypts these ciphertexts. Since $\mathcal{P}$ knows Λ, parties can obtain the IT-MAC $[PAD(\Lambda)]$.

Fig. 8. Justvengers (Part V): ZKP protocol for the batched disjunctive statement over $\mathbb{F}$ in the $\{\mathcal{F}_{\mathsf{Com}}, \mathcal{F}_{\mathsf{VOLE}}\}$-hybrid (Figs. 2 and 3) model.

Protocol $\Pi_{\mathsf{Justvengers}}$, Part VI

Verification.

20. **Parties verify the opened vanishing polynomial.** Parties *locally* compute the following IT-MAC:

$$
\begin{aligned}
&[PAD(\Lambda)] \\
&+\sum_{k=1}^{n_\times} \zeta^k([L_k(\Lambda)R_k(\Lambda)] - [O_k(\Lambda)]) + \sum_{k=1}^{n_{in}} \zeta^{n_\times+1} [IN_k(\Lambda)TV_k(\Lambda)] \\
&+\sum_{k=1}^{n_\times} \zeta^{n_\times+1} [L_k(\Lambda)TV_{n_{in}+k}(\Lambda)] + \sum_{k=1}^{n_\times} \zeta^{n_\times+1} \left[R_k(\Lambda)TV_{n_{in}+n_\times+k}(\Lambda)\right] \\
&+\sum_{k=1}^{n_\times} \zeta^{n_\times+1} \left[O_k(\Lambda)TV_{n_{in}+2n_\times+k}(\Lambda)\right] + \zeta^{n_\times+1} \left[TV_{n_{in}+3n_\times+1}(\Lambda)\right] \\
&+\sum_{i=1}^{B} \zeta^{n_\times+1+i} [MK_i(\Lambda)(MK_i(\Lambda)-1)] \\
&+\zeta^{n_\times+B+2}\left(\sum_{i=1}^{B} [MK_i(\Lambda)] - 1\right) \\
&+\zeta^{n_\times+B+3}\left(\sum_{k=1}^{n_{in}+3n_\times+1} \gamma^{k-1} [TV_k(\Lambda)] - \sum_{i=1}^{B} h_i [MK_i(\Lambda)]\right)
\end{aligned}
$$

Then $\mathcal{P}$ opens the committed value to $\mathcal{V}$. If the value is not $VP(\Lambda)$, $\mathcal{V}$ aborts.

21. **Parties verify polynomial multiplications.** Parties execute LPZK (see Sect. 2.5) to verify the following multiplication of IT-MAC triples:

$$
\begin{aligned}
&\{[L_k(\Lambda)], [R_k(\Lambda)], [L_k(\Lambda)R_k(\Lambda)]\}_{k\in[n_\times]} \\
&\{[IN_k(\Lambda)], [TV_k(\Lambda)], [IN_k(\Lambda)TV_k(\Lambda)]\}_{k\in[n_{in}]} \\
&\{[L_k(\Lambda)], [TV_{n_{in}+k}(\Lambda)], [L_k(\Lambda)TV_{n_{in}+k}(\Lambda)]\}_{k\in[n_\times]} \\
&\left\{[R_k(\Lambda)], \left[TV_{n_{in}+n_\times+k}(\Lambda)\right], \left[R_k(\Lambda)TV_{n_{in}+n_\times+k}(\Lambda)\right]\right\}_{k\in[n_\times]} \\
&\left\{[O_k(\Lambda)], \left[TV_{n_{in}+2n_\times+k}(\Lambda)\right], \left[O_k(\Lambda)TV_{n_{in}+2n_\times+k}(\Lambda)\right]\right\}_{k\in[n_\times]} \\
&\{[MK_i(\Lambda)], [MK_i(\Lambda)-1], [MK_i(\Lambda)(MK_i(\Lambda)-1)]\}_{i\in[B]}
\end{aligned}
$$

22. **Parties verify committed inputs.** For each $k \in [n_{in}]$, $\mathcal{P}$ proves to $\mathcal{V}$ that $\left[c_{k,0}^{(in)}\right] + \sum_{j=1}^{R-1} \Lambda^j \left[c_{k,j}^{(in)}\right] - [IN_k(\Lambda)]$ commits to a zero.

Output. If $\mathcal{V}$ aborted earlier, he outputs (`false`); otherwise, he outputs (`true`).

Fig. 9. Justvengers (Part VI): ZKP protocol for the batched disjunctive statement over $\mathbb{F}$ in the $\{\mathcal{F}_{\mathsf{Com}}, \mathcal{F}_{\mathsf{VOLE}}\}$-hybrid (Figs. 2 and 3) model.

4.2 Analysis and Variants

In this section, we present the main theorem. Due to space constraints, we defer its simulation-based proof to the full version. We also analyze $\Pi_{\mathsf{Justvengers}}$'s efficiency and discuss several variants that trade off between (concrete) efficiency, underlying assumptions, and soundness error.

Theorem 1 (main). *If the* AHE *scheme satisfies the CPA security, circuit privacy, and linear targeted malleability along with G is a pseudorandom generator,* $\Pi_{\mathsf{Justvengers}}$ *(Figs. 4 and 9) UC-realizes* $\mathcal{F}_{\mathsf{ZK}}^{R,B}$ *(Fig. 1) in the* $\{\mathcal{F}_{\mathsf{Com}}, \mathcal{F}_{\mathsf{VOLE}}\}$*-hybrid model (Figs. 2 and 3) in the presence of a static adversary.*

Cost Analysis. We tally the cost of Justvengers:

- **$\mathcal{F}_{\mathsf{Com}}$ Hybrid**: $\mathcal{V}$ commits to and opens λ bits whereas $\mathcal{P}$ commits to and opens $2B+3n_{in}+10n_\times+2$ AHE ciphertexts.
- **$\mathcal{F}_{\mathsf{VOLE}}$ Hybrid**: Generating $Rn_{in}+2B+3n_{in}+10n_\times+3$ VOLE correlations.
- **Communication**: Besides hybrid calls, $\mathcal{V}$ sends $2R-2$ AHE ciphertexts and 5 $\mathbb{F}$ elements (including one implicitly used in the LPZK check) whereas $\mathcal{P}$ sends Rn_{in} $\mathbb{F}$ elements to commits input coefficients, $2R-1$ $\mathbb{F}$ elements to open the aggregated vanishing polynomial, and $n_{in}+3$ $\mathbb{F}$ elements as proofs in the verification phase.
  Clearly, if $n_{in} = \mathcal{O}(1)$, the total communication is $\mathcal{O}(R+B+C)$ even in the plain model by assuming the hardness of LPN (Lemma 2 and see [WYY+22] for how to efficiently instantiate AHE and $\mathcal{F}_{\mathsf{Com}}$).
- **Round**: Justvengers clearly achieves constant-round complexity.
- **$\mathcal{P}$'s Computation**: The dominant cost in $\mathcal{P}$'s computation arises from two sources: (1) $\mathcal{O}(BC)$ field operations to generate the B topology vectors, as described in Batchman, and (2) NTT-based polynomial interpolation as in Antman. Since each polynomial has degree $\mathcal{O}(R)$, interpolation requires $\mathcal{O}(R \log R)$ field operations per polynomial. With a total of $\mathcal{O}(B+C)$ polynomials to generate, the overall computational complexity for $\mathcal{P}$ is $\mathcal{O}(BC + (B+C)R\log R)$ field operations.
- **$\mathcal{V}$'s Computation**: The dominant cost in $\mathcal{V}$'s computation arises from two sources: (1) $\mathcal{O}(BC)$ field operations to generate the B topology vectors, as described in Batchman, and (2) $\mathcal{O}(R \log R)$ field operations to verify that the degree-$\mathcal{O}(R)$ polynomial $VP(\cdot)$ vanishes at R points via NTT. Thus, the overall computational complexity for $\mathcal{V}$ is $\mathcal{O}(BC + R\log R)$ field operations.

Variants. We present two variants of our protocol that may offer practical improvements, while preserving the same asymptotic complexity:

1. **Replacing Each Powers Vector with a Uniform Vector**: In our construction, $\mathcal{V}$ uses a uniform field element and its powers to define the linear combination challenge (i.e., via universal hashing). Alternatively, $\mathcal{V}$ can sample and send a fully uniform vector to perform the linear combination. While this increases communication, it decreases the soundness error. This is a common technique, as discussed in both Antman [WYY+22] and Batchman [YHH+23a].

2. **Leveraging a Random Oracle:** The linear combination can alternatively be derived by expanding a PRG seed (modeled as a random oracle). This reduces communication overhead but introduces an additional soundness error term associated with the use of the RO. This is again a common technique, as discussed in both Antman [WYY+22] and Batchman [YHH+23a]. An additional communication optimization can be achieved using a random oracle. Specifically, checking that a set of IT-MACs are zero can be reduced to computing a running hash—$\mathcal{P}$ only needs to send the final digest rather than individual zero proofs. This technique, known as the CheckZero procedure in Antman [WYY+22], is a standard optimization used in nearly all VOLE-based ZK protocols (and beyond, such as SPDZ MPC [DPSZ12]).

4.3 Soldering Repetitions

Recall that a batched disjunctive statement is uninformative if the witnesses across repetitions are uncorrelated—if $\mathcal{P}$ can prove a single repetition, simply reusing the same witness across all R instances offers no meaningful guarantee. This has concrete implications—e.g., when using the batched disjunctive statements to model a sequence of CPU steps, the instruction executed in each step depends on the results of prior computation, requiring (extended) witness consistency across repetitions.

In this section, we show how Justvengers can support this by showing how a concrete correlated constraint can be supported. $\mathcal{P}$ aims to prove to $\mathcal{V}$ in ZK that, for each $j \in [R] \setminus \{1\}$, the first input of the j-th repetition is equal to the first multiplication output of the $(j-1)$-th repetition.

Casting this to polynomial encodings, this means $\mathcal{P}$ has to prove in ZK that

$$\forall j \in [R] \setminus \{1\}, IN_1(\alpha_j) = O_1(\alpha_{j-1})$$

This type of cross-repetition constraint can be handled using the "sacrifice" technique [DPSZ12]. In particular, $\mathcal{P}$ generates two random polynomials $r_1(\cdot)$ and $r_2(\cdot)$ such that the desired relation holds over them. Then, $\mathcal{P}$ reveals the one-time padded polynomials $\phi IN_1(\cdot) + r_1(\cdot)$ and $\phi O_1(\cdot) + r_2(\cdot)$ to $\mathcal{V}$, who issues a uniform $\phi \xleftarrow{\$} \mathbb{F}$ and verifies that the revealed two polynomials satisfy the intended constraint. ZK is ensured by the random padding.

We note that this "sacrifice" technique is also exploited by Antman, and in fact, Justvengers implicitly applies it in the batched vanishing polynomial check.

Acknowledgments. This work is supported in part by the Visa research award and the NSF awards CNS-2246354, and CCF-2217070. The author sincerely thanks David Heath and Chenkai Weng for their insightful discussions and valuable feedback, as well as the TCC'25 reviewers for their thoughtful and constructive comments.

References

[BBD+23] Baum, C., et al.: Publicly verifiable zero-knowledge and post-quantum signatures from VOLE-in-the-head. In: Handschuh, H., Lysyanskaya, A. (eds.) CRYPTO 2023, Part V. LNCS, vol. 14085, pp. 581–615. Springer, Cham (2023). https://doi.org/10.1007/978-3-031-38554-4_19

[BBMH+21] Baum, C., Braun, L., Munch-Hansen, A., Razet, B., Scholl, P.: Appenzeller to brie: efficient zero-knowledge proofs for mixed-mode arithmetic and Z2k. In: Vigna, G., Shi, E. (eds.) ACM CCS 2021, pp. 192–211. ACM Press (2021)

[BBMHS22] Baum, C., Braun, L., Munch-Hansen, A., Scholl, P.: Moz$\mathbb{Z}_{2^k}$arella: efficient vector-OLE and zero-knowledge proofs over $\mathbb{Z}_{2^k}$. In: Dodis, Y., Shrimpton, T. (eds.) CRYPTO 2022, Part IV. LNCS, vol. 13510, pp. 329–358. Springer, Cham (2022). https://doi.org/10.1007/978-3-031-15985-5_12

[BCC+24] Bui, D., et al.: An efficient ZK compiler from SIMD circuits to general circuits. J. Cryptol. **38**(1), 10 (2024)

[BCG+14] Ben-Sasson, E., et al.: Zerocash: decentralized anonymous payments from bitcoin. In: 2014 IEEE Symposium on Security and Privacy, pp. 459–474. IEEE Computer Society Press (2014)

[BCG+19] Boyle, E., Couteau, G., Gilboa, N., Ishai, Y., Kohl, L., Scholl, P.: Efficient pseudorandom correlation generators: silent OT extension and more. In: Boldyreva, A., Micciancio, D. (eds.) CRYPTO 2019, Part III. LNCS, vol. 11694, pp. 489–518. Springer, Cham (2019). https://doi.org/10.1007/978-3-030-26954-8_16

[BCGI18] Boyle, E., Couteau, G., Gilboa, N., Ishai, Y.: Compressing vector OLE. In: Lie, D., Mannan, M., Backes, M., Wang, X. (eds.) ACM CCS 2018, pp. 896–912. ACM Press (2018)

[BCI+22] Bitansky, N., Chiesa, A., Ishai, Y., Ostrovsky, R., Paneth, O.: Succinct non-interactive arguments via linear interactive proofs. J. Cryptol. **35**(3), 15 (2022)

[BDOZ11] Bendlin, R., Damgård, I., Orlandi, C., Zakarias, S.: Semi-homomorphic encryption and multiparty computation. In: Paterson, K.G. (ed.) EUROCRYPT 2011. LNCS, vol. 6632, pp. 169–188. Springer, Heidelberg (2011). https://doi.org/10.1007/978-3-642-20465-4_11

[BDSW23] Baum, C., Dittmer, S., Scholl, P., Wang, X.: SoK: vector OLE-based zero-knowledge protocols. DCC **91**(11), 3527–3561 (2023)

[Bea95] Beaver, D.: Precomputing oblivious transfer. In: Coppersmith, D. (ed.) CRYPTO 1995. LNCS, vol. 963, pp. 97–109. Springer, Heidelberg (1995). https://doi.org/10.1007/3-540-44750-4_8

[BFKL94] Blum, A., Furst, M., Kearns, M., Lipton, R.J.: Cryptographic primitives based on hard learning problems. In: Stinson, D.R. (ed.) CRYPTO 1993. LNCS, vol. 773, pp. 278–291. Springer, Heidelberg (1994). https://doi.org/10.1007/3-540-48329-2_24

[BGV12] Brakerski, Z., Gentry, C., Vaikuntanathan, V.: (Leveled) fully homomorphic encryption without bootstrapping. In: Goldwasser, S. (ed.) ITCS 2012, pp. 309–325. ACM (2012)

[BMRS21] Baum, C., Malozemoff, A.J., Rosen, M.B., Scholl, P.: Mac'n'Cheese: zero-knowledge proofs for boolean and arithmetic circuits with nested disjunctions. In: Malkin, T., Peikert, C. (eds.) CRYPTO 2021. LNCS, vol.

12828, pp. 92–122. Springer, Cham (2021). https://doi.org/10.1007/978-3-030-84259-8_4

[Can01] Canetti, R.: Universally composable security: a new paradigm for cryptographic protocols. In: 42nd FOCS, pp. 136–145. IEEE Computer Society Press (2001)

[CDS94] Cramer, R., Damgård, I., Schoenmakers, B.: Proofs of partial knowledge and simplified design of witness hiding protocols. In: Desmedt, Y.G. (ed.) CRYPTO 1994. LNCS, vol. 839, pp. 174–187. Springer, Heidelberg (1994). https://doi.org/10.1007/3-540-48658-5_19

[DEGL+23] Dittmer, S., et al.: Boosting the performance of high-assurance cryptography: parallel execution and optimizing memory access in formally-verified line-point zero-knowledge. In: Meng, W., Jensen, C.D., Cremers, C., Kirda, E. (eds.) ACM CCS 2023, pp. 2098–2112. ACM Press (2023)

[DILO22] Dittmer, S., Ishai, Y., Lu, S., Ostrovsky, R.: Improving line-point zero knowledge: two multiplications for the price of one. In: Yin, H., Stavrou, A., Cremers, C., Shi, E. (eds.) ACM CCS 2022, pp. 829–841. ACM Press (2022)

[DIO21] Dittmer, S., Ishai, Y., Ostrovsky, R.: Line-point zero knowledge and its applications. In: Tessaro, S. (ed.) ITC 2021. LIPIcs, vol. 199, pp. 5:1–5:24. Schloss Dagstuhl (2021)

[DL78] DeMillo, R.A., Lipton, R.J.: A probabilistic remark on algebraic program testing. Inf. Process. Lett. **7**(4), 193–195 (1978)

[DPSZ12] Damgård, I., Pastro, V., Smart, N., Zakarias, S.: Multiparty computation from somewhat homomorphic encryption. In: Safavi-Naini, R., Canetti, R. (eds.) CRYPTO 2012. LNCS, vol. 7417, pp. 643–662. Springer, Heidelberg (2012). https://doi.org/10.1007/978-3-642-32009-5_38

[FDNZ21] Fang, Z., Darais, D., Near, J.P., Zhang, Y.: Zero knowledge static program analysis. In: Vigna, G., Shi, E. (eds.) ACM CCS 2021, pp. 2951–2967. ACM Press (2021)

[GGHAK22] Goel, A., Green, M., Hall-Andersen, M., Kaptchuk, G.: Stacking sigmas: a framework to compose Σ-protocols for disjunctions. In: Dunkelman, O., Dziembowski, S. (eds.) EUROCRYPT 2022, Part II. LNCS, vol. 13276, pp. 458–487. Springer, Cham (2022). https://doi.org/10.1007/978-3-031-07085-3_16

[GHAK24] Goel, A., Hall-Andersen, M., Kaptchuk, G.: Dora: a simple approach to zero-knowledge for RAM programs. In: Luo, B., Liao, X., Xu, J., Kirda, E., Lie, D. (eds.) ACM CCS 2024, pp. 869–883. ACM Press (2024)

[GHAKS23] Goel, A., Hall-Andersen, M., Kaptchuk, G., Spooner, N.: Speed-stacking: fast sublinear zero-knowledge proofs for disjunctions. In: Hazay, C., Stam, M. (eds.) EUROCRYPT 2023, Part II. LNCS, vol. 14005, pp. 347–378. Springer, Cham (2023). https://doi.org/10.1007/978-3-031-30617-4_12

[GMR85] Goldwasser, S., Micali, S., Rackoff, C.: The knowledge complexity of interactive proof-systems (extended abstract). In: 17th ACM STOC, pp. 291–304. ACM Press (1985)

[HHK+24] Hazay, C., Heath, D., Kolesnikov, V., Venkitasubramaniam, M., Yang, Y.: LogRobin++: optimizing proofs of disjunctive statements in VOLE-based ZK. In: Chung, K.-M., Sasaki, Yu. (eds.) ASIACRYPT 2024, Part V. LNCS, vol. 15488, pp. 367–401. Springer, Singapore (2024). https://doi.org/10.1007/978-981-96-0935-2_12

[HK20] Heath, D., Kolesnikov, V.: Stacked garbling for disjunctive zero-knowledge proofs. In: Canteaut, A., Ishai, Y. (eds.) EUROCRYPT 2020. LNCS, vol. 12107, pp. 569–598. Springer, Cham (2020). https://doi.org/10.1007/978-3-030-45727-3_19

[HY24] Hazay, C., Yang, Y.: Toward malicious constant-rate 2PC via arithmetic garbling. In: Joye, M., Leander, G. (eds.) EUROCRYPT 2024, Part V. LNCS, vol. 14655, pp. 401–431. Springer, Cham (2024). https://doi.org/10.1007/978-3-031-58740-5_14

[HYDK21] Heath, D., Yang, Y., Devecsery, D., Kolesnikov, V.: Zero knowledge for everything and everyone: fast ZK processor with cached ORAM for ANSI C programs. In: 2021 IEEE Symposium on Security and Privacy, pp. 1538–1556. IEEE Computer Society Press (2021)

[IOS23] Ishai, Y., Ostrovsky, R., Shah, A.: Succinct arguments for RAM programs via projection codes. In: Handschuh, H., Lysyanskaya, A. (eds.) CRYPTO 2023, Part II. LNCS, vol. 14082, pp. 159–192. Springer, Cham (2023). https://doi.org/10.1007/978-3-031-38545-2_6

[IOS25] Ishai, Y., Ostrovsky, R., Shah, A.: Zero-knowledge RAM: doubly efficient and black-box. In: Fehr, S., Fouque, P.-A. (eds.) EUROCRYPT 2025, Part IV. LNCS, vol. 15604, pp. 363–395. Springer, Cham (2025). https://doi.org/10.1007/978-3-031-91134-7_13

[IP07] Ishai, Y., Paskin, A.: Evaluating branching programs on encrypted data. In: Vadhan, S.P. (ed.) TCC 2007. LNCS, vol. 4392, pp. 575–594. Springer, Heidelberg (2007). https://doi.org/10.1007/978-3-540-70936-7_31

[JKO13] Jawurek, M., Kerschbaum, F., Orlandi, C.: Zero-knowledge using garbled circuits: how to prove non-algebraic statements efficiently. In: Sadeghi, A.-R., Gligor, V.D., Yung, M. (eds.) ACM CCS 2013, pp. 955–966. ACM Press (2013)

[KPR18] Keller, M., Pastro, V., Rotaru, D.: Overdrive: making SPDZ great again. In: Nielsen, J.B., Rijmen, V. (eds.) EUROCRYPT 2018. LNCS, vol. 10822, pp. 158–189. Springer, Cham (2018). https://doi.org/10.1007/978-3-319-78372-7_6

[KZG10] Kate, A., Zaverucha, G.M., Goldberg, I.: Constant-size commitments to polynomials and their applications. In: Abe, M. (ed.) ASIACRYPT 2010. LNCS, vol. 6477, pp. 177–194. Springer, Heidelberg (2010). https://doi.org/10.1007/978-3-642-17373-8_11

[LAH+22] Luo, N., Antonopoulos, T., Harris, W. R., Piskac, R., Tromer, E., Wang, X.: Proving UNSAT in zero knowledge. In: Yin, H., Stavrou, A., Cremers, C., Shi, E. (eds.) ACM CCS 2022, pp. 2203–2217. ACM Press (2022)

[LHLA25] Liu, M., Heng, Y., Lu, X., Au, M.H.: JesseQ: efficient zero-knowledge proofs for circuits over any field . In: 2025 IEEE Symposium on Security and Privacy (SP), Los Alamitos, CA, USA, pp. 3161–3179. IEEE Computer Society (2025)

[LJA+22] Luo, N., Judson, S., Antonopoulos, T., Piskac, R., Wang, X.: ppSAT: towards two-party private SAT solving. In: Butler, K.R.B., Thomas, K. (eds.) USENIX Security 2022, pp. 2983–3000. USENIX Association (2022)

[LKA+24] Luick, D., et al.: ZKSMT: a VM for proving SMT theorems in zero knowledge. In: Balzarotti, D., Xu, W. (eds.) USENIX Security 2024. USENIX Association (2024)

[LWS+24] Luo, N., Weng, C., Singh, J., Tan, G., Raykova, M., Piskac, R.: Privacy-preserving regular expression matching using TNFA. In: Garcia-Alfaro, J., Kozik, R., Choraś, M., Katsikas, S. (eds.) ESORICS 2024, Part II. LNCS, vol. 14983, pp. 225–246. Springer, Cham (2024). https://doi.org/10.1007/978-3-031-70890-9_12

[LWX+23] Li, X., Weng, C., Yongxin, X., Wang, X., Rogers, J.: Zksql: verifiable and efficient query evaluation with zero-knowledge proofs. Proc. VLDB Endow. **16**(8), 1804–1816 (2023)

[LXY24a] Lin, F., Xing, C., Yao, Y.: Interactive line-point zero-knowledge with sublinear communication and linear computation. In: Chung, K.-M., Sasaki, Yu. (eds.) ASIACRYPT 2024, Part V. LNCS, vol. 15488, pp. 337–366. Springer, Singapore (2024). https://doi.org/10.1007/978-981-96-0935-2_11

[LXY24b] Lin, F., Xing, C., Yao, Y.: More efficient zero-knowledge protocols over $\mathbb{Z}_{2^k}$ via Galois rings. In: Reyzin, L., Stebila, D. (eds.) CRYPTO 2024, Part IX. LNCS, vol. 14928, pp. 424–457. Springer, Cham (2024). https://doi.org/10.1007/978-3-031-68400-5_13

[LXZ21] Liu, T., Xie, X., Zhang, Y.: zkCNN: zero knowledge proofs for convolutional neural network predictions and accuracy. In: Vigna, G., Shi, E. (eds.) ACM CCS 2021, pp. 2968–2985. ACM Press (2021)

[NNOB12] Nielsen, J.B., Nordholt, P.S., Orlandi, C., Burra, S.S.: A new approach to practical active-secure two-party computation. In: Safavi-Naini, R., Canetti, R. (eds.) CRYPTO 2012. LNCS, vol. 7417, pp. 681–700. Springer, Heidelberg (2012). https://doi.org/10.1007/978-3-642-32009-5_40

[Sch80] Schwartz, J.T.: Fast probabilistic algorithms for verification of polynomial identities. J. ACM (JACM) **27**(4), 701–717 (1980)

[SGRR19] Schoppmann, P., Gascón, A., Reichert, L., Raykova, M.: Distributed vector-OLE: improved constructions and implementation. In: Cavallaro, L., Kinder, J., Wang, X., Katz, J. (eds.) ACM CCS 2019, pp. 1055–1072. ACM Press (2019)

[WYKW21] Weng, C., Yang, K., Katz, J., Wang, X.: Wolverine: fast, scalable, and communication-efficient zero-knowledge proofs for boolean and arithmetic circuits. In: 2021 IEEE Symposium on Security and Privacy, pp. 1074–1091. IEEE Computer Society Press (2021)

[WYX+21] Weng, C., Yang, K., Xie, X., Katz, J., Wang, X.: Mystique: efficient conversions for zero-knowledge proofs with applications to machine learning. In: Bailey, M., Greenstadt, R. (eds.) USENIX Security 2021, pp. 501–518. USENIX Association (2021)

[WYY+22] Weng, C., Yang, K., Yang, Z., Xie, X., Wang, X.: AntMan: interactive zero-knowledge proofs with sublinear communication. In: Yin, H., Stavrou, A., Cremers, C., Shi, E. (eds.) ACM CCS 2022, pp. 2901–2914. ACM Press (2022)

[Yan25] Yang, Y.: Justvengers: batched VOLE ZK disjunctions in $\mathcal{O}(R+B+C)$ communication. Cryptology ePrint Archive, Paper 2025/936 (2025)

[Yao86] Yao, A.C.-C.: How to generate and exchange secrets (extended abstract). In: 27th FOCS, pp. 162–167. IEEE Computer Society Press (1986)

[YH24] Yang, Y., Heath, D.: Two shuffles make a RAM: improved constant overhead zero knowledge RAM. In: Balzarotti, D., Xu, W. (eds.) USENIX Security 2024. USENIX Association (2024)

[YHH+23a] Yang, Y., Heath, D., Hazay, C., Kolesnikov, V., Venkitasubramaniam, M.: Batchman and robin: batched and non-batched branching for interactive ZK. In: Meng, W., Jensen, C.D., Cremers, C., Kirda, E. (eds.) ACM CCS 2023, pp. 1452–1466. ACM Press (2023)

[YHH+23b] Yang, Y., Heath, D., Hazay, C., Kolesnikov, V., Venkitasubramaniam, M.: Batchman and robin: batched and non-batched branching for interactive ZK. Cryptology ePrint Archive, Report 2023/1257 (2023)

[YHH+24] Yang, Y., Heath, D., Hazay, C., Kolesnikov, V., Venkitasubramaniam, M.: Tight ZK CPU: batched ZK branching with cost proportional to evaluated instruction. In: Luo, B., Liao, X., Xu, J., Kirda, E., Lie, D. (eds.) ACM CCS 2024, pp. 3095–3109. ACM Press (2024)

[YHKD22] Yang, Y., Heath, D., Kolesnikov, V., Devecsery, D.: EZEE: epoch parallel zero knowledge for ANSI C. In: 2022 IEEE European Symposium on Security and Privacy, pp. 109–123. IEEE Computer Society Press (2022)

[YSWW21] Yang, K., Sarkar, P., Weng, C., Wang, X.: QuickSilver: efficient and affordable zero-knowledge proofs for circuits and polynomials over any field. In: Vigna, G., Shi, E. (eds.) ACM CCS 2021, pp. 2986–3001. ACM Press (2021)

[YWL+20] Yang, K., Weng, C., Lan, X., Zhang, J., Wang, X.: Ferret: fast extension for correlated OT with small communication. In: Ligatti, J., Ou, X., Katz, J., Vigna, G. (eds.) ACM CCS 2020, pp. 1607–1626. ACM Press (2020)

[Zip79] Zippel, R.: Probabilistic algorithms for sparse polynomials. In: International Symposium on Symbolic and Algebraic Manipulation, pp. 216–226. Springer (1979)

Four-Round Statistical Non-malleable Zero-Knowledge

Susumu Kiyoshima(✉)

NTT Social Informatics Laboratories, Tokyo, Japan
susumu.kiyoshima@ntt.com

Abstract. We present a 4-round statistical non-malleable zero-knowledge (NMZK) argument in the plain model under standard hardness assumptions. Our construction can be based on any collision-resistant hash function and injective one-way function, and it guarantees simulation extractability in the delayed-input one-many setting. Before this work, 4-round constructions were known for computational NMZK but not for statistical NMZK.

1 Introduction

Non-malleable Zero-Knowledge. *Non-malleable zero-knowledge* (NMZK) [14] is a notion of zero-knowledge defined in man-in-the-middle settings. In the most basic setting, NMZK is defined against an adversary that interacts with an honest prover and an honest verifier, and the goal is to guarantee that the interaction with the prover does not help the adversary prove a related statement to the verifier. In a work by Pass and Rosen [40], this goal is formalized by requiring the existence of a *simulator-extractor*, which simulates the adversary's view while also extracting a witness for the statement that the adversary proves. The rationale behind this formalization is that given such a simulator-extractor, a stand-alone simulator can prove the same statement as the man-in-the-middle adversary by using the extracted witness.

A central topic that has been extensively studied about NMZK is the round complexity. Regarding the asymptotic round complexity, the initial construction by Dolev, Dwork, and Naor [14] has logarithmic round complexity, and Barak [1] achieved asymptotically optimal round complexity by providing a constant-round construction using sub-exponentially hard collision-resistant hash functions. Soon after, Pass and Rosen [40] gave a constant-round construction using standard (polynomially hard) collision-resistant hash functions. Finally, Goyal [19] and Lin and Pass [31] gave constant-round constructions using one-way functions. Regarding the exact round complexity, Goyal et al. [23] gave a 4-round construction using one-way functions. (Having 4 rounds is optimal even for non-NM zero-knowledge proof/arguments in the case of black-box zero-knowledge [18].) Ciampi et al. [10] gave a 4-round construction in the *delayed-input setting* using collision-resistant hash functions. (In the delayed-input setting, the statement to be proven is determined in the last round of the protocol.)

B. Applebaum and H. Lin (Eds.): TCC 2025, LNCS 16271, pp. 138–170, 2026.
https://doi.org/10.1007/978-3-032-12290-2_5

Finally, Ciampi et al. [8] gave a 4-round construction in the delayed-input, *one-many* setting using one-way functions. (In the one-many setting, the adversary interacts with a single prover and polynomially many verifiers).

Statistical Non-malleable Zero-Knowledge. *Statistical non-malleable zero-knowledge (SNMZK)* is a version of NMZK where the simulated view must be statistically close to the real view.[1] It naturally inherits strong security guarantees from statistical ZK in the stand-alone setting. (For example, security is not compromised even if the underlying hardness assumptions are broken after the protocol executions [34][2].)

It is known that asymptotically optimal round complexity can be achieved even in the case of SNMZK. Indeed, the aforementioned constant-round construction by Pass and Rosen [40] guarantees SNMZK, and their construction can be extended to satisfy SNMZK in the one-many setting [39]. However, the exact round complexity of SNMZK arguments remains largely unexplored. In particular, whether 4-round SNMZK arguments can be obtained under standard cryptographic assumptions is unknown.

1.1 Our Result

We present the following result regarding 4-round SNMZK arguments.

Theorem (informal). *Assume the existence of collision-resistant hash functions and injective one-way functions. Then, there exists a statistical non-malleable zero-knowledge argument in the delayed-input, one-many setting.*

This result is obtained using black-box simulation techniques. Thus, like prior results on 4-round computational NMZK [8,10,23], this result matches the 4-round lower bound of black-box ZK. An interesting question left open by this result is whether a 4-round SNMZK argument can be constructed from collision-resistant hash functions (without additionally relying on injective one-way functions).

1.2 Additional Related Work

Let us review additional related work that studies NMZK in the plain model (i.e., the model where trusted setups like common reference strings are unavailable).

Concurrent non-malleable zero-Knowledge (concurrent NMZK) [2] is a version of NMZK where man-in-the-middle adversaries can interact with polynomially many provers and verifiers. Concurrent NMZK has been extensively studied [2,30,32,36,41], and there even exist works that achieve *statistical concurrent non-malleable zero-knowledge* [27,35]. However, the exact round complexity of concurrent NMZK remains largely unexplored. A major obstacle is that even

[1] The man-in-the-middle adversary is restricted to a probabilistic polynomial-time machine, and only the distinguisher is computationally unbounded.

[2] To break computational soundness, cheating provers need to break the underlying hardness assumptions during protocol executions.

obtaining constant-round concurrent (non-NM) zero-knowledge arguments currently requires strong hardness assumptions (e.g., those on which the existence of indistinguishability obfuscation can be based) [5,6,16,37].

Some recent works have investigated NMZK with practical efficiency [3,26]. This paper focuses on establishing a feasibility result and does not aim to optimize practical efficiency.

2 Technical Overview

2.1 Overall Approach

We begin by outlining the main challenge in constructing 4-round SNMZK arguments. Recall that in the definition of NMZK, a simulator-extractor must simulate the man-in-the-middle adversary's view while also extracting a witness for the statement that the adversary proves.[3] We call the interaction between the honest prover and the adversary the *left interaction*, and the interaction between the adversary and the honest verifier the *right interaction*.

The main tool used in the existing 4-round computational NMZK arguments [8,10,23] is *non-malleable (NM) commitment schemes* [14]. At a high level, NM commitment schemes guarantee that when a man-in-the-middle adversary interacts with an honest sender and an honest receiver, the value committed to by the adversary is independent of the value committed to by the honest sender. In this technical overview, we adopt the following (slightly stronger) CCA-style definition: any adversary cannot break the hiding property even given access to computationally unbounded "committed-value oracle" (which interacts with the adversary as a receiver and then returns the adversary the committed value of the commitment that the adversary provides).

What is common in the existing 4-round computational NMZK arguments is that NM commitments are made by the prover. In particular, in the existing 4-round computational NMZK arguments, NM commitments are made by the prover in a way that different values are committed in the real execution and the simulation. For example, in the constructions of [10,23], a witness for the statement is committed to in the real execution while a junk value (such as an all-0 string) is committed to in the simulation. At a very high level, when the prover makes NM commitments in this way, NMZK can be argued as follows. Suppose a man-in-the-middle adversary proves the validity of a statement in the right interaction by committing to a valid witness in an NM commitment. Then, the non-malleability of the NM commitment guarantees that when the left interaction is switched to simulation (and therefore the committed value of the NM commitment is switched to a junk value in the left interaction), the adversary continues to commit to a valid witness in the right interaction. Thus,

[3] In this overview, we focus on the one-one NMZK setting (where the adversary interacts with an honest prover and an honest verifier) rather than the one-many NMZK setting (where the adversary interacts with an honest prover and polynomially many honest verifiers).

a desired simulator-extractor can be obtained by considering a simulator that extracts the committed value of the NM commitment in the right interaction.

A challenge we face is that using NM commitment schemes in this way inherently prevents the simulation from being statistically indistinguishable. Specifically, the problem is that NM commitment schemes must be statistically binding by definition.[4] When a different value is committed in the real execution and the simulation, a computationally unbounded distinguisher can easily distinguish them by extracting the committed values of the NM commitments by brute force.

Fortunately, this problem has already been addressed in the context of asymptotically round-efficient statistical concurrent NMZK arguments [27]. At a high level, the idea is to have the verifier make NM commitments (rather than having the prover do so).[5] When only the verifier makes NM commitments, the statistical binding of the NM commitments is unproblematic for statistical simulation. Furthermore, by having the verifier make NM commitments in a trapdoor generation phase (where a trapdoor is set up for simulation), we can guarantee that the left and right interactions have independent trapdoors. This property can be used to obtain a desired simulator-extractor by showing that any man-in-the-middle adversary cannot cheat in the right interaction even when the left interaction is simulated using the trapdoor.

Naturally, our approach to 4-round SNMZK involves combining this technique with those developed for 4-round computational NMZK arguments.

2.2 Constant-Round Construction

First, we describe our construction without optimizing its round complexity. The starting point is the well-known approach by Feige and Shamir [15] for round-efficient ZK arguments. Recall that, in the case of statistical ZK, the Feige–Shamir approach can be implemented using following three components: a one-way permutation (OWP), a witness-indistinguishable proof of knowledge (WIPOK), and a statistically witness-indistinguishable argument of knowledge (SWIAOK).[6] Since our approach is to have the verifier make NM commitments, we consider combining the first two components with NM commitment schemes. Concretely, we consider the following construction for statement $x \in \mathbf{L}$.

1. **Trapdoor generation.** The verifier uses an NM commitment scheme twice to commit to two random strings, r_0 and r_1. Let i-τ_0 and i-τ_1 be the resulting commitments. Let dec_0 and dec_1 be the corresponding decommitments.
2. **Verifier proof.** The verifier uses the NM commitment scheme twice to commit to dec_0 and dec_1, resulting in two commitments, o-τ_0 and o-τ_1. Then,

[4] Non-malleability is not well-defined unless the value committed to by the adversary is uniquely determined.

[5] The idea of having the verifier make NM commitments has also been used for computational NMZK and a related primitive, for different purposes from ours [3,4,25].

[6] For simplicity, we focus on the case that the latter two satisfy *special soundness*. That is, a valid witness can be extracted from any two accepting transcripts if their commit messages are identical and their challenge messages are different.

the verifier uses a WIPOK system to prove knowledge of $\beta \in \{0,1\}$ and $\mathsf{dec} \in \{0,1\}^*$ such that (i) dec is a valid decommitment of i-τ_β and (ii) o-τ_β is a correct commitment to dec. (The witness used by the verifier is chosen randomly from $(0, \mathsf{dec}_0)$ or $(1, \mathsf{dec}_1)$.)
3. **Prover proof.** The prover uses an SWIAOK system to prove $x \in \mathbf{L}$ or knowledge of a valid decommitment of i-τ_b for some $b \in \{0,1\}$.

In the following, we call the NM commitments in the trapdoor generation phase the *inner NM commitments*, and the NM commitments in the verifier proof phase the *outer NM commitments.*

Case 1: NMZK in Asynchronous Message Scheduling. As a warm-up, let us analyze SNMZK in the setting where the messages in the left and right interactions are scheduled as shown in Fig. 1 (left). Consider a natural simulator-extractor that (i) simulates the left interaction using the extractor of the WIPOK system to obtain a witness for the SWIAOK system and (ii) extracts a witness for the statement in the right interaction using the extractor of the SWIAOK system. Statistical indistinguishability of the simulation can be shown in the standard manner by relying on the knowledge soundness of the WIPOK system and the statistical WI of the SWIAOK system. Regarding witness extractability, assume for contradiction that the simulator-extractor fails to extract a witness for the statement in the right interaction with non-negligible probability. Then, the knowledge soundness of the SWIAOK system guarantees that a valid decommitment of one of the two inner NM commitments is extracted with non-negligible probability. In addition, the witness indistinguishability of the WIPOK system guarantees that $\exists \widetilde{\beta}^* \in \{0,1\}$ s.t. the following event, BAD, occurs with non-negligible probability.

- **Event Bad:** The WIPOK system in the right interaction is completed using the decommitment of the $\widetilde{\beta}^*$-th inner NMCom commitment as the witness, and the simulator-extractor extracts a valid decommitment of the $(1-\widetilde{\beta}^*)$-th inner NM commitment in the SWIAOK system.

That is, with non-negligible probability, the extracted decommitment is for the inner NM commitment that was not used to complete the WIPOK system. Furthermore, since the simulator-extractor simulates the left interaction by using a decommitment of one of the two inner NM commitments, it follows from an averaging argument that $\exists b^* \in \{0,1\}$ such that with non-negligible probability, BAD occurs while the simulator-extractor simulates the left interaction using a decommitment of the b^*-th inner NM commitment. Then, consider the following hybrid experiments.

- In the first hybrid, the witness used for SWIAOK in the left interaction is obtained by extracting the committed value of the b^*-th outer NM commitment by brute force (rather than using the extractor of the WIPOK system). Note that when the simulator-extractor obtains a decommitment of the b^*-th inner NM commitment from the extractor of the WIPOK system, the

knowledge soundness of the WIPOK system guarantees that the same decommitment must be committed in the b^*-th outer NM commitment (and thus can be extracted by brute force). Thus, even in this hybrid, BAD occurs with non-negligible probability.
– In the second hybrid, the value committed in the $(1 - \widetilde{\beta}^*)$-th outer NM commitment in the right interaction is switched to an all-0 string.
The (CCA-style) non-malleability of the NM commitment scheme guarantees that even in this hybrid, BAD occurs with non-negligible probability.

Since the decommitment of the $(1 - \widetilde{\beta}^*)$-th inner NM commitment is no longer used in the right interaction in the second hybrid, we can break the non-malleability of the $(1 - \widetilde{\beta}^*)$-th inner NM commitment whenever BAD occurs.

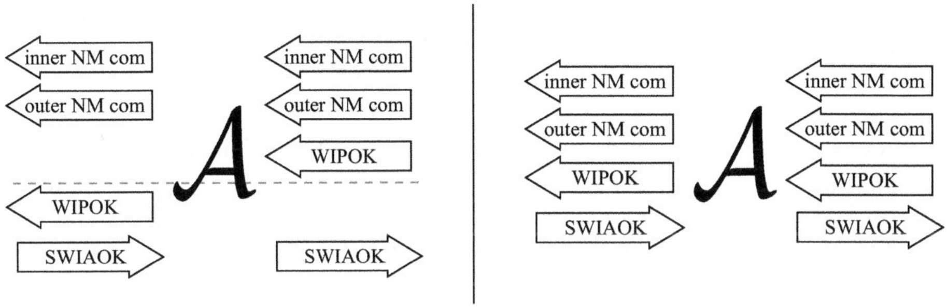

Fig. 1. Asynchronous schedule (left) and synchronous schedule (right). In the synchronous schedule, the adversary sends each message in the left interaction immediately after receiving the corresponding message in the right interaction, and vice versa. In the asynchronous schedule, the left and right interactions are synchronized except for the WIPOK part, where the WIPOK part in the left interaction starts after the WIPOK part in the right interaction completes.

Case 2: NMZK in Synchronous Message Scheduling. As a more interesting case, consider the setting where the messages in the left and right interactions are scheduled synchronously as shown in Fig. 1 (right).

In this case, the above analysis fails when we attempt to show the existence of $\widetilde{\beta}^*$ such that BAD occurs with non-negligible probability. To see this, recall that simulating the left interaction involves rewinding the WIPOK system in the left interaction. In the synchronized scheduling, rewinding the left WIPOK system inherently involves rewinding the right WIPOK system. Thus, the existence of $\widetilde{\beta}^*$ as above does not follow readily from the witness indistinguishability of the WIPOK system.

To address this issue, we adopt a technique from prior work on 4-round computational NMZK arguments. Concretely, we adapt a technique from Ciampi et al. [9]. In Ciampi et al., a problem that is closely related to the above is addressed by designing a specific construction of WIPOK. Their WIPOK system is a careful combination of several low-level primitives (such as a non-interactive commitment scheme and an honest-verifier zero-knowledge system), and the security of their 4-round NMZK argument is analyzed by directly considering reductions to the security of these low-level primitives. We define a WIPOK system that satisfies key properties of their WIPOK system, and integrate it into our construction and analysis in a (somewhat) modular fashion.[7]

Concretely, we consider the following 3-round special-purpose WIPOK system. It is tailored for the statement of the form $x_0 \in \mathbf{L} \vee x_1 \in \mathbf{L}$ (where both $x_0 \in \mathbf{L}$ and $x_1 \in \mathbf{L}$ have a unique witness), and it has the following "delayed-input" syntax that uses x_0 and x_1 only in the last round.

– For every $\beta \in \{0,1\}$, $(x_\beta, w_\beta) \in \mathbf{R_L}$, and $x_{1-\beta} \in \{0,1\}^{|x_\beta|}$,

$$\Pr\left[\mathsf{WIPOK.V_D}(x_0, x_1, \tau) = 1 \middle| \begin{array}{l} (\mathsf{wi}_1, \mathsf{st}) \leftarrow \mathsf{WIPOK.P}_1(1^{|x_\beta|}, \beta) \\ \mathsf{wi}_2 \leftarrow \mathsf{WIPOK.V}(1^{|x_\beta|}) \\ \mathsf{wi}_3 \leftarrow \mathsf{WIPOK.P}_2(\mathsf{st}, x_0, x_1, w_\beta, \mathsf{wi}_2) \\ \tau := (\mathsf{wi}_1, \mathsf{wi}_2, \mathsf{wi}_3) \end{array}\right] = 1.$$

Furthermore, its witness indistinguishability is established through a series of hybrid experiments, and some of the hybrid experiments are indistinguishable even against rewinding adversaries. Concretely, there exists a hybrid prover $(\mathsf{WIPOK}.\widehat{\mathsf{P}}_1, \mathsf{WIPOK}.\widehat{\mathsf{P}}_2)$ satisfying the following.

1. The hybrid prover $(\mathsf{WIPOK}.\widehat{\mathsf{P}}_1, \mathsf{WIPOK}.\widehat{\mathsf{P}}_2)$ follows the same syntax as the real prover $(\mathsf{WIPOK.P}_1, \mathsf{WIPOK.P}_2)$ except that $\mathsf{WIPOK}.\widehat{\mathsf{P}}_2$ needs to have witnesses for both of the sub-statements x_0, x_1 regardless of the value β. That is, it works as $\mathsf{wi}_3 \leftarrow \mathsf{WIPOK}.\widehat{\mathsf{P}}_2(\mathsf{st}, x_0, x_1, w_0, w_1, \mathsf{wi}_2)$.
2. The indistinguishability between the hybrid prover $(\mathsf{WIPOK}.\widehat{\mathsf{P}}_1, \mathsf{WIPOK}.\widehat{\mathsf{P}}_2)$ and the real prover $(\mathsf{WIPOK.P}_1, \mathsf{WIPOK.P}_2)$ can be shown using an auxiliary prover algorithm $\mathsf{WIPOK}.\widehat{\mathsf{P}}_{1.5}$ as follows.

$$\begin{aligned} &(\mathsf{WIPOK}.\widehat{\mathsf{P}}_1, \mathsf{WIPOK}.\widehat{\mathsf{P}}_2) \\ &\equiv ((\mathsf{WIPOK.P}_1, \mathsf{WIPOK}.\widehat{\mathsf{P}}_{1.5}), \mathsf{WIPOK}.\widehat{\mathsf{P}}_2) \quad (1) \\ &\equiv (\mathsf{WIPOK.P}_1, (\mathsf{WIPOK}.\widehat{\mathsf{P}}_{1.5}, \mathsf{WIPOK}.\widehat{\mathsf{P}}_2)) \quad (2) \\ &\approx (\mathsf{WIPOK.P}_1, \mathsf{WIPOK.P}_2) \quad (3) \end{aligned}$$

That is, (i) the execution of $\mathsf{WIPOK}.\widehat{\mathsf{P}}_1$ can be decomposed into a sequential execution of $\mathsf{WIPOK.P}_1$ and $\mathsf{WIPOK}.\widehat{\mathsf{P}}_{1.5}$ as shown in (1), (ii) the execution of $\mathsf{WIPOK}.\widehat{\mathsf{P}}_{1.5}$ can be deferred until the last round as shown in (2),[8] and (iii) a

[7] Ciampi et al. [7] makes a similar attempt at modularization, resulting in a different formalization (called *non-malleable honest-verifier zero-knowledge with respect to commitment*).

[8] Specifically, $\mathsf{WIPOK}.\widehat{\mathsf{P}}_{1.5}$ only generates auxiliary information to be used in $\mathsf{WIPOK}.\widehat{\mathsf{P}}_2$ (without generating anything related to the message to be sent to the verifier in the first round). Thus, any (non-rewinding) verifier cannot detect whether $\mathsf{WIPOK}.\widehat{\mathsf{P}}_{1.5}$ is executed in the first round or in the last round.

sequential execution of $\mathsf{WIPOK}.\widehat{\mathsf{P}}_{1.5}$ and $\mathsf{WIPOK}.\widehat{\mathsf{P}}_2$ is indistinguishable from $\mathsf{WIPOK}.\mathsf{P}_2$ as shown in (3).

3. The hybrid prover $(\mathsf{WIPOK}.\widehat{\mathsf{P}}_1, \mathsf{WIPOK}.\widehat{\mathsf{P}}_2)$ satisfies witness indistinguishability even against rewinding adversaries. That is, any cheating verifier cannot tell whether $\mathsf{WIPOK}.\widehat{\mathsf{P}}_1$ runs on input $\beta = 0$ or $\beta = 1$ even given multiple responses from $\mathsf{WIPOK}.\widehat{\mathsf{P}}_2$.[9]

Note that given the hybrid prover as above, the witness indistinguishability indeed follows from a simple hybrid argument: first switch the real prover to the hybrid one, next flip the value of β, and finally switch back the hybrid prover to the real one. (The second step of this hybrid argument holds even against rewinding adversaries.)

Using the above special-purpose WIPOK system, we analyze the synchronous case as follows. Recall that in the asynchronous case, we considered a hybrid argument where (i) in the first hybrid, two witnesses are available for the WIPOK system in the right interaction, whereas (ii) in the last hybrid, only a single witness is available. Based on this observation, we modify our construction so that the verifier completes the WIPOK system using the hybrid prover algorithms $(\mathsf{WIPOK}.\widehat{\mathsf{P}}_1, \mathsf{WIPOK}.\widehat{\mathsf{P}}_2)$. Thus, an honest verifier uses both of the decommitments of the two inner NM commitments for the WIPOK system. On the positive side, this modification enables us to show the existence of $\widetilde{\beta}^*$ such that BAD occurs with non-negligible probability. (The key point is that the hybrid prover of the special-purpose WIPOK system is witness indistinguishable even against rewinding adversaries). On the negative side, this modification requires us to consider an additional hybrid experiment where we switch the hybrid prover $(\mathsf{WIPOK}.\widehat{\mathsf{P}}_1, \mathsf{WIPOK}.\widehat{\mathsf{P}}_2)$ to the real prover $(\mathsf{WIPOK}.\mathsf{P}_1, \mathsf{WIPOK}.\mathsf{P}_2)$. (Otherwise, the decommitment of the $(1 - \widetilde{\beta}^*)$-th inner NM commitment remains to be used in the right interaction, and therefore we cannot derive a contradiction in the last hybrid.) Given that the hybrid prover and the real prover are not guaranteed to be indistinguishable against rewinding adversaries, it might appear that we have not made any progress. A key point to overcome this difficulty is that we do not require indistinguishability against rewinding adversaries here. To see this, observe that, as evidenced in the analysis of the asynchronous case, we will later replace the rewinding extraction with brute-force extraction in the left interaction. That is, the WIPOK system in the left interaction is not rewound in later hybrids. This observation suggests that we only need to replace the hybrid prover with the real one in the "main thread" and do not need to replace them in the "look-ahead threads" that are generated during the rewinding of the left WIPOK system (cf. Fig. 2, top left and right).[10] In

[9] This property does not contradict the proof-of-knowledge property since the hybrid prover has witnesses for both sub-statements. In particular, rewinding the hybrid prover results in extracting witnesses for both sub-statements x_0, x_1, and thus, is useless for determining the value of β.

[10] This technique is first introduced in the context of *security with super-polynomial-time simulation* by Garg et al. [17]. (Subsequently, it is also used in the context of NMZK by Ciampi et al. [9].)

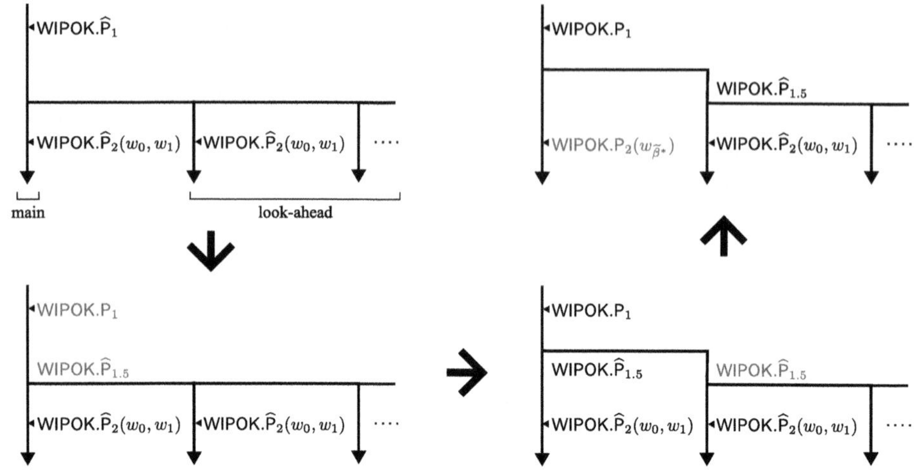

Fig. 2. Sequence of hybrids where the hybrid prover of the WIPOK system is removed from the main thread.

other words, we do not need to worry about using the hybrid prover in the look-ahead threads because the look-ahead threads will disappear in later hybrids when we switch the rewinding extraction to brute-force extraction. Concretely, first, we decompose $\mathsf{WIPOK}.\widehat{\mathsf{P}}_1$ into $(\mathsf{WIPOK}.\mathsf{P}_1, \mathsf{WIPOK}.\widehat{\mathsf{P}}_{1.5})$, and next, use an averaging argument to show that BAD occurs with non-negligible probability even when the main thread and the look-ahead threads use different executions of $\mathsf{WIPOK}.\widehat{\mathsf{P}}_{1.5}$ (cf. Fig. 2, bottom left and right). Then, we rely on the indistinguishability between $(\mathsf{WIPOK}.\widehat{\mathsf{P}}_{1.5}, \mathsf{WIPOK}.\widehat{\mathsf{P}}_2)$ and $\mathsf{WIPOK}.\mathsf{P}_2$ to show that BAD occurs with non-negligible probability even when $(\mathsf{WIPOK}.\widehat{\mathsf{P}}_{1.5}, \mathsf{WIPOK}.\widehat{\mathsf{P}}_2)$ is switched to $\mathsf{WIPOK}.\mathsf{P}_2$ in the main thread (cf. Fig. 2, top right). The rest of the analysis can proceed as in the asynchronous case since the decommitment of the $(1 - \widetilde{\beta}^*)$-th inner NM commitment is no longer used in the right interaction in the main thread.

2.3 4-Round Construction

Finally, we explain how to reduce the round complexity to 4.

The idea is simple: we run all the components of our construction in parallel. As mentioned above, the special-purpose WIPOK system requires only 3 rounds. Since there exist a 3-round NM commitment scheme [21,22] and a 4-round delayed-input SWIAOK system [28], we can reduce the round complexity to 4 by running all the components in parallel. (There are several minor issues that need to be addressed. For example, the decommitments of the inner NM commitments must be fixed in the first round so that they can be committed to in the outer NM commitments in parallel. Fortunately, the existing 3-round NM commitments [21,22] have a commit-challenge-response structure and therefore have the required property.)

The analysis is largely the same as before. Indeed, the synchronous case can be analyzed in the same way as above. For the asynchronous case, when the round complexity is reduced to 4, there are only a limited number of ways to schedule the messages in the left and right interactions, and each of them can be handled without difficulty.

We conclude this technical overview by noting that our construction can be instantiated using any collision-resistant hash function and injective one-way function. The special-purpose WIPOK system can be instantiated using any injective one-way function [9], the 3-round NM commitment scheme with the required properties can be instantiated using any injective one-way function [21, 22], and the 4-round delayed-input SWIAOK system can be instantiated using any collision-resistant hash function [13,24,28].

3 Preliminaries

We use λ to denote the security parameter, and use ε to denote the empty string. For any NP language $\mathbf{L}$, we use $\mathbf{R_L}$ to denote the corresponding witness relation. For any instance $x \in \mathbf{L}$, we use $\mathbf{R_L}(x)$ to denote the set of all witnesses for $x \in \mathbf{L}$. For any pair of probabilistic interactive Turing machines (P, V) and any $x, y, z \in \{0,1\}^*$, we use $\langle P(y), V(z)\rangle(x)$ to denote the random variable representing the output of V in an interaction between $P(x, y)$ and $V(x, z)$. We assume the reader has basic knowledge of cryptography, such as the definitions of statistical/computational indistinguishability, one-way functions, pseudorandom generators, and (public-coin) interactive proofs/arguments. We say that an interactive proof (resp., argument) is a *tag-based interactive proof (resp., argument)* if the prover and the verifier additionally take a string called a *tag* as common input.

3.1 Adaptive-Input Interactive Proofs/Arguments

We recall the definition of *adaptive-input interactive proofs/arguments* [11,12, 28], i.e., interactive proofs/arguments such that (i) the statement being proven is used only in the last round and (ii) the security holds even against adversaries selecting the statement adaptively. For concreteness, we focus on 4-round constructions with public verifiability.

Basic Security. We begin by recalling basic security notions.

Definition 1 (adaptive-input interactive proofs/arguments). *Let $\mathbf{L}$ be an NP language. A tuple of PPT Turing machines* $(\mathsf{P}_1, \mathsf{P}_2, \mathsf{V}_1, \mathsf{V}_2, \mathsf{V}_\mathsf{D})$ *is called a* (4-round) adaptive-input interactive proof (resp, argument) for $\mathbf{L}$ *if it satisfies the following.*

Delayed-input completeness. *For every* $(x, w) \in \boldsymbol{R_L}$,

$$\Pr\left[\mathsf{V_D}(x,\tau)=1 \;\middle|\; \begin{array}{l} (\mathsf{msg}_1, \mathsf{st}_V) \leftarrow \mathsf{V}_1(1^{|x|}) \\ (\mathsf{msg}_2, \mathsf{st}_P) \leftarrow \mathsf{P}_1(1^{|x|}, \mathsf{msg}_1) \\ \mathsf{msg}_3 \leftarrow \mathsf{V}_2(\mathsf{st}_V, \mathsf{msg}_2) \\ \mathsf{msg}_4 \leftarrow \mathsf{P}_2(\mathsf{st}_P, x, w, \mathsf{msg}_3) \\ \tau := (\mathsf{msg}_1, \dots, \mathsf{msg}_4) \end{array}\right] = 1.$$

Adaptive-input soundness. *For every pair of computationally unbounded (resp., PPT) Turing machines* $(\mathcal{P}_1, \mathcal{P}_2)$*, there exists a negligible function* negl *such that for every* $\lambda \in \mathbb{N}$ *and* $z \in \{0,1\}^*$,

$$\Pr\left[\begin{array}{l} x \notin \boldsymbol{L} \\ \wedge\ \mathsf{V_D}(x,\tau)=1 \end{array} \;\middle|\; \begin{array}{l} (\mathsf{msg}_1, \mathsf{st}_V) \leftarrow \mathsf{V}_1(1^{\lambda}) \\ (\mathsf{msg}_2, \mathsf{st}_{\mathcal{P}}) \leftarrow \mathcal{P}_1(1^{\lambda}, \mathsf{msg}_1, z) \\ \mathsf{msg}_3 \leftarrow \mathsf{V}_2(\mathsf{st}_V, \mathsf{msg}_2) \\ (x, \mathsf{msg}_4) \leftarrow \mathcal{P}_2(\mathsf{st}_{\mathcal{P}}, \mathsf{msg}_3) \\ \tau := (\mathsf{msg}_1, \dots, \mathsf{msg}_4) \end{array}\right] \le \mathsf{negl}(\lambda).$$

In the above, the messages msg_2*,* msg_3*, and* msg_4 *are called the* commit, challenge, *and* response *messages.* ◊

Remark 1. In the case of public-coin adaptive-input interactive proof/argument, the syntax of the verifier is simplified by removing st_V from the output of V_1 and only giving $1^{|x|}$ to V_2 as input. ◊

Additional Security. Next, we recall several additional security notions. First, we provide the definition of *adaptive-input computational special soundness.* The following definition is based on the definition of *computational special soundness* by Pass [38] and the definition of *adaptive-input special soundness* by Ciampi et al. [12].

Definition 2 (adaptive-input computational special soundness). *Let* $\Pi = (\mathsf{P}_1, \mathsf{P}_2, \mathsf{V}_1, \mathsf{V}_2, \mathsf{V_D})$ *be a public-coin adaptive-input interactive argument for an NP language* $\boldsymbol{L}$*. Then,* Π *is said to satisfy* adaptive-input computational special soundness *if there exists a deterministic polynomial-time Turing machine* Ext *(called the* extractor*) such that for every pair of PPT Turing machines* $(\mathcal{P}_1, \mathcal{P}_2)$*, there exists a negligible function* negl *such that for every* $\lambda \in \mathbb{N}$ *and* $z \in \{0,1\}^*$,

$$\Pr\left[\begin{array}{l} \forall b \in \{0,1\} : \mathsf{V_D}(x_b, \tau_b) = 1 \\ \wedge\ (x_0, w_0) \notin \boldsymbol{R_L} \end{array} \;\middle|\; \begin{array}{l} \mathsf{msg}_1 \leftarrow \mathsf{V}_1(1^{\lambda}) \\ (\mathsf{msg}_2, \mathsf{st}_{\mathcal{P}}) \leftarrow \mathcal{P}_1(1^{\lambda}, \mathsf{msg}_1, z) \\ \forall b \in \{0,1\} : \mathsf{msg}_{b,3} \leftarrow \mathsf{V}_2(1^{\lambda}) \\ (x_0, \mathsf{msg}_{0,4}, x_1, \mathsf{msg}_{1,4}) \leftarrow \mathcal{P}_2(\mathsf{st}_{\mathcal{P}}, \mathsf{msg}_{0,3}, \mathsf{msg}_{1,3}) \\ \forall b \in \{0,1\} : \tau_b := (\mathsf{msg}_1, \mathsf{msg}_2, \mathsf{msg}_{b,3}, \mathsf{msg}_{b,4}) \\ w_0 := \mathsf{Ext}(x_0, \tau_0, x_1, \tau_1) \end{array}\right] \le \mathsf{negl}(\lambda).$$

◊

Next, we recall the definition of *adaptive-input statistical witness indistinguishability.*

Definition 3 (adaptive-input statistical WI). *Let* $\Pi = (\mathsf{P}_1, \mathsf{P}_2, \mathsf{V}_1, \mathsf{V}_2, \mathsf{V}_\mathsf{D})$ *be an adaptive-input interactive argument for an NP language* $\boldsymbol{L}$*. Then,* Π *is called* adaptive-input statistical witness-indistinguishable (WI) *if for every triple of computationally unbounded Turing machines* $(\mathcal{V}_1, \mathcal{V}_2, \mathcal{V}_3)$*, there exists a negligible function* negl *such that for every* $\lambda \in \mathbb{N}$ *and* $z \in \{0,1\}^*$*, the random variable* out *satisfies* $\Pr[\mathsf{out} = 1] \leq 1/2 + \mathsf{negl}(\lambda)$ *in the following experiment.*

1. *Compute* $(\mathsf{msg}_1, \mathsf{st}_{\mathcal{V},1}) \leftarrow \mathcal{V}_1(1^\lambda, z)$*,* $(\mathsf{msg}_2, \mathsf{st}_P) \leftarrow \mathsf{P}_1(1^\lambda, \mathsf{msg}_1)$*, and* $(\mathsf{msg}_3, x, w_0, w_1, \mathsf{st}_{\mathcal{V},2}) \leftarrow \mathcal{V}_2(\mathsf{st}_{\mathcal{V},1}, \mathsf{msg}_2)$*. If* $|x| \neq \lambda \vee \exists b \in \{0,1\}$ *s.t.* $(x, w_b) \notin \boldsymbol{R_L}$*, abort.*
2. *Sample a random bit* $\beta \in \{0,1\}$ *and compute* $\mathsf{msg}_4 \leftarrow \mathsf{P}_2(\mathsf{st}_P, x, w_\beta, \mathsf{msg}_3)$*.*
3. *Compute* $\widetilde{\beta} \leftarrow \mathcal{V}_3(\mathsf{st}_{\mathcal{V},2}, \mathsf{msg}_4)$ *and let* $\mathsf{out} = 1$ *if and only if* $\widetilde{\beta} = \beta$*.* ◊

Finally, we provides an instantiation that satisfies the above two additional security notions.

Theorem 1. *Assume the existence of a collision-resistant hash function family. Then, there exists a 4-round public-coin adaptive-input interactive argument that satisfies both adaptive-input computational special soundness and adaptive-input statistical witness indistinguishability.*

Proof (sketch). It suffices to instantiate the delayed-input argument of knowledge of Lapidot and Shamir [28] with a 2-round statistically hiding commitment scheme (which can be obtained from any collision-resistant hash function [13,24]) and use a trick by Ciampi et al. [9, Appendix C.1] to obtain delayed-input computational special soundness. □

3.2 Statistical Non-malleable Zero-Knowledge

We recall the definition of *non-malleable zero-knowledge* [14]. Following recent work [3,8,10,23], we use the definition based on the notion of *simulation extractability* [40] (which is known to imply the original definition of non-malleable zero-knowledge [14]). Below, we provide the statistical zero-knowledge version of the definition in the *one-many* setting [39] with a weak form of *adaptive input selection* [29]. (See Remark 2 below for details about adaptive input selection.) The text below is adapted from [27,29].

Let $\langle P, V \rangle$ be a tag-based, adaptive-input interactive argument for an NP language $\mathbf{L}$. For a man-in-the-middle adversary $\mathcal{A}$, let us consider a probabilistic experiment in which $\mathcal{A}$ participates in the following single left and multiple right interactions.

- In the left interaction, $\mathcal{A}$ interacts with an honest prover of $\langle P, V \rangle$ and verifies the validity of a statement x using a tag tag.

- In the right interactions, $\mathcal{A}$ interacts with honest verifiers of $\langle P, V \rangle$ and proves the validity of statements $\widetilde{x}_1, \ldots, \widetilde{x}_m$ using tags $\widetilde{\mathsf{tag}}_1, \ldots, \widetilde{\mathsf{tag}}_m$.

More concretely, the experiment proceeds as follows. Prior to the interactions, all parties in the experiment receive as common input the security parameter λ in unary, and $\mathcal{A}$ also receives as auxiliary input $z \in \{0,1\}^*$. Then, $\mathcal{A}$ starts interacting with the prover and the verifiers in the left and right interactions while fully controlling the message schedule. (In particular, $\mathcal{A}$ can run the left and right interactions concurrently.) In the left (resp., each right) interaction, the tag $\mathsf{tag} \in \{0,1\}^\lambda$ (resp., $\widetilde{\mathsf{tag}}_i \in \{0,1\}^\lambda$) is selected by $\mathcal{A}$ at the beginning of the interaction, and the statement $x \in \{0,1\}^\lambda$ (resp., $\widetilde{x}_i \in \{0,1\}^\lambda$) is selected by $\mathcal{A}$ at the time of sending the last verifier (resp., prover) message to the honest party. The witness used by the honest prover in the left interaction is chosen by a *witness-selecting machine* M. Specifically, M is a PPT Turing machine such that when $\mathcal{A}$ selects the statement x in the left interaction, M takes as input the statement x, the current view of $\mathcal{A}$, and an auxiliary input z', and then picks a witness w as the private input to the honest prover. Let $\mathsf{view}_{\mathcal{A},M}(\lambda, z, z')$ be the random variable representing the joint view of $\mathcal{A}$ and the honest verifiers in the above experiment. Let us say that the pair (z, z') of auxiliary inputs is *good* if in the above experiment, (i) $\mathcal{A}$ always selects a true statement of length λ in the left interaction and (ii) M always picks a valid witness for the validity of the statement selected by $\mathcal{A}$. Let $Z_{\mathcal{A},M}(\lambda)$ be the set of good auxiliary-input pairs. Then, roughly speaking, $\langle P, V \rangle$ is *one-many statistical non-malleable zero-knowledge (SNMZK) with weak adaptive-input selection* if for every PPT adversary $\mathcal{A}$ and witness-selecting machine M, there exists a PPT machine called the *simulator-extractor* such that for every λ and every good (z, z'), the simulator-extractor can statistically simulate the view of $\mathcal{A}$ in the above experiment while extracting witnesses for the statements proven by $\mathcal{A}$ in the accepted right interactions. The formal definition is given below.

Definition 4. *A tag-based adaptive-input interactive argument $\langle P, V \rangle$ for an NP language $\boldsymbol{L}$ is said to be* one-many statistical non-malleable zero-knowledge with weak adaptive input selection *if for every polynomial $m(\cdot)$ and every PPT man-in-the-middle adversary $\mathcal{A}$ that participates in at most $m = m(\lambda)$ right interactions, there exists an expected polynomial-time Turing machine $\mathcal{SE}$ (called the* simulator-extractor*) such that for every PPT witness-selecting machine M, the following hold.*

1. ***Statistical simulation.*** *Let $\mathsf{sim\text{-}view}(\lambda, z)$ be a random variable representing the first output of $\mathcal{SE}(1^\lambda, z)$. Then, for every sequence $\{(z_\lambda, z'_\lambda)\}_{\lambda \in \mathbb{N}}$ such that $(z_\lambda, z'_\lambda) \in Z_{\mathcal{A},M}(\lambda)$, the ensembles $\{\mathsf{view}_{\mathcal{A},M}(\lambda, z_\lambda, z'_\lambda)\}_{\lambda \in \mathbb{N}}$ and $\{\mathsf{sim\text{-}view}(\lambda, z_\lambda)\}_{\lambda \in \mathbb{N}}$ are statistically indistinguishable.*
2. ***Witness extraction.*** *For every $\lambda \in \mathbb{N}$ and $(z, z') \in Z_{\mathcal{A},M}(\lambda)$, the following holds. Let $(\mathsf{view}, \{\widetilde{w}_i\}_{i \in [m]})$ denote the output of $\mathcal{SE}(\lambda, z)$. Let $\widetilde{x}_1, \ldots, \widetilde{x}_m$ be the statements of the right interactions in view, and let tag and $\widetilde{\mathsf{tag}}_1, \ldots, \widetilde{\mathsf{tag}}_m$ be the tags of the left and the right interactions in view. Then, except with*

negligible probability, it holds $(\widetilde{x}_i, \widetilde{w}_i) \in \boldsymbol{R_L}$ *for every* $i \in [m]$ *such that the* i*-th right interaction is accepting and* $\widetilde{\mathsf{tag}}_i \neq \mathsf{tag}$. ◊

Remark 2. The above formalization of adaptive input selection is weaker than the original one [29] because the original formalization considers the case where the witness-selecting machine is computationally unbounded and takes the views of all the parties (including the honest ones) as input. In other words, we focus on the case where a witness for the left statement x can be computed efficiently by using a "super witness" z'. (See [29, Section 1] for more discussion.) ◊

3.3 Synchronous Non-malleable Commitments

We recall the definition of *non-malleable commitment schemes* [14]. The following definition is based on the definition by Lin et al. [33]. For concreteness, we focus on 3-round constructions with public verifiability[11] in the synchronous-message setting.

Definition 5. *A tuple of PPT Turing machines* $(\mathsf{NMC.S}_1, \mathsf{NMC.S}_2, \mathsf{NMC.R}, \mathsf{NMC.R}_\mathsf{D})$ *is called a* 3-round synchronous non-malleable commitment scheme *if it satisfies the following.*

Correctness. *For every* $\lambda \in \mathbb{N}$, $\mathsf{tag} \in \{0,1\}^\lambda$, *and* $m \in \{0,1\}^\lambda$,

$$\Pr\left[\mathsf{NMC.R_D}(\tau, \mathsf{dec}) = m \;\middle|\; \begin{array}{l} (\mathsf{nm}_1, \mathsf{dec}, \mathsf{st}) \leftarrow \mathsf{NMC.S}_1(1^\lambda, \mathsf{tag}, m) \\ \mathsf{nm}_2 \leftarrow \mathsf{NMC.R}(1^\lambda, \mathsf{tag}, \mathsf{nm}_1) \\ \mathsf{nm}_3 \leftarrow \mathsf{NMC.S}_2(\mathsf{st}, \mathsf{nm}_2) \\ \tau := (\mathsf{nm}_1, \mathsf{nm}_2, \mathsf{nm}_3) \end{array}\right] = 1.$$

Statistical binding. *For every pair of computationally unbounded Turing machines* $(\mathcal{S}_1, \mathcal{S}_2)$, *there exists a negligible function* negl *such that for every* $\lambda \in \mathbb{N}$ *and* $z \in \{0,1\}^*$,

$$\Pr\left[\begin{array}{l} m \neq \bot \wedge m' \neq \bot \\ \wedge\ \mathsf{NMC.R_D}(\tau, \mathsf{dec}) = m \\ \wedge\ \mathsf{NMC.R_D}(\tau, \mathsf{dec}') = m' \end{array} \;\middle|\; \begin{array}{l} (\mathsf{tag}, \mathsf{nm}_1, \mathsf{st}) \leftarrow \mathcal{S}_1(1^\lambda, z) \\ \mathsf{nm}_2 \leftarrow \mathsf{NMC.R}(1^\lambda, \mathsf{tag}, \mathsf{nm}_1) \\ (\mathsf{nm}_3, m, \mathsf{dec}, m', \mathsf{dec}') \leftarrow \mathcal{S}_2(\mathsf{st}, \mathsf{nm}_2) \\ \tau := (\mathsf{nm}_1, \mathsf{nm}_2, \mathsf{nm}_3) \end{array}\right] \leq \mathsf{negl}(\lambda).$$

Synchronous non-malleability. *For any tuple of PPT Turing machines* $\mathcal{A} = (\mathcal{A}_0, \mathcal{A}_1, \mathcal{A}_2, \mathcal{A}_3, \mathcal{A}_D)$, *there exists a negligible function* negl *such that for any* $\lambda \in \mathbb{N}$ *and* $z \in \{0,1\}^*$, *the random variable* out *satisfies* $\Pr[\mathsf{out} = 1] \leq 1/2 + \mathsf{negl}(\lambda)$ *in the following experiment.*

Initialization. *Compute* $(m, \mathsf{tag}, \mathsf{st}_{\mathcal{A},0}) \leftarrow \mathcal{A}_0(1^\lambda, z)$, *where* $m \in \{0,1\}^\lambda$, $\mathsf{tag} \in \{0,1\}^\lambda$.[12] *Then, let* m^* *be defined as follows: sample a random bit* $b \in \{0,1\}$; *if* $b = 0$, *let* $m^* := m$; *otherwise, let* $m^* := m'$ *for a random string* $m' \in \{0,1\}^\lambda$.

---

[11] That is, decommitment verification does not require the receiver's internal state.

[12] If $m \notin \{0,1\}^\lambda$ or $\mathsf{tag} \notin \{0,1\}^\lambda$, then m and tag are redefined to be arbitrary default values of length λ.

Round 1. *Compute* $(\mathsf{nm}_1, \mathsf{dec}, \mathsf{st}_S) \leftarrow \mathsf{NMC.S}_1(1^\lambda, \mathsf{tag}, m^*)$ *and* $(\widetilde{\mathsf{tag}}, \widetilde{\mathsf{nm}}_1, \mathsf{st}_{\mathcal{A},1}) \leftarrow \mathcal{A}_1(\mathsf{st}_{\mathcal{A},0}, \mathsf{nm}_1)$.

Round 2. *Compute* $\widetilde{\mathsf{nm}}_2 \leftarrow \mathsf{NMC.R}(1^\lambda, \widetilde{\mathsf{tag}}, \widetilde{\mathsf{nm}}_1)$ *and* $(\mathsf{nm}_2, \mathsf{st}_{\mathcal{A},2}) \leftarrow \mathcal{A}_2(\mathsf{st}_{\mathcal{A},1}, \widetilde{\mathsf{nm}}_2)$.

Round 3. *Compute* $\mathsf{nm}_3 \leftarrow \mathsf{NMC.S}_2(\mathsf{st}_S, \mathsf{nm}_2)$ *and* $(\mathsf{st}_{\mathcal{A},3}, \widetilde{\mathsf{nm}}_3) \leftarrow \mathcal{A}_3(\mathsf{st}_{\mathcal{A},2}, \mathsf{nm}_3)$.

Final output. *Let* $\widetilde{m}$ *be the committed value of* $\widetilde{\tau} := (\widetilde{\mathsf{nm}}_1, \widetilde{\mathsf{nm}}_2, \widetilde{\mathsf{nm}}_3)$ *defined as follows: let* $\widetilde{M} := \{\widetilde{m} \mid \exists \widetilde{\mathsf{dec}}$ *s.t.* $\mathsf{NMC.R_D}(\widetilde{\tau}, \widetilde{\mathsf{dec}}) = \widetilde{m}\}$; *if* $\mathsf{tag} = \widetilde{\mathsf{tag}}$ *or* $|\widetilde{M}| \neq 1$, *let* $\widetilde{m} := \perp$; *otherwise, let* $\widetilde{m}$ *be the unique value such that* $\widetilde{m} \in \widetilde{M}$. *Then, compute* $b' \leftarrow \mathcal{A}_D(\mathsf{st}_{\mathcal{A},3}, \widetilde{m})$ *and let* $\mathsf{out} := 1$ *if and only if* $b' = b$. ◊

We note that the above definition uses somewhat unconventional syntax where the decommitment verification algorithm $\mathsf{NMC.R_D}$ outputs either the committed value (when given a valid decommitment) or $\perp$ (when given an invalid decommitment). We also note that synchronous non-malleability trivially implies the following hiding property.

Computational hiding. For any tuple of PPT Turing machines $\mathcal{R} = (\mathcal{R}_0, \mathcal{R}_1, \mathcal{R}_\mathsf{D})$, there exists a negligible function negl such that for any $\lambda \in \mathbb{N}$ and $z \in \{0,1\}^*$, the random variable out satisfies $\Pr[\mathsf{out} = 1] \leq 1/2 + \mathsf{negl}(\lambda)$ in the following experiment.

Initialization. Compute $(m, \mathsf{tag}, \mathsf{st}_{\mathcal{R},0}) \leftarrow \mathcal{R}_0(1^\lambda, z)$, where $m \in \{0,1\}^\lambda$, $\mathsf{tag} \in \{0,1\}^\lambda$. Then, let m^* be defined as follows: sample a random bit $b \in \{0,1\}$; if $b = 0$, let $m^* := m$; otherwise, let $m^* := m'$ for a random string $m' \in \{0,1\}^\lambda$.

Rounds 1, 2, 3. Compute $(\mathsf{nm}_1, \mathsf{dec}, \mathsf{st}_S) \leftarrow \mathsf{NMC.S}_1(1^\lambda, \mathsf{tag}, m^*)$, $(\mathsf{nm}_2, \mathsf{st}_{\mathcal{R},1}) \leftarrow \mathcal{R}_1(\mathsf{st}_{\mathcal{R},0}, \mathsf{nm}_1)$, and $\mathsf{nm}_3 \leftarrow \mathsf{NMC.S}_2(\mathsf{st}_S, \mathsf{nm}_2)$.

Final output. Compute $b' \leftarrow \mathcal{R}_D(\mathsf{st}_{\mathcal{R},1}, \mathsf{nm}_3)$ and let $\mathsf{out} := 1$ if and only if $b' = b$.

As mentioned in Sect. 2.3, we require a non-malleable commitment scheme that satisfies an additional property.

Theorem 2. *Assume the existence of injective one-way functions. Then, there exists a 3-round synchronous non-malleable commitment scheme satisfying the following property.*

Unique decommitment candidate. *There exists a deterministic Turing machine* $\mathsf{NMC.R_{D,weak}}$ *satisfying the following.*

Uniqueness. *For every* $\mathsf{nm}_1 \in \{0,1\}^*$, $|\{\mathsf{dec} \mid \mathsf{NMC.R_{D,weak}}(\mathsf{nm}_1, \mathsf{dec}) = 1\}| \leq 1$.

Correctness. *For every* $\tau = (\mathsf{nm}_1, \mathsf{nm}_2, \mathsf{nm}_3) \in (\{0,1\}^*)^3$ *and* dec *such that* $\mathsf{NMC.R_D}(\tau, \mathsf{dec}) \neq \perp$, *it holds* $\mathsf{NMC.R_{D,weak}}(\mathsf{nm}_1, \mathsf{dec}) = 1$.

Soundness. *For every computationally unbounded Turing machine* $\mathcal{A}$ *and every* $\lambda \in \mathbb{N}$, $\mathsf{tag} \in \{0,1\}^\lambda$, $m \in \{0,1\}^\lambda$, *and* $z \in \{0,1\}^*$,

$$\Pr\left[\begin{array}{l|l} \exists \mathsf{dec}' \ s.t. & (\mathsf{nm}_1, \mathsf{dec}, \mathsf{st}) \leftarrow \mathsf{NMC.S}_1(1^\lambda, \mathsf{tag}, m) \\ \mathsf{NMC.R}_{\mathsf{D,weak}}(\mathsf{nm}_1, \mathsf{dec}') = 1 & \mathsf{nm}_2 \leftarrow \mathcal{A}(1^\lambda, \mathsf{tag}, \mathsf{nm}_1, z) \\ \wedge\ \mathsf{nm}_3 \neq \bot & \mathsf{nm}_3 \leftarrow \mathsf{NMC.S}_2(\mathsf{st}, \mathsf{nm}_2) \\ \wedge\ \mathsf{NMC.R}_\mathsf{D}(\tau, \mathsf{dec}') \neq m & \tau := (\mathsf{nm}_1, \mathsf{nm}_2, \mathsf{nm}_3) \end{array}\right] = 0.$$

Furthermore, when a commitment is made on security parameter λ *and message length* λ*, the length of the corresponding decommitment is* λ*.*

Proof. The first part follows from [20, Claim 5 and Theorem 1], where the unique decommitment candidate property can be verified by inspecting the protocol description in [20, Figure 2]. The furthermore part can also be verified by inspection. (See the full version of this paper for details.) □

4 Tool: Special-Purpose WIPOK System

We present the main tool that we use in our 4-round SNMZK argument system. As described in Sect. 2, it is a 3-round public-coin proof of knowledge for statements of the form $x_0 \in \mathbf{L} \vee x_1 \in \mathbf{L}$, and we require it to satisfy a certain rewinding security notion. We start by defining the syntax of such 3-round proof of knowledge systems and their basic security.

Definition 6. *Let* $\boldsymbol{L}$ *be an NP language. A tuple of PPT Turing machines* $(\mathsf{WIPOK.P}_1, \mathsf{WIPOK.P}_2, \mathsf{WIPOK.V}, \mathsf{WIPOK.V}_\mathsf{D})$ *is called a* 3-round adaptive-input OR-indistinguishable special-sound proof *for* $\boldsymbol{L}$ *if it satisfies the following.*

Delayed-input correctness. *For every* $\beta \in \{0,1\}$, $(x_\beta, w_\beta) \in \boldsymbol{R_L}$, *and* $x_{1-\beta} \in \{0,1\}^{|x_\beta|}$,

$$\Pr\left[\mathsf{WIPOK.V}_\mathsf{D}(x_0, x_1, \tau) = 1 \left| \begin{array}{l} (\mathsf{wi}_1, \mathsf{st}) \leftarrow \mathsf{WIPOK.P}_1(1^{|x_\beta|}, \beta) \\ \mathsf{wi}_2 \leftarrow \mathsf{WIPOK.V}(1^{|x_\beta|}) \\ \mathsf{wi}_3 \leftarrow \mathsf{WIPOK.P}_2(\mathsf{st}, x_0, x_1, w_\beta, \mathsf{wi}_2) \\ \tau := (\mathsf{wi}_1, \mathsf{wi}_2, \mathsf{wi}_3) \end{array}\right.\right] = 1.$$

Delayed-input special soundness. *There exists a deterministic polynomial-time Turing machine* Ext *(called the* extractor*) and a polynomial-time computable function* $\mathsf{EQ} : \{0,1\}^* \times \{0,1\}^* \mapsto \{0,1\}$ *such that the following hold.*

1. *For every* $\lambda \in \mathbb{N}$,

$$\Pr\left[\mathsf{EQ}(\mathsf{wi}_{0,2}, \mathsf{wi}_{1,2}) = 1 \left| \begin{array}{l} \mathsf{wi}_{0,2} \leftarrow \mathsf{WIPOK.V}(1^\lambda) \\ \mathsf{wi}_{1,2} \leftarrow \mathsf{WIPOK.V}(1^\lambda) \end{array}\right.\right] \le \frac{1}{2^\lambda}.$$

2. *Fix any* $x_b = (x_{b,0}, x_{b,1}) \in (\{0,1\}^*)^2$ *and* $\tau_b := (\mathsf{wi}_{b,1}, \mathsf{wi}_{b,2}, \mathsf{wi}_{b,3}) \in (\{0,1\}^*)^3$ *for each* $b \in \{0,1\}$*. Suppose it holds* $|x_0| = |x_1|$, $\mathsf{wi}_{0,1} = \mathsf{wi}_{1,1}$, $\mathsf{EQ}(\mathsf{wi}_{0,2}, \mathsf{wi}_{1,2}) = 0$, *and* $\mathsf{V}_\mathsf{D}(x_{b,0}, x_{b,1}, \tau_b) = 1$ *for every* $b \in \{0,1\}$*. Then,* $\mathsf{Ext}(x_0, \tau_0, x_1, \tau_1)$ *outputs a value* w *such that* $\exists \beta \in \{0,1\} : (x_{\beta,0}, w) \in \boldsymbol{R_L}$.

Adaptive-input OR indistinguishability. *For every pair of PPT Turing machines* $(\mathcal{V}_1, \mathcal{V}_2)$, *there exists a negligible function* negl *such that for every* $\lambda \in \mathbb{N}$ *and* $z \in \{0,1\}^*$, *the random variable* out *satisfies* $\Pr[\mathsf{out} = 1] \leq 1/2 + \mathsf{negl}(\lambda)$ *in the following experiment.*

1. *Sample a random bit* $\beta \in \{0,1\}$ *and compute* $(\mathsf{wi}_1, \mathsf{st}_P) \leftarrow \mathsf{WIPOK.P}_1(1^\lambda, \beta)$.
2. *Compute* $(\mathsf{wi}_2, \{x_b, w_b\}_{b\in\{0,1\}}, \mathsf{st}_\mathcal{V}) \leftarrow \mathcal{V}_1(1^\lambda, \mathsf{wi}_1, z)$. *If* $\exists b \in \{0,1\}$ *s.t.* $(x_b, w_b) \notin \boldsymbol{R_L} \vee |x_b| \neq \lambda$, *abort.*
3. *Compute* $\mathsf{wi}_3 \leftarrow \mathsf{WIPOK.P}_2(\mathsf{st}, x_0, x_1, w_\beta, \mathsf{wi}_2)$.
4. *Compute* $\widetilde{\beta} \leftarrow \mathcal{V}_2(\mathsf{st}_\mathcal{V}, \mathsf{wi}_3)$ *and let* $\mathsf{out} = 1$ *if and only if* $\widetilde{\beta} = \beta$.

Remark 3. The adaptive-input OR indistinguishability is weaker than the standard witness indistinguishability since it only requires indistinguishability between a proof generated with a witness for $x_0 \in \mathbf{L}$ and a proof generated with a witness for $x_1 \in \mathbf{L}$. $\diamondsuit$

Next, we summarize the required rewinding security notion in the following theorem.

Theorem 3. *Let* $\boldsymbol{L}$ *be an NP language, and assume the existence of injective one-way functions. Then, there exists a 3-round adaptive-input OR-indistinguishable special-sound proof,* $\mathsf{WIPOK} = (\mathsf{WIPOK.P}_1, \mathsf{WIPOK.P}_2, \mathsf{WIPOK.V}, \mathsf{WIPOK.V}_\mathsf{D})$, *for* $\boldsymbol{L}$. *Furthermore, there exists a pair of PPT Turing machines* $(\mathsf{WIPOK.}\widehat{\mathsf{P}}_1, \mathsf{WIPOK.}\widehat{\mathsf{P}}_2)$ *and an additional PPT Turing machine* $\mathsf{WIPOK.}\widehat{\mathsf{P}}_{1.5}$ *satisfying the following.*

Delayed-input correctness of hybrid prover. *For every* $\beta \in \{0,1\}$, $(x_0, w_0) \in \boldsymbol{R_L}$, *and* $(x_1, w_1) \in \boldsymbol{R_L}$ *such that* $|x_0| = |x_1|$,

$$\Pr\left[\mathsf{WIPOK.V}_\mathsf{D}(x_0, x_1, \tau) = 1 \;\middle|\; \begin{array}{l} (\mathsf{wi}_1, \mathsf{st}, \mathsf{aux}) \leftarrow \mathsf{WIPOK.}\widehat{\mathsf{P}}_1(1^{|x_\beta|}, \beta) \\ \mathsf{wi}_2 \leftarrow \mathsf{WIPOK.V}(1^{|x_\beta|}) \\ \mathsf{wi}_3 \leftarrow \mathsf{WIPOK.}\widehat{\mathsf{P}}_2(\mathsf{st}, \mathsf{aux}, x_0, x_1, w_0, w_1, \mathsf{wi}_2) \\ \tau := (\mathsf{wi}_1, \mathsf{wi}_2, \mathsf{wi}_3) \end{array}\right] = 1.$$

Indistinguishability between real and hybrid provers.

1. *For every* $\lambda \in \mathbb{N}$ *and* $\beta \in \{0,1\}$, *the following two distributions are identically distributed.*

$$\left\{(\mathsf{wi}_1, \mathsf{st}, \mathsf{aux}) \;\middle|\; \begin{array}{l} (\mathsf{wi}_1, \mathsf{st}) \leftarrow \mathsf{WIPOK.P}_1(1^\lambda, \beta) \\ \mathsf{aux} \leftarrow \mathsf{WIPOK.}\widehat{\mathsf{P}}_{1.5}(1^\lambda, \beta) \end{array}\right\},$$

$$\left\{(\mathsf{wi}_1, \mathsf{st}, \mathsf{aux}) \mid (\mathsf{wi}_1, \mathsf{st}, \mathsf{aux}) \leftarrow \mathsf{WIPOK.}\widehat{\mathsf{P}}_1(1^\lambda, \beta)\right\}.$$

2. *For every PPT Turing machine $\mathcal{D}$, there exists a negligible function* negl *such that for every* $(x_0, w_0) \in \boldsymbol{R_L}$, $(x_1, w_1) \in \boldsymbol{R_L}$, $\beta \in \{0,1\}$, $(\mathsf{wi}_1, \mathsf{st}) \in \mathsf{WIPOK.P}_1(1^{|x_\beta|}, \beta)$, $\mathsf{wi}_2 \in \{0,1\}^*$, *and* $z \in \{0,1\}^*$ *such that* $|x_0| = |x_1|$,

$$\left| \begin{array}{l} \Pr\left[\mathcal{D}(\mathsf{params}, \mathsf{wi}_3) = 1 \mid \mathsf{wi}_3 \leftarrow \mathsf{WIPOK.P}_2(\mathsf{st}, x_0, x_1, w_\beta, \mathsf{wi}_2)\right] \\ -\Pr\left[\mathcal{D}(\mathsf{params}, \mathsf{wi}_3) = 1 \,\middle|\, \begin{array}{l} \mathsf{aux} \leftarrow \mathsf{WIPOK}.\widehat{\mathsf{P}}_{1.5}(1^{|x_\beta|}, \beta) \\ \mathsf{wi}_3 \leftarrow \mathsf{WIPOK}.\widehat{\mathsf{P}}_2(\mathsf{st}, \mathsf{aux}, x_0, x_1, w_0, w_1, \mathsf{wi}_2) \end{array}\right] \end{array} \right| \le \mathsf{negl}(|x_\beta|),$$

where $\mathsf{params} := (x_0, x_1, w_0, w_1, \beta, \mathsf{wi}_1, \mathsf{wi}_2, \mathsf{st}, z)$.[13]

Adaptive-input (rewinding) OR-indistinguishability of hybrid prover. *For every PPT oracle Turing machine $\mathcal{V}$, there exists a negligible function* negl *such that for every* $\lambda \in \mathbb{N}$ *and* $z \in \{0,1\}^*$,

$$\Pr\left[\beta = \widetilde{\beta} \,\middle|\, \begin{array}{l} \beta \leftarrow \{0,1\} \\ (\mathsf{wi}_1, \mathsf{st}, \mathsf{aux}) \leftarrow \mathsf{WIPOK}.\widehat{\mathsf{P}}_1(1^\lambda, \beta) \\ \widetilde{\beta} \leftarrow \mathcal{V}^{\mathcal{O}(\mathsf{st}, \mathsf{aux}, \cdot)}(1^\lambda, \mathsf{wi}_1, z) \end{array}\right] \le \frac{1}{2} + \mathsf{negl}(\lambda),$$

where the oracle $\mathcal{O}$ is defined as follows.

- $\underline{\mathcal{O}(\mathsf{st}, \mathsf{aux}, x_0, x_1, w_0, w_1, \mathsf{wi}_2)}$: *If* $|x_b| = \lambda$ *and* $(x_b, w_b) \in \boldsymbol{R_L}$ *for every* $b \in \{0,1\}$, *return* $\mathsf{WIPOK}.\widehat{\mathsf{P}}_2(\mathsf{st}, \mathsf{aux}, x_0, x_1, w_0, w_1, \mathsf{wi}_2)$. *Otherwise, return* $\perp$.

As stated in Sect. 2, Theorem 3 can be proved by using the WIPOK system given by Ciampi et al. [9]. (We provide a proof in the full version of this paper.) In the following, we give a lemma that we use in the analysis of our 4-round SNMZK argument. Intuitively, the lemma formalizes the argument sketched in Fig. 2 in Sect. 2.2.

Lemma 1. *Fix any computationally unbounded Turing machine $\mathcal{A}_1$ and pair of PPT Turing machines $(\mathcal{A}_2, \widehat{\mathcal{A}}_2)$ such that for every $\lambda \in \mathbb{N}$, $\beta \in \{0,1\}$, and $z \in \{0,1\}$, $\mathcal{A}_1$ is well-behaving in the following sense.*

$$\Pr\left[\begin{array}{l} |\mathsf{st}_\mathcal{A}| \le \mathsf{poly}(\lambda) \\ \wedge\ \forall b \in \{0,1\} : |x_b| = \lambda \wedge (x_b, w_b) \in \boldsymbol{R_L} \end{array} \,\middle|\, \begin{array}{l} (\mathsf{wi}_1, \mathsf{st}, \mathsf{aux}) \leftarrow \mathsf{WIPOK}.\widehat{\mathsf{P}}_1(1^\lambda, \beta) \\ (x_0, x_1, w_0, w_1, \mathsf{wi}_2, \mathsf{st}_\mathcal{A}) \leftarrow \mathcal{A}_1(1^\lambda, \mathsf{wi}_1, z) \end{array}\right] = 1.$$

Also, let $\mathcal{O}$ be the following oracle.

- $\underline{\mathcal{O}(\mathsf{st}, \mathsf{aux}, x_0, x_1, w_0, w_1, \mathsf{wi}_2)}$: *If* $|x_b| = \lambda$ *and* $(x_b, w_b) \in \boldsymbol{R_L}$ *for every* $b \in \{0,1\}$, *return* $\mathsf{WIPOK}.\widehat{\mathsf{P}}_2(\mathsf{st}, \mathsf{aux}, x_0, x_1, w_0, w_1, \mathsf{wi}_2)$. *Otherwise, return* $\perp$.

Then, there exists a negligible function negl *such that for any polynomial p, there exists a polynomial q such that for every $\lambda \in \mathbb{N}$, $\beta \in \{0,1\}$, and $z \in \{0,1\}^*$, if it holds*

$$\Pr\left[\begin{array}{l} \mathcal{A}_2(\mathsf{st}_\mathcal{A}, \mathsf{wi}_3) = 1 \\ \wedge\ \widehat{\mathcal{A}}_2^{\mathcal{O}(\mathsf{st}, \mathsf{aux}, \cdot)}(\mathsf{st}_\mathcal{A}) = 1 \end{array} \,\middle|\, \begin{array}{l} (\mathsf{wi}_1, \mathsf{st}, \mathsf{aux}) \leftarrow \mathsf{WIPOK}.\widehat{\mathsf{P}}_1(1^\lambda, \beta) \\ (x_0, x_1, w_0, w_1, \mathsf{wi}_2, \mathsf{st}_\mathcal{A}) \leftarrow \mathcal{A}_1(1^\lambda, \mathsf{wi}_1, z) \\ \mathsf{wi}_3 \leftarrow \mathsf{WIPOK}.\widehat{\mathsf{P}}_2(\mathsf{st}, \mathsf{aux}, x_0, x_1, w_0, w_1, \mathsf{wi}_2) \end{array}\right] \ge \frac{1}{p(\lambda)}, \quad (4)$$

[13] Note that aux is not given to $\mathcal{D}$.

then it also holds

$$\Pr\left[\begin{array}{l} \mathcal{A}_2(\mathsf{st}_{\mathcal{A}}, \mathsf{wi}_3) = 1 \\ \wedge\ \widehat{\mathcal{A}}_2^{\mathcal{O}(\mathsf{st},\mathsf{aux},\cdot)}(\mathsf{st}_{\mathcal{A}}) = 1 \end{array} \middle| \begin{array}{l} (\mathsf{wi}_1, \mathsf{st}, \mathsf{aux}) \leftarrow \mathsf{WIPOK}.\widehat{\mathsf{P}}_1(1^\lambda, \beta) \\ (x_0, x_1, w_0, w_1, \mathsf{wi}_2, \mathsf{st}_{\mathcal{A}}) \leftarrow \mathcal{A}_1(1^\lambda, \mathsf{wi}_1, z) \\ \mathsf{wi}_3 \leftarrow \mathsf{WIPOK}.\mathsf{P}_2(\mathsf{st}, x_0, x_1, w_\beta, \mathsf{wi}_2) \end{array}\right] \geq \frac{1}{q(\lambda)} - \mathsf{negl}(\lambda). \quad (5)$$

We emphasize that the oracle $\mathcal{O}$ remains to use hybrid prover algorithm $\mathsf{WIPOK}.\widehat{\mathsf{P}}_2$ in (5). (In the terminology used in Sect. 2.2, adversary $\mathcal{A}_2$ represents the "main thread" and $\widehat{\mathcal{A}}_2$ represents the "look-ahead threads"). We prove Lemma 1 by formalizing the argument sketched in Sect. 2.2. The proof is given in the full version of this paper.

5 Our 4-Round SNMZK Argument

In this section, we prove our main result.

Theorem 4. *Assume the existence of collision-resistant hash functions and injective one-way functions. Then, for any NP language* $\boldsymbol{L}$*, there exists a 4-round adaptive-input interactive argument that satisfies one-many statistical non-malleable zero-knowledge with weak adaptive input selection.*

To prove Theorem 4, we prove the following lemma.

Lemma 2. *Assume the existence of the following building blocks.*

- *A 3-round synchronous non-malleable commitment scheme* $\mathsf{NMC} = (\mathsf{NMC.S}_1, \mathsf{NMC.S}_2, \mathsf{NMC.R})$ *that satisfies the unique decommitment candidate property described in Theorem 2. Let* $\mathsf{NMC.R}_{\mathsf{D,weak}}$ *be the predicate that is guaranteed to exist by the unique decommitment candidate property.*
- *A 4-round public-coin adaptive-input argument* $\mathsf{SWIAOK} = (\mathsf{SWIAOK.P}_1, \mathsf{SWIAOK.P}_2, \mathsf{SWIAOK.V}_1, \mathsf{SWIAOK.V}_2, \mathsf{SWIAOK.V}_{\mathsf{D}})$ *that satisfies both adaptive-input computational special-soundness and adaptive-input statistical witness indistinguishability. Let* $\mathsf{SWIAOK.Ext}$ *be the extractor that is guaranteed to exist by the adaptive-input computational special soundness.*
- *A 3-round adaptive-input OR-indistinguishable special-sound proof* $\mathsf{WIPOK} = (\mathsf{WIPOK.P}_1, \mathsf{WIPOK.P}_2, \mathsf{WIPOK.V}, \mathsf{WIPOK.V}_{\mathsf{D}})$ *that satisfies the additional properties defined in Theorem 3. Let* $\mathsf{WIPOK.Ext}$ *and* $\mathsf{WIPOK.EQ}$ *be the extractor and predicate that are guaranteed to exist by the adaptive-input special soundness.*

Then, for any NP language $\boldsymbol{L}$*, there exists a 4-round adaptive-input interactive argument that satisfies one-many statistical non-malleable zero-knowledge with weak adaptive input selection.*

Since the building blocks listed in Lemma 2 can be constructed from any collision-resistant hash function and injective one-way function (cf. Theorem 2, Theorem 1, and Theorem 3), Lemma 2 implies Theorem 4. Thus, we focus on proving Lemma 2 below.

5.1 Protocol Description

The formal description of our 4-round SNMZK argument, $\langle P, V\rangle = (\mathsf{P}_1, \mathsf{P}_2, \mathsf{V}_1, \mathsf{V}_2, \mathsf{V}_\mathsf{D})$, is given below.

4-round SNMZK argument $\langle P, V\rangle = (\mathsf{P}_1, \mathsf{P}_2, \mathsf{V}_1, \mathsf{V}_2, \mathsf{V}_\mathsf{D})$

Let $(x, w) \in \mathbf{R_L}$ be an instance of an NP language $\mathbf{L}$ and a corresponding witness. Let $\lambda := |x|$ denote the security parameter. Let $\mathsf{tag} \in \{0,1\}^\lambda$ be a string representing the tag.

Round 1. $\mathsf{V}_1(1^\lambda, \mathsf{tag})$:

1. $\forall b \in \{0,1\}$: Compute $(\mathsf{i\text{-}nm}_{b,1}, \mathsf{i\text{-}dec}_b, \mathsf{i\text{-}st}_{\mathsf{nm},b}) \leftarrow \mathsf{NMC.S}_1(1^\lambda, \mathsf{tag}, r_b)$ for a random string $r_b \leftarrow \{0,1\}^\lambda$.
2. $\forall b \in \{0,1\}$: Compute $(\mathsf{o\text{-}nm}_{b,1}, \mathsf{o\text{-}dec}_b, \mathsf{o\text{-}st}_{\mathsf{nm},b}) \leftarrow \mathsf{NMC.S}_1(1^\lambda, \mathsf{tag}, \mathsf{i\text{-}dec}_b)$.
3. Compute $(\mathsf{wi}_1, \mathsf{st}_\mathsf{wi}, \mathsf{aux}_\mathsf{wi}) \leftarrow \mathsf{WIPOK}.\widehat{\mathsf{P}}_1(1^{\lambda_V}, \beta)$ for a random bit $\beta \leftarrow \{0,1\}$, where λ_V is the length of the statements $x_{V,0}, x_{V,1} \in \mathbf{L}_V$ defined in Round 3.
4. Compute $\mathsf{swi}_1 \leftarrow \mathsf{SWIAOK.V}_1(1^{\lambda_P})$, where λ_P is the length of the statement $x_P \in \mathbf{L}_P$ defined in Round 4.
5. Output $\mathsf{msg}_1 := (\{\mathsf{i\text{-}nm}_{b,1}, \mathsf{o\text{-}nm}_{b,1}\}_{b\in\{0,1\}}, \mathsf{wi}_1, \mathsf{swi}_1)$ and $\mathsf{st}_V := (\{\mathsf{i\text{-}st}_{\mathsf{nm},b}, \mathsf{o\text{-}st}_{\mathsf{nm},b}\}_{b\in\{0,1\}}, \mathsf{st}_\mathsf{wi}, \mathsf{aux}_\mathsf{wi})$.

Round 2. $\mathsf{P}_1(1^\lambda, \mathsf{tag}, \mathsf{msg}_1)$:

1. Compute the responses to $\{\mathsf{i\text{-}nm}_{b,1}, \mathsf{o\text{-}nm}_{b,1}\}_{b\in\{0,1\}}$, wi_1, and swi_1 as follows.
   - $\forall b \in \{0,1\}$: $\mathsf{i\text{-}nm}_{b,2} \leftarrow \mathsf{NMC.R}(1^\lambda, \mathsf{tag}, \mathsf{i\text{-}nm}_1)$.
   - $\forall b \in \{0,1\}$: $\mathsf{o\text{-}nm}_{b,2} \leftarrow \mathsf{NMC.R}(1^\lambda, \mathsf{tag}, \mathsf{o\text{-}nm}_1)$.
   - $\mathsf{wi}_2 \leftarrow \mathsf{WIPOK.V}(1^{\lambda_V})$.
   - $(\mathsf{swi}_2, \mathsf{st}_\mathsf{swi}) \leftarrow \mathsf{SWIAOK.P}_1(1^{\lambda_P}, \mathsf{swi}_1)$.
2. Output $\mathsf{msg}_2 := (\{\mathsf{i\text{-}nm}_{b,2}, \mathsf{o\text{-}nm}_{b,2}\}_{b\in\{0,1\}}, \mathsf{wi}_2, \mathsf{swi}_2)$ and $\mathsf{st}_P := \mathsf{st}_\mathsf{swi}$.

Round 3. $\mathsf{V}_2(\mathsf{st}_V, \mathsf{msg}_2)$:

1. Compute the responses to $\{\mathsf{i\text{-}nm}_{b,2}, \mathsf{o\text{-}nm}_{b,2}\}_{b\in\{0,1\}}$ as follows.
   - $\forall b \in \{0,1\}$: $\mathsf{i\text{-}nm}_{b,3} \leftarrow \mathsf{NMC.S}_2(\mathsf{i\text{-}st}_{\mathsf{nm},b}, \mathsf{i\text{-}nm}_{b,2})$.
   - $\forall b \in \{0,1\}$: $\mathsf{o\text{-}nm}_{b,3} \leftarrow \mathsf{NMC.S}_2(\mathsf{o\text{-}st}_{\mathsf{nm},b}, \mathsf{o\text{-}nm}_{b,2})$.
2. Compute the response to wi_2 by $\mathsf{wi}_3 \leftarrow \mathsf{WIPOK}.\widehat{\mathsf{P}}_2(\mathsf{st}_\mathsf{wi}, \mathsf{aux}_\mathsf{wi}, x_{V,0}, x_{V,1}, w_{V,0}, w_{V,1}, \mathsf{wi}_2)$, where $x_{V,b} := (\mathsf{i}\text{-}\tau_b, \mathsf{o}\text{-}\tau_b)$, $\mathsf{i}\text{-}\tau_b := (\mathsf{i\text{-}nm}_{b,1}, \mathsf{i\text{-}nm}_{b,2}, \mathsf{i\text{-}nm}_{b,3})$, $\mathsf{o}\text{-}\tau_b := (\mathsf{o\text{-}nm}_{b,1}, \mathsf{o\text{-}nm}_{b,2}, \mathsf{o\text{-}nm}_{b,3})$, and $w_{V,b} := (\mathsf{i\text{-}dec}_b, \mathsf{o\text{-}dec}_b)$ for each $b \in \{0,1\}$. Here, $x_{V,b}$ is viewed as an instance of the following language $\mathbf{L}_V$.

$$\mathbf{L}_V := \left\{ (\mathsf{i}\text{-}\tau, \mathsf{o}\text{-}\tau) \;\middle|\; \begin{array}{l} \exists(\mathsf{i\text{-}dec}, \mathsf{o\text{-}dec}) \text{ s.t.} \\ \mathsf{NMC.R_D}(\mathsf{i}\text{-}\tau, \mathsf{i\text{-}dec}) \neq \bot \\ \wedge\ \mathsf{NMC.R_D}(\mathsf{o}\text{-}\tau, \mathsf{o\text{-}dec}) = \mathsf{i\text{-}dec} \neq \bot \end{array} \right\}.$$

3. Compute the response to swi_2 by $\mathsf{swi}_3 \leftarrow \mathsf{SWIAOK.V}_2(1^{\lambda_P})$.

4. Output $\mathsf{msg}_3 := (\{\text{i-}\mathsf{nm}_{b,3}, \text{o-}\mathsf{nm}_{b,3}\}_{b\in\{0,1\}}, \mathsf{wi}_3, \mathsf{swi}_3)$.

Round 4. $\mathsf{P}_2(\mathsf{st}_P, x, w, \mathsf{msg}_3)$:

1. Check whether $\mathsf{WIPOK.V_D}(x_{V,0}, x_{V,1}, \tau_{\mathsf{wi}}) \stackrel{?}{=} 1$, where $\tau_{\mathsf{wi}} := (\mathsf{wi}_1, \mathsf{wi}_2, \mathsf{wi}_3)$. If the check fails, abort.
2. Compute $\mathsf{swi}_4 \leftarrow \mathsf{SWIAOK.P_2}(\mathsf{st_{swi}}, x_P, w, \mathsf{swi}_3)$, where $x_P := (x, \text{i-}\mathsf{nm}_{0,1}, \text{i-}\mathsf{nm}_{1,1})$. Here, x_P is viewed as an instance of the language $\mathbf{L}_P := \{(x, \text{i-}\mathsf{nm}_{0,1}, \text{i-}\mathsf{nm}_{1,1}) \mid x \in \mathbf{L} \vee (\text{i-}\mathsf{nm}_{0,1}, \text{i-}\mathsf{nm}_{1,1}) \in \mathbf{L}_{\mathsf{td}}\}$, where $\mathbf{L}_{\mathsf{td}} := \{(\text{i-}\mathsf{nm}_{0,1}, \text{i-}\mathsf{nm}_{1,1}) \mid \exists(b, \mathsf{dec}) \text{ s.t. } \mathsf{NMC.R_{D,weak}}(\text{i-}\mathsf{nm}_{b,1}, \mathsf{dec}) = 1\}$.
3. Output $\mathsf{msg}_4 := \mathsf{swi}_4$.

Verification. $\mathsf{V_D}(x, (\mathsf{msg}_1, \ldots, \mathsf{msg}_4))$ outputs 1 if and only if $\mathsf{SWIAOK.V_D}(x_P, \tau_{\mathsf{swi}}) = 1$ for $\tau_{\mathsf{swi}} := (\mathsf{swi}_1, \mathsf{swi}_2, \mathsf{swi}_3, \mathsf{swi}_4)$.

For each $b \in \{0,1\}$, we call $\text{i-}\tau_b = (\text{i-}\mathsf{nm}_{b,1}, \text{i-}\mathsf{nm}_{b,2}, \text{i-}\mathsf{nm}_{b,3})$ the *b-th inner* NMC *commitment*, and $\text{o-}\tau_b = (\text{o-}\mathsf{nm}_{b,1}, \text{o-}\mathsf{nm}_{b,2}, \text{o-}\mathsf{nm}_{b,3})$ the *b-th outer* NMC *commitment.* The delayed-input completeness and adaptive-input soundness of $\langle P, V\rangle$ can be analyzed in a standard manner (see the full version of this paper). Below, we prove the one-many statistical non-malleable zero-knowledge weak adaptive input selection.

5.2 Description of Simulator-Extractor

As explained in Sect. 2, our simulator-extractor simulates the left interaction using the extractor of WIPOK and extracts a witness in each accepting right interaction using the extractor of SWIAOK. Before describing how it works formally, let us mention two technical detailed omitted in Sect. 2. First, when the extractor of WIPOK is used, our simulator-extractor keeps rewinding the adversary until it obtains two (rather than one) additional accepting transcripts, and the extractor is invoked on these two additional transcripts. At a high level, using the extractor in this way makes the rewinding process almost independent of the rest of the simulator-extractor, thereby making it easy to use Lemma 1 (the technical lemma shown on WIPOK in Sect. 4).[14] Second, when the extractor of SWIAOK is used for each right interaction, our simulator-extractor keeps rewinding the adversary until it obtains an additional accepting transcript in which the left interaction is competed in the same way as before. (For example, if the left interaction was completed using the 0-th inner NMC commitment for SWIAOK before the rewinding, our simulator-extractor tries to obtain an accepting transcript in which the left interaction is again completed using the 0-th inner NMC commitment for SWIAOK.) Using the extractor in this way simplifies the analysis of witness extractability.

[14] Specifically, the rewinding process only determines which of the two inner NMC commitments are used by the simulator-extractor for the simulation of the SWIAOK proof.

Formally, for any PPT man-in-the-middle adversary $\mathcal{A}$ and a polynomial m such that $\mathcal{A}$ participates in at most $m(\lambda)$ right interactions, our simulator-extractor, $\mathcal{SE}$, works as follows.

Simulator-extractor $\mathcal{SE}$.

Simulation part. On input $(1^\lambda, z)$, the simulator-extractor $\mathcal{SE}$ internally invokes $\mathcal{A}(1^\lambda, z)$ and emulates the left and right interactions for $\mathcal{A}$ in the following way.

In each right interaction, $\mathcal{SE}$ interacts with $\mathcal{A}$ using the honest verifier algorithms. That is, $\mathcal{SE}$ interacts with $\mathcal{A}$ in the i-th right interaction as follows. (In what follows, we denote Round j of the i-th right interaction by Round i-j for each $j \in \{1, \dots, 4\}$.)

Round i-1. Receiving $\widetilde{\mathsf{tag}}_i$, compute $(\widetilde{\mathsf{msg}}_{i,1}, \widetilde{\mathsf{st}}_{V,i}) \leftarrow \mathsf{V}_1(1^\lambda, \widetilde{\mathsf{tag}}_i)$ and send $\widetilde{\mathsf{msg}}_{i,1}$ to $\mathcal{A}$.

Round i-2. Receiving $\widetilde{\mathsf{msg}}_{i,2}$, compute $\widetilde{\mathsf{msg}}_{i,3} \leftarrow \mathsf{V}_2(\widetilde{\mathsf{st}}_{V,i}, \widetilde{\mathsf{msg}}_{i,2})$ and send $\widetilde{\mathsf{msg}}_{i,3}$ to $\mathcal{A}$.

In the left interaction, $\mathcal{SE}$ interacts with $\mathcal{A}$ as follows.

Round 2. Receiving $(\mathsf{tag}, \mathsf{msg}_1)$, compute $(\mathsf{msg}_2, \mathsf{st}_P) \leftarrow \mathsf{P}_1(1^\lambda, \mathsf{tag}, \mathsf{msg}_1)$ and send msg_2 to $\mathcal{A}$.

Round 4. Receiving (x, msg_3), do the following.

4:1 Like the honest prover, check whether msg_3 is accepting, i.e., whether $\mathsf{WIPOK.V_D}(x_{V,0}, x_{V,1}, \tau_{\mathsf{wi}}) \stackrel{?}{=} 1$ for the WIPOK statements $x_{V,0}, x_{V,1}$ and transcript τ_{wi} defined based on $(\mathsf{msg}_1, \mathsf{msg}_2, \mathsf{msg}_3)$. If the check fails, abort the left interaction.

4:2 If the check passes, repeat the following until the condition described below is met.

Left rewinding. Rewind $\mathcal{A}$ to the point just before sending msg_2 to $\mathcal{A}$ in Round 2. Then, sample a new Round-2 message msg'_2 using $\mathsf{P}_1(1^\lambda, \mathsf{tag}, \mathsf{msg}_1)$ with fresh randomness, send msg'_2 to $\mathcal{A}$, and continue interacting with $\mathcal{A}$ until obtaining a new Round-3 message msg'_3. (During the interaction with $\mathcal{A}$, the right interactions are simulated as before using fresh randomness.)

The condition for breaking the loop is to find *two* new accepting Round-3 messages $\mathsf{msg}'_3, \mathsf{msg}''_3$. Let msg'_2 denote the Round-2 message that is sent to $\mathcal{A}$ when obtaining msg'_3. Let $(x'_{V,0}, x'_{V,1})$ and τ'_{wi} denote the WIPOK statements and transcript defined based on $(\mathsf{msg}_1, \mathsf{msg}'_2, \mathsf{msg}'_3)$. Let msg''_2, $(x''_{V,0}, x''_{V,1})$, and τ''_{wi} be defined similarly w.r.t. msg''_3. (At the end of this step, the state of $\mathcal{A}$ is restored to the one that $\mathcal{A}$ had before the above rewinding.)

4:3 Compute $w_V := \mathsf{WIPOK.Ext}((x'_{V,0}, x'_{V,1}), \tau'_{\mathsf{wi}}, (x''_{V,0}, x''_{V,1}), \tau''_{\mathsf{wi}})$. If $\exists \beta \in \{0,1\}$ s.t. $(x'_{V,\beta}, w_V) \in \mathbf{R}_{\mathbf{L}_V}$, parse w_V as $(\mathsf{i\text{-}dec}, \mathsf{o\text{-}dec})$ and let $w_{\mathsf{td}} := (\beta, \mathsf{i\text{-}dec})$. If there is no such β, output fail and abort.

4:4 Compute $\mathsf{swi}_4 \leftarrow \mathsf{SWIAOK.P}_2(\mathsf{st}_{\mathsf{swi}}, x_P, w_{\mathsf{td}}, \mathsf{swi}_3)$ by using w_{td} with the SWIAOK prover state $\mathsf{st}_{\mathsf{swi}}$, statement x_P, and challenge swi_3 that are defined based on $(x, \mathsf{msg}_1, \mathsf{msg}_2, \mathsf{msg}_3)$. Then, send $\mathsf{msg}_4 := \mathsf{swi}_4$ to $\mathcal{A}$.

Let sim-view be the joint view of $\mathcal{A}$ and the honest verifiers emulated in the above. We call the execution of $\mathcal{A}$ recorded in sim-view the *main thread*, and the executions of $\mathcal{A}$ generated during the left rewinding the *left look-ahead threads.* We call w_{td} (the witness used for SWIAOK in Step 4:4) the *trapdoor witness.*

Extraction part. After completing the simulation part, $\mathcal{SE}$ defines candidate witnesses $\{\widetilde{w}_i\}_{i\in[m(\lambda)]}$ in the following way. For each $i \in [m(\lambda)]$ such that the i-th right interaction is rejecting or uses the same tag as the left interaction, $\mathcal{SE}$ lets $\widetilde{w}_i := \bot$. For every other i, $\mathcal{SE}$ does the following. Let $\widetilde{x}_i$ and $\widetilde{\mathsf{msg}}_{i,4}$ denote the statement and message sent by $\mathcal{A}$ in Round i-4.

i:1 Repeat the following until the condition described below is met.
Right rewinding. Rewind $\mathcal{A}$ to the point just before sending $\widetilde{\mathsf{msg}}_{i,3}$ to $\mathcal{A}$ in Round i-3. Then, define a new Round-3 message $\widetilde{\mathsf{msg}}'_{i,3}$ as follows: parse $\widetilde{\mathsf{msg}}_{i,3}$ as $\widetilde{\mathsf{msg}}_{i,3} = (\{\widetilde{\mathsf{i\text{-}nm}}_{b,3}, \widetilde{\mathsf{o\text{-}nm}}_{b,3}\}_{b\in\{0,1\}}, \widetilde{\mathsf{wi}}_3, \widetilde{\mathsf{swi}}_3)$; then, sample a new challenge message $\widetilde{\mathsf{swi}}'_3 \leftarrow \mathsf{SWIAOK.V}_2(1^{\lambda_P})$ for SWIAOK and let $\widetilde{\mathsf{msg}}'_{i,3} := (\{\widetilde{\mathsf{i\text{-}nm}}_{b,3}, \widetilde{\mathsf{o\text{-}nm}}_{b,3}\}_{b\in\{0,1\}}, \widetilde{\mathsf{wi}}_3, \widetilde{\mathsf{swi}}'_3)$. Then, send $\widetilde{\mathsf{msg}}'_{i,3}$ to $\mathcal{A}$ and continue interacting with $\mathcal{A}$ until obtaining a new Round 4 message $\widetilde{\mathsf{msg}}'_{i,4}$ along with a new statement $\widetilde{x}'_i$ in Round i-4. (During the interaction with $\mathcal{A}$, the left and other right interactions are simulated as before using fresh randomness, including the left rewinding in Step 4:2.)

Let us call the interactions with $\mathcal{A}$ during the right rewinding the *right look-ahead threads.* Then, roughly speaking, the condition for breaking the loop is to find a right look-ahead thread in which the i-th right interaction is accepting *and* the left interaction is completed in the same way as in the main thread. Formally, the condition for breaking the loop is defined as follows. In the main and right look-ahead threads, for each $b \in \{0,1\}$, let EVENT_b denote the event that (i) the i-th right interaction is accepting and (ii) Round 4 of the left interaction is scheduled after Round i-3 and is completed using a witness of the form $(b, *)$ for SWIAOK. Similarly, let EVENT_2 denote the event that (i) the i-th right interaction is accepting and (ii) either Round 4 of the left interaction is scheduled before Round i-3 or the left interaction is aborted. Let $k^* \in \{0,1,2\}$ be such that event EVENT_{k^*} occurs in the main thread. Then, the condition for breaking the loop is to find a right look-ahead thread in which event EVENT_{k^*} occurs.

i:2 Compute $\widetilde{w}_{P,i} := \mathsf{SWIAOK.Ext}(\widetilde{x}_{P,i}, \widetilde{\tau}_{\mathsf{swi},i}, \widetilde{x}'_{P,i}, \widetilde{\tau}'_{\mathsf{swi},i})$ for (i) the SWIAOK statement $\widetilde{x}_{P,i}$ and transcript $\widetilde{\tau}_{\mathsf{swi},i}$ defined based on $(\widetilde{x}_i, \widetilde{\mathsf{msg}}_{i,1}, \widetilde{\mathsf{msg}}_{i,2}, \widetilde{\mathsf{msg}}_{i,3}, \widetilde{\mathsf{msg}}_{i,4})$ and (ii) the SWIAOK statement $\widetilde{x}'_{P,i}$ and transcript $\widetilde{\tau}'_{\mathsf{swi},i}$ defined based on $(\widetilde{x}'_i, \widetilde{\mathsf{msg}}_{i,1}, \widetilde{\mathsf{msg}}_{i,2}, \widetilde{\mathsf{msg}}'_{i,3}, \widetilde{\mathsf{msg}}'_{i,4})$. If $(\widetilde{x}_{P,i}, \widetilde{w}_{P,i}) \in \mathbf{R}_{\mathbf{L}_P}$, let $\widetilde{w}_i := \widetilde{w}_{P,i}$. Otherwise, let $\widetilde{w}_i := \bot_{\mathsf{fail}}$.

Final output. After completing the extraction part, $\mathcal{SE}$ outputs $(\mathsf{sim\text{-}view}, \{\widetilde{w}_i\}_{i \in [m(\lambda)]})$.

We analyze the witness extractability of $\mathcal{SE}$ below. (The analyses of the running time and statistical simulation property are given in the full version of this paper.) Fix any PPT man-in-the-middle adversary $\mathcal{A}$ and a polynomial m such that $\mathcal{A}$ participates in at most $m(\lambda)$ right interactions. Fix any PPT witness-selecting machine M.

5.3 Witness Extractability of Simulator-Extractor

For each $i \in [m(\lambda)]$, let us say that event BAD_i occurs in the execution of $\mathcal{SE}$ if (i) $\mathcal{SE}$ does not abort, (ii) in the main thread, the i-th right interaction is accepting and uses a different tag from the left interaction, and (iii) the i-th extracted witness $\widetilde{w}_i$ is not a valid witness for the i-th right statement $\widetilde{x}_i$. Assume for contradiction that there exists a polynomial q such that for infinitely many $\lambda \in \mathbb{N}$, there exist $(z, z') \in Z_{\mathcal{A},M}(\lambda)$ and $i^* \in [m(\lambda)]$ such that BAD_{i^*} occurs with probability at least $1/q(\lambda)$. Fix any such q, λ, (z, z'), and i^*. For simplicity (and without loss of generality), we assume that $\mathcal{A}$ schedules the messages in the left and right interactions in the following way.

- Round 4 of every right interaction is scheduled at the end of the experiment.
- Round 2 of the left interaction is scheduled immediately after Round 1 of the left interaction, and Round 4 of the left interaction is scheduled immediately after Round 3 of the left interaction.[15]
- Round 1 of each right interaction is scheduled immediately after the point where $\mathcal{A}$ selects a tag for the corresponding right interaction, and Round 3 of each right interaction is scheduled immediately after Round 2 of the corresponding right interaction.

Under this assumption, the i^*-th right interaction must be scheduled in one of the following ways.[16]

Schedule 1. Rounds 1 and 2 of the left interaction are scheduled between Rounds i^*-1 and i^*-2, and Rounds 3 and 4 of the left interaction are scheduled between Rounds i^*-3 and i^*-4. (In other words, the i^*-th right interaction is synchronized with the left interaction.)

[15] In other words, no messages belonging to the right interactions are scheduled between Rounds 1 and 2 (resp., 3 and 4) of the left interaction.

[16] When the left interaction is aborted, we think the left interaction is completed at the point of being aborted by exchanging empty messages for the remaining rounds.

Schedule 2. Round 2 of the left interaction is scheduled before the beginning of the i^*-th right interaction, and Rounds 3 and 4 of the left interaction are scheduled between Rounds i^*-3 and i^*-4.
Schedule 3. Round 4 of the left interaction is scheduled before Round i^*-2.
Schedule 4. Round 1 of the left interaction is scheduled after Round i^*-3.

For each $j \in \{1, \ldots, 4\}$, let $\mathsf{BAD}_{i^*,j}$ denote the event that (i) BAD_{i^*} occurs and (ii) the i^*-th right interaction is scheduled in Schedule j in the main thread. Since we have $\Pr[\mathsf{BAD}_{i^*}] \geq 1/q(\lambda)$, there exists $j^* \in \{1, \ldots, 4\}$ such that $\Pr[\mathsf{BAD}_{i^*,j^*}] \geq 1/4q(\lambda)$.

Synchronous Case ($j^* = 1$). We focus on the case that $\Pr[\mathsf{BAD}_{i^*,1}] \geq 1/4q(\lambda)$. (The other cases can be analyzed analogously; see the full version of this paper.) We start by making several simplifications to $\mathcal{SE}$. Consider the following hybrid simulator-extractors $\mathcal{SE}_1, \ldots, \mathcal{SE}_5$.

1. $\mathcal{SE}_1$ is identical to $\mathcal{SE}$ except that $\mathcal{SE}_1$ outputs fail and aborts if the i^*-th right interaction is not scheduled in Schedule 1 in the main thread.
2. $\mathcal{SE}_2$ is identical to $\mathcal{SE}_1$ except that in the extraction part, $\mathcal{SE}_2$ lets $\widetilde{w}_i := \bot$ for every $i \neq i^*$ and skips every step related to such $\widetilde{w}_i$ (i.e., Steps i:1 and i:2 for every $i \neq i^*$).
3. $\mathcal{SE}_3$ is identical to $\mathcal{SE}_2$ except that when defining the i^*-th witness $\widetilde{w}_{i^*}$ in the extraction part, $\mathcal{SE}_3$ only generates a single right look-ahead thread (rather than keep generating right look-ahead threads until EVENT_{k^*} occurs in the current right look-ahead thread, where recall that $k^* \in \{0, 1, 2\}$ is such that EVENT_{k^*} occurs in the main thread). If EVENT_{k^*} occurs in the unique right look-ahead thread, $\mathcal{SE}_3$ defines $\widetilde{w}_{i^*}$ as in $\mathcal{SE}_2$. Otherwise, $\mathcal{SE}_3$ outputs fail and aborts.
4. $\mathcal{SE}_4$ is identical to $\mathcal{SE}_3$ except that in the right look-ahead thread, $\mathcal{SE}_4$ completes SWIAOK in the left interaction by reusing the witness that it used in the main thread. Specifically, consider the case that EVENT_0 or EVENT_1 occurs in the main thread. From the definitions of EVENT_0 and EVENT_1, it follows that in the main thread, Round 4 of the left interaction is successfully completed after Round i^*-3 by extracting a witness w_{td} for SWIAOK using the left rewinding and $\mathsf{WIPOK.Ext}$. Then, when completing Round 4 of the left interaction in the right look-ahead thread, $\mathcal{SE}_4$ no longer re-executes the left rewinding and $\mathsf{WIPOK.Ext}$ to obtain a (potentially different) witness for SWIAOK; instead, it simply reuses w_{td}. Furthermore, in the right look-ahead thread, $\mathcal{SE}_4$ no longer checks whether EVENT_{k^*} occurs. Instead, $\mathcal{SE}_4$ checks whether a new accepting message is obtained in Round i^*-4: if yes, $\mathcal{SE}_4$ defines the i^*-th witness $\widetilde{w}_{i^*}$ as in $\mathcal{SE}_3$ using $\mathsf{SWIAOK.Ext}$; if no, $\mathcal{SE}_4$ outputs fail and aborts. ($\mathcal{SE}_4$ also outputs fail and aborts if w_{td} is not a valid witness for SWIAOK in the right look-ahead thread.)
5. $\mathcal{SE}_5$ is identical to $\mathcal{SE}_4$ except that $\mathcal{SE}_5$ only generates two left look-ahead threads in the simulation part (rather than keep generating left look-ahead threads until obtaining two new accepting Round-3 messages). If two new accepting Round-3 messages are obtained in the two left look-ahead threads,

$\mathcal{SE}_5$ completes the simulation part as in $\mathcal{SE}_4$. Otherwise, $\mathcal{SE}_5$ outputs fail and aborts.

It is not difficult to see that $\mathsf{BAD}_{i^*,1}$ still occurs with non-negligible probability in the final hybrid simulator-extractor $\mathcal{SE}' := \mathcal{SE}_5$. For completeness, we prove the following in the full version of this paper.

Claim 1. *There exists a polynomial q' (determined based on q) such that event $\mathsf{BAD}_{i^*,1}$ occurs with probability at least $1/q'(\lambda)$ in $\mathcal{SE}'$.*

Since the extraction part is only performed for the i^*-th right interaction in $\mathcal{SE}'$, in what follows we refrain from mentioning i^* in our notation. (For example, when we say "the right interaction," we refer to the i^*-th right interaction, and we write BAD_1 rather than $\mathsf{BAD}_{i^*,1}$.) We comment that $\mathcal{SE}'$ runs in strict polynomial time because it generates only a fixed number of threads.

Next, we observe that the extracted witness $\widetilde{w}$ is computationally independent of the bit $\widehat{\beta}$ that $\mathcal{SE}'$ uses for $\mathsf{WIPOK}.\widehat{\mathsf{P}}_1$ in Round 1 of the right interaction.

Claim 2. *Let $\widetilde{\beta}$ denote the bit used by $\mathcal{SE}'$ for $\mathsf{WIPOK}.\widehat{\mathsf{P}}_1$ in Round 1 of the right interaction, and let $\{\widetilde{\mathsf{i\text{-}nm}}_{b,1}\}_{b\in\{0,1\}}$ denote the NMC messages sent by $\mathcal{SE}'$ in Round 1 of the right interaction. Let us say that event $\widehat{\mathsf{BAD}}$ occurs in an execution of $\mathcal{SE}'$ if (i) BAD_1 occurs and (ii) the extracted witness $\widetilde{w}$ is a valid witness for $(\widetilde{\mathsf{i\text{-}nm}}_{0,1}, \widetilde{\mathsf{i\text{-}nm}}_{1,1}) \in \boldsymbol{L}_{\mathsf{td}}$ and of the form $(1-\widetilde{\beta}, *)$. Then, there exists a polynomial $\widehat{q}$ (determined based on q') such that when λ is sufficiently large, event $\widehat{\mathsf{BAD}}$ occurs with probability at least $1/\widehat{q}(\lambda)$.*

Proof. We show that $\widehat{\mathsf{BAD}}$ occurs with probability roughly half of the probability that BAD_1 occurs. By definition, when BAD_1 occurs (and therefore the extracted witness $\widetilde{w}$ is not a valid witness for $\widetilde{x} \in \mathbf{L}$), either $\widetilde{w} = \bot_{\mathsf{fail}}$ or $\widetilde{w}$ is a valid witness for $(\widetilde{\mathsf{i\text{-}nm}}_{0,1}, \widetilde{\mathsf{i\text{-}nm}}_{1,1}) \in \mathbf{L}_{\mathsf{td}}$. First, we have $p_{\mathsf{fail}} := \Pr\left[\mathsf{BAD}_1 \wedge \widetilde{w} = \bot_{\mathsf{fail}}\right] \leq \mathsf{negl}(\lambda)$ because of the adaptive-input computational special soundness of SWIAOK.[17] To analyze the case that $\widetilde{w}$ is a valid witness for $(\widetilde{\mathsf{i\text{-}nm}}_{0,1}, \widetilde{\mathsf{i\text{-}nm}}_{1,1}) \in \mathbf{L}_{\mathsf{td}}$, let us define p (resp., p') to be the probability that (i) BAD_1 occurs and (ii) $\widetilde{w}$ is a valid witness for $(\widetilde{\mathsf{i\text{-}nm}}_{0,1}, \widetilde{\mathsf{i\text{-}nm}}_{1,1}) \in \mathbf{L}_{\mathsf{td}}$ and of the form $(1-\widetilde{\beta}, *)$ (resp., $(\widetilde{\beta}, *)$). Then, we have $|p - p'| \leq \mathsf{negl}(\lambda)$ because of the adaptive-input rewinding OR-indistinguishability of the hybrid prover of WIPOK.[18] Now, using $p_{\mathsf{fail}} + p + p' = \Pr\left[\mathsf{BAD}_1\right] \geq 1/q'(\lambda)$, we obtain $\Pr\left[\widehat{\mathsf{BAD}}\right] = p \geq (1/q'(\lambda) - \mathsf{negl}(\lambda))/2$. □

[17] To see that the left rewinding in $\mathcal{SE}'$ does not interfere with the adaptive-input computational special soundness of SWIAOK, observe that the left rewinding can only require sampling a new challenge message for SWIAOK (which can be done without knowing the internal state of the SWIAOK verifier since SWIAOK is a public-coin protocol).

[18] We require the rewinding version of the adaptive-input OR-indistinguishability since the left rewinding can require sampling new response messages for WIPOK. To see that the right rewinding is not problematic, observe that the right look-ahead thread reuses the same WIPOK response message as the main thread.

We proceed to case analysis depending on which trapdoor witness is used to complete SWIAOK of the left interaction in the main thread. For each $\beta \in \{0,1\}$, let us say that event $\widehat{\mathsf{BAD}}_\beta$ occurs if (i) $\widehat{\mathsf{BAD}}$ occurs and (ii) SWIAOK of the left interaction is completed using a witness of form $w_{\mathsf{td}} = (\beta, *)$ in the main thread. Similarly, let us say that event $\widehat{\mathsf{BAD}}_2$ occurs if (i) $\widehat{\mathsf{BAD}}$ occurs and (ii) the left interaction is aborted in the main thread. Given Claim 2, there exists $k^* \in \{0,1,2\}$ such that $\widehat{\mathsf{BAD}}_{k^*}$ occurs with probability at least $1/3\widehat{q}(\lambda)$. In the following, we focus on the case $k^* \in \{0,1\}$. (The case of $k^* = 2$ can be handled analogously.)

Next, we design a series of hybrid experiments in which $\mathcal{SE}'$ is gradually modified, and we show that $\widehat{\mathsf{BAD}}_{k^*}$ occurs with non-negligible probability in each hybrid.

- Hybrid H_0 is the experiment where $\mathcal{SE}'(1^\lambda, z)$ is executed. From the observation above, $\widehat{\mathsf{BAD}}_{k^*}$ occurs with probability at least $\varepsilon_0 := 1/3\widehat{q}(\lambda)$ in H_0.
- Hybrid H_1 is identical to H_0 except that in the main thread, the WIPOK response message $\widetilde{\mathsf{wi}}_3$ in the right interaction is computed by $\widetilde{\mathsf{wi}}_3 \leftarrow \mathsf{WIPOK.P}_2(\widetilde{\mathsf{st}}_{\mathsf{wi}}, \widetilde{x}_{V,0}, \widetilde{x}_{V,1}, \widetilde{w}_{V,\widetilde{\beta}}, \widetilde{\mathsf{wi}}_2)$ using the real prover algorithm.[19]
- Hybrid H_2 is identical to H_1 except in how the trapdoor witness w_{td} is computed in the simulation part. Concretely, when the Round-3 message msg_3 is accepting in the left interaction in the main thread, the left look-ahead threads are no longer generated (and therefore $\mathsf{WIPOK.Ext}$ is no longer executed either), and w_{td} is computed by brute force as follows.
  1. Extract the committed values of the k^*-th outer NMC commitment by brute force. If the k^*-th outer NMC commitment is invalid (i.e., cannot be decommitted to any value), output fail and abort. Otherwise, let $\mathsf{i\text{-}dec}$ denote the extracted value.
  2. Let $w_{\mathsf{td}} := (k^*, \mathsf{i\text{-}dec})$.
- Hybrid H_3 is identical to H_2 except that in the main thread, the $(1-\widetilde{\beta})$-th outer NMC commitment in the right interaction is computed by committing to a random string.

Claim 3. *$\widehat{\mathsf{BAD}}_{k^*}$ occurs in H_1 with probability at least $\varepsilon_1 := (\varepsilon_0/2)^3 - \mathsf{negl}(\lambda)$.*

Proof. Recall that H_1 differs from H_0 in that the real prover algorithm of WIPOK is used in Round 3 of the right interaction in the main thread (while the hybrid prover algorithm remains to be used in the left look-ahead threads). We show this claim by relying on Lemma 1 (the property shown for WIPOK in Sect. 4).

Informally, we use Lemma 1 as follows. Recall that Lemma 1 is stated about three Turing machines, one is executed to obtain intermediate information $\mathsf{st}_\mathcal{A}$ and the remaining two are executed independently of each other on input $\mathsf{st}_\mathcal{A}$. Accordingly, we consider decomposing the execution of H_0 (resp., H_1) into three components.

[19] We emphasize that the switch to the real prover algorithm is made only in the main thread. In the left look-ahead threads, the WIPOK response message in the right interaction is computed as in H_1, i.e., using the hybrid prover algorithm.

- The first component runs the main thread until the point just before completing Round 3 of the right interaction (more concretely, just before obtaining the WIPOK response message $\widetilde{\mathsf{wi}}_3$ in the right interaction).
- Given the partial transcript generated by the first component, the second component obtains a trapdoor witness w_{td} by generating two left look-ahead threads and invoking WIPOK.Ext.
- Given the partial transcript generated by the first component and the trapdoor witness w_{td} generated by the second component, the third component runs the rest of the main thread (starting from the generation of the WIPOK response message $\widetilde{\mathsf{wi}}_3$ in the right interaction) and the subsequent extraction part of $\mathcal{SE}'$.

Note that H_0 and H_1 differ only in the third component, where a message obtained by the hybrid prover of WIPOK is used in H_0 while a message obtained by the real prover is used in H_1. We cannot use Lemma 1 yet since the second and third components are not independent (the third component receives the trapdoor witness w_{td} from the second component). Toward using Lemma 1, we observe that since we have $\Pr\left[\widehat{\mathsf{BAD}}_{k^*}\right] \geq \varepsilon_0$ in H_0, the following occur with probability at least ε_0 when H_0 is decomposed as above.

- In the first component, the k^*-th inner NMC commit message $\mathsf{i\text{-}nm}_{k^*,1}$ in Round 1 of the left interaction uniquely determines a decommitment candidate $\mathsf{i\text{-}dec}$ satisfying $\mathsf{NMC.R}_{\mathsf{D,weak}}(\mathsf{i\text{-}nm}_{k^*,1}, \mathsf{i\text{-}dec}) = 1$.
- In the second component, a valid trapdoor witness w_{td} of the form $(k^*, *)$ is obtained, and furthermore, it satisfies $w_{\mathsf{td}} = (k^*, \mathsf{i\text{-}dec})$ for $\mathsf{i\text{-}dec}$ determined in the first component.[20]
- In the third component, after the execution of $\mathcal{SE}'$ is completed by using $w_{\mathsf{td}} = (k^*, \mathsf{i\text{-}dec})$ for SWIAOK in the left interaction, $\widehat{\mathsf{BAD}}_{k^*}$ occurs in the emulated execution of $\mathcal{SE}'$.

Now, observe that the above remains to hold even when the third component is executed independently of the second one as follows: instead of having it use the trapdoor witness that is extracted in the second component, have it use the trapdoor witness that is defined based on the decommitment candidate that is determined in the first component. Now that the second and the third components become independent, we can use Lemma 1 to show that the above occurs with non-negligible probability even in H_1, which implies that $\widehat{\mathsf{BAD}}_{k^*}$ occurs in H_1 with non-negligible probability.

Formally, to use Lemma 1, we consider the following Turing machines.

- $\mathcal{A}_1(1^\lambda, \mathsf{wi}_1, z)$ internally invokes $\mathcal{SE}'$ and emulates H_0 with the following differences.
  - In the main thread, wi_1 is forwarded as the WIPOK commit message in Round 1 of the right interaction.

[20] To see the furthermore part, observe that by the uniqueness of valid decommitment candidates, a valid trapdoor witness of the form $(k^*, *)$ must be equal to $(k^*, \mathsf{i\text{-}dec})$.

- In the main thread, when inner NMC commit messages $\{\mathsf{i\text{-}nm}_{b,1}\}_{b\in\{0,1\}}$ are obtained in Round 1 of the left interaction, a decommitment candidate $\mathsf{i\text{-}dec}$ such that $\mathsf{NMC.R}_{\mathsf{D,weak}}(\mathsf{i\text{-}nm}_{k^*,1}, \mathsf{i\text{-}dec}) = 1$ is obtained by brute force.
- The emulation of H_0 is suspended at the point where the WIPOK response message is to be computed in Round 3 of the right interaction in the main thread. Let $\widetilde{x}_{V,0}, \widetilde{x}_{V,1}, \widetilde{w}_{V,0}, \widetilde{w}_{V,1}, \widetilde{\mathsf{wi}}_2$ be the WIPOK statements etc. that are to be used to generate the WIPOK response message, and let $\mathsf{st}_{\mathcal{SE}}$ be the current state of $\mathcal{SE}'$.

Then, $\mathcal{A}_1$ lets $\mathsf{st}_{\mathcal{A}} := (\mathsf{st}_{\mathcal{SE}}, \mathsf{i\text{-}dec})$ and outputs $(\widetilde{x}_{V,0}, \widetilde{x}_{V,1}, \widetilde{w}_{V,0}, \widetilde{w}_{V,1}, \widetilde{\mathsf{wi}}_2, \mathsf{st}_{\mathcal{A}})$.

– $\widehat{\mathcal{A}}_2^{\mathcal{O}(\mathsf{st},\mathsf{aux},\cdot)}(\mathsf{st}_{\mathcal{A}})$ parses $\mathsf{st}_{\mathcal{A}}$ as $\mathsf{st}_{\mathcal{A}} := (\mathsf{st}_{\mathcal{SE}}, \mathsf{i\text{-}dec})$ and continues the emulation of H_0 as follows.
  1. Using $\mathsf{st}_{\mathcal{SE}}$, reconstruct the main thread until the point just before Round 2 of the left interaction.
  2. Obtain a trapdoor witness w_{td} by generating two left look-ahead threads and running $\mathsf{WIPOK.Ext}$ as in H_0, where the oracle $\mathcal{O}$ is used whenever a new WIPOK response message is required in the left look-ahead threads.

  Then, $\widehat{\mathcal{A}}_2$ outputs 1 if and only if the trapdoor witness w_{td} satisfies $w_{\mathsf{td}} = (k^*, \mathsf{i\text{-}dec})$.
– $\mathcal{A}_2(\mathsf{st}_{\mathcal{A}}, \mathsf{wi}_3)$ parses $\mathsf{st}_{\mathcal{A}}$ as $\mathsf{st}_{\mathcal{A}} := (\mathsf{st}_{\mathcal{SE}}, \mathsf{i\text{-}dec})$ and continues the emulation of H_0 as follows.
  1. Using $\mathsf{st}_{\mathcal{SE}}$, reconstruct the main thread until the point at which the WIPOK response message is to be computed in Round 3 of the right interaction. Then, complete Round 3 of the right interaction by using wi_3 as the WIPOK response message.
  2. Emulate the rest of H_0 honestly except that in the main thread, if the Round-3 message msg_3 in the left interaction is accepting, then Round 4 is completed by using $(k^*, \mathsf{i\text{-}dec})$ as the witness for SWIAOK (without generating left look-ahead threads).

  Then, $\mathcal{A}_2$ outputs 1 if and only if $\widehat{\mathsf{BAD}}_{k^*}$ occurs.

Note that when wi_3 is computed by the hybrid prover of WIPOK, the adversary $(\mathcal{A}_1, \widehat{\mathcal{A}}_2, \mathcal{A}_2)$ perfectly emulates H_0 when a trapdoor witness of the form $(k^*, *)$ is obtained in the left interaction. Thus, we have

$$\Pr\left[\begin{array}{l} \mathcal{A}_2(\mathsf{st}_{\mathcal{A}}, \mathsf{wi}_3) = 1 \\ \wedge\ \widehat{\mathcal{A}}_2^{\mathcal{O}(\mathsf{st},\mathsf{aux},\cdot)}(\mathsf{st}_{\mathcal{A}}) = 1 \end{array} \middle| \begin{array}{l} (\mathsf{wi}_1, \mathsf{st}, \mathsf{aux}) \leftarrow \mathsf{WIPOK}.\widehat{\mathsf{P}}_1(1^\lambda, \beta) \\ (x_0, x_1, w_0, w_1, \mathsf{wi}_2, \mathsf{st}_{\mathcal{A}}) \leftarrow \mathcal{A}_1(1^\lambda, \mathsf{wi}_1, z) \\ \mathsf{wi}_3 \leftarrow \mathsf{WIPOK}.\widehat{\mathsf{P}}_2(\mathsf{st}, \mathsf{aux}, x_0, x_1, w_0, w_1, \mathsf{wi}_2) \end{array}\right] \geq \varepsilon_0.$$

Thus, we can use Lemma 1 to obtain

$$\Pr\left[\begin{array}{l} \mathcal{A}_2(\mathsf{st}_{\mathcal{A}}, \mathsf{wi}_3) = 1 \\ \wedge\ \widehat{\mathcal{A}}_2^{\mathcal{O}(\mathsf{st},\mathsf{aux},\cdot)}(\mathsf{st}_{\mathcal{A}}) = 1 \end{array} \middle| \begin{array}{l} (\mathsf{wi}_1, \mathsf{st}, \mathsf{aux}) \leftarrow \mathsf{WIPOK}.\widehat{\mathsf{P}}_1(1^\lambda, \beta) \\ (x_0, x_1, w_0, w_1, \mathsf{wi}_2, \mathsf{st}_{\mathcal{A}}) \leftarrow \mathcal{A}_1(1^\lambda, \mathsf{wi}_1, z) \\ \mathsf{wi}_3 \leftarrow \mathsf{WIPOK.P}_2(\mathsf{st}, x_0, x_1, w_\beta, \mathsf{wi}_2) \end{array}\right]$$
$$\geq \left(\frac{\varepsilon_0}{2}\right)^3 - \mathsf{negl}(\lambda). \quad (6)$$

Note that when wi_3 is computed by the real prover of WIPOK, the adversary $(\mathcal{A}_1, \widehat{\mathcal{A}}_2, \mathcal{A}_2)$ perfectly emulates H_1 when a trapdoor witness of the form $(k^*, *)$ is obtained in the left interaction. Thus, from (6), $\widehat{\mathsf{BAD}}_{k^*}$ occurs in H_1 with probability at least $\varepsilon_1 := (\varepsilon_0/2)^3 - \mathsf{negl}(\lambda)$. □

Claim 4. *$\widehat{\mathsf{BAD}}_{k^*}$ occurs in H_2 with probability at least $\varepsilon_2 := \varepsilon_1$.*

Proof. By definition, when msg_3 is rejecting, H_2 is identical to H_1. We therefore focus on the case that msg_3 is accepting, and we show that when $\widehat{\mathsf{BAD}}_{k^*}$ occurs in H_1, the same trapdoor witness w_{td} is used in H_1 and H_2. Suppose $\widehat{\mathsf{BAD}}_{k^*}$ occurs in H_1. Let $w^*_{\mathsf{td}} = (k^*, \mathsf{i\text{-}dec}^*)$ denote the witness used in H_1 in Round 4 of the left interaction in the main thread. By the way in which w^*_{td} is defined, $\mathsf{i\text{-}dec}^*$ is guaranteed to be the (unique) committed value of the k^*-th outer NMC commitment. Thus, when the committed value of the k^*-th outer NMC commitment is extracted by brute force, the extracted value agrees with $\mathsf{i\text{-}dec}^*$. Thus, even when the trapdoor witness w^*_{td} is computed by brute force as in H_2, event $\widehat{\mathsf{BAD}}_{k^*}$ occurs with probability at least ε_1. □

Claim 5. *$\widehat{\mathsf{BAD}}_{k^*}$ occurs in H_3 with probability at least $\varepsilon_3 := \varepsilon_4 - \mathsf{negl}(\lambda)$.*

Proof. This claim follows directly from the synchronous non-malleability of NMC since the brute-force extraction can be efficiently emulated in the non-malleability security experiment. (To see that the left rewinding is not problematic, observe that the left look-ahead threads are no longer generated in H_2 and H_3. To see that the right rewinding is not problematic, observe that the right look-ahead thread reuses the same NMC response message as the main thread). □

Now, we derive a contradiction by breaking the non-malleability of NMC using H_3. Toward this end, it suffices to consider a man-in-the-middle adversary that internally emulates H_3 while (i) using the external committer to generate the $(1-\widetilde{\beta})$-th inner NMC commitment in the right interaction and (ii) using the external receiver for the k^*-th outer NMC commitment in the left interaction. Since this adversary perfectly emulates the experiment H_3, event $\widehat{\mathsf{BAD}}_{k^*}$ occurs in the internally emulated experiment H_3 with non-negligible probability. Furthermore, when event $\widehat{\mathsf{BAD}}_{k^*}$ occurs in the internally emulated experiment H_3, the adversary can obtain the value that the external committer committed to. Thus, the adversary can trivially break the non-malleability of NMC.[21]

---

[21] Note that the $(1-\widetilde{\beta})$-th inner NMC commitment in the right interaction only needs to be non-malleable with the b^*-th outer NMC in the left interaction, and it does not need to be non-malleable with the inner NMC commitments in the left interaction. Because of this asymmetry, the inner commitments actually do not need to satisfy full-fledged non-malleability. (For example, if the outer NMC commitments satisfy a sufficiently strong extractability property, we can use any non-interactive commitment scheme for the inner commitments.) We chose to use NMC for the inner commitment for simplicity.

References

1. Barak, B.: Constant-round coin-tossing with a man in the middle or realizing the shared random string model. In: 43rd FOCS, pp. 345–355. IEEE Computer Society Press (2002). https://doi.org/10.1109/SFCS.2002.1181957
2. Barak, B., Prabhakaran, M., Sahai, A.: Concurrent non-malleable zero knowledge. In: 47th FOCS, pp. 345–354. IEEE Computer Society Press (2006). https://doi.org/10.1109/FOCS.2006.21
3. Botta, V., Ciampi, M., Orsini, E., Siniscalchi, L., Visconti, I.: Black-box (and fast) non-malleable zero knowledge. In: Reyzin, L., Stebila, D. (eds.) CRYPTO 2024, Part IX. LNCS, vol. 14928, pp. 458–490. Springer, Cham (2024). https://doi.org/10.1007/978-3-031-68400-5_14
4. Chatterjee, R., Liang, X., Pandey, O.: Improved black-box constructions of composable secure computation. In: Czumaj, A., Dawar, A., Merelli, E. (eds.) ICALP 2020. LIPIcs, vol. 168, pp. 28:1–28:20. Schloss Dagstuhl (2020). https://doi.org/10.4230/LIPIcs.ICALP.2020.28
5. Chung, K.M., Lin, H., Pass, R.: Constant-round concurrent zero knowledge from P-certificates. In: 54th FOCS, pp. 50–59. IEEE Computer Society Press (2013). https://doi.org/10.1109/FOCS.2013.14
6. Chung, K.M., Lin, H., Pass, R.: Constant-round concurrent zero-knowledge from indistinguishability obfuscation. In: Gennaro, R., Robshaw, M.J.B. (eds.) CRYPTO 2015, Part I. LNCS, vol. 9215, pp. 287–307. Springer, Heidelberg (2015). https://doi.org/10.1007/978-3-662-47989-6_14
7. Ciampi, M., Orsini, E., Siniscalchi, L.: Four-round black-box non-malleable schemes from one-way permutations. In: Kiltz, E., Vaikuntanathan, V. (eds.) TCC 2022, Part II. LNCS, vol. 13748, pp. 300–329. Springer, Cham (2022). https://doi.org/10.1007/978-3-031-22365-5_11
8. Ciampi, M., Ostrovsky, R., Siniscalchi, L., Visconti, I.: Delayed-input non-malleable zero knowledge and multi-party coin tossing in four rounds. In: Kalai, Y., Reyzin, L. (eds.) TCC 2017, Part I. LNCS, vol. 10677, pp. 711–742. Springer, Cham (2017). https://doi.org/10.1007/978-3-319-70500-2_24
9. Ciampi, M., Ostrovsky, R., Siniscalchi, L., Visconti, I.: Delayed-input non-malleable zero knowledge and multi-party coin tossing in four rounds. Cryptology ePrint Archive, Report 2017/931, Version 20181022:155022 (2017). https://eprint.iacr.org/2017/931. A preprint version of [8]
10. Ciampi, M., Ostrovsky, R., Siniscalchi, L., Visconti, I.: Four-round concurrent non-malleable commitments from one-way functions. In: Katz, J., Shacham, H. (eds.) CRYPTO 2017, Part II. LNCS, vol. 10402, pp. 127–157. Springer, Cham (2017). https://doi.org/10.1007/978-3-319-63715-0_5
11. Ciampi, M., Persiano, G., Scafuro, A., Siniscalchi, L., Visconti, I.: Improved OR-composition of sigma-protocols. In: Kushilevitz, E., Malkin, T. (eds.) TCC 2016, Part II. LNCS, vol. 9563, pp. 112–141. Springer, Heidelberg (2016). https://doi.org/10.1007/978-3-662-49099-0_5
12. Ciampi, M., Persiano, G., Scafuro, A., Siniscalchi, L., Visconti, I.: Online/offline OR composition of sigma protocols. In: Fischlin, M., Coron, J.S. (eds.) EUROCRYPT 2016, Part II. LNCS, vol. 9666, pp. 63–92. Springer, Heidelberg (2016). https://doi.org/10.1007/978-3-662-49896-5_3
13. Damgård, I., Pedersen, T.P., Pfitzmann, B.: On the existence of statistically hiding bit commitment schemes and fail-stop signatures. J. Cryptol. **10**(3), 163–194 (1997). https://doi.org/10.1007/s001459900026

14. Dolev, D., Dwork, C., Naor, M.: Nonmalleable cryptography. SIAM J. Comput. **30**(2), 391–437 (2000). https://doi.org/10.1137/S0097539795291562
15. Feige, U., Shamir, A.: Witness indistinguishable and witness hiding protocols. In: 22nd ACM STOC, pp. 416–426. ACM Press (1990). https://doi.org/10.1145/100216.100272
16. Freitag, C., Komargodski, I., Pass, R.: Non-uniformly sound certificates with applications to concurrent zero-knowledge. In: Boldyreva, A., Micciancio, D. (eds.) CRYPTO 2019, Part III. LNCS, vol. 11694, pp. 98–127. Springer, Cham (2019). https://doi.org/10.1007/978-3-030-26954-8_4
17. Garg, S., Goyal, V., Jain, A., Sahai, A.: Concurrently secure computation in constant rounds. In: Pointcheval, D., Johansson, T. (eds.) EUROCRYPT 2012. LNCS, vol. 7237, pp. 99–116. Springer, Heidelberg (2012). https://doi.org/10.1007/978-3-642-29011-4_8
18. Goldreich, O., Krawczyk, H.: On the composition of zero-knowledge proof systems. SIAM J. Comput. **25**(1), 169–192 (1996). https://doi.org/10.1137/S0097539791220688
19. Goyal, V.: Constant round non-malleable protocols using one way functions. In: Fortnow, L., Vadhan, S.P. (eds.) 43rd ACM STOC, pp. 695–704. ACM Press (2011). https://doi.org/10.1145/1993636.1993729
20. Goyal, V., Pandey, O., Richelson, S.: Textbook non-malleable commitments. Cryptology ePrint Archive, Report 2015/1178, Version 20170521:195131 (2015). https://eprint.iacr.org/2015/1178. A preprint version of [21]
21. Goyal, V., Pandey, O., Richelson, S.: Textbook non-malleable commitments. In: Wichs, D., Mansour, Y. (eds.) 48th ACM STOC, pp. 1128–1141. ACM Press (2016). https://doi.org/10.1145/2897518.2897657
22. Goyal, V., Richelson, S.: Non-malleable commitments using Goldreich-Levin list decoding. In: Zuckerman, D. (ed.) 60th FOCS, pp. 686–699. IEEE Computer Society Press (2019). https://doi.org/10.1109/FOCS.2019.00047
23. Goyal, V., Richelson, S., Rosen, A., Vald, M.: An algebraic approach to non-malleability. SIAM J. Comput. **50**(5), 1537–1579 (2021). https://doi.org/10.1137/16M1073595
24. Halevi, S., Micali, S.: Practical and provably-secure commitment schemes from collision-free hashing. In: Koblitz, N. (ed.) CRYPTO 1996. LNCS, vol. 1109, pp. 201–215. Springer, Heidelberg (1996). https://doi.org/10.1007/3-540-68697-5_16
25. Jain, A., Pandey, O.: Non-malleable zero knowledge: black-box constructions and definitional relationships. In: Abdalla, M., De Prisco, R. (eds.) SCN 2014. LNCS, vol. 8642, pp. 435–454. Springer, Cham (2014). https://doi.org/10.1007/978-3-319-10879-7_25
26. Kim, A., Liang, X., Pandey, O.: A new approach to efficient non-malleable zero-knowledge. In: Dodis, Y., Shrimpton, T. (eds.) CRYPTO 2022, Part IV. LNCS, vol. 13510, pp. 389–418. Springer, Cham (2022). https://doi.org/10.1007/978-3-031-15985-5_14
27. Kiyoshima, S.: Statistical concurrent non-malleable zero-knowledge from one-way functions. J. Cryptol. **33**(3), 1318–1361 (2020). https://doi.org/10.1007/s00145-020-09348-x
28. Lapidot, D., Shamir, A.: Publicly verifiable non-interactive zero-knowledge proofs. In: Menezes, A.J., Vanstone, S.A. (eds.) CRYPTO 1990. LNCS, vol. 537, pp. 353–365. Springer, Heidelberg (1991). https://doi.org/10.1007/3-540-38424-3_26
29. Lin, H., Pass, R.: Concurrent non-malleable zero knowledge with adaptive inputs. In: Ishai, Y. (ed.) TCC 2011. LNCS, vol. 6597, pp. 274–292. Springer, Heidelberg (2011). https://doi.org/10.1007/978-3-642-19571-6_17

30. Lin, H., Pass, R.: Constant-round non-malleable commitments from any one-way function. In: Fortnow, L., Vadhan, S.P. (eds.) 43rd ACM STOC, pp. 705–714. ACM Press (2011). https://doi.org/10.1145/1993636.1993730
31. Lin, H., Pass, R.: Constant-round nonmalleable commitments from any one-way function. J. ACM **62**(1) (2015). https://doi.org/10.1145/2699446
32. Lin, H., Pass, R., Tseng, W.L.D., Venkitasubramaniam, M.: Concurrent non-malleable zero knowledge proofs. In: Rabin, T. (ed.) CRYPTO 2010. LNCS, vol. 6223, pp. 429–446. Springer, Heidelberg (2010). https://doi.org/10.1007/978-3-642-14623-7_23
33. Lin, H., Pass, R., Venkitasubramaniam, M.: Concurrent non-malleable commitments from any one-way function. In: Canetti, R. (ed.) TCC 2008. LNCS, vol. 4948, pp. 571–588. Springer, Berlin, Heidelberg (2008). https://doi.org/10.1007/978-3-540-78524-8_31
34. Müller-Quade, J., Unruh, D.: Long-term security and universal composability. J. Cryptol. **23**(4), 594–671 (2010). https://doi.org/10.1007/s00145-010-9068-8
35. Orlandi, C., Ostrovsky, R., Rao, V., Sahai, A., Visconti, I.: Statistical concurrent non-malleable zero knowledge. In: Lindell, Y. (ed.) TCC 2014. LNCS, vol. 8349, pp. 167–191. Springer, Heidelberg (2014). https://doi.org/10.1007/978-3-642-54242-8_8
36. Ostrovsky, R., Pandey, O., Visconti, I.: Efficiency preserving transformations for concurrent non-malleable zero knowledge. In: Micciancio, D. (ed.) TCC 2010. LNCS, vol. 5978, pp. 535–552. Springer, Heidelberg (2010). https://doi.org/10.1007/978-3-642-11799-2_32
37. Pandey, O., Prabhakaran, M., Sahai, A.: Obfuscation-based non-black-box simulation and four message concurrent zero knowledge for NP. In: Dodis, Y., Nielsen, J.B. (eds.) TCC 2015, Part II. LNCS, vol. 9015, pp. 638–667. Springer, Heidelberg (2015). https://doi.org/10.1007/978-3-662-46497-7_25
38. Pass, R.: Limits of provable security from standard assumptions. In: Fortnow, L., Vadhan, S.P. (eds.) 43rd ACM STOC, pp. 109–118. ACM Press (2011). https://doi.org/10.1145/1993636.1993652
39. Pass, R., Rosen, A.: Concurrent nonmalleable commitments. SIAM J. Comput. **37**(6), 1891–1925 (2008). https://doi.org/10.1137/060661880
40. Pass, R., Rosen, A.: New and improved constructions of nonmalleable cryptographic protocols. SIAM J. Comput. **38**(2), 702–752 (2008). https://doi.org/10.1137/060671553
41. Venkitasubramaniam, M.: On adaptively secure protocols. In: Abdalla, M., De Prisco, R. (eds.) SCN 2014. LNCS, vol. 8642, pp. 455–475. Springer, Cham (2014). https://doi.org/10.1007/978-3-319-10879-7_26

Space-Deniable Proofs

Jesko Dujmovic[1], Christoph U. Günther[2(✉)], and Krzysztof Pietrzak[2]

[1] Helmholtz Center for Information Security and Saarland University, Saarbrücken, Germany
jesko.dujmovic@cispa.de

[2] Institute of Science and Technology Austria, Klosterneuburg, Austria
{cguenthe,pietrzak}@ista.ac.at

Abstract. We introduce and construct a new proof system called *Non-interactive Arguments of Knowledge or Space* (NArKoS), where a space-bounded prover can convince a verifier they know a secret, while having access to sufficient space allows one to forge indistinguishable proofs without the secret.

An application of NArKoS are space-deniable proofs, which are proofs of knowledge (say for authentication in access control) that are sound when executed by a lightweight device like a smart-card or an RFID chip that cannot have much storage, but are deniable (in the strong sense of online deniability) as the verifier, like a card reader, can efficiently forge such proofs.

We construct NArKoS in the random oracle model using an OR-proof combining a sigma protocol (for the proof of knowledge of the secret) with a new proof system called *simulatable Proof of Transient Space* (simPoTS). We give two different constructions of simPoTS, one based on labelling graphs with high pebbling complexity, a technique used in the construction of memory-hard functions and proofs of space, and a more practical construction based on the verifiable space-hard functions from TCC'24 where a prover must compute a root of a sparse polynomial. In both cases, the main challenge is making the proofs efficiently simulatable.

1 Introduction

Proofs of Knowledge. Many cryptographic primitives are based on some hard NP-relation $\mathcal{R}$, where given an instance x it's hard to find a witness w such that $(x, w) \in \mathcal{R}$ is in the relation. One example is the discrete logarithm (DL) assumption where $(h, w) \in \mathcal{R}$ if $h = g^w$ where g is some generator of a prime order group. For DL and similar assumptions there's an elegant proof system, due to Schnorr [30], to show knowledge of the witness in zero-knowledge. Such proofs can be directly used as an authentication protocol. One can also make them non-interactive via the Fiat-Shamir heuristic [21], this way getting a signature scheme.

Proofs of (Sequential) Work. Instead of proving that one knows some secret witness, some cryptographic schemes are based on proof systems that certify that

B. Applebaum and H. Lin (Eds.): TCC 2025, LNCS 16271, pp. 171–202, 2026.
https://doi.org/10.1007/978-3-032-12290-2_6

the prover spent some physical resource. The best known example are proofs of work (PoW) due to their usage in the Bitcoin blockchain. The Bitcoin PoW is very simple: the prover, upon receiving a challenge c, must find a nonce π such that the hash $H(c, \pi)$ is below some difficulty, say it starts with d zeros. Assuming H behaves like a random function, an expected 2^d evaluations of H are necessary to find a proof.

Another popular resource for proof systems is *sequential* work, where the prover must perform some sequential computation. Here, having large parallelism should not allow the prover to find a proof any faster. Proofs of sequential work have found numerous applications as they can be used to enforce sufficient time has passed between the prover receiving a challenge, and them finding a proof.

OR-Proofs. The above-mentioned protocol by Schnorr to prove knowledge of a discrete logarithm is a so called Σ-protocol, which is a class of protocols which have particularly nice properties. In particular, the verifier must only send a uniformly random challenge $c \leftarrow_{\$} \mathcal{C}$. Exploiting this structure, Cramer et al. [14] showed how compile Σ protocols into "OR-proofs", where given two statements x_0, x_1, the prover can convince the verifier that they know a witness w such that either (x_0, w) *or* (x_1, w) is in the relation. The main idea is very simple: if the prover knows a witness for x_b, it simulates a transcript for x_{b-1}, which contains some challenge c_{b-1}. Now the prover and verifier basically run the protocol for x_0 and x_1 in parallel, but the verifier sends just one challenge c, and the prover can choose any challenges c_0 and c_1 as long as $c_0 \oplus c_1 = c$. Thus, they can use the simulated c_{b-1} while using $c_b = c \oplus c_{b-1}$ as the actual challenge in the proof of knowledge for x_b.

While originally the goal of or-proofs was to hide which of several witnesses a prover knows, one can use this idea to combine different protocols. In particular, one can combine a standard proof of knowledge with a proof that some resource was wasted. This was first done by Baldimtsi et al. [8] who construct *Indistinguishable Proofs of Work or Knowledge* for proofs of work. Arun et al. [4] construct *short lived proofs and signatures*, which combines a proof of knowledge with a proof of sequential work, concretely, a verifiable delay function (VDF).[1]

Short-Lived Proofs. A short-lived signature as constructed by Arun et al. [4] certifies that the signer either knew the secret signing key, or that they computed a VDF. By choosing the difficulty for the VDF so that computing it requires, say at least a day, one gets a signature which is sound for a day, but after that becomes deniable as anyone could have computed it by solving the VDF rather than using a secret signing key. While one can achieve deniability for signatures in other ways, e.g., by using ephemeral keys that are regularly made public, short-lived signatures are appealing as they achieve deniability automatically after some time, without the signer having to take any action.

[1] A verifiable delay function (VDF) is a proof of sequential work with the additional property that the output is unique. The uniqueness property is actually not relevant for their construction, but existing VDFs have nice algebraic structure which makes using them convenient in or-proofs.

Unfortunately, short-lived signatures or proofs do not achieve the strong notion of *online* deniability, where the judge (i.e., the party to be convinced by the verifier that an interaction with the prover took place) is in contact with the prover during protocol execution. Even in an offline attack, where the verifier must record some digital evidence that later will convince a judge, deniability of short-lived primitives can be broken if the prover has access to an unpredictable public randomness beacon and a time-stamping service (both are provided by blockchains): The verifier derives the challenge from the randomness beacon and then immediately time-stamps the short-lived proof. This convinces a judge as the prover could not have had enough time to forge the proof.

Space Deniable Proofs. In this work we construct what can be called space-deniable proofs. As short-lived proofs are only sound for some time (assuming they have not been time-stamped), space-deniable proofs are only sound if we assume the prover does not have large space. Concretely, for some space bound S which is a protocol parameter, the protocol is sound assuming the verifier has less than S space, while it's deniable if the judge cannot be convinced that the verifier has less than S space.

Such an assumption is realistic in settings where the proof is executed by some light-weight devices like smart-cards or RFID chips. For example, consider access control using smart-cards, here the smart card stores some secret key sk while the reader knows the public key pk. Smart-cards can only store a few hundred KB, so a reader interacting with the card can safely assume it doesn't have, say 100 MB. At the same time, a judge interacting with the reader cannot assume the reader does not have 100s of MB of memory, and thus could fake the interaction with the smart card without the secret-key, even in an online setting where the judge is communicating with the reader during protocol execution.

As another application consider product tracking using RFID chips. Using a space-deniable protocol will still allow verifying tags, but this tracking would not allow creating any digital evidence about the interaction with a tag.

Our space-deniable proofs are simple challenge response protocols, whether such protocols exist, i.e., "can a two-flow non-interactive protocol achieve online deniability" has been stated as an open problem in [12], and we answer this question affirmatively in the setting where the prover is space bounded.

Non-interactive Arguments of Knowledge or Space (NArKoS). We call the new proof system allowing for space-deniable proofs as outline above *Non-Interactive Arguments of Knowledge or Space*, or NArKoS. The two main algorithms in this proof systems are Prove, which takes as input a public value with the witness $(x, w) \in \mathcal{R}$ (think of a public and secret key) and an auxiliary input aux (think of it as a random challenge), and outputs a proof π. The Verify algorithm, given as input x, aux and π, will accept such proofs.

Instead of using Prove, there's another algorithm Forge that can compute proofs without the witness w, but it requires significant space captured by a parameter S. The proofs computed by Prove and Forge must be indistinguishable, in our constructions they will be statistically close.

Note that this proof system is zero-knowledge as Forge is basically a simulator as required by the definition of zero-knowledge, though it needs large space. For completeness, we also provide a highly efficient simulator Sim which samples proofs without knowing w and using only low space, but it is given the ability to select the challenge. Looking ahead, our construction relies on the Fiat-Shamir [21] heuristic and thus uses a random oracle. We emphasize that Forge does not program the random oracle, while Sim naturally needs to.

Simulatable Proofs of Transient Space. To construct NArKoS we follow the blueprint from [4,8], and combine a Σ-protocol with a proof system for the resource of interest, space in our case, through an OR-proof [14]. To be used in an OR-proof, the proof system for space should satisfy the following properties.

Public-coin: The verifier sends just one uniformly random challenge.
Soundness: The honest prover needs S space, while no prover can make the verifier accept with somewhat less than S space.
Simulatable: Transcripts can be simulated using little space.

The last property is used in OR-proofs [14] so one can't distinguish which of the two transcripts was created using the secret, and which one was simulated. In a NArKoS however, one of the two cases doesn't prove knowledge of anything, just access to space. Thus we require that there's a simulator that produces transcripts with little space. Much like the zero-knowledge simulators for Σ protocols, the simulator has the advantage that it does not have to compute the transcript in order.

Another property that is not needed for the OR-composition, but relevant for deniability, is that computing proofs should be highly parallelizable. That is, while computing a proof requires large space, it can be done quickly. This ensures that NArKoS does *not* also become a "short-lived proof" [4], as then it would not be online deniable (i.e., deniable assuming the judge interacts with the verifier during the protocol). Even worse, it would not be offline deniable assuming the verifier can timestamp (as discussed above). Let us remark that it is generically possible to achieve deniability even if proof computation takes a long time: The prover, after receiving the challenge, must simply wait with his reply for the duration it would take the verifier to simulate a proof. If the computation is highly sequential, the resulting delay could make the protocol impractical.

We formally capture the above properties in a proof system *Simulatable Proofs of Transient Space* (simPoTS) in Sect. 4. One caveat is that we must relax the public-coin property. The reason is that our main construction is based on the space-hardness of finding roots of sparse polynomials [17], which is not public-coin (we'll discuss this in detail later, but informally, the reason is that a random polynomial will not necessarily have a root). This is not an issue, however, as we can use the Fiat-Shamir heuristic with minor tweaks to get a NArKoS.

Interactive Arguments of Knowledge or Space (ArKoS). The applications of space-deniability we outlined above require interaction. For example, smart-card-based authentication relies on the verifier's interactive challenge to ensure that the smart-card must compute the proof at the time of authentication. In general, we assume that any application of space-deniable proofs will want the proofs to be bound to some specific time, interaction, session, etc. Otherwise, it cannot be ruled out that the space-constrained device just always responds with a single, precomputed proof that was forged on a space-unconstrained device.

So far, however, we have only constructed *non-interactive* ArKoS, which are not bound to any interaction by definition. Recall that the non-interactivity stems from our usage of a tweaked Fiat-Shamir heuristic, which we applied to an OR-proof [14] of a sigma protocol and a simPoTS. To get an interactive ArKoS, one might hope to simply forgo the Fiat-Shamir heuristic and use the OR-proof directly. Unfortunately, this does not work:

In the interactive setting, the verifier picks an unpredictable, uniformly random challenge. The simPoTS, however, is not necessarily public-coin, so the challenge might not have a solution. This breaks space-deniability as no transcript can be forged for this challenge.

Fortunately, though, we can modify our NArKoS to get an interactive ArKoS. Recall that Fiat-Shamir derives the challenge using a random oracle. We can bind the resulting Fiat-Shamir challenge to an interaction by simply also inputting the interactive challenge to the random oracle. This results in a two-move protocol where the verifier interactively sends a uniformly random challenge, and the prover responds with a NArKoS that depends on the interactive challenge. Note that the interactive challenge may be replaced by some other unpredictable value that is sufficiently binding for the application (e.g., using the output of a public randomness beacon binds the proof to a certain time).

Summary and Outline. What we have described so far certainly sounds a bit strange since we first construct a non-interactive protocol and only then make it interactive. To recap, our construction goes as follows:

1. We construct simulatable proofs of transient space (simPoTS), which may be private-coin (cf. Sect. 4).
2. We then combine simPoTS with any sigma protocol using OR-proofs [14]. The resulting protocol almost looks like a sigma protocol, but does not due to simPoTS having private-coin challenges.
3. To handle these private-coin challenges, we apply a tweaked version of Fiat-Shamir, resulting in a non-interactive protocol (cf. Sect. 7).
4. We then turn the protocol interactive again by using the interactive challenge (or any other unpredictable value) as an extra input to the random oracle used for Fiat-Shamir (cf. Sect. 7.5).

We follow this idiosyncratic route because it allows us to use an efficient simPoTS construction. In this work, we give two simPoTS constructions. The first is based on labelling hard-to-pebble graphs (cf. Sect. 5). While it is public-coin (and would thus directly yield an interactive ArKoS via an OR-proof), it unfortunately has fairly large proofs, making it impractical. Our second construction is based on the verifiable space-hard functions of Döttling et al. [17] (cf. Sect. 6). It is much more practical, but it is not public-coin, so we need to follow the above route.

2 Technical Overview

We will now give a short technical outline of our two simulatable Proof of Transient Space (simPoTS) constructions. While the first (based on graph labeling) is public-coin, the second (based on finding roots of spare polynomials) is private-coin. We then show how a simPoTS is complied into a Non-interactive Argument of Knowledge or Space (NArKoS).

2.1 Pebbling-Based SimPoTS

The first natural simPoTS construction builds on the ideas of [5,27], who build proofs of transient space from hard-to-pebble directed acyclic graphs (DAGs). Without going into details, this means the following. Consider assigning a label ℓ_v to every vertex v:

$$\ell_v = \mathcal{H}(v, \ell_{p_1}, \ldots, \ell_{p_d}) \tag{1}$$

where $\mathcal{H}$ is a random oracle and the ℓ_{p_i} are the labels of v's parents. If the DAG is space-hard, then any algorithm computing the labels of sufficiently many sinks must use a lot of space.

Omitting some details, [5,27] turn hard-to-pebble graphs into a PoTS in the following way:

1. The prover labels the graph using this random oracle and sends a Merkle commitment to all labels to the verifier.
2. The verifier challenges the prover to open the labels of some randomly chosen vertices, together with the labels of their parents. The number of requested vertices depends on the specific graph.
3. The prover responds with the openings, and the verifier checks that the labels of these vertices were computed according to Eq. (1).

The check in Item 2 ensures that the committed labels are "mostly correctly computed", and in this case, the space hardness of the graph implies that computing the labels required significant space.

This protocol, however, is not simulatable because the prover's first message depends only on the random oracle and the graph, and computing it requires large space by construction. Moreover here a simulator cannot simply output a wrong commitment, as a distinguisher could simply recompute it and check whether it's correct. We fix this by slightly modifying the construction and randomizing the labels of the graph. In particular, we change Eq. (1) to $\ell_v = \mathcal{H}(v, r_v, \ell_{p_1}, \ldots, \ell_{p_d})$ where $r_v \leftarrow_\$ \{0,1\}^{2\lambda}$.

This turns the Merkle commitment from being perfectly binding to (almost) perfectly hiding. Now the proof is simulatable because opening some labels only reveals "local" information that cannot be checked against the unopened labels. So the simulator, who is given the verifier's challenge vertices in advance, can sample fake labels for the vertices to be opened that are only locally consistent with the graph. This does not pebble the graph, and is possible in low space. The simulator then produces a Merkle commitment where it can only open these fake labels. This is also possible in low space by randomly sampling all labels of intermediary vertices in the Merkle tree that are part of opening proofs for the fake labels.

2.2 First Attempt at ArKoS

With the pebbling-based simPoTS we can create an ArKoS for an NP-relation $\mathcal{R}$. We follow prior knowledge-or-resource constructions [4,8] and use the technique of Cramer et al. [14] to prove OR-statements. Given a statement x of $\mathcal{R}$, it proceeds as follows:

1. The prover sends first messages a_1 and a_2 of the sigma protocol and the simPoTS, respectively.
2. The verifier responds with uniformly random challenge c.
3. The prover responds with c_1 and c_2 such that $c_1 \oplus c_2 = c$, and third messages z_1 and z_2. The verifier checks that (a_1, c_1, z_1) verifies as a sigma protocol transcript for the statement x and that (a_2, c_2, z_2) is a valid simPoTS transcript.

By construction, the prover has control over either c_1 or c_2 but not both. This means, it can either simulate the sigma protocol or the simPoTS transcript in Item 1 and honestly execute the other one. Hence, in terms of completeness, a prover may succeed if it knows the witness w for the statement x, or if it uses a lot of space.

To see why this is also sound, consider a low-space adversary $\mathcal{A}$ that wins with probability 1 (for simplicity). We will use $\mathcal{A}$ to either extract a witness for x or break the space-hardness of simPoTS. The reduction runs $\mathcal{A}$ twice and uses rewinding. In the first run of $\mathcal{A}$ it gets transcripts (a_1, c_1, z_1) and (a_2, c_2, z_2) for the sigma and simPoTS protocol, respectively. Then, the reduction receives the challenge c^* from the simPoTS game. It then rewinds $\mathcal{A}$ and runs with the challenge $c' = c_1 \oplus c^*$. This results in transcripts (a'_1, c'_1, z'_1) and (a'_2, c'_2, z'_2). If $c_1 \neq c'_1$ we get a witness by the sigma protocol's special soundness. Otherwise, $c_1 = c'_1$, so $c'_2 = c' \oplus c'_1 = c^*$ by construction, which allows us to break simPoTS on challenge c^*.

2.3 Root-Finding-Based SimPoTS

A major downside of the pebbling-based simPoTS is that the proofs are rather large. To get sufficient soundness from the simPoTS we need to open many labels committed to using the Merkle tree. For reasonable parameters, a proof will be several MB in size.

Our second simPoTS is based on the space-hardness of root-finding in sparse polynomials [17]. Their sparse root finding assumption almost directly implies a PoTS.

They conjecture that finding a zero in a polynomial

$$p(X) = X^d + a_0 + a_1 X + \sum_{i=2}^{\lambda} a_i X^{e_i}$$

over some exponentially-sized finite field $\mathbb{F}$, where $e_1, \ldots, e_\lambda \leftarrow_\$ [d-1]$, a_0, $\ldots, a_\lambda \leftarrow_\$ \mathbb{F}$ requires approximately as much space as storing a degree $d-1$ polynomial. The implied simPoTS is of the following form

1. The verifier samples a polynomial $p(X)$ as above and sends it to the prover.
2. The prover computes a root x (i.e., $p(x) = 0$) and sends x to the verifier.
3. The verifier checks whether $p(x) = 0$.

However, this has two issues. First, it is not complete as $p(X)$ may have no roots; we can only prove that $p(X)$ has a root with constant probability. Second, we cannot simulate it without using a lot of space.

To fix these issues, we consider a private-coin challenger. It samples $p'(X)$ as above, computes $y' = p'(x)$ for $x \leftarrow_\$ \mathbb{F}$, and outputs $p(X) = p'(X) - y'$. This has at least one root, namely x, and while it changes the distribution, it does not affect the space-hardness [17, Lem. 15]. Furthermore, the simulator can sample the challenge $p(X)$ in the same way. This way they sample a challenge together with a solution.

2.4 Handling Private-Coin simPoTS

Since simPoTS might be private-coin, we cannot create an ArKoS as above anymore. When forging the proof using a lot of space, the challenge c_2 will be uniformly random (and thus not identically distributed to private-coin challenger outputs). We circumvent this issue by requiring that simPoTS has the following property: Given a list of uniformly-random challenges, there exists an efficient challenge-selection algorithm that outputs a challenge from this list, and the challenge it outputs is identically-distributed to challenges output by the private-coin challenger. When using Fiat-Shamir, this allows us to create a non-interactive ArKoS where the forger can try different first messages until one simPoTS challenge is correctly distributed.

Conceptually, this is similar to *Fiat-Shamir with aborts* [25], which also tries different first message until the resulting transcript fulfills a certain condition. Since checking the condition in [25] just depends on the transcript, deciding whether to re-try does not require any state. In our case, however, the condition of whether the challenge is correctly distributed *does* require keeping state.

Intuitively, the challenge-selection algorithm first samples a reference polynomial using the private-coin challenger, counts its roots, and then iterates over the list of uniformly-random challenges until it finds one with the same number of roots. This suffices to ensure that challenges output by private-coin challenger and the challenge-selection algorithm have the same distribution.

2.5 Knowledge Soundness

Prior work [4,8] analyzed the following version of knowledge soundness: If the (malicious) prover convinces the verifier with non-negligible probability, then extraction is possible with non-negligible. They prove this by showing that if prover convinces the verifier with probability η, then extraction is possible with probability $\approx \eta^2$, which follows from a forking argument.

We improve upon this analysis by considering knowledge soundness in the sense of Bellare and Goldreich [10]: If the prover convinces the verifier on statement x with probability $\eta(x) > \kappa(\lambda)$, then there exists an expected polynomial time extractor that outputs a witness with probability at least $\eta(x) - \kappa(\lambda)$. Here, the extractor has rewinding black-box accesses to the prover and one step counts as one prover call. This definition is harder to show because of its tight connection between the prover's and the extractor's probability. In particular, it does not allow for the quadratic loss incurred above.

We show that our construction satisfies such a stronger notion of knowledge soundness. We will use a slight variation that allows us to capture preprocessing [15]. Mapped to the smart card example from before, it intuitively states: It is hard to create a smart card whose probability of convincing the reader η is sufficiently high (i.e., $\eta > \kappa$), but the extraction only succeeds with low probability (i.e., less than $\eta - \kappa$).

Please refer to the full version [18, § 8] for details.

3 General Preliminaries

3.1 Notation

λ is the security parameter, which we usually use implicitly. $\log(\cdot)$ denotes the logarithm in base 2, $|\cdot|$ the size of a set or bit length of an object, $[n] = \{1, \ldots, n\}$, and $[a, b] = \{a, a+1, \ldots, b\}$.

$x \leftarrow_{\$} \mathcal{X}$ denotes sampling x uniformly at random from the set $\mathcal{X}$. $x \leftarrow \mathsf{A}(\cdots)$ denotes the output of a probabilistic algorithm, $x = \mathsf{A}(\cdots)$ the output from a deterministic one. We write $x \in \mathsf{A}(\cdots)$ to describe all x that are in the support of a probabilistic algorithm $\mathsf{A}(\cdots)$.

For two distributions, we write $\approx_c$ or $\approx_s$ if they are computationally or statistically close, respectively. In definitions, we use $\approx_{s/c}$ if both are acceptable. If the distributions are identical, we use $\equiv$.

We use the usual Landau notation (e.g., $O(\cdot)$) and shorthands such as $\mathrm{poly}(\cdot)$, $\mathrm{negl}(\cdot)$, and $\mathrm{non-negl}(\cdot)$. We typeset vectors in bold $\boldsymbol{v} = (v_1, \ldots, v_n)$, sets in calligraphic letters (e.g., $\mathcal{X}$), and algorithms in sans-serif (e.g., A). Exceptions are the adversary $\mathcal{A}$ and the random oracle $\mathcal{H}$.

Commonly used abbreviations are: Polynomial time (PT), probabilistic polynomial time (PPT), random oracle (RO), and random oracle model (ROM).

3.2 Time and Space

$\mathrm{Time}(\mathsf{A}(x))$ measures the wall-clock time of an algorithm A on input x. We allow the adversary to have parallelism p, mostly p being polynomial in λ. In this case, $\mathrm{Time}(\mathcal{A}(x))$ still measures the wall-clock time of $\mathcal{A}$ and *not* the total number of computation steps.

$\mathrm{Space}(\mathsf{A}(x))$ captures the maximum amount of space used by an algorithm A on input x. Here, also the input counts, i.e., $\mathrm{Space}(\mathsf{A}(x)) \geq |x|$. Also note that $\mathrm{Space}(\mathsf{A}(x)) \leq \mathrm{Time}(\mathsf{A}(x)) \cdot p$.

We omit the input x when it is clear from context. $\mathrm{Time}(\mathsf{A}_1, \mathsf{A}_2) \leq T$ denotes that $\mathrm{Time}(\mathsf{A}_1) \leq T$ and $\mathrm{Time}(\mathsf{A}_2) \leq T$; similarly for $\mathrm{Space}(\mathsf{A}_1, \mathsf{A}_2)$.

3.3 Protocols

In this work, we consider protocols where a prover interacts with a verifier. The verifier sends challenges from some challenge space $\mathcal{C}$. Throughout, $\mathcal{C}$ will be an additive group to allow for disjunctions (in the style of Cramer et al. [14]) later on. We also define when a protocol is public or private coin.

Definition 1 (Challenge space). *A challenge space $\mathcal{C}(\lambda)$ is an additive finite Abelian group whose elements $c \in \mathcal{C}(\lambda)$ are of size at most $|c| \leq \mathrm{poly}(\lambda)$.*

Definition 2 (Public/private coin). *A protocol is* public-coin *if the verifier's randomness may be made public without affecting soundness. Conversely, a protocol is* private-coin *if the verifier's randomness must stay private.*

Often, the prover proves knowledge of a witness w for a statement x of an NP-relation $\mathcal{R}$. We also define *hard* NP-relations, which means there is a way to sample statements $(x, w) \leftarrow \mathcal{R}(\lambda)$ such that finding w given x is hard on average. Note that we often omit the security parameter λ and just write $\mathcal{R}$, especially if hardness is not a concern.

Definition 3 (NP-relations). *We call a relation $\mathcal{R}(\lambda)$ an NP-relation if $|x| \leq \mathrm{poly}(\lambda)$ and $|w| \leq \mathrm{poly}(\lambda)$, and checking membership $(x, w) \in \mathcal{R}$ takes $\mathrm{poly}(\lambda)$ time.*

Overloading notation, let $(x, w) \leftarrow \mathcal{R}(\lambda)$ denote a PPT algorithm sampling statement-witness pairs such that $(x, w) \in \mathcal{R}(\lambda)$. We call $\mathcal{R}(\lambda)$ a hard *NP-relation if for all PPT adversaries $\mathcal{A}$ there exists a negligible function $\mathrm{negl}(\cdot)$ such that*

$$\Pr\left[(x, w) \in \mathcal{R}(\lambda) \mid x \leftarrow \mathcal{R}(\lambda); w \leftarrow \mathcal{A}(x)\right] \leq \mathrm{negl}(\lambda).$$

A sigma protocol for an NP-language $\mathcal{R}$ proves knowledge of a witness w given a statement x in zero-knowledge. It has three rounds (where a round is a message send from one party to the other) and it is public coin, which means the verifier uses public random coins to sample a uniform challenge from $\mathcal{C}$. The *first message* is a, the *challenge* c, and the *third message* z. Together (a, c, z) form a *transcript*.

Definition 4 (Σ-protocol). *A Σ-protocol for an NP-relation $\mathcal{R}$ is a three-round public-coin protocol. It is defined by the PPT algorithms $(\mathsf{P}_1, \mathsf{P}_2, \mathsf{V}, \mathsf{Sim})$ and a challenge space $\mathcal{C}(\lambda)$:*

- $\mathsf{P}_1(x, w) \rightarrow a$: *On input of a statement x and witness w, outputs a value a.*

- $\mathsf{P}_2(x, w, c) \rightarrow z$: *On input of a statement x, witness w, and challenge c, outputs a value z.*
- $\mathsf{V}(x, a, c, z) = d$: *On input of a statement x, value a, challenge c, and value z, deterministically outputs a decision $d \in \{\mathsf{acc}, \mathsf{rej}\}$.*
- $\mathsf{Sim}(x, c) \rightarrow (a, z)$: *On input statement x and challenge c, outputs the rest of a transcript (x, a, c, z).*

A Σ-protocol fulfills the following properties:

- ***Perfect completeness:*** *For any statement-witness pair $(x, w) \in \mathcal{R}$ it holds that*

$$\Pr\left[\mathsf{acc} = \mathsf{V}(x, a, c, z) \mid a \leftarrow \mathsf{P}_1(x, w); c \leftarrow_\$ \mathcal{C}(\lambda); z \leftarrow \mathsf{P}_2(x, w, c)\right] = 1$$

where the probability is taken over the choice of c, and the coins of $\mathsf{P}_1/\mathsf{P}_2$.
- ***Special soundness*** *There exists a deterministic PT extractor Ext taking a statement x and two transcripts (a, c, z) and (a, c', z') with identical first message a but different challenges $c \neq c'$ that both verify (i.e., $\mathsf{V}(x, a, c, z) = \mathsf{V}(x, a, c', z') = \mathsf{acc}$) as input, and outputs a witness $w = \mathsf{Ext}(x, a, c, z, c', z')$ such that $(x, w) \in \mathcal{R}$.*
- ***Special honest verifier zero-knowledge (SHVZK)*** *There exists a PPT simulator $\mathsf{Sim}(x, c)$ such that, for any statement-witness pair $(x, w) \in \mathcal{R}$, it holds that the transcripts of simulated and real executions are computationally/statistically close, i.e.,*

$$\left\{(a, z) \,\middle|\, \begin{array}{c} c \leftarrow_\$ \mathcal{C}(\lambda) \\ (a, z) \leftarrow \mathsf{Sim}(x, c) \end{array}\right\} \approx_{c/s} \left\{(a, z) \,\middle|\, \begin{array}{l} a \leftarrow \mathsf{P}_1(x, w) \\ c \leftarrow_\$ \mathcal{C}(\lambda) \\ z \leftarrow \mathsf{P}_2(x, w, c) \end{array}\right\}.$$

We say the Σ-protcol has computational/statistical SHVZK.

4 Simulatable Proofs of Transient Space

A simulatable proof of transient space (simPoTS) is a three-move interactive protocol. It convinces the verifier that the prover used a certain amount of space at some point during the interaction. It is simulatable in a sense similar to a sigma protocol's HVZK: There exists a simulator outputting transcripts that verify and are statistically-close to a transcript from a real interaction.

We will first define the primitive and then give two constructions. The first, dubbed GL (for Graph Labelling), is based on labeling space-hard graphs, like previous approaches to proofs of (transient) space (e.g., [20]). The second, dubbed SRF (for Sparse Root Finding) relies on the hardness of finding roots of sparse polynomials [17].

Unfortunately, SRF cannot be implemented in a public-coin manner. Intuitively, we can only guarantee that a uniform polynomial has a root with constant probability. Thus, we allow simPoTS to be private-coin, but require that it is reasonably efficient to pick an identically-distributed challenge from a list of uniformly random ones. Formally, there exists an algorithm with access to a list of uniformly random challenges, and that algorithm outputs a list index in expected PPT. Note that public-coin protocols (like GL) trivially fulfill this property.

4.1 Definition

Definition 5 (Simulatable proof of transient space). *A simulatable proof of transient space (simPoTS) is a three-round (potentially private-coin) protocol. It is defined by the algorithms* $(\mathsf{Setup}, \mathsf{P}_1, \mathsf{C}, \mathsf{P}_2, \mathsf{V}, \mathsf{Sim}, \mathsf{CSel})$ *and a challenge space* $\mathcal{C} = \mathcal{C}(\lambda)$*:*

- $\mathsf{Setup}(S) \to \mathsf{pp}$*: On input of a space bound* S *outputs public parameters* pp*.*
- $\mathsf{P}_1(\mathsf{pp}) \to (\mathsf{st}, a)$*: On input of public parameters* pp *outputs a state* st *and first message* a*.*
- $\mathsf{C}(\mathsf{pp}) \to c$*: On input of public parameters* pp *outputs a challenge* $c \in \mathcal{C}$*.*
- $\mathsf{P}_2(\mathsf{pp}, \mathsf{st}, a, c) \to z$*: On input of public parameters* pp*, state* st*, first message* a*, and challenge* c*, outputs a third message* z*.*
- $\mathsf{V}(\mathsf{pp}, a, c, z) = d$*: On input of public parameters* pp*, and transcript* (a, c, z)*, deterministically outputs a decision* $d \in \{\mathsf{acc}, \mathsf{rej}\}$*.*
- $\mathsf{Sim}(\mathsf{pp}) \to (a, c, z)$*: On input of public parameters* pp*, outputs a transcript* (a, c, z)*.*
- $\mathsf{CSel}(\mathsf{pp}, \mathcal{L}) \to c$*: On input of public parameters* pp *and a list* $\mathcal{L}$*, outputs a challenge* c*.*

A simPoTS fulfills the following properties:

- ***Perfect completeness:*** *For all polynomials* $S(\cdot)$ *and all* λ*, it holds that*

$$\Pr\left[\mathsf{acc} = \mathsf{V}(\mathsf{pp}, a, c, z) \;\middle|\; \begin{aligned} \mathsf{pp} &\leftarrow \mathsf{Setup}(S(\lambda)) \\ (\mathsf{st}, a) &\leftarrow \mathsf{P}_1(\mathsf{pp}) \\ c &\leftarrow \mathsf{C}(\mathsf{pp}) \\ z &\leftarrow \mathsf{P}_2(\mathsf{pp}, \mathsf{st}, a, c) \end{aligned}\right] = 1$$

  where the probability is taken over the randomness of C*,* P_1*, and* P_2*.*
- ***Efficiency:*** *There exists a polynomial* $\mathrm{poly}(\cdot)$ *such that, for all polynomials* $S(\cdot)$*, it holds that* $\mathrm{Time}(\mathsf{Setup}, \mathsf{V}, \mathsf{C}) \leq \mathrm{poly}(\lambda, \log S(\lambda))$ *and* $\mathrm{Time}(\mathsf{P}_1, \mathsf{P}_2) \leq \mathrm{poly}(\lambda, S(\lambda))$*.*
- ***Space-hardness:*** *SimPoTS is space-hard with gap* $0 < \varepsilon < 1$ *if, for a sufficiently large polynomial* $S(\cdot)$ *and security parameter* λ*, all PPT adversaries* $\mathcal{A} = (\mathcal{A}_0, \mathcal{A}_1, \mathcal{A}_2)$ *where* $\mathcal{A}_1$ *and* $\mathcal{A}_2$ *have* $\mathrm{poly}(\lambda)$ *parallelism and* $\mathrm{Space}(\mathcal{A}_1)$*,* $\mathrm{Space}(\mathcal{A}_2) \leq (1 - \varepsilon) \cdot S(\lambda)$*, there exists a negligible function* $\mathrm{negl}(\cdot)$ *such that*

$$\Pr\left[\mathsf{acc} = \mathsf{V}(\mathsf{pp}, a, c, z) \;\middle|\; \begin{aligned} \mathsf{pp} &\leftarrow \mathsf{Setup}(S(\lambda)) \\ (\mathsf{st}_0) &\leftarrow \mathcal{A}_0(\mathsf{pp}) \\ (\mathsf{st}_1, a) &\leftarrow \mathcal{A}_1(\mathsf{pp}, \mathsf{st}_0) \\ c &\leftarrow_{\$} \mathcal{C}(\lambda) \\ z &\leftarrow \mathcal{A}_2(\mathsf{pp}, \mathsf{st}_1, a, c) \end{aligned}\right] \leq \mathrm{negl}(\lambda) \qquad (2)$$

where the probability is taken over the randomness of Setup, $c \leftarrow_{\$} \mathcal{C}(\lambda)$, *and* $\mathcal{A}$.

- ***Public challenge selection:*** *Let* $\mathcal{L}\colon \mathbb{N} \to \mathcal{C}(\lambda)$ *represent an infinite list of uniformly random challenges. There exists a polynomial* $\mathrm{poly}(\cdot)$, *such that, for every polynomial* $S(\cdot)$ *and* $\mathsf{pp} \in \mathsf{Setup}(S(\lambda))$, *it holds that*

$$\mathbb{E}[\mathrm{Time}(\mathsf{CSel}(\mathsf{pp}, \mathcal{L}))] \leq \mathrm{poly}(\lambda, S(\lambda))$$

and CSel *outputs an integer* $j \in \mathbb{N}$ *such that*

$$\{c \mid c \leftarrow \mathsf{C}(\mathsf{pp})\} \equiv \{\mathcal{L}(j) \mid j \leftarrow \mathsf{CSel}(\mathsf{pp}, \mathcal{L})\}\,.$$

- ***Statistical honest-verifier simulatability:*** *There exists a polynomial* $\mathrm{poly}(\cdot)$ *such that, for all polynomials* $S(\cdot)$ *and* $\mathsf{pp} \in \mathsf{Setup}(S(\lambda))$, *it holds that*

$$\mathrm{Time}(\mathsf{Sim}(\mathsf{pp})) \leq \mathrm{poly}(\lambda, \log S(\lambda))$$
$$eUnALT$$

and

$$\{(a,c,z) \mid (a,c,z) \leftarrow \mathsf{Sim}(\mathsf{pp})\} \approx_s \left\{ (a,c,z) \;\middle|\; \begin{array}{r} (\mathsf{st}, a) \leftarrow \mathsf{P}_1(\mathsf{pp}) \\ c \leftarrow \mathsf{C}(\mathsf{pp}, a) \\ z \leftarrow \mathsf{P}_2(\mathsf{pp}, \mathsf{st}, c) \end{array} \right\}.$$

Remark 1 (Space-hardness). One may have noticed that we only require space-hardness for uniformly random challenges in Eq. (2). These are not necessarily close to the actual distribution produced by the challenger C. However, since we also require public challenge selection, the challenges produced by C cannot be too far from uniformly random ones to affect the hardness meaningfully.

Remark 2 (Public challenge selection). Public challenge selection may be viewed as a formalization of protocols that abort in a stateful manner. Usually, protocols with aborts are public-coin but have non-perfect completeness. When applying, e.g., Fiat-Shamir, the protocol is re-run until it succeeds. This requires that aborts are independent. Looking ahead, however, SRF (our construction based on polynomial root finding) requires stateful aborts to have the correct distribution.

5 Construction 1: Graph Labeling

In this section, we describe a simPoTS based on graph labelling denoted by GL. Our construction essentially follows the construction paradigm for proof of (persistent/transient) space introduced by Dziembowski et al. [20]. The prover's first message is a Merkle commitment, and the challenge asks the prover to prove that $\mathrm{poly}(\lambda)$-many labels are consistent with the prescribed graph. To make this simulatable, we simply randomize each label.

5.1 Preliminaries

Commitments and Merkle Trees. We will implicitly use the following *folklore commitments* in the random oracle model (ROM): $\phi = \mathcal{H}(r, m)$ is a commitment to message $m \in \{0,1\}^{\text{poly}(\lambda)}$ with randomness $r \leftarrow_\$ \{0,1\}^{2\lambda}$ using the random oracle (RO) $\mathcal{H}\colon \{0,1\}^* \to \{0,1\}^\lambda$. To open ϕ to m it is sufficient to provide r. In the ROM, this commitment is *computationally binding* (No $\mathcal{A}$ making a polynomial number of $\mathcal{H}$ queries can find tuples $(m, r) \neq (m', r')$ where $\mathcal{H}(m, r) = \mathcal{H}(m', r')$ except with negligible probability) and *statistically hiding* (ϕ reveals almost no information about m to even to an unbounded $\mathcal{A}$) [13, Lem. 17.1.1 & Lem. 17.3.1].

We will also use *Merkle trees* as vector commitments. In short, Merkle trees interpret each vector element as the leaf of a binary tree, and define non-leaf nodes to be the hash of its children. The root of the tree is the commitment ϕ. See, e.g., [13, §18] for a detailed description.

Merkle trees use a hash function which we model as a RO with λ bit outputs. In this case, they are *computationally binding* [13, Lem. 18.4.1]. Also, commitments are λ and proofs $O(\lambda \log n)$ bits for vectors of length n.

We will use the following syntax for Merkle trees, which allows us to open a set of indices I at once:

- $\mathsf{Merkle.Commit}(\boldsymbol{v}) \to \phi$ commits to a vector $\boldsymbol{v} = (v_1, \ldots, v_n)$.
- $\mathsf{Merkle.BatchOpen}(\boldsymbol{v}, \phi, I) \to \pi$ outputs a proof π attesting that v_i is the opening of ϕ at index i for all $i \in I$.
- $\mathsf{Merkle.BatchVerify}(\phi, \pi, (v_i)_{i \in I}, I) \to \{\mathsf{acc}, \mathsf{rej}\}$ verifies whether v_i is the opening of ϕ at index i for all $i \in I$.

Graphs and Graph Pebbling. Consider a direct acyclic graph (DAG) G with maximum indegree d. We denote its vertices by $V(G)$ and its sink vertices by $\text{Sinks}(G)$. We denote the parents $(p_1, \ldots, p_i)$, $i \leq d$ of a vertex $v \in V(G)$ by $\text{parents}_G(v)$.

Graph pebbling is an umbrella term comprising various games on a graph G. At each point a vertex is either pebbled or not. The game proceeds in rounds, where in each round one can place and/or remove pebbles from some vertices, but must adhere to the pebbling rules of the game. A sequence of such moves induces a *pebbling sequence* $\boldsymbol{P} = (P_0, \ldots, P_T)$ consisting of *pebbling configurations* $P_i \subseteq V(G)$, where P_i contains the vertices pebbled after round i. We say the pebbling sequence $\boldsymbol{P}$ *pebbles* v if $\{v\} \subseteq P_0 \cup \cdots \cup P_T$, i.e., vertex v is pebbled at some point.

The different pebbling games differ by which moves are allowed. In this paper, we consider the classical black pebbling game: Let $P_0 \subseteq V(G)$ be some initial pebbling configuration, and consider the move from P_i to P_{i+1}. In a move we may remove any number of pebbles, we can also place pebbles, but we may only pebble a node v if all its parents are pebbled in the current configuration, thus $P_{i+1} \subseteq P_i \cup \{v \ : \text{parents}_G(v) \in P_i\}$. We may also bound the parallelism, i.e., the number of pebbles placed in a round, by some parameter p, in which case we add the extra rule $|P_{i+1} \setminus P_i| \leq p$.

Fixing a set of rules, a graph G and a game, it is sometimes possible to characterize pebbling sequences that win the game. For example, lower bounding the time T or the number of pebbles $\max_i |P_i|$ that *any* pebbling sequence must use. This makes graph pebbling useful for the design and analysis of cryptographic schemes, e.g., memory-hard functions (MHFs) [3] or proofs of space (PoSpace) [20].

Graph Labeling. Cryptographic schemes should be implementable in practice, but pebbles are only mathematical objects. Thus, *labels* are used instead. Each $v \in V(G)$ vertex has a label $\ell_v \in \mathsf{Labels}$. It is computed by applying a *labeling function* $L\colon V(G) \times \mathsf{Labels}^{\leq d} \to \mathsf{Labels}$ to the labels of v's parents, i.e., $\ell_v = L(v, \ell_{p_1}, \ldots, \ell_{p_i})$ where $(p_1, \ldots, p_i) = \mathsf{parents}_G(v)$ with $i \leq d$ (the maximum indegree of G).

A popular labeling function is $L(v, \ell_1, \ldots, \ell_i) = \mathcal{H}(v, \ell_1, \ldots, \ell_i)$ where $\mathcal{H}$ is a RO and $0 \leq i < d$. For certain games, pebbling lower bounds transfer directly to the ROM. Examples of such games capture the games used for data-independent memory-hard functions [3] (but not data-dependent ones [1]), memory-bound functions [19], bandwidth-hard functions [11,28]. For PoSpace [22,26] pebbling lower bounds translate to the ROM if the metric is parallel time complexity [26].

Remark 3. For simplicity, we will assume that L takes *exactly* d (i.e., the maximum indegree of G) labels as input, and that $\mathsf{parents}_G$ always returns *exactly* d vertices. This is without loss of generality as one can, e.g., define $\mathsf{parents}_G$ to output 0 for the remaining values and define $\ell_0 = 0 \cdots 0$.

Pebbling Adversaries. Unfortunately, generically transferring pebbling lower bounds to the ROM is not known for all games relevant for cryptography. For example, data-dependent memory-hard functions [2] or PoSpace (counting overall cost) [20,27,29]. Sometimes one can prove the desired bound in the ROM directly (e.g., [2,7]), but often restricting the adversary is the best one can do using known techniques (e.g., [20,27,29]).

The restriction essentially requires that the adversary may only store labels in their entirety instead of, e.g., the XOR of two labels. This means that even though the adversary plays a labeling game in the ROM, it acts as if it were playing the corresponding pebbling game instead. Thus, pebbling lower bounds directly apply to this restricted class of adversaries, and still rule out a large class of natural attack strategies.

Looking ahead, the game capturing simPoTS also has no known way of transferring pebbling lowerbounds to the ROM. Thus, we also restrict the adversary like prior works above.

Definition 6 (Pebbling adversary). *Let $\mathcal{A} = (\mathcal{A}_0, \mathcal{A}_1)$ be an adversary with access to a random oracle $\mathcal{H}\colon \{0,1\}^* \to \{0,1\}^\lambda$. We say $\mathcal{A}$ is an adversary* in the pebbling model *if*

- *$\mathcal{A}_0$ adaptively performs Q queries $q_1, \ldots, q_Q$ to $\mathcal{H}$ and outputs a state st_0. It must be of the form $\mathsf{st}_0 = (\tau, h_1, \ldots, h_k)$ where $\tau \in \{0,1\}^*$ is an arbitrary*

bit string that does not depend on $\mathcal{H}$, *and the* $h_i \in \{0,1\}^\lambda$ *are responses to* $\mathcal{A}_0$*'s queries, i.e.,* $\{h_1, \ldots, h_k\} \subseteq \{\mathcal{H}(q_1), \ldots, \mathcal{H}(q_Q)\}$.
- $\mathcal{A}_1$ *proceeds in rounds making* p *queries in parallel.* $\mathcal{A}_{1,i}(\mathsf{st}_{i-1})$ *receives the state of the* $i-1$*th round and outputs a state* $\mathsf{st}_{1,i}$*. These states have the above form where the* h_i *must be query responses from any previous round.*

This definition implies that a pebbling adversary $\mathcal{A}$ cannot do better than the corresponding pebbling lower bounds. That is, if any pebbling requires at least space of n pebbles, then $\mathcal{A}$ needs at least $n\lambda$ bits of space.

Space-Hard Graphs. We will rely on graphs that have high space complexity. Loosely speaking, pebbling a random sink requires a high amount of pebbles at some point with probability at least 1/2.

Definition 7 (α-space-hard graphs). *Let* $\{G_{n,\lambda}\}_{n,\lambda \in \mathbb{N}}$ *be an efficiently sampleable family of DAGs with constant indegree* d*,* n *sources,* n *sinks, and* $\text{poly}(n, \lambda)$ *vertices in total. For* $\alpha \in [0,1]$*, we call such a family* α-space-hard *if, with overwhelming probability over* n*,*

- ***α-Space-hardness:*** *For any pebbling configuration* P_0 *of size* $|P_0| \leq \alpha n$*, there exists a subset of sinks* $U \subseteq \text{Sinks}(G_{n,\lambda})$ *of size* $|U| \geq n/2$ *such that, for any pebbling sequence* $\boldsymbol{P} = (P_0, \ldots, P_T)$ *with parallelism* p*, pebbling a sink* $v \in U$*, there either exists an* $i \in [T]$ *such that* $|P_i| > \alpha n$*, or* $\boldsymbol{P}$ *requires* $T \cdot p \geq 2^\lambda$*.*[2]
- ***Locally-navigable:*** *Computing the parents of a vertex* $v \in V(G_{n,\lambda})$ *takes at most* $\text{poly}(\lambda, \log n)$ *time.*

Such graphs have been used for PoPS and PoTS before, e.g., [5] used stacked superconcentrators [24]. A practical option are stacked expander graphs [27], which achieve this definition [27, Thm. 6]. They consist of $\lambda + 1$ layers with n vertices each where each layer is connected to the next one by a bipartite expander graph. This amounts to $(\lambda + 1)n$ vertices total, and the structure allows pebbling one layer after another, so with $2n$ pebbles at most.

Remark 4. Making each layer a depth-robust graph improves constants [22,29] (i.e., the space-hardness guarantee is closer to the honest pebbling cost). These improvements are important for, e.g., proofs of replication [22]. In our applications, better constants do not matter that much. For example, in space-deniable signatures one targets the amount of space S below which soundness should hold, so the signature forging algorithm will need space $(1/\alpha) \cdot S$. Since honest signers only simulate having space, they are not meaningfully affected by differences in α. Only signature forgers must expend more resources.

5.2 Construction

---

[2] In principle, we only require that $|U| \geq \beta n$ for some constant β. Since [27] achieves $\beta = 0.5$, we do not introduce another parameter to reduce clutter.

$\mathsf{GL.Setup}(S)$

$n = S(\lambda)/\lambda$
Fix any δ obeying $\delta < \alpha$
Sample a graph $G = G_{n,\lambda}$ (with vertices $V = V(G)$)
Output $\mathsf{pp} = (G, \delta)$

$\mathsf{GL.P}_1(\mathsf{pp} = (G, \delta))$

For node $i \in [V]$ in topographical order:
  $r_i \leftarrow_\$ \{0,1\}^{2\lambda}$
  $(p_1, \ldots, p_d) = \text{parents}_G(i)$
  $\ell_i = \mathcal{H}(i, r_i, \ell_{p_1}, \ldots, \ell_{p_d})$
Set $\boldsymbol{\ell} = (\ell_1, \ldots, \ell_{|V|})$ and $\boldsymbol{r} = (r_1, \ldots, r_{|V|})$
$\phi = \mathsf{Merkle.Commit}(\boldsymbol{\ell})$
Output $\mathsf{st} = (\boldsymbol{\ell}, \boldsymbol{r})$ and $a = \phi$

$\mathsf{GL.C}(\mathsf{pp} = (G, \delta))$

$\kappa = (\lambda|V|)/(\delta n)$
Sample and $(c_1, \ldots, c_\kappa) \leftarrow_\$ V^\kappa$ and $(c_{\kappa+1}, \ldots, c_{\kappa+\lambda}) \leftarrow_\$ \text{Sinks}(G)^\lambda$
Output $\boldsymbol{c} = (c_1, \ldots, c_{\kappa+\lambda})$

$\mathsf{GL.P}_2(\mathsf{pp} = (G, \delta), \mathsf{st} = (\boldsymbol{\ell}, \boldsymbol{r}), a = \phi, \boldsymbol{c} = (c_1, \ldots, c_{\kappa+\lambda}))$

For challenge $i \in [\kappa + \lambda]$:
  $(p_1, \ldots, p_d) = \text{parents}_G(c_i)$
  Open $\pi_i = \mathsf{Merkle.BatchOpen}(\phi, \boldsymbol{\ell}, (c_i, p_1, \ldots, p_d))$
  $\boldsymbol{z}_i = (r_{c_i}, \ell_{c_i}, \ell_{p_1}, \ldots, \ell_{p_d}, \pi_i)$
Output $\boldsymbol{z} = (\boldsymbol{z}_1, \ldots, \boldsymbol{z}_{\kappa+\lambda})$

$\mathsf{GL.V}(\mathsf{pp} = (G, \delta), a = \phi, \boldsymbol{c} = (c_1, \ldots, c_{\kappa+\lambda}), \boldsymbol{z} = (\boldsymbol{z}_1, \ldots, \boldsymbol{z}_{\kappa+\lambda}))$

For challenge $i \in [\kappa + \lambda]$:
  Parse $\boldsymbol{z}_i = (r_{c_i}, \ell_{c_i}, \ell_{p_1}, \ldots, \ell_{p_d}, \pi_i)$
  If $\mathsf{Merkle.BatchVerify}(\phi, \pi_i, (\ell_{p_1}, \ldots, \ell_{p_d}), \text{parents}_G(c_i)) = \mathsf{rej}$, output rej
  If $\ell_{c_i} \neq \mathcal{H}(c_i, r_{c_i}, \ell_{p_1}, \ldots, \ell_{p_d})$, output rej
Output acc

$\mathsf{GL.Sim}(C)$

$\boldsymbol{c} = c_1, \ldots, c_{\kappa+\lambda} \leftarrow \mathsf{GL.C}(G)$
For $c_i \in (c_1, \ldots, c_\kappa)$ in topographical order:
  $r_i \leftarrow \{0,1\}^{2\lambda}$.
  $(p_1, \ldots, p_d) = \text{parents}_G(c_i)$
  For any $j \in [d]$, if ℓ_{p_j} is undefined: Define $\ell_{p_j} \leftarrow_\$ \{0,1\}^\lambda$
  Define $\ell_{c_i} = \mathcal{H}(c_i, r_{c_i}, \ell_{p_1}, \ldots, \ell_{p_d})$
Compute Merkle commitment ϕ that is consistent with all defined ℓ_{c_i}
Compute opening proofs $\boldsymbol{z}_i$ for all defined ℓ_{c_i}
Output $(a = \phi, \boldsymbol{c}, z = (\boldsymbol{z}_1, \ldots, \boldsymbol{z}_{\kappa+\lambda}))$

Fig. 1. Pseudocode of the graph-labeling construction GL.

The pseudocode of GL is given in Fig. 1 and explained below.

$\mathsf{GL.Setup}$ samples a graph $G_{n,\lambda}$ with $n = S(\lambda)/\lambda$. This graph belongs to α-space-hard family as defined above in Definition 7. For ease of notation, we call this graph G and its vertices $V = V(G)$. It also specifies a protocol constant $\delta < \alpha$. The smaller δ, the higher the space-hardness, but also the message size.

The prover $\mathsf{GL.P}_1$ computes a labelling $\boldsymbol{\ell} = (\ell_1, \ldots, \ell_{|V|})$ of this graph according to $\mathcal{H}$. In contrast to prior works (such as, e.g., [20]), these labels are randomized by including random values r_i. The prover then commits to $\boldsymbol{\ell}$, resulting in the Merkle commitment ϕ.

The prover then receives a uniformly random challenge which consists of $\kappa \in \text{poly}(\lambda)$ many nodes, λ of which are sinks. Formally, the challenge space is $\mathcal{C}(\lambda) = V^{\kappa} \times \text{Sinks}(G)^{\lambda}$. Since the challenge is chosen uniformly at random and public-coin, $\mathsf{GL.CSel}(\mathsf{pp}, \mathcal{L})$ is trivial: It outputs the first entry of the list $\mathcal{L}$.

Given $\mathbf{c} = (c_1, \ldots, c_{\kappa+\lambda})$, the prover will output all the information showing that the labels ℓ_{c_i} are consistent with the commitment ϕ. That is, it opens ϕ at the position of all parents of c_i.[3]

The verifier $\mathsf{GL.V}$ uses the information provided by the prover to check the consistency of all labels $\ell_{c_i}, \ldots, \ell_{c_{\kappa+\lambda}}$. It checks whether all openings of ϕ are correct, and whether the label was correctly computed using H.

The simulator $\mathsf{GL.Sim}$ initially samples a list of challenges c_i. This allows it to cheat by only caring about the consistency of the labels corresponding to these challenges. To this end, it iterates over the challenge indices in topological order, setting yet-to-be-defined labels to random values. This ensures that all labels that will be opened appear consistent. It then creates a Merkle commitment ϕ such that it can open these labels at the correct position (note that it cannot open any other position).[4] This suffices to simulate a transcript.

Theorem 1. GL *is a simPoTS as in Definition 5 when instantiating* $G_{S(\lambda),\lambda}$ *with an* α*-space-hard family of DAGs (Definition 7) and modelling* $\mathcal{H}$ *as a RO. Here, space-hardness holds against pebbling adversaries (cf. Sect. 5.1) with a gap of* $\varepsilon = (\alpha - \delta)$ *where* $\delta < \alpha$ *is a constant.*

We prove Theorem 1 using Lemmas 1 to 3 below.

Lemma 1. GL *is* 1*-complete and efficient.*

Proof. Completeness follows because the prover computes consistent labels for all vertices, and the verifier only checks that all the challenge vertices are labelled consistently.

For efficiency, note that G fulfills Definition 7, so it can be sampled efficiently and has $\text{poly}(S(\lambda), \lambda)$ many vertices. It follows that Setup and P_1 (especially the number of loop iterations) are efficient. By choice of $\kappa \in \text{poly}(\lambda)$, for a constant δ and the fact that Merkle commitments are constant size with logarithmic opening proofs, C, P_2 and V are also efficient. □

[3] In principle, proving consistency of $c_{\kappa+1}, \ldots, c_{\kappa+\lambda}$ is not necessary; the labels just have to be opened. While this would make the protocol concretely more efficient, we keep the presentation simple.

[4] We do not describe this in detail to keep the pseudocode simple.

Lemma 2. GL *is statistically honest-verifier simulatable.*

Proof. First, note V cannot distinguish between P and Sim since all the labels V opens are consistent with ϕ by construction of Sim, and all labels are folklore commitments (Sect. 5.1), so the real and simulated labels are statistically indistinguishable. Second, we argue that Sim is efficient. Here, observe that computing Lines 2 to 6 only takes poly(λ) time since it iterates $\kappa \in \text{poly}(\lambda)$ times and each parents_G call takes poly($\lambda, \log S$) time since G is locally-navigatable (Definition 7). During this, Sim only stores the labels $\kappa + \lambda$, corresponding randomness and (random) co-path values. In total, this is poly($\lambda, \log(S(\lambda))$ since the tree has depth $\log(S(\lambda))$. □

Lemma 3. GL *is space-hard with gap* $\varepsilon = (\alpha - \delta)$ *for some constant* $\delta < \alpha$ *under the assumptions of Theorem 1.*

GL is essentially a proof of persistent space as defined in [20,27] where everyone stores the same file. Thus, space-hardness essentially follows from their proofs. There is only one difference: Their labels are not randomized, so only one label is consistent with a commitment ϕ (assuming the Merkle tree's binding property is not violated). In contrast, GL's labels are randomized, but each label is a folklore commitment (Sect. 5.1), which is also binding. Thus, our proof essentially follows [20,27].

Proof of Lemma 3. Consider an adversary $\mathcal{A} = (\mathcal{A}_0, \mathcal{A}_1, \mathcal{A}_2)$ that breaks space-hardness with gap ε with non-negligible probability (over the randomness of $\mathcal{A}$, Setup and C). We will show that this contradicts the space-hardness guarantee of G. By an averaging argument, we may consider $\mathcal{A}$ to be deterministic by fixing the randomness to some good value.

Assume for now that the commitment ϕ output by $\mathcal{A}_1$ is correct (i.e., as computed by P_1). If the $\mathcal{A}$ does not break the Merkle tree's or any of the labels'—recall they are folklore commitments—binding property, $\mathcal{A}$ can open ϕ to (at most) one label at index $i \in [n]$. We will assume that binding is not broken as this may happen with at most negligible probability.

Recall that the family of distributions on DAGs $\{G_{n,\lambda}\}_\lambda$ is α-space-hard. So, except for negligible probability, Setup returns a graph G where more than half of all sinks cannot be pebbled in less than 2^λ pebbling moves using less than αn pebbles where $n = S(\lambda)/\lambda$. In the pebbling model, accounting for the above assumption that ϕ is binding, α-space hardness implies that $\mathcal{A}_2$ pebbles a sink that is expensive to pebble except for probability $2^{-\lambda}$. Pebbling an expensive sink needs at least $\alpha n \lambda = \alpha S(\lambda)$ bits of space or at least 2^λ sequential time. Thus, $\mathcal{A}_2$, a polynomial time algorithm with polynomial parallelism, cannot break space-hardness (in the pebbling model) with more than negligible probability, assuming that the commitments are correct.

Now consider $\mathcal{A}_1$ potentially outputting malformed commitment $\tilde{\phi}$. As above, since folklore commitments and Merkle trees are binding, for every position $i \in [V(G)]$, $\mathcal{A}_1$ may open $\tilde{\phi}$ to (at most) one pair $\tilde{r}_i$ and $\tilde{\ell}_i$ for every $i \in [n]$ (except for negligible probability). We call vertex i *consistent with* $\tilde{\phi}$ if $\tilde{\ell}_i =$

$\mathcal{H}(i, \tilde{r}_i, \tilde{\ell}_{p_1}, \ldots, \tilde{\ell}_{p_d})$ where the p_i are the parents of vertex i in G. Since $\mathcal{A}_2$ has to prove consistency of $\kappa = \lambda |V| / (\delta n)$ vertices chosen uniformly at random, at most δn vertices are not consistent with $\tilde{\phi}$ except with exponentially small probability $e^{-\lambda}$. Since the labels of these vertices might have concise representation, we give $\mathcal{A}_2$ this many pebbles for free [20,27]. As a consequence, $\mathcal{A}_2$ must use $(\alpha - \delta)n$ pebbles or $(\alpha - \delta)S(\lambda)$ bits space except for negligible probability. □

6 Construction 2: Finding Roots of Sparse Polynomials

The following construction, which we denote by SRF, is based on the assumption of Döttling et al. [17] that finding roots of sparse polynomials is hard. It achieves better concrete parameters than GL.

6.1 Preliminaries

The assumption below follows from [17, Ass. 1 and Rem. 2].

Assumption 1 (Sparse Root-Finding [17, adapted]**).** *We define the space-hardness of finding a root in a polynomial from distribution $\mathcal{D}_{\lambda,S}$ as follows: Root-Finding is hard with a gap $0 < \varepsilon < 1$ if, for all sufficiently large polynomials $S(\cdot)$ and PPT adversaries $\{\mathcal{A}_\lambda\}_{\lambda \in \mathbb{N}}$ with $\mathrm{Space}(\mathcal{A}_\lambda) \leq (1-\varepsilon) \cdot S(\lambda)$, there exists a negligible function* negl *such that*

$$\Pr\left[p(x^*) = 0 \,\middle|\, \begin{matrix} p(X) \leftarrow \mathcal{D}_{\lambda,S(\lambda)} \\ x^* \leftarrow \mathcal{A}_\lambda(p(X)) \end{matrix}\right] = \mathrm{negl}(\lambda)$$

where the probability is taken over the randomness of $\mathcal{D}$ and $\mathcal{A}$.

Remark 5. The definition of Döttling et al. [17] considers non-uniform adversaries. In the rest of the paper, we only consider uniform ones.

To make our assumption more concrete we state a candidate distribution $\mathcal{D}$ (cf. Fig. 2) as suggested in [17, Def. 3]. Let $\mathbb{F}$ be a finite field of prime order $\Omega(2^\lambda)$ over which the polynomials are defined, and $d = \lceil S / \log |\mathbb{F}| \rceil$.

Distribution $\mathcal{D}_{\lambda,S}$
01 Set $d = \lceil S / \log |\mathbb{F}| \rceil$
02 Sample $e_2, \ldots, e_\lambda \leftarrow\!\!\$\ [d-1]^{\lambda-2}$ uniformly at random
03 Sample $a_0, \ldots a_\lambda \leftarrow\!\!\$\ \mathbb{F}^\lambda$ uniformly at random
04 Output the polynomial $X^d + a_0 + a_1 X + \sum_{i=2}^{\lambda} a_i X^{e_i}$

Fig. 2. Distribution $\mathcal{D}_{\lambda,S}$.

$c \leftarrow \mathsf{SRF.C}()$
Sample $p(x) \leftarrow \mathcal{D}$ Sample $x \leftarrow_\$ \mathbb{F}$ uniformly at random Let $y \leftarrow p(x)$ Output $(p(X), y)$

$c \leftarrow \mathsf{SRF.CSel}(\mathcal{L})$

$(p'(X), y') \leftarrow \mathsf{SRF.C}()$
Compute R', the set of preimages of y' with respect to p', i.e., the roots of $p'(X) - y'$
Initialize $i = 1$
Loop:
    Parse $(p(X), y) = \mathcal{L}(i)$
    Compute R, the set of preimages of y with respect to p, i.e., the roots of $p(X) - y$
    If $\lvert R' \rvert = \lvert R \rvert$ output i

$\mathsf{SRF.P_2}(c = (p(X), y))$
Compute R, the set of preimages of y with respect to p. I.e. $R = p^{-1}(y)$ If $\lvert R \rvert = 0$ output $\perp$ Sample $z \leftarrow_\$ R$ uniformly at random Output z

$\mathsf{SRF.V}(p(X), y, x)$
Ensure $p(x) \stackrel{?}{=} y$, else output rej Output acc

$\mathsf{SRF.Sim}()$
Sample $p(x) \leftarrow \mathcal{D}$ Sample $x \leftarrow_\$ \mathbb{F}$ uniformly at random Let $y = p(x)$ Output $(a = \perp, c = y, z = x)$

Fig. 3. Pseudocode of the root-finding construction SRF.

6.2 Construction

Let $\mathcal{D} = \mathcal{D}_{\lambda,S}$ be a distribution over polynomials for which Assumption 1 holds. The pseudocode of SRF is given in Fig. 3 and explained below. Note that SRF.Setup and $\mathsf{SRF.P_1}$ do nothing. This proof of transient space is a two message protocol. We keep the same notation for consistency's sake.

SRF.C samples a random point in the field and evaluates the polynomial $p(X)$ on it. This effectively defines the challenge polynomial $p(X) - y$.

SRF.CSel initially runs SRF.C and computes the number of preimages. It then iterates over the uniformly random tuples $(p(X), y)$ in the list and outputs it if y has the same number of preimages relative of $p(X)$.

The prover $\mathsf{SRF.P}_2$ outputs a root of the challenge polynomial $p(X)-y$. Note that such a root exists by construction of SRF.C.

The verifier SRF.V checks whether the prover's output is actually a root of the challenge polynomial.

SRF.Sim the simulator picks a random point and evaluates the polynomial $p(X)$ on it. This procedure is almost the same as SRF.C.

Theorem 2. SRF *is a complete simPoTS as in Definition 5 when instantiating* $G_{S(\lambda),\lambda}$.

Lemma 4. SRF *is space hard under the condition that sparse root finding is hard for the distribution* $\mathcal{D}$ *(Assumption 1).*

Proof. From [17, Lem. 15] follows that if an adversary compute a root for $p(X) - p(x)$ over random choice of x with probability ε then it can compute a root for $p(X) - y$ with probability $\geq \varepsilon/d$ over the random choice of y. Hardness of computing the root of $p(X) - y$ follows directly from Assumption 1. □

Lemma 5. SRF *is complete.*

Proof. Completeness follows because by definition of SRF.C there exists an $x \in \mathbb{F}$ such that $p(x) = y$ for the challenge y. □

Lemma 6. SRF *has public challenge selection.*

Proof. This follows from Claims 1 and 2 below. □

Claim 1. SRF.CSel the expected runtime in polynomial in d and λ.

Proof. Because $p(X)$ is a degree d polynomial it can have at most d roots. Therefore, the expected runtime of SRF.CSel is

$$\begin{aligned}
&\mathbb{E}[\text{Time}(\mathsf{CSel})] \\
&= \sum_{s\in[d]} \Pr_{x'\leftarrow\$\mathbb{F},p'\leftarrow\mathcal{D}}[|p'^{-1}(p'(x'))| = s] \cdot 1/ \Pr_{y\leftarrow\$\mathbb{F},p\leftarrow\mathcal{D}}[|p^{-1}(y)| = s] \cdot \text{Time}(\mathcal{R})
\end{aligned}$$

where $\mathcal{R}$ is one run of the loop in Lines 4 to 7.

From $p(X)$ being a degree d polynomial and the polynomial identity lemma follows that for every $y \in \mathbb{F}$ there are $m \leq d$ different values $x_1, \ldots, x_m$ such that $p(x_1) = \cdots = p(x_m) = y$. Therefore, for any $s \in [d]$ we have

$$\Pr_{x'\leftarrow\$\mathbb{F}}[|p^{-1}(p(x'))| = s] \leq d \Pr_{y\leftarrow\$\mathbb{F}}[|p^{-1}(y)| = s],$$

and thus

$$\begin{aligned}
&\mathbb{E}[\text{Time}(\mathsf{CSel})] \\
&\leq \sum_{s\in[d]} \Pr_{x'\leftarrow\$\mathbb{F},p'\leftarrow\mathcal{D}}[|p'^{-1}(p'(x'))| = s] \cdot d/ \Pr_{x\leftarrow\$\mathbb{F},p\leftarrow\mathcal{D}}[|p^{-1}(p(x))| = s] \cdot \text{Time}(\mathcal{R}) \\
&= d^2 \cdot \text{Time}(\mathcal{R}).
\end{aligned}$$

Because $\text{Time}(\mathcal{R})$ is polytime in d and λ we have $\mathbb{E}[\text{Time}(\mathsf{CSel})]$ is polynomial. □

Claim 2. SRF.CSel's output is identically distributed to SRF.C's output.

Proof. Fix any $p^*(X)$ in the support of $\mathcal{D}$, any $s \in [d]$, and any $y^* \in \mathbb{F}$ such that $|p^{*-1}(y^*)| = s$. We want to show that

$$\begin{aligned} &\Pr\left[p(X) = p^*(X) \wedge y = y^* \mid (p(X), y) \leftarrow \mathsf{CSel}(\mathcal{L})\right] \\ =&\Pr\left[p(X) = p^*(X) \wedge y = y^* \mid (p(X), y) \leftarrow \mathsf{C}\right]. \end{aligned}$$

Let $\mathcal{P} = \{y \mid y \in \mathbb{F} \wedge |p^{*-1}(y)| = s\}$. By construction of C, it follows that

$$\begin{aligned} &\Pr\left[p(X) = p^*(X) \wedge y = y^* \mid (p(X), y) \leftarrow \mathsf{C}\right] \\ =&\Pr\left[y = y^* \,\middle|\, \begin{array}{l} (p(X), y) \leftarrow \mathsf{C} \\ p(X) = p^*(X) \\ |p^{-1}(y)| = s \end{array}\right] \cdot \Pr\left[|p^{-1}(y)| = s \,\middle|\, \begin{array}{l} (p(X), y) \leftarrow \mathsf{C} \\ p(X) = p^*(X) \end{array}\right] \\ &\cdot \Pr\left[p(X) = p^*(X) \mid (p(X), y) \leftarrow \mathsf{C}\right] \\ =&\frac{1}{|\mathcal{P}|} \cdot \Pr\left[|p^{-1}(y)| = s \mid (p(X), y) \leftarrow \mathsf{C}\right] \end{aligned} \tag{3}$$

where the second equality follows from the fact that there are $s \cdot |\mathcal{P}|$ equally-likely choices for x in Line 2 of C obeying $p^{*-1}(p(x)) = s$, and s of them map to y^*.

Similarly, by construction of CSel, it holds that

$$\begin{aligned} &\Pr\left[p(X) = p^*(X) \wedge y = y^* \mid (p(X), y) \leftarrow \mathsf{CSel}(\mathcal{L})\right] \\ =&\Pr\left[y = y^* \,\middle|\, \begin{array}{l} (p(X), y) \leftarrow \mathsf{CSel}(\mathcal{L}) \\ p(X) = p^*(X) \\ |p^{-1}(y)| = s \end{array}\right] \cdot \Pr\left[|p^{-1}(y)| = s \,\middle|\, \begin{array}{l} (p(X), y) \leftarrow \mathsf{CSel}(\mathcal{L}) \\ p(X) = p^*(X) \end{array}\right] \\ &\cdot \Pr\left[p(X) = p^*(X) \mid (p(X), y) \leftarrow \mathsf{CSel}(\mathcal{L})\right] \\ =&\frac{1}{|\mathcal{P}|} \cdot \Pr\left[|p^{-1}(y)| = s \mid (p(X), y) \leftarrow \mathsf{CSel}(\mathcal{L})\right] \end{aligned} \tag{4}$$

where the second equality follows from fact that there are $|\mathcal{P}|$ many choices for y obeying $p^{*-1}(y) = s$, and each y is equally likely as $\mathcal{L}$ given to CSel contains uniformly random ys.

The claim now follows from Eqs. (3) and (4), and the fact that

$$\Pr\left[|p^{-1}(y)| = s \mid (p(X), y) \leftarrow \mathsf{C}\right] = \Pr\left[|p^{-1}(y)| = s \mid (p(X), y) \leftarrow \mathsf{CSel}(\mathcal{L})\right]$$

for any $s \in [d]$ by construction of CSel. □

Lemma 7. SRF *is simulatable.*

Proof. For $(a, c, z) \leftarrow \mathsf{Sim}()$ and $c' \leftarrow \mathsf{C}()$, $z' \leftarrow \mathsf{P}_2(c')$ we have (a, c, z) and $(\bot, c', z')$ follow the same distribution. $c = (p(X), y)$ and $c' = (p'(X), y')$ are sampled identically and z and z' are uniform under the condition that $p(z) = c$ and $p'(z') = c'$ respectively. □

7 Space-Deniable Non-interactive Arguments

We will define **N**on-interactive **Ar**guments of **K**nowledge or **S**pace (NArKoS). They are zero-knowledge argument for some relation $\mathcal{R}$ that can be forged given sufficient space.

Our construction is essentially a disjunction (in the style of Cramer et al. [14]) between a Σ-protocol and a simulatable proof of transient space made non-interactive using Fiat-Shamir [21]. This almost directly yields a space-deniable signature scheme when used with a hard NP-relation [21]. Previous resource-deniable designs used the same approach (work [8] and sequential time [4]), and our definition is inspired by theirs.

Note that we also include auxiliary data aux in our definition. We will later use this for signatures and interactive ArKoS.

7.1 Definition

Definition 8 (Space-deniable non-interactive argument). *A non-interactive argument of knowledge or space (NArKoS) for an NP-relation $\mathcal{R}$ is defined by the algorithms* $(\mathsf{Setup}, \mathsf{Prove}, \mathsf{Forge}, \mathsf{Verify}, \mathsf{Sim})$.

- $\mathsf{Setup}(S) \to \mathsf{pp}$*: On input of a space bound S outputs public parameters* pp.
- $\mathsf{Prove}(\mathsf{pp}, \mathsf{aux}, x, w) \to \pi$*: On input public parameters* pp*, auxiliary data* aux*, statement x, and witness w, outputs a proof π.*
- $\mathsf{Forge}(\mathsf{pp}, \mathsf{aux}, x) \to \pi$*: On input public parameters* pp*, auxiliary data* aux*, and statement x, outputs a proof π.*
- $\mathsf{Verify}(\mathsf{pp}, \mathsf{aux}, x, \pi) = d$*: On input of public parameters* pp*, auxiliary data* aux*, statement x, and proof π, deterministically outputs a decision* $d \in \{\mathsf{acc}, \mathsf{rej}\}$.
- $\mathsf{Sim}(\mathsf{pp}, \mathsf{aux}, x) \to \pi$*: On input of public parameters* pp*, auxiliary data* aux*, and statement x, outputs a proof π.*

A NArKoS fulfills the following properties:

- ***Perfect completeness:*** *For all polynomials $S(\cdot)$, auxiliary data* aux*, and statement-witness pairs $(x, w) \in \mathcal{R}$ it holds that*

$$\Pr\left[\mathsf{acc} = \mathsf{Verify}(\mathsf{pp}, \mathsf{aux}, x, \pi) \;\middle|\; \begin{array}{r}\mathsf{pp} \leftarrow \mathsf{Setup}(S(\lambda)) \\ \pi \leftarrow \mathsf{Prove}(\mathsf{pp}, \mathsf{aux}, x, w)\end{array}\right] = \mathsf{acc}$$

  where the probability is taken over the randomness of Setup *and* Prove.
- ***Efficiency:*** *There exists a polynomial* $\mathrm{poly}(\cdot)$ *such that, for all polynomials $S(\cdot)$ and statement-witness pairs $(x, w) \in \mathcal{R}$ it holds that* $\mathrm{Time}(\mathsf{Setup}, \mathsf{Verify}) \leq \mathrm{poly}(\lambda, \log S(\lambda))$ *and* $\mathrm{Time}(\mathsf{Prove}) \leq \mathrm{poly}(\lambda, \log S(\lambda))$.
- ***Space-hard soundness:*** *NArKoS has space-hard soundness with space gap $0 < \varepsilon < 1$ if, for all sufficiently large polynomials $S(\cdot)$, auxiliary data* aux*, statement-witness pairs $(x, w) \in \mathcal{R}$, and all PPT adversaries $\mathcal{A}$ with* $\mathrm{poly}(\lambda)$

parallelism, and $\mathrm{Space}(\mathcal{A}) \leq (1-\varepsilon)\cdot S(\lambda)$*, there exists a PPT extractor* Ext *with rewinding oracle access to* $\mathcal{A}$ *such that the following holds: If*

$$\Pr\left[\mathsf{acc} = \mathsf{Verify}(\mathsf{pp}, \mathsf{aux}, x, \pi) \;\middle|\; \begin{matrix} \mathsf{pp} \leftarrow \mathsf{Setup}(S(\lambda)) \\ \pi \leftarrow \mathcal{A}(\mathsf{pp}, \mathsf{aux}, x) \end{matrix}\right] \geq \mathrm{non}-\mathrm{negl}(\lambda)$$

for some non-negligible function $\mathrm{non}-\mathrm{negl}(\cdot)$*, then* $\mathsf{Ext}^{\mathcal{A}}(\mathsf{pp}, x)$ *and outputs a witness* w *with non-negligible probability, i.e.,*

$$\Pr\left[(x, w) \in \mathcal{R} \mid w \leftarrow \mathsf{Ext}^{\mathcal{A}}(\mathsf{pp}, x)\right] \geq \mathrm{non}-\mathrm{negl}(\lambda)$$

for some non-negligible function $\mathrm{non}-\mathrm{negl}(\cdot)$.

- ***Honest-verifier zero-knowledge (HVZK):*** *There exists a polynomial* $\mathrm{poly}(\cdot)$ *such that, for all polynomials* $S(\cdot)$*, auxiliary data* aux*, and statements* $(x, \cdot) \in \mathcal{R}$*, it holds that* Sim *uses little space, i.e.,*

$$\mathrm{Time}(\mathsf{Sim}(\mathsf{pp}, \mathsf{aux}, x)) \leq \mathrm{poly}(\lambda, \log S(\lambda)),$$

and it holds that the transcripts of simulated and real executions are computationally/statistically close, i.e.,

$$\left\{\pi \;\middle|\; \begin{matrix} \mathsf{pp} \leftarrow \mathsf{Setup}(S(\lambda)) \\ \pi \leftarrow_{\$} \mathsf{Sim}(\mathsf{pp}, \mathsf{aux}, x) \end{matrix}\right\} \approx_{c/s} \left\{(a, c, z) \;\middle|\; \begin{matrix} \mathsf{pp} \leftarrow \mathsf{Setup}(S(\lambda)) \\ \pi \leftarrow_{\$} \mathsf{Prove}(\mathsf{pp}, \mathsf{aux}, x, w) \end{matrix}\right\}.$$

We say NArKoS has computational/statistical HVZK.

- ***Forgeability:*** *For all polynomials* $S(\cdot)$*, auxiliary data* aux*, statement-witness pairs* $(x, w) \in \mathcal{R}$*, and* $\mathsf{pp} \in \mathsf{Setup}(S(\lambda))$ *it holds that*

$$\mathbb{E}[\mathrm{Time}(\mathsf{Forge}(\mathsf{pp}, \mathsf{aux}, x))] \leq \mathrm{poly}(\lambda, S(\lambda)),$$

and the distributions produced by Prove *and* Forge *are computationally/statistically close, i.e.,*

$$\left\{\pi \;\middle|\; \begin{matrix} \mathsf{pp} \leftarrow \mathsf{Setup}(S(\lambda)) \\ \pi \leftarrow_{\$} \mathsf{Prove}(\mathsf{pp}, \mathsf{aux}, x, w) \end{matrix}\right\} \approx_{c/s} \left\{\pi \;\middle|\; \begin{matrix} \mathsf{pp} \leftarrow \mathsf{Setup}(S(\lambda)) \\ \pi \leftarrow_{\$} \mathsf{Forge}(\mathsf{pp}, \mathsf{aux}, x) \end{matrix}\right\}.$$

We say NArKoS has computational/statistical space-deniability.

7.2 Construction

Our construction Σ-OR is a disjunction of a sigma protocol Σ and a simPoTS $\mathsf{simPoTS}$, made non-interactive using Fiat-Shamir. Due to the disjunction, we require that Σ and $\mathsf{simPoTS}$ have the same challenge space $\mathcal{C}$ (we discuss the compatibility of our simPoTS constructions in Sect. 7.4). The pseudocode of Σ-OR is given in Fig. 4 and described below.

Σ-OR.Setup(S)

Output pp $\leftarrow$ simPoTS.Setup(S)

Σ-OR.Prove(pp, aux, x, w)

$a_1 \leftarrow \Sigma.\mathsf{P}_1(x, w)$
$(a_2, c_2, z_2) \leftarrow$ simPoTS.Sim(pp)
$c = \mathcal{H}(\mathsf{pp}, \mathsf{aux}, x, a_1, a_2)$
$c_1 = c + c_2$
$z_1 \leftarrow \Sigma.\mathsf{P}_2(x, w, c_1)$
Output $\pi = (a_1, a_2, c_1, z_1, z_2)$

Σ-OR.Forge(pp, aux, x)

(st, a_2) $\leftarrow$ simPoTS.P_1(pp)
Lazily sample list $\mathcal{L}(i)$ defined as
  $c_1^{(i)} \leftarrow_\$ \mathcal{C}(\lambda)$
  $(a_1^{(i)}, z_1^{(i)}) \leftarrow \Sigma.\mathsf{Sim}(\mathsf{pp}, x, c_1^{(i)})$
  $c^{(i)} = \mathcal{H}(\mathsf{pp}, \mathsf{aux}, x, a_1^{(i)}, a_2)$
  Return $c_2^{(i)} = c^{(i)} + c_1^{(i)}$
$j \leftarrow$ simPoTS.CSel(pp, $\mathcal{L}$)
$z_1 \leftarrow$ simPoTS.P_2(pp, st, $c_2^{(j)}$)
Output $\pi = (a_1^{(j)}, a_2, c_1^{(j)}, z_1^{(j)}, z_2)$

Σ-OR.Verify(pp, aux, $x, \pi = (a_1, a_2, c_1, z_1, z_2)$)

$c = \mathcal{H}(\mathsf{pp}, \mathsf{aux}, x, a_1, a_2)$
$c_2 = c + c_1$
If $\Sigma.\mathsf{V}(x, a_1, c_1, z_1) =$ simPoTS.V(pp, a_2, c_2, z_2) $=$ acc output acc, else rej

Σ-OR.Sim(pp, aux, x)

$c \leftarrow_\$ \mathcal{C}(\lambda)$
$(a_2, c_2, z_2) \leftarrow$ simPoTS.Sim(pp)
$c_1 = c + c_2$
$(a_1, z_1) \leftarrow \Sigma.\mathsf{Sim}(\mathsf{pp}, x, c_1)$
Program $\mathcal{H}(\mathsf{pp}, \mathsf{aux}, x, a_1, a_2) = c$
Output $\pi = (a_1, a_2, c_1, z_1, z_2)$

Fig. 4. Pseudocode of Σ-OR.

Setup generates simPoTS parameters.

Prove generates the first message a_1 of Σ and simulates a transcript (a_2, c_2, z_2) for simPoTS. It derives a challenge c using $\mathcal{H}(\cdots, a_1, a_2)$, and defines the challenge $c_1 = c + c_2$. It resumes Σ on c_1 and outputs both transcripts.

Forge is similar to Prove but instead executes simPoTS honestly, while simulating Σ. Since simPoTS might be private-coin, we have to rely on simPoTS.CSel to pick an appropriate challenge. To this end, we have to provide a list $\mathcal{L}$ that contains uniformly-random challenges. We lazily sample each element of $\mathcal{L}$ by simulating Σ on a new challenge $c_1 \leftarrow_{\$} \mathcal{C}$, deriving the challenge $c = \mathcal{H}(\cdots)$, and defining $c_2 = c + c_1$. After CSel outputs a list index, we resume $\mathsf{simPoTS}$ with that challenge and output the transcripts.

Verify simply checks that both transcripts verify.

Sim picks a challenge $c \leftarrow_{\$} \mathcal{C}$ and runs the simulators of $\mathsf{simPoTS}$ to get a challenge c_2. It then sets $c_1 = c + c_2$ and runs $\Sigma.\mathsf{Sim}(x, c_1)$. After programming the RO $\mathcal{H}(\cdots) = c$ it outputs the transcript.

Theorem 3. *If Σ is a Σ-protocol for an NP-relation $\mathcal{R}$ with challenge space $\mathcal{C}$ and $\mathsf{simPoTS}$ is a simulatable PoTS with the same challenge space $\mathcal{C}$, then Σ-OR is a space-deniable non-interactive argument in the random oracle model.*

We prove Theorem 3 using Lemmas 8 to 11 below.

Lemma 8. *Under the assumptions of Theorem 3, Σ-OR is perfectly complete and efficient.*

Proof. Perfect completeness follows from Σ's perfect completeness and $\mathsf{simPoTS}$'s statistical honest-verifier simulatability. Efficiency follows from the $\mathsf{simPoTS}$'s efficiency and the fact that all of Σ's algorithms are in PPT. □

Lemma 9. *Under the assumptions of Theorem 3 and assuming that Σ-$\mathsf{OR.Sim}$ can program the random oracle $\mathcal{H}$, Σ-OR is computationally or statistically honest-verifier zero-knowledge depending on whether Σ is computationally or statistically SHVZK.*

Proof. Note that Σ-$\mathsf{OR.Sim}$ programs the RO $\mathcal{H}$ correctly to a uniformly random value. Its polynomial runtime and the computational (resp. statistical) indistinguishability of the distributions follows from Σ's SHVZK and $\mathsf{simPoTS}$ statistical honest-verifier simulatability. □

Lemma 10. *Under the assumptions of Theorem 3, Σ-OR is computationally or statistically space-deniable depending on whether Σ is computationally or statistically SHVZK.*

Proof. First, note that Σ-$\mathsf{OR.Forge}$ runs in expected PPT since $\Sigma.\mathsf{Sim}$ is a PPT algorithm and $\mathsf{simPoTS.CSel}$ runs in expected PPT.

Second, computational (resp. statistical) indistinguishability of the distributions follows from a series of hybrids: First, on the left-hand side, replace $\mathsf{simPoTS.Sim}$ by a non-simulated execution of the protocol. This is statistically close by $\mathsf{simPoTS}$'s statistical honest-verifier simulatability. Second, replace the challenger $\mathsf{simPoTS.C}$ by $\mathsf{simPoTS.CSel}$, and fix $c_1 \leftarrow_{\$} \mathcal{C}(\lambda)$ first instead of c_2. This can be achieved by defining a list $\mathcal{L}'$ similar to $\mathcal{L}$ (Lines 3 to 7 in Σ-$\mathsf{OR.Forge}$) but where Σ is still executed correctly (and not simulated). Since c_2 is distributed uniformly, $\mathsf{simPoTS.CSel}$ will output a $c_2^{(j)}$ that is distributed identically to the outputs of $\mathsf{simPoTS.C}$ by $\mathsf{simPoTS}$'s public challenge selection. Last, simulate Σ which is precisely the distribution on the right-hand side. This is computationally (resp. statistically) close by Σ's SHVZK. □

Lemma 11. *For sufficiently large polynomials $S(\lambda)$, if* simPoTS *is space-hard with gap ε, then there exists an $\varepsilon \lesssim \varepsilon' < 1$ such that Σ-*OR *has space-hard soundness with gap ε'.*

Proof. Suppose $\mathcal{A}$ produces an accepting proof π with non-negl. probability $\eta(\lambda)$ and makes at most $Q \in \text{poly}(\lambda)$ queries to the random oracle $\mathcal{H}$. We construct an adversary $\mathcal{B}$ with black-box rewinding access to $\mathcal{A}$ that either extracts a witness w given only the statement x or breaks the space-hardness of simPoTS. Without loss of generality, we omit the auxiliary data aux in the remainder of the proof.

$\mathcal{B}(\mathsf{pp}, x)$ receives as input pp from the simPoTS game. It first fixes some randomness for $\mathcal{A}$, which it will use for both rewindings. To do this space efficiently, it picks $r \leftarrow_\$ \{0,1\}^\lambda$ and queries $\mathcal{H}(r, i)$ on-demand. In total, this requires $2\lambda + O(\log \lambda)$ bits (the latter to store the counter i).

Then, $\mathcal{B}$ runs $\mathcal{A}(\mathsf{pp}, x)$ once, proxying queries to the random oracle $\mathcal{H}$. It receives π which defines two transcripts (a_1, c_1, z_1) and (a_2, c_2, z_2). For now, assume that π verifies.

$\mathcal{B}$ uses a_2 to receive the simPoTS game challenge c_{simPoTS}, computes $\hat{c} = c_{\mathsf{simPoTS}} + c_1$ and discards all values except $\hat{c}$, a_1, a_2. This adds an overhead of poly(λ) bits.

It now rewinds and runs $\mathcal{A}(\mathsf{pp}, x)$ again with the same randomness. It also proxies queries to $\mathcal{H}$, except for programming the query $\mathcal{H}(\mathsf{pp}, \mathsf{aux}, x, a_1, a_2) = \hat{c}$. In the end, $\mathcal{A}$ outputs a new proof π'; again assume that π' verifies.

For now, assume that the transcripts defined by π' have the shape (a_1, c_1', z_1') and (a_2, c_2', z_2'), i.e., a_1 and a_2 are as in the previous transcript. We distinguish two cases: If $c_1 = c_1'$, then $c_2 = c_{\mathsf{simPoTS}}$ by our choice of $\hat{c}$. Since π' and thus z_2' verify $\mathcal{B}$ breaks space-hardness of simPoTS. If $c_1 \neq c_1'$, then $\mathcal{B}$ can extract a witness w for x by Σ's special soundness.

It is clear that $\mathcal{B}$ runs in PPT. Its space overhead over $\mathcal{A}$ is $2\lambda + O(\log \lambda) +$ poly(λ) where the last term depends on the first message sizes and the challenge size of the constituent protocols. So if $S(\lambda)$ is sufficiently large, namely $(1 - \varepsilon) \cdot S(\lambda) > 2\lambda + O(\log \lambda) + \text{poly}(\lambda)$, then there exists an $\varepsilon' < 1$ such that is $\mathcal{B}$ uses at most $(1 - \varepsilon') \cdot S(\lambda)$ space in total. That is, $\mathcal{B}$ is an adversary against simPoTS with space gap ε'.

Let us analyze the probability that $\mathcal{B}$ extracts a witness. The probability that π and π' verify, and that a_1 and a_2 stay the same is at least $\eta(\lambda)^2/Q$. This follows from the local forking lemma [9]. Since breaking space-hardness of simPoTS happens with at most negligible probability, $\mathcal{B}$ extracts a witness with probability at least $\eta(\lambda)^2/Q - \text{negl}(\lambda)$ which is non-negligible by assumption on $\eta(\cdot)$. □

7.3 Space-Deniable Signatures

The Σ-OR construction almost directly gives a space-deniable signature scheme using a common design pattern [21]: A public-private key pair is a statement-witness pair of a hard NP-relation, i.e., $(\mathsf{pk}, \mathsf{sk}) = (x, w) \leftarrow \mathcal{R}(\lambda)$. To sign a message m, run $\pi \leftarrow \mathsf{Prove}(\mathsf{pp}, \mathsf{aux} = m, x = \mathsf{pk}, w = \mathsf{sk})$ where $\mathsf{aux} = m$

importantly. Space-hard soundness of Σ-OR now implies that any algorithm that forges signatures with non-negligible probability allows us to recover the secret key, but this is not possible by the hardness of $\mathcal{R}$.

7.4 Challenge Space Compatibility

We assumed that the challenge spaces of Σ and simPoTS are equal, but the challenge spaces of GL and simPoTS are rather non-standard. There exist generic composition methods, e.g., repeating Σ in parallel to increase $\Sigma.\mathcal{C}$'s size, or using primitives like partially-binding vector commitments [23]. However, our schemes GL and SRF may be modified to be directly compatible with a wide range of Σ protocols.

GL.C samples a list of vertices, but these can be derived using a PRG. This has no impact GL.Sim as it can produce messages a and z given any challenge c.

Using a PRG for SRF.C does not work since SRF.Sim chooses the challenge itself. However, we can use two observations to do better. First, SRF.Sim does not need control over the full challenge, but only a part of it, namely $y \in \mathbb{F}$.[5] Second, $\mathsf{SRF.P}_1$ always outputs a fixed first message $a_1 = \bot$. Therefore, we can modify Σ-OR to derive two challenges $c \in \mathbb{F}$ and $c_p \in \mathcal{D}$ where only the first challenge c needs to be modified. This can be achieved using domain-separated ROs, e.g., $c = \mathcal{H}(0, \mathsf{pp}, \mathsf{aux}, x, a_1, \bot)$ and $c_p = \mathcal{H}(1, \mathsf{pp}, \mathsf{aux}, x, a_1, \bot)$. Thus, SRF is compatible with any sigma protocol with challenge space $\Sigma.\mathcal{C} = \mathbb{F}$. For example, $\mathbb{F} = \mathbb{Z}_q$ works for the discrete-logarithm relation (e.g., space-deniable Schnorr signatures).

7.5 Interactive Arguments

A NArKoS may be turned into an interactive ArKoS generically, similarly to how we implemented signatures. The first message is empty, i.e., $a = \bot$, the verifier's challenge is $c \leftarrow_\$ \{0,1\}^\lambda$, and the third message is $\pi \leftarrow \mathsf{Prove}(\mathsf{pp}, \mathsf{aux} = c, x, w)$ or $\pi \leftarrow \mathsf{Forge}(\mathsf{pp}, \mathsf{aux} = c, x)$. In contrast to the NArKoS definition, this construction allows for space-unbounded PPT preprocessing (like the definition of simPoTS, Definition 5). This is because c acts as a salt [16].

One might wonder whether it is possible to also use the interactive version of the disjunction directly (i.e., without Fiat-Shamir). In general, the answer is "no" because it breaks deniability as we cannot implement Forge anymore. The reason is that simPoTS may be private-coin and only offer public challenge selection (i.e., we can select a correctly distributed challenge from a list of uniformly random challenges). While we can lazily sample such a list using Fiat-Shamir (cf. Lines 3 to 7 in Σ-OR.Forge), we only get a single fixed challenge in the interactive setting.

---

[5] Recall that the challenge is a polynomial $p(X) \leftarrow \mathcal{D}$ over the field $\mathbb{F}$ and a coefficient $y \in \mathbb{F}$. The goal is to find a root of $p(X) - y$. Thus, SRF.Sim works for *any* polynomial $p(X)$ as long as it can control y.

Let us note that if simPoTS is public-coin (e.g., the graph-labeling construction GL), then we can use the interactive disjunction directly. The properties and proofs are mostly unchanged except for two details:

First, the simulator now does not need to program the random oracle. It is not hard to see that Σ-OR.Sim achieves *special* HVZK as it works for any given challenge.

Second, while our only public-coin construction GL is in the ROM, this need not be the case in general. In the plain model, the proof of Lemma 11 (space-hard soundness) needs to be adapted. The reason is that it relies on the RO to keep the space overhead of the reduction low. This is not an issue, however, as we can replace the random oracle by a PRF. Auerbach et al. [6] used this technique in the context of memory-tight reductions (to analyze, e.g., RSA-FDH).

Acknowledgments. Jesko Dujmovic: Funded by the European Union (ERC, LACONIC, 101041207). Views and opinions expressed are however those of the author(s) only and do not necessarily reflect those of the European Union or the European Research Council. Neither the European Union nor the granting authority can be held responsible for them.

Christoph U. Günther and Krzysztof Pietrzak: This research was funded in whole or in part by the Austrian Science Fund (FWF) 10.55776/F85. For open access purposes, the author has applied a CC BY public copyright license to any author-accepted manuscript version arising from this submission.

References

1. Alwen, J., Chen, B., Kamath, C., Kolmogorov, V., Pietrzak, K., Tessaro, S.: On the complexity of scrypt and proofs of space in the parallel random oracle model. In: Fischlin, M., Coron, J.-S. (eds.) EUROCRYPT 2016. LNCS, vol. 9666, pp. 358–387. Springer, Heidelberg (2016). https://doi.org/10.1007/978-3-662-49896-5_13
2. Alwen, J., Chen, B., Pietrzak, K., Reyzin, L., Tessaro, S.: `Scrypt` is maximally memory-hard. In: Coron, J.-S., Nielsen, J.B. (eds.) EUROCRYPT 2017. LNCS, vol. 10212, pp. 33–62. Springer, Cham (2017). https://doi.org/10.1007/978-3-319-56617-7_2
3. Alwen, J., Serbinenko, V.: High parallel complexity graphs and memory-hard functions. In: Servedio, R.A., Rubinfeld, R. (eds.) 47th ACM STOC, pp. 595–603. ACM Press (2015). https://doi.org/10.1145/2746539.2746622
4. Arun, A., Bonneau, J., Clark, J.: Short-lived zero-knowledge proofs and signatures. In: Agrawal, S., Lin, D. (eds.) ASIACRYPT 2022, Part III. LNCS, vol. 13793, pp. 487–516. Springer, Cham (2022). https://doi.org/10.1007/978-3-031-22969-5_17
5. Ateniese, G., Bonacina, I., Faonio, A., Galesi, N.: Proofs of space: when space is of the essence. In: Abdalla, M., De Prisco, R. (eds.) SCN 2014. LNCS, vol. 8642, pp. 538–557. Springer, Cham (2014). https://doi.org/10.1007/978-3-319-10879-7_31
6. Auerbach, B., Cash, D., Fersch, M., Kiltz, E.: Memory-tight reductions. In: Katz, J., Shacham, H. (eds.) CRYPTO 2017. LNCS, vol. 10401, pp. 101–132. Springer, Cham (2017). https://doi.org/10.1007/978-3-319-63688-7_4

7. Auerbach, B., Günther, C.U., Pietrzak, K.: Trapdoor memory-hard functions. In: Joye, M., Leander, G. (eds.) EUROCRYPT 2024, Part III. LNCS, vol. 14653, pp. 315–344. Springer, Cham (2024). https://doi.org/10.1007/978-3-031-58734-4_11
8. Baldimtsi, F., Kiayias, A., Zacharias, T., Zhang, B.: Indistinguishable proofs of work or knowledge. In: Cheon, J.H., Takagi, T. (eds.) ASIACRYPT 2016. LNCS, vol. 10032, pp. 902–933. Springer, Heidelberg (2016). https://doi.org/10.1007/978-3-662-53890-6_30
9. Bellare, M., Dai, W., Li, L.: The local forking lemma and its application to deterministic encryption. In: Galbraith, S.D., Moriai, S. (eds.) ASIACRYPT 2019. LNCS, vol. 11923, pp. 607–636. Springer, Cham (2019). https://doi.org/10.1007/978-3-030-34618-8_21
10. Bellare, M., Goldreich, O.: On defining proofs of knowledge. In: Brickell, E.F. (ed.) CRYPTO 1992. LNCS, vol. 740, pp. 390–420. Springer, Heidelberg (1993). https://doi.org/10.1007/3-540-48071-4_28
11. Blocki, J., Ren, L., Zhou, S.: Bandwidth-hard functions: Reductions and lower bounds. In: Lie, D., Mannan, M., Backes, M., Wang, X. (eds.) ACM CCS 2018, pp. 1820–1836. ACM Press (2018). https://doi.org/10.1145/3243734.3243773
12. Celi, S., Symeonidis, I.: The current state of denial. In: Privacy Enhancing Technologies Symposium (2020)
13. Chiesa, A., Yogev, E.: Building Cryptographic Proofs from Hash Functions (2024). https://github.com/hash-based-snargs-book
14. Cramer, R., Damgård, I., Schoenmakers, B.: Proofs of partial knowledge and simplified design of witness hiding protocols. In: Desmedt, Y.G. (ed.) CRYPTO 1994. LNCS, vol. 839, pp. 174–187. Springer, Heidelberg (1994). https://doi.org/10.1007/3-540-48658-5_19
15. Damgård, I., Fujisaki, E.: A statistically-hiding integer commitment scheme based on groups with hidden order. In: Zheng, Y. (ed.) ASIACRYPT 2002. LNCS, vol. 2501, pp. 125–142. Springer, Heidelberg (2002). https://doi.org/10.1007/3-540-36178-2_8
16. Dodis, Y., Guo, S., Katz, J.: Fixing cracks in the concrete: random oracles with auxiliary input, revisited. In: Coron, J.-S., Nielsen, J.B. (eds.) EUROCRYPT 2017. LNCS, vol. 10211, pp. 473–495. Springer, Cham (2017). https://doi.org/10.1007/978-3-319-56614-6_16
17. Döttling, N., Dujmovic, J., Joux, A.: Space-lock puzzles and verifiable space-hard functions from root-finding in sparse polynomials. In: Boyle, E., Mahmoody, M. (eds.) TCC 2024, Part III. LNCS, vol. 15366, pp. 431–459. Springer, Cham (2024). https://doi.org/10.1007/978-3-031-78020-2_15
18. Dujmovic, J., Günther, C.U., Pietrzak, K.: Space-deniable proofs. Cryptology ePrint Archive, Paper 2025/1723 (2025). https://eprint.iacr.org/2025/1723
19. Dwork, C., Naor, M., Wee, H.: Pebbling and proofs of work. In: Shoup, V. (ed.) CRYPTO 2005. LNCS, vol. 3621, pp. 37–54. Springer, Heidelberg (2005). https://doi.org/10.1007/11535218_3
20. Dziembowski, S., Faust, S., Kolmogorov, V., Pietrzak, K.: Proofs of space. In: Gennaro, R., Robshaw, M. (eds.) CRYPTO 2015. LNCS, vol. 9216, pp. 585–605. Springer, Heidelberg (2015). https://doi.org/10.1007/978-3-662-48000-7_29
21. Fiat, A., Shamir, A.: How to prove yourself: practical solutions to identification and signature problems. In: Odlyzko, A.M. (ed.) CRYPTO 1986. LNCS, vol. 263, pp. 186–194. Springer, Heidelberg (1987). https://doi.org/10.1007/3-540-47721-7_12
22. Fisch, B.: Tight proofs of space and replication. In: Ishai, Y., Rijmen, V. (eds.) EUROCRYPT 2019. LNCS, vol. 11477, pp. 324–348. Springer, Cham (2019). https://doi.org/10.1007/978-3-030-17656-3_12

23. Goel, A., Green, M., Hall-Andersen, M., Kaptchuk, G.: Stacking sigmas: a framework to compose Σ-protocols for disjunctions. In: Dunkelman, O., Dziembowski, S. (eds.) EUROCRYPT 2022, Part II. LNCS, vol. 13276, pp. 458–487. Springer, Cham (2022). https://doi.org/10.1007/978-3-031-07085-3_16
24. Lengauer, T., Tarjan, R.E.: Asymptotically tight bounds on time-space trade-offs in a pebble game. J. ACM **29**(4), 1087–1130 (1982). https://doi.org/10.1145/322344.322354
25. Lyubashevsky, V.: Fiat-Shamir with aborts: applications to lattice and factoring-based signatures. In: Matsui, M. (ed.) ASIACRYPT 2009. LNCS, vol. 5912, pp. 598–616. Springer, Heidelberg (2009). https://doi.org/10.1007/978-3-642-10366-7_35
26. Pietrzak, K.: Proofs of catalytic space. In: Blum, A. (ed.) ITCS 2019, vol. 124, pp. 59:1–59:25. LIPIcs (2019). https://doi.org/10.4230/LIPIcs.ITCS.2019.59
27. Ren, L., Devadas, S.: Proof of space from stacked expanders. In: Hirt, M., Smith, A. (eds.) TCC 2016. LNCS, vol. 9985, pp. 262–285. Springer, Heidelberg (2016). https://doi.org/10.1007/978-3-662-53641-4_11
28. Ren, L., Devadas, S.: Bandwidth hard functions for ASIC resistance. In: Kalai, Y., Reyzin, L. (eds.) TCC 2017. LNCS, vol. 10677, pp. 466–492. Springer, Cham (2017). https://doi.org/10.1007/978-3-319-70500-2_16
29. Reyzin, L.: Proofs of space with maximal hardness. In: 65th FOCS, pp. 1159–1177. IEEE Computer Society Press (2024). https://doi.org/10.1109/FOCS61266.2024.00076
30. Schnorr, C.P.: Efficient identification and signatures for smart cards. In: Brassard, G. (ed.) CRYPTO 1989. LNCS, vol. 435, pp. 239–252. Springer, New York (1990). https://doi.org/10.1007/0-387-34805-0_22

Young Researcher Award and Outstanding Paper Awards

Black-Box Crypto Is Useless for Pseudorandom Codes

Sanjam Garg[1,3](✉), Sam Gunn[1], and Mingyuan Wang[2]

[1] UC Berkeley, Berkeley, USA
{sanjamg,gunn}@berkeley.edu
[2] NYU, Shanghai, China
mingyuan.wang@nyu.edu
[3] Exponential Science Foundation, Lugano, Switzerland

Abstract. A *pseudorandom code* is a keyed error-correction scheme with the property that any polynomial number of encodings appear random to any computationally bounded adversary. We show that the pseudorandomness of any code tolerating a constant rate of random errors cannot be based on black-box reductions to almost any generic cryptographic primitive: for instance, anything that can be built from random oracles, generic multilinear groups, and virtual black-box obfuscation. Our result is *optimal*, as Ghentiyala and Guruswami (2024) observed that pseudorandom codes tolerating any sub-constant rate of random errors exist using a black-box reduction from one-way functions.

The key technical ingredient in our proof is the hypercontractivity theorem for Boolean functions, which we use to prove our impossibility in the random oracle model. It turns out that this easily extends to an impossibility in the presence of "crypto oracles," a notion recently introduced—and shown to be capable of implementing all the primitives mentioned above—by Lin, Mook, and Wichs (EUROCRYPT 2025).

1 Introduction

A *pseudorandom code* (PRC) is a keyed error-correction scheme whose codewords appear pseudorandom to any computationally bounded adversary who doesn't know the key. In other words, it is a secret-key pseudorandom encryption scheme with the additional requirement that the decoding algorithm functions even if the transmission is corrupted. Unless otherwise specified, a PRC should be robust to a *constant rate* of random errors.

PRCs were defined by [CG24], where they were shown to be equivalent to robust and undetectable watermarking for large language models. These ideas have since been used for practical watermarking of AI-generated images and videos [GZS25, YZC+25, HLLL25].

Unfortunately, despite several constructions having been proposed [CG24, GG24, GM24], every known PRC either suffers from quasipolynomial-time distinguishing attacks or relies on ad-hoc hardness assumptions. It is therefore natural to ask,

B. Applebaum and H. Lin (Eds.): TCC 2025, LNCS 16271, pp. 205–224, 2026.
https://doi.org/10.1007/978-3-032-12290-2_7

is there a fundamental barrier to constructing a pseudorandom code from generic cryptographic primitives (such as one-way functions, public-key encryption, etc.)?

1.1 Our Contribution

We answer this question in the affirmative by showing that the black-box use of virtually all cryptographic primitives cannot yield a PRC resilient to a constant fraction of errors.

Informal Theorem 1. *Relative to a random oracle, there do not exist statistically-secure pseudorandom codes tolerating any constant rate of random bit-flip errors.*[1]

There is a simple construction of pseudorandom codes tolerating any sub-constant error rate in the information-theoretic random oracle model [GG24]. Therefore, our result is essentially optimal in terms of the error rate.

In fact, this theorem actually implies much stronger separation results. In the secret-key setting, the encoder and decoder effectively share a *secret random oracle* which is not accessible to the pseudorandomness adversary.[2] The ideas of [LMW25] enable us to use this fact to prove our stronger separation.

That work introduced *crypto oracles* to prove a strong black-box impossibility result for doubly efficient private information retrieval. A crypto oracle (refer to Sect. 2.5 or Sect. 3.5) is a stateless algorithm $\mathcal{B}^{\mathcal{R}}$ with access to a secret random oracle $\mathcal{R}$. The work of [LMW25] showed that crypto oracles can implement effectively all primitives in cryptography, including idealized primitives such as virtual black-box obfuscation and generic multilinear groups.

Informal Corollary 2. *Relative to any crypto oracle, there do not exist statistically secure pseudorandom codes tolerating any constant rate of random bit-flip errors.*

It is therefore not possible to build a PRC using black-box reductions to almost any generic cryptographic primitive.

By standard techniques in black-box separation literature [IR89, RTV04], our result immediately yields a black-box separation between secret-key PRCs tolerating a constant rate of errors and any primitives implied by crypto oracles.[3]

---

[1] Random errors are the weakest error model considered in the literature. Since we are proving a lower bound, this only makes our result stronger.

[2] Note that the encoder and decoder can prepend all of their queries to the random oracle $\mathcal{R}$ with the shared secret key sk. Then $\mathcal{R}(\mathsf{sk}\|\cdot)$ is the secret random oracle.

[3] Technically, our theorem shows that pseudorandom codes resilient to a constant rate of random errors do not exist relative to any crypto oracle $\mathcal{B}^{\mathcal{R}}$ and a PSPACE oracle. Similar to prior results, this corollary is established by observing that, relative to $\mathcal{B}^{\mathcal{R}}$ and PSPACE, for any primitive $\mathcal{P}$ implied by $\mathcal{B}^{\mathcal{R}}$, $\mathcal{P}$ exists but PRCs do not exist.

Informal Corollary 3. *Pseudorandom codes resilient to a constant rate of random errors are black-box separated from all primitives implied by crypto oracles, including random oracles, virtual black-box obfuscation, and generic multilinear groups.*

1.2 Concurrent Work

An independent and concurrent work also demonstrates a black-box impossibility result for pseudorandom codes [DMR25]. Our works use similar arguments involving hypercontractivity to prove the impossibility in the random oracle model. But whereas we go on to prove our impossibility relative to any crypto oracle, they introduce an interesting new class of oracles they call *local oracles* and prove their impossibility relative to this class. A local oracle is, very roughly, one for which most outputs are unrelated to each other. As far as we know, these two oracle classes are incomparable to each other.

2 Technical Overview

If the reader is already familiar with the prior work on pseudorandom codes, it should be possible to start at Sect. 2.3.

We begin this overview by recalling the definition of a pseudorandom code (PRC) and introducing useful notation in Sect. 2.1. For a more complete discussion of PRC definitions, see, e.g. [CG24, GM24, GG24, AAC+25]. We then reproduce an argument of Ghentiyala and Guruswami [GG24] showing that there exist pseudorandom codes for any $o(1)$ rate of random errors, assuming just the existence of one-way functions.

Our impossibility proof is outlined in Sects. 2.3 to 2.5. In Sect. 2.3 we explain our proof strategy, which is to start by ruling out constructions in the random oracle model. We show how to compile out the random oracle from any PRC, yielding a statistically-secure PRC in the standard model—something that is easily seen to be impossible. We outline our analysis of this compiler in Sect. 2.4, which is the key technical component of our proof. Finally, we explain how this extends to a black-box separation from most of cryptography in Sect. 2.5, using an idea of Lin, Mook, and Wichs [LMW25].

2.1 Definitions

In this work, we are interested in pseudorandom codes with robustness to the binary symmetric channel, which introduces random bit-flips. Following the convention in Boolean analysis, we denote this channel by $\mathcal{N}_\rho$. For $\rho \in [0, 1)$ and $x \in \{0, 1\}^n$, $\mathcal{N}_\rho(x)$ replaces each bit of x with a random bit with probability $1 - \rho$. Note that $\mathcal{N}_\rho$ is the binary symmetric channel $\mathsf{BSC}_{(1-\rho)/2}$. This is the weakest model of noise considered in the literature for pseudorandom codes.

For the purposes of our overview, a *pseudorandom code* (or PRC) for $\mathcal{N}_\rho$ will be a pair of polynomial-time randomized algorithms $\mathsf{Enc}, \mathsf{Dec}$ that satisfy the following properties:

- **Completeness/robustness**: If $\mathsf{sk} \leftarrow \{0,1\}^\lambda$ is random, $c \leftarrow \mathsf{Enc}(\mathsf{sk})$, and $\tilde{c} \leftarrow \mathcal{N}_\rho(c)$, then $\mathsf{Dec}(\mathsf{sk}, c) = 1$ with probability $1 - \mathsf{negl}(\lambda)$.
- **Soundness**: For any fixed $x \in \{0,1\}^n$, we have $\Pr_{\mathsf{sk} \leftarrow \{0,1\}^\lambda}[\mathsf{Dec}(\mathsf{sk}, x) = \bot] \geqslant 1 - \mathsf{negl}(\lambda)$.
- **Pseudorandomness**: For any polynomial-time adversary $\mathcal{A}$ and any $m = \mathsf{poly}(\lambda)$,

$$\left| \Pr_{\substack{c_1,\ldots,c_m \leftarrow \mathsf{Enc}(\mathsf{sk}) \\ \mathsf{sk} \leftarrow \{0,1\}^\lambda}} [\mathcal{A}(c_1, \ldots, c_m) = 1] - \Pr_{x_1,\ldots,x_m \leftarrow \{0,1\}^n} [\mathcal{A}(x_1, \ldots, x_m) = 1] \right| \leqslant \mathsf{negl}(\lambda).$$

This definition is only the *secret-key, zero-bit* case of the more general definition of [CG24]. Since we are proving an impossibility, it only strengthens our result to consider this special case.

2.2 Low-Noise Pseudorandom Codes from Pseudorandom Functions

Before we get to our impossibility, let us recall how pseudorandom codes for $\mathcal{N}_\rho$ can be built from pseudorandom functions (PRFs) if $\rho = 1 - o(1)$. This argument is from [GG24, Section 3].

Let $\ell = (\log \lambda)/(1-\rho)$ and $\mathsf{PRF}_{\mathsf{sk}} : \{0,1\}^\ell \to \{0,1\}^\ell$ be a PRF. Our encoder $\mathsf{Enc}(\mathsf{sk})$ first samples random strings $r_1, \ldots, r_{\lambda^2} \leftarrow \{0,1\}^\ell$, then outputs

$$c = (r_1 \| \mathsf{PRF}_{\mathsf{sk}}(r_1) \| \cdots \| r_{\lambda^2} \| \mathsf{PRF}_{\mathsf{sk}}(r_{\lambda^2})).$$

The decoder, upon receiving $x = (\widetilde{r}_1 \| \widetilde{y}_1 \| \cdots \| \widetilde{r}_{\lambda^2} \| \widetilde{y}_{\lambda^2})$, simply checks if $\widetilde{y}_i = \mathsf{PRF}_{\mathsf{sk}}(\widetilde{r}_i)$ for any i.

Pseudorandomness follows from the security of the PRF and the fact that $\ell = \omega(\log \lambda)$ if $\rho = 1 - o(1)$. For soundness, suppose that x is independent of sk: Then for any i, the probability that $\widetilde{y}_i = \mathsf{PRF}_{\mathsf{sk}}(\widetilde{r}_i)$ is at most $2^{-\ell} + \mathsf{negl}(\lambda)$ by security of the PRF. If $\rho = 1 - o(1)$ then this is $\mathsf{negl}(\lambda)$, and by a union bound so is the probability that the decoder outputs 1.

For robustness to $\mathcal{N}_\rho$, suppose that $c \leftarrow \mathsf{Enc}(\mathsf{sk})$ and $\tilde{c} \leftarrow \mathcal{N}(c)$. Then $\mathsf{Dec}(\mathsf{sk}, \tilde{c}) = \bot$ only if every block $r_i \| y_i$ contains an error. Each bit is correct with probability $\frac{1+\rho}{2}$, so each block contains an error with probability $1 - \left(\frac{1+\rho}{2}\right)^{2\ell}$. The probability that every block contains an error is therefore

$$\left(1 - \left(\frac{1+\rho}{2}\right)^{2\ell}\right)^{\lambda^2} \leqslant \left(1 - \frac{\lambda^{\rho^2/2}}{\lambda^2}\right)^{\lambda^2} = \mathsf{negl}(\lambda)$$

after simplifying.

This construction works when $\rho = 1 - o(1)$, but it fundamentally breaks down if $\rho = 1 - \Omega(1)$. The issue is that pseudorandomness requires our seeds r_i to each have length at least $\ell = \omega(\log n)$ in order to avoid collisions; whereas any completeness-soundness gap requires $\ell = \mathcal{O}(\log n)$, because a constant noise rate will produce an error on a string of length ℓ with probability $1 - \exp(-\ell)$.

We show that this threshold is not a result of an insufficiently clever scheme, but a fundamental barrier. That is, while we have just seen that it is easy to build a PRC for any $o(1)$ error rate in the random oracle model, it is impossible to build a PRC for any $\Omega(1)$ error rate with black-box reductions to standard generic assumptions.

2.3 The Proof Strategy

The remainder of our overview is devoted to proving the impossibility. The bulk of the proof is showing that queries to the random oracle are not useful for constructing a PRC.

In order to show that a random oracle is not useful in a two-party (e.g., encoder and decoder) protocol against a third-party eavesdropper (e.g., pseudorandomness distinguisher), a standard methodology in the black-box separation literature is to argue that the eavesdropper can learn all the *intersection queries* [IR89,BM09]. The intersection queries are those made by both parties engaging in the protocol; if the eavesdropper knows all the intersection queries, then the participating parties cannot establish a shared secret.

However, this is not possible in our setting. Unlike every prior work we are aware of, we are in the *secret-key* setting, where the encoder and decoder share sk. The encoder and decoder can simply both query, say, sk, making sk an intersection query that the eavesdropper has no way of learning. In fact, the encoder and decoder can prevent the eavesdropper from learning any query at all by prepending sk to all of their queries. One can therefore think of our model as a *secret random oracle model*, where only the secret key holders have access to the oracle. Our approach will have to demonstrate that the noise channel makes it impossible for the encoder and decoder to put this secret random oracle to good use.

Consider an arbitrary PRC for $\mathcal{N}_\rho$, say $(\mathsf{Enc}^{\mathcal{R}}, \mathsf{Dec}^{\mathcal{R}})$, that uses a random oracle $\mathcal{R} : \{0,1\}^\lambda \to \{0,1\}$. Instead of defining an adversary, we will compile this PRC into a new one, say $(\widehat{\mathsf{Enc}}^{\mathcal{R}}, \widehat{\mathsf{Dec}}^{\mathcal{R}})$, where the decoder uses *one fewer query* to $\mathcal{R}$, at the cost of a somewhat longer secret key and a small loss in completeness.[4] By iterating this transformation, we can eliminate all queries from the decoder to the oracle—resulting in a PRC that is easily seen to be impossible: If the decoder makes no queries, then the encoder can simulate the oracle locally, and the oracle can be removed altogether. But any PRC is in particular a pseudorandom encryption scheme, which cannot have statistical security in the standard model.

So, how does our compiled scheme $(\widehat{\mathsf{Enc}}^{\mathcal{R}}, \widehat{\mathsf{Dec}}^{\mathcal{R}})$ work? Let f_{sk} be the function mapping the received string x to the first query $\mathsf{Dec}^{\mathcal{R}}(\mathsf{sk}, x)$ makes to $\mathcal{R}$. Suppose for simplicity that f_{sk} is deterministic. The basic idea of our compiled scheme is to transfer the oracle values on all queries q such that $\Pr_{x \leftarrow \{0,1\}^n}[f_{\mathsf{sk}}(x) =$

[4] In Sect. 4 we will remove all queries at once. We take the one-query-at-a-time approach in this overview because we find it conceptually somewhat simpler at this level of technicality.

$q] \geqslant \tau$ to the secret key, for some threshold $\tau = 1/\mathsf{poly}(\lambda)$. We call such queries "low entropy" and otherwise "high entropy." Since there can be at most $1/\tau$ low entropy queries, our new secret key $\widehat{\mathsf{sk}}$ is at most $\mathcal{O}(\lambda/\tau)$ bits longer than sk.

The compiled scheme will simulate $(\mathsf{Enc}^{\mathcal{R}}, \mathsf{Dec}^{\mathcal{R}})$, responding to oracle queries as follows:

- For low entropy queries, both $\widehat{\mathsf{Enc}}$ and $\widehat{\mathsf{Dec}}$ consult $\widehat{\mathsf{sk}}$.
- If the first query made by Dec is a high entropy query (that is, it is not in $\widehat{\mathsf{sk}}$), then $\widehat{\mathsf{Dec}}$ samples a fresh random response.
- For all other queries, both $\widehat{\mathsf{Enc}}$ and $\widehat{\mathsf{Dec}}$ respond according to $\mathcal{R}$.

Observe that the first oracle query made by Dec is removed in $\widehat{\mathsf{Dec}}$, so our new decoder makes one fewer query. Pseudorandomness and soundness for the compiled scheme are immediate, so we must only consider completeness. Recall the completeness experiment:

1. Sample $\widehat{\mathsf{sk}} \leftarrow \{0,1\}^{\lambda}$ uniformly at random.
2. Generate a codeword $c \leftarrow \widehat{\mathsf{Enc}}^{\mathcal{R}}(\widehat{\mathsf{sk}})$.
3. Add noise to the codeword, $\tilde{c} \leftarrow \mathcal{N}_{\rho}(c)$.
4. Apply the decoder, $\widehat{\mathsf{Dec}}^{\mathcal{R}}(\widehat{\mathsf{sk}}, \tilde{c})$. If the result is $\bot$, the experiment fails; if it is 1 then the experiment succeeds.

The only case where $(\widehat{\mathsf{Enc}}^{\mathcal{R}}, \widehat{\mathsf{Dec}}^{\mathcal{R}})$ might fail to perfectly simulate $(\mathsf{Enc}^{\mathcal{R}}, \mathsf{Dec}^{\mathcal{R}})$ is when the first query made by Dec, say q, is a high entropy query: If it happens that $\widehat{\mathsf{Enc}}$ had also queried q in Step 2, then $\widehat{\mathsf{Enc}}$ and $\widehat{\mathsf{Dec}}$ will use different values for $\mathcal{R}(q)$—potentially ruining completeness. We argue in Sect. 2.4 that the error channel $\mathcal{N}_{\rho}$ prevents $\widehat{\mathsf{Enc}}$ and $\widehat{\mathsf{Dec}}$ from making the same high entropy query.

2.4 Bounding the Error of the Compiler

Recall the function f_{sk}, which maps the string $\tilde{c}$ received in Step 4 to the first oracle query $\widehat{\mathsf{Dec}}$ makes. For this overview we assume f_{sk} is deterministic to simplify notation and terminology. If we let S be the set of high entropy queries[5] made by $\widehat{\mathsf{Enc}}^{\mathcal{R}}(\widehat{\mathsf{sk}})$ in step 2, then our aim is to show that the following probability is $\mathsf{negl}(\lambda)$:

$$\Pr_{\substack{c \leftarrow \widehat{\mathsf{Enc}}^{\mathcal{R}}(\widehat{\mathsf{sk}}) \\ \tilde{c} \leftarrow \mathcal{N}_{\rho}(c)}} [f_{\mathsf{sk}}(\tilde{c}) \in S]. \tag{1}$$

Again, if $f_{\mathsf{sk}}(\tilde{c}) \notin S$ then our compiled scheme perfectly simulates the original one, so this will complete our proof.

[5] Remember that we define high entropy queries with respect to the decoder (specifically f_{sk}). If the decoder, run on a random input, is unlikely to make q as its first query, then q is a "high entropy query" even if the encoder queries q with probability 1.

The first simplifying observation is that, while c has an unknown distribution for a given $(\widehat{\mathsf{sk}}, \mathcal{R})$, the *marginal* distribution on just $(\widehat{\mathsf{sk}}, c)$ is actually uniform. The reason is simple: If $c \leftarrow \widehat{\mathsf{Enc}}^{\mathcal{R}}(\widehat{\mathsf{sk}})$ was non-uniform conditioned on $\widehat{\mathsf{sk}}$ alone, then the decoder could (inefficiently) distinguish codewords from random strings without using $\mathcal{R}$ at all! But, as we mentioned earlier, statistically "pseudorandom" encryption is not possible in the standard model (even with an inefficient decoder). For a formal proof with quantitative bounds on the distance to uniformity, see Lemma 1.

So we have the following equivalence with Eq. (1), where the codeword is now sampled *uniformly at random* instead of using the encoder:

$$\Pr_{\substack{c \leftarrow \widehat{\mathsf{Enc}}^{\mathcal{R}}(\widehat{\mathsf{sk}}) \\ \tilde{c} \leftarrow \mathcal{N}_\rho(c)}} [f_{\mathsf{sk}}(\tilde{c}) \in S] = \Pr_{\substack{x \leftarrow \{0,1\}^n \\ \tilde{x} \leftarrow \mathcal{N}_\rho(x)}} [f_{\mathsf{sk}}(\tilde{x}) \in S].$$

The set S of high entropy queries made by the encoder clearly does not depend on the error introduced by $\mathcal{N}_\rho$. So by a union bound, if we let Q be an upper bound on the number of queries made by the decoder (so $|S| \leqslant Q$),

$$\Pr_{\substack{x \leftarrow \{0,1\}^n \\ \tilde{x} \leftarrow \mathcal{N}_\rho(x)}} [f_{\mathsf{sk}}(\tilde{x}) \in S] \leqslant Q \cdot \max_{f,g \in \mathcal{H}_\tau} \Pr_{\substack{x \leftarrow \{0,1\}^n \\ \tilde{x} \leftarrow \mathcal{N}_\rho(x)}} [f(\tilde{x}) = g(x)],$$

where $\mathcal{H}_\tau = \{f, g : \left|f^{-1}(g(x^*))\right| / 2^n \leqslant \tau \text{ for all } x^* \in \{0,1\}^n\}$, capturing the fact that every $q \in S$ is at most τ-likely to be output by f.

Now it suffices to show the following simple and completely self-contained mathematical statement: For every $\rho = 1 - \Omega(1)$ and every pair of functions $f, g \in \mathcal{H}_\tau$,

$$\Pr_{\substack{x \leftarrow \{0,1\}^n \\ \tilde{x} \leftarrow \mathcal{N}_\rho(x)}} [f(\tilde{x}) = g(x)] = \tau^{\Omega(1)}. \tag{2}$$

Since τ is an arbitrary inverse-polynomial, this will imply that Eq. (1) is $\mathsf{negl}(\lambda)$.

We will formally prove Eq. (2) using hypercontractivity later, in Lemma 2. For now, let us just try to give some basic intuition, aided by Fig. 1. What we need to show is that if two strings x and $\tilde{x}$ are each random on their own and only ρ-correlated together, then very little information can be consistently extracted from them.[6] To understand why this is true, consider the special case that $f = g$. We can view f as a partition of $\{0,1\}^n$, with a label on each cell corresponding to the output of f on any string in the cell. Since f is high entropy (i.e., $(f, f) \in \mathcal{H}_\tau$), each cell in the partition is small. The key point is that in the hypercube $\{0,1\}^n$, almost all of the probability mass is on the cell boundaries—therefore $f(x) \neq f(\tilde{x})$ with high probability. Proving that small subsets of the hypercube have mass concentrated on their boundaries is highly non-trivial, and is encapsulated in the hypercontractivity theorem.

[6] Note that it is essential that x and $\tilde{x}$ are each random on their own, as otherwise error correction would make it possible to consistently extract lots of information!.

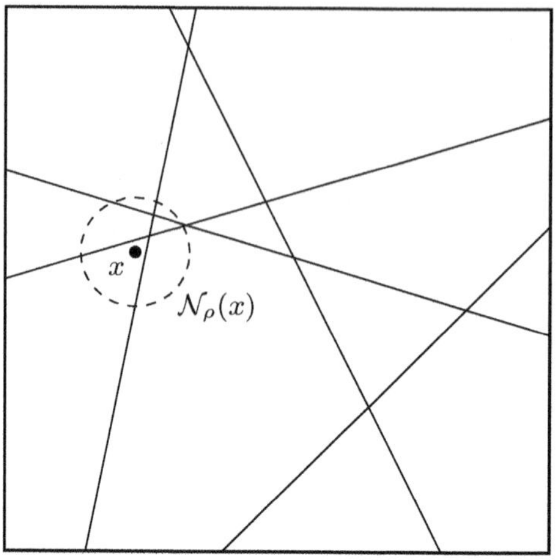

Fig. 1. The space of strings $x \in \{0,1\}^n$ received by the decoder can be partitioned according to the first oracle query $f(x)$ the decoder makes upon receiving x. Equation (2) says that in high dimensions, if every cell in the partition is small, then a small Hamming ball centered at a random string has its mass distributed across many cells—i.e., no function $g(x)$ can guess where $\tilde{x} \leftarrow \mathcal{N}_\rho(x)$ will land. Thus the noise destroys the decoder's ability to make high-entropy intersection queries.

2.5 Upgrading to a Crypto Oracle

It turns out that our random oracle impossibility easily extends to our full result by using the ideas of [LMW25]. That work introduces *crypto oracles* and shows that they are capable of implementing most generic cryptography. A crypto oracle is an efficient, stateless algorithm with access to a secret random oracle.

Because a PRC is a "secret-key" primitive—that is, the pseudorandomness adversary cannot access some secret randomness—our encoder and decoder can simply use the (public) random oracle to simulate the crypto oracle. That is, by prepending all of their queries to the random oracle with the secret key, the encoder and decoder can effectively share a secret random oracle.

Now any construction of a PRC relative to a crypto oracle $\mathcal{B}^{\mathcal{R}}$ immediately implies a PRC in the secret random oracle model, where one simply lets the encoder and decoder simulate $\mathcal{B}^{\mathcal{R}}$ using access to the secret oracle $\mathcal{R}$.[7] Consequently, our theorem immediately implies our separation result in the crypto oracle model.

[7] In a crypto oracle model, a PRC guarantees that an adversary cannot break pseudorandomness given access to $\mathcal{B}^{\mathcal{R}}$. In the compiled scheme, the adversary does not even have access to $\mathcal{B}^{\mathcal{R}}$ and, hence, can only become weaker and achieve a lower advantage.

3 Toolkit

3.1 Notation

We use λ for the security parameter and $\mathsf{negl}(\lambda)$ for a negligible function, i.e., for any polynomial $f(\lambda)$, it holds that $\mathsf{negl}(\lambda) < 1/f(\lambda)$ for all large enough λ. We use $\mathbb{N}$ to denote the set of positive integers. In this work "log" will denote the base-2 logarithm. We assume that the reader is familiar with the basic ideas of information theory, such as Shannon entropy, statistical distance, and KL divergence. For random variables X and Y, we write $H(X)$ for the binary entropy of X; $H(X|Y)$ for the binary entropy of X conditioned on Y; $\mathsf{SD}(X, Y)$ for the statistical distance (i.e. total variation distance) between X and Y; and $\mathrm{D_{KL}}(X\|Y)$ for the binary KL divergence of X from Y.

For sets $\mathcal{X}, \mathcal{Y}$, we will write $f : \mathcal{X} \to \mathcal{Y}$ and say that f is a "randomized function" if, for each $x \in \mathcal{X}$, $f(x)$ is a random variable on $\mathcal{Y}$. We use this terminology for convenience of notation; we find that the more standard approach of having f map $\mathcal{X}$ to distributions on $\mathcal{Y}$ would be cumbersome, and calling f a "randomized algorithm" is not appropriate in all of our instances.

3.2 Information Theory

In this section we prove Lemma 1, which we will use twice in our main proof: Once in order to invoke our key technical lemma, Lemma 2; and once in order to see that statistical security is impossible in the plain model. First we relate the Shannon entropy to the statistical distance from the uniform distribution.

Fact 1. *Let X be any random variable taking values in a finite set $\mathcal{S}$, and let R be a uniformly random sample from $\mathcal{S}$. If $\varepsilon = \mathsf{SD}(X, R) \leqslant 1/4$, then*

$$2\varepsilon^2 \leqslant \log|S| - H(X) \leqslant 2\varepsilon \log|S| + 2\sqrt{\varepsilon}.$$

Proof. For the inequality on the left, first observe that $\mathrm{D_{KL}}(X\|R) = \log|S| - H(X)$. Then by Pinsker's inequality, $2\varepsilon^2 \leqslant \mathrm{D_{KL}}(X\|R) \cdot \ln 2 \leqslant \mathrm{D_{KL}}(X\|R)$.

For the inequality on the right, we have $\log|S| - H(X) \leqslant 2\varepsilon\log|S| + 2\varepsilon\log(1/2\varepsilon)$ from [CT01, Theorem 16.3.2]. We simplify the second term as $2\varepsilon\log(1/2\varepsilon) \leqslant 2\varepsilon\log(1/\varepsilon) \leqslant 2\sqrt{\varepsilon}$ for $\varepsilon \leqslant 1/4$. □

We now deduce Lemma 1. Roughly, Lemma 1 states that a finite-length key can only be used to statistically hide a finite number of messages.

Lemma 1. *Let $\{\mathcal{D}_{\mathsf{k}}\}_{\mathsf{k}\in\{0,1\}^\ell}$ be a family of distributions over $\{0,1\}^n$. Let sk be a uniformly random sample from $\{0,1\}^\ell$ and let $x, x_1, \ldots, x_m$ be independent samples from $\mathcal{D}_{\mathsf{sk}}$.*

If $(x_1, \ldots, x_m)$ are jointly ε-close to uniform in statistical distance, then (sk, x) is

$$O\left(\sqrt{\varepsilon n + \sqrt{\varepsilon}/m + \ell/m}\right)$$

close to uniform in statistical distance.

Proof. Let sk be a random string from $\{0,1\}^\ell$, and let $x, x_1, \ldots, x_m$ be samples from $\mathcal{D}_{\mathsf{sk}}$. We have

$$\begin{aligned} H(x_1, \ldots, x_m) &\leqslant H(x_1, \ldots, x_m, \mathsf{sk}) \\ &= H(\mathsf{sk}) + H(x_1, \ldots, x_m | \mathsf{sk}) \\ &= \ell + m \cdot H(x|\mathsf{sk}), \end{aligned}$$

which means that $H(x|\mathsf{sk}) \geqslant (H(x_1, \ldots, x_m) - \ell)/m$.

Let R be a uniformly random sample from $\{0,1\}^{\ell+n}$. Fact 1 implies the following two inequalities:

- $\mathsf{SD}((\mathsf{sk}, x), R) \leqslant \sqrt{n + \ell - H(\mathsf{sk}, x)} = \sqrt{n - H(x|\mathsf{sk})}$, and
- $H(x_1, \ldots, x_m) \geqslant nm - 2\varepsilon nm - 2\sqrt{\varepsilon}$.

Therefore

$$\begin{aligned} \mathsf{SD}((\mathsf{sk}, x), R) &\leqslant \sqrt{n - H(x|\mathsf{sk})} \\ &\leqslant \sqrt{n - (H(x_1, \ldots, x_m) - \ell)/m} \\ &\leqslant \sqrt{n - (nm - 2\varepsilon nm - 2\sqrt{\varepsilon} - \ell)/m} \\ &= \sqrt{2\varepsilon n + 2\sqrt{\varepsilon}/m + \ell/m}, \end{aligned}$$

completing the proof. □

3.3 Pseudorandom Codes

Following [CG24], we define private-key pseudorandom codes as follows. Our impossibility result will apply to the private-key setting, which immediately implies the corresponding impossibility for the public-key setting. Therefore we omit definitions of public-key pseudorandom codes.

Definition 1 (Private-key PRC). *A* private-key $(\delta, \varepsilon, \mu)$ pseudorandom error-correcting code *over an alphabet Σ and a channel $\mathcal{E} \colon \Sigma^* \to \Sigma^*$ consists of a tuple of PPT algorithms* (KeyGen, Enc, Dec)*:*

- *A key generation algorithm* KeyGen *that samples a secret key* $\mathsf{sk} \in \{0,1\}^{\ell(\lambda)}$.
- *An encoding algorithm* Enc *that takes the secret key* $\mathsf{sk} \in \{0,1\}^{\ell(\lambda)}$ *and the message $m \in \Sigma^{k(\lambda)}$ as input and outputs a codeword $c \in \Sigma^{n(\lambda)}$.*
- *A decoding algorithm that takes the secret key* $\mathsf{sk} \in \{0,1\}^{\ell(\lambda)}$ *and a (potentially erroneous) codeword $c \in \Sigma^{n(\lambda)}$ as input and outputs a message $m \in \Sigma^{k(\lambda)} \cup \{\perp\}$.*

These algorithms must satisfy the following properties:

- **δ-Completeness (robustness).** *For any message $m \in \Sigma^k$, it holds that*

$$\Pr\left[\mathsf{Dec}(\mathsf{sk}, \widetilde{c}) = m \;\middle|\; \begin{array}{c} \mathsf{sk} \leftarrow \mathsf{KeyGen}(\cdot) \\ c \leftarrow \mathsf{Enc}(\mathsf{sk}, m) \\ \widetilde{c} \leftarrow \mathcal{E}(c) \end{array}\right] \geqslant 1 - \delta.$$

– **ε-Pseudorandomness.** *For any PPT adversary $\mathcal{A}$, it holds that*

$$\left|\Pr\left[\mathcal{A}^{\mathsf{Enc}(\mathsf{sk},\cdot)}(\cdot)=1 \mid \mathsf{sk}\leftarrow\mathsf{KeyGen}(\cdot)\right]-\Pr\left[\mathcal{A}^{\mathcal{U}(\cdot)}(\cdot)=1\right]\right|\leqslant\varepsilon,$$

where $\mathsf{Enc}(\mathsf{sk},\cdot)$ *generates fresh encodings even if the same message is queried twice and* $\mathcal{U}(\cdot)$ *is an oracle that simply outputs fresh random strings.*

– **μ-Soundness.** *For a fixed codeword $c^* \in \Sigma^n$, it holds that*

$$\Pr\left[\mathsf{Dec}(\mathsf{sk},c^*)=\bot \mid \mathsf{sk}\leftarrow\mathsf{KeyGen}(\cdot)\right]\geqslant 1-\mu.$$

We will drop the specification of δ, ε, μ in the case that they are all bounded by $\mathsf{negl}(\lambda)$.

Zero-bit PRC. We consider PRCs with only one possible message, $m = 1$, which are known as *zero-bit* PRCs and are useful for watermarking. For random errors, one can convert a zero-bit PRC to a many-bit PRC simply by concatenating codewords and random strings [CG24]. Conversely, a zero-bit PRC is immediately implied by any PRC with $k > 0$, so our impossibility result is not weakened at all by restricting to this case. We therefore drop the message in the remainder of this paper, writing $\mathsf{Enc}(\mathsf{sk})$ instead of $\mathsf{Enc}(\mathsf{sk}, 1)$. The decoder $\mathsf{Dec}(\mathsf{sk}, x)$ outputs 1 or $\bot$, indicating success or failure, respectively.

Binary Alphabet. In this work we will restrict ourselves to a binary alphabet, i.e. $\Sigma = \{0, 1\}$. Note that a pseudorandom code over large alphabet implies a pseudorandom code for binary alphabet. Since we are proving an impossibility result, this restriction only makes our lower bound stronger.

Noise Channel. In this work we will only consider the binary symmetric channel, which introduces i.i.d bit-flip errors on the codeword bits. Adversarial noise channels such as those considered in [AAC+25] can easily simulate the binary symmetric channel, so our impossibility result applies to pseudorandom codes for those channels as well. We will denote the binary symmetric channel by $\mathcal{N}_\rho$, defined as

$$\mathcal{N}_\rho(x) = x \oplus e$$

where $e \leftarrow \mathsf{Ber}((1-\rho)/2)^n$. We use $\mathsf{Ber}(p)$ to denote the Bernoulli distribution with probability p, and $\oplus$ to denote the bitwise XOR. In other words, each symbol of x is replaced by a random element with probability $1-\rho$ in $\mathcal{N}_\rho(x)$.

3.4 Boolean Analysis and Hypercontractivity

A core part of our argument makes use of Boolean analysis. We introduce minimal notation here to facilitate our proof; we refer the reader to [O'D14] for more details. For any Boolean function $f : \{0,1\}^n \to \mathbb{R}$, its ℓ-norm $\|f\|_\ell$ is defined as

$$\|f\|_\ell = \left(\mathbb{E}_x[f(x)^\ell]\right)^{1/\ell}.$$

Unless otherwise specified, expectations are assumed to be taken over the uniform distribution. For any two Boolean functions f and g, their *inner product* is defined as

$$\langle f, g \rangle = \mathbb{E}_x[f(x) \cdot g(x)].$$

By Cauchy-Schwartz, we have

$$\langle f, g \rangle \leqslant \|f\|_2 \cdot \|g\|_2.$$

We now define the *noise operator* T_ρ. For any Boolean function f, the noise operator T_ρ on the function f defines a new function $T_\rho f$ as

$$(T_\rho f)(x) = \mathbb{E}_{y \leftarrow \mathcal{N}_\rho(x)}[f(y)].$$

The following is a special case of the *hypercontractivity theorem* [KKL88].

Theorem 1 (Hypercontractivity, [KKL88]**).** *For any function $f : \{0,1\}^n \to \mathbb{R}$ and $\rho \in [0,1]$,*

$$\|T_\rho f\|_2 \leqslant \|f\|_{1+\rho^2}.$$

Hypercontractivity is the core ingredient in our main technical lemma, Lemma 2.

Lemma 2. *Let $\alpha > 0$. Suppose $f, g : \{0,1\}^n \to \mathcal{Y}$ are (randomized) functions such that, for all $x^* \in \{0,1\}^n$,*

$$\Pr\left[f(x) = g(x^*) \mid x \leftarrow \{0,1\}^n\right] \leqslant \alpha.$$

Then, for any $\rho \in [0,1]$, it holds that

$$\Pr\left[f(\widetilde{x}) = g(x) \;\middle|\; \begin{array}{l} x \leftarrow \{0,1\}^n \\ \widetilde{x} \leftarrow \mathcal{N}_\rho(x) \end{array}\right] \leqslant \alpha^{\frac{1}{2}\cdot\left(\frac{1-\rho^2}{1+\rho^2}\right)}.$$

Proof. The proof works by a careful application of Cauchy-Schwarz and hypercontractivity. For $y \in \mathcal{Y}$ and $x \in \{0,1\}^n$, let $p_y(x) = \Pr[f(x) = y]$ and

$q_y(x) = \Pr[g(x) = y]$. Let $\mathcal{Y}^* = \{y \in \mathcal{Y} : \|q_y\|_1 > 0\}$.

$$
\begin{aligned}
&\Pr\left[f(\widetilde{x}) = g(x) \;\middle|\; \begin{array}{c} x \leftarrow \{0,1\}^n \\ \widetilde{x} \leftarrow \mathcal{N}_\rho(x) \end{array} \right] \\
&= \mathbb{E}_{x \leftarrow \{0,1\}^n} \sum_{y \in \mathcal{Y}^*} q_y(x) \cdot (T_\rho p_y)(x) \\
&= \sum_{y \in \mathcal{Y}^*} \langle q_y, T_\rho p_y \rangle \\
&\leqslant \sum_{y \in \mathcal{Y}^*} \|q_y\|_2 \cdot \|T_\rho p_y\|_2 && \text{(Cauchy-Schwarz)} \\
&\leqslant \sum_{y \in \mathcal{Y}^*} \|q_y\|_2 \cdot \|p_y\|_{1+\rho^2} && \text{(Hypercontractivity)} \\
&\leqslant \sqrt{\sum_{y \in \mathcal{Y}^*} \|q_y\|_2^2} \cdot \sqrt{\sum_{y \in \mathcal{Y}^*} \|p_y\|_{1+\rho^2}^2} && \text{(Cauchy-Schwarz)} \\
&= \sqrt{\sum_{y \in \mathcal{Y}^*} \mathbb{E}_x q_y(x)^2} \cdot \sqrt{\sum_{y \in \mathcal{Y}^*} \left(\mathbb{E}_x p_y(x)^{1+\rho^2}\right)^{2/(1+\rho^2)}} \\
&\leqslant \sqrt{\sum_{y \in \mathcal{Y}^*} \mathbb{E}_x q_y(x)} \cdot \sqrt{\sum_{y \in \mathcal{Y}^*} \left(\mathbb{E}_x p_y(x)\right)^{2/(1+\rho^2)}}
\end{aligned}
$$

Letting $P(y) = \Pr_{x \leftarrow \{0,1\}^n}[f(x) = y]$ and $Q(y) = \Pr_{x \leftarrow \{0,1\}^n}[g(x) = y]$,

$$
\begin{aligned}
&= \sqrt{\sum_{y \in \mathcal{Y}^*} Q(y)} \cdot \sqrt{\sum_{y \in \mathcal{Y}^*} P(y)^{2/(1+\rho^2)}} \\
&= 1 \cdot \sqrt{\sum_{y \in \mathcal{Y}^*} P(y) \cdot P(y)^{2/(1+\rho^2)-1}} \\
&\leqslant \sqrt{\sum_{y \in \mathcal{Y}^*} P(y) \cdot \alpha^{2/(1+\rho^2)-1}} && \text{(Assumption on } f\text{)} \\
&= \alpha^{\frac{1}{2}\left(\frac{1-\rho^2}{1+\rho^2}\right)}.
\end{aligned}
$$

□

3.5 Crypto Oracles

The recent work of [LMW25] introduced "crypto oracles" for the purposes of an impossibility result for doubly-efficient private information retrieval.

Definition 2 (Crypto oracle, [LMW25]**).** *A* crypto oracle *is a function* $\mathcal{B}^{\mathcal{R}}$ *where* $\mathcal{B}$ *is a stateless, polynomial time, deterministic Turing machine with oracle access to a secret random function* $\mathcal{R} : \{0,1\}^* \to \{0,1\}$.

The same work proved the following, which we have heavily paraphrased for simplicity. See their paper for details.

Theorem 2 ([LMW25]). *There exist crypto oracles that implement:*

- *VBB obfuscation for Turing machines, and*
- *the generic multilinear group.*

4 The Impossibility

4.1 Compiling Out the Random Oracle

In this section, we present a compiler that compiles any PRC in the random oracle model into a PRC in the information-theoretic setting. The new scheme has the same soundness and pseudorandomness, but it requires a larger secret key and incurs a loss in the completeness error.

We assume $\mathsf{KeyGen}^{\mathcal{R}}$ does not make any oracle queries. This is without loss of generality because we can simply include any $\mathcal{R}$ queries/responses used by KeyGen in the secret key.

In the following lemma and proof, we leave the dependence of functions of the security parameter on the security parameter implicit, writing e.g. τ instead of $\tau(\lambda)$.

Lemma 3. *Let* $\ell, Q : \mathbb{N} \to \mathbb{N}$ *be functions of the security parameter. Let* $(\mathsf{KeyGen}, \mathsf{Enc}^{\mathcal{R}}, \mathsf{Dec}^{\mathcal{R}})$ *be any zero-bit* $(\delta, \varepsilon, \mu)$*-PRC construction in the random oracle model where* $\mathsf{Enc}^{\mathcal{R}}$ *and* $\mathsf{Dec}^{\mathcal{R}}$ *each make at most* Q *queries to* $\mathcal{R}$ *and* $\mathsf{KeyGen}(1^{\lambda})$ *outputs keys of length at most* ℓ.

Then for any $\tau : \mathbb{N} \to (0, 1)$*, there exists a* $(\delta', \varepsilon', \mu')$*-PRC construction* $(\mathsf{KeyGen}', \mathsf{Enc}', \mathsf{Dec}')$ *in the standard model where*

- $\delta' = \delta + 2^{-\lambda} \cdot Q/\tau + Q^2 \cdot \tau^{\frac{1}{2} \cdot \left(\frac{1-\rho^2}{1+\rho^2}\right)} + \mathcal{O}\left(Q^2 \cdot \sqrt{\varepsilon n}\right)$,
- $\varepsilon' = \varepsilon$,
- $\mu' = \mu$, *and*
- *the size of the new secret key is* $\ell + \mathcal{O}\left(Q \cdot \lambda^2/\tau\right)$.

Proof of Lemma 3. Our compiler is presented in Fig. 2. We now proceed to prove its properties as stated in Lemma 3.

Secret Key Size. The size of the secret key grows by the size of S, which is $\mathcal{O}\left(Q \cdot \lambda^2/\tau\right)$ by construction.

Pseudorandomness and Soundness. Observe that for the pseudorandomness (resp., soundness) property, the experiment only involves KeyGen' and the encoder Enc' (resp., the decoder Dec'). The distribution of any process involving only the encoder (resp., decoder) is identical in the compiled scheme to the original scheme. This is because *locally*, the encoder (resp., decoder) perfectly simulates the random oracle. Consequently, the pseudorandomness and soundness guarantees do not change at all.

Let $\tau \in (0,1)$ be any number. Let $(\mathsf{KeyGen}, \mathsf{Enc}^{\mathcal{R}}, \mathsf{Dec}^{\mathcal{R}})$ be a PRC in the random oracle model where $\mathsf{Dec}^{\mathcal{R}}$ makes at most $Q = Q(\lambda)$ queries to $\mathcal{R}$. We compile it into a new PRC scheme $(\mathsf{KeyGen}', \mathsf{Enc}', \mathsf{Dec}')$ in the standard model as follows.

- $\mathsf{KeyGen}'(1^\lambda)$:
  1. Sample $\mathsf{sk} \leftarrow \mathsf{KeyGen}(1^\lambda)$ and a random function $F_0 : \{0,1\}^\lambda \to \{0,1\}$.
  2. Initialize $S = \emptyset$ and repeat the following for $\lceil \lambda/\tau \rceil$ times:
     - Sample $x \leftarrow \{0,1\}^n$ and run $\mathsf{Dec}^{F_0}(\mathsf{sk}, x)$, recording each query-response pair in S.
  3. Output the new secret key as $\mathsf{sk}' = (\mathsf{sk}, S)$.
- $\mathsf{Enc}'(\mathsf{sk}')$: Parse $\mathsf{sk}' = (\mathsf{sk}, S)$ and sample a random function $F_1 : \{0,1\}^\lambda \to \{0,1\}$ that is consistent with S. Run $\mathsf{Enc}^{F_1}(\mathsf{sk})$ and output the result.
- $\mathsf{Dec}'(\mathsf{sk}', x)$: Parse $\mathsf{sk}' = (\mathsf{sk}, S)$ and sample a random function $F_2 : \{0,1\}^\lambda \to \{0,1\}$ that is consistent with S. Run $\mathsf{Dec}^{F_2}(\mathsf{sk}, x)$ and output the result.

Fig. 2. Our compiler

Completeness. If Enc^{F_1} and Dec^{F_2} do not make the same query (except for those contained in S), then the compiled scheme perfectly simulates the original scheme. Therefore, it suffices to bound the probability that Enc^{F_1} and Dec^{F_2} both query their oracles on the same point q which is not in S. We refer to such a query as an *intersection query*.

We will say that a query q is τ*-heavy* for sk, F if

$$\Pr[\mathsf{Dec}^F(\mathsf{sk}, x) \text{ queries } q \mid x \leftarrow \{0,1\}^n] \geqslant \tau.$$

Consider the PRC completeness experiment for our compiled scheme.

Completeness experiment:

1. Sample $\mathsf{sk} \leftarrow \mathsf{KeyGen}(1^\lambda)$ and a random function $F_0 : \{0,1\}^\lambda \to \{0,1\}$.
2. Initialize $S = \emptyset$ and repeat the following for $\lceil \lambda/\tau \rceil$ times:
   - Sample $x \leftarrow \{0,1\}^n$ and run $\mathsf{Dec}^{F_0}(\mathsf{sk}, x)$. Record each query-response pair in S.
3. Let $\mathsf{sk}' = (\mathsf{sk}, S)$. Sample random functions $F_1, F_2 : \{0,1\}^\lambda \to \{0,1\}$ consistent with S.
4. Compute $c \leftarrow \mathsf{Enc}^{F_1}(\mathsf{sk})$ and $\tilde{c} \leftarrow \mathcal{N}_\rho(c)$.
5. Compute $\mathsf{Dec}^{F_2}(\mathsf{sk}, \tilde{c})$.

In this experiment we define two events:

- Bad_1: This event happens when S does not contain all queries which are τ-heavy for sk, F_2.
- Bad_2: This event happens when (1) S contains all queries which are τ-heavy for sk, F_2, but (2) $\mathsf{Enc}^{F_1}(\mathsf{sk})$ and $\mathsf{Dec}^{F_2}(\mathsf{sk}, \tilde{c})$ still make an intersection query (which is not included in S).

We conclude the completeness guarantee by proving the following two bounds:

1. $\Pr[\mathsf{Bad}_1] \leqslant 2^{-\lambda} \cdot Q/\tau$. This bound will hold for every fixed choice of sk.
2. $\Pr[\mathsf{Bad}_2] \leqslant Q^2 \cdot \left(\tau^{\frac{1}{2}\cdot\left(\frac{1-\rho^2}{1+\rho^2}\right)} + \mathcal{O}\left(\sqrt{\varepsilon n}\right)\right)$. This bound will only hold on average over sk.

Bounding Bad_1. In this part we will consider sk as fixed. For any $q \in \{0,1\}^\lambda$ that is τ-heavy for sk, F_0, the probability that q is queried in any single iteration of the loop in step 2 is at least τ. Therefore, the probability that q is *never* queried throughout the $\lceil \lambda/\tau \rceil$ iterations of the loop in step 2 is at most

$$(1-\tau)^{\lceil \lambda/\tau \rceil} \leqslant 2^{-\lambda}.$$

The total number of τ-heavy queries for sk, F_0 is upper bounded by Q/τ because $\mathsf{Dec}^{F_0}(\mathsf{sk}, \cdot)$ makes at most Q queries. So by a union bound, the probability that S does not contain all the queries which are τ-heavy for sk, F_0 is at most $2^{-\lambda} \cdot Q/\tau$.

Of course, we are interested in the probability that S contains all the queries which are τ-heavy for sk, F_2 (not sk, F_0). But these two probabilities are the same because, conditioned on S, F_0 and F_2 are equal on every point in S and both uniformly random on every other point.

More formally, note that for a given sk we could equivalently define F_0 as follows:

1. Initialize $S = \emptyset$ and repeat the following for $\lceil \lambda/\tau \rceil$ times:
   - Sample $x \leftarrow \{0,1\}^n$ and run $\mathsf{Dec}^{(\cdot)}(\mathsf{sk}, x)$, simulating the oracle on-the-fly. Record each query-response pair in S.
2. Let $\mathsf{sk}' = (\mathsf{sk}, S)$. Sample a random function $F_0 : \{0,1\}^\lambda \to \{0,1\}$ consistent with S.

Since the distribution of S, F_0 does not change if we sample F_0 in this way instead, the probability that S contains all the queries which are τ-heavy for sk, F_0 does not change. However, under this method of sampling it is clear that S, F_0 is distributed identically to S, F_2, so

$$\Pr[\mathsf{Bad}_1] \leqslant 2^{-\lambda} \cdot Q/\tau.$$

Bounding Bad_2. Now we are interested in the probability that both the encoder and decoder ask a query that is not τ-heavy for sk, F_2. Whereas we bounded $\Pr[\mathsf{Bad}_1]$ for every fixed choice of sk, we will use the randomness of the entire experiment to bound $\Pr[\mathsf{Bad}_2]$.

For $i, j \in [Q]$, let $\mathsf{Bad}_2^{i,j}$ denote the event that (1) S contains all the τ-heavy queries for sk, F_2, but (2) the i-th query made by $\mathsf{Enc}^{F_1}(\mathsf{sk})$ and the j-th query made by $\mathsf{Dec}^{F_2}(\mathsf{sk}, \tilde{c})$ are both some q that is not in S. By a union bound,

$$\Pr[\mathsf{Bad}_2] \leqslant \sum_{i,j \in [Q]} \Pr\left[\mathsf{Bad}_2^{i,j}\right].$$

We will use Lemma 2 to show that, for every $i, j \in [Q]$,

$$\Pr\left[\mathsf{Bad}_2^{i,j}\right] \leqslant \tau^{\frac{1}{2}\cdot\left(\frac{1-\rho^2}{1+\rho^2}\right)} + \mathcal{O}\left(\sqrt{\varepsilon n}\right).$$

Let $f_{\mathsf{sk}'}$ be the (randomized) function with $\mathsf{sk}' = (S, \mathsf{sk})$ hardwired that maps $\tilde{c}$ to the j-th query made by $\mathsf{Dec}^{F_2}(\mathsf{sk}, \tilde{c})$. Let $h_{\mathsf{sk}'}$ be the (randomized) function with sk' hardwired that maps c to the i-th query made by $\mathsf{Enc}^{F_1}(\mathsf{sk})$, conditioned on $c \leftarrow \mathsf{Enc}^{F_1}(\mathsf{sk})$; let $g_{\mathsf{sk}'}$ be identical to $h_{\mathsf{sk}'}$ except that $g_{\mathsf{sk}'}(c)$ outputs $\perp$ whenever $h_{\mathsf{sk}'}$ outputs any query that is in S. Observe that

$$\Pr\left[\mathsf{Bad}_2^{i,j}\right] = \Pr\left[\neg\mathsf{Bad}_1 \wedge f_{\mathsf{sk}'}(\tilde{c}) = g_{\mathsf{sk}'}(c) \;\middle|\; \begin{array}{c} c \leftarrow \mathsf{Enc}^{F_1}(\mathsf{sk}) \\ \tilde{c} \leftarrow \mathcal{N}_\rho(c) \end{array}\right].$$

Applying Lemma 1, we have that $\mathsf{SD}\left((\mathsf{sk}', c \leftarrow \mathsf{Enc}(\mathsf{sk}')), (\mathsf{sk}', x \leftarrow \{0,1\}^n)\right) = \mathcal{O}\left(\sqrt{\varepsilon n}\right)$, so

$$\begin{aligned} &\Pr\left[\neg\mathsf{Bad}_1 \wedge f_{\mathsf{sk}'}(\tilde{c}) = g_{\mathsf{sk}'}(c) \;\middle|\; \begin{array}{c} c \leftarrow \mathsf{Enc}^{F_1}(\mathsf{sk}) \\ \tilde{c} \leftarrow \mathcal{N}_\rho(c) \end{array}\right] \\ &\leqslant \Pr\left[\neg\mathsf{Bad}_1 \wedge f_{\mathsf{sk}'}(\tilde{x}) = g_{\mathsf{sk}'}(x) \;\middle|\; \begin{array}{c} x \leftarrow \{0,1\}^n \\ \tilde{x} \leftarrow \mathcal{N}_\rho(x) \end{array}\right] + \mathcal{O}\left(\sqrt{\varepsilon n}\right). \end{aligned}$$

Recall that $\neg\mathsf{Bad}_1$ means S contains all the τ-heavy queries for S, F_2, and $g_{\mathsf{sk}'}(x)$ never outputs any query that is in S. Therefore, for any $x^* \in \{0,1\}^n$,

$$\Pr\left[f_{\mathsf{sk}'}(x) = g_{\mathsf{sk}'}(x^*) \mid x \leftarrow \{0,1\}^n \wedge \neg\mathsf{Bad}_1\right] \leqslant \tau.$$

Since conditioning on $\neg\mathsf{Bad}_1$ does not affect the distribution on $x \leftarrow \{0,1\}^n, \tilde{x} \leftarrow \mathcal{N}_\rho(x)$, Lemma 2 implies that

$$\begin{aligned} &\Pr\left[\neg\mathsf{Bad}_1 \wedge f_{\mathsf{sk}'}(\tilde{x}) = g_{\mathsf{sk}'}(x) \;\middle|\; \begin{array}{c} x \leftarrow \{0,1\}^n \\ \tilde{x} \leftarrow \mathcal{N}_\rho(x) \end{array}\right] \\ &\leqslant \Pr\left[f_{\mathsf{sk}'}(\tilde{x}) = g_{\mathsf{sk}'}(x) \;\middle|\; \begin{array}{c} x \leftarrow \{0,1\}^n \\ \tilde{x} \leftarrow \mathcal{N}_\rho(x) \\ \neg\mathsf{Bad}_1 \end{array}\right] \\ &\leqslant \tau^{\frac{1}{2}\cdot\left(\frac{1-\rho^2}{1+\rho^2}\right)}, \end{aligned}$$

completing the proof. □

4.2 The Main Theorem

Let $\mathcal{R} : \{0,1\}^\lambda \to \{0,1\}$ be a random oracle which is only given to the algorithms of the pseudorandom code. That is, we do not assume that pseudorandomness holds against adversaries who are allowed to access $\mathcal{R}$. We are now prepared to prove the following theorem.

Theorem 3. *Let* $(\mathsf{KeyGen}^{\mathcal{R}}, \mathsf{Enc}^{\mathcal{R}}, \mathsf{Dec}^{\mathcal{R}})$ *be a zero-bit* $(\delta, \varepsilon, \mu)$ *pseudorandom error-correcting code making queries to a secret random oracle* $\mathcal{R}$*. Suppose that the code is robust to the* ρ*-noise channel, and that the number of queries made by one execution of* $\mathsf{KeyGen}^{\mathcal{R}}$*,* $\mathsf{Enc}^{\mathcal{R}}$*, and* $\mathsf{Dec}^{\mathcal{R}}$ *is at most* Q*. Then*

$$\delta + \mu \geqslant 1 - Q^2 \cdot \lambda^{-\omega(1-\rho)} - \mathcal{O}\left(Q^2\sqrt{\varepsilon n}\right).$$

Proof. We first remove any oracle queries made by $\mathsf{KeyGen}^{\mathcal{R}}$ by sampling the responses at random and including them in the secret key. If $\mathsf{Enc}^{\mathcal{R}}$ or $\mathsf{Dec}^{\mathcal{R}}$ tries to make any query whose response is included in the secret key, it uses the stored response instead of consulting $\mathcal{R}$. This transformation does not change the parameters of our PRC at all, except to increase the length of the secret key by a polynomial in λ.

Next, we apply Lemma 3 using $\tau = \lambda^{-c}$, where $c > 0$ is any constant. This yields a statistically-pseudorandom $(\delta', \varepsilon, \mu)$-PRC construction $(\mathsf{KeyGen}', \mathsf{Enc}', \mathsf{Dec}')$ in the standard model with

$$\delta' = \delta + \mathsf{negl}(\lambda) + Q^2 \cdot \lambda^{-\frac{c}{2}\cdot\left(\frac{1-\rho^2}{1+\rho^2}\right)} + \mathcal{O}\left(Q^2 \cdot \sqrt{\varepsilon n}\right)$$

and $\mathsf{poly}(\lambda)$-length secret keys. Now by Lemma 1, PRC codewords are $\mathcal{O}(\sqrt{\varepsilon n})$-indistinguishable from random strings *even to a distinguisher provided with the secret key.* Therefore the completeness-soundness gap is $\mathcal{O}(\sqrt{\varepsilon n})$, i.e., $\delta' + \mu \geqslant 1 - \mathcal{O}(\sqrt{\varepsilon n})$. Substituting the above formula for δ' and simplifying yields the result. □

Corollary 1. *There do not exist statistically-secure pseudorandom codes for any constant-rate noise channel, relative to any crypto oracle.*

Proof. Suppose that $(\mathsf{KeyGen}^{\mathcal{O}}, \mathsf{Enc}^{\mathcal{O}}, \mathsf{Dec}^{\mathcal{O}})$ is a pseudorandom code for some $(1 - \Omega(1))$-noise channel, relative to some crypto oracle $\mathcal{O}$. Assume it is a zero-bit PRC, by always using the all-zero message and disregarding the decoder's output.

Define $(\overline{\mathsf{KeyGen}}^{\mathcal{R}}, \overline{\mathsf{Enc}}^{\mathcal{R}}, \overline{\mathsf{Dec}}^{\mathcal{R}})$ to behave identically to $(\mathsf{KeyGen}^{\mathcal{O}}, \mathsf{Enc}^{\mathcal{O}}, \mathsf{Dec}^{\mathcal{O}})$, except that they simulate $\mathcal{O}$ using oracle access to a random function $\mathcal{R}$. If $\mathcal{R}$ is secret—that is, the pseudorandomness adversary is not allowed to query $\mathcal{R}$—then $(\overline{\mathsf{KeyGen}}^{\mathcal{R}}, \overline{\mathsf{Enc}}^{\mathcal{R}}, \overline{\mathsf{Dec}}^{\mathcal{R}})$ is a pseudorandom code. We can therefore invoke Theorem 3 with $(\overline{\mathsf{KeyGen}}^{\mathcal{R}}, \overline{\mathsf{Enc}}^{\mathcal{R}}, \overline{\mathsf{Dec}}^{\mathcal{R}})$ to conclude that

$$\delta + \mu \geqslant 1 - \mathsf{negl}(\lambda),$$

which means that there is a negligible completeness-soundness gap. □

Acknowledgments. Sanjam Garg is supported in part by the AFOSR Award FA9550-24-1-0156 and research grants from the Bakar Fund, Supra Inc., and the Stellar Development Foundation.

References

[AAC+25] Alrabiah, O., Ananth, P., Christ, M., Dodis, Y., Gunn, S.: Ideal pseudorandom codes. In: STOC (2025). arXiv:2411.05947

[BM09] Barak, B., Mahmoody-Ghidary, M.: Merkle puzzles are optimal — an $O(n^2)$-query attack on any key exchange from a random oracle. In: Halevi, S. (ed.) CRYPTO 2009. LNCS, vol. 5677, pp. 374–390. Springer, Heidelberg (2009). https://doi.org/10.1007/978-3-642-03356-8_22

[CG24] Christ, M., Gunn, S.: Pseudorandom error-correcting codes. In: Reyzin, L., Stebila, D. (eds.) Advances in Cryptology – CRYPTO 2024, Part VI. LNCS, Santa Barbara, CA, USA, 18–22 August 2024, vol. 14925, pp. 325–347. Springer, Cham (2024). https://doi.org/10.1007/978-3-031-68391-6_10

[CT01] Cover, T.M., Thomas, J.A.: Elements of Information Theory. Wiley, Hobojen (2001). https://doi.org/10.1002/0471200611

[DMR25] Döttling, N., Müller, A., Rajasree, M.S.: Separating pseudorandom codes from local oracles. IACR Cryptol. ePrint Arch. 1020 (2025). https://eprint.iacr.org/2025/1020

[GG24] Ghentiyala, S., Guruswami, V.: New constructions of pseudorandom codes. Cryptology ePrint Archive, Paper 2024/1425 (2024). https://eprint.iacr.org/2024/1425

[GM24] Golowich, N., Moitra, A.: Edit distance robust watermarks via indexing pseudorandom codes. In: Globersons, A., et al. (eds.) Advances in Neural Information Processing Systems 38: Annual Conference on Neural Information Processing Systems 2024, NeurIPS 2024, Vancouver, BC, Canada, 10–15 December 2024 (2024). http://papers.nips.cc/paper_files/paper/2024/hash/24c53bfa5b53fc2cf05644f5a7a26bb0-Abstract-Conference.html

[GZS25] Gunn, S., Zhao, X., Song, D.: An undetectable watermark for generative image models. In: The Thirteenth International Conference on Learning Representations, ICLR 2025, Singapore, 24–28 April 2025. OpenReview.net (2025). https://openreview.net/forum?id=jlhBFm7T2J

[HLLL25] Hu, X., Li, H., Li, J., Liu, A.: Videomark: a distortion-free robust watermarking framework for video diffusion models. CoRR arxiv:2504.16359 (2025). https://doi.org/10.48550/ARXIV.2504.16359

[IR89] Impagliazzo, R., Rudich, S.: Limits on the provable consequences of one-way permutations. In: 21st Annual ACM Symposium on Theory of Computing, Seattle, WA, USA, 15–17 May 1989, pp. 44–61. ACM Press (1989). https://doi.org/10.1145/73007.73012

[KKL88] Kahn,J., Kalai, G., Linial, N.: The influence of variables on Boolean functions (extended abstract). In: 29th Annual Symposium on Foundations of Computer Science, White Plains, NY, USA, 24–26 October 1988, pp. 68–80. IEEE Computer Society Press (1988). https://doi.org/10.1109/SFCS.1988.21923

[LMW25] Lin, W.K., Mook, E., Wichs, D.: Black box crypto is useless for doubly efficient PIR. In: Fehr, S., Fouque, P.A. (eds.) Advances in Cryptology - EUROCRYPT 2025 - 44th Annual International Conference on the Theory and Applications of Cryptographic Techniques, Madrid, Spain, 4–8 May 2025, Proceedings, Part VI. LNCS, vol. 15606, pp. 65–93. Springer, Heidelberg (2025). https://doi.org/10.1007/978-3-031-91095-1_3

[O'D14] O'Donnell, R.: Analysis of Boolean Functions. Cambridge University Press, Cambridge (2014). http://www.cambridge.org/de/academic/

subjects/computer-science/algorithmics-complexity-computer-algebra-and-computational-g/analysis-boolean-functions

[RTV04] Reingold, O., Trevisan, L., Vadhan, S.: Notions of reducibility between cryptographic primitives. In: Naor, M. (ed.) TCC 2004. LNCS, vol. 2951, pp. 1–20. Springer, Heidelberg (2004). https://doi.org/10.1007/978-3-540-24638-1_1

[YZC+25] Yang, Z., et al.: Gaussian shading++: rethinking the realistic deployment challenge of performance-lossless image watermark for diffusion models. CoRR arxiv:2504.15026 (2025). https://doi.org/10.48550/ARXIV.2504.15026

Separating Pseudorandom Codes from Local Oracles

Nico Döttling[1], Anne Müller[1,2(✉)], and Mahesh Sreekumar Rajasree[1]

[1] CISPA Helmholtz Center for Information Security, Saarbrücken, Germany
{doettling,anne.mueller}@cispa.de, srmahesh1994@gmail.com
[2] Graduate School of Computer Science, Saarland University, Saarbrücken, Germany

Abstract. Pseudorandom codes (PRCs) are error-correcting codes with the distinguishing feature that their codewords are computationally indistinguishable from random strings. Introduced by Christ and Gunn (CRYPTO 2024), PRCs have found applications in areas such as AI watermarking, where both robustness and pseudorandomness are essential. All known constructions of PRCs rely on coding-theoretic hardness assumptions. In this work, we study how inherent the use of coding-theoretic hardness is in the construction of pseudorandom codes.

We show that there is no black-box construction of PRCs with binary alphabets capable of decoding from a constant fraction of Bernoulli noise from a class of oracles we call *local* oracles. The class of local oracles includes random oracles and trapdoor permutation oracles, and can be interpreted as a meaningful notion of oracles that are not resilient against noise. Our separation result is cast in the Impagliazzo-Rudich framework and crucially relies on the Bonami-Beckner hypercontractivity theorem on the Boolean hypercube.

As a complementary result, we show that PRCs with large alphabets that can tolerate high error rates can indeed be constructed in a black-box manner from one-way functions.

Keywords: pseudorandom codes · black-box separation

1 Introduction

Both coding theory and cryptography are deeply rooted in information theory, but their objectives and principles differ in fundamental ways. Coding theory primarily addresses the challenge of reliable communication and storage of information in the presence of noise. In the problem of error correction, the goal is to encode data so that even if a portion of it is corrupted during transmission or

N. Döttling and M. S. Rajasree—Funded by the European Union (ERC, LACONIC, 101041207). Views and opinions expressed are however those of the author(s) only and do not necessarily reflect those of the European Union or the European Research Council. Neither the European Union nor the granting authority can be held responsible for them.

B. Applebaum and H. Lin (Eds.): TCC 2025, LNCS 16271, pp. 225–257, 2026.
https://doi.org/10.1007/978-3-032-12290-2_8

storage, the original message can still be recovered accurately. This is achieved by introducing *structured redundancy* into the message, which allows errors to be detected and corrected by the receiver.

The most basic task of cryptography, on the other hand, is to ensure secrecy of data. A central concept in cryptography is pseudorandomness: the idea that one can *efficiently* generate strings that are computationally indistinguishable from truly random ones. Hence pseudorandomness hides *any discernible structure*. This property underlies many cryptographic primitives, such as pseudorandom generators (PRGs), which expand short random seeds into long pseudorandom outputs. PRGs are a cornerstone of modern cryptography and are known to be constructible from the minimal assumption of one-way functions (OWFs) [Yao82, BM84, HILL99].

Pseudorandom Codes (PRCs) [CG24] are an exciting new notion that unites these two concepts which are seemingly at odds. In a nutshell, a pseudorandom code is an error correcting code in the sense that noisy codewords can be efficiently decoded from a bounded number of Hamming errors *given a secret key*. At the same time, codewords are indistinguishable from uniformly random strings to any outsider who does not possess the secret key.

This notion was first formalized by Christ and Gunn [CG24], with the purpose of studying watermarking of AI models [ZDR19, KJGR21, Aar22, KGW+23, FGJ+25, ZALW24, KTHL24]. Their work introduces a model which allows to embed data (e.g., a watermark) into machine learning models in such a way that the watermark is resilient to small perturbations (errors), yet concealed to anyone without the appropriate secret.

Constructing PRCs. Building PRCs turns out to be a highly non-trivial task [CG24, GM24, GG24, AAC+24]. The naive approach of masking codewords of a standard error correcting code with a pseudorandom function is flawed; if encoder and decoder are not synchronized (i.e. do not share a common state) this does not yield a correct scheme. The basic premise to make this approach work is to let the encoder include an encryption of such a state into the codeword. But now this state must be protected against noise, hence we also need to encode it! It turns out that this is a hen-and-egg problem: In order to build a pseudorandom code in this way we need to start with a pseudorandom random code!

To break out of this loop, current constructions of PRCs rely on strong and sometimes non-standard cryptographic assumptions *strongly related to coding theory*, such as the McEliece problem [McE78], the Learning Parity with Noise (LPN) assumption [Kea93, BFKL93], the planted XOR or planted hyperloop assumptions [BKR23] or the existence of Local Weak Pseudorandom Functions (LWPRFs) [GM24], etc. These assumptions go significantly beyond the foundational concept of one-way functions and are typically viewed as strong assumptions in the hierarchy of cryptographic assumptions, and they are *explicitly linked to coding theory*. In other words, each of these assumptions more or less explicitly conjectures that some basic construction is, in essence, a weak form of a pseudorandom code.

Given this landscape, a fundamental and natural question arises:

Can we construct pseudorandom codes from (minimal) cryptographic standard assumptions that do not relate to coding theory?

The question of identifying the minimal assumptions required for constructing cryptographic primitives lies at the heart of cryptographic theory. Understanding the weakest possible assumption not only sheds light on the intrinsic complexity of a primitive but also helps delineate the boundaries of what is cryptographically feasible. A landmark result in this direction is the seminal work of Impagliazzo and Rudich [IR89], which showed that public-key encryption schemes cannot be constructed from one-way functions using black-box techniques.

In a black-box construction of a cryptographic primitive P from an assumption A, the primitive A is accessed solely as an oracle. Its internal structure is never exploited. Concretely, Impagliazzo and Rudich [IR89] model one-way functions as random oracles, i.e. functions with a uniformly random function table over some finite domain. This framework is attractive for its generality and modularity, often leading to simpler and more broadly applicable constructions. A *black-box separation* shows that no such construction is possible: that is, if a black-box construction of P from A did exist, then there always exists an unbounded adversary breaking the security of P which is efficient in the sense that it only makes a polynomial number of queries to A. The Impagliazzo–Rudich [IR89] framework laid the foundation for a rich body of work establishing black-box separations between various cryptographic primitives, illuminating the landscape of cryptographic assumptions and revealing the limitations of black-box constructions in building advanced cryptographic functionalities [Rud88, Rud91, Sim98, GKM+00, GMR01, HR04, BMG09, BKSY11, MM11, MP12, Mat14, FR23].

1.1 Our Results

We consider the most basic setting of symmetric key pseudorandom codes against a Bernoulli channel. In a symmetric key pseudorandom code, both the encoder Encode and the decoder Decode use the same secret key sk. In a Bernoulli channel with *bias-parameter* $\rho \in [0,1]$, each transmitted bit is independently flipped with probability $\frac{1}{2} - \frac{1}{2}\rho$. More generally, we say that an error $\mathbf{e} \in \{0,1\}^n$ follows the Bernoulli distribution[1] Ber_ρ^n, if each bit e_i of $\mathbf{e}$ is independently 1 with probability $\frac{1}{2} - \frac{1}{2}\rho$. Before we describe our technical main result, we will first discuss a consequence of this result.

Theorem 1 (Informal). *For any constant ρ, there is no black-box construction of symmetric key pseudorandom codes against the Bernoulli channel with parameter ρ from random oracles or even trapdoor permutations.*

[1] Here we use the notation commonly used in the Boolean functions literature [O'D14], where the Bernoulli distribution is parametrized in terms of the bias rather than the bit-flip probability.

That is, we can black-box-separate symmetric key pseudorandom codes from the most common *generic* assumptions used in both symmetric and public key cryptography, namely one-way functions and trapdoor permutations.

Our actual separation encompasses an even larger class of oracles, namely any oracle we call *local*. Consider the following experiment. An adversary $\mathcal{A}$ makes queries q_i to an oracle $\mathcal{O}$ and obtains responses y_i. Let Z denote the set of query-response pairs (q_i, y_i). Assume now that we want to simulate the output of $\mathcal{O}$ on a query q without actually querying $\mathcal{O}$. Under what conditions on q can we simulate the output consistently with the set Z without actually knowing Z?

In the case of random oracles this condition is simple: As long as q is distinct from all q_i in the set Z, we can just choose a fresh random output y_q to simulate $\mathcal{O}$, as in this case $\mathcal{O}(q)$ itself is uniformly random and independent of Z. That is, our simulation of the random oracle is faithful as long as q is not an *intersection query*. Further observe that if we are *given back* oracle access to the random oracle $\mathcal{O}$ after simulating the response for q, we can faithfully simulate any future query q', irrespective of whether q' is an intersection query or not: If $q' = q$ we answer with y_q, otherwise we query $\mathcal{O}$ on q'.

In general, we say that an oracle $\mathcal{O}$ is *local*, if for any (adversarially generated) set Z of query-response pairs of polynomial size, there exists a set Q_{rel} of *related queries* such that $|Q_{rel}|$ is of size polynomial in $|Z|$. We further require that for any $q \notin Q_{rel}$ there is a way to simulate the response of $\mathcal{O}(q)$ without knowledge of Z and without actually querying $\mathcal{O}$, such that the simulated response is consistent with Z. Finally, we require that all future queries q' can be simulated consistently with respect to both Z and q, given oracle access to $\mathcal{O}$ (but without knowledge of Z).

While by the above discussion it is immediately clear that random oracles are local, in Sect. 4 we show that the trapdoor permutation oracle is also local.

Our main result is a separation of pseudorandom codes from any local oracle.

Theorem 2 (Informal). *For any constant ρ, there is no black-box construction of symmetric key pseudorandom codes against the Bernoulli channel with parameter ρ from a local oracle $\mathcal{O}$.*

By the above discussion Theorem 1 is immediately implied by Theorem 2.

Pseudorandom Code Oracles are not Local. It is instructive to realize *why* oracles $\mathcal{O}_{\mathsf{PRC}}$ that implement ideal pseudorandom codes are not local. Say that $\mathcal{O}_{\mathsf{PRC}}$ can decode from $r = \alpha n$ Hamming errors. If we make an encoding query m to $\mathcal{O}_{\mathsf{PRC}}$ and obtain a codeword $\mathbf{c}$, then by the error correction property of $\mathcal{O}_{\mathsf{PRC}}$ any decoding query $\mathbf{c} + \mathbf{e}$ must return m as long as the Hamming weight of $\mathbf{e}$ is smaller than r. However, there are $2^{H(\alpha)n}$ such errors $\mathbf{e}$[2], which means there is an exponential number of related queries $\mathbf{c} + \mathbf{e}$!

Consequently, one way to interpret our result is that in order to construct a pseudorandom code in a black-box way, we need to start with a primitive that is *non-local* and therefore already exhibits strong pseudorandom code-like

[2] Here H is the binary entropy function.

properties. This is consistent with our understanding of current constructions of pseudorandom codes, which essentially bootstrap pseudorandom codes with weak correctness and security properties into pseudorandom codes with strong correctness and security properties [CG24, GM24, GG24, AAC+24].

A Complementary Result. As a complementary result, we show that symmetric key pseudorandom codes over large alphabets, i.e. alphabets of size 2^λ *can* be constructed from minimal cryptographic assumptions.

Theorem 3. *Assuming one-way functions there exists a symmetric-key pseudorandom code construction over an alphabet of size* 2^λ *with code parameters approaching the Singleton bound.*

This demonstrates that the assumption of working over a small field is in fact critical for our separation.

2 Technical Overview

We will now provide a high level outline of the main ideas of our oracle separation. For concreteness assume that $\mathcal{O}$ is a random oracle and that we are given a candidate symmetric key PRC construction $\mathsf{PRC}^{\mathcal{O}} = (\mathsf{KeyGen}, \mathsf{Encode}^{\mathcal{O}}, \mathsf{Decode}^{\mathcal{O}})$ relative to $\mathcal{O}$. Without loss of generality, we assume that the key-generator KeyGen does not make any oracle queries; since we are in the symmetric key setting any $\mathcal{O}$-queries made by KeyGen can be deferred to both $\mathsf{Encode}^{\mathcal{O}}$ and $\mathsf{Decode}^{\mathcal{O}}$. Hence assume that KeyGen just outputs a uniformly random string $\mathsf{sk} \in \{0,1\}^\lambda$. $\mathsf{Encode}^{\mathcal{O}}$ and $\mathsf{Decode}^{\mathcal{O}}$ are efficient in the sense that they only make a $\mathsf{poly}(\lambda)$ number of $\mathcal{O}$-queries.

Security of such a construction holds with respect to a distinguisher $\mathcal{D}^{\mathcal{O},\mathcal{F}}$ which has access to the oracle $\mathcal{O}$ and an additional oracle $\mathcal{F}$. $\mathcal{D}$ is allowed to make a polynomial number of queries to its oracles, but is otherwise computationally unbounded, so as to model that $\mathcal{O}$ *is the only source of computational hardness* [IR89].

The goal of the distinguisher is to distinguish the following two cases:

- The oracle $\mathcal{F}$ implements $\mathsf{Encode}^{\mathcal{O}}(sk, \cdot)$ for $\mathsf{sk} \leftarrow \mathsf{KeyGen}$. I.e.g.iven a query m it outputs $\mathbf{c} = \mathsf{Encode}^{\mathcal{O}}(sk, m) \in \{0,1\}^n$, choosing fresh random coins for Encode at each query.
- The oracle $\mathcal{F}$ outputs a fresh uniformly random string $\mathbf{u} \in \{0,1\}^n$ for each query. Note that $\mathcal{F}$ is not a random oracle as querying $\mathcal{F}$ twice on the same input will lead to two independent uniformly random outputs.

We say a pseudorandom code $\mathsf{PRC}^{\mathcal{O}}$ is secure (or satisfies the pseudorandomness property), if every distinguisher $\mathcal{D}$ that makes at most $\mathsf{poly}(\lambda)$ queries has at most negligible advantage in this experiment.

We will now outline why no such candidate construction $\mathsf{PRC}^{\mathcal{O}} = (\mathsf{KeyGen}, \mathsf{Encode}^{\mathcal{O}}, \mathsf{Decode}^{\mathcal{O}})$ can meet this security notion. That is, for every such candidate construction $\mathsf{PRC}^{\mathcal{O}}$ we will construct an efficient (i.e. poly-query) distinguisher which breaks the pseudorandomness property of $\mathsf{PRC}^{\mathcal{O}}$ with $1/\mathsf{poly}(\lambda)$ advantage.

Warmup: $\mathsf{Decode}^{\mathcal{O}}$ *Makes no* $\mathcal{O}$*-Queries.* As a starting point, we observe that if $\mathsf{PRC}^{\mathcal{O}} = (\mathsf{KeyGen}, \mathsf{Encode}^{\mathcal{O}}, \mathsf{Decode}^{\mathcal{O}})$ is such that Decode does not make any $\mathcal{O}$ queries, then unsurprisingly $\mathsf{PRC}^{\mathcal{O}}$ is insecure. Recall that $|\mathsf{sk}| = \lambda$. Our distinguisher $\mathcal{D}$ queries its oracle $\mathcal{F}$ on (say) 2λ uniformly random bits $b_1, \ldots, b_{2\lambda} \in \{0,1\}$ and obtains the outputs $\mathbf{x}_1, \ldots, \mathbf{x}_{2\lambda}$. First assume that $\mathbf{x}_1, \ldots, \mathbf{x}_{2\lambda}$ are distributed uniformly. Fix any $\mathsf{sk}^* \in \{0,1\}^\lambda$. Since the $b_i \in \{0,1\}$ are chosen uniformly and are independent of the $\mathbf{x}_i$, the probability that it holds for all i that $\mathsf{Decode}(\mathsf{sk}^*, \mathbf{x}_i) = b_i$ is at most $2^{-2\lambda}$. Hence, a union-bound shows that the probability that there exists and $\mathsf{sk} \in \{0,1\}^\lambda$ with this property is at most $2^{-\lambda}$.

On the other hand, if the $\mathbf{x}_i$ are codewords of $\mathsf{PRC}^{\mathcal{O}}$, i.e. $\mathbf{x}_i = \mathsf{Encode}^{\mathcal{O}}(\mathsf{sk}, b_i)$, then it holds by the correctness of $\mathsf{PRC}^{\mathcal{O}}$ that $\mathsf{Decode}(\mathsf{sk}, \mathbf{x}_i) = b_i$. Consequently, in this case we *know* that there exists an sk such that $\mathsf{Decode}(\mathsf{sk}^*, \mathbf{x}_i) = b_i$ for all $i \in [2\lambda]$.

This observation leads to a simple distinguishing strategy: Our distinguisher $\mathcal{D}$ just brute-forces over all $\mathsf{sk} \in \{0,1\}^\lambda$; if it finds an sk which decodes all $\mathbf{x}_i$ correctly it guesses 1 (with the meaning that the oracle $\mathcal{F}$ implements $\mathsf{Encode}^{\mathcal{O}}(\mathsf{sk}, \cdot)$), otherwise 0.

Decoders with Correctness Errors. The argument in the last paragraph assumed that if we use the correct key sk, $\mathsf{Decode}^{\mathcal{O}}(\mathsf{sk}, \mathbf{x})$ will always output the correct message. The attack does not work if Decode has a correctness error. However, even if the (honest) decoder has a correctness error, the distinguisher can still measure whether a decoder works *most of the time.* Specifically, the distinguisher can count the number of indices $i \in [2\lambda]$ for which $\mathsf{Decode}(\mathsf{sk}^*, \mathbf{x}_i) = b_i$ holds. Call this number Z.

If the $\mathbf{x}_i$ are chosen uniformly, we expect Z to be close to $2\lambda/2 = \lambda$. This can be made precise using a Chernoff bound. On the other hand, if the $\mathbf{x}_i$ are codewords, we would expect Z to be closer to 2λ *often enough.* We can make this concrete using a Markov bound.

Observe that at this point none of our distinguishers so far relies on the fact that Decode can correct errors. This will become crucial in the following paragraphs.

$\mathsf{Decode}^{\mathcal{O}}$ *Makes One Single* $\mathcal{O}$*-Query.* Now consider the case that $\mathsf{Decode}^{\mathcal{O}}$ makes one single $\mathcal{O}$-query. In this case our previous argument no longer works, the distinguisher cannot brute force over all 2^λ many $\mathsf{sk} \in \{0,1\}^\lambda$ and test whether decoding works, as this would quickly exhaust its $\mathsf{poly}(\lambda)$ budget of $\mathcal{O}$-queries.

Hence, let's have a closer look at how $\mathsf{Decode}^{\mathcal{O}}$ may use its sole $\mathcal{O}$-query. The decoder gets as inputs a secret key sk and a word $\mathbf{x} \in \{0,1\}^n$ and formulates a query q for $\mathcal{O}$. Hence, we can describe this process by a function[3] $\mathsf{Quer}_{\mathsf{sk}} : \{0,1\}^n \to Q$, where Q is the input domain of $\mathcal{O}$, the *query space*. Recall that we are analyzing a decoder for the Bernoulli channel. So what happens if we obtain $\mathbf{x}$ by adding Bernoulli noise to a codeword $\mathbf{c}$? We have that $\mathsf{Decode}^{\mathcal{O}}(\mathsf{sk}, \mathbf{c}+\mathbf{e})$ queries $\mathcal{O}$ on $\mathsf{Quer}_{\mathsf{sk}}(\mathbf{c}+\mathbf{e})$ and obtains $\mathcal{O}(\mathsf{Quer}_{\mathsf{sk}}(\mathbf{c}+\mathbf{e}))$. Assume for now that $\mathcal{O}(\mathsf{Quer}_{\mathsf{sk}}(\mathbf{c}+\mathbf{e}))$ actually has an influence on the output of the decoder, if not we have essentially and oracle-free decoder and the attack discussed above applies.

Observe that the random oracle $\mathcal{O}$ itself is not noise-robust; for any error e the oracle outputs $\mathcal{O}(q)$ and $\mathcal{O}(q+e)$ are independently uniform. Now, as the Bernoulli error $\mathbf{e}$ has high entropy, we claim that in order to achieve correctness the query-function $\mathsf{Quer}_{\mathsf{sk}}$ must be noise robust! Otherwise, if $\mathsf{Quer}_{\mathsf{sk}}$ somehow allowed the error $\mathbf{e}$ to *pass through*, the response $\mathcal{O}(\mathsf{Quer}_{\mathsf{sk}}(\mathbf{c}+\mathbf{e}))$ would be completely unpredictable from the view of the encoder. In other words, as it would be very unlikely that the encoder ever queried $\mathcal{O}$ on $\mathsf{Quer}_{\mathsf{sk}}(\mathbf{c}+\mathbf{e})$, the codeword $\mathbf{c}$ is independent of this value and the decoder does not actually need to query $\mathcal{O}$, but could just locally simulate it! Hence, if this happens too frequently, the decoder does not actually need $\mathcal{O}$ and we are once again in the oracle-free decoder setting discussed above.

Hence, we conclude that the function $\mathsf{Quer}_{\mathsf{sk}}$ must be noise robust *on codewords*! How can we use this fact to construct an attack against the one-query decoder?

Strategy. Our basic high-strategy will leverage the ideas sketched in the last paragraph to construct an *equivalent decoder* that does not make use of the oracle! The discussion in the next paragraphs of this outline will be somewhat technical, so this is a good point to reflect what goals we want to achieve in each step.

- We will first establish that the only query functions $\mathsf{Quer}_{\mathsf{sk}}$ that are robust on noisy codewords are essentially *almost constant* functions, i.e. functions that produce only a small number of *heavy* queries. This argument will rely on both sophisticated Fourier-analytic properties of boolean functions (refer Sect. 5.1 and Sect. 5.2) and the pseudorandomness of $\mathsf{PRC}^{\mathcal{O}}$ (refer Lemma 4).
- Once we have established this, we can argue that *heavy queries* computed by $\mathsf{Quer}_{\mathsf{sk}}$ can be learned from the function $\mathsf{Quer}_{\mathsf{sk}}$ alone by an *offline learner*. This allows us to include query-response pairs for such heavy queries into an augmented secret key. That is, we can effectively *compile out* the single oracle query made by $\mathsf{Decode}^{\mathcal{O}}$ and the previous attack against oracle-free decoders applies. See Lemma 5 in the main section.
- If the decoder $\mathsf{Decode}^{\mathcal{O}}$ makes more $\mathcal{O}$-queries, we can compile out the oracle queries one at a time. Some care is needed to ensure that successive queries to $\mathcal{O}$ are answered consistently with the query that has been compiled out. See Theorem 9 in the main section.

[3] Assume for now that this process is deterministic. However, our techniques readily generalize to the case where $\mathsf{Quer}_{\mathsf{sk}}(\mathbf{x})$ takes additional random coins.

Noise-Robustness of Boolean Functions. We will now bound the amount of noise robustness we can expect from a query function. Towards this goal, we will make a small detour through the realm of Fourier analysis of boolean functions. We will first introduce some terminology. Fix *any* function[4] $\mathsf{Quer} : \{0,1\}^n \to Q$. We will define two quantities with respect to Quer.

- For a query $q \in Q$, we define the *global weight* of q by $\mathsf{w}(q) = \Pr_{\mathbf{u}}[\mathsf{Quer}(\mathbf{u}) = q]$, i.e. the probability that Quer outputs q when queried on a uniformly random $\mathbf{u} \leftarrow \{0,1\}^n$.
- For an $\mathbf{x} \in \{0,1\}^n$ and a query $q \in Q$ we define the *local weight* of q by $\ell_{\mathbf{x}}(q) = \Pr_{\mathbf{e}}[\mathsf{Quer}(\mathbf{x}+\mathbf{e}) = q]$, where $\mathbf{e} \leftarrow \mathsf{Ber}_\rho^n$ follows a Bernoulli distribution. Intuitively, $\ell_{\mathbf{x}}(q)$ measures how heavy q is around $\mathbf{x}$.

How are the global and the local weight of a query q related? Intuitively, if we have a query q which has *small* global weight ϵ but *large* local weight δ around a word $\mathbf{x}$, then we can think of the function Quer as exhibiting *error correcting* properties around $\mathbf{x}$; we can think of $\mathbf{x}$ as an error-correcting encoding of q which can be decoded even under noise by evaluating $\mathsf{Quer}(\mathbf{x})$.

How frequent are such *exceptional* words $\mathbf{x}$? Basic coding bounds such as the Hamming bound (aka sphere-packing bound) suggest that such $\mathbf{x}$ are extremely rare, as each of them must come with a Hamming ball around it that occupies a considerable portion of the boolean hypercube $\{0,1\}^n$.

To make this intuition concrete, we will rely on the Bonami-Beckner hypercontractivity theorem [Bon70,Bec75], a celebrated result in Fourier-analysis of Boolean functions. In broad terms the result enables us to bound higher order moments of a noisy version of a Boolean function in terms of lower order moments of the function itself. In our concrete case, the hypercontractivity theorem allows us to bound the second moment of the local weight $\ell_{\mathbf{u}}(q)$ (for a uniformly random $\mathbf{u} \in \{0,1\}^n$) in terms of the global weight $\mathsf{w}(q)$. Specifically we get for every $q \in Q$ that

$$\mathop{\mathsf{E}}_{\mathbf{u} \leftarrow \{0,1\}^n}[\ell_{\mathbf{u}}(q)^2] \leq \mathsf{w}(q)^{1+c}$$

for some constant $c \in (0,1)$ that only depends on the Bernoulli noise-rate ρ, but is independent of the query function Quer!

Now, we call an $\mathbf{x} \in \{0,1\}^n$ (ϵ, δ)-exceptional (just exceptional for short) *if there exists* a $q \in Q$ with $\mathsf{w}(q) < \epsilon$ and $\ell_{\mathbf{x}}(q) > \delta$. We can now bound the probability that a uniformly random $\mathbf{u} \leftarrow \{0,1\}^n$ is exceptional by

$$\begin{aligned}\Pr[\mathbf{u} \text{ exceptional }] &= \Pr[\exists q \in Q \text{ with } \mathsf{w}(q) < \epsilon \text{ s.t. } \ell_{\mathbf{u}}(q) > \delta] \\ &\leq \sum_{\substack{q \in Q \\ \mathsf{w}(q) < \epsilon}} \Pr[\ell_{\mathbf{u}}(q) > \delta] \\ &= \sum_{\substack{q \in Q \\ \mathsf{w}(q) < \epsilon}} \Pr[\ell_{\mathbf{u}}(q)^2 > \delta^2]\end{aligned}$$

[4] In this paragraph we will ignore that there is a secret key involved.

$$\leq \sum_{\substack{q \in Q \\ \mathsf{w}(q) < \epsilon}} \frac{\mathsf{w}(q)^{1+c}}{\delta^2},$$

where we have just used the union bound and the Markov inequality. Using the fact that $\sum_{q \in Q} \mathsf{w}(q) = \sum_{q \in Q} \Pr[\mathsf{Quer}(\mathbf{u}) = q] = 1$ we can use a basic norm-interpolation inequality to conclude that

$$\Pr[\mathbf{u} \text{ exceptional}] \leq \epsilon^c/\delta^2.$$

For the details, refer to Sect. 5.1.

Exceptionality of Codewords. So far we have established a bound that a uniformly random string $\mathbf{u} \leftarrow \{0,1\}^n$ is exceptional. However, returning to our prior discussion, what we are actually interested in is the noise-robustness of the query function $\mathsf{Quer}_{\mathsf{sk}}$ when we evaluate it on a noisy codeword $\mathbf{c} + \mathbf{e}$. As by the discussion in the last paragraph, this immediately relates to the exceptionality of $\mathbf{c}$.

We also gained the insight that exceptional words are rare under the uniform measure on $\{0,1\}^n$.

We will now translate these insights to codewords of $\mathsf{PRC}^{\mathcal{O}}$ by relying on the pseudorandomness of $\mathsf{PRC}^{\mathcal{O}}$. Specifically, we can bound the probability that a codeword $\mathbf{c}$ is exceptional with respect to the query function $\mathsf{Quer}_{\mathsf{sk}}$ (using the correct secret key sk) by

$$\Pr[\mathbf{c} \text{ exceptional}] \leq 3\epsilon^c/\delta^2.$$

In the following, let $p^* = \epsilon^c/\delta^2$. Assume towards contradiction that the probability $\Pr[\mathbf{c} \text{ exceptional}] > 3p^*$. Recall that it holds $\Pr[\mathbf{u} \text{ exceptional}] \leq p^*$. Note that if we are given a key sk we can determine whether a word $\mathbf{x}$ is exceptional *without using the oracle* $\mathcal{O}$, i.e. just check whether there is a $q \in Q$ with $\mathsf{w}(q) < \epsilon$ and $\ell_{\mathbf{x}}(q) > \delta$. The distinguisher $\mathcal{D}$ queries its challenge oracle $N \approx (|\mathsf{sk}| + \lambda)/p^* = \mathsf{poly}(\lambda)$ times, obtaining words $\mathbf{x}_1, \ldots, \mathbf{x}_N$. Now, for each *candidate key* $\mathsf{sk} \in \{0,1\}^\lambda$ it determines the number of $\mathbf{x}_i$ that are exceptional with respect to $\mathsf{Quer}_{\mathsf{sk}}$. If there exists an sk such that this number is greater than $2p^*N$ it outputs 1, otherwise it outputs a uniformly random bit. Using a Chernoff and a union-bound we can routinely show that if the $\mathbf{x}_i \in \{0,1\}^n$ are distributed uniformly, then no such sk exists, except with negligible probability $2^{-\lambda}$. On the other hand, if the $\mathbf{x}_i$ are valid codewords with respect to some key sk, then the event that we count more than $2p^*N$ exceptional words for this key sk is at least p^*. Hence we obtain a distinguisher with advantage $p^*/2 = 1/\mathsf{poly}(\lambda)$.

We conclude that the query function $\mathsf{Quer}_{\mathsf{sk}}$ behaves essentially the same on noisy codewords as it does on uniformly random words.

Compiling-Out $\mathcal{O}$-Queries. Now we have all the tools in place to provide and analyze our main technical step: Compiling out $\mathcal{O}$-queries from the decoder.

Fix a secret key sk and hence a query function $\mathsf{Quer}_{\mathsf{sk}}$. We can we compile out the $\mathcal{O}$-query from the decoder as follows:

- We will introduce an offline-learner which queries $\mathcal{O}$ on all globally ϵ-heavy queries. Then all of the corresponding query-response pairs are included in into an *augmented secret key* (together with sk). Observe that there can be at most $1/\epsilon = \mathsf{poly}(\lambda)$ many queries of global weight $> \epsilon$, hence this learner is efficient (in terms of its number of $\mathcal{O}$-queries)
- The augmented key is given to an *augmented decoder*, which proceeds as follows. Given an input $\mathbf{x}$, it first computes $q = \mathsf{Quer}_{\mathsf{sk}}(\mathbf{x})$ to determine whether q is in the list of queries that have been learned by the offline learner. If so it takes the corresponding response from the list provided in the augmented secret key. If not it *locally simulates* $\mathcal{O}$ by choosing a uniformly random output.

We will now analyze the correctness of the augmented decoder. Fix a secret key sk and thus a query function $\mathsf{Quer}_{\mathsf{sk}}$. Further fix a codeword $\mathbf{c} = \mathsf{Encode}^{\mathcal{O}}(\mathsf{sk}, b)$. Let Q_{Encode} be the set of $\mathcal{O}$-queries made by the encoder $\mathsf{Encode}^{\mathcal{O}}$ during the encoding process for $\mathbf{c}$.

Further run the offline-learner on sk to obtain an augmented secret key. When we run the augmented decoder on $\mathbf{c} + \mathbf{e}$ (for a Bernoulli error $\mathbf{e}$) the decoder formulates a query $q = \mathsf{Quer}_{\mathsf{sk}}(\mathbf{c} + \mathbf{e})$. We now distinguish 3 different cases.

1. q is globally heavy, i.e. $\mathsf{w}(q) > \epsilon$. In this case the offline-learner has made this query and the augmented decoder will find the corresponding response in the augmented secret key. Thus the simulation is perfect, i.e. the oracle-free augmented decoder and the decoder $\mathsf{Decode}^{\mathcal{O}}$ behave identically.
2. q is globally light, i.e., $\mathsf{w}(q) \leq \epsilon$ but $q \notin Q_{\mathsf{Encode}}$, i.e. q is not an intersection query between encoder and decoder. In this case the augmented decoder will simulate the oracle output locally. As the query q was not made by the encoder, this is also a perfect simulation.
3. q is globally light, i.e., $\mathsf{w}(q) \leq \epsilon$ and $q \in Q_{\mathsf{Encode}}$, i.e. q is an intersection query between encoder and decoder. From the view of the decoder, this case is indistinguishable from the second case as it does not have access to Q_{Encode}. Hence, it will locally simulate the oracle on the query q, which will however be inconsistent with the query made by the encoder. We cannot provide any guarantees in this case and need to assume that a decoding error happens.

Hence, to bound the probability of a decoding error we need to bound the probability that case 3 happens. First assume that $\mathbf{c}$ is *not* exceptional. Then it holds for any $q \in Q_{\mathsf{Encode}}$ with $\mathsf{w}(q) \leq \epsilon$ that $\ell_{\mathbf{c}}(q) < \delta$. Hence we can bound the probability that $q = \mathsf{Quer}_{\mathsf{sk}}(\mathbf{c} + \mathbf{e}) \in Q_{\mathsf{Encode}}$ via a union bound by $|Q_{\mathsf{Encode}}| \cdot \delta$. Now observe that the probability that $\mathbf{c}$ is exceptional is bounded by $3\epsilon^c/\delta^2$. Therefore, we can bound the overall probability that case 3 happens by $|Q_{\mathsf{Encode}}| \cdot \delta + \epsilon^c/\delta^2$. Since $|Q_{\mathsf{Encode}}|$ is a fixed polynomial in λ, we can control this term by choosing $\delta = 1/(|Q_{\mathsf{Encode}}|\mathsf{poly}(\lambda))$ and $\epsilon = \delta^{2/c}/\mathsf{poly}(\lambda)$ as sufficiently small inverse polynomials to achieve any desired inverse polynomial error bound.

Note that by making ϵ smaller we increase the runtime of the offline learner, which is $1/\epsilon$. This trade-off allows us to buy a smaller correctness error by increasing the runtime of the offline learner and thus the size of the augmented secret key. Finally, note that the correctness analysis provided in this paragraph crucially relies on the fact that we add noise! Hence we cannot provide a correctness guarantee for our augmented decoder for noise-free codewords.

Attacking the Augmented Decoder. We have thus shown that a decoder $\mathsf{Decode}^{\mathcal{O}}$ that makes a single oracle query can be compiled into an augmented decoder that uses an augmented (and thus longer) secret key, but does not make any oracle queries. Furthermore, this augmented decoder has a small correctness error which can, however, be controlled by increasing the size of the augmented secret key. We can thus implement the distinguisher against oracle free decoders sketched above, with the small modification that the distinguisher now needs to add noise to the $\mathbf{x}_i$ to ensure correctness of the augmented decoder.

Compiling Out Multiple $\mathcal{O}$-Queries. The final step in our argument is to deal with decoders that make multiple $\mathcal{O}$-queries. However, as suggested above, the argument for compiling out a single $\mathcal{O}$ query can be applied recursively, thus eliminating oracle queries one by one. The only slightly complicating factor in this case is that we need to ensure that *future* oracle queries made by the decoder are answered consistently. In essence, the augmented decoder has to check for each future query if it is identical to the query that has been compiled out. If so it has to respond consistently, either with a response from the augmented secret key, or with the same locally simulated response. Any fresh query will be answered by an $\mathcal{O}$-query.

This concludes the technical overview.

2.1 Related Work

Black-Box Separations. The seminal result by Impagliazzo and Rudich [IR89] (IR) famously demonstrated the impossibility of a black-box construction of key-agreement (KA) protocols from one-way permutations (OWPs). This work highlighted fundamental barriers in achieving public-key cryptography from weaker primitives.

Building on this, Rudich, in his thesis [Rud88], established a black-box separation between one-way functions (OWFs) and OWPs. This result, combined with the IR separation, implies that OWFs are also insufficient for black-box constructions of KA and other public-key primitives. Later, Rudich [Rud91] specifically showed a black-box separation between trapdoor functions (a stronger primitive often used for public-key encryption) and KA protocols.

Further delineating the cryptographic hierarchy, Simon [Sim98] demonstrated a black-box separation between OWPs and collision-resistant hash functions (CRHFs). The original IR separation itself has been subject to further investigation: Barak and Mahmoody [BMG09] presented a stronger separation (a more efficient attack in the black-box model), while Brakerski et al. [BKSY11] provided a simpler proof technique for the IR result.

Matsuda and Matsuura [MM11] showed that there is no fully black-box construction of OWPs from length-increasing injective OWFs, even if the latter are only 1-bit-increasing. Mahmoody and Pass [MP12] established that non-interactive commitment schemes cannot be constructed from OWFs in a black-box manner. Döttling and Mour [DM24] showed that any fully-black-box construction of correlation intractable hash for any t-wise independent class of relations from collision-resistant hash, or one-way permutations, must make at least $O(t)$ calls to the underlying base primitive(s).

In the quantum setting, considerable effort has focused on understanding the implications of quantum computation for these classical separations. Several works have investigated the separation between post-quantum one-way functions (PQ-OWFs) and post-quantum key-agreement (PQ-KA) protocols, including [ACC+22, BGV+23, LLLL24, LLLL25b, LLLL25a].

Constructions of Pseudorandom Codes. In their original work [CG24] defined the error-correction capabilities of the code with respect to random errors and in a follow-up work they showed that the constructions are secure with respect to adversarially sampled errors [AAC+24]. Both works consider the notion of secret-key as well as public-key PRCs. In a public-key PRC the encoding algorithm is a public-key algorithm and the decoder is a secret-key algorithm, while in a secret-key PRC both Encode and Decode rely on the secret key.

A zero-bit PRC[5] is constructed in [GM24] under the assumption of local weak PRFs which are implied by the hardness of learning log(n)-juntas over the uniform distribution of n-bit strings. A recent work shows that the problem of learning k-junta distributions is computationally equivalent to the problem of learning k-parity functions with noise [Ber25].

Further constructions of pseudorandom codes are explored in [GG24]. They construct public-key pseudorandom codes from the planted hyperloop assumption [BKR23] and PRGs and they also construct statistically secure pseudorandom codes assuming a space bounded adversary. Additionally, they provide a construction assuming only one-way functions but the scheme tolerates only $o(1)$ errors introduced by a non-adaptive error channel.

In an earlier work [KKRT16] define a notion of pseudorandom codes that differs from the work of [CG24]. Their notion of pseudorandom codes does not require efficient decoding and they do not require actual pseudorandomness. Their codewords only need to be far apart. Such a notion can be constructed from one-way functions.

2.2 Concurrent Work

In a concurrent and independent work [GGW25] also show the impossibility of black-box constructions of pseudorandom codes in the random oracle model. Their work uses similar techniques to ours such as the hypercontractivity theorem. In particular, they show the impossibility with respect to crypto oracles [LMW25], which are stateless, efficient algorithms that have access to a random oracle. To the best of our knowledge, our notion of local oracles and crypto oracles are incomparable.

[5] A zero-bit PRC can only encode a single message $m = 0$.

3 Preliminaries

Notations: Let PPT denote probabilistic polynomial-time. We denote the set of all positive integers upto n as $[n] := \{1, \ldots, n\}$. For any set S, we denote $\mathcal{P}(S)$ as the power set of S. We denote vectors/binary strings using bold font. For any two binary strings $\mathbf{x}, \mathbf{y}$, we use the notation $\mathbf{x} \| \mathbf{y}$ to denote $\mathbf{x}$ concatenated with $\mathbf{y}$. Here, x_i denotes the ith bit of $\mathbf{x}$. We denote $\mathsf{Ham}(\mathbf{x})$ as the Hamming weight of $\mathbf{x}$, i.e., the number of '1' in the binary string $\mathbf{x}$. And, $\mathsf{Ham}(\mathbf{x}, \mathbf{y})$ denotes the Hamming distance between the binary strings $\mathbf{x}$ and $\mathbf{y}$, i.e., the number of indices where $\mathbf{x}$ and $\mathbf{y}$ differ. We denote $\mathcal{B}^n_r(\mathbf{x})$ as the set $\{\mathbf{x}' \in \{0,1\}^n \| \mathsf{Ham}(\mathbf{x}, \mathbf{x}') \leq r\}$, i.e., the set of all strings with Hamming distance of r from $\mathbf{x}$. For any finite set S, $x \leftarrow S$ denotes a uniformly random element x from the set S. Similarly, for any distribution $\mathcal{D}$, $x \leftarrow \mathcal{D}$ denotes an element x drawn from distribution $\mathcal{D}$.

3.1 Probability and Linear Algebra over the Reals

Definition 1 (Bernoulli distribution). *A binary random variable $x \in \{0,1\}$ is said to follow a* ***Bernoulli distribution*** *with bias parameter $\rho \in [0,1]$, denoted as Ber_ρ, if $\Pr[x = 1] = \frac{1-\rho}{2}$. We say that $\mathbf{x} \in \{0,1\}^n$ follows Ber^n_ρ, if each component x_i of $\mathbf{x}$ independently follows Ber_ρ.*

Theorem 4 (Markov Inequality). *Let $X \in \mathbb{R}_{\geq 0}$ be a non-negative random variable with expectation $\mathsf{E}[X]$. Then it holds for any $\delta > 0$ that*

$$\Pr[X \geq \delta] \leq \mathsf{E}[X]/\delta$$

We will also use the following simple Markov-like lemma.

Lemma 1. *Let $Z \in [0,1]$ be a (discrete) random variable. Then it holds for all $t \in [0,1]$ that $\Pr[Z > t] \geq \mathsf{E}[Z] - t$.*

Proof. It holds that

$$\begin{aligned}
\mathsf{E}[Z] &= \sum_z z \cdot \Pr[Z = z] \\
&= \sum_{z \leq t} z \cdot \Pr[Z = z] + \sum_{z > t} \underbrace{z}_{\leq 1} \cdot \Pr[Z = z] \\
&\leq t \underbrace{\Pr[Z \leq t]}_{\leq 1} + \Pr[Z > t] \\
&\leq t + \Pr[Z > t],
\end{aligned}$$

It follows that $\Pr[Z > t] \geq \mathsf{E}[Z] - t$.

Theorem 5 (Chernoff bound). *Suppose $X_1, \ldots, X_n$ are independent random variables taking values in $\{0,1\}$. Let $X = \sum_{i=1}^n X_i$ denote their sum and let $\mu = \mathbb{E}[X]$ denote the sum's expected value. Then, for any $\delta \geq 0$,*

$$\Pr(X \geq (1+\delta)\mu) \leq e^{-\frac{\delta^2 \mu}{2+\delta}}$$

Claim 1. Let $r, n \in \mathbb{N}$ such that $r \leq n/2$. Then, for $\rho = 1 - \frac{r}{n}$,

$$\Pr_{\mathbf{x} \leftarrow \mathsf{Ber}_\rho^n}[\mathsf{Ham}(\mathbf{x}) \geq r] \leq e^{-r/3}$$

Proof. We have $\Pr_{\mathbf{x} \leftarrow \mathsf{Ber}_\rho^n}[x_i = 1] = \frac{r}{2n}$. Now, using Chernoff bound, we have $\mu = r/2$, and setting $\delta = 1$, we get the required bound.

Recall that over a vector space $\mathbb{R}^n$, we define the L_p norm $\|\cdot\|_p$ via

$$\|\mathbf{x}\|_p = (\sum_{i=1}^{n} |x_i|^p)^{1/p}$$

for $p \geq 1$ and $\|\mathbf{x}\|_\infty = \max_{i \in [n]} |x_i|$. We will make use of the following very basic version of the Riesz-Thorin Theorem [Tho48] that bounds $\|\mathbf{x}\|_p$ (for $1 \leq p < \infty$) in terms of $\|\mathbf{x}\|_1$ and $\|\mathbf{x}\|_\infty$.

Lemma 2 (Norm-Interpolation). *It holds for all* $1 \leq p < \infty$ *and all* $\mathbf{x} \in \mathbb{R}^n$ *that*

$$\|\mathbf{x}\|_p \leq \|\mathbf{x}\|_\infty^{1-1/p} \cdot \|\mathbf{x}\|_1^{1/p}.$$

Proof. Fix $1 \leq p < \infty$. It holds for all $\mathbf{x} \in \mathbb{R}^n$ that

$$\|\mathbf{x}\|_p^p = \sum_{i=1}^{n} |x_i|^p = \sum_{i=1}^{n} (\underbrace{|x_i|}_{\substack{\leq \max_i |x_i| \\ = \|\mathbf{x}\|_\infty}})^{p-1} \cdot |x_i| \leq \|\mathbf{x}\|_\infty^{p-1} \cdot \sum_{i=1}^{n} |x_i| = \|\mathbf{x}\|_\infty^{p-1} \cdot \|\mathbf{x}\|_1.$$

The statement follows by raising both sides to the power of $1/p$.

3.2 Secret-Key Pseudorandom Codes for Bernoulli Channel

A secret-key PRC with κ-correctness ρ-robustness is described by three algorithms ($\mathsf{KeyGen}, \mathsf{Encode}, \mathsf{Decode}$) parameterized by a secret key sk, satisfying the following criteria:

- **(Syntax)** There exist functions $s, n, d, r, r', r'' \in \mathbb{N} \to \mathbb{N}$ such that for all $\lambda \in \mathbb{N}$, $\mathsf{KeyGen} : 1^\lambda \times \{0,1\}^{r''(\lambda)} \to \{0,1\}^{s(\lambda)}$, $\mathsf{Encode} : \{0,1\}^{s(\lambda)} \times \{0,1\}^{d(\lambda)} \times \{0,1\}^{r'(\lambda)} \to \{0,1\}^{n(\lambda)}$, and $\mathsf{Decode} : \{0,1\}^{s(\lambda)} \times \{0,1\}^{n(\lambda)} \times \{0,1\}^{r(\lambda)} \to \{0,1\}^{d(\lambda)} \cup \bot$.
- **(Error correction, or robustness)** For any $\lambda \in \mathbb{N}$, message $m \in \{0,1\}^{d(\lambda)}$,

$$\Pr\left[\mathsf{Decode}(\mathsf{sk}, \mathbf{c} + \mathbf{e}) \neq m \;\middle|\; \begin{array}{r} \mathsf{sk} \leftarrow \mathsf{KeyGen}(1^\lambda) \\ \mathbf{c} \leftarrow \mathsf{Encode}(\mathsf{sk}, m) \\ \mathbf{e} \leftarrow \mathsf{Ber}_\rho^n \end{array}\right] \leq \kappa(\lambda).$$

  where the probability is over the randomness of KeyGen, Encode and error e.

– **(Pseudorandomness)** For any polynomial-time adversary $\mathcal{A}$,

$$\Pr_{\mathsf{sk}\leftarrow\mathsf{KeyGen}(1^\lambda)}\left[\mathcal{A}^{\mathsf{O}_{\mathsf{sk}}(\cdot)}(1^\lambda)=1\right] - \Pr_{U}\left[\mathcal{A}^{U(1^\lambda,\cdot)}(1^\lambda)=1\right] \leq \mathrm{negl}(\lambda),$$

where O_{sk} on any (even previously queried) input $\mathbf{m}$ samples a random $r \in \{0,1\}^{r'(\lambda)}$ and outputs $\mathsf{Encode}(\mathsf{sk}, \mathbf{m}; r)$ and U denotes an oracle that on any (even previously queried) input returns a fresh uniform string in $\{0,1\}^n$.

Remark 1. Note that robustness is defined with respect to the Bernoulli distribution. In the context of error-correcting codes, one typically specifies a decoding radius α such that any word of the form $\mathbf{c}+\mathbf{e}$, where $\mathsf{Ham}(\mathbf{e}) < \alpha n$, can be successfully decoded. By setting $\rho = 1-\alpha$, we ensure that an error vector $\mathbf{e} \leftarrow \mathsf{Ber}_\rho^n$ satisfies $\mathsf{Ham}(\mathbf{e}) < \alpha n$ with high probability, provided α is a constant. This follows from Claim 1 and the fact that for pseudorandomness, $n = O(\lambda)$.

Remark 2. In [CG24], the authors also define a property called soundness which is not significant in our work – **(Soundness)** For any fixed $\mathbf{c} \in \Sigma^{n(\lambda)}$,

$$\Pr_{\mathsf{sk}\leftarrow\mathsf{KeyGen}(1^\lambda)}\left[\mathsf{Decode}(\mathsf{sk}, \mathbf{c}) = \bot\right] \geq 1 - \mathrm{negl}(\lambda).$$

If the scheme can only encode a singular message (i.e., $k = 0$), it is called a *zero-bit PRC*. Christ and Gunn [CG24] required the soundness condition to ensure that the construction of zero-bit PRCs is non-trivial.

3.3 Black-Box Constructions and Separations

Definition 2 (Black-box Construction). *A construction of a Pseudorandom Code* $\mathsf{PRC} = (\mathsf{KeyGen}, \mathsf{Encode}, \mathsf{Decode})$ *from a family of oracle-sets* $\{\overline{\mathcal{O}}_\lambda\}$ *is* black-box *if the following properties hold for any* $\mathcal{O}$ *from the family* $\overline{\mathcal{O}}_\lambda$

– ***Construction Efficiency:*** *The algorithms* $\mathsf{KeyGen}^{\mathcal{O}}$, $\mathsf{Encode}^{\mathcal{O}}$, *and* $\mathsf{Decode}^{\mathcal{O}}$ *run in time polynomial in* $\lambda \in \mathbb{N}$ *(and input lengths) and make at most* $\mathsf{poly}(\lambda)$ *queries to* $\mathcal{O}$.
– ***Correctness:*** *For any* $\lambda \in \mathbb{N}$, *message* $m \in \{0,1\}^{d(\lambda)}$,

$$\Pr\left[\mathsf{Decode}^{\mathcal{O}}(\mathsf{sk}, \mathbf{c}+\mathbf{e}) \neq m \;\middle|\; \begin{array}{r} \mathsf{sk} \leftarrow \mathsf{KeyGen}^{\mathcal{O}}(1^\lambda) \\ \mathbf{c} \leftarrow \mathsf{Encode}^{\mathcal{O}}(\mathsf{sk}, m) \\ \mathbf{e} \leftarrow \mathsf{Ber}_\rho^n \end{array}\right] \leq \kappa(\lambda).$$

where the probability is over the randomness of $\mathsf{KeyGen}, \mathsf{Encode}$ *and error* e.
– ***Security:*** *For any (unbounded) adversary* $\mathcal{A}$ *that makes only polynomially many queries, there exists a negligible function* $\mathrm{negl}(\cdot)$ *such that for all* $\lambda \in \mathbb{N}$,

$$\Pr_{\substack{\mathcal{O}\leftarrow\overline{\mathcal{O}}_\lambda \\ \mathsf{sk}\leftarrow\mathsf{KeyGen}^{\mathcal{O}}(1^\lambda)}}\left[\mathcal{A}^{\mathcal{O}(\cdot),\mathsf{O}_{\mathsf{sk}}(\cdot)}(1^\lambda)=1\right] - \Pr_{U}\left[\mathcal{A}^{\mathcal{O}(\cdot),U(1^\lambda,\cdot)}(1^\lambda)=1\right] \leq \mathrm{negl}(\lambda),$$

where O_{sk} *on any (even previously queried) input* m, *samples a random* $r \in \{0,1\}^{r'(\lambda)}$ *and outputs* $\mathsf{Encode}^{\mathcal{O}}(\mathsf{sk}, m; r)$ *and* U *denotes an oracle that on any (even previously queried) input returns a fresh uniform string in* Σ^n.

Definition 3 (Black-box Separation). *We say a PRC is black-box separated from a family of oracle sets if for any black-box construction of a PRC from* $\{\overline{\mathcal{O}}_\lambda\}$ *there exists an (unbounded) adversary* $\mathcal{A}$ *which makes only polynomially many oracle queries, breaks the pseudorandomness of the PRC.*

4 Local Oracles

In this section, we introduce a new class of oracles, called **local oracles**. A query q is said to be *related* to a set of query-response pairs $\{(q_i, \mathcal{O}(q_i))\}_i$ if the oracle's response to q can be computed or meaningfully constrained using the information in the set. Intuitively, this captures semantic dependency among queries. An oracle is said to be local if, for any set Z of query-response pairs, the number of queries q such that q is related to Z is bounded by a polynomial in $|Z|$.

Local oracles also possess a simulation strategy for two-stage algorithms, described as follows. In the first stage, the algorithm issues a bounded number of queries, each of which is answered by the oracle. It then outputs a new query q, which is required to be unrelated to any of the previous queries. The simulator responds to q with a value r, without accessing the oracle. In the second stage, the algorithm continues interacting with the oracle. These subsequent queries are simulated by a stateful simulator that has access to the original oracle and the pair (q, r).

Because the simulator's response r may not match the oracle's actual output on q, it must carefully handle new queries. If a new query is related to (q, r), the simulator generates a consistent answer. Otherwise, it forwards the query to the oracle to ensure consistency with the responses provided in the first phase.

Definition 4. *A family of local oracles is a collection of oracle-relation pairs* $\{(\mathcal{O}_{i,\lambda}, \mathcal{R}_{i,\lambda})\}_{i,\lambda}$ *such that for each* i*, the oracle* $\mathcal{O}_{i,\lambda}$ *has domain* $\mathcal{X}_\lambda$ *and range* $\mathcal{Y}_\lambda$*, and* $\mathcal{R}_{i,\lambda}$ *is a relation between a query and a set of query-response pairs:* $\mathcal{R}_{i,\lambda} \subseteq \mathcal{X}_\lambda \times \mathcal{P}(\mathcal{Z}_{i,\lambda})$*, where* $\mathcal{Z}_{i,\lambda} = \{(x, \mathcal{O}_{i,\lambda}(x)) \mid x \in \mathcal{X}_\lambda\}$*. The following conditions must also be satisfied:*

1. ***Locality:*** *There exists a polynomial* poly *such that for any* $Z \in \mathcal{P}(\mathcal{Z}_{i,\lambda})$*, the number of queries* $q \in \mathcal{X}_\lambda$ *for which* $(q, Z) \in \mathcal{R}_{i,\lambda}$ *is at most* $\mathsf{poly}(|Z|)$*.*
2. ***Simulatability:*** *There exist an algorithm* S_1*, a* ***stateful*** *oracle-aided algorithm* S_2 *and a negligible function* $\mathrm{negl}(\cdot)$ *such that for any pair of oracle-aided algorithms* $\mathcal{A} = (\mathcal{A}_1, \mathcal{A}_2)$*, the output distributions of the following two experiments are statistically close:*
   - *Sample* $(\mathcal{O}, \mathcal{R})$ *from the distribution* $\{(\mathcal{O}_{i,\lambda}, \mathcal{R}_{i,\lambda})\}_i$*.*
   - *The adversary* $\mathcal{A}_1^{\mathcal{O}}(1^\lambda, \mathcal{R})$ *makes poly(*λ*) queries to the oracle and outputs a query* q *and internal state* $\mathsf{st}_\mathcal{A}$*. Let* T *be the set of all query-response pairs collected during* $\mathcal{A}_1$*'s execution. If* $(q, T) \in \mathcal{R}$*, abort the experiment.*
     - ***Real world:*** *Compute* $r := \mathcal{O}(q)$*, and run* $\mathcal{A}_2$ *with oracle access to* $\mathcal{O}(\cdot)$ *and input* $(1^\lambda, q, r, \mathsf{st}_\mathcal{A})$*.*

- ***Simulated world:*** *Run* S_1 *on input* q *to obtain* $(r, \mathsf{st}_\mathsf{S}) := \mathsf{S}_1(1^\lambda, q)$. *Then, run* $\mathcal{A}_2$ *with oracle access to* $\mathsf{S}_2^{\mathcal{O}}(1^\lambda, \mathsf{st}_\mathsf{S}, \cdot)$ *and input* $(1^\lambda, q, r, \mathsf{st}_\mathcal{A})$.

– *The second adversary* $\mathcal{A}_2$ *outputs a bit in* $\{0,1\}$ *after making* $\mathsf{poly}(\lambda)$ *many oracle queries.*

Let Exp^{Real} *denote a run of the experiment where* $\mathcal{A}$ *interacts with the real world and let* Exp^{Sim} *denote a run of the experiment where* $\mathcal{A}$ *interacts with the simulated world, then*

$$|\Pr[\mathsf{Exp}^{Real}(1^\lambda, \mathcal{A}) = 1] - \Pr[\mathsf{Exp}^{Sim}(1^\lambda, \mathcal{A}) = 1]| < \mathrm{negl}(\lambda)$$

This definition encompasses a wide class of oracles. Here, we explain how some common functionalities achieve the definition.

Random Oracles are Local. Consider a random oracle which is typically used to model a OWF or a OWP. Here, the relation $\mathcal{R}$ simply checks whether q is a query present as a query in Z. For an unrelated query q, the simulator $\mathsf{S}_1(q)$ returns a random $r \in \mathcal{Y}$ and sets the state as $\mathsf{st}_\mathsf{S} = (q, r)$. The simulator $\mathsf{S}_2^{\mathcal{O}}(\mathsf{st}, t)$ then responds with $\mathcal{O}(t)$ for $t \neq q$ whereas returns r for $t = q$. This simulation is exact in the case of OWFs. However, In the case of OWPs, this simulation is imperfect with negligible probability, since S_1 might choose a value r already present in the image of some previous query in Z, which could violate injectivity.

Trapdoor Permutation Oracles are Local. A more intricate example of a local oracle arises in the context of trapdoor permutations. Here, the oracle is defined as a tuple $(\mathsf{KeyGen}, \mathsf{Eval}, \mathsf{Inv})$ with the following components:

$$\mathsf{KeyGen} : \mathcal{SK} \to \mathcal{PK}, \quad \mathsf{Eval} : \mathcal{PK} \times \mathcal{M} \to \mathcal{N}, \quad \mathsf{Inv} : \mathcal{SK} \times \mathcal{N} \to \mathcal{M},$$

where KeyGen maps a secret key $\mathsf{sk} \in \mathcal{SK}$ to a public key $\mathsf{pk} \in \mathcal{PK}$, Eval evaluates the permutation under the public key, and Inv inverts it using the secret key.

The oracle $\mathcal{O}$ accepts queries of the form (mode, q), where $\mathsf{mode} \in \{\mathsf{KeyGen}, \mathsf{Eval}, \mathsf{Inv}\}$ and q belongs to the domain of the corresponding function. Suppose an adversary observes the set of query-response pairs

$$Z = \{((\mathsf{KeyGen}, \mathsf{sk}), \mathsf{pk}),\ ((\mathsf{Eval}, \mathsf{pk}, x), y)\}.$$

Then the query $(\mathsf{Inv}, \mathsf{sk}, y)$ is *related* to Z, because given both $(\mathsf{KeyGen}, \mathsf{sk}) = \mathsf{pk}$ and $(\mathsf{Eval}, \mathsf{pk}, x) = y$, one can deduce that $(\mathsf{Inv}, \mathsf{sk}, y) = x$. Thus, a simulator without oracle access cannot correctly respond to $(\mathsf{Inv}, \mathsf{sk}, y)$ unless this information is already known.

In contrast, queries that are *unrelated* to Z do not pose this issue. For example, for a fresh secret key $\mathsf{sk}' \neq \mathsf{sk}$, the simulator S_1 can simulate $(\mathsf{KeyGen}, \mathsf{sk}')$ by generating a fresh public key pk'. However, to ensure consistency across the simulation, this key pair must be retained and passed to the stateful simulator

S_2, since the second-stage adversary $\mathcal{A}_2$ may issue follow-up queries involving $(\mathsf{pk}', \mathsf{sk}')$ (e.g., $(\mathsf{Eval}, \mathsf{pk}', x)$ or $(\mathsf{Inv}, \mathsf{sk}', y)$) and expect coherent answers.

In general, a query $(\mathsf{Inv}, \mathsf{sk}, y)$ is related to Z if it is explicitly present in Z, or if both $((\mathsf{KeyGen}, \mathsf{sk}), \mathsf{pk})$ and $((\mathsf{Eval}, \mathsf{pk}, x), y)$ appear in Z. A similar statement holds for queries of the form $(\mathsf{Eval}, \mathsf{pk}, x)$. Similarly, a query $(\mathsf{KeyGen}, \mathsf{sk})$ is related to Z if it appears explicitly, or if there exist queries $((\mathsf{Eval}, \mathsf{pk}, x), y)$ and $((\mathsf{Inv}, \mathsf{sk}, y), x)$ such that $\mathsf{KeyGen}(\mathsf{sk}) = \mathsf{pk}$.

Since each pair of query-response elements in Z can relate to at most a single query, the total number of queries related to Z is bounded by $O(|Z|^2)$. This quadratic bound implies that the oracle satisfies the locality property.

Pseudorandom Code Oracles are not Local. It is important to observe that high-error-tolerant PRC oracles are *not* local. The reason is that, for a single Encode query producing a codeword $\mathbf{c}$, all Decode queries corresponding to codewords within the Hamming sphere centered at $\mathbf{c}$ are considered related. Since the number of such queries is exponential in the dimension of the codeword, the locality condition which requires only a polynomial number of related queries, cannot be satisfied.

5 Black-Box Impossibility of Pseudorandom Codes

In this section, we present the proof of Theorem 2, i.e., there does not exist a black-box construction of PRC from any local oracle $\mathcal{O}$.

For any oracle $\mathcal{O}$, let $\mathsf{PRC}^{\mathcal{O}} = (\mathsf{KeyGen}^{\mathcal{O}}, \mathsf{Encode}^{\mathcal{O}}, \mathsf{Decode}^{\mathcal{O}})$ denote a pseudorandom error-correcting code. Without loss of generality, we can assume that KeyGen does not make any oracle queries. Concretely, one simply treats its internal randomness as part of the secret key, and modifies Encode and Decode to internally run KeyGen at the start, using this randomness to generate the required key.

Theorem 6. *Let $\mathcal{O}$ be a local oracle and $\mathsf{PRC}^{\mathcal{O}} = (\mathsf{KeyGen}, \mathsf{Encode}^{\mathcal{O}}, \mathsf{Decode}^{\mathcal{O}})$ be a single-bit ρ-robust PRC where ρ is any constant between* 0 *and* 1/2. *Then, there exists an (unbounded) distinguisher $\mathcal{D}$ and a polynomial* poly *such that for all $\lambda \in \mathbb{N}$,*

- *$\mathcal{D}$ makes $\mathsf{poly}(\lambda)$ many oracle queries.*
- *$\mathcal{D}$ breaks the pseudorandomness property of $\mathsf{PRC}^{\mathcal{O}}$ with inverse polynomial advantage.*

The proof proceeds in two main steps. In the first part, we show that for any given secret key sk, there exists a corresponding augmented secret key sk' such that, for a randomly chosen (errorless) codeword c, the adversary $\mathcal{A}$ can correctly decode c using sk' **without** querying the random oracle. In the second part, we prove that no such augmented secret key sk' can successfully decode many uniformly random strings with non-negligible probability, thus allowing the adversary to distinguish between codewords and uniformly random strings. This contradicts the pseudorandomness property of the PRC.

For the first part, we need to show that every query can either be learned or simulated. To this end, we divide the queries made by the decoder into global and local queries and prove key properties in the following section.

5.1 Global and Local Heavy Queries

Let Q be a finite set and let $\mathsf{Quer} : \{0,1\}^n \times \{0,1\}^r \rightarrow Q$ be an arbitrary function which maps an input word $\mathbf{x} \in \{0,1\}^n$ and a string $r \in \{0,1\}^r$ to a *query* $\mathsf{Quer}(\mathbf{x}, r) \in Q$. We think of $r \in \{0,1\}^r$ as random coins provided to Quer. In the following, if not specified, assume that $\mathbf{u} \leftarrow \{0,1\}^n$ is chosen uniformly random, $r \leftarrow \{0,1\}^r$ are uniformly random coins and that $\mathbf{e} \leftarrow \mathsf{Ber}_\rho^n$ follows a Bernoulli distribution.

We will now define two weight functions for queries, namely a global and local weight function which assign weights to queries.

- The *global weight function* $\mathsf{w}(q)$ measures how likely it is that a uniformly random input word leads to the query q. It is defined via

$$\mathsf{w}(q) = \Pr_{\mathbf{u},r}[\mathsf{Quer}(\mathbf{u}, r) = q],$$

where the probability is taken over the uniform choice of $\mathbf{u} \leftarrow \{0,1\}^n$.
- The *local weight function* $\ell_{\mathbf{x}}(q)$ measures how likely it is that we get the query q, if we start from a fixed word $\mathbf{x}$ and add Bernoulli noise $\mathbf{e}$. It is defined by

$$\ell_{\mathbf{x}}(q) = \Pr_{\mathbf{e},r}[\mathsf{Quer}(\mathbf{x} + \mathbf{e}, r) = q],$$

where $\mathbf{e} \leftarrow \mathsf{Ber}_\rho^n$ follows a Bernoulli distribution.

We will make critical use of the Bonami-Beckner hypercontractivity inequality [Bon70, Bec75]. We will first need some terminology concerning boolean functions.

Definition 5 (L_p Norm and Smoothing of Boolean Functions). *Let $f : \{0,1\}^n \rightarrow \mathbb{R}$ be a boolean function. For a $1 \leq p < \infty$, we define the L_p-norm of f via*

$$\|f\|_{(p)} = (\mathsf{E}_{\mathbf{u}}[|f(\mathbf{u})|^p])^{1/p}$$

and

$$\|f\|_\infty = \max_{\mathbf{x} \in \{0,1\}^n} [|f(\mathbf{x})|].$$

Furthermore, for a $0 < \rho < 1/2$, the noise operator $\mathbf{T}_\rho$ *maps f to a boolean function $\mathbf{T}_\rho f : \{0,1\}^n \rightarrow \mathbb{R}$ given by*

$$(\mathbf{T}_\rho f)(\mathbf{x}) = \mathsf{E}_{\mathbf{e} \leftarrow \mathsf{Ber}_\rho^n}[f(\mathbf{x} + \mathbf{e})].$$

Note that while very similar to the standard L_p norm on $\mathbb{R}^n$, $\| f\|_{(p)}$ norm is not the same as the L_p norm on the truth table of f. The difference is a normalization factor $2^{-n/p}$, i.e. it holds for all f that

$$\|f\|_{(p)} = 2^{-n/p} \cdot \|f\|_p.$$

One effect of this normalization is that the relationship of the L_p and L_q norms reverses, i.e. while it holds for all $\mathbf{x}$ that $\|\mathbf{x}\|_q \leq \|\mathbf{x}\|_p$ for $1 \leq p < q$, it holds that $\|f\|_{(p)} \leq \|f\|_{(q)}$ for $1 \leq p < q$[6]. Hence, to avoid confusion, we opted to use a slightly different notation for $\| \cdot \|_{(p)}$.

Theorem 7 (Hypercontractivity Theorem [Bon70, Bec75, O'D14]**).** *Let $f : \{0,1\}^n \to \mathbb{R}$ be a boolean function, let $0 \leq s \leq t < \infty$ and let $0 \leq \rho \leq \sqrt{\frac{s}{t}}$. Then it holds that*

$$\|\mathbf{T}_\rho f\|_{(1+t)} \leq \|f\|_{(1+s)}.$$

We will now use the hypercontractivity theorem to relate the global and local weights defined above. The following lemma allows us to bound the r-th moment of $\ell_{\mathbf{u}}(q)$ (for a uniform $\mathbf{u} \leftarrow \{0,1\}^n$) by a low degree term in the global weight $\mathsf{w}(q)$.

Lemma 3. *Let $0 < \rho < 1$ and let $t \geq 0$. Fix a query $q \in Q$. Then it holds that*

$$\mathsf{E}_{\mathbf{u}}[\ell_{\mathbf{u}}(q)^{1+t}] \leq (\mathsf{w}(q))^{(1+t)/(1+\rho^2 t)}.$$

Furthermore, for $0 < \delta \leq 1$, we have the tail-bound

$$\Pr_{\mathbf{u}}[\ell_{\mathbf{u}}(q) \geq \delta] \leq \frac{(\mathsf{w}(q))^{(1+t)/(1+\rho^2 t)}}{\delta^{1+t}}.$$

Proof. Define the function $p_q : \{0,1\}^n \to \mathbb{R}$ by $p_q(\mathbf{x}) = \Pr_r[\mathsf{Quer}(\mathbf{x}, r) = q]$. First note that

$$(\mathbf{T}_\rho p_q)(\mathbf{x}) = \mathsf{E}_{\mathbf{e} \leftarrow \mathsf{Ber}_\rho^n}[p_q(\mathbf{x} + \mathbf{e})] = \Pr_{\mathbf{e},r}[\mathsf{Quer}(\mathbf{x} + \mathbf{e}, r) = q] = \ell_{\mathbf{x}}(q).$$

Hence it holds by hypercontractivity (Theorem 7) with $s = \rho^2 \cdot t$ (which satisfies the requirements of the theorem) that

$$\mathsf{E}_{\mathbf{u}}[\ell_{\mathbf{u}}(q)^{1+t}] = \|\mathbf{T}_\rho p_q\|_{(1+t)}^{1+t} \leq \|p_q\|_{(1+s)}^{1+t}. \tag{1}$$

It further holds that

$$\begin{aligned}
\|p_q\|_{(1+s)}^{1+s} &= \mathsf{E}_{\mathbf{u}}[p_q(\mathbf{u})^{1+s}] = \mathsf{E}_{\mathbf{u}}[\Pr_r[\mathsf{Quer}(\mathbf{u}, r) = q]^{1+s}] \\
&\leq \mathsf{E}_{\mathbf{u}}[\Pr_r[\mathsf{Quer}(\mathbf{u}, r) = q]] = \Pr_{\mathbf{u},r}[\mathsf{Quer}(\mathbf{u}, r) = q] \\
&= \mathsf{w}(q),
\end{aligned}$$

[6] This fact is easily established via the Hölder inequality.

where the inequality $\Pr_r[\mathsf{Quer}(\mathbf{u},r) = q]^{1+s} \leq \Pr_r[\mathsf{Quer}(\mathbf{u},r) = q]$ holds as $1+s > 1$ and $\Pr_r[\mathsf{Quer}(\mathbf{u},r) = q] \leq 1$. Hence, combining with (1) we obtain that

$$\mathsf{E}_{\mathbf{u}}[\ell_{\mathbf{u}}(q)^{1+t}] \leq (\mathsf{w}(q))^{(1+t)/(1+s)} = (\mathsf{w}(q))^{(1+t)/(1+\rho^2 t)}.$$

The *furthermore* part of the lemma-statement now follows routinely from the Markov-inequality (Theorem 4): As $\ell_{\mathbf{x}}(q) = \Pr_{\mathbf{e},r}[\mathsf{Quer}(\mathbf{x}+\mathbf{e},r) = q] \geq 0$, it holds that

$$\Pr_{\mathbf{u}}[\ell_{\mathbf{u}}(q) \geq \delta] = \Pr_{\mathbf{u}}[(\ell_{\mathbf{u}}(q))^{1+t} \geq \delta^{1+t}]$$
$$\leq \mathsf{E}_{\mathbf{u}}[(\ell_{\mathbf{u}}(q))^{1+t}]/\delta^{1+t} \leq (\mathsf{w}(q))^{(1+t)/(1+\rho^2 t)}/\delta^{1+t}.$$

5.2 Exceptionality

We will now define a notion of *exceptionality* for words $\mathbf{x} \in \{0,1\}^n$. In a nutshell, we call an $\mathbf{x}$ exceptional if it exhibits code-word like properties, in the sense that for such an $\mathbf{x}$ there exists a query $q \in Q$ which has low global weight but high local weight with respect to $\mathbf{x}$. Intuitively, this can be interpreted as the set $C_q = \{\mathbf{y} \in \{0,1\}^n \mid \mathsf{Quer}(\mathbf{y}) = q\}$ having a large intersection with the hamming ball around $\mathbf{x}$.

Definition 6. *Fix* $0 < \epsilon < \delta < 1$. *We say that a word* $\mathbf{x} \in \{0,1\}^n$ *is* (ϵ,δ)*-exceptional with respect to a query function* $\mathsf{Quer} : \{0,1\}^n \times \{0,1\}^r \to Q$*, in short we say the event* $\mathsf{EXC}_{\mathsf{Quer},\epsilon,\delta}(\mathbf{x})$ *happens, if there exists a query* $q \in Q$ *such that* $\mathsf{w}(q) < \epsilon$ *and* $\ell_{\mathbf{x}}(q) \geq \delta$ *(with respect to the query function* Quer*).*

Looking ahead, we will use the notion of exceptionality at the core-part of our separation, namely to argue that the probability that there are *globally non-heavy* intersection queries between encoder and decoder is necessarily low. Hence, it will suffice for our learner to learn the globally heavy queries, which are independent of the word to be decoded.

We will now use Lemma 3 to establish our main result of this section, which shows that when we choose $\mathbf{u} \leftarrow \{0,1\}^n$ uniformly random, then the probability that $\mathbf{u}$ is (ϵ,δ)-exceptional is at most $\frac{\epsilon^{(1+t)/(1+\rho^2 t)-1}}{\delta^{1+t}}$. Note that this bound is independent of $|Q|$ and even the query function Quer.

Theorem 8. *Fix an integer* $n > 0$ *and fix a* $\rho > 0$. *Fix an integer* $r > 0$*, any finite set* Q*, and any query function* $\mathsf{Quer} : \{0,1\}^n \times \{0,1\}^r \to Q$. *Let* w*,* ℓ *be defined as above.Fix any* $0 < \epsilon < \delta < 1$ *and let* $\mathsf{EXC}_{\mathsf{Quer},\epsilon,\delta}(\cdot)$ *be as defined in Definition 6. Let* $\mathbf{u} \leftarrow \{0,1\}^n$. *Then it holds that*

$$\Pr_{\mathbf{u}}[\mathsf{EXC}_{\mathsf{Quer},\epsilon,\delta}(\mathbf{u})] \leq \frac{\epsilon^{(1+t)/(1+\rho^2 t)-1}}{\delta^{1+t}}$$

Note that n and r are only stated for syntactical reasons. Before we go into the proof of the theorem, notice that the exponent $(1+t)/(1+\rho^2 t)-1$ is greater than 0 for any choice of $\rho \in (0,1)$ and any $t > 0$. Hence the choice of the concrete t will not be critical when we use Theorem 8, hence for convenience we can choose $t=1$. Note that we can control this bound by making ϵ small, which will effectively translate to making our learner learn more queries.

Proof. For notational convenience, denote $\gamma = (1+t)/(1+\rho^2 t) > 0$ in this proof. By a union-bound and Lemma 3 it holds that

$$\begin{aligned}\Pr_{\mathbf{u}}[\mathsf{EXC}_{\mathsf{Quer},\epsilon,\delta}(\mathbf{u})] &= \Pr_{\mathbf{u}}[\exists q \in Q \text{ s.t. } \mathsf{w}(q) < \epsilon \text{ and } \ell_{\mathbf{u}}(q) \geq \delta] \\ &\leq \sum_{\substack{q\in Q \\ \mathsf{w}(q)<\epsilon}} \Pr_{\mathbf{u}}[\ell_{\mathbf{u}}(q) \geq \delta] \\ &\leq \sum_{\substack{q\in Q \\ \mathsf{w}(q)<\epsilon}} \mathsf{w}(q)^{\gamma}/\delta^{1+t} \\ &= \frac{1}{\delta^{1+t}} \cdot \sum_{\substack{q\in Q \\ \mathsf{w}(q)<\epsilon}} \mathsf{w}(q)^{\gamma}.\end{aligned}$$

Now define a vector $\mathbf{w} \in \mathbb{R}^Q$ such that $w_q = \mathsf{w}(q)$ if $\mathsf{w}(q) < \epsilon$ and otherwise $w_q = 0$. By the above it holds that

$$\Pr_{\mathbf{u}}[\mathsf{EXC}_{\mathsf{Quer},\epsilon,\delta}(\mathbf{u})] \leq \frac{1}{\delta^{1+t}} \cdot \|\mathbf{w}\|_{\gamma}^{\gamma}.$$

Furthermore, since every component of $\mathbf{w}$ is ϵ-bounded (and greater equal 0) we have that

$$\|\mathbf{w}\|_{\infty} = \max_{q\in Q} |w_q| < \epsilon.$$

Finally, it holds that

$$\|\mathbf{w}\|_1 \leq \sum_{q\in Q} \mathsf{w}(q) = \sum_{q\in Q} \Pr_{\mathbf{u},r}[\mathsf{Quer}(\mathbf{u},r) = q] = 1.$$

Hence, we have that $\|\mathbf{w}\|_1 \leq 1$ and $\|\mathbf{w}\|_{\infty} < \epsilon$. By the norm-interpolation lemma (Lemma 2) we get that $\|\mathbf{w}\|_{\gamma}^{\gamma} < \epsilon^{\gamma-1}$. We conclude that

$$\Pr_{\mathbf{u}}[\mathsf{EXC}_{\mathsf{Quer},\epsilon,\delta}(\mathbf{u})] \leq \frac{\epsilon^{\gamma-1}}{\delta^{1+t}} = \frac{\epsilon^{(1+t)/(1+\rho^2 t)-1}}{\delta^{1+t}}$$

5.3 Compiling-Out Oracle Queries

We now describe how to eliminate oracle queries from the decoding algorithm, thereby obtaining an oracle-free decoder. We start by defining PRCs with an augmented decoding procedure.

Definition 7 (Augmented Decoding). *A secret-key PRC* $\mathsf{PRC}^{\mathcal{O}} = (\mathsf{KeyGen}, \mathsf{Encode}^{\mathcal{O}}, \mathsf{Decode}^{\mathcal{O}})$ *has* ***κ-augmented correctness*** *with respect to augmented decoding algorithms* $(\mathsf{LearnQuery}^{\mathcal{O}}, \mathsf{ADecode}^{\mathcal{O}})$ *if the following holds.* $\mathsf{ADecode}$ *is a* PPT *oracle algorithm and for all* $\lambda \in \mathbb{N}$,

$$\Pr\left[\mathsf{ADecode}^{\mathcal{O}}(\mathsf{sk}, \mathsf{aux}, \mathbf{c}+\mathbf{e}) \neq m \;\middle|\; \begin{array}{r} \mathsf{sk} \leftarrow \mathsf{KeyGen}(1^{\lambda}) \\ m \leftarrow \{0,1\}^d, \mathbf{e} \leftarrow \mathsf{Ber}_{\rho}^n \\ \mathbf{c} \leftarrow \mathsf{Encode}^{\mathcal{O}}(\mathsf{sk}, m) \\ \mathsf{aux} \leftarrow \mathsf{LearnQuery}^{\mathcal{O}}(\mathsf{sk}, \epsilon) \end{array}\right] \leq \kappa$$

Before we can prove our lemma for this section, we will prove a technical lemma which establishes that exceptional queries are almost as rare for codewords of pseudorandom codes as they are for uniformly random words. The basic idea is that, since we can determine exceptionality of a word *without using the oracle*, if exceptionality of codewords was noticeably different than it is for random words, we would obtain a distinguisher (without using the oracle), contradicting pseudorandomness. In the following, we will use $\mathsf{EXC}_{\mathsf{sk},\epsilon,\delta}(\mathbf{x})$ as a shorthand for $\mathsf{EXC}_{\mathsf{Quer}_{\mathsf{sk}},\epsilon,\delta}(\mathbf{x})$

Lemma 4. *Let* $\mathsf{PRC}^{\mathcal{O}} = (\mathsf{KeyGen}, \mathsf{Encode}^{\mathcal{O}}, \mathsf{Decode}^{\mathcal{O}}, \mathsf{LearnQuery}^{\mathcal{O}}, \mathsf{ADecode}^{\mathcal{O}})$ *be an augmented pseudorandom code. Fix a query function* $\mathsf{Quer}_{\mathsf{sk}'} : \{0,1\}^n \times \{0,1\}^r \to Q$ *which depends on an augmented key* $\mathsf{sk}' = (\mathsf{sk}, \mathsf{aux})$. *Let* $p^* = p^*(\epsilon, \delta) = \frac{\epsilon^{(1-\rho^2)/(1+\rho^2)}}{\delta^2}$. *Assume that* $\mathsf{sk}' = (\mathsf{sk}, \mathsf{aux})$, *where* $\mathsf{sk}' \in \{0,1\}^k$ *and* $\mathbf{c}$ *are generated as in the experiment described in Definition 7. If* $\Pr[\mathsf{EXC}_{\mathsf{sk}',\epsilon,\delta}(\mathbf{c})] > 3p^*$, *then there exists a distinguisher* $\mathcal{D}$ *distinguishing codewords of* $\mathsf{PRC}^{\mathcal{O}}$ *from the uniform distribution on* $\{0,1\}^n$ *with advantage* $\frac{1}{2}p^* - 2^{-\lambda}$ *given* $N = (k+\lambda)/p^*$ *samples, but neither* sk *nor access to* $\mathcal{O}$. *Equivalently, if* $\mathsf{PRC}^{\mathcal{O}}$ *is pseudorandom, then* $\Pr[\mathsf{EXC}_{\mathsf{sk}',\epsilon,\delta}(\mathbf{c})] \leq 3p^*$.

Note that the distinguisher $\mathcal{D}$ does not know the secret key sk. Further note that due to the oracle $\mathcal{O}$, codewords of $\mathsf{PRC}^{\mathcal{O}}$ may be arbitrarily correlated.

Proof. The distinguisher $\mathcal{D}$ proceeds as follows, given N samples $\mathbf{x}_1, \ldots, \mathbf{x}_N$ obtained from its encoding oracle. If there exists an $\mathsf{sk} \in \{0,1\}^k$ such that $\frac{1}{N}\sum_{i=1}^N \mathsf{EXC}_{\mathsf{sk},\epsilon,\delta}(\mathbf{x}_i) > 2p^*$ guess 1 with the meaning that the samples $\mathbf{x}_1, \ldots, \mathbf{x}_N$ are codewords of $\mathsf{PRC}^{\mathcal{O}}$. Otherwise output a uniformly random bit.

We will first show that if the $\mathbf{x}_1, \ldots, \mathbf{x}_N$ are chosen uniformly random, then $\mathcal{D}$ outputs a uniformly random bit, except with negligible probability $2^{-\lambda}$. Fix an $\mathsf{sk}^* \in \{0,1\}^k$ and let $\mathbf{u}_1, \ldots, \mathbf{u}_N \leftarrow \{0,1\}^n$ be chosen i.i.d. uniformly random. Then it holds that

$$\begin{aligned} \mathsf{E}_{\mathbf{u}_1,\ldots,\mathbf{u}_N}\left[\sum_{i=1}^N \mathsf{EXC}_{\mathsf{sk}^*,\epsilon,\delta}(\mathbf{u}_i)\right] &= \sum_{i=1}^N \mathsf{E}_{\mathbf{u}_i}[\mathsf{EXC}_{\mathsf{sk}^*,\epsilon,\delta}(\mathbf{u}_i)] \\ &= \sum_{i=1}^N \underbrace{\Pr_{\mathbf{u}_i}[\mathsf{EXC}_{\mathsf{sk}^*,\epsilon,\delta}(\mathbf{u}_i)]}_{=p^*} \end{aligned}$$

$$= N \cdot p^*.$$

Hence, by the Chernoff bound we obtain that

$$\Pr_{\mathbf{u}_1,\ldots,\mathbf{u}_N}[\frac{1}{N}\sum_{i=1}^{N}\mathsf{EXC}_{\mathsf{sk}^*,\epsilon,\delta}(\mathbf{u}_i) > 2\cdot p^*] = \Pr_{\mathbf{u}_1,\ldots,\mathbf{u}_N}[\sum_{i=1}^{N}\mathsf{EXC}_{\mathsf{sk}^*,\epsilon,\delta}(\mathbf{u}_i) > 2\cdot p^*\cdot N]$$
$$\leq e^{-4/3\cdot p^*\cdot N}$$
$$\leq 2^{-p^*\cdot N}$$

Hence, via a union-bound we obtain

$$\Pr[\exists \mathsf{sk}^* \in \{0,1\}^k : \frac{1}{N}\sum_{i=1}^{N}\mathsf{EXC}_{\mathsf{sk}^*,\epsilon,\delta}(\mathbf{u}_i) > 2\cdot p^*]$$
$$\leq \sum_{\mathsf{sk}^*\in\{0,1\}^k}\Pr_{\mathbf{u}_1,\ldots,\mathbf{u}_N}[\frac{1}{N}\sum_{i=1}^{N}\mathsf{EXC}_{\mathsf{sk}^*,\epsilon,\delta}(\mathbf{u}_i) > 2\cdot p^*]$$
$$\leq 2^k\cdot 2^{-p^*\cdot N} = 2^{k-p^*\cdot N}.$$

Hence, choosing $N \geq (k+\lambda)/p^*$ we get that on input $\mathbf{u}_1,\ldots,\mathbf{u}_N$, $\mathcal{D}$ outputs a uniformly random bit, except with negligible probability $2^{-\lambda}$.

Now assume that $\mathbf{c}_1,\ldots,\mathbf{c}_N$ were generated by $\mathsf{PRC}^{\mathcal{O}}$. Define that random variable

$$Z = \frac{1}{N}\sum_{i=1}^{N}\mathsf{EXC}_{\mathsf{sk}',\epsilon,\delta}(\mathbf{c}_i).$$

First note that $Z \in [0,1]$ as for all $i \in [N]$ we have $\mathsf{EXC}_{\mathsf{sk}',\epsilon,\delta}(\mathbf{c}_i) \in \{0,1\}$. Furthermore, it holds that

$$\mathsf{E}_{\mathsf{sk}',\mathcal{O},\mathbf{c}_1,\ldots,\mathbf{c}_n}[Z] = \frac{1}{N}\sum_{i=1}^{N}\mathsf{E}_{\mathsf{sk}',\mathcal{O},\mathbf{c}_i}[\mathsf{EXC}_{\mathsf{sk}',\epsilon,\delta}(\mathbf{c}_i)] = \frac{1}{N}\sum_{i=1}^{N}\underbrace{\Pr_{\mathsf{sk}',\mathcal{O},\mathbf{c}_i}[\mathsf{EXC}_{\mathsf{sk}',\epsilon,\delta}(\mathbf{c}_i)]}_{>3p^*} > 3p^*.$$

Hence it holds by Lemma 1 that $\Pr[Z > 2p^*] \geq \mathsf{E}[Z] - 2p^* > p^*$. It follows that

$$\Pr[Z > 2p^*] > p^*.$$

Hence we have that

$$\Pr[\mathcal{D}((\mathbf{c}_i)_i) = 1]$$
$$= \underbrace{\Pr[\mathcal{D}((\mathbf{c}_i)_i) = 1|Z > 2p^*]}_{=1}\Pr[Z > 2p^*] + \underbrace{\Pr[\mathcal{D}((\mathbf{c}_i)_i) = 1|Z \leq 2p^*]}_{=1/2}\Pr[Z \leq 2p^*]$$
$$= \Pr[Z > 2p^*] + \frac{1}{2}(1 - \Pr[Z > 2p^*])$$
$$= \frac{1}{2} + \frac{1}{2}\Pr[Z > 2p^*]$$

$$> \frac{1}{2} + \frac{1}{2}p^*.$$

We conclude that our distinguisher has advantage $\frac{1}{2}p^* - 2^{-\lambda}$.

Theorem 9. *Fix the oracle* $\mathcal{O} : \{0,1\}^* \to \{0,1\}^*$. *Let* $\mathsf{PRC}^{\mathcal{O}} = (\mathsf{KeyGen}, \mathsf{Encode}^{\mathcal{O}}, \mathsf{Decode}^{\mathcal{O}})$ *be a pseudorandom code with* κ*-correctness and* ρ*-robustness. Then, there exists an (unbounded) oracle algorithm* $\mathsf{LearnQuery}^{\mathcal{O}}$ *and an efficient deterministic decoder* Decode' *such that for all* $\lambda \in \mathbb{N}$, $(\mathsf{KeyGen}, \mathsf{LearnQuery}^{\mathcal{O}}, \mathsf{Encode}^{\mathcal{O}}, \mathsf{Decode}')$ *is a PRC with* $\kappa + 1/p(\lambda)$*-augmented correctness and* ρ*-robustness for any polynomial* $p(\cdot)$.

We will prove Theorem 9 via the following Lemma, which enables us to remove oracle queries iteratively.

Lemma 5. *Let* $\mathsf{PRC}^{\mathcal{O}} = (\mathsf{KeyGen}, \mathsf{Encode}^{\mathcal{O}}, \mathsf{Decode}^{\mathcal{O}})$ *be a PRC which has an augmented decoder* $(\mathsf{LearnQuery}^{\mathcal{O}}, \mathsf{ADecode}^{\mathcal{O}})$ *with correctness error* κ *and* ρ *robustness relative to an oracle* $\mathcal{O}$. *Let* $\mathsf{S} = (\mathsf{S}_1, \mathsf{S}_2^{\mathcal{O}})$ *be a simulator relative to the oracle* $\mathcal{O}$. *Assume that* $\mathsf{ADecode}$ *makes at most* ℓ $\mathcal{O}$*-queries and* KeyGen *makes no oracle queries. Then for every* $\kappa' = 1/\mathsf{poly}(\lambda)$, *there exists an augmented decoder* $(\mathsf{LearnQuery}'^{\mathcal{O}}, \mathsf{ADecode}'^{\mathcal{O}})$ *for* $\mathsf{PRC}^{\mathcal{O}}$ *with the following properties.*

1. $\mathsf{ADecode}'$ *makes* $(\ell - 1)$ $\mathcal{O}$*-queries.*
2. *For all* $\lambda \in \mathbb{N}$, $(\mathsf{KeyGen}, \mathsf{LearnQuery}^{\mathcal{O}}, \mathsf{Encode}^{\mathcal{O}}, \mathsf{ADecode}'^{\mathcal{O}})$ *is a PRC with* $\kappa + \kappa'$*-augmented correctness and* ρ*-robustness.*
3. *The number of* $\mathcal{O}$*-queries made by* $\mathsf{LearnQuery}'$ *is at most the sum of the number of* $\mathcal{O}$*-queries made by* $\mathsf{LearnQuery}$ *and* $1/\epsilon$ *where* ϵ *only depends on* κ' *and* ρ.
4. *The size of the output of* $\mathsf{LearnQuery}'$ *is atmost* $\mathsf{poly}(\lambda)/\epsilon$.

Proof. We start by describing the $\mathsf{LearnQuery}'$ and $\mathsf{ADecode}'$ algorithms.

Description of $\mathsf{LearnQuery}'$*:* On input (sk, ϵ), $\mathsf{LearnQuery}'$ proceeds as follows:

1. Run $\mathsf{aux} \leftarrow \mathsf{LearnQuery}^{\mathcal{O}}(\mathsf{sk}, \epsilon)$.
2. Set $\mathsf{sk}' = (\mathsf{sk}, \mathsf{aux})$ and let $\mathsf{Quer}_{\mathsf{sk}'} : \{0,1\}^n \times \{0,1\}^r \to Q$ be the function that computes the *first* $\mathcal{O}$ query of $\mathsf{ADecode}^{\mathcal{O}}(\mathsf{sk}, \mathsf{aux}, \cdot)$. Define the global weight function $\mathsf{w}(\cdot)$ with respect to $\mathsf{Quer}_{\mathsf{sk}'}$.
3. Let $\tilde{Q} = \{q \in Q : \mathsf{w}(q) \geq \epsilon\}$ be the set of all globally ϵ-heavy queries. Query the oracle $\mathcal{O}$ on all $q \in \tilde{Q}$ and store all query-response pairs in a list $\mathcal{L}$.
4. Define $\mathsf{aux}' = \mathsf{aux} \| \mathcal{L}$ and output aux'.

Description of $\mathsf{ADecode}'$*:* On input $(\mathsf{sk}, \mathsf{aux}', \mathbf{c})$, where aux is a list of query-response pairs. $\mathsf{ADecode}'$ does the following

1. Parse $\mathsf{aux}' = \mathsf{aux} \| \mathcal{L}$.
2. Run $\mathsf{ADecode}^{\mathcal{O}}(\mathsf{sk}, \mathsf{aux}, \mathbf{c})$ until it makes the first query q, check if the query q is in $\mathcal{L}$. If so reply with the corresponding stored response, if not then run the simulator $(y, \mathsf{st}) \leftarrow \mathsf{S}_1(q)$ and reply y.

3. If the response to the query q was taken from $\mathcal{L}$, answer the remaining $\mathcal{O}$-queries of $\mathsf{ADecode}$ normally using $\mathcal{O}$. Otherwise, if the response to q was simulated by the first simulator, i.e., $(y, \mathsf{st}) \leftarrow \mathsf{S}_1(q)$, answer the remaining queries using $\mathsf{S}_2^{\mathcal{O}}(\mathsf{st})$.
4. Output the final output of $\mathsf{ADecode}$.

Correctness of $\mathsf{ADecode}'$ *- From Exceptionality to Intersection Queries:* We will now analyze the correctness error of the augmented decoder $(\mathsf{LearnQuery}', \mathsf{ADecode}')$. First, note that the size of the set $\tilde{Q}$ is at most $1/\epsilon$. As all $q \in \tilde{Q}$ are ϵ-heavy it holds that

$$|\tilde{Q}| \cdot \epsilon \leq \sum_{q \in \tilde{Q}} \mathsf{w}(q) = \sum_{q \in \tilde{Q}} \Pr[\mathsf{Quer}_{\mathsf{sk}'}(\mathbf{u}, r) = q] = \Pr[\mathsf{Quer}_{\mathsf{sk}'}(\mathbf{u}, r) \in \tilde{Q}] \leq 1.$$

It follows that $|\tilde{Q}| \leq 1/\epsilon$. Hence, the learner $\mathsf{LearnQuery}'$ makes at most $1/\epsilon$ oracle queries and thus satisfies the efficiency requirement.

Now consider the correctness experiments of $(\mathsf{LearnQuery}, \mathsf{ADecode})$ and $(\mathsf{LearnQuery}', \mathsf{ADecode}')$. In both experiments:

- Sample an oracle $\mathcal{O}$
- Run $\mathsf{sk} \leftarrow \mathsf{KeyGen}(1^\lambda)$
- $m \leftarrow \{0,1\}^d$
- $\mathbf{c} \leftarrow \mathsf{Encode}^{\mathcal{O}}(\mathsf{sk}, m)$
- $\mathbf{e} \leftarrow \mathsf{Ber}_\rho^n$

In $(\mathsf{LearnQuery}, \mathsf{ADecode})$ we then compute

- $\mathsf{aux} \leftarrow \mathsf{LearnQuery}^{\mathcal{O}}(\mathsf{sk}, \epsilon)$
- If $\mathsf{ADecode}^{\mathcal{O}}(\mathsf{sk}, \mathsf{aux}, \mathbf{c} + \mathbf{e}) = m$ output 1, otherwise 0

Whereas in $(\mathsf{LearnQuery}', \mathsf{ADecode}')$ we continue by

- $\mathsf{aux}' \leftarrow \mathsf{LearnQuery}'^{\mathcal{O}}(\mathsf{sk}, \epsilon)$
- If $\mathsf{ADecode}'^{\mathcal{O}}(\mathsf{sk}, \mathsf{aux}, \mathbf{c} + \mathbf{e}) = m$ output 1, otherwise 0

Now let Z_{Encode} be the set of query-response pairs (q_i, y_i) made and obtained by $\mathsf{Encode}^{\mathcal{O}}(\mathsf{sk}, m)$, i.e. $\mathsf{Encode}^{\mathcal{O}}(\mathsf{sk}, m)$ has made queries q_i to $\mathcal{O}$ and obtained the responses $y_i = \mathcal{O}(q_i)$. By the locality property of $\mathcal{O}$, the size of the set $Q_{rel} \subset Q$ of queries *related* to Z_{Encode} is at most $|Q_{rel}| \leq f(|Z_{\mathsf{Encode}}|)$ for some fixed polynomial f which only depends on $\mathcal{O}$. Consequently, as $|Z_{\mathsf{Encode}}| = \mathsf{poly}(\lambda)$ we obtain that $M = |Q_{rel}| = \mathsf{poly}(\lambda)$.

Now let $q = \mathsf{Quer}_{sk'}(\mathbf{c} + \mathbf{e})$ and consider the following 3 cases:

1. q has weight $\mathsf{w}(q) \geq \epsilon$. In this case $\mathsf{LearnQuery}'^{\mathcal{O}}$ queries q, consequently a corresponding query-response pair for q is in the list $\mathcal{L}$. All further queries are answered using $\mathcal{O}$. Hence $\mathsf{ADecode}'$ simulates $\mathsf{ADecode}$ perfectly, i.e. their outputs are identically distributed.

2. q has weight $\mathsf{w}(q) < \epsilon$ but $q \notin Q_{rel}$. In this case $\mathsf{ADecode}'$ simulates the response y to query q via $(y, \mathsf{st}) \leftarrow \mathsf{S}_1(q)$. All further queries are answered via $\mathsf{S}_2^{\mathcal{O}}(\mathsf{st})$. Hence, as $q \notin Q_{rel}$ by the simulatability property of the local oracle $\mathcal{O}$ it holds that the output distribution of $\mathsf{ADecode}'$ is statistically close to that of $\mathsf{ADecode}$.
3. q has weight $\mathsf{w}(q) < \epsilon$ and $q \in Q_{rel}$. Such queries are problematic and cannot be answered consistently by $\mathsf{ADecode}'$. Call this event BAD.

By the above discussion, conditioned on $\neg\mathsf{BAD}$ the outputs of the correctness experiment of $(\mathsf{LearnQuery}', \mathsf{ADecode}')$ is identically distributed to the output of the correctness experiment of $(\mathsf{LearnQuery}, \mathsf{ADecode})$.

Thus we need to show that case 3, i.e. the event BAD only occurs with small probability. For this purpose recall the notion of exceptional queries (Definition 6). $\mathsf{EXC}_{\mathsf{Quer}_{\mathsf{sk}'},\epsilon,\delta}(\mathbf{c})$ holds, if and only if there exists a query $q \in Q$ such that $\mathsf{w}(q) < \epsilon$ and $\ell_{\mathbf{c}}(q) \geq \delta$ (both with respect to the query function $\mathsf{Quer}_{\mathsf{sk}'}$). Lemma 4 and Theorem 8 (with $t = 1$) establish that if $\mathbf{c} \leftarrow \mathsf{Encode}^{\mathcal{O}}(\mathsf{sk}', m)$ as above, then

$$\Pr[\mathsf{EXC}_{\mathsf{Quer}_{\mathsf{sk}'},\epsilon,\delta}(\mathbf{c})] \leq 3p^*(\epsilon, \delta) = 3 \cdot \frac{\epsilon^{(1-\rho^2)/(1+\rho^2)}}{\delta^2}.$$

$$\begin{aligned}\Pr[\mathsf{BAD}] &= \Pr[\mathsf{BAD}|\neg\mathsf{EXC}_{\mathsf{sk}'}(\mathbf{c})] \underbrace{\Pr[\neg\mathsf{EXC}_{\mathsf{sk}'}(\mathbf{c})]}_{\leq 1} + \underbrace{\Pr[\mathsf{BAD}|\mathsf{EXC}_{\mathsf{sk}'}(\mathbf{c})]}_{\leq 1} \underbrace{\Pr[\mathsf{EXC}_{\mathsf{sk}'}(\mathbf{c})]}_{\leq 3p^*} \\ &\leq \Pr[\mathsf{BAD}|\neg\mathsf{EXC}_{\mathsf{sk}'}(\mathbf{c})] + 3p^*.\end{aligned}$$

It remains to bound $\Pr[\mathsf{BAD}|\neg\mathsf{EXC}_{\mathsf{sk}'}(\mathbf{c})]$. Hence fix any sk' and $\mathbf{c}$ with $\mathsf{EXC}_{\mathsf{sk}',\epsilon,\delta}(\mathbf{c}) = 0$, i.e. it holds for all $q \in Q$ with $\mathsf{w}(q) < \epsilon$ that $\ell_{\mathbf{c}}(q) < \delta$, that is $\Pr_{\mathbf{e}}[\mathsf{Quer}_{\mathsf{sk}'}(\mathbf{c} + \mathbf{e}) = q] < \delta$. Note that this last probability only depends on $\mathbf{e}$. In the following fix any set Q_{rel} with $|Q_{rel}| \leq M$.

Then it holds that

$$\begin{aligned}\Pr[\mathsf{BAD}] &= \Pr[\exists q \in Q_{rel} : \mathsf{Quer}_{\mathsf{sk}'}(\mathbf{c} + \mathbf{e}) = q \text{ and } \mathsf{w}(q) < \epsilon] \\ &\leq \sum_{\substack{q \in Q_{rel} \\ \mathsf{w}(g) < \epsilon}} \underbrace{\Pr[\mathsf{Quer}_{\mathsf{sk}'}(\mathbf{c} + \mathbf{e}) = q]}_{= \ell_{\mathbf{c}}(q) < \delta} \\ &< M \cdot \delta.\end{aligned}$$

We conclude that

$$\Pr[\mathsf{BAD}] < M \cdot \delta + 3p^* = M \cdot \delta + 3 \cdot \frac{\epsilon^{(1-\rho^2)/(1+\rho^2)}}{\delta^2}.$$

Hence, to limit the additional correctness error of $(\mathsf{LearnQuery}'^{\mathcal{O}}, \mathsf{ADecode})$ (which occurs exactly when BAD happens) to a value κ^* we can choose

- $\delta = \frac{\kappa^*}{2 \cdot M}$
- $\epsilon = \left(\frac{\kappa^* \cdot \delta^2}{6}\right)^{(1+\rho^2)/(1-\rho^2)}$

which routinely yields $\Pr[\mathsf{BAD}] < \kappa^*$. Note that both δ and ϵ are polynomial in κ^* and inverse polynomial in M. Finally, notice that we can absorb the negligible correctness error resulting from Case 2 into κ' by e.g. choosing $\kappa' = \kappa^*/2$. This concludes the proof.

Proof (Proof of Theorem 9*).* Let the number of oracle queries made by $\mathsf{Decode}^{\mathcal{O}}(\mathsf{sk}, \cdot)$ be bounded by ℓ. We begin by applying Lemma 5 to the original decoding algorithm $\mathsf{Decode}^{\mathcal{O}}$. This yields a new decoding algorithm $\mathsf{ADecode}^{\mathcal{O}}$ that makes one fewer oracle query than $\mathsf{Decode}^{\mathcal{O}}$, while maintaining correctness up to an additive error of κ'. Additionally, the size of the auxiliary information required is at most $\mathsf{poly}(\lambda)/\epsilon$ because there are at most ϵ^{-1} many ϵ-global heavy queries and each query-response pair is of size $\mathsf{poly}(\lambda)$.

We apply Lemma 5 iteratively ℓ times, eventually obtaining a decoder Decode' that makes no oracle queries. Instead, all oracle responses are simulated using the auxiliary information aux.

The total size of aux is at most $\ell \cdot \mathsf{poly}(\lambda)/\epsilon$. Since Decode' simulates Decode by answering oracle queries from aux, its running time increases by at most a $\mathsf{poly}(\epsilon^{-1}, \lambda)$ factor over that of Decode. The total degradation in correctness is additive, resulting in an overall correctness error of at most $\kappa + (\ell \cdot \kappa')$.

By setting $\kappa' = 1/(\ell \cdot p(\lambda))$ where p is polynomial in the theorem statement, we obtain the necessary efficiency and probability bound. This is because ℓ and M are polynomials in λ and ϵ depends on κ', κ and ρ.

5.4 Breaking Pseudorandomness with the Oracle-Free Decoder

Theorem 10. *Let* $\mathsf{PRC}^{\mathcal{O}} = (\mathsf{KeyGen}, \mathsf{Encode}^{\mathcal{O}}, \mathsf{Decode}^{\mathcal{O}})$ *be a PRC relative to a local oracle* $\mathcal{O}$*. Let* $\mathsf{LearnQuery}^{\mathcal{O}}$ *be a unbounded algorithm and* $\mathsf{ADecode}$ *be a decoder such that the correctness error with respect to the augmented scheme* $(\mathsf{KeyGen}, \mathsf{LearnQuery}^{\mathcal{O}}, \mathsf{Encode}^{\mathcal{O}}, \mathsf{ADecode})$ *is* κ *where* $\kappa < 1/8$*. Then, there exists an unbounded distinguisher* $\mathcal{D}$ *that breaks the pseudorandomness property of* $\mathsf{PRC}^{\mathcal{O}}$ *with advantage* $\frac{1}{16} - 2^{-\lambda}$.

Proof. Assume in the following the augmented secret key sk' for $\mathsf{ADecode}$ has bitlength k. Let $M = 8(k + \lambda)$.

Consider the following distinguisher $\mathcal{D}$, which has access to an encoding oracle but does not require additional access to the oracle $\mathcal{O}$:

- Query the encoding oracle on M uniformly random bits $b_1, \dots, b_M \leftarrow \{0,1\}$ and obtain words $\mathbf{x}_1, \dots, \mathbf{x}_M$.
- Choose Bernoulli errors $\mathbf{e}_1, \dots, \mathbf{e}_M \leftarrow \mathsf{Ber}_\rho^n$
- If there exists a string $\mathsf{sk}' \in \{0,1\}^k$ such that $Z(\mathsf{sk}') = \frac{1}{M} \sum_{i=1}^{M} z_i(\mathsf{sk}') > 3/4$ output 1, otherwise output a uniformly random bit. Here, we define the binary random variables $z_i(\mathsf{sk}')$ to be 1 if $\mathsf{ADecode}(\mathsf{sk}', \mathbf{x}_i + \mathbf{e}_i) = b_i$ and otherwise 0.

We will now analyze the advantage of this distinguisher. Assume first that the oracle provided to $\mathcal{D}$ produces uniformly random strings, i.e. for all $i \in [M]$ we have $\mathbf{x}_i = \mathbf{u}_i$ for uniformly random $\mathbf{u}_i \leftarrow \{0,1\}^n$.

Fix a secret key sk'. Since the $\mathbf{u}_i$ are independent of the b_i, and therefore, for each $i \in [M]$ that $\Pr[z_i(\mathsf{sk}') = 1] = \Pr[\mathsf{ADecode}(\mathsf{sk}', \mathbf{x}_i + \mathbf{e}_i) = b_i] = 1/2$, as the b_i are chosen uniformly random from $\{0,1\}$. Furthermore, as the b_i are independent, so are the $z_i(\mathsf{sk}')$. Consequently, it holds that

$$\mathsf{E}[Z(\mathsf{sk}')] = \mathsf{E}\left[\frac{1}{M}\sum_{i=1}^{M} z_i(\mathsf{sk}')\right] = \frac{1}{M}\sum_{i=1}^{M} \underbrace{\mathsf{E}[z_i(\mathsf{sk}')]}_{=\Pr[z_i(\mathsf{sk}')=1]} = \frac{1}{M}\cdot\frac{1}{2}\cdot M = \frac{1}{2}.$$

Consequently, it holds by a Chernoff bound that

$$\Pr[Z(\mathsf{sk}') > 3/4] \leq e^{-\frac{1}{8}M} \leq 2^{-M/8} = 2^{-k-\lambda}.$$

By a union-bound, it holds that

$$\Pr[\exists \mathsf{sk}' \in \{0,1\}^k \text{ s.t. } Z(\mathsf{sk}') > 3/4] \leq 2^k \cdot 2^{-k-\lambda} = 2^{-\lambda}.$$

Thus, we conclude that in this case $\mathcal{D}$ outputs a uniformly random bit, except with negligible probability $2^{-\lambda}$.

On the other hand, assume that the oracle provided to $\mathcal{D}$ outputs well-formed codewords $\mathbf{c}_1, \ldots, \mathbf{c}_M$ encoding the bits $b_1, \ldots, b_M$. In this case it holds that

$$\mathsf{E}[Z(\mathsf{sk})] = \frac{1}{M}\sum_{i=1}^{M}\mathsf{E}[z_i(\mathsf{sk})] = \frac{1}{M}\sum_{i=1}^{M}\underbrace{\Pr[\mathsf{ADecode}(\mathsf{sk}, \mathbf{c}_i + \mathbf{e}_i) = b_i]}_{\geq 1-\kappa} = 1-\kappa > 7/8.$$

over all random choices, including sk. Noting that $Z \in [0,1]$ it follows from Lemma 1 that $\Pr[Z > 3/4] \geq \mathsf{E}[Z] - 3/4 \geq 1/8$. Note that if there exists an sk such that with $Z(\mathsf{sk}) > 3/4$, then $\mathcal{D}$ will always output 1. Thus we get

$$\begin{aligned}
&\Pr[\mathcal{D}^{\mathsf{Encode}} = 1] \\
&= \underbrace{\Pr[\mathcal{D}^{\mathsf{Encode}} = 1 | Z > 3/4]}_{=1}\Pr[Z > 3/4] + \underbrace{\Pr[\mathcal{D}^{\mathsf{Encode}} = 1 | Z \leq 3/4]}_{=1/2}\Pr[Z \leq 3/4] \\
&= \Pr[Z > 3/4] + \frac{1}{2}(1 - \Pr[Z > 3/4]) \\
&= \frac{1}{2} + \frac{1}{2}\Pr[Z > 3/4] \\
&> \frac{1}{2} + \frac{1}{16}.
\end{aligned}$$

Hence we conclude that our distinguisher has advantage $\frac{1}{16} - 2^{-\lambda}$.

6 Construction of Large-Alphabet Pseudorandom Codes from Minimal Assumptions

In this section, we present a construction for error-correcting codes from a PRP and a SKE, which in turn can be based on the minimal assumption of one-way functions. The construction avoids the impossibility result by working over a large alphabet. For error-correcting codes that work over a large alphabet, errors are introduced per symbol[7] instead of per bit.

6.1 Construction

Consider the following parameters and primitives.

- Let $q = 2^\lambda$.
- Let $\mathsf{SKE} = (\mathsf{SKE.KeyGen}, \mathsf{SKE.Enc}, \mathsf{SKE.Dec})$ be a secret-key encryption scheme that encrypts messages of any length ℓ and generates pseudorandom ciphertexts of size $\mathbb{F}_q^k$ where $k = \mathsf{poly}(\lambda, \ell)$.
- Let $\mathsf{RS} = (\mathsf{Encode}, \mathsf{Decode})$ be a $[n, k, n-k+1]$ Reed-Solomon Code.
- Let $\mathsf{PRP} = (\mathsf{PRP.KeyGen}, \mathsf{PRP.Eval})$ be a pseudorandom permutation over the space $\mathbb{F}_q^n$.

Our construction is as follows.

$\mathsf{KeyGen}(1^\lambda) \to \mathsf{sk}$: Run $\mathsf{SKE.KeyGen}(1^\lambda) \to \mathsf{sk}_1$ and $\mathsf{PRP.KeyGen}(1^\lambda) = \mathsf{sk}_2$. Output $\mathsf{sk} = (\mathsf{sk}_1, \mathsf{sk}_2)$.

$\mathsf{Encode}(m, \mathsf{sk} = (\mathsf{sk}_1, \mathsf{sk}_2)) \to \mathsf{c}$: Encrypt the message $\mathsf{SKE.Enc}(\mathsf{sk}_1, m) \to \mathsf{ct}$. Encode ct using the Reed-Solomon Code to produce $\mathsf{Encode}(\mathsf{ct}) \to \tilde{\mathsf{c}}$. Parse $\tilde{\mathsf{c}}$ as n symbols in $\mathbb{F}_q$ and apply the pseudorandom permutation to each $i \in [n]$, i.e., $\mathsf{PRP.Eval}(\mathsf{sk}_2, \tilde{\mathsf{c}}_i) = \mathsf{c}_i$. Output $\mathsf{c} = (\mathsf{c}_1, \ldots, \mathsf{c}_n)$.

$\mathsf{Decode}(\mathsf{c}, \mathsf{sk} = (\mathsf{sk}_1, \mathsf{sk}_2)) \to m/\bot$: Parse c as n symbols in $\mathbb{F}_q$ and apply the inverse pseudorandom permutation to each element: $\mathsf{PRP.Eval}(\mathsf{sk}_2, \mathsf{c}_i) = \tilde{\mathsf{c}}_i$. Decode $\tilde{\mathsf{c}} = (\tilde{\mathsf{c}}_1, \ldots, \tilde{\mathsf{c}}_n)$ using the Reed-Solomon Decoder $\mathsf{Decode}(\tilde{\mathsf{c}}) \to \mathsf{ct}$. If the decoding was unsuccessful, output $\bot$. Otherwise decrypt the ciphertext $\mathsf{SKE.Dec}(\mathsf{ct}, \mathsf{sk}_1) \to m$ and output m.

Perfect Correctness. Since a $[n, k, n-k+1]$-Reed-Solomon code achieves perfect robustness against errors below the error threshold $t = (n-k)/(2n)$, our construction achieves perfect robustness up to tn errors. The construction inherits correctness from the correctness of the SKE scheme, the Reed-Solomon code and the pseudorandom permutation. Assuming that the message is ℓ' elements of $\mathbb{F}_q$, the transmission rate of the scheme is $r = \frac{\ell'}{n}$.

Theorem 11. *Let* SKE *be a \$-CPA secure secret-key encryption scheme and let* PRP *be a secure pseudorandom permutation and let* RS *be a Reed-Solomon Code, then the above construction is pseudorandom.*

The proof can be found in the full version.

[7] An alphabet is a finite set of symbols.

References

[AAC+24] Alrabiah, O., Ananth, P., Christ, M., Dodis, Y., Gunn, S.: Ideal pseudorandom codes. arXiv preprint arXiv:2411.05947 (2024)

[Aar22] Aaronson, S.: My AI safety lecture for UT effective altruism (2022). https://scottaaronson.blog

[ACC+22] Austrin, P., Chung, H., Chung, K.M., Fu, S., Lin, Y.T., Mahmoody, M.: On the impossibility of key agreements from quantum random oracles. In: Annual International Cryptology Conference, pp. 165–194. Springer (2022)

[Bec75] Beckner, W.: Inequalities in fourier analysis. Ann. Math. **102**(1), 159–182 (1975)

[Ber25] Beretta, L.: New statistical and computational results for learning junta distributions (2025)

[BFKL93] Blum, A., Furst, M., Kearns, M., Lipton, R.J.: Cryptographic primitives based on hard learning problems. In: Stinson, D.R. (ed.) CRYPTO 1993. LNCS, vol. 773, pp. 278–291. Springer, Heidelberg (1994). https://doi.org/10.1007/3-540-48329-2_24

[BGV+23] Bouaziz, S., Grilo, A.B., Vergnaud, D., Vu, Q.H., et al.: Towards the impossibility of quantum public key encryption with classical keys from one-way functions. Cryptology ePrint Archive (2023)

[BKR23] Bogdanov, A., Kothari, P.K., Rosen, A.: Public-key encryption, local pseudorandom generators, and the low-degree method. In: Theory of Cryptography Conference, pp. 268–285. Springer (2023)

[BKSY11] Brakerski, Z., Katz, J., Segev, G., Yerukhimovich, A.: Limits on the power of zero-knowledge proofs in cryptographic constructions. In: Ishai, Y. (ed.) TCC 2011. LNCS, vol. 6597, pp. 559–578. Springer, Heidelberg (2011). https://doi.org/10.1007/978-3-642-19571-6_34

[BM84] Blum, M., Micali, S.: How to generate cryptographically strong sequences of pseudorandom bits. SIAM J. Comput. **13**(4), 850 (1984)

[BMG09] Barak, B., Mahmoody-Ghidary, M.: Merkle puzzles are optimal — an $O(n$ $^2)$-query attack on any key exchange from a random oracle. In: Halevi, S. (ed.) CRYPTO 2009. LNCS, vol. 5677, pp. 374–390. Springer, Heidelberg (2009). https://doi.org/10.1007/978-3-642-03356-8_22

[Bon70] Bonami, A.: Etude des coefficients de fourier des fonctions de l^p(g). In Annales de l'institut Fourier **20**, 335–402 (1970)

[CG24] Christ, M., Gunn, S.: Pseudorandom error-correcting codes. In: Reyzin, L., Stebila, D. (eds.) CRYPTO 2024, Part VI. LNCS, vol. 14925, pp. 325–347. Springer, Cham (2024). https://doi.org/10.1007/978-3-031-68391-6_10

[DM24] Döttling, N., Mour, T.: On the black-box complexity of correlation intractability. In: 15th Innovations in Theoretical Computer Science Conference (ITCS 2024), pp. 40-1. Schloss Dagstuhl–Leibniz-Zentrum für Informatik (2024)

[FGJ+25] Fairoze, J., Garg, S., Jha, S., Mahloujifar, S., Mahmoody, M., Wang, M.: Publicly-detectable watermarking for language models. IACR Commun. Cryptol. **1**(4) (2025)

[FR23] Fischlin, M., Rohrbach, F.: Searching for ELFs in the cryptographic forest. In: Theory of Cryptography Conference, pp. 207–236. Springer (2023)

[GG24] Ghentiyala, S., Guruswami, V.: New constructions of pseudorandom codes. arXiv preprint arXiv:2409.07580 (2024)

[GGW25] Garg, S., Gunn, S., Wang, M.: Black-box crypto is useless for pseudorandom codes. arXiv preprint arXiv:2506.01854 (2025)

[GKM+00] Gertner, Y., Kannan, S., Malkin, T., Reingold, O., Viswanathan, M.: The relationship between public key encryption and oblivious transfer. In: Proceedings 41st Annual Symposium on Foundations of Computer Science, pp. 325–335. IEEE (2000)

[GM24] Golowich, N., Moitra, A.: Edit distance robust watermarks for language models. arXiv preprint arXiv:2406.02633 (2024)

[GMR01] Gertner, Y., Malkin, T., Reingold, O.: On the impossibility of basing trapdoor functions on trapdoor predicates. In: Proceedings 42nd IEEE Symposium on Foundations of Computer Science, pp. 126–135. IEEE (2001)

[HILL99] Håstad, J., Impagliazzo, R., Levin, L.A., Luby, M.: A pseudorandom generator from any one-way function. SIAM J. Comput. **28**(4), 1364–1396 (1999)

[HR04] Hsiao, C.-Y., Reyzin, L.: Finding collisions on a public road, or do secure hash functions need secret coins? In: Franklin, M. (ed.) CRYPTO 2004. LNCS, vol. 3152, pp. 92–105. Springer, Heidelberg (2004). https://doi.org/10.1007/978-3-540-28628-8_6

[IR89] Impagliazzo, R., Rudich, S.: Limits on the provable consequences of one-way permutations. In: Proceedings of the Twenty-First Annual ACM Symposium on Theory of Computing, pp. 44–61 (1989)

[Kea93] Kearns, M.: Efficient noise-tolerant learning from statistical queries. In: Proceedings of the Twenty-Fifth Annual ACM Symposium on Theory of Computing, New York, NY, USA. Association for Computing Machinery (1993)

[KGW+23] Kirchenbauer, J., Geiping, J., Wen, Y., Katz, J., Miers, I., Goldstein, T.: A watermark for large language models. In: Krause, A., Brunskill, E., Cho, K., Engelhardt, B., Sabato, S., Scarlett, J. (eds.) Proceedings of the 40th International Conference on Machine Learning. Proceedings of Machine Learning Research, vol. 202, pp. 17061–17084. PMLR (2023)

[KJGR21] Kaptchuk, G., Jois, T.M., Green, M., Rubin, A.D.: Meteor: cryptographically secure steganography for realistic distributions. In: Proceedings of the 2021 ACM SIGSAC Conference on Computer and Communications Security, pp. 1529–1548 (2021)

[KKRT16] Kolesnikov, V., Kumaresan, R., Rosulek, M., Trieu, N.: Efficient batched oblivious PRF with applications to private set intersection. In: Proceedings of the 2016 ACM SIGSAC Conference on Computer and Communications Security, CCS 2016, pp. 818–829, New York, NY, USA. Association for Computing Machinery (2016)

[KTHL24] Kuditipudi, R., Thickstun, J., Hashimoto, T., Liang, P.: Robust distortion-free watermarks for language models. Trans. Mach. Learn. Res. (2024)

[LLLL24] Li, L., Li, Q., Li, X., Liu, Q.: How (not) to build quantum PKE in minicrypt. In: Annual International Cryptology Conference, pp. 152–183. Springer (2024)

[LLLL25a] Li, L., Li, Q., Li, X., Liu, Q.: Cryptomania vs minicrypt in a quantum world. arXiv preprint arXiv:2504.05710 (2025)

[LLLL25b] Li, L., Li, Q., Li, X., Liu, Q.: Toward the impossibility of perfect complete quantum PKE from OWFs. In: 16th Innovations in Theoretical Computer Science Conference (ITCS 2025), pp. 71–1. Schloss Dagstuhl–Leibniz-Zentrum für Informatik (2025)

[LMW25] Lin, W.-K., Mook, E., Wichs, D.: Black box crypto is useless for doubly efficient PIR. In: Fehr, S., Fouque, P.-A. (eds.) EUROCRYPT 2025, Part VI. LNCS, vol. 15606, pp. 65–93. Springer, Cham (2025). https://doi.org/10.1007/978-3-031-91095-1_3

[Mat14] Matsuda, T.: On the impossibility of basing public-coin one-way permutations on trapdoor permutations. In: Lindell, Y. (ed.) TCC 2014. LNCS, vol. 8349, pp. 265–290. Springer, Heidelberg (2014). https://doi.org/10.1007/978-3-642-54242-8_12

[McE78] McEliece, R.J.: A public-key cryptosystem based on algebraic. Coding Thv **4244**(1978), 114–116 (1978)

[MM11] Matsuda, T., Matsuura, K.: On black-box separations among injective one-way functions. In: Ishai, Y. (ed.) TCC 2011. LNCS, vol. 6597, pp. 597–614. Springer, Heidelberg (2011). https://doi.org/10.1007/978-3-642-19571-6_36

[MP12] Mahmoody, M., Pass, R.: The curious case of non-interactive commitments – on the power of black-box vs. non-black-box use of primitives. In: Safavi-Naini, R., Canetti, R. (eds.) CRYPTO 2012. LNCS, vol. 7417, pp. 701–718. Springer, Heidelberg (2012). https://doi.org/10.1007/978-3-642-32009-5_41

[O'D14] O'Donnell, R.: Analysis of boolean functions. Cambridge University Press (2014)

[Rud88] Rudich, S.: Limits on the provable consequences of one-way functions. University of California at Berkeley (1988)

[Rud91] Rudich, S.: The use of interaction in public cryptosystems. In: Feigenbaum, J. (ed.) CRYPTO 1991. LNCS, vol. 576, pp. 242–251. Springer, Heidelberg (1992). https://doi.org/10.1007/3-540-46766-1_19

[Sim98] Simon, D.R.: Finding collisions on a one-way street: can secure hash functions be based on general assumptions? In: Nyberg, K. (ed.) EUROCRYPT 1998. LNCS, vol. 1403, pp. 334–345. Springer, Heidelberg (1998). https://doi.org/10.1007/BFb0054137

[Tho48] Thorin, G.O.: Convexity theorems generalizing those of M. Riesz and Hadamard with some applications (1948)

[Yao82] Yao, A.C.: Theory and application of trapdoor functions. In: 23rd Annual Symposium on Foundations of Computer Science (SFCS 1982), pp. 80–91. IEEE (1982)

[ZALW24] Zhao, X., Ananth, P., Li, L., Wang, Y.-X.: Provable robust watermarking for AI-generated text. In: The Twelfth International Conference on Learning Representations (2024)

[ZDR19] Ziegler, Z., Deng, Y., Rush, A.M.: Neural linguistic steganography. arXiv preprint arXiv:1909.01496 (2019)

Generalized and Unified Equivalences Between Hardness and Pseudoentropy

Lunjia Hu[1(✉)] and Salil Vadhan[2]

[1] Northeastern University, Boston, MA 02115, USA
lunjia@alumni.stanford.edu
[2] Harvard University, Cambridge, MA 02138, USA
salil_vadhan@harvard.edu

Abstract. Pseudoentropy characterizations provide a quantitatively precise demonstration of the close relationship between computational *hardness* and computational *randomness*. We prove a unified pseudoentropy characterization that generalizes and strengthens previous results for both uniform and non-uniform models of computation. Our characterization holds for a general family of entropy notions that encompasses the common notions of Shannon entropy and min entropy as special cases. Moreover, we show that the characterizations for different entropy notions can be simultaneously achieved by a single, universal function that simultaneously witnesses computational hardness and computational randomness.

A key technical insight of our work is that the notion of *weight-restricted calibration* from the recent literature on algorithm fairness, along with standard computational indistinguishability (known as *multiaccuracy* in the fairness literature), suffices for proving pseudoentropy characterizations for general entropy notions. This demonstrates the power of weight-restricted calibration to enhance the classic Complexity-Theoretic Regularity Lemma (Trevisan, Tulsiani, and Vadhan, 2009) and Leakage Simulation Lemma (Jetchev and Pietrzak, 2014) and allows us to achieve an exponential improvement in the complexity dependency on the alphabet size compared to the pseudoentropy characterizations by Casacuberta, Dwork, and Vadhan (2024) based on the much stronger notion of *multicalibration*. We show that the exponential dependency on the alphabet size is inevitable for multicalibration as well as for the weaker notion of calibrated multiaccuracy.

Keywords: Pseudorandomness · Regularity Lemma · Calibration

1 Introduction

1.1 Background on Hardness–Randomness Equivalences

The close relationship between computational *hardness* and computational *randomness* is central in cryptography and complexity theory. A classic example of

The full version [21] of this paper contains all omitted proofs.

B. Applebaum and H. Lin (Eds.): TCC 2025, LNCS 16271, pp. 258–288, 2026.
https://doi.org/10.1007/978-3-032-12290-2_9

this relationship is Yao's equivalence between pseudorandomness and (maximal) unpredictability [34], one form of which is the following:

Theorem 1. *Let (X, Y) be a random variable distributed on $\{0,1\}^n \times \{0,1\}^\ell$ with $\ell = O(\log n)$. Then the following are equivalent:*

1. *$(X, Y) \approx^c (X, U_\ell)$, where $\approx^c$ denotes computational indistinguishability (against nonuniform polynomial-time algorithms).*
2. *For every nonuniform polynomial-time algorithm A,*

$$\Pr[A(X) = Y] \leq \frac{1}{2^\ell} + \mathrm{negl}(n).$$

We refer to Condition 2 as *maximal* unpredictability, because it is trivial for an efficient A to achieve prediction probability $1/2^\ell$, by just outputting a uniformly random ℓ-bit string. It is natural to ask what happens if we weaken the hardness of prediction to allow A to succeed with other probability between $1/2^\ell$ and 1. Vadhan and Zheng [31,35] showed that such weak unpredictability is equivalent to Y having high *pseudo-average-min-entropy* [18] given X.

Theorem 2. *Let (X, Y) be a random variable distributed on $\{0,1\}^n \times \{0,1\}^\ell$ with $\ell = O(\log n)$, and let $k \in [0, \ell]$. Then the following are equivalent:*

1. *There is a random variable Z on $\{0,1\}^\ell$, jointly distributed with X, such that $(X, Y) \approx^c (X, Z)$ and $\mathsf{H}_{\text{avg-min}}(Z|X) \geq k$, where $\mathsf{H}_{\text{avg-min}}$ denotes* average min-entropy *[4]:*

$$\mathsf{H}_{\text{avg-min}}(Z|X) := -\log_2 \mathbb{E}_X \left[\max_{z_X \in \{0,1\}^\ell} \Pr[Z = z_X | X] \right].$$

2. *For every nonuniform polynomial-time algorithm A,*

$$\Pr[A(X) = Y] \leq \frac{1}{2^k} + \mathrm{negl}(n),$$

where $\mathrm{negl}(n)$ *denotes a negligible function.*

As noted in [31,35], the case when Y consists of $\ell = 1$ bits is equivalent to Holenstein's optimal version of Impagliazzo's Hardcore Lemma [16,22]; the novelty in their result was proving it for all $\ell = O(\log n)$.

Now it is also natural to ask what happens if we replace the average min-entropy above with other information-theoretic measures of randomness, like conditional Shannon entropy. In this case, Vadhan and Zheng [31] gave the following characterization.

Theorem 3. *Let (X, Y) be a random variable distributed on $\{0,1\}^n \times \{0,1\}^\ell$ with $\ell = O(\log n)$, and let $k \geq 0$. Then the following are equivalent:*

1. *There is a random variable* Z *on* $\{0,1\}^\ell$, *jointly distributed with* X, *such that* $(X,Y) \approx^c (X,Z)$ *and* $\mathsf{H}_{\mathsf{Sh}}(Z|X) \geq \mathsf{H}_{\mathsf{Sh}}(Y|X) + k - \mathrm{negl}(n)$, *where* H_{Sh} *denotes the conditional Shannon entropy.*
2. *For every nonuniform, randomized polynomial-time algorithm* A,

$$\mathsf{D}_{\mathsf{KL}}((X,Y)\|(X,A(X))) \geq k - \mathrm{negl}(n),$$

where D_{KL} *denotes KL divergence (a.k.a. relative entropy).*

Here the hardness of $A(X)$ trying to predict the value of Y is replaced by $A(X)$ trying to get close (in KL divergence) to the conditional distribution of Y given X. Vadhan and Zheng [31] used Theorem 3 to give a simpler construction of pseudorandom generators from one-way functions. Their pseudorandom generator construction avoids the use of hardcore bits like Goldreich–Levin [9], which was the traditional way of converting the hardness of inverting a one-way function into pseudoentropy, as was used in the original construction of Håstad, Impagliazzo, Levin, and Luby [17].

Note that Theorem 3 is concerned with the *pseudoentropy gap* $k = \mathsf{H}_{\mathsf{Sh}}(Z|X) - \mathsf{H}_{\mathsf{Sh}}(Y|X)$, which measures how much *more* randomness Y appears to have to feasible observers in comparison to computationally unbounded ones. Correspondingly, even if $\mathsf{H}_{\mathsf{Sh}}(Y|X)$ is large, Y may still be considered "easy" in that an efficient $A(X)$ can sample accurately from the conditional distribution $Y|_X$. In contrast, the parameter k in Theorem 2 does not distinguish between the computational hardness and information-theoretic hardness in Y given X.

Aside from this difference, the two theorems are very similar in spirit and one may wonder whether there is a unified proof for them, one which ideally also generalizes to other measures of randomness (beyond min-entropy and Shannon entropy). Zheng [35] made progress in this direction, considering a wide family of entropy measures H_φ and their corresponding *Bregman divergences* D_φ (whose definition we defer to later in the introduction).

Theorem 4. *Suppose that* $\ell = O(\log n)$ *and let* $\mathsf{H}_\varphi(B|A)$ *be a function that takes a random variable* (A,B) *distributed on* $\{0,1\}^n \times \{0,1\}^\ell$ *and outputs the negative average over* $a \leftarrow A$ *of a differentiable and strictly convex function* φ *applied to the probability mass function of* $B|A = a$. *Let* D_φ *be the Bregman divergence associated with* φ. *Suppose that given a linear function* Λ, *the probability mass function* p *on* $\{0,1\}^\ell$ *that minimizes* $\Lambda(p) + \varphi(p)$ *can be computed by a nonuniform algorithm running in time* $\mathsf{poly}(n)$, *and that, given* p, *the gradient* $\nabla\varphi(p)$ *can also be computed accurately in time* $\mathsf{poly}(n)$. *Also assume that* $\sup_p \|\nabla\varphi(p)\|_\infty = \mathsf{poly}(n)$.

Let (X,Y) *be a random variable distributed on* $\{0,1\}^n \times \{0,1\}^\ell$ *with* $\ell = O(\log n)$, *and let* $k \geq 0$. *Then the following are equivalent:*

1. *There is a random variable* Z *on* $\{0,1\}^\ell$, *jointly distributed with* X, *such that* $(X,Y) \approx^c (X,Z)$ *and* $\mathsf{H}_\varphi(Z|X) \geq \mathsf{H}_\varphi(Y|X) + k - \mathrm{negl}(n)$.
2. *For every nonuniform, randomized polynomial-time algorithm* A,

$$\mathsf{D}_\varphi((X,Y)\|(X,A(X))) \geq k - \mathrm{negl}(n).$$

This theorem implies Theorem 3 as a special case, because if we take $\varphi(p) = \sum_b p_b \log p_b$, then H_φ becomes conditional Shannon entropy and D_φ becomes KL divergence.[1] Moreover, if we instead take $\varphi(p) = \|p\|_\infty := \max_b p_b$, then H_φ is equivalent (up to a monotone increasing change of variables) to average min-entropy. Unfortunately, we cannot derive Theorem 2 from Theorem 4 because this choice of φ is not differentiable, and the proof of Theorem 4 crucially relies on differentiability. However, it does at least give us generalizations to other entropy measures. In particular, taking $\varphi(p) = \sum_b p_b^2$ or $\varphi(p) = \sqrt{\sum_b p_b^2}$, $\mathsf{H}_\varphi(B|A)$ measures conditional forms of the collision probability (equivalently, Rényi entropy of order 2), which have proved useful in cryptography and algorithmic applications, for example in [3,14]. (For interpretations of D_φ in these cases, see Sect. 1.6.)

A different unification of the hardness–randomness equivalences came recently in the work of Casacuberta, Dwork, and Vadhan [1]. Inspired by the concurrent work of Dwork, Lee, Lin, and Tankala [5], they reinterpreted the Multicalibration Theorem from the algorithmic fairness literature [12,15] and showed how it gives a simpler proof of Theorems 2 and 3 when $\ell = O(1)$, along with other known results about average-case complexity and computational indistinguishability (namely, Impagliazzo's Hardcore Lemma [16,22] and the complexity-theoretic Dense Model Theorem [28]). Here is their interpretation of the Multicalibration Theorem (with some cheating, which we will correct below):

Theorem 5 (Multicalibration Theorem, informally stated). *Let (X, Y) be a random variable distributed on $\{0,1\}^n \times \{0,1\}^\ell$ with $\ell = O(\log n)$. Then there is a function $P : \{0,1\}^n \to \{0,1\}^{O(2^\ell \cdot \log n)}$ computable by a nonuniform algorithm running in time $\mathsf{poly}(n)^{2^\ell}$ such that $(X, Y) \approx^c (X, Z)$, where for every $x \in \mathsf{Supp}(X)$, we define $Z|_{X=x}$ to be identically distributed to $Y|_{P(X)=P(x)}$.*

Notice that conditioned on the value of $P(X)$, Z and X are independent of each other. This means that, conditioned on $P(X)$, (X, Z) is the "most random" random variable of the form (X, W) that is indistinguishable from (X, Y). (Since $\ell = O(\log n)$, if (X, W) is computationally indistinguishable from (X, Y), then the marginal distribution of W must be statistically indistinguishable from Y, so the only way to noticeably increase the entropy of W given X is to make W more independent of X.)

Furthermore, when $\ell = O(1)$, P is computable in nonuniform polynomial time and outputs only $O(\log n)$ bits. In this setting, we can thus derive Theorems 2,3, and 4 easily. To illustrate with Theorem 2, consider any nonuniform polynomial-time A. Since $(X, Y) \approx^c (X, Z)$, we have:

$$\Pr[A(X) = Y] \leq \Pr[A(X) = Z] + \mathrm{negl}(n) \leq 2^{-\mathsf{H}_{\text{avg-min}}(Z|X)} + \mathrm{negl}(n),$$

[1] In this case, $\|\nabla\varphi(p)\|_\infty$ is unbounded as p approaches the boundary of Δ_L, violating the boundedness assumption required by Theorem 4, but this can be addressed easily by slightly perturbing p away from the boundary (see Sect. 5).

and furthermore, we can construct an A with $\Pr[A(X) = Y] = 2^{-\mathsf{H}_{\mathsf{avg\text{-}min}}(Z|X)}$, by having $A(X)$ compute $q = P(X)$ and output $b_q = \arg\max_b \Pr[Y = b|P(X) = q]$, which we can hardwire into our nonuniform polynomial-time algorithm. We can afford to hardwire all of the b_q values since P outputs $O(\log n)$ bits and hence there are only $2^{O(\log n)} = \mathsf{poly}(n)$ choices for q. Similarly, the fact that P is computable in non-uniform polynomial time and only outputs $O(\log n)$ bits implies that Z is the random variable of maximum average min-entropy given X such that $(X, Y) \approx^c (X, Z)$.

Interestingly, for Theorem 3 and 4, we get that the polynomial-time algorithm A that minimizes the divergence $\mathsf{D}_\varphi((X, Y)\|(X, A(X)))$ simply samples from Z given X (which can be done efficiently since P is polynomial-time computable and outputs only $O(\log n)$ bits). That is, the best efficiently computable predictor for Y given X (with respect to D_φ) is *identical* to the highest-H_φ distribution Z that is indistinguishable from Y given X. Furthermore, this distribution Z is the same for all of the Bregman entropy measures H_φ (as well as for $\mathsf{H}_{\mathsf{avg\text{-}min}}$).

Correcting the Cheating. Above, we cheated on the order of quantifiers in the Multicalibration Theorem. P is not actually computable in time $\mathsf{poly}(n)^{2^\ell}$ for a fixed polynomial $\mathsf{poly}(\cdot)$. Rather, for every polynomial $p(n)$, there is a P computable in time $\mathsf{poly}(p(n))^{2^\ell}$, outputting $\log\left(\mathsf{poly}(p(n))^{2^\ell}\right)$ bits, such that Y and X are computationally indistinguishable from being independent conditioned on $P(X)$, for nonuniform distinguishers that run in time $p(n)$ and with an advantage bounded by $1/p(n)$. This corrected order of quantifiers still suffices to prove Theorems 2, 3, and 4 when $\ell = O(1)$, without modifying those theorem statements. However, the order of quantifiers does also need to be incorporated into our informal statement that the best efficiently computable predictor for Y given X (with respect to any D_φ) is *identical* to the highest-entropy distribution Z that is indistinguishable from Y given X. (We will see precise statements later.)

In summary, the Multicalibration Theorem comes close to providing a unified picture of hardness versus randomness, but it has two significant deficiencies. First, it has a factor of 2^ℓ in the *exponent* of the runtime of P, which is unfortunately necessary (as we prove in Corollary 1). Second, it is only stated and used in [1] for nonuniform complexity, whereas the prior proofs of Theorems 2, 3 had uniform-complexity analogues [32,35].

1.2 Our Contributions

In this work, we address the aforementioned deficiencies of both Theorems 4 and 5, and thereby provide a more unified and clarified understanding of hardness versus randomness. Specifically, we provide a substantial strengthening of Theorem 4 with the following features in Theorem 7:

- The convex function φ does not need to be differentiable, and thus our generalization encompasses Theorem 2.
- Our theorem applies simultaneously to a set Φ of functions φ, with a complexity blow up that depends on the (nonuniform) time needed to accurately

evaluate the (sub)gradients $\nabla\varphi$, for an arbitrary $\varphi \in \Phi$. For the specific φ needed to capture Theorems 2 and 3, as well as for conditional collision probability (Rényi 2-entropy), the complexity blow-up is just $\mathsf{poly}(2^\ell)$, which is affordable for $\ell = O(\log n)$. But if we take all possible functions φ, we get a blow-up that is doubly-exponential in ℓ, like obtained from the Multicalibration Theorem.

- Similarly to the Multicalibration Theorem, we deduce (subject to appropriate quantifiers as mentioned above) that the best efficiently computable prediction for Y given X (with respect to D_φ) is *identical* to the highest-H_φ distribution Z that is indistinguishable from Y given X. Furthermore, this distribution Z is the same for all of the $\varphi \in \Phi$.
- We state and prove a uniform-complexity generalization of our theorem in Theorem 8. This result encompasses the uniform-complexity versions of Theorems 2 and 3 as shown in [31,35] and extends Theorem 4 to the uniform-complexity setting as well (which, to our knowledge, has not been achieved in prior work). The uniform-complexity setting plays and important role in [31], which uses the uniform-complexity version of Theorem 3 to give refined constructions of pseudorandom generators from one-way functions.
- To justify the blow-up in our theorem depending on the complexity of (approximately) computing the (sub)gradients $\nabla\varphi$, we prove that a doubly-exponential dependence on ℓ is unavoidable if we do not place any computational efficiency assumptions on φ, even when Φ only contains a single convex function φ with bounded subgradients (Theorem 9). This result implies that the doubly-exponential dependence is necessary for achieving multicalibration (as well as the weaker notion of *calibrated multiaccuracy*) even when there is only a single, extremely simple distinguisher (Corollary 1).

A key insight in our work is that full-fledged multicalibration is overkill for proving Theorems 2 and 3. Instead, it suffices to use a combination of two substantially weaker notions, *multiaccuracy* and *weight-restricted calibration*. The latter notion (weight-restricted calibration) is the part that is tailored to the specific family Φ, imposing one constraint per function $\varphi \in \Phi$, leading to a complexity blow-up that depends on the maximum complexity of (the gradients of) the functions in Φ. See Sect. 1.5 for a more detailed discussion about the relationships among these notions from the algorithmic fairness literature (multicalibration, multiaccuracy, and weight-restricted calibration).

In independent works, Casacuberta, Gopalan, Kanade, and Reingold [2] and Dwork and Tankala [6] demonstrated the power of (variants of) a similar notion termed *calibrated multiaccuracy* (see Sect. 1.5 for more discussion), with Casacuberta et al. [2] giving applications in agnostic learning and to proving Impagliazzo's Hardcore Lemma (which, as mentioned earlier, is equivalent to Theorem 5 for the case $\ell = 1$) and Dwork and Tankala [6] showing that it can substitute for multicalibration in the results of [26], which characterize computational indistinguishability under repeated samples.

1.3 Notation

To describe our results and techniques more precisely, it will be convenient to switch from random-variable notation as used above to a functional notion. Let L be a positive integer, which represents 2^ℓ in the discussion above. Let $\Delta_L \subseteq [0,1]^L$ be the set of probability distributions over a label space $[L] := \{1, \ldots, L\}$, where we represent discrete probability distributions by their probability mass functions. Then our random variable (X, Y) can be represented by the probability distribution μ of X and a function $g^* : \{0,1\}^n \to \Delta_L$, where $g^*(x)$ is the distribution of $Y|_{X=x}$. Similarly, we can represent another random variable Z jointly distributed with X by a *simulator* $s : \{0,1\}^n \to \Delta_L$.

We normally would describe a distinguisher d between (X, Y) and (X, Z) as a function $d : \{0,1\}^n \times [L] \to [0,1]$. Instead, it will be convenient to describe them as functions $f : \{0,1\}^n \to [-1,1]^L$, where the y-th coordinate of $f(x)$ (denoted by $f(x)_y$) represents $1 - 2d(x,y)$. Then computational indistinguishability between (X, Y) and (X, Z) can be conveniently described as follows.

Definition 1. *Let μ be a distribution on $\{0,1\}^n$ and $g^*, s : \{0,1\}^n \to \Delta_L$. We say that g^* and s are* (T, ε)-indistinguishable *with respect to μ if for every $f : \{0,1\}^n \to [-1,1]^L$ computable in nonuniform time T, we have:*

$$|\mathbb{E}_{x \sim \mu}\left[\langle s(x) - g^*(x), f(x)\rangle\right]| \le \varepsilon,$$

where $\langle \cdot, \cdot \rangle$ denotes the standard inner product on $\mathbb{R}^L$. We write $\mathsf{Ind}_\mu(g^*; T, \varepsilon)$ to denote the class of all functions $s : \{0,1\}^n \to \Delta_L$ that are (T, ε)-indistinguishable from g^*.

From now on, we fix an arbitrary distribution μ over X and will often omit it from our notations.

We define our entropy measures as follows:

Definition 2. *Let $\varphi : \Delta_L \to \mathbb{R}$ be a convex function. For a distribution μ on $\{0,1\}^n$ and a function $g : \{0,1\}^n \to \Delta_L$, we define*

$$\mathsf{H}_\varphi(g) = -\mathbb{E}_{x \sim \mu}\left[\varphi(g(x))\right].$$

Consider what happens when we apply this definition to a μ and g^* representing a random variable (X, Y) on $\{0,1\}^n \times [L]$. If we take $\varphi(p) = \sum_b p_b \log p_b$, then $\mathsf{H}_\varphi(g^*) = \mathsf{H}_{\mathsf{Sh}}(Y|X)$. If we take $\varphi(p) = \|p\|_\infty$, then $\mathsf{H}_\varphi(g^*) = -2^{-\mathsf{H}_{\mathsf{avg\text{-}min}}(Y|X)}$, which is indeed a monotone increasing change of variables of the average min-entropy.

The divergence measures we consider are defined as follows.

Definition 3. *Let $\varphi : \Delta_L \to \mathbb{R}$ be a convex function. If φ is differentiable, then for $g^*, g : \{0,1\}^n \to \Delta_L$ and a distribution μ on $\{0,1\}^n$, we define the* Bregman divergence *as:*

$$\begin{aligned}
\mathsf{D}_\varphi(g^* \| g) &:= \mathbb{E}_{x \sim \mu}\left[\mathsf{D}_\varphi(g^*(x) \| g(x))\right] \\
&:= \mathbb{E}_{x \sim \mu}\left[\varphi(g^*(x)) - \varphi(g(x)) - \langle g^*(x) - g(x), \nabla\varphi(g(x))\rangle\right] \\
&= \mathsf{H}_\varphi(g) - \mathsf{H}_\varphi(g^*) - \mathbb{E}_{x \sim \mu}\left[\langle g^*(x) - g(x), \nabla\varphi(g(x))\rangle\right]
\end{aligned}$$

where $\nabla\varphi(v) \in \mathbb{R}^L$ *is the gradient of* φ *at* $v \in \Delta_L$*. If* φ *is not differentiable, then we replace* $\nabla\varphi(p)$ *with a fixed choice of* subgradient *of* φ *at each* $p \in \Delta_L$*. (See Sect. 2.1.)*

Consider what happens when we apply this definition to g^* and g representing random variables (X, Y) and $(X, A(X))$ on $\{0,1\}^n \times [L]$, respectively. If we take $\varphi(p) = \sum_b p_b \log p_b$, then $\mathsf{D}_\varphi(g^* \| g) = \mathsf{D}_{\mathsf{KL}}((X,Y) \| (X, A(X)))$. If we take $\varphi(p) = \|p\|_\infty - 1$, this function is not differentiable and its subgradient is not unique. We choose

$$\nabla\varphi(p) = -\mathbf{e}_{\arg\max_b p_b},$$

where $\mathbf{e}_b$ is the standard basis vector whose b-th coordinate is one, and $\arg\max_b v_b$ is the index of the largest coordinate of v. When there are multiple largest coordinates, we define $\arg\max_b v_b$ to be the smallest index of those largest coordinates. Now we have for $v^*, v \in \Delta_L$,

$$\begin{aligned} \mathsf{D}_\varphi(v^* \| v) &= \|v^*\|_\infty - \|v\|_\infty - \langle v^* - v, \mathbf{e}_{\arg\max_j v_j} \rangle \\ &= \|v^*\|_\infty - \langle v^*, \mathbf{e}_{\arg\max_j v_j} \rangle \\ &= \|v^*\|_\infty - \langle v^*_{\arg\max_j v_j} \rangle. \end{aligned}$$

Thus, we calculate the divergence between functions g^* and g as:

$$\mathsf{D}_\varphi(g^* \| g) = 2^{-\mathsf{H}_{\text{avg-min}}(Y|X)} - \Pr[Y = \arg\max_b g(X)_b].$$

Thus, minimizing $\mathsf{D}_\varphi(g^* \| g)$ over all efficiently computable g amounts to maximizing the probability that an efficiently computable $A'(x) = \arg\max_b g(x)_b$ predicts Y, aligning with Theorem 2.

For a time bound $T \geq 0$, we use $\mathsf{Time}(T)$ to denote the class of functions $g : \{0,1\}^n \to \Delta_L$ computable in non-uniform time T. For a function $r : \Delta_L \to \mathbb{R}^L$, we define

$$\|r\|_\infty := \sup_{p \in \Delta_L} \|r(p)\|_\infty.$$

With this notation in hand, we can restate Theorem 4 of Zheng as follows:

Theorem 6 (Characterization of generalized pseudoentropy [35]). *Let* $\varphi : \Delta_L \to \mathbb{R}$ *be a differentiable strictly convex function. Let* T_φ, T'_φ *be time bounds such that given a linear function* Λ *on* Δ_L*, the* $p \in \Delta_L$ *minimizing* $\varphi(p) + \Lambda(p)$ *can be computed in nonuniform time* T_φ *and that given* $p \in \Delta_L$*, the gradient* $\nabla\varphi(p)$ *can be computed in nonuniform time* T'_φ*. Then for every time bound* $T > 0$*, every* $\varepsilon \in (0,1)$*, there exists* $T' = \mathsf{poly}(T, n, L, 1/\varepsilon) + T_\varphi$ *such that for every* $g^* : X \to \Delta_L$*,*

$$\underbrace{\max_{s \in \mathsf{Ind}(g^*; T, \varepsilon)} \mathsf{H}_\varphi(s) - \mathsf{H}_\varphi(g^*)}_{\textit{pseudoentropy gap}} \geq \underbrace{\min_{g \in \mathsf{Time}(T')} \mathsf{D}_\varphi(g^* \| g)}_{\textit{hardness of approximating}}. \tag{1}$$

Conversely, for every time bound T and for every $g^* : X \to \Delta_L$, we have[2]

$$\underbrace{\max_{s\in\mathsf{Ind}(g^*;T+T'_\varphi,\varepsilon)} \mathsf{H}_\varphi(s) - \mathsf{H}_\varphi(g^*)}_{\textit{pseudoentropy gap}} \leq \underbrace{\min_{g\in\mathsf{Time}(T)} \mathsf{D}_\varphi(g^*\|g)}_{\textit{hardness of approximating}} + \varepsilon\cdot\|\nabla\varphi\|_\infty. \tag{2}$$

Theorem 6 indeed implies Theorem 4 by the following correspondences:

$$\begin{aligned} L &= 2^\ell, \\ \mathsf{H}_\varphi(g^*) &= \mathsf{H}_\varphi(Y|X), \\ \mathsf{H}_\varphi(s) &= \mathsf{H}_\varphi(Z|X), \\ \mathsf{D}_\varphi(g^*\|g) &= \mathsf{D}_\varphi((X,Y)\|(X,A(X))). \end{aligned}$$

The assumption $\ell = O(\log n)$ in Theorem 4 gives $L = \mathsf{poly}(n)$. We also have $T_\varphi, T'_\varphi = \mathsf{poly}(n)$ from the assumptions in Theorem 4. These conditions ensure that $T' = \mathsf{poly}(T, n, 1/\varepsilon)$ in Theorem 6, so we can use (1) to prove that Item newinlinkPar15item:bregmansps22 (hardness) in Theorem 4 implies Item newinlinkPar14item:bregmansps11 (pseudoentropy). Similarly, the reverse implication follows from (2).

1.4 Formal Statement of Results

We state our main results in Theorems 7, 8, and 9 below.

Non-Uniform Setting

Theorem 7. *Let $T > 0$ be a time bound and let $\varepsilon \in (0,1)$ be an error parameter. Let Φ be a family of convex functions $\varphi : \Delta_L \to \mathbb{R}$. Assume that given $v \in \Delta_L$, the subgradient $\nabla\varphi(v)$ is bounded in $[-1,1]^L$ and can be computed to ℓ_∞ accuracy $\varepsilon/4$ in nonuniform time T_Φ, for every $\varphi \in \Phi$. Then there exists*

$$T' = O\left(\frac{(T+T_\Phi)\log L}{\varepsilon^2} + L\cdot\mathsf{poly}(1/\varepsilon, \log L)\right) \tag{3}$$

such that for every $g^* : X \to \Delta_L$, there exists $s \in \mathsf{Ind}(g^*; T, \varepsilon) \cap \mathsf{Time}(T')$ such that

$$\mathsf{H}_\varphi(s) - \mathsf{H}_\varphi(g^*) \geq D_\varphi(g^*\|s) - \varepsilon \quad \textit{for every } \varphi \in \Phi. \tag{4}$$

Conversely, for every $T > 0$, there exists $T' = O(T + T_\Phi)$ such that for every $g^* : X \to \Delta_L$ and every $\varphi \in \Phi$,

$$\max_{s\in\mathsf{Ind}(g^*;T',\varepsilon/2)} (\mathsf{H}_\varphi(s) - \mathsf{H}_\varphi(g^*)) \leq \min_{g\in\mathsf{Time}(T)} \mathsf{D}_\varphi(g^*\|g) + \varepsilon. \tag{5}$$

---

[2] The dependency on $\|\nabla\varphi\|_\infty$ in (2) ensures that (2) remains invariant after scaling φ by any positive factor.

In Theorem 7, the *single* simulator s satisfies (4) for *all* $\varphi \in \Phi$, and it simultaneously achieves indistinguishability ($s \in \mathsf{Ind}(g^*; T, \varepsilon)$) and computational efficiency ($s \in \mathsf{Time}(T')$). Therefore, (4) is stronger than the following guarantee akin to (1) in Theorem 6:

$$\max_{s \in \mathsf{Ind}(g^*;T,\varepsilon)} \mathsf{H}_\varphi(s) - \mathsf{H}_\varphi(g^*) \geq \min_{g \in \mathsf{Time}(T')} D_\varphi(g^* \| g) - \varepsilon \quad \text{for every } \varphi \in \Phi.$$

Here, the entropy maximizer s on the left (the *simulator*) and the divergence minimizer g on the right (the *approximator*) can be different and can change based on the choice of φ. By contrast, in (4), the single function s *simultaneously* plays the roles of the simulator and the approximator *simultaneously* for all $\varphi \in \Phi$. This gives a rigorous confirmation for the aforementioned informal intuition from the Multicalibration Theorem (Theorem 5) that there is a close correspondence between the best efficiently computable approximator g for g^* (with respect to any D_φ) and the highest-entropy simulator s that is indistinguishable from g^*.

The increase in complexity at (3) in Theorem 7 is polynomial in $L = 2^\ell$, a significant improvement over the doubly exponential dependence on ℓ in Theorem 5. We achieve this by focusing on a class Φ of functions φ whose subgradients $\nabla\varphi$ are efficiently computable (up to small ℓ_∞ error). This efficiency assumption is naturally satisfied by common entropy notions such as the Shannon entropy ($\varphi(v) = \sum_i v_i \ln v_i$), the min entropy ($\varphi(v) = \|v\|_\infty$), and the collision probability ($\varphi(v) = \sum_i v_i^2$, see Sect. 1.6). One caveat is that Theorem 7 also requires the subgradient $\nabla\varphi(v)$ to be bounded, which is not satisfied by the Shannon entropy when v is close to the boundary of the probability simplex Δ_L. However, this turns out to be a minor issue that can be easily addressed by slightly perturbing v away from the boundary of Δ_L (see Sect. 5).

In Theorem 9 (which we present shortly), we show that some efficiency assumption on the convex functions φ is necessary to avoid an exponential dependence on L (i.e. to avoid a doubly-exponential dependence on ℓ).

In contrast to Theorem 6, our Theorem 7 does not require φ to be differentiable or strictly convex. When φ is not differentiable, its subgradient at some $v \in \Delta_L$ may not be unique, and Theorem 7 holds as long as we use any fixed choice of subgradient to define the Bregman divergence D_φ (assuming that the subgradient is bounded and can be computed up to small ℓ_∞ error in time T). Therefore, our Theorem 7 encompasses both Theorems 2 and 3.

By (5), the function $s \in \mathsf{Ind}(g^*; T, \varepsilon) \cap \mathsf{Time}(T')$ in (4) satisfies

$$\mathsf{H}_\varphi(s) - \mathsf{H}_\varphi(g^*) \geq \max_{s' \in \mathsf{Ind}(g^*;T'',\varepsilon)} (\mathsf{H}_\varphi(s') - \mathsf{H}_\varphi(g^*)) - 2\varepsilon \quad \text{for every } \varphi \in \Phi,$$

where

$$T'' = O(T' + T_\Phi) = O(T') = O\left(\frac{(T + T_\Phi)\log L}{\varepsilon^2} + L \cdot \mathsf{poly}(1/\varepsilon, \log L)\right).$$

This means that the *single* indistinguishable function $s \in \mathsf{Ind}(g^*; T, \varepsilon)$ achieves comparable or higher entropy than *every* $s' \in \mathsf{Ind}(g^*; T'', \varepsilon)$ w.r.t. *every* entropy notion H_φ for $\varphi \in \Phi$. In this sense, s is a *universal simulator* for the pseudoentropy of g^*.

Combining the two directions (4) and (5) of Theorem 7 in a different order, we get that for every time bound $T > 0$ and every $g^* : \{0,1\}^n \to \Delta_L$, there exist $T' = O(T + T_\Phi)$,

$$T'' = O\left(\frac{(T' + T_\Phi)\log L}{\varepsilon^2} + L \cdot \mathsf{poly}(1/\varepsilon, \log L)\right)$$

and a function $s \in \mathsf{Ind}(g^*; T', \varepsilon) \cap \mathsf{Time}(T'')$ such that

$$\mathsf{D}_\varphi(g^* \| s) \leq \min_{g \in \mathsf{Time}(T)} \mathsf{D}_\varphi(g^* \| g) + 2\varepsilon \quad \text{for every } \varphi \in \Phi.$$

This means that the *single* low-complexity function $s \in \mathsf{Time}(T'')$ achieves comparable or better approximation error than *every* $g \in \mathsf{Time}(T)$ w.r.t. *every* divergence notion D_φ for $\varphi \in \Phi$. In the recent learning theory literature, a function s satisfying this property is termed an *omnipredictor* [12]. Our Theorem 7 thus recovers a result of [10] showing a construction of omnipredictors based on *calibrated multiaccuracy.* (See Sect. 1.5 for more discussion.)

Uniform Setting. In Theorem 8 below, we prove a uniform version of Theorem 7 that encompasses the uniform versions of Theorems 2 and 3 in [31,35] and extends Theorem 4 also to the uniform setting (which has not been explicitly achieved in prior work). In the uniform setting, instead of having a single function $g^* : \{0,1\}^n \to [L]$, we are interested in a family of functions $g^*_{n,L} : \{0,1\}^n \to [L]$ defined for varying choices of input length n and label space size L. Theorem 7 only allows us to construct an efficiently computable function s satisfying (4) separately for each choice of (n, L), so it does not guarantee the existence of a single uniform algorithm (e.g. a Turing machine) that efficiently computes s for all choices of (n, L). Our Theorem 8 addresses this limitation.

To state Theorem 8, we use terminology similar to the uniform versions of Theorems 2 and 3 in [31,35], where we formalize a uniform distinguisher as an efficient uniform oracle $\mathcal{A}$ that, when given sample access to $g^*, g : \{0,1\}^n \to \Delta_L$ on a distribution μ,[3] aims to output a function $f : \{0,1\}^n \to [-1,1]^L$ that witnesses the violation of Definition 1:

$$\mathbb{E}_{x \sim \mu}\langle g(x) - g^*(x), f(x)\rangle > \varepsilon. \tag{6}$$

We say g is $(\mathcal{A}, \varepsilon)$-*distinguishable* from g^* if (6) holds with high probability, and otherwise we say g is $(\mathcal{A}, \varepsilon)$-indistinguishable. We defer the formal definition to Definitions 6 and 8.

Our goal is to construct an $(\mathcal{A}, \varepsilon)$-indistinguishable function s satisfying (4) using an efficient uniform algorithm that takes $\mathcal{A}$ as a subroutine, and we

[3] This means that $\mathcal{A}$ can obtain random samples $(x, y, y^*) \in \{0,1\}^n \times [L] \times [L]$, where we first draw x from μ and then independently draw $y \sim g(x), y^* \sim g^*(x)$.

still want s to satisfy (4) simultaneously for all $\varphi \in \Phi$. To achieve this, we assume that the function class $\{\nabla\varphi\}_{\varphi\in\Phi}$ is *weakly-agnostically learnable*, which is trivially satisfied when Φ only contains a single φ whose subgradient $\nabla\varphi$ can be efficiently approximated (as in Theorems 2 and 3). Roughly speaking, we assume that there is a weak-agnostic learner $\mathcal{B}$ that, when given i.i.d. data points $(v_1, z_1), \ldots, (v_m, z_m) \in \Delta_L \times [-1, 1]^L$ drawn from an unknown distribution μ', can efficiently find $r : \Delta_L \to [-1, 1]$ such that $\mathbb{E}_{(v,z)\sim\mu'}\langle z, r(v)\rangle$ is comparable with or larger than $\sup_{\varphi\in\Phi} \mathbb{E}_{(v,z)\sim\mu'}\langle z, \nabla\varphi(v)\rangle$. We defer the formal definition to Definition 10.

Theorem 8 (Uniform version of Theorem 7; informal statement of Theorem 12). *Let Φ be a class of convex functions $\varphi : \Delta_L \to \mathbb{R}$, and let μ be an arbitrary distribution on $\{0,1\}^n$. Let $\mathcal{A}$ be an arbitrary distinguishing oracle, and let $\mathcal{B}$ be an ε_1-weak agnostic learner for $\{\nabla\varphi\}_{\varphi\in\Phi}$. We can use $\mathcal{A}$ and $\mathcal{B}$ as sub-routines to construct an efficient (uniform) algorithm $\mathcal{S}$ that, given sample access to $g^* : \{0,1\}^n \to \Delta_L$ on μ, with high probability outputs a (low-complexity) function s that is $(\mathcal{A}, \varepsilon)$-indistinguishable from g^*, and such that*

$$\mathsf{H}_\varphi(s) - \mathsf{H}_\varphi(g^*) \geq D_\varphi(g^* \| s) - \varepsilon_1 \quad \textit{for every } \varphi \in \Phi.$$

Theorem 8 encompasses the uniform versions of Theorems 2 and 3 in [31,35] by choosing the entropy notion H_φ accordingly. In the uniform versions of Theorems 2 and 3, we assume that every function s' with $\mathsf{H}_\varphi(s') - \mathsf{H}_\varphi(g^*)$ exceeding some threshold β is $(\mathcal{A}, \varepsilon)$-distinguishable from g^*. Under this assumption, since the function s from Theorem 8 is $(\mathcal{A}, \varepsilon)$-indistinguishable from g^*, it must hold that $\mathsf{H}_\varphi(s) - \mathsf{H}_\varphi(g^*) \leq \beta$, which implies that $\mathsf{D}_\varphi(g^* \| s) \leq \beta + \varepsilon_1$. In this case, the algorithm $\mathcal{S}$ from Theorem 8 becomes an efficient uniform algorithm that approximates g^* within low D_φ error, exactly as needed to prove the uniform versions of Theorems 2 and 3. We remark that the uniform versions of Theorems 2 and 3 in [31,35] also have the reverse direction that can also be extended to general entropy notions H_φ to get a uniform version of the reverse direction (5) of Theorem 7. We omit this result as this generalization can be proved straightforwardly using the same proof idea as its non-uniform counterpart.

Exponential Lower Bound. In our Theorem 7, we make a computational efficiency assumption about the convex functions $\varphi \in \Phi$ corresponding to the entropy notions considered in the theorem: we assume that the subgradient function $\nabla\varphi$ can be approximated by a circuit of size at most T_Φ for every $\varphi \in \Phi$. Correspondingly, the circuit complexity of the function s guaranteed by the theorem depends polynomially on T_Φ, in addition to the polynomial dependency on T, L and $1/\varepsilon$.

In this section, we prove the following lower-bound theorem showing that some complexity assumption on φ is necessary to avoid an exponential dependency on L in the circuit complexity of s. This lower bound holds even when Φ only contains a single convex function φ and there is only a single, extremely simple distinguisher f:

Theorem 9. *For every sufficiently large positive integer n, choosing $L = n$, there exist a distribution μ over $\{0,1\}^n$, a function $g^* : \{0,1\}^n \to \Delta_L$, an $O(n)$-sized circuit $f : \{0,1\}^n \to [-1,1]^L$, and a convex function $\varphi : \Delta_L \to \mathbb{R}$ with bounded subgradient $\nabla\varphi(v) \in [-1,1]^L$ for every $v \in \Delta_L$ that satisfy the following property. Let $s : \{0,1\}^n \to \Delta_L$ be an arbitrary function that is $(\{f\}, 0.05)$-indistinguishable from g^* (i.e. $s \in \mathsf{Ind}(g^*; \{f\}, 0.05)$) and satisfies the following inequality:*

$$\mathsf{H}_\varphi(s) \geq \mathsf{H}_\varphi(g^*) - 0.05. \tag{7}$$

Then s must have circuit complexity $\exp(\Omega(n)) = \exp(\Omega(L))$. Moreover, we can simply choose f to be the identity function: $f(x) = x \in \{0,1\}^n \subseteq [-1,1]^L$ for every $x \in \{0,1\}^n$.

We would like to remark that the condition (7) is a very mild assumption. In particular, by the nonnegativity of Bregman divergences, (7) is a necessary condition for the following guarantee of our main theorem (Theorem 7):

$$\mathsf{H}_\varphi(s) - \mathsf{H}_\varphi(g^*) \geq D_\varphi(g^* \| s) - 0.05. \tag{8}$$

Therefore, Theorem 9 implies an exponential lower bound on the circuit complexity of every function $s \in \mathsf{Ind}(g^*; \{f\}, 0.05)$ that satisfies the guarantee (4) of Theorem 7, even when Φ only contains a single function φ and there is only a single, extremely simple distinguisher f (the identity function).

There is no contradiction between the $\exp(\Omega(L))$ lower bound (Theorem 9) and the $\mathsf{poly}(L)$ upper bound (Theorem 7) on the circuit complexity of s because the upper bound assumes that the convex function φ has low complexity (specifically, its subgradient can be approximated by a circuit of size T_Φ). Thus, Theorem 9 shows that some assumptions on the complexity of φ are necessary for Theorem 7 to hold, even when Φ only contains a single convex function φ.

Our proof of Theorem 9 uses coding-theoretic ideas (specifically, the existence of a sufficiently large *design*) as well as a probabilistic counting argument. See Sect. 6 for the formal proof.

As a corollary of Theorem 9, we give an exponential lower bound on the circuit complexity for achieving multiaccuracy (i.e. indistinguishability) plus weight-restricted calibration, even for a single, extremely simple distinguisher f (the identity function) and a single weight function $\nabla\varphi : \Delta_L \to [-1,1]^L$. Consequently, this lower bound also holds for stronger notions such as calibrated multiaccuracy and multicalibration. See Sect. 1.5 for a more detailed discussion about these notions from the algorithmic fairness literature (multiaccuracy, weight-restricted calibration, calibrated multiaccuracy, and multicalibration).

Corollary 1. *For every sufficiently large positive integer n, choosing $L = n$, the same distribution μ, function g^*, distinguisher f and convex function φ from Theorem 9 have the following property. Let $s : \{0,1\}^n \to \Delta_L$ be an arbitrary function satisfying the following two conditions:*

$$|\mathbb{E}_{x\sim\mu}\langle s(x) - g^*(x), f(x)\rangle| \leq 0.05, \qquad \textbf{(Indistinguishability, a.k.a. multiaccuracy)}$$
$$\mathbb{E}_{x\sim\mu}\langle s(x) - g^*(x), \nabla\varphi(s(x))\rangle \leq 0.05. \qquad \textbf{(Weight-restricted calibration)}$$

Then s must have circuit complexity $\exp(\Omega(n)) = \exp(\Omega(L))$.

1.5 Proof Idea: Regularity Lemma with Weight-Restricted Calibration

We now give a high-level description of our proof idea for the first part of Theorem 7, i.e. the forward direction (4). Our proof of the reverse direction (5) follows the same ideas as in prior work [31,35].

Our idea is very simple in hindsight. As mentioned earlier, a key difference between our guarantee (4) from previous ones (e.g. (1)) is that the same function s appears on both sides of the inequality, playing the roles of the simulator and the approximator simultaneously. This makes it natural to calculate the diference between the two sides. Specifically, using the definitions of H_φ and D_φ in Definitions 2 and 3, we obtain the following identity, which is the central technical insight of our work:

$$\underbrace{\mathsf{H}_\varphi(s) - \mathsf{H}_\varphi(g^*)}_{\text{pseudoentropy gap}} \quad - \quad \underbrace{\mathsf{D}_\varphi(g^* \| s)}_{\text{hardness of approximating}} \quad = \langle g^* - s, \nabla\varphi \circ s \rangle. \tag{9}$$

In the right-hand side of (9) and for the rest of the paper, for any two functions $g, h : \{0,1\}^n \to \mathbb{R}^L$, we define their inner product as

$$\langle g, h \rangle := \mathbb{E}_{x\sim\mu} \langle g(x), h(x) \rangle,$$

where μ is the distribution on $\{0,1\}^n$ we fix in advance.

By (9), our goal (4) simplifies to constructing s satisfying

$$\langle s - g^*, \nabla\varphi \circ s \rangle \le \varepsilon \quad \text{for every } \varphi \in \Phi, \tag{10}$$

such that s is efficiently computable and indistinguishable from g^*. In Theorem 7, we assume that $\nabla\varphi$ is bounded in $[-1,1]^L$ and can be approximated within ℓ_∞ error $\varepsilon/4$ in non-uniform time T_Φ. Thus for every $\varphi \in \Phi$, there exists $r_\varphi : \Delta_L \to [-1,1]$ computable in non-uniform time T_Φ such that $\|r_\varphi - \nabla\varphi\|_\infty \le \varepsilon/4$. This gives a sufficient condition for (10):

$$\langle s - g^*, r_\varphi \circ s \rangle \le \varepsilon/2 \quad \text{for every } \varphi \in \Phi. \quad \textbf{(Weight-restricted calibration)} \tag{11}$$

As we will explain shortly, the condition (11) is termed *weight-restricted calibration* in the recent literature on algorithmic fairness. On the other hand, the requirement that s is indistinguishable from g^* (Definition 1) amounts to

$$|\langle s - g^*, f \rangle| \le \varepsilon \quad \text{for every } f \in \mathcal{F}, \quad \textbf{(Indistinguishability, a.k.a. multiaccuracy)} \tag{12}$$

where $\mathcal{F}$ denotes the class of functions $f : \{0,1\}^n \to [-1,1]^L$ computable in non-uniform time T. Again, as we will explain below, the indistinguishability condition (11) is termed *multiaccuracy* in the recent literature on algorithmic fairness.

The first half of Theorem 7 requires us to find a function $s \in \mathsf{Ind}(g^*; T, \varepsilon) \cap \mathsf{Time}(T')$ satisfying (4). Based on the our discussion above, the requirement $s \in \mathsf{Ind}(g^*; T, \varepsilon)$ is equivalent to (12), and a sufficient condition for (4) is given by (11). Thus our goal becomes finding $s \in \mathsf{Time}(T')$ satisfying both (11) and (12).

The structure of (11) and (12) points us to previous ideas about *regularity lemmas*. Specifically, the Complexity-Theoretic Regularity Lemma of Trevisan, Tulsiani, and Vadhan [30] and its extension to $L > 2$ in the Leakage Simulation Lemma of Jetchev and Pietrzak [23], allows us to construct $s \in \mathsf{Time}(T')$ that satisfies (12) alone. This result can be proved using a boosting algorithm. We start with a simple $s : \{0,1\}^n \to \Delta_L$ (e.g. $s(x)$ is the uniform distribution over $[L]$ for every $x \in \{0,1\}^n$). Whenever s does not satisfy (12), there exists a (low-complexity) $f \in \mathcal{F}$ that witnesses this violation, which we use to update s to reduce a nonnegative potential function by a significant amount. By the nonnegativity of the potential function, there can only be a bounded number of updates, after which s has to satisfy (12). Since each $f \in \mathcal{F}$ has non-uniform complexity at most T, each update increases the complexity of s only by a bounded amount, and since the number of total updates is also bounded, we can ensure that the final s belongs to $\mathsf{Time}(T')$. Following the work of Vadhan and Zheng [32] which proves a uniform version of the regularity lemma, we apply the classic Multiplicative Weights algorithm (a special case of Mirror Descent) to extend the boosting idea from [30] to general L (see Sects. 2.2 and 2.3).

A limitation of the complexity-theoretic regularity lemmas is that they only establish (12), but we need (11) and (12) simultaneously. The two conditions (11) and (12) look very similar, with both r_φ in (11) and f in (12) having bounded non-uniform complexity. The difference is that (11) is *circular*: the "distinguishing function" $r_\varphi \circ s$ that s tries to "fool" depends on the function s itself.

A key insight from the recent algorithmic fairness literature about *multicalibration* [13,15] is that the circularity in (11) does not incur any new major technical challenge: the exact same boosting idea from the Regularity Lemma allows us to construct $s \in \mathsf{Time}(T')$ satisfying both (11) and (12), which is exactly what we need to establish Theorem 7. We view condition (11) as an instantiation of *weight-restricted calibration*, as introduced by Gopalan, Kim, Singhal, and Zhao [13].[4] This is a relaxed version of the following condition called *calibration*:

$$\mathbb{E}_{x\sim\mu}[s(x) - g^*(x)|s(x)] \approx \mathbf{0}, \quad \textbf{(Calibration)} \tag{13}$$

where $\mathbf{0} \in \mathbb{R}^L$ is the zero vector. Indeed, calibration (13) is equivalent to

$$\langle s - g^*, r \circ s\rangle \approx 0 \quad \text{for } all r : \Delta_L \to [-1,1]^L, \quad \textbf{(Equivalent def. of calibration)} \tag{14}$$

where each $r : \Delta_L \to [-1,1]^L$ is termed a *weight function* [13]. The weight-restricted calibration condition (11) is a relaxation of (full) calibration (14) in

[4] They called it *weighted calibration* (see also [11]). We modify the terminology to more clearly convey that it is a weaker condition than calibration.

that it only considers a restricted family of weight functions $\{r_\varphi\}_{\varphi\in\Phi}$ instead of all weight functions (and it replaces "≈ 0" with "$\leq \varepsilon$").

As pointed out by Dwork, Lee, Lin, and Tankala [5], the indistinguishability condition (12) (previously studied as in the Complexity-Theoretic Regularity Lemma [30]) was rediscovered in the algorithmic fairness literature under the term *multiaccuracy* [15,25] and it is natural to ask whether stronger notions from the algorithmic fairness literature have implications in complexity theory and other domains where similar regularity lemmas are used (such as graph theory and cryptography). This question has been explored by many works in recent research [1,5,19]. Our work (especially the observation (9)) demonstrates the power of adding weight-restricted calibration (11) to the standard indistinguishability / multiaccuracy condition (12) guaranteed by the regularity lemma for generalizing and strenthening pseudoentropy characterizations.

The combination of multiaccuracy (12) and (full) calibration (13) (or (14)) is termed *calibrated multiaccuracy* in [10]. That work uses calibrated multiaccuracy to achieve omniprediction more efficiently than the *multicalibration*-based approach of [12] (we discuss multicalibration in the next paragraph). The notion of multiaccuracy (12) plus weight-restricted calibration (11) (as we use in our work) is weaker than calibrated multiaccuracy and suffices to ensure omniprediction in many cases, leading to further improved sample complexity and computational efficiency even when $L = 2$ [20,27]. Independent work [2,6] demonstrates the power of (variants of) calibrated multiaccuracy for other cryptographic, complexity-theoretic, and learning-theoretic applications (as we discussed in Sect. 1.2).

As mentioned earlier, the work of Casacuberta, Dwork, and Vadhan [1] uses *multicalibration* to establish a characterization for pseudo-min-entropy and pseudo-Shannon-entropy. Introduced by [15], multicalibration is the following much stronger condition than (11), (12) and (13) combined:

$$\mathbb{E}_{x\sim\mu}[\langle s(x) - g^*(x), f(x)\rangle | s(x)] \approx 0 \quad \text{for every } f \in \mathcal{F}. \quad \textbf{(Multicalibration)}$$

A contribution of our work is to show that multicalibration is an overkill for pseudoentropy characterizations and leads to the unnecessary doubly exponential dependence on ℓ in Theorem 5 (our Corollary 1 shows that this doubly exponential dependence cannot be avoided for multicalibration and even for the weaker notion of calibrated multiaccuracy). Based on our observation (9), the much weaker condition of multiaccuracy (12) plus weight-restricted calibration (11) is sufficient even for more general entropy notions H_φ, giving the improved polynomial dependence on $L = 2^\ell$ in Theorem 7.

1.6 Examples Beyond Shannon and Min Entropy

Our pseudoentropy characterization (Theorem 7) holds for a general family Φ of entropy notions. Here we give two examples of entropy notions beyond Shannon and min entropy.

Consider the following choice of φ with its corresponding Bregman divergence:

$$\varphi(v) = \|v\|_2^2 = \sum_{i\in[L]} v_i^2, \quad \mathsf{D}_\varphi(u\|v) = \|u-v\|_2^2 = \|u\|_2^2 + \|v\|_2^2 - 2\langle u, v\rangle. \tag{15}$$

To interpret the entropy and divergence notions from this choice of φ, let us consider a pair of jointly distributed random variables $(X,Y) \in \{0,1\}^n \times [L]$ with X drawn from a distribution μ over $\{0,1\}^n$, and define $g^* : \{0,1\}^n \to \Delta_L$ so that $g^*(x)$ is the conditional distribution of Y given $X = x$. In this case, the entropy notion H_φ is the negative conditional collision probability $\mathsf{CP}(g^*(X)|X)$ used, for example, in [3] for the analysis of hash functions:

$$\mathsf{H}_\varphi(g^*) = -\mathbb{E}_{x\sim\mu}[\varphi(g^*(x))] = -\mathsf{CP}(g^*(X)|X).$$

Here,

$$\mathsf{CP}(g^*(X)|X) := \Pr[Y' = Y],$$

where (X,Y') is identically distributed as (X,Y), and Y' is conditionally independent from Y given X.

By (15), for a fixed $g^* : \{0,1\}^n \to \Delta_L$, minimizing the Bregman divergence $\mathsf{D}_\varphi(g^*\|g)$ over $g : \{0,1\}^n \to \Delta_L$ corresponds to maximizing

$$2\langle g^*, g\rangle - \mathbb{E}_{x\sim\mu}\|g(x)\|_2^2 = 2\Pr[g^*(X) = g(X)] - \mathsf{CP}(g(X)|X), \tag{16}$$

where the first term $\Pr[g^*(X) = g(X)]$ is the prediction accuracy of g w.r.t. g^* (the same as in Theorem 2):

$$\Pr[g^*(X) = g(X)] := \Pr[Y = \hat{Y}],$$

where $X \sim \mu$, and conditioned on X, we independently draw $Y \sim g^*(X), \hat{Y} \sim g(X)$. The second term on the right-hand side of (16) can be viewed as a regularizer that encourages g to have lower collision probability (and thus higher entropy H_φ). Our characterization Theorem 7 implies that the best that an efficient g can do for this regularized optimization task is equivalent to the conditional pseudo-collision-probability of $g^*(X)$ given X (i.e., the pseudo / computational analogue of $\mathsf{CP}(g^*(X)|X)$).

Similarly, we can take

$$\varphi(v) = \|v\|_2 = \sqrt{\sum_i v_i^2}, \quad \mathsf{D}_\varphi(u\|v) = \frac{\|u\|_2\|v\|_2 - \langle u, v\rangle}{\|v\|_2}$$

to get an equivalence between maximzing the following objective over efficient g

$$\Pr[g(X) = g^*(X)]/\mathsf{CP}^{1/2}(g(X)|X),$$

and the conditional pseudo-square-root-collision-probability of $g^*(X)$ given X (i.e., the pseudo / computational analogue of $\mathsf{CP}^{1/2}(g^*(X)|X)$ used, for example, in [14] to construct statistically hiding commitments and statistical zero-knowledge arguments).

2 Preliminaries

For simplicity, we consider general and abstract vectors $g, h, f \in \mathbb{R}^L$ in this section. Later we will instantiate the vector g here as the function value $g(x) \in \Delta_L \subseteq \mathbb{R}^L$ (as in Definition 1) assigned to a specific input $x \in \{0,1\}^n$, and similarly instantiate the vector f here as the function value $f(x) \in [-1,1]^L$ of a distinguisher $f : \{0,1\}^n \to [-1,1]^L$ on a specific input $x \in \{0,1\}^n$.

2.1 Convex Analysis Basics

Let $\mathcal{G} \subseteq \mathbb{R}^L$ be a non-empty bounded convex set. Let $\varphi : \mathcal{G} \to \mathbb{R}$ be a convex function on $\mathcal{G}$. We say $h \in \mathbb{R}^L$ is a *subgradient* of φ at $g \in \mathcal{G}$ if

$$\varphi(g') - \varphi(g) \geq \langle g' - g, h\rangle \quad \text{for every } g' \in \mathcal{G},$$

or equivalently,

$$\langle g, h\rangle - \varphi(g) = \max_{g' \in \mathcal{G}}(\langle g', h\rangle - \varphi(g')). \tag{17}$$

The *convex conjugate* of φ, denoted by $\psi : \mathbb{R}^L \to \mathbb{R}$, is defined as follows:

$$\psi(h) := \sup_{g \in \mathcal{G}}(\langle g, h\rangle - \varphi(g)) \quad \text{for every } h \in \mathbb{R}^L. \tag{18}$$

By the boundedness of $\mathcal{G}$ and the convexity of φ, the supremum above is always well-defined (i.e., it is neither $+\infty$ nor $-\infty$). It is easy to verify that ψ is convex and closed.[5] The *Fenchel-Young divergence* $\Gamma_{\varphi,\psi} : \mathcal{G} \times \mathbb{R}^L \to \mathbb{R}$ is defined as follows:

$$\Gamma_{\varphi,\psi}(g, h) := \varphi(g) + \psi(h) - \langle g, h\rangle \geq 0 \quad \text{for every } g \in \mathcal{G} \text{ and } h \in \mathbb{R}^L.$$

The nonnegativity of the divergence follows immediately from the definition of ψ in (18). We will often omit the subscripts and simply write Γ in place of $\Gamma_{\varphi,\psi}$. By the characterization of subgradients in (17), for any $g \in \mathcal{G}$ and $h \in \mathbb{R}^L$,

$$h \text{ is a subgradient of } \varphi \text{ at } g \iff \Gamma(g, h) = 0 \implies g \text{ is a subgradient of } \psi \text{ at } h. \tag{19}$$

Note that the converse of the second implication is not generally true when φ is discontinuous at the boundary of $\mathcal{G}$. We say a pair $(g, h) \in \mathcal{G} \times \mathbb{R}^L$ is a *conjugate pair* w.r.t. (φ, ψ) if $\Gamma_{\varphi,\psi}(g, h) = 0$.

The sub-gradient of φ at any $g \in \mathcal{G}$ may not be unique (and it may not exist when g is at the boundary of $\mathcal{G}$). When we have a pre-determined choice $\nabla\varphi(g)$ among the subgradients, we define the *Bregman divergence* $D_\varphi(g' \| g)$ as follows:

$$\begin{aligned} D_\varphi(g' \| g) := \Gamma(g', \nabla\varphi(g)) &= \varphi(g') + \psi(\nabla\varphi(g)) - \langle g', \nabla\varphi(g)\rangle \\ &= \varphi(g') - \varphi(g) - \langle g' - g, \nabla\varphi(g)\rangle, \end{aligned}$$

[5] As standard terminology in convex analysis, we say ψ is *closed* if its epigraph $\{(h, y) \in \mathbb{R}^L \times \mathbb{R} : y \geq \psi(h)\}$ is closed (see e.g. [29]).

where the last equation uses the fact that $(g, \nabla\varphi(g))$ is a conjugate pair (by the equivalence in (19)):

$$0 = \Gamma(g, \nabla\varphi(g)) = \varphi(g) + \psi(\nabla\varphi(g)) - \langle g, \nabla\varphi(g)\rangle.$$

If we additionally assume that φ is closed (which holds, for example, when φ is continuous on a closed domain $\mathcal{G}$), the supremum in (18) can always be attained by some $g \in \mathcal{G}$. Moreover, it is a standard result that for a closed convex function φ, taking convex conjugate twice gives back the same function. That is, the closedness assumption of φ ensures that φ and ψ are convex conjugates of each other:

$$\psi(h) = \max_{g\in\mathcal{G}}(\langle g, h\rangle - \varphi(g)) \quad \text{for every } h \in \mathbb{R}^L, \tag{20}$$

$$\varphi(g) = \sup_{h\in\mathbb{R}^L}(\langle g, h\rangle - \psi(h)) \quad \text{for every } g \in \mathcal{G}. \tag{21}$$

In this case, by the characterization of subgradients in (17), for any $g \in \mathcal{G}$ and $h \in \mathbb{R}^L$, the following three statements are equivalent:

1. $\Gamma(g, h) = 0$, i.e., (g, h) is a conjugate pair;
2. h is a subgradient of φ at g;
3. g is a subgradient of ψ at h.

2.2 Mirror Descent

As in the previous section, we consider a non-empty bounded convex set $\mathcal{G} \subseteq \mathbb{R}^L$ and a convex function φ defined on it, with ψ being the convex conjugate of φ. Now we additionally assume that ψ is smooth:

Definition 4 (Smoothness). *For $\lambda \geq 0$ and a norm $\|\cdot\|$ on $\mathbb{R}^L$, we say a convex function $\psi : \mathbb{R}^L \to \mathbb{R}$ is* λ-smooth *w.r.t. $\|\cdot\|$ if for every $h_0, h \in \mathbb{R}^L$, letting g_0 be a subgradient of ψ at h_0, we have*

$$\psi(h) \leq \psi(h_0) + \langle g_0, h - h_0\rangle + \frac{\lambda}{2}\|h - h_0\|^2. \tag{22}$$

If a convex function $\psi : \mathbb{R}^L \to \mathbb{R}$ is λ-smooth, it is necessarily differentiable with the *subgradient* g_0 being the *gradient* at h_0, implying the uniqueness of the subgradient. We can thus uniquely define $\nabla\psi(h_0) := g_0$.

We additionally assume that φ is a closed function on the bounded domain $\mathcal{G}$ (and recall that ψ is the convex conjugate of φ). This ensures that $\nabla\psi(h) \in \mathcal{G}$ for every $h \in \mathbb{R}^L$ because the maximizer $g \in \mathcal{G}$ in (20) achieves $\Gamma(g, h) = 0$, and thus $\nabla\psi(h) = g \in \mathcal{G}$.

The Mirror Descent algorithm runs in iterations $k = 1, \ldots, K$, where each iteration k updates a conjugate pair $(g_k, h_k) \in \mathcal{G} \times \mathbb{R}^L$ to a new conjugate pair (g_{k+1}, h_{k+1}) given a signal vector $f \in \mathbb{R}^L$ as follows:

$$\begin{aligned} h_{k+1} &\leftarrow h_k - f; \\ g_{k+1} &\leftarrow \nabla\psi(h_{k+1}). \end{aligned} \tag{23}$$

The following standard lemma is central to analyzing mirror descent. It allows us to track the progress of the update from (g_k, h_k) to (g_{k+1}, h_{k+1}) using the nonnegative quantity $\Gamma(g^*, h_k)$ as a potential function for an arbitrary $g^* \in \mathcal{G}$. The lemma shows that the potential function $\Gamma(g^*, h_k)$ must significantly decrease if $\langle g_k - g^*, f\rangle$ is large relative to $\|f\|^2$.

Lemma 1 (Mirror Descent). *Let $\varphi : \mathcal{G} \to \mathbb{R}$ be a closed convex function on a bounded convex set $\mathcal{G} \subseteq \mathbb{R}^L$, and let $\psi : \mathbb{R}^L \to \mathbb{R}$ be its convex conjugate. Assume that ψ is λ-smooth w.r.t. norm $\|\cdot\|$ for some $\lambda \geq 0$. Assume conjugate pairs $(g_k, h_k), (g_{k+1}, h_{k+1}) \in \mathcal{G} \times \mathbb{R}^L$ satisfy (23) for some $f \in \mathbb{R}^L$. Then for every $g^* \in \mathcal{G}$,*

$$\Gamma(g^*, h_k) - \Gamma(g^*, h_{k+1}) \geq \langle g_k - g^*, f\rangle - \frac{\lambda}{2}\|f\|^2. \tag{24}$$

2.3 The Multiplicative Weights Algorithm

The Multiplicative Weights algorithm is a special case of Mirror Descent when we choose $\mathcal{G} = \Delta_L$ and choose φ to be the negative Shannon entropy

$$\varphi(g) := \sum_{y=1}^{L} g_y \ln g_y \leq 0 \quad \text{for every } g = (g_1, \ldots, g_L) \in \Delta_L. \tag{25}$$

Its convex conjugate ψ is the following function:

$$\psi(h) = \ln\left(\sum_{y=1}^{L} e^{h_y}\right) \quad \text{for every } h = (h_1, \ldots, h_L) \in \mathbb{R}^L. \tag{26}$$

The gradient of ψ is the softmax function:

$$\nabla\psi(h) = \mathsf{softmax}(h) := \frac{1}{\sum_{y=1}^{L} e^{h_y}}(e^{h_1}, \ldots, e^{h_L}) \in \Delta_L.$$

Each e^{h_y} is often interpreted as the (unnormalized) *weight* on label $y \in [L]$, and the softmax function normalizes these weights to a probability distribution over $[L]$. Thus the additive update on h_y in (23) becomes a multiplicative update on the weight e^{h_y}, hence the name multiplicative weights.

Lemma 2. *The function ψ in (26) is 1-smooth in $\|\cdot\|_\infty$. Moreover, the softmax function is a 1-Lipschitz multi-variate function from $\|\cdot\|_\infty$ to $\|\cdot\|_1$. That is, for every $h, \hat{h} \in \mathbb{R}^L$,*

$$\|\mathsf{softmax}(h) - \mathsf{softmax}(\hat{h})\|_1 \leq \|h - \hat{h}\|_\infty.$$

3 Regularity Lemma with Weight-Restricted Calibration

As we discuss in Sect. 1.5, the key to proving our main theorems (Theorems 7 and 8) is to establish an enhanced regularity lemma that allows us to construct a low complexity function $s : \{0,1\}^n \to \Delta_L$ satisfying both multiaccuracy (12) and weight-restricted calibration (11). We formally state and prove this result in both the non-uniform and uniform settings.

3.1 Non-Uniform Setting

Theorem 10 (Non-Uniform Regularity Lemma with Weight-Restricted Calibration). *Let $\mathcal{F}$ be a family of functions $f : \{0,1\}^n \to [-1,1]^L$ with circuit complexity at most $T_{\mathcal{F}}$, and let $\mathcal{R}$ be a family of functions $r : \Delta_L \to [-1,1]^L$ with circuit complexity at most $T_{\mathcal{F}}$. Define $T := T_{\mathcal{F}} + T_{\mathcal{R}}$. For every distribution μ on $\{0,1\}^n$, every $g^* : \{0,1\}^n \to \Delta_L$, and every $\varepsilon \in (0, 1/2)$, there exists a simulator $s : \{0,1\}^n \to \Delta_L$ such that*

1. *s has circuit complexity*
$$O\left(\frac{T \log L}{\varepsilon^2} + L \cdot \mathsf{poly}(1/\varepsilon, \log L)\right);$$
2. *s is indistinguishable from g^* w.r.t. $\mathcal{F}$:*
$$|\langle s - g^*, f\rangle| \le \varepsilon \quad \text{for every } f \in \mathcal{F};$$
3. *s satisfies ε-weight-restricted calibration w.r.t. $\mathcal{R}$:*
$$\langle s - g^*, r \circ s\rangle \le \varepsilon \quad \text{for every } r \in \mathcal{R}.$$

We prove Theorem 10 by constructing s using Algorithm 1 based on the Multiplicative Weights technique discussed in Sect. 2.3. In particular, our analysis tracks the Fenchel-Young divergence $\Gamma = \Gamma_{\varphi,\psi}$ defined by the negative Shannon entropy φ in (25) and its convex conjugate ψ in (26). For every $g : \{0,1\}^n \to \Delta_L$ and $h : \{0,1\}^n \to \mathbb{R}$, we define

$$\Gamma(g, h) := \mathbb{E}_{x\sim\mu}[\Gamma(g(x), h(x))].$$

For any norm $\|\cdot\|$ on $\mathbb{R}^L$ and any function $h : \{0,1\}^n \to \mathbb{R}^L$, we define

$$\|h\| := \max_{x\in\{0,1\}^n} \|h(x)\|.$$

As we will show, Theorem 10 follows from Lemmas 3 and 4 below.

Lemma 3. *Algorithm 1 terminates after $k = O((\log L)/\varepsilon^2)$ updates. Moreover, the output s produced by the algorithm satisfies*

$$\begin{aligned} |\langle s - g^*, f\rangle| &\le \varepsilon \quad \text{for every } f \in \mathcal{F}, \\ \langle s - g^*, r \circ s\rangle &\le \varepsilon \quad \text{for every } r \in \mathcal{R}. \end{aligned} \tag{27}$$

Lemma 4 (Controlling circuit complexity). *There exists an implementation of Algorithm 1 such that the following holds. Assume that the classes $\mathcal{F}$ and $\mathcal{R}$ both consist of functions with circuit complexity at most T. Then for every k, the circuit complexity of $\hat{g}_k$ is at most $(k+1)(T + L \cdot \mathsf{poly}(1/\varepsilon, \log L))$, and each coordinate of $\hat{g}_k(x)$ for every $x \in \{0,1\}^n$ is represented in binary format with $O(\log(L/\varepsilon))$ bits.*

Algorithm 1: Non-uniform Regularity Lemma with Weight-Restricted Calibration

Given: *A family* $\mathcal{F}$ *of functions* $f : \{0,1\}^n \to [-1,1]^L$ *and a family* $\mathcal{R}$ *of functions* $r : \Delta_L \to [-1,1]^L$; *a function* $g^* : \{0,1\}^n \to \Delta_L$; *parameter* $\varepsilon \in (0,1)$; *distribution* μ *on* $\{0,1\}^n$;

Initialize $h_0 : \{0,1\}^n \to \mathbb{R}^L$ as the constant function where $h_0(x) = (0,\dots,0)$ for every $x \in \{0,1\}^n$;

Compute $\hat{g}_0 : \{0,1\}^n \to \Delta_L$ s.t. $\|\hat{g}_0 - g_0\|_1 \le \varepsilon/10$, where $g_0 := \mathsf{softmax} \circ h_0$;

$k \leftarrow 0$;

`updated` $\leftarrow$ `TRUE`;

while `updated` **do**

  `updated` $\leftarrow$ `FALSE`;

  if *there exists* $f \in \mathcal{F} \cup (-\mathcal{F})$ *such that* $\langle \hat{g}_k - g^*, f\rangle > \varepsilon$ **then**

    $h_{k+1} \leftarrow h_k - \varepsilon f$;

    Compute $\hat{g}_{k+1} : \{0,1\}^n \to \Delta_L$ s.t. $\|\hat{g}_{k+1} - g_{k+1}\|_1 \le \varepsilon/10$, where $g_{k+1} := \mathsf{softmax} \circ h_{k+1}$;

    $k \leftarrow k+1$;

    `updated` $\leftarrow$ `TRUE`;

  if *there exists* $r \in \mathcal{R}$ *such that* $\langle \hat{g}_k - g^*, r \circ \hat{g}_k\rangle > \varepsilon$ **then**

    $h_{k+1} \leftarrow h_k - \varepsilon\, r \circ \hat{g}_k$;

    Compute $\hat{g}_{k+1} : \{0,1\}^n \to \Delta_L$ s.t. $\|\hat{g}_{k+1} - g_{k+1}\|_1 \le \varepsilon/10$, where $g_{k+1} := \mathsf{softmax} \circ h_{k+1}$;

    $k \leftarrow k+1$;

    `updated` $\leftarrow$ `TRUE`;

return $s := \hat{g}_k$;

3.2 Uniform Setting

To formally state and prove our enhanced regularity lemma in the uniform setting, we need to extend the notions of multiaccuracy (i.e. indistinguishability) and calibration to the uniform setting. To that end, we make the following definitions.

Definition 5 (Induced Distribution). *Let* μ *be a distribution over* $\{0,1\}^n$. *For a function* $g : \{0,1\}^n \to \Delta_L$, *we define* μ_g *as the distribution of* $(x,y) \in \{0,1\}^n \times [L]$ *where we first draw* x *from* μ *and then draw* y *from the distribution* $g(x)$. *For a pair of functions* $g, g^* : \{0,1\}^n \to \Delta_L$, *we define* μ_{g,g^*} *as the distribution of* $(x,y,y^*) \in \{0,1\}^n \times [L] \times [L]$, *where we first draw* x *from* μ, *and then independently draw* $y \sim g(x), y^* \sim g^*(x)$.

Definition 6 (Distinguishing Oracle). *An* (m,T)-distinguishing oracle *is a time-*T *algorithm* $\mathcal{A}$ *that takes* m *data points* $(x_1,y_1,y_1^*),\dots,(x_m,y_m,y_m^*) \in \{0,1\}^n \times [L] \times [L]$ *as input, and outputs (a succinct description of) a function* $f : \{0,1\}^n \to [-1,1]^L$ *such that given any* $x \in \{0,1\}^n$, *the function value* $f(x) \in [-1,1]^L$ *can be evaluated in time* T.

Definition 7 (Calibration Oracle). *An* (m, T)-calibration oracle *is a time-T algorithm $\mathcal{B}$ that takes m data points $(v_1, y_1, y_1^*), \dots, (v_m, y_m, y_m^*) \in \Delta_L \times [L] \times [L]$ as input, and outputs (a succinct description of) a function $r : \Delta_L \to [-1, 1]^L$ such that given any $v \in \Delta_L$, the function value $r(v) \in [-1, 1]^L$ can be evaluated in time T.*

Definition 8 (Distinguishability). *Let μ be a distribution over $\{0, 1\}^n$ and let $\mathcal{A}$ be an (m, T)-distinguishing oracle. For a pair of functions $g, g^* : \{0, 1\}^n \to \Delta_L$, we say g is* $(\mathcal{A}, \varepsilon, \delta)$-distinguishable *from g^* if with probability at least $1 - \delta$ over the random draw of m i.i.d. data points $(x_1, y_1, y_1^*), \dots, (x_m, y_m, y_m^*) \sim \mu_{g,g^*}$ taken as input by oracle $\mathcal{A}$, the output function $f : \{0, 1\}^n \to [-1, 1]^L$ satisfies*

$$\langle g - g^*, f \rangle > \varepsilon.$$

Correspondingly, we say g is $(\mathcal{A}, \varepsilon, \delta)$-indistinguishable *from g^* if it is not $(\mathcal{A}, \varepsilon, \delta)$-distinguishable.*

Definition 9 (Calibration). *Let μ be a distribution over $\{0, 1\}^n$ and let $\mathcal{B}$ be an (m, T) calibration oracle. For a pair of functions $g, g^* : \{0, 1\}^n \to \Delta_L$, we say g is* $(\mathcal{B}, \varepsilon, \delta)$-miscalibrated *w.r.t. g^* if with probability at least $1 - \delta$ over the random draw of m i.i.d. data points $(x_1, y_1, y_1^*), \dots, (x_m, y_m, y_m^*)$ from μ_{g,g^*}, given $(g(x_1), y_1, y_1^*), \dots, (g(x_m), y_m, y_m^*)$ as input to $\mathcal{B}$, the output function $r : \Delta_L \to [-1, 1]^L$ satisfies*

$$\langle g - g^*, r \circ g \rangle > \varepsilon.$$

Correspondingly, we say g is $(\mathcal{B}, \varepsilon, \delta)$-calibrated *w.r.t. g^* if it is not $(\mathcal{B}, \varepsilon, \delta)$-miscalibrated.*

In Definitions 8 and 9 above, the success probability of an oracle can be easily amplified by independent repetition. Suppose we have an oracle with success probability $\alpha > 0$. We can construct an oracle with success probability at least $1 - \delta$ by independently running the oracle $u = O(\alpha^{-1} \log(1/\delta))$ times to ensure that with probability at least $1 - \delta/2$, at least one of the runs is successful. We can then perform a simple test using $O(\varepsilon^{-2} \log(u/\delta)))$ additional fresh data points to select a successful run with probability at least $1 - \delta/2$ (with a constant-factor loss in ε). The overall success probability is at least $1 - \delta$ by the union bound.

We are now ready to state the enhanced regularity lemma in the uniform setting:

Theorem 11 (Uniform Regularity Lemma with Weight-Restricted Calibration). *Let $\mathcal{A}$ be an (m, T) distinguishing oracle and let $\mathcal{B}$ be an (m, T) calibration oracle. Then there exists a simulating algorithm $\mathcal{S}$ using $\mathcal{A}$ and $\mathcal{B}$ as subroutines such that for every $g^* : \{0, 1\}^n \to \Delta_L$ the following holds:*

1. *Given $\varepsilon, \delta \in (0, 1/2)$ as input, $\mathcal{S}$ addtionally takes $\mathsf{poly}(m, \log L, 1/\varepsilon, \log(1/\delta))$ i.i.d. data points from μ_{g^*} as input, and returns a function $s : \{0, 1\}^n \to \Delta_L$ in time $\mathsf{poly}(m, T, L, 1/\varepsilon, \log(1/\delta))$. Moreover, given an arbitrary $x \in \{0, 1\}^n$, the function value $s(x)$ can be evaluated also in time $\mathsf{poly}(m, T, L, 1/\varepsilon, \log(1/\delta))$.*

Algorithm 2: Uniform Regularity Lemma with Weight-Restricted Calibration

1 **Given:** *An (m,T)-distinguishing oracle $\mathcal{A}$ and an (m,T)-calibration oracle $\mathcal{B}$ on domain $\{0,1\}^n$ and label space $[L]$; access to i.i.d. data points drawn from μ_{g^*} for distribution μ on $\{0,1\}^n$ and function $g^* : \{0,1\}^n \to \Delta_L$; parameters $\varepsilon \in (0,1), m' \in \mathbb{Z}_{>0}$;*
2 Initialize $h_0 : \{0,1\}^n \to \mathbb{R}^L$ as the constant function where $h_0(x) = (0,\ldots,0)$ for every $x \in \{0,1\}^n$;
3 Compute $\hat{g}_0 : \{0,1\}^n \to \Delta_L$ s.t. $\|\hat{g}_0 - g_0\|_1 \le \varepsilon/20$, where $g_0 := \mathsf{softmax} \circ h_0$;
4 $k \leftarrow 0$;
5 **updated** $\leftarrow$ TRUE;
6 **while updated do**
7   **updated** $\leftarrow$ FALSE;
8   Draw fresh i.i.d. data points $(x_1, y_1^*), \ldots, (x_m, y_m^*)$ from μ_{g^*};
9   Draw $y_i \sim \hat{g}_k(x_i)$ independently for $i = 1, \ldots, m$;
10   Invoke distinguishing oracle $\mathcal{A}$ on data points (x_i, y_i, y_i^*) and obtain its output $f : \{0,1\}^n \to [-1,1]^L$;
11   Draw fresh i.i.d. data points $(x_1, y_1^*), \ldots, (x_{m'}, y_{m'}^*)$ from μ_{g^*} ;
12   **if** $\frac{1}{m'}\sum_{i=1}^{m'} \langle \hat{g}_k(x_i) - \mathbf{e}_{y_i^*}, f(x_i)\rangle > 3\varepsilon/4$ **then**
13         $h_{k+1} \leftarrow h_k - (\varepsilon/2) f$;
14   Compute $\hat{g}_{k+1} : \{0,1\}^n \to \Delta_L$ s.t. $\|\hat{g}_{k+1} - g_{k+1}\|_1 \le \varepsilon/20$, where $g_{k+1} := \mathsf{softmax} \circ h_{k+1}$;
15         $k \leftarrow k+1$;
16   **updated** $\leftarrow$ TRUE;
17   Draw fresh i.i.d. data points $(x_1, y_1^*), \ldots, (x_m, y_m^*)$ from μ_{g^*} ;
18   Draw $y_i \sim \hat{g}_t(x_i)$ independently for $i = 1, \ldots, m$;
19   Invoke calibration oracle $\mathcal{B}$ on data points $(\hat{g}_k(x_i), y_i, y_i^*)$ and obtain its output $r : \Delta_L \to [-1,1]^L$;
20   Draw fresh i.i.d. data points $(x_1, y_1^*), \ldots, (x_{m'}, y_{m'}^*)$ from μ_{g^*} ;
21   **if** $\frac{1}{m'}\sum_{i=1}^{m'} \langle \hat{g}_k(x_i) - \mathbf{e}_{y_i^*}, r(\hat{g}_k(x_i))\rangle > 3\varepsilon/4$ **then**
22         $h_{k+1} \leftarrow h_k - (\varepsilon/2)\, r \circ \hat{g}_k$;
23   Compute $\hat{g}_{k+1} : \{0,1\}^n \to \Delta_L$ s.t. $\|\hat{g}_{k+1} - g_{k+1}\|_1 \le \varepsilon/20$, where $g_{k+1} := \mathsf{softmax} \circ h_{k+1}$;
24         $k \leftarrow k+1$;
25   **updated** $\leftarrow$ TRUE;
26 **return** $s := \hat{g}_k$;

2. *With probability at least $1-\delta$ over the random draw of the data points, the output function s is simultaneously $(\mathcal{A}, \varepsilon, \Omega(\delta\varepsilon^2/\log L))$-indistinguishable from g^* and $(\mathcal{B}, \varepsilon, \Omega(\delta\varepsilon^2/\log L))$-calibrated w.r.t. g^*.*

We prove Theorem 11 using Algorithm 2 as the simulating algorithm $\mathcal{S}$ based on the same multiplicative weights idea as Algorithm 1. The difference is that instead of directly looking for f and r as in Lines 8 and 13 of Algorithm 1, we obtain them efficiently by invoking the oracles $\mathcal{A}$ and $\mathcal{B}$ at Lines 10 and 19 in

Algorithm 2. Recall that for $y \in [L]$, we use $\mathbf{e}_y$ to denote the standard basis vector whose y-th coordinate is one. This ensures that for every $v \in \Delta_L$, we have $\mathbb{E}_{y \sim v}[\mathbf{e}_y] = v$.

Theorem 11 follows immediately from the following lemma about Algorithm 2:

Lemma 5. *For every $\varepsilon \in (0, 1/2)$, there exist $\kappa = O((\log L)/\varepsilon^2), \delta' = \Omega(\delta/\kappa), m' = O((\log(1/\delta'))/\varepsilon^2)$ such that when we run Algorithm 2 with parameters (ε, m'), with probability at least $1 - \delta$, the following holds. Algorithm 2 terminates after $k \le \kappa$ updates and returns a function $s : \{0,1\}^n \to [-1,1]^L$ that is simultaneously $(\mathcal{A}, \varepsilon, \delta')$-indistinguishable from g^* and $(\mathcal{B}, \varepsilon, \delta')$-calibrated w.r.t. g^*. Also, Algorithm 2 runs in time $\mathsf{poly}(m, T, L, 1/\varepsilon, \log(1/\delta))$, and for every $x \in \{0,1\}^n$, the function value $s(x)$ can be evaluated in time $\mathsf{poly}(m, T, L, 1/\varepsilon, \log(1/\delta))$.*

4 Generalized and Unified Pseudoentropy Characterizations

In this section, we complete the proofs of our main results Theorems 7 and 8 using the enhanced regularity lemmas Theorems 10 and 11 from the previous section.

4.1 Non-Uniform Setting

Proof (Proof of Theorem 7). For $\varphi \in \Phi$, by our assumption that every $\nabla\varphi$ can be efficiently approximated within ℓ_∞ error $\varepsilon/4$, there exists a function $r_\varphi : \Delta_L \to [-1,1]^L$ computable in nonuniform time T_Φ such that

$$\|r_\varphi(v) - \nabla\varphi(v)\|_\infty \le \varepsilon/4 \quad \text{for every } v \in \Delta_L. \tag{28}$$

By (9), the guarantee (4) is equivalent to

$$\langle s - g^*, \nabla\varphi \circ s\rangle \le \varepsilon \quad \text{for every } \varphi \in \Phi.$$

By (28), a sufficient condition for the guarantee (4) is

$$\langle s - g^*, r_\varphi \circ s\rangle \le \varepsilon/2 \quad \text{for every } \varphi \in \Phi.$$

Now the first half of Theorem 7 (up to Equation (4)) follows directly from Theorem 10, where we set $\mathcal{R} := \{r_\varphi\}_{\varphi \in \Phi}, T_\mathcal{R} := T_\Phi$, set $\mathcal{F}$ to be the family of functions $f : \{0,1\}^n \to [-1,1]^L$ with circuit complexity at most T, set $T_\mathcal{F} := T$, and replace ε with $\varepsilon/2$.

To prove the second half of Theorem 7 (i.e. the reverse direction), we note the following identity for every $g, g^*, s : \{0,1\}^n \to \Delta_L$:

$$\mathsf{D}_\varphi(g^* \| g) = \mathsf{D}_\varphi(s \| g) + \langle s - g^*, \nabla\varphi \circ g\rangle + (\mathsf{H}_\varphi(s) - \mathsf{H}_\varphi(g^*)).$$

This identity follows immediately from the definitions of H_φ and D_φ in Definitions 2 and 3. By (28) and the fact that $\mathsf{D}_\varphi(s\|g) \geq 0$, we have

$$\begin{aligned}\mathsf{D}_\varphi(g^*\|g) &\geq \langle s - g^*, \nabla\varphi \circ g\rangle + (H_\varphi(s) - H_\varphi(g^*)) \\ &\geq \langle s - g^*, r_\varphi \circ g\rangle + (H_\varphi(s) - H_\varphi(g^*)) - \varepsilon/2. \end{aligned} \tag{29}$$

Since r_φ is computable in non-uniform time T_Φ, when g is computable in non-uniform time T, we have that $r_\varphi \circ g$ is computable in non-uniform time $O(T+T_\Phi)$, so for $s \in \mathsf{Ind}(g^*, O(T + T_\Phi), \varepsilon/2)$, we have

$$\langle s - g^*, r_\varphi \circ g\rangle \geq -\varepsilon/2.$$

Plugging this into (29) proves (5).

4.2 Uniform Setting

We need the following definition to give a formal statement of Theorem 8.

Definition 10 (Weak Agnostic Calibration Oracle). *Let μ be a fixed distribution on $\{0,1\}^n$. Let $\mathcal{R}$ be a family of functions $r : \Delta_L \to [-1,1]^L$, and let $\varepsilon_1, \varepsilon, \delta \in (0,1)$ be parameters. We say an (m,T)-calibration oracle $\mathcal{B}$ is an* $(\mathcal{R}, \varepsilon_1, \varepsilon, \delta)$-weak agnostic calibration oracle *if the following holds. For every pair $g, g^* : \{0,1\}^n \to \Delta_L$, if there exists $r \in \mathcal{R}$ such that*

$$\langle g - g^*, r \circ g\rangle > \varepsilon_1,$$

then with probability at least $1 - \delta$ over the random draw of m i.i.d. data points $(x_1, y_1, y_1^*), \ldots, (x_m, y_m, y_m^*) \sim \mu_{g,g^*}$, given $(g(x_1), y_1, y_1^*), \ldots, (g(x_m), y_m, y_m^*)$ as input to $\mathcal{B}$, the output function $r_{\mathsf{output}} : \Delta_L \to [-1,1]^L$ satisfies

$$\langle g - g^*, r_{\mathsf{output}} \circ g\rangle > \varepsilon.$$

The above definition is analogous to the standard definition of weak agnostic learning [8,24]. When $\mathcal{R}$ is a finite class, we can implement an $(\mathcal{R}, \varepsilon_1, \varepsilon_1/2, \delta)$-weak agnostic calibration oracle using $m = O(\varepsilon_1^{-2} \log(|\mathcal{R}|/\delta))$ data points by performing *empirical risk minimization (ERM)*, where we output $r \in \mathcal{R}$ that maximizes the empirical correlation:

$$\frac{1}{m}\sum_{i=1}^{m} \langle g(x_i) - \mathbf{e}_{y_i^*}, r(g(x_i))\rangle.$$

The following claim follows immediately from Definitions 9 and 10:

Claim. Let $\mathcal{R}$ be a family of functions $r : \Delta_L \to \mathbb{R}^L$ and $\mathcal{B}$ be an $(\mathcal{R}, \varepsilon_1, \varepsilon, \delta)$-weak agnostic calibration oracle. For functions $g, g^* : \{0,1\}^n \to \Delta_L$, if g is $(\mathcal{B}, \varepsilon, \delta)$-calibrated w.r.t. g^*, then

$$\langle g - g^*, r \circ g\rangle \leq \varepsilon_1 \quad \text{for every } r \in \mathcal{R}.$$

Theorem 12 (Formal statement of Theorem 8). *Consider domain $\{0,1\}^n$ and label space $[L]$. Let Φ be a family of convex functions $\varphi : \Delta_L \to \mathbb{R}$. For every $\varepsilon, \delta \in (0, 1/2)$, there exists $\delta' = \Omega(\delta\varepsilon^2/\log L)$ and a simulating algorithm $\mathcal{S}$ such that the following holds for every $g^* : \{0,1\}^n \to \Delta_L$ and oracles $\mathcal{A}$ and $\mathcal{B}$:*

1. *If $\mathcal{A}$ is an (m, T) distinguishing oracle and $\mathcal{B}$ is an (m, T) calibration oracle, then $\mathcal{S}$ takes $\mathsf{poly}(m, \log L, 1/\varepsilon, \log(1/\delta))$ i.i.d. data points from μ_{g^*} as input, uses $\mathcal{A}$ and $\mathcal{B}$ as oracles, and returns a function $s : \{0,1\}^n \to \Delta_L$ in time $\mathsf{poly}(m, T, L, 1/\varepsilon, \log(1/\delta))$. Moreover, given an arbitrary $x \in \{0,1\}^n$, the function value $s(x)$ can be evaluated also in time $\mathsf{poly}(m, T, L, 1/\varepsilon, \log(1/\delta))$.*
2. *If in addition $\mathcal{B}$ is an $(\{\nabla\varphi\}_{\varphi\in\Phi}, \varepsilon_1, \varepsilon, \delta')$ weak agnostic calibration oracle for some $\varepsilon_1 > 0$, then with probability at least $1 - \delta$ over the random draw of the input data points, the output function s is $(\mathcal{A}, \varepsilon, \delta')$-indistinguishable from g^* and satisfies*

$$H_\varphi(s) - H_\varphi(g^*) \geq D_\varphi(g^* \| s) - \varepsilon_1 \quad \text{for every } \varphi \in \Phi. \tag{30}$$

Proof. By (9), the guarantee (30) is equivalent to

$$\langle s - g^*, \nabla\varphi \circ s \rangle \leq \varepsilon_1 \quad \text{for every } \varphi \in \Phi.$$

The theorem now follows directly from Theorem 11 and Sect. 4.2, where we choose $\mathcal{R} = \{\nabla\varphi\}_{\varphi\in\Phi}$.

5 Handling Unbounded Subgradients

Our Theorem 7 requires the assumption that the subgradient $\nabla\varphi$ is bounded. This assumption is not satisfied by the Shannon entropy, where $\varphi(v) = \sum v_i \ln v_i$. In this case, $\nabla\varphi(v) = (\ln(v_1), \ldots, \ln(v_L))$ becomes unbounded when some v_i approaches zero. We show that this can be easily fixed using the following more general theorem than Theorem 7. Here, we consider an arbitrary transformation $\sigma_\varphi : \Delta_L \to \Delta_L$ associated with each $\varphi \in \Phi$, and Theorem 7 is the special case when these transformations σ_φ are the identity function. We will later choose these transformations so that the subgradient $\nabla\varphi(\sigma_\varphi(v))$ at the transformed point $\sigma_\varphi(v)$ is bounded, even when $\nabla\varphi(v)$ may not be bounded.

Theorem 13. *Let $T > 0$ be a time bound and let $\varepsilon \in (0, 1)$ be an error parameter. Let Φ be a family of convex functions $\varphi : \Delta_L \to \mathbb{R}$. For every $\varphi \in \Phi$, let $\sigma_\varphi : \Delta_L \to \Delta_L$ be an arbitrary transformation. Assume that given $v \in \Delta_L$, the transformed subgradient $\nabla\varphi(\sigma_\varphi(v))$ is bounded in $[-1, 1]^L$ and can be computed to ℓ_∞ accuracy $\varepsilon/4$ in nonuniform time T_Φ, for every $\varphi \in \Phi$. Then there exists*

$$T' = O\left(\frac{(T + T_\Phi)\log L}{\varepsilon^2} + L \cdot \mathsf{poly}(1/\varepsilon, \log L)\right) \tag{31}$$

such that for every $g^* : X \to \Delta_L$*, there exists* $s \in \mathsf{Ind}(g^*; T, \varepsilon) \cap \mathsf{Time}(T')$ *such that*

$$\mathsf{H}_\varphi(\sigma_\varphi \circ s) - \mathsf{H}_\varphi(g^*) \geq D_\varphi(g^* \| \sigma_\varphi \circ s) - \varepsilon \quad \text{for every } \varphi \in \Phi. \tag{32}$$

Conversely, for every $T > 0$*, there exists* $T' = O(T + T_\Phi)$ *such that for every* $g^* : X \to \Delta_L$ *and every* $\varphi \in \Phi$*,*

$$\max_{s \in \mathsf{Ind}(g^*; T', \varepsilon/2)} (\mathsf{H}_\varphi(s) - \mathsf{H}_\varphi(g^*)) \leq \min_{g \in \mathsf{Time}(T)} \mathsf{D}_\varphi(g^* \| \sigma_\varphi \circ g) + \varepsilon. \tag{33}$$

Theorem 13 can be proved in the exact same way as Theorem 7 using the enhanced regularity lemma Theorem 10, and similarly, we can prove a generalized version of Theorem 12 using Theorem 11 to handle unbounded subgradients in the uniform setting.

The advantage of using Theorem 13 is that it only requires $\nabla\varphi(\sigma_\varphi(v))$ to be bounded after the transformation $v \mapsto \sigma_\varphi(v)$. The challenge, however, is that while (32) is stated for the transformed $\sigma_\varphi \circ s$, Theorem 13 only ensures that the un-transformed s belongs to $\mathsf{Ind}(g^*; T, \varepsilon) \cap \mathsf{Time}(T')$. This mis-alignment between s and $\sigma_\varphi \circ s$ also appears in the reverse direction (33) where we minimize the divergence of the transformed $\sigma_\varphi \circ g$ subject to the un-transformed g being in $\mathsf{Time}(T)$. Below we show how to address this mis-alignment challenge for the Shannon entropy by choosing the transformation σ_φ appropriately.

For the (negative) Shannon entropy φ in (25), define $\sigma_\varphi(v) = (1 - \varepsilon)v + \varepsilon u$, where $u = (1/L, \dots, 1/L)$ is the uniform distribution and $\varepsilon \in (0, 1/2)$. Intuitively, this transformation perturbs v away from the boundary of Δ_L. We now have $\|\nabla\varphi(\sigma_\varphi(v))\|_\infty \leq \ln(L/\varepsilon)$, so the boundedness assumption of Theorem 13 is satisfied after a multiplicative scaling of $1/\ln(L/\varepsilon)$. Moreover, we have the following implication connecting $\sigma_\varphi \circ s$ with s that addresses the mis-alignment challenge:

$$s \in \mathsf{Ind}(g^*; T, \varepsilon) \cap \mathsf{Time}(T') \Longrightarrow \sigma_\varphi \circ s \in \mathsf{Ind}(g^*; T, 3\varepsilon) \cap \mathsf{Time}(O(T' \,\mathsf{polylog}(L/\varepsilon))).$$

Indeed, it is clear that $\|\sigma_\varphi(v) - v\|_1 \leq 2\varepsilon$, so $s \in \mathsf{Ind}(g^*; T, \varepsilon)$ implies that $\sigma_\varphi \circ s \in \mathsf{Ind}(g^*; T, 3\varepsilon)$. Also, given that s can be computed in circuit complexity T', it is clear that $\sigma_\varphi \circ s$ can be computed in circuit complexity $O(T' \,\mathsf{polylog}(L/\varepsilon))$. We can similarly address the mis-alignment challenge in the reverse direction (33) using the following connection between $\sigma_\varphi \circ g$ and g:

$$\mathsf{D}_\varphi(g^* \| \sigma_\varphi \circ g) \leq \mathsf{D}_\varphi(g^* \| g) + O(\varepsilon),$$

which holds because for every $v^*, v \in \Delta_L$,

$$\mathsf{D}_\varphi(v^* \| \sigma_\varphi(v)) = \sum_i v_i^* \ln \frac{v_i^*}{\sigma_\varphi(v_i)} \leq \sum_i v_i^* \ln \frac{v_i^*}{(1-\varepsilon)v_i} = \mathsf{D}_\varphi(v^* \| v) + \ln \frac{1}{1-\varepsilon} \leq \mathsf{D}_\varphi(v^* \| v) + O(\varepsilon).$$

6 Exponential Lower Bound for a Particular Entropy Notion

We prove Theorem 9 and Corollary 1 in this section. We need the following helper lemma:

Lemma 6. *[[7]] Define $\alpha = 1/16$. Let n be a sufficiently large positive integer. Then there exist $m = \exp(\Omega(n))$ subsets $S_1, \ldots, S_m \subseteq [n] := \{1, \ldots, n\}$ such that*

1. $|S_i| \geq \alpha n$ *for every* $i = 1, \ldots, m$;
2. $|S_i \cap S_j| \leq 2\alpha^2 n$ *for every distinct* $i, j \in \{1, \ldots, m\}$;
3. $|S_i|$ *is even for every* $i = 1, \ldots, m$.

This lemma can be proved by a natural argument using the probabilistic method (see e.g. Problem 3.2 of [33]).

Acknowledgments. LH was supported by the Simons Foundation Collaboration on the Theory of Algorithmic Fairness and the Harvard Center for Research on Computation and Society. SV was supported by a Simons Investigators Award.

Disclosure of Interests. The authors have no competing interests to declare that are relevant to the content of this article.

References

1. Casacuberta, S., Dwork, C., Vadhan, S.: Complexity-theoretic implications of multicalibration. In: Proceedings of the 56th Annual ACM Symposium on Theory of Computing, STOC 2024, pp. 1071–1082, New York, NY, USA, 2024. Association for Computing Machinery
2. Casacuberta, S., Gopalan, P., Kanade, V., Reingold, O.: How global calibration strengthens multiaccuracy. arXiv preprint arXiv:2504.15206, 2025
3. Chung, K.-M., Mitzenmacher, M., Vadhan, S.: Why simple hash functions work: exploiting the entropy in a data stream. Theory Comput. **9**(30), 897–945 (2013)
4. Dodis, Y., Ostrovsky, R., Reyzin, L., Smith, A.: Fuzzy extractors: How to generate strong keys from biometrics and other noisy data. SIAM J. Comput. **38**(1), 97–139 (2008)
5. Dwork, C., Lee, D., Lin, H., Tankala, P.: From pseudorandomness to multi-group fairness and back. In: Neu, G., Rosasco, L., (eds.), Proceedings of Thirty Sixth Conference on Learning Theory, volume 195 of Proceedings of Machine Learning Research, pp. 3566–3614. PMLR, 12–15 July 2023
6. Dwork, C., Tankala, P.: Personal communication, 2025. June 2025
7. Erdös, P., Frankl, P., Füredi, Z.: Families of finite sets in which no set is covered by the union of others. Israel J. Math. **51**(1), 79–89 (1985)
8. Feldman, V.: Distribution-specific agnostic boosting. In: Yao, A.C.-C, (ed.), Innovations in Computer Science - ICS 2010, Tsinghua University, Beijing, China, 5–7 January 2010. Proceedings, pp. 241–250. Tsinghua University Press, 2010
9. Goldreich, O., Levin, L.A.: A hard-core predicate for all one-way functions. In: Proceedings of the Twenty-First Annual ACM Symposium on Theory of Computing, STOC '89, pp. 25–32, New York, NY, USA, 1989. Association for Computing Machinery
10. Gopalan, P., Hu, L., Kim, M.P., Reingold, O., Wieder, U.: Loss minimization through the lens of outcome indistinguishability. In: Kalai, Y.T. (ed.), 14th Innovations in Theoretical Computer Science Conference (ITCS 2023), volume 251 of Leibniz International Proceedings in Informatics (LIPIcs), pp. 60:1–60:20, Dagstuhl, Germany, 2023. Schloss Dagstuhl – Leibniz-Zentrum für Informatik

11. Gopalan, P., Hu, L., Rothblum, G.N.: On computationally efficient multi-class calibration. In: Agrawal, S., Roth, A. (eds.), Proceedings of Thirty Seventh Conference on Learning Theory, volume 247 of Proceedings of Machine Learning Research, pp. 1983–2026. PMLR, 30 Jun–03 Jul 2024
12. Gopalan, P., Kalai, A. T., Reingold, O., Sharan, V., Wieder, U.: Omnipredictors. In: Braverman, M. (ed.), 13th Innovations in Theoretical Computer Science Conference (ITCS 2022), volume 215 of Leibniz International Proceedings in Informatics (LIPIcs), pp. 79:1–79:21, Dagstuhl, Germany, 2022. Schloss Dagstuhl – Leibniz-Zentrum für Informatik
13. Gopalan, P., Kim, M.P., Singhal, M.A., Zhao, S.: Low-degree multicalibration. In: Loh, P.L., Raginsky, M. (eds.), Proceedings of Thirty Fifth Conference on Learning Theory, volume 178 of Proceedings of Machine Learning Research, pp. 3193–3234. PMLR, 02–05 July 2022
14. Haitner, I., Nguyen, M.H., Ong, S.J., Reingold, O., Vadhan, S.: Statistically hiding commitments and statistical zero-knowledge arguments from any one-way function. SIAM J. Comput. **39**(3), 1153–1218 (2009)
15. Hébert-Johnson, U., Kim, M., Reingold, O., Rothblum, G.: Multicalibration: calibration for the (Computationally-identifiable) masses. In: Dy, J., Krause, A. (eds.), Proceedings of the 35th International Conference on Machine Learning, volume 80 of Proceedings of Machine Learning Research, pp. 1939–1948. PMLR, 10–15 July 2018
16. Holenstein, T.: Key agreement from weak bit agreement. In: Proceedings of the Thirty-Seventh Annual ACM Symposium on Theory of Computing, STOC '05, pp. 664–673, New York, NY, USA, 2005. Association for Computing Machinery
17. Håstad, J., Impagliazzo, R., Levin, L. A., Luby, M.: A pseudorandom generator from any one-way function. SIAM J. Comput. **28**(4), 1364–1396 (1999)
18. Hsiao, C.Y., Lu, C.J., Reyzin, L.: Conditional computational entropy, or toward separating pseudoentropy from compressibility. In: Naor, M. (eds.) Advances in Cryptology - EUROCRYPT 2007. EUROCRYPT 2007. LNCS, vol. 4515. Springer, Berlin, Heidelberg (2007). https://doi.org/10.1007/978-3-540-72540-4_10
19. Hu, L., Livni-Navon, I., Reingold, O.: Generative models of huge objects. In: Ta-Shma, A. (ed.), 38th Computational Complexity Conference (CCC 2023), volume 264 of Leibniz International Proceedings in Informatics (LIPIcs), pp. 5:1–5:20, Dagstuhl, Germany, 2023. Schloss Dagstuhl – Leibniz-Zentrum für Informatik
20. Hu, L., Tian, K., Yang, C.: Omnipredicting single-index models with multi-index models. In: Proceedings of the 57th Annual ACM Symposium on Theory of Computing, STOC '25, pp. 1762–1773, New York, NY, USA, 2025. Association for Computing Machinery
21. Hu, L., Vadhan, S.: Generalized and unified equivalences between hardness and pseudoentropy. arXiv preprint arXiv:2507.05972, 2025
22. Impagliazzo, R.: Hard-core distributions for somewhat hard problems. In: Proceedings of IEEE 36th Annual Foundations of Computer Science, pp. 538–545, 1995
23. Jetchev, D., Pietrzak, K.: How to fake auxiliary input. In: Lindell, Y. (eds.) Theory of Cryptography. TCC 2014. LNCS, vol. 8349, pp. 566–590. Springer, Berlin, Heidelberg (2014). https://doi.org/10.1007/978-3-642-54242-8_24
24. Kalai, A.T., Mansour, Y., Verbin, E.: On agnostic boosting and parity learning. In: Proceedings of the Fortieth Annual ACM Symposium on Theory of Computing, STOC '08, pp. 629–638, New York, NY, USA, 2008. Association for Computing Machinery

25. Kim, M.P., Ghorbani, A., Zou, J.: Multiaccuracy: black-box post-processing for fairness in classification. In: Proceedings of the 2019 AAAI/ACM Conference on AI, Ethics, and Society, AIES '19, pp. 247–254, New York, NY, USA, 2019. Association for Computing Machinery
26. Marcussen, C., Putterman, A., Vadhan, S.: Characterizing the distinguishability of product distributions through multicalibration. arXiv preprint arXiv:2412.03562, 2024
27. Okoroafor, P., Kleinberg, R., Kim, M.P.: Near-optimal algorithms for omniprediction. arXiv preprint arXiv:2501.17205, 2025
28. Reingold, O., Trevisan, L., Tulsiani, M., Vadhan, S.: Dense subsets of pseudorandom sets. In: Proceedings of the 2008 49th Annual IEEE Symposium on Foundations of Computer Science, FOCS '08, pp. 76–85, USA, 2008. IEEE Computer Society
29. Rockafellar, R.T.: Convex Analysis, vol. 28. Princeton university press, Princeton, 1997
30. Trevisan, L., Tulsiani, M., Vadhan, S.: Regularity, boosting, and efficiently simulating every high-entropy distribution. In: Proceedings of the 2009 24th Annual IEEE Conference on Computational Complexity, CCC '09, pp. 126–136, USA, 2009. IEEE Computer Society
31. Vadhan, S., Zheng, C.J.: Characterizing pseudoentropy and simplifying pseudorandom generator constructions. In: Proceedings of the Forty-Fourth Annual ACM Symposium on Theory of Computing, STOC '12, pp. 817–836, New York, NY, USA, 2012. Association for Computing Machinery
32. Vadhan, S., Zheng, C.J.: A uniform min-max theorem with applications in cryptography. In: Canetti, R., Garay, J.A. (eds.) Advances in Cryptology – CRYPTO 2013. CRYPTO 2013. LNCS, vol. 8042, pp. 93–110. Springer, Berlin, Heidelberg (2013). https://doi.org/10.1007/978-3-642-40041-4_6
33. Vadhan, S.P.: Pseudorandomness. Found. Trends® Theor. Comput. Sci. **7**(1–3), 1–336 (2012)
34. Yao, A.C.: Theory and application of trapdoor functions. In: 23rd Annual Symposium on Foundations of Computer Science (sfcs 1982), pp. 80–91, 1982
35. Zheng, J.: A Uniform Min-Max Theorem and Characterizations of Computational Randomness. PhD thesis, Harvard University, 2014

Special Genera of Hermitian Lattices and Applications to HAWK

Guilhem Mureau(✉)

Univ Bordeaux, CNRS, Inria, Bordeaux INP, IMB, UMR 5251, Talence, France
guilhem.mureau@math.u-bordeaux.fr

Abstract. In its decisional form, the module-Lattice Isomorphism Problem (decision module-LIP) has received first attention in [12]. The authors gave a polynomial-time algorithm to distinguish spinor genera within the genus of a quadratic binary $\mathcal{O}_F$-lattice, assuming that $\mathcal{O}_F$ is a principal ideal domain. However, this algorithm would not impact cryptographic schemes based on decision module-LIP for lattices such as those employed in HAWK [5], *i.e.*, for binary $\mathcal{O}_K$-lattices equipped with a Hermitian form (with K a cyclotomic number field). Motivated by HAWK's framework, we investigate a concept that serves as an analogue of the spinor genus for Hermitian lattices, called special genus. This notion was studied by Shimura [20] who provided a complete set of invariants for describing special genera. Building on this result, we propose an algorithm to determine whether two Hermitian lattices belong to the same special genus. Specifically for HAWK's lattice and siblings, our algorithm runs in classical polynomial-time. Nevertheless we provide numerical evidence suggesting that the ability to distinguish special genera does not, in practice, constitute a significative advantage for solving decision module-LIP.

Introduction

The primary motivation for this work arises from a recent problem in lattice-based cryptography, namely the module-Lattice Isomorphism Problem (module-LIP). First introduced in [5], it is employed as a security assumption for the signature scheme and NIST candidate HAWK. It can be described informally as follows: Given the ring of integers $\mathcal{O}_F$ of a number field F and two $\mathcal{O}_F$-lattices that are *isomorphic* (*i.e.*, such that there exists a distance-preserving F-linear map that transforms one into the other), the search variant of module-LIP — the one related to HAWK's security— asks to compute such a map. In contrast, [12] investigated the decisional variant of module-LIP which entails determining if two given $\mathcal{O}_F$-lattices are isomorphic. Although this variant of module-LIP has not yet been employed for cryptographic schemes, van Woerden and Ducas built schemes based on the decisional form of the (plain) Lattice Isomorphism Problem (for Euclidean lattices and called dLIP, see [6]) which may be adapted to lattices over number fields one day.

B. Applebaum and H. Lin (Eds.): TCC 2025, LNCS 16271, pp. 289–317, 2026.
https://doi.org/10.1007/978-3-032-12290-2_10

Isomorphic lattices share several properties, such as their volume or minimal distances, and numerous algebraic invariants are also preserved under isometry. Lattices sharing these invariants are said to be in the same *genus*. However, the genus does not constitute a complete set of invariants for the isometry relation, that is, isomorphic lattices belong to the same genus but the converse does not hold in general. In [12], Ling, Liu and Mendelsohn initiated an algorithmic investigation into finer invariants beyond the genus, namely into *spinor genera*, and explored their potential applications to solve decision module-LIP. Building on results of Earnest and Estes [7], the authors proposed a quantum algorithm to distinguish spinor genera among the genus of a rank-2 *quadratic* $\mathcal{O}_F$-lattice, assuming that $\mathcal{O}_F$ is a principal ideal domain. However, as noted by the authors, this algorithm does not apply to decision module-LIP for *Hermitian* rank-2 lattices over cyclotomic fields, such as those used in [5]. Specifically, in HAWK, one considers $\mathcal{O}_K^2$, where $K = \mathbb{Q}(\zeta_m)$ is a cyclotomic field whose conductor is a power-of-two ($m \in \{512, 1024, 2048\}$), and it is endowed with the Hermitian form $\Phi\left(\begin{smallmatrix} x \\ y \end{smallmatrix}\right) = x\overline{x} + y\overline{y}$.

We emphasize that the notion of spinor genus is specific to quadratic lattices, *i.e.*, to lattices equipped with a quadratic form. Therefore the question of whether there exists similar computable invariants for (rank-2) Hermitian lattices was left open.

Contributions. We consider for the first time the *special genus* as a novel invariant for the decisional variant of module-LIP (instantiated on Hermitian lattices). Originally introduced by Shimura in [20], the special genus is specific to Hermitian lattices and, similarly to the spinor genus, it serves as an intermediate classification between the genus and isometry classes (see Fig. 1).

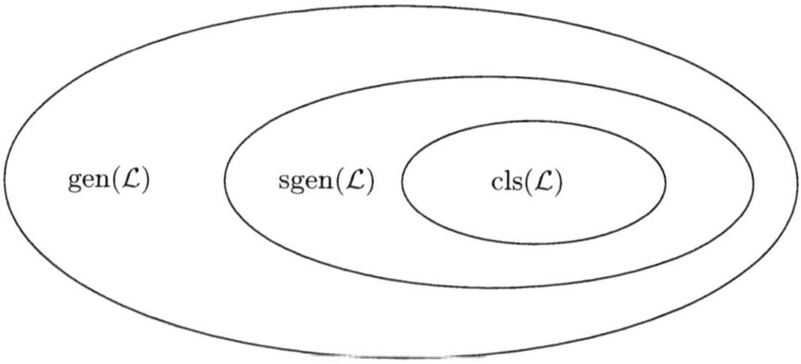

Fig. 1. The special genus of $\mathcal{L}$ fits between its genus and isometry class.

Thanks to Shimura's classification (see Theorem 2.8 and Corollary 2.11), we provide a necessary and sufficient set of conditions for determining whether two Hermitian lattices belong to the same special genus. This leads to the development of Algorithm 1, which takes as input two (pseudo-)bases of Hermitian lattices (of arbitrary rank) in the same genus, and decides if the lattices lie in the same special genus. The latter relies on a technical lemma (see Lemma 1.32) which prevents us to fully provide the time complexity of the algorithm. However for a large family of Hermitian lattices including the one we are interested in for cryptographic applications, this assumption is not needed (see Remark 3.4) and classical polynomial-time complexity is achieved.

The core of this paper concerns the use of the special genus in solving decision module-LIP. Due to the definition of the problem (see Definition 3.2), Algorithm 1 is however not suited to module-LIP's framework. To be concrete, Algorithm 1 requires pseudo-bases of Hermitian lattices as input whereas in a module-LIP instance, only pseudo-Gram matrices are known. Moreover working with pseudo-Gram matrices instead of pseudo-bases induces a lack of information and makes the computation of the special genus invariants even more difficult. Therefore we restrict ourselves to a family of Hermitian lattices which are still of interest for cryptographic applications, and for which the invariants are easier to compute. When restricting to these lattices, we are able to state Algorithm 2, whose complexity is provable. Our main contribution can be summarized as follows whereas a full statement can be found in Corollary 3.5.

Theorem (Main, Informal). For HAWK's lattice $\mathcal{O}_K^2$ over a cyclotomic number field K, there is a polynomial-time algorithm which takes as input a (pseudo-)Gram matrix corresponding to a Hermitian lattice $\mathcal{M}$, and decides whether $\mathcal{M}$ belongs to the special genus of $\mathcal{O}_K^2$.

Particular attention is adressed to the case of rank-2 Hermitian lattices, as it contains HAWK's lattice $\mathcal{H} = \mathcal{O}_K^2$. Namely in Sect. 3 we obtain estimates on the number of isomorphism classes within the genus of $\mathcal{H}$ (resp. whithin a special genus of $\mathcal{H}$). Our computations show that the special genus is indeed finer than the genus, reducing the number of classes to distinguish by a factor $2^{\Omega(d)}$ (where d is the degree of K). For cryptographic-size parameters, the comparison is summarized in Fig. 2 (assuming that all special genera contain approximately the same number of isometry classes). More details can be found in Fig. 3.

m	d	Number of isometry classes within the genus of $\mathcal{O}_K^2$	Number of isometry classes within a special genus of $\mathcal{O}_K^2$
128	64	$\simeq 2^{150}$	$\simeq 2^{130}$
256	128	$\simeq 2^{400}$	$\simeq 2^{350}$
512	256	$\simeq 2^{1050}$	$\simeq 2^{850}$ (Under GRH)

Fig. 2. Estimates for HAWK's lattice $\mathcal{O}_K^2$ over $K = \mathbb{Q}(\zeta_m)$.

Technical Overview. The question of whether two ($\mathcal{O}_K$-)Hermitian lattices $\mathcal{L}$ and $\mathcal{M}$ belong to the same special genus was answered by Shimura in [20], and Corollary 2.11 gives a complete set of conditions. The latter are divided in two types, the first one being a *global* condition on the module index $I = [\mathcal{L} : \mathcal{M}]_{\mathcal{O}_K}$, a fractional ideal of K which can be interpreted as the covolume of $\mathcal{M}$ in $\mathcal{L}$.

Precisely, a necessary condition for $\mathcal{L}$ and $\mathcal{M}$ to be in the same special genus is that $I = g \cdot \mathcal{O}_K$ is a principal ideal with $g \in K$ and $g\overline{g} = 1$. Notice that Shimura's theorem implies $I \cdot \overline{I} = \mathcal{O}_K$ as soon as $\mathcal{L}$ and $\mathcal{M}$ are in the same genus (not necessarily the same special genus). As a consequence, we can make use of Lenstra and Silverberg algorithm (see [11] or Lemma 1.35) to test efficiently if I is a principal ideal and if so, to compute a generator g with $g\overline{g} = 1$.

On the other hand there are *local* conditions to check. In our setting, $\mathcal{O}_K$ denotes the ring of integers of a number field K (*e.g.*, a cyclotomic number field) which contains a subfield F such that $\dim_F(K) = 2$. To any prime ideal $\mathfrak{p}$ of $\mathcal{O}_F$, the ring of integers of F, are associated Hermitian lattices $\mathcal{L}_\mathfrak{p}$ and $\mathcal{M}_\mathfrak{p}$, and the so-called local determinant groups $\mathbb{E}(\mathcal{L}_\mathfrak{p})$ and $\mathbb{E}(\mathcal{M}_\mathfrak{p})$ (see Subsect. 2.1 for definitions). Only a finite set of prime ideals $\mathfrak{p}$ lead to non-trivial local determinant groups —this set only depends on the genus of $\mathcal{L}$— and for each of these exceptional primes, Corollary 2.11 asks to verify a certain relation between the generator g of I and the determinant of a local isometry mapping $\mathcal{L}_\mathfrak{p}$ into $\mathcal{M}_\mathfrak{p}$. In practice, we explain how this determinant can be computed from the *Jordan decompositions* of $\mathcal{L}_\mathfrak{p}$ and $\mathcal{M}_\mathfrak{p}$, see Lemma 1.32.

As mentionned above, module-LIP deals with pseudo-Gram matrices, say $\mathbf{G}$ and $\mathbf{H}$, instead of pseudo-bases of $\mathcal{L}$ and $\mathcal{M}$. This convention introduces some complications in the computation of the special genus. First, $\mathbf{G}$ and $\mathbf{H}$ alone are not sufficient to compute the module-index I (see Lemma 1.14 for the formula). Still, we show in Proposition 3.3 that they allow to decide whether I is principal and has a generator g such that $g\overline{g} = 1$ (without even having to compute it). Sadly, the Jordan decompositions of $\mathcal{L}_\mathfrak{p}$ and $\mathcal{M}_\mathfrak{p}$ seem to be out of reach when manipulating only $\mathbf{G}$ and $\mathbf{H}$, making the local conditions above impossible to verify. Instead, we restrict ourselves to Hermitian lattices $\mathcal{L}$ having an odd rank orthogonal sublattice (*e.g.* such that $\mathbf{G}$ has a row whose non-diagonal elements are equal to zero). For these particular $\mathcal{L}$, there are no local conditions to check and deciding whether $\mathcal{M}$ is in the special genus of $\mathcal{L}$ boils down to testing if I is a principal ideal generated by an element of norm 1. This condition may seem restrictive but it contains HAWK's lattice $\mathcal{O}_K^2$, see Corollary 3.5.

Thanks to Shimura's Theorem 2.8, one can moreover compute the number of special genera within a genus. Over a cyclotomic field $K = \mathbb{Q}(\zeta_m)$, this number equals the quotient of class numbers h_K/h_F for a large family of binary Hermitian ($\mathcal{O}_K$-)lattices which includes $\mathcal{O}_K^2$. Moreover, the subfield $F = \mathbb{Q}(\zeta_m + \zeta_m^{-1})$ is known (or at least conjectured) to have $h_F = 1$ for several conductors m, including powers of two, which are relevant for cryptography. Consequently, the special genus is an invariant that refines the genus, allowing the distinction of h_K classes within the genus. This conclusion is indeed consistent with the fact that, for these particular lattices, the special genus is entirely determined by the class of the module index in the class group of K. On the other hand, Siegel's mass formulas (see [9, Chapter 4]) gives estimates on the number of isomorphism classes within the genus of a lattice. Using the obtained numbers, we get an estimate of the number of isometry classes within a special genus (assuming each contains roughly the same number). This number, although still exponential in the degree of K, represents an exponential gain compared to the number of classes in a full genus.

Impact. In [6, Section 7] the authors provided recommendations to make decision-LIP (for plain lattices) a hard problem. Since the genus is an efficiently computable invariant, a necessary condition is therefore to choose lattices within the same genus. In the case of an adaptation to Hermitian lattices over a number field, we show the necessity to choose them not only in the same genus but in the same special genus.

Although this reduces the number of classes to distinguish, the impact on decision module-LIP is very limited. Indeed, one can easily design non-isomorphic lattices lying in the same special genus. For instance, a straightforward adaptation of [6, Section 8] would be to consider $\mathcal{L} = \mathfrak{a}\mathbf{b_1} \oplus \mathfrak{b}\mathbf{b_2}$ and $\mathcal{M} = \mathbf{b_1} \oplus \mathfrak{ab}\mathbf{b_2}$, where $\mathbf{b_1} = \binom{1}{0}, \mathbf{b_2} = \binom{0}{1}$ and $\mathfrak{a}, \mathfrak{b}$ are coprime ideals of $\mathcal{O}_K$. The fact that $\mathcal{L}$ and $\mathcal{M}$ are in the same special genus is proved in Remark 3.14.

It should be noted that a large number of classes within a (special) genus does not necessarily imply that the module-LIP instance is actually hard to solve. For certain lattices enjoying remarkable geometric properties, as in HAWK (and more generally for smooth or dense lattices, see [26]), the number of classes to distinguish may be significantly reduced, taking into account that these properties must be preserved. On the contrary, the problem could be still hard for some instances, even if the (special) genus contains only few classes.

Recently, van Gent and van Woerden [24] gave a search to distinguish reduction of module-LIP for certain module lattices, extending the idea of Szydlo in [22]. Regarding the discussion above, their result combined with our partial distinguisher has, in practice, no impact on search module-LIP problem for $\mathcal{O}_K^2$ and thus on the security of HAWK.

Conclusion. The special genus is a finer invariant than the genus, which improves the current state-of-the-art on decision module-LIP. Moreover for several lattices, we show that this invariant is efficiently computable. This includes HAWK's lattice $\mathcal{O}_K^2$ over a cyclotomic field K, for which distinguishing special genera amounts to testing the principality of its module index ideal, which can be done efficiently using Lenstra and Silverberg's algorithm [11]. This paper settles the question of using the special genus in the cryptanalysis of decision module-LIP and more generally, in light of the mathematical literature, the question of finding other computable refinements of the genus for Hermitian lattices. Experiments lead in Sect. 3 suggest that despite the large number of special genera in the genus of $\mathcal{O}_K^2$, it is far from sufficient to distinguish isomorphism classes. Indeed the number of classes in a special genus seems to be still exponential in the degree of the field.

Organisation of the Paper. Section 1 provides the theoretical background for dealing with Hermitian lattices over number fields, their genera and special genera, and stating Shimura's Theorem 2.8. Particular emphasis is placed on the concept of module index, including its efficient computation, as it plays a fundamental role in the classification of special genera.

In Sect. 2, we present Shimura's Theorem 2.8 and derive from it a criterion for determining whether two Hermitian lattices belong to the same special genus, as stated in Corollary 2.11. This leads us to an algorithm (Algorithm 1) for distinguishing special genera of Hermitian lattices (given their pseudo-bases).

Finally, Sect. 3 explores the applications to the decisional variant of module-LIP. The latter is formally defined in Definition 3.2 and we adapt the previous algorithm to its framework. Algorithm 2 decides whether the module index $[\mathcal{L} : \mathcal{M}]_{\mathcal{O}_K}$ is a principal ideal generated by an element of norm 1, given only pseudo-Gram matrices of $\mathcal{L}$ and $\mathcal{M}$. In some cases, this turns out to be a complete invariant for having $\mathcal{M}$ in the special genus of $\mathcal{L}$.

Notations

For a ring R, we denote by $R^\times$ the set of invertible elements of R. The set of matrices with n rows, ℓ columns and with coefficients in R is denoted by $\mathcal{M}_{n,\ell}(R)$, or simply $\mathcal{M}_n(R)$ if $\ell = n$. The invertible elements of the ring $\mathcal{M}_n(R)$ form the group $\mathbf{GL}_n(R)$. Finally we use bold letters to denote (columns) vectors.

1 Preliminaries

This section provides the necessary background for dealing with Hermitian lattices over Dedekind domains. Our goal is to introduce key concepts such as the special genus and Shimura's Theorem 2.8, which serves as the central theoretical result. Moreover, we state some algorithmic tools that will be needed later on.

1.1 Algebraic Number Theory

Ideals. Let $\mathfrak{o}$ be a commutative and unitary domain with characteristic 0 and fraction field F. An *integral ideal* $\mathfrak{a}$ of $\mathfrak{o}$ is an additive subgroup of $\mathfrak{o}$ such that $x\mathfrak{a} \subseteq \mathfrak{a}$ for all $x \in \mathfrak{o}$. A *fractional ideal* $\mathfrak{a}$ of F is an additive subgroup of F such that $x\mathfrak{a}$ is an integral ideal of F for some $x \in F \setminus \{0\}$. We say that $\mathfrak{a}$ is *principal* if $\mathfrak{a} = x \cdot \mathfrak{o}$ consists of all multiples of some $x \in F$ by the elements of $\mathfrak{o}$. In that case x is called a *generator* of $\mathfrak{a}$ and $y \in \mathfrak{a}$ is another generator if and only if $y \in x \cdot \mathfrak{o}^\times$. The ideal *generated* by a finite subset $S \subset F$ is the smallest fractional ideal (for the inclusion) which contains S.

A *prime* ideal is an integral ideal of F, usually denoted by $\mathfrak{p}$, such that for all $x, y \in \mathfrak{o}$, $xy \in \mathfrak{p}$ implies $x \in \mathfrak{p}$ or $y \in \mathfrak{p}$. The set of prime ideals is denoted by $\mathbb{P}(\mathfrak{o})$. For any fractional ideals $\mathfrak{a}, \mathfrak{b}$, their product $\mathfrak{ab}$ is defined as the smallest fractional ideal containing all the products xy for $x \in \mathfrak{a}$ and $y \in \mathfrak{b}$. We say that $\mathfrak{b}$ *divides* $\mathfrak{a}$ whenever $\mathfrak{a} = \mathfrak{bc}$ holds for some integral ideal $\mathfrak{c}$. Finally, $\mathfrak{a}$ is *maximal* if there is no integral ideal $\mathfrak{b}$ such that $\mathfrak{a} \subsetneq \mathfrak{b}$.

Dedekind Domains. In this paper, $\mathfrak{o}$ will denote either the ring of integers of a number field F or a valutation ring obtained by completing a number field F at some prime ideal (these notions are defined below). To cover uniformly both cases, we will work with the more general notion of *Dedekind domains*. Recall that in a Dedekind domain $\mathfrak{o}$, any integral ideal $\mathfrak{a}$ is a product of finitely many prime ideals $\mathfrak{a} = \prod_i \mathfrak{p}_i^{e_i}$. Moreover this factorization is unique, up to ordering the factors. Also, any integral ideal $\mathfrak{a}$ admits an inverse, *i.e.*, there exists a fractional ideal $\mathfrak{b}$ such that $\mathfrak{a}\mathfrak{b} = \mathfrak{o}$. The inverse of $\mathfrak{a}$ will be denoted by $\mathfrak{a}^{-1}$.

Further, let $\alpha \in F$ and put $K = F[X]/(X^2 - \alpha)$. We will denote the class of X in K by $\sqrt{\alpha}$. Then K is a 2-dimensional F-algebra equipped with an involution $\bar{\cdot} : v_1\sqrt{\alpha} + v_2 \mapsto -v_1\sqrt{\alpha} + v_2$.[1] The trace and norm maps on K are defined by $\mathrm{Tr} : K \to F\,;\, a \mapsto a + \bar{a}$ and $\mathrm{N} : K \to F\,;\, a \mapsto a\bar{a}$ respectively. We define $\mathcal{O} := \{a \in K \,|\, \mathrm{Tr}(a) \in \mathfrak{o} \text{ and } \mathrm{N}(a) \in \mathfrak{o}\}$. When K is a quadratic extension of F, then $\mathcal{O}$ is the ring of integers of K and thus a Dedekind domain. Otherwise, $K \simeq F \times F$ and $\mathcal{O} \simeq \mathfrak{o} \times \mathfrak{o}$ (see [20, 2.9]). In the second case, we call fractional ideal of $\mathcal{O}$ any finitely generated $\mathfrak{o}$-module $\mathfrak{A} \subset K$ such that $\mathcal{O} \cdot \mathfrak{A} \subseteq \mathfrak{A}$. Finally, the trace (resp. norm) of a fractional ideal $\mathfrak{A} \subset K$ is the fractional ideal $\mathrm{T}(\mathfrak{A})$ (resp. $\mathrm{N}(\mathfrak{A})$) of F generated by the traces (resp. norms) of elements in $\mathfrak{A}$.

Number Fields. Let F be a *number field*, *i.e.*, an algebraic extension of the field of rational numbers $\mathbb{Q}$ with finite dimension, and let $\mathfrak{o}$ be the *ring of integers* of F. Then, F is the field of fractions of $\mathfrak{o}$ and the latter is a Dedekind domain. The set of fractional ideals of F, equipped with the multiplication of ideals, forms an abelian group denoted by $\mathcal{I}(\mathfrak{o})$. The *class group* of $\mathfrak{o}$ is then obtained as the quotient of $\mathcal{I}(\mathfrak{o})$ by the subgroup of principal ideals, and it is denoted by $\mathrm{Cl}(\mathfrak{o})$. Let $\alpha \in F \setminus F^2$ and set $K = F[X]/(X^2 - \alpha)$ as above. Then K is a number field and $\mathcal{O}$ defined as above is its ring of integers. The inverse different ideal of K/F is defined by $\mathfrak{D}^{-1} = \{a \in K \,|\, \mathrm{Tr}(a \cdot \mathcal{O}) \subseteq \mathfrak{o}\}$. Then the discriminant of K/F is the norm of the different ideal $\Delta := \mathrm{N}(\mathfrak{D})$, it is a fractional ideal of F. We will say that a prime ideal $\mathfrak{p} \in \mathbb{P}(\mathfrak{o})$ is *ramified* if it divides Δ, and that it is *unramified* otherwise. If all $\mathfrak{p} \in \mathbb{P}(\mathfrak{o})$ are unramified, then we say that K/F is unramified.

CM Number Fields. Let F be a number field of degree d, *i.e.*, with dimension d over the field of rational numbers. There are d field homomorphisms $\sigma : F \to \mathbb{C}$ called *complex embeddings*. Concretely if $F \simeq \mathbb{Q}[X]/(P)$, the complex embeddings are given by the evaluation maps $X \mapsto \alpha_i$, where the α_i's are the complex roots of P. We say that F is a *totally real* number field when $\sigma(F) \subset \mathbb{R}$ for all complex embedding σ, or equivalently if all the α_i's are real numbers. Additionally, a quadratic extension $K = F[X]/(X^2 - \alpha)$ of a totally real field F is called a *CM* (complex multiplication) number field if α is totally negative, *i.e.*, $\sigma(\alpha) < 0$ for all complex embeddings of F. We will also say that K/F is a *CM extension.*

An example largely used in cryptography are the *cyclotomic* numbers fields. The cyclotomic number field of conductor $m \geq 2$ is $K = \mathbb{Q}[X]/(\Phi_m)$, where $\Phi_m(X) \in \mathbb{Z}[X]$ is the m-th cyclotomic polynomial. Alternatively $K \simeq \mathbb{Q}(\zeta_m)$, where ζ_m is a primitive m-th root of unity. It has degree $d = \varphi(m)$, where φ

[1] K is a quadratic extension of F when α is not a square in F and it is isomorphic to $F \times F$ otherwise.

denotes Euler's totient function, and its ring of integers is $\mathcal{O} = \mathbb{Z}[X]/(\Phi_m) \simeq \mathbb{Z}[\zeta_m]$. It is a CM number field since $K = F[X]/(X^2-\alpha)$, where $F = \mathbb{Q}(\zeta_m+\zeta_m^{-1})$ is totally real and $\alpha = (\zeta_m - \zeta_m^{-1})^2 = (\zeta_m + \zeta_m^{-1})^2 - 4 \in F^\times \setminus F^{\times 2}$ is totally negative. Moreover the ramification in cyclotomic number fields is well known.

Lemma 1.1 ([27], Proposition 2.15 & [16], Chapter I, Lemma 10.1). *If $m = p^r$ is a prime power, then $\mathbb{Q}(\zeta_m)/\mathbb{Q}(\zeta_m + \zeta_m^{-1})$ is ramified at the unique prime ideal above p and unramified everywhere else. Moreover, $p \cdot \mathcal{O} = \mathfrak{P}^d$, where $\mathfrak{P} = (1 - \zeta_m) \cdot \mathcal{O}$ and $d = \varphi(p^r)$. If m is composite, then $\mathbb{Q}(\zeta_m)/\mathbb{Q}(\zeta_m + \zeta_m^{-1})$ is unramified.*

Completions. Suppose that $\mathfrak{o}$ is the ring of integers of a number field F and $K = F[X]/(X^2 - \alpha)$ is a quadratic extension of F, whose ring of integers is $\mathcal{O}$ as above. Let $\mathfrak{p} \in \mathbb{P}(\mathfrak{o})$ and $v_\mathfrak{p} : F \to \mathbb{Z} \cup \{\infty\}$ be the valuation on F defined by $v_\mathfrak{p}(x) = \max\{e \in \mathbb{Z} \mid x \cdot \mathfrak{o} \subset \mathfrak{p}^e\}$ for $x \neq 0$, and $v_\mathfrak{p}(0) = \infty$. The *completion* of F with respect to $v_\mathfrak{p}$ is a field denoted by $F_\mathfrak{p}$. Moreover $v_\mathfrak{p}$ extends to $F_\mathfrak{p}$ and the *valuation ring* associated is $\mathfrak{o}_\mathfrak{p} = \{x \in F_\mathfrak{p} \mid v_\mathfrak{p}(x) \geq 0\}$. It is a Dedekind domain with a unique prime ideal $\{x \in F_\mathfrak{p} \mid v_\mathfrak{p}(x) > 0\}$, which is still denoted by $\mathfrak{p}$. Moreover this ideal is principal and a generator of it is called a *uniformizer* of $F_\mathfrak{p}$. Consequently, any fractional ideal $\mathfrak{a}$ of $F_\mathfrak{p}$ is principal, since it is a power of $\mathfrak{p}$ (if $\mathfrak{a} \neq \{0\}$).

Let $K_\mathfrak{p} := K \otimes_F F_\mathfrak{p}$ and $\mathcal{O}_\mathfrak{p} := \mathcal{O} \otimes_\mathfrak{o} \mathfrak{o}_\mathfrak{p}$.[2] The involution $\bar{\cdot}$ on K extends to $K_\mathfrak{p}$ by $k \otimes f \mapsto \bar{k} \otimes f$, and likewise for Tr, N : $K_\mathfrak{p} \to F_\mathfrak{p}$.[3] In the case where $\mathfrak{p}$ *splits* in $\mathcal{O}$, *i.e.* when $\mathfrak{p}\mathcal{O} = \mathfrak{P}_1\mathfrak{P}_2$ with $\mathfrak{P}_1, \mathfrak{P}_2$ distinct prime ideals of $\mathcal{O}$, then we fix $\mathfrak{P} = \mathfrak{P}_i$ for some $i \in \{1, 2\}$ and a field isomorphism $K_\mathfrak{P} \simeq F_\mathfrak{p}$.[4] It yields a ring isomorphism $K_\mathfrak{p} \simeq F_\mathfrak{p} \times F_\mathfrak{p}$, $k \otimes f \mapsto (kf, \bar{k}f)$. In the same way, $\mathcal{O}_\mathfrak{p} \simeq \mathfrak{o}_\mathfrak{p} \times \mathfrak{o}_\mathfrak{p}$ (see [20, 2.9]) and we denote by $\mathfrak{P}$ as well the integral ideal of $K_\mathfrak{p}$ generated by $\mathfrak{p}$, *i.e.*, $\mathfrak{P} = \{(x, y) \mid x, y \in \mathfrak{p}\}$. Otherwise, $K_\mathfrak{p}$ is a quadratic extension of $F_\mathfrak{p}$ (in fact, $K_\mathfrak{p}$ is the completion of K at the unique prime above $\mathfrak{p}$, see [18, §1]) and $\mathcal{O}_\mathfrak{p}$ is a Dedekind domain with a unique maximal ideal, denoted by $\mathfrak{P}$.[5] In both cases, we let π be a uniformizer of $K_\mathfrak{p}$ (*i.e.*, a generator of $\mathfrak{P}$), and we fix $u_\mathfrak{p} \in \mathcal{O}_\mathfrak{p}^\times$ such that $\bar{\pi} = \pi \cdot u_\mathfrak{p}$.

1.2 Hermitian Spaces

Let V be a free K-module with finite rank n. We fix an implicit K-basis of V and we use bold letters to denote both the elements in V or their (column) coordinate vectors (in K^n), with respect to this basis.

---

[2] Since $K = F[X]/(X^2 - \alpha)$, one has $K_\mathfrak{p} = F_\mathfrak{p}[X]/(X^2 - \alpha)$.

[3] It holds that $\mathcal{O}_\mathfrak{p} = \{x \in K_\mathfrak{p} \mid \mathrm{Tr}(x) \in \mathfrak{o}_\mathfrak{p}$ and $\mathrm{N}(x) \in \mathfrak{o}_\mathfrak{p}\}$ is the integral closure of $\mathfrak{o}_\mathfrak{p}$ in $K_\mathfrak{p}$, see *e.g.*, [21, Lemma 10.147.2] with $(R, S, A, B) = (\mathfrak{o}, \mathfrak{o}_\mathfrak{p}, \mathcal{O}, K)$.

[4] $K_{\mathfrak{P}_1}$ and $K_{\mathfrak{P}_2}$ are both field extensions of $F_\mathfrak{p}$ and it follows from [16, Chapter II, §8.4] that $[K : F] = 2 = [K_{\mathfrak{P}_1} : F_\mathfrak{p}] + [K_{\mathfrak{P}_2} : F_\mathfrak{p}]$, so $[K_{\mathfrak{P}_1} : F_\mathfrak{p}] = [K_{\mathfrak{P}_2} : F_\mathfrak{p}] = 1$.

[5] In both cases, $\mathfrak{P}$ is the largest ideal $\mathfrak{p} \subseteq \mathfrak{P} \subsetneq \mathcal{O}_\mathfrak{p}$ such that $\overline{\mathfrak{P}} = \mathfrak{P}$.

Definition 1.2. *We say that V is a Hermitian space over K if it is equipped with a map $\Phi : V \times V \to K$ satisfying for any $\mathbf{v}, \mathbf{v}', \mathbf{w}, \mathbf{w}' \in V$ and $a, b \in K$,*

$$\begin{aligned}\Phi(a\mathbf{v} + b\mathbf{v}', \mathbf{w}) &= a\Phi(\mathbf{v}, \mathbf{w}) + b\Phi(\mathbf{v}', \mathbf{w}),\\ \Phi(\mathbf{v}, a\mathbf{w} + b\mathbf{w}') &= \overline{a}\Phi(\mathbf{v}, \mathbf{w}) + \overline{b}\Phi(\mathbf{v}, \mathbf{w}'),\\ \Phi(\mathbf{w}, \mathbf{v}) &= \overline{\Phi(\mathbf{v}, \mathbf{w})}.\end{aligned}$$

We also say that Φ is a Hermitian form on V. We will denote $\Phi(\mathbf{v}, \mathbf{v})$ by $\Phi(\mathbf{v})$.

Example 1.3. A relevant example for applications is when $K = \mathbb{Q}(\zeta)$ is a cyclotomic field, $F = \mathbb{Q}(\zeta + \zeta^{-1})$ its maximal totally real subfield and $V = K^n$. Then $\mathcal{O} = \mathbb{Z}[\zeta]$ and $\mathfrak{o} = \mathbb{Z}[\zeta + \zeta^{-1}]$, and the *standard Hermitian form* on K^n is defined for any $\mathbf{v} = (v_i)_{1 \le i \le n}, \mathbf{w} = (w_i)_{1 \le i \le n} \in V$ by

$$\Phi(\mathbf{v}, \mathbf{w}) = \sum_{i=1}^{n} v_i \overline{w_i}.$$

If $\mathbf{b} = \{\mathbf{v_1}, \ldots, \mathbf{v_n}\}$ is a basis of V over K, the *Gram matrix* of $\mathbf{b}$ with respect to a Hermitian form Φ on V is $G := (\Phi(\mathbf{v_i}, \mathbf{v_j}))_{1 \le i,j \le n}$. This matrix is Hermitian, *i.e.*, it is equal to its transpose-conjugate $G^* := \overline{G}^T$.

Definition 1.4. *Let Φ be a Hermitian form on V, the unitary group of (V, Φ) is*

$$\mathrm{U}(V, \Phi) = \{\sigma \in \mathbf{GL}(V) \mid \Phi(\sigma(\mathbf{v}), \sigma(\mathbf{w})) = \Phi(\mathbf{v}, \mathbf{w}) \text{ for all } \mathbf{v}, \mathbf{w} \in V\}.$$

The special unitary group of (V, Φ) is defined by

$$\mathrm{SU}(V, \Phi) = \{\sigma \in \mathrm{U}(V, \Phi) \mid \det(\sigma) = 1\}.$$

1.3 Generalities on Lattices

Let $\mathfrak{o}$ be a Dedekind domain and $(\mathfrak{o}, F, \mathcal{O}, K)$ as in Sect. 1.1, paragraph *Dedekind domains*. Further, let V be a free K-module of rank n.

Pseudo-Bases. We begin this section by giving generalities on lattices in V. Notice that the following definitions and properties do not involve any Hermitian structure on V for the moment. For more details on this topic, we refer to [3,17,20].

Definition 1.5 ($\mathcal{O}$-lattice). *An $\mathcal{O}$-lattice $\mathcal{L}$ in V is a finitely generated $\mathcal{O}$-module in V. The rank of an $\mathcal{O}$-lattice $\mathcal{L}$ in V, denoted by* rank$(\mathcal{L})$, *is the rank of the ambient space $K\mathcal{L}$ over K. We say that $\mathcal{L}$ has full rank when $K\mathcal{L} = V$, i.e., when $\mathcal{L}$ contains a K-basis of V.*

Definition 1.6 (Pseudo-basis). *Let $\mathcal{L}$ be an $\mathcal{O}$-lattice in V with rank ℓ. Suppose the existence of K-linearly independent vectors $\mathbf{v_1}, \ldots, \mathbf{v_\ell} \in V$ and fractional ideals $\mathfrak{a}_1, \ldots, \mathfrak{a}_\ell$ of K such that*

$$\mathcal{L} = \mathfrak{a}_1\mathbf{v_1} \oplus \cdots \oplus \mathfrak{a}_\ell\mathbf{v_\ell}.$$

Then the data of $\mathbf{B} = (B, \{\mathfrak{a}_i\}_{1\leq i\leq n})$, where $B = (\mathbf{v_1}|\cdots|\mathbf{v_\ell}) \in \mathcal{M}_{n,\ell}(K)$, is called a pseudo-basis of $\mathcal{L}$. Moreover when $\mathcal{O}$ is a Dedekind domain, $[\mathfrak{a}_1 \cdots \mathfrak{a}_\ell] \in \mathrm{Cl}(\mathcal{O})$ is called the Steinitz class of $\mathbf{B}$.

Remark 1.7. It is a standard fact that $\mathcal{O}$-lattices in V admit a pseudo-basis whenever $\mathcal{O}$ is a Dedekind domain (see *e.g.*, [17, Theorem 81.3]). Additionally, Shimura proved in [20, Proposition 3.2] that the same property holds for the split case $\mathcal{O} \simeq \mathfrak{o} \times \mathfrak{o}$. However, in the case where we consider *global* $\mathcal{O}$-lattices —that is, when $\mathfrak{o}$ is the ring of integers of the number field F— we will always assume that K is a field extension of F and therefore that $\mathcal{O}$ is a Dedekind domain. Accordingly, the following properties are stated only in the case where $\mathcal{O}$ is a Dedekind domain.[6]

Remark 1.8. Unless stated otherwise, we will only consider full rank $\mathcal{O}$-lattices. In particular, the matrix part of a pseudo-basis belongs to $\mathbf{GL}_n(K)$.

The results mentionned above ensure that $\mathcal{O}$-lattices always admit a pseudo-basis. In the case where $\mathcal{O}$ is a Dedekind domain, pseudo-bases corresponding to the same $\mathcal{O}$-lattice are related in the following way.

Proposition 1.9 ([3], Proposition 1.4.2). *Suppose that $\mathcal{O}$ is a Dedekind domain. Let $\mathbf{B} = (B, \{\mathfrak{a}_i\}_{1\leq i\leq n})$ be the pseudo-basis of an $\mathcal{O}$-lattice $\mathcal{L}$ in V. Then $\mathbf{C} = (C, \{\mathfrak{b}_i\}_{1\leq i\leq n})$ is a pseudo-basis of $\mathcal{L}$ if and only if there exists $U = (u_{i,j})_{1\leq i,j\leq n} \in \mathbf{GL}_n(K)$ satisfying the following properties.*

1. *$C = BU$;*
2. *$\forall i,j \in \{1,\ldots,n\}$, $u_{i,j} \in \mathfrak{a}_i\mathfrak{b}_j^{-1}$;*
3. *$\prod_{i=1}^n \mathfrak{a}_i = (\det U)\prod_{i=1}^n \mathfrak{b}_i$*

With the same notations as above, it follows from *3.* that the pseudo-bases $\mathbf{B}$ and $\mathbf{C}$ of $\mathcal{L}$ define the same Steinitz class. Thus the Steinitz class depends only on $\mathcal{L}$ and not on some pseudo-basis of it.

Definition 1.10. *Assuming $\mathcal{O}$ is a Dedekind ring, the Steinitz class of $\mathcal{L}$, denoted by $\mathrm{St}(\mathcal{L})$, is defined as the Steinitz class of $\mathbf{B}$, where $\mathbf{B}$ is any pseudo-basis of $\mathcal{L}$.*

[6] The only reason why we do not define $\mathcal{O}$-lattices exclusively for Dedekind domains $\mathcal{O}$ is to treat uniformly *local* $\mathcal{O}_\mathfrak{p}$-lattices where $\mathcal{O}_\mathfrak{p}$ is either a Dedekind domain or $\mathcal{O}_\mathfrak{p} \simeq \mathfrak{o}_\mathfrak{p} \times \mathfrak{o}_\mathfrak{p}$.

Module Index. It will appear clearly in Sect. 2 that the module index plays a fundamental role in the classification of special genera. It can be defined abstractly via the following result due to Steinitz, but we will make use of Lemma 1.14 to compute it efficiently from pseudo-bases.

Theorem 1.11 (Steinitz, [17] Theorem 81.11). *Suppose that $\mathcal{O}$ is a Dedekind domain and let $\mathcal{L}$, $\mathcal{M}$ be two (full-rank) $\mathcal{O}$-lattices in V. Then there exists a pseudo-basis $((\mathbf{v_1}|\cdots|\mathbf{v_n}), \{\mathfrak{a}_i\}_{1\le i\le n})$ of $\mathcal{L}$ and unique fractional ideals $\mathfrak{d}_1 \supseteq \cdots \supseteq \mathfrak{d}_n$ such that $((\mathbf{v_1}|\cdots|\mathbf{v_n}), \{\mathfrak{d}_i\mathfrak{a}_i\}_{1\le i\le n})$ is a pseudo-basis of $\mathcal{M}$.*

Definition 1.12. *With the same notations as in Theorem 1.11, the ideals $\mathfrak{d}_1, \ldots, \mathfrak{d}_n$ are called the invariant factors of $\mathcal{L}$ and $\mathcal{M}$. The module index of $\mathcal{M}$ in $\mathcal{L}$ is the fractional ideal*

$$[\mathcal{L} : \mathcal{M}]_{\mathcal{O}} := \prod_{i=1}^{n} \mathfrak{d}_i.$$

Remark 1.13. Notice that the module index of $\mathcal{M}$ in $\mathcal{L}$ is well defined even if $\mathcal{M}$ is not contained in $\mathcal{L}$. For instance taking $K/F = \mathbb{Q}(i)/\mathbb{Q}$ and $V = K^2$, $\mathcal{L} = \mathbb{Z}[i] + \mathbb{Z}[i]$ and $\mathcal{M} = \mathbb{Z}[i] + 2\mathbb{Z}[i]$, we have $[\mathcal{L} : \mathcal{M}]_{\mathbb{Z}[i]} = 2\mathbb{Z}[i]$ and $[\mathcal{M} : \mathcal{L}]_{\mathbb{Z}[i]} = \frac{1}{2}\mathbb{Z}[i]$.

Lemma 1.14. *Suppose that $\mathcal{O}$ is a Dedekind domain and let $\mathcal{L}$, $\mathcal{M}$ and $\mathcal{N}$ be $\mathcal{O}$-lattices in V. Then,*

1. $[\mathcal{L} : \mathcal{M}]_{\mathcal{O}} \cdot [\mathcal{M} : \mathcal{N}]_{\mathcal{O}} = [\mathcal{L} : \mathcal{N}]_{\mathcal{O}}$.

Moreover suppose that $(B, \{\mathfrak{a}_i\}_{1\le i\le n})$ and $(C, \{\mathfrak{c}_i\}_{1\le i\le n})$ are pseudo-bases of $\mathcal{L}$ and $\mathcal{M}$ respectively. Then the following properties hold

2. $[\mathcal{O}^n : \mathcal{L}]_{\mathcal{O}} = \det(B) \cdot \mathfrak{a}_1 \cdots \mathfrak{a}_n$;
3. $[\mathcal{L} : \mathcal{M}]_{\mathcal{O}} = \det(B^{-1}C) \cdot \mathfrak{a}_1^{-1}\mathfrak{b}_1 \cdots \mathfrak{a}_n^{-1}\mathfrak{b}_n$.

Proof. Notice first that the module index of $\mathcal{M}$ in $\mathcal{L}$ as defined above coincides with the ideal $\chi(\mathcal{L}, \mathcal{M})$ defined in [19, Chapter III, §1]. Hence we refer to [19, Chapter III, §1, Proposition 1] for a proof of the first property. For *2.* we apply Theorem 1.11 to $\mathcal{O}^n$ and $\mathcal{L}$: there exists a pseudo-basis $(B_0, \{\mathfrak{u}_i\}_{1\le i\le n})$ of $\mathcal{O}^n$ and fractional ideals $\mathfrak{d}_1, \ldots, \mathfrak{d}_n$ such that $(B_0, \{\mathfrak{u}_i\mathfrak{d}_i\}_{1\le i\le n})$ is a pseudo-basis of $\mathcal{L}$. Since $(I_n, \{\mathcal{O}\}_{1\le i\le n})$ is also a (pseudo-)basis of $\mathcal{O}^n$, Proposition 1.9 implies that $\det(B_0) \cdot \mathcal{O} = (\mathfrak{u}_1 \cdots \mathfrak{u}_n)^{-1}$. Similarly with $\mathcal{L}$, there exists $U \in \mathbf{GL}_n(K)$ such that $B = B_0U$ and $\det(U) \cdot \mathfrak{a}_1 \cdots \mathfrak{a}_n = \mathfrak{u}_1\mathfrak{d}_1 \cdots \mathfrak{u}_n\mathfrak{d}_n$. It yields

$$\begin{aligned}[\mathcal{O}^n : \mathcal{L}]_{\mathcal{O}} &= \mathfrak{d}_1 \cdots \mathfrak{d}_n \\ &= \det(U) \cdot (\mathfrak{u}_1 \cdots \mathfrak{u}_n)^{-1} \cdot \mathfrak{a}_1 \cdots \mathfrak{a}_n \\ &= \det(B) \cdot \mathfrak{a}_1 \cdots \mathfrak{a}_n.\end{aligned}$$

For *3.*, notice that *1.* implies $[\mathcal{L} : \mathcal{M}]_{\mathcal{O}} = [\mathcal{L} : \mathcal{O}^n]_{\mathcal{O}} \cdot [\mathcal{O}^n : \mathcal{M}]_{\mathcal{O}}$ and $[\mathcal{L} : \mathcal{O}^n]_{\mathcal{O}} = [\mathcal{O}^n : \mathcal{L}]_{\mathcal{O}}^{-1}$. The result then follows from *2.*

□ We state an immediate corollary of *3.* which will be useful in Sect. 3.

Corollary 1.15. *Suppose that $\mathcal{O}$ is a Dedekind domain and let $\mathcal{L}$ and $\mathcal{M}$ be $\mathcal{O}$-lattices in V. Then, the module index $[\mathcal{L} : \mathcal{M}]_{\mathcal{O}}$ is a principal ideal if and only if* $\mathrm{St}(\mathcal{L}) = \mathrm{St}(\mathcal{M})$.

Proof. This follows from Lemma 1.14, property *3.*

□

1.4 Hermitian Lattices

Suppose that V is equipped with a Hermitian form Φ. This form can be restricted to $\mathcal{O}$-lattices in V, giving rise to several geometrical features. In what follows, we will refer to $\mathcal{O}$-lattices in (V, Φ) as *Hermitian lattices in* (V, Φ). First we define an analog of Gram matrices for Hermitian lattices. It will be the central object studied in module-LIP.

Definition 1.16. *Let $\mathbf{B} = (B, \{\mathfrak{a}_i\}_{1 \le i \le n})$ be the pseudo-basis of a Hermitian lattice $\mathcal{L}$ in (V, Φ). The pseudo-Gram matrix associated to $\mathbf{B}$ is the pseudo-matrix*

$$\mathbf{G} = ((\Phi(\mathbf{v_i}, \mathbf{v_j}))_{1 \le i,j \le n}, \{\mathfrak{a}_i\}_{1 \le i \le n}) .$$

Example 1.17. Taking $V = K^n$ with the standard Hermitian form, the pseudo-Gram matrix associated to $\mathbf{B} = (B, \{\mathfrak{a}_i\}_{1 \le i \le n})$ is $\mathbf{G} = (G, \{\mathfrak{a}_i\}_{1 \le i \le n})$, where $G = B^* B$. Hence one recovers the definition given in [15, Definition 3.6].

Definition 1.18. *Let $\mathcal{L}$ be a Hermitian lattice in (V, Φ).*

1. *The dual of $\mathcal{L}$ is*
$$\mathcal{L}^{\#} := \{\mathbf{v} \in V \mid \Phi(\mathbf{v}, \mathcal{L}) \subset \mathcal{O}\},$$
it is a Hermitian lattice in (V, Φ) as well.
2. *If $\mathcal{L} = \mathfrak{a}\mathcal{L}^{\#}$ holds for some fractional ideal $\mathfrak{a}$ of $\mathcal{O}$, then $\mathcal{L}$ is said to be $\mathfrak{a}$-modular.*
3. *The scale of $\mathcal{L}$, denoted by $\mathfrak{s}(\mathcal{L})$, is the $\mathcal{O}$-ideal generated by $\{\Phi(\mathbf{v}, \mathbf{w}) \mid \mathbf{v}, \mathbf{w} \in \mathcal{L}\}$.*
4. *The norm of $\mathcal{L}$, denoted by $\mathfrak{n}(\mathcal{L})$, is the $\mathfrak{o}$-ideal generated by $\{\Phi(\mathbf{v}, \mathbf{v}) \mid \mathbf{v}, \mathbf{v} \in \mathcal{L}\}$.*

Remark 1.19 ([9], Remark 2.3.4). Let $\mathcal{L}$ be a Hermitian lattice in (V, Φ) with pseudo-basis $((\mathbf{v}_1 | \cdots | \mathbf{v}_n), \{\mathfrak{a}_i\}_{1 \le i \le n})$. Denote by $(\mathbf{v}_1^{\#}, \dots, \mathbf{v}_n^{\#})$ the basis of V which is dual to $(\mathbf{v}_1, \dots, \mathbf{v}_n)$ with respect to Φ. Then a pseudo-basis for $\mathcal{L}^{\#}$ is

$$\mathcal{L}^{\#} = (\overline{\mathfrak{a}_1})^{-1} \mathbf{v}_1^{\#} \oplus \cdots \oplus (\overline{\mathfrak{a}_n})^{-1} \mathbf{v}_n^{\#} . \tag{1}$$

Moreover, the scale and norm can be computed efficiently from a pseudo-Gram matrix $\mathbf{G} = ((g_{i,j})_{1 \le i,j \le n}, \{\mathfrak{a}_i\}_{1 \le i \le n})$ of $\mathcal{L}$. Indeed, one has

$$\mathfrak{s}(\mathcal{L}) = \sum_{1 \le i,j \le n} g_{i,j} \mathfrak{a}_i \overline{\mathfrak{a}_j} \quad \text{and} \quad \mathfrak{n}(\mathcal{L}) = \sum_{i=1}^{n} g_{i,i} \mathrm{N}(\mathfrak{a}_i) \; + \sum_{1 \le i < j \le n} \mathrm{Tr}(g_{i,j} \mathfrak{a}_i \overline{\mathfrak{a}_j}).$$

In [15] and over totally real number fields, the norm of $\mathcal{L}$ was called the "Gram ideal" of $\mathcal{L}$. We stick to the first one which is more standard in the litterature.

Genera and Classes. From now on, suppose furthermore that $\mathfrak{o}$ is the ring of integers of a number field F and K is a quadratic extension as before. Recall that $\mathcal{O}$ is the ring of integers of K. Let $\mathfrak{p} \in \mathbb{P}(\mathfrak{o})$ and set $V_\mathfrak{p} = V \otimes_K K_\mathfrak{p}$. Scalar extension extends the form Φ to $V_\mathfrak{p}$, turning $(V_\mathfrak{p}, \Phi)$ into a Hermitian space over $K_\mathfrak{p}$.[7] Therefore $(\mathfrak{o}_\mathfrak{p}, F_\mathfrak{p}, \mathcal{O}_\mathfrak{p}, K_\mathfrak{p}, V_\mathfrak{p})$ falls within the scope of the previous paragraphs.

Finally, we let $\mathcal{L}$ be a Hermitian lattice in (V, Φ) and set $\mathcal{L}_\mathfrak{p} := \mathcal{L} \otimes_\mathcal{O} \mathcal{O}_\mathfrak{p}$. Then, $\mathcal{L}_\mathfrak{p}$ defines a Hermitian ($\mathcal{O}_\mathfrak{p}$-)lattice in $(V_\mathfrak{p}, \Phi)$.

Definition 1.20. *Two Hermitian lattices $\mathcal{L}$, $\mathcal{L}' \subset (V, \Phi)$ are said to be isometric if there exists $\sigma \in \mathrm{U}(V, \Phi)$ such that $\mathcal{L}' = \sigma(\mathcal{L})$. We write $\mathcal{L} \simeq_\mathcal{O} \mathcal{L}'$ when $\mathcal{L}$ and $\mathcal{L}'$ are isometric. The isometry class of $\mathcal{L}$ is*

$$\mathrm{cls}(\mathcal{L}) = \{\textit{Hermitian lattices } \mathcal{M} \textit{ in } (V, \Phi) \,|\, \mathcal{L} \simeq_\mathcal{O} \mathcal{M}\},$$

and the automorphism group of $\mathcal{L}$ is the subgroup of $\mathrm{U}(V, \Phi)$ given by $\mathrm{Aut}(\mathcal{L}) = \{\sigma \in \mathrm{U}(V, \Phi) \,|\, \sigma(\mathcal{L}) = \mathcal{L}\}$. On the other hand, the genus of $\mathcal{L}$ is

$$\mathrm{gen}(\mathcal{L}) = \{\textit{Hermitian lattices } \mathcal{M} \textit{ in } (V, \Phi) \,|\, \forall\, \mathfrak{p} \in \mathbb{P}(\mathfrak{o}),\ \mathcal{L}_\mathfrak{p} \simeq_{\mathcal{O}_\mathfrak{p}} \mathcal{M}_\mathfrak{p}\}.$$

Remark 1.21. There is an inclusion $\mathrm{cls}(\mathcal{L}) \subseteq \mathrm{gen}(\mathcal{L})$ but it is in general strict. Also, the number of isomorphism classes in a genus is finite (see [9, Theorem 2.4.5]).

Definition 1.22 (Class number of $\mathcal{L}$). *The class number of a Hermitian lattice $\mathcal{L}$ in (V, Φ) is the number of isometry classes in $\mathrm{gen}(\mathcal{L})$. It is denoted by $h(\mathcal{L})$.*

Jordan Decompositions. Locally, $\mathcal{L}_\mathfrak{p}$ is almost orthogonal in the sense that it is an orthogonal sum of rank one or two sublattices. This splitting is essentially unique and it gives a description of $\mathrm{gen}(\mathcal{L})$, as $\mathfrak{p}$ runs in $\mathbb{P}(\mathfrak{o})$. Recall that for each $\mathfrak{p} \in \mathbb{P}(\mathfrak{o})$, we define $\mathfrak{P}$ as the largest ideal of $\mathcal{O}_\mathfrak{p}$ which contains $\mathfrak{p}$ and such that $\overline{\mathfrak{P}} = \mathfrak{P}$.

Definition 1.23. *An orthogonal sum $\bigoplus_{i=1}^t \mathcal{L}_i$ of Hermitian lattices in $(V_\mathfrak{p}, \Phi)$ is called a Jordan decomposition if the $\mathcal{L}_i$'s are $\mathfrak{P}^{s_i}$-modular with $s_1 < s_2 < \cdots < s_t$. Two Jordan decompositions $\bigoplus_{i=1}^t \mathcal{L}_i$ and $\bigoplus_{i=1}^{t'} \mathcal{L}_i'$ are said to be of the same Jordan type if $t = t'$ and the following properties are satisfied:*

1. *$\mathcal{L}_i$ and $\mathcal{L}_i'$ have the same rank.*
2. *$\mathfrak{s}(\mathcal{L}_i) = \mathfrak{s}(\mathcal{L}_i')$.*
3. *$\mathfrak{n}(\mathcal{L}_i)\mathcal{O} = \mathfrak{s}(\mathcal{L}_i)$ if and only if $\mathfrak{n}(\mathcal{L}_i')\mathcal{O} = \mathfrak{s}(\mathcal{L}_i')$.*

Proposition 1.24 ([9], Theorem 3.3.3). *For any Hermitian lattice $\mathcal{L}$ in (V, Φ) and $\mathfrak{p} \in \mathbb{P}(\mathfrak{o})$, the Hermitian lattice $\mathcal{L}_\mathfrak{p}$ in $(V_\mathfrak{p}, \Phi)$ admits a Jordan decomposition $\mathcal{L}_\mathfrak{p} = \bigoplus_{i=1}^t \mathcal{L}_i$. Moreover any two Jordan decompositions of $\mathcal{L}_\mathfrak{p}$ are of the same type.*

[7] The form Φ is extended to $V_\mathfrak{p} = V \otimes_K K_\mathfrak{p}$ by putting $\Phi(\mathbf{v} \otimes k_1, \mathbf{w} \otimes k_2) := \Phi(\mathbf{v}, \mathbf{w}) \cdot k_1 \cdot \overline{k_2}$..

Remark 1.25. It follows from [9, Algorithm 3.3.2] that the components appearing in a Jordan decomposition have rank at most two. We will refer to these sublattices as the *Jordan blocks* of the decomposition. With the notations of Definition 1.23, $\mathcal{L}_i$ is the orthogonal sum of the Jordan blocks which are $\mathfrak{P}^{s_i}$-modular.

Remark 1.26. Except if $\mathfrak{p}$ is a ramified prime, a Jordan type of $\mathcal{O}_\mathfrak{p}$-lattices fully determines a local isometry class. In other words, two Hermitian lattices $\mathcal{L}, \mathcal{M} \subset (V, \Phi)$ are locally isomorphic at $\mathfrak{p}$ (*i.e.*, $\mathcal{L}_\mathfrak{p} \simeq_{\mathcal{O}_\mathfrak{p}} \mathcal{M}_\mathfrak{p}$) if and only if $\mathcal{L}_\mathfrak{p}$ and $\mathcal{M}_\mathfrak{p}$ are of the same Jordan type (see [9, Theorem 3.3.6, 4]).

The $\mathfrak{P}^s$-modular Hermitian lattices in $(V_\mathfrak{p}, \Phi)$ admit an orthogonal basis, except in a few cases. Moreover, a Gram matrix can be made explicit (*c.f.*, [9, Proposition 3.3.5]). Exceptions occur when $\mathfrak{p}$ is ramified, giving rise to rank-two Hermitian lattices in $(V_\mathfrak{p}, \Phi)$. To cover these exceptions we will need the following definition.

Definition 1.27. *For $k \in \mathbb{N}$, we denote by $H(k)$ the (isometry) class of rank-two Hermitian lattices in $(V_\mathfrak{p}, \Phi)$ whose Gram matrix is $\begin{pmatrix} 0 & \pi^k \\ \overline{\pi}^k & 0 \end{pmatrix}$.*

1.5 Algorithmic Considerations

Lemma 1.28. *There is a polynomial-time algorithm that given pseudo-bases* **B** *and* **C** *of (full rank) $\mathcal{O}$-lattices $\mathcal{L}$ and $\mathcal{M}$ in V, computes the module index $[\mathcal{L} : \mathcal{M}]_\mathcal{O}$.*

Proof. Let us write $\mathbf{B} = (B, \{\mathfrak{a}_i\}_{1\le i\le n})$ and $\mathbf{C} = (C, \{\mathfrak{b}_i\}_{1\le i\le n})$ for the pseudo-bases given as input. According to Lemma 1.14 *3.*, the module index can be computed as $[\mathcal{L} : \mathcal{M}]_\mathcal{O} = \det(B^{-1}C) \cdot \mathfrak{a}_1^{-1}\mathfrak{b}_1 \cdots \mathfrak{a}_n^{-1}\mathfrak{b}_n$. This is done in polynomial-time in the size of **B** and **C**.

□

Lemma 1.29 ([9], Algorithm 3.3.2). *Let $\mathcal{L}$ be a Hermitian lattice in (V, Φ) and $\mathfrak{p} \in \mathbb{P}(\mathfrak{o})$. There is an algorithm that given a pseudo-basis of $\mathcal{L}$ and $\mathfrak{p}$, computes a Jordan decomposition of $\mathcal{L}_\mathfrak{p}$. Moreover, the output is a sum of orthogonal sublattices of $\mathcal{L}_\mathfrak{p}$ with rank at most two.*

Remark 1.30. Notice that Algorithm 3.3.2 from [9] can be performed on input $\mathfrak{p}$ and a pseudo-Gram matrix **G** of $\mathcal{L}$ instead of pseudo-basis. The output is then a Gram matrix of a Jordan decomposition of $\mathcal{L}_\mathfrak{p}$.

Remark 1.31. Although the complexity of this algorithm is not discussed in [9], Lemma 3.3.4 from *loc. cit.* may be used to show that, when $2 \notin \mathfrak{p}$, the running time is polynomial in the size of its input. In [9, Section 3.3.2] the case $2 \in \mathfrak{p}$ is treated, and the computation of several invariants allows one to obtain a Jordan decomposition.

In the following we provide an algorithm for computing the determinant of a local isometry between two isomorphic $\mathcal{O}_\mathfrak{p}$-lattices, up to some precision. This computation will be needed for Algorithm 1, for which we will not provide a complexity analysis. Let us specify that for cryptographic applications, our Algorithm 2 does not rely on this step. Moreover, for the latter, we will be able to prove a polynomial complexity.

Lemma 1.32. *Let* (V, Φ) *a Hermitian space and* $\mathfrak{p} \in \mathbb{P}(\mathfrak{o})$. *Given two pseudo-bases of Hermitian* $\mathcal{O}$*-lattices* $\mathcal{L}, \mathcal{M} \subset (V, \Phi)$ *in the same genus, there exists an algorithm for computing* $\det(\sigma_\mathfrak{p}) \pmod{\mathfrak{P}^e}$ *for any* $e \in \mathbb{N}_{>0}$, *where* $\sigma_\mathfrak{p}$ *is an element of* $\mathrm{U}(V_\mathfrak{p}, \Phi)$ *mapping* $\mathcal{L}_\mathfrak{p}$ *on* $\mathcal{M}_\mathfrak{p}$.

Proof. For simplicity (and practical interest), we make a proof only when $V = K^n$ is equipped with the Hermitian form $\sum_i x_i\overline{y_i}$. The algorithm starts by computing a basis $\{b_1, b_2\}$ of $\mathcal{O}_\mathfrak{p}$ over $\mathfrak{o}_\mathfrak{p}$.[8] From the pseudo-bases $\mathbf{B}$ and $\mathbf{C}$ of $\mathcal{L}$ and $\mathcal{M}$, the algorithm computes bases $B_\mathfrak{p}$ and $C_\mathfrak{p}$ of $\mathcal{L}_\mathfrak{p}$ and $\mathcal{M}_\mathfrak{p}$ respectively. By assumption, $\mathcal{L}_\mathfrak{p} \simeq_{\mathcal{O}_\mathfrak{p}} \mathcal{M}_\mathfrak{p}$ so there exist $\Sigma_\mathfrak{p} \in \mathbf{GL}_n(K_\mathfrak{p})$ and $U_\mathfrak{p} = (u_{i,j})_{1\le i,j\le n} \in \mathbf{GL}_n(\mathcal{O}_\mathfrak{p})$ such that $\Sigma_\mathfrak{p} B_\mathfrak{p} = C_\mathfrak{p} U_\mathfrak{p}$ and $\Sigma_\mathfrak{p}^* \Sigma_\mathfrak{p} = \mathrm{Id}$. Our goal is to output $\det(\Sigma_\mathfrak{p}) \pmod{\mathfrak{P}^e}$ for such a matrix $\Sigma_\mathfrak{p}$. The algorithm then computes the Gram matrices $G_\mathfrak{p} = {B_\mathfrak{p}}^* B_\mathfrak{p}$ and $H_\mathfrak{p} = {C_\mathfrak{p}}^* C_\mathfrak{p}$ associated to these bases. Scaling if necessary $B_\mathfrak{p}$ and $C_\mathfrak{p}$ by a common power of π, one may assume that $G_\mathfrak{p}$ and $H_\mathfrak{p}$ have their coefficients in $\mathcal{O}_\mathfrak{p}$. Because of the relation between $B_\mathfrak{p}$ and $C_\mathfrak{p}$, it holds that

$$G_\mathfrak{p} = U_\mathfrak{p}^* H_\mathfrak{p} U_\mathfrak{p}, \tag{2}$$

where $G_\mathfrak{p}, H_\mathfrak{p} \in \mathcal{M}_n(\mathcal{O}_\mathfrak{p})$ and $U_\mathfrak{p} \in \mathbf{GL}_n(\mathcal{O}_\mathfrak{p})$ is unknown. Morever writing the coordinates of the $u_{i,j}$'s in the basis $\{b_1, b_2\}$, one can transform Eq. (2) into a system of polynomial equations $\mathbf{f}(\mathbf{u}) = \mathbf{0}$ whose indeterminates lie in $\mathfrak{o}_\mathfrak{p}$. The algorithm solves this system modulo $\mathfrak{p}^e$, *i.e.*, it seeks for solutions with shape $f_0 + pf_1 + \cdots + f_{e-1}p^{e-1}$, where p is a uniformizer of $\mathfrak{o}_\mathfrak{p}$ and the f_i's run through a (finite) set of representatives for $\mathfrak{o}_\mathfrak{p}/\mathfrak{p}$. This can be done naively by an exhaustive search. Once a solution has been found, one obtains a solution $\widetilde{U}_\mathfrak{p}$ to $G_\mathfrak{p} = \widetilde{U}_\mathfrak{p}^* H_\mathfrak{p} \widetilde{U}_\mathfrak{p} \pmod{\mathfrak{p}^e\mathcal{O}}$.[9] However this solution modulo $\mathfrak{p}^e\mathcal{O}$ might not lift to a solution of Eq. (2) in $\mathcal{O}_\mathfrak{p}$. To avoid this issue, we rely on a multivariable version of Hensel's lemma (see [1]): if the solution modulo $\mathfrak{p}^e\mathcal{O}$ we found cannot be lifted, the algorithm computes another one. It may happen that no solution modulo $\mathfrak{p}^e$ can be lifted. In such cases, the algorithm computes solutions modulo $\mathfrak{p}^{e+1}, \mathfrak{p}^{e+2}$, and so on until the lifting condition is satisfied.[10] Ultimately, the

[8] Recall that $\mathfrak{o}_\mathfrak{p}$ is a principal ideal domain so $\mathcal{O}_\mathfrak{p}$ must be free over $\mathfrak{o}_\mathfrak{p}$.

[9] Notice that $\mathfrak{p}^e\mathcal{O} = b_1\mathfrak{p}^e + b_2\mathfrak{p}^e$.

[10] The existence of a solution to Eq. (2) guarantees that there are solutions modulo $\mathfrak{p}^k$ for any k, but in some exceptional cases none of these solutions may be guaranteed to lift. In fact this is the case if all the solutions in $\mathcal{O}_\mathfrak{p}$ are multiple roots of $\mathbf{f}$. In this highly unlikely case, one possible solution would be to randomize the system by sampling some $V_\mathfrak{p} \in \mathbf{GL}_n(\mathcal{O}_\mathfrak{p})$ and trying to solve $G_\mathfrak{p} = U_\mathfrak{p}^* H'_\mathfrak{p} U_\mathfrak{p}$ where $H'_\mathfrak{p} := V_\mathfrak{p}^* H_\mathfrak{p} V_\mathfrak{p}$.

algorithm computes a solution $\widetilde{U}_{\mathfrak{p}}$ modulo $\mathfrak{p}^{e+k}$ for some $k \in \mathbb{N}_{>0}$. Since $\mathfrak{P}^e$ divides $\mathfrak{p}^{e+k}$, it finally outputs $\det(C_{\mathfrak{p}}B_{\mathfrak{p}}^{-1})\det(\widetilde{U}_{\mathfrak{p}}) \pmod{\mathfrak{P}^e}$.[11]

□

Remark 1.33. Although at this stage we are not concerned with efficiency, we describe a less naive way to solve the equation $G_{\mathfrak{p}} = \widetilde{U}_{\mathfrak{p}}^* H_{\mathfrak{p}} \widetilde{U}_{\mathfrak{p}} \pmod{\mathfrak{P}^e}$, at least when the prime $\mathfrak{p}$ is unramified. Under this hypothesis, Jordan decompositions for $\mathcal{L}_{\mathfrak{p}}$ and $\mathcal{M}_{\mathfrak{p}}$ are orthogonal bases (see [9, Lemma 3.3.4]) which can be computed thanks to Lemma 1.29. Therefore, one obtains Gram matrices $G_{\mathfrak{p}}$ and $H_{\mathfrak{p}}$ which are diagonal. Still with the assumption that $\mathfrak{p}$ is unramified, the norm map $\mathrm{N} : \mathcal{O}_{\mathfrak{p}}^{\times} \to \mathfrak{o}_{\mathfrak{p}}^{\times}$ is surjective (see [19, Chapter V, §2]) so there must exists a solution $U_{\mathfrak{p}}$ to Eq. (2) which is diagonal.

Example 1.34. We illustrate the previous algorithm on an example. Let us take $(\mathfrak{o}, F, \mathcal{O}, K) = (\mathbb{Z}, \mathbb{Q}, \mathbb{Z}[i], \mathbb{Q}(i))$ and $\mathcal{L}$ (resp. $\mathcal{M}$) the $\mathcal{O}$-lattice in K^2 with basis $B = \left(\begin{smallmatrix} 2+2i & 0 \\ 0 & 3i \end{smallmatrix}\right)$ (resp. with basis $C = \left(\begin{smallmatrix} 3-2i & 3+3i \\ 4+3i & -3+3i \end{smallmatrix}\right)$). We choose $p = e = 3$ and $\mathfrak{P} = 3 \cdot \mathcal{O}$. Then, $\{1, i\}$ is a basis of $\mathcal{O}_{\mathfrak{p}}$ over $\mathfrak{o}_{\mathfrak{p}}$. Our objective is to compute $\det(\Sigma_{\mathfrak{p}}) \pmod{27}$, where $\Sigma_{\mathfrak{p}}$ maps $\mathcal{L}_p$ on $\mathcal{M}_p$ and $\Sigma_{\mathfrak{p}}^* \Sigma = \mathrm{Id}$.

Following the notations in the proof of Lemma 1.32 and the remark above, we notice that $B = B_p$ is already a Jordan decomposition $\mathcal{L}_1 \oplus \mathcal{L}_2$ of $\mathcal{L}_p$, where $\mathcal{L}_1 = \left(\begin{smallmatrix} 2+2i \\ 0 \end{smallmatrix}\right) \cdot \mathcal{O}_p$ is unimodular, and $\mathcal{L}_2 = \left(\begin{smallmatrix} 0 \\ 3i \end{smallmatrix}\right) \cdot \mathcal{O}_p$ is $\mathfrak{P}^2$-modular. Further, a Jordan decomposition of $\mathcal{M}_p$ is obtained by Gram-Schmidt orthogonalization: if we denote the columns of C by c_1, c_2, then $C_p = (c_1'|c_2')$, where $c_1' = c_1$ and

$$c_2' = c_2 - \frac{c_1^* c_2}{c_1^* c_1} c_1 = \begin{pmatrix} \frac{21}{19} + \frac{3}{19}i \\ -\frac{3}{19} - \frac{15}{19}i \end{pmatrix}.$$

Moreover the Gram matrices are $G_p = \left(\begin{smallmatrix} 8 & 0 \\ 0 & 9 \end{smallmatrix}\right)$ and $H_p = \left(\begin{smallmatrix} 38 & 0 \\ 0 & 36/19 \end{smallmatrix}\right)$. In particular, one checks that $\mathcal{L}_p$ and $\mathcal{M}_p$ are of the same Jordan type (*c.f.*, Definition 1.23) and [9, Theorem 3.3.6] ensures that $\mathcal{L}_p$ and $\mathcal{M}_p$ are isometric over $\mathcal{O}_p$. According to the previous remark, there exists a solution $U_p = \left(\begin{smallmatrix} u_1+u_2i & 0 \\ 0 & u_3+u_4i \end{smallmatrix}\right)$ to $H_p = U_p^* G_p U_p$, where $u_1, u_2, u_3, u_4 \in \mathfrak{o}_p = \mathbb{Z}_3$ and $(u_1 + u_2 i)(u_3 + u_4 i) \in \mathcal{O}_p^{\times}$. Modulo 27 we have:

$$G_p = U_p^* H_p U_p \pmod{27} \iff \begin{pmatrix} 8 & 0 \\ 0 & 9 \end{pmatrix} = \begin{pmatrix} 38\mathrm{N}(u_1 + u_2 i) & 0 \\ 0 & \frac{36}{19}\mathrm{N}(u_3 + u_4 i) \end{pmatrix} \pmod{27}$$
$$\iff \begin{cases} {u_1}^2 + {u_2}^2 = 13 \pmod{27} \\ {u_3}^2 + {u_4}^2 = 25 \pmod{27}. \end{cases}$$

Let $f_1(U_1, U_2) = {U_1}^2 + {U_2}^2 - 13$ and $f_2(U_3, U_4) = {U_3}^2 + {U_4}^2 - 25$. Then the system above is equivalent to $f_1(U_1, U_2) = 0 \pmod{27}$ and $f_2(U_3, U_4) = 0 \pmod{27}$. Moreover for the solution $\mathbf{u}_0 = (3, 2, 21, 4)$, we compute $(\nabla f_1)(3, 2) = (6, 4)$

[11] Since $\Sigma_{\mathfrak{p}} B_{\mathfrak{p}} = C_{\mathfrak{p}} U_{\mathfrak{p}}$ and $\det(\Sigma_{\mathfrak{p}}), \det(U_{\mathfrak{p}}) \in \mathcal{O}_{\mathfrak{p}}^{\times}$, we know that $\det(C_{\mathfrak{p}} B_{\mathfrak{p}}^{-1}) \in \mathcal{O}_{\mathfrak{p}}^{\times}$ as well. Morever, the latter can be computed with arbitrary precision from $B_{\mathfrak{p}}$ and $C_{\mathfrak{p}}$.

and $(\nabla f_2)(21,4) = (42,8)$. With the notations of [4], one has $|f_1(3,2)|_3 < ||(\nabla f_1)(3,2)||_3^2$ and $|f_2(21,4)|_3 < ||(\nabla f_2)(21,4)||_3^2$ and Theorem 2.1 of *loc. cit.* ensures that $\mathbf{u}_0$ can be lifted to a solution of $f_1(U_1,U_2) = f_2(U_3,U_4) = 0$ in $\mathbb{Z}_3^4$. Consequently, a solution modulo 27 is $\widetilde{U}_p = \begin{pmatrix} 3+2i & 0 \\ 0 & 21+4i \end{pmatrix}$ and the algorithm outputs $\det(C'_p B_p^{-1}) \det(\widetilde{U}_p) \pmod{27} = 1 \pmod{27}$. Indeed, one can check that $\Sigma_p = \frac{1}{2}\begin{pmatrix} 1+i & -1-i \\ 1-i & 1-i \end{pmatrix}$ is unitary, has determinant 1 and maps it $\mathcal{L}_p$ on $\mathcal{M}_p$.

A key ingredient will be an algorithm originally due to Gentry and Szydlo [8], latter revisited by Lenstra and Silverberg [11] for solving efficiently the Principal Ideal Problem (PIP) in K. Testing if an ideal is principal (and if so computing a generator) is known as a hard algorithmic problem (for classical computers only, polynomial-time complexity can be achieved given access to a quantum computer, see [1]). However there is an important speedup when one is given the relative norm of a generator as an extra information, reaching classical polynomial-time complexity.

Lemma 1.35 ([11], Theorem 1.3). *Let K/F be a CM extension. There exists a deterministic polynomial-time algorithm* `LenstraSilverberg` *that given a $\mathbb{Z}$-basis of $\mathcal{O}$, the ring of integers of K, a fractional ideal I of K and an element $w \in F$ satisfying $I \cdot \overline{I} = w \cdot \mathcal{O}$, decides whether there exists $v \in K$ such that $I = v \cdot \mathcal{O}$ and $v\overline{v} = w$, and if so computes such an element v. Moreover if no such v exists, the algorithm returns "False".*

2 Special Genera

Let $(\mathfrak{o}, F, \mathcal{O}, K, V, \Phi)$ be as in Sect. 1.4 and let $\mathcal{L}$ be a Hermitian lattice in (V, Φ). Suppose furthermore that K/F is a CM extension of number fields and $\mathfrak{o}$ (resp. $\mathcal{O}$) is the ring of integers of F (resp. of K).

Definition 2.1 (Special genus). *A Hermitian lattice $\mathcal{M}$ in (V, Φ) is in the special genus of $\mathcal{L}$ if there exists $\sigma \in \mathrm{U}(V, \Phi)$ and for all $\mathfrak{p} \in \mathbb{P}(\mathfrak{o})$, there exists $\varphi_\mathfrak{p} \in \mathrm{SU}(V_\mathfrak{p}, \Phi)$ such that $\mathcal{M}_\mathfrak{p} = \sigma(\varphi_\mathfrak{p}(\mathcal{L}_\mathfrak{p}))$.*[12]

Remark 2.2. If $\mathcal{M}$ is in the special genus of $\mathcal{L}$, then $\mathcal{M}$ is *a fortiori* in $\mathrm{gen}(\mathcal{L})$. Moreover being in the same special genus defines an equivalence relation $\sim$ on $\mathrm{gen}(\mathcal{L})$.

Definition 2.3 (Special class number). *The equivalence class of $\mathcal{L}$ for $\sim$ will be denoted by $\mathrm{sgen}(\mathcal{L})$. Further, the number of special genera in $\mathrm{gen}(\mathcal{L})$ is a finite number called the special class number of $\mathcal{L}$ and denoted by $sh(\mathcal{L})$.*[13]

[12] Notice that $\sigma \in \mathrm{U}(V, \Phi)$ can be extended to $V_\mathfrak{p} = V \otimes_K K_\mathfrak{p}$ by $\sigma(\mathbf{v} \otimes k) := \sigma(\mathbf{v}) \otimes k$.

[13] The finiteness of the class number $h(\mathcal{L})$ implies that there are only finitely many special genera in $\mathrm{gen}(\mathcal{L})$.

2.1 Shimura's Theorem

In [20], Shimura gave a complete set of invariants for the relation $\sim$ on gen($\mathcal{L}$). Morally it is given by the module index and the local determinant groups, for a few prime ideals. We follow Kirschmer's presentation [9, Section 5.4.2].

Definition 2.4. *Let $\mathcal{I}(\mathcal{O})$ be the group of fractional ideals of $\mathcal{O}$ with subgroups*

$$J = \{\mathfrak{a} \in \mathcal{I}(\mathcal{O}) \mid \mathfrak{a}\overline{\mathfrak{a}} = \mathcal{O}\} \quad \text{and} \quad J_0 = \{g\mathcal{O} \mid g \in K^\times,\, g\overline{g} = 1\}. \tag{3}$$

For $\mathfrak{p} \in \mathbb{P}(\mathfrak{o})$, we define the subgroups of $\mathcal{O}_\mathfrak{p}^\times$:

$$\begin{gathered} \mathbb{E}_{\mathfrak{p},0} = \{\varepsilon \in \mathcal{O}_\mathfrak{p}^\times \mid \varepsilon\overline{\varepsilon} = 1\} \quad ; \quad \mathbb{E}_{\mathfrak{p},1} = \{\overline{\varepsilon}\varepsilon^{-1} \mid \varepsilon \in \mathcal{O}_\mathfrak{p}^\times\} \\ \text{and} \quad \mathbb{E}(\mathcal{L}_\mathfrak{p}) = \{\det(\sigma) \mid \sigma \in \operatorname{Aut}(\mathcal{L}_\mathfrak{p})\}. \end{gathered} \tag{4}$$

The set $\mathbb{E}(\mathcal{L}_\mathfrak{p})$ will be refered as the local determinant group of $\mathcal{L}$ at $\mathfrak{p}$.

Notice that we have inclusions $J_0 \leq J \leq \mathcal{I}(\mathcal{O})$ and $\mathbb{E}_{\mathfrak{p},1}, \mathbb{E}(\mathcal{L}_\mathfrak{p}) \leq \mathbb{E}_{\mathfrak{p},0}$. The following proposition shows how to compute the local determinant groups from a Jordan decomposition.

Proposition 2.5. *Let $\mathfrak{p} \in \mathbb{P}(\mathfrak{o})$ and $\mathfrak{P} \in \mathcal{I}(\mathcal{O})$ above $\mathfrak{p}$ as is Sect. 1.4.*

1. *If $\mathfrak{p}$ is unramified in K or if $\mathcal{L}_\mathfrak{p}$ has a Jordan block of odd rank, then*

$$\mathbb{E}(\mathcal{L}_\mathfrak{p}) = \mathbb{E}_{\mathfrak{p},0}.$$

2. *If $\mathfrak{p}$ is ramified in K and $2 \notin \mathfrak{p}$, then*

$$\mathbb{E}(\mathcal{L}_\mathfrak{p}) = \begin{cases} \mathbb{E}_{\mathfrak{p},0} & \text{if } \mathcal{L}_\mathfrak{p} \text{ has a } \mathfrak{P}^i\text{-modular Jordan block for some } i \text{ even;} \\ \mathbb{E}_{\mathfrak{p},1} & \text{otherwise.} \end{cases}$$

3. *If $\mathfrak{p}$ is ramified in K and $2 \in \mathfrak{p}$, set $e := v_\mathfrak{P}(\mathfrak{D})$.[14] Then,*

$$\mathbb{E}(\mathcal{L}_\mathfrak{p}) = \begin{cases} \mathbb{E}_{\mathfrak{p},1} & \text{if } m = \operatorname{rank}(\mathcal{L}_\mathfrak{p}) \text{ is even and } \mathcal{L}_\mathfrak{p} \simeq \bigoplus_{i=1}^{m/2} H(s_i) \text{ with } s_i = e \pmod 2 \\ & \text{for all } 1 \leq i \leq \frac{m}{2} \text{ c.f., Definition 1.27;} \\ \mathbb{E}_{\mathfrak{p},0} & \text{otherwise.} \end{cases}$$

Proof. Cases *1.* and *2.* can be found in [20] or [9, Proposition 5.4.13]. For the ramified dyadic case, this was proven by Kirschmer in [10, Theorem 3.7]. □

We need a few more definitions to state Shimura's theorem.

---

[14] Recall that $\mathfrak{D}$ is the different ideal of K/F, defined in Sect. 1. Moreover in the ramified case, [10, Lemma 3.1] ensures that $v_\mathfrak{P}(\mathfrak{D}) = v_\mathfrak{P}(\pi - \overline{\pi})$.

Definition 2.6. *Let* $\mathrm{Cl}(\mathcal{O})$ *be the class group of* $\mathcal{O}$, *we put*

$$\mathrm{C}_0 := \{[\mathfrak{a}] \in \mathrm{Cl}(\mathcal{O}) \mid \overline{\mathfrak{a}} = \mathfrak{a}\} \leq \mathrm{Cl}(\mathcal{O}).$$

It is generated by $\{[\mathfrak{P}] \in \mathrm{Cl}(\mathcal{O}) \mid \mathfrak{P}$ *is ramified in* $\mathcal{O}\} \cup \{[\mathfrak{a}\mathcal{O}] \mid [\mathfrak{a}] \in \mathrm{Cl}(\mathfrak{o})\}$.

Definition 2.7. *Let* $P(\mathcal{L})$ *be the set of* $\mathfrak{p} \in \mathbb{P}(\mathfrak{o})$ *such that* $\mathbb{E}(\mathcal{L}_\mathfrak{p}) = \mathbb{E}_{\mathfrak{p},1}$. *We define*

1. $\mathbb{E}(\mathcal{L}) = \prod_{\mathfrak{p}\in P(\mathcal{L})} \mathbb{E}_{\mathfrak{p},0}/\mathbb{E}_{\mathfrak{p},1}$;
2. $R = \{(\varepsilon\mathbb{E}_{\mathfrak{p},1})_{\mathfrak{p}\in P(\mathcal{L})} \in \mathbb{E}(\mathcal{L}) \mid \varepsilon \in \mathcal{O}^\times$ *such that* $\varepsilon\overline{\varepsilon} = 1\}$;
3. $H = \{(\varepsilon\mathcal{O}, (\varepsilon\mathbb{E}_{\mathfrak{p},1})_{\mathfrak{p}\in P(\mathcal{L})} \in J \times \mathbb{E}(\mathcal{L}) \mid \varepsilon \in K^\times$ *such that* $\varepsilon\overline{\varepsilon} = 1\}$.

The set $\mathbb{E}(\mathcal{L})$ *will be refered as the determinant group of* $\mathcal{L}$.

Theorem 2.8 (Shimura, [18] Theorem 2.10). *The map*

$$\Psi : \mathrm{gen}(\mathcal{L}) \longrightarrow J \times \mathbb{E}(\mathcal{L}) \quad ; \quad \mathcal{M} \longmapsto ([\mathcal{L} : \mathcal{M}]_\mathcal{O}, (\det(\sigma_\mathfrak{p})\mathbb{E}_{\mathfrak{p},1})_{\mathfrak{p}\in P(\mathcal{L})}), \tag{5}$$

where we choose $\sigma_\mathfrak{p} \in \mathrm{U}(V_\mathfrak{p}, \Phi)$ *such that* $\mathcal{M}_\mathfrak{p} = \sigma_\mathfrak{p}(\mathcal{L}_\mathfrak{p})$ *for all* $\mathfrak{p} \in P(\mathcal{L})$, *is well defined and it induces a bijection between the set of special genera in* $\mathrm{gen}(\mathcal{L})$ *and* $(J \times \mathbb{E}(\mathcal{L}))/H$. *Moreover, the number of special genera in* $\mathrm{gen}(\mathcal{L})$ *is*

$$sh(\mathcal{L}) = [J : J_0] \cdot [\mathbb{E}(\mathcal{L}) : R] = [\mathrm{Cl}(\mathcal{O}) : \mathrm{C}_0] \cdot [\mathbb{E}(\mathcal{L}) : R]. \tag{6}$$

Remark 2.9. The map Ψ from Eq. 5 is well defined in the sense that it does not depend on the choice of $\sigma_\mathfrak{p}$. Indeed if we choose another isometry $\sigma'_\mathfrak{p}$ mapping $\mathcal{L}_p$ on $\mathcal{M}_p$, then $\sigma'_\mathfrak{p} = \sigma_\mathfrak{p} \circ \tau_\mathfrak{p}$, where $\tau_\mathfrak{p} \in \mathrm{Aut}(\mathcal{L}_\mathfrak{p})$. In particular, $\det(\tau_\mathfrak{p}) \in \mathbb{E}_{\mathfrak{p},1}$ (because $\mathfrak{p} \in P(\mathcal{L})$) and $\det(\sigma'_\mathfrak{p}) = \det(\sigma_\mathfrak{p})\det(\tau_\mathfrak{p}) = \det(\sigma_\mathfrak{p}) \pmod{\mathbb{E}_{\mathfrak{p},1}}$.

Remark 2.10. By Shimura's theorem, the module index $I = [\mathcal{L} : \mathcal{M}]_\mathcal{O}$ belongs to J, *i.e.*, it satisfies $I \cdot \overline{I} = \mathcal{O}$ whenever $\mathcal{L}$ and $\mathcal{M}$ are in the same genus. Further, asking for I to be a principal ideal is a necessary condition for having $\mathcal{M} \in \mathrm{sgen}(\mathcal{L})$.

Corollary 2.11. *Let* $\mathcal{M} \in \mathrm{gen}(\mathcal{L})$ *and for all* $\mathfrak{p} \in P$, *let us fix* $\sigma_\mathfrak{p} \in \mathrm{U}(V_\mathfrak{p}, \Phi)$ *such that* $\mathcal{M}_\mathfrak{p} = \sigma_\mathfrak{p}(\mathcal{L}_\mathfrak{p})$. *Then we have* $\mathcal{M} \in \mathrm{sgen}(\mathcal{L})$ *if and only if there exists* $\varepsilon \in K$ *such that* $\varepsilon\overline{\varepsilon} = 1$ *and*

$$\begin{cases} [\mathcal{L} : \mathcal{M}]_\mathcal{O} = \varepsilon \cdot \mathcal{O}; \\ \det(\sigma_\mathfrak{p}) = \varepsilon \pmod{\mathbb{E}_{\mathfrak{p},1}}, \text{ for all } \mathfrak{p} \in P(\mathcal{L}). \end{cases} \tag{7}$$

Proof. Observe that $\Psi(\mathcal{L}) = (\mathcal{O}, (\mathbb{E}_{\mathfrak{p},1})_{\mathfrak{p}\in P(\mathcal{L})}) \in H$. It follows from Theorem 2.8 implies that $\mathcal{M} \in \mathrm{sgen}(\mathcal{L})$ if and only if $\Psi(\mathcal{M}) \in H$.

□

2.2 An Algorithm to Distinguish Special Genera

In [18], Schiemann turned Theorem 2.8 into an algorithmic method for computing representatives of the special genera in $\mathrm{gen}(\mathcal{L})$ (see also [9, Algorithm 5.4.15]).[15] Based on Corollary 2.11, we build an algorithm to decide if $\mathcal{M} \in \mathrm{gen}(\mathcal{L})$ belongs to $\mathrm{sgen}(\mathcal{L})$. This reduces to checking if the two conditions in Eq.

Algorithm 1: Distinguish $\mathrm{sgen}(\mathcal{L})$ within $\mathrm{gen}(\mathcal{L})$

Input:
- $\mathbb{Z}$-bases of $\mathfrak{o}$ and $\mathcal{O}$;
- $\alpha \in F^\times$ such that $K = F[X]/(X^2 - \alpha)$ is a CM number field;
- Basis of a n-dimensional vector space V;
- Hermitian form $\Phi : V \to K$;
- The list $Q = \{\mathfrak{p} \in \mathbb{P}(\mathfrak{o}) \mid \mathfrak{p} \text{ ramifies in } K\}$ and the different ideal $\mathfrak{D}$;
- Pseudo-bases of Hermitian lattices $\mathcal{L}$, $\mathcal{M}$ in (V, Φ) with $\mathcal{M} \in \mathrm{gen}(\mathcal{L})$.

Output:
- 1 if $\mathcal{M} \in \mathrm{sgen}(\mathcal{L})$;
- 0 otherwise.

Compute the module index $I := [\mathcal{L} : \mathcal{M}]_{\mathcal{O}}$. `// c.f., Lemma 1.28`
Run `LenstraSilverberg` on input $(\mathcal{O}, I, 1)$. `// c.f., Lemma 1.35`
if *the output is "False"* **then**
    Return 0. `// The first condition in Equation (7) is not satisfied`
    else
        It returns $\varepsilon \in K$ such that $I = \varepsilon \cdot \mathcal{O}$ and $\varepsilon\bar{\varepsilon} = 1$.
    end
end
for $\mathfrak{p}$ *in* Q **do**
    Compute Jordan decompositions of $\mathcal{L}_\mathfrak{p}$ and $\mathcal{M}_\mathfrak{p}$. `// c.f., Lemma 1.29`
    Decide whether $\mathbb{E}(\mathcal{M}_\mathfrak{p}) = \mathbb{E}_{\mathfrak{p},0}$ or $\mathbb{E}(\mathcal{M}_\mathfrak{p}) = \mathbb{E}_{\mathfrak{p},1}$. `// c.f., Proposition 2.5`
    if $\mathbb{E}(\mathcal{M}_\mathfrak{p}) = \mathbb{E}_{\mathfrak{p},1}$ **then**
        Add $\mathfrak{p}$ to P.
    end
end
if $P = \{\}$ **then**
    Return 1. `// The second condition in Equation 7 is empty.`
    else
        for $\mathfrak{p}$ *in* P **do**
            Compute $\det(\sigma_\mathfrak{p}) \pmod{\mathfrak{P}^e}$, where $\sigma_\mathfrak{p}(\mathcal{L}_\mathfrak{p}) = \mathcal{M}_\mathfrak{p}$ is a local isometry and $e = v_\mathfrak{P}(\mathfrak{D})$. `// c.f., Lemma 1.32`
            if $\det(\sigma_\mathfrak{p})\varepsilon^{-1} - 1 \notin \mathfrak{P}^e$ **then**
                Return 0. `// c.f., Lemma 2.12`
            end
        end
    end
end
Return 1.

---

(7) are satisfied. The main trick is to use Lenstra and Silverberg algorithm (see Lemma 1.35) to test the first condition efficiently.

Before proving that Algorithm 1 is correct, we explain how the local conditions in Eq. (7) can be checked. This is done along with the loop starting at Step 19.

For $\mathfrak{p} \in P(\mathcal{L})$, the determinant of a local isometry mapping $\mathcal{L}_\mathfrak{p}$ on $\mathcal{M}_\mathfrak{p}$ can be computed with the desired precision thanks to Lemma 1.32. Then, the local condition at $\mathfrak{p}$ asks for the value of $\det(\sigma_\mathfrak{p})\varepsilon^{-1}$ modulo $\mathbb{E}_{\mathfrak{p},1}$.[16] We rely on the following result.

Lemma 2.12 (**[10], Lemma 3.5**). *Suppose that* $\mathfrak{p} \in \mathbb{P}(\mathfrak{o})$ *ramifies in* K. *Then,*

$$\mathbb{E}_{\mathfrak{p},1} = \{\varepsilon \in \mathbb{E}_{\mathfrak{p},0} \mid \varepsilon - 1 \in \mathfrak{P}^e\},$$

where e *is the* $\mathfrak{P}$*-adic valuation of* $\mathfrak{D}$.

Consequently, if $\det(\sigma_\mathfrak{p})$ is known with precision e, one can compute $\det(\sigma_\mathfrak{p})\varepsilon^{-1} \pmod{\mathfrak{P}^e}$ (recall that $\varepsilon \in K \hookrightarrow K_\mathfrak{p}$ is known exactly) and Lemma 2.12 (materialized by Step 21) gives the answer.

Moreover, let us mention that the $\mathfrak{P}$-adic valuation $\mathfrak{D}$ can be determined *a priori* (see [10, §3] for a description).

Proposition 2.13. *On input* $(\mathfrak{o}, \mathcal{O}, \alpha, V, \Phi)$, *the list* Q *of ramified prime ideals in* K/F, *the different ideal* $\mathfrak{D}$ *and pseudo-bases of Hermitian lattices* $\mathcal{L}$, $\mathcal{M}$ *in* (V, Φ) *with* $\mathcal{M} \in \operatorname{gen}(\mathcal{L})$, *Algorithm 1 outputs 1 if* $\mathcal{M} \in \operatorname{sgen}(\mathcal{L})$ *and 0 otherwise.*

Proof. Recall that $\mathcal{M} \in \operatorname{sgen}(\mathcal{L})$ if and only if all conditions in Eq. 7 are satisfied. At Step 4, the algorithm outputs 0 only if the first condition is not satisfied. By the end of the loop starting at Step 9, the set P is precisely equal to $P(\mathcal{L})$, *c.f.*, Definition 2.7. Therefore if P is in fact empty, there are no local conditions to check so we are guaranteed that $\mathcal{M} \in \operatorname{sgen}(\mathcal{L})$. Otherwise, for each $\mathfrak{p} \in P$, Step 21 tests if $\det(\sigma_\mathfrak{p}) = \varepsilon \pmod{\mathbb{E}_{\mathfrak{p},1}}$, which is the local condition given by Eq. 7 at $\mathfrak{p}$. By the end of the loop starting at Step 19, and if the algorithm has not returned 0, then all the conditions are satisfied and $\mathcal{M}$ belongs to the special genus of $\mathcal{L}$.

□

Remark 2.14. A rigorous complexity analysis of Algorithm 1 is set aside, since the complexity of Step 20 is unknown. Except for the latter (and Step 10 if $2 \in \mathfrak{p}$, see Remark 1.31), all the other steps can be executed in polynomial time in the size of the input. Moreover notice that the list Q given as input may be hard to compute for arbitrary fields. Nonetheless for cyclotomic fields $K = \mathbb{Q}(\zeta_m)$, Lemma 1.1 ensures that Q is either empty (if m is composite) or contains only one prime ideal, which is completely determined (if m is a prime power).

[15] Precisely, Schiemann's algorithm computes a set of representatives for the isometry classes in $\operatorname{gen}(\mathcal{L})$, by first computing representatives for the special genera and then iterating a neighbouring method on it.

[16] It follows from [9, Remark 5.4.12, 2.] that the quotient group $\mathbb{E}_{\mathfrak{p},0}/\mathbb{E}_{\mathfrak{p},1}$ has two elements and a system of representatives is given by $\{1, \overline{\pi}\pi^{-1}\} = \{1, u_\mathfrak{p}\}$.

3 Consequences on Module-LIP

In this section we expose the cryptographic motivation and applications behind the study of special genera and Algorithm 1. We fix $m \in \mathbb{N}_{>0}$ and a primitive m-th root of unity ζ_m, and we set $K = \mathbb{Q}(\zeta_m) \simeq \mathbb{Q}[X]/(\Phi_m)$ to be the cyclotomic field with conductor m and degree $d = \varphi(m)$. The maximal order of K is $\mathcal{O} = \mathbb{Z}[\zeta_m]$. Further, let $F = \mathbb{Q}(\zeta_m + \zeta_m^{-1})$ and $\mathfrak{o} = \mathbb{Z}[\zeta_m + \zeta_m^{-1}]$.

As mentionned in Sect. 1, K/F is a CM extension of number fields thus $(\mathfrak{o}, F, \mathcal{O}, K)$ falls under the scope of Sect. 2. Finally we let $n \in \mathbb{N}_{>0}$ and $V = K^n$ endowed with the standard Hermitian form $\Phi(\mathbf{v}, \mathbf{w}) = \sum_{i=1}^{n} v_i \overline{w_i}$.

3.1 Search and Decision Module-LIP

The (search variant of the) module-Lattice Isomorphism Problem (module-LIP) has been defined in a more general framework than the one presented here, see [15]. Let us recall the notion of pseudo-Gram matrix given in Definition 1.16. In particular for any pseudo-Gram matrix $\mathbf{G} = (G, \{\mathfrak{a}_i\}_{1 \le i \le n})$, there always exists an underlying $B \in \mathbf{GL}_n(K)$ such that $G = B^*B$.[17] Following [15, Section 3.1], we say that two pseudo-Gram matrices $\mathbf{G} = (G, \{\mathfrak{a}_i\}_{1 \le i \le n})$ and $\mathbf{H} = (H, \{\mathfrak{b}_i\}_{1 \le i \le n})$ are *congruent* whenever there exists $U = (u_{i,j})_{1 \le i,j \le n} \in \mathbf{GL}_n(K)$ such that $H = U^*GU$ and *2.* and *3.* of Proposition 1.9 are satisfied. Such a matrix U, called a *congruence matrix* between $\mathbf{G}$ and $\mathbf{H}$.

Definition 3.1. (search-modLIP$_K^{\mathbf{B}}$, Definition 3.11 [15]). *Let* $\mathbf{B}$ *be a pseudo-basis of a Hermitian lattice* $\mathcal{L}$ *in* (V, Φ)*, and* $\mathbf{G}$ *the pseudo-Gram matrix associated to* $\mathbf{B}$*. Let* $\mathbf{H}$ *be a pseudo-Gram matrix congruent to* $\mathbf{G}$*. Then the (worst-case) search module Lattice Isomorphism Problem with parameters* K *and* $\mathbf{B}$ *(search-modLIP$_K^{\mathbf{B}}$) and input* $\mathbf{H}$*, is to compute a congruence matrix between* $\mathbf{G}$ *and* $\mathbf{H}$*.*

On the other hand, the decisional variant has been defined previously but only for Euclidean lattices (called dLIP, see [6, Section 2.2]). Its definition is naturally adapted for Hermitian lattices in (V, Φ).

Definition 3.2. (decision-modLIP$_K^{\mathbf{B}}$). *Let* $\mathbf{B}$ *be a pseudo-basis of a Hermitian lattice* $\mathcal{L}$ *in* (V, Φ)*, and* $\mathbf{G}$ *the pseudo-Gram matrix associated to* $\mathbf{B}$*. Let* $\mathbf{H}$ *be a pseudo-Gram matrix. Then the decision module Lattice Isomorphism Problem with parameters* K *and* $\mathbf{B}$ *(decision-modLIP$_K^{\mathbf{B}}$) and input* $\mathbf{H}$*, is to decide if* $\mathbf{G}$ *and* $\mathbf{H}$ *are congruent.*

---

[17] In [15], pseudo-Gram matrices are defined more generally for *module-lattices* in $(K_{\mathbb{R}})^n$, where $K_{\mathbb{R}} = K \otimes_{\mathbb{Q}} \mathbb{R}$. A subtle point in this setting is that a (pseudo)-Gram matrix G with coefficients in K is not necessarily associated with a Hermitian lattice $\mathcal{L} \subset K^n$, *i.e.*, a factorization $G = B^*B$ with $B \in \mathbf{GL}_n(K)$ may not exist. However, such a (Cholesky) factorization is always possible over $K_{\mathbb{R}}$, see [15, Lemma 3.10].

An important observation is that $\mathbf{G}$ and $\mathbf{H}$ are congruent if and only if they are associated to pseudo-bases of isomorphic Hermitian lattices in (V, Φ). Thanks to this rephrasing, there is a well defined notion of genus (resp. special genus) for pseudo-Gram matrices, *i.e.*, we say that $\mathbf{G}$ and $\mathbf{H}$ are in the same *genus*, denoted $\mathbf{H} \in \mathrm{gen}(\mathbf{G})$ (resp. *special genus*, denoted $\mathbf{H} \in \mathrm{sgen}(\mathbf{G})$) when they are associated to pseudo-bases of Hermitian lattices in the same genus (resp. special genus).

3.2 An Algorithm for HAWK's Lattice

Given $\mathbf{G}$ and $\mathbf{H}$, one can decide whether $\mathbf{H}$ is in $\mathrm{gen}(\mathbf{G})$ by computing and comparing Jordan decompositions (see Lemma 1.29 and Remark 1.30). Thus in order to make decision-modLIP$_K^{\mathbf{B}}$ a hard problem, the input $\mathbf{H}$ has to be chosen in the genus of $\mathbf{G}$. Now concerning the special genus, unfortunately Algorithm 1 is not suited to the setting of decision-modLIP, since the computation of $[\mathcal{L} : \mathcal{M}]_{\mathcal{O}}$, where $\mathcal{L}$ (resp. $\mathcal{M}$) is associated to $\mathbf{G}$ (resp. $\mathbf{H}$), in Step 1 requires pseudo-bases of $\mathcal{L}$ and $\mathcal{M}$.[18] As a consequence, we relax the conditions in Corollary 2.11. Concretely, we put aside the local conditions and we focus on testing if $[\mathcal{L} : \mathcal{M}]_{\mathcal{O}}$ is a principal ideal generated by an element of norm 1; a necessary condition for having $\mathcal{M} \in \mathrm{sgen}(\mathcal{L})$, according to Theorem 2.8 and Remark 2.10.

In fact the local conditions in Corollary 2.11 only have a negligible contribution in the size of $sh(\mathcal{L}) = [\mathrm{Cl}(\mathcal{O}) : \mathrm{C}_0] \cdot [\mathbb{E}(\mathcal{L}) : R]$ (see Eq. (6)). Indeed, $[\mathbb{E}(\mathcal{L}) : R] \leq \#\mathbb{E}(\mathcal{L}) \leq 2^{\#P(\mathcal{L})}$ and $P(\mathcal{L})$ is contained in the set of primes of F which ramify in K. For cyclotomic fields, there is at most one ramified prime ideal (see Lemma 1.1) so $[\mathbb{E}(\mathcal{L}) : R] \leq 2$. Moreover using only pseudo-Gram matrices, we show how Lenstra and Silverberg's algorithm (Lemma 1.35) allows to decide whether $[\mathcal{L} : \mathcal{M}]_{\mathcal{O}}$ is a principal ideal generated by an element of norm 1 (although it does not give access to any generator).

Proposition 3.3. *Let K be a cyclotomic number field and $\mathbf{G} = (G, \{\mathfrak{a}_i\}_{1 \leq i \leq n})$, $\mathbf{H} = (H, \{\mathfrak{b}_i\}_{1 \leq i \leq n}) \in \mathrm{gen}(\mathbf{G})$ be pseudo-Gram matrices associated to Hermitian lattices $\mathcal{L}$ and $\mathcal{M}$ in K^n. On input $\mathbf{G}$ and $\mathbf{H}$, Algorithm 2 decides whether the module index $[\mathcal{L} : \mathcal{M}]_{\mathcal{O}}$ is a principal ideal generated by an element of norm 1. Moreover, the algorithm runs in polynomial-time in the size of the input.*

Proof. Recall from Corollary 1.15 that $[\mathcal{L} : \mathcal{M}]_{\mathcal{O}}$ is principal if and only if $\mathrm{St}(\mathcal{L}) = \mathrm{St}(\mathcal{M})$, *i.e.*, if and only if $[\mathfrak{a}_1 \cdots \mathfrak{a}_n] = [\mathfrak{b}_1 \cdots \mathfrak{b}_n]$ in $\mathrm{Cl}(\mathcal{O})$. We introduce $J := \det(B^{-1}C) \cdot [\mathcal{L} : \mathcal{M}]_{\mathcal{O}}$. Thanks to Lemma 1.14, J equals $\det(G^{-1}H) \cdot \prod_i \mathfrak{a}_i^{-1}\mathfrak{b}_i$. Hence it is a fractional ideal of K efficiently computable from $\mathbf{G}$ and $\mathbf{H}$. We compute $J \cdot \overline{J} = \det(G^{-1}H) \cdot [\mathcal{L} : \mathcal{M}]_{\mathcal{O}} \cdot \overline{[\mathcal{L} : \mathcal{M}]_{\mathcal{O}}}$ and according to Theorem 2.8 and Remark 2.10, we have $[\mathcal{L} : \mathcal{M}]_{\mathcal{O}} \cdot \overline{[\mathcal{L} : \mathcal{M}]_{\mathcal{O}}} = \mathcal{O}$ so $J \cdot \overline{J} = \det(G^{-1}H) \cdot \mathcal{O}$.

One observes that J is principal if and only if $[\mathcal{L} : \mathcal{M}]_{\mathcal{O}}$ is, and it has a generator of norm $\det(G^{-1}H)$ if and only if $[\mathcal{L} : \mathcal{M}]_{\mathcal{O}}$ has a generator of norm

[18] We emphasize that computing a factorization of H in $\mathbf{GL}_n(K)$ is in general a hard task. A so-called Cholesky factorization of G is efficiently computable, but it has usually its coefficients in $K_{\mathbb{R}} = K \otimes_{\mathbb{Q}} \mathbb{R}$ instead of K, see [15, Proposition 3.4].

Algorithm 2: Decide if $[\mathcal{L} : \mathcal{M}]_{\mathcal{O}}$ is generated by an element of norm 1

Input: • Pseudo-Gram matrices $\mathbf{G} = (G, \{\mathfrak{a}_i\}_{1 \le i \le n})$ and $\mathbf{H} = (H, \{\mathfrak{b}_i\}_{1 \le i \le n})$ of (unknown) Hermitian lattices $\mathcal{L}$, $\mathcal{M}$ with $\mathbf{H} \in \mathrm{gen}(\mathbf{G})$.

Output: • 1 if $[\mathcal{L} : \mathcal{M}]_{\mathcal{O}}$ is principal;
• 0 otherwise.

Set $\gamma = \det(G^{-1}H)$ and build the fractional ideal $J = \gamma \cdot \mathfrak{a}_1^{-1}\mathfrak{b}_1 \cdots \mathfrak{a}_n^{-1}\mathfrak{b}_n$.
Run `LenstraSilverberg`(J, γ). `// c.f., Lemma 1.35`
if *the output is False* **then**
  Return 0. `// The first condition in Equation (7) is not verified`
  else
    It returns $\eta \in K$ such that $J = \eta \cdot \mathcal{O}$ and $\eta\overline{\eta} = \gamma$.
    Return 1.
  end
end

1. Since a basis of J is known, as well as a generator of $J \cdot \overline{J}$, then a call to Lenstra and Silverberg algorithm (Lemma 1.35) on input $(J, \det(G^{-1}H))$ allows to conclude.

□

Remark 3.4. Interestingly, the set $P(\mathcal{L})$ can be shown to be empty for several Hermitian lattices, including HAWK's lattice $\mathcal{O}^2$. As a result, there are no local conditions to verify for these lattices, and Algorithm 2 alone suffices to determine whether two such Hermitian lattices lie in the same special genus.

Corollary 3.5 (HAWK). *Let K be a cyclotomic number field. Suppose that* $\mathbf{B}$ *is a pseudo-basis of HAWK's lattice* $\mathcal{O}^2$ *and* $\mathbf{G}$ *is the pseudo-Gram matrix associated. Let* $\mathbf{H}$ *be an input of decision-modLIP*$^{\mathbf{B}}_{K}$. *Then on input* $\mathbf{B}$ *and* $\mathbf{H}$, *Algorithm 2 decides in polynomial-time whether* $\mathbf{H} \in \mathrm{sgen}(\mathbf{G})$.

Proof. If a Hermitian lattice $\mathcal{L}$ admits an orthogonal decomposition $\mathcal{L} = \mathcal{L}_1 \perp \mathcal{L}_2$ in which $\mathcal{L}_1$ has rank one, then each completion $\mathcal{L}_{\mathfrak{p}}$ contains a Jordan block of odd rank. In this case, Proposition 2.5 implies that $P(\mathcal{L})$ is empty. By Corollary 2.11, deciding whether a lattice $\mathcal{M} \in \mathrm{gen}(\mathcal{L})$ belongs to the special genus $\mathrm{sgen}(\mathcal{L})$ reduces to checking whether the ideal index $[\mathcal{L} : \mathcal{M}]_{\mathcal{O}}$ is principal and generated by an element of norm 1. For such lattices, we conclude that Algorithm 2 correctly distinguishes $\mathrm{sgen}(\mathcal{L})$ within $\mathrm{gen}(\mathcal{L})$. In particular, this immediately applies to HAWK's lattice $\mathcal{O}^2$.

□

3.3 Numerical Estimates for HAWK's Lattice

Ultimately, we take a closer look at HAWK's lattice $\mathcal{O}^2$. For this specific lattice, we compute exactly the number $sh(\mathcal{O}^2)$ of special genera contained in its genus, using Equation (6). Subsequently, we derive bounds on $h(\mathcal{L})$, the number of isometry classes within the genus of $\mathcal{O}^2$. Taken together, these results provide numerical evidence that distinguishing special genera within $\mathrm{gen}(\mathcal{O}^2)$ offers limited advantage for solving the decision module-LIP problem (for the parameter K and lattice $\mathcal{O}^2$).

Proposition 3.6. *Let K be the cyclotomic number field of conductor m and with maximal totally real subfield F. The number of special genera in $\mathrm{gen}(\mathcal{O}^2)$ equals*

$$sh(\mathcal{O}^2) = \frac{h_K}{h_F}, \tag{8}$$

where h_K (resp. h_F) is the class number of K (resp. F).

Proof. Recall from Theorem 2.8 that $sh(\mathcal{O}^2) = [\mathrm{Cl}(\mathcal{O}) : \mathrm{C}_0] \cdot [\mathbb{E}(\mathcal{O}^2) : R]$. We compute these two factors individually. Recall the notations for $\mathrm{Cl}(\mathcal{O})$ and C_0 from Definition 2.6. In our case, C_0 is generated by the classes $[\mathfrak{a}\mathcal{O}]$ where $\mathfrak{a} \in \mathcal{I}(\mathfrak{o})$ and eventually if m is a prime power, the class of the unique ramified prime $\mathfrak{P}$. But $\mathfrak{P} = (1-\zeta_m)\cdot\mathcal{O}$ (see Lemma 1.1) so $[\mathfrak{P}] = [\mathcal{O}]$ and $[\mathrm{Cl}(\mathcal{O}) : \mathrm{C}_0] = h_K/h_F$. For the second term, Remark 3.4 yields $[\mathbb{E}(\mathcal{O}^2) : R] = 1$. □

Remark 3.7. More generally for a rank-2 Hermitian lattice $\mathcal{L}$ in K^2, the same proof as above shows that $sh(\mathcal{L}) \in \{\frac{h_K}{h_F}, \frac{2h_K}{h_F}\}$ (this is because $[\mathbb{E}(\mathcal{L}) : R] \leq \#\mathbb{E}(\mathcal{L}) \leq 2$).

Remark 3.8. Even if it means to assume GRH, $h_F = 1$ holds for several conductors m including a lot of primes and all power-of-two up to 512 (see [14] and [13]). More generally for power-of-two conductors, Weber conjectured that $h_F = 1$ always holds.

One the other hand, bounds on $h(\mathcal{O}^2)$, *i.e.*, the number of isometry classes in the genus of $\mathcal{O}^2$, can be obtained by computing the *mass* of $\mathcal{O}^2$. In full generality, the mass of a Hermitian lattice is defined as follows.

Definition 3.9. *Let $\mathcal{L}$ be a Hermitian lattice in (V, Φ). The mass of $\mathcal{L}$ is*

$$\mathrm{Mass}(\mathcal{L}) := \sum_{\mathcal{L}'} \frac{1}{\#(\mathrm{Aut}(\mathcal{L}'))},$$

where the sums ranges on a set of representatives for the isometry classes in $\mathrm{gen}(\mathcal{L})$.

Remark 3.10. Estimates on the automorphism groups $\mathrm{Aut}(\mathcal{L}')$ yield bounds on $h(\mathcal{L})$ in terms of $\mathrm{Mass}(\mathcal{L})$. For instance since $\mu(K)$ embeds in $\mathrm{Aut}(\mathcal{L}')$ for any Hermitian lattice $\mathcal{L}'$, the lower bound $\#(\mathrm{Aut}(\mathcal{L}')) \geq \#(\mu(K)) = m$ holds, giving

$\mathrm{Mass}(\mathcal{L}) \leq h(\mathcal{L})/m$.[19] For rank-2 Hermitian lattices, Chevignard *et al.* proved in [2, Theorem 3.12] the upper bound $\mathrm{Aut}(\mathcal{L}') \leq 32d^2m$. Altogether we obtain

$$\mathfrak{B}_- := m \cdot \mathrm{Mass}(\mathcal{L}) \leq h(\mathcal{L}) \leq 32d^2\, m \cdot \mathrm{Mass}(\mathcal{L}) =: \mathfrak{B}_+, \tag{9}$$

for any rank-2 Hermitian lattice $\mathcal{L}$.

Moreover the mass of $\mathcal{L}$ can be computed using a formula due to Siegel. We specialize this formula to rank-2 Hermitian lattices in K^2.

Theorem 3.11 (Siegel's mass formula, [9], **Proposition 4.2.7** *3.***).** *Let $\mathcal{L}$ be a rank-2 Hermitian lattice in K^2. Then,*

$$\mathrm{Mass}(\mathcal{L}) = \frac{1}{2^{d-1}} \cdot \prod_{\mathfrak{p}\in\mathbb{P}(\mathfrak{o})} \lambda(\mathcal{L}_\mathfrak{p}) \cdot \left|\frac{\zeta_K}{\zeta_F}(0)\right| \cdot |\zeta_F(-1)|\,, \tag{10}$$

where the local factors $\lambda(\mathcal{L}_\mathfrak{p})$ are defined in [9, Definition 4.2.6] and ζ_F, ζ_K are the Dedekind zeta functions of F and K respectively.

The computation of $\mathrm{Mass}(\mathcal{O}^2)$ was done by van Gent [25] for power-of-two conductors $m \in \{512, 1024, 2048\}$. For completeness, we generalize [25, Lemma 4] to any conductor.

Lemma 3.12 ([25], **Lemma 4**). *Let $\mathfrak{p} \in \mathbb{P}(\mathfrak{o})$. Then,*

$$\lambda({\mathcal{O}_\mathfrak{p}}^2) = \begin{cases} \frac{1}{2}(p+1) & \text{if } m = p^r \text{ and } \mathfrak{p} \text{ is the unique ramified prime above } p; \\ 3 & \text{if } m = 2^r \text{ and } \mathfrak{p} \text{ is the unique ramified prime above } 2; \\ 1 & \text{otherwise.} \end{cases}$$

Proof. The formula for the local factors is given by [9, Lemma 4.2.9], for which $m_0 = 2$ and $m_1 = 0$. Suppose first that the conductor m is composite. Then by Lemma 1.1, $\mathfrak{p}$ is unramified and the local factor is either equal to $\binom{2}{2}_2 = 1$ (split case) or to $|\binom{2}{2}_{-2}| = 1$ (inert case). Now assume that $m = p^r$ with p an odd prime number. If $p \notin \mathfrak{p}$, the same computation as before gives $\lambda({\mathcal{O}_\mathfrak{p}}^2) = 1$. Otherwise $\mathfrak{p}$ is the unique prime ideal above p and the local factors equals $\frac{1}{2}(p+1)\binom{1}{0}_{p^2} = \frac{1}{2}(p+1)$. Finally the case of power-of-two conductors was treated in [25, Lemma 4] (for arbitrary rank).

□

Together with Eq. (9), we obtain an estimation on the class number of $\mathcal{L}$. We do the computations for power-of-two conductors $m \in \{128, 256, 512, 1024\}$ but also for the prime $m = 131$ and $m = 134$. These conductors are taken such that $h_F = 1$ (see [28] and [14] for the values of h_K), in order to maximize $sh(\mathcal{O}^2)$. We obtain the following results using the same PARI/GP [23] code as in [25].

[19] The roots of unity $\mu(K)$ embed in $\mathrm{Aut}(\mathcal{L}')$ by the diagonal mapping $\mu \mapsto \mathrm{diag}(\mu, \ldots, \mu)$.

m	d	$\log_2(\mathfrak{B}_-)$	$\log_2(\mathfrak{B}_+)$	$\log_2(\frac{h_K}{h_F})$
128	64	138	155	18
134	66	123	154	20
256	128	397	416	63
131	130	387	420	65
512	256	1040	1062	182 (GRH)
1024	512	2564	2607	?

Fig. 3. Bit size estimations for the bounds on $h(\mathcal{O}^2)$ and $\frac{h_K}{h_F} = sh(\mathcal{O}^2)$.

Remark 3.13. The results above for $\mathcal{O}^2$ do not differ much for an arbitrary rank-2 Hermitian lattice $\mathcal{L}$. Indeed the special class number of $\mathcal{L}$ is either equal to h_K/h_F or $2h_K/h_F$ if $[\mathbb{E}(\mathcal{L}) : R] = 2$, and [25, Corollary 6] states the inequality $\text{Mass}(\mathcal{L}) \geq \frac{1}{3}\,\text{Mass}(\mathcal{O}^2)$ so the class number of $\mathcal{L}$ cannot be way smaller.

Remark 3.14. We conclude this section by giving an example of $\mathcal{O}$-lattices which are not isomorphic but belong to the same special genus. Let $\mathcal{L} = \mathfrak{a}\mathbf{b_1} \oplus \mathfrak{b}\mathbf{b_2}$ and $\mathcal{M} = \mathbf{b_1} \oplus \mathfrak{a}\mathfrak{b}\mathbf{b_2}$, where $\mathbf{b_1} = \left(\begin{smallmatrix}1\\0\end{smallmatrix}\right), \mathbf{b_2} = \left(\begin{smallmatrix}0\\1\end{smallmatrix}\right)$ and $\mathfrak{a}, \mathfrak{b} \subset K$ are coprime integral ideals. If $\mathfrak{p} \in \mathbb{P}(\mathfrak{o})$ does not divide $\mathfrak{a}$ or $\mathfrak{b}$, then $\mathcal{L}_\mathfrak{p} \simeq_{\mathcal{O}_\mathfrak{p}} \mathcal{O}_\mathfrak{p}\mathbf{b_1} \oplus \mathcal{O}_\mathfrak{p}\mathbf{b_2} \simeq_{\mathcal{O}_\mathfrak{p}} \mathcal{M}_\mathfrak{p}$. Now if $\mathfrak{p}$ divides $\mathfrak{a}$, one has $\mathcal{L}_\mathfrak{p} \simeq_{\mathcal{O}_\mathfrak{p}} \mathfrak{p}^{v_\mathfrak{p}(\mathfrak{a})}\mathbf{b_1} \oplus \mathcal{O}_\mathfrak{p}\mathbf{b_2} \simeq_{\mathcal{O}_\mathfrak{p}} \mathcal{M}_\mathfrak{p}$, because $\mathfrak{p} \nmid \mathfrak{b}$. In the same way, $\mathcal{L}_\mathfrak{p} \simeq_{\mathcal{O}_\mathfrak{p}} \mathcal{M}_\mathfrak{p}$ if $\mathfrak{p} \mid \mathfrak{b}$. Therefore, $\mathcal{L}$ and $\mathcal{M}$ are in the same genus. Moreover, the Steinitz class of $\mathcal{L}$ and $\mathcal{M}$ are both equal to $[\mathfrak{a}\mathfrak{b}]$ so Remark 3.4 gives the claim.

Acknowledgement. The author would like to express its gratitude to Alice Pellet-Mary and Renaud Coulangeon for helpful disscusions and comments on the draft. Thanks to Marius Kirschmer for answering technical questions. Thanks also to the anonymous reviewers for relevant comments and suggestions on the draft. The author was supported by the France 2030 program, managed by the French National Research Agency under grant agreement No. ANR-22-PETQ-0008 PQTLS.

References

1. Biasse, J.F., Song, F.: Efficient quantum algorithms for computing class groups and solving the principal ideal problem in arbitrary degree number fields. In: Proceedings of the Twenty-seventh Annual ACM-SIAM Symposium on Discrete Algorithms, pp. 893–902. SIAM (2016)
2. Chevignard, C., Fouque, P.-A., Mureau, G., Pellet-Mary, A., Wallet, A.: A reduction from hawk to the principal ideal problem in a quaternion algebra. Cryptology ePrint Archive (2024)
3. Cohen, H.: Advanced Topics in Computational Number Theory, vol. 193. Springer Science & Business Media (2012)

4. Conrad, K.: A multivariable Hensel's lemma. In: Lecture Note (2020). http://kconrad.math.uconn.edu/blurbs
5. Ducas, L., Postlethwaite, E.W., Pulles, L.N., van Woerden, W.: Hawk: module lip makes lattice signatures fast, compact and simple. In: International Conference on the Theory and Application of Cryptology and Information Security, pp. 65–94. Springer (2022)
6. Ducas, L., van Woerden, W.: On the lattice isomorphism problem, quadratic forms, remarkable lattices, and cryptography. In: Annual International Conference on the Theory and Applications of Cryptographic Techniques, pp. 643–673. Springer (2022)
7. Earnest, A.G., Estes, D.R.: Class groups in the genus and spinor genus of binary quadratic lattices. Proc. Lond. Math. Soc. **3**(1), 40–52 (1980)
8. Gentry, C., Szydlo, M.: Cryptanalysis of the revised NTRU signature scheme. In: International Conference on the Theory and Applications of Cryptographic Techniques, pp. 299–320. Springer (2002)
9. Kirschmer, M.: Definite quadratic and Hermitian forms with small class number. RWTH Aachen University, Habilitation (2016)
10. Kirschmer, M.: Determinant groups of Hermitian lattices over local fields. Arch. Math. **113**(4), 337–347 (2019)
11. Lenstra Jr., H.W., Silverberg, A.: Testing isomorphism of lattices over CM-orders. SIAM J. Comput. **48**(4), 1300–1334 (2019)
12. Ling, C., Liu, J., Mendelsohn, A.: On the spinor genus and the distinguishing lattice isomorphism problem. In: International Conference on the Theory and Application of Cryptology and Information Security, pp. 329–358. Springer (2024)
13. Miller, J.C.: Class numbers of totally real fields and applications to the weber class number problem. arXiv preprint: arXiv:1405.1094 (2014)
14. Miller, J.C.: Real cyclotomic fields of prime conductor and their class numbers ii (algebraic number theory and related topics 2014) **64**, 19–32 (2017)
15. Mureau, G., Pellet-Mary, A., Pliatsok, G., Wallet, A.: Cryptanalysis of rank-2 module-lip in totally real number fields. In: Annual International Conference on the Theory and Applications of Cryptographic Techniques, pp. 226–255. Springer (2024)
16. Neukirch, J.: Algebraic Number Theory, vol. 322. Springer Science & Business Media (2013)
17. O'Meara, O.T.: Introduction to Quadratic Forms, vol. 117. Springer (2013)
18. Schiemann, A.: Classification of hermitian forms with the neighbour method. J. Symb. Comput. **26**(4), 487–508 (1998)
19. Serre, J.-P.: Local Fields, vol. 67. Springer Science & Business Media (2013)
20. Shimura, G.: Arithmetic of unitary groups. Ann. Math. **79**(2), 369–409 (1964)
21. The Stacks Project Authors. Stacks Project (2018). https://stacks.math.columbia.edu
22. Szydlo, M.: Hypercubic lattice reduction and analysis of GGH and NTRU signatures. In: International Conference on the Theory and Applications of Cryptographic Techniques, pp. 433–448. Springer (2003)
23. The PARI Group, Univ. Bordeaux. PARI/GP version 2.16.2 (2024). http://pari.math.u-bordeaux.fr/
24. van Gent, D., van Woerden, W.: A search to distinguish reduction for the isomorphism problem on direct sum lattices. Cryptology ePrint Archive (2025)
25. van Gent, D.M.H.: A note on the genus of the hawk lattice. Cryptology ePrint Archive (2025)

26. van Woerden, W.: Dense and smooth lattices in any genus. In: International Conference on the Theory and Application of Cryptology and Information Security, pp. 386–417. Springer (2024)
27. Washington, L.C.: Introduction to Cyclotomic Fields, vol. 83. Springer Science & Business Media (2012)
28. Wikipedia. Cyclotomic field — Wikipedia, the free encyclopedia (2025). http://en.wikipedia.org/w/index.php?title=Cyclotomic%20field&oldid=1263364879

Differential Privacy

Differentially Private Learning Beyond the Classical Dimensionality Regime

Cynthia Dwork[1], Pranay Tankala[1](✉), and Linjun Zhang[2]

[1] Harvard University, Cambridge, MA 02138, USA
pranay_tankala@g.harvard.edu

[2] Rutgers University, New Brunswick, NJ 08901, USA

Abstract. We initiate the study of differentially private learning in the *proportional dimensionality regime*, in which the number of data samples n and problem dimension d approach infinity at rates proportional to one another, meaning that $d/n \to \delta$ as $n \to \infty$ for an arbitrary, given constant $\delta \in (0, \infty)$. This setting is significantly more challenging than that of all prior theoretical work in high-dimensional differentially private learning, which, despite the name, has assumed that $\delta = 0$ or is sufficiently small for problems of sample complexity $O(d)$, a regime typically considered "low-dimensional" or "classical" by modern standards in high-dimensional statistics.

We provide sharp theoretical estimates of the error of several well-studied differentially private algorithms for robust linear regression and logistic regression, including output perturbation, objective perturbation, and noisy stochastic gradient descent, in the proportional dimensionality regime. The $1 + o(1)$ factor precision of our error estimates enables a far more nuanced understanding of the price of privacy of these algorithms than that afforded by existing, coarser analyses, which are essentially vacuous in the regime we consider. Using our estimates, we discover a previously unobserved "double descent"-like phenomenon in the training error of objective perturbation for robust linear regression. We also identify settings in which output perturbation outperforms objective perturbation on average, and vice versa.

To prove our main theorems, we introduce—and strengthen, to handle perturbations required for privacy—several probabilistic tools that have not previously been used to analyze differentially private learning algorithms, such as a modern Gaussian comparison inequality and recent universality laws with origins in statistical physics.

Keywords: Differential privacy · High-dimensional statistics

1 Introduction

Over the past two decades, a groundbreaking line of research has demonstrated the limitations of classical statistical theory for modern high-dimensional supervised learning problems [15,28,47,97]. For example, although the classical theory of logistic regression predicts that the maximum likelihood estimator is

B. Applebaum and H. Lin (Eds.): TCC 2025, LNCS 16271, pp. 321–355, 2026.
https://doi.org/10.1007/978-3-032-12290-2_11

asymptotically unbiased with variance given by the inverse Fisher information, these predictions fail dramatically in the *proportional dimensionality regime*, in which the number data samples n and problem dimension d approach infinity at rates proportional to one another. However, this proportional high-dimensional regime is highly relevant in modern data science, where technological advances give rise to datasets with feature dimensions comparable to, or even exceeding, sample sizes. Indeed, in genomic, neuroscience, and image data from various domains, the dimensionality d of the data is often larger than n. A number of statistical techniques have been developed to address these challenges [13,14,36,37,45,53,54,105].

In this paper, we initiate the study of *differentially private* learning in the proportional dimensionality regime. Prior to our work, it was not even clear that *anything* non-trivial can be achieved in this regime. As an illustrative example, consider the task of fitting a d-dimensional linear regression model to n labeled data samples $(\boldsymbol{x}_i, y_i) \in \mathbb{R}^d \times \mathbb{R}$. For simplicity, suppose that $\boldsymbol{\beta}^\star \in [-1,+1]^d$ denotes the unknown regression coefficients, that the feature vectors $\boldsymbol{x}_i$ are sub-gaussian with covariance $\frac{1}{d}\boldsymbol{I}_d$, and that the labels y_i have constant variance given $\boldsymbol{\beta}^\star$ and $\boldsymbol{x}_i$. In this setting, there exists an $(\varepsilon_{\mathrm{DP}}, \delta_{\mathrm{DP}})$-differentially private algorithm [71], such that for any sufficiently small $\alpha > 0$, the algorithm's output $\widehat{\boldsymbol{\beta}}$ has error[1] $\frac{1}{d}\|\widehat{\boldsymbol{\beta}} - \boldsymbol{\beta}^\star\|^2 \leq \alpha^2$ with probability 99%, and the algorithm only uses a sample of size

$$n \leq O\bigg(\frac{d}{\alpha^2} + \frac{d + \log(1/\delta_{\mathrm{DP}})}{\alpha\varepsilon_{\mathrm{DP}}}\bigg) \cdot \mathrm{polylog}\Big(\frac{1}{\alpha}\Big).$$

Although this sample complexity upper bound is tight up to polylogarithmic factors [26], it yields vacuous error bounds in the proportional regime[2]. In the absence of knowledge of the constant suppressed by the $O(\cdot)$ notation, this bound on α is no better than that of the trivial estimator $\widehat{\boldsymbol{\beta}}_{\mathrm{trivial}} = \boldsymbol{0}$, which has error

$$\frac{1}{d}\|\widehat{\boldsymbol{\beta}}_{\mathrm{trivial}} - \boldsymbol{\beta}^\star\|^2 = \frac{1}{d}\|\boldsymbol{\beta}^\star\|^2 \leq 1.$$

Therefore, the above-mentioned upper bound leaves unanswered the question of whether the algorithm in question exhibits a nontrivial privacy-utility tradeoff in the proportional regime, unless the constant δ to which d/n converges is sufficiently small, a regime considered "low-dimensional" or "classical" by modern standards [103][3].

Adapting – with some effort (to handle the introduction of privacy-ensuring noise) – powerful recent techniques from probability and statistical physics, we

[1] The factor of $1/d$ in the estimation error is appropriate because the $\boldsymbol{x}_i$ have covariance $\frac{1}{d}\boldsymbol{I}_d$.

[2] Even with $(\varepsilon_{\mathrm{DP}}, \delta_{\mathrm{DP}}) = (1, 1/n^2)$, this bound only guarantees $\alpha \leq O(1)$ because $d/n = \Theta(1)$.

[3] Similar issues arise in other recent works on private linear regression, which assume either that $n = \widetilde{O}(d)$ or in some cases $n = O(d)$ for a suppressed, unoptimized constant factor [20,22,91,101,106].

obtain sharp $1+o(1)$ precision estimates of the error of well-studied differentially private algorithms for robust linear regression and logistic regression, including objective perturbation [32], output perturbation [42], and noisy gradient descent [11,94][4]. We discover a far more nuanced picture of the price of privacy of these algorithms than that afforded by existing, coarser analyses which are essentially vacuous in the regime we consider, yielding discovery of settings in which output perturbation outperforms objective perturbation on average, and vice versa.

Our Contributions.

(1) Initiate the study of differentially private learning in the proportional dimensionality regime;
(2) Obtain sharp asymptotic error bounds, enabling a more nuanced understanding of central, widely studied, algorithms;
(3) Discover previously unseen phenomena in the relationships among these algorithms, as well as in their training error, as the ratio δ varies;
(4) Introduce, for the first time, powerful modern statistical techniques to the analysis of differentially private algorithms;
(5) Strengthen tools, originally developed for high-dimensional regularized M-estimation introduced in [53,54,98], to cope with random perturbations introduced for privacy.

Our finding that objective perturbation, output perturbation, and a simple version of gradient descent yield nontrivial utility even in the proportional regime gives us hope that privacy will not become an unaffordable luxury in very high dimension statistical analysis. In addition, it suggests the tantalizing possibility of extending the techniques deployed herein to more recent differentially private learning algorithms, extending the advances made in those algorithms to the proportional dimensionality regime.

1.1 Results Overview

Our first main contribution is the first tight utility analysis of several differentially private learning algorithms in the proportional dimensionality regime. We determine the utility, including the optimal constants, of three prominent private estimation algorithms:

(1) In Sects. 1.1 and 1.1, we determine the error of the objective perturbation algorithm, due to [32,65]. Our bounds are tight up to a $1 \pm n^{-\Omega(1)}$ factor for robust linear regression and a $1 \pm e^{-(\log n)^{\Omega(1)}}$ factor for logistic regression, and they depend in nuanced ways on the problem parameters, such as $\varepsilon_{\mathrm{DP}}$, δ_{DP}, and the dimensionality ratio δ. Using these estimates, we discover

[4] In the proportional dimensionality regime, it is necessary to go beyond standard $O(d/n)$ or $O(\sqrt{d/n})$ convergence rates; instead, a more refined approach, relying on the solution to a system of nonlinear equations, is used to capture the nuanced dependence on d/n.

a previously unobserved "double descent"-like phenomenon in the *training error* of objective perturbation for robust linear regression, which is distinct from the better-known double descent curve for the *test error* of non-private linear regression.
In Sect. 1.1, we also give a refined privacy bound for the objective perturbation algorithm, which extends the analysis of [87] to arbitrarily small regularization strengths $\lambda > 0$ and perturbation magnitudes $\nu > 0$.

(2) In Sect. 1.1, we determine similarly tight error estimates for the output perturbation algorithm, due to [32,42]. Using our estimates, we show that the relative performance of objective perturbation and output perturbation is more nuanced than suggested by previous work. Indeed, while some prior analyses [32,65] suggest that objective perturbation is better overall, we identify some parameter settings for which output perturbation does better on average.

(3) In Sect. 1.1, we determine the error of a version of the noisy stochastic gradient descent algorithm (DP-SGD) of [11,94] that is restricted to a constant number of iterations. These estimates are accurate up to a $1 + o(1)$ factor, and they apply to certain variants of robust linear regression and logistic regression.

Our second main contribution is the introduction of two powerful techniques from the high-dimensional statistics literature that have not previously been used to analyze differentially private learning algorithms. The first technique is the *Convex Gaussian Minimax Theorem* (CGMT) of [96,99], which relates certain min-max optimization problems defined in terms of Gaussian random *matrices* in $\mathbb{R}^{n\times d}$ to simpler problems defined in terms of Gaussian random *vectors* in $\mathbb{R}^n$ and $\mathbb{R}^d$. The second technique is the *universality law* of [53,54], which allow us to apply CGMT to a wide range of non-Gaussian data distributions, including bounded data arising from the feature- or gradient-clipping subroutines of differentially private algorithms. Both CGMT and universality were developed to analyze non-private estimators, and a major part of our proofs, which we sketch in Sect. 1.2, is ensuring that the differentially private algorithms of interest to us satisfy the technical requirements needed to apply these techniques.

Utility of Objective Perturbation for Robust Linear Regression. Our first result is a sharp utility analysis in the proportional regime of the classic *objective perturbation* algorithm for empirical risk minimization, which was introduced for pure differential privacy by [32], extended to approximate differential privacy by [65], and studied further in several subsequent theoretical and empirical works [59,60,82,87]. Given a data set $(\boldsymbol{x}_1, y_1), \ldots, (\boldsymbol{x}_n, y_n) \in \mathbb{R}^d \times \mathbb{R}$ and a loss function $\ell(\boldsymbol{\beta}; (\boldsymbol{x}, y))$, the algorithm samples $\boldsymbol{\xi} \sim \mathcal{N}(\mathbf{0}, \boldsymbol{I}_d)$ and outputs

$$\widehat{\boldsymbol{\beta}} = \operatorname*{argmin}_{\boldsymbol{\beta}\in\mathbb{R}^d} \sum_{i=1}^{n} \ell(\boldsymbol{\beta}; (\boldsymbol{x}_i, y_i)) + \frac{\lambda}{2}\|\boldsymbol{\beta}\|^2 + \nu\langle \boldsymbol{\xi}, \boldsymbol{\beta}\rangle. \qquad (*)$$

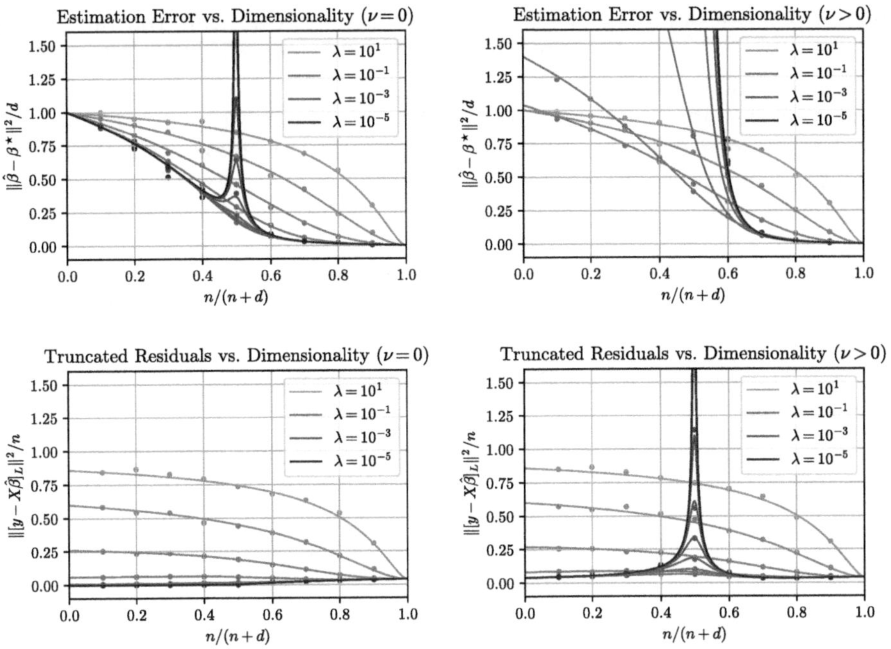

Fig. 1. Theorem 1's predictions of the *estimation error* and *truncated residuals* of objective perturbation with Huber loss. Larger $\delta \in (0,\infty)$ corresponds to smaller $n/(n+d) \in (0,1)$. Curves indicate theoretical predictions, and dots indicate the mean over 100 simulations of the algorithm on synthetic data with $n \times d = 1000$. In the left plots, the perturbation magnitude is $\nu = 0$, corresponding to the non-private case, but in the right plots, $\nu = 1/5$. All plots use $L = 10$, $\kappa = 1$, $\boldsymbol{\beta}^\star \sim \mathcal{N}(\mathbf{0}, \kappa^2 \boldsymbol{I}_d)$, $\boldsymbol{\varepsilon}^\star \sim \mathcal{N}(\mathbf{0}, (1/5)^2 \boldsymbol{I}_n)$, $\boldsymbol{X} \sim \frac{1}{\sqrt{d}}\text{Uniform}(\{-1,+1\}^{n\times d})$, and $\boldsymbol{y} = \boldsymbol{X}\boldsymbol{\beta}^\star + \boldsymbol{\varepsilon}^\star$.

We call $\lambda > 0$ and $\nu > 0$ the *regularization* and *perturbation* strengths, respectively.

Our first result concerns the error of objective perturbation for *robust linear regression*, in which the standard squared loss function for linear regression is replaced with the L-Lipschitz *Huber loss* function, due to [58], defined as $\ell(\boldsymbol{\beta}; (\boldsymbol{x}, y)) = H_L(y - \langle \boldsymbol{x}, \boldsymbol{\beta} \rangle)$, where

$$H_L(r) = \begin{cases} \frac{1}{2}r^2 & \text{if } |r| \le L \\ L|r| - \frac{1}{2}L^2 & \text{if } |r| \ge L. \end{cases}$$

We consider data $(\boldsymbol{X}, \boldsymbol{y}) \in \mathbb{R}^{n\times d} \times \mathbb{R}^n$ generated from a *linear model*, meaning that there exists a ground-truth vector $\boldsymbol{\beta}^\star \in \mathbb{R}^d$ and error vector $\boldsymbol{\varepsilon}^\star \in \mathbb{R}^n$ independent of $\boldsymbol{X}$ for which $\boldsymbol{y} = \boldsymbol{X}\boldsymbol{\beta}^\star + \boldsymbol{\varepsilon}^\star$. We also assume for the utility analysis that the feature matrix $\boldsymbol{X}$ is average-case in a certain sense, which is standard in the differentially private estimation literature. For concreteness, in our informally stated Theorem 1 below, the reader can imagine that the entries are independent, random elements of $\{-1/\sqrt{d}, +1/\sqrt{d}\}$, but the full version, Theorem 10 in Sect. 3, will apply to various distributions with different conditions on the means and variances. As always, privacy holds in a worst-case sense and requires no distributional assumptions. We state the privacy bound in terms of *zero-concentrated* differential privacy (zCDP), due to [25,44], which we define in Sect. 2. We also use the abbreviation $[r]_L = \min(L, \max(-L, r))$ for scalars $r \in \mathbb{R}$ and $L > 0$.

Theorem 1 (Informal Version of Theorem 10). *Let $(\sigma^\star, \tau^\star)$ denote the solution to the following system of two scalar equations in two variables (σ, τ), which we write in terms of $L, \lambda, \nu, \delta \in (0, \infty)$, dummy variables $Z_1, Z_2 \overset{iid}{\sim} \mathcal{N}(0,1)$, and $\kappa^2 = \frac{1}{d}\|\boldsymbol{\beta}^\star\|^2$ and $\varepsilon^2 = \frac{1}{n}\|\boldsymbol{\varepsilon}^\star\|^2$ as follows:*

$$\sigma^2 = \tau^2 \left(\frac{1}{\delta} \mathbb{E} \left[\frac{\sigma Z_1 + \varepsilon Z_2}{1+\tau} \right]_L^2 + \lambda^2 \kappa^2 + \nu^2 \right),$$

$$\tau = \frac{1}{\lambda\delta} \left(\delta - \frac{\tau}{1+\tau} \Pr\left[-L < \frac{\sigma Z_1 + \varepsilon Z_2}{1+\tau} < L \right] \right).$$

The output $\widehat{\boldsymbol{\beta}}$ of the objective perturbation algorithm with Huber loss satisfies ρ_{DP}-zCDP for a constant $\rho_{\mathrm{DP}} = \rho_{\mathrm{DP}}(L, \lambda, \nu)$ independent of n that is finite for any $L, \lambda, \nu \in (0, \infty)$. If the data are generated from a linear model as $n \to \infty$ and $d/n \to \delta$, then w.h.p., $\widehat{\boldsymbol{\beta}}$ has estimation error

$$\frac{1}{d}\|\widehat{\boldsymbol{\beta}} - \boldsymbol{\beta}^\star\|^2 = (\sigma^\star)^2 \pm n^{-\Omega(1)}.$$

As already discussed, standard $O(d/n)$ or $O(\sqrt{d/n})$ error rates are vacuous in the proportional regime, so Theorem 1 instead captures the nuanced dependence on d/n through a small system of nonlinear, scalar equations that depend on δ. Roughly speaking, these two equations arise from the first-order optimality conditions of a min-max formulation of Eq. $(*)$ as $n \to \infty$ and $d/n \to \delta$; we sketch this argument in the technical overview in Sect. 1.2 but defer the full proof to Sect. 3[5]. To quickly gain intuition for these equations, it is instructive to consider simplified versions that arise in the limit as $L \to \infty$ or $\nu \to 0$ or $\lambda \to 0$ even though, strictly speaking, our theorem only holds for fixed values of $L, \lambda, \nu \in (0, \infty)$.

First, consider the limit as $\nu \to 0$, which corresponds to removing the random linear perturbation term that was introduced for privacy. In this case, we recover a result in Sect. 5.2 of [98] for non-private ridge regression with Gaussian features, which was later extended to subgaussian features by Theorem 3.12 of [54]. Indeed, these works characterize the error of the non-private, ridge regularized

[5] This form of Theorem 1 relies on a technical assumption (Definition 13), which is a *relaxation* of the coordinate-wise i.i.d. assumption in [98]. Removing this assumption gives a set of equations that are possibly more difficult to interpret and to numerically solve.

Huber regressor via the solution to a pair of equations in (σ, τ), which match ours in the case of $\nu = 0$. In Fig. 1, we numerically compare the solution to our equations with $\nu > 0$ to those of prior work with $\nu = 0$ to precisely quantify the price of privacy paid by objective perturbation for robust linear regression.

Next, consider the limit $L \to \infty$, which corresponds to approximating Huber loss by squared loss. In this case, the equations simplify substantially:

$$\sigma^2 = \tau^2 \left(\frac{1}{\delta} \cdot \frac{\sigma^2 + \varepsilon^2}{(1+\tau)^2} + \lambda^2 \kappa^2 + \nu^2 \right), \qquad \tau = \frac{1}{\lambda \delta} \left(\delta - \frac{\tau}{1+\tau} \right).$$

In the non-private case ($\nu = 0$), solving for the error $\sigma^\star$ in the limit as $\lambda \to 0$ yields

$$(\sigma^\star)^2 \to \begin{cases} \frac{\delta}{1-\delta} \varepsilon^2 & \text{if } \delta < 1, \\ \frac{1}{\delta - 1} \varepsilon^2 + \frac{\delta - 1}{\delta} \kappa^2 & \text{if } \delta > 1. \end{cases}$$

Similarly, in the private case ($\nu > 0$), in the limit as $\lambda \to 0$, the error satisfies

$$(\sigma^\star)^2 \to \begin{cases} \frac{\delta}{1-\delta} \varepsilon^2 + \frac{\delta^2}{(1-\delta)^3} \nu^2 & \text{if } \delta < 1, \\ +\infty & \text{if } \delta > 1. \end{cases}$$

In other words, in the $\delta < 1$ regime, where $n > d$ objective perturbation incurs a mild additive penalty in squared error compared to the non-private case. However, in the $\delta > 1$ regime, where $n < d$, any constant noise level $\nu > 0$, no matter how small, sends $\sigma^\star$ from a finite constant to $+\infty$, a dramatic deterioration. This behavior is exhibited in the top two estimation error plots of Fig. 1, where we see a sharp phase transition at $n/(n + d) = 1/2$ (the region to the right of this boundary corresponds to $n > d$ or $\delta < 1$, and the region to the left of this boundary corresponds to $n < d$ or $\delta > 1$). The "spike" in estimation error at $n = d$ in the non-private case is an example of the well-known *double descent* phenomenon in modern machine learning [16,17,74], and it is notable that it does not occur in private case of fixed $\nu > 0$.

However, we reach the opposite conclusion if we examine in-sample *training error* (norm of the residuals $\boldsymbol{y} - \boldsymbol{X}\widehat{\boldsymbol{\beta}}$) instead of out-of-sample *test error* (norm of $\widehat{\boldsymbol{\beta}} - \boldsymbol{\beta}^\star$). Indeed, while Theorem 1 only estimates the squared norm of $\widehat{\boldsymbol{\beta}} - \boldsymbol{\beta}^\star$, the full version (Theorem 10) will also consider various other error metrics, including ℓ^p norms for all $p \geq 1$, as well as various residual norms. Again considering the limits $L \to \infty$ and $\lambda \to 0$, Theorem 10 predicts that

$$\frac{1}{n} \|\boldsymbol{y} - \boldsymbol{X}\widehat{\boldsymbol{\beta}}\|^2 \to \begin{cases} (1-\delta)\varepsilon^2 + \frac{\delta^2}{1-\delta} \nu^2 & \text{if } \delta < 1, \\ \frac{\delta}{\delta - 1} \nu^2 & \text{if } \delta > 1. \end{cases}$$

Strikingly, this formula shows a descent-like "spike" in training error that emerges *only* in the private case. Indeed, if $\nu = 0$, the residual error is 0 for $n < d$ and monotonically increases to ε^2 as n grows from d to ∞, but if $\nu > 0$, then there is a singularity at $\delta = 1$ on the order of $O(1/|\delta - 1|)$. This behavior is exhibited in the bottom two residual error plots of Fig. 1.

Remark 1. Although the incorporation of ν is the main quantitative difference between our theorem and those of [54,98], our theorem also comes with a number of qualitative advantages that will become more apparent once we have presented its full version (Theorem 10). For example, while Theorem 3.12 of [54] assumes that $\boldsymbol{\beta}^\star$ and $\boldsymbol{\varepsilon}^\star$ are random with i.i.d. coordinates, our theorem does not even require them to be random (although in the non-i.i.d. and nonrandom cases, we do require certain mild conditions on their coordinates as $n \to \infty$). Next, while [54,98] only determine the limiting value of $\frac{1}{d}\|\widehat{\boldsymbol{\beta}} - \boldsymbol{\beta}^\star\|^2$, we also use $\sigma^\star$ and $\tau^\star$ to characterize a wide range of other scalar quantities of interest regarding the algorithm's output $\widehat{\boldsymbol{\beta}}$, such as all of its ℓ^p distances to the ground-truth $\boldsymbol{\beta}^\star$, its correlation with the coefficients $\boldsymbol{\xi}$ of the random linear perturbation term, the error of its predictions $\boldsymbol{X}\widehat{\boldsymbol{\beta}}$ on the training data, and more.

Further intuition for the meaning of $\sigma^\star$ and $\tau^\star$ can be gleaned from Theorem 10, which will roughly show that, for $\boldsymbol{z} \sim \mathcal{N}(\boldsymbol{0}, \boldsymbol{I}_d)$ independent of the perturbation vector $\boldsymbol{\xi}$,

$$\widehat{\boldsymbol{\beta}} \approx (1 - \tau^\star\lambda)\boldsymbol{\beta}^\star - \tau^\star\nu\boldsymbol{\xi} + \sqrt{(\sigma^\star)^2 - (\tau^\star)^2(\lambda^2\kappa^2 + \nu^2)} \cdot \boldsymbol{z}.$$

In this form, it is clear that a larger $\sigma^\star$ leads to a larger coefficient on the $\boldsymbol{z}$ term, so $\sigma^\star$ is related to the *variance* of $\widehat{\boldsymbol{\beta}} - \boldsymbol{\beta}^\star$. Similarly, $\tau^\star$ is related to the correlations of $\widehat{\boldsymbol{\beta}}$ with both $\boldsymbol{\xi}$ and $\boldsymbol{\beta}^\star$, the latter of which is related to the *bias* of $\widehat{\boldsymbol{\beta}}$. Formalizing this intuition will be easy to do given the full version of the theorem.

Utility of Objective Perturbation for Logistic Regression. Our next result concerns *logistic regression*, where $\boldsymbol{y} \in \{0,1\}^n$. The logistic loss of $\boldsymbol{\beta}$ on a sample $(\boldsymbol{x}, y)$ is $\rho(\langle \boldsymbol{x}, \boldsymbol{\beta}\rangle)$ if $y = 0$ and $\rho(-\langle \boldsymbol{x}, \boldsymbol{\beta}\rangle)$ if $y = 1$, where $\rho(t) = \log(1 + e^t)$. We consider data $(\boldsymbol{X}, \boldsymbol{y}) \in \mathbb{R}^{n\times d} \times \{0,1\}^n$ generated from a *logistic model*, meaning that there exists $\boldsymbol{\beta}^\star \in \mathbb{R}^d$ for which $\boldsymbol{y} \sim \text{Bernoulli}(\rho'(\boldsymbol{X}\boldsymbol{\beta}^\star))$. Here, $\rho'(t) = 1/(1+e^{-t})$ is the *sigmoid* function, which outputs values between 0 and 1.

The subsequent theorem, much like the previous one, will involve a small number of scalar equations. We state them in terms of the *proximal operator* of the function $\gamma \cdot \rho$ for a scalar $\gamma > 0$, denoted $\text{prox}_{\gamma\rho}$. Intuitively, this function takes as input a point $s \in \mathbb{R}$ and outputs another point $t \in \mathbb{R}$ that approximately minimizes $\gamma\rho$ while maintaining proximity to s. For more detail, see Sect. 2 or [85].

Theorem 2 (Informal). *Let $(\alpha^\star, \sigma^\star, \gamma^\star)$ denote the solution to the following system of three scalar equations in three variables (α, σ, γ), which we write in terms of the algorithm's parameters $\lambda, \nu > 0$, the dimensionality ratio $\delta \in (0, \infty)$, dummy variables $Z_1, Z_2 \overset{iid}{\sim} \mathcal{N}(0,1)$ and $\kappa^2 = \frac{1}{d}\|\boldsymbol{\beta}^\star\|^2$, as follows:*

$$\sigma^2 = \gamma^2 \left(\frac{1}{\delta} \mathbb{E}\left[2\rho'(-\kappa Z_1)\rho'(\mathrm{prox}_{\gamma\rho}(\kappa\alpha Z_1 + \sigma Z_2))^2 \right] + \nu^2 \right),$$

$$\alpha = -\frac{1}{\delta} \mathbb{E}[2\rho''(-\kappa Z_1)\mathrm{prox}_{\gamma\rho}(\kappa\alpha Z_1 + \sigma Z_2)],$$

$$\gamma = \frac{1}{\lambda\delta} \left(\delta - 1 + \mathbb{E}\left[\frac{2\rho'(-\kappa Z_1)}{1 + \gamma\rho''(\mathrm{prox}_{\gamma\rho}(\kappa\alpha Z_1 + \sigma Z_2))} \right] \right).$$

The output $\widehat{\boldsymbol{\beta}}$ of the objective perturbation algorithm with logistic loss satisfies ρ_{DP}-zCDP for a constant $\rho_{\mathrm{DP}} = \rho_{\mathrm{DP}}(\lambda, \nu)$ independent of n that is finite for any $\lambda, \nu \in (0, \infty)$. If the data are generated from a logistic model as $n \to \infty$ and $d/n \to \delta$, then w.h.p., $\widehat{\boldsymbol{\beta}}$ has estimation error

$$\frac{1}{d}\|\widehat{\boldsymbol{\beta}} - \boldsymbol{\beta}^\star\|^2 = (1 - \alpha^\star)^2\kappa^2 + (\sigma^\star)^2 \pm e^{-(\log n)^{\Omega(1)}}.$$

Much like our results for robust linear regression, Theorem 2 is a differentially private analogue of existing, non-private results in the literature. Taking $\nu \to 0$, we recover Theorem 2 of [89] for regularized logistic regression with Gaussian features, which was later extended to subgaussian features by Theorem 4.3 of [53]. Taking $\lambda \to 0$ as well, we recover the landmark result of [97] on the behavior of the (non-regularized) MLE, up to some minor differences in notation and scaling. In Sect. 1.2, we sketch the proof of Theorem 2. In the extended version of our paper, we state a rigorous version of the theorem, provide a complete proof, and visualize the predictions. We remark that the full version of the theorem will also have some qualitative advantages over prior results akin to those discussed in Remark 1.

As in the previous section, further intuition for the meaning of $\alpha^\star$, $\sigma^\star$, and $\gamma^\star$ can be gleaned from the full version of Theorem 2, which will roughly show that, for $\boldsymbol{z} \sim \mathcal{N}(\mathbf{0}, \boldsymbol{I}_d)$ independent of $\boldsymbol{\xi}$,

$$\widehat{\boldsymbol{\beta}} \approx \alpha^\star\boldsymbol{\beta}^\star - \gamma^\star\nu\boldsymbol{\xi} + \sqrt{(\sigma^\star)^2 - (\gamma^\star\nu)^2} \cdot \boldsymbol{z}.$$

Consequently, $\alpha^\star$ is related to the bias of $\widehat{\boldsymbol{\beta}}$ and $\sigma^\star$ is related to the variance of the debiased estimate $\widehat{\boldsymbol{\beta}} - \alpha^\star\boldsymbol{\beta}^\star$. Similarly, $\gamma^\star$ is related to the correlation of $\widehat{\boldsymbol{\beta}}$ with $\boldsymbol{\xi}$.

Privacy of Objective Perturbation with Small $\boldsymbol{\lambda}$. Theorems 1 and 2 precisely determine the utility of objective perturbation as a function of λ and ν, but these informal statements leave the algorithm's privacy loss parameter $\rho_{\mathrm{DP}}(\lambda, \nu)$ unspecified. The following result allows us to quantify the privacy-utility tradeoff of the algorithm, which we visualize in Fig. 2:

Theorem 3 (Informal). *If ℓ is an L-Lipschitz, s-smooth, generalized linear model (GLM) loss, then objective perturbation satisfies ρ_{DP}-zCDP for*

$$\rho_{\mathrm{DP}} = \log\left(1 + \frac{s}{\lambda}\right) + \frac{L^2}{2\nu^2} + \sqrt{\frac{2}{\pi}} \cdot \frac{L}{\nu}.$$

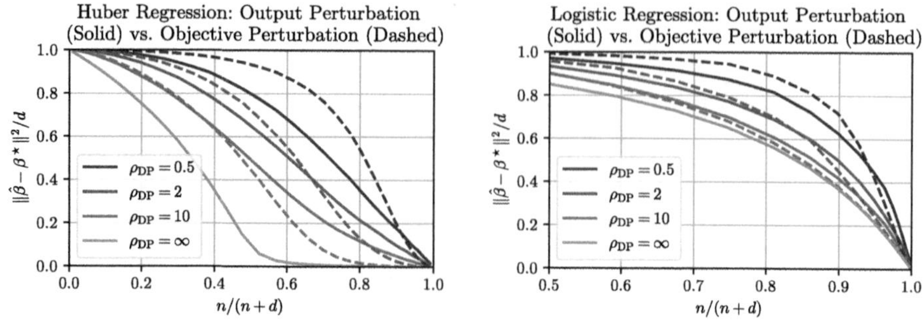

Fig. 2. Privacy-utility tradeoffs obtained by searching over feasible (λ, ν) satisfying a given zCDP privacy budget ρ_{DP} to minimize error (c.f. Theorem 3). Left: Comparison of output perturbation (Corollary 1) and objective perturbation (Theorem 1) on Huber regression with $L = 1$, $\boldsymbol{\varepsilon}^\star \sim \mathcal{N}(\mathbf{0}, (1/10)^2 \boldsymbol{I}_n)$. Right: Comparison of output perturbation (Corollary 2) and objective perturbation (Theorem 2) for logistic regression. In both plots, $\kappa = 1$, $\boldsymbol{\beta}^\star \sim \mathcal{N}(\mathbf{0}, \kappa^2 \boldsymbol{I}_d)$.

In the extended version of our paper, we give a full statement and proof of this theorem. There, we also prove even tighter $(\varepsilon_{\text{DP}}, \delta_{\text{DP}})$-DP guarantees. Importantly, our DP guarantees hold for any fixed $\lambda, \nu > 0$ and do not degrade as $n, d \to \infty$. Our proofs refine closely related arguments of [87], which establish only privacy in the case where $\lambda > s$ (e.g. $s = 1$ for robust linear regression, or $s = 1/4$ for logistic regression). Note that the privacy loss ρ_{DP} shrinks to 0 as $\lambda, \nu \to \infty$.

Utility of Output Perturbation. Our results on objective perturbation can easily be modified to characterize the utility of *output perturbation*, an even more foundational differentially private algorithm due to [40], which samples $\boldsymbol{\xi} \sim \mathcal{N}(\mathbf{0}, \boldsymbol{I}_d)$ and outputs

$$\widehat{\boldsymbol{\beta}} = \left(\operatorname*{argmin}_{\boldsymbol{\beta} \in \mathbb{R}^d} \sum_{i=1}^{n} \ell(\boldsymbol{\beta}; (\boldsymbol{x}_i, y_i)) + \frac{\lambda}{2} \|\boldsymbol{\beta}\|^2 \right) + \nu \boldsymbol{\xi}.$$

Here, the perturbation comes in the form of an additive noise term, rather than a random linear term in the objective. Extracting the ν^2 term from the systems of equations of Theorem 1 and Theorem 2 yields the following two corollaries, respectively.

Figure 2 uses these corollaries, along with the theorems of Sects. 1.1 and 1.1, to compare the privacy-utility tradeoffs of output perturbation and objective perturbation. Interestingly, for many privacy levels ρ_{DP}, neither algorithm's error curve lies strictly below the other, suggesting that their relative performance *depends* on the dimensionality ratio δ. In other words, while prior work suggests that objective perturbation is generally the better algorithm of the two, Fig. 2 tells a more complicated story, albeit one that is highly dependent on the chosen privacy bounds.

We give formal statements of these corollaries in the extended version of our paper, where we also verify their predictions against simulated data.

Corollary 1 (Informal). *Let* $(\sigma^\star, \tau^\star)$ *denote the solution to the system of equations from Theorem 1 under the substitution* $\nu = 0$*. Then, under the same conditions as Theorem 1, the estimation error of the perturbed output* $\widehat{\boldsymbol{\beta}}$ *satisfies, w.h.p.,*

$$\frac{1}{d}\|\widehat{\boldsymbol{\beta}} - \boldsymbol{\beta}^\star\|^2 = (\sigma^\star)^2 + \nu^2 \pm n^{-\Omega(1)}.$$

Corollary 2 (Informal). *Let* $(\alpha^\star, \sigma^\star, \gamma^\star)$ *denote the solution to the system of equations from Theorem 2 under the substitution* $\nu = 0$*. Then, under the same conditions as Theorem 2, the estimation error of the perturbed output* $\widehat{\boldsymbol{\beta}}$ *satisfies, w.h.p.,*

$$\frac{1}{d}\|\widehat{\boldsymbol{\beta}} - \boldsymbol{\beta}^\star\|^2 = (1-\alpha^\star)^2\kappa^2 + (\sigma^\star)^2 + \nu^2 \pm e^{-(\log n)^{\Omega(1)}}.$$

Utility of Noisy Stochastic Gradient Descent. The *noisy stochastic gradient descent* (a.k.a. DP-SGD) algorithm, which adds independent Gaussian noise to each iteration of SGD, is the cornerstone of modern, differentially private machine learning [1]. In the extended version of our paper, we present results for DP-SGD that parallel our results for objective perturbation (Theorems 1 and 2) and for output perturbation (Corollaries 1 and 2). These results for DP-SGD follow directly from a black-box reduction to powerful, recent results in the non-private literature [50,53], and we validate them against simulated data. As such, we view this section more as a valuable point of reference than as a major technical contribution of our own. The results also come with some limitations. For example, certain technical requirements inherited from [50] prevent us from studying the standard formulations of robust linear regression and logistic regression, let alone the broad range of convex and non-convex optimization problems to which DP-SGD is typically applied. Also, the system of equations now has size $O(T^2)$ for T steps of DP-SGD, where T must be held constant as $n \to \infty$ and $d/n \to \delta$. Overcoming these obstacles is a promising direction for future work.

1.2 Technical Overview

In this section, we sketch the proofs of Theorems 1 and 2, our main results on objective perturbation. We carry out these proofs in the extended version of our paper. As already discussed, our results for output perturbation are direct corollaries of these theorems, and our results for noisy stochastic gradient descent are similarly straightforward given prior results in the literature. Ultimately, for each of the three algorithms under consideration, we need two things:

- A *privacy proof*, which must hold for worst-case data points $(\boldsymbol{x}_i, y_i)$. These may be arbitrary points in $B_R(\mathbf{0}) \times \mathbb{R}$ in the case of robust linear regression, or arbitrary points in $B_R(\mathbf{0}) \times \{0, 1\}$ in the case of logistic regression, where $B_R(\mathbf{0})$ denotes the ball of radius R centered at the origin in $\mathbb{R}^d$, i.e. $B_R(\mathbf{0}) = \{\boldsymbol{x} \in \mathbb{R}^d : \|\boldsymbol{x}\| \le R\} \subseteq \mathbb{R}^d$.

- A *utility proof*, which only needs to hold for data points $(\boldsymbol{x}_i, y_i)$ sampled independently from an appropriate distribution over $B_R(\mathbf{0}) \times \mathbb{R}$ in the case of robust linear regression, or over $B_R(\mathbf{0}) \times \{0, 1\}$ in the case of logistic regression.

Our privacy proofs build on ones that exist in the differential privacy literature, and we will hence inherit various boundedness requirements from those works [9,25,87]. Specifically, to apply our privacy analysis to robust linear regression and logistic regression, for which the gradient of the loss function scales in magnitude with $\|\boldsymbol{x}\|$, we require the constraint that $\boldsymbol{x}_1, \ldots, \boldsymbol{x}_n \in B_R(\mathbf{0})$. This constraint can either be assumed as a priori knowledge, or enforced via a projection of unconstrained data in $\mathbb{R}^d$ onto $B_R(\mathbf{0})$. Bounding the norm of each $\boldsymbol{x}_i$ leads to a bound on the objective function's sensitivity, which ultimately yields our bound on the algorithm's privacy loss parameters $(\varepsilon_{\mathrm{DP}}, \delta_{\mathrm{DP}})$ or ρ_{DP}.

Our utility proofs for objective perturbation are substantially more complex and comprise our main technical contribution. In these proofs, we initially focus on Gaussian features: $\boldsymbol{x}_1, \ldots, \boldsymbol{x}_n \overset{iid}{\sim} \mathcal{N}\big(\mathbf{0}, \frac{1}{d}\boldsymbol{I}_d\big)$. The Gaussian distribution is not supported on $B_R(\mathbf{0})$, so we clearly must relax this assumption eventually. Nevertheless, Gaussianity is a fruitful starting point since it enables the use of a Gaussian comparison inequality called the *Convex Gaussian Minimax Theorem* (CGMT), as discussed earlier in the introduction. We provide the formal statement of CGMT, along with a more detailed explanation of how it is used, in Sect. 2.2.

Since our aim is to apply CGMT, the first step of our proof is to reformulate the objective perturbation algorithm as min-max optimization of the form

$$\widehat{\boldsymbol{\beta}} = \operatorname*{argmin}_{\boldsymbol{u} \in \mathcal{S}_{\boldsymbol{u}}} \max_{\boldsymbol{v} \in \mathcal{S}_{\boldsymbol{v}}} \underbrace{\langle \boldsymbol{X}\boldsymbol{u}, \boldsymbol{v} \rangle + \psi(\boldsymbol{u}, \boldsymbol{v})}_{Q_{\boldsymbol{u},\boldsymbol{v}}}.$$

Here, $\mathcal{S}_{\boldsymbol{u}} \subseteq \mathbb{R}^d$ and $\mathcal{S}_{\boldsymbol{v}} \subseteq \mathbb{R}^n$ are constraint sets, $\boldsymbol{X} = [\boldsymbol{x}_1 \cdots \boldsymbol{x}_n]^\top \in \mathbb{R}^{n \times d}$ denotes the feature matrix, which we also call the *design matrix*, and $\psi : \mathcal{S}_{\boldsymbol{u}} \times \mathcal{S}_{\boldsymbol{v}} \to \mathbb{R}$ is a convex-concave function that may depend on the ground-truth $\boldsymbol{\beta}^\star$, the regression errors $\boldsymbol{\varepsilon}^\star$, and the perturbation vector $\boldsymbol{\xi}$, but may *not* depend on $\boldsymbol{X}$. We call ψ the *mean function* because $\mathbb{E}[Q_{\boldsymbol{u},\boldsymbol{v}}] = \psi(\boldsymbol{u}, \boldsymbol{v})$, where the expectation is taken only over the randomness of $\boldsymbol{X}$.

At this point, we have expressed $\widehat{\boldsymbol{\beta}}$ in terms of the extrema of $Q_{\boldsymbol{u},\boldsymbol{v}}$ over $\boldsymbol{u} \in \mathcal{S}_{\boldsymbol{u}}$ and $\boldsymbol{v} \in \mathcal{S}_{\boldsymbol{v}}$. For the regression problems that we consider, the term $\psi(\boldsymbol{u}, \boldsymbol{v})$ will be very simple, so the main obstacle to optimizing $Q_{\boldsymbol{u},\boldsymbol{v}}$ by hand is the presence of the random matrix in the bilinear term $\langle \boldsymbol{X}\boldsymbol{u}, \boldsymbol{v} \rangle$. Essentially, CGMT enables us to replace the Gaussian random matrix $\boldsymbol{X} \in \mathbb{R}^{n \times d}$ with two standard Gaussian random vectors $\boldsymbol{g} \in \mathbb{R}^d$ and $\boldsymbol{h} \in \mathbb{R}^n$, after which solving the min-max optimization by hand becomes a straightforward matter of calculus. Taking the derivatives of this *auxiliary optimization* with respect to $\boldsymbol{u} \in \mathbb{R}^d$ and $\boldsymbol{v} \in \mathbb{R}^n$ and setting them equal to zero, while keeping in mind the constraint sets $\mathcal{S}_{\boldsymbol{u}}$ and $\mathcal{S}_{\boldsymbol{v}}$, yields a system of $n + d$ equations in $n + d$ variables characterizing the behavior of both this auxiliary optimizer and its corresponding dual variable. Ultimately, the guarantee of CGMT is that over the randomness of $\boldsymbol{X}$, the solution to this auxiliary problem is indistinguishable from the solution $\widehat{\boldsymbol{\beta}}$ to the original problem with respect to a wide range of *pseudo-Lipschitz* test functions. To complete the proof in the case of Gaussian features, we show that this system of first-order optimality equations reduces to a fixed-size system of *scalar* equations (two equations in two variables in the case of robust linear regression, or three equations in three variables in the case of logistic regression) in the limit as $n \to \infty$ with $d/n \to \delta$.

At this point, all that remains is to relax the Gaussianity assumption on $\boldsymbol{X}$, which we emphasize is crucial for the analysis of any differentially private algorithm that assumes its input is bounded in $B_R(\mathbf{0})$ or incorporates data clipping as a subroutine. To this end, we draw on recent, powerful theoretical results that formalize the notion of *universality* from statistical physics [53,54]. Informally speaking, universality is the idea that certain global properties of a system, such as the estimation error $\frac{1}{d}\|\widehat{\boldsymbol{\beta}} - \boldsymbol{\beta}^{\star}\|^2$, should not depend too heavily on the local details of the system, such as the distribution of the entries of $\boldsymbol{X}$.

The first universality law we leverage is Corollary 2.6 of [54], which we call *CGMT universality.* This result asserts that even when $\boldsymbol{X}$ is not Gaussian, the distribution of the extrema of $Q_{\boldsymbol{u},\boldsymbol{v}}$ over $\boldsymbol{u} \in \mathcal{S}_{\boldsymbol{u}}$ and $\boldsymbol{v} \in \mathcal{S}_{\boldsymbol{v}}$ is essentially unchanged upon replacing $\boldsymbol{X}$ with a matrix $\boldsymbol{X}'$ with a few matching moments in the definition of $Q_{\boldsymbol{u},\boldsymbol{v}}$. Taking $\boldsymbol{X}' = \boldsymbol{G}$ to be Gaussian allows us to apply CGMT even to non-Gaussian $\boldsymbol{X}$ drawn from any isotropic distribution over $B_R(\mathbf{0})$ with independent (not necessarily identically distributed!) entries. We believe our results can be extended to nonisotropic distributions, as well, which is a point we revisit in Sect. 3. Applying CGMT universality requires several technical conditions on the original optimization problem to be verified. For our purposes, this roughly amounts to showing that the output $\widehat{\boldsymbol{\beta}}$ of the objective perturbation algorithm satisfies $\|\widehat{\boldsymbol{\beta}}\|_\infty \le n^{o(1)}$. We prove this using a leave-one-feature-out perturbation argument, a result that may be of independent interest.

Although CGMT universality as it appears in [54] is exactly what we need to analyze the objective perturbation with robust linear loss, frustratingly, it cannot be directly applied to logistic regression. The reason is that, in the case of the logistic loss, even the initial step of reformulating the perturbed objective as $Q_{\boldsymbol{u},\boldsymbol{v}} = \langle \boldsymbol{X}\boldsymbol{u}, \boldsymbol{v}\rangle + \psi(\boldsymbol{u},\boldsymbol{v})$ requires the assumption of Gaussianity to ensure the independence of the first and second terms, a requirement for CGMT. Consequently, we need a universality law that addresses the perturbed logistic objective function in its original form, before transforming it into $Q_{\boldsymbol{u},\boldsymbol{v}}$. For this, we use the more recent universality law of [53], called *generalized first-order method* (GFOM) universality. To apply GFOM universality, we first construct a sequence of "σ-smoothed" iterates $\boldsymbol{\beta}_\sigma^{(t)}$ for $t \in \mathbb{N}$ and $\sigma > 0$ that start at $\boldsymbol{\beta}^{(0)} = \mathbf{0}$ but rapidly converge to $\widehat{\boldsymbol{\beta}}$ as $t \to \infty$ and $\sigma \to 0$. These iterates are *not* part of the objective perturbation algorithm, but rather exist solely for the purpose of analysis, as they fit the description of a smooth "generalized first-order method" put forward in [31]. GFOM universality tells us that the behavior of these iterates (and hence their limit $\widehat{\boldsymbol{\beta}}$) is unchanged upon replacing $\boldsymbol{X}$ with a Gaussian matrix $\boldsymbol{G}$ with matching dimensions and a few matching moments. Our application of

GFOM universality to the perturbed logistic objective mirrors an argument of [53] in the non-private case. The key differences arise in verifying that various technical conditions still hold in the presence of the randomness introduced for privacy.

Ultimately, universality allows us to reconcile the Gaussian design assumptions of CGMT analysis with the necessarily different data distributions encountered by differentially private algorithms, including output perturbation, objective perturbation, and noisy stochastic gradient descent. In terms of our final error bounds, CGMT universality, which we use for robust linear regression, incurs only an additive $n^{-\Omega(1)}$ penalty. GFOM universality, which we use for logistic regression, incurs only an additive $e^{-(\log n)^{\Omega(1)}}$ penalty.

1.3 Related Work

The concurrent work [18] and subsequent work [19] also study differentially private learning in the proportional and overparameterized regimes, with a focus on private gradient descent. While our results and those of [19] both pertain to regression with $n \propto d$, they study a different version of the algorithm than we do. While we consider several passes of full batch gradient descent, they consider a single pass of stochastic gradient descent (i.e. no data is reused across iterations). Their analysis also takes into consideration the effect of various hyperparameters, like the clipping level and learning rate schedule, and explicitly allows for nonisotropic feature distributions. The results of [18], in contrast, are not directly comparable to ours, as they concern overparameterized 2-layer neural networks with $n \gg d$, rather than regression with $n \propto d$.

Prior to our paper, many works studied algorithms for differentially private regression, but they did not provide substantive guarantees in the proportional dimensionality regime as we do [7,11,20,22,32,41,65,71,77,90,91,101,107]. Others studied the $d \gg n$ regime but required *sparsity* assumptions [26,27,49,64,73,95,110]. Since we do not assume sparsity, these works are not comparable to ours. Under sparsity assumptions, the analogous challenge would be to analyze the regime where n is proportional to the $s \log(d/s)$ where s is the sparsity level—the fact that this is the "effective dimension" can be argued via sample complexity, via ε-nets, or via the statistical dimension of [6]. Other works consider $d \gg n$ under the assumption that the data approximately lies in a $d' \ll n$ dimensional subspace [33] (see also [3,75] regarding robust, rather than private, estimation). Privacy analyses we build on include the works of [9,25,87,88].

At a technical level, the closest prior work to ours can be found in the non-private statistics literature. As discussed in Sects. 1.1 and 1.1, our main theorems generalize prior results of [53,54,89,98] by weakening their assumptions and accommodating the noise introduced for privacy. We carry out numerical comparisons between our error estimates and the estimates of these works in Fig. 1 and more (see the extended version of our paper). Our proofs also rely on tools from the non-private statistics literature that have not previously appeared in the privacy literature. The Convex Gaussian Minimax Theorem is based on the classical inequalities of [52,93], but it was only recently presented in its current form and applied to modern statistical problems [30,34,35,57,69,72,76,80,96,98,99,104,108]. Prior to this, a leading technique for analysis in the proportional dimensionality regime was the *approximate message passing* (AMP) framework of [13,36]. The universality laws we use are from [53,54], but there are many works on this topic [2,12,38,39,45,46,66,79,83,84].

1.4 Discussion

Although we focus on convex problems in this paper, the universality results for generalized first-order methods that we leverage [53] are not limited to convex objectives. Similarly, the AMP technique [36], which predates CGMT and can tackle a broader range of problems, has also been used to study non-convex problems in the proportional regime. The results of [50], which we use in a black box fashion in the DP-SGD section of the extended version of our paper, are also not limited to convex objectives, applying to any generalized first-order method of a certain type. For this reason, we view our work as a starting point for the eventual study of privacy-preserving algorithms for non-convex or highly structured deep learning models in the proportional dimensionality regime.

We are hopeful that these ideas can be extended to yield insights for the proportional parameter regime for other heavily studied problems in differentially private estimation, such as: heavy-tailed moment estimation [4,55,63,70], Gaussian parameter estimation [5,8,21,56,61,62,67,68,70], high-dimensional hypothesis testing and selection [24,29,51,81,86], and empirical risk minimization [11,32,65]. Progress on these problems, where the world of non-private estimation is moving ahead, is essential if privacy is not to become an unaffordable luxury.

2 Preliminaries

Throughout this paper, when working with an infinite sequence indexed by $n \in \mathbb{N}$, which may be a sequence of scalars, vectors, matrices, functions, or subsets of $\mathbb{R}^n$, we will often refer to the sequence as though it were a single object of that type. For example, when referring to the problem dimension d, it should be understood that d is not merely a scalar, but rather a scalar sequence $d(n)$ (equivalently, d_n) indexed by n.

Consequently, by the *proportional dimensionality regime*, we mean the setting in which

$$\lim_{n\to\infty} \frac{d(n)}{n} = \delta,$$

where we denote the given dimensionality ratio by $\delta \in (0, \infty)$. In the proportional regime, any scalar sequence $f(n)$ satisfying $f(n) = \Theta(n^c)$ for a fixed constant $c > 0$ also satisfies $f(n) = \Theta(d^c)$, and vice versa. For consistency, when presented with such a notational choice, we shall always choose to express asymptotic bounds in terms of n, not d.

2.1 Differential Privacy

The algorithms we study in this paper all satisfy differential privacy (DP), the accepted definition of rigorous privacy protection for data analysis. We focus on the notion of *approximate*, or (ε, δ)-differential privacy with respect to the *add/remove-one* notion of adjacency:

Definition 1 ([42]). *Given a universe $\mathcal{X}$, we say data sets $\boldsymbol{x}, \boldsymbol{x}' \in \mathbb{N}^{\mathcal{X}}$ are* adjacent *if $\|\boldsymbol{x} - \boldsymbol{x}'\|_1 = 1$. We say a randomized algorithm $\mathcal{A} : \mathbb{N}^{\mathcal{X}} \to \mathcal{Y}$ satisfies* $(\varepsilon_{\mathrm{DP}}, \delta_{\mathrm{DP}})$-differential privacy *if for all adjacent $\boldsymbol{x}, \boldsymbol{x}' \in \mathcal{X}^n$ and subsets $Y \subseteq \mathcal{Y}$,*

$$\Pr[\mathcal{A}(\boldsymbol{x}) \in Y] \leq e^{\varepsilon_{\mathrm{DP}}} \Pr[\mathcal{A}(\boldsymbol{x}') \in Y] + \delta_{\mathrm{DP}}.$$

We shall also require two other, related notions of differential privacy, known as *Rényi* and *zero-concentrated* DP, that have been used in major real-world deployments of DP. They are both defined in terms of the *Rényi divergence* of order $\alpha_{\mathrm{DP}} > 1$ between two distributions P and Q over $\mathcal{Y}$:

$$D_{\alpha_{\mathrm{DP}}}(P\|Q) = \frac{1}{\alpha_{\mathrm{DP}} - 1} \log \mathop{\mathbb{E}}_{y \sim P} \log \left(\frac{P(y)}{Q(y)}\right)^{\alpha_{\mathrm{DP}}-1}.$$

Definition 2 (RDP, [78]**).** *Given $\alpha_{\mathrm{DP}} > 1$ and $\varepsilon_{\mathrm{DP}} \geq 0$, we say a randomized algorithm $\mathcal{A} : \mathbb{N}^{\mathcal{X}} \to \mathcal{Y}$ satisfies* $(\alpha_{\mathrm{DP}}, \varepsilon_{\mathrm{DP}})$-Rényi DP *(RDP) if for all adjacent data sets $\boldsymbol{x}, \boldsymbol{x}' \in \mathcal{X}^n$,*

$$D_{\alpha_{\mathrm{DP}}}(\mathcal{A}(\boldsymbol{x})\|\mathcal{A}(\boldsymbol{x}')) \leq \varepsilon_{\mathrm{DP}}.$$

Importantly, it is known that $(\alpha_{\mathrm{DP}}, \varepsilon_{\mathrm{DP}})$-RDP implies $\left(\varepsilon_{\mathrm{DP}} + \frac{\log(1/\delta_{\mathrm{DP}})}{\alpha_{\mathrm{DP}}-1}, \delta_{\mathrm{DP}}\right)$-DP for any $0 < \delta_{\mathrm{DP}} < 1$ [78].

Definition 3 (zCDP, [25]**).** *We say a randomized algorithm $\mathcal{A} : \mathbb{N}^{\mathcal{X}} \to \mathcal{Y}$ satisfies* ρ_{DP}-zero-concentrated DP *(zCDP) if $\mathcal{A}$ satisfies $(\alpha_{\mathrm{DP}}, \rho_{\mathrm{DP}} \cdot \alpha_{\mathrm{DP}})$-RDP for all $\alpha_{\mathrm{DP}} > 1$.*

We use $\varepsilon_{\mathrm{DP}}, \delta_{\mathrm{DP}}, \alpha_{\mathrm{DP}}, \rho_{\mathrm{DP}}$ to refer to an algorithm's privacy parameters, rather than $\varepsilon, \delta, \alpha, \rho$, in order to avoid confusion with other variable names. These include the regression errors ε, the dimensionality ratio δ, the bias variable α, and the function ρ used to define the logistic loss. For more background on differential privacy, including the motivation behind the definition, the protections it provides, interpretations of the privacy parameters, privacy composition theorems, and more, we refer the reader to [43,100].

We collect here a handful of recent privacy analyses from the DP literature that we will repeatedly use in our paper. The first two results concern the *Gaussian mechanism* $\mathcal{A}(\boldsymbol{x}) = f(\boldsymbol{x}) + \boldsymbol{z}$ where $\boldsymbol{z} \sim \mathcal{N}(\boldsymbol{0}, \nu^2 \boldsymbol{I}_d)$ [40]. To state the result, which we will eventually use to analyze the output perturbation algorithm, recall that a function $f : \mathcal{X}^n \to \mathbb{R}^d$ has ℓ^2 sensitivity at most Δ if $\|f(\boldsymbol{x}) - f(\boldsymbol{x}')\| \leq \Delta$ for all adjacent $\boldsymbol{x}, \boldsymbol{x}' \in \mathcal{X}^n$.

Theorem 4 (Lemma 2.5 of [25]). *If $f : \mathbb{N}^{\mathcal{X}} \to \mathbb{R}^d$ has ℓ^2 sensitivity at most Δ, then the Gaussian mechanism w.r.t. f satisfies ρ_{DP}-zCDP for $\rho_{\text{DP}} = \frac{\Delta^2}{2\nu^2}$.*

Theorem 5 (Theorem 8 of [9]). *If $f : \mathbb{N}^{\mathcal{X}} \to \mathbb{R}^d$ has ℓ^2 sensitivity at most Δ, then for any $\varepsilon_{\text{DP}} \geq 0$ and $\delta_{\text{DP}} \in [0,1]$, the Gaussian mechanism w.r.t. f satisfies $(\varepsilon_{\text{DP}}, \delta_{\text{DP}})$-DP if and only if*

$$\delta \geq \text{HockeyStick}\left(\varepsilon_{\text{DP}}, \frac{\Delta}{\nu}\right) = \Phi\left(\frac{\Delta}{2\nu} - \frac{\varepsilon_{\text{DP}}\nu}{\Delta}\right) - e^{\varepsilon_{\text{DP}}}\Phi\left(-\frac{\Delta}{2\nu} - \frac{\varepsilon_{\text{DP}}\nu}{\Delta}\right).$$

The name "HockeyStick" comes from the term *hockey stick divergence*, defined for $\varepsilon_{\text{DP}} \geq 0$ and distributions P and Q on $\mathbb{R}$ as $H_{e^{\varepsilon_{\text{DP}}}}(P\|Q) = \int_{-\infty}^{\infty} \max(0, P(x) - e^{\varepsilon_{\text{DP}}}Q(x))\, dx$. As we have defined it, HockeyStick$(\varepsilon_{\text{DP}}, \Delta/\nu)$ measures this divergence between $P = \mathcal{N}(\Delta, \nu^2)$ and $Q = \mathcal{N}(0, \nu^2)$, which only depends on Δ and ν through their ratio Δ/ν.

The next result we state is a recent privacy analysis of objective perturbation from [87]. Although we will not use this result directly in our paper, this result and its proof are the starting point from which our own privacy analysis in the extended version of our paper proceeds. Indeed, the statement and proof of our privacy result will be very similar to that of [87]. The key difference is that ours will apply to any regularization strength $\lambda > 0$ and perturbation strength $\nu > 0$, but that of [87] requires $\lambda > s$ for some strictly positive s depending on the smoothness of the loss function.

The result of [87], which we now state, concerns loss functions of the form $\ell(\boldsymbol{\beta}; (\boldsymbol{x}, y)) = \ell_0(\langle \boldsymbol{x}, \boldsymbol{\beta} \rangle, y)$ for a function $\ell_0 : \mathbb{R}^2 \to \mathbb{R}$. Such loss functions are called *generalized linear model* (GLM) loss functions, and as the authors of [87] emphasize, most privacy proofs for objective perturbation in the DP literature require this GLM assumption, even if they do not state it explicitly.[6]

Theorem 6 (Theorems 3.1 and 3.2 of [87]). *Suppose that $\ell_0 : \mathbb{R}^2 \to \mathbb{R}$ satisfies $|\partial_1 \ell_0(\eta, y)| \leq L$ and $0 \leq \partial_1^2 \ell_0(\eta, y) \leq s$ for some constants $L, s > 0$ and for all $\eta, y \in \mathbb{R}$. Then objective perturbation (Algorithm 1) with $R = 1$, any $\lambda, \nu > 0$, and the GLM loss function $\ell(\boldsymbol{\beta}; (\boldsymbol{x}, y)) = \ell_0(\langle \boldsymbol{x}, \boldsymbol{\beta} \rangle, y)$ satisfies $(\varepsilon_{\text{DP}}, \delta_{\text{DP}})$-differential privacy for any $\varepsilon_{\text{DP}} \geq 0$ and*

$$\delta_{\text{DP}} = \begin{cases} 2 \cdot \text{HockeyStick}(\widetilde{\varepsilon}_{\text{DP}}, \frac{L}{\nu}) & \text{if } \widehat{\varepsilon}_{\text{DP}} \geq 0, \\ (1 - e^{\widehat{\varepsilon}_{\text{DP}}}) + 2e^{\widehat{\varepsilon}_{\text{DP}}} \cdot \text{HockeyStick}\left(\frac{L^2}{2\nu^2}, \frac{L}{\nu}\right) & \text{otherwise,} \end{cases}$$

where we set $\widetilde{\varepsilon}_{\text{DP}} = \varepsilon_{\text{DP}} - |\log(1 - s/\lambda)|$ and $\widehat{\varepsilon}_{\text{DP}} = \widetilde{\varepsilon}_{\text{DP}} - L^2/2\nu^2$, provided that $\lambda > s$.

---

[6] The statement of Theorem 6 is *not* identical to the statements of Theorems 3.1 and 3.2 in [87] because we have corrected a few typos in their statement: first, in the (ε, δ)-DP bound, we have added absolute value signs around the term $\log(1 - s/\lambda)$ in the definition of $\tilde{\varepsilon}$. Similarly, we have added a factor of 2 in the denominator of $L^2/2\nu^2$. The absolute value signs and the factor of 2 are both present throughout the proof of Theorem 3.1 of [87], and are only omitted in the theorem's statement.

The algorithm also satisfies $(\alpha_{\mathrm{DP}}, \varepsilon_{\mathrm{DP}})$*-Rényi differential privacy for any* $\alpha_{\mathrm{DP}} > 1$ *and*

$$\varepsilon_{\mathrm{DP}} = -\log\left(1 - \frac{s}{\lambda}\right) + \frac{L^2}{2\nu^2} + \frac{1}{\alpha_{\mathrm{DP}} - 1} \log \mathbb{E}_{X \sim \mathcal{N}\left(0, \frac{L^2}{\nu^2}\right)} \left[e^{(\alpha_{\mathrm{DP}}-1)|X|}\right].$$

2.2 Convex Gaussian Minimax Theorem

In this section, we present the Convex Gaussian Minimax Theorem (CGMT), due to [96,99], which will play a key role in our analysis of objective perturbation.

As discussed in the technical overview in Sect. 1.2, CGMT allows us to better understand the optimizers of a certain class of min-max optimization problems that are defined in terms of a Gaussian random matrix $\boldsymbol{G} \in \mathbb{R}^{n \times d}$. The theorem relates the original problem to an *auxiliary* optimization problem in which the random matrix $\boldsymbol{G}$ has been replaced with two random vectors $\boldsymbol{g} \in \mathbb{R}^d$ and $\boldsymbol{h} \in \mathbb{R}^n$, whose dimensions match the number of columns and rows of $\boldsymbol{G}$, respectively. Remarkably, the theorem shows that the optimum value of the original problem, which is a scalar-valued function of $\boldsymbol{G}$, has a similar distribution to the optimum value of the auxiliary problem, which is a scalar-valued function of $(\boldsymbol{g}, \boldsymbol{h})$ that is much easier to determine directly via calculus. The main assumption needed for CGMT is that the original min-max problem is convex-concave and depends bilinearly on $\boldsymbol{G}$.

At first glance, it may seem that knowing the optimum value of the original problem is not very useful. After all, in the proof sketch we outlined in Sect. 1.2, what we really wanted to understand was the *optimizer* $\widehat{\boldsymbol{\beta}}$, which is the location at which the optimum value is achieved. It turns out that by carefully choosing the constraint sets of the problem to which CGMT is applied, we can get our hands on a remarkable number of quantitative properties about $\widehat{\boldsymbol{\beta}}$. For example, suppose we would like to show that the estimation error of $\widehat{\boldsymbol{\beta}}$ with respect to the ground-truth $\boldsymbol{\beta}^\star$ is approximately $(\sigma^\star)^2$ in the limit. To do so, consider a small slack factor $\varepsilon_n > 0$ and define the constraint set

$$\mathcal{S}_{\varepsilon_n} = \left\{\boldsymbol{\beta} \in \mathbb{R}^d : \left|\frac{1}{d}\|\boldsymbol{\beta} - \boldsymbol{\beta}^\star\|^2 - (\sigma^\star)^2\right| \geq \varepsilon_n\right\}.$$

If we can show that, with high probability, the optimum value of the auxiliary problem over $\mathcal{S}_{\varepsilon_n}$ is strictly larger than the optimum value of the auxiliary problem over $\mathbb{R}^d$, then by CGMT, the same must be true of original problem. Since $\widehat{\boldsymbol{\beta}}$ is the optimizer of the original problem, this would allow us to conclude that with high probability, $\widehat{\boldsymbol{\beta}} \notin \mathcal{S}_{\varepsilon_n}$, so $\frac{1}{d}\|\widehat{\boldsymbol{\beta}} - \boldsymbol{\beta}^\star\|^2 = (\sigma^\star)^2 \pm \varepsilon_n$.

Nothing about the previous example is particularly specific to ℓ^2 estimation error, which suggests (correctly) that the argument can be carried out for a wide range of test functions. It turns out that we will be able to handle a broad class of *pseudo-Lipschitz* test functions. We will be able to handle slack factors on the order of $\varepsilon_n = n^{-\Omega(1)}$ in the case of robust linear regression, or $\varepsilon_n = e^{-(\log n)^{\Omega(1)}}$ in the case of logistic regression, both of which satisfy $\varepsilon_n \to 0$ as $n \to \infty$.

Theorem 7 (Convex Gaussian Minimax Theorem, [96,99]). *Given compact sets $\mathcal{S}_u \subseteq \mathbb{R}^d$ and $\mathcal{S}_v \subseteq \mathbb{R}^n$, a continuous function $\psi : \mathcal{S}_u \times \mathcal{S}_v \to \mathbb{R}$, a matrix $\boldsymbol{G} \in \mathbb{R}^{n\times d}$, and vectors $\boldsymbol{g} \in \mathbb{R}^d$, $\boldsymbol{h} \in \mathbb{R}^n$, consider the following two random variables indexed by $\boldsymbol{u} \in \mathcal{S}_u$ and $\boldsymbol{v} \in \mathcal{S}_v$:*

$$\begin{aligned} Q_{\boldsymbol{u},\boldsymbol{v}} &= \langle \boldsymbol{G}\boldsymbol{u}, \boldsymbol{v}\rangle + \psi(\boldsymbol{u},\boldsymbol{v}) \\ Q'_{\boldsymbol{u},\boldsymbol{v}} &= \|\boldsymbol{u}\|\langle \boldsymbol{h}, \boldsymbol{v}\rangle - \|\boldsymbol{v}\|\langle \boldsymbol{g}, \boldsymbol{u}\rangle + \psi(\boldsymbol{u},\boldsymbol{v}). \end{aligned}$$

We call $Q_{\boldsymbol{u},\boldsymbol{v}}$ and $Q'_{\boldsymbol{u},\boldsymbol{v}}$ the primary and auxiliary objective functions. *If $\boldsymbol{G}$, $\boldsymbol{g}$, and $\boldsymbol{h}$ all have independent $\mathcal{N}(0,\sigma^2)$ entries for some $\sigma > 0$, then:*

(a) For any threshold $t \in \mathbb{R}$,

$$\Pr\left[\min_{\boldsymbol{u}\in\mathcal{S}_u}\max_{\boldsymbol{v}\in\mathcal{S}_v} Q_{\boldsymbol{u},\boldsymbol{v}} < t\right] \le 2\Pr\left[\min_{\boldsymbol{u}\in\mathcal{S}_u}\max_{\boldsymbol{v}\in\mathcal{S}_v} Q'_{\boldsymbol{u},\boldsymbol{v}} < t\right].$$

(b) If $\mathcal{S}_u$ and $\mathcal{S}_v$ are convex and ψ is convex-concave on $\mathcal{S}_u \times \mathcal{S}_v$, then for any threshold $t \in \mathbb{R}$,

$$\Pr\left[\min_{\boldsymbol{u}\in\mathcal{S}_u}\max_{\boldsymbol{v}\in\mathcal{S}_v} Q_{\boldsymbol{u},\boldsymbol{v}} > t\right] \le 2\Pr\left[\min_{\boldsymbol{u}\in\mathcal{S}_u}\max_{\boldsymbol{v}\in\mathcal{S}_v} Q'_{\boldsymbol{u},\boldsymbol{v}} > t\right].$$

2.3 Universality

Here, we state the two key universality laws from prior work that we will use in our analyses. The first result is Corollary 2.6 of [54], which we call CGMT universality. We have slightly rephrased the statement for clarity, at the cost of generality (e.g. by assuming that the mean function ψ is differentiable). We will eventually use this result in our analyses of objective perturbation and output perturbation for robust linear regression. As we discussed earlier in the technical overview of Sect. 1.2, this result allows us to extend CGMT analysis to non-Gaussian design matrices, as long as we have a few finite, matching moments.

Theorem 8 (CGMT Universality: Corollary 2.6 of[54]). *Consider random matrices $\boldsymbol{A}, \boldsymbol{B} \in \mathbb{R}^{n\times d}$ with independent entries satisfying the following three moment conditions as $n \to \infty$ with $d = \Theta(n)$:*

(1) $\mathbb{E}\,\boldsymbol{A}_{ij} = \mathbb{E}\,\boldsymbol{B}_{ij} = 0$ for all $i \in [n]$ and $j \in [d]$.
(2) $\mathbb{E}\,\boldsymbol{A}_{ij}^2 = \mathbb{E}\,\boldsymbol{B}_{ij}^2 = 1$ for all $i \in [n]$ and $j \in [d]$.
(3) $\max_{i\in[n]}\max_{j\in[d]}\ \mathbb{E}|\boldsymbol{A}_{ij}|^3 + \mathbb{E}|\boldsymbol{B}_{ij}|^3 = O(1)$.

Let $\mathcal{S}_u \subseteq [-L_u, L_u]^d$ and $\mathcal{S}_v \subseteq [-L_v, L_v]^n$ be measurable sets with $L_u, L_v \ge 1$, and set $L = L_u + L_v$. Let $\psi : \mathbb{R}^d \times \mathbb{R}^n \to \mathbb{R}$ be a differentiable function with

$$\mathscr{M} = \max_{\boldsymbol{u}\in[-L,+L]^d}\ \max_{\boldsymbol{v}\in[-L,+L]^n} \|\nabla\psi(\boldsymbol{u},\boldsymbol{v})\|_1.$$

Finally, consider the following random variables indexed by $\boldsymbol{u} \in \mathcal{S}_{\boldsymbol{u}}$ *and* $\boldsymbol{v} \in \mathcal{S}_{\boldsymbol{v}}$*:*

$$Q^{\boldsymbol{A}}_{\boldsymbol{u},\boldsymbol{v}} = \frac{1}{n^{3/2}}\langle \boldsymbol{A}\boldsymbol{u}, \boldsymbol{v}\rangle + \psi(\boldsymbol{u}, \boldsymbol{v}) \quad \textit{and} \quad Q^{\boldsymbol{B}}_{\boldsymbol{u},\boldsymbol{v}} = \frac{1}{n^{3/2}}\langle \boldsymbol{B}\boldsymbol{u}, \boldsymbol{v}\rangle + \psi(\boldsymbol{u}, \boldsymbol{v}).$$

Then, for all thresholds $t \in \mathbb{R}$*, all gaps* $g > 0$*, and all* $\omega \geq n$*,*

$$\Pr\left[\min_{\boldsymbol{u}\in\mathcal{S}_{\boldsymbol{u}}} \max_{\boldsymbol{v}\in\mathcal{S}_{\boldsymbol{v}}} Q^{\boldsymbol{A}}_{\boldsymbol{u},\boldsymbol{v}} < t\right] - \Pr\left[\min_{\boldsymbol{u}\in\mathcal{S}_{\boldsymbol{u}}} \max_{\boldsymbol{v}\in\mathcal{S}_{\boldsymbol{v}}} Q^{\boldsymbol{B}}_{\boldsymbol{u},\boldsymbol{v}} < t + g\right]$$
$$= O\left(\left(1 + \frac{1}{g^3}\right)\left(\frac{\mathscr{M}}{\omega} + \frac{L^2 \log^{2/3}(L\omega)}{n^{1/6}}\right)\right).$$

The second result we build on is Theorem 3.2 of [53], namely generalized first-order method (GFOM) universality. This result establishes universality for a broad class of iterative methods, called *first-order methods*, involving a random design matrix $\boldsymbol{X}$. The result ensures that many *pseudo-Lipschitz* summaries of such iterates (see Sect. 2.4 for a definition of pseudo-Lipschitz) are essentially unchanged upon replacing $\boldsymbol{X}$ with a Gaussian matrix $\boldsymbol{G}$ of the same shape. As discussed in the technical overview of Sect. 1.2, this will prove useful for our analysis of objective perturbation and output perturbation for logistic regression, as well our DP-SGD results for both robust linear regression and logistic regression.

We have modified the statement slightly from the version that appeared in [53] to allow vector-valued iterates and different test functions per coordinate, changes that require only minimal, syntactic changes in the proof. Before stating the GFOM universality theorem, we give a formal definition of general first order methods:

Definition 4. *Given* $\boldsymbol{u}^{(1)}, \ldots, \boldsymbol{u}^{(t)} \in \mathbb{R}^{m\times k}$*, let* $\boldsymbol{u}^{(s)}_i \in \mathbb{R}^k$ *be the* i^{th} *row of* $\boldsymbol{u}^{(s)}$*. Let* $\boldsymbol{u}^{(1:t)} \in \mathbb{R}^{t\times m\times k}$ *be the tensor comprising* $\boldsymbol{u}^{(s)}$ *for* $s \in [t]$*. Define* $\boldsymbol{u}^{(1:t)}_i \in \mathbb{R}^{t\times k}$ *similarly. Given functions* $F_1, \ldots, F_m : \mathbb{R}^{t\times k} \to \mathbb{R}^k$*, let* $F(\boldsymbol{u}^{(1:t)}) \in \mathbb{R}^{m\times k}$ *be the matrix with* i^{th} *row* $F_i(\boldsymbol{u}^{(1:t)}_i) \in \mathbb{R}^k$*.*

Definition 5. *A* general first order method *(GFOM) consists of a matrix* $\boldsymbol{X} \in \mathbb{R}^{n\times d}$*, an* initialization $(\boldsymbol{u}^{(0)}, \boldsymbol{v}^{(0)}) \in \mathbb{R}^{d\times k} \times \mathbb{R}^{n\times \ell}$ *with* $k, \ell = O(1)$ *and* $d = \Theta(n)$*, and functions* $F^{(t)}_{1j}, F^{(t)}_{2j} : \mathbb{R}^{t\times k} \to \mathbb{R}^k$*,* $G^{(t)}_{1i} : \mathbb{R}^{t\times \ell} \to \mathbb{R}^\ell$*, and* $G^{(t)}_{2i} : \mathbb{R}^{(t+1)\times \ell} \to \mathbb{R}^\ell$ *for all* $t \in \mathbb{N}$*,* $i \in [n]$*, and* $j \in [d]$*. Its* iterates *are*

$$\begin{aligned} \boldsymbol{u}^{(t)} &= \boldsymbol{X} F^{(t)}_1(\boldsymbol{v}^{(0:t-1)}) + G^{(t)}_1(\boldsymbol{u}^{(0:t-1)}) \in \mathbb{R}^{d\times k}, \\ \boldsymbol{v}^{(t)} &= \boldsymbol{X}^\top G^{(t)}_2(\boldsymbol{u}^{(0:t)}) + F^{(t)}_2(\boldsymbol{v}^{(0:t-1)}) \in \mathbb{R}^{n\times \ell}. \end{aligned} \tag{1}$$

Theorem 9 (GFOM Universality, Theorem 3.2 of [53]). *Consider random matrices* $\boldsymbol{A}, \boldsymbol{B} \in \mathbb{R}^{n\times d}$ *with independent entries satisfying the following conditions as* $n \to \infty$ *with* $d = \Theta(n)$*:*

- $\mathbb{E}\,\boldsymbol{A}_{ij} = \mathbb{E}\,\boldsymbol{B}_{ij} = 0$ *for all* $i \in [n]$ *and* $j \in [d]$*.*

- $\mathbb{E}\, \boldsymbol{A}_{ij}^2 = \mathbb{E}\, \boldsymbol{B}_{ij}^2$ *for all* $i \in [n]$ *amd* $j \in [d]$.
- $\max_{i\in[n]} \max_{j\in[d]} \|\boldsymbol{A}_{ij}\|_{\psi_2} + \|\boldsymbol{B}_{ij}\|_{\psi_2} = O(n^{-1/2})$.

Also consider a GFOM satisfying the following condition for some $\Lambda \geq 2$*, stated in terms of the* Lipschitz norm $\|f\|_{\mathrm{Lip}} = \inf\{L \in \mathbb{R} : f is L-Lipschitz\}$ *of a function* f*:*

$$\max_{s\in[t]} \max_{q\in\{1,2\}} \max_{i\in[n]} \max_{j\in[d]} \|F_{qi}^{(t)}\|_{\mathrm{Lip}} + \|G_{qj}^{(t)}\|_{\mathrm{Lip}} + |F_{qi}^{(t)}(0)| + |G_{qj}^{(t)}(0)| \leq \Lambda.$$

Let $\boldsymbol{u}^{(t)}(\boldsymbol{X})$ *and* $\boldsymbol{v}^{(t)}(\boldsymbol{X})$ *denote the output of this GFOM with matrix* $\boldsymbol{X}$*. Then, for any collection of* Λ*-pseudo-Lipschitz functions* $\psi_{1j} : \mathbb{R}^{t\times k} \to \mathbb{R}$ *and* $\psi_{2i} : \mathbb{R}^{t\times \ell} \to \mathbb{R}$ *of order* p*, for any* $q \in \mathbb{N}$*, there exists* $C > 0$ *such that*

$$\mathbb{E}\left|\frac{1}{d}\sum_{j=1}^{d}\left(\psi_{1j}(\boldsymbol{u}_j^{(1:t)}(\boldsymbol{A})) - \psi_{1j}(\boldsymbol{u}_j^{(1:t)}(\boldsymbol{B}))\right)\right|^q$$
$$+\,\mathbb{E}\left|\frac{1}{n}\sum_{i=1}^{n}\left(\psi_{2i}(\boldsymbol{v}_i^{(1:t)}(\boldsymbol{A})) - \psi_{2i}(\boldsymbol{v}_i^{(1:t)}(\boldsymbol{B}))\right)\right|^q$$
$$\leq (\Lambda \log(n)(1 + \|\boldsymbol{u}^{(0)}\|_\infty + \|\boldsymbol{v}^{(0)}\|_\infty))^{Ct^3} n^{-1/(Ct^3)}.$$

Note that in Theorem 9, if the initialization $(\boldsymbol{u}^{(0)}, \boldsymbol{v}^{(0)})$ is random, then the conclusion of the theorem still holds even after conditioning on the value of $(\boldsymbol{u}^{(0)}, \boldsymbol{v}^{(0)})$.

2.4 Mathematical Miscellany

Basic Definitions. We write vectors, matrices, and higher-order tensors in boldface. Given $m \in \mathbb{N}$, we write $[m] = \{1, 2, \ldots, m\}$. Given a vector $\boldsymbol{x} \in \mathbb{R}^n$ and $p \geq 1$, we write $\|\boldsymbol{x}\|_p = (\sum_{i=1}^n |x_i|^p)^{1/p}$ and $\|\boldsymbol{x}\|_\infty = \max_{i\in[n]}|x_i|$ (by Hölder's inequality, if $p < q$, then $\|\boldsymbol{x}\|_q \leq \|\boldsymbol{x}\|_p \leq n^{\frac{1}{p}-\frac{1}{q}}\|\boldsymbol{x}\|_q$). Given a matrix $\boldsymbol{A} \in \mathbb{R}^{n\times m}$, we define $\|\boldsymbol{A}\|_{r\to s} = \max_{\|\boldsymbol{x}\|_r\leq 1}\|\boldsymbol{A}\boldsymbol{x}\|_s$ and $\|\boldsymbol{A}\|_p = \|\boldsymbol{A}\|_{p\to p}$. By default, we let $\|\boldsymbol{x}\| = \|\boldsymbol{x}\|_2$ and $\|\boldsymbol{A}\| = \|\boldsymbol{A}\|_2$. Given $\boldsymbol{x}, \boldsymbol{y} \in \mathbb{R}^n$, we write $\boldsymbol{x} \odot \boldsymbol{y} = (x_1y_1, \ldots, x_ny_n) \in \mathbb{R}^n$ for their entrywise (a.k.a. Hadamard) product. Given a set $\mathcal{S} \subseteq \mathbb{R}^n$, a scalar $c \in \mathbb{R}$ and a vector $\boldsymbol{x} \in \mathbb{R}^n$, we write $\boldsymbol{x} + c \cdot \mathcal{S} = \{\boldsymbol{x} + c\boldsymbol{y} : \boldsymbol{y} \in \mathcal{S}\}$ for the rescaled and translated version of $\mathcal{S}$.

Definition 6. $f : \mathbb{R}^m \to \mathbb{R}$ *is* L-pseudo-Lipschitz of order k *if for all* $\boldsymbol{a}, \boldsymbol{b} \in \mathbb{R}^m$*,*

$$|f(\boldsymbol{a}) - f(\boldsymbol{b})| \leq L(1 + \|\boldsymbol{a}\| + \|\boldsymbol{b}\|)^{k-1}\|\boldsymbol{a} - \boldsymbol{b}\|.$$

We say f *is* pseudo-Lipschitz *if there exist* $L \geq 0$ *and* $k \in \mathbb{N}$ *for which* f *is* L*-pseudo-Lipschitz of order* k*. We say* f *is* L-Lipschitz *if it is* L*-pseudo-Lipschitz of order* 1*. Let*

$$\|f\|_{\mathrm{Lip}} = \inf\{L \in \mathbb{R} : f \textit{ is } L \textit{ -Lipschitz}\}.$$

The canonical example of an order-k pseudo-Lipschitz function is $f(\boldsymbol{x}) = \|\boldsymbol{x}\|^k$. Observe that if f is L-pseudo-Lipschitz of order k, there exists $L' > 0$ such that $|f(\boldsymbol{x})| \leq L'(1 + \|\boldsymbol{x}\|^k)$. We will often use the fact that $(1 + \|\boldsymbol{a}\| + \|\boldsymbol{b}\|)^{k-1} \leq (3\max\{1, \|\boldsymbol{a}\|, \|\boldsymbol{b}\|\})^{k-1} \leq O_k(1 + \|\boldsymbol{a}\|^{k-1} + \|\boldsymbol{b}\|^{k-1})$.

High-Dimensional Probability. We collect some notation, definitions, and lemmas from probability that we will repeatedly use. For more detail, we refer the reader to [102].

First, we say a sequence of events E_n holds *with high probability (w.h.p.)* if $\Pr[E_n] \geq 1 - n^{-\Omega(1)}$, or merely *asymptotically almost surely (a.a.s.)* if $\Pr[E_n] \geq 1 - o(1)$. We say a sequence of random variables $x_1, x_2, \ldots \in \mathbb{R}$ *converges in probability to the random variable* $x_0 \in \mathbb{R}$, written $x_n \xrightarrow{P} x_0$, if for all $c > 0$, we have that a.a.s., $|x_n - x_0| \leq c$. Given $\boldsymbol{p} \in [0,1]^n$, we will denote by $\text{Bernoulli}(\boldsymbol{p})$ the distribution over $\{0,1\}^n$ with independent, $\text{Bernoulli}(p_i)$ coordinates. We will denote the standard Gaussian PDF and CDF by φ and Φ, respectively. Given a vector $\boldsymbol{\mu} \in \mathbb{R}^n$ and positive semidefinite matrix $\boldsymbol{\Sigma} \in \mathbb{R}^{n \times n}$, we will denote the multivariate Gaussian distribution with mean $\boldsymbol{\mu}$ and covariance $\boldsymbol{\Sigma}$ by $\mathcal{N}(\boldsymbol{\mu}, \boldsymbol{\Sigma})$. The key properties of the standard Gaussian distribution that we will use are its rotational invariance and Gaussian integration by parts, also known as Stein's lemma:

Lemma 1 (Rotational Invariance). *If* $\boldsymbol{z} \sim \mathcal{N}(\boldsymbol{0}, \boldsymbol{I}_n)$ *and* $\boldsymbol{Q} \in \mathbb{R}^{n \times n}$ *is orthogonal* ($\boldsymbol{Q}^{-1} = \boldsymbol{Q}^\top$)*, then* $\boldsymbol{Qz} \sim \mathcal{N}(\boldsymbol{0}, \boldsymbol{I}_n)$*, as well.*

Lemma 2 (Stein's Lemma). *If* $Z \sim \mathcal{N}(0,1)$ *and* $g : \mathbb{R} \to \mathbb{R}$ *is differentiable, then* $\mathbb{E}[g(Z)Z] = \mathbb{E}[g'(Z)]$ *if both expectations exist.*

We also require the following notion of subgaussianity.

Definition 7 (Subgaussian Norm). *The* subgaussian norm *of a random variable* $X \in \mathbb{R}$ *is*

$$\|X\|_{\psi_2} = \inf\left\{c > 0 \;\middle|\; \mathbb{E}[e^{(X/c)^2}] \leq 2\right\}.$$

We say X *is* subgaussian *if* $\|X\|_{\psi_2} < \infty$.

One can check that if $X \sim \mathcal{N}(0,1)$, then $\|X\|_{\psi_2} = \Theta(1)$. Moreover, we have $\|X\|_{\psi_2} = O(1)$ if and only if $\Pr[|X| > t] < 2\exp(-\Omega(t^2))$. Importantly, the subgaussian norm has the following relationship to projection onto a unit vector:

Lemma 3. *If the random vector* $\boldsymbol{x} \in \mathbb{R}^d$ *has independent, subgaussian components satisfying* $\|x_1\|_{\psi_2}, \ldots, \|x_d\|_{\psi_2} \leq \sigma$ *and* $\boldsymbol{u} \in \mathbb{R}^n$ *is independent of* $\boldsymbol{x}$ *with* $\|\boldsymbol{u}\| = 1$*, then*

$$\|\langle \boldsymbol{x}, \boldsymbol{u} \rangle\|_{\psi_2} = O(\sigma).$$

Convex Analysis. We now briefly review some concepts from convex analysis that we will frequently use. For the most basic definitions of convexity, as well as more detail on the concepts discussed here, we refer the reader to [23,85].

Definition 8 (Subdifferential). *The* subdifferential *of a function* $f : \mathbb{R}^n \to \mathbb{R}$ *at a point* $\boldsymbol{x} \in \mathbb{R}^n$ *is its set of* subgradients $\boldsymbol{g}$*:*

$$\partial f(\boldsymbol{x}) = \{\boldsymbol{g} \in \mathbb{R}^n : \forall \boldsymbol{y} \in \mathbb{R}^n, f(\boldsymbol{y}) \geq f(\boldsymbol{x}) + \langle \boldsymbol{g}, \boldsymbol{y} - \boldsymbol{x} \rangle\}.$$

Minimizing a (strongly convex) function amounts to finding a point $\boldsymbol{x}$ with a (nearly) vanishing subgradient $\boldsymbol{g}$:

Lemma 4 (Convex Minimization). *For any $f : \mathbb{R}^n \to \mathbb{R}$, the point $\boldsymbol{x} \in \mathbb{R}^n$ is a global minimizer of f if and only if $\mathbf{0} \in \partial f(\boldsymbol{x})$. Relatedly, if f is m-strongly convex and $\boldsymbol{g} \in \partial f(\boldsymbol{x})$, then*

$$f(\boldsymbol{x}) - \inf_{\boldsymbol{y} \in \mathbb{R}^n} f(\boldsymbol{y}) \le \frac{1}{2m} \|\boldsymbol{g}\|^2.$$

We shall repeatedly use the minimax theorem, a cornerstone result of game theory.

Lemma 5 (Sion's Minimax Theorem, [92]). *Suppose $\mathcal{S}_x \subseteq \mathbb{R}^d$ and $\mathcal{S}_y \subseteq \mathbb{R}^n$ are convex and the function $f : \mathbb{R}^d \times \mathbb{R}^n \to \mathbb{R}$ satisfies the following two properties:*

- *The map $\boldsymbol{x} \mapsto f(\boldsymbol{x}, \boldsymbol{y})$ is a closed, proper, convex function for all $\boldsymbol{y} \in \mathcal{S}_y$.*
- *The map $\boldsymbol{y} \mapsto -f(\boldsymbol{x}, \boldsymbol{y})$ is a closed, proper, convex function for all $\boldsymbol{x} \in \mathcal{S}_x$.*

If either $\mathcal{S}_x$ or $\mathcal{S}_y$ is compact, then

$$\inf_{\boldsymbol{x} \in \mathcal{S}_x} \sup_{\boldsymbol{y} \in \mathcal{S}_y} f(\boldsymbol{x}, \boldsymbol{y}) = \sup_{\boldsymbol{y} \in \mathcal{S}_y} \inf_{\boldsymbol{x} \in \mathcal{S}_x} f(\boldsymbol{x}, \boldsymbol{y})$$

We next introduce a bit of notation that will simplify the statements of our results.

Definition 9 (Moreau Envelope, Proximal Operator). *Given $\tau \ge 0$, the* Moreau envelope *of a closed, proper, convex function f is*

$$e_f(\boldsymbol{x}; \tau) = \begin{cases} \min_{\boldsymbol{y} \in \mathbb{R}^n} \left\{ \frac{1}{2\tau} \|\boldsymbol{y} - \boldsymbol{x}\|^2 + f(\boldsymbol{y}) \right\} & \text{if } \tau > 0, \\ f(\boldsymbol{x}) & \text{if } \tau = 0. \end{cases}$$

Its proximal operator *is the point $\boldsymbol{y}$ that minimizes $e_f(\boldsymbol{x}; \tau)$:*

$$\mathrm{prox}_{\tau f}(\boldsymbol{x}) = \operatorname*{argmin}_{\boldsymbol{y} \in \mathbb{R}^n} \left\{ \frac{1}{2} \|\boldsymbol{y} - \boldsymbol{x}\|^2 + \tau f(\boldsymbol{y}) \right\}.$$

Here, the subscript τf refers to the product $\tau \cdot f$, i.e. the function f scaled by τ. In the case that $\tau = 1$, we will simply write $\mathrm{prox}_f(\boldsymbol{x})$. When $\tau = 0$, so that τf vanishes everywhere, the function $\mathrm{prox}_{\tau f}$ coincides with the identity function, i.e. $\mathrm{prox}_0(\boldsymbol{x}) = \boldsymbol{x}$.

Some remarks are in order. The proximal operator can be interpreted as a generalization of the projection operator. Indeed, suppose there is a nonempty, compact, convex set $C \subseteq \mathbb{R}^d$ for which

$$f(\boldsymbol{x}) = \begin{cases} 0 & \text{if } \boldsymbol{x} \in C \\ +\infty & \text{if } \boldsymbol{x} \notin C. \end{cases}$$

Then, f is a closed, proper, convex function and

$$\operatorname{prox}_f(\boldsymbol{x}) = \operatorname*{argmin}_{y \in C} \|\boldsymbol{y} - \boldsymbol{x}\|.$$

Alternatively, the proximal operator can be interpreted as a *backward* gradient step with step size τ. Indeed, if f is differentiable and $\boldsymbol{y} = \operatorname{prox}_{\tau f}(\boldsymbol{x})$, then

$$\boldsymbol{y} = \boldsymbol{x} - \tau \nabla f(\boldsymbol{y}).$$

For general f, we have that $\boldsymbol{y}$ is the unique point such that

$$\boldsymbol{y} \in \boldsymbol{x} - \tau \partial f(\boldsymbol{y}),$$

where ∂f denotes the subgradient (see Definition 8). A priori, it is not apparent that this equation has a unique solution for $\boldsymbol{y}$, but this follows from the definition of prox_f in Definition 9 and the strong convexity of $\frac{1}{2}\|\boldsymbol{y} - \boldsymbol{x}\|^2$. For comparison, the standard equation for a *forward* gradient step is

$$\boldsymbol{y} = \boldsymbol{x} - \tau \nabla f(\boldsymbol{x}).$$

We remark that the proximal operator has a useful relationship to the convex conjugate operation, and that its derivatives can be expressed concisely:

Definition 10 (Convex Conjugate). *The* convex conjugate *of an extended real-valued function* $f : \mathbb{R}^n \to \mathbb{R} \cup \{\pm\infty\}$ *is the convex function*

$$f^\star(\boldsymbol{y}) = \sup_{\boldsymbol{x} \in \mathbb{R}^n} \langle \boldsymbol{x}, \boldsymbol{y} \rangle - f(\boldsymbol{x}).$$

If $n = 1$ *and* f *is convex, then* $f^\star$ *is also called the* Legendre transform *of* f*, and* $(f^\star)' = (f')^{-1}$.

Lemma 6 (Biconjugation). *For a closed, proper, convex function* f*, we have* $f^{\star\star} = f$.

Lemma 7 (Proximal Operator of Conjugate). $\operatorname{prox}_{f^\star}(\boldsymbol{x}) = \boldsymbol{x} - \operatorname{prox}_f(\boldsymbol{x})$.

Lemma 8 (Moreau Envelope Derivatives, [89]).

$$\nabla_{\boldsymbol{x}} e_f(\boldsymbol{x}; \tau) = \frac{\boldsymbol{x} - \operatorname{prox}_{\tau f}(\boldsymbol{x})}{\tau}, \qquad \nabla_\tau e_f(\boldsymbol{x}; \tau) = -\frac{1}{2}\left\|\frac{\boldsymbol{x} - \operatorname{prox}_{\tau f}(\boldsymbol{x})}{\tau}\right\|^2$$

3 Utility of Objective Perturbation for Robust Linear Regression

In this section, we precisely characterize the privacy-utility tradeoff for the well-known objective perturbation algorithm [32,65,87] when applied to the problem of robust linear regression. The version of the algorithm that we consider is described in Algorithm 1. Before stating the main result of this section (Theorem 10), we briefly review the setup for robust linear regression, comment on the assumptions that will be necessary for our utility analysis, and give insight into the meaning of the theorem's conclusion, which is significantly stronger than in the simplified statement Theorem 1 that we gave in the introduction.

Algorithm 1. Objective Perturbation

1: **input:** design matrix $\boldsymbol{X} = [\boldsymbol{x}_1 \cdots \boldsymbol{x}_n]^\top \in \mathbb{R}^{n\times d}$ with $\|\boldsymbol{x}_i\| \le R$, response vector $\boldsymbol{y} \in \mathbb{R}^n$, loss function $\ell : \mathbb{R}^d \times \mathbb{R}^{d+1} \to \mathbb{R}$, regularization strength $\lambda > 0$, perturbation strength $\nu > 0$.

2: Randomly sample the coefficients of the linear perturbation term:

$$\boldsymbol{\xi} \sim \mathcal{N}(\boldsymbol{0}, \boldsymbol{I}_d)$$

3: Optimize the regularized and perturbed objective function:

$$\widehat{\boldsymbol{\beta}} = \operatorname*{argmin}_{\boldsymbol{\beta}\in\mathbb{R}^d} \sum_{i=1}^{n} \ell(\boldsymbol{\beta}; (\boldsymbol{x}_i, y_i)) + \frac{\lambda}{2}\|\boldsymbol{\beta}\|^2 + \nu\langle\boldsymbol{\xi}, \boldsymbol{\beta}\rangle$$

4: **return** $\widehat{\boldsymbol{\beta}}$

Robust Linear Regression Model. We are given a dataset $(\boldsymbol{X}, \boldsymbol{y})$ of n samples. In the worst case, $(\boldsymbol{x}_i, y_i)$ are arbitrary points in $\mathbb{R}^{d+1}$ with $\|\boldsymbol{x}_i\| \le R$, but in the average case, there exists a ground-truth coefficient vector $\boldsymbol{\beta}^\star \in \mathbb{R}^d$ and regression error vector $\boldsymbol{\varepsilon}^\star \in \mathbb{R}^n$ independent of $\boldsymbol{X}$ such that

$$\boldsymbol{y} = \boldsymbol{X}\boldsymbol{\beta}^\star + \boldsymbol{\varepsilon}^\star.$$

To dampen the effect of outliers in the worst-case setting, we do not seek the least squares estimate, but rather a vector $\widehat{\boldsymbol{\beta}}$ that minimizes the average *Huber loss* (robust linear loss) on the dataset:

Definition 11. *The L-Lipschitz* Huber loss *is*

$$H_L(r) = \begin{cases} \frac{1}{2}r^2 & \text{if } |r| \le L \\ L|r| - \frac{1}{2}L^2 & \text{if } |r| \ge L. \end{cases}$$

We denote the L-truncation *of* $r \in \mathbb{R}$ *by*

$$[r]_L = H_L'(r) = \begin{cases} -L & \text{if } r \le -L, \\ r & \text{if } r \in [-L, +L], \\ +L & \text{if } r \ge L. \end{cases}.$$

For $\boldsymbol{r} \in \mathbb{R}^n$, *we define* $H_L(\boldsymbol{r}) = \sum_{i=1}^n H_L(r) \in \mathbb{R}$ *and* $[\boldsymbol{r}]_L = \nabla H_L(\boldsymbol{r}) = ([r_1]_L, \ldots, [r_n]_L) \in \mathbb{R}^n$ *(Fig. 3).*

Assumptions. The main assumption for our utility analysis will be that the matrix $\boldsymbol{X}$, which we call the *design matrix* or *feature matrix*, is subgaussian in the sense defined below.

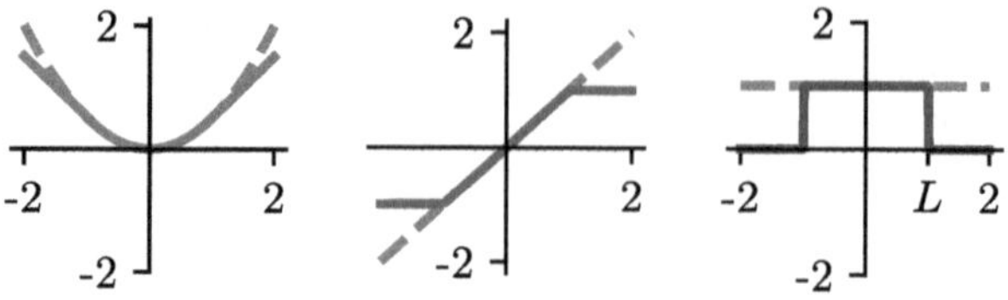

Fig. 3. The functions H_L, H'_L, and H''_L with $L = 1$.

Definition 12 (Subgaussian Design). *We say a random matrix $\boldsymbol{X} \in B_R(\mathbf{0})^n$ with $d = \Theta(n)$ follows a* subgaussian design *if its entries x_{ij} are independent and satisfy the following conditions.*

(a) For all $i \in [n]$ and $j \in [d]$, we have $\mathbb{E}[x_{ij}] = 0$ and $\mathbb{E}(x_{ij})^2 = 1/d$.
(b) $\max_{i\in[n]} \max_{j\in[d]} \|x_{ij}\|_{\psi_2} = O(1/\sqrt{n})$.

Note that any distribution supported on $\left[-\frac{R}{\sqrt{d}}, +\frac{R}{\sqrt{d}}\right]^{n\times d} \subseteq B_R(\mathbf{0})^n$ with independent, variance $1/d$ entries automatically satisfies the conditions of Definition 12. For simplicity, we have required that the variance per coordinate is precisely $1/d$, but this is merely a scaling convention, and our results extend in a straightforward manner to other isotropic distributions. In fact, given a recent line of work analyzing estimators in the proportional regime for design matrices with nonisotropic covariances or otherwise dependent entries [10,48,50,109], we suspect that the result of Theorem 10 can be further extended to nonisotropic $\boldsymbol{X}$.

More interestingly, although we do impose some mild conditions on the ground-truth $\boldsymbol{\beta}^\star$ and the regression errors $\boldsymbol{\varepsilon}^\star$, we do *not* require them to be random! This is important because several previous works indeed assume that $\boldsymbol{\beta}^\star$ and $\boldsymbol{\varepsilon}^\star$ are random with i.i.d. coordinates (e.g. [89,97], or Theorem 3.12 of [54]). We will clarify the conditions on $\boldsymbol{\beta}^\star$ and $\boldsymbol{\varepsilon}^\star$ shortly once we have defined a certain notion of convergence.

Notion of Convergence. Theorem 10 will provide estimates for a large collection of scalar quantities that one might wish to compute on the coefficient vector output by the objective perturbation algorithm, along with non-asymptotic error bounds for those estimates that hold with high probability and decay at a $n^{-\Omega(1)}$ rate. In order to state the theorem as concisely as possible, we introduce the notation $\rightsquigarrow$ to describe this type of convergence.[7]

[7] Although the $\rightsquigarrow$ abbreviation is our own, studying convergence with respect to pseudo-Lipschitz tests is certainly not new; it is considered, for example, in [13, 31,53], among many other works.

Definition 13 (Polynomial-Rate Pseudo-Lipschitz Convergence). *Consider a random variable $x_0 \in \mathbb{R}$ with finite moments of all orders and a vector $\boldsymbol{x} \in \mathbb{R}^n$. We write $\boldsymbol{x} \rightsquigarrow x_0$, if for all pseudo-Lipschitz functions $f : \mathbb{R} \to \mathbb{R}$,*

$$\exists c > 0 \quad \text{such that} \quad \Pr\left[\left|\frac{1}{n}\sum_{i=1}^{n} f(x_i) - \mathbb{E}[f(x_0)]\right| \le n^{-c}\right] \ge 1 - O(n^{-c}). \quad (2)$$

For $\boldsymbol{x} \in \mathbb{R}^m$ with $m = \Theta(n)$, we write $\boldsymbol{x} \rightsquigarrow x_0$ if (2) holds with m in place of n. Similarly, if $\boldsymbol{x}_0 \in \mathbb{R}^\ell$ and $\boldsymbol{X} = [\boldsymbol{x}_1 \cdots \boldsymbol{x}_m]^\top \in \mathbb{R}^{m\times\ell}$ for $\ell = \Theta(1)$, we write $\boldsymbol{X} \rightsquigarrow \boldsymbol{x}_0$ if (2) holds for all pseudo-Lipschitz $f : \mathbb{R}^\ell \to \mathbb{R}$ with m in place of n.

Observe that Definition 13 can be applied either to a sequence of deterministic vectors $\boldsymbol{x} \in \mathbb{R}^m$, or a sequence of random vectors $\boldsymbol{x} \in \mathbb{R}^m$. In the case of deterministic vectors, the condition that the absolute difference is bounded by n^{-c} with probability $1 - O(n^{-c})$ becomes equivalent to the condition that the absolute difference is deterministically bounded by n^{-c}. Next, observe that Definition 13 is a strengthening of the familiar notion of *convergence in distribution*, applied to the empirical distribution with mass $1/m$ on each of the coordinates of $\boldsymbol{x}$. Convergence in distribution is weaker than Definition 13 because the former only requires (2) to hold for functions f that are both bounded and Lipschitz. Also, convergence in distribution only requires an $o(1)$ convergence rate, but Definition 13 requires a much stronger $n^{-\Omega(1)}$ convergence rate. The following lemmas provide intuition for the meaning of $\boldsymbol{x} \rightsquigarrow x_0$. We defer their proofs to the extended version of our paper.

Lemma 9. *If $x_0 \in \mathbb{R}$ has finite moments and $x_1, \dots, x_m \overset{iid}{\sim} x_0$, then*

$$(x_1, \dots, x_m) \rightsquigarrow x_0.$$

Lemma 10. *If $x_0 \in \mathbb{R}$ has finite moments and $\boldsymbol{x} \rightsquigarrow x_0$, then for all $c > 0$, w.h.p., $\|\boldsymbol{x}\|_\infty \le O(n^c)$.*[8]

In the following theorem, we will phrase not only the conclusion in terms of pseudo-Lipschitz convergence, but also the assumptions on $\boldsymbol{\beta}^\star$ and $\boldsymbol{\varepsilon}^\star$. For a somewhat contrived example demonstrating the breadth of $\boldsymbol{\beta}^\star$ to which our theorem can be applied, suppose the first 50% of the coordinates of $\boldsymbol{\beta}^\star$ are deterministically equal to 0, the next 20% of the coordinates of $\boldsymbol{\beta}^\star$ are sampled i.i.d. from $\mathcal{N}(-3, 16)$, and the final 30% deterministically comprise an arithmetic progression starting at -10 and ending at 10. In this example, we have that $\boldsymbol{\beta}^\star \rightsquigarrow \beta_0^\star$ a.s., where $\beta_0^\star \in \mathbb{R}$ follows a mixture distribution of a point mass at 0, the distribution $\mathcal{N}(-3, 16)$, and the uniform distribution on $[-10, 10]$. To verify the condition (2) with respect to, say, $f(t) = t^2$, one can check that w.h.p., $\frac{1}{d}\|\boldsymbol{\beta}^\star\|^2 = \mathbb{E}(\beta_0^\star)^2 \pm O(n^{-1/2})$, where

$$\mathbb{E}(\beta_0^\star)^2 = 50\% \cdot 0 + 20\% \cdot (3^2 + 16) + 30\% \cdot \frac{1}{12}(10 - (-10))^2 = 15.$$

[8] Moreover, if $\boldsymbol{x} \in \mathbb{R}^m$ is deterministic and $\boldsymbol{x} \rightsquigarrow x_0$, then $\|\boldsymbol{x}\|_\infty \le n^{o(1)}$ holds deterministically.

For an example of $\boldsymbol{\beta}^\star \in \mathbb{R}^d$ that our theorem does *not* handle, consider $\boldsymbol{\beta}^\star = (\sqrt{d}, 0, \ldots, 0)$. On the one hand, the empirical distribution of the coordinates of this $\boldsymbol{\beta}^\star$ converges in distribution to the point mass at $\mathbf{0}$, so if $\boldsymbol{\beta}^\star$ were to converge with respect to pseudo-Lipschitz tests, it would also have to be toward the point mass at $\mathbf{0}$. On the other hand, we have $\frac{1}{d}\|\boldsymbol{\beta}^\star\|^2 = 1 \neq 0 \pm n^{-\Omega(1)}$, so $\boldsymbol{\beta}^\star$ fails to satisfy the condition (2) for $f(t) = t^2$.

We are now ready to state and prove the main theorem of this section.

Theorem 10. *Let $\widehat{\boldsymbol{\beta}}$ denote the output of Algorithm 1 with parameters $R, \lambda, \nu > 0$ and instantiated with the L-Lipschitz Huber loss function:*

$$\ell(\boldsymbol{\beta}; (\boldsymbol{x}, y)) = H_L(y - \langle \boldsymbol{x}, \boldsymbol{\beta} \rangle).$$

(a) **(Privacy)** *$\widehat{\boldsymbol{\beta}}$ satisfies $(\varepsilon_{\mathrm{DP}}, \delta_{\mathrm{DP}})$-differential privacy for any $\varepsilon_{\mathrm{DP}} \geq 0$ and*

$$\delta_{\mathrm{DP}} = \begin{cases} 2 \cdot \mathrm{HockeyStick}(\widetilde{\varepsilon}_{\mathrm{DP}}, \frac{LR}{\nu}) & \text{if } \widehat{\varepsilon}_{\mathrm{DP}} \geq 0, \\ (1 - e^{\widehat{\varepsilon}_{\mathrm{DP}}}) + 2e^{\widehat{\varepsilon}_{\mathrm{DP}}} \cdot \mathrm{HockeyStick}\left(\frac{L^2R^2}{2\nu^2}, \frac{LR}{\nu}\right) & \text{otherwise,} \end{cases}$$

where we set $\widetilde{\varepsilon}_{\mathrm{DP}} = \varepsilon_{\mathrm{DP}} - \log(1 + R^2/\lambda)$ and $\widehat{\varepsilon}_{\mathrm{DP}} = \widetilde{\varepsilon}_{\mathrm{DP}} - L^2R^2/2\nu^2$.

(b) **(Utility)** *Suppose the following hold for some $\boldsymbol{\beta}^\star \in \mathbb{R}^d$ and $\boldsymbol{\varepsilon}^\star \in \mathbb{R}^n$ as $n \to \infty$ and $d/n \to \delta$:*

(i) $\mathbf{X} \in B_R(\mathbf{0})^n \subseteq \mathbb{R}^{n \times d}$ follows a subgaussian design and $\boldsymbol{y} = \mathbf{X}\boldsymbol{\beta}^\star + \boldsymbol{\varepsilon}^\star$.

(ii) There exist random variables $\beta_0^\star, \varepsilon_0^\star \in \mathbb{R}$ such that $\boldsymbol{\beta}^\star \rightsquigarrow \beta_0^\star$ and $\boldsymbol{\varepsilon}^\star \rightsquigarrow \varepsilon_0^\star$.

Suppose there exist $\sigma^\star, \tau^\star > 0$ solving the following system of two scalar equations in two variables (σ, τ), which we write in terms of a dummy variable $Z \sim \mathcal{N}(0, 1)$ and $\kappa^2 = \mathbb{E}(\beta_0^\star)^2$ as

$$\sigma^2 = \tau^2 \left(\frac{1}{\delta} \mathbb{E} \left[\frac{\sigma Z + \varepsilon_0^\star}{1 + \tau} \right]_L^2 + \lambda^2 \kappa^2 + \nu^2 \right), \tag{3a}$$

$$\tau = \frac{1}{\lambda \delta} \left(\delta - \frac{\tau}{1 + \tau} \Pr \left[-L < \frac{\sigma Z + \varepsilon_0^\star}{1 + \tau} < L \right] \right). \tag{3b}$$

Then, in terms of $(\sigma^\star, \tau^\star)$, the estimation error $\widehat{\boldsymbol{\beta}} - \boldsymbol{\beta}^\star$ satisfies, for $\xi_0 \sim \mathcal{N}(0, 1)$,

$$(\boldsymbol{\beta}^\star, \boldsymbol{\xi}, \widehat{\boldsymbol{\beta}} - \boldsymbol{\beta}^\star) \rightsquigarrow \left(\beta_0^\star, \ \xi_0, \ \tau^\star \left(\sqrt{\frac{1}{\delta} \mathbb{E} \left[\frac{\sigma^\star Z + \varepsilon_0^\star}{1 + \tau^\star} \right]_L^2} Z - \lambda \beta_0^\star - \nu \xi_0 \right) \right).$$

Similarly, the L-truncated prediction error $[\boldsymbol{y} - \mathbf{X}\widehat{\boldsymbol{\beta}}]_L$ satisfies

$$(\boldsymbol{\varepsilon}^\star, [\boldsymbol{y} - \mathbf{X}\widehat{\boldsymbol{\beta}}]_L) \rightsquigarrow \left(\varepsilon_0^\star, \ \left[\frac{\sigma^\star Z + \varepsilon_0^\star}{1 + \tau^\star} \right]_L \right).$$

Several remarks about Theorem 10 are in order. First, we comment that part (a), whose proof we defer to the extended version of our paper, is a variant of Theorem 3.1 in [87] (for convenience, we included a statement of that prior result in Sect. 2). Essentially, part (a) establishes a link between any constant values of $L, \lambda, \nu > 0$ and a family of $(\varepsilon_{\mathrm{DP}}, \delta_{\mathrm{DP}})$-DP privacy guarantees. In the extended version of our paper, we also give a single-parameter ρ_{DP}-zCDP privacy guarantee with a constant $\rho_{\mathrm{DP}} = \rho_{\mathrm{DP}}(L, \lambda, \nu)$, which is arguably easier to interpret but not as tight.

Next, we comment that part (b), whose proof will appears in the extended version of our paper, yields several interesting corollaries about the behavior of $\widehat{\boldsymbol{\beta}}$ when combined with Definition 13. For example, suppose we would like to know the *bias* of $\widehat{\boldsymbol{\beta}}$. If we take the order-2 pseudo-Lipschitz function $f(\beta^\star, u) = (\beta^\star)^2 + \beta^\star u$, then Theorem 10(b) with Definition 13 tells us that the average value of f over the coordinates of $(\boldsymbol{\beta}^\star, \widehat{\boldsymbol{\beta}} - \boldsymbol{\beta}^\star)$ can be approximated by the expected value of f over the randomness of $(\beta_0^\star, \tau^\star(\sigma_v^\star Z - \lambda\beta_0^\star - \nu\xi_0))$ for an appropriate constant $\sigma_v^\star > 0$. Since Z, $\beta_0^\star$, and ξ_0 are independent, we deduce that with high probability over the design matrix $\boldsymbol{X}$ and the randomness $\boldsymbol{\xi}$ of the algorithm,

$$\frac{1}{d}\langle \widehat{\boldsymbol{\beta}}, \boldsymbol{\beta}^\star \rangle = \frac{1}{d}\sum_{j=1}^{d} f(\beta_j^\star, \widehat{\beta}_j - \beta_j^\star) = \mathbb{E}[(\beta_0^\star)^2 + \beta_0^\star \cdot \tau^\star(\sigma_v^\star Z - \lambda\beta_0^\star - \nu\xi_0)] \pm n^{-\Omega(1)}$$
$$= (1 - \tau^\star\lambda)\kappa^2 \pm n^{-\Omega(1)}.$$

It is apparent from Eq. (3b) that $1 - \tau^\star\lambda \in (0, 1)$. Therefore, we deduce that $\widehat{\boldsymbol{\beta}}$ is positively correlated with $\boldsymbol{\beta}^\star$, but "shrunk" toward $\mathbf{0}$ by a factor of $1 - \tau^\star\lambda \pm n^{-\Omega(1)}$. This is intuitively what we would expect given that the regularization term $\frac{\lambda}{2}\|\boldsymbol{\beta}\|^2$ is centered at the origin.

Similarly, suppose we are interested in the *mean squared error* of $\widehat{\boldsymbol{\beta}}$. If we take the order-2 pseudo-Lipschitz function $f(u) = u^2$, then by Theorem 10(b) and Definition 13, with high probability,

$$\frac{1}{d}\|\widehat{\boldsymbol{\beta}} - \boldsymbol{\beta}^\star\|^2 = \frac{1}{d}\sum_{j=1}^{d} f(\widehat{\beta}_j - \beta_j^\star) = \mathbb{E}(\tau^\star(\sigma_v^\star Z - \lambda\beta_0^\star - \nu\xi_0))^2 \pm n^{-\Omega(1)}$$
$$= (\tau^\star)^2((\sigma_v^\star)^2 + \lambda^2\kappa^2 + \nu^2) \pm n^{-\Omega(1)}.$$

By Eq. (3a), the above expression is precisely $(\sigma^\star)^2 \pm n^{-\Omega(1)}$, so we deduce that the root mean squared error of $\boldsymbol{\beta}^\star$ is precisely $\sigma^\star \pm n^{-\Omega(1)}$. Similar computations can be carried out in this manner to determine, for example, the correlation of $\widehat{\boldsymbol{\beta}}$ with the perturbation vector $\boldsymbol{\xi}$ or the fact that the residual error of the predictions $\boldsymbol{X}\widehat{\boldsymbol{\beta}}$ satisfies, w.h.p.,

$$\frac{1}{n}\left\|[\boldsymbol{y} - \boldsymbol{X}\widehat{\boldsymbol{\beta}}]_L\right\|^2 = \mathbb{E}\left[\frac{\sigma^\star Z + \varepsilon_0^\star}{1 + \tau^\star}\right]_L^2 \pm n^{-\Omega(1)}.$$

The previous two examples both measure utility using squared ℓ^2 norm, but this was arbitrary. Indeed, by choosing different pseudo-Lipschitz test functions, we could just as easily have expressed many other possible utility metrics, including $\frac{1}{d}\|\widehat{\boldsymbol{\beta}} - \boldsymbol{\beta}^\star\|_p^p$ or $\frac{1}{n}\|[\boldsymbol{y} - \boldsymbol{X}\widehat{\boldsymbol{\beta}}]_L\|_p^p$ for any $p \geq 1$, in terms of $(\sigma^\star, \tau^\star)$. We validate these corollaries against synthetic data in Fig. 1.

Next, we remark that Eqs. (3a), (3b) can be simplified if one assumes approximately Gaussian errors. Indeed, if $\varepsilon_0^\star \sim \mathcal{N}(0, \sigma_\varepsilon^2)$ for some $\sigma_\varepsilon > 0$, then we have

$$\frac{\sigma Z + \varepsilon_0^\star}{1+\tau} \sim \mathcal{N}\left(0, \frac{\sigma^2 + \sigma_\varepsilon^2}{(1+\tau)^2}\right).$$

Thus, we can express the variance of its L-truncation, as well as the probability it falls in the interval $[-L, +L]$, using rescaled versions of the following formulas for the truncated Gaussian distribution: if $Z \sim \mathcal{N}(0,1)$ and $s > 0$, then in terms of the standard Gaussian PDF φ and CDF Φ,

$$\Pr[sZ \in [-L, +L]] = 2\Phi(L/s) - 1.$$

$$\mathbb{E}[(sZ)^2 \mid sZ \in [-L, +L]] = s^2\left(1 - \frac{2(L/s)\varphi(L/s)}{2\Phi(L/s) - 1}\right).$$

4 Extended Paper With Proofs

For the extended version of our paper, see https://arxiv.org/abs/2411.13682.

Acknowledgments. This work was supported in part by Simons Foundation Grant 733782, Cooperative Agreement CB20ADR0160001 with the United States Census Bureau, and NSF CAREER DMS-2340241.

References

1. Abadi, M., et al.: Deep learning with differential privacy. In: ACM Conference on Computer and Communications Security (CCS) (2016)
2. Abbasi, E., Salehi, F., Hassibi, B.: Universality in learning from linear measurements. In: Conference on Neural Information Processing Systems (NeurIPS) (2019)
3. Abdalla, P., Zhivotovskiy, N.: Covariance estimation: optimal dimension-free guarantees for adversarial corruption and heavy tails. J. Eur. Math. Soc. (2024)
4. Agarwal, S., Kamath, G., Majid, M., Mouzakis, A., Silver, R., Ullman, J.: Private mean estimation with person-level differential privacy. In: ACM-SIAM Symposium on Discrete Algorithms (SODA) (2024)
5. Alabi, D., Kothari, P.K., Tankala, P., Venkat, P., Zhang, F.: Privately estimating a gaussian: efficient, robust, and optimal. In: ACM Symposium on Theory of Computing (STOC) (2023)
6. Amelunxen, D., Lotz, M., McCoy, M.B., Tropp, J.A.: Living on the edge: phase transitions in convex programs with random data. Inf. Inference J. IMA **3**(3), 224–294 (2014)
7. Amin, K., Joseph, M., Ribero, M., Vassilvitskii, S.: Easy differentially private linear regression. In: International Conference on Learning Representations (ICLR) (2023)

8. Ashtiani, H., Liaw, C.: Private and polynomial time algorithms for learning gaussians and beyond. In: Conference on Learning Theory (COLT) (2022)
9. Balle, B., Wang, Y.: Improving the gaussian mechanism for differential privacy: analytical calibration and optimal denoising. In: International Conference on Machine Learning (ICML) (2018)
10. Bao, Z., Han, Q., Xu, X.: A leave-one-out approach to approximate message passing (2023)
11. Bassily, R., Smith, A.D., Thakurta, A.: Private empirical risk minimization: efficient algorithms and tight error bounds. In: IEEE Symposium on Foundations of Computer Science (FOCS) (2014)
12. Bayati, M., Lelarge, M., Montanari, A.: Universality in polytope phase transitions and message passing algorithms. Ann. Appl. Probab. **25**(2), 753–822 (2015)
13. Bayati, M., Montanari, A.: The dynamics of message passing on dense graphs, with applications to compressed sensing. IEEE Trans. Inf. Theory **57**(2), 764–785 (2011)
14. Bayati, M., Montanari, A.: The lasso risk for gaussian matrices. IEEE Trans. Inf. Theory **58**(4), 1997–2017 (2011)
15. Bean, D., Bickel, P.J., El Karoui, N., Yu, B.: Optimal m-estimation in high-dimensional regression. Proc. Natl. Acad. Sci. **110**(36), 14563–14568 (2013)
16. Belkin, M., Hsu, D., Ma, S., Mandal, S.: Reconciling modern machine-learning practice and the classical bias–variance trade-off. Proc. Natl. Acad. Sci. **116**(32), 15849–15854 (2019)
17. Belkin, M., Hsu, D., Xu, J.: Two models of double descent for weak features. SIAM J. Math. Data Sci. **2**(4), 1167–1180 (2020)
18. Bombari, S., Mondelli, M.: Privacy for free in the overparameterized regime. Proc. Natl. Acad. Sci. **122**(15), e2423072122 (2025)
19. Bombari, S., Seroussi, I., Mondelli, M.: Better rates for private linear regression in the proportional regime via aggressive clipping. CoRR abs/2505.16329 (2025)
20. Brown, G., et al.: Insufficient statistics perturbation: stable estimators for private least squares. In: Conference on Learning Theory (COLT) (2024)
21. Brown, G., Hopkins, S., Smith, A.: Fast, sample-efficient, affine-invariant private mean and covariance estimation for subgaussian distributions. In: Conference on Learning Theory (COLT) (2023)
22. Brown, G.R., Dvijotham, K.D., Evans, G., Liu, D., Smith, A., Guha Thakurta, A.: Private gradient descent for linear regression: tighter error bounds and instance-specific uncertainty estimation. In: International Conference on Machine Learning (ICML) (2024)
23. Bubeck, S.: Convex optimization: algorithms and complexity. Found. Trends Mach. Learn. **8**(3–4), 231–357 (2015)
24. Bun, M., Kamath, G., Steinke, T., Wu, Z.S.: Private hypothesis selection. In: Conference on Neural Information Processing Systems (NeurIPS) (2019)
25. Bun, M., Steinke, T.: Concentrated differential privacy: simplifications, extensions, and lower bounds. In: Hirt, M., Smith, A.D. (eds.) Theory of Cryptography Conference (TCC) (2016)
26. Cai, T.T., Wang, Y., Zhang, L.: The cost of privacy: optimal rates of convergence for parameter estimation with differential privacy. Ann. Stat. **49**(5), 2825–2850 (2021)
27. Cai, T.T., Wang, Y., Zhang, L.: Score attack: a lower bound technique for optimal differentially private learning (2023)

28. Candès, E.J., Sur, P.: The phase transition for the existence of the maximum likelihood estimate in high-dimensional logistic regression. Ann. Stat. **48**(1), 27–42 (2020)
29. Canonne, C.L., Kamath, G., McMillan, A., Smith, A., Ullman, J.: The structure of optimal private tests for simple hypotheses. In: ACM Symposium on Theory of Computing (STOC) (2019)
30. Celentano, M., Montanari, A., Wei, Y.: The Lasso with general Gaussian designs with applications to hypothesis testing. Ann. Stat. **51**(5), 2194–2220 (2023)
31. Celentano, M., Montanari, A., Wu, Y.: The estimation error of general first order methods. In: Conference on Learning Theory (COLT) (2020)
32. Chaudhuri, K., Monteleoni, C., Sarwate, A.D.: Differentially private empirical risk minimization. J. Mach. Learn. Res. **12**(29), 1069–1109 (2011)
33. Dagan, Y., Jordan, M.I., Yang, X., Zakynthinou, L., Zhivotovskiy, N.: Dimension-free private mean estimation for anisotropic distributions. In: Neural Information Processing Systems (NeurIPS) (2024)
34. Deng, Z., Kammoun, A., Thrampoulidis, C.: A model of double descent for high-dimensional binary linear classification. Inf. Inference J. IMA **11**(2), 435–495 (2021)
35. Dhifallah, O., Lu, Y.M.: A precise performance analysis of learning with random features (2020)
36. Donoho, D.L., Maleki, A., Montanari, A.: Message-passing algorithms for compressed sensing. Proc. Natl. Acad. Sci. **106**(45), 18914–18919 (2009)
37. Donoho, D.L., Maleki, A., Montanari, A.: The noise-sensitivity phase transition in compressed sensing. IEEE Trans. Inf. Theory **57**(10), 6920–6941 (2011)
38. Dudeja, R., Lu, Y.M., Sen, S.: Universality of approximate message passing with semirandom matrices. Ann. Probab. **51**(5), 1616–1683 (2023)
39. Dudeja, R., Sen, S., Lu, Y.M.: Spectral universality in regularized linear regression with nearly deterministic sensing matrices. IEEE Trans. Inf. Theory **70**(11), 7923–7951 (2024)
40. Dwork, C., Kenthapadi, K., McSherry, F., Mironov, I., Naor, M.: Our data, ourselves: privacy via distributed noise generation. In: International Conference on the Theory and Applications of Cryptographic Techniques (EUROCRYPT) (2006)
41. Dwork, C., Lei, J.: Differential privacy and robust statistics. In: ACM Symposium on Theory of Computing (STOC) (2009)
42. Dwork, C., McSherry, F., Nissim, K., Smith, A.D.: Calibrating noise to sensitivity in private data analysis. In: Theory of Cryptography Conference (TCC) (2006)
43. Dwork, C., Roth, A.: The algorithmic foundations of differential privacy. Found. Trends Theor. Comput. Sci. **9**(3–4), 211–407 (2014)
44. Dwork, C., Rothblum, G.N.: Concentrated differential privacy (2016)
45. El Karoui, N.: Asymptotic behavior of unregularized and ridge-regularized high-dimensional robust regression estimators: rigorous results (2013)
46. El Karoui, N.: On the impact of predictor geometry on the performance on high-dimensional ridge-regularized generalized robust regression estimators. Probab. Theory Related Fields **170**(1), 95–175 (2018)
47. Fan, Y., Demirkaya, E., Lv, J.: Nonuniformity of p-values can occur early in diverging dimensions. J. Mach. Learn. Res. **20**(77), 1–33 (2019)
48. Fan, Z.: Approximate message passing algorithms for rotationally invariant matrices. Ann. Stat. **50**(1), 197–224 (2022)

49. Georgiev, K., Hopkins, S.B.: Privacy induces robustness: information-computation gaps and sparse mean estimation. In: Conference on Neural Information Processing Systems (NeurIPS) (2024)
50. Gerbelot, C., Troiani, E., Mignacco, F., Krzakala, F., Zdeborová, L.: Rigorous dynamical mean-field theory for stochastic gradient descent methods. SIAM J. Math. Data Sci. **6**(2), 400–427 (2024)
51. Gopi, S., Kamath, G., Kulkarni, J., Nikolov, A., Wu, Z.S., Zhang, H.: Locally private hypothesis selection. In: Conference on Learning Theory (COLT) (2020)
52. Gordon, Y.: Some inequalities for gaussian processes and applications. Israel J. Math. **50**(4), 265–289 (1985)
53. Han, Q.: Entrywise dynamics and universality of general first order methods (2024)
54. Han, Q., Shen, Y.: Universality of regularized regression estimators in high dimensions. Ann. Stat. **51**(4), 1799–1823 (2023)
55. Hopkins, S.B., Kamath, G., Majid, M.: Efficient mean estimation with pure differential privacy via a sum-of-squares exponential mechanism. In: ACM Symposium on Theory of Computing (STOC) (2022)
56. Hopkins, S.B., Kamath, G., Majid, M., Narayanan, S.: Robustness implies privacy in statistical estimation. In: ACM Symposium on Theory of Computing (STOC) (2023)
57. Hu, H., Lu, Y.M.: Slope for sparse linear regression: asymptotics and optimal regularization. IEEE Trans. Inf. Theory **68**(11), 7627–7664 (2022)
58. Huber, P.J.: Robust estimation of a location parameter. Ann. Math. Stat. **35**(1), 73–101 (1964)
59. Iyengar, R., Near, J.P., Song, D., Thakkar, O., Thakurta, A., Wang, L.: Towards practical differentially private convex optimization. In: IEEE Symposium on Security and Privacy (2019)
60. Jain, P., Thakurta, A.G.: (near) dimension independent risk bounds for differentially private learning. In: International Conference on Machine Learning (ICML) (2014)
61. Kamath, G., Li, J., Singhal, V., Ullman, J.: Privately learning high-dimensional distributions. In: Conference on Learning Theory (COLT) (2019)
62. Kamath, G., Mouzakis, A., Singhal, V., Steinke, T., Ullman, J.: A private and computationally-efficient estimator for unbounded gaussians. In: Proceedings of Thirty Fifth Conference on Learning Theory (COLT) (2022)
63. Kamath, G., Singhal, V., Ullman, J.: Private mean estimation of heavy-tailed distributions. In: Conference on Learning Theory (COLT) (2020)
64. Kent, A., Berrett, T.B., Yu, Y.: Rate optimality and phase transition for user-level local differential privacy (2024)
65. Kifer, D., Smith, A., Thakurta, A.: Private convex empirical risk minimization and high-dimensional regression. In: Conference on Learning Theory (COLT) (2012)
66. Korada, S.B., Montanari, A.: Applications of the lindeberg principle in communications and statistical learning. IEEE Trans. Inf. Theory **57**(4), 2440–2450 (2011). https://doi.org/10.1109/TIT.2011.2112231
67. Kothari, P., Manurangsi, P., Velingker, A.: Private robust estimation by stabilizing convex relaxations. In: Conference on Learning Theory (COLT) (2022)
68. Kuditipudi, R., Duchi, J., Haque, S.: A pretty fast algorithm for adaptive private mean estimation. In: Conference on Learning Theory (COLT) (2023)
69. Liang, T., Sur, P.: A precise high-dimensional asymptotic theory for boosting and minimum-ℓ_1-norm interpolated classifiers. Ann. Stat. **50**(3), 1669–1695 (2022)

70. Liu, X., Kong, W., Kakade, S.M., Oh, S.: Robust and differentially private mean estimation. In: Conference on Neural Information Processing Systems (NeurIPS) (2021)
71. Liu, X., Kong, W., Oh, S.: Differential privacy and robust statistics in high dimensions. In: Conference on Learning Theory (COLT) (2022)
72. Loureiro, B., et al.: Learning curves of generic features maps for realistic datasets with a teacher-student model. In: Conference on Neural Information Processing Systems (NeurIPS) (2021)
73. Ma, Y., Jia, K., Yang, H.: Better locally private sparse estimation given multiple samples per user. In: International Conference on Machine Learning (ICML) (2024)
74. Mei, S., Montanari, A.: The generalization error of random features regression: precise asymptotics and the double descent curve. Commun. Pure Appl. Math. **75**(4), 667–766 (2022)
75. Minasyan, A., Zhivotovskiy, N.: Statistically optimal robust mean and covariance estimation for anisotropic gaussians. Math. Stat. Learn. **8**(1–2), 33–69 (2025). https://doi.org/10.4171/MSL/48
76. Miolane, L., Montanari, A.: The distribution of the Lasso: uniform control over sparse balls and adaptive parameter tuning. Ann. Stat. **49**(4), 2313–2335 (2021)
77. Mir, D.J.: Differential privacy: an exploration of the privacy-utility landscape. Ph.D. thesis, Rutgers University (2013)
78. Mironov, I.: Rényi differential privacy. In: IEEE Computer Security Foundations Symposium (CSF) (2017)
79. Montanari, A., Nguyen, P.M.: Universality of the elastic net error. In: 2017 IEEE International Symposium on Information Theory (ISIT), pp. 2338–2342 (2017). https://doi.org/10.1109/ISIT.2017.8006947
80. Montanari, A., Ruan, F., Sohn, Y., Yan, J.: The generalization error of max-margin linear classifiers: benign overfitting and high dimensional asymptotics in the overparametrized regime (2023)
81. Narayanan, S.: Private high-dimensional hypothesis testing. In: Conference on Learning Theory (COLT) (2022)
82. Neel, S., Roth, A., Vietri, G., Wu, Z.S.: Oracle efficient private non-convex optimization. In: International Conference on Machine Learning (ICML) (2020)
83. Oymak, S., Tropp, J.A.: Universality laws for randomized dimension reduction, with applications. Inf. Inference J. IMA **7**(3), 337–446 (2017)
84. Panahi, A., Hassibi, B.: A universal analysis of large-scale regularized least squares solutions. In: Conference on Neural Information Processing Systems (NeurIPS) (2017)
85. Parikh, N., Boyd, S.P.: Proximal algorithms. Found. Trends Optim. **1**(3), 127–239 (2014)
86. Pour, A.F., Ashtiani, H., Asoodeh, S.: Sample-optimal locally private hypothesis selection and the provable benefits of interactivity. In: Conference on Learning Theory (COLT) (2024)
87. Redberg, R., Koskela, A., Wang, Y.: Improving the privacy and practicality of objective perturbation for differentially private linear learners. In: Conference on Neural Information Processing Systems (NeurIPS) (2023)
88. Redberg, R., Wang, Y.: Privately publishable per-instance privacy. In: Conference on Neural Information Processing Systems (NeurIPS) (2021)
89. Salehi, F., Abbasi, E., Hassibi, B.: The impact of regularization on high-dimensional logistic regression. In: Conference on Neural Information Processing Systems (NeurIPS) (2019)

90. Sheffet, O.: Differentially private ordinary least squares. In: International Conference on Machine Learning (ICML) (2017)
91. Sheffet, O.: Old techniques in differentially private linear regression. In: International Conference on Algorithmic Learning Theory (2019)
92. Sion, M.: On general minimax theorems. Pac. J. Math. **8**(1), 171–176 (1958)
93. Slepian, D.: The one-sided barrier problem for gaussian noise. Bell Syst. Tech. J. **41**(2), 463–501 (1962). https://doi.org/10.1002/j.1538-7305.1962.tb02419.x
94. Song, S., Chaudhuri, K., Sarwate, A.D.: Stochastic gradient descent with differentially private updates. In: IEEE Global Conference on Signal and Information Processing (GlobalSIP) (2013)
95. Steinke, T., Ullman, J.R.: Tight lower bounds for differentially private selection. In: IEEE Symposium on Foundations of Computer Science (FOCS) (2017)
96. Stojnic, M.: A framework to characterize performance of lasso algorithms (2013)
97. Sur, P., Candès, E.J.: A modern maximum-likelihood theory for high-dimensional logistic regression. Proc. Natl. Acad. Sci. **116**(29), 14516–14525 (2019)
98. Thrampoulidis, C., Abbasi, E., Hassibi, B.: Precise error analysis of regularized m-estimators in high dimensions. IEEE Trans. Inf. Theory **64**(8), 5592–5628 (2018)
99. Thrampoulidis, C., Oymak, S., Hassibi, B.: Regularized linear regression: a precise analysis of the estimation error. In: Conference on Learning Theory (COLT) (2015)
100. Vadhan, S.P.: The complexity of differential privacy. In: Lindell, Y. (ed.) Tutorials on the Foundations of Cryptography, pp. 347–450. Springer (2017)
101. Varshney, P., Thakurta, A., Jain, P.: (nearly) optimal private linear regression for sub-gaussian data via adaptive clipping. In: Conference on Learning Theory (COLT) (2022)
102. Vershynin, R.: High-Dimensional Probability: An Introduction with Applications in Data Science. Cambridge Series in Statistical and Probabilistic Mathematics. Cambridge University Press (2018)
103. Wainwright, M.J.: High-Dimensional Statistics: A Non-Asymptotic Viewpoint. Cambridge Series in Statistical and Probabilistic Mathematics. Cambridge University Press (2019)
104. Wang, S., Weng, H., Maleki, A.: Does SLOPE outperform bridge regression? Inf. Inference J. IMA **11**(1), 1–54 (2021)
105. Wang, T., Zhong, X., Fan, Z.: Universality of approximate message passing algorithms and tensor networks. Ann. Appl. Probab. **34**(4), 3943–3994 (2024)
106. Wang, Y.: Revisiting differentially private linear regression: optimal and adaptive prediction & estimation in unbounded domain. In: Conference on Uncertainty in Artificial Intelligence (UAI) (2018)
107. Wang, Y.X., Fienberg, S., Smola, A.: Privacy for free: posterior sampling and stochastic gradient Monte Carlo. In: International Conference on Machine Learning (ICML) (2015)
108. Zhang, X., Zhou, H., Ye, H.: A modern theory for high-dimensional cox regression models (2022)
109. Zhao, Q., Sur, P., Candès, E.J.: The asymptotic distribution of the MLE in high-dimensional logistic models: arbitrary covariance. Bernoulli **28**(3), 1835–1861 (2022)
110. Zhou, M., Wang, T., Chan, T.H.H., Fanti, G., Shi, E.: Locally differentially private sparse vector aggregation. In: IEEE Symposium on Security and Privacy (2022)

Differentially Private Compression and the Sensitivity of LZ77

Jeremiah Blocki[1(✉)], Seunghoon Lee[2], and Brayan Sebastián Yepes-Garcia[3]

[1] Purdue University, West Lafayette, USA
jblocki@purdue.edu
[2] University of Waterloo, Waterloo, Canada
seunghoon.lee@uwaterloo.ca
[3] Universidad Nacional de Colombia, Bogotá, Colombia
byepesg@unal.edu.co

Abstract. We initiate the study of differentially private data-compression schemes motivated by the insecurity of the popular "Compress-Then-Encrypt" framework. Data compression is a useful tool which exploits redundancy in data to reduce storage/bandwidth when files are stored or transmitted. However, if the contents of a file are confidential then the *length* of a compressed file might leak confidential information about the content of the file itself. Encrypting a compressed file does not eliminate this leakage as data encryption schemes are only designed to hide the *content* of confidential message instead of the *length* of the message. In our proposed *Differentially Private Compress-Then-Encrypt* framework, we add a random positive amount of padding to the compressed file to ensure that any leakage satisfies the rigorous privacy guarantee of (ϵ, δ)-differential privacy. The amount of padding that needs to be added depends on the sensitivity of the compression scheme to small changes in the input, i.e., to what degree can changing a single character of the input message impact the length of the compressed file. While some popular compression schemes are highly sensitive to small changes in the input, we argue that effective data compression schemes do not necessarily have high sensitivity. Our primary technical contribution is analyzing the fine-grained sensitivity of the LZ77 compression scheme (IEEE Trans. Inf. Theory 1977) which is one of the most common compression schemes used in practice. We show that the global sensitivity of the LZ77 compression scheme has the upper bound $\mathcal{O}(W^{2/3}\log n)$ where $W \leq n$ denotes the size of the sliding window. When $W = n$, we show the lower bound $\Omega(n^{2/3}\log^{1/3} n)$ for the global sensitivity of the LZ77 compression scheme which is tight up to a sublogarithmic factor.

1 Introduction

Data compression algorithms exploit redundancy in data to compress files before storage or transmission. Lossless compression schemes are widely used in

S. Lee—Work done primarily while Seunghoon was at Purdue University.

B. Applebaum and H. Lin (Eds.): TCC 2025, LNCS 16271, pp. 356–386, 2026.
https://doi.org/10.1007/978-3-032-12290-2_12

contexts such as ZIP archives (Deflate [9]) and web content compression by Google (Brotli [2]). In the Compress-Then-Encrypt framework, a message w is first compressed to obtain a (typically shorter) file $y = \texttt{Compress}(w)$ and then encrypted to obtain a ciphertext $c = \mathsf{E}_K(y)$. Intuitively, compression is used to reduce bandwidth, and encryption is used to protect the file contents from eavesdropping attacks before it is transmitted over the internet.

While encryption protects the *content* of the underlying plaintext message y, there is no guarantee that the ciphertext c will hide the *length* of the underlying plaintext y. For example, AES-GCM [4] is the most widely used symmetric key encryption scheme, but the ciphertext leaks the *exact* length of the underlying plaintext[1]. Unfortunately, the length of the compressed message y can leak information about the *content* of the original uncompressed file. For example, suppose that the original message was $w =$"`The top secret password is: password.`" An eavesdropping attacker who intercepts the AES-GCM ciphertext c would be able to infer the length $|\texttt{Compress}(w)|$ and could use this information to eliminate many incorrect password guesses, i.e., if $|\texttt{Compress}(w')| \neq |\texttt{Compress}(w)|$ where $w' =$"`The top secret password is: [guess]`" then the attacker could immediately infer that this particular password guess is incorrect.

The observation that the length of a compressed file can leak sensitive information about the *content* has led to several real-world exploits. For example, the CRIME (Compression Ratio Info-leak Made Easy) attack [24] exploits compression length leakage to hijack TLS sessions [12]. Similarly, the BREACH (Browser Reconnaissance and Exfiltration via Adaptive Compression of Hypertext) attack [14] against the HTTPS protocol exploits compression in the underlying HTTP protocol. Despite its clear security issues, the "Compress-then-Encrypt" framework continues to be used as a tool to reduce bandwidth overhead. There have been several heuristic proposals to address this information leakage. One proposal [22] is static analysis to identify/exclude sensitive information before data compression. However, it is not always clear *a priori* what information should be considered sensitive. Heal the Breach [21] pads compressed files by a random amount to mitigate leakage and protect against the CRIME/BREACH attacks. While this defense is intuitive, there will still be some information leakage and there are no rigorous privacy guarantees. This leads to the following question:

Can one design a compression scheme which provides rigorous privacy guarantees against an attacker who learns the compressed file's length?

Differential Privacy (DP) [10] has emerged as a gold standard in privacy-preserving data analysis due to its rigorous mathematical guarantees and strong composition results. Given $\epsilon > 0$ and $\delta \in (0, 1)$, a randomized algorithm $\mathcal{A}$ is called (ϵ, δ)-*differentially private* if for every pair of neighboring datasets $\mathfrak{D}$ and

[1] Any efficient encryption scheme must at least leak some information about the length of the underlying plaintext. Otherwise, the ciphertext of a short message (e.g., "hi") would need to be longer than the longest possible message supported by the protocol (e.g., a 4GB movie).

$\mathfrak{D}'$ and for all sets S of possible outputs, we have $\Pr[\mathcal{A}(\mathfrak{D}) \in S] \le e^\epsilon \cdot \Pr[\mathcal{A}(\mathfrak{D}') \in S] + \delta$. Typically, ϵ is a small constant and the additive loss δ should be negligible (if $\delta = 0$ then we can simply say that $\mathcal{A}$ satisfies ϵ-*DP*). In our context, we are focused on leakage from the length of a compressed file. We say that an compression algorithm $\texttt{Compress}$ is (ϵ, δ)-*differentially private* if for every pair of neighboring strings w and w' (e.g., differing in one symbol) and all $S \subseteq \mathbb{N}$ we have $\Pr[|\texttt{Compress}(w)| \in S] \le e^\epsilon \cdot \Pr[|\texttt{Compress}(w')| \in S] + \delta$. Intuitively, suppose that w denotes the original message and w' denotes the message after replacing a sensitive character by a special blank symbol. Differential privacy ensures that an attacker who observes the length of the compressed file will still be unlikely to distinguish between w and w'. DP composition ensures that the attacker will also be unlikely to distinguish between the original string w and a string w'' where *every* symbol of a secret password has been replaced—provided that the secret password is not too long.

We first note that the Heal the Breach proposal [21] does not necessarily satisfy differential privacy. For example, Lagarde and Perifel [16] proved that the LZ78 compression algorithm [18] is highly sensitive to small bit changes. In particular, there exists nearby strings $w \sim w'$ (i.e., $|w| = |w'|$ and $|\{i : w[i] \ne w'[i]\}| = 1$) of length n such that $|\texttt{Compress}_{\mathsf{LZ78}}(w)| = o(n)$ and $|\texttt{Compress}_{\mathsf{LZ78}}(w')| = \Omega(n)$. In particular, to prevent an eavesdropping attacker from distinguishing between w and w', the length of the padding would need to be at least $\Omega(n)$. Heal the Breach [21] adds a much smaller amount of padding $o(n)$.

Notations. For a positive integer n, we define $[n] := \{1, \ldots, n\}$. Unless otherwise noted, we will use n as the length of a string throughout the paper. We use Σ to denote a set of alphabets and $w \in \Sigma^n$ to denote a string of length n and we let $w[i] \in \Sigma$ denote the ith character of the string. Given two strings $w, w' \in \Sigma^n$, we use $\texttt{Ham}(w, w') = |\{i : w[i] \ne w'[i]\}|$ to denote the *hamming distance* between w and w', i.e., the number of indices where the strings do not match. We say that two strings w and w' are *adjacent* (or *neighbors*) if $\texttt{Ham}(w, w') = 1$ and we use $w \sim w'$ to denote this. We use $|w|$ to denote the length of a string, i.e., for any string $w \in \Sigma^n$ we have $|w| = n$. We use $w \circ w'$ to denote the concatenation of two strings w and w'. Given a character $c \in \Sigma$ and an integer $k \ge 1$, we use c^k to denote the character c repeated k times. Formally, we define $c^1 := c$ and $c^{i+1} := c \circ c^i$. Unless otherwise noted, we assume that all log's have base 2, i.e., $\log x := \log_2 x$.

1.1 Our Contributions

In this paper, we initiate the study of differentially private compression schemes focusing especially on the LZ77 compression algorithm [17]. We first provide a general transformation showing how to make any compression scheme differentially private by adding a random amount of padding which depends on the global sensitivity (the worst-case difference in the compressed length when one input symbol is modified; see Definition 2 for the formal definition) of the compression scheme. The transformation will yield an efficient compression scheme as long as the underlying compression scheme has low global sensitivity. Second, we demonstrate that good compression schemes do not inherently have high global sensitivity by demonstrating that Kolmogorov compression has low global sensitivity. Third, we analyze the global sensitivity of the LZ77 compression scheme providing an upper/lower bound that is tight up to the sublogarithmic factor of $\log^{2/3} n$.

1.1.1 Differentially Private Transform for Compression Algorithms

We provide a general framework to transform any compression scheme `Compress` into a differentially private compression algorithm $\texttt{DPCompress}(w, \epsilon, \delta)$ by adding a random positive amount of padding to $\texttt{Compress}(w)$, where the amount of padding p depends on the privacy parameters ϵ and δ as well as the global sensitivity of the underlying compression algorithm `Compress`. More concretely, we show that $A_{\epsilon,\delta}(w) := \texttt{DPCompress}(w, \epsilon, \delta)$ is (ϵ, δ)-differentially private, i.e., the length leakage is (ϵ, δ)-differentially private. The expected amount of padding added is $\mathcal{O}\left(\frac{\texttt{GS}_{\texttt{Compress}}}{\epsilon} \ln(\frac{1}{2\delta})\right)$ (see Definition 2 for the definition of the global sensitivity $\texttt{GS}_{\texttt{Compress}}$). Thus, as long as $\texttt{GS}_{\texttt{Compress}} \ll n$, it is possible to achieve a compression ratio $|\texttt{DPCompress}(w, \epsilon, \delta)|/n = |\texttt{Compress}(w)|/n + o(1)$ that nearly matches `Compress`. See Sect. 3 for details.

1.1.2 Idealized Compression Schemes Have Low Sensitivity

While the LZ78 [18] compression algorithm has high global sensitivity, we observe that compression schemes achieving optimal compression ratios do not inherently have high global sensitivity. In particular, we argue that Kolmogorov compression has low global sensitivity, i.e., at most $\mathcal{O}(\log n)$ where n denotes the string length parameter. While Kolmogorov compression is uncomputable, it is known to achieve a compression rate that is *at least as good* as any compression algorithm. We also construct a *computable* variant of Kolmogorov compression that preserves the global sensitivity, i.e., the global sensitivity of the computable variant of Kolmogorov compression is also $\mathcal{O}(\log n)$. See Sect. 6 for details.

1.1.3 Global Sensitivity of the LZ77 Compression Scheme

Our primary technical contribution is to analyze the global sensitivity of the LZ77 compression algorithm [17]. The LZ77 algorithm includes a tunable parameter $W \leq n$ for the size of the sliding window. Selecting smaller W reduces the algorithm's space footprint, but can result in worse compression rates because the algorithm can only exploit redundancy within this window. We provide an almost tight upper and lower bound of the global sensitivity of the LZ77 compression scheme. In particular, we prove that the global sensitivity of the LZ77 compression scheme for strings of length n is upper bounded by $\mathcal{O}(W^{2/3} \log n)$ where $W \leq n$ is the length of the sliding window. When $W = n$ the global sensitivity is lower bounded by $\Omega(n^{2/3} \log^{1/3} n)$ matching our upper bound up to a sublogarithmic factor of $\log^{2/3} n$. We hope that our initial paper inspires follow-up research analyzing the global sensitivity of other compression schemes.

Theorem 1 (informal). *Let* $\mathsf{LZ77}$ *be the LZ77 compression scheme for strings of length* n *with a sliding window size* $W \leq n$. *Then* $\mathsf{GS}_{\mathsf{LZ77}} = \mathcal{O}(W^{2/3} \log n)$ *and, when* $W = n$, $\mathsf{GS}_{\mathsf{LZ77}} = \Omega(n^{2/3} \log^{1/3} n)$. *(See Theorem 3 and Theorem 5.)*

At a high level, the upper bound analysis considers the relationship between the blocks generated by running the LZ77 compression for two neighboring strings $w \sim w'$. Let $B_1, \ldots, B_t$ (resp. $B'_1, \ldots, B'_{t'}$) denote the blocks generated when we run LZ77 with input w (resp. w') where block B_i (resp. B'_k) encodes the substring $w[s_i, f_i]$ (resp. $w'[s'_k, f'_k]$). We prove that if $s_i \leq s'_k \leq f_i$ (block B'_k starts inside block B_i) then $f'_{k+1} \geq f_i$. In particular, this means that for every block B_i there are *at most two* blocks from $B'_1, \ldots, B'_{t'}$ that "start inside" B_i. We can then argue that the difference in compression lengths is proportional to t_2 where $t_2 = |\{i \leq t : |\{k \leq t' : s_i \leq s'_k \leq f_i\}| = 2\}|$ denotes the number of "type-2" blocks, i.e., B_i which have two blocks that start inside it. Finally, we can upper bound $t_2 = \mathcal{O}\left(n^{2/3}\right)$ when $W = n$ or $t_2 = \mathcal{O}\left(W^{2/3}\right)$ when $W < n$.

The lower bound works by constructing a string which (nearly) maximizes t_2. See Sect. 4 and Sect. 5 for details.

1.2 Related Work

There has been extensive work on developing efficient compression algorithms. Huffman coding [15] encodes messages symbol by symbol—symbols that are used most frequently are encoded by shorter binary strings in the prefix-free code. Lempel and Ziv [17,18] developed multiple algorithms, and Welch [30] later proposed LZW as an improved implementation of [18]. Our work primarily focuses on analyzing the LZ77 compression algorithm [17] since it is one of the most common lossless compression algorithms used in practice. Deflate [9] is a lossless compression scheme that combines LZ77 compression [17] and Huffman coding [15] and is a key algorithm used in ZIP archives. The LempelZivMarkov chain algorithm (LZMA) is used in the 7z format of the 7-Zip archiver and it uses a modification of the LZ77 compression. Brotli [2] also uses the LZ77 compression with Huffman coding and the 2nd-order context modeling.

Several prior papers have studied the sensitivity of compression schemes [1, 13,16] to small input changes. Lagarde and Perifel [16] studied the multiplicative sensitivity of the LZ78 compression algorithm [18], and their result implies that the additive (i.e., global) sensitivity can be as large as $\Omega(n)$. Giuliani et al. [13] showed that the additive sensitivity of the Burrows-Wheeler Transform with Run-Length Encoding can be as large as $\Omega(\sqrt{n})$—upper bounding the additive sensitivity remains an open question.

Most closely related to ours is the work of Akagi et al. [1] who studied the additive and multiplicative sensitivity of several compression schemes including Kolmogorov and LZ77. Akagi et al. [1] proved that Kolmogorov compression has additive sensitivity $\mathcal{O}(\log n)$. We extend this result to a computable variation of Kolmogorov compression in Sect. 6. For LZ77, they proved that the additive sensitivity is lower bounded by $\Omega(\sqrt{n})$ when the window size is $W = \Omega(n)^2$. We prove that the additive sensitivity is lower bounded by $\widetilde{\Omega}(n^{2/3})$. Finally, they prove that the (local) additive sensitivity of LZ77 is *at most* $\mathcal{O}(z)$ where z is the length of the compressed file. Unfortunately, this result does not even imply that the global sensitivity is $o(n)$ because z can be as large as $z = \Omega(n)$ when the file is incompressible. By contrast, we prove that the global sensitivity is upper bounded by $\mathcal{O}\left(W^{2/3}\log n\right)$ which is tight up to logarithmic factors and is at most $\mathcal{O}\left(n^{2/3}\log n\right)$ even when $W = \Omega(n)$.

Degabriele [8] introduced a formal model for length-leakage security of compressed messages with random padding. While Degabriele [8] did not use differential privacy as a security notion, his analysis suggests that DP friendly distributions such as the Laplace distribution and Gaussian distribution minimized the leakage. Song [26] analyzed the (in)security of compression schemes against attacks such as cookie-recovery attacks and used the additive sensitivity of a compression scheme to upper bound the probability of successful attacks. Neither work [8,26] formalized the notion of a differentially private compression scheme as we do in Sect. 3.

Ratliff and Vadhan introduced a framework for differential privacy against timing attacks [23] to deal with information leakage that could occur when the running time of a (randomized) algorithm might depend on the sensitive input. They propose to introduce random positive delays after an algorithm is finished. The length of this delay will depend on the sensitivity of the algorithm's running time to small changes in the input. While our motivation is different, there are similarities: they analyze the sensitivity of an algorithm's running time while we analyze the sensitivity of a compression algorithm with respect to the length of the file. They introduce a random positive delay while proposing to add a random positive amount of padding to the compressed file.

2 Preliminaries

Definition 1 (Lossless Compression). *Let Σ, Σ' be sets of alphabets. A* lossless compression scheme *consists of two functions* `Compress` $: \Sigma^* \rightarrow (\Sigma')^*$ *and* `Decompress` $: (\Sigma')^* \rightarrow \Sigma^*$. *We require that for all string $w \in \Sigma^*$ we have* `Decompress`(`Compress`$(w)) = w$.

Global Sensitivity of Compression Scheme. Global sensitivity helps us understand how much the output of a function can change when its input is slightly modified. Recall that two strings $w, w' \in \Sigma^n$ are neighbors (denoted $w \sim w'$) if the Hamming Distance between these two strings is at most one, i.e.,

[2] Bannai et al. [3] also lower bounds the additive sensitivity of LZ77 by $\Omega(\sqrt{n})$ as well though the primary focus in [3] is on efficiently updating the compressed file after rotations instead of analyzing additive sensitivity.

$|\{i : w[i] \neq w'[i]\}| \leq 1$. In the context of compression schemes, the global sensitivity of a compression scheme is defined as the largest difference in the compression length when we compress two neighboring strings $w \sim w'$.

Definition 2 (Local/Global Sensitivity). *Let Σ, Σ' be sets of alphabets. The* local sensitivity *of the compression algorithm* $\texttt{Compress} : \Sigma^* \rightarrow (\Sigma')^*$ *at $w \in \Sigma^n$ is defined as* $\texttt{LS}_{\texttt{Compress}}(w) := \max_{w' \in \Sigma^n : w \sim w'} ||\texttt{Compress}(w)| - |\texttt{Compress}(w')||$, *and the* global sensitivity *of the compression algorithm for strings of length n is defined as* $\texttt{GS}_{\texttt{Compress}}(n) := \max_{w \in \Sigma^n} \texttt{LS}_{\texttt{Compress}}(w)$. *If it is clear from context, then one can omit the parameter n (length of a string) and simply write* $\texttt{GS}_{\texttt{Compress}}$ *to denote the global sensitivity.*

Understanding the global sensitivity of a compression algorithm is a crucial element of designing a differentially private compression scheme. While there is a large line of work using global sensitivity [5,6,11,19,20,25,27–29,31,32] to design differentially private mechanisms, to the best of our knowledge, no prior work has studied the construction of differentially private compression schemes.

In our context, the amount of random padding added to a compressed file will scale with the global sensitivity of the compression algorithm. While Lagarde and Perifel [16] were not motivated by privacy or security, their analysis of LZ78 implies that the global sensitivity of this compression algorithm is $\Omega(n)$. Thus, to achieve differential privacy, the random padding would need to be very long, i.e., at least $\Omega(n)$. This would immediately negate any efficiency gains since, after padding, the compressed file would not be shorter than the original file!

LZ77 Compression Scheme. The LZ77 compression algorithm [17] takes as input a string $w \in \Sigma^n$ and outputs a sequence of blocks $B_1, \ldots, B_k$ where each block $B_i = [q_i, \ell_i, c_i]$ is a tuple consisting of two non-negative integers q_i and ℓ_i and a character $c_i \in \Sigma$. Intuitively, if blocks $B_1, \ldots, B_{i-1}$ encode the first ctc characters of w then the block $B_i = [q_i, \ell_i, c_i]$ encodes the next $\ell_i + 1$ characters of w. In particular, if we have already recovered $w[1, \mathsf{ctc}]$ then the decoding algorithm can recover the substring $w[\mathsf{ctc}+1, \mathsf{ctc}+\ell_i+1] = w[q_i, q_i+\ell_i-1] \circ c_i$ can be recovered by copying ℓ_i characters from $w[1, \mathsf{ctc}]$ beginning at index q_i and then appending the character c_i. The compression algorithm defines the first block as $B_1 = [0, 0, w[1]]$ (where $w[i]$ denotes the ith character of w) and then initializes counters $\mathsf{ctb} = 2$ and $\mathsf{ctc} = 1$. Intuitively, the counter ctb indicates that we will output block B_{ctb} next and the parameter ctc counts the numbers of characters of w that have already been encoded by blocks $B_1, \ldots, B_{\mathsf{ctb}-1}$. In general, to produce the ctb^{th} block we will find the longest prefix of $w[\mathsf{ctc}+1, n]$ that is a substring of $w[\max\{1, \mathsf{ctc}-W+1\}, \mathsf{ctc}]$, where $W \leq n$ denotes the size of the sliding window—the algorithm only stores W most recent characters to save space. If the character $w[\mathsf{ctc}+1]$ is not contained in $w[\max\{1, \mathsf{ctc}-W+1\}, \mathsf{ctc}]$ then we will simply set $B_{\mathsf{ctb}} = [0, 0, w[\mathsf{ctc}+1]]$ and increment the counters ctb and ctc. Otherwise, suppose that the longest such prefix has length $\ell_{\mathsf{ctb}} > 0$ then for some z such that $\max\{0, \mathsf{ctc}-W\} + \ell_{\mathsf{ctb}} \leq z \leq \mathsf{ctc}$ we have $w[\mathsf{ctc}+1, \mathsf{ctc}+$

	B_1	B_2	B_3	B_4	B_5
w	a	ab	abc	d	$babca$

Initialize: $B_1 = [0, 0, a]$, $\mathsf{ctb} = 2$, and $\mathsf{ctc} = 1$

Intermediate Steps:

ctb	ctc	ℓ_{ctb}	z	B_{ctb}	updated ctb	updated ctc
2	1	1	1	$[1, 1, b]$	3	3
3	3	2	3	$[2, 2, c]$	4	6
4	6	0	N/A	$[0, 0, d]$	5	7
5	7	4	6	$[3, 4, a]$	6	12

Output: $(B_1 = [0, 0, a], B_2 = [1, 1, b], B_3 = [2, 2, c], B_4 = [0, 0, d], B_5 = [3, 4, a])$

Fig. 1. Example of Running the LZ77 Compression for a string $w =$ "$aababcdbabca$".

$\ell_{\mathsf{ctb}}] = w[z - \ell_{\mathsf{ctb}} + 1, z]$. Then we set $B_{\mathsf{ctb}} = [z - \ell_{\mathsf{ctb}} + 1, \ell_{\mathsf{ctb}}, w[\mathsf{ctc} + \ell_{\mathsf{ctb}} + 1]]$, increment ctb, and update $\mathsf{ctc} = \mathsf{ctc} + \ell_{\mathsf{ctb}} + 1$. We terminate the algorithm if $\mathsf{ctc} = n$ (i.e., the entire string has been encoded) and then output the blocks $(B_1, \ldots, B_{\mathsf{ctb}-1})$. See Fig. 1 for a toy example of running the LZ77 compression for a string $w =$ "$aababcdbabca$" $\in \Sigma^{12}$ with $\Sigma = \{a, b, c, d\}$ and $W = n$.

The decompression works straightforwardly as follows: (1) Given the compression $(B_1, \ldots, B_t)$, parse $B_1 = [0, 0, c_1]$ and initialize the string $w =$ "c_1". (2) For $i = 2$ to t, parse $B_i = [q_i, \ell_i, c_i]$ and convert it into a string v: if $q_i = \ell_i = 0$ then $v := c_i$; otherwise, $v := w[q_i, q_i + \ell_i - 1] \circ c_i$. Then update $w \leftarrow w \circ v$.

The LZ77 compression scheme described above is called the *non-overlapping (i.e., without self-referencing)* LZ77. In the non-overlapping LZ77, it is always the case that $q_i + \ell_i - 1 \leq \mathsf{ctc}$ (so that the substring that we copy from the previous encoding does not overlap with the current encoding). We still obtain a valid compression scheme if we allow for the case $q_i + \ell_i - 1 > \mathsf{ctc}$, and we refer to this scheme as LZ77 compression with self-referencing. We focus on the non-overlapping LZ77 in the main body of this paper. However, as we demonstrate in Appendix A.2, our techniques extend to LZ77 with self-referencing.

3 Differentially Private Compression

This section presents a general framework that transforms any compression scheme $\texttt{Compress} : \Sigma^* \to (\Sigma')^*$ to another compression scheme called $\texttt{DPCompress} : \Sigma^* \times \mathbb{R} \times \mathbb{R} \to (\Sigma')^*$ such that for any $\epsilon > 0$ and $\delta \in (0, 1)$, the algorithm $A_{\epsilon,\delta}(w) := \texttt{DPCompress}(w, \epsilon, \delta)$ is a (ϵ, δ)-differentially private compression algorithm as defined formally in Definition 3.

Definition 3. *We say that a randomized compression algorithm* $A : \Sigma^* \to (\Sigma')^*$ *is* (ϵ, δ)-differentially private *if for every* $n \geq 1$, *every pair of neighboring strings* $w \sim w' \in \Sigma^n$ *and all* $S \subseteq \mathbb{N}$ *we have*

$$\Pr[|A(w)| \in S] \leq e^{\epsilon} \cdot \Pr[|A(w')| \in S] + \delta \ .$$

Intuitively, $\texttt{DPCompress}(w, \epsilon, \delta)$ works by running $\texttt{Compress}(w)$ and adding a random amount of padding. In particular, $\texttt{DPCompress}(w, \epsilon, \delta)$ outputs $\texttt{Compress}(w) \circ 0 \circ 1^{p-1}$ where p is a random variable defined as follows: $p = \max\{1, \lceil Z + k \rceil\}$: where $Z \sim \text{Lap}(\texttt{GS}_{\texttt{Compress}}/\epsilon)$ is a random variable following Laplace distribution with mean 0 and scale parameter $\texttt{GS}_{\texttt{Compress}}/\epsilon$ and $k = \frac{\texttt{GS}_{\texttt{Compress}}}{\epsilon} \ln(\frac{1}{2\delta}) + \texttt{GS}_{\texttt{Compress}} + 1$ is a constant (see Algorithm 1). The decompression algorithm works straightforwardly as it is easy to remove padding $0 \circ 1^{p-1}$ even though one does not know p, i.e., given the compressed string $\texttt{DPCompress}(w, \epsilon, \delta) = \texttt{Compress}(w) \circ 0 \circ 1^{p-1}$, we could start removing 1's from the right until we see 0. After removing the 0 as well, we get $\texttt{Compress}(w)$. Now we could obtain w by calling $\texttt{Decompress}(\texttt{Compress}(w))$.

Intuitively, the output $Z + |\texttt{Compress}(w)|$ preserves ϵ-DP since this is just the standard Laplacian Mechanism and the output $\lceil Z + |\texttt{Compress}(w)| + k \rceil = |\texttt{Compress}(w)| + \lceil Z + k \rceil$ also preserves ϵ-DP since it can be viewed as post-processing applied to a DP output. Finally, note that by our choice of k we have $\Pr[p \neq \lceil Z + k \rceil] = \Pr[Z + k \leq 0] \leq \delta$. It follows that the output $|\texttt{Compress}(w)| + p$ preserves (ϵ, δ)-DP, as shown in Theorem 2.

Algorithm 1. $\texttt{DPCompress}(w, \epsilon, \delta)$

Input: w, ϵ, δ
Output: Differentially Private Padded Data.
$Z \leftarrow \text{Lap}\left(\frac{\texttt{GS}_{\texttt{Compress}}}{\epsilon}\right)$
$k \leftarrow \frac{\texttt{GS}_{\texttt{Compress}}}{\epsilon} \ln(\frac{1}{2\delta}) + \texttt{GS}_{\texttt{Compress}} + 1$
$p \leftarrow \max\{1, \lceil Z + k \rceil\}$
Return $\texttt{pad}(\texttt{Compress}(w), p) := \texttt{Compress}(w) \circ 0 \circ 1^{p-1}$

Theorem 2. *Define* $A_{\epsilon,\delta}(w) := \texttt{DPCompress}(w, \epsilon, \delta)$ *then, for any* $\epsilon, \delta > 0$, *the algorithm* $A_{\epsilon,\delta}$ *is a* (ϵ, δ)*-differentially private compression scheme.*

The proof of Theorem 2 is straightforward using standard DP techniques and therefore is deferred to the full version [7].

On average, the amount of padding added is approximately $k = \frac{\texttt{GS}_{\texttt{Compress}}}{\epsilon} \ln(\frac{1}{2\delta}) + \texttt{GS}_{\texttt{Compress}} + 1$. If $k = o(n)$ then it will still be possible for $\texttt{DPCompress}$ to achieve efficient compression ratios, i.e., $|\texttt{DPCompress}(w, \epsilon, \delta)|/n = |\texttt{Compress}(w)|/n + o(1)$. On the other hand, if $k = \Omega(n)$ then the padding alone will prevent us from achieving a compression ratio of $o(1)$. Thus, our hope is to find practical compression schemes with global sensitivity $\texttt{GS}_{\texttt{Compress}} = o(n)$—LZ78 [18] does not satisfy these criteria [16]. This motivates our study of the global sensitivity of the LZ77 compression scheme [17]—see Sect. 4 for details.

4 Upper Bound for the Global Sensitivity of LZ77

Recall that in Sect. 3, we provided the framework to convert any compression scheme to a (ϵ, δ)-DP compression scheme by adding a random amount of padding $p = \max\{1, \lceil Z + k \rceil\}$, where $Z \sim \text{Lap}(\texttt{GS}_{\texttt{Compress}}/\epsilon)$ and $k = \frac{\texttt{GS}_{\texttt{Compress}}}{\epsilon} \ln(\frac{1}{2\delta}) + \texttt{GS}_{\texttt{Compress}} + 1$ is a constant. We observed that as long as $k = o(n)$, we can still argue that DPCompress achieves efficient compression ratios, i.e., $|\texttt{DPCompress}(w, \epsilon, \delta)| / n = |\texttt{Compress}(w)| / n + o(1)$. That was the motivation to find practical compression schemes with global sensitivity $o(n)$. We argue that the LZ77 compression scheme [17] satisfies this property. For simplicity of exposition, we will assume that $W = n$ in most of our analysis and then briefly explain how the analysis changes when $W < n$. In particular, we prove that the global sensitivity of the LZ77 compression scheme is $\mathcal{O}\left(W^{2/3} \log n\right)$ or $\mathcal{O}\left(n^{2/3} \log n\right)$ when $W = n$.

4.1 Analyzing the Positions of Blocks

Recall that LZ77 [17] with the compression function $\texttt{Compress} : \Sigma^* \to (\Sigma')^*$ outputs a sequence of blocks $B_1, \ldots, B_t$ where each block is of the form $B_i = [q_i, \ell_i, c_i]$ such that $0 \le q_i, \ell_i < n$ are nonnegative integers and $c_i \in \Sigma$ is a character. This implies that for a string $w \in \Sigma^n$, it takes $2\lceil \log n \rceil + \lceil \log |\Sigma| \rceil$ bits to encode each block and this is the same for all the blocks. Therefore, the length of compression is proportional to the number of blocks t, i.e., we have $|\texttt{Compress}(w)| = t(2\lceil \log n \rceil + \lceil \log |\Sigma| \rceil)$. Let $B'_1, \ldots, B'_{t'}$ denotes the blocks when compressing w' instead of w. Our observation above tells us that to analyze the global sensitivity of the LZ77 compression scheme, it is crucial to understand the upper/lower bound of $t' - t$ (WLOG we can assume $t' \ge t$ since we can always change the role of w and w') where t (resp. t') is the number of blocks in $\texttt{Compress}(w)$ (resp. $\texttt{Compress}(w')$) for neighboring strings $w \sim w' \in \Sigma^n$.

To analyze the difference between the number of blocks $t' - t$, it is helpful to introduce some notation. First, since $w \sim w'$ we will use $j \le n$ to denote the unique index such that $w[j] \ne w'[j]$—note that $w[i] = w'[i]$ for all $i \ne j$. Second, the block $B_i = [q_i, \ell_i, c_i]$ can be viewed intuitively as an instruction for the decompression algorithm to locate the substring $w[q_i, q_i + \ell_i - 1]$ from the part of w that we have already decompressed, copy this substring and append it to the end of the of the decompressed file followed by the character c_i. While the inputs q_i and ℓ_i tell us where to copy *from* it is also useful to let $s_i := 1 + \sum_{r=1}^{i-1} (\ell_r + 1)$ and $f_i := \sum_{r=1}^{i} (\ell_r + 1)$ denote the location where the block is copied *to*, i.e., we have $w[s_i, f_i] = w[q_i, q_i + \ell_i - 1] \circ c_i$.

We say that block B'_k starts inside block B_i if $s_i \le s'_k \le f_i$ and we indicate this with the predicate $\mathsf{StartInside}(i, k) := 1$. Otherwise, if $s'_k < s_i$ or $s'_k > f_i$ then we have $\mathsf{StartInside}(i, k) := 0$. Our key technical insight is that if $\mathsf{StartInside}(i, k) = 1$ then for block B'_{k+1} we must have $f'_{k+1} \ge f_k$. In particular, for later blocks $B'_{k'}$ with $k' > k$ we will have $s'_{k'} > f_i$ so $\mathsf{StartInside}(i, k') = 0$. In particular, if we let $\mathcal{M}_i := \{k \in [t'] : \mathsf{StartInside}(i, k) = 1\}$ then Lemma 1 tells us that one of three cases applies: (1) $\mathcal{M}_i = \emptyset$, (2) $\mathcal{M}_i = \{k\}$ for some $k \le t'$, or (3) $\mathcal{M}_i = \{k, k+1\}$ for some $k < t'$. In any case, we have $|\mathcal{M}_i| \le 2$. This has already been proven by Akagi et al. [1], but for the sake of completeness, we include our proof in the full version [7].

Lemma 1 [1]. *Let* $\texttt{Compress} : \Sigma^* \to (\Sigma')^*$ *be the LZ77 compression algorithm and* $w, w' \in \Sigma^n$ *such that* $w \sim w'$. *Let* $(B_1, ..., B_t) \leftarrow \texttt{Compress}(w)$ *and* $(B'_1, ..., B'_{t'}) \leftarrow \texttt{Compress}(w')$. *Then for all* $i \in [t]$, *either* $\mathcal{M}_i = \emptyset$ *or* $\mathcal{M}_i = [i_1, i_2]$ *for some* $i_1 \leq i_2 \leq i_1 + 1$. *In particular,* $|\mathcal{M}_i| \leq 2, \forall i \in [t]$.

Now we can partition the blocks $B_1, \ldots, B_t$ into three sets based on the size of $\mathcal{M}_i$. In particular, let $\mathcal{B}_m := \{i : |\mathcal{M}_i| = m\}$ for $m \in \{0, 1, 2\}$—Lemma 1 implies that $\mathcal{B}_m = \emptyset$ for $m \geq 3$. To upper bound $t' - t$, it is essential to *count the number of type-2 blocks*. Let $t_m = |\mathcal{B}_m|$ be the number of type-m blocks for $m = 0, 1, 2$. Then we have the following claim.

Claim 1. *Let* $\texttt{Compress} : \Sigma^* \to (\Sigma')^*$ *be the LZ77 compression function and* w, w' *be strings of length* n *and* $w \sim w'$. *Let* $(B_1, \ldots, B_t) \leftarrow \texttt{Compress}(w)$ *and* $(B'_1, \ldots, B'_{t'}) \leftarrow \texttt{Compress}(w')$. *Then* $t' - t \leq t_2$.

Proof. We observe $t_0 + t_1 + t_2 = t$ by Lemma 1 and since there are m blocks in $(B'_1, \ldots, B'_{t'})$ that start inside type-m blocks in $(B_1, \ldots, B_t)$ for $m = 0, 1, 2$, we have $t' = \sum_{m=0}^{2} m \cdot t_m = t_1 + 2t_2$, which implies that $t' - t = t_2 - t_0 \leq t_2$.

Claim 1 implies that $||\texttt{Compress}(w)| - |\texttt{Compress}(w')|| \leq (t' - t)(2\lceil \log n \rceil + \lceil \log |\Sigma| \rceil) \leq t_2(2\lceil \log n \rceil + \lceil \log |\Sigma| \rceil)$ since it takes $2\lceil \log n \rceil + \lceil \log |\Sigma| \rceil$ bits to encode each block (see Claim 8 in Appendix A.1). Hence, upper bounding the number of type-2 blocks t_2 would allow us to upper bound the global sensitivity of the LZ77 compression.

4.2 Counting Type-2 Blocks Using Uniqueness of Offsets

We can effectively count the number of type-2 blocks by considering the location of the unique index j such that $w[j] \neq w'[j]$ and show that the number of type-2 blocks is at most $\mathcal{O}(n^{2/3})$ as stated in Lemma 2.

Lemma 2. *Let* $\texttt{Compress} : \Sigma^* \to (\Sigma')^*$ *be the LZ77 compression function and* w, w' *be strings of length* n *and* $w \sim w'$. *Let* $(B_1, \ldots, B_t) \leftarrow \texttt{Compress}(w)$ *and* $(B'_1, \ldots, B'_{t'}) \leftarrow \texttt{Compress}(w')$. *Then* $t_2 \leq \frac{\sqrt[3]{9}}{2} n^{2/3} + \frac{\sqrt[3]{3}}{2} n^{1/3} + 1$.

Proof Sketch. We only give the proof sketch here and the formal proof can be found in Appendix A.2. To prove Lemma 2, we show the following helper claims.

- First, we show that if B_i is a type-2 block then either $s_i \leq j \leq f_i$ or $q_i \leq j < q_i + \ell_i$ should hold (see Claim 9 in Appendix A.2). Intuitively, any type-2 block B_i with $s_i > j$ is constructed by copying the longest possible substring *from* a section around the index j i.e., $j \in [q_i, q_i + \ell_i)$. Type-2 blocks cannot occur before the strings diverge at index j i.e., if $f_i < j$ then B_i is not a type-2 block.
- Second, we show that if blocks $B_{i_1} = [q_{i_1}, \ell_{i_1}, c_{i_1}]$ and $B_{i_2} = [q_{i_2}, \ell_{i_2}, c_{i_2}]$ are both type-2 blocks with $s_{i_1}, s_{i_2} > j$ then $(q_{i_1}, \ell_{i_1}) \neq (q_{i_2}, \ell_{i_2})$ (see Claim 10 in Appendix A.2). In particular, the pair (q_i, ℓ_i) must be *unique* for each type-2 block and, if $s_i > j$, then we must have $j \in [q_i, q_i + \ell_i)$ by our observation above.

- Finally, followed by the uniqueness of offsets from the previous claim, we can show that the number of type-2 blocks with length ℓ is at most ℓ by pigeonhole principle, i.e., if $\mathcal{B}_2^\ell := \{i \in \mathcal{B}_2 : \ell_i = \ell\}$ and if $s_{i^*} \le j \le f_{i^*}$ for some $i^* \in [t]$, then $|\mathcal{B}_2^\ell| \le \ell$ for all $\ell \ne \ell_{i^*}$ and $|\mathcal{B}_2^{\ell_{i^*}}| \le \ell_{i^*} + 1$ (see Claim 11 in Appendix A.2).

Let $x_\ell := |\mathcal{B}_2^\ell|$ denote the number of type-2 blocks with length ℓ. The total number of type-2 blocks is given by the sum $\sum_\ell x_\ell$. If we try to maximize $\sum_\ell x_\ell$ subject to the constraints that $x_\ell \le \ell$ (for all $\ell \ne \ell_{i^*}$), $x_{\ell_{i^*}} \le \ell_{i^*} + 1$, and $\sum_\ell x_\ell(\ell+1) \le n$, we obtain a solution where we set $x_\ell = \ell$ for $\ell \le z$ with $\ell \ne \ell_{i^*}$ (and set $x_{\ell_{i^*}} = \ell_{i^*} + 1$ if $\ell_{i^*} \le z$) and $x_\ell = 0$ for $\ell > z$ by a simple swapping argument (see the formal proof in Appendix A.2 for details). Note that x_z could be less than z, i.e., for the threshold z, we have $x_z = c$ for some $0 < c \le z$. To find the threshold z, we observe that $\left[\sum_{\ell=0}^{z-1} \ell(\ell+1)\right] + x_z(z+1) = \sum_{\ell\ge 0} x_\ell(\ell+1) \le n$. Simplifying the sum, we have $\left[\sum_{\ell=0}^{z-1} \ell(\ell+1)\right] + x_z(z+1) = \frac{1}{3}(z-1)z(z+1) + x_z(z+1) \ge z^3/3$ where the last inequality follows because $x_z \ge 1$. Thus, we have $z^3 \le 3n$ and $z \le \sqrt[3]{3n}$. Setting this value of z, we have $t_2 \le \left(\sum_{\ell=0}^{\sqrt[3]{3n}} \ell\right) + 1 = \frac{\sqrt[3]{9}}{2} n^{2/3} + \frac{\sqrt[3]{3}}{2} n^{1/3} + 1$. □

While we focus on analyzing the global sensitivity of the *non-overlapping* LZ77 compression scheme, one can easily extend the results to the LZ77 with self-referencing and achieve the same upper bound for $t_2 = \mathcal{O}\left(n^{2/3}\right)$. See Appendix A.3 for details.

We remark that this is a key result to upper bound the global sensitivity of the LZ77 compression scheme from our previous discussion that it takes $\mathcal{O}(\log n)$ bits to encode each block. Since the number of type-2 blocks is $\mathcal{O}(n^{2/3})$ and $t' - t$ is bounded by the number of type-2 blocks, we can combine those results and conclude that the global sensitivity of the LZ77 compression scheme is upper bounded by $\mathcal{O}(n^{2/3} \log n)$, as stated in Theorem 3.

Theorem 3. *Let* $\texttt{Compress} : (\Sigma)^* \to (\Sigma')^*$ *be the LZ77 compression function with unbounded sliding window size* $W = n$. *Then*

$$\mathsf{GS}_{\texttt{Compress}} \le \left(\frac{\sqrt[3]{9}}{2} n^{2/3} + \frac{\sqrt[3]{3}}{2} n^{1/3} + 1\right)(2\lceil \log n\rceil + \lceil \log |\Sigma|\rceil) = \mathcal{O}\left(n^{2/3}\log n\right).$$

Proof. Let $(B_1, \ldots, B_t) \leftarrow \texttt{Compress}(w)$ and $(B_1', \ldots, B_{t'}') \leftarrow \texttt{Compress}(w')$. By Claim 1 and Lemma 2, we have $t' - t \le t_2 \le \frac{\sqrt[3]{9}}{2} n^{2/3} + \frac{\sqrt[3]{3}}{2} n^{1/3} + 1$. We know $|\texttt{Compress}(w)| = t(2\lceil \log n\rceil + \lceil \log|\Sigma|\rceil)$ and $|\texttt{Compress}(w')| = t'(2\lceil \log n\rceil + \lceil \log|\Sigma|\rceil)$. Hence, $||\texttt{Compress}(w)| - |\texttt{Compress}(w')|| = |t - t'|(2\lceil \log n\rceil + \lceil \log|\Sigma|\rceil) \le \left(\frac{\sqrt[3]{9}}{2} n^{2/3} + \frac{\sqrt[3]{3}}{2} n^{1/3} + 1\right)(2\lceil \log n\rceil + \lceil \log|\Sigma|\rceil)$. Since this inequality hold for arbitrary $w \sim w'$ of length n, we have

$$\begin{aligned}\mathsf{GS}_{\texttt{Compress}} &= \max_{w\in\Sigma^n} \max_{w'\in\Sigma^n : w\sim w'} ||\texttt{Compress}(w)| - |\texttt{Compress}(w')|| \\ &\le \left(\frac{\sqrt[3]{9}}{2} n^{2/3} + \frac{\sqrt[3]{3}}{2} n^{1/3} + 1\right)(2\lceil \log n\rceil + \lceil \log|\Sigma|\rceil) = \mathcal{O}\left(n^{2/3}\log n\right).\end{aligned}$$

□

For the LZ77 with self-referencing, Lemma 1 essentially still holds except that we might have one type-3 block (i.e., $t_3 = 1$), i.e., the block containing the edited position j—see [1, p.18]. Thus, the global sensitivity of the LZ77 with self-referencing would be bounded by $\mathcal{O}(t_2 \log n + 2t_3 \log n) = \mathcal{O}(t_2 \log n + 2 \log n) = \mathcal{O}\left(n^{2/3} \log n\right)$. See Theorem 6 in Appendix A.3 for details.

4.3 Bounded Sliding Window ($W < n$)

The analysis for the case when $W < n$ is very similar. When $W < n$ then we obtain an additional constraint on any type-2 block as stated in Claim 2.

Claim 2. *Let* $\texttt{Compress} : (\Sigma)^* \to (\Sigma')^*$ *be the LZ77 compression function with sliding window size* W *and* $w \sim w'$ *be strings of length* n *with* $w[j] \neq w'[j]$. *Let* $(B_1, \ldots, B_t) \leftarrow \texttt{Compress}(w)$ *and* $(B'_1, \ldots, B'_{t'}) \leftarrow \texttt{Compress}(w')$. *If* $B_i \in \mathcal{B}_2$ *then* $s_i \leq j + W$.

The proof of Claim 2 is elementary and can be found in Appendix A.4. Claim 2 tells us that there is no type-2 block that starts after $j + W$. Prior constraints still apply: we still have $f_i \geq j$ for type-2 blocks B_i and if $s_i \geq j$ then we must have $j \in [q_i, q_i + \ell_i)$. In particular, we can have at most ℓ type-2 blocks of length ℓ and, if $s_i \geq j$, we must have $j \in [q_i, q_i + \ell_i)$. Letting x_ℓ denote the number of type-2 blocks of length ℓ (excluding any block B_i such that $j \in [s_i, f_i]$ or such that $f_i > j + W$ if any such type-2 blocks exist[3]) we now obtain the constraint that $\sum_\ell (\ell + 1) x_\ell \leq 3W$ instead of the prior constraint that $\sum_\ell (\ell + 1) x_\ell \leq n$. Maximizing $\sum_\ell x_\ell$ subject to the above constraint, as well as the prior constraints that $x_\ell \leq \ell$ for all ℓ, we can now obtain a tighter upper bound $t_2 = \mathcal{O}\left(W^{2/3}\right)$ instead of $t_2 = \mathcal{O}\left(n^{2/3}\right)$. This leads to the following result.

Theorem 4. *Let* $\texttt{Compress} : (\Sigma)^* \to (\Sigma')^*$ *be the LZ77 compression function with sliding window size* W. *Then* $\texttt{GS}_{\texttt{Compress}} \leq \left(\frac{\sqrt[3]{81}}{2} W^{2/3} + \frac{\sqrt[3]{9}}{2} W^{1/3} + 3\right) (2\lceil \log n \rceil + \lceil \log |\Sigma| \rceil) = \mathcal{O}\left(W^{2/3} \log n\right)$.

Essentially the same result holds for the LZ77 with self-referencing as well; see Theorem 7 in Appendix A.4 for details.

In practice, many implementations of LZ77 set $W \ll n$ to minimize space usage. In addition to minimizing space usage, these implementations also reduce the global sensitivity of the compression algorithm.

5 Lower Bound for the Global Sensitivity of LZ77

In Sect. 4, we proved that the upper bound for the global sensitivity of the LZ77 compression algorithm $\texttt{Compress}$ is $O(n^{2/3} \log n)$ with window size $W = n$.

[3] Observe that we exclude *at most* two blocks since there can be *at most* one type-2 block B_i with $f_i > j + W$ and there can be *at most* one type two block B_i with $j \in [s_i, f_i]$.

One could ask if this is a tight bound, i.e., if we can prove the matching *lower bound* for the global sensitivity of `Compress` as well. This section proves the almost-matching lower bound up to a sub-logarithmic factor. In particular, we show that the global sensitivity of the LZ77 compression algorithm is $\Omega(n^{2/3}\log^{1/3} n)$. To prove the lower bound, we need to give example strings $w \sim w'$ of length n that achieves $||\texttt{Compress}(w)| - |\texttt{Compress}(w')|| = \Omega(n^{2/3}\log^{1/3} n)$, since this implies $\texttt{GS}_{\texttt{Compress}} = \max_{x\in\Sigma^n} \max_{x'\in\Sigma^n : x\sim x'} ||\texttt{Compress}(x)| - |\texttt{Compress}(x')|| \geq ||\texttt{Compress}(w)| - |\texttt{Compress}(w')|| = \Omega(n^{2/3}\log^{1/3} n)$. In this section, we will give the construction of such example strings w and w'.

5.1 String Construction

Consider an encoding function $\mathsf{E} : \mathbb{Z} \to \{0,1\}^*$ that maps integers to binary strings. Then for a positive integer $m \in \mathbb{Z}$, we have an injective encoding of the number set $\mathcal{S} := \{0, 1, \ldots, m\}$ using $\lceil \log m \rceil$ bits, i.e., $\mathsf{E}(i) \neq \mathsf{E}(j)$ if $i, j \in \mathcal{S}$ and $i \neq j$. For example, if $m = 2^q - 1$ for some positive integer q, we could encode the elements of $\mathcal{S}$ as follows:

$$\mathsf{E}(0) = 0^{\lceil \log m \rceil}, \mathsf{E}(1) = 0^{\lceil \log m \rceil - 1}1, \mathsf{E}(2) = 0^{\lceil \log m \rceil - 2}10, \ldots, \mathsf{E}(m) = 1^{\lceil \log m \rceil}.$$

Now, consider a quinary alphabet $\Sigma = \{0, 1, 2, 3, 4\}$ and define a string

$$S_{\ell,u} := \mathsf{E}(m-u+1)^2 \circ \mathsf{E}(m-u+2)^2 \circ \cdots \circ \mathsf{E}(m)^2 \circ 2 \circ \mathsf{E}(m+1)^2 \circ \cdots \circ \mathsf{E}(m-u+\ell)^2$$

in Σ^* for $2 \leq \ell \leq m$ and $1 \leq u \leq \ell - 1$. Here, $(\cdot)^2$ denotes the concatenation of the string itself twice, i.e., $\mathsf{E}(\cdot)^2 = \mathsf{E}(\cdot) \circ \mathsf{E}(\cdot)$. We define a procedure called $\mathsf{QuinStr}(m)$ which takes as input a positive integer $m \in \mathbb{Z}$ and outputs two quinary strings as follows.

The Construction of Two Quinary Strings $\mathsf{QuinStr}(m)$.

1. Compute two quinary strings S_w and $S_{w'}$ where

$$S_w := \mathsf{E}(1)^2 \circ \cdots \circ \mathsf{E}(m)^2 \circ 2 \circ \mathsf{E}(m+1)^2 \circ \cdots \circ \mathsf{E}(2m)^2 \circ 4, \text{ and}$$
$$S_{w'} := \mathsf{E}(1)^2 \circ \cdots \circ \mathsf{E}(m)^2 \circ 3 \circ \mathsf{E}(m+1)^2 \circ \cdots \circ \mathsf{E}(2m)^2 \circ 4.$$

2. Compute two quinary strings $w := S_w \circ S$ and $w' := S_{w'} \circ S$, where

$$S = S_{2,1} \circ 4 \circ S_{3,2} \circ 4 \circ S_{3,1} \circ 4 \circ \ldots \circ S_{m,m-1} \circ 4 \circ \ldots \circ S_{m,1} \circ 4.$$

3. Output (w, w').

Claim 3 tells us that the strings w and w' outputted by the procedure $\mathsf{QuinStr}(m)$ has equal length $\Theta(m^3 \log m)$. Since the proof is elementary, we defer the proof of Claim 3 to Appendix B.

Claim 3. *Let $m \in \mathbb{N}$ and $(w, w') \leftarrow \mathsf{QuinStr}(m)$. Then $|w| = |w'| = \Theta(m^3 \log m)$. In particular, for $m \geq 4$, $\frac{2}{3}m^3\lceil \log m \rceil < |w| = |w'| < m^3\lceil \log m \rceil$.*

5.2 Analyzing the Sensitivity of QuinStr(m)

A central step in our sensitivity analysis for QuinStr(m) is precisely counting the type-2 blocks produced by the LZ77 compression scheme, as we did in Sect. 4. Lemma 3 shows that for $(w, w') \leftarrow \mathsf{QuinStr}(m)$, we have $|\mathcal{B}_2| = \frac{(m-1)m}{2} - (\lfloor \frac{m}{2} \rfloor - 1)$. Intuitively, we first show that for $w = S_w \circ S$, there is no type-2 block for the blocks compressing S_w. Then the main insight is that we carefully crafted strings w and w' such that the marker symbol '4' becomes the endpoint for each block in $\mathtt{Compress}(w)$ for the tail part S of $w = S_w \circ S$. By repeating each encoding twice, we can ensure that most of the occurrences of $S_{\ell,u} \circ 4$ yield type-2 blocks, with an edge case (addressed in Claim 7) that makes the block in $\mathcal{B}_1$ but this happens for only about $m/2$ blocks. Consequently, despite these few exceptions, the overall count of type-2 blocks remains quadratic in m.

Lemma 3. *Let $m \in \mathbb{N}$ and $(w, w') \leftarrow \mathsf{QuinStr}(m)$ and let $\mathtt{Compress} : \Sigma^* \rightarrow (\Sigma')^*$ be the LZ77 compression algorithm. Let $(B_1, \ldots, B_t) \leftarrow \mathtt{Compress}(w)$ and $(B'_1, \ldots, B'_{t'}) \leftarrow \mathtt{Compress}(w')$. Then $|\mathcal{B}_0| = 0$ and $|\mathcal{B}_2| = \frac{(m-1)m}{2} - (\lfloor \frac{m}{2} \rfloor - 1)$.*

Proof. Recall that $w = S_w \circ S$ and $w' = S_{w'} \circ S$, where

- $S_w = \mathsf{E}(1)^2 \circ \cdots \circ \mathsf{E}(m)^2 \circ 2 \circ \mathsf{E}(m+1)^2 \circ \cdots \circ \mathsf{E}(2m)^2 \circ 4$,
- $S_{w'} = \mathsf{E}(1)^2 \circ \cdots \circ \mathsf{E}(m)^2 \circ 3 \circ \mathsf{E}(m+1)^2 \circ \cdots \circ \mathsf{E}(2m)^2 \circ 4$, and
- $S = S_{2,1} \circ 4 \circ S_{3,2} \circ 4 \circ S_{3,1} \circ 4 \circ \ldots \circ S_{m,m-1} \circ 4 \circ \ldots \circ S_{m,1} \circ 4$, where
- $S_{\ell,u} := \mathsf{E}(m-u+1)^2 \circ \mathsf{E}(m-u+2)^2 \circ \cdots \circ \mathsf{E}(m)^2 \circ 2 \circ \mathsf{E}(m+1)^2 \circ \cdots \circ \mathsf{E}(m-u+\ell)^2$ for $2 \le \ell \le m$ and $1 \le u \le \ell - 1$.

We first observe that $w \sim w'$. Define $S_w^F := \mathsf{E}(1)^2 \circ \cdots \circ \mathsf{E}(m)^2 \circ 2$ (resp. $S_{w'}^F := \mathsf{E}(1)^2 \circ \cdots \circ \mathsf{E}(m)^2 \circ 3$) to be the first-half substring of S_w (resp. of $S_{w'}$), and $S_w^L = S_{w'}^L := \mathsf{E}(m+1)^2 \circ \cdots \circ \mathsf{E}(2m)^2 \circ 4$ to be the last-half substring of S_w (or $S_{w'}$ since they are indeed identical). It is useful to define a notation $\mathsf{str}(B_k)$ for a block B_k, which denotes the substring of w represented by the block B_k, i.e., for $B_k = [q_k, \ell_k, c_k]$, $\mathsf{str}(B_k) := w[q_k, q_k + \ell_k - 1] \circ c_k$.

Let B_{i_1} be the first block such that S_w^F becomes a substring of $\mathsf{str}(B_1) \circ \mathsf{str}(B_2) \circ \ldots \circ \mathsf{str}(B_{i_1})$, and similarly, let $B'_{i'_1}$ be the first block such that $S_{w'}^F$ becomes a substring of $\mathsf{str}(B'_1) \circ \mathsf{str}(B'_2) \circ \ldots \circ \mathsf{str}(B'_{i'_1})$. Then we observe the following:

(1) $B_{i_1} = [q_{i_1}, \ell_{i_1}, 2]$, i.e., $\mathsf{str}(B_{i_1})$ ends with 2 (which is the last character in S_w^F), since 2 never showed up before as all the encodings are binary strings, it has to be added to the dictionary as a new character,
(2) $B_i = B'_i$ for all $i \in [i_1 - 1]$, as we are compressing the identical strings until we see 2 in S_w^F (and 3 in $S_{w'}^F$), and
(3) $i_1 = i'_1$ and $B'_{i_1} = [q_{i_1}, \ell_{i_1}, 3]$, since two strings S_w^F and $S_{w'}^F$ are identical except for the very last character.

Now let B_{i_2} be the first block such that S_w^L becomes a substring of $\mathsf{str}(B_{i_1+1}) \circ \mathsf{str}(B_{i_1+2}) \circ \ldots \circ \mathsf{str}(B_{i_2})$, and similarly, let $B'_{i'_2}$ be the first block such that $S_{w'}^L$ becomes a substring of $\mathsf{str}(B'_{i_1+1}) \circ \mathsf{str}(B'_{i_1+2}) \circ \ldots \circ \mathsf{str}(B'_{i'_2})$. Then we observe the following:

(4) $i_2 = i'_2$ and $B_i = B'_i$ for all $i \in [i_1+1, i_2]$, since $i_1 = i'_1$ from observation 3 and we have $S^L_w = S^L_{w'}$ while they do not contain 2 or 3, and
(5) $B_{i_2} = [q_{i_2}, \ell_{i_2}, 4]$, since 4 never showed up before in our compression.

From the observations above, we have that $B_i \in \mathcal{B}_1$ for all $i \in [i_2]$. Now we are left with the blocks $(B_{i_2+1}, \ldots, B_t)$ compressing the last part S of w and the blocks $(B'_{i_2+1}, \ldots, B'_{t'})$ compressing the last part S of w'. For the blocks $(B_{i_2+1}, \ldots, B_t)$, we observe that each block ends at the next '4' because each $S_{\ell,u}$ (for $2 \le \ell \le m$ and $1 \le u \le \ell - 1$) is contained in the former part of w (which was S_w) but 4 only shows up in S_w followed by $\mathsf{E}(2m)^2$ while $S_{\ell,u}$ cannot contain $\mathsf{E}(2m)$. Hence, we observe the following:

(6) $\mathsf{str}(B_{i_2+1}) = S_{2,1} \circ 4, \mathsf{str}(B_{i_2+2}) = S_{3,2} \circ 4$, and so on. To see this, we recall that $S_{\ell,u} := \mathsf{E}(m-u+1)^2 \circ \mathsf{E}(m-u+2)^2 \circ \cdots \circ \mathsf{E}(m)^2 \circ 2 \circ \mathsf{E}(m+1)^2 \circ \cdots \circ \mathsf{E}(m-u+\ell)^2$. Because of '2' in the middle of each $S_{\ell,u}$ and '4' at the end of each $S_{\ell,u} \circ 4$, we observe that $S_{\ell,u} \circ 4$ cannot be copied from a previous position in S.
(7) In general, $\mathsf{str}\left(B_{i_2 + \frac{(\ell-2)(\ell-1)}{2} + (\ell-u)}\right) = S_{\ell,u} \circ 4$, for $2 \le \ell \le m$ and $1 \le u \le \ell - 1$. Intuitively, the blocks are numbered by iterating over $\ell = 2, \ldots, m$, and for each ℓ, iterating over $u = \ell - 1, \ldots, 1$ in reverse order. This indeed covers all the blocks from $B_{i_2+1}, \ldots, B_t$ (See Claim 4 and observation 8).
(8) Furthermore, we can observe that $t = i_2 + (1+2+\ldots+(m-1)) = i_2 + \frac{(m-1)m}{2}$.

Claim 4. *For any integer $m \ge 2$, the function $f(\ell, u) := \frac{(\ell-2)(\ell-1)}{2} + (\ell - u)$ defined over integers ℓ and u such that $2 \le \ell \le m$ and $1 \le u \le \ell - 1$ is injective, and its range is $[\frac{(m-1)m}{2}]$.*

The proof of Claim 4 is elementary by induction on m, and hence, we defer the proof to Appendix B. What we are interested in is whether each B_i, for $i_2 + 1 \le i \le t$, belongs to $\mathcal{B}_0$, $\mathcal{B}_1$, or $\mathcal{B}_2$. In Claim 5, we prove that the blocks are mostly in $\mathcal{B}_2$ and the rest of the blocks are in $\mathcal{B}_1$, meaning that $\mathcal{B}_0 = \emptyset$. In particular, we prove that for $2 \le \ell \le m$ and $1 \le u \le \ell - 1$, $B_{i_2 + \frac{(\ell-2)(\ell-1)}{2} + (\ell-u)} \in \mathcal{B}_1$ if and only if all of these conditions hold: (1) $\ell > 2$, (2) ℓ is even, and (3) $u = \ell/2$.

Claim 5. *For $2 \le \ell \le m$ and $1 \le u \le \ell - 1$,*

- $B_{i_2 + \frac{(\ell-2)(\ell-1)}{2} + (\ell-u)} \in \mathcal{B}_1$ *if and only if $\ell > 2, 2 \mid \ell$, and $u = \ell/2$;*
- *Otherwise* $B_{i_2 + \frac{(\ell-2)(\ell-1)}{2} + (\ell-u)} \in \mathcal{B}_2$.

We will give the proof of Claim 5 below and finish the proof of Lemma 3 first for readability. By Claim 5, since there are only $\lfloor \frac{m}{2} \rfloor - 1$ of such pairs of (ℓ, u) (satisfying $\ell > 2, 2 \mid \ell$, and $u = \ell/2$), we observe that $|\mathcal{B}_2| = \frac{(m-1)m}{2} - (\lfloor \frac{m}{2} \rfloor - 1)$. Since we have that $B_i \in \mathcal{B}_1$ for all $i \in [i_2]$, we have $\mathcal{B}_0 = \emptyset$ and therefore $|\mathcal{B}_0| = 0$. This completes the proof of Lemma 3.

Proof of Claim 5. Recall that $S = S_{2,1} \circ 4 \circ S_{3,2} \circ 4 \circ S_{3,1} \circ 4 \circ \ldots \circ S_{m,m-1} \circ 4 \circ \ldots \circ S_{m,1} \circ 4$ and $\mathsf{str}(B_{i_2+1}) = S_{2,1} \circ 4$, $\mathsf{str}(B_{i_2+2}) = S_{3,2} \circ 4$, $\mathsf{str}(B_{i_2+3}) =$

$S_{3,1} \circ 4, \ldots, \mathsf{str}(B_t) = S_{m,1} \circ 4$. For each $S_{\ell,u}$, we observe that $S_{\ell,u}$ is *not* a substring of $S_{w'}$. Hence, we see that each block B_i (for $i_2+1 \le i \le t$) is roughly split into two blocks for the blocks of $\texttt{Compress}(w')$ unless it could copy beyond the character 4. To observe the cases when this happens, for each $S_{\ell,u}$, it is helpful to define:

- $S^F_{\ell,u} := \mathsf{E}(m-u+1)^2$ denotes the very first encoding concatenation that shows in $S_{\ell,u}$,
- $S^{F,(1/2)}_{\ell,u} := \mathsf{E}(m-u+1)$ denotes the very first encoding in $S_{\ell,u}$ (i.e., half of $S^F_{\ell,u}$),
- $S^L_{\ell,u} := \mathsf{E}(m-u+\ell)^2$ denotes the very last encoding concatenation that shows in $S_{\ell,u}$, and
- For $k > u$, $S^{(k)}_{\ell,u} := \mathsf{E}(m-u+1)^2 \circ \mathsf{E}(m-u+2)^2 \circ \ldots \circ \mathsf{E}(m)^2 \circ 2 \circ \mathsf{E}(m+1)^2 \circ \ldots \circ \mathsf{E}(m-u+k)^2$ denotes the first k encoding concatenations that shows in $S_{\ell,u}$.

Then we observe the following claims. Since proofs of Claim 6 and Claim 7 are elementary, we defer the proofs to Appendix B.

Claim 6. *$S^L_{\ell,u} \circ 4 \circ S^F_{\ell,u-1}$ does not repeat for different ℓ and u such that $3 \le \ell \le m$ and $2 \le u \le \ell - 1$.*

Claim 6 tells us that, due to the injectivity of the encoding, any block in $\texttt{Compress}(w')$ containing a portion of $S^L_{\ell,u}$ along with the delimiter '4' must finish at $S^{F,(1/2)}_{\ell,u}$ in the worst case. In particular, note that $S^L_{\ell,u} = \mathsf{E}(m-u+\ell)^2 = S^L_{\ell+1,u+1}$ for $3 \le \ell < m$ and $2 \le u < \ell - 1$. Moreover, we have $S^{F,(1/2)}_{\ell,u-1} = \mathsf{E}(m-u+2)$ and $S^{F,(1/2)}_{\ell+1,u} = \mathsf{E}(m-u+1)$, which can agree on all but the final bit (e.g., $S^{F,(1/2)}_{\ell,u-1} = 00\cdots 00$ and $S^{F,(1/2)}_{\ell+1,u} = 00\cdots 01$). Without the repetition of each encoding, a block might incorporate nearly the entire $S^{F,(1/2)}_{\ell+1,u}$ except for the last bit. Consequently, by having this last bit as a new character, $S_{\ell,u-1} \circ 4$ would be placed in $\mathcal{B}_1$. Repeating the encoding twice eliminates this possibility and we can ensure that the scenario described in Claim 7 is the only case where type-1 blocks would occur. Again, see Appendix B for the proof of Claim 7.

Claim 7. *For $2 \le \ell \le \lfloor \frac{m}{2} \rfloor - 1$, $S^L_{\ell,1} \circ 4 \circ S_{\ell+1,\ell}$ repeats at $S^L_{2\ell,\ell+1} \circ 4 \circ S^{(\ell+1)}_{2\ell,\ell}$.*

Let's go back to the proof of Claim 5. By Claim 7, we can see that the block of the form $B_{i_2+\frac{(2\ell-2)(2\ell-1)}{2}+(2\ell-\ell)}$ which satisfies

$$\mathsf{str}\left(B_{i_2+\frac{(2\ell-2)(2\ell-1)}{2}+(2\ell-\ell)}\right) = S_{2\ell,\ell} \circ 4,$$

is in $\mathcal{B}_1$, and all of the other blocks beyond B_{i_2} are in $\mathcal{B}_2$. This completes the proof of Claim 5. □

Taken altogether, we can lower bound the global sensitivity of the LZ77 compression scheme as stated in Theorem 5 below.

Theorem 5. *Let* $\texttt{Compress} : \Sigma^* \rightarrow \Sigma'^*$ *be the LZ77 compression function. Then* $\texttt{GS}_{\texttt{Compress}} \geq 4^{-1/3} \cdot n^{2/3} \log^{1/3} n = \Omega(n^{2/3} \log^{1/3} n)$.

Proof. Let $(w, w') \leftarrow \mathsf{QuinStr}(m)$ and let $|w| = |w'| = n$. By Claim 3, we have $|w| = |w'| = \Theta(m^3 \log m)$ and therefore $n = \Theta(m^3 \log m)$. Furthermore, Claim 3 tells us that there exists some α with $\frac{2}{3} \leq \alpha \leq 1$ such that $n = \alpha m^3 \log m$. Now let $(B_1, \ldots, B_t) \leftarrow \texttt{Compress}(w)$ and $(B'_1, \ldots, B'_{t'}) \leftarrow \texttt{Compress}(w')$. Recall that if we look at the proof of Claim 1, it tells us that $t' - t = |\mathcal{B}_2| - |\mathcal{B}_0|$. From Lemma 3, we have $|\mathcal{B}_0| = 0$ and $|\mathcal{B}_2| = \frac{(m-1)m}{2} - (\lfloor \frac{m}{2} \rfloor - 1)$, which implies that $t' - t = \frac{(m-1)m}{2} - (\lfloor \frac{m}{2} \rfloor - 1)$. We know $|\texttt{Compress}(w)| = t(2\lceil \log n \rceil + \lceil \log |\Sigma| \rceil)$ and $|\texttt{Compress}(w')| = t'(2\lceil \log n \rceil + \lceil \log |\Sigma| \rceil)$, we have

$$\begin{aligned} \texttt{GS}_{\texttt{Compress}} &\geq ||\texttt{Compress}(w)| - |\texttt{Compress}(w')|| \\ &= |t - t'| \left(2\lceil \log n \rceil + \lceil \log |\Sigma| \rceil\right) \\ &= |t - t'| \left(2 \left\lceil \log(\alpha m^3 \log m) \right\rceil + \lceil \log |\Sigma| \rceil\right) \\ &\geq \frac{m^2}{4} \cdot 4 \log m = m^2 \log m \ . \end{aligned}$$

Furthermore, since we have $n = \alpha m^3 \log m$ for some $\frac{2}{3} \leq \alpha \leq 1$, we observe that

$$\begin{aligned} m^2 \log m = m^2 \cdot \frac{n}{\alpha m^3} &= \frac{n}{\alpha} \cdot \frac{1}{m} = \frac{n}{\alpha} \cdot \frac{\alpha^{1/3} \cdot \log^{1/3} m}{n^{1/3}} \\ &\geq \left(\frac{n}{\alpha}\right)^{2/3} \cdot 4^{-1/3} \cdot \log^{1/3} n \\ &\geq 4^{-1/3} \cdot n^{2/3} \log^{1/3} n, \end{aligned}$$

where the first inequality comes from the observation $\log n = \log \alpha + 3 \log m + \log\log m \leq 4 \log m$ and the second inequality comes from $(1/\alpha) \geq 1$. Hence,

$$\texttt{GS}_{\texttt{Compress}} \geq m^2 \log m \geq 4^{-1/3} \cdot n^{2/3} \log^{1/3} n,$$

which completes the proof.

6 Is High Sensitivity Inevitable?

Based on the results of Lagarde and Perifel [16], one might wonder whether or not any effective compression mechanism will necessarily have *high* global sensitivity. We argue that this is not necessarily the case by considering *Kolmogorov compression.* The Kolmogorov compression of an input string w is simply the encoding of the minimum-size Turing Machine M such that the Turing Machine M will eventually output w when run with an initially empty input tape. It is also easy to see that the Kolmogorov compression scheme has low global sensitivity $\mathcal{O}(\log n)$ for strings of length n as was previously noted in [1]. Let $\texttt{KC} : \Sigma^* \rightarrow \mathfrak{M}$ be the Kolmogorov compression where $\mathfrak{M}$ is the set of all Turing machines. For a string $w \in \Sigma^n$, suppose that $\mathtt{KC}(w) = M \in \mathfrak{M}$. Then for a string $w' \sim w$ that differs on the ith bit, one can obtain M' which outputs w' by (1) running M to obtain w, and (2) changing the ith character of w to obtain w'. Then the description of M' needs the description of M and i plus some constant. Since it takes $\log n$ bits to encode i, It follows that $\mathtt{KC}(w') \leq |M'| \leq |M| + \mathcal{O}(\log n) = \mathtt{KC}(w) + \mathcal{O}(\log n)$. In particular, the global sensitivity of Kolmogorov compression is upper bounded $\mathcal{O}(\log n)$. While Kolmogorov compression is not computable, when it comes to efficient compression ratios, Kolmogorov compression is at least as effective as any other compression scheme, i.e., for any compression scheme `Compress` there is a universal constant C such that $|\mathtt{KC}(w)| \leq C + |\mathtt{Compress}(w)|$ for all string $w \in \Sigma^*$.[4] Thus, the goal of designing a compression algorithm with low global sensitivity does not need to be inconsistent with the goal of designing a compression algorithm that achieves good compression rates.

We note that one can construct a *computable* variant of Kolmogorov compression CKC that preserves low global sensitivity and is competitive with any efficiently computable compression algorithm although the compression algorithm CKC itself is computationally inefficient. Instead of outputting the minimum-size Turing machine, one can output the *minimum-score* Turing machine M followed by $1 \circ 0^{\log t_M}$ (where t_M is the running time of the machine M), where the *score* of a Turing machine M is defined as $\mathsf{Score}(M) := |M| + 1 + \log t_M$.[5] Since the length of the compression becomes the score of the minimum-score Turing machine, one can similarly argue that this computable variant of Kolmogorov compression has global sensitivity $\mathcal{O}(\log n)$. To see that the compression scheme is computable, note that any string w of length n will have compression length at most $\mathcal{O}(n + \log n)$, i.e., the machine M_w which hardcodes w and copies it to the output tape in $\mathcal{O}(n)$ has $\mathsf{Score}(M_w) = \mathcal{O}(n + \log n)$. Thus, to find the turing machine M minimizing $\mathsf{Score}(M)$ we only need to enumerate Turing machines with description length at most $\mathcal{O}(n + \log n)$ and we only need to run each of these TMs for at most $2^{\mathcal{O}(n+\log n)}$ steps since machines that run longer than this cannot have minimum score. While the compression take exponential time, it is computable as the total amount of work is finite.

It is also easy to see that the compression rate for our computable variant of Kolmogorov compression is at least as good as *any* efficiently computable compression algorithm, i.e., for any compression scheme `Compress` running in time $\mathcal{O}(n^c)$ for some constant c and *any* string $w \in \Sigma^n$ we have $|\mathtt{CKC}(w)| \leq$

[4] The Turing Machine M can implement any decompression algorithm. We can hardcode $z = \mathtt{Compress}(w)$ to obtain a new machine M_z which simulates M on the input z to recover w.

[5] Briefly, any string w of length n will have compression length at most $\mathcal{O}(n + \log n)$, i.e., consider the machine M_w which hardcodes w and copies it to the output tape in $\mathcal{O}(n)$ steps we have $\mathsf{Score}(M_w) = \mathcal{O}(n + \log n)$. Thus, to find the minimum score TM, we only need to enumerate Turing machines with description length at most $\mathcal{O}(n + \log n)$ and we only need to run each of these TMs for at most $2^{\mathcal{O}(n+\log n)}$ steps. This will take exponential time, but the total amount of work is still finite and hence the compression algorithm is computable.

$|\texttt{Compress}(w)| + \log n^c + \mathcal{O}(1) = |\texttt{Compress}(w)| + \mathcal{O}(\log n)$. This implies that a computable compression scheme which achieves good compression ratios does not necessarily have high global sensitivity.

Proposition 1. *Let* $\texttt{CKC} : \Sigma^* \to \mathfrak{M} \times \{0,1\}^*$ *be the computable variant of Kolmogorov compression. Then* $\texttt{GS}_{\texttt{CKC}}(n) = \mathcal{O}(\log n)$.

Proof Sketch. (See Appendix C for a more rigorous proof.) For a string $w \in \Sigma^n$, suppose that $\texttt{CKC}(w) = (M, 1 \circ 0^{t_M})$ where M is the minimum-score Turing Machine that outputs w running in time t_M. For $w' \sim w$ that differs on the ith bit, one can obtain a Turing Machine M' that outputs w' by running M to obtain w and then changing the ith character of w to obtain w'. Then the running time of M' is $t_{M'} = t_M + \mathcal{O}(n)$. Furthermore, the description of M' needs the description of M plus i plus some constant, which implies $|M'| \le |M| + \mathcal{O}(\log n)$ since it takes $\log n$ bits to encode i.

Let $\texttt{CKC}(w') = (M'', 1 \circ 0^{t_{M''}})$ where M'' is the minimum-score Turing Machine that outputs w' with running time $t_{M''}$. Then by definition, we have $\mathsf{Score}(M'') \le \mathsf{Score}(M')$. Hence,

$$\begin{aligned}|\texttt{CKC}(w')| &= |M''| + 1 + \log t_{M''} = \mathsf{Score}(M'') \le \mathsf{Score}(M') = |M'| + 1 + \log t_{M'} \\ &\le |M| + \mathcal{O}(\log n) + \log(t_M + \mathcal{O}(n)) \le |M| + \log t_M + \mathcal{O}(\log n) \\ &= |\texttt{CKC}(w)| + \mathcal{O}(\log n),\end{aligned}$$

which implies $\texttt{GS}_{\texttt{CKC}}(n) = \max_{w \in \Sigma^n} \max_{w' : w \sim w'} ||\texttt{CKC}(w)| - |\texttt{CKC}(w')|| = \mathcal{O}(\log n)$. Note that $\log(t_M + \mathcal{O}(n)) \le \max\{\log t_M, \log \mathcal{O}(n)\} + 1$ and the last inequality above holds whatever the maximum is between $\log t_M$ and $\log \mathcal{O}(n)$. □

Appendices

A Upper Bound for the Global Sensitivity of the LZ77 Compression Scheme: Missing Proofs

Definition 4. *Let* $\texttt{Compress} : \Sigma^* \to (\Sigma')^*$ *be the LZ77 compression scheme and* w, w' *be strings of length* n. *Let* $(B_1, \ldots, B_t) \leftarrow \texttt{Compress}(w)$ *and* $(B'_1, \ldots, B'_{t'}) \leftarrow \texttt{Compress}(w')$. *Then we say that for* $k \in [t']$, *the block* B'_k starts inside B_i, $i \in [t]$, *if and only if* $s_i \le s'_k \le f_i$.

We can also define a predicate $\mathsf{StartInside} : \mathbb{Z} \times \mathbb{Z} \to \{0,1\}$ *for the blocks above, where*

$$\mathsf{StartInside}(i,k) := \begin{cases} 1 \text{ if } i \in [t] \wedge k \in [t'] \wedge s_i \le s'_k \le f_i, \text{ and} \\ 0 \text{ otherwise.} \end{cases}$$

That is, $\mathsf{StartInside}(i,k) = 1$ *if and only if* B'_k *starts inside* B_i. *Let* $\mathcal{M}_i$ *be the set of indices of blocks for compressing* w' *which start inside* B_i *defined as follows:* $\mathcal{M}_i := \{k \in [t'] : \mathsf{StartInside}(i,k) = 1\}$. *We further define* $\mathcal{B}_m$ *to be the set of indices* $i \in [t]$ *(of blocks for compressing* w*) where the length of the set* $\mathcal{M}_i$ *equals* m, *i.e.,* $\mathcal{B}_m = \{i \in [t] : |\mathcal{M}_i| = m\}$.

A.1 Analyzing the Positions of Blocks

Claim 8. *Let* $\texttt{Compress} : (\Sigma)^* \rightarrow (\Sigma')^*$ *be the LZ77 compression function and* w, w' *be strings of length* n *and* $w \sim w'$. *Then* $||\texttt{Compress}(w)| - |\texttt{Compress}(w')|| \leq t_2(2\lceil\log n\rceil + \lceil\log|\Sigma|\rceil)$.

Proof of Claim 8. Let $(B_1, \ldots, B_t) \leftarrow \texttt{Compress}(w)$ and $(B'_1, \ldots, B'_{t'}) \leftarrow \texttt{Compress}(w')$. We first observe that there are t blocks in $\texttt{Compress}(w)$ and encoding each block we need $2\lceil\log n\rceil + \lceil\log|\Sigma|\rceil$ bits, since each block consists of two integers q_i and ℓ_i, and one character c_i with $0 \leq q_i, \ell_i \leq n-1$ and $c_i \in \Sigma$. Hence, $|\texttt{Compress}(w)| = t(2\lceil\log n\rceil + \lceil\log|\Sigma|\rceil)$. and $|\texttt{Compress}(w')| = t'(2\lceil\log n\rceil + \lceil\log|\Sigma|\rceil)$. Then, $|\texttt{Compress}(w)| - |\texttt{Compress}(w')| = |t - t'|\,|2\lceil\log n\rceil + \lceil\log|\Sigma|\rceil|$. By Claim 1 above, we observe that $|t - t'| \leq t_2$. Hence, we have
$||\texttt{Compress}(w)| - |\texttt{Compress}(w')|| \leq t_2(2\lceil\log n\rceil + \lceil\log|\Sigma|\rceil)$. □

A.2 Counting Type-2 Blocks for LZ77

Reminder of Lemma 2. *Let* $\texttt{Compress} : \Sigma^* \rightarrow (\Sigma')^*$ *be the LZ77 compression function and* w, w' *be strings of length* n *and* $w \sim w'$. *Let* $(B_1, \ldots, B_t) \leftarrow \texttt{Compress}(w)$ *and* $(B'_1, \ldots, B'_{t'}) \leftarrow \texttt{Compress}(w')$. *Then* $t_2 \leq \frac{\sqrt[3]{9}}{2}n^{2/3} + \frac{\sqrt[3]{3}}{2}n^{1/3} + 1$.

Proof of Lemma 2. To prove Lemma 2, we need the following claims.

Claim 9. *If* $i \in \mathcal{B}_2$ *then either (1)* $s_i \leq j \leq f_i$ *or (2)* $j - \ell_i < q_i \leq j$.

Proof. We first observe that it has to be either $j \geq s_i$ or $j < s_i$.

- If $j \geq s_i$, then we want to show that $s_i \leq j \leq f_i$. Suppose for contradiction that $j > f_i$. Then we have $w[1, f_i] = w'[1, f_i]$, i.e., two substrings are identical. Hence, by definition of the LZ77 compression algorithm, the block constructions are also the same, i.e., $s_i = s'_i$ and $f_i = f'_i$, where s'_i and f'_i denote the starting and finishing index for the block B'_i for compressing w'. This implies that $\mathcal{M}_i = \{i\}$ and $i \in \mathcal{B}_1$. Contradiction since $i \in \mathcal{B}_2$. Hence, we have $s_i \leq j \leq f_i$ if $j \geq s_i$.
- If $j < s_i$, then we want to show that $j - \ell_i < q_i \leq j$, i.e., $q_i \leq j < q_i + \ell_i$. Suppose for contradiction that $j \notin [q_i, q_i + \ell_i - 1]$. Then we have

$$w[s_i, f_i - 1] = w[q_i, q_i + \ell_i - 1] = w'[q_i, q_i + \ell_i - 1] = w'[s_i, f_i - 1]. \quad (1)$$

  Let k be the smallest element in $\mathcal{M}_i$, i.e., $s_i \leq s'_k \leq f_i$ but $s'_{k-1} < s_i$.
  - ∘ If $s'_k = f_i$, then if there is another $k' \in \mathcal{M}_i$ with $k' \neq k$, then by choice of k, we have $k < k'$ and therefore $s'_{k'} > f'_k > s'_k = f_i$. Hence, $|\mathcal{M}_i| = 1$ and $i \in \mathcal{B}_1$. Contradiction!

∘ If $s_i \leq s'_k \leq f_i - 1$, then from Eq. (1) and from the fact that $f_i = s_i + \ell_i$, we observe that the substring $w'[s_i, f_i - 1]$ can be obtained by shifting the substring $w'[q_i, q_i + \ell_i - 1]$ by $s_i - q_i$. Hence,

$$\begin{aligned} w'[s'_k, f_i - 1] &= w'[s'_k, s_i + \ell_i - 1] \\ &= w'[s'_k - (s_i - q_i), s_i + \ell_i - 1 - (s_i - q_i)] \\ &= w'[q_i + (s'_k - s_i), q_i + \ell_i - 1], \end{aligned}$$

which implies that $f'_k \geq f_i$ by definition of the LZ77 compression algorithm. If there is another $k' \in \mathcal{M}_i$ with $k' \neq k$, then by choice of k, we have $k < k'$ and therefore $s'_{k'} > f'_k \geq f_i$. Hence, $|\mathcal{M}_i| = 1$ and $i \in \mathcal{B}_1$. Contradiction!

Hence, we have $j \in [q_i, q_i + \ell_i - 1]$ and therefore $q_i \leq j < q_i + \ell_i$ if $j < s_i$.

Taken together, we can conclude that if $i \in \mathcal{B}_2$ then either $s_i \leq j \leq f_i$ or $q_i \leq j < q_i + \ell_i$ must hold.

□

Claim 10. *If* $i_1, i_2 \in \mathcal{B}_2$ *then* $(q_{i_1}, \ell_{i_1}) \neq (q_{i_2}, \ell_{i_2})$.

Proof. Intuitively, we prove the claim by contradiction. Suppose there exists $i_1, i_2 \in \mathcal{B}_2$ such that $(q_{i_1}, \ell_{i_1}) = (q_{i_2}, \ell_{i_2})$. Then for the first block of `Compress`(w') that starts inside B_{i_2}, we can copy a substring until at least the end of B_{i_2} either from $w'[q_{i_2}, q_{i_2} + \ell_{i_2} - 1]$ or from B_{i_1} since at least one of them does not contain the differing index j by Claim 9. We remark that the same intuition applies for the LZ77 with self-referencing as well—see Claim 13 in Appendix A.3 for details. Below we give the formal proof of Claim 10.

Suppose for contradiction that there exist distinct $i_1, i_2 \in \mathcal{B}_2$ such that $(q_{i_1}, \ell_{i_1}) = (q_{i_2}, \ell_{i_2})$. Without loss of generality, let $i_1 < i_2$. Now, we consider the following cases:

- *Case 1:* $j < s_{i_1}$. Since $i_1 < i_2$, we observe that $j < s_{i_1} < s_{i_2}$. Let $k \in \mathcal{M}_{i_2}$ be the *smallest* element in $\mathcal{M}_{i_2}$. Since $q_{i_1} = q_{i_2}$ and $\ell_{i_1} = \ell_{i_2}$ and $j < s_{i_1}$, we have $w[q_{i_1}, q_{i_1} + \ell_{i_1} - 1] = w[s_{i_1}, f_{i_1} - 1] = w'[s_{i_1}, f_{i_1} - 1]$ and $w[q_{i_2}, q_{i_2} + \ell_{i_2} - 1] = w[s_{i_2}, f_{i_2} - 1] = w'[s_{i_2}, f_{i_2} - 1]$. Therefore, we have

$$w'[s'_k, f_{i_2} - 1] = w'[s_{i_1} + (s'_k - s_{i_2}), f_{i_1} - 1]. \tag{2}$$

  We claim $f'_k \geq f_{i_2}$. Suppose for contradiction that $f'_k < f_{i_2}$. By definition of LZ77, $w'[s'_k, f'_k - 1]$ is the longest substring of $w'[1, s'_k - 1]$ starting at s'_k. However, Eq. (2) implies that $w'[s'_k, f_{i_2} - 1]$ is also a substring of $w'[1, s'_k - 1]$ which is *longer than* $w'[s'_k, f'_k - 1]$, which is a contradiction. Hence, we have $f'_k \geq f_{i_2}$.
  If there is another $k' \in \mathcal{M}_{i_2}$ such that $k' \neq k$ then, by choice of k, we have $k < k'$ and therefore $s'_{k'} > f'_k \geq f_{i_2}$. This contradicts the definition of $\mathcal{M}_{i_2}$ since block $B'_{k'}$ does not start inside block B_{i_2}. It follows that $|\mathcal{M}_{i_2}| \leq 1$ and therefore $i_2 \in \mathcal{B}_1$. This is a contradiction!

- *Case 2:* $j \geq s_{i_1}$. We then observe $s_{i_1} \leq j < f_{i_1}$ (if $f_{i_1} \leq j$ then only one block would have started inside B_{i_1} by observing $w[s_{i_1}, f_{i_1} - 1] = w'[s_{i_1}, f_{i_1} - 1]$, hence $i \in \mathcal{B}_1$, which is a contradiction since $i \in \mathcal{B}_2$). And since we assumed $i_1 < i_2$, we further have $s_{i_1} \leq j < f_{i_1} < s_{i_2}$. Now since $s_{i_2} > j$, by Claim 9, we have $q_{i_2} \leq j < q_{i_2} + \ell_{i_2}$. Since $q_{i_1} = q_{i_2}$ and $\ell_{i_1} = \ell_{i_2}$ by our assumption, we then have $q_{i_1} \leq j < q_{i_1} + \ell_{i_1}$. This is a contradiction since $s_{i_1} \leq j < f_{i_1}$!

Taken together, we can conclude that if $i_1, i_2 \in \mathcal{B}_2$ then $(q_{i_1}, \ell_{i_1}) \neq (q_{i_2}, \ell_{i_2})$.

Claim 11. *Let* $\mathcal{B}_2^\ell := \{i \in \mathcal{B}_2 : \ell_i = \ell\}$ *and suppose that* $s_{i^*} \leq j \leq f_{i^*}$ *for some* $i^* \in [t]$. *Then* $|\mathcal{B}_2^\ell| \leq \ell$ *for all* $\ell \neq \ell_{i^*}$, *and* $|\mathcal{B}_2^{\ell_{i^*}}| \leq \ell_{i^*} + 1$.

Proof. We first observe from Claim 9 that if $i \in \mathcal{B}_2$, either $s_i \leq j \leq f_i$ or $j - \ell_i < q_i \leq j$ holds. Let $i^* \in [t]$ be the unique index such that $s_{i^*} \leq j \leq f_{i^*}$.

- If $\ell \neq \ell_{i^*}$, then for all $i \in \mathcal{B}_2^\ell$, we have $j - \ell_i < q_i \leq j$ since $j \notin [s_i, f_i]$ for all $i \in \mathcal{B}_2^\ell$. Suppose for contradiction that there exists some $\ell' \neq \ell_{i^*}$ such that $|\mathcal{B}_2^{\ell'}| \geq \ell' + 1$. Then we have at least $\ell' + 1$ i's such that $j - \ell' < q_i \leq j$. Then by the pigeonhole principle, there exists some $i_1, i_2 \in \mathcal{B}_2^{\ell'}$ such that $q_{i_1} = q_{i_2}$, which implies that $(q_{i_1}, \ell_{i_1} = \ell') = (q_{i_2}, \ell_{i_2} = \ell')$. Contradiction by Claim 10! Hence, $|\mathcal{B}_2^\ell| \leq \ell$ for all $\ell \neq \ell_{i^*}$.
- If $\ell = \ell_{i^*}$, then we clearly see $i^* \in \mathcal{B}_2^{\ell_{i^*}}$. Then what is remained to show is that $|\mathcal{B}_2^{\ell_{i^*}} \setminus \{i^*\}| \leq \ell_{i^*}$. For all $i \in \mathcal{B}_2^{\ell_{i^*}} \setminus \{i^*\}$, we have $j - \ell_i < q_i \leq j$ since $s_{i^*} \leq j \leq f_{i^*}$. Now by the previous case analysis, we have $|\mathcal{B}_2^{\ell_{i^*}} \setminus \{i^*\}| \leq \ell_{i^*}$. Hence, $|\mathcal{B}_2^{\ell_{i^*}}| \leq \ell_{i^*} + 1$. □

Let's get back to the proof of Lemma 2. We first observe that block B_i has length $\ell_i + 1$ and the string length is n. Hence, we have $\sum_{i \in \mathcal{B}_2} (\ell_i + 1) \leq n$. Furthermore, we observe that for $i \in \mathcal{B}_2^\ell$, the length of block B_i is $\ell + 1$. Therefore,

$$\sum_{i \in \mathcal{B}_2} (\ell_i + 1) = \sum_{\ell} \sum_{i \in \mathcal{B}_2^\ell} (\ell + 1) = \sum_{\ell} |\mathcal{B}_2^\ell| \, (\ell + 1) \leq n.$$

Let $x_\ell := |\mathcal{B}_2^\ell|$. Observe that $t_2 \leq \sum_\ell x_\ell$. Thus, to bound t_2 we want to maximize $\sum_\ell x_\ell$ subject to the constraints that (here, $i^* \in [t]$ is the *unique* index where $s_{i^*} \leq j \leq f_{i^*}$)

(1) $x_\ell \leq \ell$ for all $\ell \neq \ell_{i^*}$ and $x_{\ell_{i^*}} \leq \ell_{i^*} + 1$, and
(2) $\sum_\ell x_\ell (\ell + 1) \leq n$.

It is clear that the maximum is obtained by setting x_ℓ the maximum possible value for all $\ell \leq z$ (set $x_\ell = \ell$ for all $\ell \leq z$ with $\ell \neq \ell_{i^*}$, and set $x_{\ell_{i^*}} = \ell_{i^*} + 1$ if $\ell_{i^*} \leq z$) and $x_\ell = 0$ for all $\ell > z$ for some threshold value z. It is followed by a simple swapping argument. Let $c_\ell = \ell$ if $\ell \neq \ell_{i^*}$ and $c_{\ell_{i^*}} = \ell_{i^*} + 1$. Suppose we have a feasible solution $(x_0, \ldots, x_{n-1})$ which satisfies the constraints and we have $0 < x_{\ell_1} < c_{\ell_1}$ and $0 < x_{\ell_2} < c_{\ell_2}$ with $\ell_1 < \ell_2$. Now define a new set of solution $(x'_0, \ldots, x'_{n-1})$ where $x'_{\ell_1} = x_{\ell_1} + 1, x'_{\ell_2} = x_{\ell_2} - 1$, and $x'_i = x_i$ for all

$i \neq \ell_1, \ell_2$. Then we observe that $0 \leq x'_\ell \leq c_\ell$ for all $\ell = 0, 1, \ldots, n-1$, and furthermore,

$$\begin{aligned}\sum_\ell x'_\ell(\ell+1) &= x'_{\ell_1}(\ell_1+1) + x'_{\ell_2}(\ell_2+1) + \sum_{\ell \neq \ell_1, \ell_2} x'_\ell(\ell+1) \\ &= (x_{\ell_1}+1)(\ell_1+1) + (x_{\ell_2}-1)(\ell_2+1) + \sum_{\ell \neq \ell_1, \ell_2} x_\ell(\ell+1) \\ &= \sum_\ell x_\ell(\ell+1) + (\ell_1 - \ell_2) < \sum_\ell x_\ell(\ell+1) \leq n,\end{aligned}$$

which implies that $(x'_0, \ldots, x'_{n-1})$ is also a feasible solution. We can repeat these swaps to keep the solution feasible but with a higher value in x_ℓ for a smaller index ℓ, and finally, with having x_ℓ the maximum possible value for all $\ell \leq z$ for some threshold z. Note that x_z could be less than z, i.e., for the threshold z, we have $x_z = c$ for some $0 < c \leq z$.

To find the threshold z, we first observe that $\left[\sum_{\ell=0}^{z-1} \ell(\ell+1)\right] + x_z(z+1) = \sum_{\ell \geq 0} x_\ell(\ell+1) \leq n$ by condition (2). Simplifying the sum we have $\left[\sum_{\ell=0}^{z-1} \ell(\ell+1)\right] + x_z(z+1) = \frac{1}{3}(z-1)z(z+1) + x_z(z+1) \geq z^3/3$ where the last inequality follows because $x_z \geq 1$. Thus, we have $z^3 \leq 3n$ and $z \leq \sqrt[3]{3n}$. Setting this value of z, we have

$$t_2 \leq \sum_\ell x_\ell \leq \left(\sum_{\ell=0}^{\sqrt[3]{3n}} \ell\right) + 1 = \frac{\sqrt[3]{9}}{2} n^{2/3} + \frac{\sqrt[3]{3}}{2} n^{1/3} + 1,$$

where the addition of 1 in the inequality above comes from the case if $\ell_{i^*} \leq z$.

A.3 Counting Type-2 Blocks for LZ77 with Self-Referencing

For the LZ77 compression scheme with self-referencing, we can prove an analogous claim as stated in Lemma 4.

Lemma 4. *Let* $\texttt{Compress}_{\texttt{SR}} : \Sigma^* \to (\Sigma')^*$ *be the LZ77 compression function with self-referencing and* $w \sim w'$ *be strings of length* n*. Let* $(B_1, \ldots, B_t) \leftarrow \texttt{Compress}_{\texttt{SR}}(w)$ *and* $(B'_1, \ldots, B'_{t'}) \leftarrow \texttt{Compress}_{\texttt{SR}}(w')$*. Then* $t_2 \leq \frac{\sqrt[3]{9}}{2} n^{2/3} + \frac{\sqrt[3]{3}}{2} n^{1/3} + 1$.

Following a similar proof strategy to Sect. 4.2, we verify that the same claims hold for LZ77 with self-referencing as well.

Claim 12. *For LZ77 with self-referencing, if* $i \in \mathcal{B}_2$ *then either (1)* $s_i \leq j \leq f_i$ *or (2)* $j - \ell_i < q_i \leq j$.

Proof. Since the only difference between the non-overlapping LZ77 and the LZ77 with self-referencing is that we allow for $\ell_i + q_i - 1 >$ ctc and this does not affect the proof at all, we can follow the exact same proof of Claim 9.

□

Claim 13. *For LZ77 with self-referencing, if $i_1, i_2 \in \mathcal{B}_2$ then $(q_{i_1}, \ell_{i_1}) \neq (q_{i_2}, \ell_{i_2})$.*

Proof. We can follow a similar proof strategy with Claim 10, except that since we are considering LZ77 with self-referencing, in Case 1, $w'[s'_k, f'_k - 1]$ becomes the longest substring of $w'[1, f'_k - 1]$. However, Eq. (2) implies that $w'[s'_k, f_{i_2} - 1]$ is also a substring of $w'[1, s'_k - 1]$, which is a substring of $w'[1, f'_k - 1]$. This is a contradiction since $w'[s'_k, f'_k - 1]$ does *not* become the longest substring of $w'[1, f'_k - 1]$. Hence, we have the same conclusion that $f'_k \geq f_{i_2}$, and the rest of the proof follows the same as Claim 10.

□

Claim 14. *For LZ77 with self-referencing, let $\mathcal{B}_2^\ell := \{i \in \mathcal{B}_2 : \ell_i = \ell\}$ and suppose that $s_{i^*} \leq j \leq f_{i^*}$ for some $i^* \in [t]$. Then $|\mathcal{B}_2^\ell| \leq \ell$ for all $\ell \neq \ell_{i^*}$, and $|\mathcal{B}_2^{\ell_{i^*}}| \leq \ell_{i^*} + 1$.*

Proof. Since the proof of Claim 11 relied on Claim 9 and Claim 10 along with the pigeonhole principle, we can follow the same proof strategy relying on Claim 12 and Claim 13 instead.

□

Proof of Lemma 4. Since the proof of Lemma 2 did not exploit the restriction that the non-overlapping LZ77 has, we can follow the same proof of Lemma 2.

Theorem 6. *Let $\texttt{Compress}_{\texttt{SR}} : (\Sigma)^* \to (\Sigma')^*$ be the LZ77 compression function with self-referencing, with unbounded sliding window size $W = n$. Then*

$$\mathrm{GS}_{\texttt{Compress}_{\texttt{SR}}} \leq \left(\frac{\sqrt[3]{9}}{2} n^{2/3} + \frac{\sqrt[3]{3}}{2} n^{1/3} + 3 \right) (2\lceil \log n \rceil + \lceil \log |\Sigma| \rceil) = \mathcal{O}\left(n^{2/3} \log n\right).$$

Proof. As discussed in Sect. 4.1, we see that Lemma 1 essentially holds similarly for the self-referencing case except that there might be one type-3 block (i.e., $t_3 \leq 1$), i.e., the block containing the edited position j, as stated in [1, p.18]. Thus, we have $t = t_0 + t_1 + t_2 + t_3$ and we further observe that $t' = \sum_{m=0}^{3} m \cdot t_m = t_1 + 2t_2 + 3t_3$ which is similar to Claim 1. Hence, $t' - t = 2t_3 + t_2 - t_0 \leq t_2 + 2t_3 \leq t_2 + 2$. Hence, by Lemma 4,

$$\begin{aligned} ||\texttt{Compress}(w)| - |\texttt{Compress}(w')|| &= |t - t'|(2\lceil \log n \rceil + \lceil \log |\Sigma| \rceil) \\ &\leq \left(\frac{\sqrt[3]{9}}{2} n^{2/3} + \frac{\sqrt[3]{3}}{2} n^{1/3} + 3 \right) (2\lceil \log n \rceil + \lceil \log |\Sigma| \rceil). \end{aligned}$$

Since this inequality hold for arbitrary $w \sim w'$ of length n, we have

$$\begin{aligned} \mathrm{GS}_{\texttt{Compress}} &= \max_{w \in \Sigma^n} \max_{w' \in \Sigma^n \text{ s.t. } w \sim w'} ||\texttt{Compress}(w)| - |\texttt{Compress}(w')|| \\ &\leq \left(\frac{\sqrt[3]{9}}{2} n^{2/3} + \frac{\sqrt[3]{3}}{2} n^{1/3} + 3 \right) (2\lceil \log n \rceil + \lceil \log |\Sigma| \rceil) = \mathcal{O}\left(n^{2/3} \log n\right). \end{aligned}$$

□

A.4 Bounded Sliding Window

Reminder of Claim 2. *Let* $\texttt{Compress} : (\Sigma)^* \to (\Sigma')^*$ *be the LZ77 compression function with sliding window size* W *and* $w \sim w'$ *be strings of length* n *with* $w[j] \neq w'[j]$. *Let* $(B_1, \ldots, B_t) \leftarrow \texttt{Compress}(w)$ *and* $(B'_1, \ldots, B'_{t'}) \leftarrow \texttt{Compress}(w')$. *If* $B_i \in \mathcal{B}_2$ *then* $s_i \leq j + W$.

Proof. Let $B_i = [q_i, \ell_i, c_i]$ such that $s_i > j + W$. Then we will show that $B_i \in \mathcal{B}_0 \cup \mathcal{B}_1$.

- If $B_i \in \mathcal{B}_0$ then we clearly have $B_i \in \mathcal{B}_0 \cup \mathcal{B}_1$.
- If $B_i \notin \mathcal{B}_0$ then let B'_k be the first block that starts inside B_i. We argue that $f'_k \geq f_i$, which implies that $B_i \in \mathcal{B}_1$. Suppose for contradiction that $f'_k < f_i$. Then we have that $w'[s'_k, f'_k - 1]$ is the longest substring of $w'[\max\{1, s'_k - W\}, s'_k - 1]$ that starts at s'_k.
  Since $s_i > j + W$, we have that $j < s_i - W$ and therefore $w[q_i, q_i + \ell_i - 1] = w'[q_i, q_i + \ell_i - 1]$ since we only look at the previous W characters when finding the longest substring to construct B_i. Hence,
$$\begin{aligned} w'[q_i + (s'_k - s_i), q_i + \ell_i - 1] &= w[s_i + (s'_k - s_i), f_i - 1] \\ &= w[s'_k, f_i - 1] \\ &= w'[s'_k, f_i - 1]. \end{aligned}$$
  Furthermore, since $q_i \geq s_i - W$ by definition of LZ77, we observe $q_i + (s'_k - s_i) \geq s'_k - W$, meaning that $w'[s'_k, f_i - 1]$ is also a substring of $w'[\max\{1, s'_k - W\}, s'_k - 1]$ that starts at s'_k. But since $f'_k < f_i$, $w'[s'_k, f_i - 1]$ is a *longer* substring of $w'[\max\{1, s'_k - W\}, s'_k - 1]$ that starts at s'_k than $w'[s'_k, f'_k - 1]$. Contradiction! This contradiction is due to the assumption that $f'_k < f_i$. Hence, we have $f'_k \geq f_i$ and therefore $B_i \in \mathcal{B}_1$. Therefore, $B_i \in \mathcal{B}_0 \cup \mathcal{B}_1$.

Finally, if $B_i \in \mathcal{B}_2$ then $B_i \notin \mathcal{B}_0 \cup \mathcal{B}_1$, hence we have $s_i \leq j + W$.

□

Theorem 7. *Let* $\texttt{Compress}_{\texttt{SR}} : (\Sigma)^* \to (\Sigma')^*$ *be the LZ77 compression function with self-referencing, with sliding window size* W. *Then*

$$\mathsf{GS}_{\texttt{Compress}_{\texttt{SR}}} \leq \left(\frac{\sqrt[3]{81}}{2} W^{2/3} + \frac{\sqrt[3]{9}}{2} W^{1/3} + 5 \right) (2\lceil \log n \rceil + \lceil \log |\Sigma| \rceil) = \mathcal{O}\left(W^{2/3} \log n \right).$$

B Lower Bound for the Global Sensitivity of the LZ77 Compression Scheme: Missing Proofs

Reminder of Claim 3. *Let* $m \in \mathbb{N}$ *and* $(w, w') \leftarrow \mathsf{QuinStr}(m)$. *Then* $|w| = |w'| = \Theta(m^3 \log m)$. *In particular, for* $m \geq 4$, $\frac{2}{3} m^3 \lceil \log m \rceil < |w| = |w'| < m^3 \lceil \log m \rceil$.

Proof. We first observe that $|w| = |w'|$ since they only differ by one character (2 and 3 in S_w and $S_{w'}$, respectively). We then observe that $|S_w| = 4m\lceil\log m\rceil + 2$ since we have $4m$ encodings with length $\lceil\log m\rceil$ each along with the character 2 and 4, which has length 1 each. And similarly, for $2 \le \ell \le m$ and $1 \le u \le \ell - 1$, we observe that $|S_{\ell,u}| = 2\ell\lceil\log m\rceil + 1$. Hence,

$$\begin{aligned}
|w| &= |S_w| + \sum_{\ell=2}^{m}\sum_{u=1}^{\ell-1}(1 + |S_{\ell,u}|) \\
&= 4m\lceil\log m\rceil + 2 + \sum_{\ell=2}^{m}\sum_{u=1}^{\ell-1}(2 + 2\ell\lceil\log m\rceil) \\
&= 4m\lceil\log m\rceil + 2 + \sum_{\ell=2}^{m}\left[2(\ell-1) + 2\ell(\ell-1)\lceil\log m\rceil\right] \\
&= 4m\lceil\log m\rceil + 2 + (m-1)m + \lceil\log m\rceil \cdot \frac{2}{3}\left(m^3 - m\right) \\
&= \frac{2}{3}m^3\lceil\log m\rceil + \frac{10}{3}m\lceil\log m\rceil + (m-1)m + 2.
\end{aligned}$$

It is clear that $|w| > \frac{2}{3}m^3\lceil\log m\rceil$ since the term $\frac{10}{3}m\lceil\log m\rceil + (m-1)m + 2$ is always positive for $m \ge 1$. Now we consider the upper bound. For $m = 4$, we can directly show that $\frac{2}{3}m^3\lceil\log m\rceil + \frac{10}{3}m\lceil\log m\rceil + (m-1)m + 2 = \frac{378}{3} < 128 = m^3\lceil\log m\rceil$. For $m \ge 5$, we have $m^2 \ge 25$ and $5(m-1)m + 10 < 5(m-1)m + 5m = 5m^2 \le m^3$, which implies

$$\begin{aligned}
|w| &= \frac{2}{3}m^3\lceil\log m\rceil + \frac{10}{3}m\lceil\log m\rceil + (m-1)m + 2 \\
&= \frac{2}{3}m^3\lceil\log m\rceil + \frac{10}{25}\cdot\frac{25}{3}m\lceil\log m\rceil + \frac{1}{5}\left[5(m-1)m + 10\right] \\
&< \frac{2}{3}m^3\lceil\log m\rceil + \frac{10}{25}\cdot\frac{1}{3}m^3\lceil\log m\rceil + \frac{1}{5}m^3 \\
&< \frac{2}{3}m^3\lceil\log m\rceil + \frac{10}{25}\cdot\frac{1}{3}m^3\lceil\log m\rceil + \frac{1}{5}m^3\lceil\log m\rceil = m^3\lceil\log m\rceil.
\end{aligned}$$

Taken together, we can conclude that $|w| = |w'| = \Theta(m^3\log m)$.

Reminder of Claim 4. *For any integer $m \ge 2$, the function*

$$f(\ell, u) := \frac{(\ell-2)(\ell-1)}{2} + (\ell - u)$$

defined over integers ℓ and u such that $2 \le \ell \le m$ and $1 \le u \le \ell - 1$ is injective, and its range is $[\frac{(m-1)m}{2}]$.

Proof. We prove this by induction on m. For the base case ($m = 2$), the domain of the function f only consists of a single element $\{(2, 1)\}$, therefore the function is clearly injective and $f(2, 1) = 1$ shows that its range is $[1] = [\frac{(m-1)m}{2}]$. Now suppose that the claim holds for some $m = m'$ and consider the case where

$m = m'+1$. By inductive hypothesis, we already know that $f(\ell, u)$ is an injective function for $2 \le \ell \le m'$ and $1 \le u \le \ell - 1$ and its range is $[\frac{(m'-1)m'}{2}]$. When $\ell = m'+1$ and $1 \le u \le \ell - 1 = m'$, we observe that

$$f(\ell, u) = f(m'+1, u) = \frac{(m'-1)m'}{2} + (m'+1-u),$$

hence the output of the function is all different for different u's, and its range is $[\frac{(m'-1)m'}{2}+1, \frac{(m'-1)m'}{2}+m'] = [\frac{(m'-1)m'}{2}+1, \frac{m'(m'+1)}{2}]$. Since $[\frac{(m'-1)m'}{2}]$ and $[\frac{(m'-1)m'}{2}+1, \frac{m'(m'+1)}{2}]$ are mutually exclusive, we can conclude that the function is still injective over integers ℓ and u such that $2 \le \ell \le m'+1$ and $1 \le u \le \ell - 1$, and its range is $[\frac{(m'-1)m'}{2}] \cup [\frac{(m'-1)m'}{2}+1, \frac{m'(m'+1)}{2}] = [\frac{m'(m'+1)}{2}]$, which concludes the proof.

□

Reminder of Claim 6. *$S^L_{\ell,u} \circ 4 \circ S^F_{\ell,u-1}$ does not repeat for different ℓ and u such that $3 \le \ell \le m$ and $2 \le u \le \ell - 1$.*

Proof. We have $S^L_{\ell,u} = \mathsf{E}(m - u + \ell)^2$ and $S^F_{\ell,u-1} = \mathsf{E}(m - u + 2)^2$. Since the pairs $(-u+\ell, -u+2)$ for $3 \le \ell \le m$ and $2 \le u \le \ell - 1$ are all distinct, the claim holds.

□

Reminder of Claim 7. *For $2 \le \ell \le \lfloor \frac{m}{2} \rfloor - 1$, $S^L_{\ell,1} \circ 4 \circ S_{\ell+1,\ell}$ repeats at $S^L_{2\ell,\ell+1} \circ 4 \circ S^{(\ell+1)}_{2\ell,\ell}$.*

Proof. We observe that

$$\begin{aligned} S^L_{2\ell,\ell+1} \circ 4 \circ S^{(\ell+1)}_{2\ell,\ell} &= \mathsf{E}(m - (\ell+1) + 2\ell)^2 \circ 4 \circ \mathsf{E}(m - \ell + 1)^2 \circ \ldots \circ \mathsf{E}(m)^2 \circ 2 \circ \mathsf{E}(m+1)^2 \\ &= \mathsf{E}(m - 1 + \ell)^2 \circ 4 \circ \mathsf{E}(m - \ell + 1)^2 \circ \ldots \circ \mathsf{E}(m)^2 \circ 2 \circ \mathsf{E}(m+1)^2 \\ &= S^L_{\ell,1} \circ 4 \circ S_{\ell+1,\ell}, \end{aligned}$$

which completes the proof.

□

C Rigorous Proof for Proposition 1

Here we give a mathematically rigorous proof of Proposition 1.

Reminder of Proposition 1. *Let $\mathtt{CKC} : \Sigma^* \to \mathfrak{M} \times \{0,1\}^*$ be the computable variant of Kolmogorov compression. Then $\mathtt{GS}_{\mathtt{CKC}}(n) = \mathcal{O}(\log n)$.*

Proof. For a string $w \in \Sigma^n$, suppose that $\mathtt{CKC}(w) = (M, 1 \circ 0^{t_M})$, i.e., M is the minimum-score Turing Machine that outputs w running in time t_M. For $w' \sim w$ that differs on the ith bit, one can obtain a Turing Machine M' that outputs w' as follows:

- Run M to obtain w, and
- Flip the ith bit of w to obtain w'.

Then the running time of M' is $t_{M'} = t_M + \mathcal{O}(n)$, meaning that there exist a constant $C_1 > 0$ and a positive integer n_1 such that for all $n \geq n_1$ we have $t_{M'} \leq t_M + C_1 n$. Furthermore, the description of M' needs the description of M plus i plus some constant, which implies $|M'| \leq |M| + \mathcal{O}(\log n)$ since it takes $\log n$ bits to encode i. Also, this means that there exist a constant $C_2 > 0$ and a positive integer n_2 such that for all $n \geq n_2$ we have $|M'| \leq |M| + C_2 \log n$.

Let $\mathtt{CKC}(w') = (M'', 1 \circ 0^{t_{M''}})$, i.e., M'' is the minimum-score Turing Machine that outputs w' with running time $t_{M''}$. Then by definition, we have $\mathsf{Score}(M'') \leq \mathsf{Score}(M')$. Hence, for all $n \geq \max\{n_1, n_2\}$ we have

$$\begin{aligned}|\mathtt{CKC}(w')| &= |M''| + 1 + \log t_{M''} \\ &= \mathsf{Score}(M'') \\ &\leq \mathsf{Score}(M') \\ &= |M'| + 1 + \log t_{M'} \\ &\leq |M| + C_2 \log n + 1 + \log(t_M + C_1 n).\end{aligned}$$

Now we consider the two cases:

(1) If $t_M \geq C_1 n$, then for all $n \geq \max\{n_1, n_2, 2\}$ we have (recall that log is base 2)

$$\begin{aligned}|\mathtt{CKC}(w')| &\leq |M| + C_2 \log n + 1 + \log(t_M + C_1 n) \\ &\leq |M| + C_2 \log n + 1 + \log(2t_M) \\ &= |M| + 1 + \log t_M + 1 + C_2 \log n \\ &\leq |M| + 1 + \log t_M + (C_2 + 1) \log n \\ &= |\mathtt{CKC}(w)| + (C_2 + 1) \log n.\end{aligned}$$

Hence, $\mathtt{GS}_{\mathtt{CKC}}(n) = \max_{w \in \Sigma^n} \max_{w': w \sim w'} ||\mathtt{CKC}(w)| - |\mathtt{CKC}(w')|| \leq (C_2+1) \log n$ for all $n \geq \max\{n_1, n_2, 2\}$, which implies $\mathtt{GS}_{\mathtt{CKC}}(n) = \mathcal{O}(\log n)$.

(2) If $t_M < C_1 n$, then for all $n \geq \max\{n_1, n_2, 2C_1\}$ we have

$$\begin{aligned}|\mathtt{CKC}(w')| &\leq |M| + C_2 \log n + 1 + \log(t_M + C_1 n) \\ &\leq |M| + C_2 \log n + 1 + \log(2C_1 n) \\ &= |M| + 1 + (C_2 + 2) \log n \\ &\leq |M| + 1 + \log t_M + (C_2 + 2) \log n \\ &= |\mathtt{CKC}(w)| + (C_2 + 2) \log n.\end{aligned}$$

Hence, $\mathtt{GS}_{\mathtt{CKC}}(n) = \max_{w \in \Sigma^n} \max_{w': w \sim w'} ||\mathtt{CKC}(w)| - |\mathtt{CKC}(w')|| \leq (C_2+2) \log n$ for all $n \geq \max\{n_1, n_2, 2C_1\}$, which implies $\mathtt{GS}_{\mathtt{CKC}}(n) = \mathcal{O}(\log n)$.

□

References

1. Akagi, T., Funakoshi, M., Inenaga, S.: Sensitivity of string compressors and repetitiveness measures. Inf. Comput. **291**(C) (2023)
2. Alakuijala, J., Szabadka, Z.: Brotli Compressed Data Format. RFC 7932 (2016)
3. Bannai, H., Charalampopoulos, P., Radoszewski, J.: Maintaining the size of LZ77 on semi-dynamic strings. In: Inenaga, S., Puglisi, S.J. (eds.) 35th Annual Symposium on Combinatorial Pattern Matching (CPM 2024). Leibniz International Proceedings in Informatics (LIPIcs), Dagstuhl, Germany, vol. 296, pp. 3:1–3:20. Schloss Dagstuhl – Leibniz-Zentrum für Informatik (2024)
4. Black, D.L., McGrew, D.: Using Authenticated Encryption Algorithms with the Encrypted Payload of the Internet Key Exchange version 2 (IKEv2) Protocol. RFC 5282 (2008)
5. Blocki, J., Grigorescu, E., Mukherjee, T.: Privately estimating graph parameters in sublinear time. In: Bojańczyk, M., Merelli, E., Woodruff, D.P. (eds.) 49th International Colloquium on Automata, Languages, and Programming (ICALP 2022). Leibniz International Proceedings in Informatics (LIPIcs), Dagstuhl, Germany, vol. 229, pp. 26:1–26:19. Schloss Dagstuhl – Leibniz-Zentrum für Informatik (2022)
6. Blocki, J., Grigorescu, E., Mukherjee, T., Zhou, S.: How to make your approximation algorithm private: a black-box differentially-private transformation for tunable approximation algorithms of functions with low sensitivity. In: Megow, N., Smith, A. (eds.) Approximation, Randomization, and Combinatorial Optimization. Algorithms and Techniques (APPROX/RANDOM 2023). Leibniz International Proceedings in Informatics (LIPIcs), Dagstuhl, Germany, vol. 275, pp. 59:1–59:24. Schloss Dagstuhl – Leibniz-Zentrum für Informatik (2023)
7. Blocki, J., Lee, S., Yepes-Garcia, B.S.: Differentially private compression and the sensitivity of LZ77. Cryptology ePrint Archive, Paper 2025/1733 (2025)
8. Degabriele, J.P.: Hiding the lengths of encrypted messages via gaussian padding. In: Vigna, G., Shi, E. (eds.) ACM CCS 2021, pp. 1549–1565. ACM Press (2021)
9. Deutsch, L.P.: DEFLATE Compressed Data Format Specification version 1.3. RFC 1951 (1996)
10. Dwork, C., McSherry, F., Nissim, K., Smith, A.: Calibrating noise to sensitivity in private data analysis. In: Halevi, S., Rabin, T. (eds.) TCC 2006. LNCS, vol. 3876, pp. 265–284. Springer, Heidelberg (2006). https://doi.org/10.1007/11681878_14
11. Farias, V.A.E., Brito, F.T., Flynn, C., Machado, J.C., Srivastava, D.: Differentially private multi-objective selection: pareto and aggregation approaches (2025)
12. Fisher, D.: CRIME Attack Uses Compression Ratio of TLS Requests as Side Channel to Hijack Secure Sessions. ThreatPost. Accessed 13 Sept 2012
13. Giuliani, S., Inenaga, S., Lipták, Z., Romana, G., Sciortino, M., Urbina, C.: Bit catastrophes for the burrows-wheeler transform. In: Drewes, F., Volkov, M. (eds.) DLT 2023. LNCS, vol. 13911, pp. 86–99. Springer, Cham (2023). https://doi.org/10.1007/978-3-031-33264-7_8
14. Gluck, Y., Harris, N., Prado, A.: BREACH: Reviving the CRIME Attack (2013). https://breachattack.com/
15. Huffman, D.A.: A method for the construction of minimum-redundancy codes. Proc. IRE **40**(9), 1098–1101 (1952)
16. Lagarde, G., Perifel, S.: Lempel-ziv: a "one-bit catastrophe" but not a tragedy. In: Proceedings of the Twenty-Ninth Annual ACM-SIAM Symposium on Discrete Algorithms, pp. 1478–1495. SIAM (2018)

17. Lempel, A., Ziv, J.: A universal algorithm for sequential data compression. IEEE Trans. Inf. Theory **23**(3), 337–343 (1977)
18. Lempel, A., Ziv, J.: Compression of individual sequences via variable-rate coding. IEEE Trans. Inf. Theory **24**(5), 530–536 (1978)
19. Liu, S., Cao, Y., Murakami, T., Liu, J., Yoshikawa, M.: CARGO: crypto-assisted differentially private triangle counting without trusted servers. In: 2024 IEEE 40th International Conference on Data Engineering (ICDE), Los Alamitos, CA, USA, pp. 1671–1684. IEEE Computer Society (2024)
20. Lu, Z., Asghar, H.J., Kaafar, M.A., Webb, D., Dickinson, P.: A differentially private framework for deep learning with convexified loss functions. IEEE Trans. Inf. Forensics Secur. **17**, 2151–2165 (2022)
21. Palacios, R., Fernández-Portillo, A.F., Sánchez-Úbeda, E.F., García-De-Zúñiga, P.: HTB: a very effective method to protect web servers against breach attack to https. IEEE Access **10**, 40381–40390 (2022)
22. Paulsen, B., Sung, C., Peterson, P.A., Wang, C.: Debreach: mitigating compression side channels via static analysis and transformation. In: 2019 34th IEEE/ACM International Conference on Automated Software Engineering (ASE), pp. 899–911. IEEE (2019)
23. Ratliff, Z., Vadhan, S.: A framework for differential privacy against timing attacks. arXiv preprint arXiv:2409.05623 (2024)
24. Rizzo, J., Duong, T.: The CRIME attack. Presentation at Ekoparty 2012 (2012)
25. Sheng, W., Chen, J., Hu, C., Cai, B., Han, M., Yu, J.: Differentially private distance query with asymmetric noise (2025)
26. Song, Y.: Refined techniques for compression side-channel attacks. Master's thesis, ETH Zürich (2024)
27. Tětek, J.: Additive noise mechanisms for making randomized approximation algorithms differentially private. In: Kumar, A., Ron-Zewi, N. (eds.) Approximation, Randomization, and Combinatorial Optimization. Algorithms and Techniques (APPROX/RANDOM 2024). Leibniz International Proceedings in Informatics (LIPIcs), Dagstuhl, Germany, vol. 317, pp. 73:1–73:20. Schloss Dagstuhl – Leibniz-Zentrum für Informatik (2024)
28. Ünsal, A., Önen, M.: Chernoff information as a privacy constraint for adversarial classification. In: 2024 60th Annual Allerton Conference on Communication, Control, and Computing, pp. 1–8 (2024)
29. Wang, H., Zhao, D., Wang, H.: Dynamic global sensitivity for differentially private contextual bandits. In: Proceedings of the 16th ACM Conference on Recommender Systems, RecSys 2022, pp. 179–187. Association for Computing Machinery, New York (2022)
30. Welch, T.: A technique for high-performance data compression. Computer **17**(6), 8–19 (1984)
31. Wicker, M., et al.: Certification for differentially private prediction in gradient-based training (2024)
32. Zhang, M., Liu, X., Yin, L.: Sensitivity estimation for differentially private query processing (2023)

Securing Unbounded Differential Privacy Against Timing Attacks

Zachary Ratliff(✉) and Salil Vadhan

Harvard University, Cambridge, MA, USA
zacharyratliff@g.harvard.edu, salil_vadhan@harvard.edu

Abstract. Recent works [9,25] have started to theoretically investigate how we can protect differentially private programs against timing attacks, by making the joint distribution the output and the runtime differentially private (JOT-DP). However, the existing approaches to JOT-DP have some limitations, particularly in the setting of unbounded DP (which protects the size of the dataset and applies to arbitrarily large datasets). First, the known conversion of pure DP programs to pure JOT-DP programs in the unbounded setting [9] (a) incurs a constant additive increase in error probability (and thus does not provide vanishing error as $n \to \infty$) (b) produces JOT-DP programs that fail to preserve the computational efficiency of the original pure DP program and (c) is analyzed in a toy computational model in which the runtime is defined to be the number of coin flips. For approximate JOT-DP, an efficient conversion with vanishing error in the RAM model is known [17,25], but only applies to programs that run in $O(n)$ time on datasets of size n, as linear runtime is implied by "timing stability," the timing analogue of global sensitivity. In this work, we overcome these limitations. Specifically:

1. We show that the error required for pure JOT-DP in the unbounded setting depends on the model of computation.
   - In a randomized RAM model where the dataset size n is given (or can be computed in constant time) and we can generate random numbers (not just random bits) in constant time, polynomially small error probability is necessary and sufficient.
   - If n is not given or we only have a random-bit generator, an (arbitrarily small) constant error probability is necessary and sufficient.
2. The aforementioned positive results are proven by efficient procedures to convert any pure JOT-DP program P in the upper-bounded setting to a pure JOT-DP program P' in the unbounded setting, such that the output distribution of P' is γ-close in total variation distance to that of P, where γ is either an arbitrarily small constant or polynomially small, depending on the model of computation.

Keywords: Differential Privacy · Timing Attacks · Side Channels

B. Applebaum and H. Lin (Eds.): TCC 2025, LNCS 16271, pp. 387–414, 2026.
https://doi.org/10.1007/978-3-032-12290-2_13

1 Introduction

Timing side-channel attacks, in which an attacker measures the runtime of an algorithm to infer otherwise private information, have proven to be a highly effective method for breaking modern cryptographic systems. These attacks have been used to extract signing keys from cryptographic processors [20], recover private keys from remote TLS servers [3,4,10,11], and leak sensitive information from hidden hardware states (e.g., Spectre [19] and Meltdown [22]).

Early research on timing attacks focused on identifying and mitigating timing side-channels in cryptographic implementations. However, the growing adoption of *differential privacy* (DP) [14]—an influential framework for privacy-preserving data analysis, used in applications such as analyzing user behavior [16,23] and releasing aggregate statistics [1,2]—has introduced new avenues for timing attacks. Differential privacy achieves its protections by adding carefully calibrated noise to computations, ensuring that the output of a query is not too sensitive to the addition or removal of a single data point. However, researchers have already identified that the runtime of user-defined queries [5,17] and noise samplers [18] can severely violate the promises of differential privacy. Thus, recent research has begun to theoretically investigate *timing-private* DP programs, which ensure that the joint distribution of the output and runtime satisfies differential privacy [9,25].

Definition 1 ((ε, δ)-Joint Output/Timing Privacy [9,25]**).** *Let $\mathcal{X}$ be a dataset space with an adjacency relation, $\mathcal{E}$ be a set of execution environments for a computational model, $\mathcal{Y}$ be an output space, $\mathcal{T} \subseteq \mathbb{R}^{\geq 0}$ a set of possible runtimes in the model, and $P : \mathcal{X} \times \mathcal{E} \to \mathcal{Y} \times \mathcal{E}$ a randomized program in the model. Then we say that P is (ε, δ)-*jointly output/timing-private *(JOT-DP) if for all adjacent $x, x' \in \mathcal{X}$, all pairs of input-compatible execution environments* $\texttt{env}, \texttt{env}' \in \mathcal{E}$, *and all $S \subseteq \mathcal{Y} \times \mathcal{T}$*

$$\Pr[(Y, T) \in S] \leq e^{\varepsilon} \cdot \Pr[(Y', T') \in S] + \delta$$

where $Y = \texttt{out}(P(x, \texttt{env}))$ and $T_P(x, \texttt{env})$ denote the output and runtime of P respectively (and defined similarly for Y' and T'). When $\delta = 0$, we say that P achieves pure *JOT-DP, and when $\delta > 0$, we say that P achieves* approximate *JOT-DP. The dataset space $\mathcal{X}$ and its adjacency relation determine whether the program achieves JOT-DP in the* bounded *(the number of records $n = |x|$ in a dataset $x \in \mathcal{X}$ is fixed and publicly known),* unbounded *($|x|$ can be arbitrarily large and is intended to remain private), or*upper-bounded *(upper bound on $|x|$ is publicly known, but $|x|$ should remain private subject to the upper bound) settings.*

The above notion of timing privacy requires that the joint distribution of the program P's output and runtime when executed in the environment $\texttt{env}$ satisfies the standard definition of differential privacy. Informally, the execution environment represents the state of the computer before execution, for example, the contents of memory. We give further background on execution environments in Sect. 2.

Beyond its role in data analysis, DP has recently emerged as a valuable tool for designing more practical and efficient cryptographic systems. For instance, metadata-private messaging systems have leveraged weaker DP guarantees to improve performance over purely cryptographic approaches [21, 26]. Similarly, the concept of *differential obliviousness*, which extends DP-like guarantees to the memory access patterns of a process, has been proposed as a lightweight alternative to oblivious RAM [13]. Apple has even adopted DP in their implementation of *enhanced visual search* as a more efficient method of anonymizing user queries [6, 7]. Thus, there is a pressing need to understand the extent to which DP implementations can be protected from timing attacks.

1.1 Limitations of Prior Approaches

One general technique suggested by Haeberlen, Pierce, and Narayan [17] and formalized and generalized by Ratliff and Vadhan [25], for constructing JOT-DP programs involve first establishing a bound on the program's *timing stability*, which is the timing equivalent of global sensitivity. Once this bound is established, the output release is delayed by an amount sampled from a distribution, scaled according to the timing stability and the desired privacy level. However, this technique seems to inherently result in *approximate* privacy ($\delta > 0$) because it can only add non-negative "noise" to the program's runtime. It is possible to achieve *pure* ($\delta = 0$) JOT-DP in the bounded-DP (or upper-bounded DP) setting, where the maximum size of the input is known and public, by padding execution to the worst case runtime. However, in the *unbounded* DP setting, where the size of the program's input is unknown and must be protected by differential privacy, achieving JOT-DP for non-trivial programs introduces several interesting challenges.

First, Ben Dov, David, Naor, and Tzalik [9] show that pure DP programs in the unbounded setting can be converted into JOT-DP programs, but the conversion results in a constant additive increase in error probability (and thus does not provide vanishing error as the dataset size $n \to \infty$). It remains unknown whether one must tolerate this constant probability of constant additive error, or if it is possible to construct pure JOT-DP programs that maintain the same asymptotic accuracy guarantees as their non-timing-private versions (which typically have error probability that tends to 0 as the dataset size n grows). Furthermore, the conversion technique of [9] can produce in a JOT-DP program that is inefficient, even if the original pure DP program is efficient. The reason being that constructing the sampler for the JOT-DP program requires computing the probabilities of all possible outputs of the original program, which may take exponential time even if the original program runs in expected polynomial time.

For approximate JOT-DP, the previously mentioned technique of adding random delays can achieve vanishing error, but it is only applicable to programs that are timing stable, which implies an $O(n)$ runtime on datasets of size n. Consequently, in the unbounded DP setting, this approach cannot ensure timing privacy for common DP algorithms with superlinear runtimes. For example, the *smooth-sensitivity median* algorithm [24] for differentially private median computation requires sorting the input data, which incurs a $\Omega(n \log n)$ runtime for any comparison-based sorting algorithm. Thus, in the unbounded DP setting, no method is currently known for constructing even *approximately* JOT-DP analogues of DP algorithms that require superlinear runtime.

1.2 Our Results

In this work, we address the above limitations and introduce new techniques for constructing differentially private programs in the unbounded setting that are secure against timing attacks. We adopt the RAM model of computation with a random number generator, which we view as more natural than the model used by Ben Dov et al. [9] (see Sect. 2). Their results used a toy computational model equipped solely with a random bit generator, where the total runtime was measured by the number of random bits generated before halting. Additionally, since we focus on the unbounded setting of differential privacy, we do not utilize the Word RAM model, as its finite word size[1] imposes constraints on addressable memory and, consequently, on input size. However, we note that our transformations do not rely on the RAM model's capability to generate integers that are super-polynomially large in the program's runtime.

Within the RAM model of computation, we answer an open question by Ben Dov et al. [9] and construct an efficient procedure for converting any pure DP program P in the *upper-bounded* setting (see Definition 1) to a pure JOT-DP program P' for the unbounded setting whose output distribution differs by at most a constant β in total variation distance from P.

Theorem 2 (Pure JOT-DP RAM programs in the Unbounded Setting). *For all $0 < \beta < 1$, $\varepsilon > 0$, $\varepsilon' > \varepsilon$, and ε-JOT-DP RAM programs $P : \mathcal{X} \times \mathcal{E} \to \mathcal{Y} \times \mathcal{E}$ in the* upper-*bounded setting, there exists a ε'-JOT-DP RAM program $P' : \mathcal{X} \times \mathcal{E} \to \mathcal{Y} \times \mathcal{E}$ for the unbounded setting such that*

$$\left\| \mathtt{out}(P(x, \mathtt{env})) - \mathtt{out}(P'(x, \mathtt{env})) \right\|_{TV} < \beta$$

Furthermore, the mechanism $P'(x, \mathtt{env})$ is simply an explicit algorithm that makes one oracle call to P on a truncation of x along with an additional computation that takes time $O(|x|)$ with probability at least $1 - \beta - O(|x|^{-c})$ for some constant $c > 0$.

Given the above result, we can convert pure JOT-DP programs with superlinear runtime in the upper-bounded setting into pure JOT-DP programs in the unbounded setting. Note that the requirement that P has a pure JOT-DP implementation in the upper-bounded setting is not overly restrictive, as many useful

[1] The Word RAM model sometimes defines the word size ω as $\omega = O(\log n)$, where n is the program's input length. However, this introduces additional complexities, as the word size itself may reveal information about the input length.

programs have such implementations (for example, by padding all executions to the maximum runtime on datasets of size within the upper bound). This resolves the open problem of Ben Dov et al. [9].

Note that Theorem 2 allows for a constant additive error in the output with constant probability, even as $n \to \infty$. This raises the question of whether such an error is unavoidable, a question we address in this work. Specifically, we show that the answer depends on the computational model starting with the following lower bound:

Theorem 3 (Lower Bound for Pure JOT-DP Programs). *Let $P : \mathcal{X} \times \mathcal{E} \to \mathbb{N} \times \mathcal{E}$ be a ε-JOT-DP program in the unbounded setting for some computational model, and that releases an estimate of its true input length. Let $t_0 = O(1)$ be the expected runtime of P on the empty dataset, and $p_{t_0}(n) \leq 1$ be the smallest non-zero probability such that $Z \sim$ Bernoulli$(p_{t_0}(n))$ can be sampled in time $2 \cdot t_0$ when P is executed on a dataset consisting of n records equal to a fixed value (e.g., 0). Then $\exists c$ such that $\forall x \in \mathcal{X}, |x| \geq c$:*

$$\Pr\left[\left|\mathtt{out}(P(x, \mathtt{env})) - n\right| > n - c\right] > p_{t_0}(n)$$

for $n = |x|$ as $n \to \infty$.

The above theorem gives a *computational-model-dependent* lower bound on the achievable utility for pure JOT-DP programs. In particular, with probability at least $p_{t_0}(n)$, the program will output a useless result (since the error is of the order $O(n)$). If our computational model includes only a coin-tossing function as in the BDNNT model (Sect. 2), then $p(n) \geq 2^{-2 \cdot t_0}$, so the error probability is at least a constant. On the other hand, we show that in a randomized RAM model of computation where the input length is given as part of the input, we can achieve error that decays inverse polynomially in the input length (Sect. 4).

Theorem 4 (Pure JOT-DP RAM Programs in the Unbounded Setting). *For all $\varepsilon > 0$, $\varepsilon' > \varepsilon$, and ε-DP RAM programs $P : \mathcal{X} \times \mathcal{E} \to \mathcal{Y} \times \mathcal{E}$ in the upper-bounded setting, there exists a ε'-JOT-DP RAM program $P' : \mathcal{X} \times \mathcal{E} \to \mathcal{Y} \times \mathcal{E}$ for the unbounded setting satisfying $\forall x \in \mathcal{X}$ of length n, $\forall$ input-compatible $\mathtt{env} \in \mathcal{E}$, $\forall c \geq 2$:*

$$\left\|\mathtt{out}(P(x, \mathtt{env})) - \mathtt{out}(P'(x, \mathtt{env}))\right\|_{TV} < O\left(\frac{1}{n^c}\right)$$

Furthermore, the mechanism $P'(x, \mathtt{env})$ is an explicit algorithm that makes one oracle call to P on a truncation of x along with an additional computation that takes time $O(|x|)$ with high probability.

In particular, we obtain the following pure JOT-DP implementation of the Laplace mechanism.

Corollary 1 (Pure JOT-DP Laplace Mechanism). *For all $\varepsilon > 0$, and all $c > 0$, there exists an ε-JOT-DP RAM program $P : \mathcal{X} \times \mathcal{E} \to \mathcal{Y} \times \mathcal{E}$ for releasing sums in the unbounded setting such that for all datasets $x \in \mathcal{X}$:*

$$\Pr\left[\left|\mathtt{out}(P(x, \mathtt{env})) - \sum x_i\right| \geq \frac{C \cdot \ln(n)}{\varepsilon}\right] < O\left(\frac{1}{n^c}\right)$$

where $n = |x|$ is the size of the dataset, and $C > 0$ is a universal constant.

Theorem 4 shows that we can construct *pure* JOT-DP sums in the randomized RAM model that achieve comparable privacy guarantees to the standard ε-DP Laplace mechanism. While the error probability is not exponentially decaying as in the standard (non-timing-private) Laplace mechanism, the JOT-DP mechanism still ensures that the error vanishes at a polynomial rate. This is an improvement over the constant error bound given by Ben Dov et al. [9] and Theorem 2, and is the best possible by Theorem 3 since $p_{t_0}(n) \geq n^{-2^{2 \cdot t_0}}$ (Sect. 4).

1.3 Techniques

We introduce a new technique for constructing *pure* JOT-DP programs in the unbounded setting (Sect. 3). Specifically, both Theorem 2 and Theorem 4 are obtained by (a) constructing a pure JOT-DP program that coarsely estimates its input length, (b) truncating the dataset based on this estimate, and (c) running an upper-bounded pure JOT-DP program using the estimate as the upper bound on dataset size.

Informally, the coarse estimation procedure repeatedly queries whether the input length exceeds some threshold, where the threshold doubles in each round, continuing until the answer is "no." Because the query responses must satisfy differential privacy, each has an associated error probability. However, this error can be made arbitrarily small.

To achieve the bound for RAM programs in Theorem 4, we leverage the fact that the input length n is known in advance, allowing the error parameter to explicitly depend on n. Specifically, the algorithm uses an adaptive sampling procedure that repeatedly flips a biased coin, starting with an initial success probability of $1/(n+k)^c$ for constants c and k. After each unsuccessful flip, the success probability is updated to $1/(n-i+k)^c$ until it reaches a fixed probability of $1/k^c$. Flipping continues until the first success, at which point the algorithm outputs the total number of flips. Importantly, this ensures (a) the runtime is exactly determined by the output, and (b) the output itself is an ε-DP estimate of the input length, making the algorithm ε-JOT-DP. Using this adaptive sampler as a building block, we construct pure JOT-DP RAM programs that achieve the bound from Theorem 4. Our construction is optimal in terms of its failure probability (i.e., it achieves error probability that vanishes at a polynomial rate). In particular, Theorem 3 establishes that this decay rate is the best achievable within the RAM model, and in fact, weaker computational models can only achieve a constant error probability.

To establish the lower bound in Theorem 3, we analyze the output support of a pure DP program in the unbounded setting conditioned on halting within time $t \leq 2t_0$, where t_0 is the expected runtime of the program on the empty input. Our argument relies on the observation that even when the database is very long, the mechanism must with some probability behave exactly as it does on the empty database. On the empty database the mechanism halts within time $2 \cdot t_0$ with high probability, and thus the same behavior must occur with positive probability on the long database. By the definition of JOT-DP, the output support conditioned on halting within this time bound must be finite and identical across all inputs. We further show that every output in this finite support provides poor utility for most inputs. Nonetheless, the mechanism must output an element from this finite set with probability at least $p_{t_0}(n)$, where $p_{t_0}(n)$ is the smallest non-zero probability computable by a program running in time $2t_0$. Together, our results demonstrate that in many reasonable computational models, pure JOT-DP programs in the unbounded setting necessarily incur an added utility cost to maintain their timing privacy guarantees.

2 Preliminaries

RAM Model. Throughout this work, we will use the idealized RAM model of computation. The RAM model consists of an infinite sequence of memory cells, each capable of storing arbitrarily large natural numbers. Variables are stored in registers and RAM programs can perform a set of basic operations for arithmetic (addition, subtraction, multiplication, and integer division), Boolean logic (AND, OR, NOT), and reading/writing memory. They also allow conditional jumps (e.g., **if** CONDITIONAL **goto** LINE), which implement standard control flow constructs such as **if** and **if/else** statements. Additionally, we allow our RAM programs to use randomness by executing a `RAND`(n) instruction to uniformly sample an integer from $\{0, \ldots, n\}$. The runtime of a RAM program is defined as the number of basic instructions[2] executed before the program halts, meaning that the set of possible runtime values $\mathcal{T}$ corresponds to the natural numbers $\mathbb{N}$. We also include a built-in variable `input_len` and `input_ptr` (respectively `output_len` and `output_ptr`), which stores the length of the program's input and its location in memory respectively (and similarly for the program's output).

We also consider a variant of the randomized RAM model where the program lacks direct access to the input length (i.e., `input_len` is not initialized). This model is strictly weaker than the one described above, as the program must compute the input length during execution if needed. In this model, the end of the input is marked in memory by a special delimiter symbol reserved for indicating the end of the input.

RAM$_{\mathbf{BDDNT}}$. Earlier work by Ben Dov et al. [9] used a computational model where randomness is provided by a simple coin-tossing function (i.e., a draw

[2] We count conditional branching instructions and randomness sampling as basic instructions taking one time step.

from Bernoulli(1/2)), and runtime is measured solely by the number of coin tosses performed. This is in contrast to our RAM model, where a call to `RAND(n)` samples a random integer from $\{0, \ldots, n\}$ and runtime is measured by the total number of instructions executed before halting. Consequently, when discussing the main results of Ben Dov et al. in Sect. 3, we denote by $\mathrm{RAM}_{\mathrm{BDDNT}}$ the RAM model in which randomness is restricted to calls to a simple Bernoulli(1/2) sampler and runtime is measured by the total number of such calls.

Execution Environments. The runtime of a program on a given input is often highly dependent on the program's *execution environment.* For example, a program executing on x86 hardware will have runtime that can be influenced by concurrent processes executing on the system, the state of the branch predictor (if the hardware supports speculative execution), the cache state, and various other forms of resource contention that might occur on the system. Thus, we always consider a program's runtime to be a function of both the input and some execution environment $\mathtt{env} \in \mathcal{E}$ representing the machines initial state before executing the program. For example, the set of execution environments $\mathcal{E}$ for RAM programs includes all possible memory configurations and initial values of built-in variables.

Definition 2 (RAM Execution Environment). *The* execution environment `env` *of a RAM program is the infinite sequence* $(v_0, v_1, \ldots,)$ *such that* $M[i] = v_i$ *for all* i *along with the values stored by the built-in variables such as* `input_ptr` *and* `input_len`*,* `output_ptr`*, and* `output_len`*.*

We note that while the execution environment significantly influences program runtimes in practice, throughout this paper, we will work with RAM programs whose runtime and output distributions are jointly independent of the execution environment. Additionally, we emphasize that not every execution environment is *compatible* with a given input. For example, a RAM program that processes a length-n string consisting entirely of 1's may be incompatible with a RAM environment where memory has been zeroed out. We say that $P(x, \mathtt{env})$ is undefined for such environments `env` that are incompatible with an input x. Consequently, our definitions are often quantified over all pairs of inputs $x \in \mathcal{X}$ and *input-compatible* execution environments $\mathtt{env} \in \mathcal{E}$.

The Bounded, Upper-Bounded, and Unbounded Settings. Differential privacy is defined with respect to an input space $\mathcal{X}$, where inputs typically consist of $n \geq 0$ records drawn from some domain $\mathcal{D}$. Formally, we define the input space as $\mathcal{X} = \bigcup_{n=0}^{\infty} \mathcal{D}^n$. Two inputs $x, x' \in \mathcal{X}$ are said to be *adjacent* with respect to a dataset distance metric $d_{\mathcal{X}}$ if $d_{\mathcal{X}}(x, x') \leq 1$.

We can distinguish between different settings of differential privacy according to whether the program's input size is considered public information. In the *bounded* setting, the input length is assumed to be publicly known. Consequently, privacy guarantees do not extend to hiding the dataset size. This assumption simplifies the defense against timing attacks, as execution can often be padded to match the worst-case runtime for inputs of a given length. A stronger flavor of DP is the *upper-bounded* setting, where only an upper bound $n_{\max}$ on the program's input length is assumed to be public. This setting is commonly encountered in practice, as one can typically establish a conservative upper limit on the dataset size. Similarly to the bounded setting, one can often pad execution up to a worst case runtime[3] in the upper-bounded setting to protect against timing attacks. However, the strongest privacy guarantee is provided by the *unbounded* setting, in which the input length is intended to be kept private and can be arbitrarily large.

In both the upper-bounded and unbounded settings, adjacency is often defined using an *insert-delete* distance.

Definition 3 (Insert-Delete Distance). *For $x \in \mathcal{D}^*$, an insertion to x is an addition of an element z to a location in x resulting in a new input $x' = [x_1, \ldots, x_i, z, x_{i+1}, \ldots, x_n]$. Likewise, a deletion from x is the removal of an element from a location i, giving a new input $x' = [x_1, \ldots, x_{i-1}, x_{i+1}, \ldots, x_n]$. We define the* insert-delete distance, *denoted d_{ID}, of inputs $x, x' \in \mathcal{D}^*$ to be the minimum number of insertion and deletion operations needed to transform x into x'.*

Throughout this paper, we operate within the unbounded setting of differential privacy and will therefore implicitly use d_{ID} as the adjacency relation in all definitions and theorems.

Properties of JOT-DP Programs. We will frequently use the fact that DP programs with constant-time execution on all inputs are also JOT-DP.

Lemma 1 (Constant-Time JOT-DP Programs [25]). *If a program $P : \mathcal{X} \times \mathcal{E} \to \mathcal{Y} \times \mathcal{E}$ is ε-DP in its output and there exists a constant c such that $T_P(x, \texttt{env}) = c$ for all $x \in \mathcal{X}$ and $\texttt{env} \in \mathcal{E}$, then P is ε-JOT-DP.*

We will also make use of programs P that are the composition of JOT-DP programs P_1 and P_2. Such programs P are constructed by *chaining* together P_1 such that its output along with its unaltered input are fed as the input to program P_2.

Lemma 2 (Sequential Composition of JOT-DP RAM Programs [25]). *Let $P_1 : \mathcal{X} \times \mathcal{E} \to \mathcal{Y} \times \mathcal{E}$ be an ε_1-JOT-DP RAM program. Let $P_2 : \mathcal{X} \times \mathcal{E} \to \mathcal{Z} \times \mathcal{E}$ be an ε_2-JOT-DP RAM program. Then the sequentially composed program $P_2 \otimes P_1 : \mathcal{X} \times \mathcal{E} \to (\mathcal{Y} \times \mathcal{Z}) \times \mathcal{E}$ that executes P_1 on the input x followed by P_2 on input x is $(\varepsilon_1 + \varepsilon_2)$-JOT-DP.*

Finally, we review the Discrete Laplace distribution.

Definition 4 (Discrete Laplace Distribution). *The* Discrete Laplace distribution *with shift $\mu \in \mathbb{N}$ and scale $s > 0$, is supplied a $x \in \mathbb{Z}$, has the probability mass function:*

$$p(x \mid \mu, s) = \frac{e^{1/s} - 1}{e^{1/s} + 1} \cdot e^{-|x-\mu|/s}$$

[3] However, in practice, this approach may be inefficient, as the program's worst-case runtime for inputs of length $n_{\max}$ could be prohibitively long.

The cumulative distribution function (CDF) is given by:

$$F(x \mid \mu, s) = \begin{cases} \frac{e^{1/s}}{e^{1/s}+1} \cdot e^{-(\mu-x)/s}, & \text{if } x \leq \mu, \\ 1 - \frac{1}{e^{1/s}+1} \cdot e^{-(x-\mu)/s}, & \text{if } x > \mu. \end{cases}$$

Throughout this paper, we will often use a *censored*[4] version of the Discrete Laplace distribution, which we denote by $\texttt{CensoredDiscreteLaplace}(\mu, s, \ell, u)$. This distribution is additionally parameterized by lower and upper bounds ℓ and u so that $X \sim \text{DiscreteLaplace}(\mu, s)$ is clamped to the range $[\ell, u]$.

Lemma 3 (Censored Discrete Laplace is DP [15]**).** *Let x, x' be adjacent datasets, $\ell, u \in \mathbb{N}$ for $\ell \leq u$, $f : \mathcal{X} \to \mathbb{Z}$ a function with global sensitivity Δ, and $\varepsilon > 0$. Then $M(x) = \texttt{CensoredDiscreteLaplace}(\mu = f(x), s = \Delta/\varepsilon, \ell, u)$ is ε-DP.*

We remark that constant-time instantiations of the censored Discrete Laplace distribution are known [8,25]. Using Lemma 3 and the fact that we can implement the censored Discrete Laplace mechanism to run in fixed time that depends only on s, ℓ, and u, we obtain a JOT-DP version of $\texttt{CensoredDiscreteLaplace}$ (by Lemma 1).

Lemma 4 (Censored Discrete Laplace is JOT-DP). *Let x, x' be adjacent datasets, $\ell, u \in \mathbb{N}$ for $\ell \leq u$, $f : \mathcal{X} \to \mathbb{Z}$ a function with global sensitivity Δ, and $\varepsilon > 0$. Then there exists a RAM program $P : \mathcal{X} \times \mathcal{E} \to \mathcal{Y} \times \mathcal{E}$ such that $P(x, \texttt{env})$ samples from $\texttt{CensoredDiscreteLaplace}(\mu = f(x), s = \Delta/\varepsilon, \ell, u)$ in time $O(u)$ and achieves ε-JOT-DP.*

3 Pure Timing-Private Programs

In this section, we characterize pure JOT-DP programs in the unbounded setting. To begin, we reintroduce a result from Ben Dov et al. [9] for the $\text{RAM}_{\text{BDDNT}}$ model of computation (described in Sect. 2).

Theorem 1 (Ben Dov et al. [9]**).** *Let $P : \mathcal{X} \times \mathcal{E} \to \mathcal{Y} \times \mathcal{E}$ be any ε-DP RAM_{BDDNT} program. For any $\beta > 0$, $\varepsilon' > \varepsilon$ there exists a ε'-JOT-DP RAM_{BDDNT} program $P' : \mathcal{X} \times \mathcal{E} \to \mathcal{Y} \times \mathcal{E}$ such that for all $x \in \mathcal{X}$, $\texttt{env} \in \mathcal{E}$:*

$$\Big\| \texttt{out}(P(x, \texttt{env})) - \texttt{out}(P'(x, \texttt{env})) \Big\|_{TV} < \beta$$

Theorem 1 is promising in that it suggests one can achieve pure JOT-DP as long as one is willing to tolerate a constant error probability. However, the authors left as an open question whether the pure JOT-DP program P' can maintain the computational efficiency of P. We give a positive answer to this question for a wide class of programs (namely, programs that have pure JOT-DP implementations in the upper-bounded setting).

[4] The literature also refers to this as the Truncated Geometric Mechanism [15].

Program 1 . General Construction for Pure JOT-DP Programs in the Unbounded Setting

Input: A dataset x, privacy parameter $\varepsilon' > 0$, failure parameter $\beta > 0$, and ε-JOT-DP program P for the upper-bounded setting.

Output: The output of P when executed on the input x truncated to $\hat{n}$ records where $\hat{n}$ is a ε'-DP count on the size of x.

1: $\varepsilon' = \varepsilon'/2$;
2: $\beta' = \beta/2$;
3: $m = \frac{2}{\varepsilon'} \cdot \lceil \ln(\frac{1}{\beta'}) \rceil$;
4: **while True do**
5:     Scan first m rows of input and set $\mu = \min\{n, m\}$; `//note that` $n = |x|$
6:     $s = 1/\varepsilon'$;
7:     $\ell = 0$; `//lower bound for censored Discrete Laplace mechanism`
8:     $u = m$; `//upper bound for censored Discrete Laplace mechanism`
9:     $\hat{n} =$ `CensoredDiscreteLaplace`(μ, s, ℓ, u);
10:     **if** $\hat{n} < \frac{m}{2}$ **then**
11:         $s = 1/\varepsilon$;
12:         $\hat{x} =$ `Truncate`(x, m); `//Truncates dataset to` m `records if` $|x| > m$
13:         run $P^m(\hat{x})$; `//`P `in the` m`-upperbounded setting`
14:         **return** output of $P(\hat{x})$;
15:     **else**
16:         $\varepsilon' = \varepsilon'/2$;
17:         $\beta' = \beta'/2$;
18:         $m = \frac{2}{\varepsilon'} \cdot \lceil \ln(\frac{1}{\beta'}) \rceil$;

We start with the construction described by Program 1, which first computes a pure JOT-DP *over*-estimate of a program's input length that holds with arbitrarily small probability β. Intuitively, Program 1 scans its input m_i entries at a time, where m_i depends only on the parameters ε', β, and i, and m_{i+1} is roughly $2m_i$. In each iteration, the program releases a DP count on the first m_i entries of the input (i.e., a DP count on m_i if $m_i < |x|$, and a DP count on $|x|$ otherwise) and stops scanning the input once it releases a count less than $m_i/2$. This step consumes ε' of the privacy budget to generate the coarse estimate m_k, which serves as an upper bound on the input size with high probability. Once this estimate is determined, the input is truncated (if necessary) in time that depends only on the differentially private overestimate m_k. Finally, the program P^m is executed on the transformed dataset $\hat{x}$, where P^m is the program P restricted to inputs of length at most m_k.

Lemma 5. *Let $P' : \mathcal{X} \times \mathcal{E} \rightarrow \mathcal{Y} \times \mathcal{E}$ be the RAM program implementing Program 1 for a RAM program $P : \mathcal{X} \times \mathcal{E} \rightarrow \mathcal{Y} \times \mathcal{E}$ that is ε-JOT-DP in the upper-bounded setting. Then P' achieves $(\varepsilon + \varepsilon')$-JOT-DP in the unbounded setting.*

Proof. We can interpret the program P' as the composition of two subprograms. The first, $P_{(\texttt{line 13})}$, executes the loop until iteration k, transforms the input dataset into a new dataset $\hat{x} = \texttt{Truncate}(x, m_k)$ containing at most m_k records, and then outputs the bound m_k. By construction, if $d_{\text{ID}}(x, x') \leq 1$ then so are $d_{\text{ID}}(\hat{x}, \hat{x}') \leq 1$ since Truncate is 1-stable.[5] The second subprogram, P^m, is the execution of P on the truncated dataset $\hat{x}$ in the upper bounded setting, where inputs are guaranteed to have length at most $m = m_k$. Thus, the overall privacy argument reduces to showing that $P_{\texttt{(line 13)}}$ is ε'-JOT-DP. If this is established, then the program P' is simply the composition of two JOT-DP programs: $P_{\texttt{(line 13)}}$ in the unbounded setting, and P^m in the upper bounded setting (which is ε-JOT-DP by assumption). By basic composition, and the fact that the upper bound m is itself DP, the composed program satisfies $(\varepsilon + \varepsilon')$-JOT-DP.

To reason about the privacy of $P_{\texttt{(line 13)}}$, consider the following mental experiment. Define P_{inf} to be the program that never halts and continues executing the loop forever (i.e., the "if" clause is dropped and only the "else" clause is ever executed). On each iteration i, the program invokes the censored Discrete Laplace mechanism with parameters $\varepsilon_i = \varepsilon'/2^i$ and $\beta_i = \beta/2^i$, producing both a noisy count $\widehat{n}_i$ and a runtime value $\widehat{t}_i$. Thus, for each iteration i we can consider the pair $(\widehat{n}_i, \widehat{t}_i)$. By Lemma 4, each such iteration is ε_i-JOT-DP. Hence for every k and neighboring datasets x and x' we obtain

$$\begin{aligned} D_\infty\Big(((\widehat{n}_1, \widehat{t}_1), \ldots, (\widehat{n}_k, t_k)) \,\|\, ((\widehat{n}'_1, \widehat{t}'_1), \ldots, (\widehat{n}'_k, \widehat{t}'_k))\Big) &\leq \sum_{i=1}^{k} \varepsilon_i \\ &\leq \sum_{i=1}^{\infty} \varepsilon_i \\ &= \varepsilon' \end{aligned}$$

We now make use of the following lemma.

Lemma 6 (Van Erven and Harremoës [27]). *Let $P^1, P^2, \ldots$ and $Q^1, Q^2, \ldots$ be consistent sequences of probability distributions on $(\Omega^1, \Gamma^1), (\Omega^2, \Gamma^2), \ldots$, where, for $n = 1, 2, \ldots, \infty$, (Ω^n, Γ^n) is the direct product of the first n measurable spaces in the infinite sequence $(\Omega_1, \Gamma_1), (\Omega_2, \Gamma_2), \ldots$. Then for any $\alpha \in (0, \infty]$*

$$\lim_{n \to \infty} D_\alpha(P^n \| Q^n) = D_\alpha(P^\infty \| Q^\infty)$$

By Lemma 6, as $k \to \infty$ the max divergence of the k-prefix distributions converges to that of the full infinite sequence. Since each prefix divergence is bounded by ε', the limiting divergence is also at most ε'. Thus we may view the thought experiment program P_{inf} as a limiting mechanism that is itself ε'-JOT-DP.

Now note that the actual program $P_{\texttt{(line 13)}}$ is obtained by post processing the output/runtime pairs of P_{inf}. It examines the sequence $((\widehat{n}_1, \widehat{t}_1), (\widehat{n}_2, \widehat{t}_2), \ldots)$

[5] A function $f : \mathcal{X} \to \mathcal{X}$ that maps datasets to datasets is c-stable if for all $x, x' \in \mathcal{X}$, $d_{\text{ID}}(f(x), f(x')) \leq c \cdot d_{\text{ID}}(x, x')$.

and truncates it to the first k entries according to a stopping condition (i.e., comparing $\widehat{n}_k$ with m_k, where m_k depends only on the public parameters ε' and β). The total runtime of $P_{(\texttt{line 13})}$ is then a deterministic function of the first k runtime values $\widehat{t}_1, \ldots, \widehat{t}_k$, together with the fixed overhead of the loop structure, since each iteration executes a constant number of additional instructions besides the call to the censored Discrete Laplace mechanism. By post-processing, $P_{(\texttt{line 13})}$ is also ε'-JOT-DP. Consequently, P' is the composition of two JOT-DP programs, $P_{(\texttt{line 13})}$ and P^m. By the basic composition theorem (Lemma 2), it follows that the overall program satisfies $(\varepsilon + \varepsilon')$-JOT-DP.

Lemma 7. *Let $P' : \mathcal{X} \times \mathcal{E} \to \mathcal{Y} \times \mathcal{E}$ be the program implementing Program 1 for a program $P : \mathcal{X} \times \mathcal{E} \to \mathcal{Y} \times \mathcal{E}$ that is ε-JOT-DP in the upper-bounded setting. Then P' returns the output of P on dataset x with probability at least $1 - \beta$.*

Proof. We first consider the case where Program 1 terminates on loop iteration k with $m_k < |x|$. In this scenario, $\hat{x} = \texttt{Truncate}(x, m_k)$ and $|\hat{x}| < |x|$ so the program returns the output of P on the first m_k entries of x. The probability of this occurring is given by

$$\Pr\left[\hat{n}_i < \frac{m_i}{2}\right] \le e^{-m_i \cdot \varepsilon_i / 2} \le \beta_i$$

for $\hat{n}_i \sim \texttt{CensoredDiscreteLaplace}(\mu = m_i, s = 1/\varepsilon_i, \ell = 0, u = m_i)$ by the CDF of the Discrete Laplace distribution and the fact that $m_i \ge \frac{2}{\varepsilon_i} \cdot \ln(1/\beta_i)$. We union bound over the k invocations of the mechanism:

$$\begin{aligned}\sum_{i=1}^{k} \Pr\left[\hat{n}_i < \frac{m_i}{2}\right] &\le \sum_{i=1}^{\infty} \beta_i \\ &= \sum_{i=1}^{\infty} \frac{\beta}{2^i} \\ &= \beta \sum_{i=1}^{\infty} \frac{1}{2^i} \\ &= \beta\end{aligned}$$

We now condition on Program 1 halting on loop iteration k where $m_k \ge |x|$. In this case, $\hat{x} = x$ since $\texttt{Truncate}(x, m_k)$ does not alter x when $m_k > |x|$. Thus P' returns the output of P executed on x and the claim follows.

We now prove that for every pure JOT-DP program in the upper-bounded setting, we can obtain a pure JOT-DP program in the unbounded setting.

Theorem 2 (Pure JOT-DP in the Unbounded Setting). *For all $0 < \beta < 1$, $\varepsilon > 0$, $\varepsilon' > \varepsilon$, and ε-JOT-DP RAM programs $P : \mathcal{X} \times \mathcal{E} \to \mathcal{Y} \times \mathcal{E}$ in the* upper-*bounded setting, there exists a ε'-JOT-DP RAM program $P' : \mathcal{X} \times \mathcal{E} \to \mathcal{Y} \times \mathcal{E}$ for the unbounded setting such that*

$$\left\| \texttt{out}(P(x, \texttt{env})) - \texttt{out}(P'(x, \texttt{env})) \right\|_{TV} < \beta$$

Furthermore, the mechanism $P'(x, \texttt{env})$ *is simply an explicit algorithm that makes one oracle call to* P *on a truncation of* x *along with an additional computation that takes time* $O(|x|)$ *with probability at least* $1 - \beta - O(|x|^{-c})$ *for some constant* $c > 0$.

Proof. The proof follows from Lemma 5 and Lemma 7. In particular, given P, we construct the program P' as described in Program 1 so that P' is ε'-JOT-DP for $\varepsilon' > \varepsilon$. What remains to be shown is that, with high probability, P' runs in time $O(|x|)$ before making the oracle call to P.

There are two cases. We first consider the case where $m_k < |x|$. As shown in Lemma 7, this happens with probability:

$$\begin{aligned} \sum_{i=1}^{\infty} \Pr\left[\hat{n}_i < \frac{m_i}{2}\right] &\leq \sum_{i=1}^{\infty} e^{-m_i \cdot \varepsilon_i / 2} \\ &\leq \sum_{i=1}^{\infty} \beta_i \\ &= \beta \end{aligned}$$

where $\hat{n}_i \sim \texttt{CensoredDiscreteLaplace}(\mu = m_i, s = 1/\varepsilon_i, \ell = 0, u = m_i)$. Thus, we consider the case where $m_k > |x|$ and show that P' stops looping when $m_k = O(|x|)$ with high probability. First, observe that

$$\begin{aligned} \frac{m_k}{m_{k-1}} &= \frac{\frac{2^k}{\varepsilon'} \cdot \left\lceil \log \frac{2^k}{\beta} \right\rceil}{\frac{2^{k-1}}{\varepsilon'} \cdot \left\lceil \log \frac{2^{k-1}}{\beta} \right\rceil} \\ &= 2 \cdot \frac{r+1}{r} \end{aligned}$$

for $r = k - 1 + \left\lceil \log(1/\beta) \right\rceil \geq 1$. Thus,

$$2 \leq \frac{m_k}{m_{k-1}} \leq 4$$

Therefore, during each iteration of the loop, we increase the number of input entries scanned by at least a factor of 2 and at most a factor of 4. Now, consider the index k such that $m_k > |x|$ but $m_{k-1} \leq |x|$. Then $|x| < m_k \leq 4 \cdot |x|$. Furthermore, there exists a $j \geq k$ such that $4 \cdot |x| \leq m_j \leq 16 \cdot |x|$. Note that during this loop iteration we have $\hat{n}_j \sim$ `CensoredDiscreteLaplace`$(\mu = |x|, s = 1/\varepsilon_j, \ell = 0, u = m_j)$ and

$$\Pr\left[\hat{n}_j > \frac{m_j}{2}\right] = 1 - F\left(\frac{m_j}{2} \mid \mu = |x|, s = 1/\varepsilon_j\right) \leq e^{-\Theta(\log|x|)} \leq |x|^{-O(1)}$$

where F is the CDF of the Discrete Laplace distribution. Thus, with probability at least $1-\beta-O(n^{-c})$ for some constant $c > 0$, P' stops looping on iteration $j = O(\log|x|)$ where $m_j = O(|x|)$. The runtime of each loop iteration is dominated by the time it takes to sample from `CensoredDiscreteLaplace`$(\mu, s, \ell, u = m_i)$, which can be bounded by $O(m_i)$ (Lemma 4), where u starts at m_1 and at least doubles during each iteration up to $m_j = O(|x|)$. It follows that, with high probability, P' runs in time $O(|x|)$ before making the oracle call to P and terminating.

Theorem 2 shows that for any DP RAM program P, it is possible to efficiently construct a JOT-DP variant P' with comparable privacy guarantees, incurring at most a β increase in error probability. In other words, the modified program $P'(x)$ may return inaccurate results with probability at most β higher than $P(x)$. However, the construction used in Theorem 2 does not extend to the $\text{RAM}_{\text{BDDNT}}$ model, as it relies on sampling from a Censored Discrete Laplace distribution using a constant number of coin flips. This sampling is possible only if all output probabilities are dyadic, but Lemma 12 shows that no nontrivial Censored Discrete Laplace distribution has this property. Consequently, even in the bounded DP setting, one cannot implement the standard Laplace mechanism with *perfect* timing privacy guarantees, as can be done in the RAM model. Fortunately, we demonstrate that replacing the sampling from the Censored Discrete Laplace distribution in line 9 of Program 1 with sampling from a closely related distribution whose probability masses are entirely dyadic ensures that Theorem 2 also holds in the $\text{RAM}_{\text{BDDNT}}$ model (see Appendix).

Whether the constant additive increase in error probability β is unavoidable even in the RAM model remains an open question. In the next section, we establish a lower bound on the achievable utility of pure JOT-DP programs in the unbounded setting.

4 A Lower Bound for JOT-DP Programs

A key question that arises from Theorem 2 (Sect. 3) is whether the constant additive error in the output, which occurs with constant probability even as the input size n grows, is unavoidable. In this section, we address this question, exploring the inherent limitations of JOT-DP programs. We begin by establishing a lower bound, demonstrating that the achievable utility for pure JOT-DP programs depends on the computational model.

Theorem 3 (Lower Bound for JOT-DP Programs). *Let $P : \mathcal{X} \times \mathcal{E} \to \mathbb{N} \times \mathcal{E}$ be a ε-JOT-DP program in the unbounded setting for some computational model, and that releases an estimate of its true input length. Let $t_0 = O(1)$ be the* *expected runtime of P on the empty dataset, and $p_{t_0}(n) \leq 1$ be the smallest non-zero probability such that $Z \sim Bernoulli(p_{t_0}(n))$ can be sampled in time $2 \cdot t_0$ when P is executed on a dataset consisting of n records equal to a fixed value (e.g., 0). Then $\exists c$ such that $\forall x \in \mathcal{X}, |x| \geq c$:*

$$\Pr\left[\left|\mathtt{out}(P(x, \mathtt{env})) - n\right| > n - c\right] > p_{t_0}(n)$$

for $n = |x|$ as $n \to \infty$.

Proof. Let $P : \mathcal{X} \times \mathcal{E} \to \mathcal{Y} \times \mathcal{E}$ be a ε-JOT-DP program for releasing an estimate on the length of its input. Let $\mathbb{E}[T_P(\lambda, \mathtt{env}_\lambda)] = t_0$ where $t_0 = O(1)$ and λ is the empty dataset and $\mathtt{env}_\lambda$ is an input-compatible execution environment. Let $p_{t_0}(n) \leq 1$ be the smallest probability such that $Z \sim Bernoulli(p_{t_0}(n))$ is sampleable in time $2 \cdot t_0$ when P is executed on a dataset consisting of n copies of a fixed record.

Observe that $\Pr[T_P(\lambda, \mathtt{env}_\lambda) < 2 \cdot t_0] \geq 1/2$ by Markov's inequality. Furthermore, let

$$S = \mathrm{supp}(\mathtt{out}(P(\lambda, \mathtt{env}_\lambda)) | T_P(\lambda, \mathtt{env}_\lambda) \leq 2 \cdot t_0)$$

Note that S is finite since $P(\lambda, \mathtt{env}_\lambda)$ can only generate a finite number of outputs within $2 \cdot t_0$ time steps. We can set $c = \max_{y \in S} y$. Then $\forall n \geq c, y \in S$ it follows that

$$|y - n| \geq n - c$$

By pure JOT-DP, we have that for all x

$$\mathrm{supp}(\mathtt{out}(P(x, \mathtt{env})) | T_P(x, \mathtt{env}) \leq 2 \cdot t_0) = S$$

Thus, we have $\Pr\left[|\mathtt{out}(P(x, \mathtt{env})) - n| > n - c\right] > p_{t_0}(n)$ where $n = |x|$.

Theorem 3 establishes that the achievable utility of pure JOT-DP programs in the unbounded setting depends on the computational model. For example, in the randomized RAM model, as we have defined it, where the program receives its input length n as part of the input, then $p_{t_0}(n) \geq n^{-2^{2 \cdot t_0}}$ implying that $p_{t_0}(n)$ vanishes as $n \to \infty$. This can be realized, for instance, by a RAM program that applies repeated squaring to the input length and then invokes a random number generator on the result. Conversely, if the RAM program *does not* receive its input length n as part of its input (e.g., as described in Sect. 2), the best achievable bound[6] is $p_{t_0}(n) \geq 2^{-O(2^{2t_0})}$, which only guarantees a constant failure probability. In the next section, we present explicit constructions of pure JOT-DP RAM programs in the unbounded setting where $p(n)$ vanishes as $n \to \infty$.

[6] Obtainable by starting with a constant and performing repeated squaring.

4.1 Pure JOT-DP RAM Programs in the Unbounded Setting

We now present a general construction for converting a JOT-DP RAM program P in the upper-bounded setting into a JOT-DP RAM program P' in the unbounded setting. Notably, P' achieves an error probability that matches the best achievable bound (up to constant factors) within the RAM model, as established by the lower bound in Theorem 3. Intuitively, our construction follows a similar approach to Program 1, but leverages the fact that the program has access to the input length n. The program begins by computing a coarse estimate of the dataset size, ensuring with high probability that this estimate serves as a valid upper bound on the input length $|x|$. Given this upper bound, we then apply the same technique as in Program 1, truncating the dataset if necessary before executing the upper-bounded JOT-DP program P.

Program 2 takes as input a dataset $x \in \mathcal{D}^*$ and outputs an estimate of the dataset size using an adaptive coin-flipping process. The program initializes a biased coin with a success probability of $1/(n+k)^c$ for constants c and k. It then repeatedly flips the coin until the first success, recording the total number of flips as the output. On the $(i+1)$th flip, the success probability is adjusted to $1/(n-i+k)^c$, and this adjustment continues until the success probability reaches a fixed value of $1/k^c$, at which point the bias is no longer updated. Thus, the PMF of the output of Program 2 is given below.

$$f_{(n,c)}(i) = \begin{cases} \frac{1}{(n-i+k)^c} \cdot \prod_{j=0}^{x-1} \left(1 - \frac{1}{(n-j+k)^c}\right) & \text{if } 0 \le i \le n, \\ \mathrm{Geom}_{\frac{1}{k^c}}(i-n) \cdot \prod_{j=0}^{n-1} \left(1 - \frac{1}{(n-j+k)^c}\right) & \text{if } i > n \end{cases}$$

where $\mathrm{Geom}_p(i)$ is the PMF of the Geometric distribution defined as:

$$\mathrm{Geom}_p(i) = \begin{cases} (1-p)^{i-1} \cdot p & \text{if } i \in \{1, 2, 3, \dots\}, \\ 0 & \text{otherwise.} \end{cases}$$

Importantly, the runtime of Program 2 is fully determined by its output. Thus, if the program's output satisfies ε-DP, it is also true that the program will satisfy ε-JOT-DP.

Lemma 8. *For all $c \ge 2$, $k \ge 2$, the RAM program $P : \mathcal{X} \times \mathcal{E} \to \mathbb{N} \times \mathcal{E}$ described in Program 2 is ε-JOT-DP in the unbounded setting where* $\varepsilon = 2c \cdot \ln\left(\frac{k+1}{k-1}\right)$.

Proof. Let $p_n(j) = 1/(n-j+k)^c$ and observe that

$$p_{n+1}(j+1) = \frac{1}{(n+1-j-1+k)^c} = \frac{1}{(n-j+k)^c} = p_n(j)$$

and therefore for all $y < n$

$$\prod_{j=0}^{y} \left(\frac{1-p_n(j)}{1-p_{n+1}(j)}\right) = \frac{1-p_n(y)}{1-p_{n+1}(0)} \le \frac{(n+1+k)^c}{(n+1+k)^c - 1} \le \frac{k^c}{k^c-1}$$

Program 2. A RAM Program for Approximate Timing-Private Counts

Input: A dataset x occupying memory locations $M[0], \ldots, M[\texttt{input\_len} - 1]$. The values $c, k \geq 2$ are hardcoded constants.

Output: A noisy estimate of the input length $|x|$.

```
n = input_len;
count = 0;
flag = 0;
while flag == 0 do
   v = n − count;  //Note the RAM model rounds negative numbers to 0
   b = v + k;
   B = 1;
   for j = 0, ..., (c − 1) do
      B = B · b;  //compute the value b^c
   r = RAND(B − 1);
   if r == 0 then
      flag = 1;
   else
      count = count + 1;

return count;
```

and similarly

$$\prod_{j=0}^{y}\left(\frac{1-p_{n+1}(j)}{1-p_n(j)}\right) = \frac{1-p_{n+1}(0)}{1-p_n(y)} \leq \frac{(n-y+k)^c}{(n-y+k)^c-1} \leq \frac{k^c}{k^c-1}$$

We now consider the ratio of PMFs.

Case 1 $(y \leq n)$**:**

$$\begin{aligned}
\frac{f_n(y)}{f_{n+1}(y)} &= \frac{p_n(y)}{p_{n+1}(y)} \cdot \prod_{j=0}^{y-1}\left(\frac{1-p_n(j)}{1-p_{n+1}(j)}\right) \\
&= \frac{p_n(y)}{p_{n+1}(y)} \cdot \frac{1-p_n(y-1)}{1-p_{n+1}(0)} \\
&\leq \left(\frac{(n+1-y+k)^c}{(n-y+k)^c}\right) \cdot \frac{k^c}{k^c-1} \\
&\leq \frac{(k+1)^c}{k^c} \cdot \frac{k^c}{k^c-1} \\
&\leq \frac{(k+1)^c}{k^c-1} \\
&\leq \left(\frac{k+1}{k-1}\right)^{2c}
\end{aligned}$$

Similarly,

$$\begin{aligned}
\frac{f_{n+1}(y)}{f_n(y)} &= \frac{p_{n+1}(y)}{p_n(y)} \cdot \prod_{j=0}^{y-1} \left(\frac{1-p_{n+1}(j)}{1-p_n(j)} \right) \\
&= \frac{p_{n+1}(y)}{p_n(y)} \cdot \left(\frac{1-p_{n+1}(0)}{1-p_n(y-1)} \right) \\
&= \frac{(n-y+k)^c}{(n+1-y+k)^c} \cdot \left(\frac{k^c}{k^c-1} \right) \\
&\leq \frac{(n-y+1+k)^c}{(n-y+1+k)^c-1} \\
&\leq \frac{(k+1)^c}{(k+1)^c-1} \\
&\leq \frac{(k+1)^c}{k^c-1} \\
&\leq \left(\frac{k+1}{k-1} \right)^{2c}
\end{aligned}$$

Case 2 ($y > n$)**:**

$$\begin{aligned}
\frac{f_n(y)}{f_{n+1}(y)} &= \frac{\mathrm{Geom}(p=\frac{1}{k^c}, y-n)}{\mathrm{Geom}(p=\frac{1}{k^c}, y-n-1)} \cdot \left(\frac{1}{1-p_{n+1}(n)} \right) \cdot \prod_{j=0}^{n-1} \left(\frac{1-p_n(j)}{1-p_{n+1}(j)} \right) \\
&= \left(\frac{k^c}{k^c} \right) \cdot \frac{(1-\frac{1}{k^c})^{y-n-1}}{(1-\frac{1}{k^c})^{y-n-2}} \cdot \left(\frac{(k+1)^c}{(k+1)^c-1} \right) \cdot \left(\frac{1-p_n(n-1)}{1-p_{n+1}(0)} \right) \\
&\leq \frac{(k+1)^c}{(k+1)^c-1} \cdot \left(\frac{k^c}{k^c-1} \right) \\
&\leq \left(\frac{k+1}{k-1} \right)^{2c}
\end{aligned}$$

and similarly,

$$\begin{aligned}
\frac{f_{n+1}(y)}{f_n(y)} &= \frac{\mathrm{Geom}(p=\frac{1}{k^c}, y-n-1)}{\mathrm{Geom}(p=\frac{1}{k^c}, y-n)} \cdot (1-p_{n+1}(n)) \cdot \prod_{j=0}^{n-1} \left(\frac{1-p_{n+1}(j)}{1-p_n(j)} \right) \\
&\leq \frac{k^c}{k^c-1} \cdot \left(\frac{1-p_{n+1}(0)}{1-p_n(n-1)} \right) \\
&\leq \frac{k^c}{k^c-1} \cdot \left(\frac{k^c}{k^c-1} \right) \\
&\leq \left(\frac{k+1}{k-1} \right)^{2c}
\end{aligned}$$

It follows that the program is ε-DP for $\varepsilon = 2c \cdot \ln\left(\frac{k+1}{k-1}\right)$. Furthermore, observe that the runtime of this program is a deterministic function of its output. Specifically,

$$T_P(x, \mathtt{env}) = 5 + (\mathtt{out}(P(x, \mathtt{env})) + 1) \cdot (7 + 2(c-1))$$

Since there exists a deterministic function f such that $T_P(x, \mathtt{env}) = f(\mathtt{out}(P(x, \mathtt{env})))$, if $\mathtt{out}(P(x, \mathtt{env}))$ is ε-DP, then by post-processing, $(\mathtt{out}(P(x, \mathtt{env})), T_P(x, \mathtt{env}))$ must also satisfy ε-DP. Thus, the claim follows.

We now describe how to set k appropriately. By Lemma 8, we have

$$\varepsilon \geq 2c \cdot \ln\left(\frac{k+1}{k-1}\right) = 2c \cdot \ln\left(1 + \frac{2}{k-1}\right)$$

When k is large, we can use the approximation that $\ln(1+x) \approx x$ for small x, and therefore

$$\begin{aligned} \varepsilon &= 2c \cdot \ln\left(1 + \frac{2}{k-1}\right) \\ &\approx 2c \cdot \frac{2}{k-1} \\ &= \frac{4c}{k-1} \end{aligned}$$

Rearranging the inequality, it suffices to choose $k = O(c/\varepsilon)$ and then run Program 2 to obtain a JOT-DP estimate of the input length of a RAM program. We now demonstrate that this estimate is sufficiently accurate to derive an *upper bound* on the input length, where the probability that the upper bound is less than the true length of the input decays inverse polynomially in n.

Lemma 9. *For all $c \geq 2, k \geq 2$, the RAM program $P : \mathcal{X} \times \mathcal{E} \to \mathbb{N} \times \mathcal{E}$ described in Program 2 outputs an estimate $\hat{y} = \mathtt{out}(P(x, \mathtt{env}))$ of $|x| = n$ that satisfies*

$$\Pr\left[\hat{y} < \frac{n}{2}\right] \leq O\left(\frac{1}{n^{c-1}}\right)$$

Proof. Let $n = |x|$ and $\hat{y} = \mathtt{out}(P(x, \mathtt{env}))$ be the output of Program 2. We have that

$$\begin{aligned} \Pr[\hat{y} < \frac{n}{2}] &= \sum_{i=1}^{\frac{n}{2}} \left(p_n(i) \prod_{j=0}^{i-1} (1 - p_n(j))\right) \\ &\leq \sum_{i=1}^{\frac{n}{2}} p_n(i) \qquad \text{(union bound)} \\ &\leq \frac{n}{2} \cdot p_n\left(\frac{n}{2}\right) \\ &= \frac{\frac{n}{2}}{(\frac{n}{2} + k)^c} \\ &\leq O\left(\frac{1}{n^{c-1}}\right) \end{aligned}$$

and the claim follows.

Program 3. JOT-DP RAM Program for the Unbounded Setting

Input: A dataset x, and a privacy parameter $\varepsilon_1 > 0$. The program P is hardcoded into line 4

Output: The output of P on input x truncated to $\hat{n}$ entries where $\hat{n}$ is a noisy upper bound on $|x|$

1: Set $\hat{n}$ to the output of Program 2 with constants k and c such that $k = O(c/\varepsilon_1)$;
2: $\hat{n} = 2 \cdot \hat{n}$;
3: $\hat{x} = \texttt{Truncate}(x, \hat{n})$; `// returns the first` $\hat{n}$ `entries of` x `if` $|x| > \hat{n}$
4: run ε_2-JOT-DP program $P^{\hat{n}}(\hat{x})$ and return the result

By Lemma 9, we can set $m = 2 \cdot \hat{y}$, ensuring that with probability $O(1/n^{c-1})$, we have $m \geq |x|$. We can then apply the same technique as in Sect. 3 and compose Program 2 with an arbitrary RAM program P that is JOT-DP in the upper-bounded setting. We describe the general construction in Program 3.

Lemma 10. *For all $c \geq 2$, $k \geq 2$, the RAM program $P : \mathcal{X} \times \mathcal{E} \to \mathbb{N} \times \mathcal{E}$ described in Program 2 runs in time $O(n)$ with probability at least $1 - (1 - \frac{1}{k^c})^n$, where $n = |x|$.*

Proof. The runtime of Program 2 is a deterministic function of its output. Specifically,

$$\begin{aligned} T_P(x, \texttt{env}) &= 5 + (\texttt{out}(P(x, \texttt{env})) + 1) \cdot (6 + 2(c - 1)) \\ &= O(\texttt{out}(P(x, \texttt{env}))) \end{aligned}$$

Thus, it suffices to show that $\Pr[\texttt{out}(P(x, \texttt{env})) \leq 2n]$ holds with high probability. Observe that:

$$\begin{aligned} \Pr[\texttt{out}(P(x, \texttt{env})) > 2n] &\leq \mathrm{Geom}\left(p = \frac{1}{k^c}, n\right) \\ &\leq \left(1 - \frac{1}{k^c}\right)^n \end{aligned}$$

Theorem 4 (Pure JOT-DP RAM Programs). *For all $\varepsilon > 0$, $\varepsilon' > \varepsilon$, and ε-DP RAM programs $P : \mathcal{X} \times \mathcal{E} \to \mathcal{Y} \times \mathcal{E}$ in the upper-bounded setting, there exists a ε'-JOT-DP RAM program $P' : \mathcal{X} \times \mathcal{E} \to \mathcal{Y} \times \mathcal{E}$ for the unbounded setting satisfying $\forall x \in \mathcal{X}$ of length n, $\forall$ input-compatible $\texttt{env} \in \mathcal{E}$, $\forall c \geq 2$:*

$$\Big\| \texttt{out}(P(x, \texttt{env})) - \texttt{out}(P'(x, \texttt{env})) \Big\|_{TV} < O\left(\frac{1}{n^c}\right)$$

Furthermore, the mechanism $P'(x, \texttt{env})$ is an explicit algorithm that makes one oracle call to P on a truncation of x along with an additional computation that takes time $O(|x|)$ with high probability.

Proof. The proof follows a similar structure to that of Theorem 2. In line 1 of Program 3, a noisy estimate $\hat{n}$ of $n = |x|$ is obtained by executing Program 2. By Lemma 8, Program 2 satisfies ε_1-JOT-DP in the unbounded setting. Furthermore, lines 2–3 can be executed in a fixed number of instructions. Thus, we represent lines 1–3 of Program 3 as the ε_1-JOT-DP program $P_{\texttt{(line 3)}}$.

Next, we consider the composition of $P_{\texttt{(line 3)}}$ with the ε_2-JOT-DP program P. By sequential composition, it follows that Program 3 is ε'-JOT-DP in the unbounded setting, where $\varepsilon' = \varepsilon_1 + \varepsilon_2$. What remains to be shown are the accuracy and runtime guarantees of Program 3.

By Lemma 10, we have that, with high probability, Program 3 runs in time $O(n)$ before making a single oracle call to P on a truncated version of x. Observe that, conditioned on $\hat{n} > \frac{n}{2}$ in line 1, we have $\hat{x} = x$ after executing line 3. Thus, Program 3 returns the output of the ε-JOT-DP program P on input x. By Lemma 9, Program 2 in line 1 returns an estimate $\hat{n}$ such that

$$\Pr\left[\hat{n} < \frac{n}{2}\right] = O\left(\frac{1}{n^{c-1}}\right)$$

Therefore, after executing line 2 so that $\hat{n} = 2 \cdot \hat{n}$, it follows that $\hat{n} > |x|$ with probability at least $1 - O(\frac{1}{n^{c-1}})$. Conditioning on this case, $\hat{x} = x$ after executing line 3, and therefore Program 3 will return the output of $P^{\hat{n}}$ on input x, where $P^{\hat{n}}$ accepts inputs of length at most $\hat{n}$ and satisfies $\hat{n} > |x|$.

Corollary 1 (Pure JOT-DP Laplace Mechanism). *For all $\varepsilon > 0$, and all $c > 0$, there exists an ε-JOT-DP RAM program $P : \mathcal{X} \times \mathcal{E} \to \mathcal{Y} \times \mathcal{E}$ for releasing sums in the unbounded setting such that for all datasets $x \in \mathcal{X}$:*

$$\Pr\left[\left|\texttt{out}(P(x, \texttt{env})) - \sum x_i\right| \geq \frac{C \cdot \ln(n)}{\varepsilon}\right] < O\left(\frac{1}{n^c}\right)$$

where $n = |x|$ is the size of the dataset, and $C > 0$ is a universal constant.

Proof Fix $c \geq 2$. Let M be the Censored Discrete Laplace mechanism that adds noise drawn from a Discrete Laplace distribution and clips the output to lie within the bounds $\ell = 0$ and $u = \Delta \cdot U$, where U is an upper bound on the input length and each $x_i \in [0, \Delta]$. By Lemma 4, there exists an ε'-JOT-DP RAM program $P_{\text{Lap}} : \mathcal{X} \times \mathcal{E} \to \mathcal{Y} \times \mathcal{E}$ that implements M, and furthermore P_{Lap} is a ε'-JOT-DP RAM program for the upper-bounded setting since it accepts inputs of length at most U. Let Z denote the output of the censored Discrete Laplace program P_{Lap}. Because $Z \sim \texttt{CensoredDiscreteLaplace}(\mu = \sum x_i, s = \Delta/\varepsilon', \ell = 0, u = \Delta \cdot U)$, we have

$$\Pr[|Z - \mu| \geq t] \leq \exp\left(-\frac{\varepsilon' \cdot t}{\Delta}\right)$$

Applying Theorem 4 with $\varepsilon > \varepsilon'$ gives an ε-JOT-DP RAM program $P : \mathcal{X} \times \mathcal{E} \to \mathcal{Y} \times \mathcal{E}$ such that, for every x of length n and every input-compatible env

$$\left\|\texttt{out}(P_{\text{Lap}}(x, \texttt{env})) - \texttt{out}(P(x, \texttt{env}))\right\|_{TV} = O(n^{-c})$$

Thus, by a union bound:

$$\Pr\left[\left|\texttt{out}(P(x, \texttt{env})) - \sum_{i=1}^{n} x_i\right| \geq t\right] \leq \exp\left(-\frac{\varepsilon' \cdot t}{\Delta}\right) + O(n^{-c})$$

We choose $t = \Delta \cdot c \ln n/\varepsilon'$ so that

$$\Pr\left[\left|\texttt{out}(P(x, \texttt{env})) - \sum_{i=1}^{n} x_i\right| \geq t\right] \leq \frac{1}{n^c} + O(n^{-c}) = O(n^{-c})$$

Thus, setting $C = \Delta \cdot c \cdot \varepsilon/\varepsilon'$ and substituting $t = C \ln n/\varepsilon$:

$$\Pr\left[\left|\texttt{out}(P(x, \texttt{env})) - \sum_{i=1}^{n} x_i\right| \geq \frac{C \ln n}{\varepsilon}\right] < O(n^{-c})$$

Acknowledgments. This work was supported in part by Cooperative Agreement CB20ADR0160001 with the Census Bureau and Salil Vadhan's Simons Investigator Award. Portions of the work were completed while Salil Vadhan was a Visiting Researcher in the School of Computer Science at the University of Sydney and at the Sydney Mathematical Research Institute.

A Appendix

We show that programs that attempt to avoid *all* information leakage through their runtime (i.e., $T_P(x, \texttt{env}) \equiv T_P(x', \texttt{env}')$ for all $x, x' \in \mathcal{D}^*$ and $\texttt{env}, \texttt{env}' \in \mathcal{E}$) will experience some loss in utility. In particular, we show that programs for computing means will exhibit a constant additive error in their output even as the length of the input $n \to \infty$. This result suggests that some portion of the program's privacy budget must be allocated to privatizing the program's runtime.

Lemma 11. *Let $P : \mathcal{X} \times \mathcal{E} \to \mathcal{Y} \times \mathcal{E}$ be a ε-DP RAM program for computing the mean $\frac{1}{|x|}\sum_{i=1} x_i$ such that $T_P(x, \texttt{env}) \equiv T_P(x', \texttt{env}')$ for all $x, x' \in \{0,1\}^*$ and input-compatible* $\texttt{env}, \texttt{env}' \in \mathcal{E}$*. Then for every $0 < \beta < 1$, there exists a dataset x and a constant α such that*

$$\Pr\left[\left|\texttt{out}(P(x, \texttt{env})) - \frac{1}{|x|}\sum x_i\right| > \alpha\right] > \beta$$

Proof. Let F be the cumulative distribution function of the runtime random variable $T_P(x, \texttt{env})$. We pick $p > 0$ and let $t = F^{-1}(1-p)$. Then $\Pr[T_P(x, \texttt{env}) > t] = p$. When $T_P(x, \texttt{env}) \leq t$, the program can read at most t entries of the input. By lower bounds for samplers [12], for every $0 < \beta < 1$, there exists an input x such that, conditioned on reading at most t locations of x, the algorithm fails to output an α-accurate estimate $\hat{\mu}$ of $\mu = \frac{1}{|x|}\sum x_i$ with probability at least β for

$$\alpha = \Omega\left(\sqrt{\frac{\log(1/\beta)}{t}}\right)$$

Thus, without conditioning, the program fails to output an α-accurate estimate of μ with probability at least $\beta - p$. We take $\beta = 2p$ so that t is a fixed constant and hence so is α.

Lemma 12 (No Fully-Dyadic Censored Discrete Laplace). *Fix integers $\ell < \mu < u$ and a scale $s > 0$. Let Z be the Discrete Laplace random variable with shift $\mu \in \mathbb{Z}$, censored to the support $\{\ell, \ell+1, \ldots, \mu, \mu+1, \ldots, u\}$:*

$$\Pr[Z = k] = \begin{cases} F(\ell \mid \mu, s) & \text{if } k = \ell \\ p(k \mid \mu, s) & \text{if } \ell < k < u \\ 1 - F(u-1 \mid \mu, s) & \text{if } k = u \\ 0 & \text{otherwise} \end{cases}$$

where

$$p(k \mid \mu, s) = \frac{e^{1/s} - 1}{e^{1/s} + 1} \cdot e^{-|k-\mu|/s}$$

$$F(x \mid \mu, s) = \begin{cases} \frac{e^{1/s}}{e^{1/s}+1} \cdot e^{-(\mu - x)/s} & \text{if } x \leq \mu \\ 1 - \frac{1}{e^{1/s}+1} \cdot e^{-(x-\mu)/s} & \text{if } x > \mu \end{cases}$$

If the support contains at least four points, then there exists a $k \in \{\ell, \ell+1, \ldots, \mu, \mu+1, \ldots, u\}$ such that:

$$\Pr[Z = k] \notin \left\{\tfrac{t}{2^N} : t, N \in \mathbb{N}\right\}$$

That is, there is at least one output mass that is non-dyadic.

Proof. Let $q = e^{-1/s} \in (0, 1)$ and $c = \dfrac{1-q}{1+q}$. For every interior index $\ell < k < u$ we have

$$\Pr[Z = k] = c \cdot q^{|k-\mu|}$$

Case 1: q is dyadic. Write $q = m/2^N$ with $1 \leq m < 2^N$ odd. Then

$$c = \frac{1-q}{1+q} = \frac{2^N - m}{2^N + m}$$

whose denominator $2^N + m$ is not a power of two, so c is non-dyadic. Because $\ell < \mu < u$, it follows that $\Pr[Z = \mu] = c$ is a non-dyadic mass.

Case 2: q *is not* dyadic. Write $q = r/d$ in lowest terms. Since q is not dyadic, the denominator d is not a power of two, so it contains at least one odd prime factor. Because the support has ≥ 4 points, either $\ell < \mu+1 < u$ or $\ell < \mu-1 < u$. Assume $\ell < \mu + 1 < u$ (the other side is symmetric). Then

$$\Pr[Z = \mu + 1] = c \cdot q = \frac{d-r}{d+r} \cdot \frac{r}{d}$$

Let j be the odd prime dividing d. Because $\gcd(r, d) = 1$, j does not divide r. Consequently j does not divide $(d - r)$ or $(d + r)$. Thus the denominator $d \cdot (d+r)$ contains at least one factor j, whereas the numerator $r \cdot (d-r)$ contains none. After cancelling the greatest common divisor, a power of j remains in the denominator, so the reduced fraction is not of the form $t/2^N$. Hence $\Pr[Z = \mu+1]$ is non-dyadic.

Lemma 13 (Finite-Coin Sampler for Censored Dyadic Symmetric Geometric). *Let integers $\ell < \mu < u$ and $p \in (0, 1)$ (dyadic rational) be given. Draw one unbiased coin for a sign $S \in \{-1, +1\}$ and draw $G \sim \mathrm{Geom}(p)$. Define a Dyadic Symmetric Geometric random variable as:*

$$Z = \begin{cases} \mu - G & \text{if } S = -1 \\ \mu + 1 + G & \text{if } S = +1 \end{cases}$$

Then a Censored *Dyadic Symmetric Geometric random variable*

$$Y = \max\{\ell, \min\{Z, u\}\}$$

is exactly sampleable with a finite (constant) number of unbiased coin flips under the RAM$_{\text{BDDNT}}$ model.

Proof. Flip one unbiased coin to choose a sign $S \in \{-1, +1\}$ and draw $G \sim \mathrm{Geom}(p)\big|_0^m$, the geometric distribution with parameter $p = 2^{-k}$ clamped to $\{0, 1, \ldots, m\}$ where $m = \max\{\mu - \ell, u - \mu\}$. Each Bernoulli($p$) trial in the geometric sampler can be implemented using exactly k unbiased coins, so the clamped geometric draw uses at most $k \cdot (m+1)$ coin flips. Together with the one coin for S, the entire sampling procedure uses at most $1 + k \cdot (m + 1)$ unbiased coins. Once S and G are drawn, define $Y = \mu - G$ if $S = -1$ and $Y = \mu + 1 + G$ if $S = +1$. The value Y is a sample from the clamped Dyadic Symmetric Geometric distribution centered at μ and clamped to $[\ell, u]$ as desired. Therefore, Y is sampleable with a finite (constant) number of unbiased coin flips under the RAM$_{\text{BDDNT}}$ model.

Lemma 14 (Censored Dyadic Symmetric Geometric Mechanism is DP). *Fix integers* $\ell < \mu < u$ *and let* $\mu' = \mu + 1$. *Let* $p \in (0,1)$ *be any dyadic rational. Let* $Z \sim \mathrm{DTG}_{\mu,p}$ *and* $Z' \sim \mathrm{DSG}_{\mu',p}$ *be samples from the (unclamped) Dyadic Symmetric Geometric distribution centered at* μ *and* μ'*, respectively. Let* $Y = \max\{\ell, \min\{Z, u\}\}$ *and* $Y' = \max\{\ell, \min\{Z', u\}\}$. *Then for every* $y \in \mathbb{Z} \cap [\ell, u]$ *we have*

$$\frac{\Pr[Y = y]}{\Pr[Y' = y]} \leq \frac{1}{1-p} \quad \textit{and} \quad \frac{\Pr[Y' = y]}{\Pr[Y = y]} \leq \frac{1}{1-p}$$

so the mechanism is ε*-differentially private with*

$$\varepsilon = \ln\left(\tfrac{1}{1-p}\right)$$

Proof. We analyze the *unclamped* Dyadic Symmetric Geometric random variables Z and Z'. Generate Z by flipping one unbiased coin for a sign $S \in \{-1, +1\}$ and drawing $G \sim \mathrm{Geom}(p)$, setting $Z = \mu - G$ if $S = -1$ and $Z = \mu + 1 + G$ if $S = +1$. Generate Z' in the same way but with center $\mu' = \mu + 1$. For every $z \in \mathbb{Z}$ the shift of the center changes the probability mass by *at most* a single factor of $q = 1 - p$, so

$$\frac{\Pr[Z = z]}{\Pr[Z' = z]} \leq q^{-1} \quad \text{and} \quad \frac{\Pr[Z' = z]}{\Pr[Z = z]} \leq q^{-1}$$

Since the ratio for Z and Z' is bounded by $1/(1-p)$, the random variables Z and Z' are ε–differentially private with

$$\varepsilon = \ln\left(\tfrac{1}{1-p}\right)$$

The outputs $Y = \max\{\ell, \min\{Z, u\}\}$ and $Y' = \max\{\ell, \min\{Z', u\}\}$ are obtained from Z and Z' by deterministic clamping, which is a post-processing operation. Consequently the same bound holds for every $y \in \mathbb{Z} \cap [\ell, u]$ and the clamped mechanism is also ε–DP.

Theorem 5 (Pure JOT-DP *RAM*$_{BDDNT}$ Programs in the Unbounded Setting). *For all* $0 < \beta < 1$, $\varepsilon > 0$, $\varepsilon' > \varepsilon$, *and* ε*-JOT-DP RAM*$_{BDDNT}$ *programs* $P : \mathcal{X} \times \mathcal{E} \to \mathcal{Y} \times \mathcal{E}$ *in the* upper-*bounded setting, there exists a* ε'*-JOT-DP RAM*$_{BDDNT}$ *program* $P' : \mathcal{X} \times \mathcal{E} \to \mathcal{Y} \times \mathcal{E}$ *for the unbounded setting such that*

$$\left\| \mathtt{out}(P(x, \mathtt{env})) - \mathtt{out}(P'(x, \mathtt{env})) \right\|_{TV} < \beta$$

Furthermore, the mechanism $P'(x, \mathtt{env})$ *is simply an explicit algorithm that makes one oracle call to* P *on a truncation of* x *along with an additional computation that takes time* $O(|x|)$ *with probability at least* $1 - \beta - O(|x|^{-c})$ *for some constant* $c > 0$.

Proof. By replacing the call to `CensoredDiscreteLaplace` in Program 1 with the Censored Dyadic Symmetric Geometric Mechanism `CDSG`, we obtain an equivalent result for Theorem 2 in the $\mathrm{RAM}_{\mathrm{BDDNT}}$ model. This follows directly from Lemma 13 and Lemma 14 which give the needed ε_i-DP mechanism that executes in constant-time during each iteration of the program's loop. The rest of the proof follows identically to the proof of Theorem 2. In particular, during each iteration of the loop, when $m_i \geq (2/\varepsilon_i) \cdot \ln(1/\beta_i)$ we can round $p = 1 - e^{-\varepsilon_i}$ up to the nearest dyadic rational. Then when $m_i < |x|$, we have that for $\hat{n}_i = \mathtt{CDSG}(\mu = m_i, p = 1 - e^{-\varepsilon_i}, \ell = 0, u = m_i)$:

$$\Pr\left[\hat{n}_i < \tfrac{m_i}{2}\right] = \frac{(1-p)^{\frac{m_i}{2}}}{2} \leq e^{-m_i \cdot \varepsilon_i/2} \leq \beta_i$$

as desired. Furthermore, if we let iteration j be the first iteration when $m_j > 4 \cdot |x|$, then for $\hat{n}_j = \mathtt{CDSG}(\mu = |x|, p = 1 - e^{-\varepsilon_j}, \ell = 0, u = m_j)$:

$$\Pr\left[\hat{n}_j > \tfrac{m_j}{2}\right] = \frac{(1-p)^{\frac{m_j}{2} - |x|}}{2} \leq e^{-\varepsilon_j \cdot |x|} \leq e^{-\Theta(\log |x|)} \leq |x|^{-\Theta(1)}$$

Thus, with high probability the program halts on iteration j, and therefore the runtime analysis follows exactly to that of Theorem 2.

References

1. Abowd, J.M.: The us census bureau adopts differential privacy. In: Proceedings of the 24th ACM SIGKDD International Conference on Knowledge Discovery & Data Mining, pp. 2867–2867 (2018)
2. Aktay, A., et al.: Google covid-19 community mobility reports: anonymization process description (version 1.1). arXiv preprint arXiv:2004.04145 (2020)
3. Al Fardan, N.J., Paterson, K.G.: Lucky thirteen: breaking the TLS and DTLs record protocols. In: 2013 IEEE Symposium on Security and Privacy, pp. 526–540. IEEE (2013)
4. Albrecht, M.R., Paterson, K.G.: Lucky microseconds: a timing attack on amazon's s2n implementation of TLS. In: Fischlin, M., Coron, J.-S. (eds.) EUROCRYPT 2016. LNCS, vol. 9665, pp. 622–643. Springer, Heidelberg (2016). https://doi.org/10.1007/978-3-662-49890-3_24
5. Andrysco, M., Kohlbrenner, D., Mowery, K., Jhala, R., Lerner, S., Shacham, H.: On subnormal floating point and abnormal timing. In: 2015 IEEE Symposium on Security and Privacy, pp. 623–639. IEEE (2015)
6. Apple: Privacy-preserving machine learning with homomorphic encryption (2024). https://machinelearning.apple.com/research/homomorphic-encryption. Accessed 19 Jan 2025
7. Asi, H., et al.: Scalable private search with wally. arXiv preprint arXiv:2406.06761 (2024)
8. Balcer, V., Vadhan, S.: Differential privacy on finite computers. J. Priv. Confidentiality **9**, 2 (2019)

9. Ben Dov, Y., David, L., Naor, M., Tzalik, E.: Resistance to timing attacks for sampling and privacy preserving schemes. In: 4th Symposium on Foundations of Responsible Computing (FORC 2023). Schloss Dagstuhl-Leibniz-Zentrum für Informatik (2023)
10. Brumley, B.B., Tuveri, N.: Remote timing attacks are still practical. In: Atluri, V., Diaz, C. (eds.) ESORICS 2011. LNCS, vol. 6879, pp. 355–371. Springer, Heidelberg (2011). https://doi.org/10.1007/978-3-642-23822-2_20
11. Brumley, D., Boneh, D.: Remote timing attacks are practical. Comput. Netw. **48**(5), 701–716 (2005)
12. Canetti, R., Even, G., Goldreich, O.: Lower bounds for sampling algorithms for estimating the average. Inf. Process. Lett. **53**(1), 17–25 (1995)
13. Chan, T.H.H., Chung, K.M., Maggs, B., Shi, E.: Foundations of differentially oblivious algorithms. ACM J. ACM (JACM) **69**(4), 1–49 (2022)
14. Dwork, C., McSherry, F., Nissim, K., Smith, A.: Calibrating noise to sensitivity in private data analysis. In: Halevi, S., Rabin, T. (eds.) TCC 2006. LNCS, vol. 3876, pp. 265–284. Springer, Heidelberg (2006). https://doi.org/10.1007/11681878_14
15. Ghosh, A., Roughgarden, T., Sundararajan, M.: Universally utility-maximizing privacy mechanisms. SIAM J. Comput. **41**(6), 1673–1693 (2012)
16. Greenberg, A., et al.: Apple's "differential privacy" is about collecting your data–but not your data. Wired **13**(1) (2016)
17. Haeberlen, A., Pierce, B.C., Narayan, A.: Differential privacy under fire. In: 20th USENIX Security Symposium (USENIX Security 2011) (2011)
18. Jin, J., McMurtry, E., Rubinstein, B.I., Ohrimenko, O.: Are we there yet? Timing and floating-point attacks on differential privacy systems. arXiv preprint arXiv:2112.05307 (2021)
19. Kocher, P., et al.: Spectre attacks: exploiting speculative execution. Commun. ACM **63**(7), 93–101 (2020)
20. Kocher, P.C.: Timing attacks on implementations of Diffie-Hellman, RSA, DSS, and other systems. In: Koblitz, N. (ed.) CRYPTO 1996. LNCS, vol. 1109, pp. 104–113. Springer, Heidelberg (1996). https://doi.org/10.1007/3-540-68697-5_9
21. Lazar, D., Gilad, Y., Zeldovich, N.: Karaoke: distributed private messaging immune to passive traffic analysis. In: 13th USENIX Symposium on Operating Systems Design and Implementation (OSDI 2018), pp. 711–725 (2018)
22. Lipp, M., et al.: Meltdown. arXiv preprint arXiv:1801.01207 (2018)
23. Messing, S., et al.: Facebook Privacy-Protected Full URLs Data Set (2020). https://doi.org/10.7910/DVN/TDOAPG
24. Nissim, K., Raskhodnikova, S., Smith, A.: Smooth sensitivity and sampling in private data analysis. In: Proceedings of the Thirty-Ninth Annual ACM Symposium on Theory of Computing, pp. 75–84 (2007)
25. Ratliff, Z., Vadhan, S.: A framework for differential privacy against timing attacks. In: Proceedings of the 2024 on ACM SIGSAC Conference on Computer and Communications Security, pp. 3615–3629 (2024)
26. Van Den Hooff, J., Lazar, D., Zaharia, M., Zeldovich, N.: Vuvuzela: scalable private messaging resistant to traffic analysis. In: Proceedings of the 25th Symposium on Operating Systems Principles, pp. 137–152 (2015)
27. Van Erven, T., Harremos, P.: Rényi divergence and kullback-leibler divergence. IEEE Trans. Inf. Theory **60**(7), 3797–3820 (2014)

Cryptography with Weak Privacy

Amos Beimel[1(✉)], Yuval Ishai[2,3], Eyal Kushilevitz[2], and Hanjun Li[4]

[1] Ben Gurion University, Be'er Sheva, Israel
amos.beimel@gmail.com
[2] Technion, Haifa, Israel
[3] AWS, New York, USA
[4] Carnegie Mellon University, Pittsburgh, USA

Abstract. We initiate a systematic study of information-theoretic cryptography with *weak privacy*, only requiring that the adversary cannot rule out any possible secret. For a parameter $0 < p \leq 1$, we say that a primitive has p-weak privacy (p-WP) if for every possible view V and inputs x_1, x_2, the ratio between the probabilities of the adversary observing V on x_1 and on x_2 is at least p. This generalizes both perfect privacy, which is p-WP for $p = 1$, and a previous "combinatorial" notion of privacy, which is p-WP for *some* $p > 0$. We obtain the following main results.

- **Positive results.** We present efficient WP constructions for generalized secret sharing, decomposable randomized encodings, and the related notions of garbling schemes and PSM protocols, as well as interactive secure multiparty computation protocols in the plain model and in the OT-hybrid model. For secret sharing, we settle a question of Beimel and Franklin (TCC 2007), showing that every n-party access structure admits a WP scheme with per-party share size $O(n)$. When all unauthorized sets have constant size, we get a p-WP scheme with constant share size and $p \geq 1/\text{poly}(n)$.
- **Negative result.** For decomposable randomized encodings, we show that a previous lower bound technique of Ball et al. (ITCS 2020) applies also to the WP notion. Together with our upper bound, this shows that the optimal WP garbling size of the worst-case $f : \{0,1\}^n \to \{0,1\}$ is $\tilde{\Theta}(n^2)$.
- **Application.** While WP may seem like an unrealistically weak security notion, we demonstrate its usefulness towards achieving traditional security guarantees. Concretely, under the standard LPN assumption, we show that any p-WP secret-sharing scheme with inverse-polynomial p implies a *computationally secure* secret-sharing scheme for a related access structure. Together with our positive results for WP secret sharing, this implies a super-polynomial improvement of the share size for a natural class of access structures.

1 Introduction

Information-theoretic cryptography is an area full of big open questions. For the widely studied problem of information-theoretic secure multiparty computation (MPC), there are still exponential gaps between the best upper and lower bounds on the communication required for computing general functions $f : \{0,1\}^n \to \{0,1\}$ [9]. Similarly,

B. Applebaum and H. Lin (Eds.): TCC 2025, LNCS 16271, pp. 415–447, 2026.
https://doi.org/10.1007/978-3-032-12290-2_14

for the problem of realizing a general monotone access structure Γ by a secret-sharing scheme, there are still exponential gaps between the best known lower bound on the share size [21] and the best known upper bounds, in spite of significant recent progress on the upper bounds front [2,4,37–39].

Motivated by this state of affairs, it is natural to consider simpler "toy versions" of the above open questions. In this work, we revisit these questions by considering a very weak notion of security that only insists on *possible deniability*, in the sense that no admissible secret can be ruled out by the adversary. Can the above exponential gaps be closed in this simpler setting?

Weak Privacy. More concretely, we consider the following notion of weak secrecy which is inspired by differential privacy. For $0 < p \leq 1$, we say that a primitive is *p-weakly private*, or p-WP for short, if for any possible view V of the adversary and any two "equivalent" inputs x_1, x_2,

$$\Pr[\text{ The adversary sees } V \text{ on input } x_1] \geq p \cdot \Pr[\text{ The adversary sees } V \text{ on input } x_2].$$

For example, in the context of secret-sharing schemes, the view of an adversary consists of the shares of an unauthorized set of parties, and the inputs are any two secrets. This is similar to the definition of pure differential privacy of Dwork, McSherry, Nissim, and Smith [24] except for considering all pairs of admissible inputs rather than only pairs of neighboring inputs. However, in the differential privacy literature, the parameter p is typically viewed as a constant.[1] In contrast, we typically consider small values $p > 0$ that vanish with the instance size n (e.g., $1/n$ or even $1/2^n$). While potentially leaking a lot of information about the inputs, WP implementations of cryptographic primitives still leave some small ambiguity and hence a possible room for deniability.

Jumping ahead, we will later use the fact that a p-WP view of a secret bit b can be simulated from the output of a *binary symmetric channel* that flips b with probability $\delta = p/(1+p)$ [32], which is close to p when p is small. This motivates the specific distance metric that we use. In contrast, the standard notion of security with statistical distance $0 \leq \varepsilon \leq 1$ can only guarantee a similar simulation from the output of a *binary erasure channel* that erases b with probability $\delta = 1 - \varepsilon$ [40].

Example 1.1 (WP private information retrieval). In a 2-server private information retrieval (PIR) protocol [19], two servers hold an n-bit database and a user wants to retrieve the i-th bit of the database without disclosing i to each server. The best known 2-server PIR protocol with perfect privacy has communication $2^{\tilde{O}(\sqrt{\log n})}$ [23]. We next describe a simple WP 2-server PIR protocol with much better efficiency; the user, on index i, with probability $1/2$ sends i to the first server and a random index $j \neq i$ to the second server and with probability $1/2$ sends i to the second server and a random index $j \neq i$ to the first server. Each server sends the bit of the database specified by the message it gets. The probability that a server gets the index j when the user's index is j is $1/2$ and the probability that a server gets the index j when the user's index is $i \neq j$ is $1/2(n-1)$; thus, the protocol is $\frac{1}{n-1}$-WP.

[1] Since here we consider a minimal notion of privacy, we use a different parameterization than in the differential privacy literature; namely, p-WP corresponds to ε-DP for $\varepsilon = \ln(1/p)$.

In the extreme, we consider a "combinatorial" notion of secrecy, sometimes referred to as *weak privacy* (WP), which only requires that it is *never* the case that an adversary can rule out an input with *absolute certainty*. Equivalently, WP is p-WP for an arbitrary $p > 0$. Such a combinatorial notion of secrecy was already studied for different cryptographic problems. Beimel and Franklin [8] studied weakly private secret-sharing schemes, requiring that any set of shares which is possible for an unauthorized set of parties on one secret s is also possible on any other secret s' (i.e., the two share distributions have equal supports, though the probabilities can be very different). Beaver, Haber, and Winkler [7] considered key agreement from correlated randomness, where they only require weak privacy, i.e., every key is *possible* given the communication that is exchanged between the parties.

Motivation. Beyond the theoretical interest in WP as a natural notion of security, we study this notion for three additional reasons. The first two also apply to the "combinatorial" notion of weak privacy, while the third critically depends on the quantitative notion of p-WP we introduce in this work.

- STRONGER NEGATIVE RESULTS. Since weak privacy relaxes perfect privacy, ruling out weak privacy yields stronger negative results that apply to the *combinatorics* of the problem at hand. Beimel and Franklin [8] give several examples of cryptographic tasks where weak privacy and perfect privacy have essentially the same power; this gives a more complete picture of the feasibility of such tasks. For example, Shannon's classic result [42] that in any perfect encryption scheme the key length is at least the length of the message only requires weak privacy (i.e., that given an encryption, all messages are possible). As another example, Kushilevitz [36] characterized the functions that can be computed with perfect privacy by two semi-honest parties; in particular, a function can be computed in this model with perfect privacy if and only if it can be computed with weak privacy.
- GUIDING RESEARCH EFFORTS. When considering challenging open questions about perfect privacy, studying the simpler combinatorial notion of weak privacy is a natural first step. In particular, WP lower bounds (while stronger) are typically simple to obtain whenever they exist. In light of this, strong *upper bounds* for weak privacy can be useful in ruling out such a combinatorial approach to lower bounds. For example, for the case of the 2-out-of-n threshold access structure, Beimel and Franklin showed that 2 bits per share suffice for a weakly-private secret sharing of a 1-bit secret, compared to the $\Theta(\log n)$ share size required for a (standard) perfectly private scheme for this access structure [14,17,33,41]. Alternatively, if improved WP upper bounds turn out to be challenging, this may suggest that the barrier towards progress is combinatorial in nature.
- BOOSTING WP TO STANDARD SECURITY. Somewhat surprisingly, we will demonstrate that in some cases p-WP security with an inverse-polynomial p can serve as a useful step towards new results for standard cryptographic primitives satisfying the usual notion of security.

1.1 Our Contribution

Motivated by the above, we initiate a systematic study of WP security for some of the central primitives in information-theoretic cryptography. In a nutshell, we obtain three types of results:

- Positive results. We present efficient WP constructions for secret-sharing schemes realizing general access structures, decomposable randomized encodings (and the related notions of garbling schemes and PSM protocols), and secure two-party and multi-party computation with and without correlated randomness.
- Negative result. For the case of decomposable randomized encodings, we show that a previous lower bound technique of Ball, Holmgren, Ishai, Liu, and Malkin [6] applies also to the relaxed WP notion. This leads to an almost tight bound on the WP complexity of this and related primitives.
- Application. We show how to leverage our positive results on WP secret sharing for general access structures to improve the state of the art on *computational* secret sharing for a natural class of access structures (under a standard cryptographic assumption).

We now give a more detailed account of our results, starting with the case of secret sharing.

WP Secret-Sharing Schemes. In a secret-sharing scheme [14,31,41], there is a dealer holding a secret (for simplicity, a bit) that she wants to distribute among a set of parties. This is done by giving each party a string (called the share) such that only some pre-defined subsets of the n parties can recover the secret from their shares; the collection of authorized sets is called an access structure. In a perfect secret-sharing scheme, the probability of any possible shares of an unauthorized set (a set not in the access structure) given that the secret is 0 is equal to the probability that these shares are generated for the secret 1. Our WP definition allows for the probabilities of the shares for the two secrets 0, 1 to be different, but it bounds the ratio between them. Formally, for $0 < p \leq 1$, the notion of p-WP requires that for every unauthorized set A, any possible collection of shares $\langle \mathsf{sh}_j \rangle_{p_i \in A}$, and any secret $s \in \{0, 1\}$ we have:

$$\begin{aligned} &\Pr[\text{ The shares generated for } A \text{ on the secret } s \text{ are } \langle \mathsf{sh}_j \rangle_{p_i \in A}] \\ &\quad \geq p \cdot \Pr[\text{ The shares generated for } A \text{ on the secret } \overline{s} \text{ are } \langle \mathsf{sh}_j \rangle_{p_i \in A}]. \end{aligned}$$

In particular, $p = 1$ gives perfect privacy, while any positive $p > 0$ gives weak privacy. We present our results for secret-sharing schemes in Sect. 3. The main result is a p-WP secret-sharing scheme with linear share size, for every access structure. When all unauthorized sets are of constant size, we get p which is inverse-polynomial; otherwise, it can be exponentially small. More generally:

Informal Theorem 1 (WP secret sharing for general access structures). *Let Γ be an n-party access structure in which all unauthorized sets are of size at most t. Then, there is a p-WP secret-sharing scheme (for 1-bit secrets) that realizes Γ with per-party share size $O(t)$, where $p = \Omega(n^{-t})$ if t is constant and $p = 2^{-O(t \log(n/t))}$ for general $t = t(n)$.*

Access structures where the size of the maximal unauthorized sets is $t = 2$ are known as forbidden graph access structures [43]. The best known perfect secret-sharing scheme for n-party forbidden graph access structures has shares of size $2^{\tilde{O}(\sqrt{\log n})}$ [38]. We construct a $1/n^2$-WP scheme for them with share size $O(1)$. For general n-party access structures, the best known perfect secret-sharing scheme has shares of size $2^{0.58n}$ [4]. We construct a $1/2^{\Theta(n)}$-WP scheme for them with share size $O(n)$. This solves an open problem of Beimel and Franklin [8].

We shortly recall previous results on weakly-private secret-sharing schemes. The work of Beimel and Franklin [8], which served as the starting point for our work, defined and studied weakly-private secret-sharing schemes. When combined with [4], their construction yield, for every access structure, a WP secret-sharing scheme for sharing a long q-bit secrets with share size $q + 2^{0.58n}$; that is, their scheme has information ratio 1 for large values of q. In contrast, we construct such schemes with share size $q + O(n)$. Beimel and Franklin [8] also constructed WP t-out-of-n secret-sharing schemes with share size $O(t)$, which improves upon perfect secret-sharing schemes when $t < \log n$. In addition, Beimel and Franklin proved that the share size in any weakly-private t-out-of-n secret-sharing scheme is at least $\Omega(\min\{t, \log\log\log(n-t)\})$. This implies that the share size in weakly-private secret-sharing schemes for the worst access structure is $\Omega(\log\log\log(n)) = \omega(1)$. A related notion of differentially-private secret-sharing schemes was previously studied by Talwar [44], where a differentially-private n-out-of-n secret-sharing scheme of vectors of norm at most 1 was constructed.

WP Decomposable Randomized Encoding. We then turn to apply this notion of weak privacy in the context of Decomposable Randomized Encoding (DRE) (see [3]). A DRE can be viewed as a simple information-theoretic variant of a garbling scheme [12,45], or alternatively as an n-party Private Simultaneous Message (PSM) protocol [26,30] in which each party holds only one input bit.

More formally, a randomized encoding of a function $f : \{0,1\}^n \to \{0,1\}$ is a randomized function $\textsc{Enc}$ that, given an input $x \in \{0,1\}^n$, outputs an encoding $\hat{y} \leftarrow \textsc{Enc}(x;r)$ of $f(x)$ while hiding all other information about x. That is, (1) one can recover $f(x)$ from the encoding $\hat{y}$, i.e., there is a decoding procedure $\textsc{Dec}$ such that $\textsc{Dec}(\textsc{Enc}(x;r)) = x$, and (2) $\textsc{Enc}(x;r)$ and $\textsc{Enc}(x';r)$ are equally distributed for every x, x' such that $f(x') = f(x)$. Of course, $\textsc{Enc}(x)$ can always output $f(x)$; however, usually the goal is to use a randomized function $\textsc{Enc}$ that is easier to compute than the original function f. We consider a scenario in which $x = (x_1, \ldots, x_n)$ is distributed between n parties, i.e., the i-th party holds x_i and there is no central authority that can compute $\textsc{Enc}(x)$. In a *decomposable randomized encoding (DRE)*, each party locally computes $\textsc{Enc}_i(x_i;r)$ such that $\textsc{Enc}(x;r) = (\textsc{Enc}_1(x_1;r), \ldots, \textsc{Enc}_n(x_n;r))$ is a randomized encoding of x (note that all local encoding have access to the same randomness r). The best known DRE for an arbitrary function $f : \{0,1\}^n \to \{0,1\}$ is of size $\text{poly}(n) \cdot 2^{n/2}$ [5,9,10]. We consider p-WP decomposable randomized encodings, where the privacy requirement is relaxed, requiring that $\Pr[\,\textsc{Enc}(x;r) = \widehat{y}\,] \geq p \cdot \Pr[\,\textsc{Enc}(x';r) = \widehat{y}\,]$, for every x, x' such that $f(x) = f(x')$ and every $\hat{y}$. We show how to construct efficient WP randomized encoding for arbitrary functions.

Informal Theorem 2 (Upper bound for WP DRE). *Let $f : \{0,1\}^n \to \{0,1\}$ be a function. There is a $2^{-O(n)}$-WP decomposable randomized encoding for f with encoding size $\tilde{O}(n^2)$.*

We also prove nearly matching lower bounds for WP randomized encoding of some explicit functions, showing that the encoding size in the above theorem is tight up to a logarithmic factor. This lower bound is the same as the lower bound of Ball et al. [6], which is the best known lower bound for statistical randomized encoding; our proof is an adaptation of the proof of Ball et al., showing that weak privacy suffices to prove the lower bound. We note that our result is incomparable to the results of Ball et al., as their proof applies to the incomparable notion of statistical privacy and allows error in the correctness.

Informal Theorem 3 (Lower bound for WP DRE). *There exist explicit functions $f : \{0,1\}^n \to \{0,1\}$ such that, for every $p > 0$, any p-WP decomposable randomized encoding for f has size $\Omega(n^2/\log n)$.*

WP Secure MPC Protocols. We construct WP k-party secure multiparty computation protocols, for any function $f : (\{0,1\}^n)^k \to \{0,1\}$, that are secure against a semi-honest adversary. We construct such protocols in two settings. First, we consider the plain model and assume that there is an honest majority, i.e., the adversary controls less than $k/2$ parties. Second, we consider the case where there is no guarantee of an honest majority, i.e., the adversary can control any subset of parties. In this case, for many functions, MPC protocols do not exist in the plain model even if we require weak privacy; the impossibility results of [20,36] hold also assuming weak privacy. We, therefore, consider the OT-hybrid model, i.e., in each step of the protocol a pair of parties can give inputs to an ideal computation of the oblivious transfer (OT) functionality and the first party gets its output.[2] The p-WP property for these two models is defined analogously to the case of DRE described above. We obtain the following results.

Informal Theorem 4 (Upper bound for WP MPC protocols). *Let $f : (\{0,1\}^n)^k \to \{0,1\}$ be a function.*

- *There is a $2^{-O(kn)}$-WP secure k-party protocol for f in the plain model assuming an honest majority, in which the communication complexity is* $\text{poly}(k) \cdot n$.
- *There is a $2^{-O(kn)}$-WP secure k-party protocol for f in the OT-hybrid model secure against any number of semi-honest parties, in which the communication complexity and the number of calls to OT are* $\text{poly}(k) \cdot n$.

Beimel and Malkin [11] proved that in any secure 2-party protocol for the equality function with inputs of size n (and for other functions) the OT complexity is $\Omega(n)$; this lower bound holds also for weakly-private 2-PC protocols and implies a lower bound of $\Omega(kn)$ for some functions $f : (\{0,1\}^n)^k \to \{0,1\}$ (e.g., $f(x_1,\ldots,x_k) = 1$ if

[2] In an ideal computation of OT, the first party's input is $i \in \{0,1\}$, the second party's input is a pair of bits b_0, b_1, the first party gets output b_i without learning any information about $b_{\bar{i}}$ and the second party does not learn any information about i.

$x_1 \circ \cdots \circ x_{k/2} = x_{k/2+1} \circ \cdots \circ x_k$ for an even k). This implies that our weakly-private protocols in the OT-hybrid model are optimal up to a factor of poly(k).

We next review the best known protocols with perfect privacy for this task, starting with the OT-hybrid model and then moving to the plain model with honest majority. Beimel et al. [9] showed that every function $f : (\{0,1\}^n)^2 \to \{0,1\}$ can be computed by a secure 2-PC protocol in the OT-hybrid model, where the OT and communication complexities are $2^{\tilde{O}(\sqrt{n})}$ (this is achieved by plugging the PIR protocol of [23] in the protocol of [9]). For $k > 2$, the best k-party MPC protocol in the OT-hybrid model for a function $f : (\{0,1\}^n)^k \to \{0,1\}$ is the GMW protocol [29], where the OT and communication complexities are poly$k$ times the size of the best Boolean circuit computing f; for almost all functions this results in a protocol with OT and communication complexities $2^{O(kn)}$.

The best known secure 3-PC protocol for a function $f : (\{0,1\}^n)^3 \to \{0,1\}$ in the plain model assuming at most one semi-honest party has communication complexities $2^{\tilde{O}(\sqrt[3]{n})}$ (this is achieved by plugging the PIR protocol of [28] in the 2-PC protocol of [9] with correlated randomness and transforming it into a secure 3-party protocol in the plain model). For $k > 3$, the best k-party MPC protocol for a function $f : (\{0,1\}^n)^k \to \{0,1\}$ in the plain model is the BGW protocol [13], where the communication is poly$k$ times the size of the best Arithmetic circuit computing f; for almost all functions this results in a protocol with communication complexity $2^{O(kn)}$.

Computational Secret-Sharing Schemes for Composed Gap Access Structures. Finally, we present a somewhat unexpected application of our new WP secret-sharing schemes. While it may seem that WP security is unrealistically weak, we show that this notion (with inverse-polynomial p) can be leveraged towards improving the efficiency of *standard* computational secret sharing for a natural class of access structures. In fact, we obtain an exponential improvement over the best known information-theoretic secret-sharing schemes for the same access structures. Recall that in computational secret-sharing schemes [1,35,46], the sharing and reconstruction are efficient, and a computationally-bounded adversary cannot learn information from the shares of an unauthorized set.

We consider "composed gap access structures." To explain what this means, recall the notion of ramp secret-sharing schemes [15], which generalize threshold schemes. Ramp schemes (also known as gap threshold schemes) are parameterized by the number of parties n and two integers $0 \le \alpha \le \beta \le 1$; it is required that every set of less than αn parties should not learn any information about the secret, while every set of size at least βn parties can reconstruct the secret. This scheme realizes a partially-defined access structure, i.e., there are no requirements on sets of parties whose size is at least αn and less than βn. We consider a composed gap access structure, where we replace each party in the ramp scheme by an access structure; that is, we are given m access structures $\Gamma_1, \ldots, \Gamma_m$ on disjoint sets of parties $P_1, \ldots, P_m$ and parameters $0 \le \alpha \le \beta \le 1$ and consider a composed gap access structure $\mathrm{Gap}_{\alpha,\beta}(\Gamma_1, \ldots, \Gamma_m)$, which is a partially defined access structure such that:

- A set B is authorized if it is authorized in at least βm access structures, i.e., $|\{i : B \cap P_i \in \Gamma_i\}| \ge \beta m$.

- A set A is unauthorized if it is authorized in less than αm access structures, i.e., $|\{i : A \cap P_i \in \Gamma_i\}| < \alpha m$.

As in ramp schemes, we do not have any requirements on sets C such that $\alpha m \leq |\{i : C \cap P_i \in \Gamma_i\}| < \beta m$ (i.e., they can either reconstruct the secret, learn no information about the secret, or learn partial information about the secret). Composed-gap access structures are used in [2,4] to construct the best known schemes for arbitrary access structures; in their construction, each Γ_i has exponentially many parties, while we only construct schemes where each Γ_i has a logarithmic number of parties.

Our computational secret-sharing schemes are based on the hardness of the learning parity with noise (LPN) problem [16]. The (decisional) LPN assumption roughly says that, for a public random linear code generated by a random matrix $C \in \mathbb{F}_2^{O(k)\times k}$, it is hard to distinguish between a noisy encoding $Cx + e$ of a random message $x \in \mathbb{F}_2^k$ and a uniformly random vector in $\mathbb{F}_2^{O(k)}$. Concretely, we assume that each coordinate of the error vector e is independently sampled from a Bernoulli distribution with parameter $1/\sqrt{k}$. In fact, LPN is widely conjectured to hold even if we take a Bernoulli distribution with parameter $1/k^c$ for any constant $0 < c < 1$.

Informal Theorem 5 (Computational secret-sharing schemes for composed gap). *Let α, β be constants such that $\beta > 1/2$ and $0 \leq \alpha \leq 1 - h(\beta)$. There exists a constant γ such that assuming that $\mathrm{LPN}(k, \gamma/\sqrt{k})$ holds, the following computational secret-sharing schemes exist:*

- *A scheme with share size $O(1)$ for the family of access structures $\mathrm{Gap}_{\alpha,\beta}(\Gamma_1, \ldots, \Gamma_m)$, where each Γ_i is a forbidden graph access structure with $m^{1/4}$ parties.*
- *A scheme with share size $\log m$ for the family of access structures $\mathrm{Gap}_{\alpha,\beta}(\Gamma_1, \ldots, \Gamma_m)$, where each Γ_i is an access structure with $0.1 \cdot \log m$ parties.*

We next compare the above computational schemes to the best known perfect secret-sharing schemes for composed gap access structures. For $\beta = 1$ and a constant $\alpha < 1$, there is a perfect secret-sharing scheme for composed gap access structures for forbidden graph access structures with 1-bit shares (see the full version). For other cases, the known perfect schemes are much less efficient than the computational schemes; for composed gap forbidden graph access structures, the best scheme we can construct has share size $2^{\tilde{O}(\sqrt{\log n})}$ and for the gap composition of arbitrary access structures, the best scheme we can construct has share size $n^{0.058-o(1)}$. That is, for the latter case, there is an exponential gap in the share size of our WP secret-sharing scheme and the best known perfect secret-sharing scheme.

Open Problems. We initiated a systematic study of WP variants of central cryptographic primitives. In addition to extending this study to other primitives, our results leave several natural open problems.

- What is the biggest $p \leq 1$ such that there are p-WP secret-sharing schemes for arbitrary access structures with polynomial share size? As the best known lower bound on the share size for perfect secret-sharing schemes is $\Omega(n/\log(n))$ [21], we cannot rule out that perfect secret-sharing schemes (i.e., $p = 1$) with polynomial share size exist for every access structure.

- Are there WP secret-sharing schemes for arbitrary access structures with share size $o(n)$?
- Graph access structures are access structures in which the minimal authorized sets are of size two (however, unauthorized sets can be big). The best upper bound on the share size for graph access structures is $O(n/\log n)$ [25], which is better than our construction applied to graph access structures, when there are large independent sets in the graph. Are there more efficient WP secret-sharing schemes for graph access structures?
- Beimel and Franklin [8] constructed $1/n$-WP 2-out-of-n threshold secret-sharing schemes with share size 2, leaving the case of large thresholds open. Is there a WP $(n-1)$-out-of-n threshold secret-sharing scheme with share size $o(\log n)$?
- Finally, it would be interesting to find additional applications of WP security in mainstream cryptography.

1.2 Technical Overview

Weakly Private Secret Sharing for Arbitrary Access Structures

Warm-Up. A forbidden graph access structure [43] is an access structure in which all maximal unauthorized sets are of size 2. We start with a simple $\Theta(1/n^2)$-WP secret-sharing scheme realizing any forbidden graph access structure with 1-bit shares but with imperfect reconstruction. In this scheme, an authorized set either reconstructs the correct value or it outputs $\perp$ (it never outputs an incorrect value for the secret). The scheme is simple: to share a secret $s \in \{0,1\}$, the dealer chooses with uniform distribution a maximal unauthorized set $\{p_{i_1}, p_{i_2}\}$ (of size 2) and two bits r_1, r_2, gives the secret s as the share to all parties not in $\{p_{i_1}, p_{i_2}\}$, gives r_1 to party p_{i_1}, and gives r_2 to p_{i_2}. Reconstruction by an authorized set $B \in \Gamma$ is as follows: if the shares of all parties in B are the same value b, then the parties in B output b as the secret; otherwise, they output $\perp$. Since Γ is monotone, $B \setminus \{p_{i_1}, p_{i_2}\} \neq \emptyset$ and at least one party in B gets the secret as its share and so the reconstruction never errs.[3] For the WP property of the scheme, consider an unauthorized set $A \notin \Gamma$. With probability greater than $1/n^2$, this set is chosen by the dealer and the shares of the two parties in the set are uniformly distributed in $\{0,1\}^2$. Thus, the probability of each vector of shares in $\{0,1\}^2$ is at least $O(1/n^2)$; in particular, the scheme is $O(1/n^2)$-WP.

A $1/O(n^2)$-WP Secret-Sharing Scheme for Forbidden Graphs. In the scheme described above, when a minimal authorized set B gets two different shares, it does not know which one of them is the correct secret. To get perfect correctness, still with constant size shares, we add a mechanism that enables any authorized set to identify a party holding the correct value. This is done using a tournament $G_0 = (V_0, E_0)$[4] such that

[3] The probability that an authorized set B outputs $\perp$ can be reduced to $O(1/n)$; see details in Sect. 3.2.

[4] A directed graph $G_0 = (V_0, E_0)$ is a tournament if for every distinct $u, v \in V_0$ either $(u, v) \in E_0$ or $(v, u) \in E_0$ (but not both).

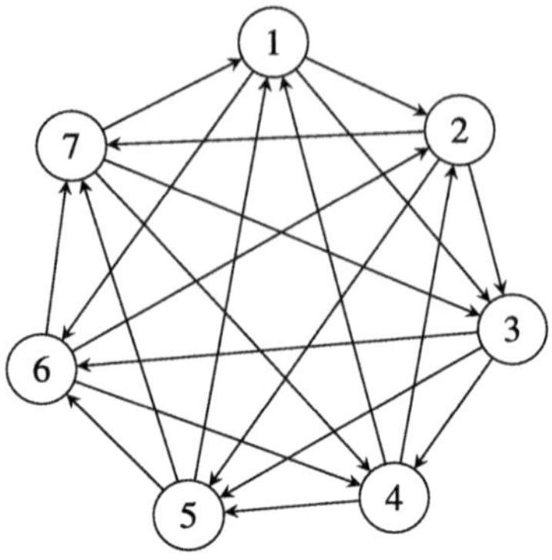

Fig. 1. A 2-dominated graph with 7 vertices.

for every $v_1, v_2 \in V_0$ there is a vertex $u \neq v_1, v_2$ such that $(u, v_1), (u, v_2) \in E_0$, i.e., u "dominates" v_1, v_2. Such a tournament, called a 2-dominated graph, is described in Fig. 1; it has 7 vertices. For each pair of vertices, there is a unique vertex that dominates them. For example, $(1, 2), (1, 6) \in E_0$; thus, vertex 1 dominates vertices 2, 6.

We use a 2-dominated graph $G_0 = (V_0, E_0)$ to construct a perfectly correct WP secret-sharing scheme for a forbidden graph access structure determined by an n-vertex graph $G = (V, E)$ as follows:

- On secret $s \in \{0, 1\}$, the dealer chooses at random, with uniform distribution, a maximal unauthorized set $A = \{p_i, p_j\}$, uniformly distributed vertices $v_i, v_j \in V_0$, and uniformly distributed secrets $s_i, s_j \in \{0, 1\}$.
- Let $u \neq v_i, v_j$ be a vertex in G_0 that dominates v_1, v_2; for every $p_\ell \notin A$ let $s_\ell = s$ and $v_\ell = u$.
- The share of p_ℓ, for $\ell \in [n]$, is $\langle s_\ell, v_\ell \rangle$.
- Reconstruction for a minimal authorized set $B = \{p_{i_1}, p_{i_2}\} \in \Gamma$ holding shares $\langle s_{i_1}, v_{i_1} \rangle$ and $\langle s_{i_2}, v_{i_2} \rangle$: If $v_{i_1} = v_{i_2}$ or $(v_{i_1}, v_{i_2}) \in E_0$ output s_{i_1}, otherwise output s_{i_2}.

We first explain why the reconstruction is always correct. By the monotonicity of Γ, we have $B \setminus A \neq \emptyset$. If $p_{i_1}, p_{i_2} \notin A$, then they both hold the share $\langle s, u \rangle$ and the reconstruction outputs the correct secret s. If $p_{i_1} \notin A$ and $p_{i_2} \in A$, then party p_{i_1} holds the share $\langle s, u \rangle$, party p_{i_2} holds the share $\langle s_{i_2}, v_{i_2} \rangle$, and $(u, v_{i_2}) \in E_0$, and the reconstruction outputs the correct secret $s = s_{i_1}$. If $p_{i_1} \in A$ and $p_{i_2} \notin A$, then party p_{i_1} holds the share $\langle s_{i_1}, v_{i_1} \rangle$, party p_{i_2} holds the share $\langle s, u \rangle$, and $(v_{i_1}, u) \notin E_0$ (since G_0 is a tournament and $(u, v_{i_1}) \in E_0$); again, the reconstruction outputs the correct secret $s = s_{i_2}$.

We claim that this scheme is $1/O(n^2)$-WP. We first argue that the scheme is weakly private. Let $A' = \{p_{i'}, p_{j'}\}$ be a maximal unauthorized set. Every pair of shares $\langle s_{i'}, v_{i'} \rangle, \langle s_{j'}, v_{j'} \rangle \in (\{0, 1\} \times V_0)^2$ is possible, for every secret s, when the dealer chooses $A = A'$ as the random unauthorized set, chooses these shares as the shares of A', takes a vertex u such that $(u, v_{i'}), (u, v_{j'}) \in E_0$ (such u exists by the properties of G_0), and gives the share $\langle s, u \rangle$ to all the other parties. Since the probability of each vector of shares is at least $\frac{1}{\binom{n}{2}\cdot(|V_0|\cdot 2)^2} = \frac{1}{O(n^2)}$, the scheme is $1/O(n^2)$-WP.

A WP Secret-Sharing Scheme for Arbitrary Access Structures with Share Size O(n). Our WP secret-sharing scheme for arbitrary access structures Γ is a generalization of the scheme for forbidden graphs. Let $t < n$ be the maximum size of an unauthorized set. We use a tournament $G_0 = (V_0, E_0)$ such that for every $W \subset V_0$ of size t there is a vertex $u \in V_0$ that dominates all vertices in W, i.e., $(u, v) \in E_0$ for every $v \in W$. We prove that a random tournament with $O(t^2 2^t)$ vertices has this property with high probability. The share of each party contains a secret and a vertex of the tournament, i.e., the share length is $O(t) = O(n)$. A simple implementation of this idea will result in a $2^{-O(n^2)}$-WP secret-sharing scheme. We describe a better distribution on the vertices and secrets given to the parties in A that results in a $2^{-O(n)}$-WP secret-sharing scheme in Sect. 3.

LPN and Computational Secret Sharing Schemes for Composed Access Structures. We construct computational secret-sharing schemes for composed gap access structures based on the hardness of the learning parity with noise (LPN) problem. To present the ideas of our construction, we consider in the introduction an access structure $\text{Gap}_{\alpha,\beta}(\Gamma_1, \ldots, \Gamma_m)$, where each access structure Γ_i is an arbitrary access structure with $0.1 \log m$ parties.

A simple way to construct a scheme for this access structure is to first share the secret in a ramp secret-sharing scheme with m parties such that any set of at least βm parties can reconstruct the secret and any set of less than αm parties learns no information on the secret, and then share the i-th share (for $1 \leq i \leq m$) independently using a perfect secret-sharing scheme realizing Γ_i. The best known implementation of this scheme for the above access structures, using the perfect secret-sharing scheme of [4], will result in a secret-sharing scheme with share size $m^{0.058}$.

We construct a computational secret-sharing scheme for the gap access structure with share size $O(\log m)$; this scheme is secure under the LPN assumption. Our scheme uses a random matrix C over $\mathbb{F}_2^{cm \times m}$ (for some constant $c < 1$) to implement the ramp secret-sharing scheme, i.e., the shares are generated by sampling a random $x \in \mathbb{F}_2^{ck}$ and computing the shares as Cx; by [18] this is a ramp secret-sharing scheme. We now share the i-th share using a $\frac{1}{m^2}$-WP secret-sharing scheme. We show that the uncertainty of the secret in a WP secret-sharing scheme implies the computational security of this scheme. The technical challenge in the security proof is to take a noisy vector $y = Cx+e$, where each coordinate of e is independently sampled using the Bernoulli distribution with parameter $\frac{1}{m^2}$, and to construct shares of non-authorized sets for the vector Cx in the WP secret-sharing schemes for $\Gamma_1, \ldots, \Gamma_m$. This is done by using a lemma about differential privacy [32] that states that the output of a differentially-private algorithm $\mathcal{A}(z)$ with a binary input z can be simulated as $g(y)$, where $y = z + e$ for e sampled from a Bernoulli distribution.

Weakly Private Decomposable Randomized Encoding and MPC

A Construction of WP DRE for All Functions with Communication $\tilde{O}(n^2)$. We describe below how to construct a WP decomposable randomized encoding (DRE) for an arbitrary function $f : \{0, 1\}^n \to \{0, 1\}$. The idea of our construction is to design a mechanism g that reveals the input x almost all the time, but with some (small) probability reveals a random input x', under the condition that $f(x') = f(x)$. Intuitively, the output of this mechanism satisfies our desired WP property as, given only the output of the mechanism, one cannot be sure whether it is the actual input x or some randomly sampled x' satisfying $f(x') = f(x)$. We then implement such a mechanism g securely via an existing DRE scheme with standard security from [34]; as g is a fairly simple function, it has an efficient DRE with standard security. Intuitively, this ensures that the final encoding reveals only the mechanism output, which satisfies our WP requirement.

In more detail, our WP encoding function $\textsc{Enc}(x)$ is described below. We first sample a uniformly distributed string $w \in \{0, 1\}^n$ (where w is a guess of the input x) and then choose a uniformly distributed string $w' \in \{0, 1\}^n$ such that $f(w) = f(w')$. The WP decomposable randomized encoding is computed as follows:

- Run a standard DRE encoding for the function $g(x, w, w')$ that outputs w' if the guess is correct, i.e. indeed $x = w$, and outputs x otherwise. Then, output the encoding of the function $g(x, w, w')$.

The WP decoding function Dec runs the standard DRE decoding algorithm to recover either the original x or the randomly sampled w'. It then outputs the evaluation of f over the recovered output of g; i.e., x or w'. Note that the evaluation result is correct in either case of $f(x)$ or $f(w') = f(w = x)$.

Notably, we only apply a fully secure DRE on a simple function g whose complexity depends only on the input length n, and not on the function f. Plugging in an existing DRE construction from [34], we obtain a construction with size $\tilde{O}(n^2)$. We show that the construction satisfies p-WP for $p = 2^{-O(n)}$ in Sect. 5.1.

An Almost Matching Lower Bound. In the full version, we show that the lower bound of $\Omega(n^2/\log n)$ for DREs in [6] still holds even assuming only p-WP privacy, for some positive $p > 0$. We outline the arguments here of a weaker result, that is, there is an explicit function g such that in any DRE of g there exists a j such that the size of the encoding $\textsc{Enc}_j$ is $\Omega(n/\log n)$.

Consider the function $g : \{0, 1\}^{n+\log n} \rightarrow \{0, 1\}$, where we parse the input of g as an n bit string $x = (x_1, \ldots, x_n)$ and an index $i \in [n]$ (this is a $\log n$-bit string) and define $g(x, i) = x_i$. Let $\textsc{Enc}$ be a DRE of g. Fix an input $x \neq 0^n, 1^n$ and a random string r; for $1 \leq j \leq n$ let $\hat{y}_j = \textsc{Enc}_j(x_j; r)$ (that is, $\hat{y}_j$ is the local encoding of x_j with r). Let $z \in \{0, 1\}^n$ be any string. By the choice of x, there is some i such that $x_i = z_1$; thus, $g(x, i) = g(z, 1)$. The weak privacy implies that the local encodings $\hat{y}_1, \ldots, \hat{y}_n$ are possible given z, that is, there is some r_z such that $\hat{y}_j = \textsc{Enc}_j(z_j; r_z)$ for $1 \leq j \leq n$. To conclude, $\hat{y}_1, \ldots, \hat{y}_n$ (without the encodings of i) do not rule out any n-bit string.

We use the above facts to describe z by the encoding $\textsc{Enc}_{n+\ell}$ for $1 \leq \ell \leq \log n$ as follows (forgetting any privacy requirements). For every $z \in \{0, 1\}^n$, fix r_z as above; for $1 \leq \ell \leq \log n$ and $b \in \{0, 1\}$, let $\hat{y}_{\ell,b} = \textsc{Enc}_{\ell+n}(b, r_z)$ (that is, we consider all possibilities of the encoding of the bits of an index $i = (i_1, \ldots, i_{\log(n)})$ with the string r_z). The correctness requirement implies that for every $i = (i_1, \ldots, i_{\log(n)})$ given $\hat{y}_j$ for $1 \leq j \leq n$ and $\langle \hat{y}_{\ell,i_b} \rangle_{1 \leq \ell \leq \log n}$ one can recover z_i. In other words, given the fixed encodings $\langle \hat{y}_j \rangle_{1 \leq j \leq n}$ and the $2 \log n$ encodings $\langle \hat{y}_{\ell,b} \rangle_{1 \leq \ell \leq \log n, b \in \{0,1\}}$ one can recover the entire string z. This implies that for at least one z the size of $\langle \hat{y}_{\ell,b} \rangle_{1 \leq \ell \leq \log n, b \in \{0,1\}}$ is at least n; i.e., there is at least one ℓ such that the size of $\textsc{Enc}_{n+\ell}$ is at least $n/2 \log n$.

A Construction of WP MPC Protocols for All Functions. In this paper, we construct WP MPC protocols secure against semi-honest parties in two models: (1) protocols assuming an honest majority in the plain model, and (2) protocols secure against any number of semi-honest parties in the OT-hybrid model. The idea of the protocols is similar to the DRE construction, where to securely compute $f : (\{0,1\}^n)^k \to \{0,1\}$ the parties reveal their input $x_1, \ldots, x_k$ almost all the time; however, with some (small) probability they reveal a random input $y_1, \ldots, y_k$, under the condition that $f(x_1, \ldots, x_k) = f(y_1, \ldots, y_k)$. To implement this idea, we define a simple functionality g and use known perfect MPC protocols of [13,29] to compute g.

To be concrete, we consider here the two-party case and the OT-hybrid model (all cases are detailed in Sect. 5.2; we denote the two parties by Alice and Bob. Given a function $f : (\{0,1\}^n)^2 \to \{0,1\}$, we define the function $g : \left((\{0,1\}^n)^4 \times \{0,1\}\right)^2 \to (\{0,1\}^n)^2$, where $g((x_0, x_1^0, y_0^0, y_1^0, r_0), (x_1, x_0^1, y_0^1, y_1^1, r_1))$ is computed as follows:

- If $r_0 = r_1$ (where $r_0, r_1 \in \{0,1\}$), $x_1^0 = x_1$, and $f(x_0, x_1^0) = f(y_0^0, y_1^0)$, then output y_0^0, y_1^0,
- If $r_0 \neq r_1$, $x_0^1 = x_0$, and $f(x_0^1, x_1) = f(y_0^1, y_1^1)$, then output y_0^1, y_1^1,
- Otherwise, output x_0, x_1.

The protocol for computing $f(x_0, x_1)$ is as follows: Alice (resp. Bob) samples with a uniform distribution $x_1^0, y_0^0, y_1^0 \in \{0,1\}^n$ and $r_0 \in \{0,1\}$ (resp., $x_0^1, y_0^1, y_1^1 \in \{0,1\}^n$ and $r_1 \in \{0,1\}$). Thereafter, the parties execute a secure 2-party protocol in the OT-hybrid model computing $g((x_0, x_1^0, y_0^0, y_1^0, r_0), (x_1, x_0^1, y_0^1, y_1^1, r_1))$, get the output z_0, z_1 of g, and output $f(z_0, z_1)$.

To understand the function g, the inputs x_0, x_1 are the true inputs of the parties (i.e., the parties want to compute $f(x_0, x_1)$), the input x_1^0 is Alice's guess of Bob's input, and y_0^0, y_1^0 are the random inputs that (with small probability) will replace the true inputs; the condition $f(x_0, x_1^0) = f(y_0^0, y_1^0)$ (resp., $f(x_0^1, x_1) = f(y_0^1, y_1^1)$) ensures the correctness of the protocol. The inputs r_0, r_1 provide the privacy. Namely, to prove the weak privacy of the view of Bob, we consider inputs x_0, x_0', x_1 such that $f(x_0, x_1) = f(x_0', x_1)$. The most likely output of g when Alice and Bob hold x_0, x_1 is x_0, x_1. However, x_0, x_1 can also be the output of g as seen by Bob when Alice and Bob hold x_0', x_1; if Alice and Bob choose random inputs such that $r_0 = r_1$, $x_1^0 = x_1$, $y_0^0 = x_0$, and $y_1^0 = x_1$, then $g((x_0', x_1, x_0, x_1, r_0), (x_1, x_0^1, y_0^1, y_0^1, r_0)) = (x_0, x_1)$.

We next explain how to construct a perfect 2-PC for g. First note that Alice (resp., Bob) can locally check if $f(x_0, x_1^0) = f(y_0^0, y_1^0)$ (resp., $f(x_0^1, x_1) = f(y_0^1, y_1^1)$). Given this information, the function g can be computed by a Boolean circuit of size $O(n)$ with gates of fan-in 2; thus, the GMW protocol [29] can be used to compute g in the OT-hybrid model, using $O(n)$ calls to OT.

Organization. For lack of space, most of the proofs are removed to the full version.

2 Preliminaries

Notation. Given a finite set A, we use the notation $y \leftarrow A$ to denote assigning y a value chosen uniformly at random from A. Similarly, for a randomized algorithm Alg, we write $y \leftarrow \text{Alg}(x)$ to denote assigning y the output of Alg on input x. The *binary entropy function* is $h : [0, 1] \to [0, 1]$, defined as $h(x) = -x \log x - (1 - x) \log(1 - x)$ for all $x \in (0, 1)$, with $h(0) = h(1) = 0$.

2.1 Information-Theoretic Secret-Sharing Schemes

In this section, we present definitions related to Information-Theoretic (IT) Secret-Sharing Schemes.

Definition 2.1 (Partial access structures). *Let $P = \{p_1, \ldots, p_n\}$ be a set of parties. A* partial access structure *is a pair of collections of sets $\Gamma = (\Gamma_{\text{no}}, \Gamma_{\text{yes}})$, where $\Gamma_{\text{no}}, \Gamma_{\text{yes}} \subseteq 2^P$ such that $\emptyset \notin \Gamma_{\text{yes}}$ and $B \not\subseteq A$ for every $A \in \Gamma_{\text{no}}, B \in \Gamma_{\text{yes}}$. Sets in Γ_{yes} are called* authorized *and sets in Γ_{no} are called* unauthorized. *If $\Gamma_{\text{no}} \cup \Gamma_{\text{yes}} = 2^P$, we say that Γ is a complete access structure, or just an access structure, and will denote it by $\Gamma = \Gamma_{\text{yes}}$.*

We only have a minimal consistency requirement on partial access structures, i.e., an authorized set in Γ_{yes} will be able to reconstruct the secret; thus, it cannot be contained in an unauthorized set in Γ_{no} that should not get "too much" information on the secret.

A secret-sharing scheme is a randomized mapping that, given a secret s, outputs n strings called shares such that any authorized set of parties can reconstruct the secret from its shares. We consider a security requirement that we call weakly private, denoted WP; a secret-sharing scheme is p-WP (for $p \in [0, 1]$) if, for any unauthorized set A, the probability of any shares of A given one secret is at least p times the probability of those shares given any other secret.

Definition 2.2 (Weakly private (WP) secret-sharing schemes). *A* secret-sharing scheme *with domain of secrets S such that $|S| \geq 2$ and domains of shares $S_1, S_2, \ldots, S_n$ is a randomized mapping Π that takes as input a secret $s \in S$ and outputs an n-tuple $\langle \mathsf{sh}_1, \ldots, \mathsf{sh}_n \rangle \in S_1 \times S_2 \times \cdots \times S_n$. For a set $A \subseteq P$, we denote $\Pi_A(s)$ as the restriction of $\Pi(s)$ to its A-entries (i.e., the shares of the parties in A; namely, $\langle \mathsf{sh}_i \rangle_{p_i \in A}$).*

Given a secret-sharing scheme Π, define the size of the secret *as $\log |S|$, the* share size *of party p_j as $\log |S_j|$, the* max share size *as $\max_{1 \leq j \leq n} \{\log |S_j|\}$, and the* total share size *as $\sum_{j=1}^{n} \log |S_j|$.*

Let $0 < p \leq 1$. We say that Π is a p-WP secret-sharing scheme realizing an access structure $\Gamma = (\Gamma_{\text{no}}, \Gamma_{\text{yes}})$ if the following two requirements hold:

Perfect Correctness. The secret s can be reconstructed by any authorized set of parties. That is, for any set $B = \{p_{i_1}, \ldots, p_{i_{|B|}}\} \in \Gamma_{\text{yes}}$ there exists a reconstruction function $\text{Recon}_B : S_{i_1} \times \cdots \times S_{i_{|B|}} \to S$ *such that* $\text{Recon}_B(\Pi_B(s)) = s$, *for every secret $s \in S$ and every randomness of Π.*

p-WP. Every unauthorized set cannot learn "too much" information about the secret from its shares. Formally, for any set $A = \{p_{i_1}, \ldots, p_{i_{|T|}}\} \in \Gamma_{\text{no}}$, every two secrets $s_1 \neq s_2 \in S$, and every vector of shares $\langle \mathsf{sh}_{i_1}, \ldots, \mathsf{sh}_{i_{|A|}} \rangle \in S_{i_1} \times \cdots \times S_{i_{|A|}}$,

$$\Pr[\, \Pi_A(s_1) = \langle s_j \rangle_{p_j \in A} \,] \geq p \cdot \Pr[\, \Pi_A(s_2) = \langle s_j \rangle_{p_j \in A} \,].$$

A secret-sharing scheme is a perfect secret-sharing scheme if it is 1-WP. A secret-sharing scheme is a weakly private secret-sharing scheme if it is p-WP for some $p > 0$.

Our definition of privacy is inspired by the definition of (pure) ε-differential privacy, a notion introduced by Dwork, McSherry, Nissim, and Smith [24]; since we deal with very weak privacy, we use a different parameterization; namely, p-WP corresponds to $\varepsilon = \ln(1/p)$.

2.2 Computational and Statistical Secret-Sharing Schemes

In this section we define *computational* secret-sharing schemes (resp., *statistical* secret-sharing schemes), that is, secret-sharing schemes in which the sharing and reconstruction are efficient, and no polynomial-time adversary (resp., any unbounded adversary) can learn non-negligible information about the secret from the shares of any unauthorized set of parties. When defining "efficiency", it is important to consider the way the access structure is represented. Following [1], we start with an abstract definition of a representation model for access structures.

Definition 2.3 (Representation model). *A* representation model *is a polynomial time computable function* $U : \{0,1\}^* \times 2^{\{p_1,p_2,\ldots\}} \to \{0,1,*\}$, *where the input of* U *is a "program"* Prog *and a set* A*;* Prog *represents a partial access structure as follows: if* $U(\text{Prog}, A) = 1$ *then* A *is authorized, if* $U(\text{Prog}, A) = 0$ *then* A *is unauthorized, and if* $U(\text{Prog}, C) = *$, *there are no requirements for* C. *We assume that each* Prog *specifies the number of parties* n *in the access structure (i.e.,* $U(\text{Prog}, C) = *$ *if* $C \nsubseteq \{p_1, \ldots, p_n\}$*) and assume that* $|\text{Prog}| \geq n$.

We now define computational secret-sharing schemes. For simplicity, we assume here that the secret is a single bit. This can always be generalized to sharing an ℓ-bit secret by independently sharing each bit of the secret. Moreover, using a symmetric encryption scheme, the amortized cost of sharing long secrets can be improved.

Definition 2.4 (Computational secret sharing – Syntax and correctness). *A computational secret-sharing (CSS) scheme for a representation model* U *consists of a pair of algorithms* CSS = (CSS.Share, CSS.Recon) *with the following syntax.*

Sharing. CSS.Share(Prog, s) $\to$ $(\mathsf{sh}_0, \mathsf{sh}_1, \ldots, \mathsf{sh}_n)$ *(where* n *denotes the number of parties in* Prog*) is a randomized poly-time algorithm that takes as input a program* Prog *and a secret* $s \in \{0,1\}$ *and outputs* $n+1$ *shares* $\mathsf{sh}_0, \mathsf{sh}_1, \ldots, \mathsf{sh}_n$, *where* sh_0 *is public information and* sh_i, *for* $1 \leq i \leq n$, *is the share of party* p_i.

Reconstruction. CSS.Recon(Prog, A, sh_0, $(\mathsf{sh}_i)_{p_i \in A}$) $\to$ s *is a deterministic poly-time algorithm that takes as input a program* Prog, *a set* $A \subseteq \{p_1, \ldots, p_n\}$ *(where* n *denotes the number of parties in* Prog*), the public share, and the shares of the parties in* A. *The algorithm outputs a value* $s \in \{0,1\}$.

We say that CSS *is* correct *(with respect to* U*) if there is a negligible function* $\varepsilon(n)$ *such that for every program* Prog *and a set* $A \subseteq \{p_1, \ldots, p_n\}$ *such that* $\text{Prog}(A) = 1$ *(where* n *denotes the number of parties in* Prog*), the process of invoking* CSS.Share(Prog, s) *and then invoking* CSS.Recon(Prog, A, sh_0, $(\mathsf{sh}_i)_{p_i \in A}$) *(with the shares* sh_i *generated by* CSS.Share*) returns* s *with probability at least* $1 - \varepsilon(n)$.

Definition 2.5 (Computational and statistical secret-sharing schemes – Security). *Consider the following game between a non-uniform poly-time adversary $\mathcal{A}$ and a challenger:*

1. *The adversary $\mathcal{A}$ on input 1^n chooses a program* Prog, *representing an n-party access structure, and a set $A \subseteq \{p_1, \ldots, p_n\}$ such that* $\text{Prog}(A) = 0$ *and sends them to the challenger.*
2. *The challenger chooses a secret bit $s \leftarrow_U \{0, 1\}$ uniformly at random. It computes* $(\mathsf{sh}_0, \mathsf{sh}_1, \ldots, \mathsf{sh}_n) \leftarrow \text{CSS.S}\text{HARE}(\text{Prog}, s)$ *and sends* $\mathsf{sh}_0, (\mathsf{sh}_i)_{p_i \in A}$ *to the adversary.*
3. *The adversary outputs a bit s'.*

The adversary wins the game if $s' = s$.

We say that CSS *is* computationally secure *if, for every non-uniform poly-time adversary $\mathcal{A}$, there exists a negligible function $\varepsilon(n)$ such that the probability that $\mathcal{A}$ wins the above game is at most $1/2 + \varepsilon(n)$. We say that* CSS *is* statistically secure *if the above holds for every unbounded adversary $\mathcal{A}$.*

2.3 Useful Access Structures

We will use the following access structures in the sequel.

Definition 2.6 (Forbidden graph access structures). *Given an undirected graph $G = (V, E)$, define the partial access structure $\Gamma_G = \langle \Gamma_{G,\text{no}}, \Gamma_{G,\text{yes}} \rangle$ whose parties are V and the collections are $\Gamma_{G,\text{no}} = \{\{u, v\} : (u, v) \notin E\}$ and $\Gamma_{G,\text{yes}} = \{\{u, v\} : (u, v) \in E\}$, that is, each set of size 2 is either authorized or unauthorized; it is authorized if and only if it is an edge in the graph. There are no additional requirements for sets of size larger than 2.*

Ramp secret-sharing schemes generalize threshold secret-sharing schemes. In a t-private, k-correct ramp secret-sharing scheme, sets of parties of size at least k should be able to reconstruct the secret, while sets of parties of size at most t should get no information on the secret. There are no requirements on sets with more than k parties but less than t parties. Allowing a gap between t and k results in schemes that are more efficient than threshold secret-sharing schemes. Ramp secret-sharing schemes were first presented by Blakley and Meadows [15], and were used to construct efficient secure multiparty computation (MPC) protocols, starting in the work of Franklin and Yung [27].

Definition 2.7 (Ramp secret-sharing schemes). *Let $0 \leq t < k \leq n$. A secret-sharing scheme is a t-private, k-correct* ramp secret-sharing scheme *if it realizes the following partial access structure $\Gamma_{\text{ramp}} = (\Gamma_{\text{ramp,no}}, \Gamma_{\text{ramp,yes}})$, where $\Gamma_{\text{ramp,no}} = \{A \subset \{p_1, \ldots, p_n\} : |A| \leq t\}$ and $\Gamma_{\text{ramp,yes}} = \{A \subset \{p_1, \ldots, p_n\} : |A| \geq k\}$.*

2.4 Binary Symmetric Channels (BSC) and WP Secret-Sharing Schemes

A δ-BSC channel is a randomized mapping with domain $\{0, 1\}$ that for every $s \in \{0, 1\}$ outputs $\overline{s}$ with probability δ and outputs s with probability $1 - \delta$; i.e., with probability δ the value of the bit is flipped. The following lemma is a special case of a result of [32]; this lemma asserts that a p-WP secret-sharing scheme with a binary secret can be simulated from a BSC channel whose input is a secret.

Lemma 2.8. *Let Π be a randomized mapping with a domain $\{0,1\}$ and range O, and let $0 \le p \le 1$. If, for every $o \in O$ and every $s \in \{0,1\}$,*

$$\Pr[\Pi(s) = o] \ge p \cdot \Pr[\Pi(\overline{s}) = o], \tag{1}$$

then Π can be simulated from a δ-BSC channel BSC(s)*, for $\delta = \frac{p}{1+p}$. That is, there is a randomized mapping g with domain $\{0,1\}$ such that, for every $o \in O$ and every $s \in \{0,1\}$,*

$$\Pr[\Pi(s) = o] = \Pr[g(\mathrm{BSC}(s)) = o]. \tag{2}$$

Furthermore, if for every $s \in \{0,1\}$ and $o \in 0$, the probability $\Pr[\Pi(s) = o]$ can be efficiently computed, then g can be efficiently computed.

2.5 LPN and Random Linear Error-Correcting Codes

Our computational secret-sharing schemes are based on the hardness of the learning parity with errors (LPN) problem; i.e., a noisy encoding of a random string using a random linear error-correcting code is indistinguishable from a random string. We next provide some background on random linear error-correcting codes and the LPN problem.

Given an $[m+1, k, d]$ linear error-correcting code C over a finite field $\mathcal{K}$, define the m-party secret-sharing scheme LSSS(C), where to share a secret $s \in \mathcal{K}$, one chooses a random codeword $y = (y_0, \dots, y_m)$ such that $y_0 = s$ and the share of party p_i is y_i.

Theorem 2.9 ([18]). *Let C be an $[m+1, k, d]$-code over a finite field $\mathcal{K}$ whose dual code has distance $d^\perp$. Then LSSS(C) is a linear $(d^\perp - 2)$-private, $(m - d + 2)$-correct ramp secret-sharing scheme.*

Theorem 2.10 ([18]). *Let $0 < \delta < 1/2$. The distance of a random linear code over $\mathbb{F}_2$ of length m and dimension k is at least δm except with probability $2^{k-m(1-h(\delta))}$.*

In the LPN problem, a random linear error-correcting code $C \in \mathbb{F}_2^{m\times k}$ and an information word x are uniformly and independently sampled, a noisy codeword $y = (y_1, \dots, y_m)$ is computed as $y = Cx + e$, where each coordinate of e is sampled from a Bernoulli distribution. The LPN assumption assumes that the distribution C, y is indistinguishable from the distribution C, u, where u is a uniformly distributed string. For the security of our computational secret-sharing schemes, we need a version of the LPN problem in which the first $\alpha \cdot m$ coordinates of the noise vector e are 0, that is, we consider a version of the LPN problem in which the first αm coordinates of the codeword are exposed without noise. We show that this version is equivalent to the standard LPN assumption where there is no exposure.

Definition 2.11 (Learning parity with noise (LPN) with known coordinates). *Let k be the dimension, $m(k)$ be the number of samples, i.e., the length of the code word, $\mu(k)$ be the error rate, and α be the exposure parameter (where $k, m(k) \in \mathbb{N}$ and $0 \le$*

$\mu(k), \alpha < 1$). The learning parity with noise assumption LPN$(m(k), \mu(k), \alpha)$ *assumes the following distributions to be computationally indistinguishable*

$$\{(C, Cx + e)\}_k \approx_c \{(C, u)\}_k,$$

where the public matrix C, the random word u, and the secret vector x are sampled at random as $C \leftarrow \mathbb{F}_2^{m\times k}$, $u \leftarrow \mathbb{F}_2^{m(k)}$, $x \leftarrow \mathbb{F}_2^k$, and the error vector $e = (e_1, \ldots, e_m)$ is computed such that $e_1 = \cdots = e_{\lfloor \alpha\cdot m(k)\rfloor} = 0$ and each e_i, for $\lfloor \alpha \cdot m(k)\rfloor + 1 \le i \le m(k)$, is independently sampled from a Bernoulli distribution with parameter $\mu(k)$. We denote LPN$(m(k), \mu(k), 0)$ *by* LPN$(m(k), \mu(k))$.

It was observed by Dodis et al. [22] (see comment on Page 5) that the LPN$(m(k), \mu(k), \alpha)$ assumption is implied by the LPN assumption without exposure, i.e., the standard LPN assumption (with smaller parameters as stated in the next lemma). In particular, LPN$(m(k) = O(k), \mu = 1/\Omega(\sqrt{k}))$ implies LPN$(m(k) = ck, \mu = 1/\Omega(\sqrt{k}), \alpha)$ for any constants $c \cdot \alpha < 1$. This follows from the fact that linear leakage of the LPN secret is equivalent to leaking bits of the secret, which effectively reduces its secret dimension. For completeness, the proof of the following lemma can be found in the full version of this paper.

Lemma 2.12. *Let c, α be constants such that $c > 1$ and $\alpha c < 1$ and let $c' = (1 - \alpha)c/(1 - \alpha c)$. If the* LPN$(c'k, \mu(k/(1 - \alpha c)))$ *assumption holds, then the* LPN$(ck, \mu(k), \alpha)$ *assumption holds.*

Remark 2.13. We can consider a version in which a set $I \subset [m]$ of size αm is chosen by an adversary prior to seeing C, and the noise vector e is chosen such that $e_i = 0$ for every $i \in I$ and each e_i for $i \notin I$ is independently sampled with a Bernoulli distribution with parameter $\mu(k)$. This version can be trivially transformed to the version of the problem discussed in Definition 2.11, where given I and C, y one permutes the rows of C and y such that the I-rows in C are permuted to the first αm rows.

2.6 Decomposable Randomized Encodings

We next define decomposable randomized encoding schemes, also known as garbling schemes and private simultaneous messages protocols. We take the definition from [6] and extend it with our weak privacy requirement.

Definition 2.14 (Decomposable randomized encodings). *A randomized encoding for a function $f : \{0, 1\}^n \to Y$ consists of a "randomness" distribution $\mathcal{R}$, an encoding algorithm* Enc $: \{0, 1\}^n \times \mathcal{R} \to \{0, 1\}^\ell$*, and a decoding algorithm* Dec $: \{0, 1\}^\ell \to \mathcal{Y}$*, where ℓ is called the size of the randomized encoding.*

Perfect Correctness. The value of $f(x)$ can be computed from the encoding. That is, for any input $x \in \{0, 1\}^n$, for every $r \in \mathcal{R}$

$$\text{Dec}(\text{Enc}(x; r)) = f(x).$$

p-WP. For any inputs $x_1, x_2 \in \{0, 1\}^n$ such that $f(x_1) = f(x_2)$, and any encoding $\widehat{y} \in \{0, 1\}^\ell$,

$$\Pr_{r\leftarrow\mathcal{R}}[\,\text{Enc}(x_1; r) = \widehat{y}\,] \ge p \cdot \Pr_{r\leftarrow\mathcal{R}}[\,\text{Enc}(x_2; r) = \widehat{y}\,].$$

Decomposability. Each output bit of $\textsc{Enc}(x; r)$ *is determined by* r *and one bit of* x*; that is, there are functions* $\textsc{Enc}_1, \dots, \textsc{Enc}_n : \{0,1\} \times \mathcal{R} \to \{0,1\}^\ell$ *such that for every* $x = \langle x_1, \dots, x_n \rangle \in \{0,1\}^n$ *and every* $r \in \mathcal{R}$, $\textsc{Enc}(x; r) = \langle \textsc{Enc}_1(x_1; r), \dots, \textsc{Enc}_n(x_n; r) \rangle$. *The size of a decomposable randomized encoding is*

$$\max_{1 \le i \le n, b \in \{0,1\}, r \in \mathcal{R}} |\textsc{Enc}_i(b; r)|.$$

A WP decomposable randomized encoding is a p*-WP decomposable randomized encoding for some positive* $p > 0$*, and a (standard) decomposable randomized encoding is a* 1*-WP decomposable randomized encoding.*

Note that in a DRE, all local encoding functions use the same random string r. Efficient constructions of decomposable randomized encoding were given in [5,9,10, 30,34]; we will use the following result of Kolesnikov [34].

Lemma 2.15 (Decomposable randomized encoding for boolean formulas [34]**).** *There exists a decomposable randomized encoding for any Boolean formula* $f : \{0,1\}^n \to \{0,1\}$ *with size* $O(2^d d^2 \log d)$*, where* d *is the depth of* f.

2.7 WP MPC Protocols

We consider k-party protocols for semi-honest parties both in the plain model and in the OT-hybrid model. In the plain model, the k parties $\{1, \dots, k\}$ exchange messages on secure and private point-to-point channels. In the OT-hybrid model, in addition, in each step of the protocol, any ordered pair of parties can use an ideal blackbox that computes the oblivious transfer function, that is, the input of the first party is an index $i \in \{0,1\}$, the input of the second party is two bits i_0, i_1, the first party gets as an output i_b, and the second party gets no output. The view of a coalition of parties T in a protocol Π in the plain model, denoted $\text{View}_T(x_1, \dots, x_k)$, is a random variable consisting of the inputs of the parties in the set, their randomness, and the communication exchanged between the parties in the coalition and the parties not in the coalition. In the OT-hybrid mode, the view also contains the outputs of the OT blackboxes given to the parties in the coalition.

In a k-party WP MPC protocol, the p-weak privacy requirement is as follows: For every coalition $T \subseteq \{1, \dots, k\}$ such that $|T| \le t$, every inputs $x_1, \dots, x_k, x'_1, \dots, x'_k$ such that $x_i = x'_i$ for every $i \in T$ and $f(x_1, \dots, x_k) = f(x'_1, \dots, x'_k)$, and every possible view view_T of the parties in T,

$$\Pr_{(r_i)_{i \notin T}} [\ \text{View}_T(x_1, \dots, x_k) = \text{view}_T\ ] \ge p \cdot \Pr_{(r_i)_{i \notin T}} [\ \text{View}_T(x'_1, \dots, x'_k) = \text{view}_T\ ].$$

3 Constructions of WP Secret-Sharing Schemes

In this section, we present a WP secret-sharing scheme for an arbitrary access structure with share size $O(t) + q$, where t is the maximum size of an unauthorized set and q is the length of the secrets. As a warm-up, we describe two simple schemes with binary secrets for forbidden graphs (i.e., access structures in which every maximal unauthorized set has size 2). In the first scheme, correctness is perfect and the share size is 1; however, the scheme does not provide weak privacy. The second is $1/O(n^2)$-WP; however, the correctness is not perfect.

3.1 Warm-Up: A Simple Construction for Forbidden Graphs

We start with a very simple secret-sharing scheme for forbidden graphs Γ, described in Fig. 2. This scheme has perfect correctness, but is *not* weakly private and it only offers some "average case" security: any unauthorized set of size 2 with a small probability ($\geq 1/n^2$ for an n-party access structure) will not get any information on the secret; however, in all other cases, this set will learn everything (i.e., the value of s). Although this scheme provides little security, it is used in the full version to construct a secret-sharing scheme with statistical security for a composed gap access structure.

Input: a secret $s \in \{0, 1\}$.

1. Choose with uniform distribution an unauthorized set $\{p_{i_1}, p_{i_2}\} \notin \Gamma$.
2. The share of each p_j, where $j \neq i_1, i_2$, is s.
3. The share of p_{i_1} and p_{i_2} is 2.

Reconstruction for $B \in \Gamma$: Take a $p_i \in B$ whose share is in $\{0, 1\}$ and output the share of this party.

Fig. 2. A simple non-private secret-sharing scheme for forbidden graphs.

We next explain the correctness and security of the secret-sharing scheme described in Fig. 2. For the correctness, note that if the share of a party is a value in $\{0, 1\}$, then this value is the secret. Let B be an authorized set. Since $\{p_{i_1}, p_{i_2}\}$ is unauthorized, there is a party $p_i \in B \setminus \{p_{i_1}, p_{i_2}\}$; the share of such p_i is the secret s and this is the value reconstructed in the scheme. For the security, consider an unauthorized set $\{u, v\} \notin \Gamma$. With probability at least $1/n^2$, this set is chosen in Step 1; in this case, the parties get no information about the secret.

3.2 A WP Scheme for Forbidden Graphs with Imperfect Correctness

We next present in Fig. 3 a $O(1/n^2)$-WP secret-sharing scheme for forbidden graphs in which any authorized set reconstructs the correct secret with a high probability of at least $1 - 2/n$; with the remaining probability, it outputs $\perp$ (i.e., the reconstruction never errs). The advantage of this scheme is that the share of each party is a bit.

Lemma 3.1. *The scheme described in Fig. 3 is a $2/3n^2$-WP secret-sharing scheme with binary shares in which an authorized set reconstructs the correct secret with probability $1 - O(1/n)$ and with the remaining probability outputs $\perp$.*

3.3 A Construction with Perfect Reconstruction for Arbitrary Access Structures

Let Γ be an access structure in which all unauthorized sets are of size at most t. In Fig. 4, we present a WP secret-sharing scheme realizing any such Γ (with perfect correctness). The scheme uses t-dominated graphs as defined in Definition 3.2.

Input: a secret $s \in \{0, 1\}$.

1. Choose with uniform distribution $i_1, i_2 \in [n]$ such that $i_1 \neq i_2$.
2. The share of each p_j, where $j \neq i_1, i_2$, is s.
3. If $\{p_{i_1}, p_{i_2}\} \in \Gamma$ then the shares of p_{i_1} and p_{i_2} are s.
4. If $\{p_{i_1}, p_{i_2}\} \notin \Gamma$ then
   (a) with probability $1/3$ the shares of p_{i_1} and p_{i_2} are $\overline{s}$,
   (b) with probability $1/3$ the share of p_{i_1} is $\overline{s}$ and the share of p_{i_2} is s,
   (c) with probability $1/3$ the share of p_{i_1} is s and the share of p_{i_2} is $\overline{s}$.

Reconstruction for a minimal $B \in \Gamma$: If both parties in B hold the same share, then output this common value; otherwise, output $\perp$.

Fig. 3. A $2/3n^2$-WP secret-sharing scheme for forbidden graphs.

Definition 3.2 (t-dominated graphs). *Let $G = (V, E)$ be a directed graph without antiparallel edges and let $1 \leq t < |V|$ be an integer. We say that a vertex u dominates a set $W \subset V$ if $(u, v) \in E$ for every $v \in W$. We say that a directed graph $G = (V, E)$ is a t-dominated graph if for every $W \subset V$ such that $|W| = t$ there exists a vertex $u \in V \setminus W$ that dominates W.*

For example, a directed cycle with 3 vertices is a 1-dominated graph, and in Fig. 1 we describe a 2-dominated graph with 7 vertices. We can always assume that a t-dominated graph is a tournament (i.e., for every $u, v \in V$ either $(u, v) \in E$ or $(v, u) \in E$ (but not both).

Remark 3.3. If a graph has a dominating set of size t, then it is not t-dominated. Recall that every tournament with N vertices has a dominating set of size $\log N$ (such a set can be constructed by the greedy algorithm using the fact that in every N-vertex tournament there is a vertex with out-degree $(N-1)/2$). Thus, in every t-dominated graph, there are at least 2^t vertices.

In Fig. 4, we describe a p-WP secret-sharing scheme for an arbitrary access structure that uses a t-dominated graph G, where t is the maximum size of an unauthorized set in the access structure. In this scheme to share a secret $s \in \{0, 1\}^q$, we choose a uniformly distributed maximal unauthorized set A (of size at most t); the share of each party in the set A is a random secret and a random vertex from G. We take some vertex u that dominates all the vertices in the shares of the parties in A and the share of each party not in A is $\langle s, u\rangle$, i.e., the secret that is shared and the dominating vertex. To achieve weak privacy, we can choose the vertex and secret of each party in A independently with uniform distribution. To achieve p-WP for a smaller p, we choose the vertices and secrets of the parties in A using a more involved process (see Procedure ChooseVertices in Fig. 4). For example, for an arbitrary n-party access structure, the naive way of choosing vertices and secrets will result in a $1/2^{O(n^2)}$-WP scheme, while using Procedure ChooseVertices results in a $1/2^{O(n)}$-WP scheme.

Input: a secret $s \in \{0,1\}^q$.

1. Let t be the maximum size of an unauthorized set and $G = (V, E)$ be a t-dominated graph.
2. Choose with uniform distribution a maximal unauthorized set $A \notin \Gamma$, and choose, using Procedure ChooseVertices, $|A|$ vertices $\langle v_j \rangle_{p_j \in A}$ and $|A|$ secrets $\langle s_j \rangle_{p_j \in A}$.
3. Let u be the lexicographically first vertex that dominates $\{v_j\}_{p_j \in A}$.
4. For every $p_i \notin A$ let $s_j = s$ and $v_j = u$.
5. The share of p_j is $\langle s_j, v_j \rangle$.

Reconstruction by a set $B \in \Gamma$ holding shares $\langle\langle s_j, v_j \rangle\rangle_{p_j \in B}$: Find $p_i \in B$ such that v_i dominates $\{v_j\}_{p_j \in B} \setminus \{v_i\}$ in G and output s_i.[a]

Procedure ChooseVertices:

1. Let $C = A$, $k = 0$.
2. While $C \neq \emptyset$ do:
   (a) Set $k = k + 1$.
   (b) Choose with uniform distribution a subset $C_k \subseteq C$, a vertex $w_k \in V$, and a secret σ_k.
   (c) Set $C = C \setminus C_k$ and $v_j = w_k$, $s_j = \sigma_k$ for every $p_j \in C_k$.

[a] If all vertices have the same vertex v, then v dominates $\{v_j\}_{p_j \in B} \setminus \{v_i\} = \emptyset$.

Fig. 4. A WP secret-sharing scheme for an arbitrary access structure.

Theorem 3.4 (WP secret sharing for general access structures). *Let Γ be an access structure in which all unauthorized sets are of size at most t and $G = (V, E)$ be a t-dominated graph. Assume that Γ contains M maximal unauthorized sets. The scheme described in Fig. 4 is a $\frac{1}{2M|V|2^{q+t}}$-WP secret-sharing scheme realizing Γ with a q-bit secret and share size $\lceil \log(|V|) \rceil + q$.*

Proof. We first prove the correctness of the scheme. Let $B \in \Gamma$ be an authorized set holding shares $\langle\langle s_j, v_j \rangle\rangle_{p_j \in B}$ and let A be the set chosen in Step 2. By the monotonicity of Γ, there exists $p_i \in B \setminus A$. Every party $p_i \in B \setminus A$ holds the share $\langle s, u \rangle$, where s is the correct secret and u dominates $\{v_j\}_{p_j \in A}$ – all vertices appearing in shares of A; in particular, u dominates $\{v_j\}_{p_j \in B \cap A} = \{v_j\}_{p_j \in B} \setminus \{u\}$. Clearly, for every $p_j \in B \cap A$, the vertex v_j does not dominate u. Thus, a $p_i \in B \setminus A$ is chosen and the secret in its share is the correct secret.

We next prove the privacy of the scheme. As a warm-up, we first prove weak privacy. Let A be a maximal unauthorized set of parties. Let $\langle\langle s_j, v_j \rangle\rangle_{p_j \in A}$ be any vector of shares in $\{0,1\}^q \times V$. We prove that this vector of shares has a positive probability for every secret $s \in \{0,1\}^q$. With positive probability, the set A is chosen in Step 2 of the scheme and Procedure ChooseVertices partitions the set A to sets $C_1, \ldots, C_{|A|}$, each set containing exactly one element. In this case, $\langle\langle s_j, v_j \rangle\rangle_{p_j \in A}$ are chosen with probability

$1/(2^q \cdot |V|)^{|A|}$ as the shares of A. Furthermore, as G is t-dominated and $|A| \leq t$, there exists a vertex that dominates $\{v_j\}_{p_j \in A}$; i.e., the shares $\langle\langle s_j, v_j \rangle\rangle_{p_j \in A}$ can be completed to a vector of shares of all parties.

In the full version of this paper, we prove that the scheme is p-WP for the p claimed in the theorem. □

In Sect. 3.3, we provide constructions of t-dominated graphs, as summarized in the next lemma. The number of vertices in the first construction $\tilde{O}(2^t)$. Our second construction is strongly explicit, i.e., we construct a graph with $2^{O(t \log t)}$ vertices such that for every pair of vertices u, v, each one described by $O(t \log t)$ bits, one can check in time poly(t) if $(u, v) \in E$.

Lemma 3.5. *For every t, there exists a t-dominated graph with $O(t^2 \cdot 2^t)$ vertices. Furthermore, for every t, there exists a strongly explicit t-dominated graph with $2^{O(t \log t)}$ vertices.*

Using Lemma 3.5 in Theorem 3.4, we obtain the following corollary.

Corollary 3.6 (WP secret sharing for general access structures). *Let Γ be an access structure in which all unauthorized sets are of size at most t and let $p = \frac{1}{O\left(\binom{n}{\min\{t,n/2\}} t^2 2^{2t} 2^q\right)}$. There is a p-WP secret-sharing scheme realizing Γ with a q-bit secret and share size $O(t) + q$.*

In the special case of forbidden graphs in which $t = 2$ and binary secrets (i.e., $q = 2$), the share size is $O(1)$ and the scheme is $1/O(n^2)$-WP. That is, the scheme achieves the same parameters as the scheme of Sect. 3.2, up to constant factors; however, the scheme in this subsection has perfect correctness. For an arbitrary n-party access structure, we get a $2^{-O(n)}$-WP secret-sharing scheme with share size $O(n) + q$.

Constructions of t-Dominated Graphs. We next provide two constructions of t-dominated graphs, proving Lemma 3.5.

First Construction. We prove that a random tournament with $N = O(t^2 \cdot 2^t)$ is t-dominated with high probability. Formally, let $N = O(t^2 \cdot 2^t)$, $V = [N]$ and for each $1 \leq i < j \leq N$ independently choose with a uniform distribution if $(i, j) \in E$ or $(j, i) \in E$. Fix a set W of size t and a vertex $u \notin V$. The probability that u dominates W is 0.5^t. Thus, the probability that there is no vertex that dominates W is

$$\left(1 - \frac{1}{2^t}\right)^{N-t} = \left(\left(1 - \frac{1}{2^t}\right)^{2^t}\right)^{O(t^2)} \leq e^{-O(t^2)}.$$

By the union bound, the probability that there is some W of size t that is not dominated by any vertex is less than

$$N^t e^{-O(t^2)} = (O(t^2 2^t))^t e^{-O(t^2)} = 2^{-(O(1)-1)t^2 + O(t \log t)} \ll 1.$$

This implies that for every t there is a t-dominated graph with $O(t^2 \cdot 2^t)$ vertices.

Second Construction. The second construction is strongly explicit; however, the number of vertices is $2^{O(t \log t)}$, which is larger than the number of vertices in the first construction. The idea of the construction is that each vertex is assigned a label r (taken from a domain of size $O(t^2)$) and a set T of t labels; there is an edge from vertex $\langle r, T\rangle$ to vertex $\langle r', T'\rangle$ if $r' \in T$ and $r \notin T'$. In other words, each vertex is assigned t labels that it dominates.

Formally, we construct the following graph $G = (V, E)$, where for every $r \in [t^2+t+1]$ and every set $T \subset [t^2+t+1] \setminus \{r\}$ of size t there is a vertex $\langle r, T\rangle$ and $(\langle r, T\rangle, \langle r', T'\rangle) \in E$ if $r' \in T$ and $r \notin T'$ (in particular, G does not contain anti-parallel edges). We next show that G is t-dominated. Let $\langle r_1, T_1\rangle, \ldots, \langle r_t, T_t\rangle$ be any set of t vertices. Take T as any set of size T that contains $r_1, \ldots, r_t$ (e.g., if $r_1, \ldots, r_t$ are distinct, then $T = \{r_1, \ldots, r_t\}$) and take r as any element in $[t^2+t+1] \setminus (T \cup T_1 \cup \cdots \cup T_t)$ (since $|T \cup T_1 \cup \cdots \cup T_t| \leq (t+1)t$, such r exists). Clearly, $\langle r, T\rangle$ dominates $\langle r_1, T_1\rangle, \ldots, \langle r_t, T_t\rangle$. The number of vertices in G is $(t^2+t+1)\binom{t^2+t}{t} = 2^{O(t \log t)}$.

4 Composed Gap Access Structures

In this section, we construct *computational* secret-sharing schemes for gap access structures, as defined below. Our schemes use information-theoretic WP schemes, as those constructed in Sect. 3.3, and their security is based on the LPN assumption.

Next, we define a composition operation between m access structures $\Gamma_1, \ldots, \Gamma_m$; for parameters $0 \leq \alpha < \beta \leq 1$, we define the composition of these access structures as a ramp scheme where the authorized sets are those that are authorized in at least β fraction of the m access structures, and the unauthorized sets are those that are authorized in less than an α fraction.

Definition 4.1. *Given m fully defined access structures $\Gamma_1, \ldots, \Gamma_m$ on sets of parties $P_1, \ldots, P_m$ (respectively) and two real numbers $0 \leq \alpha \leq \beta \leq 1$, the composed gap access structure* $\mathrm{Gap}_{\alpha,\beta}(\Gamma_1, \ldots, \Gamma_m)$ *is the partially defined access structure $\Gamma = \langle \Gamma_{\mathrm{no}}, \Gamma_{\mathrm{yes}}\rangle$, where $B \in \Gamma_{\mathrm{yes}}$ if and only if $|\{i : B \cap P_i \in \Gamma_i\}| \geq \beta m$ and $A \in \Gamma_{\mathrm{no}}$ if and only if $|\{i : A \cap P_i \in \Gamma_i\}| < \alpha m$.*

We will concentrate on the following two families of composed gap access structures:

- Let $P_1, \ldots, P_m$ be disjoint sets of parties of size $\ell = O(\sqrt{m/\log m})$, and let $\Gamma_1, \ldots, \Gamma_m$ be forbidden graph access structures with parties $P_1, \ldots, P_m$, respectively; the number of parties in the composed access structure is $n = m\ell < m^{3/2}$. This family can be realized by a perfect secret-sharing scheme (even when $\alpha = \beta$), where we first share the secret using Shamir's βm-out-of-m secret-sharing scheme, producing shares $\mathsf{sh}_1, \ldots, \mathsf{sh}_m$, and share each sh_i with the secret-sharing scheme of [38] realizing the graph access structure Γ_i. The resulting share size is $2^{\tilde{O}(\sqrt{\log n})}$. We will construct a computational secret-sharing scheme for this access structure with shares of size $O(1)$ (under the LPN assumption).

– Let $P_1, \ldots, P_m$ be disjoint sets of parties of size $\ell = 0.1 \log m$, and let $\Gamma_1, \ldots, \Gamma_m$ be any access structures with parties $P_1, \ldots, P_m$, respectively; the number of parties in the composed access structure is $n = m\ell = O(m \log m)$. This family can be realized by a perfect secret-sharing scheme (even when $\alpha = \beta$), where we first share the secret using Shamir's βm-out-of-m secret-sharing scheme, producing shares $\mathsf{sh}_1, \ldots, \mathsf{sh}_m$, and share each sh_i with the secret-sharing scheme of [4] realizing the access structure Γ_i. The resulting share size is greater than $2^{0.58\ell} = n^{0.058-o(1)}$. We will construct a computational secret-sharing scheme for this access structure with shares of size $O(\log n)$ (under the LPN assumption).

In Fig. 5, we describe a computational secret-sharing scheme realizing $\mathrm{Gap}_{\alpha,\beta}(\Gamma_1, \ldots, \Gamma_m)$ for constants α, β such that $\beta > 0.5$ and $\alpha \leq 1 - h(\beta)$. The security of our scheme holds under the LPN assumption, i.e., the intractability assumption $\mathrm{LPN}(c'k, \gamma'/\sqrt{k})$ for some constants $c', \gamma' > 0$. We consider a family of access structures, where for every n an n-party access structure in this family is defined by composing access structures $\Gamma_1, \ldots, \Gamma_m$ such that each Γ_i is an access structure with a disjoint set of parties that can be realized by a p-WP secret-sharing scheme Π_i for $p = 1/O(\sqrt{m})$. We will use Lemma 2.8 to simulate this scheme. That is, we would like to share a bit z_i; however, we are only given a noisy version $y_i = \frac{p}{1+p}\text{-BSC}(z_i)$, that is $\Pr[y_i = z_i] = 1/(p+1)$ and $\Pr[y_i = 1 - z_i] = p/(p+1)$. By Lemma 2.8, there is a function $g_i(y_i)$ generating the shares of $A \cap P_i$ for a secret z_i from its noisy version y_i. We require that the sharing of the secret and the reconstructing of the secret from shares of any authorized set can be done in $\mathrm{poly}(m)$ time. Furthermore, to be able to compute $g(y_i)$ efficiently, we require that for every secret $s \in \{0, 1\}$, every set $A \notin \Gamma_i$, and every possible shares $\langle \mathsf{sh}_j \rangle_{p_j \in A}$, the probability $\Pr[\Pi_A(s) = \langle \mathsf{sh}_j \rangle_{p_j \in A}]$ can be computed in $\mathrm{poly}(m)$ time. We refer to such a scheme as a simulatable p-WP secret-sharing scheme.

Input: a secret $s \in \{0, 1\}$.

1. Let $m = m(n)$, c be a constant such that $1/(1 - h(\beta)) < c < 1/\alpha$, and $k = (m+1)/c$.
2. Share s using a random binary code; that is, choose a random matrix $C \leftarrow \mathbb{F}_2^{(m+1)\times k}$ and a random $x \leftarrow \mathbb{F}_2^k$ such that the zero coordinate of Cx is s and let $\mathsf{sh}_1, \ldots, \mathsf{sh}_m$ be the last m coordinates of Cx.
3. For every $1 \leq i \leq m$, share sh_i among the parties in P_i using a $1/O(\sqrt{m})$-WP secret-sharing scheme realizing the access structure Γ_i; the share of each $p_j \in P_i$ is its share in this scheme. The public information sh_0 is C.

Fig. 5. A computational secret-sharing scheme for $\mathrm{Gap}_{\alpha,\beta}(\Gamma_1, \ldots, \Gamma_m)$ for access structures $\Gamma_1, \ldots, \Gamma_m$, where Γ_i is an access structure with disjoint set of parties P_i that can be realized by a $1/O(\sqrt{m})$-simulatable WP secret-sharing scheme, assuming the hardness of LPN.

Theorem 4.2 (WP-based composed gap secret sharing). *Let α, β be constants such that $\beta > 1/2$ and $0 \leq \alpha \leq 1 - h(\beta)$, c be a constant such that $1/(1 - h(\beta)) < c < 1/\alpha$,* *and* $p : \mathbb{N} \to [0, 1]$ *be a function such that* $p(m) \geq \gamma / \sqrt{m}$ *for some constant* $\gamma > 1$. *There exist constants* $c', \gamma' > 0$ *such that assuming that* $\mathrm{LPN}(c'k, \gamma' / \sqrt{k})$ *holds, there is a computational secret-sharing scheme with share size* $s(m)$ *realizing the family of composed access structures* $\mathrm{Gap}_{\alpha,\beta}(\Gamma_1, \ldots, \Gamma_m)$*, where every* Γ_i *is an access structure that can be realized by a simulatable* $p(m)$*-WP secret-sharing scheme with share size* $s(m)$.

We next consider the two families of composed access structures discussed in the beginning of Sect. 4.

Corollary 4.3. *Let* $\beta > 1/2$ *and* $\alpha < 1 - h(\beta)$. *There are constants* $c', \gamma' > 0$ *such that assuming that* $\mathrm{LPN}(c'k, \gamma' / \sqrt{k})$ *holds, there is a computational secret-sharing scheme with share size* $O(1)$ *for the family of access structures* $\mathrm{Gap}_{\alpha,\beta}(\Gamma_1, \ldots, \Gamma_m)$*, where each* Γ_i *is a forbidden graph access structure with* $\ell(m) = m^{1/4}$ *disjoint parties.*

Corollary 4.4. *Let* $\beta > 1/2$ *and* $\alpha < 1 - h(\beta)$. *There are constants* $c', \gamma' > 0$ *such that assuming that* $\mathrm{LPN}(c'k, \gamma' / \sqrt{k})$ *holds, there is a computational secret-sharing scheme with share size* $\log m$ *for the family of access structures* $\mathrm{Gap}_{\alpha,\beta}(\Gamma_1, \ldots, \Gamma_m)$*, where each* Γ_i *is an access structure with* $\ell(m) = 0.1 \log m$.

Remark 4.5. For composition of forbidden graph access structures, there is a variant of the above scheme in which the shares are a bit. The scheme is obtained from the scheme described in Fig. 5 by using the simpler scheme described in Fig. 3 as the WP scheme in Step 3 (instead of the scheme described in Fig. 4). This results in a scheme with 1-bit shares. As the scheme described in Fig. 3 is $1/O(\ell^2)$-WP, the resulting scheme is secure under the intractability of $\mathrm{LPN}(c'k, \gamma' / \sqrt{k})$. In the full version, we show that for $\beta' = \Omega(m^{-0.75})$ any authorized set $B \in \mathrm{Gap}_{\alpha,\beta+\beta'}(\Gamma_1, \ldots, \Gamma_m)$ can reconstruct the secret with high probability. We do not know how to generalize these ideas for composition of arbitrary access structures, as we do not know how to generalize the scheme described in Fig. 3 to arbitrary access structures while having small reconstruction error.

5 Weakly Private Decomposable Randomized Encoding and MPC Protocols

In this section we construct WP decomposable randomized encoding (DRE) (see Sect. 5.1) and WP MPC protocols (see Sect. 5.2).

5.1 A WP Decomposable Randomized Encoding (DRE)

We next show that every function $f : \{0, 1\}^n \to \{0, 1\}$ has a WP DRE of size $\tilde{O}(n^2)$ and prove that there are explicit functions f such that every WP DRE for f is of size $\Omega(n^2 / \log n)$. As mentioned in the introduction, the notion of DRE is closely related to notions such as garbling and n-party PSM protocols.

We start with our positive result, where we construct a very efficient WP DRE for any $f : \{0, 1\}^n \to \{0, 1\}$, by constructing a DRE for a related function g. The idea is that the function g is, on one hand, very simple and hence has a very efficient perfect DRE (independently of the complexity of f) and, on the other hand, g's output allows computing f with some (weak) level of privacy.

- Define the function $g : \{0,1\}^n \times \{0,1\}^n \times \{0,1\}^n \to \{0,1\}^n$ as

$$g(x, w, w') = \begin{cases} w' & \text{if } x = w, \\ x & \text{otherwise,} \end{cases}$$

  and let $\textsc{Enc}_g, \textsc{Dec}_g$ be a decomposable randomized encoding for g.
- $\textsc{Enc}(x; R)$: parse $R = (R_1, w, w')$, where $w, w' \in \{0,1\}^n$, the string w is uniformly distributed, and w' is a uniformly distributed string such that $f(w) = f(w')$. Output $\widehat{y} \leftarrow \textsc{Enc}_g(x, w, w'; R_1)$.
- $\textsc{Dec}(\widehat{y})$: run $\textsc{Dec}_g(\widehat{y})$ to recover x^* and output $y = f(x^*)$.

Fig. 6. A WP decomposable randomized encoding for any function $f : \{0,1\}^n \to \{0,1\}$ with $O(n^2 \cdot \log^2 n \cdot \log\log n)$ size.

Theorem 5.1. *Let $f : \{0,1\}^n \to \{0,1\}$ be a function. The randomized encoding scheme for f, described in Fig. 6, is a p-WP DRE for $p = 2^{-O(n)}$, and has size $\ell \leq O(n^2 \cdot \log^2 n \cdot \log\log n)$.*

An $\Omega(n^2/\log n)$ Size Lower Bound. Our next goal is to show that the complexity of the above WP DRE scheme is essentially optimal for some functions f. We start with some notations.

Function Restrictions. For a subset $S \subseteq [n]$ with complement $\overline{S}$ and a partial input $z \in \{0,1\}^{\overline{S}}$, let $f_{S|z}$ denote the restriction of f on S via z:

$$f_{S|z}(x) := f(x'), \text{ where } x \in \{0,1\}^S, \text{ and } x'^{(i)} = \begin{cases} x^{(i)} & \text{if } i \in S \\ z^{(i)} & \text{otherwise.} \end{cases}$$

Let $g_S(f)$ count the (log of) number of distinct, non-constant restrictions of f on S:

$$g_S(f) := \log(\#\{f_{S|z} : z \subset \{0,1\}^{\overline{S}}, f_{S|z} \text{ not constant}\}).$$

Given a DRE scheme, let $\textsc{Enc}_S$ denote the output bits that are determined by the input bits at positions in S. Let $\ell_S \leq \ell$ denote the number of such output bits. For example, for a partial input $z \in \{0,1\}^{\overline{S}}$ and randomness R, we write $\widehat{y_{\overline{S}}} = \textsc{Enc}_{\overline{S}}(z; R)$ and say $\widehat{y_{\overline{S}}}$ is a partial encoding with respect to z. The bit-length of the partial encoding is denoted by $\ell_{\overline{S}} = |\hat{y}_{\overline{S}}|$.

We first show in the following claim that WP privacy of a DRE scheme requires a partial encoding $\hat{y}_{\overline{S}}$ with respect to some partial input $z_1 \in \{0,1\}^{\overline{S}}$ to be explainable by any other partial input z_2, as long as $f_{S|z_1}$ and $f_{S|z_2}$ are not constant.

Claim 5.2 (WP of partial inputs). *Let $\mathcal{R}, \textsc{Enc}, \textsc{Dec}$ be a WP decomposable randomized encoding for some function $f : \{0,1\}^n \to \{0,1\}$. For any $S \subseteq [n]$, partial inputs*

$z_1, z_2 \in \{0,1\}^{\overline{S}}$ *such that the restrictions* $f_{S|z_1}$, $f_{S|z_2}$ *are not constant, and any partial encoding* $\widehat{y_{\overline{S}}} \in \{0,1\}^{\ell_{\overline{S}}}$,

$$\Pr_{R \leftarrow \mathcal{R}}[\mathrm{Enc}_{\overline{S}}(z_1; R) = \widehat{y_{\overline{S}}}] > 0 \implies \Pr_{R \leftarrow \mathcal{R}}[\mathrm{Enc}_{\overline{S}}(z_2; R) = \widehat{y_{\overline{S}}}] > 0.$$

Proof. Since $f_{S|z_1}$ is non-constant, in particular not constantly zero, there exists an extension $x_1 \in \{0,1\}^n$ to the partial input $z_1 \in \{0,1\}^{\overline{S}}$ such that $f(x_1) = 1$. Similarly, there also exists an extension x_2 to the partial input z_2 such that $f(x_2) = 1$.

$$f(x_1) = f(x_2), \quad \text{and for } i \in \overline{S}, \quad x_1^{(i)} = z_1^{(i)}, x_2^{(i)} = z_2^{(i)}.$$

By assumption, there exists $R_1 \in \mathcal{R}$ such that $\mathrm{Enc}_{\overline{S}}(z_1; R_1) = \widehat{y_{\overline{S}}}$. Let $\widehat{y} = \mathrm{Enc}(x_1; R_1)$. It suffices to show that $\Pr_{R_2 \leftarrow \mathcal{R}}[\mathrm{Enc}(x_2; R_2) = \widehat{y}] > 0$, as the event $\mathrm{Enc}(x_2, R_2) = \widehat{y}$ implies $\mathrm{Enc}_{\overline{S}}(z_2; R_2) = \widehat{y_{\overline{S}}}$. The desired inequality follows from WP (for any $p > 0$):

$$\Pr_{R_2 \leftarrow \mathcal{R}}[\mathrm{Enc}(x_2; R_2) = \widehat{y}] \geq p \cdot \Pr_{R_1 \leftarrow \mathcal{R}}[\mathrm{Enc}(x_1; R_1) = \widehat{y}] > 0.$$

□

Building onto the previous claim, we next show that the bit-length of a partial encoding ℓ_S is at least $g_S(f)/2$, where $g_S(f)$ counts the log of the number of non-constant restrictions to S.

Claim 5.3 (Size lower-bound for partial encodings). *Let* $\mathcal{R}$, Enc, Dec *be a WP decomposable randomized encoding for some function* $f : \{0,1\}^n \to \{0,1\}$. *For any* $S \subseteq [n]$, *we have* $2\ell_S \geq g_S(f)$.

Proof. Consider any $S \subseteq [n]$. If there are no non-constant restrictions on S, then we have $g_S(f) = 0$ and we are done. Otherwise, let $\widehat{y_{\overline{S}}}$ be a partial encoding that can explain all partial inputs $z \in \{0,1\}^{\overline{S}}$ such that $f_{S|z}$ are non-constant:

$$\forall z \in \{0,1\}^{\overline{S}} \text{ s.t. } f_{S|z} \text{ not constant,} \quad \exists R \text{ s.t. } \mathrm{Enc}_{\overline{S}}(z, R) = \widehat{y_{\overline{S}}}. \tag{3}$$

(Such a partial encoding can be obtained by choosing an arbitrary partial input z_1 such that $f_{S|z_1}$ is non-constant, an arbitrary randomness R_1, and computing $\widehat{y_{\overline{S}}} = \mathrm{Enc}_{\overline{S}}(z_1; R_1)$. By Claim 5.2, $\widehat{y_{\overline{S}}}$ also explains all other partial input z_2 such that $f_{S|z_2}$ is non-constant.)

For every such z, R that explains $\widehat{y_{\overline{S}}}$ (as in (3)), we examine the possible extensions to $\widehat{y_{\overline{S}}}$ into a complete encoding:

$$\mathrm{Ext}_{S,R} := \{\mathrm{Enc}_{\{i\}}(b, R) : i \in S, b \in \{0,1\}\}. \tag{4}$$

By decomposability of the DRE scheme, the extension to $\widehat{y_{\overline{S}}}$ from a partial encoding w.r.t. $z \in \{0,1\}^{\overline{S}}$ into a complete encoding w.r.t. $x \in \{0,1\}^n$ is exactly obtained by choosing $\mathrm{Enc}_{\{i\}}(x^{(i)}, R)$ from the materials $\mathrm{Ext}_{S,R}$ computed above in (4). Then by the correctness of the DRE scheme, this extended encoding w.r.t. x can be decoded by Dec to recover $f(x)$. Therefore, the materials $\mathrm{Ext}_{S,R}$, together with $\widehat{y_{\overline{S}}}$, determine the truth table of $f_{S|z}$.

In summary, we showed that for every partial input z one can compute a set of materials $\text{Ext}_{S,R}$ that determine the truth table of $f_{S|z}$, as long as $f_{S|z}$ is non-constant. This implies the bit-length of $\text{Ext}_{S,R}$ to be at least $g_S(f)$. Therefore, we can conclude

$$|\text{Ext}_{S,R}| = 2\ell_S \geq g_S(f).$$

□

Finally, we rely on known results taken from [6] to conclude a $\Omega(n^2/\log n)$ lower bound on the size of WP DRE schemes.

Fact 5.4. *Let V denote any partition of $[n]$. There exist explicit functions $f : \{0,1\}^n \to \{0,1\}$ such that* $\max_V \sum_{S \in V} g_S(f) \geq \Omega(n^2/\log n)$.

Theorem 5.5. *There exist explicit functions $f : \{0,1\}^n \to \{0,1\}$ such that any WP-decomposable randomized encoding for f has size $\ell \geq \Omega(n^2/\log n)$.*

Proof. Note that for any partition V of $[n]$, we have $\ell = \sum_{S \in V} \ell_S$. The lower bound follows from Claim 5.3 and Fact 5.4. □

5.2 WP MPC Protocols

We next present WP MPC protocols with communication complexity $O(nk)$ secure against a semi-honest adversary. We construct protocols in two models: (1) in the plain model assuming honest majority, and (2) in the OT-hybrid model, where there is no bound on the number of semi-honest parties. Both protocols have the same structure, similar to our DRE construction above. That is, given a function $f : (\{0,1\}^n)^k \to \{0,1\}$, which k parties want to compute, they instead compute a related function g, which is much simpler to compute than f, but leaks some information. This function g is computed by a perfect MPC protocol.

Formally, let $1 \leq t \leq k$ be an upper bound on the number of semi-honest parties. For simplicity of the notations, we assume that the k parties in the protocol are parties $0, \ldots, k-1$. Define the function $g_{k,t} : \left((\{0,1\}^n)^{2k+1} \times \{0,\ldots,t\}\right)^{t+1} \times (\{0,1\}^n)^{k-t-1} \to (\{0,1\}^n)^k$, where the input of the j-th party for $0 \leq j \leq t$ is $x_j, (x_\ell^j, y_\ell^j)_{0 \leq \ell \leq k-1}, r_j$, the input of the j-th party for $t \leq j \leq k-1$ is x_j, and the value of $g_{k,t}$ on these inputs is computed as follows: Let $i = \sum_{0 \leq j \leq t-1} r_j \bmod (t+1)$; If $f(x_0^i, \ldots, x_{k-1}^i) = f(x_0, \ldots, x_{k-1})$ and $x_j^i = x_j$ for $0 \leq j \leq k-1$ then output $y_0^i, \ldots, y_{k-1}^i$, else output $x_0, \ldots, x_{k-1}$.

Lemma 5.6. *If $\Pi_{g_{k,t}}$ is a perfect t-private protocol for $g_{k,t}$, then Protocol Π_f described in Fig. 7 is a $\frac{1}{(t+1)2^{2kt}}$-WP MPC protocol for f.*

To construct an MPC protocol for f, we need to explain which MPC protocol $\Pi_{g_{k,t}}$ we use. Note that, for each $0 \leq j \leq t$, the equality $f(x_0^j, \ldots, x_{k-1}^j) = f(y_0^j, \ldots, x_{k-1}^j)$ can be locally computed without any communication. Using this information, the function $g_{k,t}$ can be computed by a Boolean or Arithmetic circuit with fan-in 2 and size $\text{poly}(k) \cdot n$.

If we assume an honest majority, we can use the BGW protocol [13] to compute $g_{k,\lceil (k+1)/2 \rceil}$. The communication complexity of the BGW protocol is polynomial in the

Protocol $\Pi_f(x_0, \ldots, x_{k-1})$: Let $\Pi_{g_{k,t}}$ be a perfect t-private protocol for $g_{k,t}$.

1. The j-th party, for $0 \le j \le t-1$, samples with uniform distribution $(x_\ell^j, y_\ell^j)_{0 \le \ell \le k-1} \in (\{0,1\}^n)^{2k}$ and $r_j \in \{0, \ldots, t\}$.
2. Secularly compute
$$g\Big(\big(x_0, (x_\ell^0, y_\ell^0)_{0\le\ell\le k-1}, r_0\big), \ldots, \big(x_t, (x_\ell^t, y_\ell^t)_{0\le\ell\le k-1}, r_t\big), x_{t+1}, \ldots, x_{k-1}\Big)$$
using $\Pi_{g_{k,t}}$; get output $z_0, \ldots, z_{k-1}$.
3. Output $f(z_0, \ldots, z_{k-1})$.

Fig. 7. A WP k-party protocol for a function $f : (\{0,1\}^n)^k \to \{0,1\}$, in the $g_{k,t}$-hybrid model.

number of parties and linear in the size of the arithmetic circuit; this results in a protocol with communication complexity poly$k \cdot n$ for f.

Without any assumptions on the number of semi-honest parties, we can use the GMW protocol [29] to compute $g_{k,k-1}$ in the OT hybrid model. The number of OT calls in the GMW protocol is polynomial in the number of parties and linear in the size of the Boolean circuit; this results in a protocol for f with poly$k \cdot n$ OT calls.
Thus, we obtain the following:

Theorem 5.7. *Let* $f : (\{0,1\}^n)^k \to \{0,1\}$ *be a function. Then,*

- *There is a* 2^{2kn}*-WP secure k-party protocol for f assuming an honest majority with communication complexity* poly$k \cdot n$.
- *There is a* 2^{2kn}*-WP secure k-party protocol for f in the OT-hybrid model in which the number of calls to OT is* poly$k \cdot n$.

Remark: Similar protocols can be constructed for general k-private, k-party MPC with correlated randomness, by using k-out-of-k secret sharing of the values. In this case, the input $\mathbf{x} = (x^1, \ldots, x^k)$ is of total length $k \cdot n$, and sharing two such inputs $\mathbf{x}_1$ and $\mathbf{x}_2$ among the k parties will lead to $O(k^2 n)$ communication and correlated-random complexity.

Acknowledgments. Amos Beimel is partially supported by ISF grant 1614/25. He is co-funded by the European Union (ERC, NFITSC, 101097959). Views and opinions expressed are, however, those of the author(s) only and do not necessarily reflect those of the European Union or the European Research Council. Neither the European Union nor the granting authority can be held responsible for them. Yuval Ishai is supported by ISF grant 3527/24, BSF grant 2022370, and ISF-NSFC grant 3127/23. This paper is not associated with Amazon. Eyal Kushilevitz is supported by ISF grant 3527/24 and BSF grant 2022370.

References

1. Applebaum, B., Beimel, A., Ishai, Y., Kushilevitz, E., Liu, T., Vaikuntanathan, V.: Succinct computational secret sharing. In: STOC 2023, pp. 1553–1566. ACM (2023)

2. Applebaum, B., Beimel, A., Nir, O., Peter, N.: Better secret sharing via robust conditional disclosure of secrets. In: STOC 2020, pp. 280–293. ACM (2020)
3. Applebaum, B., Ishai, Y., Kushilevitz, E.: How to garble arithmetic circuits. In: Ostrovsky, R. (ed.) Proceedings of the 52th IEEE Symposium on Foundations of Computer Science, pp. 120–129. IEEE Computer Society (2011). https://doi.org/10.1109/FOCS.2011.40
4. Applebaum, B., Nir, O.: Upslices, downslices, and secret-sharing with complexity of 1.5^n. In: Malkin, T., Peikert, C. (eds.) CRYPTO 2021. LNCS, vol. 12827, pp. 627–655. Springer, Cham (2021). https://doi.org/10.1007/978-3-030-84252-9_21
5. Assouline, L., Liu, T.: Multi-party PSM, revisited: - improved communication and unbalanced communication. In: Nissim, K., Waters, B. (eds.) TCC 2021. LNCS, vol. 13043, pp. 194–223. Springer, Cham (2021). https://doi.org/10.1007/978-3-030-90453-1_7
6. Ball, M., Holmgren, J., Ishai, Y., Liu, T., Malkin, T.: On the complexity of decomposable randomized encodings, or: how friendly can a garbling-friendly PRF be? In: Vidick, T. (ed.) 11th ITCS. LIPIcs, vol. 151, pp. 86:1–86:22. Schloss Dagstuhl - Leibniz-Zentrum für Informatik (2020). https://doi.org/10.4230/LIPICS.ITCS.2020.86
7. Beaver, D., Haber, S., Winkler, P.: On the isolation of a common secret. In: Graham, R.L., Nesetril, J., Butler, S. (eds.) The Mathematics of Paul Erdős II, pp. 21–38. Springer, Cham (2013). https://doi.org/10.1007/978-1-4614-7254-4_3
8. Beimel, A., Franklin, M.: Weakly-private secret sharing schemes. In: Vadhan, S.P. (ed.) TCC 2007. LNCS, vol. 4392, pp. 253–272. Springer, Heidelberg (2007). https://doi.org/10.1007/978-3-540-70936-7_14
9. Beimel, A., Ishai, Y., Kumaresan, R., Kushilevitz, E.: On the cryptographic complexity of the worst functions. In: Lindell, Y. (ed.) TCC 2014. LNCS, vol. 8349, pp. 317–342. Springer, Heidelberg (2014). https://doi.org/10.1007/978-3-642-54242-8_14
10. Beimel, A., Kushilevitz, E., Nissim, P.: The complexity of multiparty PSM protocols and related models. In: Nielsen, J.B., Rijmen, V. (eds.) EUROCRYPT 2018. LNCS, vol. 10821, pp. 287–318. Springer, Cham (2018). https://doi.org/10.1007/978-3-319-78375-8_10
11. Beimel, A., Malkin, T.: A quantitative approach to reductions in secure computation. In: Naor, M. (ed.) TCC 2004. LNCS, vol. 2951, pp. 238–257. Springer, Heidelberg (2004). https://doi.org/10.1007/978-3-540-24638-1_14
12. Bellare, M., Hoang, V.T., Rogaway, P.: Foundations of garbled circuits. In: Yu, T., Danezis, G., Gligor, V.D. (eds.) The ACM Conference on Computer and Communications Security, CCS 2012, Raleigh, NC, USA, 16–18 October 2012, pp. 784–796. ACM (2012). https://doi.org/10.1145/2382196.2382279
13. Ben-Or, M., Goldwasser, S., Wigderson, A.: Completeness theorems for noncryptographic fault-tolerant distributed computations. In: 20th STOC, pp. 1–10 (1988)
14. Blakley, G.R.: Safeguarding cryptographic keys. In: Proceedings of the 1979 AFIPS National Computer Conference. AFIPS Conference proceedings, vol. 48, pp. 313–317. AFIPS Press (1979)
15. Blakley, G.R., Meadows, C.: Security of ramp schemes. In: Blakley, G.R., Chaum, D. (eds.) CRYPTO 1984. LNCS, vol. 196, pp. 242–268. Springer, Heidelberg (1985). https://doi.org/10.1007/3-540-39568-7_20
16. Blum, A., Furst, M., Kearns, M., Lipton, R.J.: Cryptographic primitives based on hard learning problems. In: Stinson, D.R. (ed.) CRYPTO 1993. LNCS, vol. 773, pp. 278–291. Springer, Heidelberg (1994). https://doi.org/10.1007/3-540-48329-2_24
17. Cascudo, I., Cramer, R., Xing, C.: Bounds on the threshold gap in secret sharing and its applications. IEEE Trans. Inf. Theory **59**(9), 5600–5612 (2013)
18. Chen, H., Cramer, R., Goldwasser, S., de Haan, R., Vaikuntanathan, V.: Secure computation from random error correcting codes. In: Naor, M. (ed.) EUROCRYPT 2007. LNCS, vol. 4515, pp. 291–310. Springer, Heidelberg (2007). https://doi.org/10.1007/978-3-540-72540-4_17

19. Chor, B., Goldreich, O., Kushilevitz, E., Sudan, M.: Private information retrieval. In: Proceedings of the 36th IEEE Symposium on Foundations of Computer Science, pp. 41–51 (1995). Journal version: J. ACM **45**, 965–981 (1998)
20. Chor, B., Kushilevitz, E.: A zero-one law for Boolean privacy. SIAM J. Discret. Math. **4**(1), 36–47 (1991)
21. Csirmaz, L.: The size of a share must be large. In: De Santis, A. (ed.) EUROCRYPT 1994. LNCS, vol. 950, pp. 13–22. Springer, Heidelberg (1995). https://doi.org/10.1007/BFb0053420
22. Dodis, Y., Kalai, Y.T., Lovett, S.: On cryptography with auxiliary input. In: Mitzenmacher, M. (ed.) Proceedings of the 41st ACM Symposium on the Theory of Computing, pp. 621–630. ACM (2009). https://doi.org/10.1145/1536414.1536498
23. Dvir, Z., Gopi, S.: 2-server PIR with sub-polynomial communication. In: 47th STOC, pp. 577–584 (2015)
24. Dwork, C., McSherry, F., Nissim, K., Smith, A.: Calibrating noise to sensitivity in private data analysis. In: Halevi, S., Rabin, T. (eds.) TCC 2006. LNCS, vol. 3876, pp. 265–284. Springer, Heidelberg (2006). https://doi.org/10.1007/11681878_14
25. Erdös, P., Pyber, L.: Covering a graph by complete bipartite graphs. Discret. Math. **170**(1–3), 249–251 (1997)
26. Feige, U., Kilian, J., Naor, M.: A minimal model for secure computation. In: 26th STOC, pp. 554–563 (1994)
27. Franklin, M.K., Yung, M.: Communication complexity of secure computation. In: Proceedings of the 24th ACM Symposium on the Theory of Computing, pp. 699–710 (1992)
28. Ghasemi, F., Kopparty, S., Sudan, M.: Improved PIR schemes using matching vectors and derivatives. In: Proceedings of the 57th ACM Symposium on the Theory of Computing (2025)
29. Goldreich, O., Micali, S., Wigderson, A.: How to play any mental game. In: Proceedings of the 19th ACM Symposium on the Theory of Computing, pp. 218–229 (1987)
30. Ishai, Y., Kushilevitz, E.: Private simultaneous messages protocols with applications. In: 5th Israel Symposium on Theory of Computing and Systems, pp. 174–183 (1997)
31. Ito, M., Saito, A., Nishizeki, T.: Secret sharing schemes realizing general access structure. In: Globecom 1987, pp. 99–102 (1987). Journal version: Multiple assignment scheme for sharing secret. J. Cryptol. **6**(1), 15–20 (1993)
32. Kairouz, P., Oh, S., Viswanath, P.: Differentially private multi-party computation: optimality of non-interactive randomized response. CoRR abs/1407.1546 (2014). http://arxiv.org/abs/1407.1546
33. Kilian, J., Nisan, N.: Private communication (1990)
34. Kolesnikov, V.: Gate evaluation secret sharing and secure one-round two-party computation. In: Roy, B. (ed.) ASIACRYPT 2005. LNCS, vol. 3788, pp. 136–155. Springer, Heidelberg (2005). https://doi.org/10.1007/11593447_8
35. Krawczyk, H.: Secret sharing made short. In: Stinson, D.R. (ed.) CRYPTO 1993. LNCS, vol. 773, pp. 136–146. Springer, Heidelberg (1994). https://doi.org/10.1007/3-540-48329-2_12
36. Kushilevitz, E.: Privacy and communication complexity. SIAM J. Discret. Math. **5**(2), 273–284 (1992)
37. Liu, T., Vaikuntanathan, V.: Breaking the circuit-size barrier in secret sharing. In: 50th STOC, pp. 699–708 (2018)
38. Liu, T., Vaikuntanathan, V., Wee, H.: Conditional disclosure of secrets via non-linear reconstruction. In: Katz, J., Shacham, H. (eds.) CRYPTO 2017. LNCS, vol. 10401, pp. 758–790. Springer, Cham (2017). https://doi.org/10.1007/978-3-319-63688-7_25
39. Liu, T., Vaikuntanathan, V., Wee, H.: Towards breaking the exponential barrier for general secret sharing. In: Nielsen, J.B., Rijmen, V. (eds.) EUROCRYPT 2018. LNCS, vol. 10820, pp. 567–596. Springer, Cham (2018). https://doi.org/10.1007/978-3-319-78381-9_21

40. Maurer, U., Pietrzak, K., Renner, R.: Indistinguishability amplification. In: Menezes, A. (ed.) CRYPTO 2007. LNCS, vol. 4622, pp. 130–149. Springer, Heidelberg (2007). https://doi.org/10.1007/978-3-540-74143-5_8
41. Shamir, A.: How to share a secret. Commun. ACM **22**, 612–613 (1979)
42. Shannon, C.E.: Communication theory of secrecy systems. Bell Syst. Tech. J. **28**(4), 656–715 (1949)
43. Sun, H.M., Shieh, S.P.: Secret sharing in graph-based prohibited structures. In: INFOCOM 1997, pp. 718–724 (1997)
44. Talwar, K.: Differential secrecy for distributed data and applications to robust differentially secure vector summation. In: 3rd Symposium on Foundations of Responsible Computing, FORC 2022. LIPIcs, vol. 218, pp. 7:1–7:16. Schloss Dagstuhl - Leibniz-Zentrum für Informatik (2022). https://doi.org/10.4230/LIPICS.FORC.2022.7
45. Yao, A.C.: How to generate and exchange secrets. In: Proceedings of the 27th IEEE Symposium on Foundations of Computer Science, pp. 162–167 (1986)
46. Yao, A.C.: Unpublished manuscript (1989). Presented at Oberwolfach and DIMACS Workshops

Timed Cryptography and Verifiable Random Function

Time/Space Tradeoffs for Generic Attacks on Delay Functions

Kasper Green Larsen[1] and Mark Simkin[1,2(✉)]

[1] Aarhus University, Aarhus, Denmark
larsen@cs.au.dk, mark@univariate.org
[2] Flashbots, George Town, Cayman Islands

Abstract. Delay functions have the goal of being inherently slow to compute. They have been shown to be useful for generating public randomness in distributed systems in the presence of a dishonest majority of network participants; a task that is impossible to solve without such functions, due to Cleve's seminal impossibility result (STOC 1986). Currently, little is known on how to construct secure delay functions or how to analyze the security of newly proposed candidate constructions.

In this work, we explore the time/space tradeoffs of generic attacks for a large class of potential delay function designs. We consider delay functions F^T, which are computed as

$$F^T := \underbrace{F(\dots F(F}_{T}(x))\dots),$$

where $F : [N] \to [N]$ is some round function, in the presence of an adversary, who is given an advice string of some bounded size, has oracle access to F, and would like to compute F^T on a random input x using less than T sequential oracle calls.

We show that for both random and arbitrary functions F there exist non-trivial adversaries, who successfully evaluate F^T using only $T/4$ sequential calls to oracle F, when given a large enough advice string. We also show that there exist round functions F for which the adversary cannot compute F^T using less than $T/2$ sequential queries, unless they receive a large advice string or they can perform a large number of oracle queries to F in parallel.

1 Introduction

Delay functions, first introduced by Goldschlag and Stubblebine [GS98], are functions that are inherently slow to compute, no matter how much parallel computing power is available. Slightly more formally, these are functions that cannot be evaluated by low depth circuits, unless the circuit size is super-polynomial related to the input length. Treating the depth of a circuit as a proxy for the physical time needed to evaluate the corresponding function and assuming that parties in a distributed network can measure time, has fascinating consequences in both theoretical and applied cryptography.

B. Applebaum and H. Lin (Eds.): TCC 2025, LNCS 16271, pp. 451–477, 2026.
https://doi.org/10.1007/978-3-032-12290-2_15

Boneh et al. [BBBF18], for example, show that delay functions allow for overcoming Cleve's impossibility result [Cle86], which states that n parties cannot flip an unbiased coin in a distributed network, when half or more of the processors are faulty.[1] Being able to flip coins securely in the presence of a dishonest majority is of significant importance for modern day blockchains and following the results of Boneh et al., several constructions of randomness beacons based on delay functions have been proposed [CMB23]. Motivated by the application outlined above and various other ones in the context of blockchains, delay functions have received a significant amount of interest [BBBF18, Pie19, Wes19, EFKP20, MSW20, RS20, ARS24] in recent years.

Unfortunately, right now we do not know how to construct delay functions that are as secure and as efficient as one might hope for and our ability to assess the security of new candidate delay functions is quite limited. Broadly speaking, there are two main approaches for assessing their security and both of them are constrained in their power.

The *reductionist approach* is to base the security of a given delay function upon the presumed hardness of some computational problem. This approach presupposes that there are "good" problems to reduce to, but as of now this does not seem to be the case. Delay functions built upon the assumption that repeated squaring in groups of unknown order cannot be parallelized, an assumption introduced by Cai et al. [CLSY93], all face practical obstacles. They either rely on a trusted setup or require performing highly efficient (low depth) arithmetic operations over class groups, which are hard to implement in practice. Alternatively, delay functions can be built upon the sole assumption that certain non-parallelizable languages and one-way functions exist [ARS24], but the practicality of the resulting constructions remains yet to be seen.

The *cryptanalytic approach* is try and break a given candidate delay function and to declare it secure, when no meaningful attacks have been found for a sufficiently long time. In recent years, several new delay function designs have been proposed by different researchers [BBBF18, DMPS19, LM23, KMT22], but many of these proposed constructions have been broken shortly after their initial publication [PT24, BFH+24, DDJ24]. Although these attacks are bad news for the delay functions they target, they may also provide valuable insights for developing new, more secure designs, serving as guiding principles for future delay functions.

The existing attacks [BBBF18, PT24, BFH+24, DDJ24] specifically target the algebraic structure underlying the delay functions they consider, thus they provide somewhat limited insights into what more general design principles for delay functions could be.

1.1 Our Contribution

In this work we put on our cryptanalytic hat and explore time/space tradeoffs for generic attacks on a large class of delay functions. Specifically, we focus on

[1] The general idea of using time-based cryptography to overcome Cleve's impossibility originally appeared in the work of Boneh and Naor [BN00].

delay functions F^T that are comprised of a round function $F : [N] \to [N]$ with $[N] := \{0, \ldots, N-1\}$, which is repeatedly applied to itself. In other words, we consider delay functions with arbitrary round functions of the form

$$F^T := \underbrace{F(\ldots F(F(x)) \ldots)}_{T}.$$

This class of delay functions encompasses virtually all existing candidate delay functions, with the exception of a recent work by Abram, Roy, and Simkin [ARS24]. We consider an adversary $\mathcal{A} = (\mathcal{A}_0, \mathcal{A}_1)$, who has oracle access to the function F and who aims to evaluate $F^T(x)$ on a random challenge x using less than T sequential calls to the oracle F. The adversary $\mathcal{A}_0$ is initially allowed to perform an unbounded preprocessing step, which is independent of the challenge x, and return an advice string of size S. This advice string along with a random challenge x is then given to $\mathcal{A}_1$, who aims to output $F^T(x)$ using at most $\widetilde{T}$ with $\widetilde{T} < T$ sequential oracle calls to F, where during each call the adversary can evaluate F in at most P different points in parallel.

In this work, we explore the relationship between all of the involved parameters, namely between the size S of the advice string, the number of required and sufficient oracle calls $T, \widetilde{T}, P$, and the size of the domain N. We show several somewhat complementary results.

First, using rather simple attack ideas, we show that non-trivial adversaries exist for random and arbitrary functions. For example, we show that for some range of parameters, there exists an efficient adversary for arbitrary F that successfully computes F^T using $\widetilde{T} = T/4$ sequential oracle calls with constant success probability. Slightly more formally, this result is captured in the theorem statement below.

Theorem 1 (Informal). *For any round function $F : [N] \to [N]$, any $T \in \mathbb{N}$, there exists an adversary $\mathcal{A} = (\mathcal{A}_0, \mathcal{A}_1)$ that outputs an advice string of size $S = \mathcal{O}\left(\frac{N \lg N}{T}\right)$, makes at most $\widetilde{T} = T/4$ sequential and at most P parallel queries, such that and*

$$\Pr\left[\mathcal{A}_1(x, \sigma) = F^T(x) : \sigma \leftarrow \mathcal{A}_0(F)\right] > 1/2,$$

where the probability is taken over the choice of $x \in [N]$ and the random coins of the adversary.

The above theorem tells us that for some parameter ranges we have successfully found an adversarial strategy that works, but it leaves open the question, whether there are much better attacks for arbitrary functions F.

Using an encoding argument, a proof technique that has been used with great success in data structure lower bounds [PD06, PV10, Lar12a, Lar12b, BL13, VZ13, CKL18, LS20, LY20, LLYZ23], we show that there is a limit to how successful an adversary can be. Concretely, we show that there exist round functions for which *any* adversary that wants to do less than $T/2$ sequential oracle calls needs to have a large advice string and/or needs to perform many parallel oracle calls.

Proving this statement is rather involved and constitutes the main technical contribution of this work. Slightly more formally, we get the following theorem.

Theorem 2 (Informal). *There exist round functions $F : [N] \to [N]$, such that for any adversary $\mathcal{A} = (\mathcal{A}_0, \mathcal{A}_1)$ with*

$$\Pr\left[\mathcal{A}_1(x, \sigma) = F^T(x) : \sigma \leftarrow \mathcal{A}_0(F)\right] > 1/2,$$

either the number of sequential queries $\widetilde{T} \geq T/2$ or (roughly speaking) it must hold that

$$(S + \widetilde{T})\widetilde{T}P = \Omega(N).$$

Are These Attacks Practical? We note that the goal of this work is to explore the asymptotic landscape of time/space tradeoffs for generic attacks on delay functions. We have not optimized the hidden constants in our results and leave tightening hidden constants and exploring the practicality of the proposed attacks for future work.

1.2 Related Works

Several works [RSS20, KLX20, RS20] investigate the computational hardness of the repeated squaring assumption of Cai et al. [CLSY93]. Rotem, Segev, and Shahaf [RSS20] rule out a large class of potential constructions of delay functions from known-order cyclic groups. Katz, Loss, and Xu [KLX20] as well as Rotem and Segev [RS20] show that under certain simplifying assumptions reducing the sequential time needed for performing repeated squaring in groups of unknown order is as hard as factoring. Boneh et al. [BBBF18] investigate delay functions based on certain types of permutation polynomials and explore several kinds of algebraic attacks on those. Peikert and Tang [PT24] show that a new hardness assumption over lattices, introduced by Lai and Malavolta [LM23] with the goal of constructing delay functions, is false. All these works have a focus that is different from ours, as we care about generic attacks, whereas these works focus on highly specific algebraic structures.

Several different attacks and their time/space tradeoffs have also been explored in the context of a specific, by now defunct, candidate delay function called Minroot [LMP+23]. Ideas underlying some of these attacks are similar to those underlying our attacks on arbitrary round functions, but whereas their attacks and analysis focuses on Minroot specifically (in an idealized model), we show that this type of attack can be made to work for arbitrary round functions (without an idealized model).

Somewhat more loosely related, but similar in spirit is the topic of function inversion [Hel80]. Here, an adversary is given oracle access to a function F, can perform an unbounded preprocessing step to output an advice string of length S and is then asked to invert F on a random output y, i.e. the adversary is given y and asked to find an x, such that $F(x) = y$, while making as few queries to the oracle F as possible. In his seminal work, Hellman [Hel80] proved that non-trivial time/space tradeoffs exist for random functions and suggested that they also exist for arbitrary functions. A subsequent work by Fiat and Naor [FN91] has then rigorously proven the time/space tradeoffs for arbitrary functions. More recently, this topic has seen a renewed interest [CK19,CHM20,GGPS23], which has led to new bounds.

We stress that despite their superficial similarities, function inversion and our model in this work are fundamentally different; especially when it comes to proving limits on the power of adversaries in the respective settings. Lower bounds in function inversion need to argue that, given some advice string of bounded size, the adversary has to make at least some number of oracle queries *in total* to compute the output. In our setting, the output can be computed using only T sequential queries, but we need to prove that an adversary cannot compute it using significantly less that T *sequential* queries, unless it effectively queries most of the domain using parallel queries.

2 Model

Definition 1 (Iterated Functions). *Let $T \in \mathbb{N}$ and let $F : [N] \to [N]$ be a function. We define*

$$F^T := \underbrace{F(\ldots F(F}_{T}(x))\ldots)$$

to be the T-wise iterated function with round function F.

Definition 2 (Parallel and Sequential Oracle Queries). *Let $\mathcal{A}$ be an algorithm with query access to oracle $\mathcal{O}$. Separate queries by $\mathcal{A}$ to $\mathcal{O}$ are said to be sequential, if they happen one after another. They are said to be parallel, if they happen simultaneously. Any algorithm $\mathcal{A}$ is allowed to do both types of queries.*

Definition 3 ($(S, P, \widetilde{T})$-admissible adversaries). *Let $S, P, \widetilde{T} \in \mathbb{N}$. An adversary $\mathcal{A} = (\mathcal{A}_0, \mathcal{A}_1)$ is said to be $(S, P, \widetilde{T})$-admissible, if $\mathcal{A}_0$ on some given input always returns a bit string of length at most S and if $\mathcal{A}_1$ with access to oracle $\mathcal{O}$ makes at most P parallel queries at once in a single round and at most $\widetilde{T}$ sequential rounds of queries.*

Definition 4 (Sequentiality). *Let $S, P, T \in \mathbb{N}$, let $\epsilon \in \mathbb{R}$ with $0 \leq \epsilon \leq 1$, and let $F : [N] \to [N]$ be a round function. We say iterated function F^T is (S, P, ϵ)-secure against, if for all $(S, P, \epsilon T)$-admissible adversaries $\mathcal{A} := (\mathcal{A}_0, \mathcal{A}_1)$, it holds that*

$$\Pr\left[\mathsf{Exp}^{\mathsf{SEQ}}_{\mathcal{A},F,T} = 1\right] \leq \frac{1}{2},$$

where experiment $\mathsf{Exp}^{\mathsf{SEQ}}_{\mathcal{A}}$ is depicted in Fig. 1 and where the probability is taken over the random choice of the challenge.

$\mathsf{Exp}^{\mathsf{SEQ}}_{\mathcal{A},F,T}$

$\sigma \leftarrow \mathcal{A}_0(F)$
$x \leftarrow [N]$
$y \leftarrow \mathcal{A}_1^F(\sigma, x)$
if $y = F^T(x)$
  return 1
else
  return 0

Fig. 1. The delay function sequentiality experiment

Definition 5 (Evaluation Trace). *Let* $T \in \mathbb{N}$, *let* $F : [N] \to [N]$, *and let* $x \in [N]$. *The evaluation trace of iterated function* F^T *on input* x *is defined as*

$$\text{TRACE}(F^T, x) := \{x, F(x), F(F(x)), \ldots, F^T(x)\}.$$

3 Upper Bounds

In this section, we present several simple adversarial strategies. In Sect. 3.1, we show that when F is random and when the number of required iterations T is large enough, then exists an adversary that can compute F^T in $T/4$ steps using no preprocessing at all. In Sect. 3.2, we then go on to consider arbitrary round functions F. First we show in Theorem 3 that a sufficient amount of space allows for an adversary for arbitrary F that uses no parallelism, but only does $T/4$ sequential queries. We then show in Theorem 5 how to exploit parallelism to reduce the size of the required advice string at the cost of also now requiring the adversary to perform $3T/4$ sequential steps.

3.1 Random Round Functions

Definition 6. *Let* $F : [N] \to [N]$ *be a uniformly random function. Then for any* $T \geq 8 \cdot \sqrt{N}$, *the iterated function* F^T *is not* $(0, 1, 1/4)$*-secure, i.e. there exists a* $(0, 1, T/4)$*-admissible adversary* $\mathcal{A}$ *with*

$$\Pr\left[\mathsf{Exp}^{\mathsf{SEQ}}_{\mathcal{A},F,T} = 1\right] > \frac{1}{2}.$$

Proof. To prove the theorem, we will construct an adversary which correctly computes the output of F^T using at most $T/4$ many sequential queries to oracle F. The idea behind the attack is very simple. Consider the (directed) functional graph of F, i.e. the graph (V, E) with vertices $V := \{1, \ldots, N\}$ and edges $E := \{(u, v) \mid u \in \mathbb{N} \wedge F(u) = v\}$. Evaluating F on a point x corresponds to walking along an edge in the corresponding functional graph. Our attacker will simply hope that the given challenge x is either directly on a cycle or on a path into a cycle, such that walking $T/4$ steps on the graph starting from x will complete a full walk over the cycle. If this is the case, then the adversary does not need to perform any more queries to the oracle F, since computing F^T just corresponds to running laps on the cycle that is known after $T/4$ sequential queries.

For an input $x \in [N]$, let E_x be the indicator variable that is one, if there exists $i \in [T/4]$ with $F^i(x) \in \textsc{Trace}(F^{i-1}, x)$, where $\textsc{Trace}(F^0, x) := x$. For x and $i \in [T/4]$, let $E_{x,i}$ be the indicator variable that is one, if $F^i(x) \in \textsc{Trace}(F^{i-1}, x)$. We observe that

$$\Pr[E_x] = \Pr\left[E_{x,1} \vee \cdots \vee E_{x,T/4}\right] = 1 - \Pr\left[\neg E_{x,1} \wedge \cdots \wedge \neg E_{x,T/4}\right].$$

Since F is a uniformly random function, it holds that

$$\begin{aligned}
&\Pr\left[\neg E_{x,1} \wedge \cdots \wedge \neg E_{x,T/4}\right] \\
&= \Pr\left[\neg E_{x,1}\right] \cdot \Pr\left[\neg E_{x,2} \mid \neg E_{x,1}\right] \cdots \Pr\left[\neg E_{x,T/4} \mid \neg E_{x,1} \wedge \cdots \wedge \neg E_{x,T/4-1}\right] \\
&= \prod_{i=1}^{T/4} \left(1 - \frac{i}{N}\right) \leq \prod_{i=1}^{T/4} e^{-i/N} = e^{-1/N \cdot \sum_{i=1}^{T/4} i} \leq e^{-\frac{T^2}{32N}}.
\end{aligned}$$

Plugging in the bound for T from the theorem statement, we get that

$$\Pr[E_x] \geq 1 - e^{-2} > 1/2.$$

Finally, we observe that, if E_x happens, then

$$F^T(x) \in \textsc{Trace}(F^T, x) = \textsc{Trace}(F^{T/4}, x),$$

and the adversary can simply retrieve the output $F^T(x)$ from the already computed partial trace, without querying the oracle F any more. □

3.2 Arbitrary Round Functions

Theorem 3. *For any $T \in \mathbb{N}$ and any $F : [N] \to [N]$, there exists a $(\frac{8N \lg N}{T}, 1, T/4)$-admissible adversary $\mathcal{A}$ with*

$$\Pr\left[\mathsf{Exp}^{\mathsf{SEQ}}_{\mathcal{A},F,T} = 1\right] > \frac{1}{2}.$$

Proof. To prove the theorem statement, we construct a $(\frac{8N \lg N}{T}, 1, T/4)$-admissible adversary $\mathcal{A} = (\mathcal{A}_0, \mathcal{A}_1)$. During preprocessing, adversary $\mathcal{A}_0$ picks $x_i \in [N]$ for $i \in [4N/T]$ independently and uniformly at random and stores $(x_i, F^{3T/4}(x_i))$. The advice string σ is the set of these pairs. The bit length of the advice string produced by $\mathcal{A}_0$ is $\frac{8N \lg N}{T}$.

Upon receiving a challenge $x \in [N]$, adversary $\mathcal{A}_1$ checks whether advice σ contains the pair $(x, F^{3T/4}(x))$. If σ contains the pair, then $\mathcal{A}_1$ uses $T/4$ sequential calls to oracle F to compute $F^T(x)$ from the stored value $F^{3T/4}(x)$. If σ does not contain the pair, then $\mathcal{A}_1$ computes $F(x)$ and checks whether σ contains $(F(x), F^{3T/4}(F(x))$ and proceeds as above. $\mathcal{A}_1$ repeats this process until they match a pair in σ or until they compute $F^{T/4}(x)$ from x using $T/4$ sequential calls. If no pair was matched at this point, then $\mathcal{A}_1$ checks whether $\left|\text{TRACE}(F^{T/4}, x)\right| < T/4+1$. If this is the case, then the evaluation trace contains repeated values, meaning that the iterated evaluation is in a cycle in the functional graph of F and thus $\mathcal{A}_1$ can compute $F^T(x)$ from the existing trace, without querying the oracle F any further. If, however, $\left|\text{TRACE}(F^{T/4}, x)\right| = T/4+1$, then $\mathcal{A}_1$ outputs $\perp$ and aborts. It is clear that $\mathcal{A}_1$ either correctly computes $F^T(x)$ with $T/4$ sequential calls to F or outputs $\perp$.

Let us analyze the success probability of the adversary above. Let hit be the event that for some value $z \in \text{TRACE}(F^{T/4}, x)$, it holds that $(z, F^{T/4}(z)) \in \sigma$ and without loss of generality, we now assume that $\left|\text{TRACE}(F^{T/4}, x)\right| = T/4 + 1$, as the adversary wins trivially otherwise. To win the sequentiality security experiment, the adversary needs

$$\Pr[\mathsf{hit}] > 1/2,$$

where the probability is taken over the random choices of $\mathcal{A}_0$ and the choice of the challenge x.

To analyze this probability, we observe that the choice of σ is independent of x and the corresponding evaluation trace. We can therefore consider the equivalent experiment of first picking x, computing the corresponding evaluation trace up to $T/4$, and then selecting pairs for σ uniformly at random. Then, we get that

$$\Pr[\neg\mathsf{hit}] < \left(1 - \frac{(T/4)}{N}\right)^{4N/T} \leq \left(e^{-T/4}\right)^{4/T} = e^{-1} < 1/2.$$

Thus it follows that the adversary $\mathcal{A}$ will be successful with probability strictly greater than half. □

Corollary 4. *Let $T \in \mathbb{N}$. For any iterated function $F^T : [N] \to [N]$ that is $(S, 1, 1/4)$-secure, it must hold that $S \cdot T \in \mathcal{O}(N \lg N)$.*

Let us now explore how the ability to do parallel queries can be exploited.

Theorem 5. *Let $T, P \in \mathbb{N}$ and let $S = 6(N/T - P)\lg N$. For any round function $F : [N] \to [N]$, there exists a $(S, P+1, 2T/3)$-admissible adversary $\mathcal{A}$ with*

$$\Pr\left[\mathsf{Exp}^{\mathsf{SEQ}}_{\mathcal{A},F,T} = 1\right] > \frac{1}{2}.$$

Proof. To prove the theorem statement, we construct a $(S, P+1, 2T/3)$-admissible adversary $\mathcal{A} = (\mathcal{A}_0, \mathcal{A}_1)$. During preprocessing, adversary $\mathcal{A}_0$ picks $x_i \in [N]$ for $i \in [3N/T - P]$ independently and uniformly at random and stores $(x_i, F^{T/3}(x_i))$. The advice string σ is the set of these pairs. The bit length of the advice string produced by $\mathcal{A}_0$ is $2\lg N\,(3N/T - P)$.

Upon receiving challenge x, adversary $\mathcal{A}_1$ picks $x_1, \ldots, x_P \in [N]$ independently and uniformly at random. Then, $\mathcal{A}_1$ computes $F^{T/3}(x), F^{T/3}(x_1), \ldots, F^{T/3}(x_P)$ using $T/3$ sequential and $P+1$ parallel queries to oracle F. Let

$\tilde{\sigma} := \sigma \cup \{(x_i, F^{T/3}(x_i)) \mid i \in [P]\}$ be the set containing all pairs computed during preprocessing and computed now.

Now for $i \in [T/3]$, the adversary $\mathcal{A}_1$ iteratively keeps computing $F^{T/3+i}(x)$ and checking whether $(F^{T/3+i}(x), F^{T2/3+i}(x))$ is contained in $\tilde{\sigma}$. If, for some $i \in [T/3]$ such a pair is found, the adversary skips from $F^{T/3+i}(x)$ to $F^{T2/3+i}(x)$ and computes $F^T(x)$ from there on honestly. If no such pair is found in these $T/3$ steps (and the evaluation did not end up in a cycle in the functional graph), then $\mathcal{A}_1$ outputs $\perp$ and aborts. If the adversary is successful, it is clear that $\mathcal{A}_1$ makes $2T/3$ sequential queries to F.

The analysis of the adversary's success probability is basically the same as in the previous proof. Let hit be the event that for some value in $z \in \{F^{T/3+1}(x), \ldots, F^{2T/3}(x)\}$, it holds that $(z, F^{T/3}(z)) \in \tilde{\sigma}$. To win the sequentiality security experiment, the adversary needs

$$\Pr[\mathsf{hit}] > 1/2,$$

where the probability is taken over the random choices of $\mathcal{A}_0$, $\mathcal{A}_1$, and the choice of the challenge x.

$$\begin{aligned}\Pr[\neg\mathsf{hit}] &= \left(1 - \frac{(T/3)}{N}\right)^{(3N/T-P)+P} = \left(1 - \frac{(T/3)}{N}\right)^{3N/T} \leq \left(e^{-T/3}\right)^{3/T} \\ &= e^{-1} < 1/2.\end{aligned}$$

Thus it follows that the adversary $\mathcal{A}$ will be successful with probability strictly greater than half. □

Corollary 6. *Let $T, P \in \mathbb{N}$. For any iterated function $F^T : [N] \to [N]$ that is $(S, P+1, 2/3)$-secure, it must hold that $(S+P) \cdot T \in \mathcal{O}(N \lg N)$.*

4 Lower Bound

After having established that adversaries with large enough advice and sufficient sequential and parallel time can win the iterated function security experiment with probability greater than $1/2$ no matter the round function F, let us now show the converse. That is, there exist functions F for which the adversary cannot evaluate F^T using $\widetilde{T} \leq T/2$ sequential oracle calls, unless they have many bits of advice and/or perform many calls in parallel.

For the purpose of this lower bound, it will be convenient to view the adversary $\mathcal{A}$ as a data structure D of $S \ll N$ bits, such that for a uniform random $x \in [N]$, it allows for quickly computing $F^T(x)$. We require D to return the correct result on a random input with probability at least $1/2$. We now show the following theorem.

Theorem 7. *For $N \geq c$, where $c \in \mathbb{N}$ is a large enough constant, there exists a functions $F : [N] \to [N]$, such that any data structure D that answers queries $F^T(x)$ on uniformly random inputs x correctly with probability at least $1/2$, must either have $\widetilde{T} \geq T/2$ or satisfy*

$$(S + \widetilde{T} \lg N) \max\{\widetilde{T} P \lg^5(\widetilde{T}), T\} = \Omega(N).$$

To prove the theorem statement, let us define a hard distribution over round functions F.

Hard Input Distribution. Let the round function $\mathbf{F}$ be obtained by drawing a uniform random permutation π with a single cycle over the elements $\{1,\ldots,N-1\}$ and letting $\mathbf{F}(0)=\pi(1)$, $\mathbf{F}(\mathbf{F}(0))=\pi(2)$, $\mathbf{F}^k(0)=\pi(k)$ for $1\leq k\leq N-1$ and $\mathbf{F}^N(0)=0$. The function $\mathbf{F}$ is thus obtained by drawing a uniform random directed cycle on the elements/nodes $[N]$ and letting $\mathbf{F}(x)$ be the successor of the node x on the cycle.

Henceforth, we thus think of the problem as if we are given a uniform random directed cycle on the elements $[N]$ as input, and we get to store S bits. A query is a uniform random element $x\in[N]$. We then have $\widetilde{T}$ (sequential) rounds of evaluating the successor of P nodes. The goal is to determine the T-th successor of x along the cycle. We use $\mathbf{F}^i(x)$ to denote the i-th successor of x along the cycle.

Proof Framework. We now introduce the main ideas and general framework used to prove our lower bound. On an intuitive level, if $\widetilde{T}<T$, then the data structure has an insufficient number of rounds of oracle calls to $\mathbf{F}$ to merely follow the "successor pointers" on the cycle, starting from x, then $\mathbf{F}(x)$, $\mathbf{F}(\mathbf{F}(x))$ and so forth. Hence it must either "guess" intermediate nodes between x and $\mathbf{F}^T(x)$ by randomly querying elements in $[N]$, or it must use the S bits of advice to store "short cuts". The former strategy requires a large number of total queries, i.e. $\widetilde{T}\cdot P$ must be large. The latter strategy requires many advice bits, i.e. S must be large. To formalize this, we want to argue that without many queries and advice, the data structure must be very *lucky* if it is to correctly compute $\mathbf{F}^T(x)$. Turning this into a solid argument is however far from trivial. Our approach for doing so is based on an *encoding argument*, a technique which has been used to great success in data structure lower bounds, see e.g. [PD06,PV10,Lar12a,Lar12b, BL13,VZ13,CKL18,LS20,LY20,LLYZ23].

The general idea of an encoding argument is to show that an efficient data structure D implies an efficient binary encoding of a randomly chosen input cycle/function $\mathbf{F}$. We view such an encoding as consisting of two parts, an *encoder* and a *decoder*. The encoder receives $\mathbf{F}$ as input and must send a prefix-free message to the decoder. The decoder must be able to uniquely recover $\mathbf{F}$ from the message. If $H(\cdot)$ denotes binary Shannon entropy, then it follows from Shannon's source coding theorem that the expected length of the message must be at least $H(\mathbf{F})=\lg((N-1)!)$ bits. The key step is now to show that a too efficient data structure D, can be used to give an encoding into fewer bits, yielding an information theoretic contradiction.

To simplify our proof, we make two further modifications to this framework. First, our lower bound holds also for randomized data structures D that errs with probability up to $1/2$ on any given input-query pair (F,x). By Yao's principle (fixing the random coins), this also implies the existence of a deterministic data structure with the same $\widetilde{T},P,S$ that errs with probability at most $1/2$ over the random choice of $\mathbf{F}$ and a uniform random query $\mathbf{X} \in [N]$. We thus assume D is a deterministic data structure with this property.

Next, it will be convenient for the encoder and decoder to agree on a set of random queries. We thus let the encoder and decoder share access to B uniform random and independently chosen elements $\mathbf{X}_1, \ldots, \mathbf{X}_B \in [N]$ for a $B \leq N/(8\widetilde{T})$ to be chosen later. By independence, we have $H(\mathbf{F} \mid \mathbf{X}_1, \cdots, \mathbf{X}_B) = H(\mathbf{F}) = \lg((N-1)!)$. It follows that any prefix free encoding of $\mathbf{F}$ must use at least $\lg((N-1)!)$ bits in expectation, even if the encoder and decoder share access to $\mathbf{X}_1, \ldots, \mathbf{X}_B$.

4.1 Overall Encoding Scheme

With the encoding framework introduced above, we now present the overall ideas in our encoding scheme. Our strategy is to show that being able to answer the random queries $\mathbf{X}_1, \ldots, \mathbf{X}_B$ on $\mathbf{F}$ reveals $\tilde{\Omega}(B)$ bits of information about $\mathbf{F}$. If a data structure D has only S bits of advice, this will eventually lead to a contradiction if B is sufficiently larger than S. However for this claim to be true, we need that many of the queries $\mathbf{X}_1, \ldots, \mathbf{X}_B$ are answered correctly, and that the queries are *sufficiently different*. Intuitively, if $\mathbf{X}_i$ and $\mathbf{X}_j$ are two queries close to each other on the cycle defining $\mathbf{F}$, then answering both of them may reuse evaluations of $\mathbf{F}$ and thus reveal little or no new information. With these considerations in mind, we thus define an *interesting input.*

Definition 7. *We say that* $\mathbf{F}, \mathbf{X}_1, \ldots, \mathbf{X}_B$ *is an* interesting input *for a data structure* D *with* $\widetilde{T}$ *sequential queries, if there exists* $m \geq B/8$ *distinct indices* $i_1, \ldots, i_m \in \{1, \ldots, B\}$ *such that* $\mathbf{X}_{i_j}$ *is answered correctly by* D *on input* $\mathbf{F}$ *for every* i_j *and* $\mathbf{X}_{i_j} \neq \mathbf{F}^k(\mathbf{X}_h)$ *for any* $1 \leq k \leq 2\widetilde{T}$ *and* $h \neq i_j$. *We say such an index* i_j *is* useful.

Notice the crucial property of our definition requiring that $\mathbf{X}_{i_j} \neq \mathbf{F}^k(\mathbf{X}_h)$ for any $1 \leq k \leq 2\widetilde{T}$. This ensures that even if D evaluates $\mathbf{F}(\mathbf{X}_i)$ in round one for every i, then $\mathbf{F}(\mathbf{F}(\mathbf{X}_i))$ in round two and so forth for $\widetilde{T}$ rounds, there will be no overlap in the discovered nodes as the $\mathbf{X}_i$'s are spaced by at least $2\widetilde{T}$ on the cycle. We will later show that many inputs are interesting.

In our encoding, we will consider the function evaluations $\mathbf{F}(X)$ made by the data structure D implemented on $\mathbf{F}$ when the queries are $\mathbf{X}_1, \ldots, \mathbf{X}_B$. Let us denote by $\mathbf{Y}_1^i, \ldots, \mathbf{Y}_{B \cdot P}^i \in [N]$ the list of function evaluations made by D in the i-th sequential round when answering the queries $\mathbf{X}_1, \ldots, \mathbf{X}_B$. That is, in the i-th round, D evaluates $\mathbf{F}(\mathbf{Y}_1^i), \ldots, \mathbf{F}(\mathbf{Y}_{BP}^i)$. We order the evaluations such that $(i,j) < (i',j')$ if either $i < i'$ or if $i = i'$ and $j < j'$.

With the interpretation of $\mathbf{F}$ as a cycle, each function evaluation $\mathbf{F}(\mathbf{Y}_j^i)$ made by D *discovers* one directed edge $(\mathbf{Y}_j^i, \mathbf{F}(\mathbf{Y}_j^i))$ on the cycle. We define the *view* $\mathbf{V}_j^i$ of D after evaluations $\mathbf{Y}_1^1, \ldots, \mathbf{Y}_{j-1}^i$ as all discovered edges $(\mathbf{Y}_{j'}^{i'}, \mathbf{F}(\mathbf{Y}_{j'}^{i'}))$ after the function evaluations $\mathbf{F}(\mathbf{Y}_{j'}^{i'})$ with $(1,1) \leq (i',j') < (i,j)$.

The edges in a view $\mathbf{V}_j^i$ naturally reveal *chains* of nodes on the cycle corresponding to $\mathbf{F}$. The first element on a chain is called the *head*, and is the only element on the chain for which its predecessor in $\mathbf{F}$ has not yet been discovered (the predecessor of an X is the Y such that $\mathbf{F}(Y) = X$). The *tail* is likewise the only element on the chain for which its successor has not been discovered. For a node $X \in [N]$, we let $\mathbf{c}_j^i(X)$ denote the list of nodes on the chain containing X in $\mathbf{V}_j^i$. The list is ordered in the natural ordering with the head first and the tail last. Observe that in the view $\mathbf{V}_1^1$ corresponding to before any function evaluations are made, all nodes X reside in a singleton chain $\mathbf{c}_1^1(X) = X$. We need to also count the number of nodes on the chain from X and until the tail of the chain. Let $\mathbf{t}_j^i(X)$ denote this number of nodes. Note that $\mathbf{t}_j^i(X) = 1$ if X is the tail of $\mathbf{c}_j^i(X)$ and $\mathbf{t}_j^i(X) = |\mathbf{c}_j^i(X)|$ if X is the head.

With these definitions, we now take two alternative approaches to encoding $\mathbf{F}$ depending on the chains in the *final view* $\mathbf{V}^\infty := \mathbf{V}_{BP+1}^{\widetilde{T}}$. Note that the final view corresponds to when the data structure D has finished answering all queries $\mathbf{X}_1, \ldots, \mathbf{X}_B$. For an interesting input $\mathbf{F}, \mathbf{X}_1, \ldots, \mathbf{X}_B$, let $\mathcal{I} = \{\mathbf{I}_1, \ldots, \mathbf{I}_{B/8}\}$ be the first (i.e. of smallest values) $B/8$ useful indices. If at least half the indices $j \in \mathcal{I}$ have $|\mathbf{t}^\infty(\mathbf{X}_j)| := |\mathbf{t}_{BP+1}^{\widetilde{T}}(\mathbf{X}_j)| = |\mathbf{t}_1^{\widetilde{T}+1}(\mathbf{X}_j)| > 2\widetilde{T}$, then we say the final view has *long chains*. Otherwise, we say it has *short chains*. We present a different encoding in these two cases. The overall encoding strategy described above is shown as Algorithm 1, where $\mathrm{bin}(z)$ for an integer z promised to be in $[2^k]$ is a length-k binary encoding of the integer z and $a \circ b$ is the concatenation of binary strings a and b.

The encoding procedure is accompanied by a decoding/reconstruction procedure, shown as Algorithm 2. In the decoding procedure, we use the notation $b[i]$ for a binary string $b \in \{0,1\}^*$ to denote the i-th bit of b, with $b[0]$ being the first bit. We use the notation $b[i:j]$ to denote $b[i] \circ \cdots \circ b[j]$ and we use $b[i:\infty]$ to denote the suffix of b starting at the i-th bit.

In the next sections, we give the two encoding and decoding procedures for the cases of short and long chains. The number of bits used by the two encoding procedures is shown in the following the lemmas.

Lemma 8. *If $N \geq 2^7$, $B\widetilde{T}P \leq N/4$ and $B(T+1) \leq N$, then the encoding length of* EncodeShortChains *is no more than*

$$\lg((N-1)!) + 6 + 2\lg N - B/16$$

bits.

Lemma 9. *If $B\widetilde{T}P \lg^5(4\widetilde{T}) \leq N/2^{20}$, then the encoding length of* Encode-LongChains *is no more than*

$$\lg((N-1)!) + 1 + \widetilde{T}(1 + \lg N) - B/32$$

bits.

We will prove the two results in the following sections and instead proceed to analyse the expected length of the encoding and derive the lower bound.

Algorithm 1: ENCODE$(F, X_1, \ldots, X_B, D)$

Input: Function $F : [N] \to [N]$ corresponding to a cycle, queries $X_1, \ldots, X_B \in [N]$, data structure D.
Result: Prefix free encoding of F (binary string).
Build D on F.
if $(F, X_1, \ldots, X_B)$ *is not an interesting input for* D **then**
  Interpret F as an integer f in $[(N-1)!]$.
  return $0 \circ \text{bin}(f)$
Let a be the S bits of advice of D on input F.
Let $\mathcal{I} = \{I_1, \ldots, I_{B/8}\}$ be the first $B/8$ useful indices in $\{1, \ldots, B\}$.
Execute all queries $X_1, \ldots, X_B$ on D and compute views V_j^i for all $1 \le i \le \widetilde{T}$ and $1 \le j \le BP + 1$.
Let $L \subseteq \mathcal{I}$ be the set of indices $j \in \mathcal{I}$ such that $|t^\infty(X_j)| > 2\widetilde{T}$.
if $|L| < B/16$ **then**
  return $10 \circ a \circ$ ENCODESHORTCHAINS$(F, X_1, \ldots, X_B, \mathcal{I} \setminus L, D)$
else
  return $11 \circ a \circ$ ENCODELONGCHAINS$(F, X_1, \ldots, X_B, L, D)$

Algorithm 2: DECODE$(b, X_1, \ldots, X_B, D)$

Input: binary string $b \in \{0,1\}^*$ with $b =$ENCODE$(F, X_1, \ldots, X_B, D)$ for some $F : [N] \to [N]$ corresponding to a cycle, queries $X_1, \ldots, X_B \in [N]$, data structure D.
Result: The function $F : [N] \to [N]$.
if $b[0] = 0$ **then**
  Interpret $b[1:\infty]$ as an integer f in $[(N-1)!]$.
  return F *corresponding to* f
Let $a = b[2 : 1 + S]$.
if $b[1] = 0$ **then**
  return DECODESHORTCHAINS$(b[2+S, \infty], a, X_1, \ldots, X_B, D)$
else
  return DECODELONGCHAINS$(b[2+S, \infty], a, X_1, \ldots, X_B, D)$

First, observe that ENCODE adds $2 + S$ bits to encoding produced by either ENCODESHORTCHAINS or ENCODELONGCHAINS. The savings of $B/16$ or $B/32$ in Lemma 8 and Lemma 9 must be enough to make up for this as well as the additional bits in the two lemmas. We thus set $B = 32(S + \widetilde{T}(1 + \lg N) + 22)$. We conclude that either $(S + \widetilde{T} \lg N)\widetilde{T} P \lg^5(\widetilde{T}) = \Omega(N)$, or $(S + \widetilde{T} \lg N)T = \Omega(N)$, or both encodings use no more than $\lg((N-1)!) - 22$ bits.

Assume for the sake of contradiction that the encodings use no more than $\lg((N-1)!) - S - 22$ bits. If E denotes the event that the random input $\mathbf{F}, \mathbf{X}_1, \ldots, \mathbf{X}_B$ is interesting, the expected length of the encoding is the bounded by

$$
\begin{aligned}
&1 + (1 - \Pr[E])(1 + \lg((N-1)!)) + \Pr[E](S + \lg((N-1)!) - S - 22) \\
\le &2 + \lg((N-1)!) - \Pr[E]22.
\end{aligned}
$$

We now invoke the following observation to show that the input is interesting with good probability:

Observation 8. *For any data structure D, the random input $\mathbf{F}, \mathbf{X}_1, \ldots, \mathbf{X}_B$ is an interesting input with probability at least $1/7$.*

Inserting this bound for $\Pr[E]$ gives an expected encoding length of at most $2 + \lg((N-1)!) - 22/7 < \lg((N-1)!)$, i.e. a contradiction. We thus conclude that either $(S + \widetilde{T} \lg N)\widetilde{T} P \lg^5(\widetilde{T}) = \Omega(N)$, or $(S + \widetilde{T} \lg N)T = \Omega(N)$. This proves Theorem 7.

We conclude this section by proving the above observation regarding the probability of obtaining an interesting input.

Proof (of Observation 8). Consider a fixed index $i \in \{1, \dots, B\}$. Since $\mathbf{X}_i$ is uniform random in $[N]$, it follows from the guarantees of D that $\mathbf{X}_i$ is answered correctly with probability at least 1/2 over the choice of $\mathbf{F}$. At the same time, conditioned on $\mathbf{X}_1, \dots, \mathbf{X}_{i-1}, \mathbf{X}_{i+1}, \dots, \mathbf{X}_B$, we have that $\mathbf{X}_i$ is still uniform random in N. Hence $\mathbf{X}_i \neq \mathbf{F}^k(\mathbf{X}_h)$ for all $1 \leq k \leq 2p$ and $h \neq i$ with probability at least $(N - 2B\widetilde{T})/N = 1 - 2B\widetilde{T}/N \geq 1 - 1/4$. A union bound implies that $\mathbf{X}_i$ is both answered correctly and has $\mathbf{X}_i \neq \mathbf{F}^k(\mathbf{X}_h)$ for all $1 \leq k \leq t$ and $h \neq i$ with probability at least 1/4 (i.e. i is useful). The expected number of useful i is thus at least $B/4$. This also implies that the expected number of i that is not useful is no more than $3B/4$. By Markov's inequality, the probability that there are more than $7B/8$ i that are not useful is thus at most $(3/4)/(7/8) = 6/7$.

4.2 Encoding with Short Chains

In this section, we describe the encoding and decoding procedures for the case when the final view has short chains. Recall that this implies the existence of a subset $\mathcal{I}' \subseteq \mathcal{I}$ with $|\mathcal{I}'| = B/16$ such that for all $j \in \mathcal{I}'$, we have $|t^\infty(X_j)| \leq 2\widetilde{T}$. The key observation is that for every $j \in \mathcal{I}'$, the chain $t^\infty(X_j)$ containing X_j in the final view is different from the chain $t^\infty(F^T(X_j))$ containing the answer $F^T(X_j)$ to the query X_j. This is because T is assumed larger than $2\widetilde{T}$ and less than $2\widetilde{T}$ nodes succeed X_j on its chain. That they are on different chains intuitively means that the answer to the query X_j reveals new information not discovered while evaluating the function F. This is precisely what we exploit to compress F. In our encoding, we assume an ordering on the chains in a view V_j^i. The concrete ordering is not important, as long as it is consistent with the ordering used in decoding. One choice could be to order them based on the indices of the head of the chains, i.e. a smaller index head means earlier in the ordering.

The encoding procedure is shown as Algorithm 3 and we will describe the ideas in the encoding by referring to the pseudocode.

The first part of EncodeShortChains (Algorithm 3) constructs the data structure D and executes the queries to compute the different views V_j^i (lines 1–2). We then select the first $B/16$ indices $\mathcal{I}' \subseteq \mathcal{I}$. Recall that when Encode invokes EncodeShortChains, the list $\mathcal{I}$ contains indices j of queries that are answered correctly and where $|t^\infty(X_j)| \leq 2\widetilde{T} < T$. In line 4 we then encode these indices $\mathcal{I}'$ such that the decoder will be able to recover these indices.

In lines 5–11 we now encode the final view V^∞ such that the decoder may reconstruct this view. The way we encode it, is to simply write down the edges discovered while D performs the function evaluations $F(Y_j^i)$ during its execution. This will allow the decoder to simulate the execution of D as well. Up to this point, there is no saving of bits in the encoding.

Algorithm 3: ENCODESHORTCHAINS($F, X_1, \ldots, X_B, \mathcal{I}, D$)

Input: Function $F : [N] \to [N]$ corresponding to a cycle, queries $X_1, \ldots, X_B \in [N]$, indices $\mathcal{I} \subseteq \{1, \ldots, B\}$ with $|\mathcal{I}| \geq B/16$, data structure D.
Result: Prefix free encoding of F (binary string).

1 Build D on F.
2 Execute all queries $X_1, \ldots, X_B$ on D and compute views V_j^i for all $1 \leq i \leq \widetilde{T}$ and $1 \leq j \leq BP$.
3 Let $\mathcal{I}' \subseteq \mathcal{I}$ be the first $B/16$ indices in $\mathcal{I}$.
4 Let $b \leftarrow \text{bin}(\mathcal{I}')$ be a binary encoding of $\mathcal{I}'$ as a subset of the indices $\{1, \ldots, B\}$ using $\lceil \lg \binom{B}{B/16} \rceil$ bits.
5 Let $m \in [N]$ be the number of chains in V^∞. Update $b \leftarrow b \circ \text{bin}(m)$.
6 Let L be an initially empty list of indices.
7 **for** $i = 1, \ldots, \widetilde{T}$ **do**
8 **for** $j = 1, \ldots, BP$ **do**
9   **if** *Y_j^i is the tail of the chain $c_j^i(Y_j^i)$* **then**
10   Append the rank r_j^i of $c_j^i(F(Y_j^i))$ among all chains in $V_j^i \setminus \{c_j^i(Y_j^i)\}$ to L.
11 Interpret the list L as a number $\ell \in [(N-1)(N-2)\cdots m]$ and update $b \leftarrow b \circ \text{bin}(\ell)$.
12 Let $V^\star \leftarrow V^\infty$ equal the final view and $c^\star(X)$ denote the chain in $V^\star$ containing a node $X \in [N]$.
13 Let K be an initially empty list of indices.
14 **for** $i = 1, \ldots, B/16$ **do**
15 Let j be the i-th index in $\mathcal{I}'$.
16 **while** $c^\star(X_j) \neq c^\star(F^T(X_j))$ **do**
17   Let $x \leftarrow t^\star(X_j)$ denote the number of nodes from X_j and until the tail of $c^\star(X_j)$.
18   Let $y \leftarrow |c^\star(F^T(X_j))| - t^\star(F^T(X_j))$ denote the number of nodes from the head and up just before $F^T(X_j)$ in $c^\star(F^T(X_j))$.
19   **if** $x + y = T$ **then**
20   Add the edge from the tail of $c^\star(X_j)$ to the head of $c^\star(F^T(X_j))$ and merge the chains in $V^\star$.
21   **else**
22   Append the rank in $V^\star \setminus \{c^\star(X_j)\}$ of the chain whose head is the successor of the tail in $c^\star(X_j)$ to K. Then merge the two chains in $V^\star$ by inserting the corresponding edge.
23 Update $b \leftarrow b \circ \text{bin}(|K|)$ with $|K| \in [N]$.
24 Interpret the list K as a number $k \in [(m-1)(m-2)\cdots(m-|K|)]$ and update $b \leftarrow b \circ \text{bin}(k)$.
25 $b \leftarrow b \circ$ ENCODEREMAININGVIEW($F, V^\star$).
26 **return** b

Algorithm 4: ENCODEREMAININGVIEW($F, V^\star$)

Input: $F : [N] \to [N]$ corresponding to a cycle, view $V^\star$ consistent with F.
Result: Prefix free encoding of F from $V^\star$.

Let L be an initially empty list of indices.
Let $n \leftarrow |V^\star| - 1$.
for $i = 1, \ldots, n$ **do**
 Let c_1 be the chain in $V^\star$ with the smallest rank.
 Append the rank in $V^\star \setminus \{c_1\}$ of the chain whose head is the successor of the tail in c_1 to L. Then merge the two chains in $V^\star$ by inserting the corresponding edge.
Interpret the list L as a number $\ell \in [(|V^\star|-1)(|V^\star|-2)\cdots 1]$.
return $\text{bin}(\ell)$

Lines 12–23 if where we finally exploit that D managed to answer the queries while not connecting the chains $c^\infty(X_j)$ and $c^\infty(F^T(X_j))$. Concretely, the for-

Algorithm 5: DecodeShortChains($b, a, X_1, \ldots, X_B, D$)

Input: binary string $b \in \{0,1\}^*$ with $b =$ EncodeShortChains($F, a, X_1, \ldots, X_B, \mathcal{I} \setminus L, D$) for some $F : [N] \to [N]$ corresponding to a cycle, advice a of data structure D on input F, queries $X_1, \ldots, X_B \in [N]$, data structure D.
Result: The function $F : [N] \to [N]$.

1 Read and remove first $\lceil \lg \binom{B}{B/16} \rceil$ bits of b to recover $\mathcal{I}'$.
2 Read and remove first $\lceil \lg N \rceil$ bits of b to recover $m = |V^\infty|$.
3 Read and remove first $\lceil \lg((N-1)!/(m-1)!) \rceil$ bits of b to recover L.
4 **for** $i = 1, \ldots, \widetilde{T}$ **do**
5 From a, queries $X_1, \ldots, X_B$, $Y_j^{i'}$ and $F(Y_j^{i'})$ with $i' < i$, simulate D to determine all Y_j^i, i.e. all function evaluation made by D in sequential round i. This also determines the view V_{BP+1}^{i-1} (end of round $i-1$).
6 **for** $j = 1, \ldots, BP$ **do**
7 **if** *Y_j^i is the tail of the chain $c_j^i(Y_j^i)$* **then**
8 Read and remove the first element r_j^i of L. We learn that $F(Y_j^i)$ is the head of the chain of rank r_j^i in $V_j^i \setminus \{c_j^i(Y_j^i)\}$. We can thus compute $F(Y_j^i)$ and the next view V_{j+1}^i.
9 Let $V^\star \leftarrow V^\infty$ equal the final view.
10 From simulating D on queries X_j, compute $F^T(X_j)$ for every $j \in \mathcal{I}'$.
11 Read and remove first $\lceil \lg N \rceil$ bits to recover $|K|$.
12 Read and remove first $\lceil \lg((m-1)!/(m-|K|-1)!) \rceil$ bits to recover K.
13 **for** $i = 1, \ldots, B/16$ **do**
14 Let j be the i-th index in $\mathcal{I}'$.
15 **while** $c^\star(X_j) \neq c^\star(F^T(X_j))$ **do**
16 Let $x \leftarrow t^\star(X_j)$.
17 Let $y \leftarrow |c^\star(F^T(X_j))| - t^\star(F^T(X_j))$.
18 **if** $x + y = T$ **then**
19 Add the edge from the tail of $c^\star(X_j)$ to the head of $c^\star(F^T(X_j))$ and merge the chains in $V^\star$.
20 **else**
21 Remove the first element from K. This determines the chain whose head is the successor of the tail in $c^\star(X_j)$. Then merge the two chains in $V^\star$ by inserting the corresponding edge.
22 **return** DecodeRemainingView*($b, V^\star$)*

Algorithm 6: DecodeRemainingView($b, V^\star$)

Input: binary string $b \in \{0,1\}^*$, view $V^\star$ consistent with F.
Result: The function $F : [N] \to [N]$.

1 Read the $\lceil \lg((|V^\star| - 1)! \rceil$ bits in b to recover L.
2 Let $n \leftarrow |V^\star| - 1$.
3 **for** $i = 1, \ldots, n$ **do**
4 Let c_1 be the chain in $V^\star$ with the smallest rank.
5 Remove the first element r of L and interpret it as the rank in $V^\star \setminus \{c_1\}$ of the chain whose head is the successor of the tail in c_1 to L. Then merge the two chains in $V^\star$ by inserting the corresponding edge.
6 **return** *The unique function F consistent with the single chain in $V^\star$*

loop iterations over all the queries in $\mathcal{I}'$ in turn. For each one, it repeatedly merges chains (lines 16–22) until X_j and $F^T(X_j)$ are on the same chain. The crucial point is that when the number of elements succeeding X_j on its chain, plus the number of elements up to and including $F^T(X_j)$ on its chain equals T, then we know that there must be an edge from the tail of the chain containing X_j to the head of the other chain. This saves us the encoding of an edge, i.e. the information is contained in the answer to the query. The second crucial point is that we save the encoding of one edge for every single index in $\mathcal{I}'$. This is because the indices in $\mathcal{I}'$ are *useful* and thus spaced by at least T. Furthermore, all edges inserted in the while-loop for a fixed X_j are inserted between X_j and $F^T(X_j)$.

Finally, we complete the encoding in line 25 by invoking ENCODEREMAININGVIEW. This process simply encodes how to merge the remaining chains using $\lceil \lg((|V^\star| - 1)!) \rceil$ bits for a view $V^\star$ with $|V^\star|$ many chains.

With the above in mind, the decoding procedure is shown as Algorithm 5.

We briefly discuss it while refering to the pseudocode. In lines 1–3, we read off $\mathcal{I}'$, $|V^\infty|$ and the list L produced by ENCODESHORTCHAINS. Lines 4–9 now simulates the execution of the data structure D on queries $X_1, \ldots, X_B$ on the function F. Note that this is done without direct access to F. Instead, since the decoding procedure is provided with the advice bits a, it can first determine all function evaluations that D would make in the first sequential round. That is, we know $Y_1^1, \ldots, Y_{BP}^1$. Now in order to simulate D, we need to know the answer to all the function evaluations $F(Y_i^1)$. But this information is precisely what is stored in L. Once we know the results of all function evaluation in the first sequential round, we can continue simulating D for the second round and so forth until completion. This obtains the final view V^∞. Furthermore, and critically, we also finish simulating D on all the queries. Since all queries in $\mathcal{I}'$ are answered correctly by D, the decoding procedure now knows $F^T(X_j)$ for every $j \in \mathcal{I}'$ (line 10).

In lines 11–21 we now re-execute all the merges of chains that ENCODESHORTCHAINS performed (in lines 14–22 of that procedure). The key observation here is that we know the query answers and thus can still carry out the test $x + y = T$?. We thus reconstruct $V^\star$ as it was during encoding, just before invoking ENCODEREMAININGVIEW. We feed this $V^\star$ to DECODEREMAININGVIEW, which merely reads off the merges necessary to reduce the number of chains in $V^\star$ to one. This also uniquely determines the function F.

We have thus argued correctness of our encoding and decoding procedure for handling views with short chains. Let us next analyse the size of the encoding.

Encoding Size with Short Chains. Examining the ENCODESHORTCHAINS procedure, we see that it writes

$$\begin{aligned}
&\left\lceil \lg \binom{B}{B/16} \right\rceil + 2\lceil \lg N \rceil + \left\lceil \lg \left(\frac{(N-1)!}{(m-1)!} \right) \right\rceil + \left\lceil \lg \left(\frac{(m-1)!}{(m-|K|-1)!} \right) \right\rceil \\
&+\lceil \lg((|V^\star|-1)!) \rceil \\
\leq& 6 + \lg \binom{B}{B/16} + 2\lg N + \lg \left(\frac{(N-1)!}{(m-1)!} \right) + \lg \left(\frac{(m-1)!}{(m-|K|-1)!} \right) \\
&+ \lg((|V^\star|-1)!) \\
\leq& 6 + (B/16)\lg(16e) + 2\lg N + \lg \left(\frac{(N-1)!}{(m-|K|-1)!} \right) + \lg((|V^\star|-1)!)
\end{aligned}$$

bits, where $V^\star$ here denotes the $V^\star$ that is passed to the procedure ENCODEREMAININGVIEW. Now observe that $|V^\star| = m - |K| - B/16$. This is because the loop in lines 13–21 of EncodeShortChains performs precisely $|K|$ merges that add an element to K and one merge for each index $i \in \mathcal{I}'$ which does not add to K. As mentioned earlier, this is precisely where our saving comes from. The above is thus upper bounded by

$$\begin{aligned}&6 + (B/16)\lg(16e) + 2\lg N + \lg\left(\frac{(N-1)!}{(m-|K|-1)!}\right)\\&+\lg((m-|K|-B/16-1)!)\\&\leq \lg((N-1)!) + 6 + (B/16)\lg(16e) + 2\lg N - (B/16)\lg(m-|K|-B/16).\end{aligned}$$

Since m is the number of chains in the final view V^∞ and D performs at most $B\widetilde{T}P$ function evaluations throughout the encoding procedure, we have $m \geq N - B\widetilde{T}P$. At the same time, we have that the loop in lines 14–22 of EncodeShortChains only adds elements to K when merging chains within the first T steps of X_j on the cycle for $j \in \mathcal{I}'$. Hence $|K| \leq (B/16)T$. We thus get a number of bits of at most

$$\lg((N-1)!) + 6 + 2\lg N - (B/16)\lg((N - B\widetilde{T}P - (B/16)(T+1))/(16e)).$$

If $N \geq 2^7$, $B\widetilde{T}P \leq N/4$ and $B(T+1) \leq N$, then $\lg((N - B\widetilde{T}P - (B/16)(T+1))/(16e)) \geq \lg((N/2)/(16e)) \geq 1$ and the above is at most $\lg((N-1)!) + 6 + 2\lg N - (B/16)$. This completes the proof of Lemma 8.

4.3 Encoding with Long Chains

In this section, we describe the encoding and decoding procedures for the case when the final view has long chains. Recall that this implies the existence of a subset $\mathcal{I}' \subseteq \mathcal{I}$ with $|\mathcal{I}'| = B/16$ such that for all $j \in \mathcal{I}'$, we have $|t^\infty(X_j)| > 2\widetilde{T}$. Our main observation is that chains may only grow this long if some of the function evaluations $F(Y_j^i)$ made by D return nodes on the cycle that reside on chains of length longer than 1. Since there are no more than $B\widetilde{T}P$ many chains of length longer than 1, this allows us to save bits in encoding such $F(Y_j^i)$. Unlike in the short chains case, the savings in compression size thus come from encoding the view V^∞ resulting from executing the queries $X_1, \dots, X_n$ on D.

We will next go over the steps of the encoding procedure while referring to the pseudocode shown in Algorithm 7.

Lines 1–4 are somewhat uneventful. Here we simply start by executing the queries $X_1, \dots, X_B$ on D to compute the views V_j^i. We then pick the first $B/16$ indices $\mathcal{I}'$ among the indices $\mathcal{I}$ given as argument. Recall that Encode invokes EncodeLongChains with $\mathcal{I}$ being a set of useful queries X_j with $|t^\infty(X_j)| > 2\widetilde{T}$. These are queries in which the data structure managed to grow the length of its chain by much more than one per sequential round (there are $\widetilde{T}$ sequential rounds). The encoding will exploit this and show that such long chains may be used to compress F.

In line 5, we compute the increase in the number of nodes succeeding X_j in its chain during sequential round i. The two min-expression ensures that we

Algorithm 7: $\textsc{EncodeLongChains}(F, X_1, \ldots, X_B, \mathcal{I}, D)$

Input: Function $F : [N] \to [N]$ corresponding to a cycle, queries $X_1, \ldots, X_B \in [N]$, indices $\mathcal{I} \subseteq \{1, \ldots, B\}$ with $|\mathcal{I}| \geq B/16$, data structure D.
Result: Prefix free encoding of F (binary string).

1 Build D on F.
2 Execute all queries $X_1, \ldots, X_B$ on D and compute views V_j^i for all $1 \leq i \leq \widetilde{T}$ and $1 \leq j \leq BP$.
3 Let $\mathcal{I}' \subseteq \mathcal{I}$ be the first $B/16$ indices in $\mathcal{I}$.
4 Let $b \leftarrow \text{bin}(\mathcal{I}')$ be a binary encoding of $\mathcal{I}'$ as a subset of the indices $\{1, \ldots, B\}$ using $\lceil \lg \binom{B}{B/16} \rceil$ bits.
5 Let $\ell_j^i \leftarrow \min\{2\widetilde{T}+1, t_1^{i+1}(X_j)\} - \min\{2\widetilde{T}+1, t_1^i(X_j)\}$ for each $i \in \{1, \ldots, \widetilde{T}\}$ and $j \in \{1, \ldots, B\}$.
6 **for** $j \in \mathcal{I}'$ **do**
7   Compute an index $h_j \in \{0, \ldots, \lg(\widetilde{T}) - 3\}$ such that there are at least $\Delta_{h_j} := 2^{h_j}/(h_j+1)^2$ indices q with $\ell_j^q - 1 \geq \widetilde{T}/2^{h_j+3}$ (such h_j always exists).
8   Let $S_{h_j} \subseteq \{1, \ldots, \widetilde{T}\}$ be the first Δ_{h_j} indices q with $\ell_j^q - 1 \geq \widetilde{T}/2^{h_j+3}$.
9   Update $b \leftarrow b \circ \text{bin}(h_j) \circ \text{bin}(S_{h_j})$, where $\text{bin}(S_{h_j})$ is encoded as a Δ_{h_j}-sized subset of $\{1, \ldots, \widetilde{T}\}$.
10 **for** $i = 1, \ldots, \widetilde{T}$ **do**
11   Let L_i be an initially empty list of indices.
12   Let $V' \leftarrow V_1^i$ and use $c'(X)$ and $t'(X)$ as the equivalent definitions of c_j^i and t_j^i for the view V'.
13   **for** $j \in \mathcal{I}'$ **do**
14   **if** $i \in S_{h_j}$ **then**
15   **while** *$t'(X_j) \leq 2\widetilde{T}$ and the tail of $c'(X_j)$ equals Y_k^i for some k* **do**
16   Let $z \leftarrow |c'(F(Y_k^i))|$.
17                 $b \leftarrow b \circ \text{binAdapt}(\lceil \lg z \rceil)$.
18   **if** $z > 1$ **then**
19   Let $r \in [\lfloor B\widetilde{T}P/2^{\lceil \lg z \rceil - 1} \rfloor]$ be the rank of the chain $c'(F(Y_k^i))$ among all chains c in V' with $|c| \in (2^{\lceil \lg z \rceil - 1}, 2^{\lceil \lg z \rceil}]$.
20                     $b \leftarrow b \circ \text{bin}(r)$.
21   **else**
22   **if** *the singleton chain $c'(F(Y_k^i)) = F(Y_k^i)$ has $Y_\ell^i = F(Y_k^i)$ for some $\ell \in [BP]$* **then**
23                         $b \leftarrow b \circ 0 \circ \text{bin}(\ell)$.
24   **else**
25                         $b \leftarrow b \circ 1 \circ \text{bin}(F(Y_k^i))$ with $F(Y_k^i) \in [N]$.
26   Add the edge from the tail of $c'(X_j)$ to $F(Y_k^i)$ and merge the chains in V'.
27   **for** $j = 1, \ldots, BP$ **do**
28   **if** *Y_j^i is the tail of the chain $c'(Y_j^i)$* **then**
29   Append the rank r_j^i of $c'(F(Y_j^i))$ among all chains in $V' \setminus \{c'(Y_j^i)\}$ to L_i.
30   Let $m_i \in [N]$ denote $|L_i|$ and update $b \leftarrow b \circ \text{bin}(m_i)$.
31   Interpret the list L_i as a number $\ell_i \in [(|V'| + m_i - 1)(|V'| + m_i - 2) \cdots |V'|]$ and update $b \leftarrow b \circ \text{bin}(\ell_i)$
32 $b \leftarrow b \circ \textsc{EncodeRemainingView}(F, V^\infty)$.
33 **return** b

will only count an increase in number of nodes while the chain extends no more than $2\widetilde{T}$ beyond X_j. The reason for this cap, is that since the queries $j \in \mathcal{I}'$ are useful, they are spaced by at least this much on the cycle. This will guarantee that all edges/function evaluations that we exploit to compress F are disjoint for different X_j's.

In lines 6–9, we iterate over the useful $j \in \mathcal{I}'$. For each of these, we look for a "typical" increase in the number of nodes on X_j's chain. Concretely, we determine the indices h_j in line 7, guaranteeing that there are at least $\Delta_{h_j} :=$

$2^{h_j}/(h_j+1)^2$ rounds where the chain length grows by at least $\widetilde{T}/2^{h_j+3}+1$. At the end of this section, we will show that such an index h_j always exists:

Lemma 10. *If $t_1^{\widetilde{T}+1}(X_j) > 2\widetilde{T}$, then there exists an index $h_j \in \{0, \ldots, \lg(\widetilde{T}) - 3\}$ such that there are at least $\Delta_{h_j} := 2^{h_j}/(h_j+1)^2$ indices i with* $\min\{2\widetilde{T}+1, t_1^{i+1}(X_j)\} - \min\{2\widetilde{T}+1, t_1^i(X_j)\} \geq \widetilde{T}/2^{h_j+3}+1$.

We then encode a number of sequential rounds in which the chain of X_j grows by at least $\widetilde{T}/2^{h_j+3}+1$. The reason for encoding such rounds, is that it is expensive (bit-wise) to encode a round in which the chain grows. Thus the chain has to grow sufficiently much to afford encoding the round. The exact details will be clearer when we analyse the encoding length.

In lines 10–31, we now wish to encode the views V_1^i at the beginning of each sequential round. The overall goal with these steps, is to allow the decoder to recover V^∞. The encoding of sequential round i begins with going over the useful indices in $\mathcal{I}'$. For each such j, if sequential round i was one of the rounds where the increase in X_j's chain length is sufficiently large, we encode the chain merges that X_j is involved in. In particular, lines 15–26 encode all function evaluations $F(Y_k^i)$ that grow the chain of X_j. For each such function evaluation, we check the length of the chain $c'(F(Y_k^i))$ that we merge with. This length is precisely the increase in the length of X_j's chain. If we merge with a non-singleton ($z > 1$) chain, we will save bits by encoding the chain $c'(F(Y_k^i))$ as an index into the set of chains of length in $(2^{\lceil \lg z \rceil - 1}, 2^{\lceil \lg z \rceil}]$. Since any chain with a length in this interval has at least $2^{\lceil \lg z \rceil - 1}$ many edges and D makes no more than $B\widetilde{T}P$ function evaluations in total, the number of such chains is no more than $\lfloor B\widetilde{T}P/2^{\lceil \lg z \rceil - 1} \rfloor$. The crucial point is that the number of bits we spend on encoding the chain drops with the increase z in chain length. If instead we merge with a singleton chain, we check whether that chain is itself involved in a merge in sequential round i (line 22). If so, then we know that the head/tail of the singleton chain is one of the Y_ℓ^i. Since there are only BP function evaluations per sequential round, this allows us to save in the encoding length. Finally, if the singleton is not involved in a merge, we pay an expensive encoding of the chain (line 25). Fortunately, this will be made up for by the savings in other steps of the encoding.

Notice that in line 17, we encode the value $\lceil \lg z \rceil$ above using a special binAdapt(x) encoding. This encoding is prefix-free and uses a number of bits proportional to the value $x \geq 0$. It starts with $\lceil \lg(x+1) \rceil$ 0's, followed by a 1. This gives a unary encoding of $\lceil \lg(x+1) \rceil$. It then has $\lceil \lg(x+1) \rceil$ bits giving a binary encoding of x. Decoding such a number is straight forward: read bits until the first 1 is encountered. This recovers $\lceil \lg(x+1) \rceil$. Then read the next $\lceil \lg(x+1) \rceil$ bits to recover x. The number of bits used to encode an integer $x \geq 0$ is thus no more than

$$2\lceil \lg(x+1)\rceil \leq 2 + 2\lg(x+1).$$

In lines 27–29 we complete the encoding of all merges taking place in sequential round i. This is done by going over all Y_j^i that still correspond to a tail of a chain and merely encoding the successor $F(Y_j^i)$ as an index into the remaining chains. This step will make no savings in bits, but also will not lose any. The crucial point is that upon completing the encoding of one sequential round i, we have encoded all merges that occur in the round. This will allow the decoder to determine the view at the beginning of round $i+1$.

Finally, once all $\widetilde{T}$ sequential rounds have been completed, we encode the merges necessary for completing the final view V^∞ to a single chain (similarly to the short chains case).

The corresponding decoding procedure, DecodeLongChains, shown as Algorithm 8 simply reconstructs the views V_1^i in the order produced by the encoding. For completeness, we here outline the steps. First, in lines 1–4, we recover $\mathcal{I}'$, h_j and S_{h_j} for each $j \in \mathcal{I}'$. With this information, the decoding procedure can now simulate the i sequential rounds of D. In round i, we start by processing all $j \in \mathcal{I}'$ for which $i \in S_{h_j}$. Here we read off (lines 11–23) all the function evaluations/chain merges that extends the chain of X_j in round i (unless it grows beyond $2\widetilde{T}$ nodes succeeding X_j). In lines 24–28 we then decode all other function evaluations in round i. Note that decoding crucially uses in line 8 that the decoder has access to the advice a, the queries $X_1, \ldots, X_B$ and the view V_1^i. Since the view V_1^i contains all edges corresponding to function evaluations in previous sequential rounds, the decoding procedure can thus simulate D up to round i and determine all function evaluations $F(Y_j^i)$ made by D in round i. After processing sequential round i, we have recovered all function evaluations made by D in round i and thus V_1^{i+1} equals V' (as updated in line 29). Finally, we use the procedure from decoding short chains, DecodeRemainingView (Algorithm 6), to recover F.

Encoding Size with Long Chains. Analysing the encoding length with long chains is a bit more tricky than with short chains.

Examining EncodeLongChains in Algorithm 7, we first have $\lceil \lg \binom{B}{B/16} \rceil$ bits to encode $\mathcal{I}'$. For each $j \in \mathcal{I}'$, we use $\lceil \lg(\lg(\widetilde{T}) - 2) \rceil$ bits to encode h_j and $\lceil \lg \binom{\widetilde{T}}{\Delta_{h_j}} \rceil$ bits for S_{h_j}. We will argue that the remaining part of the encoding makes savings that can pay for these costs.

First, observe that upon completion of lines 10–31 in Algorithm 7, we use $\lceil \lg((|V^\infty| - 1)!) \rceil$ bits to encode the merges of the chains in V^∞. Encoding the lists L_i costs $\lceil \lg((|V_i'| + m_i - 1)!/(|V_i'| - 1)!) \rceil$, where V_i' is the value of V' upon reaching line 31 in iteration i of the for-loop. We also pay $\lceil \lg N \rceil$ to encode $|L_i|$ for each i. The key point is that if we ignore the rounding $\lceil \cdot \rceil$, then all factors in $\lg((|V^\infty| - 1)!) + \sum_i \lg((|V_i'| + m_i - 1)!/(|V_i'| - 1)!)$ correspond to terms in $\lg((N-1)!)$. Furthermore, there is precisely one term in $(N-1)!$ missing for every edge added in line 26. Moreover, each of these terms is at least $|V^\infty| \geq N - B\widetilde{T}P$

Algorithm 8: DecodeLongChains$(b, a, X_1, \ldots, X_B, D)$

Input: binary string $b \in \{0,1\}^*$ with $b =$EncodeLongChains$(F, a, X_1, \ldots, X_B, \mathcal{I} \setminus L, D)$ for some $F : [N] \to [N]$ corresponding to a cycle, advice a of data structure D on input F, queries $X_1, \ldots, X_B \in [N]$, data structure D.

Result: The function $F : [N] \to [N]$.

1 Read and remove first $\lceil \lg \binom{B}{B/16} \rceil$ bits of b to recover $\mathcal{I}'$.
2 **for** $j \in \mathcal{I}'$ **do**
3   Read and remove first $\lceil \lg(\lg(\widetilde{T}) + 2) \rceil$ bits to recover h_j.
4   Read and remove first $\lceil \lg \binom{\widetilde{T}}{\Delta_{h_j}} \rceil$ bits to recover S_{h_j}.
5 Let V_1^1 be the view with all nodes as singleton chains.
6 **for** $i = 1, \ldots, \widetilde{T}$ **do**
7   Let $V' \leftarrow V_1^i$ and use $c'(X)$ and $t'(X)$ as the equivalent definitions of c_j^i and t_j^i for the view V'.
8   From V' and the advice a, simulate D until sequential round i to determine the function evaluations $F(Y_j^i)$ it makes in round i.
9   **for** $j \in \mathcal{I}'$ **do**
10   **if** $i \in S_{h_j}$ **then**
11   **while** *$t'(X_j) \leq 2\widetilde{T}$ and the tail of $c'(X_j)$ equals Y_k^i for some k* **do**
12   Read and remove $\lceil \lg z \rceil \leftarrow |c'(F(Y_k^i))|$ from b.
13   **if** $\lceil \lg z \rceil > 0$ **then**
14   Read and remove the rank r of the chain $c'(F(Y_k^i))$ among all chains c in V' with $|c| \in (2^{\lceil \lg z \rceil - 1}, 2^{\lceil \lg z \rceil}]$ from b.
15   Add the edge from Y_k^i to the head of the chain $c'(F(Y_k^i))$ to V' and merge the two chains.
16   **else**
17   Read and remove the first bit q from b.
18   **if** $q = 0$ **then**
19   Read and remove $\lceil \lg(BP) \rceil$ bits from b to recover ℓ such that $F(Y_k^i) = Y_\ell^i$.
20   Add the edge from Y_k^i to Y_ℓ^i and merge the two chains.
21   **else**
22   Read and remove $\lceil \lg(N) \rceil$ bits from b to recover $F(Y_k^i)$.
23   Add the edge from Y_k^i to $F(Y_k^i)$ and merge the two chains.
24   Read and remove first $\lceil \lg N \rceil$ bits to recover $m_i = |L_i|$.
25   Read and remove $\lceil \lg((|V'| + m_i - 1)!/(|V'| - 1)!) \rceil$ bits from b to recover L_i.
26   **for** $j = 1, \ldots, BP$ **do**
27   **if** *Y_j^i is the tail of the chain $c'(Y_j^i)$* **then**
28   Read and remove the first element r_j^i of L_i. We learn that $F(Y_j^i)$ is the head of the chain of rank r_j^i in $V' \setminus \{c'(Y_j^i)\}$. We can thus compute $F(Y_j^i)$, insert the edge from Y_j^i to $F(Y_j^i)$ and merge the two chains in V'.
29     $V_1^{i+1} \leftarrow V'$.
30 $V^\infty \leftarrow V_1^{\widetilde{T}+1}$.
31 **return** DecodeRemainingView(b, V^∞)

large. If a total of Z edges are added in line 26, we then have

$$\lg((|V^\infty|-1)!) + \sum_i \lg((|V_i'|+m_i-1)!/(|V_i'|-1)!) \leq \lg((N-1)!) - Z\lg(N-B\widetilde{T}P).$$

Let us now partition these Z edges depending on the index $j \in \mathcal{I}'$ and $i \in S_{h_j}$ causing us to add the edges in line 26. That is, we let Z_j^i denote the number of edges added in line 26 for a fixed $j \in \mathcal{I}'$ and $i \in S_{h_j}$. We want to argue that the number of bits added to the encoding in lines 15–26 due to this fixed j and i is smaller than $Z_j^i \lg(N - B\widetilde{T}P)$.

For this argument, note that since $i \in S_{h_j}$, we have $\ell_j^i := \min\{2\widetilde{T}+1, t_1^{i+1}(X_j)\} - \min\{2\widetilde{T}+1, t_1^i(X_j)\} \geq \widetilde{T}/2^{h_j+3}+1$. The total length of the chains corresponding to the Z_j^i edges is thus at least ℓ_j^i. Consider one of these Z_j^i edges e, and let z_e denote the increase in $t'(X_j)$ due to the edge. The edge first adds binAdapt($\lceil \lg z_e \rceil$) to the encoding, which we argued above cost no more than $2+2\lg(\lceil \lg z_e \rceil + 1) \leq 2 + 2\lg\lg(4z_e)$ bits.

If $z_e > 1$, we then pay $\lceil \lg(B\widetilde{T}P/2^{\lceil \lg z_e \rceil - 1}) \rceil \leq 2 + \lg(B\widetilde{T}P) - \lg z_e$. The *saving* due to the edge e is thus at least $\lg(N - B\widetilde{T}P) - \lg(2^4 B\widetilde{T}P \lg^2(4z_e)/z_e)$ bits.

If $z_e = 1$ and we enter line 23, we pay $1 + \lceil \lg BP \rceil \leq 2 + \lg BP$ for the edge e in line 23, plus the $2 + 2\lg\lg 4 = 4$ bits from binAdapt($\lceil \lg z_e \rceil$). The edge e thus *saves* at least $\lg(N - B\widetilde{T}P) - \lg(2^6 BP)$ bits.

Comparing the two cases above, we see that the *saving per increase in* $t'(X_j)$ is $\lg(N - B\widetilde{T}P) - \lg(2^6 BP)$ in the latter case and $(\lg(N - B\widetilde{T}P) - \lg(2^4 B\widetilde{T}P\lg^2(4z_e)/z_e))/z_e$ in the former case. Since the expensive case in line 25 can only occur once (since no further merges occur for the chain), the above two cases must account for at least $\ell_j^i - 1$ of the increase in $t'(X_j)$. The total saving is smallest when this is due to a single edge with $z_e = \ell_j^i - 1 \geq \widetilde{T}/2^{h_j+3}$, giving a total saving of at least $\lg(N - B\widetilde{T}P) - \lg(2^4 B\widetilde{T}P\lg^2(4\widetilde{T})/(\widetilde{T}/2^{h_j+3})) = \lg(N - B\widetilde{T}P) - \lg(2^{h_j+7}BP\lg^2(4\widetilde{T}))$. The expensive case in line 25 may happen once, giving a *negative* saving of $\lg(N - B\widetilde{T}P) - \lg N - 1$. The Z_j^i edges for the fixed $j \in \mathcal{I}'$ and $i \in S_{h_j}$ thus give a saving of at least

$$\lg\left(\frac{(N - B\widetilde{T}P)^2}{2^{h_j+7}BP\lg^2(4\widetilde{T})N}\right)$$

bits. This happens for each of the Δ_{h_j} choices of $i \in S_{h_j}$. Also accounting for the $\lceil \lg \binom{\widetilde{T}}{\Delta_{h_j}} \rceil \leq 1 + \Delta_{h_j}\lg(e\widetilde{T}/\Delta_{h_j})$ bits spent encoding S_{h_j} now gives a saving of

$$\Delta_{h_j}\lg\left(\frac{(N - B\widetilde{T}P)^2\Delta_{h_j}}{e2^{h_j+7}\widetilde{T}BP\lg^2(4\widetilde{T})N}\right).$$

Using that $\Delta_{h_j} = 2^{h_j}/(h_j+1)^2$ and $h_j \leq \lg(\widetilde{T}) - 3$, this is at least

$$\Delta_{h_j}\lg\left(\frac{(N - B\widetilde{T}P)^2}{e2^7(h_j+1)^2\widetilde{T}BP\lg^2(4\widetilde{T})N}\right) \geq \Delta_{h_j}\lg\left(\frac{(N - B\widetilde{T}P)^2}{e2^7\widetilde{T}BP\lg^4(4\widetilde{T})N}\right).$$

If we now assume that $B\widetilde{T}P\lg^5(4\widetilde{T}) \leq N/2^{20}$, then the above saving is at least

$$\Delta_{h_j}\lg\left(\frac{(N/2)^2}{e2^7N^2/(2^{20}\lg(4\widetilde{T}))}\right) \geq \Delta_{h_j}\lg(2^7\lg(4\widetilde{T})) \geq \lg(2^7\lg(4\widetilde{T})).$$

Finally accounting for the $\lceil \lg(\lg(\widetilde{T}) - 2) \rceil \leq \lg(2\lg(\widetilde{T}))$ bits spend on encoding h_j, we get a saving of at least $\lg(2^7\lg(4\widetilde{T})) - \lg(2\lg(\widetilde{T})) \geq 6$ bits for each $i \in \mathcal{I}'$.

Recalling that we spend $\lceil \lg N \rceil$ on encoding $|L_i|$ for each i, the total encoding length is thus bounded by

$$\lg((N-1)!) + \left\lceil \lg \binom{B}{B/16} \right\rceil - 6B/16 + 1 + \widetilde{T}(1 + \lg N).$$

This is at most

$$\begin{aligned} &\lg((N-1)!) + 1 + \widetilde{T}(1 + \lg N) - (B/16)\lg(2^6/(e16)) \\ \leq &\lg((N-1)!) + 1 + \widetilde{T}(1 + \lg N) - (B/32). \end{aligned}$$

This completes the proof of Lemma 9.

The indices h_j exist (Proof of Lemma 10). Here we give the proof of Lemma 10 showing that it is possible to find the indices h_j.

Proof (of Lemma 10). Observe that for $t_1^{\widetilde{T}+1}(X_j) > 2\widetilde{T}$, we have

$$\sum_{i=1}^{\widetilde{T}} \min\{2\widetilde{T}+1, t_1^{i+1}(X_j)\} - \min\{2\widetilde{T}+1, t_1^{i}(X_j)\} \geq 2\widetilde{T}.$$

Using $\delta_i := \min\{2\widetilde{T}+1, t_1^{i+1}(X_j)\} - \min\{2\widetilde{T}+1, t_1^{i}(X_j)\}$ for short, this also implies

$$\sum_{i=1}^{\widetilde{T}} (\delta_i - 1) \geq \widetilde{T}. \tag{1}$$

Now assume for the sake of contradiction that there is no index $h_j \in \{0, \ldots, \lg(\widetilde{T}) - 3\}$ such that there are at least $\Delta_{h_j} := 2^{h_j}/(h_j+1)^2$ indices i with $\delta_i \geq \widetilde{T}/2^{h_j+3} + 1$. Then we have

$$\sum_{i=1}^{\widetilde{T}} (\delta_i - 1) = \sum_{h=1}^{\lg(\widetilde{T})-3} \sum_{i:\widetilde{T}/2^{h+3}+1 \leq \delta_i < \widetilde{T}/2^{h+2}+1} (\delta_i - 1) + \sum_{i:\delta_i \geq \widetilde{T}/2^3+1} (\delta_i - 1)\,.$$

Observe that $\Delta_0 = 1$ and thus our contradictory assumption implies that there are no indices i with $\delta_i \geq \widetilde{T}/2^3 + 1$. We thus upper bound the sum by

$$\begin{aligned} \sum_{i=1}^{\widetilde{T}} (\delta_i - 1) &\leq \sum_{h=1}^{\lg(\widetilde{T})-3} \sum_{i:\widetilde{T}/2^{h+3}+1 \leq \delta_i < \widetilde{T}/2^{h+2}+1} \left(\widetilde{T}/2^{h+2} - 1\right) \\ &\leq \sum_{h=1}^{\lg(\widetilde{T})-3} \left(2^h/(h+1)^2 - 1\right)\left(\widetilde{T}/2^{h+2} - 1\right) \\ &\leq \frac{\widetilde{T}}{4} \sum_{h=1}^{\lg(\widetilde{T})-3} \frac{1}{(h+1)^2} < \frac{\pi^2 \widetilde{T}}{24} < \widetilde{T}. \end{aligned}$$

This contradicts (1).

References

[ARS24] Abram, D., Roy, L., Simkin, M.: Time-based cryptography from weaker assumptions: randomness beacons, delay functions and more. Cryptology ePrint Archive, Report 2024/769 (2024). https://eprint.iacr.org/2024/769

[BBBF18] Boneh, D., Bonneau, J., Bünz, B., Fisch, B.: Verifiable delay functions. In: Shacham, H., Boldyreva, A. (eds.) CRYPTO 2018. LNCS, vol. 10991, pp. 757–788. Springer, Cham (2018). https://doi.org/10.1007/978-3-319-96884-1_25

[BFH+24] Biryukov, A., et al.: Cryptanalysis of algebraic verifiable delay functions. In: Reyzin, L., Stebila, D. (eds.) CRYPTO 2024. LNCS, vol. 14922, pp. 457–490. Springer, Cham (2024). https://doi.org/10.1007/978-3-031-68382-4_14

[BL13] Bringmann, K., Larsen, K.G.: Succinct sampling from discrete distributions. In: Boneh, D., Roughgarden, T., Feigenbaum, J. (eds.) 45th Annual ACM Symposium on Theory of Computing, Palo Alto, CA, USA, 1–4 June 2013, pp. 775–782. ACM Press (2013). https://doi.org/10.1145/2488608.2488707

[BN00] Boneh, D., Naor, M.: Timed commitments. In: Bellare, M. (ed.) CRYPTO 2000. LNCS, vol. 1880, pp. 236–254. Springer, Heidelberg (2000). https://doi.org/10.1007/3-540-44598-6_15

[CHM20] Chawin, D., Haitner, I., Mazor, N.: Lower bounds on the time/memory tradeoff of function inversion. In: Pass, R., Pietrzak, K. (eds.) TCC 2020. LNCS, vol. 12552, pp. 305–334. Springer, Cham (2020). https://doi.org/10.1007/978-3-030-64381-2_11

[CK19] Corrigan-Gibbs, H., Kogan, D.: The function-inversion problem: barriers and opportunities. In: Hofheinz, D., Rosen, A. (eds.) TCC 2019. LNCS, vol. 11891, pp. 393–421. Springer, Cham (2019). https://doi.org/10.1007/978-3-030-36030-6_16

[CKL18] Chakraborty, D., Kamma, L., Larsen, K.G.: Tight cell probe bounds for succinct Boolean matrix-vector multiplication. In: Diakonikolas, I., Kempe, D., Henzinger, M. (eds.) 50th Annual ACM Symposium on Theory of Computing, Los Angeles, CA, USA, 25–29 June 2018, pp. 1297–1306. ACM Press (2018). https://doi.org/10.1145/3188745.3188830

[Cle86] Cleve, R.: Limits on the security of coin flips when half the processors are faulty (extended abstract). In: Hartmanis, J. (eds.) Proceedings of the 18th Annual ACM Symposium on Theory of Computing, Berkeley, California, USA, 28–30 May 1986, pp. 364–369. ACM (1986)

[CLSY93] Cai, J., Lipton, R.J., Sedgewick, R., Yao, A.C.-C.: Towards uncheatable benchmarks. In: Proceedings of the Eight Annual Structure in Complexity Theory Conference, San Diego, CA, USA, 18–21 May 1993, pp. 2–11. IEEE Computer Society (1993). https://doi.org/10.1109/SCT.1993.336546

[CMB23] Choi, K., Manoj, A., Bonneau, J.: SoK: distributed randomness beacons. In: 44th IEEE Symposium on Security and Privacy, SP 2023, San Francisco, CA, USA, 21–25 May 2023, pp. 75–92. IEEE (2023)

[DDJ24] Döttling, N., Dujmovic, J., Joux, A.: Space-lock puzzles and verifiable space-hard functions from root-finding in sparse polynomials. In: Boyle, E., Mahmoody, M. (eds.) TCC 2024. LNCS, vol. 15366, pp. 431–459. Springer, Cham (2025). https://doi.org/10.1007/978-3-031-78020-2_15

[DMPS19] De Feo, L., Masson, S., Petit, C., Sanso, A.: Verifiable delay functions from supersingular isogenies and pairings. In: Galbraith, S.D., Moriai, S. (eds.) ASIACRYPT 2019. LNCS, vol. 11921, pp. 248–277. Springer, Cham (2019). https://doi.org/10.1007/978-3-030-34578-5_10

[EFKP20] Ephraim, N., Freitag, C., Komargodski, I., Pass, R.: Continuous verifiable delay functions. In: Canteaut, A., Ishai, Y. (eds.) EUROCRYPT 2020. LNCS, vol. 12107, pp. 125–154. Springer, Cham (2020). https://doi.org/10.1007/978-3-030-45727-3_5

[FN91] Fiat, A., Naor, M.: Rigorous time/space tradeoffs for inverting functions. In: 23rd Annual ACM Symposium on Theory of Computing, New Orleans, LA, USA, 6–8 May 1991, pp. 534–541. ACM Press (1991). https://doi.org/10.1145/103418.103473

[GGPS23] Golovnev, A., Guo, S., Peters, S., Stephens-Davidowitz, N.: Revisiting time-space tradeoffs for function inversion. In: Handschuh, H., Lysyanskaya, A. (eds.) CRYPTO 2023. LNCS, vol. 14082, pp. 453–481. Springer, Cham (2023). https://doi.org/10.1007/978-3-031-38545-2_15

[GS98] Goldschlag, D.M., Stubblebine, S.G.: Publicly verifiable lotteries: applications of delaying functions. In: Hirchfeld, R. (ed.) FC 1998. LNCS, vol. 1465, pp. 214–226. Springer, Heidelberg (1998). https://doi.org/10.1007/BFb0055485

[Hel80] Hellman, M.E.: A cryptanalytic time-memory trade-off. IEEE Trans. Inf. Theory **26**(4), 401–406 (1980)

[KLX20] Katz, J., Loss, J., Xu, J.: On the security of time-lock puzzles and timed commitments. In: Pass, R., Pietrzak, K. (eds.) TCC 2020. LNCS, vol. 12552, pp. 390–413. Springer, Cham (2020). https://doi.org/10.1007/978-3-030-64381-2_14

[KMT22] Khovratovich, D., Maller, M., Tiwari, P.R.: MinRoot: candidate sequential function for ethereum VDF. Cryptology ePrint Archive, Report 2022/1626 (2022). https://eprint.iacr.org/2022/1626

[Lar12a] Larsen, K.G.: The cell probe complexity of dynamic range counting. In: Karloff, H.J., Pitassi, T. (eds.) 44th Annual ACM Symposium on Theory of Computing, New York, NY, USA, 19–22 May 2012, pp. 85–94. ACM Press (2012). https://doi.org/10.1145/2213977.2213987

[Lar12b] Larsen, K.G.: Higher cell probe lower bounds for evaluating polynomials. In: 53rd Annual Symposium on Foundations of Computer Science, New Brunswick, NJ, USA, 20–23 October 2012, pp. 293–301. IEEE Computer Society Press (2012). https://doi.org/10.1109/FOCS.2012.21

[LLYZ23] Li, T., Liang, J., Yu, H., Zhou, R.: Tight cell-probe lower bounds for dynamic succinct dictionaries. In: 64th IEEE Annual Symposium on Foundations of Computer Science, FOCS 2023, Santa Cruz, CA, USA, 6–9 November 2023, pp. 1842–1862. IEEE (2023)

[LM23] Lai, R.W.F., Malavolta, G.: Lattice-based timed cryptography. In: Handschuh, H., Lysyanskaya, A. (eds.) CRYPTO 2023. LNCS, vol. 14085, pp. 782–804. Springer, Cham (2023). https://doi.org/10.1007/978-3-031-38554-4_25

[LMP+23] Leurent, G., et al.: Analysis of minroot (2023). https://inria.hal.science/hal-04320126/file/minrootanalysis2023.pdf

[LS20] Larsen, K.G., Simkin, M.: Secret sharing lower bound: either reconstruction is hard or shares are long. In: Galdi, C., Kolesnikov, V. (eds.) SCN 2020. LNCS, vol. 12238, pp. 566–578. Springer, Cham (2020). https://doi.org/10.1007/978-3-030-57990-6_28

[LY20] Liu, M., Yu, H.: Lower bound for succinct range minimum query. In: Makarychev, K., Makarychev, Y., Tulsiani, M., Kamath, G., Chuzhoy, J. (eds.) 52nd Annual ACM Symposium on Theory of Computing, Chicago, IL, USA, 22–26 June 2020, pp. 1402–1415. ACM Press (2020). https://doi.org/10.1145/3357713.3384260

[MSW20] Mahmoody, M., Smith, C., Wu, D.J.: Can verifiable delay functions be based on random oracles? In: Czumaj, A., Dawar, A., Merelli, E. (eds.) ICALP 2020: 47th International Colloquium on Automata, Languages and Programming. Leibniz International Proceedings in Informatics (LIPIcs), Saarbrücken, Germany, 8–11 July 2020, vol. 168, pp. 83:1–83:17. Schloss Dagstuhl - Leibniz-Zentrum fuer Informatik (2020). https://doi.org/10.4230/LIPIcs.ICALP.2020.83

[PD06] Puatracscu, M., Demaine, E.D.: Logarithmic lower bounds in the cell-probe model. SIAM J. Comput. **35**(4), 932–963 (2006). https://doi.org/10.1137/S0097539705447256

[Pie19] Pietrzak, K.: Simple verifiable delay functions. In: Blum, A. (ed.) 10th Innovations in Theoretical Computer Science Conference, ITCS 2019, San Diego, California, USA, 10–12 January 2019. LIPIcs, vol. 124, pp. 60:1–60:15. Schloss Dagstuhl - Leibniz-Zentrum für Informatik (2019)

[PT24] Peikert, C., Tang, Y.: Cryptanalysis of lattice-based sequentiality assumptions and proofs of sequential work. In: Reyzin, L., Stebila, D. (eds.) CRYPTO 2024. LNCS, vol. 14924, pp. 129–157. Springer, Cham (2024). https://doi.org/10.1007/978-3-031-68388-6_6

[PV10] Patrascu, M., Viola, E.: Cell-probe lower bounds for succinct partial sums. In: Charika, M. (ed.) 21st Annual ACM-SIAM Symposium on Discrete Algorithms, Austin, TX, USA, 17–19 January 2010, pp. 117–122. ACM-SIAM (2010). https://doi.org/10.1137/1.9781611973075.11

[RS20] Rotem, L., Segev, G.: Generically speeding-up repeated squaring is equivalent to factoring: sharp thresholds for all generic-ring delay functions. In: Micciancio, D., Ristenpart, T. (eds.) CRYPTO 2020. LNCS, vol. 12172, pp. 481–509. Springer, Cham (2020). https://doi.org/10.1007/978-3-030-56877-1_17

[RSS20] Rotem, L., Segev, G., Shahaf, I.: Generic-group delay functions require hidden-order groups. In: Canteaut, A., Ishai, Y. (eds.) EUROCRYPT 2020. LNCS, vol. 12107, pp. 155–180. Springer, Cham (2020). https://doi.org/10.1007/978-3-030-45727-3_6

[VZ13] Verbin, E., Zhang, Q.: The limits of buffering: a tight lower bound for dynamic membership in the external memory model. SIAM J. Comput. **42**(1), 212–229 (2013). https://doi.org/10.1137/110842211

[Wes19] Wesolowski, B.: Efficient verifiable delay functions. In: Ishai, Y., Rijmen, V. (eds.) EUROCRYPT 2019. LNCS, vol. 11478, pp. 379–407. Springer, Cham (2019). https://doi.org/10.1007/978-3-030-17659-4_13

Constrained Verifiable Random Functions Without Obfuscation and Friends

Nicholas Brandt[1], Miguel Cueto Noval[2], Christoph U. Günther[2], Akin Ünal[2(✉)], and Stella Wohnig[3,4]

[1] ETH Zurich, Zurich, Switzerland
nicholas.brandt@inf.ethz.ch
[2] Institute of Science and Technology Austria, Klosterneuburg, Austria
{mcuetono,cguenthe,auenal}@ista.ac.at
[3] CISPA Helmholtz Institute for Information Security, Saarbrücken, Germany
stella.wohnig@cispa.de
[4] Saarland University, Saarbrücken, Germany

Abstract. CVRFs are PRFs that unify the properties of verifiable and constrained PRFs. Since they were introduced concurrently by Fuchsbauer and Chandran-Raghuraman-Vinayagamurthy in 2014, it has been an open problem to construct CVRFs without using heavy machinery such as multilinear maps, obfuscation or functional encryption.

We solve this problem by constructing a prefix-constrained verifiable PRF that does not rely on the aforementioned assumptions. Essentially, our construction is a verifiable version of the Goldreich-Goldwasser-Micali PRF. To achieve verifiability we leverage degree-2 algebraic PRGs and bilinear groups. In short, proofs consist of intermediate values of the Goldreich-Goldwasser-Micali PRF raised to the exponents of group elements. These outputs can be verified using pairings since the underlying PRG is of degree 2.

We prove the selective security of our construction under the *Decisional Square Diffie-Hellman* (DSDH) assumption and a new assumption, which we dub *recursive Decisional Diffie-Hellman* (recursive DDH).

We prove the soundness of recursive DDH in the generic group model assuming the hardness of the Multivariate Quadratic (MQ) problem and a new variant thereof, which we call MQ+.

Last, in terms of applications, we observe that our CVRF is also an exponent (C)VRF in the plain model. Exponent VRFs were recently introduced by Boneh et al. (Eurocrypt'25) with various applications to threshold cryptography in mind. In addition to that, we give further applications for prefix-CVRFs in the blockchain setting, namely, stake-pooling and compressible randomness beacons.

1 Introduction

Pseudorandom Functions (PRFs) allow for the generation of bit strings that are indistinguishable from true random coins, thereby constituting a central cryptographic building block. Concretely, a PRF is a keyed *deterministic* function that

B. Applebaum and H. Lin (Eds.): TCC 2025, LNCS 16271, pp. 478–511, 2026.
https://doi.org/10.1007/978-3-032-12290-2_16

has to be indistinguishable from a truly random function for any party that does not know the secret key of the PRF. Goldreich, Goldwasser & Micali [29] showed how to construct PRFs from *Pseudorandom Generators* (PRGs). In contrast to PRFs, PRGs only need to generate a polynomial number of pseudorandom bits from a truly random key and can be instantiated from one-way functions [32,40].

A popular line of research augments PRFs with additional properties. In this work, we will study two useful properties for PRFs: *constrainability* and *verifiability.*

A *Constrained PRF* (CPRF) [14,15,38] allows deriving constrained keys from the root secret key. While a constrained key enables one to evaluate the CPRF on a proper subset $\mathcal{X} \subsetneq \{0,1\}^\ell$ of its input domain, the security of the CPRF guarantees that a constrained key does not reveal anything about the CPRF on inputs outside $\mathcal{X}$. This delegates the power of the CPRF hierarchically.

By design, outputs of a PRF cannot be *trusted* by third parties, as checking the correctness of a potential output of a PRF requires access to its secret key. This limits the use-case of plain PRFs to inherently trusted settings. *Verifiable Random Functions* (VRFs) [45] are PRFs that solve this problem by tying a public verification key to the secret key and accompanying outputs by proofs of correctness. Without a proof, any output of the VRF must be indistinguishable from random coins, even given the verification key. However, with the corresponding proof, correctness of the output can be easily checked. To be practical in trustless settings, VRFs must satisfy a very strong soundness property called *unique provability*, which asserts that even for malformed verification keys (and adversarially programmed random oracles) it is not possible to prove the correctness of two different output values (for the same input).

Since both primitives, CPRFs and VRFs, enjoy simple instantiations, one might assume that a natural construction could be made to achieve both *constrainability* and *verifiability*, at the same time. Quite surprisingly, however, the construction of PRFs that are both, constrained and verifiable, turned out to be quite involved. In 2014, Fuchsbauer [28] and Chandran, Raghuraman & Vinayagamurthy [19] put forth the notion of *constrained verifiable PRFs* (CVRFs) that unify CPRFs and VRFs. CVRFs are versatile tools. For example, prefix-constrained CVRFs imply hierarchical identity-based signature algorithms with unique pseudorandom signatures. Both works devised candidates based on multilinear maps (mmaps), a heavy tool. Subsequent works [24,41,42,55] tried to relax this assumption, but still relied on indistinguishability Obfuscation (iO) or functional encryption (FE) [23].

Naturally, the heavy machinery of iO, mmaps and FE yield impractical constructions that are hard to understand and implement. Hence, we raise the following decade-long open question:

Can we construct constrained verifiable PRFs from simple cryptographic building blocks?

1.1 Our Candidate

In this work, we answer the above question positively. Concretely, we devise a candidate construction for prefix-constrained verifiable PRFs, which only makes use of bilinear groups and algebraic PRGs of degree 2. Those are PRGs whose outputs are computed by quadratic multivariate polynomials.

The Starting Point. Recall the (constrained) PRF construction of Goldreich, Goldwasser & Micali [29]. It uses a length-doubling PRG $G\colon \{0,1\}^n \to \{0,1\}^{2n}$ where we let G_0 and G_1 be the functions computing the first and last n output bits of G, respectively. The value of the PRF F on a point $x = x_1 \cdots x_\ell \in \{0,1\}^\ell$ is given by

$$F_{\mathsf{sk}}(x) := G_x(\mathsf{sk}) := G_{x_\ell}(G_{x_{\ell-1}}(\cdots(G_{x_2}(G_{x_1}(\mathsf{sk})))))$$

where $\mathsf{sk} \leftarrow \{0,1\}^n$ is the secret key of the PRF. Given the simplicity of this construction, its security follows from a simple hybrid argument. In addition, F is already a prefix-constrained PRF [14,15,38]. Indeed, given a constrained key $\mathsf{sk}_w = G_w(\mathsf{sk})$ for a prefix $w \in \{0,1\}^{\ell'}$, one can compute any value $F_{sk}(wx')$, while the pseudorandomness of G implies that a value $F_{\mathsf{sk}}(x)$ still looks random as long as w is not a prefix of $x \in \{0,1\}^\ell$.

A First Attempt at Adding Verifiability. As a first step, we take the CPRF of Goldreich, Goldwasser & Micali [29] and move it to an algebraic setting to allow for verifiability. To this end, let $e\colon \mathbb{G}_1^2 \to \mathbb{G}_2$ be a bilinear pairing of groups $\mathbb{G}_1 = \langle \mathsf{g}_1 \rangle$ and $\mathbb{G}_2 = \langle \mathsf{g}_2 \rangle$ of prime order p. Further, let $G\colon \mathbb{Z}_p^n \to \mathbb{Z}_p^{2n}$ now be a PRG that outputs values computed by quadratic multivariate polynomials over $\mathbb{Z}_p$. Again, we subdivide $G = (G_0, G_1)$ into two parts computing the left and right half of its output.[1] Since G is quadratic, it is possible to compute the *target* group elements $\mathsf{g}_2^{G_0(\boldsymbol{s})}, \mathsf{g}_2^{G_1(\boldsymbol{s})} \in \mathbb{G}_2^n$ when given *source* group elements $\mathsf{g}_1^{\boldsymbol{s}} = (\mathsf{g}_1^{s_1}, \ldots, \mathsf{g}_1^{s_n}) \in \mathbb{Z}_p^n$ by using the bilinear pairing e. In other words, we can evaluate the PRG G in the exponents of group elements, however, this will necessitate a transition from $\mathbb{G}_1$ to $\mathbb{G}_2$.

We draw the secret key sk of the CPRF F as a seed for G, i.e. $\mathsf{sk} \leftarrow\!\!\$\ \mathbb{Z}_p^n$. Consequently, F_{sk} outputs now vectors $F_{\mathsf{sk}}(x) = G_{x_{\ell-1}}(\cdots(G_{x_1}(\mathsf{sk}))) \in \mathbb{Z}_p^n$. To allow for verification, we introduce the verification key $\mathsf{vk} = \mathsf{g}_2^{\mathsf{sk}}$, a vector of group elements whose exponents are the elements of sk, and supply a proof π with every output $F_{\mathsf{sk}}(x)$. The proof π consists of a list of group elements

$$\pi_0 = \mathsf{g}_1^{\mathsf{sk}}, \pi_1 = \mathsf{g}_1^{G_{x_1}(\mathsf{sk})}, \pi_2 = \mathsf{g}_1^{G_{x_2}(G_{x_1}(\mathsf{sk}))}, \ldots, \pi_\ell = \mathsf{g}_1^{G_{x_\ell}(\cdots(G_{x_1}(\mathsf{sk})))}.$$

Given π, we can verify the correctness of the output $F_{\mathsf{sk}}(x)$ of our CPRF as follows: we first verify the soundness of the first vector of group elements $\pi_0 \in \mathbb{G}_1^n$ by checking $e(\pi_0, \mathsf{g}_1) = \mathsf{vk}$. Subsequently, we verify the correctness of π_i by asserting the equality $e(\pi_i, \mathsf{g}_1) = \mathsf{g}_2^{G_{x_i}(\cdots(G_{x_1}(\mathsf{sk})))}$, where we compute $\mathsf{g}_2^{G_{x_i}(\cdots(G_{x_1}(\mathsf{sk})))}$

[1] Because of technical reasons, we will actually choose a fresh PRG $G^{(i)} : \mathbb{Z}_p^n \to \mathbb{Z}_p^{2n}$ for every layer $i \in [\ell]$ of the binary tree underlying our construction later.

by evaluating G_{x_i} at the exponents of π_{i-1}. Finally, we verify the correct evaluation of F_{sk} at x by ensuring that $\mathsf{g}_1^{F_{\mathsf{sk}}(x)} = \pi_\ell$ holds. This approach enables the uniqueness of output elements, even under a malformed verification key vk, proof π and PRG G. Thus, it fulfills the very strict requirement of *unique provability* which is necessary for VRFs. Additionally, the simplicity of this construction allows constraining a constrained key even further, fulfilling the notion of *delegability* [19]. On top of that, constrained keys themselves can be verified and fulfil again unique provability.

An Issue with the First Attempt and the Solution. While the first attempt is verifiable, a keen eye will have noticed that the above construction is *not* pseudorandom. To demonstrate this, consider the case $\ell = 2$. The proof $\pi = (\pi_0, \pi_1, \pi_2)$ for the output $F_{\mathsf{sk}}(00)$ contains the value $\pi_1 = \mathsf{g}_1^{G_0(\mathsf{sk})}$. It can be used to compute $\mathsf{g}_2^{G_1(G_0(\mathsf{sk}))}$, which suffices to verify the other output $F_{\mathsf{sk}}(01)$. In general, this leads to a simple attack where an adversary queries a proof for 0^ℓ and challenges the pseudorandomness of F at $0^{\ell-1}1$.

To solve this problem, we redefine the output of the CVRF F as

$$F_{\mathsf{sk}}(x) = \mathsf{g}_2^{\boldsymbol{y}^2} \in \mathbb{G}_2^n \quad \text{where} \quad \boldsymbol{y} = G_{x_\ell}(\cdots(G_{x_1}(\mathsf{sk}))).$$

($\boldsymbol{y}^2 = (y_1^2, \ldots, y_n^2)$ denotes the vector of squares of entries of $\boldsymbol{y} = (y_1, \ldots, y_n) \in \mathbb{Z}_p^n$.) This output can still be verified using π by checking that $F_{\mathsf{sk}}(x) = e(\pi_\ell, \pi_\ell)$ while intuitively ensuring pseudorandomness under the *Decisional Square Diffie-Hellman* (DSDH) assumption.[2] (An example for input lengths of $\ell = 2$ is given in Fig. 1.)

Indeed, this change invalidates the given counterexample for $\ell = 2$, as DSDH implies that the output $F_{\mathsf{sk}}(01) = \mathsf{g}_2^{G_1(G_0(\mathsf{sk}))^2}$ stays pseudorandom even if an adversary can obtain $\mathsf{g}_2^{G_1(G_0(\mathsf{sk}))}$.

Unfortunately, fully proving the selective[3] security of the CVRF F remains challenging. The reason lies in the fact that F commits to the root secret key sk in two ways: by the verification key $\mathsf{vk} = \mathsf{g}_2^{\mathsf{sk}}$, a vector of group elements, and by constrained keys $G_w(\mathsf{sk})$, vectors over $\mathbb{Z}_p$. This prohibits typical reduction techniques of, e.g., the generic group model, and makes it hard to hop between different games by using the pseudorandomness of G. Indeed, sk is committed to in such a rigid way that it is impossible for a reduction to directly replace some values of F by randomness behind the scenes without the adversary noticing.

1.2 Contribution

Proving the pseudorandomness of the CVRF F is non-trivial and requires new techniques. As a first step, we modularize the proof by a new tool, which we

[2] The decisional square Diffie-Hellman problem (in the target group $\mathbb{G}_2$) consists in distinguishing $(\mathsf{g}_2, \mathsf{g}_2^a, \mathsf{g}_2^{a^2})$ and $(\mathsf{g}_2, \mathsf{g}_2^a, \mathsf{g}_2^r)$ for $a, r \leftarrow_\$ \mathbb{Z}_p$.

[3] In this work, we focus only on the selective security of CVRFs, where an adversary has to commit to a challenge point $x^* \in \{0,1\}^\ell$ before it sees a verification key. Proving the adaptive security is out of scope as it requires intricate rewinding techniques [34].

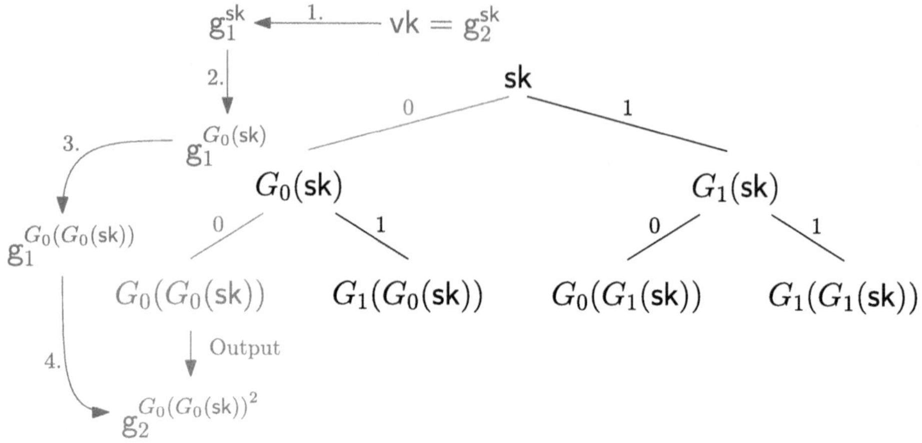

Fig. 1. Illustration of our construction for 2 bit inputs. For the sake of example, it shows the evaluation on input 00 by highlighting the corresponding path and output in orange. The verification key vk, the proof $\pi = (\pi_0, \pi_1, \pi_2)$, and the four iterative verification steps are depicted in pink. All verification steps rely on the pairing e, especially steps 2 and 3, which evaluate the degree-2 PRG in the exponent using e. (Color figure online)

dub the *recursive Decisional Diffie-Hellman* (recursive DDH) assumption. This assumption (detailed in the technical overview) asserts that an *a posteriori* challenge must be hard if an *a priori* challenge is hard. From this assumption and DSDH, the pseudorandomness of F follows, leading to our first main result:

Theorem 1. *Under the decisional square Diffie-Hellman and the recursive decisional Diffie-Hellman assumption, F is a selectively secure prefix-constrained verifiable random function.*

As a next step and second result, we prove the soundness of recursive DDH in Maurer's *Generic Group Model* [44] assuming the hardness of MQ and MQ+. MQ is a standard assumption capturing the hardness of solving multivariate quadratic equation systems. For example, multiple NIST post-quantum digital signatures candidates are based on it. MQ+ is a new assumption introduced by us that is closely related to MQ. We will discuss MQ and MQ+ in the technical overview, and analyze attacks on recursive DDH, MQ and MQ+ in the full version [17, App. A].

Theorem 2. *In the generic group model, the recursive DDH assumption is implied by the MQ and the MQ+ assumption.*

Finally, we optimize the verification algorithm, reducing the amount of pairings computed by the verifier to $O(\ell n)$. For $n = \ell = 256$, the optimized verification only needs 66049 symmetric pairings. To get a ballpark performance estimate, evaluating these pairings takes about 4.5 minutes on a laptop.[4] In short, the verifier does not check n quadratic equations individually, but instead only checks a random linear combination of them. This introduces a negligible error probability that only depends on the verifier's coins. Thus, it does not go against the spirit of unique provability. For details, we refer to the full version [17, App. B].

1.3 Technical Overview

We will first sketch the security of our CVRF F under our novel recursive DDH assumption, and then prove the hardness of recursive DDH in the generic group model under two falsifiable and contained assumptions, MQ and MQ+.

Fresh PRGs per Layer. Before we sketch our proofs of the pseudorandomness of F, we point out an additional technicality. In our actual construction of F, we use a fresh algebraic degree-2 PRG $G^{(i)} = (G_0^{(i)}, G_1^{(i)}) : \mathbb{Z}_p^n \to \mathbb{Z}_p^{2n}$ for every layer $i \in [\ell]$. This means, the coefficients of the quadratic polynomials computing the functions $G^{(1)}, \ldots, G^{(\ell)}$ are all distributed uniformly and independently at random. Consequently, we define the value of F at input $x = x_1 \cdots x_\ell$ by

$$F_{\mathsf{sk}}(x) := \mathsf{g}_2^{\boldsymbol{y}^2} \text{ where } \boldsymbol{y} = G_x(\mathsf{sk}) := G_{x_\ell}^{(\ell)}(G_{x_{\ell-1}}^{(\ell-1)}(\cdots(G_{x_2}^{(2)}(G_{x_1}^{(1)}(\mathsf{sk}))))),$$

with $\boldsymbol{y}^2 = (y_1^2, \ldots, y_n^2)$. Constrained keys for prefixes $w = w_1 \cdots w_{\ell'}$ are computed by

$$\mathsf{sk}_w := G_w(\mathsf{sk}) = G_{w_{\ell'}}^{(\ell')}(G_{w_{\ell'-1}}^{(\ell'-1)}(\cdots(G_{w_2}^{(2)}(G_{w_1}^{(1)}(\mathsf{sk}))))).$$

Because of this change, we can always assume in the selective security game that an adversary submits 0^ℓ as challenge point x^*, at which it has to distinguish the value of F from uniform random group elements. Indeed, if $x^* \neq 0^\ell$, we can simply swap $G_0^{(i)}$ and $G_1^{(i)}$ whenever $x_i^* \neq 0$.

The Recursive Decisional Diffie-Hellman Assumption. The *recursive Decisional Diffie-Hellman* (recursive DDH) assumption states that, for each sampler Samp, a certain challenge stays hard even if we hand out more, seemingly useless, auxiliary information. Concretely, let $e\colon \mathbb{G}_1^2 \to \mathbb{G}_2$ be a bilinear map of groups and Samp be a PPT algorithm that on input $1^\lambda, p, n$ outputs three *hint* functions $h_0\colon \mathbb{Z}_p^n \to \mathbb{Z}_p^{m_0}$, $h_1\colon \mathbb{Z}_p^n \to \mathbb{Z}_p^{m_1}$, $h_2\colon \mathbb{Z}_p^n \to \mathbb{Z}_p^{m_2}$ and a *challenge* function $c\colon \mathbb{Z}_p^n \to \mathbb{Z}_p^n$.

The recursive DDH assumption states for each sampler Samp that, if $\mathsf{g}_2^{c(\boldsymbol{s})}$ is pseudorandom given

$$(c, h_0, h_1, h_2), \qquad h_0(\boldsymbol{s}), \qquad \mathsf{g}_1^{h_1(\boldsymbol{s})}, \qquad \mathsf{g}_2^{h_2(\boldsymbol{s})}, \qquad \mathsf{g}_2^{\boldsymbol{s}},$$

[4] RELIC's [5] benchmarks for the 1536-bit supersingular elliptic curve preset result in 4.1 ms per pairing on an Apple MacBook Pro (2021).

then $\mathsf{g}_2^{c(\boldsymbol{s}')}$ is pseudorandom given

$$\begin{array}{llllll} & (c, h_0, h_1, h_2), & h_0(\boldsymbol{s}'), & \mathsf{g}_1^{h_1(\boldsymbol{s}')}, & \mathsf{g}_2^{h_2(\boldsymbol{s}')}, & \mathsf{g}_2^{\boldsymbol{s}'}, \\ \textbf{and} & (G_0, G_1), & G_1(\boldsymbol{x}), & \mathsf{g}_1^{\boldsymbol{x}}, & & \end{array}$$

where we draw $\boldsymbol{s}, \boldsymbol{x} \leftarrow \mathbb{Z}_p^n$, $(c, h_0, h_1, h_2) \leftarrow \mathsf{Samp}(1^\lambda, p, n)$ and set $\boldsymbol{s}' = G_0(\boldsymbol{x})$ for two uniformly random maps $G_0, G_1 : \mathbb{Z}_p^n \to \mathbb{Z}_p^n$ computed by multivariate quadratic polynomials. We will call the first decisional problem the if-*challenge*, and the second decisional problem the then-*challenge*.

Let us explain the soundness of this assumption intuitively: The if-challenge states that the auxiliary information $h_0(\boldsymbol{s}), \mathsf{g}_1^{h_1(\boldsymbol{s})}$, $\mathsf{g}_2^{h_2(\boldsymbol{s})}$ and $\mathsf{g}_2^{\boldsymbol{s}}$ do not help at distinguishing $\mathsf{g}_2^{c(\boldsymbol{s})}$ from a vector of n random group elements of $\mathbb{G}_2$. This implies, in particular, that $\mathsf{g}_2^{c(\boldsymbol{s})}$, while it is correlated with the auxiliary information, cannot be simply algebraically derived from the other group elements $\mathsf{g}_1^{h_1(\boldsymbol{s})}$, $\mathsf{g}_2^{h_2(\boldsymbol{s})}$, $\mathsf{g}_2^{\boldsymbol{s}}$, even when knowing $h_0(\boldsymbol{s})$ in plain. The then-part of the assumption postulates that $\mathsf{g}_2^{c(\boldsymbol{s})}$ stays pseudorandom, even if $\boldsymbol{s} = G_0(\boldsymbol{x})$ is now sampled as the left-hand output of the PRG G, and even if we additionally give the adversary the corresponding right-hand output $G_1(\boldsymbol{x})$ in plain and the seed of the PRG $\mathsf{g}_1^{\boldsymbol{x}}$ as source group elements. Hence, recursive DDH simply states that a certain group vector stays pseudorandom even if we hand out more information, $\mathsf{g}_1^{\boldsymbol{x}}$ and $G_1(\boldsymbol{x})$, to the distinguisher. Note if we would hand out only one of $\{\mathsf{g}_1^{\boldsymbol{x}}, G_1(\boldsymbol{x})\}$, the correctness of the assumption would easily follow.[5]

Unfortunately, giving a reduction of the if-problem to the then-problem becomes challenging as soon as one hands out both additional auxiliary elements $\mathsf{g}_1^{\boldsymbol{x}}$ and $G_1(\boldsymbol{x})$. While it is intuitively clear that both vectors together do not help at distinguishing $\mathsf{g}_2^{c(\boldsymbol{s})}$ from random group elements, the above techniques fail at proving this, since we are committed to the PRG-seed $\boldsymbol{x}$ in two different ways (as group elements $\mathsf{g}_1^{\boldsymbol{x}}$ and as plain numbers $G_1(\boldsymbol{x})$). For now, we postpone the discussion of how we solve this conundrum and continue to show the application of recursive DDH.

Proving Security under Recursive DDH. The recursive DDH assumption gives an elegant way to prove the pseudorandomness of our CVRF F. Let $\mathcal{A}$ be a selective adversary that, at the start of the game, sends a challenge point $x^* \in \{0,1\}^\ell$ to a challenger $\mathcal{C}$. As explained above, we can assume $x^* = 0^\ell$ without loss of generality. $\mathcal{C}$ has to respond by sending $\mathcal{A}$ a verification key vk, constrained[6] keys $\mathsf{sk}_1, \mathsf{sk}_{01}, \ldots, \mathsf{sk}_{0^{\ell-2}1}$ (for all non-prefixes of 0^ℓ), the output

[5] For example, if the adversary only receives $G_1(\boldsymbol{x})$ as additional auxiliary information, we can invoke (in the absence of $\mathsf{g}_1^{\boldsymbol{x}}$) the pseudorandomness of $G = (G_0, G_1)$, and replace $\boldsymbol{s} = G_0(\boldsymbol{x})$ and $G_1(\boldsymbol{x})$ in the distribution by uniformly random vectors $\boldsymbol{r}_1, \boldsymbol{r}_2 \leftarrow_\$ \mathbb{Z}_p^n$, which immediately reduces the if-challenge to the then-challenge.

[6] Note that from those values, $\mathcal{A}$ can compute all other possible queries on its own. Further, since constrained keys, evaluation values and proofs are generated deterministically, $\mathcal{A}$ does not profit from querying the same value multiple times.

value $F_{\mathsf{sk}}(0^{\ell-1}1)$, and finally proofs $\pi_1, \ldots, \pi_\ell$ for the correctness of the aforementioned constrained keys and output value. Here, $\mathsf{sk} = \boldsymbol{s} \leftarrow \mathbb{Z}_p^n$ is a uniformly random vector. The verification key is given by $\mathsf{vk} = \mathrm{g}_2^{\boldsymbol{s}}$. The output at $0^{\ell-1}1$ is given by

$$F_{\mathsf{sk}}(0^{\ell-1}1) = \mathrm{g}_2^{\boldsymbol{y}^2} \quad \text{for} \quad \boldsymbol{y} = G_1^{(\ell)}(G_0^{(\ell-1)}(\cdots(G_0^{(1)}(\boldsymbol{s})))).$$

The constrained keys are all vectors in $\mathbb{Z}_p^n$ of shape

$$G_1^{(1)}(\boldsymbol{s}), \qquad G_1^{(2)}(G_0^{(1)}(\boldsymbol{s})), \qquad \ldots, \qquad G_1^{(\ell-1)}(G_0^{(\ell-2)}(\cdots(G_0^{(1)}(\boldsymbol{s})))),$$

while the proof elements are vectors of group elements given by

$$\pi_0 = \mathrm{g}_1^{\boldsymbol{s}}, \qquad \pi_1 = \mathrm{g}_1^{G_0^{(1)}(\boldsymbol{s})}, \qquad \ldots, \qquad \pi_\ell = \mathrm{g}_1^{G_1^{(\ell)}(G_0^{(\ell-1)}(\cdots(G_0^{(1)}(\boldsymbol{s}))))}.$$

Let us first consider the base-case of $\ell = 0$. In this case, our CVRF has exactly one possible input (the empty word ϵ), and $\mathcal{A}$ only gets the verification key $\mathrm{g}_2^{\boldsymbol{s}}$, while it has to distinguish the only possible output value $F_{\mathsf{sk}}(\epsilon) = \mathrm{g}_2^{\boldsymbol{s}^2}$ from random group elements.[7] Obviously, the pseudorandomness of our CVRF for $\ell = 0$ is equivalent to the decisional square Diffie-Hellman problem and, therefore, follows directly from the corresponding assumption.

The pseudorandomness of our construction for $\ell = 1$ follows now by applying recursive DDH. Indeed, by letting $c(\boldsymbol{s}) = \boldsymbol{s}^2$ be the squaring function and defining all hint functions h_0, h_1, h_2 to be empty (and letting $G^{(\ell)} = (G_0^{(\ell)}, G_1^{(\ell)})$ be the PRG randomly sampled by the assumption), recursive DDH implies directly that $F_{\mathsf{sk}}(0) = \mathrm{g}_2^{G_0^{(\ell)}(\boldsymbol{x})^2}$ is pseudorandom given $G_1^{(\ell)}(\boldsymbol{x})$ and $\pi_{\ell-1} = \mathrm{g}_1^{\boldsymbol{x}}$. Since $\mathcal{A}$ can compute $\mathsf{vk} = \mathrm{g}_2^{\boldsymbol{x}}$, $\pi_\ell = \mathrm{g}_1^{G_1^{(\ell)}(\boldsymbol{x})}$ and $F_{\mathsf{sk}}(1) = \mathrm{g}_2^{G_1^{(\ell)}(\boldsymbol{x})^2}$ from this data, recursive DDH implies now the pseudorandomness of our construction for input lengths $\ell = 1$. (Note that the secret key is now called $\boldsymbol{x}$ instead of $\boldsymbol{s}$.)

Applying recursive DDH a second time, now with $\ell = 2$, $h_0(\boldsymbol{s})$ being the empty function, $h_1(\boldsymbol{s}) = G_1^{(\ell)}(\boldsymbol{s})$, $h_2(\boldsymbol{s}) = G_1^{(\ell)}(\boldsymbol{s})^2$ and $c(\boldsymbol{s}) = G_0^{(\ell)}(\boldsymbol{s})^2$, yields that $F_{\mathsf{sk}}(00) = \mathrm{g}_2^{c(\boldsymbol{s})} = \mathrm{g}_2^{c(G_0^{(\ell-1)}(\boldsymbol{x}))} = \mathrm{g}_2^{G_0^{(\ell)}(G_0^{(\ell-1)}(\boldsymbol{x}))^2}$ stays pseudorandom, for $\boldsymbol{s} = G_0^{(\ell-1)}(\boldsymbol{x})$, even when given

$$\pi_\ell = \mathrm{g}_1^{h_1(\boldsymbol{s})} = \mathrm{g}_1^{G_1^{(\ell)}(G_0^{(\ell-1)}(\boldsymbol{x}))}, \qquad F_{\mathsf{sk}}(01) = \mathrm{g}_2^{h_2(\boldsymbol{s})} = \mathrm{g}_2^{G_1^{(\ell)}(G_0^{(\ell-1)}(\boldsymbol{x}))^2},$$
$$\mathsf{sk}_1 = G_1^{(\ell-1)}(\boldsymbol{x}), \qquad \pi_{\ell-1} = \mathrm{g}_1^{\boldsymbol{x}}.$$

Again, $\mathcal{A}$ can compute the remaining element $\mathsf{vk} = \mathrm{g}_2^{\boldsymbol{x}}$ on its own, hence, the pseudorandomness of our CVRF for $\ell = 2$. Applying recursive DDH a third time will imply the pseudorandomness of our CVRF for inputs of length $\ell = 3$, and

[7] The proof of the correctness of $F_{\mathsf{sk}}(\epsilon)$ is given by the group element vector $\mathrm{g}_1^{\boldsymbol{s}}$. However, since $\ell = 0$, $\mathcal{A}$ can challenge the pseudorandomness of the CVRF at one point and, hence, not receive this proof element.

so on. Hence, the security of our CVRF candidate in the selective pseudorandomness game for inputs of length ℓ follows directly by the decisional square Diffie-Hellman assumption and ℓ applications of our recursive DDH assumption.

Proving Recursive DDH in the Generic Group Model. We will sketch now how to prove the soundness of the recursive DDH assumption in Maurer's Generic Group Model (GGM) [44].[8] First, let us give a high-level overview: We perform two game hops to remove the additional auxiliary information given in the then-challenge. The first game hop replaces $\mathrm{g}_1^{\boldsymbol{x}}$ by dummy-elements. Since we are committed to $\mathrm{g}_1^{\boldsymbol{x}}$ by $G_1(\boldsymbol{x})$ and $\mathrm{g}_2^{\boldsymbol{s}} = \mathrm{g}_2^{G_0(\boldsymbol{x})}$, we cannot use the standard GGM technique of replacing $\mathrm{g}_1^{\boldsymbol{x}}$ by uniformly random group elements. Instead, we answer group queries using a carefully designed algebraic procedure. Omitting details for now, it allows us to invoke MQ+ to argue that the adversary cannot detect this change. After removing $\mathrm{g}_1^{\boldsymbol{x}}$, we perform a second game hop and replace $\boldsymbol{s} = G_0(\boldsymbol{x})$ and $G_1(\boldsymbol{x})$ by uniform randomness. The indistinguishability of both games follows directly from the MQ assumption. In the last game, $\boldsymbol{s}$ has been sampled uniformly at random and $\mathrm{g}_1^{\boldsymbol{x}}, G_1(\boldsymbol{x})$ have been removed. Now, we finish the security proof of recursive DDH by reducing the if-problem to this game.

Next, we introduce and discuss the MQ and MQ+ assumptions, and then give a more elaborated proof sketch of the soundness of recursive DDH in the GGM under MQ and MQ+.

MQ and MQ+. The decisional *Multivariate Quadratic* (MQ) problem is a post-quantum assumption on the hardness of solving random systems of multivariate quadratic equations. It is used to construct non-interactive zero-knowledge proofs [22] and underlies the security of a large proportion of candidates [4,7–9] in NIST's standardization process for additional post-quantum signatures. MQ+ is a computational assumption, similar to MQ, that requires an adversary to extract a simple non-trivial relationship about the solution of a random quadratic equation system. While the MQ+ problem is likely not equivalent to the MQ problem, we will present some intuitive arguments why MQ+ should be hard whenever MQ is hard in the full version [17, App. A.2]. Essentially, if there would be an MQ+ solver that outputs fresh solutions for MQ+, we could leverage it to a solving algorithm for MQ (under some assumptions).

For our construction, we need to assume, at a minimum, that G is a PRG. Indeed, otherwise an adversary could invert $G_1(\boldsymbol{x})$ and break the then-challenge, while the if-challenge might still be intractable for it. Note that we sample G as a function where each output is computed by a uniformly random quadratic polynomial $g \in \mathbb{Z}_p[X_1, \ldots, X_n]$ over $\mathbb{Z}_p$ in n variables. Distinguishing outputs of G from uniform randomness constitutes exactly the decisional MQ problem.

[8] Remember that in the GGM a generic adversary obtains handles for group elements, which only allow it to perform group and pairing operations. In Maurer's GGM, those handles are deterministic and given by increasing register addresses. As alternative model, one can also consider Shoup's GGM [50] where handles are uniformly random bit strings.

Now, the *MQ+* problem is intuitively similar. Formally, the MQ+ assumption states that it is hard for a PPT adversary, when given $2n$ uniformly random degree-2 polynomials $g_1, \ldots, g_{2n} \in \mathbb{Z}_p[X_1, \ldots, X_n]$, which compute $G : \mathbb{Z}_p^n \to \mathbb{Z}_p^{2n}$ for example, and their values $g_1(\boldsymbol{x}), \ldots, g_{2n}(\boldsymbol{x})$ on a secret point $\boldsymbol{x} \leftarrow_\$ \mathbb{Z}_p^n$, to find an additional quadratic polynomial $h \in \mathbb{Z}_p[X_1, \ldots, X_n]$ that vanishes on $\boldsymbol{x}$ but is linearly independent of $g_1(X) - g_1(\boldsymbol{x}), \ldots, g_{2n}(X) - g_{2n}(\boldsymbol{x})$. Let us explain this: when given $g_1, \ldots, g_{2n}$ and $g_1(\boldsymbol{x}), \ldots, g_{2n}(\boldsymbol{x})$, it is trivial to find new polynomials that vanish on $\boldsymbol{x}$, even if we do not know $\boldsymbol{x}$. Indeed, any linear combination $h(X) = \alpha_1 \cdot (g_1(X) - g_1(\boldsymbol{x})) + \cdots + \alpha_{2n} \cdot (g_{2n}(X) - g_{2n}(\boldsymbol{x}))$ must be zero at $\boldsymbol{x}$. On the other hand, finding a degree-2 polynomial h that vanishes on $\boldsymbol{x}$ and does not lie in the space spanned by $g_1(X) - g_1(\boldsymbol{x}), \ldots, g_{2n}(X) - g_{2n}(\boldsymbol{x})$ would give us a new and non-trivial information about the solution of the equation system $g_1(X) = g_1(\boldsymbol{x}), \ldots, g_{2n}(X) = g_{2n}(\boldsymbol{x})$. Indeed, if we would be able to solve the MQ+ problem $O(n^2)$ times with fresh and independent solutions $h_1, h_2 \ldots$, we could simply linearize the quadratic equation system and solve it trivially. We will postpone cryptanalysis of MQ and MQ+ for now, and continue with showing how both assumptions imply recursive DDH in the generic group model.

Proof Sketch. Let Samp be an efficient probabilistic sampling algorithm that on input $1^\lambda, p, n$ outputs functions $c\colon \mathbb{Z}_p^n \to \mathbb{Z}_p^n$, $h_0\colon \mathbb{Z}_p^n \to \mathbb{Z}_p^{m_0}$, $h_1\colon \mathbb{Z}_p^n \to \mathbb{Z}_p^{m_1}$, $h_2\colon \mathbb{Z}_p^n \to \mathbb{Z}_p^{m_2}$. To prove the soundness of the assumption, we need to reduce the hardness of the if-challenge, which consists of distinguishing $\mathbf{g}_2^{c(\boldsymbol{s})}$ from random group elements when given $h_0(\boldsymbol{s})$, $\mathbf{g}_1^{h_1(\boldsymbol{s})}$ and $\mathbf{g}_2^{h_2(\boldsymbol{s})}$, to the hardness of the then-challenge, which consists of distinguishing $\mathbf{g}_2^{c(\boldsymbol{s})}$ from random group elements when given $h_0(\boldsymbol{s})$, $\mathbf{g}_1^{h_1(\boldsymbol{s})}$, $\mathbf{g}_2^{h_2(\boldsymbol{s})}$ and additionally $\mathbf{g}_1^{\boldsymbol{x}}$, $G_1(\boldsymbol{x})$ where $\boldsymbol{s} = G_0(\boldsymbol{x})$ (for a uniformly random quadratic map $G = (G_0, G_1)\colon \mathbb{Z}_p^n \to \mathbb{Z}_p^{2n}$).

Let G_0 be the game between an adversary $\mathcal{A}$ and a then-challenger Ch. To prove the recursive DDH assumption, we need to change G_0 to a game to which the if-challenge can be directly reduced.

Step 1: Removing $\mathbf{g}_1^{\boldsymbol{x}}$. As a first step, we would like to replace the group elements $\mathbf{g}_1^{\boldsymbol{x}}$ given to the adversary by random group elements or dummy elements, which are devoid of any information about $\boldsymbol{x}$. The problem, however, is that we are committed to $\boldsymbol{x}$ in two different ways: by $\mathbf{g}_2^{\boldsymbol{s}} = \mathbf{g}_2^{G_0(\boldsymbol{x})}$ and by $G_1(\boldsymbol{x})$. Indeed, replacing $\mathbf{g}_1^{\boldsymbol{x}}$ naively by group elements $\mathbf{g}_1^{\boldsymbol{x}'}$, for $\boldsymbol{x} \neq \boldsymbol{x}' \in \mathbb{Z}_p^n$, can directly be detected by $\mathcal{A}$ by applying G_0 or G_1 in the exponent of $\mathbf{g}_1^{\boldsymbol{x}'}$ and comparing the result with $\mathbf{g}_2^{G_0(\boldsymbol{x})}$ or $G_1(\boldsymbol{x})$.

To solve this problem, let $g_1, \ldots, g_{2n} \in \mathbb{Z}_p[X_1, \ldots, X_n]$ be the quadratic polynomials computing G. Additionally, since $\mathcal{A}$ is generic, we model each of its group queries by polynomials on the exponents of its given group elements. This means, $\mathcal{A}$ can only submit group queries in the form of polynomials f to its group oracle. Whenever $\mathcal{A}$ submits such a query f, Ch has to tell $\mathcal{A}$ if f does vanish on the exponents of the given group elements. Given the bilinearity of the involved groups, all of those polynomials are quadratic.

Our novel technique for the first hybrid step consists in replacing $\mathsf{g}_1^{\boldsymbol{x}} = (\mathsf{g}_1^{x_1}, \ldots, \mathsf{g}_1^{x_n})$ by dummy-elements $\mathsf{g}_1^{X} = (\mathsf{g}_1^{X_1}, \ldots, \mathsf{g}_1^{X_n})$ and by devising an *algebraic algorithm* for answering group queries of the adversary. Concretely, in this new game, which we call G_1, Ch tells $\mathcal{A}$ that an equality-check[9] $f \in \mathbb{Z}_p[X_1, \ldots, X_n]$ passes on the exponents of $\mathsf{g}_1^{\boldsymbol{x}}$, i.e. $f(\boldsymbol{x}) = 0$, if it lies in the $\mathbb{Z}_p$-vector space

$$V := \mathrm{span}_{\mathbb{Z}_p}[g_1(X) - s_1, \ldots, g_n(X) - s_n, g_{n+1}(X) - w_1, \ldots, g_{2n}(X) - w_n]$$

spanned by $g_1(X) - s_1, \ldots, g_n(X) - s_n$, $g_{n+1}(X) - w_1, \ldots, g_{2n}(X) - w_n \in \mathbb{Z}_p[X]$ where $\boldsymbol{s} = G_0(\boldsymbol{x})$ denotes the left-hand and $\boldsymbol{w} := G_1(\boldsymbol{x})$ the right-hand output of $G(\boldsymbol{x})$.

To prove that $\mathcal{A}$ cannot distinguish between G_0 and G_1, we invoke the MQ+ assumption. Indeed, $\mathcal{A}$ can only distinguish between both games if it can come up with a query f that passes in one game and fails in the other one. Since $(\boldsymbol{s}, \boldsymbol{w}) = G(\boldsymbol{x})$, we must have $f(\boldsymbol{x}) = 0$ whenever $f \in V$. Hence, to notice a difference, $\mathcal{A}$ must output a query f that passes in G_0 ($f(\boldsymbol{x}) = 0$), but fails in G_1 ($f \notin V$). Such a polynomial f is exactly a solution to the MQ+ problem with respect to $G = (G_0, G_1)$, which asks for a non-trivial degree-2 polynomial that vanishes on $\boldsymbol{x}$. Assuming the hardness of MQ+, we can deduce that $\mathcal{A}$ can not distinguish between the *honest* way of answering group queries in G_0 and our novel algebraic way of answering queries in G_1.

Step 2: Removing $G_1(\boldsymbol{x})$. In G_2, we switch $(\boldsymbol{s}, \boldsymbol{w})$ from $(G_0(\boldsymbol{x}), G_1(\boldsymbol{x}))$ to two uniformly random vectors in $\mathbb{Z}_p^n$. Indistinguishability follows directly from the normal MQ assumption. Indeed, after Step 1, all group elements given to $\mathcal{A}$ (and thus all information $\mathcal{A}$ can determine by generic group queries) do not depend on $\boldsymbol{x}$, but only on $(G_0(\boldsymbol{x}), G_1(\boldsymbol{x}))$.

Step 3: Reducing the if-Challenge to G_2. Finally, in G_2, $\boldsymbol{w}$ is uniformly random and independent of $\boldsymbol{s}$ and all other information given to $\mathcal{A}$. Additionally, $\mathcal{A}$ is given simulated group elements g_1^{X} instead of the real group elements $\mathsf{g}_1^{\boldsymbol{x}}$. At this point, we can reduce the if-challenge to G_2 by simulating all extra information ($\mathsf{g}_1^{\boldsymbol{x}}$ and $G_1(\boldsymbol{x})$) the then-adversary $\mathcal{A}$ would receive. There are some technicalities involved in how group queries of $\mathcal{A}$ are handled, as a reduction does not know $\boldsymbol{s}$ in plain. However, these issues can be solved by algebraically decomposing the group queries of $\mathcal{A}$. Refer to the full proof in Sect. 5 for details.

Cryptanalysis of Our Assumptions. Security hinges on our new recursive DDH assumption. In this work, recursive DDH only functions as an intermediate

[9] Note that $\mathcal{A}$'s equality checks must actually involve more variables. In fact, besides $X_1, \ldots, X_n$, f should contain variables $S_1, \ldots, S_n$ representing the exponents of $\mathsf{g}_2^{\boldsymbol{s}} \in \mathbb{G}_2^n$, variables $C_1, \ldots, C_n$ representing the exponents of $\mathsf{g}_2^{c(\boldsymbol{s})} \in \mathbb{G}_2^n$, variables $H_1^{(1)}, \ldots, H_{m_1}^{(1)}$ representing the exponents of $\mathsf{g}_1^{h_1(\boldsymbol{s})} \in \mathbb{G}_1^{m_1}$ and variables $H_1^{(2)}, \ldots, H_{m_2}^{(2)}$ representing the exponents of $\mathsf{g}_2^{h_2(\boldsymbol{s})} \in \mathbb{G}_2^{m_2}$. To keep this exposition simple, we neglect this fact and consider here group queries of $\mathcal{A}$ that only involve the elements $\mathsf{g}_1^{\boldsymbol{x}}$.

step to prove the security of our construction, and we can prove the soundness of our assumption in an idealized model under MQ and MQ+.

While MQ is a well-studied standard assumption in cryptography, MQ+ is a novel variation of it. While there is no direct reduction from MQ to MQ+, the hardness of the MQ+ problem should be comparable to the hardness of the MQ problem. Indeed, XL-style attacks [20,21,46,47,54], which are based on computing *Macaulay matrices*, should not be faster on MQ+ than on MQ, and any efficient algorithm for solving MQ+ would, intuitively, imply a fast solving algorithm for MQ. We refer to the full version [17, App. A] for detailed cryptanalytic discussions on recursive DDH, MQ and MQ+.

On Generic Constructions. Finally, let us address the question if it is possible to construct CVRFs generically from Non-Interactive Zero-Knowledge proofs (NIZKs) and CPRFs. First, we want to point out that NIZKs, and other primitives depending on random oracles or common reference strings, are infeasible for this task, as the very strict requirement of unique provability needs to hold, even for *malformed* oracles and reference strings. However, in the plain model, one may still ask if it is possible to enhance CPRFs with verifiability by using non-interactive witness-indistinguishable proofs (NIWIs). Prior works [11,30] constructed VRFs from NIWIs, puncturable PRFs and commitments. It is possible to extend these constructions to CVRFs, however, with significant drawbacks on security (and efficiency given the sizes of the involved NIWI proofs). The crux lies in the path-invariance Definition 6, respectively, the lack thereof. Path-invariance is a technical property that allows us to significantly simplify the security game for CVRFs. A NIWI-based CVRF (following the blueprint of [11,30]) not only fails to be path-invariant, it is also not possible to prove it secure in more elaborate security games that better reflect reality; refer to the full version [17, App. C].

Applications. We discuss three potential applications of our construction and of CVRFs in general. These are Exponent VRFs [12], stake pooling, and compressible randomness beacons [31]. Due to space constraints we defer the details to the full version [17, § 1.4].

1.4 Related Work

CPRFs have been introduced by [14,15,38]. Notably, [14] gave instantiations for constraints specified by arbitrary circuits, assuming mmaps. CPRFs for inputs of unbounded length and constraints specified by Turing machines have been given by [2,26] using iO.

The first candidate VRFs have been constructed by [45] assuming the hardness of factoring. Important VRFs have been put forth by Lysyanskaya [43] and Dodis & Yampolskiy [27], which described two styles of pairing-based VRFs. Most pairing-based VRFs use q-type assumptions [1,6,13,27,35–37,43,48,53] to achieve small proof sizes, or are based on DLIN [33,39,49]. [16] showed that it is hard for a pairing-based VRF to achieve constant-size proofs and assumptions at the same time. It is possible to construct VRFs generically from NIWIs [10,30]

Initially, [19,28] constructed CVRFs based on the CPRFs of [14]. They achieve bit-fixing and circuit constraints using mmaps. Subsequent CVRF candidates also enjoy circuit constrainability and use iO: [41] achieves selective security, [42] extends their security notion and [55] achieves adaptive security under iO. Additionally, [24,25] construct CVRFs for unbounded inputs. An exception is [23], which constructs CVRFs from functional encryption (which is equivalent to iO up to subexponential loss). In comparison, our construction only supports less expressive constraints, but builds upon significantly simpler building blocks.

2 Preliminaries

Notation. Denote by $\lambda \in \mathbb{N}$ the security parameter. We denote the output of deterministic and probabilistic algorithms by $y = D(x)$ and $y \leftarrow P(x)$, respectively. Denote by $x \leftarrow\!\!\$\ X$ that x is sampled uniformly at random from the set X. Denote by $2^X = \{A : A \subseteq X\}$ the power set of X. Set $[n] := \{x \in \mathbb{N} : 1 \leq x \leq n\}$ where $\mathbb{N} = \{1, 2, 3, \ldots\}$ is the set of natural numbers.

We denote elements of cyclic groups $\mathbb{G}, \mathbb{G}_1, \mathbb{G}_2$ of order p by monospaced letters $\mathtt{g}, \mathtt{g}_1, \mathtt{g}_2$. Given a vector $\boldsymbol{x} = (x_1, \ldots, x_n) \in \mathbb{Z}_p^n$ and a group element $\mathtt{h} \in \mathbb{G}$, we denote by $\mathtt{h}^{\boldsymbol{x}}$ the vector of group elements $(\mathtt{h}^{x_1}, \ldots, \mathtt{h}^{x_n}) \in \mathbb{G}^n$.

For a bit $b \in \{0,1\}$, set $\overline{b} = 1 - b$. We denote the length of a bit string $x \in \{0,1\}^*$ by $|x|$. Let ϵ be the empty word of length 0 and note that $\{0,1\}^0 = \{\epsilon\}$. For $\ell \in \mathbb{N}$, we write $\{0,1\}^\ell$ to denote the bit strings of length ℓ. By $\{0,1\}^{\leq \ell}$ we denote the set of all bit strings of length at most ℓ, including ϵ. We denote string concatenation by $x \cdot y$ and sometimes write xy to avoid clutter. Given a bit string $x \in \{0,1\}^\ell$, we denote its bits by $x = x_1 \cdots x_\ell$. A bit string $x \in \{0,1\}^*$ is a *prefix* of a bit string $y \in \{0,1\}^*$ if there exists $w \in \{0,1\}^*$ such that $x \cdot w = y$.

On Groups. We will consider a definition of symmetric bilinear groups akin to certified bilinear groups as given in [33].

Definition 1 (Symmetric Bilinear Groups). *A (symmetric)* bilinear group, *is a pair of cyclic groups $\mathbb{G}_1, \mathbb{G}_2$ of prime order p with generators $\mathtt{g}_1$, $\mathtt{g}_2$ and a map $e\colon \mathbb{G}_1 \times \mathbb{G}_1 \to \mathbb{G}_2$ s.t. the following holds: e is bilinear, i.e., $e(\mathtt{g}_1^a, \mathtt{g}_1^b) = e(\mathtt{g}_1, \mathtt{g}_1)^{ab}$ for all $a, b \in \mathbb{Z}$, and e is perfect, i.e., $e(\mathtt{g}_1, \mathtt{g}_1) = \mathtt{g}_2$. We require that e and the group operations on $\mathbb{G}_1$ and $\mathbb{G}_2$ are efficiently computable.*

As a small technicality, we additionally require $\mathbb{G}_1, \mathbb{G}_2$ to have unique, recognizable representations of its elements. That is for each element $\mathtt{h}_1 \in \mathbb{G}_1$, there is a canonical encoding as a bit string $\langle \mathtt{h}_1 \rangle_1$. Further, there is a verification algorithm $\mathsf{GrpVfy}_1(s)$, *which on input of a supposed bit-string description of an element s outputs 0 or 1. The encoding is uniquely recognizable in the sense that* $\mathsf{GrpVfy}_1(s) = 1$ *implies that there is $a \in \mathbb{Z}_p$ such that $s = \langle \mathtt{g}_1^a \rangle_1$. The same holds respectively for an encoding $\langle \mathtt{h}_2 \rangle_2$ and a verification algorithm* $\mathsf{GrpVfy}_2(s)$ *in $\mathbb{G}_2$. When referring to a group element $\mathtt{h}$ in $\mathbb{G}_1$ or $\mathbb{G}_2$ as input in the following, we will implicitly mean its unique encoding, which is implicitly checked to be a valid group element encoding at the beginning of each algorithm.*

In this work, we use Maurer's generic model [44] for bilinear groups. Concretely, access to the elements and operations on the two groups $\mathbb{G}_1, \mathbb{G}_2$ (isomorphic to $\mathbb{Z}_p$) with a non-trivial bilinear (symmetric) pairing $e\colon \mathbb{G}_1 \times \mathbb{G}_1 \to \mathbb{G}_2$ are hidden behind oracles. Further, instead of real group elements, a generic adversary is given handles which only point to elements used by the oracles to perform group operations. Whenever a group query is made to an oracle to perform a certain group operation, handles for the involved group elements and possibly a number in $\mathbb{Z}_p$ has to be supplied. In Maurer's original model, the oracle will then respond with a handle for a new group element (which will be stored internally) and a list of pairs of handles which point to equal group elements.

We will deviate here from Maurer's original model by making equality checks explicit. First note that the adversaries in our setting do not need to output group elements. Instead, they only need to output bits. Hence, we also do not need to give them handles for new group elements after performing group operations. To make this precise, we will define generic adversaries as algorithms that receive handles for group elements as inputs and may only query if some degree-2 polynomial over the exponents of the group elements vanishes. This means, the generic adversary can only query if some computation on its group elements yields the trivial group element, or if two of its computed group elements collide. We model this by allowing it to submit degree-2 polynomials to some oracle, which tells the adversary if the polynomial would vanish on the exponents of the group elements.

The difference between Maurer's original model and our interpretation of it is polynomial: in Maurer's original model, an adversary needs to query q group operations to receive the result of $(q+n)^2$ equality checks, where n is the number of received group elements at the start of the experiment. In our variation, the adversary needs to perform $(q+n)^2$ equality checks, which is by a polynomial amount larger than q.

Definition 2 (Generic Adversaries). *An adversary is called* generic *if it works as follows: At the beginning of a security game, the generic adversary receives a number of source group element handles, let's say* $\mathsf{g}_1^{x_1}, \ldots, \mathsf{g}_1^{x_n}$ *and* $\mathsf{g}_2^{y_1}, \ldots, \mathsf{g}_2^{y_m}$*, where* g_1 *and* g_2 *are fixed generators of* $\mathbb{G}_1$ *and* $\mathbb{G}_2$*, respectively, with* $e(\mathsf{g}_1, \mathsf{g}_1) = \mathsf{g}_2$*. It may now only query equality checks, which are modelled by* $h \in \mathbb{Z}_p[X_1, \ldots, X_n, Y_1, \ldots, Y_m]$*, which must have the shape*

$$h(X, Y) = \sum_{i,j=1}^{n} \alpha_{i,j} X_i X_j + \sum_{k=1}^{m} \beta_k Y_k$$

for some $\alpha_{i,j}, \beta_k \in \mathbb{Z}_p$. Whenever the simulator of the group receives such a polynomial h, it has to reply with "$h(\boldsymbol{x}, \boldsymbol{y}) = 0$" if $h(x_1, \ldots, x_n, y_1, \ldots, y_m) = 0$. (This means, the equality check passes.) Otherwise, the simulator has to reply with "$h(\boldsymbol{x}, \boldsymbol{y}) \neq 0$".

On Pseudorandom Functions

Definition 3 (Constrained Pseudorandom Function). *A constrained* pseudorandom function *(CPRF) with input domain $\mathcal{X} = \mathcal{X}(\lambda)$, output codomain $\mathcal{Y} = \mathcal{Y}(\lambda)$, and set of efficiently representable constraints $\mathcal{C} = \mathcal{C}(\lambda) \subseteq 2^{\mathcal{X}}$ where $\emptyset \in \mathcal{C}$ is a tuple* $\mathsf{CPRF} = (\mathsf{Setup}, \mathsf{Constrain}, \mathsf{Eval})$ *of three (probabilistic) polynomial-time algorithms*

$\mathsf{Setup}(1^\lambda) \rightarrow \mathsf{sk}_\emptyset$: *Given a unary encoded security parameter, samples a secret key $\mathsf{sk}_\emptyset$, which may evaluate all inputs $\mathcal{X}$.*
$\mathsf{Constrain}(\mathsf{sk}_C, C') = \mathsf{sk}_{C'}$: *Given a secret key sk_C with constraint $C \in \mathcal{C}$ and a constraint $C' \in \mathcal{C}$, outputs the constrained secret key $\mathsf{sk}_{C'}$ or $\perp$.*
$\mathsf{Eval}(\mathsf{sk}_C, x) = y$: *Given a secret key sk_C with constraint $C \in \mathcal{C}$ and an input $x \in \mathcal{X}$, outputs $y \in \mathcal{Y}$ or $\perp$. This algorithm needs to be deterministic.*

A CPRF has to fulfill the following properties:

d**-Delegability:** *For any constraints $\emptyset = C_0 \subseteq \cdots \subseteq C_d$ with $C_i \in \mathcal{C}$, any $x \in \mathcal{X} \setminus C_d$ and any $\mathsf{sk}_{C_0} \leftarrow \mathsf{Setup}(1^\lambda)$ it holds that*

$$\mathsf{Eval}(\mathsf{sk}_{C_0}, x) = \cdots = \mathsf{Eval}(\mathsf{sk}_{C_d}, x)$$

where $\mathsf{sk}_{C_1} = \mathsf{Constrain}(\mathsf{sk}_{C_0}, C_1)$, ..., $\mathsf{sk}_{C_d} = \mathsf{Constrain}(\mathsf{sk}_{C_{d-1}}, C_d)$.

(t, q, d, μ)**-Selective Pseudorandomness:** *Consider the following game parameterized by λ that is played by an adversary $\mathcal{A}$ making at most q queries:*

1. *Sample* $\mathsf{sk}_\emptyset \leftarrow \mathsf{Setup}(1^\lambda)$ *and* $b \leftarrow_\$ \{0,1\}$.
2. *$\mathcal{A}$ outputs a list of constraint queries $((C_i^h)_{h=0}^{d_i})_{i \in [q_1]}$ where $0 \leq d_i \leq d$ and $\emptyset = C_i^0 \subseteq C_i^1 \subseteq \cdots \subseteq C_i^{d_i}$.*
3. *$\mathcal{A}$ outputs a list of input queries $(x_j, (C_j^h)_{h=0}^{d_j})_{j \in [q_2]}$ where $0 \leq d_j \leq d$ and $\emptyset = C_j^0 \subseteq C_j^1 \subseteq \cdots \subseteq C_j^{d_j}$, $x_j \notin C_j^{d_j}$.*
4. *$\mathcal{A}$ outputs a challenge input $(x^*, (C^h)_{h=0}^{d^*})$ where $0 \leq d^* \leq d$ and $\emptyset = C^0 \subseteq C^1 \subseteq \cdots \subseteq C^{d^*}$, $x^* \notin C^{d^*}$.*
5. *Set* $\mathsf{sk}_{C_i^0} = \mathsf{sk}_\emptyset$ *and* $\mathsf{sk}_{C_j^0} = \mathsf{sk}_\emptyset$ *in the following. $\mathcal{A}$ receives* $(\mathsf{sk}_{C_i^{d_i}})_{i \in [q_1]}$ *where* $\mathsf{sk}_{C_i^h} \leftarrow \mathsf{Constrain}(\mathsf{sk}_{C_i^{h-1}}, C_i^h)$ *for $h \in [d_i]$.*
6. *$\mathcal{A}$ receives* $(y_j = \mathsf{Eval}(\mathsf{sk}_{C_j^{d_j}}, x_j))_{j \in [q_2]}$ *where* $\mathsf{sk}_{C_j^h} \leftarrow \mathsf{Constrain}(\mathsf{sk}_{C_j^{h-1}}, C_j^h)$ *for $h \in [d_j]$. and we set $C_j^0 = \emptyset$.*
7. *$\mathcal{A}$ receives y_b^* where* $y_0^* = \mathsf{Eval}(\mathsf{sk}_{C^{d^*}}, x^*)$ *and* $\mathsf{sk}_{C^h} \leftarrow \mathsf{Constrain}(\mathsf{sk}_{C^{h-1}}, C^h)$ *for $h \in [d^*]$ and $y_1^* \leftarrow_\$ \mathcal{Y}$.*
8. *$\mathcal{A}$ outputs a guess b^*.*

We say "$\mathcal{A}$ wins" if and only if $b = b^*$, $q_1 + q_2 \leq q$, $C^{h-1} \subseteq C^h$ for $h \in [d^*]$, $x^* \in C_i^{d_i}$ for all $i \in [q_1]$, and $x_j \neq x^*$ for all $j \in [q_2]$. The advantage *of $\mathcal{A}$ in the above game is*

$$\mathrm{Adv}_{\mathsf{CPRF}}^{\mathcal{A}}(\lambda) = \Pr[\mathcal{A} \text{ wins}] - 1/2$$

where the probability is taken over the randomness of $\mathcal{A}$ and the game. CPRF *is* (t, q, d, μ)-selective pseudorandom *if, for every $\mathcal{A}$ running in time at most $t(\lambda)$ making at most $q(\lambda)$ queries, it holds that $\mathrm{Adv}_{\mathsf{CPRF}}^{\mathcal{A}}(\lambda) \leq \mu(\lambda)$.*

We call CPRF delegable *if it is d-delegable for every* $d \in \text{poly}(\lambda)$*, and* (t, d, μ)-selective pseudorandom *if it is* (t, q, d, μ)-selective pseudorandom *for every* $q \in \text{poly}(\lambda)$.

Definition 4 (Puncturable CPRF). *A CPRF with input domain* $\mathcal{X}$ *and set of constraints* $\mathcal{C}$ *is* puncturable *if* $\{x\} \in \mathcal{C}$ *for every* $x \in \mathcal{X}$.

Definition 5 (Constrained Verifiable Pseudorandom Function). *A* constrained verifiable pseudorandom function *(CVRF) with public parameter space* $\mathcal{P} = \mathcal{P}(\lambda)$*, input domain* $\mathcal{X} = \mathcal{X}(\lambda)$*, output codomain* $\mathcal{Y} = \mathcal{Y}(\lambda)$*, and set of constraints* $\mathcal{C} = \mathcal{C}(\lambda) \subseteq 2^{\mathcal{X}}$ *where* $\emptyset \in \mathcal{C}$ *is a tuple* $\mathsf{CVRF} = (\mathsf{Setup}, \mathsf{Constrain}, \mathsf{Eval}, \mathsf{Verify}, \mathsf{VerifyC})$ *of five (probabilistic) polynomial-time algorithms*

$\mathsf{Setup}(1^\lambda) \to (\mathsf{pp}, \mathsf{sk}_\emptyset, \mathsf{vk}, \pi_\emptyset)$*: Given a unary encoded security parameter, samples public parameters* $\mathsf{pp} \in \mathcal{P}$*, secret key* $\mathsf{sk}_\emptyset$*, verification key* vk*, and proof* $\pi_\emptyset$.[10]

$\mathsf{Constrain}_{\mathsf{pp}}(\mathsf{sk}_C, \pi_C, C') \to (\mathsf{sk}_{C'}, \pi_{C'})$*: Given a secret key* sk_C *with constraint* $C \in \mathcal{C}$*, proof* π_C*, and a constraint* $C' \in \mathcal{C}$*, outputs the constrained secret key* $\mathsf{sk}_{C'}$ *and proof* $\pi_{C'}$*, or* $\perp$.

$\mathsf{Eval}_{\mathsf{pp}}(\mathsf{sk}_C, \pi_C, x) \to (y, \pi)$*: Given a secret key* sk_C *with constraint* $C \in \mathcal{C}$ *and an input* $x \in \mathcal{X}$*, outputs* $y \in \mathcal{Y}$ *and proof* π*, or* $\perp$*. The computation of* y *needs to be deterministic.*

$\mathsf{VerifyC}_{\mathsf{pp}}(\mathsf{vk}, C, \mathsf{sk}_C, \pi_C) = b$*: Given the verification key* vk*, constraint* $C \in \mathcal{C}$*, constrained secret key* sk_C*, and proof* π_C*, outputs* $b \in \{\mathsf{ACCEPT}, \mathsf{REJECT}\}$.

$\mathsf{Verify}_{\mathsf{pp}}(\mathsf{vk}, x, y, \pi) = b$*: Given the verification key* vk*, input* $x \in \mathcal{X}$*, output* $y \in \mathcal{Y}$*, and proof* π*, outputs* $b \in \{\mathsf{ACCEPT}, \mathsf{REJECT}\}$.

A CVRF has to fulfill the following properties:

d-Delegability: *For any constraints* $\emptyset = C_0 \subsetneq \cdots \subsetneq C_d$ *with* $C_i \in \mathcal{C}$*, and* $x \in \mathcal{X} \setminus C_d$ *it holds that*

$$\Pr\left[\begin{matrix}\mathsf{VerifyC}_{\mathsf{pp}}(\mathsf{vk}, C_0, \mathsf{sk}_{C_0}, \pi_{C_0}) = \cdots = \mathsf{VerifyC}_{\mathsf{pp}}(\mathsf{vk}, C_d, \mathsf{sk}_{C_d}, \pi_{C_d}) = \\ \mathsf{Verify}_{\mathsf{pp}}(\mathsf{vk}, x, y_0, \pi_0) = \cdots = \mathsf{Verify}_{\mathsf{pp}}(\mathsf{vk}, x, y_d, \pi_d) = \mathsf{ACCEPT}\end{matrix}\right] = 1$$

where the probability is over $(\mathsf{pp}, \mathsf{sk}_{C_0}, \mathsf{vk}, \pi_{C_0}) \leftarrow \mathsf{Setup}(1^\lambda)$*, and* $(\mathsf{sk}_{C_i}, \pi_{C_i}) \leftarrow \mathsf{Constrain}(\mathsf{sk}_{C_{i-1}}, \pi_{C_{i-1}}, C_i)$ *and* $(y_i, \pi_i) \leftarrow \mathsf{Eval}_{\mathsf{pp}}(\mathsf{sk}_{C_i}, \pi_{C_i}, x)$ *for* $i \in [d]$.

Unique Provability: *For all (even malformed) public parameters* pp*, verification keys* vk*, and proofs* π, π' *as well as all inputs* $x \in \mathcal{X}$ *and outputs* $y, y' \in \mathcal{Y}$*, it holds that*

$$\mathsf{Verify}_{\mathsf{pp}}(\mathsf{vk}, x, y, \pi) = \mathsf{Verify}_{\mathsf{pp}}(\mathsf{vk}, x, y', \pi') = \mathsf{ACCEPT} \implies y = y'.$$

[10] The proof $\pi_\emptyset$ is a formality that allows us to streamline definitions and syntax. $\pi_\emptyset$ can be seen as part of $\mathsf{sk}_\emptyset$.

Functionality Binding: *For all (even malformed) public parameters* pp*, verification keys* vk*, secret keys* $\mathsf{sk}_C, \mathsf{sk}'_C$ *and proofs* π_C, π'_C *the following holds: If*

$$\mathsf{VerifyC}_{\mathsf{pp}}(\mathsf{vk}, C, \mathsf{sk}_C, \pi_C) = \mathsf{VerifyC}_{\mathsf{pp}}(\mathsf{vk}, C, \mathsf{sk}'_C, \pi'_C) = \mathsf{ACCEPT},$$

then, for all inputs $x \in \mathcal{X} \setminus C$*, for all* $(y, \pi) \leftarrow \mathsf{Eval}(\mathsf{sk}_C, \pi_C, x)$ *and* $(y', \pi') \leftarrow \mathsf{Eval}(\mathsf{sk}'_C, \pi'_C, x)$ *it holds that* $y = y'$.

(t, q, d, μ)**-Selective Pseudorandomness:** *Consider the following game parameterized by* λ *that is played by an adversary* $\mathcal{A}$ *making at most* q *queries:*

1. *Sample* $(\mathsf{pp}, \mathsf{sk}_\emptyset, \mathsf{vk}, \pi_\emptyset) \leftarrow \mathsf{Setup}(1^\lambda)$ *and* $b \leftarrow_{\$} \{0,1\}$.
2. $\mathcal{A}$ *outputs a list of constraint queries* $((C_i^h)_{h=0}^{d_i})_{i\in[q_1]}$ *where* $0 \le d_i \le d$ *and* $\emptyset = C_i^0 \subseteq C_i^1 \subseteq \cdots \subseteq C_i^{d_i}$.
3. $\mathcal{A}$ *outputs a list of input queries* $(x_j, (C_j^h)_{h=0}^{d_j})_{j\in[q_2]}$ *where* $0 \le d_j \le d$ *and* $\emptyset = C_j^0 \subseteq C_j^1 \subseteq \cdots \subseteq C_j^{d_j}$, $x_j \notin C_j^{d_j}$.
4. $\mathcal{A}$ *outputs a challenge input* $(x^*, (C^h)_{h=0}^{d^*})$ *where* $0 \le d^* \le d$ *and* $\emptyset = C^0 \subseteq C^1 \subseteq \cdots \subseteq C^{d^*}$, $x^* \notin C^{d^*}$.
5. $\mathcal{A}$ *receives* pp *and* vk.
6. *For* $i \in [q_1]$ *and* $h \in [d_i]$*, sample* $(\mathsf{sk}_{C_i^h}, \pi_{C_i^h}) \leftarrow \mathsf{Constrain}(\mathsf{sk}_{C_i^{h-1}}, \pi_{C_i^{h-1}}, C_i^h)$. $\mathcal{A}$ *receives* $(\mathsf{sk}_{C_i^{d_i}}, \pi_{C_i^{d_i}})_{i\in[q_1]}$.
7. *For* $j \in [q_2]$ *and* $h \in [d_j]$*, sample* $(\mathsf{sk}_{C_j^h}, \pi_{C_j^h}) \leftarrow \mathsf{Constrain}(\mathsf{sk}_{C_j^{h-1}}, \pi_{C_j^{h-1}}, C_j^h)$ *and* $(y_j, \pi_j) \leftarrow \mathsf{Eval}(\mathsf{sk}_{C_j^{d_j}}, \pi_{C_j^{d_j}}, x_j)$. $\mathcal{A}$ *receives* $(y_j, \pi_j)_{j\in[q_2]}$.
8. *For* $h \in [d^*]$*, sample* $(\mathsf{sk}_{C^h}, \pi_{C^h}) \leftarrow \mathsf{Constrain}(\mathsf{sk}_{C^{h-1}}, \pi_{C^{h-1}}, C^h)$ *and* $(y_0^*, \pi_0^*) \leftarrow \mathsf{Eval}(\mathsf{sk}_{C^{d^*}}, \pi_{C^{d^*}}, x^*)$. *Sample* $y_1^* \leftarrow_{\$} \mathcal{Y}$. $\mathcal{A}$ *receives* y_b^*.
9. $\mathcal{A}$ *outputs a guess* b^*.

We say "$\mathcal{A}$ *wins" if and only if* $b = b^*$, $q_1 + q_2 \le q$, $x^* \in C_i^{d_i}$ *for all* $i \in [q_1]$*, and* $x_j \ne x^*$ *for all* $j \in [q_2]$. *The* advantage *of* $\mathcal{A}$ *in the above game is*

$$\mathrm{Adv}^{\mathcal{A}}_{\mathsf{CVRF}}(\lambda) = \Pr[\mathcal{A} \ \ wins] - 1/2$$

where the probability is taken over the randomness of $\mathcal{A}$ *and the game.* CVRF *is* (t, q, d, μ)-selective pseudorandom *if, for every* $\mathcal{A}$ *running in time at most* $t(\lambda)$ *making at most* $q(\lambda)$ *queries, it holds that* $\mathrm{Adv}^{\mathcal{A}}_{\mathsf{CVRF}}(\lambda) \le \mu(\lambda)$.

We call CVRF delegable *if it is* d*-delegable for every* $d \in \mathrm{poly}(\lambda)$*, and* (t, d, μ)-selective pseudorandom *if it is* (t, q, d, μ)-selective pseudorandom *for every* $q \in \mathrm{poly}(\lambda)$.

Definition 6 (Path-Invariance). CVRF *is* path-invariant *if we have for all constraints* $C_1 \subseteq C_2$ *and* $x \in \mathcal{X} \setminus C_1$ *the following equalities of distributions:*

$$\mathsf{Constrain}_{\mathsf{pp}}(\mathsf{sk}_\emptyset, \pi_\emptyset, C_2) \equiv \mathsf{Constrain}_{\mathsf{pp}}(\mathsf{sk}_{C_1}, \pi_{C_1}, C_2),$$
$$\mathsf{Eval}_{\mathsf{pp}}(\mathsf{sk}_\emptyset, \pi_\emptyset, x) \equiv \mathsf{Eval}_{\mathsf{pp}}(\mathsf{sk}_{C_1}, \pi_{C_1}, x)$$

where $(\mathsf{pp}, \mathsf{sk}_\emptyset, \mathsf{vk}, \pi_\emptyset) \leftarrow \mathsf{Setup}(1^\lambda)$ *and* $(\mathsf{sk}_{C_1}, \pi_{C_1}) \leftarrow \mathsf{Constrain}(\mathsf{sk}_\emptyset, \pi_\emptyset, C_1)$.

Remark 1. The notion of path-invariance (Definition 6) for CVRFs has been introduced by Fuchsbauer [28] under the name *constraint-hiding.* It is easy to see that path-invariance implies ∞-delegability. Additionally, it allows to us significantly simplify the security games of Definitions 3 and 5. Indeed, these selective pseudorandomness games allow for involved queries of repeated or nested constraining. Such queries correspond to complex scenarios where multiple parties might receive constrained keys and further constrain them. If the underlying CPRF resp. CVRF scheme is path-invariant, the keys, proofs and outputs the adversary receives are completely independent of their constraint history. Hence, when making queries, the adversary does not need to submit chain of constraints $(C^h)_{h=0}^d$ and the challenger can compute all keys, proofs and keys directly from the root secret key $\mathsf{sk}_\emptyset$.

The construction we give in Sect. 3 is path-invariant in the strongest possible way, as all outputs, proofs and constrained keys of it are determined deterministically by its verification key. This allows us to greatly simplify its security proof by omitting all constraint histories submitted by the adversary.

Definition 7 (Prefix-Constrained CPRFs and CVRFs). *A CPRF or CVRF with input domain $\mathcal{X} = \{0,1\}^\ell$ is* prefix-constrained *if, for every $x \in \{0,1\}^{\leq \ell}$,*

$$\{y \in \{0,1\}^\ell \mid x \text{ is not a prefix of } y\} \in \mathcal{C}.$$

For $C = \{y \in \{0,1\}^\ell \mid x \text{ is not a prefix of } y\}$, we will usually denote the outputs of $\mathsf{Constrain}(\mathsf{sk}_\emptyset, \pi_\emptyset, C)$ by (sk_x, π_x) instead of (sk_C, π_C).

On Quadratic Polynomials. We will introduce here some notation on polynomials of degree 2 that will span through this work.

Definition 8. *Let $n, p \in \mathbb{N}$. A* **degree-2** *map $F : \mathbb{Z}_p^n \longrightarrow \mathbb{Z}_p^n$ is a map whose outputs are computed by n polynomials $f_1, \ldots, f_n \in \mathbb{Z}_p[X_1, \ldots, X_n]$ of degree ≤ 2. Denote the set of all degree-2 maps by*

$$Q_{p,n} := \{F : \mathbb{Z}_p^n \to \mathbb{Z}_p^n \mid F \text{ is a degree-2 map}\}.$$

In this work, we will sometimes refer to $Q_{p,n}$ as Q, whenever p, n are clear from context.

Definition 9. *For $\ell \in \mathbb{N}$, denote by $Q_{p,n}^{\ell \times 2}$ the set of lists of ℓ pairs of functions in $Q_{p,n}$. We will denote an element $\mathcal{G} \in Q_{p,n}^{\ell \times 2}$ by*

$$\mathcal{G} = ((G_0^{(1)}, G_1^{(1)}), \ldots, (G_0^{(\ell)}, G_1^{(\ell)}))$$

where $G_0^{(1)}, \ldots, G_0^{(\ell)}, G_1^{(1)}, \ldots, G_1^{(\ell)} \in Q_{p,n}$ are all degree-2 maps from $\mathbb{Z}_p^n$ to $\mathbb{Z}_p^n$. Further, for a bit string $x = x_1 \cdots x_{\ell'} \in \{0,1\}^{\leq \ell}$, we set

$$G_x := G_{x_{\ell'}}^{(\ell')} \circ \cdots \circ G_{x_1}^{(1)} : \mathbb{Z}_p^n \to \mathbb{Z}_p^n.$$

For the sake of completeness, let G_ϵ denote the identity function on $\mathbb{Z}_p^n$.

Finally, let $e\colon \mathbb{G}_1 \times \mathbb{G}_1 \to \mathbb{G}_2$ be a bilinear pairing with generators $\mathbf{g}_1 \in \mathbb{G}_1$, $\mathbf{g}_2 \in \mathbb{G}_2$. For a degree-2 map $F \in Q$, we define an efficiently computable function $e_F : \mathbb{G}_1^n \to \mathbb{G}_2^n$ as follows: let $f_1, \dots, f_n \in \mathbb{Z}_p[X_1, \dots, X_n]$ be the polynomials that compute the outputs of F. Decompose each f_i as

$$f_i = \sum_{1 \le j \le k \le n} c_{j,k}^{(i)} \cdot X_j X_k + \sum_{j \in [n]} c_{0,j}^{(i)} \cdot X_j + c_{0,0}^{(i)}$$

with coefficients $c_{j,k}^{(i)} \in \mathbb{Z}_p$. Then, the output of e_F on input $\mathbf{g}_1^{\mathbf{s}}$ is given by $e_F(\mathbf{h}_1, \dots, \mathbf{h}_n) = (\mathbf{h}_1', \dots, \mathbf{h}_n')$ where

$$\mathbf{h}_i' := \left(\prod_{1 \le j \le k \le n} e(\mathbf{h}_j, \mathbf{h}_k)^{c_{j,k}^{(i)}} \right) \cdot \left(\prod_{j \in [n]} e(\mathbf{h}_j, \mathbf{g}_1)^{c_{0,j}^{(i)}} \right) \cdot \mathbf{g}_2^{c_{0,0}^{(i)}}.$$

Note that we have $e_F(\mathbf{g}_1^{\mathbf{s}}) = \mathbf{g}_2^{F(\mathbf{s})}$ for $\mathbf{s} \in \mathbb{Z}_p^n$.

3 Our CVRF Construction

Our construction draws inspiration from the CPRF of Goldreich, Goldwasser and Micali [29] (GGM-CPRF). The GGM-CPRF's input domain is $\{0,1\}^\ell$ and, conceptually, it may be viewed as a binary tree of depth ℓ. Each node is identified by a bit string $x \in \{0,1\}^{\le \ell}$ where the root node is ϵ, and the children of a node x are $x0$ and $x1$, respectively. The set of leafs is $\{0,1\}^\ell$. Additionally, each node has a label associated with it, and these labels are defined inductively by a length-doubling PRG $G = (G_0, G_1)$. The label of the root node is the CPRF's root secret keys sk_ϵ. The labels of other nodes are computed recursively: the labels of the left and right child result by applying G_0 and G_1 to the parent's label, respectively. In the GGM-CPRF, constrained keys correspond to the labels of inner nodes, while outputs correspond to the labels of leaf nodes.

Our CVRF construction (denoted by CVRF) shares the input domain $\{0,1\}^\ell$ and PRG-defined tree structure with the GGM-CPRF. To enable verification, however, our construction differs in several aspects:

1. Our PRGs are degree-2 polynomials over $\mathbb{Z}_p$ in n variables (as explained in Definition 8). Additionally, for each level of the tree, we use a *fresh* PRG $G^{(i)} \leftarrow_\$ Q^2$ that is sampled uniformly and independently of all other PRGs.
2. Due to our choice of PRGs, each node's label is a value in $\mathbb{Z}_p^n$. In particular, the root secret key sk_ϵ is a uniformly random vector $\mathbf{s} \leftarrow_\$ \mathbb{Z}_p^n$.
3. While constrained keys are the labels of inner nodes as in the GGM-CPRF, outputs are not the labels of leaf nodes directly, but a function of them. In particular, outputs are vectors of group elements in $\mathbb{G}_2^n$ where, on input $x \in \{0,1\}^\ell$, the output is $\mathbf{g}_2^{G_x(\mathbf{s})^2}$ (where $G_x(\mathbf{s})$ is the label of the leaf node x by the notational shorthand introduced in Definition 9, and $G_x(\mathbf{s})^2$ is the vector of squares of entries of $G_x(\mathbf{s})$).

4. To enable verification of constrained keys and outputs, nodes not only have a label, but also a proof element associated to them.
   (a) The verification key is $\mathsf{vk} = \mathsf{g}_2^{\mathsf{sk}_\epsilon} = \mathsf{g}_2^{s}$.
   (b) Each node $x \in \{0,1\}^{\leq \ell}$ has the proof element $\mathsf{g}_1^{G_x(s)}$ associated to it.
5. Each constrained key or output is accompanied by the proof elements along the path from the root node to itself. Since the labels are inductively defined via degree-2 polynomials, the proof elements enable efficient verification by using the pairing e.

Given this high-level overview, we give the pseudocode of CVRF in Fig. 2. To avoid redundant code, CVRF uses internally the helper algorithms HelperEval and HelperVerify, which are called whenever outputs and constrained keys are generated and verified, respectively.

Theorem 3. CVRF *fulfills* Delegability, Unique Provability *and* Functionality Binding *(Definition 5). In addition, it is* path-invariant *(Definition 6).*

Proof. Delegability follows almost directly from the fact that HelperVerify accepts outputs of HelperEval by construction and the fact that HelperEval and HelperVerify do not differentiate between root and constrained secret keys. *Path-invariance* also follows by construction since HelperEval is deterministic.

As for *Unique Provability* and *Functionality Binding*, we will show that, for any input $x \in \{0,1\}^{\leq \ell}$, and any verification key $\mathsf{vk} \in \mathbb{G}_2^n$ there is a unique input $(\pi_x \in (\mathbb{G}_1^n)^{\ell'}, \tilde{\pi}^{(\ell')} \in \mathbb{G}_1^n)$ resulting in $\mathsf{HelperVerify}(\mathsf{vk}, x, \pi_x, \tilde{\pi}^{(\ell')}) = \mathsf{ACCEPT}$.

This directly implies the unique provability as Verify only accepts an input $\boldsymbol{y}$ if it fulfills $\boldsymbol{y} = e(\tilde{\pi}^{(\ell')}, \tilde{\pi}^{(\ell')})$ for a thus unique $\tilde{\pi}^{(\ell')}$ predetermined by HelperVerify. Regarding functionality binding, we can actually show the stronger notion, that for any constraint $x \in \{0,1\}^{<\ell}$ constrained keys $\mathsf{sk}_x, \mathsf{sk}'_x$ and proofs π_x, π'_x, $\mathsf{VerifyC}_{\mathsf{pp}}(\mathsf{vk}, x, \mathsf{sk}_x, \pi_x) = \mathsf{VerifyC}_{\mathsf{pp}}(\mathsf{vk}, x, \mathsf{sk}'_x, \pi'_x) = \mathsf{ACCEPT}$ already implies that $\mathsf{sk}_x = \mathsf{sk}'_x$. This follows in the same way as unique provability, as VerifyC only accepts a key sk_x if it conforms to $\mathsf{g}_1^{\mathsf{sk}_x} = \tilde{\pi}^{(\ell')}$ for this unique value $\tilde{\pi}^{(\ell')}$.

Let us now show that there is one unique accepting input to HelperVerify. Consider any $\mathsf{pp} = ((G_0^{(i)}, G_1^{(i)})_{i=1}^{\ell})$ and any $\mathsf{vk} \in \mathbb{G}_2^n$. Let $\ell' \leq \ell$ and $x \in \{0,1\}^{\ell'}$. Suppose we are given two proofs $\pi_1 = (\tilde{\pi}_1^{(i)})_{i=0}^{\ell'-1}$ and $\pi_2 = (\tilde{\pi}_2^{(i)})_{i=0}^{\ell'-1} \in (\mathbb{G}_1^n)^{\ell'}$ with corresponding inputs $\tilde{\pi}_1^{(\ell')}$ and $\tilde{\pi}_2^{(\ell')}$ that both result in ACCEPT (we use the subscripts 1 and 2 to differentiate between the two executions of HelperVerify). We will show by induction on $0 \leq i \leq \ell'$ that $\tilde{\pi}_1^{(i)} = \tilde{\pi}_2^{(i)} = \mathsf{g}_1^{G_{x_1 \ldots x_i}(\mathsf{sk}_\epsilon)}$ for all i.

For the base case $i = 0$ it holds that $\tilde{\pi}_1^{(0)} = \tilde{\pi}_2^{(0)} = \mathsf{g}_1^{\mathsf{sk}_\epsilon} = \mathsf{g}_1^{G_\epsilon(\mathsf{sk}_\epsilon)}$ as otherwise the comparison with vk in Line 2 would not pass. For the induction step assume that $\tilde{\pi}_1^{(i-1)} = \tilde{\pi}_2^{(i-1)} = \mathsf{g}_1^{G_{x_1 \ldots x_{i-1}}(\mathsf{sk}_\epsilon)}$ holds. By the check in Line 4, $G_{x_i}^{(i)}$ is a degree-2 map, so the output of the pairing e in Line 5 is well-defined. The check in Line 5 ensures that $\tilde{\pi}_1^{(i)} = \tilde{\pi}_2^{(i)} = \mathsf{g}_1^{G_{x_1 \ldots x_i}(\mathsf{sk}_\epsilon)}$, completing the proof. □

$\mathsf{CVRF.Setup}(1^\lambda)$:

Sample $\boldsymbol{s} \leftarrow\!\!\$\ \mathbb{Z}_p^n$; Set $\mathsf{sk}_\epsilon = \boldsymbol{s}$
Set $\mathsf{vk} = \mathbf{g}_2^{\boldsymbol{s}}$
Sample degree-2 maps $\mathcal{G} \leftarrow\!\!\$\ Q_{p,n}^{\ell\times 2}$; Set $\mathsf{pp} = \mathcal{G}$
Output $(\mathsf{pp}, \mathsf{sk}_\epsilon, \mathsf{vk}, \pi_\epsilon = \emptyset)$

$\mathsf{HelperEval}_{\mathsf{pp}}(\mathsf{sk}_{x'} \in \mathbb{Z}_p^n, \pi_{x'} \in (\mathbb{G}_1^n)^{\ell'}, x \in \{0,1\}^{\ell''})$:

Check that $|x'| = \ell' \leq \ell'' \leq \ell$; otherwise, abort
Parse $\pi_{x'} = (\tilde{\pi}^{(i)})_{i=0}^{\ell'-1}$, $\mathsf{pp} = ((G_0^{(i)}, G_1^{(i)}))_{i=1}^{\ell}$, and $\boldsymbol{s}_{\ell'} = \mathsf{sk}_{x'}$
For $i \in \{\ell', \ldots, \ell''-1\}$:
  Set $\tilde{\pi}^{(i)} = \mathbf{g}_1^{\boldsymbol{s}_i}$
  Set $\boldsymbol{s}_{i+1} = G_{x_i}^{(i)}(\boldsymbol{s}_i)$
Output $(\boldsymbol{y} = \boldsymbol{s}_{\ell''}, \pi_x = (\tilde{\pi}^{(i)})_{i=0}^{\ell''-1})$

$\mathsf{CVRF.Constrain}_{\mathsf{pp}}(\mathsf{sk}_{x'} \in \mathbb{Z}_p^n, \pi_{x'} \in (\mathbb{G}_1^n)^{\ell'}, x \in \{0,1\}^{<\ell})$:

Check whether x' is a prefix of x and $|x| < \ell$; else, abort
Output $(\mathsf{sk}_x, \pi_x) \leftarrow \mathsf{HelperEval}_{\mathsf{pp}}(\mathsf{sk}_{x'}, \pi_{x'}, x)$

$\mathsf{CVRF.Eval}_{\mathsf{pp}}(\mathsf{sk}_{x'} \in \mathbb{Z}_p^n, \pi_{x'} \in (\mathbb{G}_1^n)^{\ell'}, x \in \{0,1\}^{\ell})$:

Check whether x' is a prefix of x and $|x| = \ell$; else, abort
$(\hat{\boldsymbol{y}}, \pi_x) \leftarrow \mathsf{HelperEval}_{\mathsf{pp}}(\mathsf{sk}_{x'}, \pi_{x'}, x)$
Output $(\boldsymbol{y} = \mathbf{g}_2^{\hat{\boldsymbol{y}}^2}, \pi = (\pi_x, \mathbf{g}_1^{\hat{\boldsymbol{y}}}))$ where $(\hat{\boldsymbol{y}}_1, \ldots, \hat{\boldsymbol{y}}_n)^2 = (\hat{\boldsymbol{y}}_1^2, \ldots, \hat{\boldsymbol{y}}_n^2) \in \mathbb{Z}_p^n$

$\mathsf{HelperVerify}_{\mathsf{pp}}(\mathsf{vk} \in \mathbb{G}_2^n, x \in \{0,1\}^{\ell'}, \pi_x \in (\mathbb{G}_1^n)^{\ell'}, \tilde{\pi}^{(\ell')} \in \mathbb{G}_1^n)$:

Parse $\pi_x = (\tilde{\pi}^{(i)})_{i=0}^{\ell'-1}$ and $\mathsf{pp} = ((G_0^{(i)}, G_1^{(i)}))_{i=1}^{\ell}$
If $\mathsf{vk} \neq e(\tilde{\pi}^{(0)}, \mathbf{g}_1)$, output REJECT
For $1 \leq i \leq \ell'$:
  If $G_{x_i}^{(i)}$ is not a degree-2 map, output REJECT
  If $e(\tilde{\pi}^{(i)}, \mathbf{g}_1) \neq e_{G_{x_i}^{(i)}}(\tilde{\pi}^{(i-1)})$, output REJECT
Output ACCEPT

$\mathsf{CVRF.VerifyC}_{\mathsf{pp}}(\mathsf{vk} \in \mathbb{G}_2^n, x \in \{0,1\}^{\ell'}, \mathsf{sk}_x \in \mathbb{Z}_p^n, \pi_x \in (\mathbb{G}_1^n)^{\ell'})$:

If $\ell' \geq \ell$, output REJECT
Output $\mathsf{HelperVerify}_{\mathsf{pp}}(\mathsf{vk}, x, \pi_x, \mathbf{g}_1^{\mathsf{sk}_x})$

$\mathsf{CVRF.Verify}_{\mathsf{pp}}(\mathsf{vk} \in \mathbb{G}_2^n, x \in \{0,1\}^{\ell}, \boldsymbol{y} \in \mathbb{G}_2^n, \pi = (\pi_x \in (\mathbb{G}_1^n)^{\ell}, \tilde{\pi}^{(\ell)} \in \mathbb{G}_1^n))$:

If $\mathsf{HelperVerify}_{\mathsf{pp}}(\mathsf{vk}, x, \pi_x, \tilde{\pi}^{(\ell)}) =$ REJECT, output REJECT
If $e(\tilde{\pi}^{(\ell)}, \tilde{\pi}^{(\ell)}) = \boldsymbol{y}$, output ACCEPT; else REJECT

Fig. 2. Pseudocode of CVRF.

4 Security Proof by Recursive Assumptions

4.1 Diffie-Hellman Assumptions

The security of our efficient construction in Sect. 3 is based on two assumptions. The first one assumes the hardness of the Decisional Square Diffie-Hellman (DSDH) problem over a cyclic group $\mathbb{G}$ of order p with generator g, which consists in distinguishing a pair of the form $(\mathsf{g}^a, \mathsf{g}^b)$ where $a, b \leftarrow\!\!\$\ \mathbb{Z}_p$ from a pair $(\mathsf{g}^a, \mathsf{g}^{a^2})$ where $a \leftarrow\!\!\$\ \mathbb{Z}_p$.

Definition 10 (DSDH Assumption). *Fix $n \in \mathrm{poly}(\lambda)$, a prime $p \leq 2^{\mathrm{poly}(\lambda)}$ and a cyclic group $\mathbb{G}$ of order p with generator $\mathsf{g} \in \mathbb{G}$.*

For an adversary $\mathcal{A}$, we define its advantage at solving the Decisional Square Diffie-Hellman Problem *(DSDH) problem in $\mathbb{G}$ by*

$$\mathrm{Adv}^{\mathcal{A}}_{\mathsf{DSDH}}(\lambda) := \Big| \Pr_{a,b \leftarrow \$ \mathbb{Z}_p^n}[\mathcal{A}(\mathsf{g}^a, \mathsf{g}^b) = 1] - \Pr_{a \leftarrow \$ \mathbb{Z}_p^n}[\mathcal{A}(\mathsf{g}^a, \mathsf{g}^{a^2}) = 1] \Big|.$$

For non-negative functions $t = t(\lambda), \mu = \mu(\lambda)$, the Decisional Square Diffie-Hellman assumption (t, μ)-DSDH *states that we have $\mathrm{Adv}^{\mathcal{A}}_{\mathsf{DSDH}} \leq \mu$ for all algorithms $\mathcal{A}$ that run in time at most t.*

Note that the DSDH assumption is usually stated for $n = 1$. Since DSDH is rerandomizable, there is a tight reduction of the corresponding problem from the case $n = 1$ to the case $n > 1$.

We now state our novel *Recursive Decisional Diffie-Hellman* assumption. It consists of two challenges: an if-challenge and a then-challenge. The assumption postulates that for every adversary $\mathcal{A}_{\mathsf{then}}$ for the then-challenge, there exists an adversary for the if-challenge of comparable time complexity and advantage. In other words, if the if-challenge is hard, then the then-challenge has to be hard, too. Assumptions of this structure are already known in the lattice-setting as evasive Learning With Errors assumptions [18,51,52] and in the pairing setting [3] However, we note that this assumption is just a cornerstone for the security proof of our CVRF, as we prove the assumption sound in the GGM under falsifiable contained assumptions.

Assumption 1 (Recursive DDH). *Fix $n, m_1, m_2 \in \mathrm{poly}(\lambda)$, a prime $p \leq 2^{\mathrm{poly}(\lambda)}$ and a bilinear pairing $e : \mathbb{G}_1 \times \mathbb{G}_1 \to \mathbb{G}_2$ of groups of order p with generators $\mathsf{g}_1 \in \mathbb{G}_1$, $\mathsf{g}_2 \in \mathbb{G}_2$. Let* Samp *be an algorithm that on input $1^\lambda, p, n$, outputs descriptions of*

1. *an efficiently computable function $c : \mathbb{Z}_p^n \to \mathbb{Z}_p^n$,*
2. *an efficiently computable function $h_0 : \mathbb{Z}_p^n \to \mathbb{Z}_p^{m_0}$,*
3. *an efficiently computable function $h_1 : \mathbb{Z}_p^n \to \mathbb{Z}_p^{m_1}$,*
4. *and an efficiently computable function $h_2 : \mathbb{Z}_p^n \to \mathbb{Z}_p^{m_2}$.*

For an adversary $\mathcal{A}_{\mathsf{if}}$, we define its advantage in the if*-challenge by*

$$\begin{aligned}\mathrm{Adv}^{\mathcal{A}_{\mathsf{if}}}_{\mathsf{if}} = |&\Pr[\mathcal{A}_{\mathsf{if}}(c, h_0, h_1, h_2, h_0(\boldsymbol{s}), \mathsf{g}_1^{h_1(\boldsymbol{s})}, \mathsf{g}_2^{h_2(\boldsymbol{s})}, \mathsf{g}_2^{\boldsymbol{s}}, \mathsf{g}_2^{c(\boldsymbol{s})}) = 1] \\ &- \Pr[\mathcal{A}_{\mathsf{if}}(c, h_0, h_1, h_2, h_0(\boldsymbol{s}), \mathsf{g}_1^{h_1(\boldsymbol{s})}, \mathsf{g}_2^{h_2(\boldsymbol{s})}, \mathsf{g}_2^{\boldsymbol{s}}, \mathsf{g}_2^{\boldsymbol{r}}) = 1]|\end{aligned}$$

where the probabilities are taken over $(c, h_0, h_1, h_2) \leftarrow \mathsf{Samp}(1^\lambda, p, n)$, $\boldsymbol{s} \leftarrow_\$ \mathbb{Z}_p^n$ *and* $\boldsymbol{r} \leftarrow_\$ \mathbb{Z}_p^n$. *For an adversary* $\mathcal{A}_{\mathsf{then}}$, *we define its advantage in the* then-*challenge by* $\mathrm{Adv}_{\mathsf{then}}^{\mathcal{A}_{\mathsf{then}}} =$

$$|\Pr[\mathcal{A}_{\mathsf{then}}(c, h_0, h_1, h_2, G_0, G_1, h_0(\boldsymbol{s}), \mathrm{g}_1^{h_1(\boldsymbol{s})}, \mathrm{g}_2^{h_2(\boldsymbol{s})}, \mathrm{g}_2^{\boldsymbol{s}}, \mathrm{g}_1^{\boldsymbol{x}}, G_1(\boldsymbol{x}), \mathrm{g}_2^{c(\boldsymbol{s})}) = 1]$$
$$- \Pr[\mathcal{A}_{\mathsf{then}}(c, h_0, h_1, h_2, G_0, G_1, h_0(\boldsymbol{s}), \mathrm{g}_1^{h_1(\boldsymbol{s})}, \mathrm{g}_2^{h_2(\boldsymbol{s})}, \mathrm{g}_2^{\boldsymbol{s}}, \mathrm{g}_1^{\boldsymbol{x}}, G_1(\boldsymbol{x}), \mathrm{g}_2^{\boldsymbol{r}}) = 1]|$$

where $\boldsymbol{s} = G_0(\boldsymbol{x})$, *and the probabilities are over* $(c, h_0, h_1, h_2) \leftarrow \mathsf{Samp}(1^\lambda, p, n)$, $\boldsymbol{x} \leftarrow_\$ \mathbb{Z}_p^n$, $G_0, G_1 \leftarrow_\$ Q_{p,n}$ *and* $\boldsymbol{r} \leftarrow_\$ \mathbb{Z}_p^n$.

Finally, fix non-negative functions $t = t(\lambda)$, $q = q(\lambda)$, $\mu = \mu(\lambda)$. *The* Recursive Decisional Diffie-Hellman *assumption* (t, q, μ)-rDDH *states that for all samplers of the above form that run in time* t *and for all* then-*adversaries* $\mathcal{A}_{\mathsf{then}}$, *there exists an* if-*adversary* $\mathcal{A}_{\mathsf{if}}$ *s.t.*

$$\mathrm{Adv}_{\mathsf{if}}^{\mathcal{A}_{\mathsf{if}}}(\lambda) \geq \mathrm{Adv}_{\mathsf{then}}^{\mathcal{A}_{\mathsf{then}}}(\lambda) - \mu(\lambda) \quad \text{and} \quad \mathrm{time}(\mathcal{A}_{\mathsf{if}}) \leq \mathrm{time}(\mathcal{A}_{\mathsf{then}}) + q.$$

Note that we state the recursive DDH assumption in an additive manner, i.e., the advantage and time complexity of the postulated if-adversary $\mathcal{A}_{\mathsf{if}}$ only deteriorate by additive amounts. This makes the assumption very strong. We justify this by proving in Theorem 5 that any *generic* adversary on the then-challenge implies a *generic* adversary on the if-challenge with only small additive overhead.

4.2 Security Under the Recursive Decisional Diffie-Hellman

Theorem 4. *Let* $t = t(\lambda), q = q(\lambda), \mu = \mu(\lambda), \mu' = \mu'(\lambda)$. *Under the* $(t + \ell q + \ell n t_{\mathsf{pair}}, \mu)$-*Decisional Square Diffie-Hellman for the target group* $\mathbb{G}_2$ *and* (t', q, μ')-*Recursive Decisional Diffie-Hellman assumptions* $\mathsf{CVRF}\colon \{0,1\}^\ell \to \mathbb{G}_2^n$ *is* $(t, \mu + \mu'\ell)$-*selectively-secure, where* $t' = \Theta(\ell n^3 \log_2 p)$ *and* t_{pair} *is the time complexity to evaluate* $e : \mathbb{G}_1^2 \to \mathbb{G}_2$ *once.*

Proof of Theorem 4. We will consider the *Selective Constrained Pseudorandomness* game (cf. Definition 5) for different input lengths $\mathsf{idx} \leq \ell$. As explained in Remark 1, we consider a simplified, but equivalent security game, where the constraint-history of every query is omitted. By $\mathcal{A}_{\mathsf{idx}}$ we denote the adversary playing the game with inputs of length $0 \leq \mathsf{idx} \leq \ell$; its advantage is denoted by $\mathrm{Adv}_{\mathsf{CVRF-idx}}^{\mathcal{A}_{\mathsf{idx}}}$. Under the (t', q, μ')-rDDH assumption, the following claim holds:

Claim 1. For all $1 \leq \mathsf{idx} \leq \ell$, the existence of an adversary $\mathcal{A}_{\mathsf{idx}}$ for CVRF with input length idx which runs in time at most $t + (\ell - \mathsf{idx})(q + n t_{\mathsf{pair}})$ and has advantage $\mathrm{Adv}_{\mathsf{CVRF-idx}}^{\mathcal{A}_{\mathsf{idx}}}$, implies the existence of an adversary $\mathcal{A}_{\mathsf{idx}-1}$ for CVRF with input length $\mathsf{idx}-1$ that runs in time at most $t + (\ell - \mathsf{idx} + 1)(q + n t_{\mathsf{pair}})$ and has advantage $\mathrm{Adv}_{\mathsf{CVRF-idx}}^{\mathcal{A}_{\mathsf{idx}}} \leq \mathrm{Adv}_{\mathsf{CVRF-(idx-1)}}^{\mathcal{A}_{\mathsf{idx}-1}} + \mu'$ provided that the (t', q, μ')-rDDH assumption holds.

We defer the claim's proof for now and prove the theorem's statement first. Consider the adversary $\mathcal{A}_\ell$ that we are interested in. Suppose that it runs in time at most t. After ℓ applications of Claim 1 to $\mathcal{A}_\ell$, we arrive at $\mathcal{A}_0$.

Observe that $\mathcal{A}_0$ is an adversary against the *Selective Constrained Pseudorandomness* game (cf. Definition 5) for input length 0. Since the input space only contains the empty word ϵ, $\mathcal{A}_0$ must challenge $x^* = \epsilon$. As a consequence, it must distinguish whether a value $\boldsymbol{y}^*$ is equal to $\mathsf{g}_2^{\mathsf{sk}_\epsilon^2}$ (i.e., an output of CVRF) or uniformly random while only receiving $\mathsf{vk} = \mathsf{g}_2^{\mathsf{sk}_\epsilon}$ from the game. I.e., $\mathcal{A}_0$ must solve the DSDH problem.

Moreover, $\mathcal{A}_0$ runs in time at most $t + \ell(q + nt_{\mathsf{pair}})$ since we applied Claim 1 ℓ times. This together with the $(t + \ell(q + nt_{\mathsf{pair}}), \mu)$-$\mathsf{DSDH}$ assumption implies that $\mathrm{Adv}^{\mathcal{A}_0}_{\mathsf{CVRF}-0} \leq \mu$. As a consequence, (again, recalling the ℓ applications of Claim 1), $\mathrm{Adv}^{\mathcal{A}_\ell}_{\mathsf{CVRF}-\ell} \leq \mu + \mu'\ell$ holds completing the proof. □

Proof of Claim 1. For $\mathsf{idx} \in \{1, \dots, \ell\}$, let $\mathcal{A}_{\mathsf{idx}}$ be an adversary for CVRF with inputs of length idx. In the following, we suppose that $\mathcal{A}_{\mathsf{idx}}$ runs in time at most $t + (\ell - \mathsf{idx})(q + nt_{\mathsf{pair}})$. Further, we assume that $\mathcal{A}_{\mathsf{idx}}$ always challenges $x^* = 0 \cdots 0 \in \{0,1\}^{\mathsf{idx}}$. This is without loss of generality since the view of $\mathcal{A}_{\mathsf{idx}}$ is statistically identical (up to reordering terms) for each input $x^* \in \{0,1\}^{\mathsf{idx}}$. Indeed, we sample a fresh and independent PRG $(G_0^{(i)}, G_1^{(i)}) \leftarrow\!\!\$\; Q^2$ for every layer of the tree, so if $\mathcal{A}_{\mathsf{idx}}$ were to submit a challenge point $x^* \neq 0^{\mathsf{idx}}$, we could simply swap $G_0^{(i)}$ and $G_1^{(i)}$ whenever $x_i^* = 1$. Further, we assume—again without loss of generality—that $\mathcal{A}_{\mathsf{idx}}$ requests, besides the verification key vk, the constrained keys for the prefixes $1, 01, \dots, 0^{\mathsf{idx}-2}1$ and the evaluation of CVRF at $0^{\mathsf{idx}-1}1$ (all including corresponding proofs). Indeed, from this information, $\mathcal{A}$ can evaluate CVRF anywhere except 0^{idx} on its own. Further, since CVRF is path-invariant and generates proofs and keys deterministically, $\mathcal{A}$ does not learn anything by repeatedly requesting the same evaluation or constrained key.

So, $\mathcal{A}_{\mathsf{idx}}$ receives the following information from its challenger: First, $\mathsf{pp}, \mathsf{vk}, \pi_\epsilon$ as sampled by $(\mathsf{pp}, \mathsf{sk}_\epsilon, \mathsf{vk}, \pi_\epsilon) \leftarrow\!\!\$\; \mathsf{Setup}(1^\lambda)$. Here, $\mathsf{pp} = \mathcal{G} \leftarrow\!\!\$\; Q_{p,n}^{\mathsf{idx} \times 2}$, $\mathsf{sk} = \mathsf{sk}_\epsilon \leftarrow\!\!\$\; \mathbb{Z}_p^n$, $\mathsf{vk} = \mathsf{g}_2^{\mathsf{sk}_\epsilon}$, and $\pi_\epsilon = \emptyset$ where an element $\mathcal{G} \in Q_{p,n}^{\mathsf{idx} \times 2}$ is of the form

$$\mathcal{G} = ((G_0^{(1)}, G_1^{(1)}), \dots, (G_0^{(\mathsf{idx})}, G_1^{(\mathsf{idx})}))$$

with each $G_b^{(j)} : \mathbb{Z}_p^n \to \mathbb{Z}_p^n$ being a degree 2-map. Remember that we set

$$G_\epsilon(\boldsymbol{s}) := \boldsymbol{s} \quad \text{and} \quad G_x(\boldsymbol{s}) := G_{x_{\mathsf{idx}'}}^{(\mathsf{idx}')}(\cdots (G_{x_1}^{(1)}(\boldsymbol{s})))$$

for a bit string $x = x_1 \cdots x_{\mathsf{idx}'} \in \{0,1\}^{\leq \mathsf{idx}}$. Second, it also receives the outputs of its Eval- and $\mathsf{Constrain}$-queries, given by

$$(\boldsymbol{y}, \pi) = \mathsf{Eval}_{\mathsf{pp}}(\mathsf{sk}_\epsilon, \pi_\epsilon, 0^{\mathsf{idx}-1}1) \quad \text{and} \quad (\mathsf{sk}_i, \pi_i) = \mathsf{Constrain}_{\mathsf{pp}}(\mathsf{sk}_\epsilon, \pi_\epsilon, 0^{i-1}1) \tag{1}$$

for $i \in [\mathsf{idx} - 1]$. Note that the outputs of Eval are of shape $\boldsymbol{y} = \mathsf{g}_2^{\hat{\boldsymbol{y}}^2}$ and $\pi = (\hat{\pi}, \mathsf{g}_1^{\hat{\boldsymbol{y}}})$ where $\hat{\pi} = (\mathsf{g}_1^{G_{0^i}(\mathsf{sk}_\epsilon)})_{i \in [\mathsf{idx}-1]}$ and $\hat{\boldsymbol{y}} = G_{0^{\mathsf{idx}-1}1}(\mathsf{sk}_\epsilon)$. The constrained keys are of the form $\mathsf{sk}_i = G_{0^{i-1}1}(\mathsf{sk}_\epsilon)$ and the proofs are $\pi_i = (\mathsf{g}_1^{G_{0^j}(\mathsf{sk}_\epsilon)})_{j \in [i-1]}$.

$\mathsf{Samp}_{\mathsf{idx}}(1^\lambda, p, n)$

Sample $(G_0^{(i)}, G_1^{(i)})_{i \in [\mathsf{idx}-1]} \leftarrow_{\$} Q_{p,n}^{(\mathsf{idx}-1)\times 2}$.

Output $\{G_0^{(j)}, G_1^{(j)}\}_{j=1}^{\mathsf{idx}-1}$. This acts as a description of the following functions:

- $c_{\mathsf{idx}-1} \colon \mathbb{Z}_p^n \to \mathbb{Z}_p^n$ defined as $c_{\mathsf{idx}-1}(\cdot) = G_{0^{\mathsf{idx}-1}}(\cdot)^2$.
- $h_{0,\mathsf{idx}-1} \colon \mathbb{Z}_p^n \to \mathbb{Z}_p^{n\cdot(\mathsf{idx}-2)}$ defined as $h_{0,\mathsf{idx}-1}(\cdot) = (G_{0^j 1}(\cdot))_{j=0}^{\mathsf{idx}-3}$, which can be computed using the degree-2 maps $\{G_0^{(j)}, G_1^{(j)}\}_{j=1}^{\mathsf{idx}}$.
- $h_{1,\mathsf{idx}-1} \colon \mathbb{Z}_p^n \to \mathbb{Z}_p^{n\cdot\mathsf{idx}}$ defined as $h_{1,\mathsf{idx}-1}(\cdot) = ((G_{0^j}(\cdot))_{j=0}^{\mathsf{idx}-2}, G_{0^{\mathsf{idx}-2}1}(\cdot))$.
- $h_{2,\mathsf{idx}-1} \colon \mathbb{Z}_p^n \to \mathbb{Z}_p^n$ defined as $h_{2,\mathsf{idx}-1}(\cdot) = G_{0^{\mathsf{idx}-2}1}(\cdot)^2$.

Fig. 3. Pseudocode of $\mathsf{Samp}_{\mathsf{idx}}$.

We invoke the Recursive DDH (cf. Assumption 1) assumption to show that the existence of $\mathcal{A}_{\mathsf{idx}}$ implies the existence of $\mathcal{A}_{\mathsf{idx}-1}$ as defined in the claim's statement. Concretely, we define a sampler $\mathsf{Samp}_{\mathsf{idx}}$ in Fig. 3 such that $\mathcal{A}_{\mathsf{then}} = \mathcal{A}_{\mathsf{idx}}$ which guarantees the existence of $\mathcal{A}_{\mathsf{if}} = \mathcal{A}_{\mathsf{idx}-1}$ by the assumption. Recall that $\mathcal{A}_{\mathsf{if}}$ has to distinguish between

$$(c, h_0, h_1, h_2, G_0, G_1, h_0(\boldsymbol{s}), \mathsf{g}_1^{h_1(\boldsymbol{s})}, \mathsf{g}_2^{h_2(\boldsymbol{s})}, \mathsf{g}_2^{\boldsymbol{s}}, \mathsf{g}_2^{c(\boldsymbol{s})})$$

and

$$(c, h_0, h_1, h_2, G_0, G_1, h_0(\boldsymbol{s}), \mathsf{g}_1^{h_1(\boldsymbol{s})}, \mathsf{g}_2^{h_2(\boldsymbol{s})}, \mathsf{g}_2^{\boldsymbol{s}}, \mathsf{g}_2^{\boldsymbol{r}})$$

for $\boldsymbol{s} \leftarrow_{\$} \mathbb{Z}_p^n$ and $\boldsymbol{r} \leftarrow_{\$} \mathbb{Z}_p^n$. The crucial observation is that $\mathcal{A}_{\mathsf{if}}$ with $\boldsymbol{s} = \mathsf{sk}_\epsilon$ is an adversary against the CVRF construction with input length $\mathsf{idx} - 1$ (up to rearrangement of inputs): The description of (c, h_0, h_1, h_2) is $(G_0^{(i)}, G_1^{(i)})_{i \in [\mathsf{idx}-1]}$ which is equal to the public parameters $\mathsf{pp}_{\mathsf{idx}-1}$ for $\mathcal{A}_{\mathsf{idx}-1}$. The values $h_{0,\mathsf{idx}-1}(\boldsymbol{s})$, $\mathsf{g}_1^{h_{1,\mathsf{idx}-1}(\boldsymbol{s})}$ and $\mathsf{g}_2^{h_{2,\mathsf{idx}-1}(\boldsymbol{s})}$ represent the information $\mathcal{A}_{\mathsf{idx}-1}$ receives from its Eval and $\mathsf{Constrain}$ queries, analogously to the information in Eq. (1) sent to $\mathcal{A}_{\mathsf{idx}}$. Second, $c_{\mathsf{idx}-1}(\boldsymbol{s})$ is precisely the output of CVRF on challenge point $x^* = 0^{\mathsf{idx}-1}$. Finally, $\mathsf{g}_1^{\boldsymbol{s}}$ in the if-challenge equals the verification key vk, which $\mathcal{A}_{\mathsf{idx}-1}$ receives.

Let us now consider $\mathcal{A}_{\mathsf{then}}$. It has to distinguish between

$$(c, h_0, h_1, h_2, G_0, G_1, h_0(\boldsymbol{s}), \mathsf{g}_1^{h_1(\boldsymbol{s})}, \mathsf{g}_2^{h_2(\boldsymbol{s})}, \mathsf{g}_2^{\boldsymbol{s}}, \mathsf{g}_1^{\boldsymbol{x}}, G_1(\boldsymbol{x}), \mathsf{g}_2^{c(\boldsymbol{s})})$$

and

$$(c, h_0, h_1, h_2, G_0, G_1, h_0(\boldsymbol{s}), \mathsf{g}_1^{h_1(\boldsymbol{s})}, \mathsf{g}_2^{h_2(\boldsymbol{s})}, \mathsf{g}_2^{\boldsymbol{s}}, \mathsf{g}_1^{\boldsymbol{x}}, G_1(\boldsymbol{x}), \mathsf{g}_2^{\boldsymbol{r}})$$

when $\boldsymbol{x} \leftarrow_{\$} \mathbb{Z}_p^n$, $(G_0, G_1) \leftarrow_{\$} Q_{p,n}$, $\boldsymbol{r} \leftarrow_{\$} \mathbb{Z}_p^n$ and $\boldsymbol{s} = G_0(\boldsymbol{x})$. Now, $\mathcal{A}_{\mathsf{then}}$ is *almost* equal to $\mathcal{A}_{\mathsf{idx}}$, only incurring an additive overhead of $O(n)$. For this, note that G_0, G_1 play the role of $G_0^{(0)}, G_1^{(0)}$ in the construction, while the maps $G_0^{(i)}, G_1^{(i)}$ output by the sampler $\mathsf{Samp}_{\mathsf{idx}}(1^\lambda, p, n)$ play the role of $G_0^{(i+1)}, G_1^{(i+1)}$ in the construction. As a consequence, the verification key needs to be $\mathsf{g}_2^{\boldsymbol{x}}$ which can be computed from $\mathsf{g}_1^{\boldsymbol{x}}$ by evaluating n pairings.

To summarize, (t', q, μ')-rDDH implies that, if $\mathcal{A}_{\mathsf{idx}}$ exists, then there also exists $\mathcal{A}_{\mathsf{idx}-1}$ with $\mathcal{A}_{\mathsf{idx}-1}(\lambda) \geq \mathcal{A}_{\mathsf{idx}}(\lambda) - \mu'$ and $\mathrm{time}(\mathcal{A}_{\mathsf{idx}-1}) \leq \mathrm{time}(\mathcal{A}_{\mathsf{idx}}) + q + nt_{\mathsf{pair}}$, which completes the proof. □

5 Proving Recursive DDH in the Generic Group Model

Notation. For $d \in \mathbb{N}$, denote by $\mathbb{Z}_p[X]^{\leq d}$ the space of all polynomials $h(X_1, \ldots, X_n)$ of degree $\leq d$. Further, denote by $\mathbb{Z}_p[X]^d$ the space of all homogeneous polynomials of degree exactly d.

Further, for maps $G_1, \ldots, G_\ell \in Q$, denote by $\mathrm{span}_{\mathbb{Z}_p}[G_1, \ldots, G_\ell] \subseteq \mathbb{Z}_p[X]^{\leq 2}$ the space generated by all polynomials that compute the outputs of $G_1, \ldots, G_\ell$.

In this section, we prove the security of the recursive DDH Assumption (Assumption 1) in Maurer's generic group model under the following two assumptions:

Assumption 2 (MQ). *The* ***(decisional) multivariate quadratic*** *assumption (t, μ)-$\mathsf{MQ}_{p,n}$ states that we have for all adversaries $\mathcal{A}$ running in time t*

$$|\Pr[\mathcal{A}((G_0, G_1), (G_0(\boldsymbol{x}), G_1(\boldsymbol{x}))) = 1] - \Pr[\mathcal{A}((G_0, G_1), \boldsymbol{y}) = 1]| \leq \mu$$

where we draw $G_0, G_1 \leftarrow_{\$} Q$, $\boldsymbol{x} \leftarrow_{\$} \mathbb{Z}_p^n$ and $\boldsymbol{y} \leftarrow_{\$} \mathbb{Z}_p^{2n}$.

Assumption 3 (MQ+). *Let p be prime. The* ***multivariate quadratic plus*** *assumption (t, μ)-$\mathsf{MQ+}_{p,n}$ states that we have for all adversaries $\mathcal{A}$ running in time t*

$$\Pr\left[\begin{array}{l} h \in \mathbb{Z}_p[X_1, \ldots, X_n]^{\leq 2}, h(\boldsymbol{x}) = 0, \\ h \notin \mathrm{span}_{\mathbb{Z}_p}[G_0(X) - G_0(\boldsymbol{x}), G_1(X) - G_1(\boldsymbol{x})] \end{array}\right] - \frac{2}{p} \leq \mu$$

where we draw $G_0, G_1 \leftarrow_{\$} Q$, $\boldsymbol{x} \leftarrow_{\$} \mathbb{Z}_p^n$ and $h \leftarrow \mathcal{A}((G_0, G_1), (G_0(\boldsymbol{x}), G_1(\boldsymbol{x})))$.

Note that we require the adversary's success probability in MQ+ to be by a noticeable amount μ to be larger than $2/p$. The reason is that there exists a default adversary that has a success probability of exactly $2/p$ by simply outputting a random polynomial outside $\mathrm{span}_{\mathbb{Z}_n}[G_0(X) - G_0(\boldsymbol{x}), G_1(X) - G_1(\boldsymbol{x})]$. For example, if we always output $h(X) = (X_1 - z_1)(X_2 - z_2)$ for some $z_1, z_2 \in \mathbb{Z}_p$, then h will vanish on $\boldsymbol{x} \leftarrow_{\$} \mathbb{Z}_p^n$ with probability $2/p$. On the other hand, for any *fixed* polynomial h, the probability that h vanishes on $\boldsymbol{x} \leftarrow_{\$} \mathbb{Z}_p^n$ is bounded by $2/p$. For exponential p, the success probability of such adversaries is negligible, however, for polynomial p, its success probability is noticable. Hence, we need to set the advantage of an MQ+-solver to be its success probability minus the probability of *guessing randomly correct.*

Additionally, we require the modulus p to be prime. This requirement is necessary as MQ+ can be solved with success probability larger than $2/p$ if p is composite. For example, if p is even, then the polynomial $h(X) = \frac{p}{2} \cdot X_1$ vanishes on $\boldsymbol{x} \leftarrow_{\$} \mathbb{Z}_p$ with probability at least $1/2$. We give more details on the cryptanalysis of MQ+ in the full version [17, App. A.2].

Theorem 5. *Let* Samp *be a sampling algorithm with time complexity t'' for Assumption 1 that outputs functions h_0, h_1, h_2, c that can be evaluated in time t''. Let $\mathcal{A}_{\mathsf{then}}$ be a generic adversary against the* then*-challenge of Assumption 1 with advantage $\mu + q\mu_{\mathsf{MQ+}} + \mu_{\mathsf{MQ}} + \frac{2n+3q}{p}$ and time complexity t that makes q group-queries (in the sense of Definition 2). Assume (t', μ_{MQ})-$\mathsf{MQ}_{p,n}$ and $(t', \mu_{\mathsf{MQ+}})$-$\mathsf{MQ+}_{p,n}$ for $t' = t + t'' + O(qn^6)$.*

Then, there exists an adversary $\mathcal{A}_{\mathsf{if}}$ on the if*-challenge of Assumption 1 that makes q group-queries and has an advantage of μ and a time complexity of t'.*

To prove Theorem 5, we will argue by hybrid games given in Fig. 4. Each game is defined by two algorithms $(\mathsf{G}_i^{\mathcal{A}_{\mathsf{then}}}, \mathsf{R})$ that share the same state. $\mathsf{G}_i^{\mathcal{A}_{\mathsf{then}}}$ sets up the experiment and runs $\mathcal{A}_{\mathsf{then}}$. Since $\mathcal{A}_{\mathsf{then}}$ is generic, it does not receive real group elements, instead it receives handles that we represent by dummy group elements with formal variables as exponents: $\mathsf{g}_1^{H^{(1)}} = (\mathsf{g}_1^{H_1^{(1)}}, \dots, \mathsf{g}_1^{H_{m_1}^{(1)}})$ represents the group element vector $\mathsf{g}_1^{h_1(\boldsymbol{s})} \in \mathbb{G}_1^{m_1}$, $\mathsf{g}_2^{H^{(2)}} = (\mathsf{g}_1^{H_1^{(1)}}, \dots, \mathsf{g}_1^{H_{m_2}^{(1)}})$ represents $\mathsf{g}_2^{h_2(\boldsymbol{s})} \in \mathbb{G}_2^{m_2}$, $\mathsf{g}_2^{S} = (\mathsf{g}_2^{S_1}, \dots, \mathsf{g}_2^{S_n})$ represents $\mathsf{g}_2^{\boldsymbol{s}} \in \mathbb{G}_2^n$, $\mathsf{g}_1^{X} = (\mathsf{g}_1^{X_1}, \dots, \mathsf{g}_1^{X_n})$ represents $\mathsf{g}_1^{\boldsymbol{x}} \in \mathbb{G}_1^n$ and $\mathsf{g}_2^{C} = (\mathsf{g}_2^{C_1}, \dots, \mathsf{g}_2^{C_n})$ represents $\mathsf{g}_2^{\boldsymbol{c}}$. Since $\mathcal{A}_{\mathsf{then}}$ is generic (in the sense of 2), it can only interact with the group element handles by making explicit group queries. For this end, it has to call the oracle R on a quadratic function $f \in \mathbb{Z}_p[H^{(1)}, H^{(2)}, S, X, C]$. To ensure that the adversary only multiplies the exponents of source group elements with each other, R rejects any f that is not *admissible* where the space of admissible polynomials is defined as

$$A := \mathrm{span}_{\mathbb{Z}_p}[V_1 \cdot V_2 \mid V_1, V_2 \in \{1, H_1^{(1)}, \dots, H_{m_1}^{(1)}, X_1, \dots, X_n\}] \\ + \mathrm{span}_{\mathbb{Z}_p}[H_1^{(2)}, \dots, H_{m_2}^{(2)}, S_1, \dots, S_n, C_1, \dots, C_n].$$

Additionally, denote by $B \subseteq A$ the subspace of all admissible polynomials in which the monomials $(X_j \cdot X_k)_{j,k \in [n]}$, do not appear

$$B := \mathrm{span}_{\mathbb{Z}_p}[1, X_1, \dots, X_n] + \mathrm{span}_{\mathbb{Z}_p}[X_i \cdot H_j^{(1)} \mid i \in [n], j \in [m_1]] \\ + \mathrm{span}_{\mathbb{Z}_p}[H_i^{(1)} \cdot H_j^{(1)} \mid i, j \in [m_1]] \\ + \mathrm{span}_{\mathbb{Z}_p}[H_1^{(2)}, \dots, H_{m_2}^{(2)}, S_1, \dots, S_n, C_1, \dots, C_n].$$

Lemma 1. *For $i \in [q]$, the advantage of $\mathcal{A}_{\mathsf{then}}$ at distinguishing G_{i-1} and G_i is bounded by $\frac{2}{p} + \mu_{\mathsf{MQ+}}$. I.e., $|\Pr[\mathsf{G}_{i-1}^{\mathcal{A}_{\mathsf{then}}}(1^\lambda) = 1] - \Pr[\mathsf{G}_i^{\mathcal{A}_{\mathsf{then}}}(1^\lambda) = 1]| \le \frac{2}{p} + \mu_{\mathsf{MQ+}}$.*

Proof. Let $f_1, \dots, f_q$ be the group queries made by $\mathcal{A}_{\mathsf{then}}$. G_{i-1} and G_i only differ in how they handle the i-th query f_i. We can distinguish three cases:

1. If $f_i(h_1(\boldsymbol{s}), h_2(\boldsymbol{s}), \boldsymbol{x}, \boldsymbol{s}, \boldsymbol{c}) \neq 0$, then $\mathsf{R}(f_i)$ will reply with 0 in both games.
2. If $f_i(h_1(\boldsymbol{s}), h_2(\boldsymbol{s}), X, \boldsymbol{s}, \boldsymbol{c}) \in \mathrm{span}_{\mathbb{Z}_p}[G_0(X) - \boldsymbol{s}, G_1(X) - \boldsymbol{w}]$, then $\mathsf{R}(f_i)$ will reply with 1 in both games.

Game $\mathsf{G}_i^{\mathcal{A}_{\mathsf{then}}}(1^\lambda)$, $i \in \{0, \dots, q+2\}$, with adversary $\mathcal{A}_{\mathsf{then}}$:

Initialize generic groups $\mathbb{G}_1 = \langle \mathrm{g}_1 \rangle$, $\mathbb{G}_2 = \langle \mathrm{g}_2 \rangle$
Set $j = 0$
Sample $b \leftarrow_\$ \{0,1\}$
Sample $(c, h_0, h_1, h_2) \leftarrow \mathsf{Samp}(1^\lambda, p, n)$
Sample $\boldsymbol{x} \leftarrow_\$ \mathbb{Z}_p^n$, $G_0, G_1 \leftarrow_\$ Q_{p,n}$
If $i \leq q$, set $\boldsymbol{s} = G_0(\boldsymbol{x})$ and $\boldsymbol{w} = G_1(\boldsymbol{x})$
If $i \geq q+1$, sample $\boldsymbol{s}, \boldsymbol{w} \leftarrow_\$ \mathbb{Z}_p^n$
If $b = 1$, sample $\boldsymbol{c} \leftarrow_\$ \mathbb{Z}_p^n$; else, set $\boldsymbol{c} = c(\boldsymbol{s})$
Run $b' \leftarrow \mathcal{A}_{\mathsf{then}}^{\mathsf{R}}(c, h_0, h_1, h_2, G_0, G_1, h_0(\boldsymbol{s}), \mathrm{g}_1^{H^{(1)}}, \mathrm{g}_2^{H^{(2)}}, \mathrm{g}_2^{S}, \mathrm{g}_1^{X}, \boldsymbol{w}, \mathrm{g}_2^{C})$
Return 1, if $b = b'$; else, return 0

Group Query Subroutine $\mathsf{R}(f \in \mathbb{Z}_p[H^{(1)}, H^{(2)}, X, S, C])$:

Increase $j = j + 1$
If f is not admissible or $j > q$, return $\perp$
If $j > i \leq q+1$, do the following:
    If $f(h_1(\boldsymbol{s}), h_2(\boldsymbol{s}), \boldsymbol{x}, \boldsymbol{s}, \boldsymbol{c}) = 0$, return 1; else, return 0;
If $j \leq i \leq q+1$, do the following:
    If $f(h_1(\boldsymbol{s}), h_2(\boldsymbol{s}), X, \boldsymbol{s}, \boldsymbol{c}) \in \mathrm{span}_{\mathbb{Z}_p}[G_0(X) - \boldsymbol{s}, G_1(X) - \boldsymbol{w}]$, return 1
    Else, return 0
If $i = q+2$, do the following:
    Compute $f' \in B$ s.t. $f - f' \in \mathrm{span}_{\mathbb{Z}_p}[G_0(X) - S, G_1(X) - \boldsymbol{w}]$
    If such an f' does not exist, return 0
    Draw $\boldsymbol{x}' \leftarrow_\$ \mathbb{Z}_p^n$
    If $f'(h_1(\boldsymbol{s}), h_2(\boldsymbol{s}), \boldsymbol{x}', \boldsymbol{s}, \boldsymbol{c}) = 0$, return 1; else, return 0

Fig. 4. Hybrid Games for the proof of Theorem 5. Lines whose execution depends on the index i of the current hybrid have a gray background.

3. If $f_i(h_1(\boldsymbol{s}), h_2(\boldsymbol{s}), \boldsymbol{x}, \boldsymbol{s}, \boldsymbol{c}) = 0$ and $f_i(h_1(\boldsymbol{s}), h_2(\boldsymbol{s}), X, \boldsymbol{s}, \boldsymbol{c}) \notin \mathrm{span}_{\mathbb{Z}_p}[G_0(X) - \boldsymbol{s}, G_1(X) - \boldsymbol{w}]$, then $\mathsf{R}(f_i)$ will reply with 1 in G_{i-1}, but with 0 in G_i.

It follows that $\mathcal{A}_{\mathsf{then}}$'s advantage at distinguishing G_{i-1} and G_i is bounded by the probability of the last case occurring. Let us call this probability α.

To reduce the MQ+-problem to the problem of distinguishing G_{i-1} and G_i, we consider the following reduction: $\mathcal{R}$ receives $(G_0, G_1, G_0(\boldsymbol{x}), G_1(\boldsymbol{x}))$ from an MQ+-challenger Ch. It sets $\boldsymbol{s} = G_0(\boldsymbol{x})$, $\boldsymbol{w} = G_1(\boldsymbol{x})$ and simulates G_{i-1} for $\mathcal{A}_{\mathsf{then}}$ by sampling $(c, h_0, h_1, h_2) \leftarrow \mathsf{Samp}(1^\lambda)$, $b \leftarrow \{0,1\}$, and computing $c(\boldsymbol{s}), h_0(\boldsymbol{s}), h_1(\boldsymbol{s}), h_2(\boldsymbol{s})$. Note that $\mathcal{R}$ can evaluate the first $i-1$ calls of the R-oracle, since $\mathcal{R}$ is able to decide if

$$f_j(h_1(\boldsymbol{s}), h_2(\boldsymbol{s}), X, \boldsymbol{s}, \boldsymbol{c}) \in \mathrm{span}_{\mathbb{Z}_p}[G_0(X) - \boldsymbol{s}, G_1(X) - \boldsymbol{w}]$$

for $j < i$. Once $\mathcal{A}_{\mathsf{then}}$ calls R for the i-th time with f_i, $\mathcal{R}$ stops the simulation and sends $f'(X) := f_i(h_1(\boldsymbol{s}), h_2(\boldsymbol{s}), X, \boldsymbol{s}, \boldsymbol{c})$ to $\mathsf{Ch}_{\mathsf{MQ+}}$. With probability α, f' is a correct MQ+-solution, as we have

$$f'(\boldsymbol{x}) = 0, \qquad \text{but} \qquad f'(X) \notin \mathrm{span}_{\mathbb{Z}_p}[G_0(X) - G_0(\boldsymbol{x}), G_1(X) - G_1(\boldsymbol{x})].$$

Hence, we have $|\Pr[\mathsf{G}_{i-1}^{\mathcal{A}_{\mathsf{then}}}(1^\lambda) = 1] - \Pr[\mathsf{G}_{i}^{\mathcal{A}_{\mathsf{then}}}(1^\lambda) = 1]| \leq \alpha \leq \mu_{\mathsf{MQ+}} + \frac{2}{p}$. □

Lemma 2. *The advantage of* $\mathcal{A}_{\mathsf{then}}$ *at distinguishing* G_q *and* G_{q+1} *is bounded by* μ_{MQ}. *I.e.,* $|\Pr[\mathsf{G}_{q}^{\mathcal{A}_{\mathsf{then}}}(1^\lambda) = 1] - \Pr[\mathsf{G}_{q+1}^{\mathcal{A}_{\mathsf{then}}}(1^\lambda) = 1]| \leq \mu_{\mathsf{MQ}}$.

Proof. Let $\mathcal{R}$ be a reduction that receives $(G_0, G_1) \leftarrow_{\$} Q$ and $(\boldsymbol{s}, \boldsymbol{w})$ from an MQ-challenger Ch. $\mathcal{R}$ simulates the games G_q and G_{q+1} for $\mathcal{A}_{\mathsf{then}}$ by computing $h_0(\boldsymbol{s}), h_1(\boldsymbol{s}), h_2(\boldsymbol{s}), c(\boldsymbol{s})$, sampling $b \leftarrow_{\$} \{0,1\}$ and setting $\boldsymbol{c}$ to either $c(\boldsymbol{s})$ or sampling it uniformly at random. Note that $\mathcal{R}$ can answer each group query made by $\mathcal{A}$ to R, as it can check if $f(h_1(\boldsymbol{s}), h_2(\boldsymbol{s}), X, \boldsymbol{s}, \boldsymbol{c}) \in \mathrm{span}_{\mathbb{Z}_p}[G_0(X) - \boldsymbol{s}, G_1(X) - \boldsymbol{w}]$.

Now, if the vector $(\boldsymbol{s}, \boldsymbol{w})$ that $\mathcal{R}$ received from Ch equals $(G_0(\boldsymbol{x}), G_1(\boldsymbol{x}))$ for some $\boldsymbol{x} \leftarrow_{\$} \mathbb{Z}_p^n$, then $\mathcal{R}$ simulates the game G_q for $\mathcal{A}_{\mathsf{then}}$. On the other hand, if $(\boldsymbol{s}, \boldsymbol{w}) \leftarrow_{\$} \mathbb{Z}_p^n$ has been sampled uniformly at random, then $\mathcal{R}$ simulates the game G_{q+1} for $\mathcal{A}_{\mathsf{then}}$. Hence, $\mathcal{R}$ can use the difference in $\mathcal{A}_{\mathsf{then}}$'s win-probability to decide its decisional MQ-problem. Hence, we have $|\Pr[\mathsf{G}_{q}^{\mathcal{A}_{\mathsf{then}}}(1^\lambda) = 1] - \Pr[\mathsf{G}_{q+1}^{\mathcal{A}_{\mathsf{then}}}(1^\lambda) = 1]| \leq \mu_{\mathsf{MQ}}$. □

Lemma 3. *Let* $n \geq 3$. *Over the randomness of* $(G_0, G_1) \leftarrow_{\$} Q$, *we have*

$$\Pr[\exists \boldsymbol{s}, \boldsymbol{w} \in \mathbb{Z}_p^n, \exists f \in \mathrm{span}_{\mathbb{Z}_p}[G_0(X) - \boldsymbol{s}, G_1(X) - \boldsymbol{w}] \mid f \neq 0, \deg f \leq 1] \leq \frac{2n}{p}.$$

Proof. Let $\boldsymbol{s}, \boldsymbol{w} \in \mathbb{Z}_p^n$ be arbitrary and let $g_1, \ldots, g_{2n} \in \mathbb{Z}_p[X]^{\leq 2}$ be the polynomials computing $(G_0(X) - \boldsymbol{s}, G_1(X) - \boldsymbol{w})$. Denote by $g_1^\top, \ldots, g_{2n}^\top \in \mathbb{Z}_p[X]^2$ their top terms, i.e., $g_i^\top$ is the homogeneous degree-2 part of g_i. Note that $g_1^\top, \ldots, g_{2n}^\top$ are independent of $\boldsymbol{s}$ and $\boldsymbol{w}$. The space $\mathrm{span}_{\mathbb{Z}_p}[G_0(X) - \boldsymbol{s}, G_1(X) - \boldsymbol{w}]$ can only contain a degree-1 polynomial if the top parts cancel out, i.e., if there is some $\alpha \in \mathbb{Z}_p^{2n}$, $\alpha \neq 0$, s.t. $\alpha_1 \cdot g_1^\top(X) + \cdots + \alpha_{2n} \cdot g_{2n}^\top(X) = 0$. Since G_0, G_1 are uniformly at random sampled from Q, the top terms $g_1^\top, \ldots, g_{2n}^\top$ are distributed uniformly at random in $\mathbb{Z}_p[X]^2$. The vector space dimension of $\mathbb{Z}_p[X]^2$ is given by $\dim_{\mathbb{Z}_p}(\mathbb{Z}_p[X]^2) = \binom{n+1}{2}$. Since $\binom{n+1}{2} \geq 2n$, by a Schwartz-Zippel argument, the probability that the terms $g_1^\top, \ldots, g_{2n}^\top$ are linearly dependent is bounded by $2n/p$. □

Lemma 4. *The advantage of* $\mathcal{A}_{\mathsf{then}}$ *at distinguishing* G_{q+1} *and* G_{q+2} *is bounded by* $(2n + q)/p$. *I.e.,* $|\Pr[\mathsf{G}_{q+1}^{\mathcal{A}_{\mathsf{then}}}(1^\lambda) = 1] - \Pr[\mathsf{G}_{q+2}^{\mathcal{A}_{\mathsf{then}}}(1^\lambda) = 1]| \leq (2n + q)/p$.

Proof. G_{q+1} and G_{q+2} only differ in how they handle group queries. We cnegligible.

Because of Lemma 3, with probability $\geq 1 - 2n/p$, the function $(G_0, G_1) \leftarrow_{\$} Q^2$ is sampled such that $\mathrm{span}_{\mathbb{Z}_p}[G_0(X) - \boldsymbol{s}, G_1(X) - \boldsymbol{w}]$ contains no polynomials that are linear in the X-variables (for all $\boldsymbol{s}, \boldsymbol{w} \in \mathbb{Z}_p^n$). In this case, we claim that the statistical distance between the outputs of R in both games are bounded by $1/p$.

Let $f \in A$. First, assume $f \notin B + \text{span}_{\mathbb{Z}_p}[G_0(X) - S, G_1(X) - \boldsymbol{w}]$. In this case, R outputs 0 in G_{q+2} We claim that R in G_{q+1} must also output 0, as $f(h_1(\boldsymbol{s}), h_2(\boldsymbol{s}), X, \boldsymbol{s}, \boldsymbol{c}) \notin \text{span}_{\mathbb{Z}_p}[G_0(X) - \boldsymbol{s}, G_1(X) - \boldsymbol{w}]$. Indeed, modulo B we can eliminate all monomials of f that are not of shape $X_j \cdot X_k$, $j, k \in [n]$, and deduce $f \notin \text{span}_{\mathbb{Z}_p}[G_0(X), G_1(X)] + B$. Now, if $f(h_1(\boldsymbol{s}), h_2(\boldsymbol{s}), X, \boldsymbol{s}, \boldsymbol{c}) \in \text{span}_{\mathbb{Z}_p}[G_0(X) - \boldsymbol{s}, G_1(X) - \boldsymbol{w}]$, we could again eliminate all monomials that are not $X_j \cdot X_k$, and extract the contradicting statement $f \in \text{span}_{\mathbb{Z}_p}[G_0(X), G_1(X)] + B$. Hence, R must also output 0 in G_{q+1}.

Now, let $f' \in B$ s.t. $f - f' \in \text{span}_{\mathbb{Z}_p}[G_0(X) - S, G_1(X) - \boldsymbol{w}]$. Because of Lemma 3, $\text{span}_{\mathbb{Z}_p}[G_0(X) - \boldsymbol{s}, G_1(X) - \boldsymbol{w}]$ does not contain degree-1 polynomials. Hence, the degree-2 polynomial $f(h_1(\boldsymbol{s}), h_2(\boldsymbol{s}), X, \boldsymbol{s}, \boldsymbol{c})$ can only lie in $\text{span}_{\mathbb{Z}_p}[G_0(X) - \boldsymbol{s}, G_1(X) - \boldsymbol{w}]$ if the degree-1 polynomial $f'(h_1(\boldsymbol{s}), h_2(\boldsymbol{s}), X, \boldsymbol{s}, \boldsymbol{c})$ is zero. By a Schwartz-Zippel argument, we have $f'(h_1(\boldsymbol{s}), h_2(\boldsymbol{s}), X, \boldsymbol{s}, \boldsymbol{c}) = 0$ if $f'(h_1(\boldsymbol{s}), h_2(\boldsymbol{s}), \boldsymbol{x}', \boldsymbol{s}, \boldsymbol{c}) = 0$ for $\boldsymbol{x}' \leftarrow_{\$} \mathbb{Z}_p^n$, except with probability $1/p$. Since the output of R in G_{q+1} and G_{q+2} depends on $f(h_1(\boldsymbol{s}), h_2(\boldsymbol{s}), X, \boldsymbol{s}, \boldsymbol{c}) \in \text{span}_{\mathbb{Z}_p}[G_0(X) - \boldsymbol{s}, G_1(X) - \boldsymbol{w}]$ and $f'(h_1(\boldsymbol{s}), h_2(\boldsymbol{s}), \boldsymbol{x}', \boldsymbol{s}, \boldsymbol{c}) = 0$, respectively, the statistical distance in its output behavior is bounded by $1/p$. □

Proof of Theorem 5. Let $\mathcal{A}_{\mathsf{then}}$ be an adversary on the then-challenge of Assumption 1 with time complexity t and advantage $\mu + q\left(\mu_{\mathsf{MQ+}} + \frac{2}{p}\right) + \mu_{\mathsf{MQ}} + \frac{2n+q}{p}$. Because of Lemmas 1, 2 and 4, $\mathcal{A}_{\mathsf{then}}$'s advantage at winning G_{q+2} is at least μ.

Let Ch be a challenger for the if-challenge of Assumption 1. We give a reduction $\mathcal{R}$ that gets challenged by Ch and simulates the then-game for $\mathcal{A}_{\mathsf{then}}$. Let $\mathbb{A}_1 = \langle \mathsf{a}_1 \rangle$, $\mathbb{A}_2 = \langle \mathsf{a}_2 \rangle$ be the p-order groups used by Ch. At the start of the if-game, Ch samples $\boldsymbol{s} \leftarrow_{\$} \mathbb{Z}_p^n$, $b \leftarrow_{\$} \{0,1\}$ and $(h_0, h_1, h_2, c) \leftarrow \mathsf{Samp}(1^\lambda)$. If $b = 0$, it sets $\boldsymbol{c} = c(\boldsymbol{s})$, otherwise, it samples $\boldsymbol{c} \leftarrow_{\$} \mathbb{Z}_p^n$. It initializes $\mathcal{R}$ by sending $c, h_0, h_1, h_2, h_0(\boldsymbol{s}), \mathsf{a}_1^{h_1(\boldsymbol{s})}, \mathsf{a}_2^{h_2(\boldsymbol{s})}, \mathsf{a}_2^{\boldsymbol{s}}, \mathsf{a}_2^{\boldsymbol{c}}$ to it.

As $\mathcal{R}$ cannot control $\mathbb{A}_1, \mathbb{A}_2$, it has to set up its own generic groups $\mathbb{G}_1 = \langle \mathsf{g}_1 \rangle$, $\mathbb{G}_2 = \langle \mathsf{g}_2 \rangle$. $\mathcal{R}$ samples $G_0, G_1 \leftarrow_{\$} Q$, $\boldsymbol{w} \leftarrow_{\$} \mathbb{Z}_p^n$ and sends $c, h_0, h_1, h_2, G_0, G_1$, $h_0(\boldsymbol{s}), \mathsf{g}_1^{H^{(1)}}, \mathsf{g}_2^{H^{(2)}}, \mathsf{g}_2^{S}, \mathsf{g}_1^{X}, \boldsymbol{w}, \mathsf{g}_2^{\boldsymbol{c}}$ to $\mathcal{A}_{\mathsf{then}}$, while simulating game G_{q+2} to $\mathcal{A}_{\mathsf{then}}$.

Whenever $\mathcal{A}_{\mathsf{then}}$ makes an admissible group query $f \in A$, $\mathcal{R}$ computes the output of $\mathsf{R}(f)$ as follows: $\mathcal{R}$ computes the polynomial $f' \in B$ s.t. $f - f' \in \text{span}_{\mathbb{Z}_p}[G_0(X) - S, G_1(X) - \boldsymbol{w}]$ (if such an f' does not exist, $\mathcal{R}$ returns 0), samples $\boldsymbol{x}' \leftarrow_{\$} \mathbb{Z}_p^n$ and checks the equality $f'(h_1(\boldsymbol{s}), h_2(\boldsymbol{s}), \boldsymbol{x}', \boldsymbol{s}, \boldsymbol{c}) = 0$ by verifying $\mathsf{a}_2^{f'(h_1(\boldsymbol{s}), h_2(\boldsymbol{s}), \boldsymbol{x}', \boldsymbol{s}, \boldsymbol{c})} = \mathsf{a}_2^0$. $\mathcal{R}$ can indeed verify this equality of group elements as it is given the group elements $\mathsf{a}_1^{h_1(\boldsymbol{s})}, \mathsf{a}_2^{h_2(\boldsymbol{s})}, \mathsf{a}_2^{\boldsymbol{s}}, \mathsf{a}_2^{\boldsymbol{c}}$ by Ch and knows $\boldsymbol{x}'$ in plain.

Finally, note that, for each group query made by $\mathcal{A}_{\mathsf{then}}$, $\mathcal{R}$ makes exactly one group query to Ch. Hence, $\mathcal{R}$ makes at most q group queries in total. □

Acknowledgments. We thank Jonas Steinbach and Gertjan De Mulder for helpful discussions on BIP 32, Dennis Hofheinz and Julia Kastner for helpful discussions on early prototypes of our CVRF, and Klaus Kraßnitzer for running pairing benchmarks on his MacBook Pro.

Christoph U. Günther: This research was funded in whole or in part by the Austrian Science Fund (FWF) 10.55776/F85. For open access purposes, the author has applied

References

1. Abdalla, M., Catalano, D., Fiore, D.: Verifiable random functions from identity-based key encapsulation. In: Joux, A. (ed.) EUROCRYPT 2009. LNCS, vol. 5479, pp. 554–571. Springer, Heidelberg (2009). https://doi.org/10.1007/978-3-642-01001-9_32
2. Abusalah, H., Fuchsbauer, G., Pietrzak, K.: Constrained PRFs for unbounded inputs. In: Sako, K. (ed.) CT-RSA 2016. LNCS, vol. 9610, pp. 413–428. Springer, Cham (2016). https://doi.org/10.1007/978-3-319-29485-8_24
3. Agrawal, S., Wichs, D., Yamada, S.: Optimal broadcast encryption from LWE and pairings in the standard model. In: Pass, R., Pietrzak, K. (eds.) TCC 2020. LNCS, vol. 12550, pp. 149–178. Springer, Cham (2020). https://doi.org/10.1007/978-3-030-64375-1_6
4. Akiyama, R., et al.: QR-UOV. Technical report, National Institute of Standards and Technology (2024). https://csrc.nist.gov/Projects/pqc-dig-sig/round-2-additional-signatures
5. Aranha, D.F., Gouvêa, C.P.L.: RELIC is an Efficient LIbrary for Cryptography. https://github.com/relic-toolkit/relic
6. Belenkiy, M., Chase, M., Kohlweiss, M., Lysyanskaya, A.: Compact E-cash and simulatable VRFs revisited. In: Shacham, H., Waters, B. (eds.) Pairing 2009. LNCS, vol. 5671, pp. 114–131. Springer, Heidelberg (2009). https://doi.org/10.1007/978-3-642-03298-1_9
7. Benadjila, R., Bouillaguet, C., Feneuil, T., Rivain, M.: MQOM — MQ on my Mind. Technical report, National Institute of Standards and Technology (2024). https://csrc.nist.gov/Projects/pqc-dig-sig/round-2-additional-signatures
8. Beullens, W., Campos, F., Celi, S., Hess, B., Kannwischer, M.J.: MAYO. Technical report, National Institute of Standards and Technology (2024). https://csrc.nist.gov/Projects/pqc-dig-sig/round-2-additional-signatures
9. Beullens, W., et al.: UOV — Unbalanced Oil and Vinegar. Technical report, National Institute of Standards and Technology (2024). https://csrc.nist.gov/Projects/pqc-dig-sig/round-2-additional-signatures
10. Bitansky, N.: Verifiable random functions from non-interactive witness-indistinguishable proofs. In: Kalai, Y., Reyzin, L. (eds.) TCC 2017. LNCS, vol. 10678, pp. 567–594. Springer, Cham (2017). https://doi.org/10.1007/978-3-319-70503-3_19
11. Bitansky, N.: Verifiable random functions from non-interactive witness-indistinguishable proofs. J. Cryptol. **33**(2), 459–493 (2019). https://doi.org/10.1007/s00145-019-09331-1
12. Boneh, D., Haitner, I., Lindell, Y., Segev, G.: Exponent-VRFs and their applications. In: Fehr, S., Fouque, P.A. (eds.) EUROCRYPT 2025, pp. 195–224. Springer, Cham (2025). https://doi.org/10.1007/978-3-031-91098-2_8
13. Boneh, D., Montgomery, H.W., Raghunathan, A.: Algebraic pseudorandom functions with improved efficiency from the augmented cascade. In: Al-Shaer, E., Keromytis, A.D., Shmatikov, V. (eds.) ACM CCS 2010, pp. 131–140. ACM Press (2010). https://doi.org/10.1145/1866307.1866323

14. Boneh, D., Waters, B.: Constrained pseudorandom functions and their applications. In: Sako, K., Sarkar, P. (eds.) ASIACRYPT 2013. LNCS, vol. 8270, pp. 280–300. Springer, Heidelberg (2013). https://doi.org/10.1007/978-3-642-42045-0_15
15. Boyle, E., Goldwasser, S., Ivan, I.: Functional signatures and pseudorandom functions. In: Krawczyk, H. (ed.) PKC 2014. LNCS, vol. 8383, pp. 501–519. Springer, Heidelberg (2014). https://doi.org/10.1007/978-3-642-54631-0_29
16. Brandt, N., Hofheinz, D., Kastner, J., Ünal, A.: The price of verifiability: lower bounds for verifiable random functions. In: Kiltz, E., Vaikuntanathan, V. (eds.) TCC 2022, Part II. LNCS, vol. 13748, pp. 747–776. Springer, Cham (2022). https://doi.org/10.1007/978-3-031-22365-5_26
17. Brandt, N., Noval, M.C., Günther, C.U., Ünal, A., Wohnig, S.: Constrained verifiable random functions without obfuscation and friends. Cryptology ePrint Archive, Paper 2025/1045 (2025). https://eprint.iacr.org/2025/1045
18. Brzuska, C., Ünal, A., Woo, I.K.Y.: Evasive LWE assumptions: definitions, classes, and counterexamples. In: Chung, K.M., Sasaki, Y. (eds.) ASIACRYPT 2024, Part IV. LNCS, vol. 15487, pp. 418–449. Springer, Singapore (2024). https://doi.org/10.1007/978-981-96-0894-2_14
19. Chandran, N., Raghuraman, S., Vinayagamurthy, D.: Constrained pseudorandom functions: verifiable and delegatable. Cryptology ePrint Archive, Report 2014/522 (2014). https://eprint.iacr.org/2014/522
20. Cheng, C.-M., Chou, T., Niederhagen, R., Yang, B.-Y.: Solving quadratic equations with XL on parallel architectures. In: Prouff, E., Schaumont, P. (eds.) CHES 2012. LNCS, vol. 7428, pp. 356–373. Springer, Heidelberg (2012). https://doi.org/10.1007/978-3-642-33027-8_21
21. Courtois, N., Klimov, A., Patarin, J., Shamir, A.: Efficient algorithms for solving overdefined systems of multivariate polynomial equations. In: Preneel, B. (ed.) EUROCRYPT 2000. LNCS, vol. 1807, pp. 392–407. Springer, Heidelberg (2000). https://doi.org/10.1007/3-540-45539-6_27
22. Dao, Q., Jain, A., Jin, Z.: Non-interactive zero-knowledge from LPN and MQ. In: Reyzin, L., Stebila, D. (eds.) CRYPTO 2024, Part IX. LNCS, vol. 14928, pp. 321–360. Springer, Cham (2024). https://doi.org/10.1007/978-3-031-68400-5_10
23. Datta, P.: Constrained pseudorandom functions from functional encryption. Theor. Comput. Sci. **809**, 137–170 (2020). https://doi.org/10.1016/j.tcs.2019.12.004. https://www.sciencedirect.com/science/article/pii/S0304397519307662
24. Datta, P., Dutta, R., Mukhopadhyay, S.: Constrained pseudorandom functions for unconstrained inputs revisited: achieving verifiability and key delegation. In: Fehr, S. (ed.) PKC 2017. LNCS, vol. 10175, pp. 463–493. Springer, Heidelberg (2017). https://doi.org/10.1007/978-3-662-54388-7_16
25. Datta, P., Dutta, R., Mukhopadhyay, S.: Constrained pseudorandom functions for turing machines revisited: how to achieve verifiability and key delegation. Algorithmica **81**(9), 3245–3390 (2019). https://doi.org/10.1007/s00453-019-00576-7
26. Deshpande, A., Koppula, V., Waters, B.: Constrained pseudorandom functions for unconstrained inputs. In: Fischlin, M., Coron, J.-S. (eds.) EUROCRYPT 2016. LNCS, vol. 9666, pp. 124–153. Springer, Heidelberg (2016). https://doi.org/10.1007/978-3-662-49896-5_5
27. Dodis, Y., Yampolskiy, A.: A verifiable random function with short proofs and keys. In: Vaudenay, S. (ed.) PKC 2005. LNCS, vol. 3386, pp. 416–431. Springer, Heidelberg (2005). https://doi.org/10.1007/978-3-540-30580-4_28

28. Fuchsbauer, G.: Constrained verifiable random functions. In: Abdalla, M., De Prisco, R. (eds.) SCN 2014. LNCS, vol. 8642, pp. 95–114. Springer, Cham (2014). https://doi.org/10.1007/978-3-319-10879-7_7
29. Goldreich, O., Goldwasser, S., Micali, S.: How to construct random functions. J. ACM **33**(4), 792–807 (1986). https://doi.org/10.1145/6490.6503
30. Goyal, R., Hohenberger, S., Koppula, V., Waters, B.: A generic approach to constructing and proving verifiable random functions. In: Kalai, Y., Reyzin, L. (eds.) TCC 2017. LNCS, vol. 10678, pp. 537–566. Springer, Cham (2017). https://doi.org/10.1007/978-3-319-70503-3_18
31. Hansen, A.B., Nielsen, J.B., Simkin, M.: Ocash: fully anonymous payments between blockchain light clients. In: Jager, T., Pan, J. (eds.) PKC 2025, pp. 169–202. Springer, Cham (2025). https://doi.org/10.1007/978-3-031-91832-2_6
32. Håstad, J., Impagliazzo, R., Levin, L.A., Luby, M.: A pseudorandom generator from any one-way function. SIAM J. Comput. **28**(4), 1364–1396 (1999)
33. Hofheinz, D., Jager, T.: Verifiable random functions from standard assumptions. In: Kushilevitz, E., Malkin, T. (eds.) TCC 2016. LNCS, vol. 9562, pp. 336–362. Springer, Heidelberg (2016). https://doi.org/10.1007/978-3-662-49096-9_14
34. Hofheinz, D., Kastner, J., Klein, K.: The power of undirected rewindings for adaptive security. In: Handschuh, H., Lysyanskaya, A. (eds.) CRYPTO 2023, Part II. LNCS, vol. 14082, pp. 725–758. Springer, Cham (2023). https://doi.org/10.1007/978-3-031-38545-2_24
35. Hohenberger, S., Waters, B.: Constructing verifiable random functions with large input spaces. In: Gilbert, H. (ed.) EUROCRYPT 2010. LNCS, vol. 6110, pp. 656–672. Springer, Heidelberg (2010). https://doi.org/10.1007/978-3-642-13190-5_33
36. Jager, T.: Verifiable random functions from weaker assumptions. In: Dodis, Y., Nielsen, J.B. (eds.) TCC 2015. LNCS, vol. 9015, pp. 121–143. Springer, Heidelberg (2015). https://doi.org/10.1007/978-3-662-46497-7_5
37. Katsumata, S.: On the untapped potential of encoding predicates by arithmetic circuits and their applications. In: Takagi, T., Peyrin, T. (eds.) ASIACRYPT 2017. LNCS, vol. 10626, pp. 95–125. Springer, Cham (2017). https://doi.org/10.1007/978-3-319-70700-6_4
38. Kiayias, A., Papadopoulos, S., Triandopoulos, N., Zacharias, T.: Delegatable pseudorandom functions and applications. In: Sadeghi, A.R., Gligor, V.D., Yung, M. (eds.) ACM CCS 2013, pp. 669–684. ACM Press (2013). https://doi.org/10.1145/2508859.2516668
39. Kohl, L.: Hunting and gathering – verifiable random functions from standard assumptions with short proofs. In: Lin, D., Sako, K. (eds.) PKC 2019. LNCS, vol. 11443, pp. 408–437. Springer, Cham (2019). https://doi.org/10.1007/978-3-030-17259-6_14
40. Levin, L.A.: One-way functions and pseudorandom generators. In: 17th ACM STOC, pp. 363–365. ACM Press (1985). https://doi.org/10.1145/22145.22185
41. Liang, B., Li, H., Chang, J.: Constrained verifiable random functions from indistinguishability obfuscation. In: Au, M.-H., Miyaji, A. (eds.) ProvSec 2015. LNCS, vol. 9451, pp. 43–60. Springer, Cham (2015). https://doi.org/10.1007/978-3-319-26059-4_3
42. Liu, M., Zhang, P., Wu, Q.: A novel construction of constrained verifiable random functions. Secur. Commun. Netw. **2019**(1), 4187892 (2019). https://doi.org/10.1155/2019/4187892
43. Lysyanskaya, A.: Unique signatures and verifiable random functions from the DH-DDH separation. In: Yung, M. (ed.) CRYPTO 2002. LNCS, vol. 2442, pp. 597–612. Springer, Heidelberg (2002). https://doi.org/10.1007/3-540-45708-9_38

44. Maurer, U.: Abstract models of computation in cryptography. In: Smart, N.P. (ed.) Cryptography and Coding 2005. LNCS, vol. 3796, pp. 1–12. Springer, Heidelberg (2005). https://doi.org/10.1007/11586821_1
45. Micali, S., Rabin, M.O., Vadhan, S.P.: Verifiable random functions. In: 40th FOCS, pp. 120–130. IEEE Computer Society Press (1999). https://doi.org/10.1109/SFFCS.1999.814584
46. Mohamed, M.S.E., Ding, J., Buchmann, J.: Algebraic cryptanalysis of MQQ public key cryptosystem by MutantXL. Cryptology ePrint Archive, Report 2008/451 (2008). https://eprint.iacr.org/2008/451
47. Mohamed, M.S.E., Mohamed, W.S.A.E., Ding, J., Buchmann, J.: *MXL2*: solving polynomial equations over GF(2) using an improved mutant strategy. In: Buchmann, J., Ding, J. (eds.) PQCrypto 2008. LNCS, vol. 5299, pp. 203–215. Springer, Heidelberg (2008). https://doi.org/10.1007/978-3-540-88403-3_14
48. Niehues, D.: Verifiable random functions with optimal tightness. In: Garay, J.A. (ed.) PKC 2021. LNCS, vol. 12711, pp. 61–91. Springer, Cham (2021). https://doi.org/10.1007/978-3-030-75248-4_3
49. Roşie, R.: Adaptive-secure VRFs with shorter keys from static assumptions. In: Camenisch, J., Papadimitratos, P. (eds.) CANS 2018. LNCS, vol. 11124, pp. 440–459. Springer, Cham (2018). https://doi.org/10.1007/978-3-030-00434-7_22
50. Shoup, V.: Lower bounds for discrete logarithms and related problems. In: Fumy, W. (ed.) EUROCRYPT 1997. LNCS, vol. 1233, pp. 256–266. Springer, Heidelberg (1997). https://doi.org/10.1007/3-540-69053-0_18
51. Tsabary, R.: Candidate witness encryption from lattice techniques. In: Dodis, Y., Shrimpton, T. (eds.) CRYPTO 2022, Part I. LNCS, vol. 13507, pp. 535–559. Springer, Cham (2022). https://doi.org/10.1007/978-3-031-15802-5_19
52. Wee, H.: Optimal broadcast encryption and CP-ABE from evasive lattice assumptions. In: Dunkelman, O., Dziembowski, S. (eds.) EUROCRYPT 2022, Part II. LNCS, vol. 13276, pp. 217–241. Springer, Cham (2022). https://doi.org/10.1007/978-3-031-07085-3_8
53. Yamada, S.: Asymptotically compact adaptively secure lattice IBEs and verifiable random functions via generalized partitioning techniques. In: Katz, J., Shacham, H. (eds.) CRYPTO 2017. LNCS, vol. 10403, pp. 161–193. Springer, Cham (2017). https://doi.org/10.1007/978-3-319-63697-9_6
54. Yang, B.-Y., Chen, J.-M.: All in the XL family: theory and practice. In: Park, C., Chee, S. (eds.) ICISC 2004. LNCS, vol. 3506, pp. 67–86. Springer, Heidelberg (2005). https://doi.org/10.1007/11496618_7
55. Zan, Y., Li, H., Xu, H.: Adaptively secure constrained verifiable random function. In: Yung, M., Chen, C., Meng, W. (eds.) Science of Cyber Security, pp. 367–385. Springer, Cham (2023). https://doi.org/10.1007/978-3-031-45933-7_22

Provably Memory-Hard Proofs of Work with Memory-Easy Verification

Jeremiah Blocki(✉) and Nathan Smearsoll

Purdue University, West Lafayette, IN 47907, USA
{jblocki,nsmearso}@purdue.edu

Abstract. A Proof of Work (PoW) is an important construction for spam-mitigation and distributed consensus protocols. Intuitively, a PoW is a short proof that is easy for the verifier to check but moderately expensive for a prover to generate. However, existing proofs of work are not egalitarian in the sense that the amortized cost to generate a PoW proof using customized hardware is often several orders of magnitude lower than the cost for an honest party to generate a proof on a personal computer. Because Memory-Hard Functions (MHFs) appear to be egalitarian, there have been multiple attempts to construct Memory-Hard Proofs of Work (MHPoW) which require memory-hard computation to generate, but are efficient to verify. Biryukov and Khovratovich (Usenix, 2016) developed a MHPoW candidate called Merkle Tree Proofs (MTP) using the Argon2d MHF. However, they did not provide a formal security proof and Dinur and Nadler (Crypto, 2017) found an attack which exploited the data-dependencies of the underlying Argon2d graph.

We revisit the security of the MTP framework and formally prove, in the parallel random oracle model, that the MTP framework is sound when instantiated with a suitable *data-independent* Memory-Hard Function (iMHF). We generically lower bound the cumulative memory cost (cmc) of any prover for the protocol by the pebbling cost of the *ex-post facto* graph. We also prove that, as long as the underlying graph of the original iMHF is sufficiently depth-robust, the *ex-post facto* graph will have high cumulative memory cost—except with negligible probability. In particular, if we instantiate the iMHF with DRSample then we obtain a MHPoW with the following properties: (1) An honest prover for the protocol can run in sequential time $O(N)$, (2) The proofs have size $\texttt{polylog}(N)$ and can be verified in time $\texttt{polylog}(N)$ (3) Any malicious prover who produces a valid proof must incur high cmc at least $\Omega\left(\frac{N^2}{\log N}\right)$. We also develop general pebbling attacks which we use to show that (1) any iMHF based MHPoW using the MTP framework has proof size at least $\Omega\left(\log^2 N/\log\log N\right)$, and (2) at least $\tilde{\Omega}(N^{0.32})$ when the iMHF is instantiated with Argon2i, the data-independent version of Argon2.

1 Introduction

Proofs of Work (PoWs), originally introduced by [26] to combat spam email, allow a prover to convince a verifier that they have spent significant computa-

B. Applebaum and H. Lin (Eds.): TCC 2025, LNCS 16271, pp. 512–544, 2026.
https://doi.org/10.1007/978-3-032-12290-2_17

tional work in evaluating a function upon some string, such as an email message or list of transactions on a blockchain. In the spam reduction application, before sending an e-mail χ the sender would generate a proof of work $\pi_\chi = \texttt{Prove}(\chi)$ for the string χ and send both χ and π_χ to the recipient. The recipient would discard the email χ unless the proof of work for is valid i.e., $\texttt{Verify}(\chi, \pi_\chi) = 1$. Importantly, it should be moderately expensive to generate a proof π_χ for a string χ, but the final proof π_χ should be short and inexpensive to verify. PoWs can also be used to protect against distributed denial of service attacks and in many blockchain based distributed consensus protocols.

Hashcash [11] is one of the simplest and most natural PoW schemes and the backbone of the Bitcoin consensus mechanism. Fixing a cryptographic hash function $\mathcal{H} : \{0,1\}^* \rightarrow \{0,1\}^\lambda$ and a hardness parameter κ the Hashcash PoW algorithm $\texttt{Prove}^{\mathcal{H}}(\chi, \kappa)$ simply searches for a string π_χ such that $\mathcal{H}(\chi, \pi_\chi)$ has κ leading 0's i.e., $\mathcal{H}(\chi, \pi_\chi) = x \circ 0^\kappa$ for some string $x \in \{0,1\}^{\lambda-\kappa}$. The parameter κ controls the hardness of the PoW i.e., in the random oracle model any (possibly malicious) proving algorithm will need to make 2^κ queries in expectation to generate a valid proof for χ. The Hashcash verification algorithm is incredibly efficient. Given a proof π_χ the verification algorithm $\texttt{Verify}^{\mathcal{H}}(\chi, \pi_\chi, \kappa)$ simply computes $y = H(\chi, \pi_\chi)$ and checks that y has κ leading 0's.

Unfortunately, the Hashcash PoW is not egalitarian—meaning that the cost of generating a proof of work on customized hardware can be orders of magnitude cheaper than the cost of generating a proof on a personal computer. For example, Application-Specific Integrated Circuits (ASICs) for computing the SHA-256 hashing algorithm are four to five orders of magnitude more energy efficient than the CPU on a state of the art personal computer e.g., see [32,35]. This is highly undesirable for applications like spam mitigation as there is no good way to tune the hardness parameter κ. Either it becomes prohibitively expensive for legitimate senders to generate a proof of work on their personal computer, or it will be relatively cheap for a spamming attacker to generate proofs of work on a customized ASIC.

Biryukov and Khovratovich [15] proposed developing egalitarian proofs of work: proofs of work where the cost of generating a proof using customized hardware is not significantly better than on general-purpose hardware. Motivated by the observation that memory costs tend to be egalitarian across different architectures they introduced a candidate *memory-hard* proof of work (MHPoW) called Merkle Tree Proofs (MTP) which combined Merkle Trees (MTs) with the Argon2 Memory-Hard Function [13]. Intuitively, the prover first runs the Argon2 evaluation algorithm on input χ to generate N memory blocks $L_1, \ldots, L_N$ using a random oracle $\mathcal{H}$ where $N = 2^n$ denotes the running time parameter. Then the prover computes the root τ of a Merkle Tree commitment to the labels $L_1, \ldots, L_N$, and applies the Fiat-Shamir paradigm to generate k challenges $c_1, \ldots, c_k$ by hashing the root τ e.g., $c_i = 1 + (\mathcal{H}(i, \tau) \mod N)$. For each challenge c_i, the prover uses the Merkle Tree to prove that the label c_i is locally consistent by revealing L_{c_i} and any dependent label value L_u which was used to compute L_{c_i}. The final proof π_χ consists of the Merkle Tree root τ along with the Merkle Tree openings for each challenge label L_{c_i} and depended labels.

The MTP construction [15] seems to be natural as the Argon2 MHF is believed to have maximal cumulative memory complexity $\Omega(N^2)$, and the challenges ensure that almost all labels are computed in the expected way. However, [15] did not prove that their MTP construction satisfied any formal notion of memory-hardness. Dinur and Nadler [25] found an attack on MTP which significantly reduces the cost of generating a proof e.g., by a factor of 55, 000. Biryukov and Khovratovich [14] proposed a different MHPoW candidate called Equihash along with an argument that the construction was secure. However, Alcock and Ren [1] demonstrated a flaw in the security analysis of Equihash raising questions about whether or not Equihash is truly memory-hard/egalitarian. This leads us to our central question:

Can a memory-hard proof of work scheme be designed which is provably secure?

One naive solution to designing egalitarian memory-hard proofs of work would be to simply have the prover compute a memory-hard function f with the input χ and send the output $\pi = f(\chi)$ to the verifier. We have constructions of memory-hard functions which are *provably* memory-hard (i.e., have high cumulative memory complexity) such as SCRYPT [7] and DRSample [4] in the parallel random oracle model. While this solution ensures that any prover that generates a valid MHPoW would need to perform memory-hard computation, the problem is that the verifier would also need to perform expensive memory-hard computation.

An alternate solution would be to have the prover compute $y = f(\chi)$ and then generate a succinct non-interactive argument of knowledge (SNARK [12]) π_χ proving that the output is correct. However, the overhead would likely be quite high in practice. Furthermore, it is not clear that the solution would still be egalitarian. In particular, the cost for an honest party to generate the SNARK proof π_χ is substantially higher than the cost to evaluate the MHF $f(\chi)$ i.e., prover costs would dominated by the cost to generate the SNARK. The cumulative memory cost to generate the SNARK proof π_χ would likely be substantially lower for a parallel attacker using customized hardware making the overall solution non-egalitarian.

Another alternative solution would be to use trapdoor memory-hard functions such as td-SCRYPT [16]. Auerbach et al. [10] proved that, without the trapdoor, the cumulative memory complexity was at least $\Omega(N^2/\log N)$ and Blocki and Lee [18] improved the lower bound to $\Omega(N^2)$. Any party who has the trapdoor can evaluate the function at substantially reduced cost $\tilde{O}(N)$. Thus, a verifier who has the trapdoor could validate the claim that $y = f(\chi)$ at greatly reduced cost. However, the solution no longer qualifies as a proof of work because there is no efficient public verifier i.e., verifiers that do not have the trapdoor will need perform memory-hard computation to check that $y = f(\chi)$. If the prover wants a proof that can be efficiently checked by two different verifiers s/he would need to generate two separate proofs. Furthermore, even for a verifier that has the trapdoor, the solution is not as efficient as we would like. Ideally we would like the MHPoW verification algorithm to run in time $O(\texttt{polylog}(N))$. By contrast, computing the td-SCRYPT function with the trapdoor requires at least $\Omega(N)$ steps.

Scientific understanding of memory-hard functions has advanced significantly over the past decade, including in formal mathematical definitions to quantify "memory-hardness" [6,9,35], techniques to analyze memory-hard functions [2,3,5,8,17,21], and techniques to construct memory-hard functions. Alwen and Serbinekno [9] pointed out that the classical notion of space-time complexity is not suitable for defining memory-hardness [4,5,17]. In particular, a function with high space-time complexity does not necessarily have high amortized space-time complexity i.e., a parallel attacker may be able to evaluate the function on multiple inputs without any increase to its space-time costs. Thus, Alwen and Serbinekno [9] introduced the notion of cumulative memory complexity to quantify the amortized space-time complexity of a memory-hard function.

While the definition of cumulative memory complexity (or equivalently amortized space-time complexity) extends naturally to the Memory-Hard Proof of Work setting, we still lack techniques to analyze the security of MHPoW candidates. Alwen and Serbinenko also proved that—in the parallel random oracle model—the cumulative memory complexity of a data-independent memory hard function (iMHF) $f_{G,\mathcal{H}}$, a class which provides natural resistance to side-channel attacks, is fully captured by the cumulative pebbling cost of the underlying data-dependency graph G. This powerful connection between cumulative memory complexity and graph pebbling greatly simplifies the task of cryptanalyzing iMHF candidates and has been exploited both to develop attacks on iMHF candidates [2,3,5,8,17,21], and to develop iMHFs [4,5,17] with provably high cumulative memory complexity by constructing depth-robust graphs with provably high cumulative pebbling cost. However, it is unclear whether or not one could establish a similar connection between graph pebbling and the cumulative memory complexity of a MHPoW. This leads us to our second question:

Can we relate the cumulative memory complexity of a MHPoW to the pebbling cost of its DAG?

1.1 Our Contributions

We prove that the Merkle tree proofs framework yields a secure memory-hard proof of work when instantiated with a suitable data-independent memory hard function. A data-independent memory-hard function $f_{G,H}$ can be specified using a random oracle $H : \{0,1\}^* \to \{0,1\}^\lambda$ and a Directed Acyclic Graph (DAG) G with N nodes and constant indegree. Applying the Merkle Tree Proofs framework to $f_{G,H}$ with security parameter k and label size λ, we obtain a MHPoW $(\texttt{Prove}^H, \texttt{Verify}^H)$ such that (1) the honest prover algorithm $\texttt{Prove}^H(\chi, N)$ has cmc at most $O(N^2\lambda)$ and generates a proof of size $O(k\lambda \log N)$, (2) the honest verifier makes $O(k \log N)$ queries to the hash function $H : \{0,1\}^* \to \{0,1\}^\lambda$ and (3) except with negligible probability, any dishonest prover $\texttt{Prove}'$ in the parallel random oracle model must incur cumulative memory complexity at least $\mathsf{cmc}(\mathtt{Prove}') = \Omega(\mathsf{cc}(G-S)\lambda)$ where $|S| \leq N\lambda/k$. Here, $G-S$ denotes the graph G after removing all nodes in $S \subseteq V(G)$ and any incident edges. The notation $\mathsf{cc}(G-S)$ denotes the cumulative pebbling cost of the best parallel pebbling of $G-S$.

For an iMHF $f_{G,H}$ Alwen and Serbinenko [9] proved that $\mathsf{cmc}(f_{G,H}) = \Omega(\mathsf{cc}(G)\lambda)$ i.e., any evaluation algorithm for $f_{G,H}$ has cumulative memory cost lower bounded directly by the cumulative pebbling cost of G. In our setting a cheating prover may never actually compute $f_{G,H}$ i.e., because the verifier cannot double check all of the prover's computations a cheating prover may make up the values for some intermediate labels without getting caught. However, we can conclude that $\mathsf{cmc}(\mathtt{Prove}') \geq \Omega\left(\min_{S:|S|\leq N\lambda/k} \mathsf{cc}(G-S)\lambda\right)$. Thus, a suitable iMHF DAG G should have the property that $\mathsf{cc}(G-S)$ is large for all reasonably large sets $S \subseteq V(G)$. We show that this property hold as long as the graph G is instantiated by a depth-robust graph such as DRSample [4]. In particular, the DRSample graph has the property that, for some suitable constant $c > 0$ and any set S of at most $|S| \leq \frac{cN}{\log N}$ nodes, the subgraph $G' = G - S$ still has cumulative complexity $\Omega\left(\frac{N^2}{\log N}\right)$, which is asymptotically equivalent to the original DRSample graph G [4,17]. Thus, setting $k = O(\lambda \log N)$ we obtain a MHPoW with proof size $O(\lambda^2 \log^2 N)$ such that the verifier only makes $O(\lambda \log^2 N)$ queries to the random oracle H. Any cheating prover $\mathtt{Prove}'$ must incur cmc at least $\Omega\left(\frac{N^2\lambda}{\log N}\right)$.

We also show that instantiating the MTP MHPoW framework with the Argon2i [13] graph G yields provable guarantees. However, the proof size must be larger, and the cmc guarantee will be much weaker e.g., if we are willing to tolerate a proof size of $\Omega\left(N^{1/3}\lambda\right)$ then we can ensure that any cheating prover incurs cmc at least $\widetilde{\Omega}\left(N^{5/3}\lambda\right)$.

Finally, we analyze the inherent limitations of MTP-style constructions by developing pebbling-based attacks on MTP MHPoWs. The attacker first picks a set S of nodes to "delete" from the graph and then finds a low-cost pebbling for $G-S$. As long as the set $|S| \leq N/k$ is not too big we can construct a cheating prover $\mathtt{Prove}'$ which succeeds with constant probability and has cumulative memory complexity at most $\mathsf{cmc} \leq \mathsf{cc}(G-S)\lambda$. Thus, by finding pebbling attacks we can lower bound the parameter k (number of challenges) and the size of the proof necessary to prevent attacks with lower than desired cumulative memory complexity. Specific findings include the following:

- In general, for any DAG G with N nodes and constant indegree, if $k = o(\log N/\log\log N)$ then there is a set $|S| \leq N/k$ such that $\mathsf{cc}(G-S) = o(N^2/\log^c N)$ for any constant $c \geq 1$. In particular, for any graph G that we use to instantiate our MTP-style MHPoW our proof size must be at least $\Omega(\lambda \log^2 N/\log\log N)$ or else there will be a cheating prover with lower cumulative memory complexity than we hope e.g., $\mathsf{cmc} = o(N^2\lambda/\log^{1000} N)$.
- For the Argon2i DAG [13] we show that for any $k \geq 1$ there is a set $|S| \leq N/k$ such that $\mathsf{cc}(G-S) = O(Nk^{12/5})$. If $k = o\left(N^{5/18}\right)$ then $\mathsf{cc}(G-S) = o(N^{5/3})$

and the cc bound approaches N as k grows smaller. Thus, when instantiating our MTP MHPoW with Argon2i we must pick an undesirably large k (leading to larger proof sizes) just to ensure the cmc is not $O(\lambda N \operatorname{polylog} N)$.

1.2 Related Work

Merkle Trees and Their Applications to Proofs of Space and Proofs of Sequential Work. A Merkle Tree, introduced by [31], is a short commitment to a large set of strings. Given a particular commitment, one can later reveal any of the strings used, to show that their value was indeed committed to. Merkle Trees have been used previously to construct Proofs of Space (PoS) [27] and Proofs of Sequential Work (PoSWs) [30]. Constructions of PoS [27] and PoSWs [30] are similar to our construction of a Memory-Hard Proof of Work. In particular, constructions of PoSWs [23,30] and PoS [27,34] involve using a directed acyclic graph and a cryptographic hash function (Random Oracle) to generate labels for each node in the graph. Similarly to our construction, the prover commits to the labels using a Merkle Tree structure then proves to the verifier that most nodes in the graph are *locally consistent* i.e., when challenged to prove that a node v is locally consistent the prover will use the Merkle Tree to reveal the label of node v as well as the labels of v's parents. In both cases these consistency challenges can be generated non-interactively by invoking the Fiat-Shamir paradigm—Proofs of Space require a separate interactive audit phase where the verifier periodically challenges the prover to confirm that the prover has still allocated space on its hard disk. One can formally prove that PoSWs constructions [23,30] are secure in the parallel random oracle model—these proofs were later extended to the parallel quantum random oracle model [19,22]. While the notion of PoSW security is quite different from Memory-Hard Proofs of Work some of analysis techniques are useful in our context e.g., the notion of a "bad-order" event in the analysis of [23] and the partial Merkle Tree extraction technique from [19].

Merkle Tree Proofs. Biryukov and Khovratovich [15] proposed the first candidate construction of a Memory-Hard Proof of Work called Merkle Tree Proofs following a similar approach to prior constructions of PoSW [30] and PoS [27,34]. One important distinction for their construction was that the prover used their data-dependent MHF Argon2d to generate the initial labels committed to by the Merkle Tree. Because Argon2d is data-dependent the directed acyclic graph is not fixed a priori and the directed edges in the graph are dependent on intermediate labels. Biryukov and Khovratovich [15] did not provide any rigorous security proofs for their construction, and Dinur and Nadler [25] later gave an attack on MTP which exploited the fact that a malicious prover could modify the edge structure in a data-dependent graph by performing precomputation and then selectively modifying several of the intermediate labels to advantageously control to edge structure. The attack of Dinur and Nadler [25] highlights the importance of rigorous security proofs for MHPoWs. We demonstrate the the Merkle Tree Proof framework used by Biryukov and Khovratovich [15] is sound as long as the underlying graph is fixed a priori (i.e., cannot be adversarially modified) and is sufficiently depth-robust.

Memory-Hard Functions. The notion of a Memory-Hard Proof of Work is similar to that of a standard Memory-Hard Function. Alwen and Serbinenko [9] gave the first rigorous security definitions and proofs for a memory-hard function. In particular, they introduced the notion of *cumulative memory cost (cmc)* to model the *amortized space-time* complexity of a function. Their security analysis provided a more general pebbling reduction showing that the cmc of data-independent Memory-Hard Functions was fully characterized by the pebbling cost of the underlying DAG. Alwen and Blocki [2] showed that *any* directed acyclic graph with N nodes and constant indegree had cumulative pebbling complexity at most $O(N^2 \log\log N/\log N)$ and that known iMHF candidates such as Argon2i (winner of the password hashing competition[1]) had substantially lower cumulative pebbling complexity. On the positive side Alwen et al. [4,5] constructed depth-robust graphs with constant indegree and cumulative pebbling complexity *at least* $\Omega(N^2/\log N)$. These depth-robust graph are also useful for constructing Memory-Hard Proofs of Work.

1.3 Technical Overview

Our central technical contribution is to provide an extractor argument linking the cumulative memory complexity of a Memory Hard Proof of Work constructed using the Merkle Tree Proof framework to the pebbling complexity of the underlying directed acyclic graph G in the Parallel Random Oracle Model (pROM). Previously, Alwen and Serbinenko provided a similar extractor argument linking the cumulative memory complexity of a data-independent Memory Hard Function to the cumulative pebbling complexity of the underlying DAG G in the pROM. We begin by reviewing the extractor argument of [9] highlighting additional challenges that arise in our PoW context and how we overcome them.

Review: Parallel Pebbling, the Parallel Random Oracle Model, and Graph Labeling. Given a graph $G = (V = [N], E)$ with nodes $V = \{1, \ldots, N = 2^n\}$ given in topological order, a random oracle H, and an input string χ, we can label each vertex of G as follows: we label the first node $\ell_1 = H(\chi, 1)$, then label each node v with incoming edges from $\{u_1, \ldots, u_k\} = \{u : (u,v) \in E\} \doteq \mathsf{parents}(v, G)$ by computing $\ell_v = H(\chi, v, \ell_{u_1}, \ldots, \ell_{u_k})$. A pebbling $P = (P_0, P_1, \ldots, P_t)$ of G is a sequence of sets $P_0, P_1, P_2, \ldots, P_t \subseteq P_t$ such that (1) $P_0 = \{\}$, (2) $\forall i < t, v \in P_{i+1} \setminus P_i$ we have $\mathsf{parents}(v, G) \doteq \{u : (u,v) \in E\} \subseteq P_i$ and (3) $V \subseteq \bigcup_i P_i$. Intuitively, each node $v \in V$ in the graph represents an intermediate data label ℓ_v generated during the computation of an iMHF $f_{G,H}$ and edges represent data dependencies between these labels e.g., if $\ell_v = H(v, \ell_{v-1}, \ell_u)$ then the graph G would include directed edges $(v-1, v)$ and (u, v). Placing a pebbling on node v corresponds to computing label ℓ_v and storing it in memory,

[1] https://www.password-hashing.net/.

and pebbling constraint (2) corresponds to the natural requirement that labels ℓ_{v-1} and ℓ_u need to be available before computing ℓ_v. Constraint (1) implies that we begin computation without any of the labels in memory and constraint (3) requires that every label is computed eventually since we must eventually compute the label of the final sink node N. The cumulative pebbling cost of a pebbling is $\mathsf{cc}(P) \doteq \sum_i |P_i|$ and the cumulative pebbling cost of a graph G is $\mathsf{cc}(G) \doteq \min_P \mathsf{cc}(P)$ where the minimum is taken over all legal parallel pebblings of the graph G, i.e., $\mathsf{cc}(G)$ is the cumulative pebbling cost of the best parallel pebbling of G.

Computation in the Parallel Random Oracle Model takes place over rounds. A pROM algorithm $A(\sigma_0)$ begins execution in round $i = 0$ with an initial input state $\sigma_0 = (\tau_0, \{\})$. The algorithm then performs arbitrary computation before outputting a new state τ_1 and a batch of random oracles queries Q_1. The queries $Q_1 = \{x_{1,1}, \ldots, x_{1,z_1}\}$ are then submitted to the random oracle H to obtain responses $H(Q_1) = \{H(x_{1,1}), \ldots, H(x_{1,z_1})\}$. In round $i = 1$ we set $\sigma_1 = (\tau_1, H(Q_1))$ and $A(\sigma_1)$ may again perform arbitrary computation before outputting τ_2 and a new batch of ROM queries Q_2. More generally, in round i we run $A(\sigma_i = (\tau_i, H(Q_i))$ to generate our new state τ_{i+1} and batch of queries Q_{i+1}. Fixing the input χ, random oracle H and any random coins R used by our algorithm A we obtain a sequence of states $\mathtt{trace}(A, H, \chi, R) = \sigma_0, \sigma_1, \ldots, \sigma_t$ called the execution trace. The cumulative memory cost of an execution trace is $\mathsf{cmc}(\mathtt{trace}(A, H, \chi, R)) = \sum_{i=1}^{t} |\sigma_i|$ where $|\sigma_i|$ denotes size of the state at time i (# bits).

Review of Alwen and Serbinenko. Alwen and Serbinenko [9] showed that for any pROM algorithm A which computes $f_{G,H}(x)$ correctly with probability at least ϵ (the randomness is taken over the selection of the random oracle $H : \{0,1\}^* \rightarrow \{0,1\}^\lambda$ and any random coins R) that we will have $\mathsf{cmc}(\mathtt{trace}(A, H, \chi, R)) \geq c \cdot \mathsf{cc}(G) \cdot \lambda$ with probability $\epsilon - \mu(\lambda)$ for some negligible function $\mu(\ldots)$ and some constant $c > 0$. To prove this, Alwen and Serbinenko [9] first introduce the notion of an ex-post facto pebbling of G which can be extracted from the execution trace $\mathtt{trace}(A, H, \chi, R)$. In particular, for each node v they track rounds where the label ℓ_v appears as an input to a random oracle query and rounds where the "prelabel" $\mathtt{prelabel}(v, H) \doteq (\chi, v, \ell_{v_1}, \ldots, \ell_{v_\delta})$ is submitted as a query to the random oracle—the output of this query will be $H(\chi, v, \ell_{v_1}, \ldots, \ell_{v_\delta})$. A node v is said to be "needed" in round i if the label ℓ_v will be used as part of a random oracle input before the label ℓ_v will be generated as an output and we use the notation $\mathsf{need}(i) \subseteq V$ to denote the set of nodes that are needed during round i.

Alwen and Serbinenko define the ex-post facto pebbling by setting $P_i = \mathsf{need}(i)$ and they prove that, except with negligible probability, the ex-post facto pebbling is legal[2]. To complete their proof Alwen and Serbinenko argue that,

[2] The pebbling might be illegal if for some node v the label ℓ_v is used as a random oracle input before it appears as the output to a random oracle query. However, the probability of such an "out-of-order" event occurring is easily shown to be negligible.

except with negligible probability, we will have $|\sigma_i| \geq c\lambda|P_i|$ for all rounds i, i.e., the number $|P_i|$ of pebbles at round i is upper bounded by the state size $|\sigma_i|$.

To argue this, they give an extractor which, given a state σ_i and a short hint h, can extract $|P_i|$ query-output pairs without ever having submitted them as a query. Essentially, the extractor will simulate the pROM algorithm A with the initial state σ_i knowing that for every node $v \in P_i$ with parents $u_1, \ldots, u_\delta$ the corresponding label $\ell_v = H(\texttt{prelab}(v, H))$ will appear as an input to a future random oracle query made by A before its prelabel $\texttt{prelabel}(v, H)$. The hint h will encode the index of the first query where ℓ_v appears as an input as well as the index of the first subsequent query to $\texttt{prelabel}(v, H)$ (if applicable)—if A queries $\texttt{prelabel}(v, H)$ in the future the simulator will simply respond with the extracted value ℓ_v without every querying the random oracle H. In this way the extractor can obtain $|P_i|$ input-output pairs $(\texttt{prelabel}(v, H), \ell_v = H(\texttt{prelabel}(v, H))$ for all $v \in P_i$ without ever querying the random oracle on the corresponding inputs $H(\texttt{prelabel}(v, H))$. This implies that the length of the input to the extractor must be $|\sigma_i| + |h| = \Omega(|P_i|\lambda)$. Otherwise, we would obtain a contradiction as it would be possible to compress the random oracle.

Challenge 1: Labels Are Not Fixed A Priori. Our first challenge in proving the security of MTP is that the labeling may not be fixed a priori. A proof consists of a Merkle Tree root τ', the opening of k randomly selected leaf nodes $c_1, \ldots, c_k \in V$ in the Merkle Tree along with the opening of their parents. The verifier will check that all the Merkle Tree openings are valid and then verify that each challenge node c_i is "locally consistent" i.e., if ℓ'_{c_i} denotes the revealed value from the MT opening then we expect that $\ell'_{c_i} = H(v, \chi, \ell'_{v_1}, \ldots, \ell'_{v_\delta})$ where $v_1, \ldots, v_\delta$ are the parents of node v and ℓ'_{v_i} denotes the revealed value from the MT opening of leaf node v_i. Because the verifier only checks $k \ll N$ nodes are locally consistent a proof that is accepted does not necessarily have to use the correct labels $\ell_1, \ell_2, \ldots, \ell_N$. Thus, we cannot simply follow Alwen and Serbinenko [9] to define an ex-post facto pebbling by observing when each honest label ℓ_v appears as an input (or output) of a random oracle query.

We address this first challenge by introducing the notion of an ex-post facto labeling. In particular, once a pROM algorithm A outputs the root τ' of a Merkle Tree we can extract a labeling $\ell'_1, \ldots, \ell'_n$ from τ' by examining the database D of all prior random oracle queries made by A. As long as D contains no collisions the ex-post facto labeling will be unique, and because $q \ll 2^{\lambda/2}$ the probability that D contains a collision will be negligible.

Challenge 2: Pebbling Graph is not Fixed A Priori. Once we have such an ex-post facto labeling $\ell'_1, \ldots, \ell'_n$, it would be natural to define an ex-post facto pebbling from the execution trace of our pROM algorithm A by observing when label ℓ'_v appears as an input or as an output to a random oracle query. Unfortunately, the resulting pebbling sequence $P_1, \ldots, P_t$ may not be a legal pebbling sequence for the original graph G. The problem is that some nodes in the ex-post facto labeling may not be locally consistent e.g., for a node v with parents $v_1, \ldots, v_\delta$ we might have $\ell'_v = 0^\lambda$ instead of $\ell_{v'} = H(v, \chi, \ell'_{v_1}, \ldots, \ell'_{v_k})$. Because the verifier only checks $k \ll N$ random nodes for local consistency it is certainly possible that several nodes are not locally consistent. If v is not locally consistent then it is possible that the label ℓ'_v appears out of order e.g., ℓ'_v might appear as input to a random oracle query before appearing as an output. Thus, if the edge (v, w) exists it may be possible to compute $\ell_{w'}$ without ever producing ℓ'_v as a random oracle output—even if the node w was locally consistent.

We address this challenge by introducing the notion of an ex-post facto subgraph G' of G which can be extracted from the execution trace $\texttt{trace}(A, H, \chi, R)$ of our pROM algorithm A. To define the ex-post facto subgraph G' we first introduce the notion of node colors. We call a node v *Green* if it is locally consistent and *Red* otherwise. We call the set of labels $\ell'_1, \ldots, \ell'_n$ actually used by the prover the Ex-Post-Facto Labeling (see Definition 8), and can use them to check the color of each node.

Definition 1 (Informal, see Definition 7). *Given a directed acyclic graph G with nodes $V = [N]$ and a fixed labeling $\ell'_1, \ldots, \ell'_N \in \{0,1\}^\lambda \cup \{\perp\}$ (which may or may not correspond to the honest labeling), we say that a node $v \in V$ with parents $1 \leq v_1 < \ldots < v_d \leq N$ is* Green *if and only if $\ell'_v = H(v, \ell'_{v_1}, \ell'_{v_2}, \cdots, \ell'_{v_d})$. A node that is not* Green *is called a* Red *node.*

The ex-post facto graph $G' = \texttt{EPFG}(G, \texttt{trace}(A, H, \chi, R), \chi, \tau)$ can also be called the green-only subgraph, i.e., the subgraph induced by all the nodes which are green in Definition 7. For this subgraph, all nodes are locally consistent and thus their labels and the labels of their parents form a valid input-output pair to the random oracle. We now want to show that the Ex-Post-Facto Pebbling is legal for G'.

Challenge 3: Proving that the Ex-Post-Facto Pebbling is Legal for the Ex-Post-Facto Graph. Recall that, in the context of regular iMHFs, Alwen and Serbinenko [9] showed that the ex-post-facto pebbling was a legal pebbling of the original graph G. In their context the graph G and the labels $\ell_1, \ldots, \ell_N$ are fixed a priori. In our context we want to show that the ex-post-facto pebbling is a legal pebbling of the ex-post-facto graph G'. However, because the ex-post-facto graph is not fixed a priori we cannot directly apply Alwen and Serbinenko's [9] results to conclude that the ex-post-facto pebbling is legal for G'. For example, we need to consider the ex-post-facto labeling $\ell'_1, \ldots, \ell'_N$ when we define the pebbling. However, some of the key ideas from [9] can still be adapted. In particular, we define a predicate $\mathsf{need}(v, i)$ which indicates whether the (ex-post-facto) label ℓ'_v will appear next as an input before it is an output[3] before the prelabel x'_v of node v . We will have a pebble $v \in P_i$ on node v in round i if and only if its corresponding label ℓ'_v is needed during round i.

Definition 2 (Informal, see Definition 10). *Given an execution trace $\texttt{trace}(A, H, \chi, R)$, a string $\ell' \in \{0,1\}^\lambda$, and a particular round i, we define*

[3] More precisely, if node v has parents $v_1, \ldots, v_\delta$ then we can define $x'_v = (v, \chi, \ell'_{v_1}, \ldots, \ell'_{v_\delta})$ as the prelabel of node v. Since $\ell'_v = H(x'_v)$ we would say that ℓ'_v is an output in round j if $x'_v \in Q_j$ is random oracle query during this round.

the predicate $\mathsf{need}(v,i)$ *to be true if and only if the label* ℓ'_v *will next be used as input before it appears as the output of a random oracle query.*

Definition 3 (Informal, see Definition 11**).** *Given a DAG* $G = (V,E)$ *and an execution trace* $\texttt{trace}(A,H,\chi,R)$*, we define the Ex-Post-Facto Pebbling* $P' = \mathtt{EPFP}(G, \texttt{trace}(A,H,\chi,R),\chi,\tau)$ *of the Ex-Post-Facto Graph* $P' = (P'_0, P'_1, \ldots, P'_t)$ *where* $P'_i = \{v \in V' | \mathsf{need}(v,i)\}$*.*

We then show that this Ex-Post-Facto Pebbling is, with high probability, a legal pebbling of our Ex-Post-Facto Graph by showing that any illegal moves necessitate some form of low-probability bad event (i.e., a hash collision or randomly guessing the output of a query).

Theorem 1 (Informal, see Theorem 4**).** *Except with negligible probability the Ex-Post-Facto Pebbling* $P' = \mathtt{EPFP}(G, \texttt{trace}(A,H,\chi,R),\chi,\tau)$ *is a legal pebbling of the Ex-Post-Facto Graph* $G' = \mathtt{EPFG}(G, \texttt{trace}(A, H,\chi,R),\chi,\tau)$*.*

Challenge 4: Linking cmc *and* $\mathsf{cc}(G')$. The next challenge is to argue that, except with negligible probability, $\mathsf{cmc}(\texttt{trace}(A,H,\chi,R)) = \Omega(\mathsf{cc}(P'))$ where P' is the Ex-Post-Facto Pebbling of our Ex-Post-Facto Graph. To prove this we use a similar extractor argument as Alwen and Serbinenko [9] to argue that, except with negligible probability, we have $|P'_i| \leq 4|\sigma_i|/\lambda$ for all rounds i. We show that there is an extractor which takes as input a hint of size $|\sigma_i| + |P'_i|(2\log_2 q + \log_2(\mathsf{indeg}(G)))$ and outputs $|P'_i|$ input/output pairs $\{(x'_v, \ell'_v)\}_{v \in P'_i}$ for the random oracle H without ever querying H on *any* of the inputs x'_v. Here, q denotes the number of random oracle queries that A makes and x'_v denotes the prelabel of node v i.e., given a node v with parents $v_1, \ldots, v_\delta$ in G and a fixed labeling $\ell'_1, \ldots, \ell'_N$ for each node in G we use $x'_v = \texttt{prelabel}(v) = (v, \chi, \ell'_{v_1}, \ldots, \ell'_{v_\delta})$ to denote the prelabel of node v.

Intuitively, the extractor works by simulating A from the initial state σ_i. For each node $v \in P'_i$ the hint tells us the index $h^b_v \leq q$ of the first random oracle query where label ℓ'_v appears as an input—this query x'_w will be the prelabel for another node w such that $(v,w) \in E(G')$. The hint also tells us the location h^w_v of ℓ'_v inside this prelabel—this requires $\log_2(\mathsf{indeg}(G))$ bits since w has at most $\mathsf{indeg}(G)$ parents. Thus, when the query x'_w is made the extractor can locate ℓ'_v and record the tuple $(v, \_, \ell'_v)$. The extractor must also avoid querying the random oracle H on the prelabel x'_v, which is tricky because x'_v is not known a priori. Thus, for each node $v \in P'_i$ the hint also includes the index h^a_v of the first time that the query x'_v is submitted to the random oracle. When A submits this query to H the extractor can update the tuple $(v, \_, \ell'_v)$ to (v, x'_v, ℓ'_v) and simply respond with ℓ'_v without actually forwarding the query x'_v to H. Note that by definition of P'_i we know that the label ℓ'_v will appear as an input before it is output so we can safely assume that the tuple $(v, \_, \ell'_v)$ was recorded when the query x'_v is submitted. If A submits the query x'_v to H in a future round the extractor can simply locate the tuple (v, x'_v, ℓ'_v) and respond with x'_v without querying H.

By simulating A, the extractor will eventually be able to output $|P_i'|$ input/output pairs $\{(x_v', \ell_v')\}_{v \in P_i'}$ for the random oracle H without ever querying H on *any* of the inputs x_v'. Since H is a random oracle each string ℓ_v' is a uniformly random λ-bit string which cannot be compressed. In particular, given a hint of size $\leq |P_i'|\lambda - \lambda/2$ the probability of successfully extracting $|P_i'|$ input/output pairs without querying the random oracle on any of the inputs is at most $2^{-|P_i|\lambda + (|P_i'|\lambda - \lambda/2)} \leq 2^{-\lambda/2}$. It follows that (whp) we will have $|\sigma_i| \geq |P_i'|(\lambda - 2\log_2 q - \log_2 \mathsf{indeg}(G)) - \lambda/2 \geq |P_i'|\lambda/4$. The last inequality follows under the reasonable assumption that $\log_2 q + \log_2 \mathsf{indeg}(G) \leq \lambda/2$. By applying union bounds we can conclude that (whp) $|\sigma_i| \geq |P_i'|\lambda/4$ for every round i. It follows that, except with negligible probability, $\mathsf{cmc}(\mathtt{trace}(A, H, \chi, R)) = \sum_i |\sigma_i| \geq \sum_i |P_i'|\lambda/4 \geq \mathsf{cc}(G')\lambda/4$.

Theorem 2 (Informal, see Theorem 6). *Except with negligible probability* $\mathsf{cmc}(\mathtt{trace}(A, H, \chi, R)) \geq \mathsf{cc}(G')\frac{\lambda}{4}$, *where* $G' = \mathtt{EPFG}(G, \mathtt{trace}(A, H, \chi, R), \chi, \tau)$ *is the Ex-Post-Facto Graph, and* τ *is the Merkle Tree root output by* A

Challenge 5: Lower Bounding the Pebbling Cost of the Ex-Post Facto Graph. We have seen that $\mathsf{cmc}(\mathtt{trace}(A, H, \chi, R)) \geq \mathsf{cc}(G')\lambda/4$ i.e., the cumulative memory complexity of A on input χ can be lower bounded by the cumulative pebbling complexity of the Ex-Post-Facto Graph G'. However, this lower bound is only meaningful if $\mathsf{cc}(G')$ is large. Unfortunately, it is possible that $\mathsf{cc}(G') \ll \mathsf{cc}(G)$ because G' is only a subgraph of G with all red (locally-inconsistent) nodes removed. Let S' denote the set of red nodes that were removed from G because they are not locally consistent i.e., $G' = G - S'$.

We first observe that if the number of red nodes $|S'|$ is too large, then the probability $(1 - |S'|/N)^k$ that none of the k challenges are red will be negligible. Thus, we can safely assume that $|S'| \leq e$ for some parameter $e \leq N$ that will depend on the number of challenges k.

Our goal will be to find a graph G with the property that $\forall S' \subseteq V(G)$ of size $|S'| \leq e$ the subgraph $G' = G - S'$ has high cumulative pebbling cost. We observe that depth-robust graphs satisfy this criteria. Thus, we suggest instantiating the MTP framework with a highly depth-robust graph such as DRSample [4]. We say that G is (e, d)-depth-robust if for all $S \subseteq V(G)$ of size $|S| \leq e$ the graph $G - S$ still contains a directed path of length d. Alwen et al. [5] showed that any (e, d)-depth-robust graph has cumulative pebbling complexity at least $\mathsf{cc}(G) > ed$. Furthermore, Alwen et al. [4,5] showed how to construct (e, d)-depth-robust graphs on N nodes with constant indegree for $e = \Omega(N/\log N)$ and $d = \Omega(N)$. It is easy to see that if G is $(2e, d)$-depth-robust then for any $S' \subseteq V(G)$ of size $|S'| \leq e$ the graph $G' = G - S'$ is still (e, d)-depth-robust and, therefore, $\mathsf{cc}(G - S') \geq ed$ for all $|S'| \leq e$. Thus, if G is $(2e, d)$-depth-robust we can conclude that either (1) there are at least $|S'| > e$ red nodes omitted from the Ex-Post-Facto Graph G', or (2) $\mathsf{cmc}(\mathtt{trace}(A, H, \chi, R)) \geq ed\lambda/4$ i.e., $\mathsf{cmc}(\mathtt{trace}(A, H, \chi, R)) = \Omega(N^2\lambda/\log N)$ if G is $(\Omega(N/\log N), \Omega(N))$-depth-robust.

Challenge 6: Bounding the Probability of Lucky Challenges. We just observed that when we instantiate G with a $(2e, d)$-depth-robust graph that either (1) we will have at least $|S'| > e$ red nodes, or (2) the cumulative memory complexity will be at least $ed\lambda/4$. It remains to show that we can tune the parameter k (number of challenges) to ensure that, except with negligible probability, the first outcome $|S'| > e$ will not occur. Let $x_{i,j}$ denote the jth random oracle query in round i and let $\tau_{i,j} = H(x_{i,j})$ denote the output of this query. We can interpret $\tau_{i,j}$ as the root of a Merkle Tree and let $G'_{i,j} = G - S'_{i,j}$ denote the corresponding ex-post facto graph. Intuitively, we define a "lucky query" event $\textsc{LuckyQuery}_{i,j}$ which occurs if $c_1, \ldots, c_k \notin S'_{i,j}$ where $c_z = (H(\chi, z, \tau_{i,j}) \texttt{mod} N)$ i.e., none of the k challenges are red even though $|S'_{i,j}| > e$. If $x_{i,j}$ is a fresh random oracle query we can assume that (except with negligible probability) none of the random oracle queries $H(\chi, z, \tau_{i,j})$ were submitted before $x_{i,j}$. In this case the challenges $c_1, \ldots, c_k$ can be viewed as uniformly random and probability of the event $\textsc{LuckyQuery}_{i,j}$ is at most $(1-e/N)^k$. If we set $k = (2N \ln 2\lambda)/e$ then the probability is at $2^{-\lambda}$. Union bounding over all q queries we can upper bound the probability that any lucky query occurs as $q2^{-\lambda}$. This leads to our primary result that the probability that an algorithm A produces a valid MHPoW with cumulative memory complexity below $\mathsf{cc}(G')\lambda/4$ is negligible.

Theorem 3 (Informal, see Theorem 7, Corollary 1 and 3). *Define the event* $\textsc{Success}$ *that A produces a valid MHPoW that the verifier will accept.*

$$\Pr\left[\textsc{Success} \wedge \mathsf{cmc}\left(\mathit{trace}(A, H, \chi, R)\right) < \frac{\lambda}{4}\left(\min_{S \subset V(G):|S| \leq e} (\mathsf{cc}(G - S))\right)\right] \leq \mathbf{negl}(\lambda) .$$

Furthermore, if G is $(2e, d)$-depth-robust then

$$\Pr\left[\textsc{Success} \wedge \mathsf{cmc}\left(\mathit{trace}(A, H, \chi, R)\right) < \frac{\lambda ed}{4}\right] \leq \mathbf{negl}(\lambda) .$$

When we instantiate the graph G with a $(\Omega(N/\log N), \Omega(N))$-depth-robust graph like DRSample [4] we can conclude that (WHP) any algorithm A must incur cumulative memory cost $\Omega(N^2\lambda/\log N)$ whenever it succeeds in generating a valid MHPoW.

Pebbling Attacks on Merkle Tree Memory Hard Proofs of Work. Finally, in Sect. 7 we aim to lower bound the number of challenges k required to obtain a secure MHPoW by developing pebbling attacks. Our basic observation is that the attacker can remove up to $e = N/k$ nodes from the graph G while ensuring that the probability $(1 - (N/k)/N)^k = (1 - 1/k)^k = 1/e$ of avoiding detection remains large. Let $\texttt{depth}(G, v)$ denote the length (number of nodes) in the longest directed path ending at node v in the DAG G. We first observe that if G' does not contain a directed path longer than d then G' can be pebbled in d parallel rounds by defining $P_i = \{v \in V(G') : \texttt{depth}(G', v) \leq i\}$ for each round $i \leq d$. Therefore, if $\max_{v \in V(G')} \texttt{depth}(\texttt{G}', \texttt{v}) \leq d$ then we have $\mathsf{cc}(G') \leq \sum_{i=1}^{d} |P_i| \leq dN$.

We say that a DAG G is (e, d)-reducible if it is not (e, d) depth-robust. In particular, G is (e, d)-reducible if there exists a subset $S \subseteq V(G)$ of size $|S| \le e$ such that $\max_{v \in V(G) \setminus S} \mathsf{depth}(G - S, v) < d$ i.e., $G - S$ does not contain any directed path of length d. It is known that any DAG G with constant indegree is (e_i, d_i)-reducible with $d_i = N/2^i$ and $e_i = O(Ni/\log N)$ [2]. If G has constant indegree and $k \le c \log N/\log\log N$ for a suitable constant c then we can find a set $S' \subseteq V(G)$ of size $|S'| \le N/k = O(N \log\log N/\log N)$ such that $G' = G - S$ contains no directed path of length $N/\log^8 N$. It immediately follows that $\mathsf{cc}(G') \le N^2/\log^8 N$, but the probability that the attacker avoids detection is constant. Thus, we must have $k = \Omega(\log N/\log\log N)$ if we want to obtain a MHPoW with cumulative memory complexity at least $\Omega(N^2\lambda/\log N)$.

We can develop improved attacks when G is instantiated with Argon2i which is known to be (e, d)-reducible with $d = O(N^3/e^3)$ for any parameter $e \ge N^{2/3}$ [21]. We can further improve upon the previous attack $\mathsf{cc}(G') \le d_i N$ by adapting the recursive pebbling strategy of Alwen et al. [5] against a graph that is depth-reducible at on a range of values (e_i, d_i) i.e., we can find sets $S_0, S_1, \ldots$ such that $|S_i| \le e_i$ and $G - S_i$ contains no directed path of length d_i. Alwen et al. [5] showed that if the DAG G has $\mathsf{indeg}(G) \le \delta$ and depth at most d_0 and is (e_1, d_1)-reducible with parameters e_1, d_2 such that $2d_1 N \le e_1 d_0$ and S_1 is a depth reducing set of size $|S_1| \le e_1$ such that $\mathsf{depth}(G - S_1) \le d_1$ then, starting from an initially empty pebbling configuration, the cost of pebbling any target set $T \subseteq V(G)$ within at most $2d_0$ rounds is upper bounded by $\mathsf{cc}(G, T, 2d_0) \le (4\delta + 4)e_1 d_0 + \frac{N}{e_1}\left(\max_{T' \subseteq V \setminus S_1 : |T'| \le \delta e_1} \mathsf{cc}(G - S_1, T', 2d_1)\right)$. We trivially have $\mathsf{cc}(G - S_1, T', 2d_1) \le 2d_1 N$, but if the subgraph $G - S_1$ is itself (e_2, d_2)-reducible with parameters e_2, d_2 such that $2d_2 N \le e_2 d_1$ then the result can be applied applied recursively to further reduce costs. If the original graph is (e_i, d_i)-depth-reducible for a sequence $\{(e_i, d_i)\}$ such that $2d_{i+1}N \le e_{i+1}d_i$ then we can continue recursing further to minimize pebbling costs. The key challenge is how to select a sequence $\{(e_i, d_i)\}$ to minimize cc. Alwen et al. [5] showed how to do this for Argon2iA (an earlier version of Argon2i), and Blocki and Zhou [21] showed how to do this for Argon2i. One key difference in our setting is that the first depth-reducing set $|S_0| = N/k$ is *actually* removed from the graph G to obtain the green only subgraph. Thus, we start with a graph of depth $d_0 = \mathsf{depth}(G - S_0)$ instead of $d_0 = N$. This yields a different cost optimization problem and allows us to achieve an even lower cumulative pebbling cost than [5] or [21].

2 Preliminaries

2.1 Parallel Random Oracle Model and Basic Facts

Given a oracle set $\mathbb{H}$, let A be any pROM algorithm on input x with random coins R, with parallel access to H sampled uniformly from $\mathbb{H}$.

Parallel Random Oracle Model. Computation in the parallel random oracle model proceeds in rounds. An algorithm A is an oracle algorithm with the following behavior: In round $i+1$ the algorithm A receives as input the previous state

$\sigma_i = (\tau_i, Q_i)$ as well as the responses $Y = H(Q_i) = [H(x_{i,1}), \cdots, H(x_{i,z_i})]$ to the random oracle queries $Q_i = \{x_{i,1}, \ldots, x_{i,z_i}\}$ made in the previous round. The algorithm A may then perform *arbitrary computation* [4] before outputting a new state τ_{i+1} and a new batch of random oracle queries Q_{i+1}. The initial state σ_0 encodes the initial input χ to the computation. We have $Q_0 = \{\}$. Computation ends when the algorithm A writes on a special output tape instead of making another batch of queries to the random oracle.

We say that a string s is an input at round i if for query $x_{i,j}$ we have $x_{i,j} = w_1 \| s \| w_2$ for some strings $w_1, w_2 \in \{0,1\}^*$ i.e., s is a substring of $x_{i,j}$.

The Oracle Prediction Game. A useful game for bounding probabilities under the Random Oracle Model is the "Oracle Prediction Game". In this game, an algorithm P (which may be randomized) is given access to a ROM H and a hint h of size $|h|$. P may adaptively query H by submitting a query x_i (for some $1 \leq i \leq q$ and receiving the response $y_i = H(x_i)$. At the end of execution, P outputs a set of input output pairs $S = \{(a_1, b_1), \ldots, (a_d, b_d)\}$ such that none of the inputs were previously queried, i.e. $\forall (a_d, b_d) \in S, 1 \leq i \leq q : a_d \neq x_i$, yet all the pairs are correct, i.e. $\forall (a_d, b_d) \in S : H(a_d) = b_d$. The proof of this bound is well known; see, for example, [28].

Lemma 1. *Given random coins R Let P be any predictor algorithm which receives a hint of size $|h|$, as described above. Then the probability (over the choice of H and R) that P outputs $|S|$ correct predictions of λ bits is at most $|h| 2^{-\lambda |S|}$.*

Fixing any input χ, random oracle H, and random coins R for our algorithm A we obtain a sequence of states $\sigma_0, \sigma_1 \ldots, \sigma_t$. We call this sequence the execution trace and denote it as $\texttt{trace}(A, H, \chi, R) = (\sigma_0, \ldots, \sigma_t)$—note that $\texttt{trace}(A, H, \chi, R) = (\sigma_0, \ldots, \sigma_t)$ is deterministically fixed once χ, H, R and A are specified. Following [9] we define the cumulative memory cost (cmc) of an execution trace as:

Definition 4.

$$\mathsf{cmc}(\mathit{trace}(A, H, \chi, R)) = \sum_{i=1}^{t} |\sigma_i| \ .$$

In particular, $\mathsf{cmc}(\texttt{trace})$ is the sum of the size of the states during each round.

We use $Q_i(A, H, \chi, R)$ to denote the set of queries made during round i when we fix our algorithm A, random oracle H, input χ and random coins R. We use $x_{i,j}(A, H, \chi, R)$ to denote the jth query in $Q_i(A, H, \chi, R)$. It is also convenient to define $Q_{\leq i}(A, H, \chi, R) = \bigcup_{j=1}^{i} Q_j(A, H, \chi, R)$ as the set of all random oracle queries made in rounds 1 to i and $Q(A, H, \chi, R) = \bigcup_i Q_i(A, H, \chi, R)$

[4] We do not constrain this computation in any way except that the algorithm cannot make random oracle queries in-between rounds. For example, A may run for exponential time before outputting the new state/batch of queries.

as the set of all random oracle queries made in any round. We say that a query $x_{i,j} \in Q_i(A,H,\chi,R)$ in round i is fresh if it has not been made previously i.e., $x_{i,j} \notin Q_{\leq i-1}(A,H,\chi,R)$. Note that if a query $x_{i,j}$ is fresh then $H(x_{i,j})$ can be viewed as a uniformly random string that is still yet to be sampled. We also define $q(A,H,\chi,R)$ as the total number of queries A makes i.e., $q = \sum_i |Q_i|(A,H,\chi,R)$. When A, H, χ, R are clear from the context we will often drop them from our notation and simply write Q_i, $x_{i,j}$, $Q_{\leq i}$ and Q respectively.

Bad Events. Given any pROM algorithm A we define the event $\textsc{Collision}(A,H,\chi,R)$ to denote the event that A produces a collision i.e., $\exists x_{i,j}, x_{k,\ell} \in Q(A,H,\chi,R)$ such that $x_{i,j} \neq x_{k,\ell}$ and $H(x_{i,j}) = H(x_{k,\ell})$.

We define the event $\textsc{BadOrder}_{i,j}(A,H,\chi,R)$ as the event that the jth query $x_{i,j} \in Q_i(A,H,\chi,R) \setminus Q_{\leq i-1}$ during round i is fresh and the string $H(x_{i,j})$ is a substring of some query in the set $Q_{\leq i}$.

We further define the event $\textsc{BadOrder}_i(A,H,\chi,R) = \bigcup_j \textsc{BadOrder}_{i,j}(A,H,\chi,R)$, i.e. that a bad order query occurs in round i. Finally, we define the event $\textsc{BadOrder}(A,H,\chi,R) = \bigcup_i \textsc{BadOrder}_i(A,H,\chi,R)$ as the event that there exists some round i where the event $\textsc{BadOrder}_i(A,H,\chi,R)$ occurs i.e., a bad order query occurs at any point.

It is well known that the probability of these events is bounded by $\Pr_H[\textsc{Collision}(A,H,\chi,R)] \leq \binom{q}{2}2^{-\lambda}$ and $\Pr_H[\textsc{BadOrder}(A,H,\chi,R)] \leq q^2 n 2^{-\lambda}$. The proof of these bounds can be found in the full version [20].

2.2 Graph Notation

We use $G = (V = [N], E)$ to denote a DAG with $N = 2^n$ nodes. WLOG, we assume that the vertices are already in topological order $1, 2, \ldots, N$ so that for any directed edge $(u,v) \in E$ we have $u < v$.

Basic Notation. The indegree of a node $v \in V$ is $\mathsf{indeg}(G,v) \doteq |\{u : (u,v) \in E|$ and the maximum indegree of a DAG G is $\mathsf{indeg}(G) = \max_{v \in V} \mathsf{indeg}(G,v)$. When G is clear from context we often drop G and write $\mathsf{indeg}(v)$. Given a node $v \in V$ we define $\mathsf{parents}(v,G) = \{u : (u,v) \in E(G)\}$ to be the set of all nodes u with outgoing edge to v. WLOG we assume that the set $\mathsf{parents}(v,G)$ is given in topological order i.e., $\mathtt{parents}(v) = (v_1, \ldots, v_{\mathsf{indeg}(v)})$ where $v_i < v_{i+1}$. When it is clear from context, we will drop the G and simply write $\mathsf{parents}(v)$. Given a DAG $G = (V,E)$ and a subset $S \subseteq V$ we define $G - S = (V - S, \{(u,v) \in E \text{ s.t. } u \notin S \wedge v \notin S\}$ to be the subgraph obtained by deleting all nodes in S and any incident edges. We also define $G[S] = G - (V \setminus S)$ to be the subgraph obtained by deleting all nodes *except* those in S.

Graph Pebbling. Let $G = (V,E)$ be a DAG and $T, S \subseteq V$ be node sets. Then a (legal) pebbling of G (with starting configuration S and target T) is a sequence $P = (P_0, \ldots, P_t)$ of subsets of V such that:

1. $P_0 = \emptyset$
2. Pebbles are added only when their parents already have a pebble at the end of the previous step. That is, $\forall i \in [t] \forall y \in P_i \setminus P_{i-1} \forall x \in \mathsf{parents}(y) x \in P_{i-1}$.
3. At some point every target node is pebbled (though not necessarily simultaneously). That is, $\forall x \in T \exists i \leq t x \in P_i$.

We call a pebbling of G complete if $S = \emptyset$ and T is the set of sink nodes of G.

We further define $cc(G, T, d)$ as the cost of the best parallel pebbling of G in at most d rounds which ends with pebbles on T.

The Labeling Game. Given input χ and random oracle H and a DAG G we define labels $\ell_1, \ldots, \ell_N$ where the label of the first node is $\ell_1 = H(\chi, 1)$ and the label of each internal node $v \in [N]$ with $\mathsf{parents}(v) = (v_1, \ldots, v_k)$ is computed as $\ell_v = H(\chi, v, \ell_{v_1}, \ldots, \ell_{v_k})$—note that ℓ_v can be computed once we have all of the labels $\ell_1, \ldots, \ell_{v-1}$.

In our setting an attacker may chose not to compute labels honestly. Fixing arbitrary labels $\ell'_1, \ldots, \ell'_N$ we say that node $v \in [N]$ with $\mathsf{parents}(v) = (v_1, \ldots, v_k)$ is locally consistent with respect to χ,H and $\ell'_1, \ldots, \ell'_N$ if and only if $\ell'_v = H(\chi, v, \ell'_{v_1}, \ldots, \ell'_{v_k})$.

Fixing a labeling $\boldsymbol{\ell}' = (\ell'_1, \ldots, \ell'_N)$ of our DAG $G = (V, E)$, an input χ, and a node $v \in V$ with parents $\mathsf{parents}(v) = (v_1, \ldots, v_k)$ we define $\texttt{prelabel}(v, \boldsymbol{\ell}', G, \chi) = \left(\chi, v, \ell'_{v_1}, \ldots, \ell'_{v_k}\right)$. When G, $\boldsymbol{\ell}'$ and χ are clear from context we simply write $\texttt{prelabel}(v)$.

We often find it useful to convert from a number to the binary string representing that number, especially when computing Merkle Trees. We use $\texttt{bin}(v) = \sum_{i=1}^{k} v_i 2^{i-1}$ to denote the integer corresponding to the binary string v.

3 Merkle Tree Memory Hard Proofs of Work

3.1 Definition

This work is chiefly concerned with memory-hard proofs of work; a Memory Hard Proof of Work consists of two algorithms: an honest prover `Prove` and a verifier `Verify`. Note that we define Memory-Hard Proofs of Work with respect to the random oracle model as Merkle Tree Memory-Hard Proofs of Work constructions are in the random oracle model. However, our Definition 5 easily extends to standard model by requiring that the prover and verifier ignore the random oracle.

Definition 5. *A Memory Hard Proof of Work consists of two algorithms:* `Prove` *and* `Verify`*. The prover* $\texttt{Prove}^H(\chi, N)$ *takes an input string* χ *and a hardness parameter* N*, and outputs a certificate* c*. The algorithm* $\texttt{Verify}^H(\chi, N, c')$ *takes both the original input string* χ *and hardness parameter, as well as a candidate certificate* c'*, and outputs a 1 (accept) or a 0 (reject). The Proof of Work must satisfy four properties*

1. *(Prover Efficiency) For all inputs* $\chi \in \{0,1\}^\lambda$, *hardness parameters* N, *random oracles* $H : \{0,1\}^* \rightarrow \{0,1\}^\lambda$, *and random coins* R *the algorithm* `Prove` *has* $\mathsf{cmc}(\mathit{trace}(\mathtt{Prove}, H, \chi, R)) \leq N^2\lambda$ *and terminates after at most* $O(N)$ *rounds.*
2. *(Verifier Efficiency) We say that the Memory Hard Proof of Work is* $k(N, \lambda)$ *efficient if, for all inputs* $\chi \in \{0,1\}^\lambda$, *hardness parameters* N, *random oracles* $H : \{0,1\}^* \rightarrow \{0,1\}^\lambda$, *random coins* R *and candidate certificates* c' *the algorithm* $\mathtt{Verify}^H(\chi, Nc'; R)$ *terminates after* $k(N, \lambda)$ *rounds. We will typically require that* $k(N, \lambda) = o(N)$.
3. *(Perfect Completeness) For all inputs* χ *and hardness parameters* N *we have* $\Pr\left[\mathtt{Verify}^H\left(\chi, N, \mathtt{Prove}^H(\chi, N)\right) = 1\right] = 1$ *where the randomness is taken over the selection of the random oracle* H *as well as any random coins of* `Prove` *or* `Verify`.
4. *(Soundness) We say that the Proof of Work is* $(\epsilon(N, \lambda), C(N, \lambda))$*-sound if for all inputs* χ, *hardness parameters* N, *random oracles* $H : \{0,1\}^* \rightarrow \{0,1\}^\lambda$, *random coins* R, *and adversaries* $A^H(\chi, N; R)$ *which output a candidate certificate* c', $\Pr\left[\mathtt{Verify}^H\left(\chi, N, \mathcal{A}^H(\chi, N)\right) = 1 \wedge \mathsf{cmc}(\mathit{trace}(A, H, \chi, R)) \leq C(N, \lambda)\right] \leq \epsilon(N, \lambda)$

3.2 Merkle Tree Proof Framework

The following is a folklore construction of a memory-hard proof of work, which is similar to [15]. Fix a random oracle H and a family of DAGs $\{G_N\}_{n\geq 1}$ where G_N is a DAG with N nodes $V_N = [N]$ and constant indegree. When N is clear from context we will often write G instead of G_N to simplify notation. We will also assume that $N = 2^n$ is a power of 2 to simplify presentation. The construction also utilizes a tunable parameter k (number of challenges). Intuitively, increasing k will decrease verifier efficiency, but will boost soundness.

We define a related event, Success. For a fixed graph G and random oracle H and given an input string χ, random coins R, a number of challenge rounds k, and any algorithm A, we say that $\textsc{Success}(G, H, \chi, R, A, k)$ occurs if and only $V(G, H, \chi, R, k, A(G, H, \chi, R, k))$ accepts, i.e. A produces a verified certificate. We say that A succeeds with probability α if $\Pr_H[\textsc{Success}(G, H, \chi, R, A, k)] \geq \alpha$, where the probability is taken over the choice of random oracle.

Given an input string χ, random coins R, and a number of challenge rounds k, the honest prover $\mathtt{Prove}^H(\chi, N, k)$ proceeds as follows:

1. $\mathtt{Prove}^H(\chi, N, k)$ computes the label each node $v \in V(G)$ in topological order. The label of the source node 1 is $\ell_1 = H(\chi, 1)$. One we have computed labels $\ell_1, \ldots, \ell_{v-1}$ we can compute ℓ_v by querying $\ell_v = H(\chi, v, \ell_{v_1}, \ldots, \ell_{v_k})$ where $\ell_{v_1}, \ldots, \ell_{v_k} = \mathsf{parents}(v, G_N)$ denote the parents of node v.
2. $\mathtt{Prove}^H(\chi, N, k)$ computes a Merkle Tree commitment to this labeling, producing root τ. In particular, for each $v \in \{0,1\}^n$ we write $\tau_v = \ell_{1+bin(v)}$ and for $v \in \{0,1\}^{\leq n}$ define $\tau_v = H(\chi, \tau_{v\|0}, \tau_{v\|1})$ and the root is $\tau = H(\chi, \tau_0, \tau_1)$.
3. For each $i \in [1, k]$, $\mathtt{Prove}^H(\chi, N, k)$ identifies the node $c_i = (H(\chi, i, \tau) \bmod N)$ as the ith challenge, then:

   1. `Prove` computes a Merkle Tree Reveal $\mu_i = \texttt{MerkleTreeReveal}(\mathsf{bin}(c_i))$ for the label ℓ_{c_i+1} where we define $\texttt{MerkleTreeReveal}(x = (x_1, \ldots, x_n)) = \left(\tau_x, \{\tau_{x_1 x_2 \ldots x_{j-1}\overline{x}_j}\}_{j=1}^n\right)$ where $x_1, \ldots, x_n$ denote the bits of $x \in \{0,1\}^n$ and $\overline{x}_j$ denotes the bit flip of x_j,
   2. Similarly, for each parent $v \in \mathsf{parents}(c_i + 1)$, `Prove` computes a Merkle Tree Reveal for the label $\ell_v = \tau_{\mathsf{bin}(v-1)}$ i.e., $\mu_{i,v} = \texttt{MerkleTreeReveal}(\mathsf{bin}(v-1))$. Let $L_i = \{(\ell_v, \mu_{i,v})\}_{v \in \mathsf{parents}(c_i+1)}$.
4. $\texttt{Prove}^H(\chi, N, k)$ can then output the certificate $c = \tau, \{(\ell_1, \mu_1, L_1), v, (\ell_k, \mu_k, L_k)\}$.

The corresponding verifier $\texttt{Verify}^H(\chi, R, c', k)$ proceeds as follows:

1. `Verify` identifies τ from the candidate certificate c', and computes all the challenges $c'_i = (H(\chi, i, \tau) \mod N)$.
2. For each challenge i, `Verify` separates the response into $L = \{(\ell_i, \mu_i, \{\ell_j, \mu_j\}_{j \in \mathsf{parents}(c_i+1)})\}_{i \in [1,k]}$, and runs $\textsc{MerkleTreeReveal}(\chi, i, \ell_i, \mu_i, \tau)$ on each of the reveals. If any fails, `Verify` rejects.
3. For each challenge, `Verify` checks that $\ell_v = H(\chi, v, \ell_{v_1}, \ldots, \ell_{v_k}$ holds for the labels the prover committed to. If this does not hold for any challenge, `Verify` rejects.
4. If c' passes all the above checks, `Verify` accepts.

Efficiency: The honest prover runs in sequential time $O(N + k \log N)$ and has cumulative memory complexity at most $\mathsf{cmc}(\texttt{Prove}^H(\chi, N, k)) \in O(N^2\lambda + kN\lambda)$ i.e., the honest evaluation algorithm allocates $O(N\lambda)$ space to store $O(N)$ labels and keeps these labels in memory for the duration of the compuation. Assuming that we set $k = o(N/\log N)$ the sequential running time is at most $O(N)$ and the cumulative memory complexity is at most $\mathsf{cmc}(\texttt{Prove}^H(\chi, N, k)) \in O(N^2\lambda)$. The size of the proof is $O(k\lambda \log N)$ since we must reveal $O(k)$ labels and each Merkle Tree Reveal requires $O(\lambda \log N)$ bits. The running time of the verifier is $O(k \log N)$ since the verifier must make $O(k \log N)$ queries to the hash function to verify the Merkle Tree openings and check that each revealed label is locally consistent. We will assume that $k \ll N/\log N$. Thus, the size of the proof is $o(N\lambda)$ and the running time of the verifier is $o(N)$.

Correctness: It is readily apparent that an honest prover P's certificate will always be accepted by a verifier V, so this procedure passes the correctness requirements. What remains is to prove its soundness.

4 Security Proof

In this section, we prove Theorem 6, which states that, as long as no bad events occur, the cmc of any attacker which computes a valid Memory-Hard Merkle Tree Proofs certificate is lower bounded by the minimum cc of the Ex-Post-Facto Graph.

4.1 Tracing a Merkle Tree

Merkle Tree Commitments. We utilize Merkle Tree commitments in our constructions. Given strings $x_1, \ldots, x_{2^k}$, a hash function H, and a salt s, we define the following labeling: for each string $v \in \{0,1\}^k$ we have $\ell'_v = x_{1+\mathtt{bin}(v)}$ where $\mathtt{bin}(v) = \sum_{i=1}^{k} v_i 2^{i-1}$ denotes the integer corresponding to the binary string v. For each $i \le k$ and each string $v \in \{0,1\}^i$ we define $\ell_v = H(s, \ell'_{v\|0}, \ell'_{v\|1})$. Finally, the Merkle Tree commitment to $x_1, \ldots, x_{2^m}$ is given by the root label $\ell'_\epsilon = H(s, \ell'_0, \ell'_1)$.

Tracing a Merkle Tree. In the random oracle model we can often reconstruct the entire Merkle Tree given only the root commitment ℓ'_ϵ and the salt s. In particular, suppose that the database $D = \{(x_1, y_1), \ldots, (x_q, y_q)\}$ encodes all known input/output pairs for our random oracle. We can attempt to reconstruct the Merkle Tree by looking for any $(x_i, y_i) \in D$ such that X_i takes the form $x_i = s\|w_0\|w_1$ for arbitrary strings $w_0, w_1 \in \{0,1\}^\lambda$ and $y_i = \ell'_\epsilon$. Note that as long as there are no collisions in D that there will be *at most* one such pair (x_i, y_i) in D. Once we find $(x_i, y_i) \in D$ with $y_i = \ell'_\epsilon$ and $x_i = s\|w_0\|w_1$ we can recursively trace the left (resp. right) subtree by setting $\ell'_0 = w_0$ (resp. $\ell'_1 = w_1$) and searching for $(x_j, y_j) \in D$ such that $y_j = \ell'_0$ (resp. $y_j = \ell'_1$) and x_j takes the form $x_j = s\|w'_0\|w'_1$ for arbitrary strings $w'_0, w'_1 \in \{0,1\}^\lambda$. It is of course possible that there is no pair $(x_j, y_j) \in D$ with $y_j = \ell'_0$ and x_j of the form $x_j = s\|w'_0\|w'_1$ for arbitrary strings $w'_0, w'_1 \in \{0,1\}^\lambda$. In this case we can simply set $\lambda_{0\|x} = \perp$ for all $x \in \{0,1\}^{\le m-1}$ to indicate that it is not possible to further expand the left-subtree i.e., all the other nodes in this subtree have label $\perp$.

We use $\mathtt{MT}(\tau, D, s, k)$ to denote the recursive procedure which attempts to trace a Merkle Tree of depth k with root value $\ell_\epsilon = \tau$. In particular, the procedure will output the associated label $\ell'_v \in \{0,1\}^\lambda$ for all nodes $v \in \{0,1\}^{\le k}$ in the traced Merkle Tree. It is possible that $\ell'_v = \perp$ for some nodes $v \in \{0,1\}^k$ if the Merkle Tree is incomplete. However, as long as the database D contains no collisions the output of $\mathtt{MT}(\tau, D, s, k)$ is uniquely defined.

Definition 6. *Given an execution trace $\mathtt{trace}(A, H, \chi, R)$ we can define the database $D(\mathtt{trace}(A, H, \chi, R))$ as the set of all queries made within the trace. That is, $D(\mathtt{trace}(A, H, \chi, R)) = \bigcup_i Q_i(A, H, \chi, R)$.*

Definition 7. *Given a directed acyclic graph G with nodes $V = [N]$, an input χ, and a fixed labeling $\ell'_1, \ldots, \ell'_N \in \{0,1\}^\lambda \cup \{\perp\}$ (which may or may not correspond to the honest labeling), we say that a node $v \in V$ with parents $1 \le v_1 < \ldots < v_d \le N$ is* Green *if and only if (1) $\ell'_v \ne \perp$, (2) $\ell'_{v_i} \ne \perp$ for all $i \le d$ and (3) $\ell'_v = H(\chi, v, \ell'_{v_1}, \ell'_{v_2}, \cdots, \ell'_{v_d})$. A node that is not* Green *is called a* Red *node.*

Recall that given a database D of random oracle output queries, a DAG G with $N = 2^n$ nodes, and a candidate Merkle Tree root value τ we can use $\mathtt{MT}(\tau, D(\mathtt{trace}(A, H, \chi, R)), \chi, n)$ (where χ, our input, is also used as the salt) to trace labels ℓ'_v for each node $v \in \{0,1\}^{\le n}$ in the Merkle Tree. As long as the database D contains no collisions the values ℓ'_v are uniquely determined once we fix τ, D, χ and n. In this case we can obtain a fixed labeling for our DAG G by setting $\ell'_i = \ell'_{\texttt{bin}^{-1}(i-1,n)}$ for each $i \in [N]$ where $\texttt{bin}^{-1}(i-1, n)$ denotes the binary encoding of $i-1$ as a n-bit string.

Definition 8. *Given a graph G, execution trace $\texttt{trace}(A, H, \chi, R)$, corresponding initial input χ, and a Merkle Tree root value τ, when $D = D(\texttt{trace}(A, H, \chi, R))$ we call $\ell'_1, \ldots, \ell'_n$ (as traced above) the Ex-Post-Facto Labeling of G and denote it by $\texttt{EPFL}(G, \texttt{trace}(A, H, \chi, R), \chi, \tau)$.*

Thus, assuming there are no collisions we can determine which nodes in a graph G are *Green*/*Red* given only $\texttt{trace}(A, H, \chi, R)$, χ and τ. It will be convenient to let $S_{Red}(G, \texttt{trace}(A, H, \chi, R), \chi, \tau)$ denote the set of nodes that are red.

Definition 9. *Given a graph G, execution trace $\texttt{trace}(A, H, \chi, R)$, corresponding initial input χ, and a certificate rooted at τ, we define the Ex-Post-Facto Graph G' to be the subgraph of G induced by the nodes which are green. That is, $G' = G - S_{RED}$. We denote this by $G' = \texttt{EPFG}(G, \texttt{trace}(A, H, \chi, R), \chi, \tau)$*

Tracing an Ex-Post-Facto Pebbling. Therefore, for any given graph G, execution trace $\texttt{trace}(A, H, \chi, R)$, corresponding initial input χ, and candidate Merkle Tree root τ, we begin by tracing the Merkle Tree labeling with $\texttt{MT}(\tau, D, \chi, n)$. This lets us find the Ex-Post-Facto Labeling ℓ'_v for each vertex v. Then, we find the Ex-Post-Facto Graph G', which contains only *Green* nodes with respect to the ex post facto labeling $\ell'_1, \ldots, \ell'_N$.

We now use our Ex-Post-Facto Labeling to define a pebbling of our Ex-Post-Facto Graph. In particular, for each step i in our $\texttt{trace}$ and each vertex v in G' we consider whether the corresponding label ℓ'_v will be "needed" as input to a random oracle query before the next round where this label will appear as an output. Intuitively, during round i we keep keep pebbles on the set P'_i of nodes that are "needed." Recall that, given a node v with parents $v_1, \ldots, v_\delta$, $\texttt{prelabel}(v) = (v, \chi, \ell'_{v_1}, \ldots, \ell_{v_\delta})$ denotes the prelabel of node v, i.e., the random oracle query such that $H(x'_v) = \ell'_v$.

Definition 10. *Given an execution trace $\texttt{trace}(A, H, \chi, R)$, an Ex-Post-Facto Labeling $L' = \ell'_1, \ldots, \ell'_N$, a vertex $v \in V(G')$, and a particular round i, we define the predicate $\mathsf{need}(\texttt{trace}(A, H, \chi, R), L', v, i)$ to be true if and only if the label ℓ'_v will next be used as input to a query before being output by a query. That is, $\mathsf{need}(\texttt{trace}(A, H, \chi, R), L', v, i) = 1$ if and only if (1) there exists a query $x_{j,b} \in Q_j(A, H, \chi, R)$ such that $i \le j$, and $x_{j,b} = \texttt{prelabel}(w)$ for some node w such that $(v, w) \in E(G')$, but (2) there is no $x_{k,l} \in Q_k(A, H, \chi, R)$ for any $i \le k < j$ such that $x_{k,l} = \texttt{prelabel}(v)$. For simplicity we will write $\mathsf{need}(v, i)$ instead of $\mathsf{need}(\texttt{trace}(A, H, \chi, R), L', v, i)$ When $\texttt{trace}(A, H, \chi, R)$ and L' are clear from context.*

We are now ready to define the Ex-Post-Facto Pebbling of the Ex-Post-Facto Graph.

Definition 11. *Given a DAG* $G = (V, E)$*, an execution trace* $\mathtt{trace}(A, H, \chi, R)$*, the corresponding initial input* χ*, and a Merkle Tree root* $\tau \in \{0,1\}^\lambda$ *we define the Ex-Post-Facto Pebbling* $P' = \mathtt{EPFP}(G, \mathtt{trace}(A, H, \chi, R), \chi, \tau)$ *of the Ex-Post-Facto Graph* $G' = \mathtt{EPFG}(G, \mathtt{trace}(A, H, \chi, R), \chi, \tau)$ *as follows:* $P' = (P'_0, P'_1, \dots, P'_t)$ *where* $P'_i = \{v \in V' \mid \mathsf{need}(\mathtt{trace}(A, H, \chi, R), L', v, i) = 1\}$ *where* $L' = (\ell'_1, \dots, \ell'_n) = \mathtt{EPFL}(G, \mathtt{trace}(A, H, \chi, R), \chi, \tau)$ *denotes the Ex-Post-Facto Labeling of the Ex-Post-Facto Graph* $G' = (V', E')$*.*

Consider a given graph G, algorithm A, ROM H, input string χ, and random coins R. Recall that a node v with parents $v_1, \dots, v_d$ is *Green* if it is internally consistent: it has a label ℓ'_v which can be traced from the Merkle Tree by $\mathtt{EPFL}(G, \mathtt{trace}(A, H, \chi, R), \chi, \tau)$ and that label is the hash of its parents' labels, i.e. $\ell'_v = H(\chi, v, \ell'_{v_1}, \dots, \ell'_{v_d})$. Intuitively, if v is *Green* then A must have found ℓ'_v by querying $H(\chi, v, \ell'_{v_1}, \dots, \ell'_{v_d})$. However, this intuition is not guaranteed to be correct. It is possible, albeit highly unlikely, that A simply guessed ℓ'_v, yet this guess was by sheer chance internally consistent. We call this MisColoring the node v, and give the following formal definition. The proofs of Lemma 2 and Theorem 4 can be found in the full version [20].

Definition 12. *Fix a graph* G*, algorithm* A*, input string* χ*, random coins* R *and random oracle* H*. Let* $tr = \mathtt{trace}(A, H, \chi, R)$ *be the execution trace when running* A *on* χ *and let* $\boldsymbol{\ell}' = \mathtt{EPFL}(G, tr, \chi, \tau)$ *be the Ex-Post-Facto Labeling of* G *where* τ *is the Merkle Tree root output by* A*. Given a vertex* $v \in V(G)$*, we define the event* $\textsc{MisColor}_v(G, A, H, \chi, R, \tau)$ *as the event that* v *is* Green *with respect to* $\boldsymbol{\ell}'$*,* χ*, and* G *but the string* $\mathtt{prelabel}(v, \boldsymbol{\ell}', G, \chi)$ *has never been queried i.e.,* $x_{i,j} \neq \mathtt{prelabel}(v, \boldsymbol{\ell}', G, \chi)$ *for all* i, j*. In this case we say that the vertex* v *was miscolored. We further define the event that any vertex is miscolored as*

$$\textsc{MisColor}(G, A, H, \chi, R, \tau) = \bigcup_v \textsc{MisColor}_v(G, A, H, \chi, R, \tau) .$$

Lemma 2. *Let* G *be a DAG;* $\mathtt{trace}(A, H, \chi, R)$ *be an execution trace of a pROM algorithm* A *for ROM* $H : \{0,1\}^n \to 2^\lambda$*, input* χ*, and random coins* R*;* χ *be the corresponding input to* A*; and* τ *be the Merkle Tree commitment generated. For all inputs* χ *and random coins* R *we have* $\Pr_H[\textsc{MisColor}(G, A, H, \chi, R, \tau)] \leq |V(G)| 2^{-\lambda}$*, where the probability is taken over the selection of the random oracle* H*.*

Theorem 4. *If the bad events* $\textsc{Collision}(A, H, \chi, R)$*,* $\textsc{BadOrder}(A, H, \chi, R)$*, and* $\textsc{MisColor}(G, A, H, \chi, R, \tau), \chi, \tau)$ *never occur, then* $P' = \mathtt{EPFP}(G, \mathtt{trace}(A, H, \chi, R), \chi, \tau)$ *is a legal pebbling of* $G' = \mathtt{EPFG}(G, \mathtt{trace}(A, H, \chi, R), \chi, \tau)$*.*

4.2 Extracting Input/Output Pairs from the Random Oracle

In the previous section we argued that the ex-post facto pebbling of the ex-post facto graph must be legal (as long as certain highly unlikely "bad" events do not occur). We now argue that during each round of our execution trace the size of the state σ_i is lower bounded by $|P'_i|$, i.e., the number of pebbles in the ex-post facto pebbling. We use an extractor argument to prove this. The extractor will output $|P'_i|$ input/output pairs for the random oracle without querying the random oracle at this points. Intuitively, the random oracle outputs will correspond to the ex-post facto label ℓ'_v of each node $v \in P'_i$. Recall that, by definition, for any vertex $v \in P'_i \in \mathtt{EPFP}(G, \mathtt{trace}(A, H, \chi, R), \chi, \tau)$ we have $\mathsf{need}(v, i)$ i.e., the ex-post facto label ℓ'_v will appear as an input to a future random oracle query *before* it is output. Thus, it will be possible for the extractor to extract each ex-post facto label ℓ'_v by simulating our algorithm A starting from the initial state σ_i given a small hint about which query contains each label ℓ'_v as part of the input. Since we can extract random oracle input/output pairs from σ_i without every querying these points, σ_i must be large.

Defining the Extractor. Intuition: Given any intermediate state $\sigma_i = (\tau_i, Q_i)$ of A, access to the random oracle H, an input χ, and random coins R, we can simulate A from this initial state. The goal of the extractor is to output $(\mathtt{prelabel}(v, \boldsymbol{\ell}', G, \chi), \ell'_v)$ for each node $v \in P'_i$ without every querying $\mathtt{prelabel}(v, \boldsymbol{\ell}', G, \chi)$. To simulate A we will need the *responses* to the random oracle queries Q_i. We can obtain these responses simply by submitting each query $x_{i,j} \in Q_i$ to the random oracle. However, if $x_{i,j} = \mathtt{prelabel}(v, \boldsymbol{\ell}', G, \chi)$ for some node $v \in P'_i$ then we must *not* submit this query. However, if we have already extracted ℓ'_v then it will be possible to find the output $H(x_{i,j})$ without actually making this query. Thus, for each node $v \in P'_i$ our hint will include the index of the first query where ℓ'_v appears as part of a query input as well as the index of the first query where the input is $\mathtt{prelabel}(v, \boldsymbol{\ell}', G, \chi)$—if such a query exists. Note that, by definition, ℓ'_v will appear first as input so if we do encounter a future query $\mathtt{prelabel}(v, \boldsymbol{\ell}', G, \chi)$ we will be able to respond to the query without needing to query the random oracle. If the query $\mathtt{prelabel}(v, \boldsymbol{\ell}', G, \chi)$ never occurs in our simulation of A starting at round i we can still extract $\mathtt{prelabel}(v, \boldsymbol{\ell}', G, \chi)$ by subsequently simulating A from the initial state σ_0. Note that the state σ_0 (as well as the random coins R) are entirely independent of the random oracle H and thus do not count as part of our random oracle dependent hint.

RO Dependent Hint. In addition to the initial state σ_i we will give our extractor a hint $h_i = \{(h^b_v, h^w_v, h^a_v)\}_{v \in P'_i}$. In particular, for each node v in P'_i the value $h^b_v \le q$ is the index of the first query where ℓ'_v will appear as part of the input and $h^w_v \le \mathsf{indeg}(G)$ denotes which portion of this query is ℓ'_v. Similarly, $h^a_v \le q$ denotes the index of the first query where the input is $\mathtt{prelabel}(v, \boldsymbol{\ell}', G, \chi)$ i.e., the query whose output would be ℓ'_v. Note that it is possible that this query occurs after the extractor finishes simulating A from the intermediate state σ_i and begins simulating A from the initial state σ_0 until we reach the state σ_i. The total number of random oracle queries throughout the simulation is at most q so we are still guaranteed that $h^a_v \le q$. We also note that $h^a_v > h^b_v$ since the label ℓ'_v will appear as input before it appears as output.

Formal Description of the Extractor. Given the intermediate state $\sigma_i = (\tau_i, Q_i)$ of A the extractor E first examines each query $x_{i,j} \in Q_i$. If $x_{i,j}$ is the h_v^b-th query made for any h_v^b in the hint, then ℓ'_v is the h_v^w-th parent used in this query, given by $x_{i,j}[|\chi| + \log_2(N) + h_v^w \cdot \lambda, |\chi| + \log_2(N) + (h_v^w + 1) \cdot \lambda - 1]$. E extracts this value, infers v by examining the structure of G to see which node is the h_v^w-th parent, and records the tuple $(v, \_, \ell'_v)$ to indicate that it has extracted the ex-post facto label ℓ'_v, but does not yet know $\texttt{prelabel}(v)$. Now, if $x_{i,j}$ is the h_v^a-th query made for any h_v^a in the hint, E can find the tuple $(v, \_, \ell'_v)$ and update this record to $(v, x_{i,j}, \ell'_v)$ to show that it knows both the label and prelabel for the node v. Finally, E checks whether there is some tuple of the form $(u, x_{i,j}, \ell'_u)$ in its records. If so, it does not make this query and instead sets $y_{i,j} = \ell'_u$. Otherwise, E can safely make the random oracle query and set $y_{i,j} = H(x_{i,j})$. Now that E has the random oracle responses Y_i it will continue to simulate A to get the next state $\sigma_{i+1} = (\tau_{i+1}, Q_{i+1})$.

In general when E obtains the state $\sigma_r = (\tau_r, Q_r)$ for some round $r > i$ it proceeds in the exact same manner. In particular, for each query $x_{r,j} \in Q_r$, E checks if $x_{r,j}$ is the h_v^b-th query made for any h_v^b in the hint, recording the tuple $(v, \_, \ell'_v)$ if so. E checks if $x_{r,j}$ is the h_v^a-th query made for any h_v^a in the hint, updating the record $(v, \_, \ell'_v)$ to $(v, x_{r,j}, \ell'_v)$ if so. Finally, we check whether there is a tuple of the form $(u, x_{r,j}, \ell'_u)$ in our records. If so, we do not make this query and instead set $y_{r,j} = \ell'_u$. Otherwise, we make the random oracle query and set $y_{r,j} = H(x_{r,j})$. Our extractor continues simulating A in this manner until A terminates. However, it is of course possible that we still have some tuple in our record of the form $(u, \_, \ell'_u)$ if no query of the form $x_{k,l} = \texttt{prelabel}(u)$ has been made. In this case, the extractor will continue to simulate A, beginning from the initial state $\sigma_0 = (\chi, \emptyset)$ until it reaches state σ_i at round i. During this simulation during each round $r \leq i$ we continue to check each query $x_{r,j} \in Q_r$ to see if $x_{r,j}$ is the h_j^a-th query made for any h_v^a in the hint. When this occurs we update the tuple $(v, \_, \ell'_v)$ to $(v, x_{r,j}, \ell'_v)$. We also double check every query $x_{r,j}$ to see if some tuple of the form $(u, x_{r,j}, \ell'_u)$ was previously recorded so that we can avoid querying $\texttt{prelabel}(u)$ for any node $u \in P'_i$. Finally, the extractor will locate all of the tuples of the form (u, w_u, ℓ'_u) and output the random oracle input/output pair (w_u, ℓ'_u).

We use E to denote the above extractor procedure. In particular, for any fixed graph G, algorithm A, ROM H, input χ, and random coins R, $E(G, A, H, \chi, \sigma_i \| h_i)$ takes as input a state of the algorithm σ_i and the corresponding small additional hint h_i (as described above), and outputs a set of $|P'_i|$ input-output pairs of a ROM without ever querying them. The proof of Theorem 5 can be found in the full version [20].

Theorem 5. *As long as* $\textsc{Collision}(A, H, \chi, R)$, $\textsc{BadOrder}(A, H, \chi, R)$, *and* $\textsc{MisColor}(G, A, H, \chi, R, \tau)$ *do not occur, running* $E^H(G, A, \chi, \sigma_i \| h_i)$ *will successfully extract* $|P'_i|$ *pairs* $(a_1, b_1), \ldots, (a_{|P'_i|}, b_{|P'_i|})$ *such that for all* $j \leq |P'_i|$ *(1)* $H(a_j) = b_j$ *and (2)* E *never queries* $H(a_j)$*.*

Hint Size. We must consider the required size of h_i for any round i. First, we observe that h_i contains 3 elements for each node $v_j \in |P'_i|$. Let q be the total number of queries made by A and n be the number of bits in an input to H. h^b_j uniquely identifies a query made by A, and thus requires $\log_2(q)$ bits. h^w_j identifies a parent of each vertex, and thus requires at most $\log_2(\mathsf{indeg}(G))$ bits. h^a_j once again identifies a query and requires $\log_2(q)$ bits. Thus, for each node $v_j \in |P'_i|$, h_i contains at most $\log_2\left(q^2\mathsf{indeg}(G)\right)$ bits. We can upper bound this value as at most $2\log_2(q)+\log_2(\mathsf{indeg}(G))$ bits. The total length of h_i is therefore $(2\log_2(q) + \log_2(\mathsf{indeg}(G)))\,|P'_i|$.

We will now consider when an extractor is able to succeed at the Oracle Prediction Game. There are two necessary conditions for this: the extractor must be able to extract the $|P'_i|$ input-output pairs, and the hint given to the extractor must be sufficiently small. We define this with the event IE, for an *Implausible Extraction.*

Definition 13. *Fix a graph G, pROM algorithm A, input string χ and random coins R. Given a random oracle H and an integer i denoting an execution round we define the event* $\mathrm{IE}_i(G, A, H, \chi, R)$ *(implausible extraction during round i) as the event that* $\textsc{Collision}(A, H, \chi, R)$, $\textsc{BadOrder}(A, H, \chi, R)$, *and* $\textsc{MisColor}(G, A, H, \chi, R)$ *do not occur, but* $|\sigma_i| < \frac{|P'_i|\lambda}{4}$. *We further define the event* $\mathrm{IE}(G, A, H, \chi, R) = \bigcup_i \mathrm{IE}_i(G, A, H, \chi, R)$ *as the event that there exists some round where* $|\sigma_i| < \frac{|P'_i|\lambda}{4}$.

In the full version [20] we upper bound $\Pr[\mathrm{IE}] \le t2^{-\lambda/2}$. Fix a graph G, pROM algorithm A, an input string χ, random coins R, and random oracle H. Let $tr = \mathtt{trace}(A, H, \chi, R)$ be the execution trace when running A on χ and τ be the Merkle Tree root output by A. As long as none of the bad events $\textsc{Collision}(A, H, \chi, R)$, $\textsc{BadOrder}(A, H, \chi, R)$, $\textsc{MisColor}(G, A, H, \chi, R, \tau)$, nor $\mathrm{IE}(G, A, H, \chi, R)$ occur, clearly the cumulative memory cost (cmc) of running A on χ is at least $\frac{\lambda}{4}cc(G')$, where $cc(G')$ is the cumulative pebbling cost of the Ex-Post-Facto Graph $G' = \mathtt{EPFG}(G, \mathtt{trace}(A, H, \chi, R), \chi, \tau)$. Thus, with probability $1 - (\Pr[\textsc{Collision}] + \Pr[\textsc{BadOrder}] + \Pr[\textsc{MisColor}] + \Pr[\mathrm{IE}])$, the cmc is large as long as $\mathsf{cc}(G')$ is large.

Theorem 6. *Fixing a graph G, pROM algorithm A, an input string χ, and random coins R. Then, if the bad events* $\textsc{Collision}$, $\textsc{BadOrder}$, $\textsc{MisColor}$, *and* IE *do not occur,* $\mathsf{cmc}(tr) \ge \mathsf{cc}(G')\frac{\lambda}{4}$, *where* $tr = \mathtt{trace}(A, H, \chi, R)$ *is the execution trace when running A on χ,* $G' = \mathtt{EPFG}(G, \mathtt{trace}(A, H, \chi, R), \chi, \tau)$ *is the Ex-Post-Facto Graph, and τ is the Merkle Tree root output by A.*

The proof of Theorem 6 can be found in the full version [20].

5 Lucky Certificates

In the last section we argued that cumulative memory cost can be lower bounded by the cumulative pebbling cost of the Ex-Post-Facto Pebbling. We now argue that, except with negligible probability, the Ex-Post-Facto Pebbling must be a large subgraph of the original graph G.

Definition 14. *Fix a graph G with N nodes, input string χ, random coins R, and algorithm A, a number of challenge rounds k, and a threshold β (with $0 < \beta$). Given some query $x_{i,j}$ made during round i, we define the event* $\textsc{LuckyQuery}_{i,j}(A, H, \chi, R, k, \beta)$ *as the event that the query $x_{i,j}$ is fresh and produces output string $\tau_{i,j} = H(x_{i,j})$ such that: (1) the Ex-Post-Facto Graph*[5] $G'_{i,j} = \mathtt{EPFG}(G, \mathtt{trace}(A, H, \chi, R), \chi, \tau_{i,j})$ *has at most $(1-\beta)N$ nodes - i.e. the fraction of red nodes is at least β - and (2) for each index $z \in [1, k]$, the challenge $c_z = (H(\chi, z, \tau_{i,j}) \bmod N)$ is a* Green *node in G - i.e. for the labeling $\ell'_1, \ldots, \ell'_n = \mathtt{EPFL}(G, \mathtt{trace}(A, H, \chi, R), \chi, \tau_{i,j})$ ℓ'_{c_z} is* Green, *i.e. that the query $x_{i,j}$ forms an accepted Merkle tree root. Intuitively, if the Ex-Post-Facto Graph $G'_{i,j}$ has at most $(1-\beta)N$ nodes then there are* at least *βN missing nodes and the probability that all of k of our challenges are green nodes is at most $(1-\beta)^k$. The event $\textsc{LuckyQuery}_{i,j}$ happens if all of the challenges are green even though a substantial fraction β of the nodes are red.*

In the full version [20] we upper bound the conditional probability as $\Pr_H[\textsc{LuckyQuery}(A, H, \chi, R, k, \beta) | \overline{\textsc{Collision}} \wedge \overline{\textsc{BadOrder}}] \leq q(1-\beta)^k$.

Theorem 7. *Fix a graph G with N nodes, input string χ, random coins R, and algorithm A, a number of challenges rounds k, and a threshold β (with $0 < \beta$). Given an algorithm A, if $\textsc{Success}(G, H, \chi, R, A, k)$ occurs and the bad events* $\textsc{Collision}$, $\textsc{BadOrder}$, $\textsc{MisColor}$, IE, *and* $\textsc{LuckyQuery}$ *do not occur, then* $\mathsf{cmc}(tr) \geq \frac{\lambda}{4}\left(\min_{S \subset V(G):|S| \leq \beta N}(cc(G-S))\right)$, *where $tr = \mathtt{trace}(A, H, \chi, R)$ is the execution trace when running A on χ.*

Corollary 1 follows immediately from Theorem 7 since we can upper bounded the probability that one of the bad events occurs. The proofs of Theorem 7 and Corollary 1 can be found in the full version [20].

Corollary 1. *Fix a graph G with N nodes and maximum in-degree δ, input string χ, random coins R, and algorithm A, a number of challenges rounds k, and a threshold β (with $0 < \beta$). Given an algorithm A which succeeds with probability at least α after t rounds of execution,* $\Pr_H[\mathsf{cmc}(tr) < \frac{\lambda}{4}\left(\min_{S \subset V(G)||S| \leq \beta N}(cc(G-S))\right)] \leq \alpha - \left(2^{-\lambda}\binom{q}{2} + n2^{-\lambda}q^2 + 2^{-\lambda}|V(G)| + 2^{-\lambda/2}t + q(1-\beta)^k\right)$, *where $tr = \mathtt{trace}(A, H, \chi, R)$ is the execution trace when running A on χ and probability is taken over the choice of random oracle.*

---

[5] An astute reader may notice that there is a subtle difference between calculating the Ex-Post-Facto Graph using the entire execution trace $\mathtt{trace}(A, H, \chi, R)$ versus calculating the Ex-Post-Facto Graph using the partial execution trace at the time that the query $x_{x,,i}j$ is made. However, as long as neither bad event $\textsc{Collision}(A, H, \chi, R)$ nor $\textsc{BadOrder}(A, H, \chi, R)$ occurs the Ex-Post-Facto Graph $\mathtt{EPFG}(G, \mathtt{trace}(A, H, \chi, R), \chi, \tau_{i,j})$ will be identical to the Ex-Post-Facto graph that we would have obtained by considering the partial execution trace.

6 Instantiating Merkle Tree MHPoWs

In the previous section, we proved that the cmc of any attacker which produces a valid Memory-Hard Merkle Tree with high probability proof is at least $\frac{\lambda}{4}\left(\min_{S\subset V(G)||S|\leq\beta N}\left(\mathsf{cc}(G-S)\right)\right)$. The question remaining is: can we find graphs G such that cc is large even when S is relatively large?

We say that a DAG $G=(V,E)$ is (e,d)-depth-robust if for all subsets $S\subseteq V$ the graph $G-S$ has a directed path of length at least d. Alwen et al. [5] showed that $\mathsf{cc}(G)\geq ed$ for any (e,d)-depth-robust graph. One can trivially observe that if $G=(V,E)$ is (e,d)-depth-robust and we remove $|S|<e$ nodes that the remaining graph $G'=G-S$ is still $(e-|S|,d)$-depth-robust. It immediately follows from [5] that $\mathsf{cc}(G')\geq(e-|S|)d$. Generalizing this observation,

Lemma 3. *Let $e'<e$ be given. Then for any (e,d)- depth-robust graph G we have:* $\min_{S\subseteq V:|S|\leq e'}\mathsf{cc}(G-S)\geq(e-e')d$.

In our setting we will think of S as denoted the set of red-nodes that were erased from the original graph. If we assume that the event $\textsc{LuckyQuery}(A,H,\chi,R,k,\beta)$ does not occur then $|S|\leq\beta N$. It follows that our Ex-Post-Facto Graph G' has $\mathsf{cc}(G')\geq\min_{S\subseteq V:|S|\leq\beta N}\mathsf{cc}(G-S)\geq(e-\beta N)d$. As long as we pick β such that $\beta N\leq e/2$ we have $\mathsf{cc}(G')\geq ed/2$.

Alwen et al. [4,5] constructed (e,d)-depth-robust graphs G with constant indegree, $e=\Omega(N/\log N)$ and $d=\Omega(N)$. If we allow the indegree of the graph to be $O(\log N)$ then for any constant $\epsilon>0$, Alwen et al. [6] constructed ϵ-extreme depth-robust graphs—graphs that are (e,d)-depth-robust for *any* parameters e,d such that $e+d\leq(1-\epsilon)N$. However, in practical applications we generally want constant indegree.

Finally, we instantiate our Memory-Hard Proof of Work with the family of graphs $\{G_N=([N],E_N)\}_{N=1}^{\infty}$ such that each graph G_N is $(c_3N/\log N,c_4N)$ depth-robust for fixed constants $c_3,c_4>0$. In our analysis we will set $\beta=c_3/(2\log N)$ so that $\beta N\leq c_3N/(2\log N)$ and that for any $|S|\leq\beta N$ we have $\mathsf{cc}(G-S)\geq c_3c_4N^2/(2\log N)$ i.e., the graph $G-S$ still has high cumulative pebbling cost. We instantiate the parameter k (number of challenges) as $k=\lambda(2\log N)/C_3$ to ensure that the error term $q(1-\beta)^k\leq qe^{-\lambda}$ remains negligible. The proof of Corollary 2 can be found in the full version [20].

Corollary 2. *Let G be any (e,d)-depth-robust graph with N nodes and set $k=\left(\frac{2N\ln 2}{e}\lambda\right)$. For any input string χ and any algorithm A and any string R (A's random coins). Let $\alpha_N\doteq\Pr[\textsc{Success}(G,H,\chi,R,A,k)]$ denote the probability that A succeeds taken over the selection of the random oracle H. We have $\Pr_H[\mathsf{cmc}(\mathit{trace}(A,H,\chi,R))<\frac{\lambda}{4}(ed/2)]\leq\alpha_N-f(N,q,\lambda,\alpha_N)$ where the probability is taken over the selection of H and $f(N,q,\lambda,\alpha_N)=\left(2^{-\lambda}\binom{q}{2}+n2^{-\lambda}q^2+2^{-\lambda}N+2^{-\lambda/2}t+q2^{-\lambda}\right)$ is a negligible function.*

6.1 Instantiation with DRSample

Fact 8. *There exist constants $c_1,c_2>0$ and a family of graphs $\{G_N=([N],E_N)\}_{N=1}^{\infty}$ such that for each N we have $\mathsf{indeg}(G_N)=2$ and G_N is*

$(c_1N/\log N, c_2N)$-depth-robust. In particular, for each N we have

$$\min_{S\subseteq V:|S|\leq c_1N/(2\log N)} \mathsf{cc}(G-S) = \frac{(c_1c_2/2)N^2}{\log N} .$$

The proof of Fact 8 can be found in the full version [20]. The proof of Corollary 3 follows immediately from Corollary 2. Observe that since $k = (2\lambda \log N)/c_1$ and each Merkle Tree opening is $O(\lambda \log N)$ bits the overall proof size is $O(\lambda^2 \log^2 N)$ bits which is sublinear with respect to N.

Corollary 3. *Let $\{G_N = ([N], E_N)\}_{N=1}^{\infty}$ be the family of graphs from Fact 8. Let $c_1, c_2 > 0$ be the constants such that G_N is $(c_1N/\log N, c_2N)$-depth-robust and set $k = (2\lambda \log N)/c_1$. Fix any input string χ. Let A be any algorithm, let R be any string (random coins) and let $\alpha_N \doteq \Pr[\text{SUCCESS}(G_N, H, \chi, R, A, k)]$ denote the probability that A succeeds where the randomness is taken over the selection of the random oracle H. We have*

$\Pr_H[\mathsf{cmc}(\mathit{trace}(A, H, \chi, R)) < \frac{\lambda}{4}(c_3c_4/2)N^2/\log N] \leq f(N, q, \lambda, \alpha_N)$ *where* $f(N, q, \lambda, \alpha_N) = \alpha_N - \left(2^{-\lambda}\binom{q}{2} + n2^{-\lambda}q^2 + 2^{-\lambda}N + 2^{-\lambda/2}t + qe^{-\lambda}\right)$

6.2 Instantiation with Argon 2i

We can also consider instantiating this with other families of graphs, such as those used in Argon2i. Argon 2i is (e, d)-depth-robust with $d = \tilde{\Omega}(N^3/e^3)$ for any $e \geq n^{2/3}$. If we set $k = \Omega(N\lambda/e)$, it follows from Corollary 2 that we obtain a MH Proof of work with cmc at least $\tilde{\Omega}\left(N^3/e^2\right)$.

Corollary 4. *Let $\{G_N = ([N], E_N)\}_{N=1}^{\infty}$ be the family of graphs used in Argon2i. Let $c_1, c_2 > 0$ be the constants such that G_N is $(c_1N/\log N, c_2N)$-depth-robust and set $k = (2\lambda \log N)/c_1$. Fix any input string χ. Let A be any algorithm, let R be any string (random coins) and let $\alpha_N \doteq \Pr[\text{SUCCESS}(G_N, H, \chi, R, A, k)]$ denote the probability that A succeeds where the randomness is taken over the selection of the random oracle H. We have*

$\Pr_H[\mathsf{cmc}(\mathit{trace}(A, H, \chi, R)) < \frac{\lambda}{4}\tilde{\Omega}\left(N^3/e^2\right)] \leq f(N, q, \lambda, \alpha_N)$ *where* $f(N, q, \lambda, \alpha_N) = \alpha_N - \left(2^{-\lambda}\binom{q}{2} + n2^{-\lambda}q^2 + 2^{-\lambda}N + 2^{-\lambda/2}t + qe^{-\lambda}\right)$

This means there is a trade-off when selecting our e. the greater the cmc achieved, the larger the proof size. For example, we achieve a maximal cmc lower bound by setting $e = n^{2/3}$ so that cmc is $\tilde{\Omega}\left(N^{5/3}\lambda\right)$, but the proof size $k = \Omega(N^{1/3}\lambda)$ is larger. It possible to reduce the proof size k by increasing e, but this will reduce CMC e.g., if we set $N = N^{0.9}$ then we have $k = \Omega(N^{0.1}\lambda)$ but the CMC lower bound drops to $\Omega(N^{1.2})$.

7 General Attacks on Merkle Tree Memory Hard Proofs of Work

In this section we outline general attacks on Memory Hard Proofs of Work which follow the Merkle Tree Proofs framework outlined earlier in the paper.

We show that any scheme which follows the Merkle Tree Proofs framework and uses a graph with constant indegree can be meaningfully attacked unless $k \in \omega(\log N)$ and that a scheme which uses Argon2 can be meaningfully attacked unless $k \in \Omega(N^{5/12})$. In the full paper [20] we warm up by discussing a simple attack on any (e, d)-depth reducible graph. The attack has cumulative memory cost $O(Nd\lambda + N\lambda \log N)$ and succeeds with probability at least $(1 - e/N)^k$. Intuitively, the attack exploits the observation that we can fix a depth-reducing set $|S_0| \leq e$ and assign random (a priori fixed) labels to these nodes hoping that they do not appear one of the k challenges. This corresponds to removing these nodes from G so that we only need to pebble the subgraph $G - S_0$. Since $G - S_0$ has depth at most d we trivially have $\mathsf{cc}(G - S_0) \leq Nd$.

We can further improve the above attack by adopting recursive pebbling strategy of [5]. This yields an even more efficient attack when the graph is (e_i, d_i)-reducible on a range of points (e_i, d_i).

Lemma 4. *[5, Lemma 8] Let $G = (V, E)$ be any DAG of size N, indegree δ, and $\mathsf{depth}(G) \leq d_0$. If G is (e_1, d_1) depth-reducible with parameters e_1, d_1 such that $2d_1N \leq e_1d_0$ and $d_1 \leq d_0$, then for any target set $T \subseteq V$ we have*
$$\mathsf{cc}(G, T, 2d_0) \leq (4\delta + 4)e_1d_0 + \frac{N}{e_1}\left(\max_{T' \subseteq V - S_1; |T'| \leq \delta \cdot e_1} \mathsf{cc}(G - S_1, T', 2d_1)\right),$$
where $S_1 \subseteq V$ and $|S_1| \leq e_1$ such that $\mathsf{depth}(G - S_1) \leq d_1$

Observe that we can apply Lemma 4 recursively i.e., if G is (e_2, d_2)-reducible with $2d_2N \leq e_2d_1$ and $d_2 \leq d_1$ then we can use Lemma 4 to upper bound $\mathsf{cc}(G - S_1, T', 2d_1)$. Unlike [5] we still get to "cheat" and begin by removing all nodes in S_0 for free where we will pick S_0 to be a (e_0, d_0)-reducing set of size $|S_0| \leq e_0$. We now want to pebble the remaining graph $G - S_0$ in parallel. In particular, instead of upper bounding $\mathsf{cc}(G)$ using Lemma 4 we only need to upper bound $\mathsf{cc}(G - S_0)$.

7.1 Attack on Argon2i-MTP

With high probability, an Argon2i DAG G is (e_i, d_i)-reducible with $d_i = O(N^3/e_i^3)$ for any parameter i, as shown by [21]. Thus, like [21] we can apply Lemma 4 to attack Argon2i by selecting an appropriate sequence $\{e_i\}_{i=1}^{z}$. The key difference is that [21] upper bounds $\mathsf{cc}(G)$ while in the MTP context we only need to upper bound $\mathsf{cc}(G - S_0)$ for some set $|S_0| \leq N/k$ because we can delete $O(N/k)$ nodes from G while (likely) not getting caught within k challenges. This allows us to obtain a tighter upper bound though we need to find a different sequence $\{e_i\}_{i=1}^{z}$ when applying Lemma 4—see the full version [20] for the proof of Theorem 9.

Theorem 9. *Let G be a directed acyclic graph with $N = |V|$ nodes and maximum indegree δ. Suppose that for some constant $\alpha > 0$ the graph G is (e, d)-reducible with $d = \alpha N^3/e^3$ for any $e \geq 1$. Then there is a constant $c > 0$ such that for every $k \geq 1$ there is a set $S_0 \subseteq V$ of size $|S_0| \leq N/k$ such that $\mathsf{cc}(G - S_0) \leq cNk^{12/5} = O\left(Nk^{12/5}\right)$.*

We can apply this attack to Argon2i graphs to lower bound the number of challenges k that must be included in the proof. In particular, we can apply Theorem 9 to obtain an attack on Argon2i graphs with cumulative memory cost at most $O(Nk^{12/5})$. If $k \in o(N^{.320})$ then we have an attack with $cc \in o(N^{1.768})$ which is better than any known pebbling attack on Argon2i without node deletions [21]. Similarly, if $k \in O(N^{5/18-\epsilon})$ then we have an attack with $cc \in O(N^{1.75-12\epsilon/5})$ which is provably better than *any* possible pebbling of G since [21] showed that (whp) $\mathsf{cc}(G) = \tilde{\Omega}(N^{1.75})$. To make this particular attack completely ineffective one would need to use at least $k \in \Omega\left(N^{5/12}\right)$ challenges so that this particular attack has $\mathsf{cc} \in \Omega(N^2)$. However, even if cannot delete nodes (e.g., $k = \Omega(N)$) we would achieve cc at most $\mathsf{cc}(G) = O(N^{1.768})$ due to the attack of [21].

7.2 General Attack on any MTP-Based MHPoW

Any DAG G with constant indegree is (e_i, e_i)-reducible with $e_i = iN/\log N$ and $d_i = O(N/2^i)$ for any parameter $1 \leq i \leq \log_2 N$ [2]. Thus, we can apply Lemma 4 to obtain the following general upper bound on any MTP construction which uses a static graph G with constant indegree.

Theorem 10. *Let G be any directed acyclic graph with $N = |V|$ nodes and maximum indegree δ. There is a constant $c_\delta > 0$ such that for every $k \geq 1$ there is a set $S_0 \subseteq V$ of size $|S_0| \leq N/k$ such that:*

$$\begin{cases} \mathsf{cc}(G - S_0) \leq \frac{N^2}{(\log^8 N)} & \text{if } k < \frac{c_\delta \log N}{8 \log\log N} \\ \mathsf{cc}(G - S_0) \leq \frac{c_\delta N^2 \log\log N}{2^{\frac{\log N}{c_\delta k}} \log N} & \text{otherwise} \end{cases}$$

We can apply Theorem 10 to obtain a general attack on any DAG G graphs with constant indegree whenever k is too small. Recall that in our MTP construction we set $k = \Theta(\lambda \log N)$ and achieve cc at least $\Omega(N^2/\log N)$, or equivalently cmc at least $\Omega(N^2\lambda/\log N)$. Theorem 10 indicates that the parameter k must be at least $\log N$ and this dependence cannot be eliminated without leaving the MHPoW vulnerable to attacks. For example, suppose we select $k < \frac{c_\delta \log N}{8 \log\log N}$ instead of $\Theta(\lambda \log N)$. Then we have shown an attack on any constant-indegree DAG with cumulative pebbling cost at most $O(N^2/\log^8 N)$, which is superior to any possible pebbling of a depth-robust graph G [4,5]. Suppose, on the other hand, that we select $k \geq \frac{c_\delta \log N}{8 \log\log N}$. If $k \in o(\log N)$, then we have an attack with cumulative memory complexity $\frac{N^2 \lambda \log\log N}{2^{\omega(1)} \log N}$, which is better than the best known general pebbling attack on constant indegree graphs [2]. If $k \in o\left(\frac{\log N}{\log\log\log N}\right)$, then this attack has cmc at most $\frac{N \log\log N}{\omega(\log\log N) \log N}$, which is better than best known pebbling lower bound $\Omega\left(\frac{N^2}{\log N}\right)$ [5] for any DAG G with constant indegree [4,5].

Acknowledgments. This work was supported in part by NSF CAREER Award #2047272.

References

1. Alcock, L., Ren, L.: A note on the security of equihash. In: Proceedings of the 2017 on Cloud Computing Security Workshop, CCSW 2017, pp. 51–55. Association for Computing Machinery, New York (2017). https://doi.org/10.1145/3140649.3140652
2. Alwen, J., Blocki, J.: Efficiently computing data-independent memory-hard functions. In: Robshaw, M., Katz, J. (eds.) CRYPTO 2016. LNCS, vol. 9815, pp. 241–271. Springer, Heidelberg (2016). https://doi.org/10.1007/978-3-662-53008-5_9
3. Alwen, J., Blocki, J.: Towards practical attacks on Argon2i and balloon hashing. In: 2017 IEEE European Symposium on Security and Privacy, pp. 142–157. IEEE Computer Society Press, Paris, France (2017). https://doi.org/10.1109/EuroSP.2017.47
4. Alwen, J., Blocki, J., Harsha, B.: Practical graphs for optimal side-channel resistant memory-hard functions. In: Thuraisingham, B.M., Evans, D., Malkin, T., Xu, D. (eds.) ACM CCS 2017: 24th Conference on Computer and Communications Security, pp. 1001–1017. ACM Press, Dallas, TX, USA (2017). https://doi.org/10.1145/3133956.3134031
5. Alwen, J., Blocki, J., Pietrzak, K.: Depth-robust graphs and their cumulative memory complexity. In: Coron and Nielsen [24], pp. 3–32. https://doi.org/10.1007/978-3-319-56617-7_1
6. Alwen, J., Blocki, J., Pietrzak, K.: Sustained space complexity. In: Nielsen and Rijmen [33], pp. 99–130. https://doi.org/10.1007/978-3-319-78375-8_4
7. Alwen, J., Chen, B., Pietrzak, K., Reyzin, L., Tessaro, S.: Scrypt is maximally memory-hard. In: Coron and Nielsen [24], pp. 33–62. https://doi.org/10.1007/978-3-319-56617-7_2
8. Alwen, J., et al.: On the memory-hardness of data-independent password-hashing functions. In: Kim, J., Ahn, G.J., Kim, S., Kim, Y., López, J., Kim, T. (eds.) ASIACCS 18: 13th ACM Symposium on Information, Computer and Communications Security, pp. 51–65. ACM Press, Incheon, Republic of Korea (2018). https://doi.org/10.1145/3196494.3196534
9. Alwen, J., Serbinenko, V.: High parallel complexity graphs and memory-hard functions. In: Servedio, R.A., Rubinfeld, R. (eds.) 47th Annual ACM Symposium on Theory of Computing, pp. 595–603. ACM Press, Portland, OR, USA (2015). https://doi.org/10.1145/2746539.2746622
10. Auerbach, B., Günther, C.U., Pietrzak, K.: Trapdoor memory-hard functions. In: Joye, M., Leander, G. (eds.) EUROCRYPT 2024, Part III. LNCS, vol. 14653, pp. 315–344. Springer, Cham (2024). https://doi.org/10.1007/978-3-031-58734-4_11
11. Back, A., et al.: Hashcash-a denial of service counter-measure (2002)
12. Ben-Sasson, E., Chiesa, A., Genkin, D., Tromer, E., Virza, M.: SNARKs for C: verifying program executions succinctly and in zero knowledge. In: Canetti, R., Garay, J.A. (eds.) CRYPTO 2013. LNCS, vol. 8043, pp. 90–108. Springer, Heidelberg (2013). https://doi.org/10.1007/978-3-642-40084-1_6
13. Biryukov, A., Dinu, D., Khovratovich, D.: Argon2: new generation of memory-hard functions for password hashing and other applications. In: 2016 IEEE European Symposium on Security and Privacy, pp. 292–302. IEEE Computer Society Press, Saarbrücken, Germany (2016). https://doi.org/10.1109/EuroSP.2016.31
14. Biryukov, A., Khovratovich, D.: Equihash: Asymmetric proof-of-work based on the generalized birthday problem. Cryptology ePrint Archive, Paper 2015/946 (2015). https://eprint.iacr.org/2015/946

15. Biryukov, A., Khovratovich, D.: Egalitarian computing. In: Holz, T., Savage, S. (eds.) USENIX Security 2016: 25th USENIX Security Symposium, pp. 315–326. USENIX Association, Austin, TX, USA (2016)
16. Biryukov, A., Perrin, L.: Symmetrically and asymmetrically hard cryptography. In: Takagi, T., Peyrin, T. (eds.) ASIACRYPT 2017. LNCS, vol. 10626, pp. 417–445. Springer, Cham (2017). https://doi.org/10.1007/978-3-319-70700-6_15
17. Blocki, J., Harsha, B., Kang, S., Lee, S., Xing, L., Zhou, S.: Data-independent memory hard functions: new attacks and stronger constructions. In: Boldyreva, A., Micciancio, D. (eds.) CRYPTO 2019. LNCS, vol. 11693, pp. 573–607. Springer, Cham (2019). https://doi.org/10.1007/978-3-030-26951-7_20
18. Blocki, J., Lee, S.: A tight lower bound on the TdScrypt trapdoor memory-hard function. Cryptology ePrint Archive (2024)
19. Blocki, J., Lee, S., Zhou, S.: On the security of proofs of sequential work in a post-quantum world. In: Tessaro, S. (ed.) ITC 2021: 2nd Conference on Information-Theoretic Cryptography. Leibniz International Proceedings in Informatics (LIPIcs), vol. 199, pp. 22:1–22:27. Schloss Dagstuhl - Leibniz-Zentrum fuer Informatik, Seattle, WA, USA (2021). https://doi.org/10.4230/LIPIcs.ITC.2021.22
20. Blocki, J., Smearsoll, N.: Provably memory-hard proofs of work with memory-easy verification. Cryptology ePrint Archive, Paper 2025/1456 (2025). https://eprint.iacr.org/2025/1456
21. Blocki, J., Zhou, S.: On the depth-robustness and cumulative pebbling cost of Argon2i. In: Kalai and Reyzin [29], pp. 445–465. https://doi.org/10.1007/978-3-319-70500-2_15
22. Chung, K.-M., Fehr, S., Huang, Y.-H., Liao, T.-N.: On the compressed-oracle technique, and post-quantum security of proofs of sequential work. In: Canteaut, A., Standaert, F.-X. (eds.) EUROCRYPT 2021. LNCS, vol. 12697, pp. 598–629. Springer, Cham (2021). https://doi.org/10.1007/978-3-030-77886-6_21
23. Cohen, B., Pietrzak, K.: Simple proofs of sequential work. In: Nielsen and Rijmen [33], pp. 451–467. https://doi.org/10.1007/978-3-319-78375-8_15
24. Coron, J.S., Nielsen, J.B. (eds.): EUROCRYPT 2017, Part III. LNCS, vol. 10212. Springer, Cham (2017)
25. Dinur, I., Nadler, N.: Time-memory tradeoff attacks on the MTP proof-of-work scheme. In: Katz, J., Shacham, H. (eds.) CRYPTO 2017. LNCS, vol. 10402, pp. 375–403. Springer, Cham (2017). https://doi.org/10.1007/978-3-319-63715-0_13
26. Dwork, C., Naor, M.: Pricing via processing or combatting junk mail. In: Brickell, E.F. (ed.) CRYPTO 1992. LNCS, vol. 740, pp. 139–147. Springer, Heidelberg (1993). https://doi.org/10.1007/3-540-48071-4_10
27. Dziembowski, S., Faust, S., Kolmogorov, V., Pietrzak, K.: Proofs of space. In: Gennaro, R., Robshaw, M. (eds.) CRYPTO 2015. LNCS, vol. 9216, pp. 585–605. Springer, Heidelberg (2015). https://doi.org/10.1007/978-3-662-48000-7_29
28. Dziembowski, S., Kazana, T., Wichs, D.: One-time computable self-erasing functions. In: Ishai, Y. (ed.) TCC 2011. LNCS, vol. 6597, pp. 125–143. Springer, Heidelberg (2011). https://doi.org/10.1007/978-3-642-19571-6_9
29. Kalai, Y., Reyzin, L. (eds.): TCC 2017, Part I. LNCS, vol. 10677. Springer, Cham (2017)
30. Mahmoody, M., Moran, T., Vadhan, S.P.: Publicly verifiable proofs of sequential work. In: Kleinberg, R.D. (ed.) ITCS 2013: 4th Innovations in Theoretical Computer Science, pp. 373–388. Association for Computing Machinery, Berkeley, CA, USA (2013). https://doi.org/10.1145/2422436.2422479

31. Merkle, R.C.: A digital signature based on a conventional encryption function. In: Pomerance, C. (ed.) CRYPTO 1987. LNCS, vol. 293, pp. 369–378. Springer, Heidelberg (1988). https://doi.org/10.1007/3-540-48184-2_32
32. Narayanan, A., Bonneau, J., Felten, E., Miller, A., Goldfeder, S.: Bitcoin and cryptocurrency technologies: a comprehensive introduction. Princeton University Press (2016)
33. Nielsen, J.B., Rijmen, V. (eds.) EUROCRYPT 2018, Part II. LNCS, vol. 10821. Springer, Cham (2018)
34. Pietrzak, K.: Proofs of catalytic space. In: Blum, A. (ed.) ITCS 2019: 10th Innovations in Theoretical Computer Science Conference, vol. 124, pp. 59:1–59:25. Leibniz International Proceedings in Informatics (LIPIcs), San Diego, CA, USA (2019). https://doi.org/10.4230/LIPIcs.ITCS.2019.59
35. Ren, L., Devadas, S.: Bandwidth hard functions for ASIC resistance. In: Kalai and Reyzin [29], pp. 466–492. https://doi.org/10.1007/978-3-319-70500-2_16

Secure Computation II

On the Impossibility of Actively Secure Distributed Samplers

Damiano Abram[1], Serge Fehr[2], Maciej Obremski[3], and Peter Scholl[4(✉)]

[1] The University of Edinburgh, Edinburgh, UK
[2] CWI Amsterdam and Leiden University, Amsterdam, The Netherlands
[3] National University of Singapore, Singapore, Singapore
[4] Aarhus University, Aarhus, Denmark
peter.scholl@cs.au.dk

Abstract. One-round secure computation is generally believed impossible due to the *residual function attack*: any honest-but-curious participant can replay the protocol in their head changing their input, and learn, in this way, a new output. Inputless functionalities are among the few that are immune to this problem.

This paper studies one-round, multi-party computation protocols (MPC) that implement the most natural inputless functionality: one that generates a random sample from a fixed distribution. These are called *distributed samplers*. At Eurocrypt 2022, Abram, Scholl and Yakoubov showed how to build this primitive in the semi-honest model with dishonest majority. In this work, we give a lower bound for constructing distributed samplers with a malicious adversary in the standard model. More in detail, we show that for any construction in the stand-alone model with black-box simulation, even with a CRS and honest majority, the output of the sampling protocol must have low entropy. This essentially implies that this type of construction is useless in applications. Our proof is based on an entropic argument, drawing a new connection between computationally secure MPC, information theory and learning theory.

1 Introduction

Even in the semi-honest model, any one-round computation protocol is subject to the residual function attack [HIJ+17]: any participant can replay the protocol in their head, reusing the other parties' messages in combination with a new input. From any such virtual execution, the attacker learns a new output. This is fatal for most applications, as the freshly derived outputs often leak information about the other parties' inputs. There is, however, one situation that is immune to the attack: *no-signaling* functionalities [DLN+04, DHRW16]. These are functionalities where the outputs of any subset of corrupted parties look independent of the remaining parties' inputs. For instance, any inputless functionality is no-signaling.

Work done while the authors was affiliated with Aarhus University and Bocconi University.

B. Applebaum and H. Lin (Eds.): TCC 2025, LNCS 16271, pp. 547–581, 2026.
https://doi.org/10.1007/978-3-032-12290-2_18

This paper studies one-round protocols that implement the most natural, non-trivial inputless functionality: one that generates a random sample from a fixed distribution $\mathcal{D}$. This question is also motivated from a real-word perspective. Many cryptographic protocols require public parameters to be generated in a secure manner. This is the case, for instance, with trusted parameters used in many succinct zero-knowledge proofs [BCCT12], or trusted RSA moduli used in cryptographic accumulators [Bd94]. These parameters often hide *trapdoors*, artifacts of the security proofs that, if leaked to an attacker, could completely compromise the desired security properties. For this reason, it is important that the generation of these parameters is performed correctly and securely.

A common practice is to delegate the generation of this sensitive material to trusted authorities, for instance a public institution or a private corporation: essentially, due to their reputation and accountability, we have confidence that they generate the public parameters correctly and ensure that all trapdoors remain secret. Ignoring the fact that it is debatable whether we can really trust that these institutions will not take advantage of their privileged position (remember the Snowden files), this practice inherently introduces a point of failure in the constructions: what if a cyber attack manages to breach into the servers of the trusted institution? What if they succeed in learning any of the trapdoors?

As a result, when such parameters are needed, the parties involved may wish to run a secure multi-party computation protocol to generate them, guaranteeing security and secrecy of the trapdoors as long as sufficiently many parties are honest. However, this type of setup protocol is typically expensive to carry out and coordinate. This is especially true for small end-users, normal people around the globe that only rarely need to run secure computations and, consequently, cannot easily amortise the costs of these setups.

Distributed samplers, recently introduced by Abram, Scholl and Yakoubov [ASY22, AWZ23], propose a solution to these issues by allowing parameters to be sampled using a *one-round* protocol: each party publishes a single message, after which everybody can obtain the same random sample from the desired distribution. More formally, a distributed sampler for n parties and a distribution $\mathcal{D}$ is defined by a pair of algorithms $(\mathsf{Gen}, \mathsf{Sample})$, such that given a set of messages $U_i = \mathsf{Gen}(1\!\!1^\lambda, i)$, for $i \in [n]$, one can compute a sample $R \leftarrow \mathsf{Sample}(U_1, \ldots, U_n)$[1]. The security requirement essentially states that this one-round protocol must securely realize the ideal functionality for sampling from $\mathcal{D}$.

In their work, Abram, Scholl and Yakoubov studied this primitive in the dishonest majority setting, both with passive and active security [ASY22]. Active security is particularly challenging, due to the need to handle a rushing adversary, who may choose their messages U_i *after* seeing the messages U_j of the other parties. This allows an attacker to "grind" different choices of their randomness, obtaining different U_i, until finding an output R that she likes. So, the best form of security one can hope for in this setting is a relaxation of the ideal functionality for sampling, where the adversary first obtains several samples from $\mathcal{D}$, before settling on a final output.

---

[1] λ represents the security parameter.

Table 1. Overview of the feasibility of distributed samplers in different settings. UC = universal composability; BB = stand-alone with black-box simulation; game=game-based security definition; pRO = programmable random oracle; poly/subexp = polynomial/subexponential hardness; ELF = extremely lossy function. Observe that, since our results hold in a weaker setting (i.e. honest majority with CRS and black-box simulation), our impossibility is stronger.

Security model	Setup	Corruption Threshold	Feasibility
Semi-malicious	None	Dishonest majority	poly iO + OWF [ASY22]
Malicious, UC	pRO	Dishonest majority	poly iO + OWF [ASY22]
Malicious, game	CRS	Dishonest majority	subexp iO + subexp OWF + ELF [AWZ23]
Malicious, UC	None	Dishonest majority	impossible [CKL03]
Malicious, BB	None	Dishonest majority	impossible [HV16, PVW08]
Malicious, BB	CRS	Any $t \geq \epsilon \cdot n$	impossible (Sect. 4)

Abram et al. [ASY22] constructed distributed samplers in the plain model (no CRS) for any distribution based on indistinguishability obfuscation. Their first construction is secure only against a *semi-malicious*[2] and non-rushing adversary. This was then upgraded to malicious security in the programmable random oracle model. On top of this, they showed how distributed samplers can be used for sampling arbitrary forms of *correlated randomness*, often used in MPC protocols, with a one-round protocol.

1.1 Our Results

In this work, we further explore the feasibility of distributed samplers. See Table 1 for an overview of our results and prior relevant work.

Impossibility of Distributed Samplers Without Random Oracles. We first pose the question: is it possible to build actively secure, one-time distributed samplers in the *standard model*, that is, without random oracles? As a starting point, we observe that actively secure distributed samplers cannot be built without a common reference string (CRS) in the UC model [Can01]. This is an immediate consequence of the UC impossibility for same-output probabilistic functions of [CKL03], since the function $\mathcal{D}(1\!\!1^\lambda)$ we want to compute has an unpredictable output and no inputs.

We observe also that generic actively secure distributed samplers without a CRS cannot exist even in the standalone model with black-box simulation. If that was not the case, by sequentially composing a distributed sampler with 2-round active OT protocols in the CRS model such as [PVW08], we would obtain a 3-round OT protocol with active security and black-box simulation in the plain model. The latter is known to be impossible [HV16].

[2] A semi-malicious adversary is one who follows the protocol, but may choose their random tape arbitrarily.

For this reason, we investigate the CRS model. At first glance, it seems that distributed samplers are then trivial: the CRS can directly encode a sample from the desired distribution. This solution does not even need interaction, however, interactive distributed samplers with a CRS may have some advantages over this trivial solution: the CRS could be reused multiple times, or it could be easier to generate, by being short or unstructured (i.e. a uniformly random string). We prove that, if the distributed sampler is secure against active adversaries in the stand-alone model with black-box simulation, none of the above properties can be satisfied, even if the adversary corrupts only $t = \epsilon \cdot n$ parties for any constant $\epsilon > 0$. We prove this by relying on a new kind of information-theoretic argument: by analysing the Shannon entropy diagram of the protocol, we show that any black-box simulator would fail to simulate even adversaries that follow the protocol but generate their randomness using a w-wise independent hash function (for a sufficiently large w) applied on the honest-parties messages. Essentially, at the base of the proof is the impossibility for any black-box simulator to learn the w-wise independent hash function, which would allow it to predict the adversary's randomness and simulate the protocol. Our argument therefore draws new connections between computationally secure MPC, information theory and learning theory.

All of these impossibilities come from our main result, below.

Theorem 1 (Informal, c.f. Thm. 4). *For any t-out-of-n distributed sampler that is secure against rushing adversaries in the stand-alone model with black-box simulation, we have*

$$\mathsf{H}(R \mid \sigma) = \frac{n}{t} \cdot O(\log \lambda),$$

where σ denotes the CRS and R the output of the distributed sampler.[3]

This essentially rules out this flavour of distributed sampler for all practical applications, as we discuss in the following corollaries.

Corollary 1: The Collision Probability is Large. An immediate consequence of small Shannon entropy is that the output of the distributed sampler has a high probability of a collision if the CRS is not changed. This implies that in applications where more than one sample from $\mathcal{D}$ is needed, the same CRS cannot be reused.

Corollary 2: The CRS must be Long. Less trivially, we show that this means that the CRS must be at most $O(\lambda)$ bits smaller than the Yao incompressibility entropy of $\mathcal{D}$. Recall that this roughly measures the compressed size of a sample from $\mathcal{D}$, after applying any efficient compression algorithm. As a result, the CRS must be almost as long as an output of $\mathcal{D}$, after applying compression.

[3] We use H to denote the Shannon entropy. We refer to Sect. 3 for formal definitions.

Corollary 3: The CRS must be Ugly. Finally, we show that in meaningful scenarios, the CRS must inherently be *structured*, or "ugly", meaning that it requires private coins to sample. In practice, this type of CRS must be generated by a trusted party or multi-party computation protocol, whereas obtaining a CRS that can be sampled from uniform randomness is much easier, relying only on a public source of randomness (or a hash function modeled as a random oracle).

Conclusion. Put together, the above corollaries show that, if there exists a $\omega(\log \lambda)$ multiplicative gap between the Shannon entropy of the distribution $\mathsf{H}(\mathcal{D})$ and the corruption ratio n/t, actively-secure distributed samplers with black-box simulation are essentially useless: given that the CRS can only be used once, is structured, and roughly as long as an output of $\mathcal{D}$, in practice it will most likely be no easier to generate the CRS than to just generate a sample from $\mathcal{D}$.

On the Tightness of the Lower Bound. We observe that if $\mathsf{H}(\mathcal{D}) \leq n/t \cdot O(\log \lambda)$, it is sometimes possible to build distributed samplers with black-box simulation. For instance, suppose that $\mathcal{D}$ outputs a random string in $\{0,1\}^n$. Then, if $t = O(\log \lambda)$, we can build a black-box simulatable t-out-of-n distributed sampler for $\mathcal{D}$. The protocol is simple: each party P_i broadcasts a random bit b_i. The output consists of $(b_1, \ldots, b_n)$. To simulate, it is sufficient to query a random string x from the functionality and make all honest parties output a bit according to it. Given that there are at most $O(\log \lambda)$ corrupted parties, the bits chosen by the adversary will be consistent with x with $1/\mathsf{poly}(\lambda)$ probability. In the case of an unlucky event, the simulator can simply rewind and retry with another random string received from the functionality.

How to Interpret the Impossibility. Our lower bound *must not* be read as a general impossibility for actively secure distributed samplers with non-trivial efficiency: the message we are trying to pass is that, if we want to construct such primitive, we need to rely on *non-black-box techniques* [Bar01]. As a matter of fact, the adversarial class for which we prove the impossibility of a black-box simulator is one for which we can easily build a non-black-box simulator. This is because for suitable w-wise independent hash functions, given an input-output pair (x, y), we can efficiently sample a random hash key that maps x to y. Therefore, to simulate the protocol, we can generate a transcript using a semi-honest simulator and then generate the hash key (the adversary's random tape) so that the honest messages are mapped to the simulated randomness for the adversary. Notice, however, that if we consider slightly more complex ways of generating the randomness for our honest adversary, the question of non-black-box simulation becomes immediately hard. For instance, what if we substitute the w-wise independent hash function with a PRF? What if we substitute it with a correlation-intractable hash function? Simulating any such adversary seems to intrinsically require the use of non-black-box techniques.

Notice that, even after years of research, our knowledge of the non-black-box world is still rather limited, and this is even more so in the context of non-interactive protocols. This seems to suggest that constructing non-trivial, actively secure distributed samplers is a particularly difficult task.

1.2 Related Work

Preliminary Version. A preliminary, unpublished draft of this work can be found on the IACR ePrint Archive [AOS23]. The two versions of the work differ mainly in two aspects. First, the preliminary impossibility was proven for the UC model [Can01] with full-threshold corruption. In this submission, the impossibility has been *strengthened* to the standalone model with black-box simulation and a potentially honest majority. Secondly, in the preliminary draft, we explained how to build party-dynamic distributed samplers in the random oracle model. These additional results have been moved to another work.

Game-Based Actively Secure Distributed Samplers. In [AWZ23], Abram, Waters and Zhandry presented solutions to circumvent the impossibility proven in this paper. Instead of aiming for a simulation-based security definition, they show that, using strong primitives (including subexponential iO) but no random oracle, it is possible to implement game-based definitions for distributed samplers that allow removing trusted setups in one round while preserving the hardness of search problems and the security of most protocols against active adversaries.

The lower bounds in this paper offer an argument that—notwithstanding a major advance in non-black-box simulation—the complex game-based definitions of [AWZ23] are necessary, as simulation-based security is unachievable without a random oracle. We point out that a simulation-based definition is, in principle, desirable as there exist situations for which the definitions of [AWZ23] are not sufficient. For instance, their notion of a hardness-preserving distributed sampler does not allow removing the CRS from a NIZK while preserving soundness. This is because hardness-preserving distributed samplers preserve the hardness of games only when the challenger is efficient. Their second notion of indistinguishability-preserving distributed samplers also does not work in all contexts. For example, consider the functionality $\mathcal{F}$ that provides the adversary with several RSA moduli, lets the adversary choose one of them (denote the chosen modulus by N), and then allows MPC over $\mathbb{Z}_N$ (this is an interesting setting, e.g. for using MPC tools from [OSY21] that require a trusted setup). There exists a protocol Π that, given an RSA modulus as CRS, implements $\mathcal{F}$. However, if we apply an indistinguishability-preserving distributed sampler [AWZ23] to generate the CRS, the result Π' cannot be proven to securely implement the functionality $\mathcal{F}$ using black-box techniques (following our main result).

Coin Tossing Extension. In [ADIN24], Abram et al. proved a lower-bound for statistically secure coin-tossing extension with black-box simulation using an entropic argument similar to the one we used in Theorem 4. Their setting differs from ours in two important ways. First of all, unlike us, they work with statistically secure protocols. This significantly simplifies their argument given that Shannon entropy is preserved under statistical indistinguishability. On the other hand, Shannon entropy of computationally indistinguishable random variables can assume significantly different values. The other big difference is that their impossibility holds in the dishonest majority setting, whereas our lower-bound holds even in the presence of an honest majority (making our negative result stronger).

2 Technical Overview

We now give a high-level overview of the techniques used to obtain our results.

Notation. We denote the security parameter by λ. Even when not explicitly written, we assume that all random variables depend on λ. We use bold font to denote random variables. We use $\mathsf{Supp}(\mathbf{X})$ to denote the support of the random variable $\mathbf{X}$. The symbol $\sim_c$ denotes computational indistinguishability. We indicate the bit-length of any string s by $|s|$. With an abuse of notation, we identify distributions $\mathcal{D}$ with circuits mapping uniformly random strings of bits into samples. We say that a distribution is efficient if its circuit has $\mathsf{poly}(\lambda)$ size. We represent the number of parties by n, the set of corrupted players by C, the set of honest players by H. Throughout the whole paper, we assume that n is at most a polynomial quantity in the security parameter λ. We use $\mathsf{negl}(\lambda)$ to denote an arbitrary negligible function, i.e., $\mathsf{negl}(\lambda) = \lambda^{-\omega(1)}$. We say that an event E holds with overwhelming probability if $\Pr[\neg E] \leq 1 - \mathsf{negl}(\lambda)$.

2.1 (Im)possibility of Distributed Samplers Without Random Oracle

As we motivated in the introduction, actively secure distributed samplers in the plain model with black-box simulation are impossible. In the CRS model, instead, they are trivial to build: the CRS can directly encode a sample from the underlying distribution. The result is a distributed sampler in which the parties do not even need to communicate, since they just output the CRS.

We study how interactive constructions can improve upon the trivial solution. In principle, the advantages can be multiple: the same CRS can be reused in many distributed sampler executions producing independent-looking outputs. Moreover, the CRS of distributed samplers can be nicer (i.e. easier to generate) than the direct encoding of a sample, for instance because of the smaller size, or because it is unstructured (i.e. a uniformly random string of bits). The result of our analysis is that none of the above properties can be satisfied: without a random oracle, distributed samplers with black-box simulation essentially provide no advantage over the trivial solution. In order for this impossibility to hold, we do not even need to aim for active security, it suffices that the adversary is *strongly semi-malicious*: it may adaptively choose the randomness of the corrupted parties after seeing the honest messages, but all corrupted players follow the protocol. Even more surprisingly, in the proof, we will show that no black-box simulator is able to simulate adversaries that produce the randomness of the corrupted parties deterministically, using a w-wise independent hash function for a sufficiently large w. Observe that all of these adversaries can actually be simulated very easily, but *not in a black-box manner*, intuitively, because the w-wise independent hash function is not learnable by a simulator with query complexity $< w$.

On the Unpredictability of Distributed Samplers in the CRS Model. All the negative results mentioned above are consequences of the main theorem of this work: in a strongly semi-malicious distributed sampler with black-box simulation, the Shannon entropy of the output conditioned on the CRS is $O(\log \lambda)$. Interestingly, this holds even in the honest majority setting when the corruption threshold is a constant fraction of the total number of participants.

Throughout the paper, we carefully juggle different variants of entropy, each bringing a unique set of properties we require during the proofs. Shannon entropy H has a powerful chain rule. Collision entropy H_2 gives us an elegant tool for building distinguishers, but lacks a chain rule and is not invariant under computational indistinguishability (i.e. for two computationally indistinguishable random variables, H_2 can be vastly different). Finally, Yao's entropy is the only entropy we use that remains invariant under computational indistinguishability (i.e. two computationally indistinguishable random variables have the same Yao entropy). For formal definitions please refer to Sect. 3.

Our Definition of Distributed Samplers. To understand the idea behind the result, we first recall the definition of distributed samplers with security against an active adversary [ASY22]. We consider a classical simulation-based security definition. Specifically, we work in the stand-alone model with black-box simulation [GK90,Ore87,BMO90]: we require the existence of a single PPT simulator that, given oracle access to the adversary and the functionality, should be able to reproduce an adversarial view that is consistent with the functionality's outputs. In particular, we study *computational security*: the view of the adversary in the protocol should be computationally indistinguishable from the output of the simulator even if we leak the outputs of the honest parties.

The distributed sampler functionality provides the adversary with as many samples from the underlying distribution as the adversary wants. The adversary can then select one of these, which the functionality outputs to all the honest parties. This kind of behaviour is needed to model the fact that, in the case of a rushing adversary, the corrupted parties see the honest messages before they publish their own. In other words, before committing to a choice, they can always test their candidate messages and discard them if they are not happy. Below, we sketch the definition, a more formal version can be found in Sect. 4.

Definition 1 (Distributed sampler - informal security against rushing adversaries). *Let $\mathcal{D}(\mathbb{1}^\lambda)$ be an efficiently samplable distribution and let t be a corruption threshold. An n-party actively secure (resp. strongly semi-maliciously secure) distributed sampler for $\mathcal{D}(\mathbb{1}^\lambda)$ is a one-round protocol implementing the functionality $\mathcal{F}_\mathcal{D}$ (see Fig. 1) against a static and active (resp. strongly semi-malicious) adversary corrupting up to t parties.*

THE FUNCTIONALITY $\mathcal{F}_{\mathcal{D}}$

Initialisation. On input Init from every honest party and the adversary, the functionality activates and sets $Q := \emptyset$. (Q will be used to keep track of queries.) If all the parties are honest, the functionality outputs $R \stackrel{\$}{\leftarrow} \mathcal{D}(\mathbb{1}^\lambda)$ to every honest party and sends R to the adversary, then it halts.

Query. On input Query from the adversary, the functionality samples $R \stackrel{\$}{\leftarrow} \mathcal{D}(\mathbb{1}^\lambda)$ and creates a fresh label id. It sends (id, R) to the adversary and adds the pair to Q.

Output. On input $(\mathsf{Output}, \widehat{\mathsf{id}})$ from the adversary, the functionality retrieves the only pair $(\mathsf{id}, R) \in Q$ with $\mathsf{id} = \widehat{\mathsf{id}}$. Then, it outputs R to every honest party and terminates.

Fig. 1. The distributed sampler functionality for rushing adversaries

Our Adversarial Model. Our proof will only consider adversaries that behave almost completely honestly: the adversary will generate the corrupted parties' messages following the protocol execution, but will produce their randomness by running a w-wise independent hash function on the honest parties' messages and the CRS. Here, w denotes a polynomial upper bound on the number of times the simulator queries the adversary, so rewinding the adversary will give no advantage to the simulator. Notice that since we are proving a lower bound, considering very weak adversaries makes our results even stronger.

In the Real World, the Output is Easily Predictable from the CRS and the Messages of the Honest Parties. Our starting goal is to show that, in the real world, $\mathsf{H}(R|U_H, \sigma) = O(\log \lambda)$, where R denotes the output of the distributed sampler, U_H denotes the set of messages of the honest parties and σ represents the CRS. We show that if that is not the case, we would be able to distinguish between the real and the ideal world with non-negligible advantage. The attack is very simple: the distinguisher estimates the probability that, by rerunning the protocol with the same CRS, the same messages for the honest parties, but fresh messages from the corrupted parties, the output is again R.

The intuition is that such probability is significantly higher in the ideal world. Since the adversary generates the messages of the corrupted parties using the w-wise independent hash function (which is not learnable), in order to make the simulated transcript consistent with the output, the simulator needs to test it by querying the candidate CRS and the honest messages to the adversary. This means that in at least one of the w queried executions, the adversary ended up choosing R as the output. Furthermore, this is not just a random R, it must be one of the ideal samples provided by the functionality! Notice that there are polynomially many of these, let's say at most q. If the simulator wants to be sure that, in at least one of the w tested executions, the adversary chooses one of these q ideal samples, it must be that these elements have a higher-than-usual probability of getting picked. As a consequence, the distribution of R must be biased towards elements that have a high probability of being resampled.

The Final Bound. To prove that $\mathsf{H}(R|\sigma) = \frac{n}{t} \cdot O(\log \lambda)$, we rely on the following lemma, proven in Sect. 4. We believe that this result could be of independent interest. Essentially, it states that, in a one round protocol, the influence of an adversary corrupting at most t parties, is proportional to the ratio t/n.

Lemma 1 (Informal). *Let $X_1, \ldots, X_n, Y$ be random variables and suppose that $X_1, \ldots, X_n$ are all independent conditioned on Y. Let $R \leftarrow f(X_1, \ldots, X_n, Y)$ be a deterministic function. Then, for every $\tau \in [n]$, there exists a subset $S_\tau \subseteq [n]$ such that $|S_\tau| = \tau$ and*

$$\mathsf{H}(R|X_{S_\tau}, Y) \geq \frac{n-\tau}{n} \cdot \mathsf{H}(R|Y).$$

To see why this lemma implies our lower bound, observe that the output of the distributed sampler is a deterministic function of $U_1, \ldots, U_n, \sigma$. Moreover, since our adversary is almost honest, in the real world, $U_1, \ldots, U_n$ are all independent conditioned on σ. We conclude that there exists a subset H of $n-t$ elements such that

$$\frac{t}{n} \cdot \mathsf{H}(R|\sigma) \leq \mathsf{H}(R|U_H, \sigma) = O(\log \lambda).$$

Bad News for Distributed Samplers. All the results we discuss below hold in absence of a random oracle and for distributed samplers that achieve t-out-of-n security (for $t/n = \Theta(1)$) with black-box simulation against our class of almost-honest adversaries.

Distributed Sampler CRSs cannot be Used Twice. Suppose that the distribution underlying the distributed sampler has high min-entropy, i.e. $\mathsf{H}_\infty(\mathcal{D}) = \omega(\log \lambda)$. We would hope that if we run the distributed sampler twice using the same CRS, the resulting outputs look like two independent samples from $\mathcal{D}(1\!\!1^\lambda)$ and therefore, they differ with overwhelming probability. Alas! This is impossible: the first corollary of Theorem 1 is that two distributed sampler executions using the same CRS have colliding outputs with non-negligible probability.

The reason at the base of our first corollary is that, by a simple application of Jensen's inequality, the average collision entropy $\widetilde{\mathsf{H}}_2(R|\,\sigma)$ is bounded from above by $\mathsf{H}(R|\,\sigma) = O(\log \lambda)$. We recall that the average collision entropy is defined as

$$\widetilde{\mathsf{H}}_2(R|\,\sigma) := -\log\big(\Pr[R = R']\big)$$

where R and R' are two distributed sampler outputs computed using the same CRS σ and the probability is also over the randomness of σ. We conclude that $\Pr[R = R'] \geq 1/\mathsf{poly}(\lambda)$.

Distributed Sampler CRSs are Long. We prove that CRSs of strongly semi-malicious distributed samplers cannot be small: they can be at most $O(\log \lambda)$ bits shorter than the Yao entropy of the underlying distribution $\mathsf{H}_{\mathsf{Yao}}(\mathcal{D})$[4].

[4] The Yao entropy of $\mathcal{D}$ roughly measures how much a sample from $\mathcal{D}$ can be compressed in polynomial time without losing information.

We prove this result by first observing that $\mathsf{H}_{\mathsf{Yao}}(R|\,\sigma) = O(\log \lambda)$. Indeed, as we motivated in the previous paragraph, two distributed sampler executions using the same CRS have colliding outputs with non-negligible probability. We can therefore consider the Yao's compressor that outputs nothing and the associated decompressor that, provided with the CRS σ, reruns the distributed sampler protocol in its head and outputs the result R'. With $1/\mathsf{poly}(\lambda)$ probability, R' coincides with the input of the compressor.[5] This is enough to conclude that $\mathsf{H}_{\mathsf{Yao}}(R|\,\sigma) = O(\log \lambda)$.

We then show that $\mathsf{H}_{\mathsf{Yao}}(R|\,\sigma) \geq \mathsf{H}_{\mathsf{Yao}}(R) - |\sigma|$. We prove this by noticing that, given a compressor-decompressor pair (c', d') for $\mathsf{H}_{\mathsf{Yao}}(R|\,\sigma)$, we can build a compressor-decompressor pair (c, d) for $\mathsf{H}_{\mathsf{Yao}}(R)$ as follows: c provides its input R to the distributed sampler simulator, corrupting no party. It obtains a fake CRS σ' that looks like the real one. It then outputs $c'(R, \sigma')$ along with σ'. The decompressor d is exactly the same as d'. The success probability of (c, d) is the same as for (c', d') except for a negligible quantity. The size of the compressed string has however grown by $|\sigma|$ bits, increasing $\mathsf{H}_{\mathsf{Yao}}(R)$ by the same amount.

We point out that, in order to prove the above inequality, we cannot use the Yao chain rule of [KPW13, Appendix B] as their compressor for $\mathsf{H}_{\mathsf{Yao}}(R)$ has $O(2^{|\sigma|})$ size.

Distributed Sampler CRSs are Ugly. Suppose that there exists a strongly semi-malicious distributed sampler for the distribution $\mathcal{D}$ having CRS σ. We prove that it is possible to *non-interactively* and *securely* generate a sample from $\mathcal{D}$ given only σ and public random coins. In other words, if there exists a distributed sampler with nice CRS, also the underlying distribution can be encoded in a nice CRS. The second solution may be preferable as it often requires less communication. As an additional corollary, if the distributed sampler uses a URS (i.e. the CRS is a random string of bits), we can sample from $\mathcal{D}$ using just public random coins. So, in the random oracle model, we would not even need a CRS.

Our idea is that, given σ and public random coins, each party can just rerun the distributed sampler protocol with σ as CRS and the public coins as randomness for the players. The distribution result R is clearly indistinguishable from a sample from $\mathcal{D}$. However, in order to prove that this protocol is secure, we need to be able to simulate σ and the public coins, given R.

We simulate σ by feeding R to the distributed sampler simulator (we corrupt no party). Unfortunately, the simulator cannot provide us with the randomness used by the parties. We proceed by brute-force: we rerun the protocol in our head using the fake CRS and we hope that the output collides with R. If we fail, we retry sampling a new fake CRS. Once we succeed, we output the fake σ and the randomness of the parties that led to the collision.

By the first corollary of Theorem 1, we know that, *on average* over R, the collision probability is $1/\mathsf{poly}(\lambda)$. So, for a *polynomial fraction* of all possible values R, the simulation succeeds after a polynomial number of tries. For the remaining fraction of the support of $\mathcal{D}$, our approach fails, meaning that the

[5] We can make the decompressor deterministic using a PRF.

CRS and the randomness of the parties might leak too much information about the output.

In other words, the sampling protocol we described is secure only for a polynomial fraction of the support of $\mathcal{D}$. The good news is that it is possible to tell if the result of our non-interactive sampling protocol lies in the secure subset or not: the parties can locally run the simulator. If it succeeds with sufficiently high frequency, they can be sure their output is secure, otherwise, they need to discard it, generate a new σ and public coins and rerun the protocol. Since there is a polynomial fraction of the support of $\mathcal{D}$ that will not be discarded, the players need a polynomial number of attempts before succeeding. We also point out that the distribution of the outputs will be biased, but not significantly: if $\mathcal{D}$ describes the distribution of another protocol's CRS, it is still secure to use the outputs of our procedure as CRSs for such protocol.

3 Preliminaries on Entropy

In information theory, entropy is used to measure the unpredictability of random variables. After almost a century of research, several definitions have been formalised. In this section, we recall some of the important notions and the related properties. We start with Shannon's entropy [Sha48].

Definition 2 (Shannon's entropy). *Let* $\mathbf{X}$ *be a random variable having finite support. The Shannon's entropy of* $\mathbf{X}$ *is*

$$\mathsf{H}(\mathbf{X}) := -\sum_x \Pr[\mathbf{X} = x] \cdot \log\big(\Pr[\mathbf{X} = x]\big).$$

We recall also the notion of conditional Shannon's entropy, mutual information and interaction information.

Definition 3 (Conditional Shannon's entropy). *Let* $\mathbf{X}$ *and* $\mathbf{Y}$ *be random variables having finite support and let* E *be an event. The Shannon's entropy of* $\mathbf{X}$ *conditioned on* E *is*

$$\mathsf{H}(\mathbf{X}|E) := -\sum_x \Pr[\mathbf{X} = x|E] \cdot \log\big(\Pr[\mathbf{X} = x|E]\big).$$

The Shannon's entropy of $\mathbf{X}$ *conditioned on* $\mathbf{Y}$ *is instead*

$$\mathsf{H}(\mathbf{X}|\mathbf{Y}) := \sum_y \Pr[\mathbf{Y} = y] \cdot \mathsf{H}(\mathbf{X}|\mathbf{Y} = y).$$

Definition 4 (Mutual information). *Let* $\mathbf{X}$*,* $\mathbf{Y}$ *and* $\mathbf{Z}$ *be random variables. The mutual information of* $\mathbf{X}$ *and* $\mathbf{Y}$ *conditioned on* $\mathbf{Z}$ *is*

$$\mathsf{I}(\mathbf{X}; \mathbf{Y}|\mathbf{Z}) := \mathsf{H}(\mathbf{X}|\mathbf{Z}) - \mathsf{H}(\mathbf{X}|\mathbf{Y}, \mathbf{Z}).$$

Definition 5 (Interaction information). *Let* $\mathbf{X}_1, \ldots, \mathbf{X}_n$ *and* $\mathbf{Z}$ *be random variables. The interaction information of* $\mathbf{X}_1, \ldots, \mathbf{X}_n$ *conditioned on* $\mathbf{Z}$ *is defined inductively by* $\mathsf{I}(\mathbf{X}_1|\mathbf{Z}) := \mathsf{H}(\mathbf{X}_1|\mathbf{Z})$ *and*

$$\mathsf{I}(\mathbf{X}_1; \ldots; \mathbf{X}_n|\mathbf{Z}) := \mathsf{I}(\mathbf{X}_1; \ldots; \mathbf{X}_{n-1}|\mathbf{Z}) - \mathsf{I}(\mathbf{X}_1; \ldots; \mathbf{X}_{n-1}|\mathbf{X}_n, \mathbf{Z}).$$

Shannon's entropy satisfies an important property called *the strong chain rule.* We recall it below.

Theorem 2 (Strong chain rule). *Let* $\mathbf{X}$ *and* $\mathbf{Y}$ *be random variables with finite support. Then,*

$$\mathsf{H}(\mathbf{X}, \mathbf{Y}) = \mathsf{H}(\mathbf{Y}) + \mathsf{H}(\mathbf{X}|\mathbf{Y}).$$

Notice that $(\mathbf{X}, \mathbf{Y})$ is a random variable, so $\mathsf{H}(\mathbf{X}, \mathbf{Y})$ is defined as in Definition 2. We also recall the following properties of Shannon's entropy.

Lemma 2. *Let* $\mathbf{X}, \mathbf{Y}$ *and* $\mathbf{Z}$ *be random variables with finite support. Then,*

1. *If* $\mathbf{X}$ *is uniform over a set of cardinality* m, $\mathsf{H}(\mathbf{X}) = \log m$.
2. *If* $\mathbf{X}$ *is independent of* $\mathbf{Y}$, *given* $\mathbf{Z}$, $\mathsf{H}(\mathbf{X}|\mathbf{Y}, \mathbf{Z}) = \mathsf{H}(\mathbf{X}|\mathbf{Z})$ *and so* $\mathsf{I}(\mathbf{X}; \mathbf{Y}|\mathbf{Z}) = 0$.
3. $\mathsf{H}(\mathbf{X}|\mathbf{Y}, \mathbf{Z}) \leq \mathsf{H}(\mathbf{X}|\mathbf{Z})$ *and so* $\mathsf{I}(\mathbf{X}; \mathbf{Y}|\mathbf{Z}) \geq 0$.
4. *If* f *is a deterministic function,* $\mathsf{H}(f(\mathbf{X})) \leq \mathsf{H}(\mathbf{X})$.

We now recall other definitions of entropy that are used to prove our results.

Definition 6 (Max entropy). *Let* X *be a random variable with finite support, let* E *be an event. We define the max entropy of* $\mathbf{X}$ *to be*

$$\mathsf{H}_0(\mathbf{X}) = \log|\mathsf{Supp}(\mathbf{X})|.$$

We define the max entropy of $\mathbf{X}$ *conditioned on* E *to be*

$$\mathsf{H}_0(\mathbf{X}|E) = \log|\mathsf{Supp}(\mathbf{X}|E)|.$$

Definition 7 (Min entropy). *Let* $\mathbf{X}$ *be a random variable with finite support, let* E *be an event. We define the min entropy of* $\mathbf{X}$ *to be*

$$\mathsf{H}_\infty(\mathbf{X}) = -\log\big(\max_x \Pr[\mathbf{X} = x]\big).$$

We define the min entropy of X *conditioned on* E *to be*

$$\mathsf{H}_\infty(\mathbf{X}|E) = -\log\big(\max_x \Pr[\mathbf{X} = x|E]\big).$$

Finally, we recall the definition of collision entropy.

Definition 8 (Collision entropy). *Let* $\mathbf{X}$ *and* $\mathbf{Y}$ *be random variables with finite support, let* E *be an event. We define the collision entropy of* $\mathbf{X}$ *to be*

$$\mathsf{H}_2(\mathbf{X}) = -\log\Big(\sum_x \Pr[\mathbf{X} = x]^2\Big) = -\log\big(\Pr[\mathbf{X} = \mathbf{X}']\big),$$

where $\mathbf{X}'$ *is independent and identically distributed to* $\mathbf{X}$*. We define the collision entropy of* $\mathbf{X}$ *conditioned on* E *to be*

$$\mathsf{H}_2(\mathbf{X}|E) = -\log\Big(\sum_x \Pr[\mathbf{X} = x|E]^2\Big).$$

The average collision entropy of $\mathbf{X}$ *given* $\mathbf{Y}$ *is instead*

$$\widetilde{\mathsf{H}}_2(\mathbf{X}|\mathbf{Y}) = -\log\Big(\sum_{x,y} \Pr[\mathbf{Y} = y] \cdot \Pr[\mathbf{X} = x|\mathbf{Y} = y]^2\Big).$$

All the above definitions of entropy are not equivalent. For instance, Shannon's entropy can assume values that are significantly larger than min and collision entropy. The definitions are however related by the following well-known inequalities.

Theorem 3. *Let* $\mathbf{X}$ *be a random variable with finite support, let* E *be an event. We have that*

$$0 \le \mathsf{H}_\infty(\mathbf{X}) \le \mathsf{H}_2(\mathbf{X}) \le \mathsf{H}(\mathbf{X}) \le \mathsf{H}_0(\mathbf{X}),$$
$$0 \le \mathsf{H}_\infty(\mathbf{X}|E) \le \mathsf{H}_2(\mathbf{X}|E) \le \mathsf{H}(\mathbf{X}|E) \le \mathsf{H}_0(\mathbf{X}|E) \le \mathsf{H}_0(\mathbf{X}).$$

Yao's Incompressibility Entropy. All the entropy notions we recalled above are great for measuring information theoretic properties, however, they all suffer from an important disadvantage, namely, they do not behave well under computational indistinguishability. Specifically, if $\mathbf{X} \sim_c \mathbf{X}'$, the entropy of $\mathbf{X}$ can be significantly different from the entropy of $\mathbf{X}'$, it does not matter which of the above definitions we consider.

We solve this issue by relying on a notion of computational entropy [Yao82, HLR07]. We recall the definition.

Definition 9 (Yao's entropy). *Let* $(\mathbf{X}_\lambda)_{\lambda\in\mathbb{N}}$ *be an ensemble of random variables. We say that the Yao entropy of* $\mathbf{X}$ *is smaller or equal to* $k(\lambda)$*, written* $\mathsf{H}_{\mathsf{Yao}}(\mathbf{X}) \le k(\lambda)$*, if there exists a pair of polynomial sized deterministic circuits* $(c_\lambda, d_\lambda)_{\lambda\in\mathbb{N}}$ *such that*

$$\Pr[d_\lambda(c_\lambda(\mathbf{X})) = \mathbf{X}] \ge \frac{2^{\ell(\lambda)}}{2^{k(\lambda)}} - \mathsf{negl}(\lambda).$$

In the above formula, $\ell(\lambda)$ *denotes the output size of* c_λ*. The circuit* c_λ *is called a compressor, whereas* d_λ *is called a decompressor.*

In [HLR07], Hsiao, Lu and Reyzin generalised the definition to the conditional case. We recall it below.

Definition 10 (Conditional Yao's entropy). *Let* $(\mathbf{X}_\lambda)_{\lambda\in\mathbb{N}}$ *and* $(\mathbf{Y}_\lambda)_{\lambda\in\mathbb{N}}$ *be two ensembles of random variables. We say that the Yao entropy of* X *conditioned on* Y *is smaller or equal to* $k(\lambda)$*, written* $\mathsf{H}_{\mathsf{Yao}}(\mathbf{X}|\mathbf{Y}) \le k(\lambda)$*, if there exists a pair of polynomial sized deterministic circuits* $(c_\lambda, d_\lambda)_{\lambda\in\mathbb{N}}$ *such that*

$$\Pr[d(c(\mathbf{X}, \mathbf{Y}), \mathbf{Y}) = \mathbf{X}] \ge \frac{2^{\ell(\lambda)}}{2^{k(\lambda)}} - \mathsf{negl}(\lambda).$$

In the above formula, $\ell(\lambda)$ *denotes the output size of* c_λ*. The circuit* c_λ *is called a compressor, whereas* d_λ *is called a decompressor. If* $\mathsf{H}_{\mathsf{Yao}}(\mathbf{X}|\mathbf{Y}) \leq k(\lambda)$ *where* $k(\lambda)$ *is* $O(\log \lambda)$*, we will simply write that* $\mathsf{H}_{\mathsf{Yao}}(\mathbf{X}|\mathbf{Y}) = O(\log \lambda)$*.*

Essentially, Yao's incompressibility entropy measures how much it is possible to compress, in polynomial time, samples from a distribution $\mathbf{X}$ given that the outcome of the possibly correlated random variable $\mathbf{Y}$ is known.

We observe that Yao's entropy can assume values that are significantly larger than Shannon's entropy. Examples of this kind are the outputs of PRGs. In some particular cases, however, also the opposite is true. For instance, there exist distributions $\mathbf{X}$ such that $\mathsf{H}_\infty(\mathbf{X}) = O(\log \lambda)$ but $\mathsf{H}(\mathbf{X}) = \omega(\log \lambda)$. For all such $\mathbf{X}$, we have $\mathsf{H}_{\mathsf{Yao}}(\mathbf{X}) = O(\log \lambda)$ (consider the compressor that outputs the empty string and the decompressor that outputs the most likely element).

The following well-known lemma formalises the fact that Yao's entropy preserves under computational indistinguishability.

Lemma 3. *Let* $(\mathbf{X}_\lambda, \mathbf{Y}_\lambda)_{\lambda \in \mathbb{N}}$ *and* $(\mathbf{X}'_\lambda, \mathbf{Y}'_\lambda)_{\lambda \in \mathbb{N}}$ *be two ensembles of random variables such that* $(\mathbf{X}_\lambda, \mathbf{Y}_\lambda) \sim_c (\mathbf{X}'_\lambda, \mathbf{Y}'_\lambda)$*. Then,* $\mathsf{H}_{\mathsf{Yao}}(\mathbf{X}|\mathbf{Y}) \leq k(\lambda)$ *if and only if* $\mathsf{H}_{\mathsf{Yao}}(\mathbf{X}'|\mathbf{Y}') \leq k(\lambda)$*.*

We highlight that Yao's entropy is not the only notion of computational entropy [Rey11,HILL99,HLR07]. Among all the studied notions, it is however the one assuming highest values [HLR07]. We decided to use Yao's entropy exactly for this reason, making the results presented in this paper as strong as possible.

4 Impossibility of Distributed Samplers Without Random Oracle

We now present and prove our main theorem, namely that in a strong semi-malicious distributed sampler $\mathsf{H}(R|\sigma) = O(\log \lambda)$. The idea was sketched in the technical overview (see Sect. 2.1).

We start by describing what an n-party distributed sampler with black-box simulation is.

Definition 11 (Syntax of distributed samplers). *Let* $\mathcal{D}(1\!\!1^\lambda)$ *be an efficiently samplable distribution. An* n*-party distributed sampler for* $\mathcal{D}(1\!\!1^\lambda)$ *consists of a triple of PPT algorithms* $(\mathsf{CRS}, \mathsf{Gen}, \mathsf{Sample})$ *with the following syntax:*

- CRS *is randomised, it takes as input the security parameter* $1\!\!1^\lambda$ *and outputs a CRS* σ*.*
- Gen *is randomised and takes as input the security parameter* $1\!\!1^\lambda$*, a CRS* σ *and the index of the party* j *running the procedure. The output is a distributed sampler message* U_j *and secret information* r_j*.*
- Sample *is deterministic and takes as input a CRS* σ*,* n *distributed sampler messages* $U_1, \dots, U_n$*, the index of a party* j *and the relative secret information* r_j*. The output is a sample* R *from the distribution* $\mathcal{D}(1\!\!1^\lambda)$*.*

We say that the distributed sampler has public output if Gen *always outputs* $r_j = \bot$.

Definition 12 (t-out-of-n distributed sampler with black-box simulation). *Let $\mathcal{C}$ be an adversarial class and let $t \leq n$. We say that an n-party distributed sampler* (CRS, Gen, Sample) *for the distribution $\mathcal{D}(\mathbb{1}^\lambda)$ is t-out-of-n secure against $\mathcal{C}$ with black-box simulation if there exists a uniform PPT simulator* Sim *such that, for every polynomial function $q(\lambda)$, uniform adversary $\mathcal{A} \in \mathcal{C}$ requiring $q(\lambda)$ random coins, auxiliary information ψ and every subset $H \subseteq [n]$ such that $|H| \geq n - t$, the following distributions are computationally indistinguishable*

$$\left\{ \begin{array}{c|l} & \rho \xleftarrow{\$} \{0,1\}^{q(\lambda)} \\ & \sigma \xleftarrow{\$} \mathsf{CRS}(\mathbb{1}^\lambda) \\ (R_j)_{j \in H} & \\ \sigma, U_H, \rho & \forall j \in H : (U_j, r_j) \xleftarrow{\$} \mathsf{Gen}(\mathbb{1}^\lambda, \sigma, j) \\ & U_C \leftarrow \mathcal{A}(\mathbb{1}^\lambda, \sigma, U_H, \psi; \rho) \\ & \forall j \in H : R_j \leftarrow \mathsf{Sample}(\sigma, U_1, \dots, U_n, j, r_j) \end{array} \right\}$$

$$\left\{ \begin{array}{c|l} (R_j)_{j \in H} & (\widehat{\mathsf{id}}, U_H, \sigma, \rho) \xleftarrow{\$} \mathsf{Sim}^{\mathcal{A}, \mathcal{F}_\mathcal{D}}(\mathbb{1}^\lambda, H, \psi) \\ \sigma, U_H, \rho & \forall j \in H : R_j \leftarrow R_{\widehat{\mathsf{id}}} \end{array} \right\}$$

Notice that Sim *is given oracle access to $\mathcal{A}$ and $\mathcal{F}_\mathcal{D}$ (see Fig. 1). This means that it can query $\mathcal{A}$, multiple times, on any input $(\mathbb{1}^{\lambda'}, \sigma', U'_H, \rho')$ and see the corresponding response. Furthermore,* Sim *can ask $\mathcal{F}_\mathcal{D}$ for samples. We use $R_{\widehat{\mathsf{id}}}$ to denote the sample produced by $\mathcal{F}_\mathcal{D}$ associated with the label $\widehat{\mathsf{id}}$. If such sample does not exist, we set $R_{\widehat{\mathsf{id}}} := \bot$.*

Remark 1. There is a technicality we need to pay attention to: what if the simulator runs in time $p(\lambda) < q(\lambda)$? It would be impossible for the simulator to query the adversary even once, let alone outputting the randomness ρ at the end of its execution. This fact was already observed by Bellare, Micali and Ostrovsky in [BMO90]. To solve the issue, they proposed the following modification: suppose that the simulator is equipped with two random tapes, one for itself and one for the adversary (which is provided with $q(\lambda)$ random coins). The simulator is allowed to read and modify the random tape of the adversary as long as its total running time does not exceed $p(\lambda)$ (in particular, the simulator can touch at most $p(\lambda)$ bits on the adversary's tape). Each time the simulator queries $\mathcal{A}$, the adversary is run using the randomness present on its random tape at that particular moment. Moreover, the randomness ρ output by the simulator will be the one present on the adversary's random tape at the end of the simulator's execution.

There are other ways this problem could be addressed, for instance, by setting an upper-bound on the size of the random tape of the adversary. Even if it is unclear whether all these definitions are equivalent, we believe that our impossibility can be extended (perhaps, with some non-trivial argument) also to these models. The reason why we chose this particular definition of black-box simulation is that it is the one that allows us to prove, in the most direct way, an intuition common to all black-box simulation settings: if the simulator rewinds the adversary on some new input, the adversary generates its answer using independent looking randomness.

Definition 13 (Strong semi-malicious security). *We say that a distributed sampler is strongly semi-maliciously secure if it is secure against the class of uniform adversaries that, after receiving σ, U_H and auxiliary information ψ, output $(U_j)_{j\in C}$ where*

$$\forall j \in C : U_C \leftarrow \mathsf{Gen}(\mathbb{1}^\lambda, \sigma, j; \rho_j), \qquad (\rho_j)_{j\in C} \xleftarrow{\$} \mathcal{M}(\mathbb{1}^\lambda, \sigma, U_H, \psi)$$

and $\mathcal{M}$ is a PPT algorithm.

Theorem 4. *Let $\mathcal{D}(\mathbb{1}^\lambda)$ be an efficient distribution. In a strongly semi-maliciously secure, t-out-of-n distributed sampler for $\mathcal{D}(\mathbb{1}^\lambda)$ with black-box simulation, we have that $\mathsf{H}(R_i \,|\, \sigma) = \frac{n}{t} \cdot O(\log \lambda)$ for any $i \in [n]$, where R_i denotes the output of party P_i.*

Before proving the above theorem, we state and prove the following lemma about information theory.

Lemma 4. *Let $\mathbf{X}_1, \dots, \mathbf{X}_n, \mathbf{Y}$ be random variables such that $\mathbf{X}_1, \dots, \mathbf{X}_n$ are all independent conditioned on $\mathbf{Y}$. Let f be a deterministic function of $\mathbf{X}_1, \dots, \mathbf{X}_n, \mathbf{Y}$. Then, if we denote $f(\mathbf{X}_1, \dots, \mathbf{X}_n, \mathbf{Y})$ by $\mathbf{R}$, we have that, for every $t \in [n]$, there exists $S \subseteq [n]$ such that $|S| = t$ and*

$$\mathsf{H}(\mathbf{R}|\mathbf{X}_S, \mathbf{Y}) \geq \frac{n-t}{n} \cdot \mathsf{H}(\mathbf{R}|\mathbf{Y})$$

Proof. Fix a subset $S' \subseteq [n]$ such that $|S'| = t-1$. Consider also disjoint subsets $S_0, S_1 \subseteq [n]$. Due to the independence between $\mathbf{X}_1, \dots, \mathbf{X}_n$ conditioned on $\mathbf{Y}$, we have that, for any $i \in S_1$,

$$\begin{aligned}
&\mathsf{I}(\mathbf{R}; \mathbf{X}_{S_1}|\mathbf{X}_{S_0}, \mathbf{Y})\\
&\overset{5}{=}\mathsf{I}(\mathbf{R}; \mathbf{X}_i|\mathbf{X}_{S_0}, \mathbf{Y}) + \mathsf{I}(\mathbf{R}; \mathbf{X}_{S_1\setminus\{i\}}|\mathbf{X}_{S_0\cup\{i\}}, \mathbf{Y})\\
&\overset{5}{=}\mathsf{I}(\mathbf{R}; \mathbf{X}_i|\mathbf{X}_{S_0}, \mathbf{Y}) + \mathsf{I}(\mathbf{R}; \mathbf{X}_{S_1\setminus\{i\}}|\mathbf{X}_{S_0}, \mathbf{Y}) - \mathsf{I}(\mathbf{R}; \mathbf{X}_{S_1\setminus\{i\}}; \mathbf{X}_i|\mathbf{X}_{S_0}, \mathbf{Y})\\
&\overset{5}{=}\mathsf{I}(\mathbf{R}; \mathbf{X}_i|\mathbf{X}_{S_0}, \mathbf{Y}) + \mathsf{I}(\mathbf{R}; \mathbf{X}_{S_1\setminus\{i\}}|\mathbf{X}_{S_0}, \mathbf{Y}) - \Big(\mathsf{I}(\mathbf{X}_{S_1\setminus\{i\}}; \mathbf{X}_i|\mathbf{X}_{S_0}, \mathbf{Y}) - \mathsf{I}(\mathbf{X}_{S_1\setminus\{i\}}; \mathbf{X}_i|\mathbf{R}, \mathbf{X}_{S_0}, \mathbf{Y})\Big)\\
&\overset{2.2}{=}\mathsf{I}(\mathbf{R}; \mathbf{X}_i|\mathbf{X}_{S_0}, \mathbf{Y}) + \mathsf{I}(\mathbf{R}; \mathbf{X}_{S_1\setminus\{i\}}|\mathbf{X}_{S_0}, \mathbf{Y}) + \mathsf{I}(\mathbf{X}_{S_1\setminus\{i\}}; \mathbf{X}_i|\mathbf{R}, \mathbf{X}_{S_0}, \mathbf{Y})\\
&\overset{2.3}{\geq}\mathsf{I}(\mathbf{R}; \mathbf{X}_i|\mathbf{X}_{S_0}, \mathbf{Y}) + \mathsf{I}(\mathbf{R}; \mathbf{X}_{S_1\setminus\{i\}}|\mathbf{X}_{S_0}, \mathbf{Y}).
\end{aligned}$$

By recursively applying the bound above to the term $\mathsf{I}(\mathbf{R}; \mathbf{X}_{S_1\setminus\{i\}}|\mathbf{X}_{S_0}, \mathbf{Y})$, we conclude that

$$\mathsf{I}(\mathbf{R}; \mathbf{X}_{S_1}|\mathbf{X}_{S_0}, \mathbf{Y}) \geq \sum_{i\in S_1} \mathsf{I}(\mathbf{R}; \mathbf{X}_i|\mathbf{X}_{S_0}, \mathbf{Y})$$

and so

$$\begin{aligned}
\mathsf{H}(\mathbf{R}|\mathbf{X}_{S'},\mathbf{Y}) &\overset{2.2}{=} \mathsf{I}(\mathbf{R};\mathbf{X}_{[n]\setminus S'}|\mathbf{X}_{S'},\mathbf{Y}) \\
&\geq \sum_{i\notin S'} \mathsf{I}(\mathbf{R};\mathbf{X}_i|\mathbf{X}_{S'},\mathbf{Y}) \\
&\overset{4}{=} (n-t+1)\cdot \mathsf{H}(\mathbf{R}|\mathbf{X}_{S'},\mathbf{Y}) - \sum_{i\notin S'} \mathsf{H}(\mathbf{R}|\mathbf{X}_{S'\cup\{i\}},\mathbf{Y}).
\end{aligned}$$

This proves that $(n-t)\cdot \mathsf{H}(\mathbf{R}|\mathbf{X}_{S'},\mathbf{Y}) \leq \sum_{i\notin S'} \mathsf{H}(\mathbf{R}|\mathbf{X}_{S'\cup\{i\}},\mathbf{Y})$ and therefore

$$\begin{aligned}
\sum_{|S'|=t-1} (n-t)\cdot \mathsf{H}(\mathbf{R}|\mathbf{X}_{S'},\mathbf{Y}) \leq &\sum_{|S'|=t-1}\sum_{i\notin S'} \mathsf{H}(\mathbf{R}|\mathbf{X}_{S'\cup\{i\}},\mathbf{Y}) \\
&= t\cdot \sum_{|S|=t} \mathsf{H}(\mathbf{R}|\mathbf{X}_S,\mathbf{Y}).
\end{aligned}$$

Notice that the last equality follows from the fact that, given S such that $|S| = t$, there are t ways to choose S' and $i \notin S'$ such that $S = S' \cup \{i\}$. In other words, in the sum on the left, $\mathsf{H}(\mathbf{R}|\mathbf{X}_S,\mathbf{Y})$ gets added t times. Now, with an inductive argument over t, we obtain that

$$\begin{aligned}
\sum_{|S|=t} \mathsf{H}(\mathbf{R}|\mathbf{X}_S,\mathbf{Y}) &\geq \frac{n-t}{t}\cdot \sum_{|S|=t-1} \mathsf{H}(\mathbf{R}|\mathbf{X}_S,\mathbf{Y}) \\
&\vdots \\
&\geq \frac{n-t}{t}\cdot\frac{n-t+1}{t-1}\cdots\frac{n-1}{1}\cdot \mathsf{H}(\mathbf{R}|\mathbf{Y}).
\end{aligned}$$

Finally, by an averaging argument, we conclude that there exists S such that $|S| = t$ and

$$\mathsf{H}(\mathbf{R}|\mathbf{X}_S,\mathbf{Y}) \geq \frac{\binom{n-1}{t}}{\binom{n}{t}}\cdot \mathsf{H}(\mathbf{R}|\mathbf{Y}) = \frac{n-t}{n}\cdot \mathsf{H}(\mathbf{R}|\mathbf{Y}).$$

□

We are finally ready to prove Theorem 4.

Proof. Throughout the proof, we view $\boldsymbol{\sigma}$ and $\mathbf{U}_H$ as random variables, i.e., functions of the randomness of the various algorithms involved in the considered settings: real world, ideal world and a hybrid world, we are about to introduce.

Since the simulator runs in polynomial time, there exists a polynomial upper bound $q(\lambda)$ on the number of samples the simulator queries to the functionality. Let $\mathbf{Q}$ be the random variable describing the set containing the responses to these queries. There exists also a polynomial upper bound on the number of times the simulator queries the adversary, let this be $w(\lambda)$. Finally, there exists a polynomial upper bound $\ell(\lambda)$ on the number of bits on the adversary's random tape that are read or modified by the simulator. Without loss of generality, we can make three assumptions regarding the simulator. The first one is that it issues all its queries to the functionality at the beginning of its execution. The second one is that it never outputs a tuple $(\widehat{\mathsf{id}}, U_H, \sigma, \rho)$ without first having queried $\mathcal{A}$ on (U_H, σ, ρ). The last one is that the simulator never queries the adversary twice on the same value.

We consider the uniform adversary that follows the protocol but generates the randomness it feeds into Gen using a $w(\lambda)$-wise independent hash function applied on $(\mathbf{U}_H, \boldsymbol{\sigma})$. The hash key for such hash function is obtained by ignoring the first $\ell(\lambda)$ bits of the adversary's randomness. Notice that, from the simulator's perspective, the hash key is random, because it cannot read nor modify past the $\ell(\lambda)$-th element in the string.

We therefore consider a hybrid world obtained by modifying the ideal world: the queries of the simulator to the adversary will be now generated without using the w-wise independent hash function, but just using uniform randomness provided on a new tape not accessible to the simulator. More specifically, the queries of the simulator will now be generated by a stateful machine making sure that identical queries are answered in the same way, and new queries are answered using fresh randomness. From the perspective of the simulator, this hybrid is identical to the ideal world. Indeed, previously, the view of the simulator was independent of the w-wise independent hash key used by the adversary (the simulator could not even read such key). So, given that the adversary was queried at most $w(\lambda)$ times, all responses were generated with independent, uniform randomness. In this hybrid world, our probability space $\varXi$ will be the union of three probability subspaces: the one defined by the randomness of the simulator, the one defined by the randomness of the functionality and the one defined randomness of the new hybrid adversary.

Let $(\mathbf{U}^i_H, \boldsymbol{\sigma}^i, \boldsymbol{\rho}^i)$ be random variables describing the i-th query of the simulator to the adversary $\mathcal{A}$[6]. Let $\mathbf{U}^i_C$ be the random variable corresponding to the answer. Notice that, since our adversary generates the messages of the corrupted parties following the protocol, we can also define the random variables $(\mathbf{r}^i_j)_{j \in C}$ representing the secret information obtained by the corrupted parties during the generation of $\mathbf{U}^i_C$. Since there exists a unique $\boldsymbol{\mu} \in [w]$ such that $(\boldsymbol{\sigma}, \mathbf{U}_H) = (\boldsymbol{\sigma}^{\boldsymbol{\mu}}, \mathbf{U}^{\boldsymbol{\mu}}_H)$, we define $\mathbf{U}_C$ as the random variable $\mathbf{U}^{\boldsymbol{\mu}}_C$. Similarly, for every $j \in C$, we define the random variable $\mathbf{r}_j$ as $\mathbf{r}^{\boldsymbol{\mu}}_j$.

Assume that Gen requires $L(\lambda)$ bits of randomness. Take $k \in \mathbb{N}$ such that $t \cdot L \leq \lambda^k$. Consider a constant $T \in \mathbb{N}$. Let ι be the index of a fixed corrupted party, we define the random variable $\mathbf{R}_\iota$ as $\mathsf{Sample}(\boldsymbol{\sigma}, \mathbf{U}_H, \mathbf{U}_C, \iota, \mathbf{r}_\iota)$. Independently of the world we are working on, we consider an auxiliary probability space $\varXi_{\mathsf{aux}}$ providing uniform randomness (independent of the one used by the various actors in the protocol and in the simulation). We denote the probability measure over

[6] Notice that we are not fixing the values of these variables, we are just giving a name to the functions that map the randomness in $\varXi$ to the i-th query of the simulator to the adversary.

such space by $\Pr_{\mathsf{aux}}$. For any values $\widehat{R}, \widehat{U}_H, \widehat{\sigma}$, we define the following quantities:

$$p(\widehat{R}, \widehat{U}_H, \widehat{\sigma}) := \Pr_{\mathsf{aux}}\left[\mathsf{Sample}(\widehat{\sigma}, \widehat{U}_H, \mathbf{U}_C, \iota, \mathbf{r}_\iota) = \widehat{R} \,\middle|\, \forall j \in C: \quad (\mathbf{U}_j, \mathbf{r}_j) \xleftarrow{\$} \mathsf{Gen}(1\!\!1^\lambda, \widehat{\sigma}, j)\right]$$
$$p_T(\lambda) := \Pr\left[p(\mathbf{R}_\iota, \mathbf{U}_H, \boldsymbol{\sigma}) < \lambda^{-T}\right]$$

Notice that $p(\mathbf{R}_\iota, \mathbf{U}_H, \boldsymbol{\sigma})$ is a random variable over the probability space Ξ.

Claim 41. *For any $T \in \mathbb{N}$, in the real world, we have*

$$\mathsf{H}(\mathbf{R}_\iota | \mathbf{U}_H, \mathbf{r}_H, \boldsymbol{\sigma}) \leq O(\lambda^k) \cdot p_T(\lambda) + T \cdot \log \lambda$$

Proof of the Claim. Let $\mathbf{E}$ be the random variable that is equal to 1 when $p(\mathbf{R}_\iota, \mathbf{U}_H, \boldsymbol{\sigma}) \geq \lambda^{-T}$, 0 otherwise. We observe that

$$\begin{aligned}
&\mathsf{H}(\mathbf{R}_\iota | \mathbf{U}_H, \mathbf{r}_H, \boldsymbol{\sigma}) \\
&\overset{2.4}{=} \mathsf{H}(\mathbf{R}_\iota, \mathbf{E} | \mathbf{U}_H, \mathbf{r}_H, \boldsymbol{\sigma}) \\
&\overset{2}{=} \mathsf{H}(\mathbf{R}_\iota | \mathbf{E}, \mathbf{U}_H, \mathbf{r}_H, \boldsymbol{\sigma}) + \mathsf{H}(\mathbf{E} | \mathbf{U}_H, \mathbf{r}_H, \boldsymbol{\sigma}) \\
&\overset{3}{\leq} \mathsf{H}(\mathbf{R}_\iota | \mathbf{E}, \mathbf{U}_H, \mathbf{r}_H, \boldsymbol{\sigma}) + \mathsf{H}_0(\mathbf{E} | \mathbf{U}_H, \mathbf{r}_H, \boldsymbol{\sigma}) \\
&\overset{6}{\leq} \mathsf{H}(\mathbf{R}_\iota | \mathbf{E}, \mathbf{U}_H, \mathbf{r}_H, \boldsymbol{\sigma}) + 1 \\
&\overset{3}{=} \sum_{\widehat{\sigma}, \widehat{U}_H, \widehat{r}_H} \left(\mathsf{H}\left(\mathbf{R}_\iota \,\middle|\, \begin{matrix} \mathbf{E} = 1 \\ \mathbf{U}_H = \widehat{U}_H \\ \mathbf{r}_H = \widehat{r}_H \\ \boldsymbol{\sigma} = \widehat{\sigma} \end{matrix}\right) \cdot \Pr\begin{bmatrix} \mathbf{E} = 1 \\ \mathbf{U}_H = \widehat{U}_H \\ \mathbf{r}_H = \widehat{r}_H \\ \boldsymbol{\sigma} = \widehat{\sigma} \end{bmatrix} + \mathsf{H}\left(\mathbf{R}_\iota \,\middle|\, \begin{matrix} \mathbf{E} = 0 \\ \mathbf{U}_H = \widehat{U}_H \\ \mathbf{r}_H = \widehat{r}_H \\ \boldsymbol{\sigma} = \widehat{\sigma} \end{matrix}\right) \cdot \Pr\begin{bmatrix} \mathbf{E} = 0 \\ \mathbf{U}_H = \widehat{U}_H \\ \mathbf{r}_H = \widehat{r}_H \\ \boldsymbol{\sigma} = \widehat{\sigma} \end{bmatrix} \right) + 1 \\
&\leq \sum_{\widehat{\sigma}, \widehat{U}_H, \widehat{r}_H} \left(\mathsf{H}\left(\mathbf{R}_\iota \,\middle|\, \begin{matrix} \mathbf{E} = 1 \\ \mathbf{U}_H = \widehat{U}_H \\ \mathbf{r}_H = \widehat{r}_H \\ \boldsymbol{\sigma} = \widehat{\sigma} \end{matrix}\right) + \mathsf{H}\left(\mathbf{R}_\iota \,\middle|\, \begin{matrix} \mathbf{E} = 0 \\ \mathbf{U}_H = \widehat{U}_H \\ \mathbf{r}_H = \widehat{r}_H \\ \boldsymbol{\sigma} = \widehat{\sigma} \end{matrix}\right) \cdot \Pr\left[\mathbf{E} = 0 \,\middle|\, \begin{matrix} \mathbf{U}_H = \widehat{U}_H \\ \mathbf{r}_H = \widehat{r}_H \\ \boldsymbol{\sigma} = \widehat{\sigma} \end{matrix}\right] \right) \cdot \Pr\begin{bmatrix} \mathbf{U}_H = \widehat{U}_H \\ \mathbf{r}_H = \widehat{r}_H \\ \boldsymbol{\sigma} = \widehat{\sigma} \end{bmatrix} + 1 \\
&\overset{3}{\leq} \sum_{\widehat{\sigma}, \widehat{U}_H, \widehat{r}_H} \left(\mathsf{H}_0\left(\mathbf{R}_\iota \,\middle|\, \begin{matrix} \mathbf{E} = 1 \\ \mathbf{U}_H = \widehat{U}_H \\ \mathbf{r}_H = \widehat{r}_H \\ \boldsymbol{\sigma} = \widehat{\sigma} \end{matrix}\right) + \mathsf{H}_0\left(\mathbf{R}_\iota \,\middle|\, \begin{matrix} \mathbf{E} = 0 \\ \mathbf{U}_H = \widehat{U}_H \\ \mathbf{r}_H = \widehat{r}_H \\ \boldsymbol{\sigma} = \widehat{\sigma} \end{matrix}\right) \cdot \Pr\left[\mathbf{E} = 0 \,\middle|\, \begin{matrix} \mathbf{U}_H = \widehat{U}_H \\ \mathbf{r}_H = \widehat{r}_H \\ \boldsymbol{\sigma} = \widehat{\sigma} \end{matrix}\right] \right) \cdot \Pr\begin{bmatrix} \mathbf{U}_H = \widehat{U}_H \\ \mathbf{r}_H = \widehat{r}_H \\ \boldsymbol{\sigma} = \widehat{\sigma} \end{bmatrix} + 1 \\
&\overset{6}{=} \sum_{\widehat{\sigma}, \widehat{U}_H, \widehat{r}_H} \left(T \cdot \log \lambda + O(\lambda^k) \cdot \Pr\left[\mathbf{E} = 0 \,\middle|\, \begin{matrix} \mathbf{U}_H = \widehat{U}_H \\ \mathbf{r}_H = \widehat{r}_H \\ \boldsymbol{\sigma} = \widehat{\sigma} \end{matrix}\right] \right) \cdot \Pr\begin{bmatrix} \mathbf{U}_H = \widehat{U}_H \\ \mathbf{r}_H = \widehat{r}_H \\ \boldsymbol{\sigma} = \widehat{\sigma} \end{bmatrix} + 1 \\
&= O(\lambda^k) \cdot p_T(\lambda) + T \cdot \log \lambda.
\end{aligned}$$

The second last inequality follows from the fact that there could be at most λ^T elements $\mathbf{R}_\iota$ such that $p(\mathbf{R}_\iota, \widehat{U}_H, \widehat{\sigma}) \geq \lambda^{-T}$. Moreover, the total number of possible outputs, once conditioned on $\boldsymbol{\sigma} = \widehat{\sigma}$, is bounded from above by the total amount of randomness used by the parties. ■

Claim 42. *In the hybrid world, we have*

$$\Pr\left[p(\mathbf{R}_\iota, \mathbf{U}_H, \boldsymbol{\sigma}) < \lambda^{-T} \,\middle|\, (\widehat{\mathsf{id}}, \mathbf{U}_H, \boldsymbol{\sigma}, \boldsymbol{\rho}) \xleftarrow{\$} \mathsf{Sim}^{\mathcal{A}, \mathcal{F}_\mathcal{D}}(\mathbb{1}^\lambda)\right] \leq w(\lambda) \cdot q(\lambda) \cdot \lambda^{-T} + \mathsf{negl}(\lambda).$$

Proof of the Claim. Let E' be the event in which $\mathbf{R}_{\widehat{\mathsf{id}}} = \mathsf{Sample}(\boldsymbol{\sigma}, \mathbf{U}_H, \mathbf{U}_C, \iota, \mathbf{r}_\iota)$. Observe that, even if P_ι is corrupted, $\mathbf{r}_\iota$ is still well-defined, given that our adversary $\mathcal{A}$ follows the protocol. We notice that $\Pr[E'] = 1 - \mathsf{negl}(\lambda)$. Indeed, consider the protocol execution when no party is corrupted: in the ideal world, the functionality outputs the same sample R to all parties, therefore, with overwhelming probability, all parties output the same sample R even in the real world. Now, let's go back to our setting. Even if some of our parties are corrupted, they behave as if they were honest. So, in the real world, with overwhelming probability, the outputs of the honest parties will all be the same and will coincide with $\mathsf{Sample}(\boldsymbol{\sigma}, \mathbf{U}_H, \mathbf{U}_C, j, \mathbf{r}_j)$ for every corrupted party P_j. Notice that, as for P_ι, even if P_j is corrupted, $\mathbf{r}_j$ is still well-defined, given that we only consider adversaries that follow the protocol. We argue that, even in the ideal world (where some parties are corrupted), with overwhelming probability, the honest parties all output the same sample $\mathbf{R}$ and this will coincide with $\mathsf{Sample}(\boldsymbol{\sigma}, \mathbf{U}_H, \mathbf{U}_C, j, \mathbf{r}_j)$ for every corrupted party P_j. If that was not the case, we would have an easy way to distinguish the real world from the ideal world. We conclude by observing that, in the ideal world, the output of the honest parties is $\mathbf{R}_{\widehat{\mathsf{id}}}$. This ensures that $\Pr[E'] = 1 - \mathsf{negl}(\lambda)$. Finally, notice that the distribution of $(\boldsymbol{\sigma}, \mathbf{U}_H, \mathbf{U}_C, \mathbf{r}_C, \mathbf{R}_{\widehat{\mathsf{id}}})$ in the hybrid world is the same as in the ideal world. This proves that, even in such setting, $\Pr[E'] = 1 - \mathsf{negl}(\lambda)$.

Next, fix an $i \in [w]$. We define the random variable $\mathbf{R}^i_\iota = \mathsf{Sample}(\boldsymbol{\sigma}^i, \mathbf{U}^i_H, \mathbf{U}^i_C, \iota, \mathbf{r}^i_\iota)$. Consider any values $\widehat{Q}, \widehat{R}, \widehat{U}_H, \widehat{\sigma}$ (not random variables) such that $p(\widehat{R}, \widehat{U}_H, \widehat{\sigma}) < \lambda^{-T}$. We observe that, trivially,

$$\Pr\left[\mathsf{Sample}(\boldsymbol{\sigma}^i, \mathbf{U}^i_H, \mathbf{U}^i_C, \iota, \mathbf{r}^i_\iota) = \widehat{R} \,\middle|\, \begin{matrix} \mathbf{Q} = \widehat{Q} \\ \boldsymbol{\sigma}^i = \widehat{\sigma} \\ \mathbf{U}^i_H = \widehat{U}_H \end{matrix}\right] < \lambda^{-T}.$$

This is because, in the hybrid world, the adversary generates $\mathbf{U}^i_C$ using uniform randomness, independent of $\mathbf{Q}, \mathbf{U}^i_H$ and $\boldsymbol{\sigma}^i$. We notice that

$$\begin{aligned}
&\Pr\begin{bmatrix} p(\mathbf{R}^i_\iota, \mathbf{U}^i_H, \boldsymbol{\sigma}^i) < \lambda^{-T} \\ \mathbf{R}^i_\iota \in \mathbf{Q} \end{bmatrix} \\
&= \sum_{\widehat{Q}, \widehat{U}_H, \widehat{\sigma}} \Pr\left[\begin{matrix} p(\mathbf{R}^i_\iota, \mathbf{U}^i_H, \boldsymbol{\sigma}^i) < \lambda^{-T} \\ \mathbf{R}^i_\iota \in \mathbf{Q} \end{matrix} \,\middle|\, \begin{matrix} \mathbf{Q} = \widehat{Q} \\ \mathbf{U}^i_H = \widehat{U}_H \\ \boldsymbol{\sigma}^i = \widehat{\sigma} \end{matrix}\right] \cdot \Pr\begin{bmatrix} \mathbf{Q} = \widehat{Q} \\ \mathbf{U}^i_H = \widehat{U}_H \\ \boldsymbol{\sigma}^i = \widehat{\sigma} \end{bmatrix} \\
&\leq \sum_{\widehat{Q}, \widehat{U}_H, \widehat{\sigma}} \sum_{\substack{\widehat{R} \in \widehat{Q} \\ p(\widehat{R}, \widehat{U}_H, \widehat{\sigma}) < \lambda^{-T}}} \Pr\left[\mathsf{Sample}(\boldsymbol{\sigma}, \mathbf{U}^i_H, \mathbf{U}^i_C, \iota, \mathbf{r}^i_\iota) = \widehat{R} \,\middle|\, \begin{matrix} \mathbf{Q} = \widehat{Q} \\ \mathbf{U}^i_H = \widehat{U}_H \\ \boldsymbol{\sigma}^i = \widehat{\sigma} \end{matrix}\right] \cdot \Pr\begin{bmatrix} \mathbf{Q} = \widehat{Q} \\ \mathbf{U}^i_H = \widehat{U}_H \\ \boldsymbol{\sigma}^i = \widehat{\sigma} \end{bmatrix}
\end{aligned}$$

$$< \sum_{\widehat{Q},\widehat{U}_H,\widehat{\sigma}} \sum_{\substack{\widehat{R}\in\widehat{Q} \\ p(\widehat{R},\widehat{U}_H,\widehat{\sigma})<\lambda^{-T}}} \lambda^{-T} \cdot \Pr[\mathbf{Q} = \widehat{Q}, \mathbf{U}_H^i = \widehat{U}_H, \boldsymbol{\sigma}^i = \widehat{\sigma}]$$

$$\leq \sum_{\widehat{Q},\widehat{U}_H,\widehat{\sigma}} \sum_{\widehat{R}\in\widehat{Q}} \lambda^{-T} \cdot \Pr[\mathbf{Q} = \widehat{Q}, \mathbf{U}_H^i = \widehat{U}_H, \boldsymbol{\sigma}^i = \widehat{\sigma}]$$

$$\leq \sum_{\widehat{Q},\widehat{U}_H,\widehat{\sigma}} q(\lambda) \cdot \lambda^{-T} \cdot \Pr[\mathbf{Q} = \widehat{Q}, \mathbf{U}_H^i = \widehat{U}_i, \boldsymbol{\sigma}^i = \widehat{\sigma}]$$

$$= q(\lambda) \cdot \lambda^{-T}.$$

By union bounding over all $i \in [w]$, we conclude that

$$\Pr\left[\exists i \in [w] \text{ s.t. } \begin{array}{r} p(\mathbf{R}_\iota^i, \mathbf{U}_H^i, \boldsymbol{\sigma}^i) < \lambda^{-T} \\ \mathbf{R}_\iota^i \in \mathbf{Q} \end{array}\right] \leq w(\lambda) \cdot q(\lambda) \cdot \lambda^{-T}.$$

Finally, we terminate the proof by observing that

$$\Pr\left[p(\mathbf{R}_\iota, \mathbf{U}_H, \boldsymbol{\sigma}) < \lambda^{-T} \,\middle|\, (\widehat{\mathsf{id}}, \mathbf{U}_H, \boldsymbol{\sigma}, \boldsymbol{\rho}) \xleftarrow{\$} \mathsf{Sim}^{\mathcal{A},\mathcal{F}_\mathcal{D}}(1\!\!1^\lambda)\right]$$

$$\leq \Pr\left[p(\mathbf{R}_\iota, \mathbf{U}_H, \sigma) < \lambda^{-T} \,\middle|\, \begin{array}{l} (\widehat{\mathsf{id}}, \mathbf{U}_H, \boldsymbol{\sigma}, \boldsymbol{\rho}) \xleftarrow{\$} \mathsf{Sim}^{\mathcal{A},\mathcal{F}_\mathcal{D}}(1\!\!1^\lambda) \\ E' \end{array}\right] + \Pr[\neg E']$$

$$\leq \Pr\left[\exists i \in [w] \text{ s.t. } \begin{array}{r} p(\mathbf{R}_\iota^i, \mathbf{U}_H^i, \boldsymbol{\sigma}^i) < \lambda^{-T} \\ \mathbf{R}_\iota^i \in \mathbf{Q} \end{array} \middle| E'\right] + \Pr[\neg E']$$

$$\leq \Pr\left[\exists i \in [w] \text{ s.t. } \begin{array}{r} p(\mathbf{R}_\iota^i, \mathbf{U}_H^i, \boldsymbol{\sigma}^i) < \lambda^{-T} \\ \mathbf{R}_\iota^i \in \mathbf{Q} \end{array}\right] + 2 \cdot \Pr[\neg E']$$

$$\leq w(\lambda) \cdot q(\lambda) \cdot \lambda^{-T} + \mathsf{negl}(\lambda).$$

■

Claim 43. *In the real world,* $\mathsf{H}(\mathbf{R}_\iota \mid \mathbf{U}_H, \mathbf{r}_H, \boldsymbol{\sigma}) = O(\log \lambda)$.

Proof of the Claim. Suppose the claim is false. We pick $T > 1$ so that $w(\lambda) \cdot q(\lambda) \cdot \lambda^{-T} = O(\lambda^{-2k})$. We consider the distinguisher D that, given σ, U_H and the output R_ι, performs the following attacks

1. $\alpha \leftarrow 0$
2. for $i = 1, \ldots, \lambda^{4T}$:
   (a) $\forall j \in C: \quad (U_j', r_j') \xleftarrow{\$} \mathsf{Gen}(1\!\!1^\lambda, \sigma, j)$
   (b) $R_\iota' \leftarrow \mathsf{Sample}(\sigma, \widehat{U}_H, U_C', \iota, r_\iota')$
   (c) if $R_\iota' = R_\iota$, $\alpha \leftarrow \alpha + 1$
3. if $\alpha \geq \lambda^{3T} - \lambda^{2T+1}$, output 0
4. otherwise output 1.

Observe that the randomness of this distinguisher defines a new probability space Ξ_{D}. Let $\Pr_{\mathsf{D}}$ be the corresponding probability measure. Let $\Pr_{\mathsf{tot}}$ be the probability measure over the union of Ξ and Ξ_{D}.

By the Chernoff bound, we know that

$$\Pr_{\mathsf{D}}\left[\left|\alpha - p(\mathbf{R}_\iota, \mathbf{U}_H, \boldsymbol{\sigma}) \cdot \lambda^{4T}\right| \leq \lambda^{2T+1}\right] \geq 1 - \mathsf{negl}(\lambda).$$

So, if $p(\mathbf{R}_\iota, \mathbf{U}_H, \boldsymbol{\sigma}) \geq \lambda^{-T}$, with overwhelming probability over the randomness of the distinguisher, $\alpha \geq \lambda^{3T} - \lambda^{2T+1}$ and the algorithm outputs 0. In other words,

$$\Pr_{\mathsf{tot}}\left[\mathsf{D}(\mathbb{1}^\lambda, \boldsymbol{\sigma}, \mathbf{U}_H, \mathbf{R}_\iota) = 1 \,\middle|\, p(\mathbf{R}_\iota, \mathbf{U}_H, \boldsymbol{\sigma}) \geq \lambda^{-T}\right] \leq \mathsf{negl}(\lambda). \tag{1}$$

Now, we can upper-bound the total probability (over the randomness of the distinguisher, the simulator, the adversary and the functionality) that the distinguisher outputs 1 in the hybrid world by λ^{-2k}. Indeed, by putting together (1 and Claim 42, we have

$$\begin{aligned}
&\Pr_{\mathsf{tot}}\left[\mathsf{D}(\mathbb{1}^\lambda, \boldsymbol{\sigma}, \mathbf{U}_H, \mathbf{R}_\iota) = 1\right] \\
&\leq \Pr_{\mathsf{tot}}\left[\mathsf{D}(\mathbb{1}^\lambda, \boldsymbol{\sigma}, \mathbf{U}_H, \mathbf{R}_\iota) = 1 \,\middle|\, p(\mathbf{R}_\iota, \mathbf{U}_H, \boldsymbol{\sigma}) \geq \lambda^{-T}\right] + \Pr\left[p(\mathbf{R}_\iota, \mathbf{U}_H, \boldsymbol{\sigma}) < \lambda^{-T}\right] \\
&\leq \lambda^{-2k} + \mathsf{negl}(\lambda).
\end{aligned}$$

On the other hand, the total probability that the distinguisher outputs 1 in the real world is at least $\Theta(\lambda^{-k})$. Indeed, from Claim 41, we immediately deduce that, for every $T \in \mathbb{N}$,

$$p_T(\lambda) = \omega(\lambda^{-k}).$$

Moreover, we know that

$$\Pr\left[p(\mathbf{R}_\iota, \mathbf{U}_H, \boldsymbol{\sigma}) < \lambda^{-2T}\right] = p_{2T}(\lambda) = \omega(\lambda^{-k}).$$

Notice that, by the Chernoff bound, when $p(\mathbf{R}_\iota, \mathbf{U}_H, \boldsymbol{\sigma}) < \lambda^{-2T}$, with overwhelming probability over the randomness of the distinguisher, $\alpha < \lambda^{2T} + \lambda^{2T+1}$, which is asymptotically smaller than $\lambda^{3T} - \lambda^{2T+1}$. When this occurs, the distinguisher always outputs 1. In other words,

$$\Pr_{\mathsf{tot}}\left[\mathsf{D}(\mathbb{1}^\lambda, \boldsymbol{\sigma}, \mathbf{U}_H, \mathbf{R}_\iota) = 1 \,\middle|\, p(\mathbf{R}_\iota, \mathbf{U}_H, \boldsymbol{\sigma}) < \lambda^{-2T}\right] \geq 1 - \mathsf{negl}(\lambda).$$

To conclude,

$$\begin{aligned}
\Pr_{\mathsf{tot}}\left[\mathsf{D}(\mathbb{1}^\lambda, \boldsymbol{\sigma}, \mathbf{U}_H, \mathbf{R}_\iota)\right] &\geq \Pr_{\mathsf{tot}}\left[\mathsf{D}(\mathbb{1}^\lambda, \boldsymbol{\sigma}, \mathbf{U}_H, \mathbf{R}_\iota) = 1 \,\middle|\, p(\mathbf{R}_\iota, \mathbf{U}_H, \boldsymbol{\sigma}) < \lambda^{-2T}\right] \cdot \Pr\left[p(\mathbf{R}_\iota, \mathbf{U}_H, \boldsymbol{\sigma}) < \lambda^{-2T}\right] \\
&\geq \omega(\lambda^{-k}).
\end{aligned}$$

We have just proven that the advantage of our distinguisher is non-negligible! This is a contradiction. ■

Claim 44. *In the real world,* $\mathsf{H}(\mathbf{R}_\imath \,|\, \boldsymbol{\sigma}) = O(\log \lambda)$.

Proof of the Claim. We observe that $\mathbf{R}_\imath$ is a deterministic function of $\boldsymbol{\sigma}$, $(\mathbf{U}_1, \mathbf{r}_1), \ldots, (\mathbf{U}_n, \mathbf{r}_n)$. Furthermore, $(\mathbf{U}_1, \mathbf{r}_1), \ldots, (\mathbf{U}_n, \mathbf{r}_n)$ are all independent conditioned on the CRS $\boldsymbol{\sigma}$. By applying Lemma 4, we obtain that there exists a subset $H \subseteq [n]$ such that $|H| = n - t$ and

$$\mathsf{H}(\mathbf{R}_\imath | \mathbf{U}_H, \mathbf{r}_H, \boldsymbol{\sigma}) \geq \frac{t}{n} \cdot \mathsf{H}(\mathbf{R}_\imath | \boldsymbol{\sigma}).$$

We also observe that, with overwhelming probability, we have $R_1 = \cdots = R_n$. This is because, when all the parties are honest, in the ideal world execution, the simulator outputs the same sample to all the parties. If the same did not happen with overwhelming probability even in the real world, we would obtain a successful distinguisher.

Now, pick $\imath \notin H$, and let $\mathbf{E}'$ be the random variable that is equal to 1 when $\mathbf{R}_1 = \cdots = \mathbf{R}_n$, and 0 in all other cases. We observe that

$$\begin{aligned}
&\mathsf{H}(\mathbf{R}_\imath | \mathbf{U}_H, \mathbf{r}_H, \boldsymbol{\sigma}) \\
&\overset{2}{\leq} \mathsf{H}(\mathbf{R}_\imath, \mathbf{E}' | \mathbf{U}_H, \mathbf{r}_H, \boldsymbol{\sigma}) \\
&\overset{2}{=} \mathsf{H}(\mathbf{R}_\imath | \mathbf{E}', \mathbf{U}_H, \mathbf{r}_H, \boldsymbol{\sigma}) + \mathsf{H}(\mathbf{E}' | \mathbf{U}_H, \mathbf{r}_H, \boldsymbol{\sigma}) \\
&\overset{3}{\leq} \mathsf{H}(\mathbf{R}_\imath | \mathbf{E}', \mathbf{U}_H, \mathbf{r}_H, \boldsymbol{\sigma}) + \mathsf{H}_0(\mathbf{E}' | \mathbf{U}_H, \mathbf{r}_H, \boldsymbol{\sigma}) \\
&\overset{6}{\leq} \mathsf{H}(\mathbf{R}_\imath | \mathbf{E}', \mathbf{U}_H, \mathbf{r}_H, \boldsymbol{\sigma}) + 1 \\
&\overset{3}{=} \sum_{\widehat{\sigma}, \widehat{U}_H, \widehat{r}_H} \left(\mathsf{H}\left(\mathbf{R}_\imath \,\middle|\, \begin{array}{l} \mathbf{E}' = 1 \\ \mathbf{U}_H = \widehat{U}_H \\ \mathbf{r}_H = \widehat{r}_H \\ \boldsymbol{\sigma} = \widehat{\sigma} \end{array}\right) \cdot \Pr\left[\begin{array}{l} \mathbf{E}' = 1 \\ \mathbf{U}_H = \widehat{U}_H \\ \mathbf{r}_H = \widehat{r}_H \\ \boldsymbol{\sigma} = \widehat{\sigma} \end{array}\right] + \mathsf{H}\left(\mathbf{R}_\imath \,\middle|\, \begin{array}{l} \mathbf{E}' = 0 \\ \mathbf{U}_H = \widehat{U}_H \\ \mathbf{r}_H = \widehat{r}_H \\ \boldsymbol{\sigma} = \widehat{\sigma} \end{array}\right) \cdot \Pr\left[\begin{array}{l} \mathbf{E}' = 0 \\ \mathbf{U}_H = \widehat{U}_H \\ \mathbf{r}_H = \widehat{r}_H \\ \boldsymbol{\sigma} = \widehat{\sigma} \end{array}\right] \right) + 1 \\
&\overset{3}{\leq} \sum_{\widehat{\sigma}, \widehat{U}_H, \widehat{r}_H} \left(\mathsf{H}\left(\mathbf{R}_\imath \,\middle|\, \begin{array}{l} \mathbf{E}' = 1 \\ \mathbf{U}_H = \widehat{U}_H \\ \mathbf{r}_H = \widehat{r}_H \\ \boldsymbol{\sigma} = \widehat{\sigma} \end{array}\right) \cdot \Pr\left[\begin{array}{l} \mathbf{E}' = 1 \\ \mathbf{U}_H = \widehat{U}_H \\ \mathbf{r}_H = \widehat{r}_H \\ \boldsymbol{\sigma} = \widehat{\sigma} \end{array}\right] + \mathsf{H}_0\left(\mathbf{R}_\imath \,\middle|\, \begin{array}{l} \mathbf{E}' = 0 \\ \mathbf{U}_H = \widehat{U}_H \\ \mathbf{r}_H = \widehat{r}_H \\ \boldsymbol{\sigma} = \widehat{\sigma} \end{array}\right) \cdot \Pr\left[\begin{array}{l} \mathbf{E}' = 0 \\ \mathbf{U}_H = \widehat{U}_H \\ \mathbf{r}_H = \widehat{r}_H \\ \boldsymbol{\sigma} = \widehat{\sigma} \end{array}\right] \right) + 1 \\
&\overset{6}{\leq} \sum_{\widehat{\sigma}, \widehat{U}_H, \widehat{r}_H} \left(\mathsf{H}\left(\mathbf{R}_\imath \,\middle|\, \begin{array}{l} \mathbf{E}' = 1 \\ \mathbf{U}_H = \widehat{U}_H \\ \mathbf{r}_H = \widehat{r}_H \\ \boldsymbol{\sigma} = \widehat{\sigma} \end{array}\right) \cdot \Pr\left[\begin{array}{l} \mathbf{E}' = 1 \\ \mathbf{U}_H = \widehat{U}_H \\ \mathbf{r}_H = \widehat{r}_H \\ \boldsymbol{\sigma} = \widehat{\sigma} \end{array}\right] + \lambda^k \cdot \Pr\left[\begin{array}{l} \mathbf{E}' = 0 \\ \mathbf{U}_H = \widehat{U}_H \\ \mathbf{r}_H = \widehat{r}_H \\ \boldsymbol{\sigma} = \widehat{\sigma} \end{array}\right] \right) + 1 \\
&= \sum_{\widehat{\sigma}, \widehat{U}_H, \widehat{r}_H} \left(\mathsf{H}\left(\mathbf{R}_\imath \,\middle|\, \begin{array}{l} \mathbf{E}' = 1 \\ \mathbf{U}_H = \widehat{U}_H \\ \mathbf{r}_H = \widehat{r}_H \\ \boldsymbol{\sigma} = \widehat{\sigma} \end{array}\right) \cdot \Pr\left[\begin{array}{l} \mathbf{E}' = 1 \\ \mathbf{U}_H = \widehat{U}_H \\ \mathbf{r}_H = \widehat{r}_H \\ \boldsymbol{\sigma} = \widehat{\sigma} \end{array}\right] \right) + \lambda^k \cdot \Pr[\mathbf{E}' = 0] + 1
\end{aligned}$$

$$\stackrel{3}{=} \mathsf{H}(\mathbf{R}_\iota|\mathbf{E}',\mathbf{U}_H,\mathbf{r}_H,\boldsymbol{\sigma}) - \sum_{\widehat{\sigma},\widehat{U}_H,\widehat{r}_H}\left(\mathsf{H}\left(\mathbf{R}_\iota \middle| \begin{array}{l}\mathbf{E}'=0\\ \mathbf{U}_H=\widehat{U}_H\\ \mathbf{r}_H=\widehat{r}_H\\ \boldsymbol{\sigma}=\widehat{\sigma}\end{array}\right)\cdot \Pr\begin{bmatrix}\mathbf{E}'=0\\ \mathbf{U}_H=\widehat{U}_H\\ \mathbf{r}_H=\widehat{r}_H\\ \boldsymbol{\sigma}=\widehat{\sigma}\end{bmatrix}\right) + \mathsf{negl}(\lambda)+1$$

$$\leq \mathsf{H}(\mathbf{R}_\iota|\mathbf{E}',\mathbf{U}_H,\mathbf{r}_H,\boldsymbol{\sigma}) + \mathsf{negl}(\lambda)+1$$

$$\stackrel{2.3}{\leq} \mathsf{H}(\mathbf{R}_\iota|\mathbf{U}_H,\mathbf{r}_H,\boldsymbol{\sigma}) + \mathsf{negl}(\lambda)+1.$$

Notice that H is a legitimate set of honest parties and $\iota \notin H$, so by Claim 43,

$$\mathsf{H}(\mathbf{R}_\iota|\mathbf{U}_H,\mathbf{r}_H,\boldsymbol{\sigma}) = O(\log\lambda).$$

We conclude that $\mathsf{H}(\mathbf{R}_i|\boldsymbol{\sigma}) \leq \frac{n}{t}\cdot O(\log\lambda)$.

■

□

4.1 Distributed Sampler CRSs Cannot be Used Twice

We now discuss the first consequence of Theorem 4. Suppose that our distribution $\mathcal{D}(1\!\!1^\lambda)$ has high min-entropy, i.e. $\mathsf{H}_\infty(\mathcal{D}) = \omega(\log\lambda)$. We observe that the probability that two independent samples from $\mathcal{D}(1\!\!1^\lambda)$ collide is negligible. Indeed, denoting the two independent outputs by $\mathbf{R}$ and $\mathbf{R}'$, we have

$$\Pr[\mathbf{R}=\mathbf{R}'] = 2^{-\mathsf{H}_2(\mathcal{D})} \leq 2^{-\mathsf{H}_\infty(\mathcal{D})} = 2^{-\omega(\log\lambda)}.$$

We show, however, that if we run a strongly semi-maliciously secure distributed sampler for $\mathcal{D}(1\!\!1^\lambda)$ twice using the same CRS, the outputs collide with non-negligible probability. As a consequence, we cannot hope to reuse the same CRS to generate independent looking samples.

Corollary 1. *Let $\mathcal{D}(1\!\!1^\lambda)$ be an efficiently samplable distribution. Consider a strongly semi-maliciously secure, t-out-of-n distributed sampler protocol for $\mathcal{D}(1\!\!1^\lambda)$ with black-box simulation. Suppose that $t/n = \Theta(1)$ and let $\mathbf{R}_i$ and $\mathbf{R}'_i$ denote the outputs of any party P_i in two protocol executions having the same CRS. Then, $\Pr[\mathbf{R}_i = \mathbf{R}'_i] \geq 1/\mathsf{poly}(\lambda)$.*

Proof. By Theorem 4, we know that $\mathsf{H}(\mathbf{R}_i|\boldsymbol{\sigma}) = O(\log\lambda)$. Now, we have that

$$\Pr[\mathbf{R}_i=\mathbf{R}'_i] = \sum_{\widehat{\sigma}}\Pr[\boldsymbol{\sigma}=\widehat{\sigma}]\cdot\Pr[\mathbf{R}_i=\mathbf{R}'_i|\boldsymbol{\sigma}=\widehat{\sigma}] \stackrel{8}{=} \sum_{\widehat{\sigma}}\Pr[\boldsymbol{\sigma}=\widehat{\sigma}]\cdot 2^{-\mathsf{H}_2(\mathbf{R}_i|\boldsymbol{\sigma}=\widehat{\sigma})}$$

$$\stackrel{3}{\geq} \sum_{\widehat{\sigma}}\Pr[\boldsymbol{\sigma}=\widehat{\sigma}]\cdot 2^{-\mathsf{H}(\mathbf{R}_i|\boldsymbol{\sigma}=\widehat{\sigma})}$$

We observe that $f(x) := 2^{-x}$ is a convex function, so, by Jensen's inequality

$$\Pr[\mathbf{R}_i=\mathbf{R}'_i] \geq \sum_{\widehat{\sigma}}\Pr[\boldsymbol{\sigma}=\widehat{\sigma}]\cdot 2^{-\mathsf{H}(\mathbf{R}_i|\boldsymbol{\sigma}=\widehat{\sigma})} \geq 2^{-\sum_{\widehat{\sigma}}\Pr[\boldsymbol{\sigma}=\widehat{\sigma}]\cdot\mathsf{H}(\mathbf{R}_i|\boldsymbol{\sigma}=\widehat{\sigma})} \stackrel{3}{=} 2^{-\mathsf{H}(\mathbf{R}_i|\boldsymbol{\sigma})}.$$

Observe that $2^{-\mathsf{H}(\mathbf{R}_i|\boldsymbol{\sigma})} = 1/\mathsf{poly}(\lambda)$. □

4.2 Distributed Sampler CRSs Cannot be Short

A second consequence of Theorem 4 is that the CRSs of strongly semi-maliciously secure distributed samplers cannot be short. Specifically, the bit-length of the CRS $|\sigma|$ must be at most $O(\log\lambda)$ bits shorter than $\mathsf{H}_{\mathsf{Yao}}(\mathcal{D})$.

The Yao Entropy $\mathsf{H}_{\mathsf{Yao}}(\mathbf{R}|\boldsymbol{\sigma})$ *must be Small.* Although Yao's entropy and Shannon's entropy can assume very different values, we prove that if $\mathsf{H}(\mathbf{R}|\boldsymbol{\sigma}) = O(\log\lambda)$, also $\mathsf{H}_{\mathsf{Yao}}(\mathbf{R}|\boldsymbol{\sigma}) = O(\log\lambda)$. Indeed, by Corollary 1, we know that two distributed sampler executions using the same CRS have colliding outputs with non-negligible probability. We can therefore consider the compressor that on input (R,σ) outputs the empty string and the decompressor that on input σ, runs the distributed sampler using σ as CRS, outputting the result R'. Since there is a $1/\mathsf{poly}(\lambda)$ probability that $R = R'$, we conclude that $\mathsf{H}_{\mathsf{Yao}}(\mathbf{R}|\boldsymbol{\sigma}) = O(\log\lambda)$. Observe that we can make the decompressor deterministic using a PRF.

A Chain Rule for Yao's Entropy. To conclude our argument, we show that

$$\mathsf{H}_{\mathsf{Yao}}(\mathbf{R}|\boldsymbol{\sigma}) \geq \mathsf{H}_{\mathsf{Yao}}(\mathbf{R}) - |\boldsymbol{\sigma}|. \tag{2}$$

By the security of distributed samplers in the fully honest case, $\mathbf{R}$ and $\mathcal{D}(1\!\!1^\lambda)$ are computationally indistinguishable, so, $\mathsf{H}_{\mathsf{Yao}}(\mathbf{R}) = \mathsf{H}_{\mathsf{Yao}}(\mathcal{D})$. From this, we easily deduce that $\mathsf{H}_{\mathsf{Yao}}(\mathcal{D}) - |\boldsymbol{\sigma}| \leq O(\log\lambda)$.

We highlight that in [KPW13, Appendix B], Krenn *et al.* proved the chain rule for Yao's entropy, which seems to immediately imply (2. Unfortunately, this is not the case. The idea at the base of their proof is that given a compressor-decompressor pair (c,d) for $\mathsf{H}_{\mathsf{Yao}}(\mathbf{R}|\boldsymbol{\sigma})$, we can build a new compressor-decompressor pair for $\mathsf{H}_{\mathsf{Yao}}(\mathbf{R})$ with the same success probability as (c,d). On input R, the new compressor performs a brute-force search for a σ' such that $d(c(R,\sigma'),\sigma') = R$, then it outputs $c(R,\sigma'),\sigma'$. The decompressor instead is identical to d. Since the output size of the new compressor is $|\boldsymbol{\sigma}|$ bits larger than c's, we obtain that $\mathsf{H}_{\mathsf{Yao}}(\mathbf{R}|\boldsymbol{\sigma}) \geq \mathsf{H}_{\mathsf{Yao}}(\mathbf{R}) - |\boldsymbol{\sigma}|$. Observe however that if $|\boldsymbol{\sigma}|$ is more than $O(\log\lambda)$, the new compressor does not run in polynomial time. That prevents us from using their result.

We notice that in our setting, the new compressor does not need to perform a brute-force search. Indeed, in order to obtain a σ', it can just feed R to the distributed sampler simulator for the fully honest case and pick the CRS contained in the simulated view. The latter is indistinguishable from the real CRS used for the generation of R. This allows us to prove the chain rule even if $|\boldsymbol{\sigma}|$ is more than $O(\log\lambda)$.

Corollary 2. *Suppose that* $t/n = \Theta(1)$. *If OWFs exist, the CRS* $\boldsymbol{\sigma}$ *of a strongly semi-maliciously secure, t-out-of-n distributed sampler for* $\mathcal{D}(1\!\!1^\lambda)$ *with black-box simulation must satisfy* $\mathsf{H}_{\mathsf{Yao}}(\mathcal{D}) - |\boldsymbol{\sigma}| \leq O(\log\lambda)$.

Proof. We start by proving the following claim.

Claim 45. *In the distributed sampler protocol, for any* $i \in [n]$, *we have* $\mathsf{H}_{\mathsf{Yao}}(\mathbf{R}_i|\boldsymbol{\sigma}) = O(\log\lambda)$.

Proof of the Claim. Consider the following randomised pair of compressor and decompressor:

- On input a pair (R_i, σ), the compressor c outputs the empty string.
- On input σ, the decompressor d runs the distributed sampler protocol in-its-head using σ as CRS. Then, it outputs the result R'_i.

Observe that $\Pr[d(c(\mathbf{R}_i, \boldsymbol{\sigma}), \boldsymbol{\sigma}) = \mathbf{R}_i] = \Pr[\mathbf{R}_i = \mathbf{R}'_i]$. Since $\mathbf{R}_i$ and $\mathbf{R}'_i$ are the outputs of two distributed sampler executions using the same CRS, by Corollary 1, we know that

$$\Pr[d(c(\mathbf{R}_i, \boldsymbol{\sigma}), \boldsymbol{\sigma}) = \mathbf{R}_i] = \frac{1}{\mathsf{poly}(\lambda)}$$

Now, consider the deterministic decompressor d' that performs exactly the same operations as d, but uses a PRF F to generate its randomness, i.e. d' has a random PRF key K hard-coded in its circuit and it generates its randomness by computing $F(K, \sigma)$. By the security of the PRF

$$\Pr[d'(c(\mathbf{R}_i, \boldsymbol{\sigma}), \boldsymbol{\sigma}) = \mathbf{R}_i] \geq \Pr[d(c(\mathbf{R}_i, \boldsymbol{\sigma}), \boldsymbol{\sigma}) = \mathbf{R}_i] - \mathsf{negl}(\lambda) = \frac{1}{\mathsf{poly}(\lambda)}.$$

Notice that the probability in the first term is also over $\mathbf{K}$. So,

$$\begin{aligned}\frac{1}{\mathsf{poly}(\lambda)} &\leq \Pr[d'(c(\mathbf{R}_i, \boldsymbol{\sigma}), \boldsymbol{\sigma}) = \mathbf{R}_i] = \sum_{\hat{K}} \frac{1}{|\mathbf{K}|} \cdot \Pr[d'(c(\mathbf{R}_i, \boldsymbol{\sigma}), \boldsymbol{\sigma}) = \mathbf{R}_i | \mathbf{K} = \hat{K}] \\ &\leq \max_{\hat{K}} \Pr[d'(c(\mathbf{R}_i, \boldsymbol{\sigma}), \boldsymbol{\sigma}) = \mathbf{R}_i | \mathbf{K} = \hat{K}].\end{aligned}$$

Let $\widetilde{K}$ be the value of $\hat{K}$ associated with the maximum, let $d'_{\widetilde{K}}$ be the decompressor having $K = \widetilde{K}$. We have proven that the pair $(c, d'_{\widetilde{K}})$ is successful in compressing and decompressing with probability greater than $1/\mathsf{poly}(\lambda)$. We conclude that $\mathsf{H}_{\mathsf{Yao}}(\mathbf{R}_i | \boldsymbol{\sigma}) = O(\log \lambda)$. ■

Claim 46. *In the distributed sampler protocol, for any $i \in [n]$, we have* $\mathsf{H}_{\mathsf{Yao}}(\mathbf{R}_i | \boldsymbol{\sigma}) \geq \mathsf{H}_{\mathsf{Yao}}(\mathbf{R}_i) - |\boldsymbol{\sigma}|$.

Proof of the Claim. Suppose that $\mathsf{H}_{\mathsf{Yao}}(\mathbf{R}_i | \boldsymbol{\sigma}) \leq k(\lambda)$ for some function $k(\lambda)$. Then, there exists a compressor-decompressor pair (c, d) such that

$$\Pr[d(c(\mathbf{R}_i, \boldsymbol{\sigma}), \boldsymbol{\sigma}) = \mathbf{R}_i] \geq \frac{2^\ell}{2^k} - \mathsf{negl}(\lambda).$$

We now design a new compressor $\hat{c}$ for $\mathbf{R}_i$: $\hat{c}$ feeds its input R_i to the distributed sampler simulator Sim for the fully-honest case. The latter provides a CRS σ' and the messages of all the parties. The compressor outputs $c(R_i, \sigma')$ as well as σ'.

Let $\boldsymbol{\sigma}$ be the CRS used to generate $\mathbf{R}_i$. By the security of the distributed sampler in the fully honest case, we know that the triple $(\boldsymbol{\sigma}, (\mathbf{U}_j)_{j \in [n]} (\mathbf{R}_j)_{j \in [n]})$ in the protocol is computationally indistinguishable from $(\mathsf{Sim}(\mathbb{1}^\lambda, \mathbf{R}'), (\mathbf{R}')_{j \in [n]})$

where $\mathbf{R}' \xleftarrow{\$} \mathcal{D}(\mathbb{1}^\lambda)$. We conclude that the pairs $(\mathbf{R}_i, \boldsymbol{\sigma})$ and $(\mathbf{R}_i, \boldsymbol{\sigma}')$ are also computationally indistinguishable. As a consequence,

$$\Big|\Pr[d(c(\mathbf{R}_i, \boldsymbol{\sigma}), \boldsymbol{\sigma}) = \mathbf{R}_i] - \Pr[d(c(\mathbf{R}_i, \boldsymbol{\sigma}'), \boldsymbol{\sigma}') = \mathbf{R}_i]\Big| = \mathsf{negl}(\lambda).$$

We conclude that

$$\begin{aligned}\Pr[d(\hat{c}(\mathbf{R}_i)) = \mathbf{R}_i] = \Pr[d(c(\mathbf{R}_i, \boldsymbol{\sigma}'), \boldsymbol{\sigma}') = \mathbf{R}_i] &\geq \Pr[d(c(\mathbf{R}_i, \boldsymbol{\sigma}), \boldsymbol{\sigma}) = \mathbf{R}_i] - \mathsf{negl}(\lambda)\\ &\geq \frac{2^\ell}{2^k} - \mathsf{negl}(\lambda) = \frac{2^{\ell+|\boldsymbol{\sigma}|}}{2^{k+|\boldsymbol{\sigma}|}} - \mathsf{negl}(\lambda).\end{aligned}$$

Observe that $\ell + |\boldsymbol{\sigma}|$ is the output size of $\hat{c}$. Notice also that $\hat{c}$ is not deterministic, however, we can make it so adopting the same technique used in Claim 45, i.e. by generating its randomness using a PRF. Specifically, consider the deterministic compressor $\hat{c}'$ which has a PRF key K hard-coded in its circuit and generates its randomness by computing $F(K, R_i)$, performing then the same operations as $\hat{c}$. By the security of the PRF, we have that

$$\Big|\Pr[d(\hat{c}'(\mathbf{R}_i)) = \mathbf{R}_i] - \Pr[d(\hat{c}(\mathbf{R}_i)) = \mathbf{R}_i]\Big| = \mathsf{negl}(\lambda).$$

So,

$$\Pr[d(\hat{c}'(\mathbf{R}_i)) = \mathbf{R}_i] \geq \frac{2^{\ell+|\boldsymbol{\sigma}|}}{2^{k+|\boldsymbol{\sigma}|}} - \mathsf{negl}(\lambda).$$

As in the proof of the previous claim, the probability in the first term is also over $\mathbf{K}$. So,

$$\begin{aligned}\frac{2^{\ell+|\boldsymbol{\sigma}|}}{2^{k+|\boldsymbol{\sigma}|}} - \mathsf{negl}(\lambda) \leq \Pr[d(\hat{c}'(\mathbf{R}_i)) = \mathbf{R}_i] &= \sum_{\hat{K}} \frac{1}{|\mathbf{K}|} \cdot \Pr[d(\hat{c}'(\mathbf{R}_i)) = \mathbf{R}_i | \mathbf{K} = \hat{K}]\\ &\leq \max_{\hat{K}} \Pr[d(\hat{c}'(\mathbf{R}_i)) = \mathbf{R}_i | \mathbf{K} = \hat{K}].\end{aligned}$$

Let $\widetilde{K}$ be the value of $\hat{K}$ associated with the maximum, let $\hat{c}'_{\widetilde{K}}$ be the decompressor having $\mathbf{K} = \widetilde{K}$. We have proven that the pair $(\hat{c}'_{\widetilde{K}}, d)$ succeeds in compressing and decompressing $\mathbf{R}_i$ with probability greater than $2^{\ell+|\boldsymbol{\sigma}|}/2^{k+|\boldsymbol{\sigma}|} - \mathsf{negl}(\lambda)$, so $\mathsf{H}_{\mathsf{Yao}}(\mathbf{R}_i) \leq k(\lambda) + |\boldsymbol{\sigma}|$. We conclude that $\mathsf{H}_{\mathsf{Yao}}(\mathbf{R}_i | \boldsymbol{\sigma}) \geq \mathsf{H}_{\mathsf{Yao}}(\mathbf{R}_i) - |\boldsymbol{\sigma}|$. ■

By Claims 45 and 46, we have $O(\log \lambda) = \mathsf{H}_{\mathsf{Yao}}(\mathbf{R}_i | \boldsymbol{\sigma}) \geq \mathsf{H}_{\mathsf{Yao}}(\mathbf{R}_i) - |\boldsymbol{\sigma}|$. We notice that, by the security of the distributed sampler in the fully honest case, $\mathbf{R}_i$ is computationally indistinguishable from $\mathcal{D}(\mathbb{1}^\lambda)$, so, $\mathsf{H}_{\mathsf{Yao}}(\mathbf{R}_i) = \mathsf{H}_{\mathsf{Yao}}(\mathcal{D})$. We conclude that $\mathsf{H}_{\mathsf{Yao}}(\mathcal{D}) - |\boldsymbol{\sigma}| \leq O(\log \lambda)$. □

4.3 Distributed Sampler CRSs Cannot be (too) Nice

The *niceness* of a CRS cannot be defined in a mathematical way. However, informally speaking, we can say that a CRS is nicer than another if it is easier to produce in an MPC setting, e.g. a uniformly random string of bits (i.e. a

URS) is simpler to generate than a random RSA modulus of unknown factorisation. Indeed, if we aim for security with abort, we can generate a URS using a simple commit-then-reveal approach. On the other hand, all the state-of-the-art constructions for the generation of RSA moduli rely on rejection sampling: first the parties generate secret-shared (or encrypted) candidate primes p and q, they multiply them and apply expensive (bi)primality tests on the secret-shared data [FLOP18, HMR+19, CCD+20]. After sufficiently many trials (the number depends on the size of the modulus), the players obtain a valid RSA modulus with high probability. This results in rather complex protocols.

In the previous sections, we have seen that the CRS of distributed samplers cannot be used more then once and cannot be short. These facts suggest that directly encoding a sample from $\mathcal{D}(\mathbb{1}^\lambda)$ in a CRS is probably better than relying on a distributed sampler protocol for $\mathcal{D}(\mathbb{1}^\lambda)$. At least in the first case, the parties spare one round of interaction. But what if the CRS used by the distributed sampler is nicer than any encoding of $\mathcal{D}(\mathbb{1}^\lambda)$? We prove that this cannot happen as it is always possible to non-interactively generate samples from $\mathcal{D}(\mathbb{1}^\lambda)$ using only distributed sampler CRSs and public random coins.

Non-interactive Generation of Samples from $\mathcal{D}(\mathbb{1}^\lambda)$ Using a Distributed Sampler CRS and Random Bits. In this section, we observe that a distributed sampler for $\mathcal{D}(\mathbb{1}^\lambda)$ allows us to construct an efficient deterministic function De that maps pairs consisting of a distributed sampler CRS σ and uniformly random bits r into values R that are computationally indistinguishable from $\mathcal{D}(\mathbb{1}^\lambda)$. This algorithm trivially outputs the result of the distributed sampler using σ as CRS and r as randomness for the parties. The interesting fact is that if the distributed sampler is strongly semi-maliciously secure with black-box simulation, the algorithm is efficiently invertible with non-negligible probability. Specifically, we prove that there exists an efficient PPT algorithm test, that outputs 1 with $1/\mathsf{poly}(\lambda)$ probability when run over a sample $R \xleftarrow{\$} \mathcal{D}(\mathbb{1}^\lambda)$. Moreover, if this event occurs, it is possible to efficiently find (using an algorithm En) a pair (σ, r) that looks random over $\mathsf{De}^{-1}(R)$.

In other words, if we provide the parties with a distributed sampler CRS σ and public uniformly random bits r, the parties can obtain a sample R from $\mathcal{D}(\mathbb{1}^\lambda)$ without any interaction. Furthermore, with $1/\mathsf{poly}(\lambda)$ probability, (σ, r) reveals no information in addition to what can be already inferred from R. Finally, the honest parties can tell when (σ, r) reveals too much information, having therefore the opportunity to reject R and restart.

Biases in the Distribution. Notice that the selective rejection biases the distribution of the output. However, any cryptographic protocol basing its security on R will remain secure even if R is sampled according to the biased distribution. Indeed, at least a polynomial fraction of the samples is not rejected. If the protocol was insecure in the new setting, there would be a non-negligible probability of sampling a bad R even in the original protocol, which would therefore be insecure.

Why is De *Invertible with Non-negligible Probability?* Our idea is based on the fact that in a strongly semi-malicious distributed sampler, $\mathsf{H}(\mathbf{R}|\boldsymbol{\sigma})$ is small. In other words, the CRS of the protocol describes the output with high precision. Obtaining the exact CRS used for the generation of $\mathbf{R}$ is usually hard, however, the simulator for the fully-honest case can provide us with a functionally equivalent object.

In order to completely describe $\mathbf{R}$, we need to extract also randomness $\mathbf{r}$ for the parties, so that, using $\mathbf{r}$ in conjunction with the CRS, we obtain $\mathbf{R}$. Unfortunately, the simulator cannot provide much help here. Indeed, given $(\boldsymbol{\sigma}', (\mathbf{U}_i)_{i\in[n]}) \xleftarrow{\$} \mathsf{Sim}(\mathbb{1}^\lambda, \mathbf{R})$, it is usually hard to extract the randomness $\mathbf{r}$ used to generate $(\mathbf{U}_i)_{i\in[n]}$. Actually, such $\mathbf{r}$ might not even exist. Luckily, in Corollary 1, we have proven that two executions of a strongly semi-maliciously secure distributed sampler using the same CRS have colliding outputs with $1/\mathsf{poly}(\lambda)$ probability. So, if we run the distributed sampler protocol again using $\boldsymbol{\sigma}'$ as CRS, we obtain $\mathbf{R}$ again with non-negligible probability. Clearly, in the new execution, the value of $(\mathbf{U}_i)_{i\in[n]}$ has probably changed, however, this time we know the randomness $\mathbf{r}'$ used to generate the messages.

On Average Invertibility. We observe that the probability of succeeding in inverting De is also over the outcome of $\mathbf{R}$. In other words, we just know that the *average* probability of inverting $\mathbf{R}$ is $1/\mathsf{poly}(\lambda)$. That does not mean that the overwhelming majority of values of $\mathbf{R}$ is efficiently invertible: if $\mathbf{R}$ assumes an unlucky value, we can try to invert as many times as we want without any hope of succeeding. We could prove, however, that there always exists a polynomial fraction of the space of events for which $\mathbf{R}$ is easy to invert.

We also noticed that it is possible to efficiently test if a value R is easy to invert or not. Indeed, we can just try to invert it many times, if the success frequency is lower than a certain threshold, we can reject R, otherwise, we accept it. We used the Chernoff bound to find the threshold and the maximum number of inversion attempts. In particular, we needed test to succeed with at least $1/\mathsf{poly}(\lambda)$ probability.

The Special Case of URSs. As a corollary of the result described in this section, if the distributed sampler uses a URS, it is possible to securely generate samples from $\mathcal{D}(\mathbb{1}^\lambda)$ using public random coins only. In particular, in the random oracle model, the parties can securely sample from $\mathcal{D}(\mathbb{1}^\lambda)$ without interacting and without needing any CRS.

Corollary 3. *Suppose that there exists a strongly semi-maliciously secure, t-out-of-n distributed sampler for $\mathcal{D}(\mathbb{1}^\lambda)$ with black-box simulation. Suppose that $t/n = \Theta(1)$ and let $\mathsf{CRS}(\mathbb{1}^\lambda)$ be the algorithm used to generate the CRS of the protocol. Then, there exist a deterministic polynomial algorithm* De *and PPT algorithms* En *and* test *such that*

- $\mathsf{De}(\mathsf{CRS}(\mathbb{1}^\lambda), \mathcal{U}(\mathbb{1}^\lambda)) \sim_c \mathcal{D}(\mathbb{1}^\lambda)$
- $\Pr[\mathsf{test}(\mathcal{D}(\mathbb{1}^\lambda)) = 1] \geq 1/\mathsf{poly}(\lambda)$

THE GAME $\mathcal{G}_{\mathcal{A}}^{\mathsf{Inv}}(\mathbb{1}^\lambda)$

The challenger performs the following operations

1. $b \xleftarrow{\$} \{0,1\}$
2. $\sigma \xleftarrow{\$} \mathsf{CRS}(\mathbb{1}^\lambda)$, $r \xleftarrow{\$} \mathcal{U}(\mathbb{1}^\lambda)$
3. $R \leftarrow \mathsf{De}(\sigma, r)$
4. If $\mathsf{test}(R) = 0$, go back to step 2.
5. If $b = 0$, provide the adversary with (σ, r), otherwise provide it with $\mathsf{En}(R)$.

The adversary wins if it terminates its execution outputting b.

Fig. 2. Invertibility game

– *No PPT adversary can win the game* $\mathcal{G}_{\mathcal{A}}^{\mathsf{Inv}}(\mathbb{1}^\lambda)$ *(see Fig. 2) with non-negligible advantage.*

Proof. We start by defining the algorithm De, which on input σ and random string r, runs the distributed sampler protocol using σ as CRS and r as randomness for the parties, outputting the result of party P_1.

Claim 47. $\mathsf{De}\big(\mathsf{CRS}(\mathbb{1}^\lambda), \mathcal{U}(\mathbb{1}^\lambda)\big) \sim_c \mathcal{D}(\mathbb{1}^\lambda)$

Proof of the Claim. We observe that $\mathbf{R} := \mathsf{De}\big(\mathsf{CRS}(\mathbb{1}^\lambda), \mathcal{U}(\mathbb{1}^\lambda)\big)$ is distributed exactly as the distributed sampler output. By the security of the distributed sampler, we conclude that $\mathbf{R} \sim_c \mathcal{D}(\mathbb{1}^\lambda)$. ■

We now define the PPT algorithm Inv as follows: Inv feeds the input R to the distributed sampler simulator for the fully honest case. In this way, it obtains a fake CRS σ' and messages $(U_i)_{i \in [n]}$. Finally, Inv picks a uniformly random string r and outputs (σ', r).

Claim 48. *Let* $\mathbf{R}$ *denote a sample from* $\mathcal{D}(\mathbb{1}^\lambda)$. *Then, there exists a polynomial* $q(\lambda)$ *such that*

$$\Pr[\mathsf{De}(\mathsf{Inv}(\mathbf{R})) = \mathbf{R}] \geq \frac{1}{q(\lambda)}$$

Proof of the Claim. Let $(\boldsymbol{\sigma}', \mathbf{r}) := \mathsf{Inv}(\mathbf{R})$. By the security of distributed samplers, we know that $(\boldsymbol{\sigma}', \mathbf{R})$ is computationally indistinguishable from $(\boldsymbol{\sigma}, \mathsf{De}(\boldsymbol{\sigma}, \mathbf{r}))$ where $\boldsymbol{\sigma} \xleftarrow{\$} \mathsf{CRS}(\mathbb{1}^\lambda)$ and $\mathbf{r}$ is uniformly random. We conclude that for $\mathbf{r}$ and $\mathbf{r}'$ independent and uniformly random

$$\big(\boldsymbol{\sigma}, \mathsf{De}(\boldsymbol{\sigma}, \mathbf{r}'), \mathsf{De}(\boldsymbol{\sigma}, \mathbf{r})\big) \sim_c \big(\boldsymbol{\sigma}', \mathbf{R}, \mathsf{De}(\boldsymbol{\sigma}', \mathbf{r})\big) \tag{3}$$

By Corollary 1, we know that

$$\Pr[\mathsf{De}(\boldsymbol{\sigma}, \mathbf{r}') = \mathsf{De}(\boldsymbol{\sigma}, \mathbf{r})] \geq \frac{1}{\mathsf{poly}(\lambda)}$$

We conclude that, by (3),

$$\Pr[\mathsf{De}(\mathsf{Inv}(\mathbf{R}))=\mathbf{R}]=\Pr[\mathsf{De}(\boldsymbol{\sigma}',\mathbf{r}')=\mathbf{R}]\geq\frac{1}{\mathsf{poly}(\lambda)}-\mathsf{negl}(\lambda)\geq\frac{1}{\mathsf{poly}(\lambda)}$$

■

We now define the algorithm test as follows: on input R, test checks if $\mathsf{De}(\mathsf{Inv}(R))=R$ for $4\lambda\cdot q(\lambda)$ times. If the equation is satisfied less than λ times, test outputs 0, otherwise it output 1.

In a similar way, we define En: on input R, En computes $(\sigma',r)\xleftarrow{\$}\mathsf{Inv}(R)$ and checks if $\mathsf{De}(\sigma',r)=R$. If that is the case, it outputs (σ',r). Otherwise, it repeats the operation. If the procedure fails for more than $8\lambda\cdot q(\lambda)$, En outputs $\perp$.

Claim 49.

$$\Pr[\mathsf{test}(\mathcal{D}(1\!\!1^\lambda))=1]\geq\frac{1}{8q(\lambda)}$$

Proof of the Claim. For every value x, we define $p_x:=\Pr[\mathsf{De}(\mathsf{Inv}(x))=x]$. Let $\mathbf{R}$ be a random variable denoting a sample from $\mathcal{D}(1\!\!1^\lambda)$ and notice that $p_\mathbf{R}$ is a random variable. By Claim 48, we know that

$$\mathbb{E}[p_\mathbf{R}]=\sum_x\Pr[\mathbf{R}=x]\cdot p_x=\Pr[\mathsf{De}(\mathsf{Inv}(\mathbf{R}))=\mathbf{R}]\geq\frac{1}{q(\lambda)}$$

Since $0\leq p_x\leq 1$, we have that $\mathbb{E}[p_\mathbf{R}^2]\leq\mathbb{E}[p_\mathbf{R}]$, so, by the Paley-Zygmund inequality,

$$\Pr\left[p_\mathbf{R}\geq\frac{1}{2q(\lambda)}\right]\geq\Pr\left[p_\mathbf{R}>\frac{1}{2}\mathbb{E}[p_\mathbf{R}]\right]\geq\frac{1}{4}\cdot\frac{\mathbb{E}[p_\mathbf{R}]^2}{\mathbb{E}[p_\mathbf{R}^2]}\geq\frac{1}{4}\cdot\mathbb{E}[p_\mathbf{R}]\geq\frac{1}{4q(\lambda)}$$

Define now $\Omega_{\mathsf{good}}=\{x|p_x\geq\frac{1}{2q(\lambda)}\}$. Suppose now that $x\in\Omega_{\mathsf{good}}$. If we run the check $\mathsf{De}(\mathsf{Inv}(x))=x$ for $8\lambda\cdot q(\lambda)$ times, by the Chernoff bound, we know that it succeeds more than

$$\frac{1}{2}\cdot 4\lambda q(\lambda)\cdot p_x\geq\lambda$$

times with overwhelming probability. So if $x\in\Omega_{\mathsf{good}}$, $\mathsf{test}(x)=1$ with overwhelming probability. We conclude that

$$\begin{aligned}\Pr[\mathsf{test}(\mathbf{R})=1]&\geq\Pr[\mathsf{test}(\mathbf{R})=1|\mathbf{R}\in\Omega_{\mathsf{good}}]\cdot\Pr[\mathbf{R}\in\Omega_{\mathsf{good}}]\\&\geq\min_{x\in\Omega_{\mathsf{good}}}\Pr[\mathsf{test}(x)=1]\cdot\Pr[\mathbf{R}\in\Omega_{\mathsf{good}}]\geq\frac{1}{8q(\lambda)}\end{aligned}$$

■

Claim 410. *No PPT adversary can win the game $\mathcal{G}^{\mathsf{Inv}}_{\mathcal{A}}(1\!\!1^\lambda)$ (see Fig. 2) with non-negligible advantage.*

Proof of the Claim. As in the previous claim, let $p_x := \Pr[\mathsf{De}(\mathsf{Inv}(x)) = x]$. Define now $\Omega_{\mathsf{bad}} = \{x | p_x \leq \frac{1}{8q(\lambda)}\}$. Suppose that $x \in \Omega_{\mathsf{bad}}$. If we run the check $\mathsf{De}(\mathsf{Inv}(x)) = x$ for $4\lambda \cdot q(\lambda)$ times, by the Chernoff bound, we know that it succeeds less than

$$2 \cdot 4\lambda q(\lambda) \cdot p_x \leq \lambda$$

times with overwhelming probability. So, if $x \in \Omega_{\mathsf{bad}}$, $\mathsf{test}(x) = 0$ with overwhelming probability.

Let $\mathbf{R} \xleftarrow{\$} \mathcal{D}(1\!\!1^\lambda)$. We observe that

$$\Pr[\mathsf{En}(\mathbf{R}) = \bot | \mathsf{test}(\mathbf{R}) = 1] \leq \Pr[\mathbf{R} \in \Omega_{\mathsf{bad}} | \mathsf{test}(\mathbf{R}) = 1] + \Pr[\mathsf{En}(\mathbf{R}) = \bot | \mathbf{R} \notin \Omega_{\mathsf{bad}}].$$

We know that

$$\begin{aligned} \Pr[\mathbf{R} \in \Omega_{\mathsf{bad}} | \mathsf{test}(\mathbf{R}) = 1] &\leq \frac{\Pr[\mathsf{test}(\mathbf{R}) = 1 | \mathbf{R} \in \Omega_{\mathsf{bad}}]}{\Pr[\mathsf{test}(\mathbf{R}) = 1]} \\ &\leq 8q(\lambda) \cdot \max_{x \in \Omega_{\mathsf{bad}}} \Pr[\mathsf{test}(x) = 1] = \mathsf{negl}(\lambda). \end{aligned}$$

Furthermore,

$$\Pr[\mathsf{En}(\mathbf{R}) = \bot | \mathbf{R} \notin \Omega_{\mathsf{bad}}] \geq \min_{x \notin \Omega_{\mathsf{bad}}} \Pr[\mathsf{En}(x) = \bot].$$

Notice that for every $x \notin \Omega_{\mathsf{bad}}$, $p_x > \frac{1}{8q(\lambda)}$. Observe also that En tries to invert the input up to $8\lambda \cdot q(\lambda) > \lambda / p_x$ times, so, with overwhelming probability $\mathsf{En}(x) \neq \bot$. We conclude that $\Pr[\mathsf{En}(\mathbf{R}) = \bot | \mathsf{test}(\mathbf{R}) = 1] = \mathsf{negl}(\lambda)$.

Now, suppose that $\mathsf{En}(\mathbf{R}) = (\boldsymbol{\sigma}', \mathbf{r}') \neq \bot$. We recall that $\boldsymbol{\sigma}'$ is obtained by running $\mathsf{Sim}(1\!\!1^\lambda, \mathbf{R})$, so by the security of distributed samplers $(\mathbf{R}, \boldsymbol{\sigma}') \sim_c (\mathsf{De}(\boldsymbol{\sigma}, \mathbf{r}), \boldsymbol{\sigma})$ where $\boldsymbol{\sigma} \xleftarrow{\$} \mathsf{CRS}(1\!\!1^\lambda)$ and $\mathbf{r} \xleftarrow{\$} \mathcal{U}(1\!\!1^\lambda)$. We also know that $\mathbf{r}'$ is random conditioned on satisfying $\mathsf{De}(\boldsymbol{\sigma}', \mathbf{r}') = \mathbf{R}$. In other words, $(\mathbf{R}, \boldsymbol{\sigma}', \mathbf{r}')$ is computationally indistinguishable from $(\mathsf{De}(\boldsymbol{\sigma}, \mathbf{r}), \boldsymbol{\sigma}, \mathbf{r})$. We conclude our proof observing that $(\mathbf{R}, \mathsf{En}(\mathbf{R})) \sim_c (\mathsf{De}(\boldsymbol{\sigma}, \mathbf{r}), \mathsf{En}(\mathsf{De}(\boldsymbol{\sigma}, \mathbf{r})))$. ■

□

Acknowledgments. The authors would like to thank Ivan Damgård, Jesper Buus Nielsen and Sophia Yakoubov for their feedback and support.

D.A. and P.S. were supported by the Aarhus University Research Foundation (AUFF) and the Independent Research Fund Denmark (DFF) (grant DFF-0165-00107B "C3PO"). D.A was supported by the European Research Council through an ERC Starting Grant (Grant agreement No. 101077455, ObfusQation). M.O. was supported by MOE tier 2 grant - T2EP20223-0024, and NRF award NRF- NRFI09-0005.

References

[ADIN24] Abram, D., Doerner, J., Ishai, Y., Narayanan, V.: Constant-round simulation-secure coin tossing extension with guaranteed output. In: Joye, M., Leander, G. (eds.) EUROCRYPT 2024. LNCS, vol. 14655, pp. 122–154. Springer, Cham (2024). https://doi.org/10.1007/978-3-031-58740-5_5

[AOS23] Abram, D., Obremski, M., Scholl, P.: On the (im)possibility of distributed samplers: lower bounds and party-dynamic constructions. Cryptology ePrint Archive, Paper 2023/863 (2023)
[ASY22] Abram, D., Scholl, P., Yakoubov, S.: Distributed (correlation) samplers: how to remove a trusted dealer in one round. In: Dunkelman, O., Dziembowski, S. (eds.) EUROCRYPT 2022. LNCS, vol. 13275, pp. 790–820. Springer, Cham (2022). https://doi.org/10.1007/978-3-031-06944-4_27
[AWZ23] Abram, D., Waters, B., Zhandry, M.: Security-preserving distributed samplers: how to generate any crs in one round without random oracles. In: Handschuh, H., Lysyanskaya, A. (eds.) CRYPTO 2023. LNCS, vol. 14081, pp. 489–514. Springer, Cham (2023). https://doi.org/10.1007/978-3-031-38557-5_16
[Bar01] Barak, B.: How to go beyond the black-box simulation barrier. In: 42nd FOCS. IEEE Computer Society Press (2001)
[BCCT12] Bitansky, N., Canetti, R., Chiesa, A., Tromer, E.: From extractable collision resistance to succinct non-interactive arguments of knowledge, and back again. In: ITCS 2012. ACM (2012)
[Bd94] Benaloh, J., de Mare, M.: One-way accumulators: a decentralized alternative to digital signatures. In: Helleseth, T. (ed.) EUROCRYPT 1993. LNCS, vol. 765, pp. 274–285. Springer, Heidelberg (1994). https://doi.org/10.1007/3-540-48285-7_24
[BMO90] Bellare, M., Micali, S., Ostrovsky, R.: The (true) complexity of statistical zero knowledge. In: 22nd ACM STOC. ACM Press (1990)
[Can01] Canetti, R.: Universally composable security: a new paradigm for cryptographic protocols. In: 42nd FOCS. IEEE Computer Society Press (2001)
[CCD+20] Chen, M., et al.: Multiparty generation of an RSA modulus. In: Micciancio, D., Ristenpart, T. (eds.) CRYPTO 2020. LNCS, vol. 12172, pp. 64–93. Springer, Cham (2020). https://doi.org/10.1007/978-3-030-56877-1_3
[CKL03] Canetti, R., Kushilevitz, E., Lindell, Y.: On the limitations of universally composable two-party computation without set-up assumptions. In: Biham, E. (ed.) EUROCRYPT 2003. LNCS, vol. 2656, pp. 68–86. Springer, Heidelberg (2003). https://doi.org/10.1007/3-540-39200-9_5
[DHRW16] Dodis, Y., Halevi, S., Rothblum, R.D., Wichs, D.: Spooky encryption and its applications. In: Robshaw, M., Katz, J. (eds.) CRYPTO 2016. LNCS, vol. 9816, pp. 93–122. Springer, Heidelberg (2016). https://doi.org/10.1007/978-3-662-53015-3_4
[DLN+04] Dwork, C., Langberg, M., Naor, M., Nissim, K., Reingold, O.: Succinct proofs for np and spooky interactions. Unpublished manuscript (2004)
[FLOP18] Frederiksen, T.K., Lindell, Y., Osheter, V., Pinkas, B.: Fast distributed RSA key generation for semi-honest and malicious adversaries. In: Shacham, H., Boldyreva, A. (eds.) CRYPTO 2018. LNCS, vol. 10992, pp. 331–361. Springer, Cham (2018). https://doi.org/10.1007/978-3-319-96881-0_12
[GK90] Goldreich, O., Krawczyk, H.: On the composition of zero-knowledge proof systems. In: Paterson, M.S. (ed.) ICALP 1990. LNCS, vol. 443, pp. 268–282. Springer, Heidelberg (1990). https://doi.org/10.1007/BFb0032038
[HIJ+17] Halevi, S., Ishai, Y., Jain, A., Komargodski, I., Sahai, A., Yogev, E.: Non-interactive multiparty computation without correlated randomness. In: Takagi, T., Peyrin, T. (eds.) ASIACRYPT 2017. LNCS, vol. 10626, pp. 181–211. Springer, Cham (2017). https://doi.org/10.1007/978-3-319-70700-6_7

[HILL99] Håstad, J., Impagliazzo, R., Levin, L.A., Luby, M.: A pseudorandom generator from any one-way function. SIAM J. Comput. (4) (1999)

[HLR07] Hsiao, C.-Y., Lu, C.-J., Reyzin, L.: Conditional computational entropy, or toward separating pseudoentropy from compressibility. In: Naor, M. (ed.) EUROCRYPT 2007. LNCS, vol. 4515, pp. 169–186. Springer, Heidelberg (2007). https://doi.org/10.1007/978-3-540-72540-4_10

[HMR+19] Hazay, C., Mikkelsen, G.L., Rabin, T., Toft, T., Nicolosi, A.A.: Efficient RSA key generation and threshold paillier in the two-party setting. J. Cryptol. (2) (2019)

[HV16] Hazay, C., Venkitasubramaniam, M.: What security can we achieve within 4 rounds? In: Zikas, V., De Prisco, R. (eds.) SCN 2016. LNCS, vol. 9841, pp. 486–505. Springer, Cham (2016). https://doi.org/10.1007/978-3-319-44618-9_26

[KPW13] Krenn, S., Pietrzak, K., Wadia, A.: A counterexample to the chain rule for conditional HILL entropy. In: Sahai, A. (ed.) TCC 2013. LNCS, vol. 7785, pp. 23–39. Springer, Heidelberg (2013). https://doi.org/10.1007/978-3-642-36594-2_2

[Ore87] Oren, Y.: On the cunning power of cheating verifiers: some observations about zero knowledge proofs (extended abstract). In: 28th FOCS. IEEE Computer Society Press (1987)

[OSY21] Orlandi, C., Scholl, P., Yakoubov, S.: The rise of paillier: homomorphic secret sharing and public-key silent OT. In: Canteaut, A., Standaert, F.-X. (eds.) EUROCRYPT 2021. LNCS, vol. 12696, pp. 678–708. Springer, Cham (2021). https://doi.org/10.1007/978-3-030-77870-5_24

[PVW08] Peikert, C., Vaikuntanathan, V., Waters, B.: A framework for efficient and composable oblivious transfer. In: Wagner, D. (ed.) CRYPTO 2008. LNCS, vol. 5157, pp. 554–571. Springer, Heidelberg (2008). https://doi.org/10.1007/978-3-540-85174-5_31

[Rey11] Reyzin, L.: Some notions of entropy for cryptography - (invited talk). In: Fehr, S. (ed.) ICITS 2011. LNCS, vol. 6673, pp. 138–142. Springer, Heidelberg (2011). https://doi.org/10.1007/978-3-642-20728-0_13

[Sha48] Shannon, C.E.: A mathematical theory of communication. Bell Syst. Tech. J. **27**, 623–656 (1948)

[Yao82] Yao, A.C.-C.: Theory and applications of trapdoor functions (extended abstract). In: 23rd FOCS. IEEE Computer Society Press (1982)

Scalable Multi-server Private Information Retrieval

Ashrujit Ghoshal[1(✉)], Baitian Li[2], Yaohua Ma[2], Chenxin Dai[2], and Elaine Shi[3]

[1] Indian Institute of Technology Madras, Chennai, India
ashrujit@cse.iitm.ac.in
[2] Tsinghua IIIS, Beijing, China
{lbt21,ma-yh21,daicx21}@mails.tsinghua.edu.cn
[3] Carnegie Mellon University, Pittsburgh, USA

Abstract. We revisit multi-server Private Information Retrieval (PIR), where the client interacts with S non-colluding servers. Ideally, we want a *scalable* family of multi-server PIR schemes where all the performance metrics of the scheme decrease as S increases. However, no prior work achieved scalability under any setting, and any hardness assumption.

In this paper we construct new multi-server, information-theoretically secure *scalable* PIR schemes for three natural settings. First, we give a construction where all the performance metrics scale at equal rate. Second, we give a scalable construction that minimizes the per-query bandwidth. Third, we give a scalable construction that minimizes the per-query online bottleneck cost (the maximum of the bandwidth and computation). For the first two settings, our constructions are *doubly efficient* with only a super-constant number of servers. In comparison, the best known prior works in the information-theoretic setting required super-logarithmically many servers to achieve the doubly efficient notion.

Our techniques for achieving scalable PIR also enable us to advance the state of the art in the polynomial space setting. In this setting, we show how to improve the space consumption of prior works by a polynomial factor while preserving all other metrics. Further, we show a new balancing technique that allows us to further minimize the bandwidth per query by trading off the computation and server space, thus enabling a more smooth tradeoff between the metrics and generalizing the design space.

1 Introduction

Private Information Retrieval (PIR), originally proposed by Chor et al. [12], allows a client to retrieve an entry from a public database stored on one or more server(s), without leaking its query to any individual server. PIR promises numerous applications such as private DNS [2,17,43], privately checking whether

E. Shi—Author ordering is randomized.

B. Applebaum and H. Lin (Eds.): TCC 2025, LNCS 16271, pp. 582–610, 2026.
https://doi.org/10.1007/978-3-032-12290-2_19

one's password is in some leaked password database [1,15], private contact discovery [3], private web search [22], and more.

In this paper, we revisit multi-server PIR, where a client interacts with S non-colluding servers. This setting becomes particularly interesting if adding more servers can improve the performance of PIR schemes. The holy grail is to get a *scalable* family of schemes, where the all performance metrics, including computation, bandwidth, and space decrease as we increase the number of servers.

Unfortunately, to the best of our knowledge, *no prior multi-server PIR scheme can achieve scalability under any setting and any hardness assumptions.* Classical PIR schemes without preprocessing [4,9–12,18,19,23,29,34–37,39,40,45] inherently cannot scale beyond the linear computation barrier. Specifically, Beimel, Ishai, and Malkin [5] proved that any classical PIR scheme (without preprocessing) must incur a server-side computation cost that is linear in the size of the database for every query. Intuitively, if the servers need not look at some locations to answer a client's query, then the client's interest in those locations can be ruled out, thus breaking privacy. Although recent works, pioneered by Beimel et al. [5] and Corrigan-Gibbs and Kogan [14], have shown how to overcome this linear computation barrier by introducing a *one-time preprocessing* [5,13,14,20,24,31–33,38,42,46,48], existing preprocessing schemes fail to satisfy scalability. Most existing preprocessing PIR schemes [13,14,20,24,31–33,38,42,48] are designed for a fixed number of servers (e.g., one or two), making scalability beyond their scope. While a few works [5,44,46] have explored a parameterizable number of servers, none have achieved full scalability. For example, Beimel et al. [5] and Woodruff and Yekhanin [46] showed that bandwidth and computation can scale as fast as $n^{O(1/S)}$ where S is the number of servers. However, their server space grows as rapidly as $n^{\omega(S^2/\log S)}$, which is the opposite of scaling. The concurrent and independent work of Singh et al. [44] showed how to achieve $n^{O(1/S)}$ bandwidth scaling, but their computation and client space cannot scale beyond $n^{1/2}$.

In this paper, we ask the following natural question:

Can we have multi-server PIR schemes with scalable efficiency as we increase the number of servers?

1.1 Our Main Results

We answer the above question affirmatively. Since tradeoffs exist between the bandwidth, computation, and space requirement of the PIR scheme, we present our results for three natural settings:

- *Setting 1: equal scaling.* What scalability can we achieve if we want all metrics to scale equally fast w.r.t. the number of servers? The concept of equal scaling is similar to that of "bottleneck cost" proposed in the MPC literature [8]. The idea is that as the problem size scales up, the most unscalable dimension

becomes the bottleneck. This setting is particularly of relevance when the storage, computation and network transmission costs of a system are similar.
- *Setting 2: minimize bandwidth.* How do we minimize the bandwidth consumption per query while achieving scalability in all dimensions? This setting is particularly of relevance when the network transmission costs of a system overwhelmingly dominate compute and storage costs. This was the primary setting considered in prior works such as Beimel et al. [5] and Woodruff and Yekhanin [46]; thus results in this setting allows a direct comparison with these prior works.
- *Setting 3: minimize bottleneck cost.* How do we minimize the bottleneck cost per query (i.e., the max of the bandwidth and computation) while achieving scalability in server space? This setting is particularly of relevance when storage is relatively cheap and we want to optimize the query response times, subject to being scalable.

Below, we state our main results for these three settings. Unless otherwise stated, the notation $\widetilde{O}(\cdot)$ hides polylogarithmic dependences on n and S. We also omit $O(\log S/\log n)$ terms in the exponent of n since typically $S = n^{o(1)}$.

Theorem 1 (Informal: equal scaling setting). *There exists an information-theoretic preprocessing S-server PIR scheme where each query incurs* $\widetilde{O}(n^{O(1/\log S)})$ *per-server bandwidth and computation, and* $\widetilde{O}(S \cdot n^{O(1/\log S)})$ *client computation, while requiring* $\widetilde{O}(n^{1+O(1/\log S)})$ *per-server space.*

Theorem 2 (Informal: minimizing bandwidth subject to scalable). *There is an information-theoretic preprocessing S-server PIR scheme where each query incurs* $n^{\tilde{O}(1/S)}$ *per-server bandwidth,* $n^{O(1/\log\log S)}$ *per-server computation,* $\tilde{O}(S \cdot n^{O(1/\log\log S)})$ *server computation while requiring* $n^{1+O(\log\log\log S/\log\log S)}$ *server space.*

Theorem 3 (Informal: minimizing bottleneck cost subject to scalable). *There is an information-theoretic preprocessing S-server PIR scheme where each query incurs* $n^{\tilde{O}(1/S^{1/\omega(1)})}$ *per-server bandwidth and computation,* $S \cdot n^{\tilde{O}(1/S^{1/\omega(1)})}$ *client computation while requiring* $n^{1+\tilde{O}(1/S^{1/\omega(1)})+O(\log\log n \cdot \omega(1)/\log S)}$ *server space. In the above, we abuse the notation* $\omega(1)$ *to mean an arbitrarily small super-constant function in* n.

Relation to Doubly-Efficient. In the literature [30,33], it is customary to use the term *doubly efficient* to describe a PIR scheme that achieves $n^{o(1)}$ bandwidth and computation per query, and $n^{1+o(1)}$ server space where $o(1)$ denotes any function that goes to 0 as n goes to infinity. Therefore, in Theorem 1 and Theorem 2, we achieve the notion of doubly efficient as long as S is a super-constant function in n. In Theorem 3, we would satisfy doubly efficient as long as S is super-polylogarithmic in n.

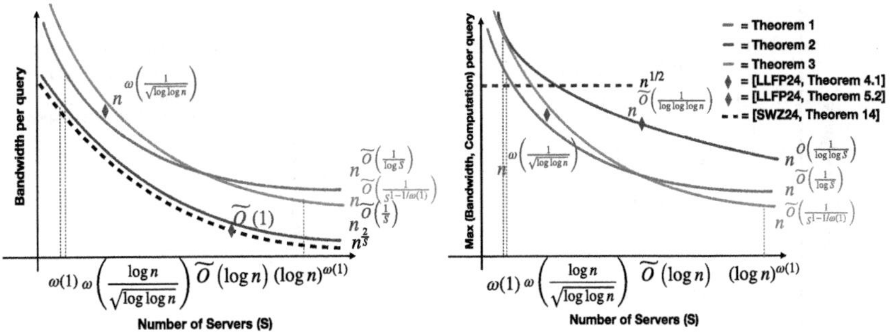

Fig. 1. Left: Graph comparing the bandwidth of our doubly efficient constructions with other multi-server preprocessing PIR schemes. **Right**: Graph comparing the online bottleneck of our doubly efficient constructions with other multi-server preprocessing PIR schemes. (Color figure online)

Graphical Illustration. To aid understanding, we plot the above results (Theorems 1 to 3), in Fig. 1. For each curve, the vertical dotted line shows when the corresponding scheme becomes doubly efficient. In this figure, we also compare with two concurrent works:

- The first construction of Lazzaretti et al. [30, Theorem 4.1] scheme is shown in Fig. 1 as the blue ♦, meaning that they are a special case of our Theorem 3. The second construction of Lazzaretti et al. [30, Theorem 5.2] scheme is shown in Fig. 1 as the purple ♦, meaning that our construction in Theorem 1 can achieve lower bandwidth and online bottleneck cost using fewer servers.
- The scheme of Singh et al. [44] is shown as the dashed black curves in Fig. 1. As mentioned earlier, their scheme does not achieve scalability in terms of computation per query, and this is why the dashed black curve in Fig. 1 (right) is a horizontal line. While all other schemes in Fig. 1 adopt server-side preprocessing, Singh et al. adopts client-side preprocessing where each client must separately participate in a preprocessing protocol with the servers during a subscription phase. As a result, Singh et al. removes the need for additional server space, at the cost of requiring approximately $n^{1/2}$ space on each client.

1.2 Additional Results and Contributions

Improved Results for the Poly-Space Setting. While our paper focuses on scalable families of PIR schemes, the previous literature on preprocessing PIR [5,46] instead asked what is the minimal bandwidth we can achieve subject to polynomial server space. We refer to this setting as the *poly-space setting.*

Our techniques for achieving scalable PIR also enable us to advance the state of the art in the poly-space setting. Specifically, we can improve the server space of Beimel et al. by a polynomial factor while approximately matching their bandwidth and computation, as stated in the following theorem.

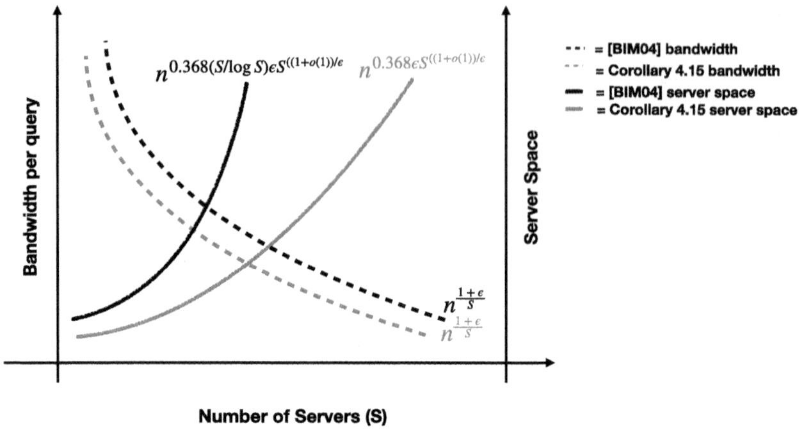

Fig. 2. Graph comparing the bandwidth and space of our polynomial space setting scheme with [5].

Theorem 4 (Informal: the poly-space setting). *For sufficiently large S, n, and sufficiently small $\epsilon > 0$, there exists an S-server PIR scheme where each query incurs $\widetilde{O}(n^{(1+\epsilon)/S})$ per-server bandwidth and computation, and $\widetilde{O}(n^{(1+\epsilon)/S} \cdot S)$ client computation, while requiring $n^{0.368\epsilon S^{(1+o(1))/\epsilon}}$ per-server space.*

In Fig. 2, we compare our scheme in the poly-space setting with that of Beimel et al. [5]. Specifically, their server space is an $S/\log S$-factor worse *in the exponent.* Further, with the same framework and different choice of parameters, we can also match the scheme with polylogarithmically many servers of Beimel et al. [5]. In Table 1, we compare the concrete efficiency of our schemes in Theorem 1, Theorem 4 and the scheme of [5, Theorem 4.3].

Table 1. Comparison of concrete efficiency of our schemes with [5, Theorem 4.3]. The numbers represent the exponent of n ignoring additive $o(1)$ factors, e.g., 0.75 means $n^{0.75+o(1)}$.

S	Theorem 1		Theorem 4		[5, Theorem 4.3]	
	Comm./Work	Storage	Comm./Work	Storage	Comm./Work	Storage
2	0.6824	1.6824	0.75	1.7735	0.75	1.7735
4	0.4541	1.4541	0.375	3.7832	0.375	5.4874
6	0.4063	1.4063	0.25	8.0230	0.25	14.0940
10	0.3258	1.3258	0.15	19.9255	0.15	51.5976
16	0.2725	1.2725	0.09	47.8135	0.09	179.0431

A Generic Balancing Technique. In all schemes mentioned so far, the download bandwidth is significantly larger than the upload bandwidth. We devise a generic technique for balancing these two costs, which reduces the total bandwidth at the cost of increased server computation. Our new balancing theorem differs in nature from the standard balancing theorem from prior literature [12]—the prior version focuses on the opposite scenario, where the upload bandwidth exceeds the download bandwidth.

Our balancing theorem is remotely related to a balancing technique described in the elegant work of Woodruff and Yekhanin [46] The main difference is that their balancing technique is tightly coupled with their specific PIR construction, and does not easily generalize. By contrast, we devise novel techniques and derive a balancing theorem that applies to *any* PIR scheme.

As an implication of this new balancing technique, we can obtain an improved 2-server PIR scheme as stated in the following theorem:

Theorem 5 (Informal: improved 2-server PIR in the poly-space setting). *Let $\epsilon \in (0,1)$ be an arbitrarily small constant. There exists an information-theoretic 2-server PIR scheme with $n^{(1+\epsilon)/3}$ bandwidth and $n^{(2+\epsilon)/3}$ computation per query, while requiring a polynomial amount of server space.*

Theorem 5 almost matches the $O(n^{1/3})$ bandwidth achieved by Woodruff and Yekhanin [46], but we significantly improve their computation cost, from $n/\mathsf{poly}\log n$ to $n^{(2+\epsilon)/3}$. There is also evidence indicating potential barriers to further bandwidth improvements. Specifically, Razborov and Yakhanin showed that $n^{1/3}$ bandwidth is optimal for a natural class of bilinear and group-based 2-server PIR schemes [41]. To date, with the exception of Dvir and Gopi [16], all known 2-server PIR schemes (in all settings) satisfy this natural characterization, including this paper.

2 Technical Roadmap

2.1 Equal Scaling in All Dimensions from Multiplicity Codes

We first construct a family of multi-server PIR schemes from *multiplicity codes* and show how to parameterize the construction to get a PIR scheme where the bandwidth, server computation and space scale at the same rate. This scheme is doubly efficient when the number of servers is superconstant.

Background: Multiplicity Codes. Multiplicity codes, introduced by Kopparty et al. [28], are a family of locally correctable codes (hence, also locally decodable codes) based on evaluations of polynomials and their derivatives. Multiplicity codes use *Hasse derivatives* which do not vanish even within a small field. A codeword for multiplicity code is obtained by evaluating an m-variate polynomial $F \in \mathbb{F}_q[X_1, \dots, X_m]$ (where q is a prime or a prime power) of total degree at most d, along with all its derivatives of order $< t$, at all points in $\mathbb{F}_m^q$. In the context of locally decodable codes, the desired properties are for it to be locally decodable with a *low number of queries*, and for it to have *high rate* and *high minimum distance*. A code is k-query locally decodable if there is an algorithm that given a codeword, can recover the i-th bit of an n-bit message for any $i \in [\![n]\!]$[1] by querying the codeword at k locations (for multiplicity codes one location of the codeword is the evaluation of F and all its derivatives at one point in $\mathbb{F}_q^m$). The rate of a code is the ratio between the length of a message and a codeword. High rate means that the length of a codeword is close to the length of a message. Minimum distance is defined as the minimum number of locations two codewords differ in. High minimum distance means that the code can correct a large fraction of errors. For multiplicity codes, setting $m = O(1)$ and $t > m^2 = O(1)$ makes them n^ϵ-query locally decodable, for some constant ϵ. Moreover, these parameters achieve constant rate and constant minimum distance. This has been the regime of interest in prior works [27,28,47] on multiplicity codes.

From Multiplicity Codes to PIR. Our goal is to construct a scalable family of S-server PIR scheme with global preprocessing using multiplicity codes of order-t evaluations of degree-d polynomials in m variables over $\mathbb{F}_q$. We encode the database DB into an m-variate polynomial F with degree d, i.e., we let $E : [\![n]\!] \to \mathbb{F}_q^m$ be the injective mapping that maps elements in $[\![n]\!]$ to their q-ary representation of length m and then using polynomial interpolation find F such that $F(E(i)) = \mathsf{DB}[i]$ for all $i \in [\![n]\!]$. Now suppose the client wants to query the database at index i such that $E(i) = \vec{u}$. The client chooses a random $\vec{v} \in \mathbb{F}_q^m$ and *distinct* and *non-zero* field elements $\lambda_0, \ldots, \lambda_{S-1}$ and sends $\vec{u} + \lambda_s \vec{v}$ to each server s where $s \in [\![S]\!]$. Each server returns to the client the value of F and all the Hasse derivatives up to order $t - 1$ evaluated at the point it received.

Define $f(\lambda) = F(\vec{u} + \lambda\vec{v})$. Now, the client can compute the Hasse derivates of f up to order $t-1$ denoted from the servers' answers using a modified version of the chain rule. Then, using *Hermite interpolation of Hasse derivatives* [7,21], the client can recover $f(0) = F(\vec{u}) = F(E(i)) = \mathsf{DB}[i]$.

In order for the above PIR construction to work, certain constraints involving the parameters m, q, d, t, S need to be satified. We list them below.

- For the encoding E to exist, we need $q^m \geq n$.
- For the polynomial F to interpolate DB, F needs at least n monomials. This entails that $\binom{m+d}{m} \geq n$.
- To make sure S distinct non-zero points are in $\mathbb{F}_q$, we need $q \geq S + 1$.
- For the Hermite interpolation to work, we need that $t \cdot S > d$.

If the multiplicity code is S-query local, and satisfies these constraints, the construction that we outline above is an S-server PIR. The rate of the multiplicity code determines the server storage, i.e., the server storage will be n times the inverse of the rate. The minimum distance of the multiplicity code does not affect any parameter of the PIR because we do not need error correction.

If we directly use parameters for multiplicity codes similar to those used in the coding theory literature (e.g., [27,28,47]), i.e., set $m = O(1)$ and $t = O(1)$,

[1] For any $n \in \mathbb{N}$, $[\![n]\!]$ denotes the set $\{0, 1, \ldots, n-1\}$.

we would get an $\Omega(n^{\epsilon})$-server PIR for any constant $\epsilon > 0$. As a PIR scheme, the number of servers is too large and thus this parameter regime is of little interest. Moreover, since we can accept polynomial server storage and do not care about error correction, we can use multiplicity codes with low rate and minimum distance close to zero. Therefore, PIR asks for a different parameter regime than the standard coding theory literature.

In order to set the parameters, q, m, d, t let us first describe how the performance of the PIR construction is affected by these parameters (we show the detailed calculation of these parameters in Sect. 4.2).

- The upload bandwidth is $O(m \log q)$, while the download bandwidth is $O\left(\binom{m+t-1}{t-1} \log q\right)$. The latter is larger since $t \geq 1$ and therefore dominates.
- The server computation is $O\left(\binom{m+t-1}{t-1} \log q\right)$.
- The client computation is $O\left(S \cdot \binom{m+t-1}{t-1} \cdot m \cdot \mathsf{poly}\log q\right) + O(\mathsf{poly}(d, \log q))$. The first term comes from the client's chain rule computation and the latter from the Hermite interpolation.
- The server storage is $O\left(\binom{m+t-1}{t-1} \cdot q^m \log q\right)$.
- The preprocessing time is $O\left(\binom{m+t-1}{t-1} \cdot q^m \cdot m \cdot \mathsf{poly}\log q\right)$.

Parameter Setting for Equal Scaling. We now set our parameters for this construction making server space, computation and bandwidth at equal rates as S grows.

- Since q^m appears in both storage and preprocessing time, and we have the constraint $q^m \geq n$, we will set $m = \lceil \log n / \log q \rceil$, the smallest possible value of m satisfying this inequality.
- For setting d, we will again choose smallest possible value that we can show satisfies $\binom{m+d}{m} \geq n$. We want to minimize this because $\mathsf{poly}(d, q)$ appears in the client computation time, and we want to reduce it.
  Note that $\binom{m+d}{m} \geq ((m+d)/m)^m$ and we have set m such that $q^m \geq n$. So, it suffices to satisfy $(m+d)/m \geq q$. We choose $d = (q-1) \cdot m$.
- Now we set q, t. We want to minimize t because $\binom{m+t-1}{m}$ grows as t grows (after we fix m). We need to satisfy the constraint $t \cdot S > d = (q-1) \cdot m$, i.e., $t > ((q-1) \cdot m)/S$. Now, the minimum value of q is $S+1$ because we need S non-zero distinct field elements $\lambda_0, \ldots, \lambda_{S-1}$ to exist. For simplicity, we assume $S+1$ is a prime or prime power for now, and set $q = S+1$ because minimizing q minimizes S. Then, we set $t = m+1$, which is the minimum value of t satisfying the aforementioned constraint.

Formally, with precise calculations where we do not assume S is a prime or a prime power, we get the following theorem.

Theorem 6. *For any S, there exists an S-server PIR scheme which achieves $O(n^{2/(\log S-1)} \log S)$ per-server bandwidth, $O(n^{2/(\log S-1)} \log S)$ per-server computation and $O(n^{2/(\log S-1)} S \log n \cdot \mathsf{poly}\log S)$ client computation per query, with $O(n^{1+2/(\log S-1)} \cdot S \cdot \mathsf{poly}\log n)$ preprocessing time and server storage.*

The details are in Sect. 4.3, and a simplified version of the theorem is stated in Theorem 1. Notice that all the per server parameters decrease with the increase in the number of servers, i.e., the scheme is scalable. Further, as long as $S = \omega(1)$, our construction is doubly efficient.

2.2 Minimizing Bandwidth Subject to Scalability

Many prior works on PIR [9,10,16,20,31,32] viewed bandwidth as the primary performance metric. In the equal-scaling scheme of Sect. 2.1, the bandwidth scales as $n^{O(1/\log S)}$. In comparison, prior works [5] showed that if we forgo scalability in the server space, the bandwidth can scale as fast as $n^{O(1/S)}$. Therefore, a meaningful question is how to minimize the bandwidth while subject to scalability.

Unfortunately, relying solely on multiplicity codes appears to limit us to a bandwidth of $n^{O(1/\log S)}$ if we require scalability in all dimensions. Specifically, there is a direct tradeoff between the bandwidth and server space, such that further reducing bandwidth would lead to a super-polynomial blowup in server space. To achieve further bandwidth reduction, we need to make m larger, which in turn allows for smaller choices of d and t. As a result, the dominant term in the bandwidth expression, $\binom{m+t-1}{t-1}$, decreases. Unfortunately, increasing m beyond $\log n/\log q$ would cause the server space (related to q^m) to become super-polynomial

To overcome this dilemma, we turn to polynomial preprocessing algorithms. Intuitively, these algorithms make more efficient use of the server space while still preserving the ability to perform fast evaluation by storing some specialized data structures whose size is much smaller than q^m. This way we can set m to be larger without making the server space superpolynomial in n.

Here, we specifically use the polynomial preprocessing algorithm from [6] which has the following guarantee: Consider a m-variate polynomial $F \in \mathbb{F}_q[X_1, \ldots, X_m]$ of *individual degree* d'—this means total degree $d \leq m \cdot d'$:

- There is an algorithm $\mathsf{Preprocess}$ that takes as input the polynomial F, runs in time $O((16 \cdot d' \cdot (\log d' + \log\log q))^m \cdot \mathsf{poly}\log(m, d', q)$ and produces a data structure $\widetilde{F}$ of size $O((16 \cdot d' \cdot (\log d' + \log\log q))^m \cdot \mathsf{poly}\log(m, d', q)$.
- Given any $\vec{x} \in \mathbb{F}_q^m$, $\widetilde{F}(\vec{x}) = F(\vec{x})$, evaluating $\widetilde{F}$ takes time $O(16^m \cdot \mathsf{poly}\log(m, d', q))$.

The servers use the above polynomial preprocessing algorithm to preprocess F and its Hasse derivatives and store the data structures. When the query is made the servers use the stored data structures to compute their answers.

We set the parameters as follows: $m \approx \log n/\log\log q, q = S + 1, d' \approx \log q$ (this makes total degree $d \approx m \log q$), $t \approx m \log q/S$, the storage is not super-polynomial in n for superconstant S. It is easy to see that these parameters satisfy the constraints. Further m is much larger than t, so $\binom{m+t-1}{t-1} \approx (m/t)^t \approx (S/\log S)^{\log n \cdot \log S/(S \log\log S)} \approx n^{\widetilde{O}(1/S)}$. Therefore, the bandwidth scales as $n^{\widetilde{O}(1/S)}$. Moreover, 16^m is $n^{O(1/\log\log S)}$, $(d')^m$ is roughly n, $(\log d' + \log\log q)^m$ is

$n^{O(\log\log\log S/\log\log S)}$. Thus the total storage is $n^{1+O(\log\log\log S/\log\log S)}$. Moreover, the server computation is dominated by the $16^m \cdot \binom{m+t-1}{t-1}$ term becomes $n^{\tilde{O}(1/S)+O(1/\log\log S)}$. As already discussed earlier, the bandwidth scales as $n^{\tilde{O}(1/S)}$. Hence, the construction is also doubly efficient for any S superconstant in n.

Above, we used rough approximations in several places as indicated by the $\approx$ signs. With precise rounding and exact inequalities, we get the following theorem in Sect. 5.

Theorem 7. *There is an S-server PIR scheme which achieves the following parameters.*

- *per-server bandwidth* $n^{O\left(\frac{\log^2 S}{S\log\log S}\right)+O\left(\frac{\log S}{\log n}\right)} \cdot \mathsf{poly}\log(n,S)$,
- *per-server computation* $n^{O\left(\frac{\log^2 S}{S\log\log S}\right)+O\left(\frac{1}{\log\log S}\right)+O\left(\frac{\log S}{\log n}\right)} \cdot \mathsf{poly}\log(n,S)$,
- *client computation* $n^{O\left(\frac{\log^2 S}{S\log\log S}\right)+O\left(\frac{\log S}{\log n}\right)} \cdot \mathsf{poly}\log(n,S)$,
- *per-server preprocessing time and storage*

$$n^{1+O\left(\frac{\log^2 S}{S\log\log S}\right)+O\left(\frac{\log\log\log S}{\log\log S}\right)+O\left(\frac{\log S}{\log n}\right)} \cdot \mathsf{poly}\log(n,S)\,.$$

A simpler version of this theorem was stated in Theorem 2.

Details on the Polynomial Data Structure. We briefly sketch the polynomial preprocessing algorithm that we use here. This algorithm in [6] which is an improvement on the fast polynomial evaluation algorithm from [25] that has been previously used in PIR constructions (e.g., [33]).

Let F be a m-variate polynomial with *individual degree* d' over $\mathbb{Z}_q$. Given $\vec{x} \in \mathbb{Z}_q^m$, we want to evaluate $F(\vec{x})$ fast. It is easy to see that since F has at most $(d'+1)^m$ monomials and the maximum value of a monomial is $(q-1)\cdot(q-1)^{md'}$, the maximum value of F over $\mathbb{Z}$ is $M = (q-1)^{md'+1}\cdot(d'+1)^m$. In the algorithm in [25] the idea is to compute primes $p_1, p_2, \ldots, p_k : \prod_{j\in[k]} p_j > M$ where $p_1 < p_2 < \ldots < p_k$. We know that we can find primes such that $p_k = O(\log M) = O(md'\log q)$. Then the algorithm stores all evaluations of $F(\vec{x}) \bmod p_j$ for all $\vec{x} \in \mathbb{Z}_{p_j}^m$ for all $j \in [k]$. In the online phase in order to compute $F(\vec{x})$, the algorithm looks up $F(\vec{x}) \bmod p_j$ for all $j \in [k]$ and uses the Chinese Remainder Theorem to compute $F(\vec{x})$ from these values. Storing all the evaluations of $F(\vec{x}) \bmod p_j$ for all $\vec{x} \in \mathbb{Z}_{p_j}^m$ for all $j \in [k]$ requires space $O(p_j^m) = O((md'\log q)^m)$. By using recursion to instead compute the values of $F(\vec{x}) \bmod p_j$ by decomposing p_j into smaller primes can make the $(\log q)^m$ factor reduce to $(\log\log q)^m$, but does not get rid of the m^m factor.

In [6], the idea is to instead find primes $p_1, p_2, \ldots, p_k : \prod_{j\in[k]} p_j^m > M$. Here, we can find these primes such that $p_j = O((\log M)/m) = O(d'\log q)$. Now, if we store all the evaluations $F(\vec{x}) \bmod p_j^m$ for all $j \in [k]$, for all $\vec{x} \in \mathbb{Z}_{p_j^m}^m$, the total storage is $O(p_j^{m^2})$, which is significantly worse than above! So, the key observation in [6] is that over $\mathbb{Z}_{p_j^m}$, the evaluation of an m-variate polynomial

F at a point $\vec{x}$ can be derived from the evaluations of the Hasse derivatives of F upto order m at another point $\vec{y}$ such that the co-ordinates of $\vec{x} - \vec{y}$ are multiples of p_j. So, it just suffices to compute the evaluations of F and its Hasse derivatives upto order m at a certain subset of $\mathbb{Z}_{p_j^m}^m$ whose size is p_j^m. This helps us get rid of the m^m factor from the storage. It however turns out, just doing this is not yet enough for the result we want. We need to again recursively compute $F(\vec{y}) \bmod p_j^m$ by again decomposing p_j into even smaller primes. That suffices to get the parameters we want for our PIR construction.

2.3 Minimizing Bottleneck Cost Subject to Scalability

In Sect. 2.2, while the bandwidth scales as $n^{\tilde{O}(1/S)}$, the online server computation is the online bottleneck and scales only as $n^{\tilde{O}(1/S)+O(1/\log\log S)}$. The server computation is also a part of the online bottleneck along with the bandwidth. So it is another natural question to minimize the online bottleneck cost subject to the construction being scalable.

To minimize the online bottleneck cost, the bandwidth and the server computation need to scale at a similar rate asymptotically. In the construction in Sect. 2.2 this was not possible because the server computation time included the time needed for evaluation of the polynomial data structure which was significantly larger than the bandwidth. To get around that, we instead need to use a polynomial preprocessing algorithm that has much faster evaluation at the cost of using more space.

So, we turn to the polynomial preprocessing algorithm from [25] which trades time off for more space compared to the algorithm in [6]. Concretely, for the algorithm in [25], the storage is $(md'(\log m + \log d' + \log\log q))^m \cdot \mathsf{poly}\log(m, d', \log q)$ and the evaluation time is $\mathsf{poly}\log(m, d', \log q)$. Since the online time is not exponential in m using this polynomial preprocessing algorithm would allow us to set parameters such that server computation time scales at a similar rate than the bandwidth. This was not possible when we used the scheme from [6] because the server computation had a 16^m term and $m \geq \log n/\log q$.

Here we choose $q = S + 1$ and $m \approx \log n \cdot \omega(1)/\log q$ where $\omega(1)$ is some superconstant function in n and it is in $o(\log n)$. We set $d' \approx S^{1/\omega(1)}$ which ensures $\binom{m+m\cdot d'}{m} \geq n$ and $t = \theta(m \cdot d'/S)$ which ensures $t \cdot S > m \cdot d'$.

This makes $\binom{m+t-1}{t-1} \approx (m/t)^t = O(S^{1-1/\omega(1)})^{\log n \cdot \omega(1)/S^{1-\omega(1)}} \approx n^{\tilde{O}(1/S^{1-\omega(1)})}$. This binomial coefficient is the dominating term in bandwidth and computation, and therefore the online bottleneck scales as $n^{\tilde{O}(1/S^{1-\omega(1)})}$. Furthermore, $m^m \approx n^{O(\log\log n \cdot \omega(1)/\log S)}$, $(d')^m \approx n$ and $(\log d' + \log m + \log\log q) \approx n^{O(\log\log n \cdot \omega(1)/\log S)}$. The term $n^{O(\log\log n \cdot \omega(1)/\log S)}$ becomes $n^{o(1)}$ when S is superpolylogarithmic in n, making the storage $n^{1+o(1)}$.

Above, we used rough approximations in several places as indicated by the $\approx$ signs. With precise rounding and exact inequalities, we get the following theorem in Sect. 5.

Theorem 8. *Let $\omega(1)$ be any superconstant function such that it is in $o(\log n)$. There is an S-server PIR scheme which achieves the following parameters.*

- *per-server bandwidth* $n^{\tilde{O}\left(\frac{1}{S^{1/\omega(1)}}\right)+O\left(\frac{\log S}{\log n}\right)} \cdot \mathsf{poly}\log(n) \cdot \log S$,
- *per-server computation* $n^{\tilde{O}\left(\frac{1}{S^{1/\omega(1)}}\right)+O\left(\frac{\log S}{\log n}\right)} \cdot \mathsf{poly}\log(n, S)$,
- *client computation* $n^{\tilde{O}\left(\frac{1}{S^{1/\omega(1)}}\right)+O\left(\frac{\log S}{\log n}\right)} \cdot \mathsf{poly}\log(n, S)$,
- *per-server preprocessing time and storage*

$$n^{1+\tilde{O}\left(\frac{1}{S^{1/\omega(1)}}\right)+O\left(\frac{\log S}{\log n}\right)+O\left(\frac{\log\log n \cdot \omega(1)}{\log S}\right)} \cdot \mathsf{poly}\log(n, S)\ .$$

A simpler version of this theorem was stated in Theorem 3.

2.4 Additional Results for the Poly-Space Setting

We next consider the setting considered in earlier works [5,46] where we focus on optimizing the bandwidth while allowing the server space to grow with respect to S as long as the server space is still polynomially bounded.

We slightly optimize our construction from Sect. 2.1 to improve the parameters for the PIR scheme. Compared to our scalable PIR family construction, here we choose a different kind of polynomial F than standard multiplicity code. Specifically we want F to be homogenous and *multi-linear*, i.e., all monomials in F have d variables and each variable has exponent one. Our encoding works as follows: we construct an injective mapping E which maps each element in $[\![n]\!]$ to an element of $\{0,1\}^m$ of hamming weight exactly d. For such a mapping to exist, we need $\binom{m}{d} \geq n$. Then we define an m-variate *multilinear homogeneous* polynomial F of degree d that satisfies $F(E(i)) = \mathsf{DB}[i]$. This makes our definition of F the same as that of Woodruff and Yekhanin [46]. We then encode the database with a multiplicity code for the polynomial F evaluated to order $< t$.

We adopt a new query and reconstruction algorithm that differs from both standard multiplicity code as well as Woodruff and Yekhanin [46]. Say the client wants to query the database at index i such that $E(i) = \vec{u}$. The client chooses a random $\vec{v} \in \mathbb{F}_q^m$. In the scalable construction the client chose S distinct non-zero field elements λ_s and sends $\vec{u} + \lambda_s \vec{v}$ to server s for $s \in [\![S]\!]$. In contrast, here we make the client choose S distinct field elements λ_s for $s \in [\![S]\!]$, but do not require all of them to be non-zero. The client sends $\lambda_s \vec{u} + \vec{v}$ to server S in this case. We can let one of the λ_s's be zero since it does not leak $\vec{u}$. This allows us to set the field size $q = S$ (assuming S is a prime, we describe the general case in the full version). This optimization helps us reduce the field size by 1 (i.e., in the scalable constructed we needed $q \geq S+1$), and since the server storage has a q^m multiplicative term, this helps us reduce the server storage by a polynomial factor.

The servers return the evaluations and all derivatives up to order $t-1$ of F at the point it received to the client. We define $f(\lambda) = F(\lambda\vec{u} + \vec{v})$. Again, the client can compute the Hasse derivates of f up to order $t-1$. Then, using *Hermite interpolation of Hasse derivatives* [7,21], the client can recover f. It turns out that the coefficient of λ^d in f is $\mathsf{DB}[i]$, which the client returns.

Here, in order to match the parameter setting in [5,46], we need to set $q = S$, $m = O(\log n)$, $d = \theta m$ for $0 \leq \theta \leq 1/2$ (we show that it is possible to choose such m, d satisfying $\binom{m}{d} \geq n$) and $t = \lceil (d+1)/S \rceil$. In Table 1, we show how this construction improves on the server space compared to [5]. Table 1 also shows how our optimization of choosing $\lambda_s \vec{u} + \vec{v}$ leads to savings in server space compared to the decoding strategy used for our scalable construction.

Remark 1 (Comparision with [46]*).* While our definition of F is same as that Woodruff and Yekhanin [46], because of their use of normal derivatives, they need to set $q > d$. Therefore, they cannot use a parameter regime like ours where $m = O(\log n), d = O(\log n)$. Instead, they use $q = S + 1, d = S, m = O(dn^{1/d})$. This makes q^m superpolynomial in n and hence their preprocessing cannot store all the evaluations and partial derivatives of F at q^m points. So, they devise a different preprocessing strategy tailored to their construction.

Further, we introduce a new balancing trick and apply it to our construction in the polynomial server space setting to generalize this construction. Using the balancing trick we can achieve a scheme where the per-server bandwidth is $n^{(1+\epsilon)/(S+1)}$, and the per-server computation is $n^{(2+\epsilon)/(S+1)}$.

We provide the details of our construction in the polynomial space setting in the full version.

2.5 A New Balancing Technique

Finally, we give an overview of our new balancing technique. Recall that for the 2-server setting, Beimel et al. [5] can achieve $n^{1/2+\varepsilon}$ bandwidth and computation per query, whereas Woodruff and Yekhanin [46] can compress the bandwidth to $n^{1/3+\varepsilon}$ but as a tradeoff, their server computation increases abruptly to $n/\mathsf{poly}\log n$ which is only slightly sublinear. An interesting question is whether we can further reduce the bandwidth while trading off computation in a more graceful manner. For example, for the special case of 2 servers, can we match the $n^{1/3+\varepsilon}$ bandwidth of Woodruff and Yekhanin but still achieve n^{δ} server computation for some constant $\delta \in (0,1)$?

To answer the above questions, we describe a new balancing trick that allows us to enable a smooth tradeoff curve between bandwidth and computation. This allows us to generalize the design space for multi-server PIR. Given a (preprocessing) PIR scheme whose upload and download bandwidths are asymmetric, we want to use a balancing trick to balance the two to minimize the bandwidth.

Naïve Balancing. In Lemma 4.4 of Beimel et al. [5], they cite a naïve balancing trick originally proposed by Chor et al. [12]. However, this naïve trick is tailored for the case when the original PIR scheme has more upload bandwidth than download bandwidth. The idea is as follows. Suppose we have a database of n bits. We can divide it into $B := n^{1-\mu}$ blocks each of length n^{μ} for some appropriate $\mu \in (0,1)$. Now, to retrieve some index $i \in [\![n]\!]$ of the database that lies in block $r := \lfloor i/n^{\mu} \rfloor$, we run a separate PIR instance to retrieve the (i mod n^{μ})-th bit of each block, treating each block as a separate database of n^{μ} size. Further, all blocks may share the same query vector; however, the server needs to send a separate response for each block. Therefore, if the original PIR scheme has $\alpha(n)$ upload bandwidth and $\beta(n)$ download bandwidth for a database of size n, then the balanced scheme would have $\alpha(n^{\mu})$ upload bandwidth, and $n^{1-\mu} \cdot \beta(n^{\mu})$ download bandwidth. This naïve balancing trick works the best if the original PIR scheme has higher upload bandwidth than download bandwidth.

Unfortunately, Beimel et al. [5]'s preprocessing PIR scheme as well as our improved version have the opposite behavior: the upload bandwidth is asymptotically smaller than the download bandwidth. In this case, this naïve balancing trick cannot reduce the bandwidth. Take their 2-serer scheme as an example: recall that it achieves $n^{(1+\epsilon)/2}$ computation and bandwidth per query. Suppose we now divide the database into $B := n^{1/3}$ blocks each of size $n^{2/3}$. Applying this balancing trick, the new bandwidth and computation per query becomes $n^{(1+\epsilon)/3} \cdot n^{1/3} = n^{(2+\epsilon)/3}$ which is worse than before.

New Balancing Technique: First Attempt. We propose a new balancing trick for the case when the original PIR has higher download bandwidth than upload bandwidth. The idea is still to divide the database into blocks. However, we now want to aggregate the answers for all blocks rather than the queries for all blocks to save the download bandwidth. To understand our idea, it helps to first think of the following flawed attempt. Suppose that all S servers use the same deterministic algorithm to answer queries. We will have the client send to each server an honestly constructed query for the relevant block r that contains the desired index, and for all non-relevant blocks, the client sends the *same* random query to all S servers. Each server computes the summation mod S of the answers of all blocks. Now, for each non-relevant block, all servers have the same answer, so they cancel out under summation mod S. Unfortunately, with this scheme, the client could only get the summation (mod S) of all answers for the relevant block r too, and it is not clear how the client can reconstruct the correct answer—specifically, to correctly recover the answer using the underlying PIR scheme, the client would need to know all S answers for the relevant block r. Likely for this exact reason, Woodruff and Yekhanin [46] came up with their own non-blackbox balancing trick that is tightly coupled with their scheme. However, their particular instantiation requires a large field size and this is one reason why they cannot achieve tighter server space and preprocessing cost.

Our Idea. Unlike Woodruff and Yekhanin [46], we salvage the above flawed attempt and devise a general balancing trick for any "natural" (preprocessing) PIR scheme whose upload bandwidth is smaller than download bandwidth. Specifically, we modify the this flawed approach such that all non-relevant cancel out while still ensuring that the client can recover all S answers for the relevant block r.

The intuition is as follows. The n-bit database is divided into $B = n^{1-\mu}$ blocks each of size n^{μ} for some appropriate $\mu \in (0, 1)$. Suppose the desired index i lies in the r-th block. Then, the client will send real queries denoted $Q_{r,0}, \ldots, Q_{r,S-1}$ for the relevant block r to the S servers, and for every non-relevant block $j \neq r$, it will send the same random query denoted $Q_{j,0}$ to all S servers. Each server will compute the answers to all blocks. For each block's answer, the server will XOR it into one of two slots, called slot 0 and slot 1 respectively. The client signals to each server which slot to encode each block's answer by sending the server a random bit per block. Our construction guarantees the following invariants:

1. For the relevant block r, at least one server XORs the answer into slot 0, and at least one server XORs the answer into slot 1. In our actual construction, we simply make server 0 XOR it in a random slot b_r, and make all other servers XOR it in slot $1 - b_r$.
2. For each non-relevant blocks $j \neq r$, all servers XOR the answer of block j in the same random slot b_j.

This construction allows the client to recover all S answers for the relevant block r. Specifically, let J_b be the set of non-relevant blocks chosen for slot $b \in \{0, 1\}$. Suppose for some server $s \in [\![S]\!]$, the relevant block r's answer is XOR'ed into slot 0. Then, server s's response is of this form:

$$\left(\bigoplus_{j \in J_0} \mathsf{ans}_j\right) \bigoplus \mathsf{ans}_{r,s}, \quad \bigoplus_{j \in J_1} \mathsf{ans}_j \tag{1}$$

In the above, $\mathsf{ans}_{r,s}$ denotes server s's answer (of the underlying PIR scheme) for the relevant block r. Further, for $j \neq r$, ans_j denotes the answer for block j of the underlying PIR scheme—since all S servers have the same answer for each non-relevant block $j \neq r$, we omit the server index in the notation ans_j. Now, suppose there exists another server s' who XORs the relevant block r's answer into slot 1, then its response to the client is of the form

$$\bigoplus_{j \in J_0} \mathsf{ans}_j, \quad \left(\bigoplus_{j \in J_1} \mathsf{ans}_j\right) \bigoplus \mathsf{ans}_{r,s'}, \tag{2}$$

Clearly, we can recover both $\mathsf{ans}_{r,s}$ and $\mathsf{ans}_{r,s'}$ from Equation (1) and Equation (2). Specifically, this can be done by XORing the two servers' answers for the each of the two slots. Generalizing this, as long as the above two conditions are satisfied, the client can recover all S answers (of the underlying PIR) for the r-th block, denoted $\{\mathsf{ans}_{r,s}\}_{s \in [\![S]\!]}$. It can now call the underlying PIR's reconstruction algorithm to reconstruct the answer for the relevant block r.

Applying the Balancing Trick. Suppose we start with a scheme with $n^{(1+\epsilon)/S}$ bandwidth and computation and $\mathsf{poly}(S)$ preprocessing cost and server space such as Beimel et al. [5] or our new scheme with improved server space. We can apply this balancing trick by choosing $\mu = S \cdot \alpha$ for any $\alpha \in [1/(S+1), 1/S]$. The resulting scheme will enjoy $O(n^{(1+\epsilon)\alpha} \log S)$ per-server bandwidth, $n^{1-(S-1-\epsilon)\alpha}$

per-server computation, and the server space and preprocessing cost are still polynomially bounded. Specifically, if we take $\alpha = 1/(S+1)$, the upload and download bandwith will be balanced (up to $1+\epsilon$ factors in the exponent). In this case, the per-server bandwidth is minimized to $n^{(1+\epsilon)/(S+1)}$, and the per-server computation is $n^{(2+\epsilon)/(S+1)}$. We provide the details of our balancing technique in the full version.

3 Definitions: S-Server PIR with Global Preprocessing

We give a formal definition of an S-server information-theoretic PIR with global preprocessing. We index the servers by $0, 1, \ldots, S-1$.

Definition 1 (S-server PIR). An S-server PIR scheme consists of the following possibly randomized algorithms:

- $\widetilde{\mathsf{DB}}_s \leftarrow \mathbf{Preproc}_s(\mathsf{DB})$: given database $\mathsf{DB} \in \{0,1\}^n$, server $s \in [\![S]\!]$ calls this algorithm to do a one-time preprocessing and computes an encoding of the database denoted $\widetilde{\mathsf{DB}}_s$.
- $st, Q_0, \ldots, Q_{S-1} \leftarrow \mathbf{Query}(n, i)$: given the database size n and a query index $i \in [\![n]\!]$, the algorithm outputs some private state st as well as $Q_0, \ldots, Q_{S-1}$ representing the query messages to be sent to each of the S servers.
- $\mathbf{Answer}_s(\widetilde{\mathsf{DB}}_s, Q_s)$: given the encoded database $\widetilde{\mathsf{DB}}_s$ and a query message Q_s of server $s \in [\![S]\!]$, this algorithm outputs the response message ans_s;
- $\mathbf{Recons}(st, \mathsf{ans}_0, \ldots, \mathsf{ans}_{S-1})$: given the private state st and the responses $\mathsf{ans}_0, \ldots, \mathsf{ans}_{S-1}$ from all the servers, this algorithm reconstructs the answer $\mathsf{DB}[i]$.

The scheme should satisfy the following properties:

Correctness. Correctness requires that the client should output the correct answer under an honest execution. Formally, we want that for any n, $\mathbf{DB} \in \{0,1\}^n$ and $i \in [\![n]\!]$,

$$\Pr\left[\begin{array}{l}\forall s \in [\![S]\!] : \widetilde{\mathsf{DB}}_s \leftarrow \mathbf{Preproc}_s(\mathsf{DB}), \\ st, Q_0, \ldots, Q_{S-1} \leftarrow \mathbf{Query}(n, i), \\ \forall s \in [\![S]\!] : \mathsf{ans}_s \leftarrow \mathbf{Answer}_s(\widetilde{\mathsf{DB}}_s, Q_s)\end{array} : \mathbf{Recons}(st, \mathsf{ans}_0, \ldots, \mathsf{ans}_{S-1}) = \mathsf{DB}[i]\right] = 1$$

Security. Security requires that any individual server's view leaks nothing about the client's desired index. Formally, for any n, S, for any $i_1, i_2 \in [\![n]\!]$ and any $s \in [\![S]\!]$, the distributions $\{Q_s : (Q_0, \ldots, Q_{S-1}) \leftarrow \mathbf{Query}(n, i_1)\}$ and $\{Q_s : (Q_0, \ldots, Q_{S-1}) \leftarrow \mathbf{Query}(n, i_2)\}$, are identical.

Further, we say that a multi-server PIR scheme is *doubly efficient* if all these conditions hold.

- **Preproc**$_s$ runs time $n^{1+o(1)}$ for all $s \in [\![S]\!]$ and its output is of size $n^{1+o(1)}$ i.e., the preprocessing time and the server storage is $n^{1+o(1)}$.
- The combined runtime of **Query**, **Recons** is $n^{o(1)}$ i.e., the client computation per query is $n^{o(1)}$.
- The runtime of **Answer**$_s$ is $n^{o(1)}$ i.e., the server computation per query is $n^{o(1)}$.
- The sum of the size of the output of **Query** and the maximum size of the output of **Answers**$_s$ for $s \in [\![S]\!]$ is $n^{o(1)}$, i.e., the per server bandwidth per query is at most $n^{o(1)}$.

4 Preprocessing PIR from Multiplicity Codes

In this section, we introduce a framework to construct a family of server-side preprocessing PIR schemes from multiplicity codes. In Sect. 4.1, we give some preliminaries about multiplicity codes. In Sect. 4.2, we present our family of PIR schemes from multiplicity codes. The parameters of the PIR construction depends on the parameters of the multiplicity code. In Sect. 4.3, we show how to set the parameters to get a new scalable family of PIR schemes where the (per-server) bandwidth and computation per query as well as the server space scale with respect to the number of servers. This new scalable family also allows us to get a doubly efficient PIR scheme with only super-constant servers. In the full version, we present some further optimizations to our construction in order to optimize the bandwidth in the polynomial space setting.

4.1 Preliminaries on Multiplicity Codes

We define $A_{k,m}$ to be the set of all vectors of non-negative integers of length m and 1-norm exactly k:

$$A_{k,m} = \{\vec{a} \in \mathbb{N}^m : \mathsf{wt}(\vec{a}) = k\}$$

where $\mathsf{wt}(\vec{a}) = \vec{a}_1 + \ldots + \vec{a}_m$ denotes the 1-norm of the vector $\vec{a}$. Let $A_{<k,m} := A_{0,m} \cup A_{1,m} \ldots \cup A_{k-1,m}$.

Further, for $d \in \mathbb{N}$, we define $A_{k,m,d}$ to be the set of all vectors of length m whose entries are in $\{0, 1, \ldots, d\}$ and have 1-norm exactly k:

$$A_{k,m,d} = \{\vec{a} \in \{0, 1, \ldots, d\}^m : \mathsf{wt}(\vec{a}) = k\}$$

We $A_{<k,m,d} := A_{0,m,d} \cup A_{1,m,d} \ldots \cup A_{k-1,m,d}$.

Given $\vec{a} := (\vec{a}_1, \ldots, \vec{a}_m) \in \mathbb{N}^m$, and a polynomial F, we define the partial derivative operator $\boldsymbol{\partial}^{\vec{a}}$ as:

$$\boldsymbol{\partial}^{\vec{a}} \circ F := \frac{\partial^{\mathsf{wt}(\vec{a})} F}{\partial X_1^{\vec{a}_1} \ldots \partial X_m^{\vec{a}_m}}$$

Henceforth, given a vector $\vec{X} := (\vec{X}_1, \ldots, \vec{X}_m)$ of variables and a vector $\vec{a} := (\vec{a}_1, \ldots, \vec{a}_m)$ of exponents, we use the following vector exponentiation notation:

$$\vec{X}^{\vec{a}} := \prod_{k=1}^{m} \vec{X}_k^{\vec{a}_k}$$

Definition 2 (Hasse derivatives). For m-variate polynomial $F \in \mathbb{F}[X_1, \ldots, X_m]$ over the field $\mathbb{F}$, the Hasse derivative of f with respect to $\vec{a} = (\vec{a}_1, \ldots, \vec{a}_m) \in \mathbb{N}^m$ is defined as

$$\overline{\partial}^{\vec{a}} \circ F = \sum_{\vec{e}=(\vec{e}_1,\ldots,\vec{e}_m)\in\mathbb{N}^m} \prod_{i=1}^{m} \binom{\vec{a}_i}{\vec{e}_i} \cdot \mathsf{Coeff}_{X_1^{\vec{e}_1}\ldots X_m^{\vec{e}_m}}(F)\vec{X}^{\vec{a}-\vec{e}}$$

where $\mathsf{Coeff}_{X_1^{\vec{e}_1}\ldots X_m^{\vec{e}_m}}(F)$ denotes the coefficient of $X_1^{\vec{e}_1} \ldots X_m^{\vec{e}_m}$ in F.

Specifically, for a univariate degree-d polynomial $f(\lambda) = \sum_{k=0}^{d} c_k \cdot \lambda^k \in \mathbb{F}[\lambda]$, we omit the vector notation and denote its r-th Hasse derivative as $\overline{\partial}^{(r)} f(\lambda) = \overline{\partial}^{(r)} \circ f(\lambda) = \sum_{k=r}^{d} c_k \cdot \binom{k}{r} \lambda^{k-r}$. If the field $\mathbb{F}$ has characteristic 0, then $\overline{\partial}^{(r)} f(\lambda) = \frac{1}{r!} f^{(r)}(\lambda)$.

Chain Rule. Given a univariate polynomial $g \in \mathbb{F}[\lambda]$, we use $g^{(k)}$ to denote the k-th derivative of g, and we use $\overline{\partial}^{(k)} g$ to denote the k-th Hasse derivative of g. We will need to use the chain rule for higher-order derivatives. We first state the chain rule for normal derivatives which was used by Woodruff and Yekhanin's PIR scheme [46], and then state the version for Hasse derivates which is the version we will need.

Lemma 1 (Chain rule for normal derivatives). *For m-variate polynomial $f(X_1, \ldots, X_m)$ over field $\mathbb{F}$, $\vec{u}, \vec{v} \in \mathbb{F}^m$, and let $g(\lambda) = f(\vec{u} + \lambda\vec{v})$ be a univariate polynomial in λ, we have*

$$g^{(k)}(\lambda) = \sum_{l_1,\ldots,l_k\in[m]} \frac{\partial^k f}{\partial X_{l_1} \quad \partial X_{l_k}} (\vec{u} + \lambda\vec{v}) \prod_{i=1}^{k} \vec{v}_{l_i}.$$

In the above, the same partial derivative may appear multiple times in the summation depending on the order of the variables; however, in the chain rule for Hasse derivatives, the same partial derivative appears only once as stated below:

Lemma 2 (Chain rule for Hasse derivatives). *For m-variate polynomial $f(X_1, \ldots, X_m)$ over field $\mathbb{F}$, let $g(\lambda) = f(\vec{u} + \lambda\vec{v})$ be a univariate polynomial in λ, we have*

$$\overline{\partial}^{(k)} g(\lambda) = \sum_{\vec{a}=(\vec{a}_1,\ldots,\vec{a}_m)\in A_{k,m}} \overline{\partial}^{\vec{a}} \circ f(\vec{u} + \lambda\vec{v}) \cdot \vec{v}^{\vec{a}}$$

Specifically, when f is a multilinear polynomial (a multivariate polynomial with individual degree 1 in each variable), clearly $\overline{\partial}^{\vec{a}} \circ f = \boldsymbol{\partial}^{\vec{a}} \circ f$ for any $\vec{a} \in A_{k,m,1}$, therefore,

$$\overline{\partial}^{(k)} g(\lambda) = \sum_{\vec{a}=(\vec{a}_1,\ldots,\vec{a}_m)\in A_{k,m,1}} \boldsymbol{\partial}^{\vec{a}} \circ f(\vec{u} + \lambda\vec{v}) \cdot \vec{v}^{\vec{a}}$$

Hermite Interpolation. It is well-known that for a polynomial f over field with characteristic 0, given sufficiently many evaluations of f and higher-order (normal) derivatives of f at some points, it suffices to reconstruct f, known as Hermite interpolation. The same holds for Hasse derivatives, the difference is that Hasse derivative version works not only on field with characteristic 0, but also arbitrary finite fields:

Lemma 3 (Hermite interpolation of Hasse derivatives [7,21]**).** *Let f be an univariate polynomial of degree d over finite field $\mathbb{F}$, and m positive integers $e_1, \ldots, e_m$ such that $e_1 + \cdots + e_m > d$. Let $\alpha_1, \ldots, \alpha_m$ be distinct elements in $\mathbb{F}$. For all $i \in [m]$ and $j \in [e_i]$, let $\overline{\partial}^{(j-1)} f(\alpha_i) = y_{i,j}$. Then, the coefficients of f can be recovered from $\{(\alpha_i, j, y_{i,j})\}_{i\in[m],j\in[e_i]}$ in time $\mathsf{poly}(d, \log|\mathbb{F}|)$.*

Multiplicity Codes. Finally, we come to the definition of multiplicity codes. We use the definition from [28].

Definition 3 (Multiplicity Code [28]**).** Let t, d, m be non-negative integers and let q be a prime power. Let $\Sigma = \mathbb{F}_q^{\binom{m+t-1}{m}} = \mathbb{F}_q^{\{\vec{a}\in A_{<t,m}\}}$. For $F(X_1, \ldots, X_m) \in \mathbb{F}_q[X_1, \ldots, X_m]$ we define the order t evaluation of F at $\vec{x}$ to be the vector $(\overline{\partial}^{\vec{a}} \circ F(\vec{x}))_{\vec{a}\in A_{<t,m}}$. The multiplicity code of order-t evaluations of degree-d polynomials in m variables over $\mathbb{F}_q$ is defined as follows. The code is over alphabet Σ and has length q^m, where the coordinates are indexed by elements of $\mathbb{F}_q^m$. For each polynomial $F(\vec{X}) \in \mathbb{F}_q[X_1, \ldots, X_m]$ with $\deg(F) \leq d$, there is a codeword given by

$$\mathbf{Encode}_{t,d,m,q}(F) = \left((\overline{\partial}^{\vec{a}} \circ F(\vec{x}))_{\vec{a}\in A_{<t,m}}\right)_{\vec{x}\in\mathbb{F}_q^m}.$$

We will prove the following claim related to multiplicity codes of order-t evaluations of degree-d polynomials in m variables over $\mathbb{F}_q$ that will be useful later.

Claim 9. *Let $t, d, m > 0$ and $S > 1$ be integers. Let q be a prime or prime power and $\vec{u}, \vec{v} \in \mathbb{F}_q^m$. Let $\lambda_0, \lambda_1, \ldots, \lambda_{S-1}$ be distinct nonzero elements of $\mathbb{F}_q$. Let $\vec{z}_s = \vec{u} + \lambda_s\vec{v}$ for $s \in [\![S]\!]$. For a polynomial $F \in \mathbb{F}_q[X_1, \ldots, X_m]$ such that $\deg(F) \leq d$, given the evaluation of $\overline{\partial}^{\vec{a}} \circ F(\vec{z}_s)$ for all $\vec{a} \in A_{<t,m}$, $s \in S$, we can recover $F(\vec{u})$ if $S \cdot t > d$.*

Proof. Let $f(\lambda) = F(\vec{u}+\lambda\vec{v})$. Using the chain rule for Hasse derivatives, we have that for all $s \in [\![S]\!]$ and $0 \le k < t$

$$\overline{\partial}^{(k)} f(\lambda_s) = \sum_{\vec{a} \in A_{k,m}} \overline{\partial}^{\vec{a}} \circ F(\vec{z_s}) \cdot \vec{v}^{\vec{a}} . \tag{3}$$

Note that given the evaluation of $\overline{\partial}^{\vec{a}} \circ F(\vec{z_s})$ for all $\vec{a} \in A_{<t,m}$, $\vec{z}_s$ for $s \in [\![S]\!]$, we can compute the right hand side of the other expression when $0 \le k < t$.

Now observe that $\deg(f) \le \deg(F) \le d$. So, it follows from Lemma 3 that we can reconstruct f by Hasse derivatives computed above as long as $S \cdot t > d$.

4.2 PIR Family from Multiplicity Codes

In this section, we present the construction of the family of PIR schemes from multiplicity codes. We start off by giving some intuition about how we use multiplicity codes to construct PIR schemes.

Our goal is to construct a scalable family of S-server PIR scheme with global preprocessing using multiplicity codes of order-t evaluations of degree-d polynomials in m variables over $\mathbb{F}_q$. We encode the database DB into an m-variate polynomial F with degree d, i.e., we let $E : [\![n]\!] \to \mathbb{F}_q^m$ be the injective mapping that maps elements in $[\![n]\!]$ to their q-ary representation of length m and then find such F using interpolation satisfying $F(E(i)) = \mathsf{DB}[i]$ for all $i \in [\![n]\!]$. Now suppose the client wants to query the database at index i such that $E(i) = \vec{u}$. The client chooses a random $\vec{v} \in \mathbb{F}_q^m$ and distinct non-zero field elements $\lambda_0, \ldots, \lambda_{S-1}$ and sends $\vec{u} + \lambda_s\vec{v}$ to server s for $s \in [\![S]\!]$. The server returns the evaluations and all derivatives up to order t of F at the point it received to the client. Using Claim 9, the client can recover $F(\vec{u}) = \mathsf{DB}[i]$.

In order to make the server's online computation efficient, we make the server store all possible evaluations and Hasse derivates of the polynomial F. To make the preprocessing phase of the server efficient, we do the following:

- In order to compute the polynomial F described above, we use the interpolation algorithm of Lin, Mook, and Wichs [33, Lemma 2.2] for encoding a database of size at most q^m elements into a m-variate polynomial F over $\mathbb{F}_q$.
  - Given the **injective** map $E : [\![n]\!] \to \mathbb{F}_q^m$ that maps elements in $[\![n]\!]$ to their q-ary representation of length m, there is an interpolation algorithm that takes $n \le q^m$ values $\{y_i\}_{i \in [\![n]\!]}$, and recovers coefficients of a polynomial $F(X_1, \ldots, X_m) \in \mathbb{F}_q[X_1, \ldots, X_m]$ with individual degree at most d' in each variable such that $F(E(i)) = y_i$ for all $i \in [\![n]\!]$. Further, the algorithm runs in time $O((d')^m \cdot m \cdot \mathsf{poly}\log(d'))$. When we have an upper bound on total degree instead of individual degree, individual degree cannot be more than $q-1$, so in that case the algorithm runs in time $O(q^m \cdot m \cdot \mathsf{poly}\log q)$.
- In order to pre-compute the evaluation of $\overline{\partial}^{\vec{a}} \circ F$ for all $\vec{a} \in A_{\le t,m}$, $\vec{(x)} \in \mathbb{F}_q^m$ we use the result from [26, Theorem 4.1] (stated below as Lemma 4), which states that given an m-variate polynomial F over prime field $\mathbb{F}_q$, we can simultaneously evaluate it at every point of $\mathbb{F}_q^m$ in almost linear time.

Lemma 4 ([26]). *There is a deterministic algorithm that takes coefficients of an m-variate polynomial F over finite field $\mathbb{F}_q$ (without loss of generality we may assume F has individual degree at most $q-1$ in each variable) as input then outputs $F(\vec{X})$ for all $\vec{X} \in \mathbb{F}_q^m$, and runs in time $O(q^m \cdot m \cdot \mathsf{poly}\log q)$.*

We give the formal description of our construction below.

S-server PIR. Our S-server PIR works as follows.

- **Preproc$_s$**: Encode database DB to m-variate polynomial F with total degree d. Concretely, we let $E : [\![n]\!] \to \mathbb{F}_q^m$ be the injective mapping that maps elements in $[\![n]\!]$ to their q-ary representation of length m, and recover F such that $F(E(i)) = \mathsf{DB}[i]$ for all $i \in [\![n]\!]$ using the interpolation techniques described by Lin et al. [33].
  For each $\vec{a} \in A_{<t,m}$, we can use the preprocessing algorithm described in Lemma 4 to pre-compute evaluation of $\overline{\partial}^{\vec{a}} \circ F$ at any point $x \in \mathbb{F}_q^m$.
- **Query**: Given query index i, the client uniformly generates $\vec{v} \in \mathbb{F}_q^m$, and sets $\vec{u} = E(i)$. Then it picks S distinct and **nonzero** elements in $\mathbb{F}_q$ called $\lambda_0, \ldots, \lambda_{S-1}$.
  For $s \in [\![S]\!]$, the client sets $\vec{z}_s = \vec{u} + \lambda_s \vec{v}$.
  The client sends $Q_s = \vec{z}_s$ to each server $s \in [\![S]\!]$.
- **Answer$_s$**: The s-th server ($s \in \{0, 1, \ldots, S\}$) parses the message received from the client as a vector $\vec{z}_s$. For each $\vec{a} \in A_{<t,m}$, it sends $\mathsf{ans}_{s,\vec{a}} = \underbrace{\overline{\partial}^{\vec{a}} \circ F(\vec{z}_s)}_{\text{precomputed during preproc}}$ back to the client.
- **Recons**:
  1. Define univariate polynomial $f(\lambda) = F(\vec{u} + \lambda\vec{v})$, clearly $\vec{z}_s = \vec{u} + \lambda_s \vec{v} = f(\lambda_s)$. Given the responses of all servers, the client computes $\overline{\partial}^{(k)} f(\lambda_s)$ for all $s \in [\![S]\!]$ and $0 \le k < t$ by:
  $$\overline{\partial}^{(k)} f(\lambda_s) = \sum_{\vec{a} \in A_{k,m}} \overline{\partial}^{\vec{a}} \circ F(\vec{z}_s) \cdot \vec{v}^{\vec{a}} = \sum_{\vec{a} \in A_{k,m}} \mathsf{ans}_{s,\vec{a}} \cdot \vec{v}^{\vec{a}}$$
  2. Reconstruct f by its Hasse derivatives. Since F has degree d, f has degree at most d. For each $s \in [\![S]\!]$, the client has already known its k-th order Hasse derivatives at point λ_s for any $0 \le k < t$. So, if $S \cdot t > d$, the client can use Hermite interpolation (Lemma 3) to reconstruct the coefficients, and output $f(0) = F(\vec{u}) = \mathsf{DB}[i]$ as the answer.

For the above to work, certain constraints need to be satisfied. We list them below.

Constraints. For database size n,

- To ensure that the *injective* mapping $E : [\![n]\!] \to \mathbb{F}_q^m$ exists, we need $q^m \ge n$.

- To ensure that a polynomial m-variate polynomial F with degree at most d interpolates n points, the number of monomials in F has to be at least n. Therefore, $\binom{m+d}{m} \geq n$.
- Since the client sends $\vec{u} + \lambda_s \vec{v}$ to server $s \in [\![S]\!]$, and since none of the λ_s can be zero (because that would leak $\vec{u}$, thus compromising privacy), the field must constant at least S non-zero elements. Therefore, $q \geq S + 1$.
- For reconstruction to work, we need $S \cdot t > d$.

Proof of Correctness. The correctness of PIR scheme immediately follows from Claim 9 above.

Proof of Security. Each server $s \in [\![S]\!]$ receives $\vec{z}_s = \vec{u} + \lambda_s \vec{v}$, the privacy follows the fact $\vec{z}_s$ is randomly distributed in $\mathbb{F}_q^m$ when $\lambda_s \neq 0$ and $\vec{v}$ is randomly sampled.

Efficiency. We now analyze the efficiency of our construction.

- **Bandwidth**: The upload bandwidth per server is $m \log q$ since the client sends an element in $\mathbb{F}_q^m$ to each server. Each server should return $|A_{<t,m}|$ elements in $\mathbb{F}_q$, and we have $|A_{<t,m}| = \binom{t+m-1}{m}$. Thus the total per-server download bandwidth is $|A_{<t,m}| \log q = \binom{m+t-1}{m} \log q$.
- **Server computation**: Each server simply sends back $|A_{<t,m}|$ stored values, so the total computation is $O\left(\binom{m+t-1}{m} \log q\right)$.
- **Client computation**: For applying the chain rule, for each server s and $\vec{a} \in A_{<t,m}$, the client should do $O(m)$ multiplications in $\mathbb{F}_q$ (where each takes $O(\mathsf{poly}\log q)$ time). This takes time $O\left(S \cdot \binom{m+t-1}{m} \cdot m \cdot \mathsf{poly}\log q\right)$. The hermite interpolation takes time $\mathsf{poly}(d, \log q)$. Therefore, total client computation is $O\left(S \cdot \binom{m+t-1}{m} \cdot m \cdot \mathsf{poly}\log q\right) + O(\mathsf{poly}(d, \log q))$.
- **Server space**: Each server runs preprocessing algorithm in Lemma 4 for $|A_{<t,m}|$ polynomials. For each polynomial, it needs to store q^m elements in $\mathbb{F}_q$, thus in total it takes space

$$|A_{<t,m}| \cdot O(q^m \log q) = \binom{m+t-1}{m} \cdot q^m \cdot \log q$$

- **Preprocessing time**: Each server needs to interpolate the polynomial F which takes time $O(q^m \cdot m \cdot \mathsf{poly}\log q)$. For each $\vec{a} \in A_{<t,m}$ $\overline{\partial}^{\vec{a}} \circ f$ can be computed in time $O(q^m \cdot m \cdot \mathsf{poly}\log q)$. Therefore, the total time foe computing these polynomials is $|A_{<t,m}| \cdot O(q^m \cdot m \cdot \mathsf{poly}\log q)$. Further, each of these polynomials are to be evaluated in q^m points. Using Lemma 4, each evaluation takes time $O(q^m \cdot m \cdot \mathsf{poly}\log q)$.
  Therefore, the total preprocessing time is

$$O((|A_{<t,m}| \cdot O(q^m \cdot m \cdot \mathsf{poly}\log q)) = O\left(\binom{m+t-1}{m} \cdot q^m \cdot m \cdot \mathsf{poly}\log q\right).$$

Theorem 10. *Let $n, S, d, m, q, t \in \mathbb{N}$ satisfy the following constraints: q is a prime or a prime power with $q \geq S+1$, $q^m \geq n$, $\binom{m+d}{m} \geq n$, $S \cdot t > d$.*

Then, there exists an S-server PIR scheme which achieves the following parameters.

- *per-server upload bandwidth $m \log q$, per-server download bandwidth $\binom{m+t-1}{m} \log q$.*
- *per-server computation $O\left(\binom{m+t-1}{m} \log q\right)$.*
- *client computation $O\left(S \cdot \binom{m+t-1}{m} \cdot m \cdot \mathsf{poly} \log q\right) + O(\mathsf{poly}(d, \log q))$.*
- *per-server storage $\binom{m+t-1}{m} \cdot q^m \cdot \log q$.*
- *per-server preprocessing time $O\left(\binom{m+t-1}{m} \cdot q^m \cdot m \cdot \mathsf{poly} \log q\right)$.*

4.3 Scaling Bandwidth, Computation and Space Equally

In this section, we show how to set the parameters for the construction in Sect. 4.2 to get a scalable family of PIR schemes where the (per-server) bandwidth and computation per query as well as the server space scale with respect to the number of servers. The scheme is same as described in Sect. 4.2, with the following parameters. Let $S(n)$ be the number of servers, we pick $S^*(n) \leq S(n)$ to be the maximum integer such that $S^*(n)+1$ is a prime (by Bertrand's postulate, $S^*(n) \in [\lfloor S(n)/2 \rfloor, S(n)]$), then use only $S^*(n)$ servers, and ignore the other servers. We set $q = S^*(n)+1$, $m = \lceil \log n / \log q \rceil$, $d = (q-1) \cdot m$ and $t = m+1$. The constraints $q \geq S+1, q^m \geq n, t \cdot S > d$ can be seen to be satisfied from the above. Note that $\binom{m+d}{d} = \binom{(q-1) \cdot m}{m} \geq (q-1)^m \geq n$. Therefore, all the constraints are satisfied. Observe that since $t = m$, it follows that $\binom{m+t-1}{t-1} \leq \binom{2m}{m} \leq 2^{2m} \leq O(n^{2/\log q})$. We now compute the performance parameters for the PIR scheme.

- **Bandwidth**: The bandwidth will be dominated by the download bandwidth. Thus, the total per-server bandwidth is bounded by $O(n^{2/\log q} \log q)$.
- **Server computation**: The total computation is that is, $O(n^{2/\log q} \log q)$.
- **Client computation**: The client computation is $O(S \cdot n^{2/\log q} \cdot \mathsf{poly} \log q \cdot \mathsf{poly} \log n + q^2 \cdot \mathsf{poly} \log q)$.
- **Server space**: Since $q^m \leq n \cdot q$, we have that the total server space is $O(n^{1+2/\log q} \cdot q \cdot \log q)$.
- **Preprocessing time**: The preprocessing time is $O(n^{1+2/\log q} \cdot q \cdot \mathsf{poly} \log n)$

Notice that our parameterization guarantees $q > S(n)/2$ and $2/\log q \leq 2/(\log S(n) - 1)$. So, we have the following theorem.

Theorem 11. *For any S, there exists an S-server PIR scheme which achieves $O(n^{2/(\log S - 1)} \log S)$ per-server bandwidth, $O(n^{2/(\log S-1)} \log S)$ per-server computation and $O(n^{2/(\log S-1)} S \log n \cdot \mathsf{poly} \log S + S^2 \cdot \mathsf{poly} \log S)$ client computation per query, with $O(n^{1+2/(\log S-1)} \cdot S \cdot \mathsf{poly} \log n)$ preprocessing time and server storage.*

For constant number servers setting, our construction shows nontrivial results about tradeoff between preprocessing time and bandwidth.

If we choose $S(n) = \omega(1)$ to be any super-constant function (e.g. $S(n) = \log^*(n)$), then we have $2/\log q = 2/\log \Omega(S(n)) = o(1)$, thus $\binom{m+t-1}{t-1}$ is bounded by $n^{o(1)}$. Moreover, the polylogarithm factor can be absorbed by $n^{o(1)}$. Therefore, we get a doubly-efficient mutli-server PIR using a superconstant number of servers. In conclusion, we have:

Corollary 1. *For any $S(n) = \omega(1)$, there exists an S-server PIR scheme where each query incurs $n^{o(1)}$ per-server bandwidth and computation and $S^2 \cdot n^{o(1)}$ client computation, while requiring $n^{1+o(1)}$ per-server preprocessing time and storage. Specifically, when $S(n) = n^{o(1)}$, the client computation is also bounded by $n^{o(1)}$.*

5 Multi-server PIR Using Multiplicity Codes and Fast Polynomial Evaluation Data Structure

In this section, we present families of PIR schemes that use multiplicity codes in conjunction with fast polynomial evaluation algorithms. In our scheme in Sect. 4, our preprocessing involved storing the evaluation of the polynomials at all points. Now, we will use fast polynomial evaluation algorithms from [6,25] where the server does not pre-compute the evaluation of the polynomials at all points, and instead stores a data structure. In the online phase, the server uses this data structure to evaluate the polynomials at the desired point.

We will construct two incomparable families of PIR schemes using two different polynomial preprocessing algorithms. We will first use the following algorithm from [6].

Theorem 12 (Polynomial preprocessing theorem from [6]). *For a m-variate polynomial $f : \mathbb{F}_q^m \to \mathbb{F}_q$ with individual degree $\leq d'$, over some finite field $\mathbb{F}_q$, then there exists algorithms* $\mathsf{PolyPreprocess}, \mathsf{EvalPoly}$ *such that*

- *The runtime of* $\mathsf{PolyPreprocess}(f)$ *is* $(16d'(\log d' + \log\log q)^m \cdot \mathsf{poly}(m, d', \log q)$
- *Let* $\widetilde{f} \leftarrow \mathsf{PolyPreprocess}(f)$, *for any* $\vec{x} \in \mathbb{F}_q^m$, $\mathsf{EvalPoly}(\widetilde{f}, \vec{x}) = f(\vec{x})$ *and the runtime of* $\mathsf{EvalPoly}(\widetilde{f}, \vec{x})$ *is* $16^m \cdot \mathsf{poly}(m, d', \log q)$.

Since [6] give an algorithm that does not have a separate preprocessing and online phase, for the sake of completeness we give a self-contained proof of this theorem in the full version.

Using this theorem will give us a family of PIR schemes where the bandwidth scales as $n^{\widetilde{O}(1/S)}$. This construction scales with respect to all parameters and minimizes bandwidth. Further, this construction is doubly efficient with a superconstant number of servers.

We will then use the following fast polynomial evaluation algorithm from [25] to get a different scheme.

Theorem 13 (Polynomial preprocessing theorem from [25]). *For a m-variate polynomial $f : \mathbb{F}_q^m \to \mathbb{F}_q$ with individual degree $\le d'$, over some finite field $\mathbb{F}_q$, then there exists algorithms* $\mathsf{PolyPreprocess}, \mathsf{EvalPoly}$ *such that*

- *The runtime of* $\mathsf{PolyPreprocess}(f)$ *is* $(md'(\log d' + \log m + \log\log q)^m \cdot \mathsf{poly}(m, d', \log q)$
- *Let* $\widetilde{f} \leftarrow \mathsf{PolyPreprocess}(f)$, *for any* $\vec{x} \in \mathbb{F}_q^m, \mathsf{EvalPoly}(\widetilde{f}, \vec{x}) = f(\vec{x})$ *and the runtime of* $\mathsf{EvalPoly}(\widetilde{f}, \vec{x})$ *is* $\mathsf{poly}(m, d', \log q)$.

Using this theorem we will get a PIR scheme where the online bottleneck (the maximum of bandwidth and computation time) scales as $n^{\frac{1}{S^{1-1/\omega(1)}}}$. Here the scaling of the online bottleneck is minimized.

The main difference of our PIR schemes here compared to that in Sect. 4.2 is that our schemes use the PolyPreprocess from the above theorems in the preprocessing phase instead of the algorithm in Lemma 4. Further, in the online phase, the server uses the data-structure obtained from the preprocessing instead of simply looking up the value. The other difference here is the polynomial F has a restriction on individual degree as opposed to total degree – we need this in order to use the fast polynomial evaluation algorithm.

We give the formal description of our construction below.

S-server PIR. Our S-server PIR works as follows.

- **Preproc$_s$**: Encode database DB to m-variate polynomial F with individual degree at most d'. Note that the total degree d is therefore at most md'. We let $E : [\![n]\!] \to \mathbb{F}_q^m$ be the injective mapping that maps elements in $[\![n]\!]$ to their q-ary representation of length m, and recover F by interpolating on the set $\{\mathsf{DB}[i]\}_{i\in[\![n]\!]}$ using the techniques described by Lin et al. [33].

  For each $\vec{a} \in A_{<t,m}$, use compute in Lemma 4 to compute $\widetilde{\overline{\partial}^{\vec{a}} \circ F} = \mathsf{PolyPreprocess}(\overline{\partial}^{\vec{a}} \circ F)$.
- **Query**: Given query index i, the client uniformly generates $\vec{v} \in \mathbb{F}_q^m$, and sets $\vec{u} = E(i)$. Then it picks S distinct and **nonzero** elements in $\mathbb{F}_q$ called $\lambda_0, \ldots, \lambda_{S-1}$.
  For $s \in [\![S]\!]$, the client sets $\vec{z}_s = \vec{u} + \lambda_s\vec{v}$.
  The client sends $Q_s = \vec{z}_s$ to each server $s \in [\![S]\!]$.
- **Answer$_s$**: The s-th server ($s \in \{0, 1, \ldots, S\}$) parses the message received from the client as a vector $\vec{z}_s$. For each $\vec{a} \in A_{<t,m}$, it sends $\mathsf{ans}_{s,\vec{a}} = \mathsf{EvalPoly}(\widetilde{\overline{\partial}^{\vec{a}} \circ F}, \vec{z}_s)$ back to the client.
- **Recons**:
  1. Define univariate polynomial $f(\lambda) = F(\vec{u} + \lambda\vec{v})$, clearly $\vec{z}_s = \vec{u} + \lambda_s\vec{v} = f(\lambda_s)$. Given the responses of all servers, the client computes $\overline{\partial}^{(k)} f(\lambda_s)$ for all $s \in [\![S]\!]$ and $0 \le k < t$ by:

$$\overline{\partial}^{(k)} f(\lambda_s) = \sum_{\vec{a}\in A_{k,m}} \overline{\partial}^{\vec{a}} \circ F(\vec{z}_s) \cdot \vec{v}^{\vec{a}} = \sum_{\vec{a}\in A_{k,m}} \mathsf{ans}_{s,\vec{a}} \cdot \vec{v}^{\vec{a}}$$

2. Reconstruct f by its Hasse derivatives. Since F has degree d, f has degree at most d. For each $s \in [\![S]\!]$, the client has already known its k-th order Hasse derivatives at point λ_s for any $0 \leq k < t$. So, if $S \cdot t > d$, the client can use Hermite interpolation (Lemma 3) to reconstruct the coefficients, and output $f(0) = F(\vec{u}) = \mathsf{DB}[i]$ as the answer.

The correctness follows from the scheme in Sect. 4.2 and the correctness of the fast polynomial evaluation algorithm. Security follows from the scheme in Sect. 4.2.

In terms of efficiency, the bandwidth and client computation remain the same as in Sect. 4.2. The online server computation, server storage and the preprocessing computation depend on the particular polynomial preprocessing scheme used.

Instantiating this scheme with the polynomial preprocessing scheme from Theorem 12 and setting parameters appropriately gives us this result.

Corollary 2. *There is a S-server PIR scheme which achieves the following parameters.*

- *per-server bandwidth* $n^{O\left(\frac{\log^2 S}{S \log\log S}\right)+O\left(\frac{\log S}{\log n}\right)} \cdot \mathsf{poly}\log(n, S)$.
- *per-server computation* $n^{O\left(\frac{\log^2 S}{S \log\log S}\right)+O\left(\frac{1}{\log\log S}\right)+O\left(\frac{\log S}{\log n}\right)} \cdot \mathsf{poly}\log(n, S)$.
- *client computation* $\left(S \cdot n^{O\left(\frac{\log^2 S}{S \log\log S}\right)+O\left(\frac{\log S}{\log n}\right)}\right) \cdot \mathsf{poly}\log(n, S)$,
- *per-server preprocessing time and storage*

$$n^{1+O\left(\frac{\log^2 S}{S \log\log S}\right)+O\left(\frac{\log\log\log S}{\log\log S}\right)+O\left(\frac{\log S}{\log n}\right)} \cdot \mathsf{poly}\log(n, S)\,.$$

For $S = \omega(1)$, this scheme has storage and preprocessing time $n^{1+o(1)}$ and online computation and bandwidth $n^{o(1)}$. Moreover, the bandwidth scales roughly $n^{\widetilde{O}(1/S)}$. Here the server computation and storage are also scalable, but their scaling is worse than the bandwidth. We defer the details of this scheme to the full version.

On the other hand, instantiating the above PIR scheme with the polynomial preprocessing scheme from Theorem 13 and setting parameters appropriately gives us this result.

Corollary 3. *Let $\omega(1)$ be any superconstant function such that it is in $o(\log n)$. There is a S-server PIR scheme which achieves the following parameters.*

- *per-server bandwidth* $n^{\widetilde{O}\left(\frac{1}{S^{1/\omega(1)}}\right)+O\left(\frac{\log S}{\log n}\right)} \cdot \mathsf{poly}\log(n) \cdot \log S$.
- *per-server computation* $n^{\widetilde{O}\left(\frac{1}{S^{1/\omega(1)}}\right)+O\left(\frac{\log S}{\log n}\right)} \cdot \mathsf{poly}\log(n, S)$.
- *client computation* $\left(S \cdot n^{\widetilde{O}\left(\frac{1}{S^{1/\omega(1)}}\right)+O\left(\frac{\log S}{\log n}\right)} + n^{O\left(\frac{\log\log n \cdot \omega(1)+\log S}{\omega(1)\cdot \log n}\right)}\right) \cdot \mathsf{poly}\log(n, S)$

– *per-server preprocessing time and storage*

$$n^{1+\tilde{O}\left(\frac{1}{S^{1/\omega(1)}}\right)+O\left(\frac{\log S}{\log n}\right)+O\left(\frac{\log\log n\cdot\omega(1)}{\log S}\right)}\cdot \mathsf{poly}\log(n,S)\ .$$

Remark 2. Observe that when S is superpolylogarithmic in n and $S \in n^{o(1)}$, the storage becomes $n^{1+o(1)}$. The bandwidth, computation parameters also become $n^{o(1)}$. Therefore, the construction is doubly efficient when S is superpolylogarithmic in n. Note that this $S \in n^{o(1)}$ is *not an additional restriction* because for $S \gg n^{o(1)}$, the total client computation and bandwidth is naturally $\gg n^{o(1)}$ and the construction cannot be doubly efficient.

We defer the details of this scheme to the full version.

Acknowledgments. We gratefully acknowledge Yuval Ishai and Henry Corrigan-Gibbs for suggesting the generic balancing technique. The version described in our paper is a slight improvement of their original idea. This work is in part supported by NSF awards 2212746, 2044679, 2128519, the DARPA SIEVE grant under a subcontract from SRI, a grant from 0xPARC, and a grant from the late Nikolai Mushegian.

References

1. https://haveibeenpwned.com/
2. Oblivious DNS over https. https://tools.ietf.org/html/draft-pauly-dprive-oblivious-doh-04
3. Technology deep dive: building a faster ORAM layer for enclaves. https://signal.org/blog/building-faster-oram/
4. Beigel, R., Fortnow, L., Gasarch, W.I.: A nearly tight bound for private information retrieval protocols. In: Electronic Colloquium on Computational Complexity (ECCC) (2003)
5. Beimel, A., Ishai, Y., Malkin, T.: Reducing the servers' computation in private information retrieval: PIR with preprocessing. J. Cryptol. **17**(2), 125–151 (2004). https://doi.org/10.1007/s00145-004-0134-y
6. Bhargava, V., Ghosh, S., Guo, Z., Kumar, M., Umans, C.: Fast multivariate multipoint evaluation over all finite fields. J. ACM **71**(3), 1–32 (2024)
7. Bhargava, V., Ghosh, S., Kumar, M., Mohapatra, C.K.: Fast, algebraic multivariate multipoint evaluation in small characteristic and applications. In: Proceedings of the 54th Annual ACM SIGACT Symposium on Theory of Computing, STOC 2022, pp. 403–415. Association for Computing Machinery, New York (2022). https://doi.org/10.1145/3519935.3519968
8. Boyle, E., Jain, A., Prabhakaran, M., Yu, C.H.: The bottleneck complexity of secure multiparty computation. In: 45th International Colloquium on Automata, Languages, and Programming (ICALP 2018), pp. 24–1. Schloss Dagstuhl–Leibniz-Zentrum für Informatik (2018)
9. Cachin, C., Micali, S., Stadler, M.: Computationally private information retrieval with polylogarithmic communication. In: EUROCRYPT, pp. 402–414 (1999)
10. Chang, Y.C.: Single database private information retrieval with logarithmic communication. In: ACISP (2004)

11. Chor, B., Gilboa, N.: Computationally private information retrieval. In: STOC (1997)
12. Chor, B., Goldreich, O., Kushilevitz, E., Sudan, M.: Private information retrieval. In: FOCS (1995)
13. Corrigan-Gibbs, H., Henzinger, A., Kogan, D.: Single-server private information retrieval with sublinear amortized time. In: Eurocrypt (2022)
14. Corrigan-Gibbs, H., Kogan, D.: Private information retrieval with sublinear online time. In: EUROCRYPT (2020)
15. Demmler, D., Rindal, P., Rosulek, M., Trieu, N.: PIR-PSI: scaling private contact discovery. Proc. Priv. Enhancing Technol. **2018**(4), 159–178 (2018)
16. Dvir, Z., Gopi, S.: 2-server PIR with subpolynomial communication. J. ACM **63**(4) (2016)
17. Feamster, N.: Oblivious DNS deployed by Cloudflare and Apple. https://medium.com/noise-lab/oblivious-dns-deployed-by-cloudflare-and-apple-1522ccf53cab
18. Gasarch, W.I.: A survey on private information retrieval. Bull. EATCS **82**, 72–107 (2004)
19. Gentry, C., Ramzan, Z.: Single-database private information retrieval with constant communication rate. In: ICALP (2005)
20. Ghoshal, A., Zhou, M., Shi, E.: Efficient pre-processing PIR without public-key cryptography. In: Eurocrypt (2024)
21. Hasse, H.: Theorie der höheren differentiale in einem algebraischen funktionenkörper mit vollkommenem konstantenkörper bei beliebiger charakteristik. Journal für die reine und angewandte Mathematik **175**, 50–54 (1936). http://eudml.org/doc/149955
22. Henzinger, A., Dauterman, E., Corrigan-Gibbs, H., , Zeldovich, N.: Private web search with Tiptoe. In: 29th ACM Symposium on Operating Systems Principles (SOSP), Koblenz, Germany (2023)
23. Henzinger, A., Hong, M.M., Corrigan-Gibbs, H., Meiklejohn, S., Vaikuntanathan, V.: One server for the price of two: simple and fast single-server private information retrieval. In: Usenix Security (2023)
24. Hoover, A., Patel, S., Persiano, G., Yeo, K.: Plinko: single-server PIR with efficient updates via invertible PRFs. IACR Cryptol. ePrint Arch. 318 (2024)
25. Kedlaya, K.S., Umans, C.: Fast modular composition in any characteristic. In: 49th Annual IEEE Symposium on Foundations of Computer Science, pp. 146–155 (2008)
26. Kedlaya, K.S., Umans, C.: Fast polynomial factorization and modular composition. SIAM J. Comput. (2011)
27. Kopparty, S.: Some remarks on multiplicity codes. Discret. Geom. Algebraic Comb. **625**(155–176), 1–1 (2013)
28. Kopparty, S., Saraf, S., Yekhanin, S.: High-rate codes with sublinear-time decoding. J. ACM (JACM) **61**(5), 1–20 (2014)
29. Kushilevitz, E., Ostrovsky, R.: Replication is not needed: single database, computationally-private information retrieval. In: FOCS (1997)
30. Lazzaretti, A., Liu, Z., Fisch, B., Papamanthou, C.: Multi-server doubly efficient PIR. Cryptology ePrint Archive, Paper 2024/829 (2024). https://eprint.iacr.org/2024/829
31. Lazzaretti, A., Papamanthou, C.: Single server PIR with sublinear amortized time and polylogarithmic bandwidth. Cryptology ePrint Archive, Paper 2022/830 (2022). https://eprint.iacr.org/2022/830
32. Lazzaretti, A., Papamanthou, C.: Treepir: sublinear-time and polylog-bandwidth private information retrieval from DDH. In: CRYPTO (2023)

33. Lin, W., Mook, E., Wichs, D.: Doubly efficient private information retrieval and fully homomorphic RAM computation from ring LWE. In: Saha, B., Servedio, R.A. (eds.) Proceedings of the 55th Annual ACM Symposium on Theory of Computing, STOC 2023, Orlando, FL, USA, 20–23 June 2023, pp. 595–608. ACM (2023). https://doi.org/10.1145/3564246.3585175
34. Lipmaa, H.: First CPIR protocol with data-dependent computation. In: ICISC (2009)
35. Melchor, C.A., Crespin, B., Gaborit, P., Jolivet, V., Rousseau, P.: High-speed private information retrieval computation on GPU. In: Proceedings of the 2008 Second International Conference on Emerging Security Information, Systems and Technologies, SECURWARE 2008, pp. 263–272. IEEE Computer Society, Washington, DC, USA (2008)
36. Melchor, C.A., Gaborit, P.: A lattice-based computationally-efficient private information retrieval protocol. IACR Cryptology ePrint Archive **2007**, 446 (2007)
37. Menon, S.J., Wu, D.J.: Spiral: fast, high-rate single-server PIR via FHE composition. In: IEEE S&P (2022)
38. Mughees, M.H., I, S., Ren, L.: Simple and practical amortized sublinear private information retrieval. Cryptology ePrint Archive, Paper 2023/1072 (2023)
39. Olumofin, F.G., Goldberg, I.: Revisiting the computational practicality of private information retrieval. In: Financial Cryptography, pp. 158–172 (2011)
40. Ostrovsky, R., Skeith, III., W.E.: A survey of single-database private information retrieval: techniques and applications. In: PKC, pp. 393–411 (2007)
41. Razborov, A.A., Yekhanin, S.: An $\omega(n^{1/3})$ lower bound for bilinear group based private information retrieval. In: 2006 47th Annual IEEE Symposium on Foundations of Computer Science (FOCS 2006), pp. 739–748 (2006). https://doi.org/10.1109/FOCS.2006.10
42. Shi, E., Aqeel, W., Chandrasekaran, B., Maggs, B.: Puncturable pseudorandom sets and private information retrieval with near-optimal online bandwidth and time. In: CRYPTO (2021)
43. Singanamalla, S., et al.: Oblivious DNS over https (ODOH): a practical privacy enhancement to DNS. In: PET Symposium (2021)
44. Singh, J., Wei, Y., Zikas, V.: Information-theoretic multi-server private information retrieval with client preprocessing. In: TCC (2024)
45. Sion, R., Carbunar, B.: On the computational practicality of private information retrieval. In: Network and Distributed Systems Security Symposium (NDSS) (2007)
46. Woodruff, D.P., Yekhanin, S.: A geometric approach to information-theoretic private information retrieval. In: 20th Annual IEEE Conference on Computational Complexity (CCC 2005), 11–15 June 2005, San Jose, CA, USA, pp. 275–284. IEEE Computer Society (2005)
47. Yekhanin, S., et al.: Locally decodable codes. Found. Trends® Theor. Comput. Sci. **6**(3), 139–255 (2012)
48. Zhou, M., Lin, W.K., Tselekounis, Y., Shi, E.: Optimal single-server private information retrieval. In: EUROCRYPT (2023)

Multi-server Doubly Efficient PIR in the Classical Model and Beyond

Arthur Lazzaretti[1], Zeyu Liu[1], Ben Fisch[1], Peihan Miao[2(✉)], and Charalampos Papamanthou[1]

[1] Yale University, New Haven, USA
{arthur.lazzaretti,zeyu.liu,benjamin.fisch, charalampos.papamanthou}@yale.edu
[2] Brown University, Providence, USA
peihan_miao@brown.edu

Abstract. A Doubly Efficient Private Information Retrieval (DEPIR) is defined as a Private Information Retrieval (PIR) scheme with both near-linear server-side preprocessing time and sublinear query time. For many years, it has been a strong open question to devise a DEPIR scheme from standard assumptions. Very recently, Lin et al. (STOC '23) devised the first single-server DEPIR scheme from standard assumptions. However, their work left one major question open: can we build a DEPIR scheme in the multi-server setting, without relying on heavy cryptographic machinery?

In this work, we discuss two different settings for multi-server DEPIR. In the non-colluding, non-communicating servers setting, we propose the first doubly efficient multi-server PIR scheme. Our scheme is information-theoretic. For a database of size N, our scheme allows servers to answer an infinite number of client queries in $N^{o(1)}$ time, after a single preprocessing phase which takes $N^{1+o(1)}$ time. Our result is only an $N^{o(1)}$ factor from the lower bound proven by Persiano and Yeo (SODA '22) for this setting. In addition, we devise a second information-theoretic PIR scheme in this setting which pushes the state of the art for the setting where the number of servers is more constrained. It achieves equally fast query times as our first scheme above, and a preprocessing time of $N^{2+o(1)}$. This scheme uses $O(\log N)$ servers. Both schemes don't require any cryptographic primitives.

Furthermore, in the setting where the servers are additionally allowed to communicate and keep a global state (which is similarly required by PIR allowing database updates), we show a family of information-theoretic DEPIR schemes which achieve $N \mathsf{polylog} N$ preprocessing time, and $\log^3 N$ communication and server time, for any number of servers k greater than three. We also discuss how introducing more servers or computational assumptions in this setting may improve concrete efficiency of the PIR. This setting of communicating servers requires online communication between servers to answer queries, in contrast to the standard multi-server PIR setting where servers only communicate to coordinate the database contents and do not communicate at query time.

B. Applebaum and H. Lin (Eds.): TCC 2025, LNCS 16271, pp. 611–641, 2026.
https://doi.org/10.1007/978-3-032-12290-2_20

1 Introduction

Private Information Retrieval (PIR) was first introduced three decades ago by Chor et al. [15] in the multi-server, information-theoretic setting. In PIR, a client holds an index $i \in [N]$, and k, non-colluding servers hold the same database $\mathsf{DB} \in \{0,1\}^N$. The goal of the protocol (informally) is to devise a way for the client to learn $\mathsf{DB}[i]$ without either server learning any information about the client's desired index i. PIR has been used as a building block for many privacy-preserving applications such as private web searches [39], privacy-enhanced Tor [63], private ad serving [1], among others.

Since the problem's original inception, many works have pushed our understanding of the PIR problem in this same setting [7,14,15,76,79] (a non-exhaustive list) as well as many different scenarios; single-server computational PIR [49], two-server computational PIR [12,32,51,52] among others [9,50,81]. Aside from the number of servers and the computational assumption on the adversary, we can also consider preprocessing or non-preprocessing schemes. Within preprocessing schemes, there are two well-known approaches, which we will denote server preprocessing and client preprocessing.

In client preprocessing, the server and client run a joint preprocessing phase after which the client stores a secret hint which can be used to perform queries to the server later in time sublinear in the database size. This requires each client to run an expensive (linear time) preprocessing phase with the server, which means the server work to server m clients is at least $m \cdot N$, where N is the database size.

On the other hand, in server preprocessing, the server runs a one-time preprocessing phase by itself and stores additional bits server-side, which it can then use to answer queries from any client in time sublinear in the database size. In this work, we focus on the server preprocessing setting (we cover a broad overview of the other settings in Sect. 1.2).

The server preprocessing paradigm has a clear advantage with respect to total server time, in the sense that the overhead for serving many clients is considerably smaller. The first family of server preprocessing schemes was introduced by Beimel et al. [7] in 2000 in the multi-server setting. They present schemes for constant and polylogarithmic number of servers, with different trade-offs, as well as a number of lower bounds. Notably, in its Journal of Cryptology version [8], the authors present the first multi-server scheme (with a polylogarithmic number of servers) in the server preprocessing model which achieves $\mathsf{polylog}(N)$ query time and $\mathsf{polylog}(N)$ communication after a preprocessing phase running in time $\mathsf{poly}(N)$.

Persiano and Yeo [69] recently tighten the lower bounds shown by Beimel et al., showing that any server preprocessing scheme in the single server setting with query time $\Omega(t)$ must have the server store a hint of at least size $\Omega(N \log N/t)$, for any number of servers.

Very recently, in a seminal paper by Lin et al. [55] which makes use of a polynomial preprocessing algorithm by Kedlaya and Umans [47] to achieve a PIR scheme which preprocesses in time $O_\lambda(N^{1+o(1)})$ and stores $O_\lambda(N^{1+o(1)})$

after which it can serve PIR queries in time $N^{o(1)}$.[1] They refer this as the *doubly efficient PIR*: in particular, the server can preprocess the database *once in nearly linear time* (e.g., $N^{1+o(1)}$), and answer an infinite number of queries from the clients very quickly (e.g., $N^{o(1)}$ time).

According to the bound by Persiano and Yeo, this is close to optimal asymptotically (only $N^{o(1)}$ factors away). After the work by Lin et al., two main questions were left open for server preprocessing PIR:

1. Can we achieve similar asymptotics in the multi-server setting without the computational assumption (i.e., information-theoretic) while minimizing the number of servers required?
2. Can we achieve doubly efficient PIR without the use heavy cryptographic primitives such as fully homomorphic encryption (FHE)?

The first question is important theoretically due to the relationship of multi-server information-theoretic PIR with other cryptographic primitives [78,79] and to push our understanding of the problem. The second question was also posed after a follow-up work by Okada et al. [66,67] showed that the scheme by Lin et al., implemented as is, still incurs astronomic empirical costs despite the very nice asymptotic efficiencies.

In this work, we answer both questions in the affirmative by providing novel families of multi-server server preprocessing scheme with near-optimal asymptotics that do not use FHE.

Specifically, we introduce three families of multi-server, server-preprocessing PIR schemes for two different settings. First, we consider the setting of multiple non-colluding and non-communicating servers holding the database. Then, we consider the setting of multi-server server preprocessing PIR schemes where the servers can additionally communicate online (note that while the standard multi-server PIR setting enforces non-communication between servers, offline communication is still required to ensure synchronization between databases).

Since our constructions do not rely on any heavy cryptographic tools (and most constructions require no cryptographic tools at all), our work is notably empirically much more efficient in practice than the work by Lin et al., given that the Algebraic Homomorphic Encryption necessary to build their PIR scheme incurs large overheads [66].

Our work pushes our understanding of multi-server server preprocessing PIR and we believe this may pave the way towards building a truly practical doubly efficient PIR constructions in both the single and multi-server settings.

We conclude our work with thoughts on important open questions to be resolved in future work, as well as briefly discuss the possibility of replacing the non-collusion or honesty assumption with the rational server assumption.

1.1 Our Results

Our results can be categorized in two settings.

[1] Or alternatively preprocess in $N^{1+\epsilon}$ time and query in $\mathsf{polylog}(N)$ time for some constant ϵ).

Table 1. Comparisons to prior works. N is the number of bits in a database, and k, ϵ are tunable constants in [8]. γ is a tunable constant satisfying $\frac{1}{k+1} \leq \gamma \leq \frac{1}{k}$ in [30]. Our $\widetilde{O}(\log(N)) = \frac{\log(N)\log\log(N)}{\log\log\log(N)}$. * : A more recent version of [30] shows how to achieve a scheme with $N^{1+o(1)}$ preprocessing and storage and $N^{o(1)}$ online time and communication (see Appendix A for more details). **: This scheme works in the setting where servers are allowed to communicate online and also maintain a global state (i.e., the database updates per query, similar to updatable PIR, which also requires database updates periodically).

Scheme	Efficiency			
	# of Servers	Preprocessing Time & Storage	Online Time	Communication
[76]	2	$\mathsf{poly}(N)$	$N/\mathsf{polylog}(N)$	$N^{1/3}$
[8]	k	$\mathsf{poly}(N)$	$O(N^{1/k+\epsilon})$	$O(N^{1/k+\epsilon})$
[30]	k	$\mathsf{poly}(N)$	$O(N^{1-\gamma(k-1)+\epsilon})$	$O(N^{\gamma+\epsilon})$
[8,30]*	$O(\mathsf{polylog}(N))$	$\mathsf{poly}(N)$	$\mathsf{polylog}N$	$\mathsf{polylog}N$
Theorem 2	$\widetilde{O}(\log(N))$	$N^{1+o(1)}$	$N^{o(1)}$	$N^{o(1)}$
Theorem 3	$o(\log(N))$	$N^{2+o(1)}$	$N^{o(1)}$	$N^{o(1)}$
Theorem 4**	3	$N\mathsf{polylog}N$	$\log^3(N)$	$\log^3(N)$

New PIR Schemes for Non-Colluding, Non-communicating Servers. First, we construct two k-server information-theoretic PIR construction with server-side preprocessing. Both are compared with the state-of-the-art prior works in information-theoretic PIR with server-side preprocessing [8,76] and the concurrent work [30] in Table 1.

In particular, our *first* scheme in this setting is a doubly efficient PIR scheme (see Definition 1) with no computational assumptions where the server computation at query time is significantly smaller than N, specifically, $N^{o(1)}$. Also, in order to satisfy the definition of doubly efficient, it means that each server's preprocessing time is near-linear in the database size N (in particular, we have $N^{1+o(1)}$). These are achieved with roughly $O(\log(N))$ servers.

In our second scheme in this setting, we demonstrate that one can further reduce the number of servers required for the scheme, at the expensive of a more costly preprocessing phase, which is no longer near linear, but $N^{2+o(1)}$. This is the first scheme to achieve $N^{o(1)}$ query time with $\mathsf{poly}(N)$ preprocessing and $o(\log N)$ servers. Note that such efficiency is also not achieved by any prior work with $o(\log(N))$ servers (even *any* $\mathsf{poly}(N)$ preprocessing time).

To transfer the doubly efficient PIR scheme of Lin et al. [55] into the information-theoretic setting, the first challenge is to find a way to hide the query without employing homomorphic encryption. In the multi-server setting, secret sharing has been a solution to hide the client query without the use of encryption [5,71]. However, it is not immediately clear how to secret share the input in a way that preserves the homomorphism necessary to evaluate the polynomial from the server side without blowing up the cost.

We therefore take a slightly different approach, inspired by the elegant result of Woodruff and Yekhanin [76], which removes the necessity for finding a secret sharing scheme with homomorphic properties. In particular, they ask each server to evaluate a single point on the polynomial representing the database, and the client can recover the database point using these evaluations. Following this work, we can apply the polynomial-preprocessing data structure considered in [55]. In more detail, we can let each server preprocess the polynomial in advance, and then evaluate the preprocessed result online.

One immediate issue, however, is that using the result in [55], the resulting scheme has relatively bad efficiency. In particular, we need the preprocessing time to be $\mathsf{poly}(N)$ or we need $\mathsf{polylog}(N)$ servers with some large hidden factor in the exponent (i.e., $\log^r(N)$ for some large r, i.e. $r > 20$).

Thus, instead, We also employ a different polynomial preprocessing technique [10] than the one used in [55]. Such new result introduces some new constraints (e.g., the characteristic of $\mathbb{F}_q$ the polynomial works over p needs to be $d^{o(1)}$ where d is the individual degree of the polynomial), and thus we need to carefully balance how the parameters are chosen to make sure the preprocessing works and achieve the desired efficiency. We expand on these in more detail in Sects. 4 and 5.

New PIR Schemes in the Multi-Server Setting with Communication. In this part of our work, we consider a setting where the database is distributed across multiple servers, and these servers are allowed to communicate and maintain state. Note here that the non-collusion assumption remains. We believe the communication among servers is a reasonable setting. Specifically, since PIR schemes assume the databases on all servers to be identical, communication is required at least to synchronize the data between all servers. The difference is that in this setting, communication is necessary at query time. Similarly, the cost of (global) statefulness is also minor, since most use cases of PIR [4,39] consider dynamic databases and require periodic updates. Thus, being stateful is not an extra requirement for updatable PIR.

Furthermore, in our construction, the cost of updating the state is not larger than the cost of serving the client query, which greatly surpasses the existing updatable PIR constructions [27,43,53].

For this setting, we show that against an unbounded adversary, $k = 3$ servers are sufficient to achieve a DEPIR scheme with $N \mathsf{poly} \log N$ preprocessing time and $\log^3(N)$ online communication and server computation time.

This family of PIR construction leverages a cryptographic primitive called distributed oblivious RAM (DORAM) [60]. Interestingly, while there have been a lot of constructions for DORAM [21–23,25,37,38,45,60,74,80], to our knowledge, there is no construction that uses DORAM to build PIR. We show that DORAM can be directly used to build PIR with essentially no overhead, and thus any concretely efficient DORAM implies a concretely efficient PIR scheme in this communicating-server setting. Also, increasing the number of servers or introducing computational assumptions can improve concrete costs. This is discussed in Sect. 6.

Comparisons with Prior Information-Theoretic PIR Works. As shown in Table 1, compared to [8] with constant k number of servers, our construction achieves better efficiency (both for preprocessing and online queries). A similar comparison can be drawn when compared to [76]. Compared to [8] with polylogarithmic number of servers, our construction achieves better preprocessing efficiency, while requiring a smaller number of servers. On the other hand, our online efficiency is slightly worse. Nonetheless, altogether, our work provides a preprocessing time and query time trade-off not achievable before.

Comparison with Concurrent and Independent Work. Some recent concurrent and independent work addresses some of the same problems we tackle in this paper. At a high level, heir scheme achieves similar complexities as ours in the settings we share, although some of their constructions generalize to a broader parameter set. Their work does not cover the communicating server setting in Theorem 6, that is unique to our work. We provide a more precise comparison between the two schemes in Appendix A.

1.2 Other Related Works

Client preprocessing PIR was first introduced in the two-server setting by Corrigan-Gibbs and Kogan [19,20,27,48,50,51,53,70,75,83,84]. As aforementioned, in this setting, the client and server jointly run a preprocessing phase and the client stores a hint which it later uses to perform queries in time sublinear in the database size. (A version where the queries run in linear time was introduced by [68] eariler.) Although the server has to run one preprocessing phase per client, one big advantage of this model is that the server stores no additional bits server-side other than the original database. In contrast, server preprocessing schemes can require quite large server storage overheads, up to 100x the size of the original database [7,55]. The original work also showed a lower bound on the efficiency of schemes in client preprocessing model. In specific, if the preprocessing phase outputs a hint of size $O(Q)$, then the query phase must at least in time $O(N/Q)$.Several works have since improved the original work by Corrigan-Gibbs et al. in terms of bandwidth [72], as well as devised single-server client preprocessing schemes with similar techniques and asymptotics [19,26,50,82].

One line of work in server preprocessing not mentioned above, by [13,42] achieved PIR schemes with $\widetilde{O}(\mathsf{poly}(N))$ preprocessing time and $\mathsf{polylog}(N)$ both client and server time per query from non-standard assumptions. Holmgren et al. [42] were actually the first to coin the term *doubly efficient PIR.* Both their work and the concurrent work by Boyle et al. [13] also consider the problem of doubly efficient PIR. We do not make comparison with these works because they both rely on non-standard assumptions to build their schemes. Specifically, the scheme in [42] relies on a Hidden Permutation with Noise (HPN) assumption and the scheme in [13] relies on a permuted puzzles assumption (a toy version of which was broken in subsequent works). We do not currently still have a good grasp on the true level of security these conjectured assumptions provide. Furthermore, these schemes rely on a trusted party to run the preprocessing. Since then, there have been no advances in this line of work which considers a trusted third party to run the preprocessing (even under standard assumptions) and it could also be an avenue towards more practical PIR (although the trusted party assumption is difficult to enforce in practice).

Other works have studied preprocessing that does not reduce asymptotic server load but performs extremely fast in practice in the single server setting [2,40,62,64]

PIR has been used as a building block for many different privacy-preserving applications, such as meta-data hiding messaging [3], private streaming [36], private contact-tracing [41], and more [4,62]. One interesting application of PIR is Oblivious Message Retrieval (OMR), a primitive introduced in [57] to address the private retrieval issue in the setting of privacy-preserving blockchains. In a very recent work [46], Jia et al. developed a multi-server OMR construction that uses PIR as a building block. Therefore, multi-server PIR can also be interesting to blockchain settings.

2 Preliminary

In this section we will cover important primitives and definitions necessary for our work.

Notation. $\mathbb{F}_q$ defines a finite field of size q. The characteristic of a finite field is the smallest positive number of copies of the field's multiplicative identity (i.e., 1) that will sum to the additive identity (i.e., 0). If q is a prime power (i.e., $q = p^\alpha$ for some prime p and $\alpha \geq 0$), the characteristic of $\mathbb{F}_q$ is p. We use $\widetilde{O}(\log(N))$ to represent $O(\log(N)\mathsf{poly}\log\log(N))$.

2.1 Private Information Retrieval

First, we define doubly efficient private information retrieval (DEPIR) formally. This definition captures the informal requirements of our client always being able to reconstruct the desired database entry at the end of the protocol, as well as the requirement that servers, individually, not learn anything about the query index picked by the client. (This is the standard definition for non-colluding, non-communicating servers.)

Definition 1 (Multi-server DEPIR with server preprocessing [16,55]). *A k-server, server preprocessing Private Information Retrieval scheme for a database of length N consists of four PPT algorithms:*

- *a preprocessing function* $\mathsf{Preprocess}$*:* $\mathsf{DB} \in \{0,1\}^N \to \widetilde{\mathsf{DB}}$*;*

- *a query function* $\mathsf{Query}: (i \in [N], j \in [k]) \rightarrow q$*;*
- *an answer functions* $\mathsf{Answer}: (\widetilde{\mathsf{DB}}, q) \rightarrow A$*;*
- *a reconstruction function* $\mathsf{Reconstruct}: a_1, \ldots, a_k \rightarrow \{0,1\}$*.*

These functions should satisfy the correctness and privacy defined below.

Correctness: *For every* $\mathsf{DB} \in \{0,1\}^N$*, let* $\widetilde{\mathsf{DB}} = \mathsf{Preprocess}(\mathsf{DB})$*. For any* $i \in [N]$*, let* $q_j \leftarrow \mathsf{Query}(i,j)$*, and* $a_j \leftarrow \mathsf{Answer}(\widetilde{\mathsf{DB}}, q_j)$*, where* $j \in [k]$*, it holds that*

$$\Pr[\mathsf{Reconstruct}(i, a_1, \ldots, a_j) = \mathsf{DB}[i]] = 1$$

Privacy: *For every* $i_1, i_2 \in [N], j \in [k]$*, and* $q \in \mathbf{Q}$ *where* $\mathbf{Q}$ *is the output space of* Query*,*

$$\Pr[\mathsf{Query}(i_1, j) = q] = \Pr[\mathsf{Query}(i_2, j) = q]$$

Then, a PIR scheme is doubly-efficient if it satisfies the following property.

Doubly Efficient: *A PIR construction is doubly efficient if it is both Preprocessing efficient and Query efficient, which are defined as follows:*

- *(Preprocessing efficient) For any database* $\mathsf{DB} \in \{0,1\}^N$*, the runtime of* $\widetilde{\mathsf{DB}} \leftarrow \mathsf{Preprocess}(\mathsf{DB})$ *and* $|\widetilde{\mathsf{DB}}|$ *are both* $N^{1+o(1)}$*.*
- *(Query efficient) For any* $i \in [N]$*, let* $q_j \leftarrow \mathsf{Query}(i,j)$*,* $a_j \leftarrow \mathsf{Answer}(\widetilde{\mathsf{DB}}, q_j)$*, for all* $j \in [k]$*, and* $\mathsf{Reconstruct}(i, a_1, \ldots, a_j)$*, it holds that:*
  1. *The total runtime of the* k *calls of* Query, Answer *and the one call of* Reconstruct *in total are* $N^{o(1)}$*.*
  2. $|(q_1, \ldots, q_k, a_1, \ldots, a_k)| = N^{o(1)}$*.*

Note that this definition naturally captures the multi-query setting since it assumes correctness for any query after the preprocessing. This definition is slightly modified from the original definition presented in [16] (and adapted according to [55] to accommodate the doubly efficient definition). For the double efficiency requirement, we additionally require the preprocessing to be at most $N^{1+o(1)}$ instead of $\mathsf{poly}(N)$ as in prior works.

PIR with Communicating and Stateful Servers. Now, we alternatively define PIR against a set of k communicating servers. The definition above is not sufficient, since the interfaces and privacy do not take communication and statefulness of the servers into consideration. While we maintain the standard definition above for our schemes in Sects. 4 and 5, we provide a new definition for the multi-server setting that allows communication.

Our new definition follows from other multi-party computation privacy notions. We allow server interaction, and define the new privacy guarantee (servers learn nothing as long as at least one participating servers is honest). In more detail, the new game asks the adversary to distinguish the view of any subset of the servers (up to $k-1$ servers) for two (adversarially picked) sequences of queries

This is captured formally below.

Definition 2 (Communicating and Stateful Multi-server DEPIR with server preprocessing).

A k-server, server preprocessing, and server communication allowed, Private Information Retrieval scheme with stateful servers for a database of length N consists of four PPT procedures:

- *A preprocessing procedure* $\mathsf{Preprocess}(\mathsf{DB} \in \{0,1\}^N) \to (\widetilde{\mathsf{DB}}_j)_{j\in[k]}$*; where server* j *holds* $\widetilde{\mathsf{DB}}_j$*;*
- *a query procedure* $\mathsf{Query}(i \in [N]) \to q_1, \ldots, q_k$*;*
- *an interactive answer procedure* $\mathsf{Answer}((\widetilde{\mathsf{DB}}_j)_{j\in[k]}, (q_j)_{j\in[k]}) \to a_1, \ldots, a_k$*; run between the k servers, servers are stateful and thus this procedure also implicitly outputs updated* $\widetilde{\mathsf{DB}}_j$ *for* $j \in [k]$*.*
- *a reconstruction procedure* $\mathsf{Reconstruct}(a_1, \ldots, a_k) \to \{0,1\}$*; this takes in the server answers and outputs the queried database bit.*

These functions should satisfy the correctness and privacy games below, as well as the efficiency requirement; for any $w, k, N \in \mathbb{N}$*,* $k \geq 2$*.*

Correctness. *For every* $\mathsf{DB} \in \{0,1\}^N$*, let* $(\widetilde{\mathsf{DB}}_j)_{j\in[k]} = \mathsf{Preprocess}(\mathsf{DB})$*. For any* $i \in [N]$*, let* $(q_j)_{j\in[k]} \leftarrow \mathsf{Query}(i)$*, and* $(a_j)_{j\in[k]} \leftarrow \mathsf{Answer}((\widetilde{\mathsf{DB}}_j)_{j\in[k]}, (q_j)_{j\in[k]})$*, it holds that*

$$\Pr[\mathsf{Reconstruct}(i, a_1, \ldots, a_k) = \mathsf{DB}[i]] \geq 1 - \mathsf{negl}(\lambda)$$

Privacy. *The following must hold for every* $\mathsf{DB} \in \{0,1\}^N$*, and for any two sequences* $i_{1,1}, \ldots, i_{1,w} \in [N]$ *and* $i_{2,1}, \ldots, i_{2,w} \in [N]$*.*

For $\alpha \in \{1,2\}$*:*

- *Let* $(\widetilde{\mathsf{DB}}_j^{\alpha})_{j\in[k]} = \mathsf{Preprocess}(\mathsf{DB})$*.*
- *For* $\beta \in [w]$*:*
  - *Let* $(q_j^{\alpha,\beta})_{j\in[k]} \leftarrow \mathsf{Query}(i_{\alpha,\beta})$*.*
  - *Let* $(a_j^{\alpha,\beta})_{j\in[k]} \leftarrow \mathsf{Answer}((\widetilde{\mathsf{DB}}_j^{\alpha})_{j\in[k]}, (q_j)_{j\in[k]})$*.*

Then, for any $j \in [k]$*, let* $\mathsf{View}_j(\alpha)$ *denote the view of server* j *when processing queries for* $i_{\alpha,1}, \ldots, i_{\alpha,w}$*. A PIR scheme is private if it holds that* $\mathsf{View}_j(1)$ *is indistinguishable from* $\mathsf{View}_j(2)$ *for all* $j \in [k]$*.*

Doubly Efficient. *Finally, a PIR scheme is doubly-efficient if it satisfies the efficiencies denoted in Definition 1 (with interfaces adapted accordingly).*

2.2 Polynomial Preprocessing

As aforementioned, our (first two) schemes will make use of polynomial preprocessing schemes, which take as input a polynomial and output a data structure that can later be used to evaluate the input polynomial much faster than a standard evaluation. Specifically, a polynomial preprocessing scheme has two algorithms. The first algorithm, preprocessing, takes in a polynomial and outputs a datastructure. The second algorithm, evaluate, takes in this data structure and any point and outputs the evaluation of the polynomial.

We restate the results from Bhargava et al. [10] as follows.[2]

Theorem 1 (Thm 6.1 in [10]). *For a m-variate polynomial $P : \mathbb{F}_q^m \to \mathbb{F}_q$ with individual degree $\leq d$, over some finite field $\mathbb{F}_q$ such that $q = p^\alpha$ for some prime $p = d^{o(1)}$ and $\alpha > 0$ then, there exists an algorithm* PolyPreProcess *such that (1) the runtime of* $\mathsf{PolyPreProcess}(P)$ *is* $(\alpha dp)^m \cdot 4^m \cdot \mathsf{poly}(\alpha, d, m, p)$*; (2) let* $\widetilde{P} \leftarrow \mathsf{PolyPreProcess}(P)$*, for any* $\vec{x} \in \mathbb{F}_q^m$*,* $\widetilde{P}(\vec{x}) = P(\vec{x})$ *and that the runtime of* $\widetilde{P}(\vec{x})$ *is* $4^m \cdot \mathsf{poly}(\alpha, d, m, p)$*.*

With appropriate parameter choices, we will be able to find a polynomial P that represents our database of N bits such that we can preprocess P into a data structure in time $O(N^{1+o(1)})$ and subsequently evaluate P at any point in time $O(N^{o(1)})$. We dive more into the exact details in Sect. 4.

2.3 Polynomial Interpolation

Notice that to be able to use the polynomial preprocessing scheme mentioned above in a PIR scheme, we need to find a polynomial that represents the database. For any $x \in \{0,1\}^N$, we need to find a polynomial P such that for any $i \in [N]$, $P(\mathsf{encode}(i)) = x_i$, for some encoding function encode to be defined later. This is the problem of polynomial interpolation. Given a set of N points, we need to fit a polynomial to these points. It is well-known that we can find a univariate polynomial of degree N that interpolates N points in time $O(N \log N)$ [29,55]. This result is also extended to the multi-variate polynomial setting, as seen in the theorem below.[3]

Lemma 1 (Lemma B.1 in [55]). *Let $\mathbb{F}_q$ be a finite field, and let $m \in \mathbb{N}$ be an integer. Let $\{y_{x_1,\ldots,x_m} \in \mathbb{F}_q\}_{(x_1,\ldots,x_m)\in\mathbb{F}_d^m}$ be any set of d^m values. Then, there is an algorithm that runs in time* $O(d^m \cdot m \cdot \mathsf{polylog}(q))$ *and recoveres the coefficients of a polynomial $f(X_1,\ldots,X_m) \in \mathbb{F}_q[X_1,\ldots,X_m]$ with individual degree less than d in each variable such that $f(x_1,\ldots,x_m) = y_{x_1,\ldots,m_m}$ for all $(x_1,\ldots,x_m) \in \mathbb{F}_q^m$.*

3 Multi-server PIR by Woodruff and Yekhanin

We first recall in detail the scheme by Woodruff and Yekhanin [76] in the k-server, no preprocessing PIR setting, which elegantly achieves large bandwidth improvements with respect to its predecessors. Our construction greatly relies on this work.

[2] This is a follow-up work to [47] which is used by [55] in their PIR construction, with slightly different asymptotics and tradeoffs. Note that [11] improves the result from [10] on some fronts, but some technical details make it unusable for our use case.

[3] Note that in [55], their lemma is stated in a prime field. However, it easily extends to any finite field, as the uni-variate polynomial interpolation used in its proof extending to multi-variate interpolation can be done in any finite field as shown in [29].

Let $h = 2k-1$ where recall k is the number of non-colluding servers available in the PIR scheme. We first define an encoding function used in [76] $\mathsf{encode} : [N] \rightarrow \mathbb{F}_p^m$ where $m = O(hN^{1/h})$ and $k < p < 2k$. We define $\mathsf{encode}(1), \ldots,$ $\mathsf{encode}(N)$ to be distinct points of hamming weight h in $\mathbb{F}_p^m$ with each individual value restricted to $\{0,1\} \subset \mathbb{F}_p$. Such encoding exists if $C(m,h) \geq N$, where C here denotes the number of combinations [6,76]. (This is database-independent but depends on public parameters such as the size of the database and the number of servers.)

Now, suppose the servers also are given along with the database an m-variate polynomial F such that for each $i \in [N]$, $F(\mathsf{encode}(i)) = \mathsf{DB}[i]$ (this can be interpolated in near-linear time).

Note F is a m-variate polynomial with a total degree of $2k-1$ which maps $\mathbb{F}_p^m \rightarrow \mathbb{F}_p$. Explicitly, F can be written as:

$$F(z_1, \ldots, z_m) = \sum_{i=1}^{N} \left(\mathsf{DB}[i] \cdot \prod_{\mathsf{encode}(i)[\ell]=1} z_\ell \right),$$

where $\mathsf{encode}(i)[\ell]$ denotes the ℓ–th element of the output of $\mathsf{encode}(i)$. One can work out that $F(\mathsf{encode}(i)) = \mathsf{DB}[i]$. Also, since each output of encode has weight h, it follows that also F has total degree at most h (at most h variable are multiplied together per term). From this setup, the client performs a query to an index $i \in [N]$ as follows:

1. Pick $\vec{v}$ uniformly at random from $\mathbb{F}_p^m$.
2. To each server $j \in [k]$, send $q_j = \mathsf{encode}(i + \lambda_j \vec{v})$, where each λ_j is a distinct non-zero element from $\mathbb{F}_q$.
3. Server j computes and returns $F(q_j)$ as well as the partial derivatives $\frac{\partial F}{\partial z_1}(q_j)$, $\ldots, \frac{\partial F}{\partial z_m}(q_j)$.

The last part of item 3 refers to the partial derivative of F with respect to variable z_i evaluated at point q_j, for each $i \in [m]$.

First, note that we can define a function $f : \mathbb{F}_q \rightarrow \mathbb{F}_q$ such that $f(\lambda_j) = F(i + \lambda_j \vec{v})$. This function has a degree at most $h = 2k-1$ because F has total degree $h = 2k-1$ as explained above. Also note that $f(0) = F(i) = \mathsf{DB}[i]$ by construction.

If it were the case that $h = k-1$, we could recover the entire function f (and thus $f(0) = \mathsf{DB}[i]$) with each server returning only $F(\mathsf{encode}(i) + \lambda_j \vec{v}) = f(\lambda_j)$ and then interpolating. However, since $h = 2k-1$, the max degree of our local polynomial f is at most $2k-1$ and therefore k points are not enough to recover $f(0)$. The observation by [76] is that we can use the fact that to interpolate a polynomial of degree $2k-1$, it suffices to know k points of the polynomial and the derivative at these same k points. Now, from the partial derivatives returned by each server, we can recover $f'(\lambda_j)$ by applying the chain rule as follows:

$$f'(\lambda_j) = \frac{\partial F(i + \lambda_j \vec{v})}{\partial \lambda} = \sum_{\ell=1}^{m} \vec{v}_\ell \cdot \frac{\partial F}{\partial z_\ell}(\mathsf{encode}(i) + \lambda_j \vec{v}).$$

Since the client knows the first element in the sum and the server returns the second part, it can therefore compute $f'(\lambda_j)$ for each $j \in [k]$ and use these along with the set of $\{f(\lambda_j)\}_{j\in[k]}$ to compute $f(0) = F(\mathsf{encode}(i) + 0 \cdot \vec{v}) = \mathsf{DB}[i]$.

With this, the client can recover $f(0) = \mathsf{DB}[i]$ the data point with k servers and $O(k^2 \log k N^{1/(2k-1)})$ of communication cost.

This scheme is the starting point for our multi-server scheme with preprocessing. Note that [76] do include mention of preprocessing PIR in their work as well, but the best they can achieve is a query time of $O(N/\log^r N)$ for some constant r. In contrast, we will pair this technique with the polynomial preprocessing techniques to achieve a query time of $N^{o(1)}$.

Below is a lemma shown along the way in [76], which we will need for our correctness proof. Essentially, it helps showing that $f(\lambda_j)$ together of the derivatives $f'(\lambda_j), \dots, f^\ell(\lambda_j)$ are enough to uniquely determine a univariate function f with degree $k \cdot \ell - 1$ for $j \in [k]$ and $k \geq 1$.

Lemma 2 (Lemma 1 in [76]). *Let $f \in \mathbb{F}_q[X]$ where $q = p^\alpha$ for some prime p and $\alpha > 0$, and $\ell \leq p - 1$. Suppose $f(X_0) = f'(X_0) = \cdots = f^\ell(X_0) = 0$, then $(X - X_0)^{\ell+1} | f$.*

4 Our First Construction

We now move to construct our multi-server doubly efficient PIR scheme. Recall that doubly efficient refers to almost linear server preprocessing time, and sublinear client query times. Note that the scheme recalled in Sect. 3 does not fit the definition since the server performs $\Omega(N)$ work per query.

Then, we pose the question of whether it is possible to utilize the recent idea in [55] to enhance the scheme in [76] preprocessing the polynomial first, and the allow the servers to serve client queries in time sublinear in the database size N. In particular, in [47], the authors show how to construct a data structure that allows one to preprocess an m-variate polynomial with individual degree $< d$ such that the preprocessing takes $\Omega(d^m \cdot m^m)$ time (and storage) and the evaluation of any arbitrary input can be done in $\mathsf{poly}(m, d, \log(q))$ time (used by Lin et al. in the PIR context in [55]).

Unfortunately, naively applying this technique to the scheme by Woodruff and Yekhanin does not achieve the desired results. Specifically, in the scheme presented, the preprocessing takes roughly $O(2^{N^{1/k}})$, since $m \approx N^{1/k}$ and $d = 2$ (each variable only has degree 1) for some constant k, Therefore, the question is: can we achieve (almost) N total preprocessing time and server-side storage while achieving (almost) constant online costs (computation and communication)?

4.1 Substituting the Function

As mentioned, the major issue is that the function evaluated by the server cannot be efficiently preprocessed. Therefore, our first idea is to replace the underlying function.

As shown in [55, Claim 4.2.1], instead, we can first encode each index $i \in [N]$ into a d-ary vector $\vec{i}$ such that $i = \sum_j \vec{i}_j \cdot d^{j-1}$ (via some deterministic encoding algorithm $\mathsf{encode}(\cdot)$). Then, we can interpolate a polynomial P with m variables and individual degree d over some finite field $\mathbb{F}_q$ for $q > d$, where $d^m \geq N$, such that $P(\vec{i}) = \mathsf{DB}[i]$.

In this case, the client instead needs to interpolate a function f with degree $d \cdot m$ (since P has m variables and each variable has degree at most d). To interpolate such a function, the client needs $d \cdot m + 1$ points, which can be obtained by $d \cdot m + 1$ servers. In [55], they provide two sets of parameter settings:

1. In the first setting, we set $d = O(\log^{2/\epsilon} N)$ and set $m = O(\epsilon \log(N)/\log\log(N))$ for some constant ϵ. In this case, the total number of servers needed is $O(\log^2(N))$ if we set $\epsilon = 2$, and the preprocessing takes $N^{1+\epsilon} = N^3$, which is $\mathsf{poly}(N)$. Alternatively, ϵ can be set smaller (e.g. 1/10), and the preprocessing becomes $N^{1.1}$ which is much closer to linear preprocessing. However, in this case, the number of servers needed is then $\log^{21}(N)$ which is quite large.
2. In the second setting, $d = 2^{O(\sqrt{\log(N)})}$ and $m = O(\sqrt{\log(N)})$. Under this setting, the preprocessing time remains $N^{1+o(1)}$ which is essentially linear. However, the total number of servers required in this case is $2^{\sqrt{\log(N)}}$, which is super-polylogarithmic, and undesirable.

Then, using this framework, it seems impossible to achieve both a polylogarithmic number of servers and an almost linear time preprocessing time. However, we notice that [10] (recalled in Theorem 1) reduces the preprocessing time of the scheme used in [55] from $d^m \cdot m^m$ to $d^m \cdot 4^m$. The requirement to use this scheme is that it only works with finite fields of small characteristic ($p = d^{o(1)}$).

By leveraging this new result, with a careful parameters selection we can achieve all of our desired asymptotics, (1) a polylogarithmic number of servers and (2) almost linear preprocessing time and (3) fast query times.

Specifically, we show in Theorem 2 that with such a new technique, and careful parameter selection, we can reduce the number of servers to $\widetilde{O}(\log(N))$, while keeping the preprocessing time $N^{1+o(1)}$, and with a query time of $N^{o(1)}$.

We formally present our scheme in Fig. 1.

Theorem 2. *The Private Information Retrieval scheme in Fig. 1 satisfies Definition 1 is doubly-efficient. In particular, it runs with efficiencies:*

- *Number of servers:* $\tilde{O}(\log(N)) = O(\frac{\log(N)\log\log(N)}{\log\log\log(N)})$.
- *Preprocess time and server storage:* $N^{1+o(1)}$.
- *Total online time:* $N^{o(1)}$.
- *Total online communication:* $N^{o(1)}$.

Proof. We prove the properties separately.

Public Parameters (set according to the proof of Theorem 2):

1. m: number of variables.
2. d: total degree of a polynomial function.
3. q: a prime power p^α for some prime p and $\alpha \in \mathbb{Z}^+$.
4. $k = dm + 1$: number of servers.
5. $\mathsf{encode}(i) \rightarrow \mathbb{F}_q^m$: deterministic mapping for $i \in [N]$ to $\mathbb{Z}_q^m$.

$\underline{\mathsf{Preprocess}(\mathsf{DB})}$:

1. Interpolate m-variate, d-degree polynomial $P : \mathbb{F}_q^m \rightarrow \mathbb{F}_q$, such that $P(\mathsf{encode}(i)) = \mathsf{DB}[i]$.
2. Compute $\widetilde{P} \leftarrow \mathsf{PolyPreProcess}(P)$.
3. Return $\widetilde{\mathsf{DB}} = \widetilde{P}$.

$\underline{\mathsf{Query}(i \in [N], j \in [k] \subset \mathbb{F}_q)}$:

1. Sample $\vec{v} \leftarrow \mathbb{F}_q^m$.
2. Compute $q_j \leftarrow j \cdot \vec{v} + \mathsf{encode}(i)$. (For simplicity, we view $[k]$ as the first k elements in $\mathbb{F}_q$.)
3. Return q_j.

$\underline{\mathsf{Answer}(\widetilde{\mathsf{DB}}, q)}$:

1. Return $\widetilde{P}(q)$.

$\underline{\mathsf{Reconstruct}(a_1, \ldots, a_k)}$:

1. Use the answer to interpolate a function $f : \mathbb{F}_q \rightarrow \mathbb{F}_q$ of degree $d \cdot m$, using $f(j) = P(j \cdot \vec{v} + \mathsf{encode}(i))$ (included in A) for $j \in [k]$ where $k = dm + 1$.
2. Return $f(0)$.

Fig. 1. Our multi-server doubly efficient PIR scheme.

Correctness: For correctness, we simply need to argue that $f(0) = P(i)$. This is simple since we have $dm + 1$ distinct points and are recovering a function f of degree dm. Follows as in [76].

Privacy: Privacy is also simple: since $\vec{v}$ is sampled uniformly at random from $\mathbb{F}_q^m$, $j \cdot \vec{v} + \mathsf{encode}(i)$ is indistinguishable from a uniformly randomly drawn vector from $\mathbb{F}_q^m$ for any $j \in [k]$ (for $[k]$ denoting k elements of $\mathbb{F}_q$).

Efficiency: Now, to prove the efficiency, we first set the parameters accordingly.

1. We set $d^m = N$ and $d = \log\log(N) = 2^{\log\log\log(N)}$, which gives $m = O(\log(N)/\log\log\log(N))$.
2. Then, we set $p = O(\log\log\log(N)) = d^{o(1)}$ (satisfying the requirement in Theorem 1).
3. Lastly, we set α such that $p^\alpha = q \geq k+1$, and thus:

$$\alpha = O(\log_p(k)) = O(\log\log(N)^{1/\log\log\log\log(N)}).$$

With these parameters, we analyze each efficiency metrics separately.

- Number of servers:

$$\begin{aligned} k &= m \cdot d \\ &= O(\log(N)\log\log(N)/\log\log\log(N)) \\ &= \tilde{O}(\log(N)) \end{aligned}$$

.

- Preprocessing time: Let's start with the preprocessing of the polynomial (line 2). Recall that from Theorem 1, the preprocessing time for a degree-d and m-variate polynomial is: $(\alpha dp)^m \cdot 4^m \cdot \mathsf{poly}(\alpha, d, m, p)$. We analyze this term by term.
  - $\alpha^m = (\log_p(k+1))^m = O(N^{1/\log\log\log\log(N)}) = N^{o(1)}$.
  - $d^m = N$.
  - $p^m = N^{\log\log\log\log(N)/\log\log\log(N)} = N^{o(1)}$.
  - $\mathsf{poly}(\alpha, d, m, p) = \mathsf{polylog}(N)$.

  Therefore, the total preprocessing time for a single function is $N^{1+o(1)}$. For $dm+1 = \mathsf{polylog}(N)$ servers, The total polynomial preprocessing time is thus $N^{1+o(1)}$.
  Now, let us move to the interpolation of the functions (line 1). As introduced in Lemma 1, the interpolation time is $N\mathsf{polylog}(N)$. Putting all these together, the preprocessing time is $N^{1+o(1)}$. Therefore, the extra storage (i.e., $|\widetilde{\mathsf{DB}}|$) is also trivially bounded by $N^{1+o(1)}$.
- Online time: The online time of the client query is simply the time for encoding, which is $O(\log(N))$. Then, for each server, the online time is to evaluate the preprocessed function. As in Theorem 1, each evaluation takes $4^m \cdot \mathsf{poly}(\alpha, d, m, p)$. Since $4^m = N^{o(1)}$ and $\mathsf{poly}(\alpha, d, m, p) = \mathsf{polylog}(N)$, the runtime of each server is $N^{o(1)}$. Since there are only $dm+1$ servers, the total runtime is also $N^{o(1)}$. Lastly, the reconstruction time is the time to reconstruct f plus the evaluation of f, which is simply bounded by $\mathsf{poly}(dm) = \mathsf{polylog}(N)$ [29]. The evaluation is also $O(dm) = \mathsf{polylog}(N)$ since the function has degree dm.
  Note that the unit of the computation cost above is the number of $\mathbb{F}_q$ operations. Note that since $q = O(\mathsf{polylog}(N))$, each $\mathbb{F}_q$ operation costs at most $\mathsf{polylog}(N)$ bit operations and thus does not affect the conclusion above.

– Online communication: The query size is simply m $\mathbb{F}_q$ elements, and thus $\mathsf{polylog}(N)$. The answer size is bounded by the total runtime of all the servers, which is thus $N^{o(1)}$. Thus, the total online communication is also $N^{o(1)}$.

With all these efficiency metrics proven, our construction indeed satisfies the definition of being *doubly efficient.*

5 Our Second Construction

Next, we explore whether we reduce the number of servers needed even further.

Recall that in [76], each server evaluates not only the interpolated function, but also the derivatives of the functions. While they only use one level of derivatives, we can naturally extend their idea to work over L levels of derivatives. In more detail, [76] shows that for an (odd) degree $2k-1$ univariate function f, it suffices to have k unique points $f(x_i) = y_i$ for $i \in [k]$ and k unique derivatives $f'(x_i) = z_i$ to uniquely determine f. We further extend their insight and show that with k points, k first derivatives, k second derivatives, and so on, up to k L-th derivatives, to uniquely determine the function with degree $k(L+1)-1$, as formally proven in the following lemma.

Lemma 3. *Suppose* $\{x_i\}, \{y_{0,i}\}, \ldots, \{y_{L,i}\}$ *are elements of some finite field* $\mathbb{F}_q$, *where* $i \in [I]$ *for some* I *greater than* 0 *and the set* $\{x_i\}$ *has size* I; *then there exists at most one polynomial* $f(x) \in \mathbb{F}_q[x]$ *of degree less than or equal to* $(L+1) \cdot I - 1$ *such that* $f(x_i) = y_{0,i}$ *and* $f^\ell(x_i) = y_{\ell,i}$ *for* $\ell \in [L-1]$ *and* f^ℓ *denotes the* ℓ*-th derivative of* f, *where* $\mathbb{F}_q$ *has characteristics* p *greater than or equal to* $L+1$.

Proof. If there exist two such polynomials $f_1(x), f_2(x)$, then let $f = f_1 - f_2$. Then, it is clear that $f(x_i) = \cdots = f^L(x_i) = 0$ for all $i \in [I]$. Thus, by Lemma 2, it holds that $\prod_{i \in [I]}(x - x_i)^{L+1} | f(x)$, implying $f(x) = 0$ since the degree of f is at most $|L+1|I-1$.

With this in mind, instead, each server calculates the partial derivatives of the interpolated polynomial P, and preprocess these derivatives as a polynomial as well. More formally, each server computes

$$\frac{\partial^\ell P}{\partial x_{z_1}, \ldots x_{z_\ell}},$$

for all $z_1, \ldots, z_\ell \in [m]^\ell$.

With L levels of derivatives, we then only need approximately dm/L servers. However, note that for each level of derivative, the number of functions that are stored at the server grows by a factor of m (as $z_1, \ldots, z_\ell \in [m]^\ell$). Thus, for L levels, there are $O(m^L)$ functions. To make the preprocessing time and online costs reasonable, we need to tune the parameters accordingly.

In Theorem 3, we show that with the careful parameter setup, we can achieve $o(\log(N))$ servers, while maintaining the online cost to be $N^{o(1)}$ and preprocessing time to be $\mathsf{poly}(N)$.

The construction of our recursive scheme is presented below in Fig. 2.

Public Parameters (set according to the proof of Theorem 3):

1. m: number of variables.
2. d: total degree of a polynomial function.
3. q: a prime power p^α for some prime p and $\alpha \in \mathbb{Z}^+$.
4. k: number of servers.
5. $\mathsf{encode}(i) \rightarrow \mathbb{F}_q^m$: deterministic mapping for $i \in [N]$ to $\mathbb{Z}_q^m$.
6. L: levels of derivatives we need.

Preprocess(DB):

1. Interpolate m-variate, d-degree polynomial $P : \mathbb{F}_q^m \rightarrow \mathbb{F}_q$, such that $P(\mathsf{encode}(i)) = \mathsf{DB}[i]$.
2. Compute $\widetilde{P} \leftarrow \mathsf{PolyPreProcess}(P)$.
3. Compute $P_{x_{z_1},\ldots,x_{z_\ell},\ell} \leftarrow \frac{\partial^\ell P}{\partial x_{z_1},\ldots,\partial x_{z_\ell}}$ for every $\ell \in [L]$, for all $(z_1, \ldots, z_\ell) \in [m]^\ell$.
4. Compute $\widetilde{P}_{x_{z_1},\ldots,x_{z_\ell},\ell} \leftarrow \mathsf{PolyPreProcess}(P_{x_{z_1},\ldots,x_{z_\ell},\ell})$.
5. Return $\widetilde{\mathsf{DB}} = (\widetilde{P}, \widetilde{P}_{x_{z_1},\ldots,x_{z_\ell},\ell})$ for all $(z_1, \ldots, z_\ell) \in [m]^\ell$ and $\ell \in [L]$.

Query($i \in [N], j \in [k] \subset \mathbb{F}_q$):

1. Sample $\vec{v} \leftarrow \mathbb{F}_q^m$.
2. Compute $q_j \leftarrow j \cdot \vec{v} + \mathsf{encode}(i)$. (For simplicity, we view $[k]$ as the first k elements in $\mathbb{F}_q$.)
3. Return q_j.

Answer($\widetilde{\mathsf{DB}}, q$) :

1. Retruen $\widetilde{P}(q)$ and $\widetilde{P}_{z_1,\ldots,z_\ell,\ell}(q)$ for all $(z_1, \ldots, z_\ell) \in [m]^\ell$ and $\ell \in [L]$.

Reconstruct($a_1, \ldots, a_k$) :

1. Use the answer to interpolate a function $f : \mathbb{F}_q \rightarrow \mathbb{F}_q$ of degree $d \cdot m$, as follows: $f(j) = P(j \cdot \vec{v} + \mathsf{encode}(i))$ (included in a_j); and

$$f^\ell(j) = \sum_{z_1,\ldots,z_\ell \in [m]^\ell} \frac{\partial^\ell P}{\partial x_{z_1}, \ldots, \partial x_{z_\ell}}(j \cdot \vec{v} + \mathsf{encode}(i)) \prod_{i \in [\ell]} \vec{v}_{z_i} \quad (1)$$

2. Return $f(0)$.

Fig. 2. Our recursive PIR scheme.

Theorem 3 (Recursive dePIR). *The Private Information Retrieval scheme in Fig. 2 satisfies Definition 1 that is query efficient. In particular, it runs with efficiencies:*

- *Number of servers:* $o(\log(N))$.
- *Preprocess time and server storage:* $N^{2+o(1)}$.
- *Total online time:* $N^{o(1)}$.
- *Total online communication:* $N^{o(1)}$.

Proof. We prove each of the properties separately. We start with the privacy and efficiency, since the correctness depends on the parameters setup analyzed in detail in the efficiency analysis.

Privacy: Privacy follows by exactly the same argument as in Theorem 2.

Efficiency: Now, to prove the efficiency, we first set the parameters accordingly.

1. We set $d^d = N$ which gives $d = \frac{\log(N)}{W(\log(N))}$ where $W(\cdot)$ is the Lambert W function [18].
2. Then, we set $m = d$.
3. And we set $L = \frac{\log(N)}{W(\log(N))^{1.5}}$.
4. Then, set $k = m \cdot d/L$.
5. Furthermore, we set prime p to be the smallest prime such that $p \geq L + 1$ (by Bertrand's postulate [65], $p = O(L)$).
6. Lastly, we set α such that $p^\alpha = q \geq k + 1$, which means:

$$\begin{aligned}\alpha &= O(\log_p(k)) \\ &= \log_p(p \cdot W(\log(N))) \\ &= 1 + \log_p(W(\log(N))) \\ &= 1 + o(1) = O(1)\,.\end{aligned}$$

With these parameters, we analyze the efficiency metrics accordingly.

- Number of servers: $k = m \cdot d/L = O(\frac{\log(N)}{\sqrt{W(\log(N))}}) = o(\log(N))$.
- Preprocessing time: Let's start with the preprocessing of each polynomial (line 2 and 4). Recall that from Theorem 1, the preprocessing time for a single function is: $(\alpha dp)^m \cdot 4^m \cdot \mathsf{poly}(\alpha, d, m, p)$. We analyze this term by term.
  - $\alpha^m = O(1)^m = N^{o(1)}$.
  - $d^m = N$ as parametrized above.
  - $p^m = O(N)$ (since $m^m = O(N)$, $p = O(L)$ and $L = o(m)$).
  - $\mathsf{poly}(\alpha, d, m, p) = \mathsf{polylog}(N)$.

Therefore, the total preprocessing time for a single function is $N^{2+o(1)}$. In total, there are at most:

$$m^L + 1 = O(N^{1/\sqrt{W(\log(N))}}) = N^{o(1)}$$

functions. Then, the total preprocessing time is $N^{2+o(1)}$.
Now, let us move to the interpolation of the functions and the calculations of the derivatives (line 1 and 3). As introduced in Lemma 1, the interpolation time is $N \cdot \mathsf{polylog}(N)$. Furthermore, computing the partial derivative over a single variable of a function is trivially bounded by $O(N)$, and since there are at most $N^{o(1)}$ partial derivatives (as calculated above), the cost is $N^{1+o(1)}$. Putting all these together, the preprocessing time is $N^{1+o(1)}$. Therefore, the extra storage is also trivially bounded by $N^{2+o(1)}$.

- Online time: The online time of the client query is trivially the time for encoding, which is $\log(N)$ Then, for each server, the online time is to evaluate the preprocessed function. As in Theorem 1, each evaluation takes $4^m \cdot \mathsf{poly}(\alpha, d, m, p)$. Since $4^m = N^{o(1)}$ and $\mathsf{poly}(\alpha, d, m, p) = \mathsf{polylog}(N)$, and there are a total of $m^L = N^{o(1)}$ evaluations, the runtime of each server is $N^{o(1)}$. Since there are only $o(\log(N))$ servers, the total runtime is also $N^{o(1)}$. Lastly, the reconstruction time is the time to reconstruct f plus the evaluation of f. Note that there are at most $N^{o(1)}$ points, we can thus recover $f(j), f'(j), f''(j), \ldots, f^L(j)$ within time $N^{o(1)}$. Lastly, using n points, we can recover function f with time $\mathsf{poly}(n)$ [29], and $n = N^{o(1)}$. The evaluation is also $O(dm) = \mathsf{polylog}(N)$ since the function has degree dm.
Again, the unit of the computation cost above is the number of $\mathbb{F}_q$ operations. However, since $q = O(\mathsf{polylog}(N))$, each $\mathbb{F}_q$ operation costs at most $\mathsf{polylog}(N)$ bit operations and thus does not affect the calculation above.
- Online communication: The query size is simply m $\mathbb{F}_q$ elements, and thus $\mathsf{polylog}(N)$. The answer size is bounded by the total runtime of all the servers, which is $N^{o(1)}$. Therefore, the total online communication for the scheme is also $N^{o(1)}$.

Correctness: Lastly, with the parameters setup, we need to argue that $f(0) = P(i)$. It is a simple application of chain rule as described in Sect. 3.

As shown in Lemma 3 (note that we set $p \geq L+1$ and thus $\mathbb{F}_q$ has characteristics $p \geq L+1$), since we have k unique points of f, k corresponding first derivatives of f, and so on, up to k corresponding L-th derivatives of f, we can uniquely determine a function f with degree $d \cdot m \leq k(L+1)-1$. The derivatives are obtained by a simple application of the chain rule (Eq. (1)).

Therefore, $f(0) = P(\mathsf{encode}(i))$.

6 Multi-server PIR from Distributed Oblivious RAM

Now, we discuss a different model for multi-server PIR. As mentioned, to the best of our knowledge, all the existing works on multi-server PIR assume that the servers do not communicate with each other can do not need to update their states per query. While this gives a weaker environment assumption, we believe that it might be too restrictive, especially since that, for the reasons we argued in Sect. 1, it is hard to fully avoid server communication and keeping states.

Given the relaxation on communication and statefulness, we show that we can achieve PIR with much better efficiency: specifically, with only 3 servers, we can achieve information-theoretic PIR with $O(\log^3(N))$ online runtime and communication with quasi-linear preprocessing.[4]

Note that for statefulness, while the servers keep a state, they do not keep a state per client, but instead keep a global state for all clients. We believe that this is a more reasonable relaxation in practice since keeping a database, especially a frequently updated database, is a global state as well. This also draws a clear difference from Oblivious RAM (ORAM), which keeps a state *per client* (and moreover requires a database per client, causing $\Omega(N \cdot M)$ storage for M clients).

The asymptotics we can achieve above, given such relaxation, dominate what can be achieved by all existing multi-server PIR constructions (including even the new ones we proposed above). The large discrepancy comes first from the number of servers, which even given a "weak" dependence on N such as $O(\log N)$ or $o(\log N)$ can be hard to satisfy for any real system. Furthermore, looking ahead, the building blocks we rely on are relatively lightweight, so the hidden constants are relatively small, and therefore this path empirically leads to very practical PIR constructions. We discuss this briefly later in the section.

Now, we will go through how to actually instantiate the PIR construction. We start from achieving our desired PIR using a trusted third party, as it helps with exposition, then show how to get rid of it.

Starting Point: A Trusted Third Party. Our key observation starts from the fact that if there exists a trusted third party, PIR can be realized using Oblivious RAM (ORAM) [34].[5] Specifically, given a server $\mathcal{S}$ and trusted party $\mathcal{T}$, we can realize PIR (with global preprocessing) as follows: the trusted party download the database DB with N entries (e.g., N bits) held by the server, encode the database into an ORAM database DB' and store it on $\mathcal{S}$ using ORAM. For a client $\mathcal{C}$, with query qry_i, send this query qry_i to $\mathcal{T}$. Then, $\mathcal{T}$ decrypts, performs an ORAM read query with $\mathcal{S}$ to obtain $\mathsf{DB}[\mathsf{qry}_i]$, and then sends $\mathsf{DB}[\mathsf{qry}_i]$ to $\mathcal{C}$. Clearly, this achieves the correctness requirement of PIR. Furthermore, privacy is guaranteed: ORAM guarantees that $\mathcal{S}$ *does not* learn anything about qry_i.[6]

Removing the Trusted Third Party. Then, the next step is to remove the trusted third party. Fortunately, using secure multi-party computation (MPC)

[4] This can be further reduced to only $\omega(\log^2(N))$ [25] but we use $O(\log^3(N))$ for simplicity.

[5] For completeness, we include a more formal description of ORAM in Appendix B.

[6] Note that a normal ORAM only protects access patterns assuming the server does not see the database contents themselves, which is easily achievable by having $\mathcal{T}$ encrypting the database and performing ORAM queries using re-randomized ciphertexts. This is widely known, so we directly assume the ORAM does not leak access patterns even when $\mathcal{S}$ can see the (encoded) database.

Public parameters: database size $\mathsf{DB} \in \{0,1\}^N$. k servers.
Procedures:

- $[\mathsf{DB}'] \leftarrow \mathsf{Init}([\mathsf{DB}])$: initialize a secret-shared encoded database DB' with the intial database DB secret shared among the k servers.
- $[\mathsf{DB}[i]], [\mathsf{DB}] \leftarrow \mathsf{Read}([i], [\mathsf{DB}'])$: takes the encoded database DB' (secret-shared aong k servers) and a secret-shared index i, and returns (1) the secret shares of $\mathsf{DB}[i]$ (the i-th item of the original database) and (2) the updated secret-shared encoded database DB' to each server.

Fig. 3. Distributed ORAM Functionality (read-only). $[x]$ denotes the secret shares of x among the k servers. For simplicity, assume this is additive secret sharing. See Appendix B for details on secret sharing.

[33,77], we can replace the trusted third party with a set of parties that can securely compute the function (given certain assumptions on their behavior, to be discussed later).

Specifically, if we replace the trusted party $\mathcal{T}$ with a set of k parties running MPC, acting as the ORAM client, we immediately obtain a $(k+1)$-server PIR. Of course, the issue is that the circuit of the MPC for ORAM query fetch is unclear: it may have size linear in N, which means that the online runtime is linear in N, making this scheme moot. However, in fact, we can indeed find a specialized MPC primitive to realize this efficiently, called *distributed ORAM.*

At a high-level, distributed ORAM (DORAM) [60] has k servers, a RAM functionality on secret-shared inputs and outputs. In more detail, DORAM participants (the k servers) jointly hold a database DB (each server holding a share of DB), and also some secret-shared index i, DORAM returns the shares of $\mathsf{DB}[i]$ to each server. More formally, it is defined in Fig. 3, adapted from [24]:

Note that we only need the read functionality of DORAM, so in Fig. 3, we only define the Read functionality. Despite the write functionality not being useful for our standard PIR functionality, it can be useful for updating database values or adding new database values in the settings where the database is dynamic. We discuss this further down in the section.[7]

From DORAM to PIR. Now, we are ready to discuss how to achieve PIR with DORAM. The construction is straightforward: we let the k servers secret share their (shared) database, and use DORAM Init to encode the database and obtain a shared $[\mathsf{DB}']$. Then, for a client with query qry, it secret shares the query, sends the shares to each server. Then, the servers use DORAM to obtain the shares of $\mathsf{DB}[\mathsf{qry}]$ (and of course the updated encoded database DB' accordingly), and

[7] The definition in [24] includes an $\mathsf{Extract}$ procedure (which extracts the original non-encoded database in the secret-sharing form) to be run periodically to re-instantiate the database for efficiency. This is not necessary in all DORAM constructions and is not relevant in the PIR setting.

Public Parameters:

1. N: database size
2. k: number of servers.

Preprocess(DB):

1. Server $j \in [k]$ obtains the share $[\mathsf{DB}]_j$ (denoting the j-th share of DB).
2. All k servers together run $[\mathsf{DB}'] \leftarrow \mathsf{Init}([\mathsf{DB}])$ (the DORAM initialization procedure) and server j stores $\widetilde{\mathsf{DB}}_j := [\mathsf{DB}']_j$.

Query($i \in [N]$):

1. Secret share i into $[i]_j$ for server $j \in [k]$.
2. $q_j := [i]_j$.

Answer($\widetilde{\mathsf{DB}}_1 = [\mathsf{DB}']_1, \ldots, \widetilde{\mathsf{DB}}_k = [\mathsf{DB}']_k, q_1 = [i]_1, \ldots, q_k = [i]_k$) :

1. k servers together run $[\mathsf{DB}[i]] \leftarrow \mathsf{Read}([\mathsf{DB}'], [i])$ and server j holds $[\mathsf{DB}[i]]_j$.
2. $a_j := [\mathsf{DB}[i]]_j$.

Reconstruct($a_1 = [\mathsf{DB}[i]]_1, \ldots, [\mathsf{DB}[i]]_k$) :

1. Reconstruct $\mathsf{DB}[i]$ via $[\mathsf{DB}[i]]$.
2. Return $\mathsf{DB}[i]$.

Fig. 4. Our DORAM-based PIR construction.

sends these shares back to the client. The client locally recovers $\mathsf{DB}[\mathsf{qry}]$ using the secret shares. We describe it formally as follows.

Theorem 4 (DORAM-based PIR). *The Private Information Retrieval scheme in Fig. 4 satisfies Definition 2. In particular, it runs with efficiencies:*

- *Number of servers: k.*
- *Preprocess time and server storage: T_{Init}.*
- *Total online time and communication: T_{Read}.*

assuming the underlying DORAM scheme (Fig. 3) with k servers, Init *runtime being T_{Init}, and* Read *runtime being T_{Read}.*

Proof. The proof is straightforward. The correctness and privacy follow directly from DORAM and secret sharing. The efficiency also directly follows since the construction essentially only uses DORAM.

Realization and Efficiency of DORAM. Since our PIR construction essentially directly follows from DORAM, an efficient DORAM construction implies an efficient PIR construction. Specifically, using GigaDORAM [25], we achieve quasi-linear preprocessing time, and $O(\log^3(N))$ online time and communication. These are asymptotically better than any existing multi-server PIR construction, including our constructions above and the concurrent work [30]. Concretely, this in fact allows us to make one PIR query against 8GB of database with only about 1ms, according to the benchmarks in [25], which is also orders of magnitude faster than any existing PIR construction. While GigaDORAM is based on computational privacy, we can also use other DORAM constructions with information-theoretic privacy achieving similar asymptotics (e.g., [24]). Malicious security can also be achieved by using [38]. Any future advances in DORAM could also greatly improve our PIR construction.

Updatable PIR. As mentioned, many PIR works are also concerned with the updates [28,43,48,52,55,61]. Luckily, our construction can deal with updates very efficiently. Specifically, DORAM, in addition, supports writes as well, which means that the servers can simply jointly use DORAM writes to update the database with $O(\log^3(N))$ time.

Further Application to Oblivious Message Retrieval. An additional application of DORAM is Oblivious Message Retrieval (OMR) [57]. Essentially, OMR works in anonymous messaging systems, where the recipient would like to retrieve the message address to them, but for a message, before performing the retrieval, only the sender knows who the recipient is, and this information should be kept confidential from anyone else. To address this issue, most existing construction as single-server [54,56–59]. There are also several two-server constructions [17,46]. However, all these constructions have *linear* online time per retrieval per recipient, even for the two-server constructions.

However, this online time can be greatly improved with DORAM. Specifically, in [44], the authors introduced a way to build OMR with trusted hardware plus ORAM. One could easily replace this trusted hardware with MPC and ORAM with DORAM. This allows a multi-server OMR construction with poly-logarithmic online time, greatly improving upon the state-of-the-art constructions asymptotically. However, whether this approach is concretely more efficient is still an open question left for future work.

7 Concluding Remarks

In this paper, we introduce three multi-server PIR constructions. Our first two constructions are more of theoretical interests, while our third construction, we believe, for the very first time, introduces a new path towards making PIR practical. As mentioned, with existing DORAM constructions, we can fetch one PIR query with only $\approx$ 1ms for an 8GB database, and the runtime growth is only $O(\log^3(N))$.

Rational Instead of Honest Servers. One interesting question to consider is the case where the servers might want to collude covertly, if it is profitable to them. In particular, as all prior works [8,30,76], our work assumes that the servers do not collude.

However, one interesting direction is to relax this assumption further. Instead of assuming all the servers to be semi-honest and not to collude with each other, can we relax this assumption to assume the servers to be rational players? In this framework, we need to prove that any rational server would not want to collude and instead follow the protocol.

A recent work [35] explored this multi-server PIR in this rational setting. At a high level, the work provides a transformation from the non-collusion model to the rational server model through a public contract. It works as follows.

When servers collude and learn any non-trivial information $f(i)$ where i is the index that the client retrieves, within a pre-determined period of time (which can be long, e.g., years), the server(s) can submit a report to show that they have learned such nontrivial information via collusion. The first server that correctly submits the report is rewarded and the rest gets punished. To avoid false reports and false accusations, the work employs additional techniques.

This same idea can be applied to our multi-server PIR constructions in practice to avoid the non-collusion assumption. According to [35], the cost of setting it up is under 10 dollars when setting up the contract using Ethereum.

Future Work. For future work, we find the following questions to be compelling:

- (Reducing the number of servers) For the non-communicating model, can we reduce the number of non-colluding servers required to a constant number (ideally 2), while maintaining our current asymptotics (or slightly relaxing the current asymptotics, e.g., allowing the preprocessing time to be $O(N^{1+\epsilon})$ for some constant ϵ)? We know of no negative results in this regard. Nevertheless, there are no known constructions even given some that achieve even close to the asymptotics above with a small, constant number of servers.
- (Computational PIR) For the non-communicating setting, can introducing (lightweight) computational assumptions (e.g. OWF) help reduce either the number of servers or the online query time for our family of schemes, without ruining the practicality? In non-preprocessing PIR, distributed point functions have enabled two-server computational PIR with $O(\log N)$ communication, which has yet to be achieved for two-server information-theoretic PIR. We think it is probable that likewise, some computational assumption may help further improve the current known asymptotics for multi-server server-preprocessing PIR.
- (Relaxing the non-collusion assumption) All multi-server PIR schemes require the assumption that the participating servers are non-colluding. However, when allowing for communication, it is not clear why we cannot achieve constructions assuming only 1-out-of-k honest party (or more generally t-out-of-k for some $t < k$). Thus, one interesting open questions is to construct DORAM with $k > 3$ assuming only 1 or $t \ll k$ honest parties without affecting the scheme's efficiency, which directly affects our PIR construction.

Acknowledgements. We thank Ran Canetti and Ling Ren for helpful discussions on alternative models for multi-server PIR. Charalampos Papamanthou and Arthur Lazzaretti were supported by NSF and Protocol Labs. Zeyu Liu was supported by Yale CADMY. Peihan Miao was supported in part by NSF, Meta, Google, and Amazon AWS.

A Discussion on the Concurrent Work

A very recent work [30] also focuses on information-theoretic multi-server PIR with server-side preprocessing.

We first note that their work does not cover the case of communicating servers. It focuses solely on the setting of k non-colluding, non-communicating servers. From Table 1, we see that asymptotically, the results from Theorem 4 dominate the results from concurrent work, however, it requires servers to communicate at query time.

In terms of comparison between our work and their work for the setting of non-communicating servers, our works compare as follows. In [30, Thm 1.3 & Appendix B], they achieve $\mathsf{poly}(N)$ preprocessing time and storage, $\mathsf{polylog}(N)$ online costs (computation and communication) with $\mathsf{polylog}(N)$ servers, which asymptotically is similar to [8, Thm 4.9] (summarized in Table 1, the fourth row).

Compared to our result in this non-communicating-server setting, our result achieves better preprocessing time than both schemes (with fewer servers), as seen in Table 1 (although our query time is slightly worse, it is not clear that either scheme can achieve our preprocessing time, even at the sacrifice of their query time).

The other results in [30] provide alternative constructions for a constant number of servers which allow finer tuning than prior works in terms of online computation and communication (see Table 1, the third row): allowing better communication by trading-off some online computation cost. On the other hand, our paper focuses on providing a tradeoff between the number of servers and the preprocessing time, for a reasonably small number of servers (roughly or less than $\log(N)$ servers), while still maintaining small online costs (i.e., $N^{o(1)}$).

In terms of techniques for this setting, our works share similarities as both are based on [70] and both use polynomial preprocessing. However, they use Hasse derivatives while we use normal derivatives, as well as different techniques and a different polynomial preprocessing scheme.

This comparison is with the version of their paper released concurrently with ours. A later version of their paper improves some of their results further. Specifically, newer version of [30] was after the original version and our original version in [31]. They achieve close to $N^{1+o(1)}$ preprocessing time and storage, close to $N^{o(1)}$ online time and communication, with $\omega(1)$ servers. This $o(1), \omega(1)$ asymptotics is a summary of all the results from [31], but for a more detailed representation, please see [31, Thm 1.1, 1.2, 1.3]. While this improves upon their older result, it is still dominated by our DORAM-based constructions. Thus, a similar conclusion can be drawn as before.

B Additional Preliminaries

Obliviosu RAM. At a high level, Oblivious RAM (ORAM) [34] allows one to hide its access pattern to a database.

Definition 3. *ORAM contains one PPT algorithm:*

- $\mathsf{data}' \leftarrow \mathsf{Access}(\mathsf{DB}, \mathsf{op}, \mathsf{a}, \mathsf{data})$: *on the input of an identifier* DB *to some database, an operation* op *that can be either* Read *or* Write, *an identifier of the data block (e.g., memory location of the data block), and a data block* data, *returns a data block* data.

Let $\mathsf{ORAM.Read}(\mathsf{DB}, \mathsf{a})$ *denote* $\mathsf{Access}(\mathsf{DB}, \mathsf{Read}, \mathsf{a}, \cdot)$ *(here* $\cdot$ *is a dummy input) and let* $\mathsf{ORAM.Write}(\mathsf{DB}, \mathsf{a}, \mathsf{data})$ *denote* $\mathsf{Access}(\mathsf{DB}, \mathsf{Write}, \mathsf{a}, \mathsf{data})$.

Let $\vec{x} = ((\mathsf{DB}, \mathsf{op}_1, \mathsf{a}_1, \mathsf{data}_1), \ldots, (\mathsf{DB}, \mathsf{op}_Q, \mathsf{a}_Q, \mathsf{data}_Q))$ *denote a data request sequence of length* Q*, where* op_i *is the operation that can be either* Read *OR* Write, a_i *is the identifier of the data block, and* data_i *is the data being written. We define ORAM construction's correctness and privacy as follows:*

- *(Correctness) On the input* $\vec{x}$*, it returns data that is consistent with* $\vec{x}$ *with probability* $\geq 1 - \mathsf{negl}(|\vec{x}|)$.
- *(Computational Privacy) Let* $A(\vec{x})$ *be a sequence of accesses given the sequence of data requests* $\vec{x}$*. An ORAM construction is computationally private if for any two data request sequences* $\vec{y}$ *and* $\vec{z}$ *of the same length, their access patterns* $A(\vec{y})$ *and* $A(\vec{z})$ *are computationally indistinguishable by PPT algorithm except for the TEE.*

As mentioned, ORAM does not consider the server's ability to see the database. However, as long as the database is encrypted and all the operations are done via rerandomized ciphertexts, the privacy guarantee is maintained even if the server can see the database. This is widely assumed as recognized in ORAM literature (e.g., [73]).

Secret Sharing. As mentioned, we use secret sharing [71] in Sect. 6. For simplicity, aligned with the DORAM definition used in [24], we use additive secret sharing. Specifically, for $x \in \{0,1\}^*$, $x = \oplus_{j\in[k]} x_j$ where $x_j \leftarrow_\$ \{0,1\}^*$ for $j \in [k-1]$. Then, $[x]_j := x_j$ is the j-th share of x.

References

1. Ahmad, I., Yang, Y., Agrawal, D., Abbadi, A.E., Gupta, T.: Addra: metadata-private voice communication over fully untrusted infrastructure (2021)
2. Ali, A., et al.: Communication–computation trade-offs in PIR, pp. 1811–1828 (2021)

3. Angel, S., Setty, S.: Unobservable communication over fully untrusted infrastructure. In: Proceedings of the 12th USENIX Conference on Operating Systems Design and Implementation, OSDI 2016, pp. 551–569. USENIX Association, USA (2016)
4. Backes, M., ate, A., Maffei, M., Pecina, K.: ObliviAd: provably secure and practical online behavioral advertising. In: 2012 IEEE Symposium on Security and Privacy, pp. 257–271 (2012). ISSN 2375-1207
5. Beimel, A., Ishai, Y.: Information-theoretic private information retrieval: a unified construction. In: Orejas, F., Spirakis, P.G., van Leeuwen, J. (eds.) ICALP 2001. LNCS, vol. 2076, pp. 912–926. Springer, Heidelberg (2001). https://doi.org/10.1007/3-540-48224-5_74
6. Beimel, A., Ishai, Y., Kushilevitz, E., Raymond, J.-F.: Breaking the O(n1(2k-1)/) barrier for information-theoretic private information retrieval, pp. 261–270 (2002)
7. Beimel, A., Ishai, Y., Malkin, T.: Reducing the servers computation in private information retrieval: PIR with preprocessing. In: Bellare, M. (ed.) CRYPTO 2000. LNCS, vol. 1880, pp. 55–73. Springer, Heidelberg (2000). https://doi.org/10.1007/3-540-44598-6_4
8. Beimel, A., Ishai, Y., Malkin, T.: Reducing the servers' computation in private information retrieval: PIR with preprocessing. J. Cryptol. **17**, 125–151 (2004)
9. Beimel, A., Stahl, Y.: Robust information-theoretic private information retrieval. J. Cryptol. **20**(3), 295–321 (2007)
10. Bhargava, V., Ghosh, S., Guo, Z., Kumar, M., Umans, C.: Fast multivariate multipoint evaluation over all finite fields. In: 2022 IEEE 63rd Annual Symposium on Foundations of Computer Science (FOCS), pp. 221–232 (2022). ISSN 2575-8454
11. Bhargava, V., Ghosh, S., Kumar, M., Mohapatra, C.K.: Fast, algebraic multivariate multipoint evaluation in small characteristic and applications. In: Proceedings of the 54th Annual ACM SIGACT Symposium on Theory of Computing, STOC 2022, pp. 403–415. Association for Computing Machinery, New York (2022)
12. Boyle, E., Gilboa, N., Ishai, Y.: Function secret sharing. In: Oswald, E., Fischlin, M. (eds.) EUROCRYPT 2015. LNCS, vol. 9057, pp. 337–367. Springer, Heidelberg (2015). https://doi.org/10.1007/978-3-662-46803-6_12
13. Boyle, E., Ishai, Y., Pass, R., Wootters, M.: Can we access a database both locally and privately? (2017)
14. Chor, B., Gilboa, N., Naor, M.: Private information retrieval by keywords (1998). Report Number: 003
15. Chor, B., Goldreich, O., Kushilevitz, E., Sudan, M.: Private information retrieval (1995)
16. Chor, B., Goldreich, O., Kushilevitz, E., Sudan, M.: Private information retrieval. In: 36th FOCS, pp. 41–50. IEEE Computer Society Press (1995)
17. Chu, H., Wang, X., Jia, Y.: Private signaling secure against actively corrupted servers. Cryptology ePrint Archive, Paper 2025/1056 (2025)
18. Corless, R., Gonnet, G., Hare, D., Jeffrey, D., Knuth, D.: On the lambert W function. Adv. Comput. Math. **5**, 329–359 (1996)
19. Corrigan-Gibbs, H., Henzinger, A., Kogan, D.: Single-server private information retrieval with sublinear amortized Time. In: Dunkelman, O., Dziembowski, S. (eds) EUROCRYPT 2022. LNCS, vol. 13276, pp. 3–33. Springer, Cham (2022). https://doi.org/10.1007/978-3-031-07085-3_1
20. Corrigan-Gibbs, H., Kogan, D.: Private information retrieval with sublinear online time. In: Canteaut, A., Ishai, Y. (eds.) EUROCRYPT 2020. LNCS, vol. 12105, pp. 44–75. Springer, Cham (2020). https://doi.org/10.1007/978-3-030-45721-1_3

21. Doerner, J., Shelat, A.: Scaling ORAM for secure computation. In: Thuraisingham, B.M., Evans, D., Malkin, T., Xu, D. (eds.) ACM CCS 2017, pp. 523–535. ACM Press (2017)
22. Faber, S., Jarecki, S., Kentros, S., Wei, B.: Three-party ORAM for secure computation. In: Iwata, T., Cheon, J.H. (eds.) ASIACRYPT 2015, Part I. LNCS, vol. 9452, pp. 360–385. Springer, Heidelberg (2015). https://doi.org/10.1007/978-3-662-48797-6_16
23. Falk, B.H., Noble, D., Ostrovsky, R.: 3-party distributed ORAM from oblivious set membership. In: Galdi, C., Jarecki, S. (eds.) SCN 2022. LNCS, vol. 13409, pp. 437–461. Springer, Cham (2022). https://doi.org/10.1007/978-3-031-14791-3_19
24. Falk, B.H., Noble, D., Ostrovsky, R.: MetaDORAM: info-theoretic distributed ORAM with less communication. Cryptology ePrint Archive, Report 2024/011 (2024)
25. Falk, B.H., Ostrovsky, R., Shtepel, M., Zhang, J.: GigaDORAM: breaking the billion address barrier. In: Calandrino, J.A., Troncoso, C. (eds.) USENIX Security 2023, pp. 3871–3888. USENIX Association (2023)
26. Fisch, B., Lazzaretti, A., Liu, Z., Papamanthou, C.: Single server PIR via homomorphic thorp shuffles. Cryptology ePrint Archive, Paper 2024/482 (2024). https://eprint.iacr.org/2024/482
27. Fisch, B., Lazzaretti, A., Liu, Z., Papamanthou, C.: ThorPIR: single server PIR via homomorphic thorp shuffles. In: Luo, B., Liao, X., Xu, J., Kirda, E., Lie, D. (eds.) ACM CCS 2024, pp. 1448–1462. ACM Press (2024)
28. Fisch, B., Lazzaretti, A., Liu, Z., Papamanthou, C.: ThorPIR: single server PIR via homomorphic thorp shuffles. In: Proceedings of the 2024 on ACM SIGSAC Conference on Computer and Communications Security, CCS 2024, pp. 1448–1462. Association for Computing Machinery, New York (2024)
29. Gathen, J.V.Z., Gerhard, J.: Modern Computer Algebra, 2nd edn. Cambridge University Press, USA (2003)
30. Ghoshal, A., Li, B., Ma, Y., Dai, C., Shi, E.: Information-theoretic multi-server PIR with global preprocessing. Cryptology ePrint Archive, Paper 2024/765 (2024). Version: 20240519:202013
31. Ghoshal, A., Li, B., Ma, Y., Dai, C., Shi, E.: Scalable multi-server private information retrieval. Cryptology ePrint Archive, Paper 2024/765 (2024)
32. Gilboa, N., Ishai, Y.: Distributed point functions and their applications. In: Nguyen, P.Q., Oswald, E. (eds.) EUROCRYPT 2014. LNCS, vol. 8441, pp. 640–658. Springer, Heidelberg (2014). https://doi.org/10.1007/978-3-642-55220-5_35
33. Goldreich, O., Micali, S., Wigderson, a.: How to play ANY mental game. In: Proceedings of the Nineteenth Annual ACM Symposium on Theory of Computing, STOC 1987, pp. 218–229. Association for Computing Machinery, New York (1987)
34. Goldreich, O., Ostrovsky, R.: Software protection and simulation on oblivious RAMs. J. ACM **43**(3), 431–473 (1996)
35. Gong, T., Henry, R., Psomas, A., Kate, A.: Relax the non-collusion assumption for multi-server PIR. In: S&P 2024 (2024)
36. Gupta, T., Crooks, N., Mulhern, W., Setty, S., Alvisi, L., Walfish, M.: Scalable and private media consumption with Popcorn. In: Proceedings of the 13th Usenix Conference on Networked Systems Design and Implementation, NSDI 2016, pp. 91–107. USENIX Association, USA (2016)
37. Hamlin, A., Varia, M.: Two-server distributed ORAM with sublinear computation and constant rounds. In: Garay, J.A. (ed.) PKC 2021, Part II. LNCS, vol. 12711, pp. 499–527. Springer, Cham (2021). https://doi.org/10.1007/978-3-030-75248-4_18

38. Hemenway, B., Noble, D., Ostrovsky, R., Shtepel, M., Zhang, J.: DORAM revisited: Maliciously secure RAM-MPC with logarithmic overhead. In: Rothblum, G.N., Wee, H. (eds.) TCC 2023, Part I. LNCS, vol. 14369, pp. 441–470. Springer, Cham (2023). https://doi.org/10.1007/978-3-031-48615-9_16
39. Henzinger, A., Dauterman, E., Corrigan-Gibbs, H., Zeldovich, N.: Private Web Search with Tiptoe. In: Proceedings of the 29th Symposium on Operating Systems Principles, SOSP 2023, pp. 396–416. Association for Computing Machinery, New York (2023)
40. Henzinger, A., Hong, M.M., Corrigan-Gibbs, H., Meiklejohn, S., Vaikuntanathan, V.: One Server for the price of two: simple and fast single-server private information retrieval, p. 27 (2022)
41. Hetz, L., Schneider, T., Weinert, C.: Scaling mobile private contact discovery to billions of users (2023). Publication info: Published elsewhere. Minor revision. ESORICS 2023
42. Holmgren, J., Canetti, R., Richelson, S.: Towards doubly efficient private information retrieval. Technical report 568 (2017)
43. Hoover, A., Patel, S., Persiano, G., Yeo, K.: Plinko: Single-server PIR with efficient updates via invertible PRFs. In: Fehr, S., Fouque, PA. (eds) EUROCRYPT 2025. LNCS, vol. 15606, pp. 3–33. Springer, Cham (2024). https://doi.org/10.1007/978-3-031-91095-1_1
44. Jakkamsetti, S., Liu, Z., Madathil, V.: Scalable private signaling. CSF 2025 (2025)
45. Jarecki, S., Wei, B.: 3PC ORAM with low latency, low bandwidth, and fast batch retrieval. In: Preneel, B., Vercauteren, F. (eds.) ACNS 2018. LNCS, vol. 10892, pp. 360–378. Springer, Cham (2018). https://doi.org/10.1007/978-3-319-93387-0_19
46. Jia, Y., Madathil, V., Kate, A.: HomeRun: high-efficiency oblivious message retrieval, unrestricted. In: CCS 2024 (2024)
47. Kedlaya, K.S., Umans, C.: Fast polynomial factorization and modular composition. SIAM J. Comput. **40**(6), 1767–1802 (2011)
48. Kogan, D., Corrigan-Gibbs, H.: Private blocklist lookups with checklist. In: 30th USENIX Security Symposium (USENIX Security 2021). USENIX Association (2021)
49. Kushilevitz, E., Ostrovsky, R.: Replication is not needed: single database, computationally-private information retrieval. In: FOCS 1997 (1997)
50. Lazzaretti, A., Papamanthou, C.: Near-optimal private information retrieval with preprocessing. In: Rothblum, G.N., Wee, H. (eds.) TCC 2023, Part II. LNCS, vol. 14370, pp. 406–435. Springer, Cham (2023). https://doi.org/10.1007/978-3-031-48618-0_14
51. Lazzaretti, A., Papamanthou, C.: TreePIR: Sublinear-time and polylog-bandwidth private information retrieval from DDH. In: Handschuh, H., Lysyanskaya, A. (eds.) CRYPTO 2023. Part II. LNCS, vol. 14082, pp. 284–314. Springer, Cham (2023). https://doi.org/10.1007/978-3-031-38545-2_10
52. Lazzaretti, A., Papamanthou, C.: Single pass client preprocessing private information retrieval. In: USENIX Security 2024 (2024)
53. Lazzaretti, A., Papamanthou, C.: Single pass client-preprocessing private information retrieval. In: Balzarotti, D. Xu, W. (eds.) USENIX Security 2024. USENIX Association (2024)
54. Lee, K., Yeo, Y.: SophOMR: improved oblivious message retrieval from SIMD-aware homomorphic compression. Cryptology ePrint Archive, Report 2024/1814 (2024)

55. Lin, W.-K., Mook, E., Wichs, D.: Doubly efficient private information retrieval and fully homomorphic RAM computation from ring LWE (2022). Report Number: 1703
56. Liu, Z., Sotiraki, K., Tromer, E., Wang, Y.: Snake-eye resistant PKE from LWE for oblivious message retrieval and robust encryption. In: Fehr, S., Fouque, P.-A. (eds.) EUROCRYPT 2025, Part III. LNCS, vol. 15603, pp. 126–156. Springer, Cham (2025). https://doi.org/10.1007/978-3-031-91131-6_5
57. Liu, Z., Tromer, E.: Oblivious message retrieval. In: Dodis, Y., Shrimpton, T. (eds.) Advances in Cryptology – CRYPTO 2022. LNCS, vol. 13507, pp. 753–783. Springer, Cham (2022). https://doi.org/10.1007/978-3-031-15802-5_26. Cryptology ePrint Archive 2021; internal citations follow the latter's numbering
58. Liu, Z., Tromer, E., Wang, Y.: Group oblivious message retrieval. In: 2024 IEEE Symposium on Security and Privacy, pp. 4367–4385. IEEE Computer Society Press (2024)
59. Liu, Z., Tromer, E., Wang, Y.: PerfOMR: oblivious message retrieval with reduced communication and computation. In: Balzarotti, D., Xu, W. (eds.) USENIX Security 2024. USENIX Association (2024)
60. Lu, S., Ostrovsky, R.: Distributed oblivious RAM for secure two-party computation. In: Sahai, A. (ed.) TCC 2013. LNCS, vol. 7785, pp. 377–396. Springer, Heidelberg (2013). https://doi.org/10.1007/978-3-642-36594-2_22
61. Ma, Y., Ke, Z., Rabin, T., Angel, S.: Incremental offline/online PIR (extended version). In: USENIX Security 2022 (2022)
62. Menon, S.J., Wu, D.J.: Spiral: fast, high-rate single-server PIR via FHE composition. In: IEEE Symposium on Security and Privacy 2022 (2022)
63. Mittal, P., Olumofin, F., Troncoso, C., Borisov, N., Goldberg, I.: PIR-Tor: scalable anonymous communication using private information retrieval (2011)
64. Mughees, M.H., Chen, H., Ren, L.: OnionPIR: response efficient single-server PIR. In: Proceedings of the 2021 ACM SIGSAC Conference on Computer and Communications Security, CCS 2021, pp. 2292–2306. Association for Computing Machinery, New York (2021)
65. Nagell, T.: Introduction to Number Theory. American Mathematical Society (1964). Google-Books-ID: Znc5EAAAQBAJ
66. Okada, H., Player, R., Pohmann, S., Weinert, C.: Towards practical doubly-efficient private information retrieval. In: Clark, J., Shi, E. (eds.) FC 2024. LNCS, vol. 14745, pp. 264–282. Springer, Cham (2025). https://doi.org/10.1007/978-3-031-78679-2_14
67. Okada, H., Player, R., Pohmann, S., Weinert, C.: On algebraic homomorphic encryption and its applications to doubly-efficient PIR. In: Fehr, S., Fouque, PA. (eds.) EUROCRYPT 2025. LNCS, vol. 15606. Springer, Cham (2025). https://doi.org/10.1007/978-3-031-91095-1_2. ISSN 1611-3349
68. Patel, S., Persiano, G., Yeo, K.: Private stateful information retrieval. In: Proceedings of the 2018 ACM SIGSAC Conference on Computer and Communications Security, CCS 2018, pp. 1002–1019. Association for Computing Machinery, New York (2018)
69. Persiano, G., Yeo, K.: Limits of preprocessing for single-server PIR. Technical Report 235 (2022)
70. Ren, L., Mughees, M.H., Sun, I.: Simple and practical amortized sublinear private information retrieval using dummy subsets. In: Luo, B., Liao, X., Xu, J., Kirda, E., Lie, D. (eds.) ACM CCS 2024, pp. 1420–1433. ACM Press (2024)
71. Shamir, A.: How to share a secret. Commun. ACM **22**(11), 612–613 (1979)

72. Shi, E., Aqeel, W., Chandrasekaran, B., Maggs, B.: Puncturable pseudorandom sets and private information retrieval with near-optimal online bandwidth and time. In: Malkin, T., Peikert, C. (eds.) CRYPTO 2021. LNCS, vol. 12828, pp. 641–669. Springer, Cham (2021). https://doi.org/10.1007/978-3-030-84259-8_22
73. Stefanov, E., et al.: Path ORAM: an extremely simple oblivious RAM protocol. J. ACM **65**(4), 18:1–18:26 (2018)
74. Vadapalli, A., Henry, R., Goldberg, I.: Duoram: a bandwidth-efficient distributed ORAM for 2- and 3-party computation. In: Calandrino, J.A., Troncoso, C. (eds.) USENIX Security 2023, pp. 3907–3924. USENIX Association (2023)
75. Wang, Z., Ren, L.: Single-server client preprocessing PIR with tight space-time trade-off. In: Fehr, S., Fouque, P.-A. (eds.) EUROCRYPT 2025, Part VI. LNCS, vol. 15606, pp. 94–122. Springer, Cham (2025). https://doi.org/10.1007/978-3-031-91095-1_4
76. Woodruff, D., Yekhanin, S.: A geometric approach to information-theoretic private information retrieval (2005)
77. Yao, A.C.: Protocols for secure computations. In: Proceedings of the 23rd Annual Symposium on Foundations of Computer Science, SFCS 1982, pp. 160–164. IEEE Computer Society, USA (1982)
78. Yekhanin, S.: Towards 3-query locally decodable codes of subexponential length. J. ACM **55**(1), 1–16 (2008)
79. Yekhanin, S.: Locally Decodable Codes and Private Information Retrieval Schemes. Information Security and Cryptography. Springer, Heidelberg (2010). https://doi.org/10.1007/978-3-642-14358-8
80. Zahur, S., et al.: Revisiting square-root ORAM: efficient random access in multi-party computation. In: 2016 IEEE Symposium on Security and Privacy, pp. 218–234. IEEE Computer Society Press (2016)
81. Zhao, L., Wang, X., Huang, X.: Verifiable single-server private information retrieval from LWE with binary errors. Inf. Sci. **546**, 897–923 (2021)
82. Zhou, M., Lin, W.-K., Tselekounis, Y., Shi, E.: Optimal single-server private information retrieval. ePrint IACR (2022)
83. Zhou, M., Lin, W.-K., Tselekounis, Y., Shi, E.: Optimal single-server private information retrieval. In: Hazay, C., Stam, M. (eds.) EUROCRYPT 2023, Part I. LNCS, vol. 14004, pp. 395–425. Springer, Cham (2023). https://doi.org/10.1007/978-3-031-30545-0_14
84. Zhou, M., Park, A., Shi, E., Zheng, W.: Piano: extremely simple, single-server PIR with sublinear server computation. In: 2023 IEEE S&P (2024)

Universally Composable Succinct Vector Commitments and Applications

Ran Canetti(✉) and Megan Chen

Boston University, Boston, USA
canetti@bu.edu

Abstract. We develop a toolbox for modular construction and analysis of *succinct, non-interactive* commitments and vector commitments in the random oracle model, while guaranteeing universally composable security. To demonstrate its power, we use the toolbox to construct and analyze a modular variant of the Kilian-Micali ZK-SNARK. Along the way we also propose a new UC formulation of a global random oracle, that avoids a weakness in existing formulations and also enables expressing more nuanced, session-specific abstractions. We hope that this toolbox will be useful for building secure applications in settings where both succinctness and non-interactivity are key.

1 Introduction

The Universally Composable Security (UC) framework [Can01,Can20] enables the specification of cryptographic tasks in an idealized way that precisely and robustly captures their security requirements, along with a modular design methodology where a given task is realized using idealized sub-tasks. Protocols are ultimately constructed by realizing all sub-tasks, potentially through further decomposition, until all sub-tasks are realized by concrete protocols.

Initially, the UC framework was used for analyzing the security of *interactive* protocols. Examples include [Can01,CF01,CK02,CLOS02,KLP05,DN03,MPR10]. For such protocols, ideal functionalities did not specify limits on the rounds of interaction in the realizing protocol and often require all parties to interact. In other words, an execution of such protocols consists of atomic operations, where in each atomic operation a party processes an incoming message and generates an outgoing one. This applies both to the security specifications (ideal functionalities) and to the analyzed protocols.

Another line of works use the UC framework to capture tasks that restrict the communication pattern of the realizing protocols to be *non-interactive*, i.e. protocols that consist of a single message sent by some party, plus local processing by the recipients. Examples include public-key encryption, digital signature, and non-interactive zero knowledge (NIZK), e.g. [CKN03,Can04,CSV16,GOS12,BFG+22,GKO+23,CF24]. However, while many non-interactive protocols are themselves often conceived in a modular way, (namely, using other cryptographic primitives as building blocks), taking advantage of the composabilility properties of the UC framework to facilitate modular construction and analysis of composite non-interactive protocols has been progressing more slowly.

This work is supported by NSF grant 2428488.

B. Applebaum and H. Lin (Eds.): TCC 2025, LNCS 16271, pp. 642–674, 2026.
https://doi.org/10.1007/978-3-032-12290-2_21

Indeed, such an endeavor is challenging, as it requires modeling the building blocks as non-interactive protocols within the UC framework, and then formulating the relevant security properties of these protocols in a way that makes them readily usable as components within other non-interactive ones. More specifically, the challenge is to formulate ideal functionalities that: (A) guarantee the desired security properties, while consisting of one party outputting a single "idealized" string that is then further processed by other non-interactive protocols, and (B) are realizable by actual non-interactive protocols. Given that realizing UC functionalities naturally requires straight-line simulation, extraction, and equivocation, this endeavor appears almost impossible.

Still, a number of works have taken on this challenge. Specifically, the UC modeling and analysis of the Signal protocol of [CJSV22] includes multiple sub-components that handle the processing of each received message and the sending of each message. Also, [CSW22] gives a UC modeling of non-interactive commitment and use it to construct non-interactive zero-knowledge protocols in the common reference string model. In both cases, the modularity enables a more general result with a simpler and more readily verifiable analysis.

1.1 Our Contributions

This work aims to enable modular construction and analysis of primitives that are both non-interactive and additionally require *succinctness*. Examples include non-interactive succinct commitments, vector commitments, accumulators, ZK-SNARKs and Proof-Carrying Code (PCD) systems, delegation of computation scheme, shared database systems, and related tasks.

Given the inherent incompatibility of succinctness, non-interactivity, and straight-line black-box simulation-extraction in the plain model, we concentrate on protocols designed and analyzed in the random oracle model. This, in turn, requires appropriate modeling of a programmable random oracle as globally shared resource within the UC framework. We thus start by providing a formulation of a programmable random oracles as a (global) ideal functionality, $\mathcal{F}_{\mathsf{GRO}}$. The new formulation avoids shortcomings of previous ones, e.g. those in [CDG+18, CF24] (also discussed in [LR22]), and may be of independent interest. We then proceed as follows:

(a) We formulate an ideal functionality, $\mathcal{F}_{\mathsf{NC}}$, that captures succinct non-interactive commitment in the presence of $\mathcal{F}_{\mathsf{GRO}}$. This builds on the non-interactive commitment of [CSW22], which models schemes in the common reference string model.
(b) We show that $\mathcal{F}_{\mathsf{NC}}$ is realized by a simple folklore succinct commitment scheme.
(c) We formulate an ideal functionality, $\mathcal{F}_{\mathsf{NVC}}$, that captures succinct non-interactive vector commitment in the presence of $\mathcal{F}_{\mathsf{GRO}}$.
(d) We show that a variant of the Merkle tree-based vector commitment, where each node is implemented using an instance of $\mathcal{F}_{\mathsf{NC}}$, *perfectly* realizes $\mathcal{F}_{\mathsf{NVC}}$.

To demonstrate the viability of our formalism, we show that the Kilian-Micali ZK-SNARK, formulated as a protocol that uses the ideal sub-component $\mathcal{F}_{\mathsf{NVC}}$, UC-realizes $\mathcal{F}_{\mathsf{NIZK}}$, where $\mathcal{F}_{\mathsf{NIZK}}$ is an adaptation of the non-interactive zero-knowledge functionality of [GOS12] to be in the presence of $\mathcal{F}_{\mathsf{GRO}}$. This application can be viewed as a modular alternative to the recent work of Chiesa and Fenzi [CF24], which shows that the

Kilian-Micali protocol UC-realizes $\mathcal{F}_{\mathsf{NIZK}}$ in the presence of a global, programmable random oracle (as formulated in [LR22]). Indeed, Chiesa and Fenzi directly analyze the entire Kilian-Micali protocol, without taking advantage of the modularity provided by the UC framework. In addition to avoiding the weakness in their formulation of $\mathcal{F}_{\mathsf{GRO}}$, our analysis obtains somewhat better concrete parameters than those obtained in [CF24], due to our modular treatment of vector commitments. (See discussion in Sect. 1.3.)

Additional potential uses of our formalism of succinct UC commitments and vector commitments include other constructions of ZK SNARKs and Proof-Carrying Data (PCD) protocols from these two primitives (such as, IOPs [BCS16] or the recent proposal of [BMNW25]). Additional candidate uses include verifiable and updatable databases (for secret data), dynamic accumulators (of secret data), and anonymous credentials (see [CF13]).

1.2 Technical Overview

We give an overview of our formalism and technical contributions.

A Weakness in Existing Programmable Global Random Oracles. The main challenge in formulating the random oracle as a global ideal functionality, $\mathcal{F}_{\mathsf{GRO}}$, within the UC framework is to preserve the validity of modular composition with the oracle as a shared object, while also preserving the model's pertinent properties, namely the ability to observe the adversary's oracle queries and determine ("program") the responses provided to the adversary.

We first demonstrate a weakness in existing formalisms (e.g. those used in [CDG+18, LR22, CF24]). Specifically, consider a protocol ρ that makes subroutine calls to some ideal functionality $\mathcal{F}$ and in addition has access to the [CDG+18, LR22, CF24] formulation of $\mathcal{F}_{\mathsf{GRO}}$. We show how ρ can use its access to the global $\mathcal{F}_{\mathsf{GRO}}$ to tell whether or not $\mathcal{F}$ was replaced by some protocol π that realizes it - thereby "bypassing" the guarantees made by the UC theorem. We further exploit this weakness of $\mathcal{F}_{\mathsf{GRO}}$ to have ρ break down as soon as $\mathcal{F}$ is replaced by π. This demonstrates that having access to [CDG+18, LR22, CF24] formulation of $\mathcal{F}_{\mathsf{GRO}}$ means that the UC theorem is no longer useful for security analysis. See more details within.

An Alternative Formulation of Global Programmable Random Oracle. We present a new $\mathcal{F}_{\mathsf{GRO}}$ formalism which avoids the weakness and also enjoys some additional attractive properties. Rather than interacting directly with the environment/adversary, our $\mathcal{F}_{\mathsf{GRO}}$ only allows ideal functionalities (i.e., machines with pid $=\perp$) to observe or program. Furthermore, each ideal functionality can only observe or program the responses to queries that encode (say, start with) the session ID of that ideal functionality.

In addition to avoiding said weakness, the new $\mathcal{F}_{\mathsf{GRO}}$ is also more expressive: first, it enables ideal functionalities to determine context-specific policies for when queries can be observed and when responses can be programmed, thus capturing more nuanced security guarantees. It also allows situations where different sessions allow different observing/programming behaviors of the random oracle. Finally, it enables ideal functionalities to be explicit about the properties they expect from the random oracle.

UC Non-interactive Shrinking Commitments. An ideal functionality that captures non-interactive commitments was recently proposed in [CSW22]. Unlike the more traditional commitment functionality of [CF01] where commitment and decommitment strings are implicit even for non-interactive commitments, here the ideal commitment functionality explicitly outputs commitment and decommitment strings to the committer in the commitment phase. This enables the modular decomposition of non-interactive protocols which involve computing on commitment strings. However, the [CSW22] formulation of commitments is geared towards realization with a common reference string. In particular, it is not realizable by protocols where the commitment string is shorter than the message.[1]

We extend the non-interactive commitment functionality of [CSW22] to interact with $\mathcal{F}_{\mathsf{GRO}}$. On the positive side, this extension enables realizations where the length of the commitment depends only on the security parameter, irrespective of the length of the message. It also allows us to use a significantly simpler formulation where each instance of the commitment functionality, $\mathcal{F}_{\mathsf{NC}}$, handles only a single commitment. (In contrast, all prior work on UC commitments have a non-global setup that is reused over multiple commitments, which in turn mandates using the more complex sub-session formalism for handling multiple commitments within the same instance of the functionality.)

On the negative side, allowing $\mathcal{F}_{\mathsf{NC}}$ to interact with the global $\mathcal{F}_{\mathsf{GRO}}$ opens the door to potential "backdoors" where $\mathcal{F}_{\mathsf{NC}}$ inadvertently leaks information to an external observer via its interaction with $\mathcal{F}_{\mathsf{GRO}}$. This danger is actually quite imminent, given that $\mathcal{F}_{\mathsf{NC}}$ uses simulator-provided code to generate strings representing ideal commitment and decommitment, and furthermore that the code can observe and program $\mathcal{F}_{\mathsf{GRO}}$. Indeed, making sure that no such "backdoors" are possible adds significant subtlety to the structure of $\mathcal{F}_{\mathsf{NC}}$. Our treatment here is inspired by that of [CDL+24].

At high level, $\mathcal{F}_{\mathsf{NC}}$ provides the following service. When asked by a committer C to commit to a message m, $\mathcal{F}_{\mathsf{NC}}$ returns to C a commitment string cm and a decommitment string dcm. When asked by anyone to verify a triple $(m', \mathsf{cm}', \mathsf{dcm}')$, $\mathcal{F}_{\mathsf{NC}}$ accepts or rejects. Both the generation of $(\mathsf{cm}, \mathsf{dcm})$ and the accept/reject response use programs that are provided by the adversary (or, simulator) and are executed by $\mathcal{F}_{\mathsf{NC}}$ in a controlled way. Overall, the security guarantees are:

Secrecy: The commitment string cm is generated independently of m. Furthermore, even though the process of generating the decommitment string dcm depends on m, it does not leak information on m to an external observer. In fact, an external observer that interacts with $\mathcal{F}_{\mathsf{NC}}$ but is given only cm, but not dcm, cannot guess (except for negligible probability) whether cm is a commitment to the message provided by the observer or else a commitment to some arbitrary fixed value.

[1] Consider a UC simulator $\mathcal{S}$ for a succinct non-interactive commitment scheme in the common reference string model. Then $\mathcal{S}$ would need to win the following game with probability negligibly close to 1: $\mathcal{S}$ first generates a simulated reference string s. Next a random n-bit message m is chosen, and $\mathcal{S}$ obtains an honestly generated commitment c to m (relative to s), where c is an n'-bit string. $\mathcal{S}$ wins if it correctly guesses m. Clearly, if $n' < n$ then $\mathcal{S}$ wins with probability at most one half.

Completeness and Consistency: When asked to verify a triple that was generated earlier by $\mathcal{F}_{\mathsf{NC}}$ in a response to a commitment request, $\mathcal{F}_{\mathsf{NC}}$ always accepts. Also, two requests to verify the same triple are always answered in the same way.

Binding and non-malleability: Any string cm can be opened to at most one message. Furthermore, whenever $\mathcal{F}_{\mathsf{NC}}$ accepts an opening $(m, \mathsf{cm}, \mathsf{dcm})$, we are guaranteed that there exists an explicitly determined earlier point in the execution, such that the state of the system at that point uniquely and efficiently determines m.

Immediate response: $\mathcal{F}_{\mathsf{NC}}$ responds to both commit and verify requests immediately, namely without the environment being activated in between request and response. This guarantees that both commitment and verification are local computational processes that do not involve interaction.

A few comments are in order: First, it may seem odd that $\mathcal{F}_{\mathsf{NC}}$ allows for a non-zero probability of guessing the plaintext and decommitment string. However, this is an inherent weakness of non-interactive commitments: a lucky guess of the correct decommitment string, given the commitment string and a conjectured value for the underlying message, will inevitably be recognized by the decommitment algorithm.

Second, the "extraction point" mentioned in the binding guarantee is determined as follows: If cm equals a value returned earlier by $\mathcal{F}_{\mathsf{GRO}}$, then the extraction point is at the first such event. Otherwise, the extraction point is the first activation of $\mathcal{F}_{\mathsf{NC}}$. This means that a protocol using $\mathcal{F}_{\mathsf{NC}}$ has the guarantee that, as soon as any party comes up with a string cm, cm can only be opened to a fixed (albeit hidden) plaintext.

We defer the descriptions of *how* $\mathcal{F}_{\mathsf{NC}}$ provides the above guarantees to the body of the paper, which also provides precise formulations of the above properties, along with formal proofs that these properties hold with respect to $\mathcal{F}_{\mathsf{NC}}$. This process of formulating mathematical claims regarding security properties *of ideal functionalities,* together with rigorous proofs of these claims, can be viewed as an additional contribution of this work.

Realizing $\mathcal{F}_{\mathsf{NC}}$. We show that the following protocol (which is implicit in [Mic00], and may be considered folklore), unconditionally UC-realizes $\mathcal{F}_{\mathsf{NC}}$: To commit to a message m, choose a random κ-bit string r, compute $c \leftarrow \mathcal{F}_{\mathsf{GRO}}(\mathsf{sid}, m, r)$, where sid is the relevant session ID for this particular commitment, and let c, r be the commitment and decommitment strings for m. To verify that r decommits c to message m with respect to session ID sid, check that $c = \mathcal{F}_{\mathsf{GRO}}(\mathsf{sid}, m, r)$. (The inclusion of sid in the input to $\mathcal{F}_{\mathsf{GRO}}$ cryptographically binds the commitment string to a specific instance. This binding is crucial for our modular analysis.)

Our proof of security is unconditional, and the simulation error is bounded by $t \cdot 2^{-\kappa} + (2t^2 + 3t) \cdot 2^{-\lambda}$, where t is the number of oracle queries made by the environment, λ is the length of $\mathcal{F}_{\mathsf{GRO}}$ outputs, and κ is the min-entropy of decommitments. The proof also trivially addresses the case of adaptive corruption of the committer. Indeed, the commitment stage is immediate (i.e., it takes a single activation), and no secret information is generated (other than the decommitment string itself, which is part of the output of the commitment stage).

UC Non-interactive Vector Commitments. Vector commitments [CF13] allow committing to a vector $\mathbf{m}$ of values, then decommitting to the values in different positions in the vector at different times. To capture the relevant security properties in an abstract way, we formulate an ideal functionality $\mathcal{F}_{\mathsf{NVC}}$ that provides the following service: when asked by a committer C to commit to a plaintext vector $\mathbf{m} \in (\Sigma \cup \bot)^n$, $\mathcal{F}_{\mathsf{NVC}}$ returns to C a commitment string cm, along with a decommitment string $\mathbf{dcm}[i]$ for each index i where $\mathbf{m}[i] \in \Sigma$. When asked by anyone to verify a tuple $(\mathsf{cm}', i', m', \mathsf{dcm}')$, in which $m' \in \Sigma$ is the claimed value of entry i' in $\mathbf{m}$ and dcm' is the claimed decommitment with respect to cm', $\mathcal{F}_{\mathsf{NVC}}$ either accepts or rejects. The security guarantees of $\mathcal{F}_{\mathsf{NVC}}$ extend those of $\mathcal{F}_{\mathsf{NC}}$ to the vector setting, as follows:

Secrecy: The commitment string cm is generated independently of the committed vector $\mathbf{m}$. Furthermore, each decommitment string $\mathbf{dcm}[i]$ is generated independently of $\{\mathbf{m}[i'] : i' \neq i\}$. In addition, even though the process of generating each decommitment string $\mathbf{dcm}[i]$ depends on $\mathbf{m}[i]$, it does not leak information on $\mathbf{m}[i]$ to an external observer: an external observer that interacts with $\mathcal{F}_{\mathsf{NVC}}$ but is given only cm and $\{\mathbf{dcm}[i'] : i' \neq i\}$, but not $\mathbf{dcm}[i]$, cannot guess (except for negligible probability) whether $\mathsf{cm}[i]$ is the message provided by the observer or else some arbitrary fixed value.

Completeness and Consistency: When asked to verify a tuple $(\mathsf{cm}, i, m, \mathsf{dcm})$ that is part of the commitmentment and decommitment information generated in the commit stage, $\mathcal{F}_{\mathsf{NVC}}$ always accepts. Furthermore, two requests to verify the same tuple are always answered in the same way.

Binding and non-malleability: Any string cm can be opened to at most one message in each coordinate. More precisely, whenever $\mathcal{F}_{\mathsf{NC}}$ accepts an opening $(\mathsf{cm}, i, m, \mathsf{dcm})$ we are guaranteed that there exists an explicitly determined earlier point in the execution such that the state of the system at that point uniquely and efficiently determines an *entire vector* $\mathbf{m} \in (\Sigma \cup \bot)^n$, where $\mathbf{m}[i] = m$.

Immediate response: $\mathcal{F}_{\mathsf{NC}}$ responds to both commit and verify requests immediately, namely without the environment being activated in between request and response. This captures the fact that both commitment and verification are local computational processes that do not involve interaction.

The above discussion of $\mathcal{F}_{\mathsf{NC}}$ is applicable here as well. In addition, we emphasize that the binding and non-malleability properties are strong ones: successful decommitment of a commitment string cm to *even a single element* (i, m) implies that the *entire* plaintext vector $\mathbf{m} \in (\Sigma \cup \bot)^n$ has been fixed at the "extraction point."

Realizing $\mathcal{F}_{\mathsf{NVC}}$. We realize $\mathcal{F}_{\mathsf{NVC}}$ using a variant of the Merkle tree construction where both the leaves and the intermediary nodes are instantiated via instances of $\mathcal{F}_{\mathsf{NC}}$. The instances of $\mathcal{F}_{\mathsf{NC}}$ that correspond to intermediary nodes have plaintext that is 2λ bits long and commitment that is λ bits long. The session ID for each instance of $\mathcal{F}_{\mathsf{NC}}$ includes the session ID of $\mathcal{F}_{\mathsf{NVC}}$, together with an identifier that indicates the position of this instance in the commitment tree.

Note that this variant is somewhat different than the standard Kilian-Micali construction, in which commitments happen only at the leaves and internal nodes are implemented via a simple shrinking hash function. Our construction incurs a small cost in commitment size, but has the advantage of being modular, namely it only needs access to $\mathcal{F}_{\mathsf{NC}}$. Furthermore, it *perfectly* realizes $\mathcal{F}_{\mathsf{NVC}}$, without any loss in security - a feature which more than compensates for the increase in commitment size, towards minimizing the overall overhead needed to obtain a given security level.

Like for plain commitment, the proof of security of this protocol trivially addresses the case of adaptive corruption of the committer: The commitment stage is immediate (i.e., it takes a single activation), and no secret information is generated other than the decommitment string itself, which is part of the output of the commitment stage.

Constructing a simulator for this protocol encounters the following technical difficulty: In order to provide the environment with a view that is identical to an execution of the protocol, the simulator code within $\mathcal{F}_{\mathsf{NVC}}$ should somehow cause $\mathcal{F}_{\mathsf{NVC}}$ to program points that correspond to the reserved spaces of the individual commitments; however, these spaces are outside the domain that $\mathcal{F}_{\mathsf{NVC}}$ is allowed to program. We get around this issue by devising a mechanism for $\mathcal{F}_{\mathsf{NVC}}$ to spawn gateway functionalities that perform the appropriate programming, while still keeping the simulator code appropriately "sandboxed". The same mechanism is used also for proving security of the application to UC SNARKS below.

Application to UC ZK SNARKs. To exhibit the usefulness of $\mathcal{F}_{\mathsf{NVC}}$, we use it to provide modular analysis of the Kilian-Micali ZK-SNARK. To this end, we first adapt the non-interactive zero knowledge functionality of [CF24] to our modeling, where the ideal functionality is the one interacting with $\mathcal{F}_{\mathsf{GRO}}$ for observing and programming.

Next, we show how to turn any honest verifier zero knowledge extractable PCP (e.g. [KPT97, IMS12]) into a ZK-SNARK along the lines of the Kilian-Micali construction.

The proof is unconditional and relatively straightforward. It makes crucial use of the fact that even a single successful opening of an element in a vector commitment implies that the entire vector has been fixed, and furthermore extracted. There are four sources of error, all inevitable: The probability of guessing a decommitment of an ideal vector commitment, the probability of finding an ideal vector commitment string that yields a bad Fiat-Shamir challenge, the soundness (or, extraction) error of the underlying PCP, and the zero knowledge error of the underlying PCP.

We also extend the analysis to provide security in case of adaptive corruption of the prover. Specifically, we define a natural extension of the notion of zero-knowledge PCP to handle adaptive corruption of the PCP prover, and argue that most existing Zero Knowledge PCPs are already adaptive zero-knowledge. We then show that, as long as the underlying PCP has the adaptive zero-knowledge property, the constructed protocol UC realizes $\mathcal{F}_{\mathsf{NIZK}}$ in the presence of adaptive corruptions.

More potential uses of $\mathcal{F}_{\mathsf{NC}}$ and $\mathcal{F}_{\mathsf{NVC}}$. While the analysis of the Kilian-Micali ZK-SNARK demonstrates the validity of the formalism, we hope that $\mathcal{F}_{\mathsf{NVC}}$ will be valuable for more modular analysis of applications that use vector commitments, or more generally Merkle trees – especially in contexts that require the combination of soundness, secrecy, and succinctness.

One natural target is modular analysis of ZK-SNARKs that are built from PCPs/IOPs and *polynomial commitments,* which is a special case of vector commitments in which the committed vector has polynomial structure. Indeed, prior work analyzes ZK-SNARKs based on polynomial commitments monolithically.

Additionally, a substantial body of literature validates [CF13]'s proposed uses of vector commitments, including: verifiable and updatable databases (for secret data), dynamic accumulators (of secret data), and anonymous credentials.

Additional schemes that make crucial use of Merkle trees and could potentially benefit from the $\mathcal{F}_{\mathsf{NVC}}$ abstraction include constructions of proofs of sequential work [MMV13, CP18], key verification for end users [MBB+15], proofs of space (or storage) [DFKP15, Pro17], and private blockchains such as Zerocash [BCG+14].

A more recent and exciting application of vector commitments is constructing incrementally verifiable computation (IVC) and proof-carrying data (PCD). The ability to model vector commitments as an ideal functionality with universal composability guarantees would naturally strengthen (and potentially simplify the analysis of) any of these applications. For example, the recent work of [BMNW25] shows how to generically construct PCDs from vector commitments and accumulators of low depth.

1.3 Additional Related Work

Other Functionalities for Non-interactive Primitives. [CDL+24] proposes a non-interactive (digital) signature functionality, which enables a modular analysis of the Dolev-Strong broadcast protocol.

Non-interactive zero-knowledge functionality $\mathcal{F}_{\mathsf{NIZK}}$. The $\mathcal{F}_{\mathsf{NIZK}}$ formulation in this work, as well as in [CF24, GKO+23, CSW22] essentially all follow that of [GOS06, GOS12]. All works have straight-line extraction; this is necessary for proving UC security. The differences are:

1. **Simulator interaction.** In [CSW22, GKO+23], $\mathcal{F}_{\mathsf{NIZK}}$ receives the simulated proof string and the extracted witness directly from the simulator, whereas in this work $\mathcal{F}_{\mathsf{NIZK}}$ runs code that was given to it by the simulator ahead of time. The latter formulation is somewhat stronger in that it formally guarantees that the proof generation and verification are done locally by the parties without network interaction. Similarly, in [CF24], the simulator's algorithms are fixed in the setup phase. The only difference is that we use the global code library $\mathcal{F}_{\mathsf{lib}}$ formalism.
2. **Multi vs. single session.** In [CSW22, GKO+23], $\mathcal{F}_{\mathsf{NIZK}}$ is multi-session (due to the use of a common reference string (CRS)), whereas in this work and in [CF24], $\mathcal{F}_{\mathsf{NIZK}}$ is single session.
3. **Interface with $\mathcal{F}_{\mathsf{GRO}}$.** In [GKO+23, CF24] and this work, the security of $\mathcal{F}_{\mathsf{NIZK}}$ is considered with respect to a global $\mathcal{F}_{\mathsf{GRO}}$ as discussed above.[2] Recall that [CF24] uses the observable and restricted programmable $\mathcal{F}_{\mathsf{GRO}}$ from [CDG+18], which has an isProgrammed interface for "detecting" whether a point was programmed by the adversary and has a consistent sid. Thus, their $\mathcal{F}_{\mathsf{NIZK}}$ (or Π_{NIZK}) invokes isProgrammed to detect bad behavior. (Further discussion of this point appears in Sect. 3 and in the full version of this paper [CC25].)

[2] In [GKO+23], there is no explicit interaction between $\mathcal{F}_{\mathsf{NIZK}}$ and $\mathcal{F}_{\mathsf{GRO}}$. In [CF24] and this work, this interaction is made explicit. However, this is only a syntactic difference due to the fact that in [GKO+23] the adversary can directly ask $\mathcal{F}_{\mathsf{GRO}}$ to observe queries as opposed to routing these requests via $\mathcal{F}_{\mathsf{NIZK}}$.

Angel-Based Security and the Shielded Simulators Framework. Formalizing the random oracle model as a global ideal functionality can be viewed as somewhat reminiscent of other frameworks for relaxing the UC model, specifically angel-based security and the shielded simulators framework [PS04, BDH+17]. However, these approaches differ from the present one in that they present the protocol in question as-is, and only modify the security experiment. In contrast (and in line with the random oracle methodology), here we only analyze an abstract version of the actual protocol (i.e. described in the presence of $\mathcal{F}_{\mathsf{GRO}}$) and say nothing about potential transitions of the analyzed protocol to fully specified ones (i.e. replacing $\mathcal{F}_{\mathsf{GRO}}$ with a protocol). In particular, general uninstantiability results for protocols in the random oracle model (such as [CGH04]) apply to our protocols as well. For more comparison with related work, see [CC25].

Organization. In this extended abstract, we only present the formalism for the programmable global random oracle Sect. 3, plus definitions and constructions for commitments (resp. Sects. 4 and 5) and vector commitments (resp. Sects. 6 and 7). For the definitions and constructions for non-interactive zero knowledge see the full version of this paper [CC25].

2 Preliminaries

We notate $[n] := \{1, \ldots, n\}$. A random variable X has min-entropy h if $\max_x \Pr[X = x] = 2^{-h}$. Let X, Y be random variables. Then, the min-entropy of X conditioned on Y is $-\log \max_{x,y} \Pr[X = x | Y = y] = \min_y H_\infty(X|Y = y)$.

UC with Global Subroutines. We use the UC model from [Can20], together with the modeling from [BCH+20] of global subroutines within the plain UC model.

$\mathcal{F}_{\mathsf{lib}}$: Global Code Library Functionality. We use a variant of the global code library functionality $\mathcal{F}_{\mathsf{lib}}$ of [CJSV22], which is explained in the full version [CC25].

3 $\mathcal{F}_{\mathsf{GRO}}$: Ideal Functionality for Global Random Oracle

We describe our proposed ideal functionality $\mathcal{F}_{\mathsf{GRO}}$ for representing a global random oracle $\{0,1\}^* \to \{0,1\}^\lambda$. (We think of λ as the security parameter.) As with prior formulations of the global random oracle (e.g. [CJS14, CDG+18, LR22, CF24]), the goal is to capture a globally available random oracle that enables observability and programmability and, at the same time, enables meaningful security-preserving protocol composition.

In prior works, the global programmable random oracle functionality allows anyone (in particular, the adversary) to program the oracle at any point that has not yet been queried. We first demonstrate that this modeling approach carries an inherent security weakness: it allows the simulator for a single protocol instance to "pollute" the random oracle everywhere, and thus create a situation where unsuspecting protocol instances experience a different state of the random oracle, depending on whether the "polluting" protocol instance is present.

Concretely, consider the formulation of programmable RO in [CDG+18], which is used in [LR22, CF24]. Let π be a protocol that UC realizes an ideal functionality $\mathcal{F}$ in the presence of the global RO. We demonstrate a toy protocol ρ that uses subroutine calls to $\mathcal{F}$, and loses all security as soon as π is substituted for $\mathcal{F}$. See details in Appendix A.

To avoid "polluting simulators," we don't allow the simulator to directly program the oracle. Instead, we only allow ideal functionalities to observe and program the global oracle; furthermore, we only allow ideal functionality to observe/program the oracle at inputs that encode the session id of that functionality. In addition to preventing widespread "pollution" of programmed points, this modeling allows an ideal functionalities to set rules for how a simulator can interact with the global random oracle at points associated with them.

More specifically, we let an ideal functionality (i.e., a machine whose party ID is $\perp$) request $\mathcal{F}_{\mathsf{GRO}}$ to "control its session identifier". Now, whenever some party P asks $\mathcal{F}_{\mathsf{GRO}}$ to evaluate the oracle at a point x that decodes to a pair $x = (\mathsf{sid}, x')$ (using some pre-determined uniquely decodable encoding scheme) and sid has a registered controller P', $\mathcal{F}_{\mathsf{GRO}}$ tells the controller that P asked x. If x is a new query, then $\mathcal{F}_{\mathsf{GRO}}$ also lets P' determine the response. See Fig. 1 for the description of $\mathcal{F}_{\mathsf{GRO}}$.

For one, observe that this formulation of $\mathcal{F}_{\mathsf{GRO}}$ gets around the "polluting" simulators weakness, as even a rogue $\mathcal{F}$ can only program points within its own input space. Furthermore, it provides for more expressive modeling of $\mathcal{F}_{\mathsf{GRO}}$, in that it allows individual ideal functionalities to judiciously delegate the ability to observe and program points under its control to its simulator, under functionality-specific criteria.

We also note that our formalism does not interfere with the ability of ideal functionalities to guarantee immediate response of any implementing protocol. In particular the processing of an oracle query always completes without having to "yield control" to the environment. This property, which is new to the present modeling of a global random oracle, is used extensively throughout.

Observing and Programming $\mathcal{F}_{\mathsf{GRO}}$. We note that the present formulation does not make a formal distinction between observing a query and "programming" the response. $\mathcal{F}_{\mathsf{GRO}}$ always allows the controller of a session ID sid to both observe and program the response for all the correctly formatted queries $x = (\mathsf{sid}, x')$. This formulation is geared towards a modeling where the controller parties are ideal functionalities, so the decisions of when and how to program become an explicit part of the security specification of the task that is modelled by the ideal functionality. For any queries $x = (\mathsf{sid}, x')$ such that sid doesn't have a controller, $\mathcal{F}_{\mathsf{GRO}}$ lazily samples the output value, as per the usual formulation of the random oracle.

Finally we define shorthand notation for querying $\mathcal{F}_{\mathsf{GRO}}$.

Definition 1. *For a query point x, the notation $\mathsf{GRO}(x)$ denotes the following:*

1. Invoke $\mathcal{F}_{\mathsf{GRO}}$ with subroutine input $(\mathtt{Eval}, x)$.
2. Receive the subroutine output $(\mathtt{EvalOutput}, y)$ from $\mathcal{F}_{\mathsf{GRO}}$.

Functionality $\mathcal{F}_{\mathsf{GRO}}$

I **Parameters:** A security parameter λ. # Length of $\mathcal{F}_{\mathsf{GRO}}$ outputs.

II **Initialization:** Upon first activation, set the below as empty (i.e. as $\bot$):
- Hist: a list of query-response pairs (x, y), in which $x \in \{0,1\}^*$ is a query point and $y \in \{0,1\}^\lambda$ is a query answer. # Function evaluation table for GRO.
- $\mathsf{Control}$: a list containing tuples of the form (sid, P), in which sid is a session ID and P is the party that controls sid.

III **Assigning control:** Receive input $(\mathtt{Control})$ from a party $P = (\mathsf{sid}, \mathsf{pid})$. If $\mathsf{pid} = \bot$, then add sid to $\mathsf{Control}$ and return $(\mathtt{Ok}, \mathsf{Hist}[\mathsf{sid}])$ to P, in which $\mathsf{Hist}[\mathsf{sid}]$ is the subset of Hist for which queries have the prefix sid. Else, return $\bot$. # If P is an ideal functionality, record sid as controlled.

IV **Evaluate:** Receive $(\mathtt{Eval}, x)$ from a party P.
- (a) If x has the form $x = (\mathsf{sid}, x')$ and P' is the controller of sid, output $(\mathtt{ProgramReq}, P, x)$ to P'.
  # Allow the party that controls sid to observe the query and program the output.
- (b) Else: # No one controls sid.
  - i. If there is no record of the form $(x, \cdot) \in \mathsf{Hist}$, then sample $y \leftarrow \{0,1\}^\lambda$ and add (x, y) to Hist. # Lazily sample the output value y.
  - ii. Output $(\mathtt{EvalOutput}, y)$ to P.

V **Program:** Receive $(\mathtt{Program}, x, y)$ from P.
- (a) If x is not of the form $x = (\mathsf{sid}, x')$ or P is not the controller of sid, then end the activation.
- (b) If there is no record of the form $(x, \cdot) \in \mathsf{Hist}$, then add (x, y) to Hist. # Only program queries without a determined output value.
- (c) Output $(\mathtt{EvalOutput}, y)$ to P, where (x, y) is the entry in Hist corresponding to x.

Fig. 1. The global random oracle functionality.

4 $\mathcal{F}_{\mathsf{NC}}$: Ideal Functionality for Non-interactive Commitment

We introduce an ideal functionality for non-interactive commitment $\mathcal{F}_{\mathsf{NC}}$ in the presence of global subroutine $\mathcal{F}_{\mathsf{GRO}}$. Our motivation for defining a *non-interactive* version of the commitment functionality is the same as in [CSW22]: to describe protocols realizing the non-interactive zero-knowledge functionality $\mathcal{F}_{\mathsf{NIZK}}$. The ideal commitment functionality $\mathcal{F}_{\mathsf{Com}}$ from [CF01] does not suffice for this task because $\mathcal{F}_{\mathsf{Com}}$ never issues commitment and decommitment strings. In contrast, the ability to further process a commitment string (specifically, to hash it, along with other information) is essential for the Kilian-Micali protocol. The ideal non-interactive commitment functionality from [CSW22] also does not suffice because it does not interact with a global random oracles and hence does not generate a succinct commitment.

Functionality $\mathcal{F}_{\mathsf{NC}}$ appears in Figs. 2 and 3. We overview of how it is structured.

Upon first activation with session ID sid, $\mathcal{F}_{\mathsf{NC}}$ first asks $\mathcal{F}_{\mathsf{GRO}}$ to take control of sid and aborts if the request does not succeed. $\mathcal{F}_{\mathsf{NC}}$ then creates an initially-empty list $\mathsf{Hist}_{\mathsf{GRO}}$ of queries to $\mathcal{F}_{\mathsf{GRO}}$ and the corresponding responses. $\mathsf{Hist}_{\mathsf{GRO}}$ will contain all the queries to $\mathcal{F}_{\mathsf{GRO}}$ made by entities other than $\mathcal{F}_{\mathsf{NC}}$ (namely, the environment) to values controlled by $\mathcal{F}_{\mathsf{NC}}$, specifically queries of the form $x = (\mathsf{sid}, x')$ and the query responses. Note that $\mathcal{F}_{\mathsf{NC}}$ instructs $\mathcal{F}_{\mathsf{GRO}}$ to return random values as the responses to all such external GRO queries, i.e. lazily sample; namely, it does not "program" any externally queried point.

Next, $\mathcal{F}_{\mathsf{NC}}$ uses a set of adversarially generated "simulator" algorithms SCode, which includes three algorithms:

- $\mathsf{Com}(\mathsf{sid}, r_{\mathsf{cm}}) \to (\mathsf{cm}, \mathsf{st})$: On input a session ID sid and randomness r_{cm}, Com outputs a commitment string cm and internal state st (to be handed over to Equiv).
- $\mathsf{Equiv}(\mathsf{sid}, \mathsf{cm}, \mathsf{st}, m, r_{\mathsf{dcm}}) \to (\mathsf{dcm}, \mathsf{State}^{\mathsf{NC}})$: On input a session ID sid, a commitment string cm, an internal state st from Com, a message m, and randomness r_{dcm} from the ideal functionality, Equiv outputs a decommitment string dcm and a committer state $\mathsf{State}^{\mathsf{NC}}$ which is returned in case of adaptive corruption.
- $\mathsf{Extr}(\mathsf{sid}, \mathsf{cm}, Q) \to (m, \mathsf{dcm})$: On input a session ID sid, a commitment cm, and a list of $\mathcal{F}_{\mathsf{GRO}}$ query-answer pairs Q, deterministically outputs a message m and a decommitment dcm.

Each instance of $\mathcal{F}_{\mathsf{NC}}$ generates only a single commitment. To account for fact that commitments can be generated by anyone and furthermore that verification of potential decommitments is a non-interactive process, $\mathcal{F}_{\mathsf{NC}}$ allows verifying (and possibly accepting) the decommitments of multiple commitment strings with the same sid.

To generate a commitment for an input message m, $\mathcal{F}_{\mathsf{NC}}$ first runs Com to generate the commitment string obliviously of m, and then runs Equiv to generate the decommitment string to m. Both Com and Equiv may program $\mathcal{F}_{\mathsf{GRO}}$, as long as the query points to be programmed have sufficient min-entropy. These conditions are enforced by ensuring that these values appear as substrings of $\mathcal{F}_{\mathsf{NC}}$'s internal randomness r_{dcm}.

To verify a tuple $(\mathsf{cm}, m, \mathsf{dcm})$, $\mathcal{F}_{\mathsf{NC}}$ first checks if it has seen cm before. If so: (A) If the supplied (m, dcm) match the values used during commitment generation, $\mathcal{F}_{\mathsf{NC}}$ accepts; (B) If the entire tuple $(\mathsf{cm}, m, \mathsf{dcm})$ was previously seen, $\mathcal{F}_{\mathsf{NC}}$ responds in a manner consistent with its previous response; and (C) $\mathcal{F}_{\mathsf{NC}}$ rejects in all other cases. If cm is a value that is new to $\mathcal{F}_{\mathsf{NC}}$, $\mathcal{F}_{\mathsf{NC}}$ provides Extr with cm and the relevant part of the recorded history $\mathsf{Hist}_{\mathsf{GRO}}$. If Extr is able to recover m and dcm given this information, then $\mathcal{F}_{\mathsf{NC}}$ accepts; else it rejects.

4.1 The Interface Between $\mathcal{F}_{\mathsf{NC}}$ and $\mathcal{F}_{\mathsf{GRO}}$

We detail the interface between $\mathcal{F}_{\mathsf{NC}}$ and $\mathcal{F}_{\mathsf{GRO}}$. While this interface adds complexity to the description of $\mathcal{F}_{\mathsf{NC}}$, we note that placing this complexity with $\mathcal{F}_{\mathsf{NC}}$ (rather than with $\mathcal{F}_{\mathsf{GRO}}$) is a design choice that makes the extent of the reliance of $\mathcal{F}_{\mathsf{NC}}$ on $\mathcal{F}_{\mathsf{GRO}}$ explicit.

$\mathcal{F}_{\mathsf{NC}}$ handles internal requests by SCode algorithms to program $\mathcal{F}_{\mathsf{GRO}}$ and also enables observing queries to $\mathcal{F}_{\mathsf{GRO}}$ made by an external party (e.g. the environment).

Programming. Algorithms in SCode may program $\mathcal{F}_{\mathsf{GRO}}$ by invoking the Program subroutine (Fig. 4), which may choose to allow or disallow the request. Specifically, this access control structure ensures that $\mathcal{F}_{\mathsf{NC}}$ is hiding and binding, even if the (adversarially-defined) algorithms in SCode program $\mathcal{F}_{\mathsf{GRO}}$. (As such, $\Phi_{\mathcal{F}}$ differs for every ideal functionality.) We formalize the checks as a predicate $\Phi_{\mathcal{F}_{\mathsf{NC}}}$ (Fig. 5) that is run by Program. Specifically, the predicate check $\Phi_{\mathcal{F}}$ has the following interface.

Functionality $\mathcal{F}_{\mathsf{NC}}$ (main)

I **Parameters:** A message alphabet Σ, a commitment length $h_{\mathsf{cm}} \in \mathbb{N}$, and a decommitment length $h_{\mathsf{dcm}} \in \mathbb{N}$.

II **Commit:** Receive input $(\texttt{Commit}, m \in \Sigma \cup \{\bot\})$ from a party C.
  (a) If this is not the first $(\texttt{Commit}, \cdot)$ input, output $(\texttt{Error})$. # Fail-close clause.
  (b) If this is the first activation, run the Initialization subroutine (Step V).
  (c) Compute $(\mathsf{cm}, \mathsf{st}) \leftarrow \mathsf{SCode.Com}(\mathsf{sid}, r_{\mathsf{cm}})$.
  # SCode.Com may program $\mathcal{F}_{\mathsf{GRO}}$ by calling Program (Figure 4).
    i. If $\mathsf{cm} \notin r_{\mathsf{cm}}$, $(\mathsf{cm}, \cdot, \cdot, \cdot, v) \in \mathsf{CState}$, or SCode.Com commits an SCodeError (Definition 4): # Error. Outputs default values when consistency is violated.
      A. Run the default committer code (Step VI) with message m.
      B. Output $(\texttt{Receipt}, \mathsf{cm}, \mathsf{dcm})$ to C.
    ii. Else, continue to next step.
  (d) If $m = \bot$: # Don't run SCode.Equiv.
    i. Set $\mathsf{dcm} := \bot$ and $\mathsf{State}^{\mathsf{NC}} := \bot$. Append $(\mathsf{cm}, m, \mathsf{dcm}, \mathsf{State}^{\mathsf{NC}}, 0)$ to CState.
  (e) Else, compute $(\mathsf{dcm}, \mathsf{State}^{\mathsf{NC}}) \leftarrow \mathsf{SCode.Equiv}(\mathsf{sid}, \mathsf{cm}, \mathsf{st}, m, r_{\mathsf{dcm}})$.
  # SCode.Equiv may program $\mathcal{F}_{\mathsf{GRO}}$ by calling Program (Figure 4).
    i. If $\mathsf{dcm} \notin r_{\mathsf{dcm}}$, SCode.Equiv or SCode.Equiv commits an SCodeError (Definition 4):
      A. Run the default committer code (Step VI) with message m.
    ii. Else, append $(\mathsf{cm}, m, \mathsf{dcm}, \mathsf{State}^{\mathsf{NC}}, 1)$ to CState. # No errors.
  (f) Output $(\texttt{Receipt}, \mathsf{cm}, \mathsf{dcm})$ to C.

III **(Adaptive) Committer Corruption:** On input $(\texttt{Corrupt})$ from the adversary $\mathcal{E}$.
  (a) If there exists $(\mathsf{cm}, m, \mathsf{dcm}, \mathsf{State}^{\mathsf{NC}}, 1) \in \mathsf{CState}$, output $(\texttt{Corrupted}, \mathsf{State}^{\mathsf{NC}})$ to $\mathcal{E}$.
  (b) Else, output $(\texttt{Corrupted}, \bot)$ to $\mathcal{E}$.

IV **Verify:** Receive input $(\texttt{Verify}, \overline{\mathsf{cm}}, \overline{m}, \overline{\mathsf{dcm}})$ from a party R.
  (a) If this is the first activation, run the Initialization subroutine (Step V).
  (b) If $(\overline{\mathsf{cm}}, \overline{m}, \overline{\mathsf{dcm}}, \cdot, v) \in \mathsf{CState}$, output $(\texttt{VerStatus}, v)$ to R (thereby ending the activation). # Enforces completeness and consistency.
  (c) If $(\mathsf{cm} = \overline{\mathsf{cm}}, m, \mathsf{dcm}, \cdot, 1) \in \mathsf{CState}$ for some $m \neq \overline{m}$, then output $(\texttt{VerStatus}, 0)$ to R. # Enforces binding.
  (d) If $(\mathsf{cm} = \overline{\mathsf{cm}}, m = \overline{m}, \mathsf{dcm}, \cdot, 1) \in \mathsf{CState}$ for some $\mathsf{dcm} \neq \overline{\mathsf{dcm}}$, then output $(\texttt{VerStatus}, 0)$ to R. # Enforces non-malleability, only allows a single decommitment.
  (e) If $(\cdot, \overline{\mathsf{cm}})$ was programmed by SCode.Com or SCode.Equiv, output $(\texttt{VerStatus}, 0)$ to R. # Prevents information leakage by adversarial SCode.Com or SCode.Equiv.
  (f) Else: # For extractability and non-malleability.
    i. Compute the set $Q \subseteq \mathsf{Hist}_{\mathsf{GRO}}$ such that $Q := \{(x, y) \mid y = \overline{\mathsf{cm}} \wedge (x, y) \in \mathsf{Hist}_{\mathsf{GRO}}\}$.
    ii. Compute $(m', \mathsf{dcm}') \leftarrow \mathsf{SCode.Extr}(\mathsf{sid}, \overline{\mathsf{cm}}, Q)$. # Only allows a single valid dcm' value.
    iii. If $m' = \bot$, $m' \neq \overline{m}$, $\mathsf{dcm}' \neq \overline{\mathsf{dcm}}$, $\overline{\mathsf{cm}} \notin r_{\mathsf{cm}}$, or SCode.Extr commits SCodeTimeError (Definition 4), set $v := 0$. Else, set $v := 1$. # Errors.
    iv. Append $(\overline{\mathsf{cm}}, \overline{m}, \overline{\mathsf{dcm}}, \bot, v)$ to CState and output $(\texttt{VerStatus}, v)$ to R.

Fig. 2. The non-interactive commitment functionality in the presence of $\mathcal{F}_{\mathsf{GRO}}$, part 1: Commit and Verify.

Functionality $\mathcal{F}_{\mathsf{NC}}$ (subroutines)

V **Initialization:** In the first activation, do: # First activation can be `Commit` or `Verify`.
  (a) Set the following variables as empty (i.e. $\bot$):
  - CState: a list of tuples $(\mathsf{cm}, m, \mathsf{dcm}, \mathsf{State}^{\mathsf{NC}}, v)$ where cm is a commitment string, $m \in \Sigma$ is a message, dcm is a decommitment string, $\mathsf{State}^{\mathsf{NC}}$ is the committer state, and $v \in \{0,1\}$ represents whether $(\mathsf{cm}, m, \mathsf{dcm})$ is valid.
  - $\mathsf{Hist}_{\mathsf{GRO}}$: a list of tuples (x, y), in which x is an externally queried point and y is the answer.
  - ActiveAlg: records which algorithm is currently interacting with $\mathcal{F}_{\mathsf{GRO}}$.

  (b) Take control of session sid (where sid is the local sid) in $\mathcal{F}_{\mathsf{GRO}}$ by sending (`Control`) to $\mathcal{F}_{\mathsf{GRO}}$, and receive a message m from $\mathcal{F}_{\mathsf{GRO}}$.# Enables observing and programming GRO.
    i. If $m = (\mathtt{Ok}, \mathsf{Hist})$ such that $\mathsf{Hist} \neq \bot$, output $\bot$. # Failure.

  (c) Send $(\mathtt{CodeRequest}, \mathcal{F}_{\mathsf{NC}})$ to $\mathcal{F}_{\mathsf{lib}}$ and receive $(\mathtt{Answer}, \mathsf{LinkedRecords})$, where
  $\mathsf{LinkedRecords} = (\mathcal{F}_{\mathsf{NC}}, \mathsf{SCode}, \cdot)$ and SCode is a tuple of algorithms $\{\mathsf{Com}, \mathsf{Equiv}, \mathsf{Extr}\}$.

  (d) Let $r_{\mathsf{cm}} \leftarrow (\{0,1\}^{h_{\mathsf{cm}}})^\lambda$, $r_{\mathsf{dcm}} \leftarrow (\{0,1\}^{h_{\mathsf{dcm}}})^\lambda$, $\widehat{r_{\mathsf{cm}}} \leftarrow (\{0,1\}^{h_{\mathsf{cm}}})^\lambda$, $\widehat{r_{\mathsf{dcm}}} \leftarrow (\{0,1\}^{h_{\mathsf{dcm}}})^\lambda$, denote the random strings of $\mathcal{F}_{\mathsf{NC}}$. # The random strings $r_{\mathsf{cm}}, r_{\mathsf{dcm}}$ will be given to SCode.Com and SCode.Equiv. $\widehat{r_{\mathsf{cm}}}, \widehat{r_{\mathsf{dcm}}}$ are for running default code.

VI **Default commit code:** # Generates strings in event of errors.
  (a) Set $\mathsf{cm} := \widehat{r_{\mathsf{cm}}}[0]$
  (b) If $m = \bot$, set $\mathsf{dcm} := \bot$. Else, set $\mathsf{dcm} := \widehat{r_{\mathsf{dcm}}}[0]$.
  (c) Append $(\mathsf{cm}, m, \mathsf{dcm}, \bot, 0)$ to CState. # Values generated with default code are not valid.

VII **External request to program the GRO:** Upon receiving $(\mathtt{ProgramReq}, P, x)$ from $\mathcal{F}_{\mathsf{GRO}}$: # This interface allows $\mathcal{F}_{\mathsf{NC}}$ to observe oracle queries.
  (a) Sample $y \leftarrow \{0,1\}^{h_{\mathsf{cm}}}$ and add $(x, y) \in \mathsf{Hist}_{\mathsf{GRO}}$.
  (b) Send subroutine input $(\mathtt{Program}, x, y)$ to $\mathcal{F}_{\mathsf{GRO}}$.

Fig. 3. The non-interactive commitment functionality in the presence of $\mathcal{F}_{\mathsf{GRO}}$, Part 2: Subroutines for initialization, default committer code, internal $\mathcal{F}_{\mathsf{GRO}}$ programming requests, and external $\mathcal{F}_{\mathsf{GRO}}$ evaluation requests.

- $\Phi_{\mathcal{F}}(\mathsf{sid}, \mathsf{ActiveAlg}, x, y) \rightarrow \{0,1\}$.
  On input the session ID of a calling party sid, the calling algorithm ActiveAlg, a $\mathcal{F}_{\mathsf{GRO}}$ query point $x \in \mathrm{Dom}(\mathcal{F}_{\mathsf{GRO}})$, and a $\mathcal{F}_{\mathsf{GRO}}$ query answer $y \in \mathrm{Cod}(\mathcal{F}_{\mathsf{GRO}})$, outputs a bit indicating whether this is a valid query to program in $\mathcal{F}_{\mathsf{GRO}}$.

For $\mathcal{F}_{\mathsf{NC}}$, $\Phi_{\mathcal{F}_{\mathsf{NC}}}$ checks that:

- Only the SCode algorithms in the **Commit** stage, specifically Com and Equiv can program $\mathcal{F}_{\mathsf{GRO}}$. While it's possible to allow Com and Equiv to also query $\mathcal{F}_{\mathsf{GRO}}$ at additional points, we do not specify this functionality because it is not required for modeling the commitment protocol of Fig. 6.

- $\mathsf{SCode.Equiv}$ only programs a single location in $\mathcal{F}_{\mathsf{GRO}}$. While it's possible to allow $\mathsf{SCode.Equiv}$ to program more locations in $\mathcal{F}_{\mathsf{GRO}}$, we elect not to do so for simplicity and since this condition suffices for proving Theorem 4.
- The SCode algorithms in the **Verify** stage (specifically, Extr) may only access adversarial queries that are made to $\mathcal{F}_{\mathsf{GRO}}$, specifically a subset Q of the list $\mathsf{Hist}_{\mathsf{GRO}}$. This prevents $\mathcal{E}$ from breaking hiding or binding, via repeatedly querying **Verify**, to either leak information about $\mathcal{F}_{\mathsf{GRO}}$ or "program" information into $\mathcal{F}_{\mathsf{GRO}}$.[3]

We note that the $\mathsf{Program}$ subroutine of Fig. 4 only handles programming requests originating from the functionality itself. See Fig. 10 for an extension of $\mathsf{Program}$ that additionally handles programming requests from sub-functionalities simulated by SCode, e.g. for simulating a composed protocol.

Observing. $\mathcal{F}_{\mathsf{NC}}$ observes and records all "adversarial" queries with prefix sid in $\mathsf{Hist}_{\mathsf{GRO}}$ in Step VII of $\mathcal{F}_{\mathsf{NC}}$; we write adversarial queries to mean any queries with prefix sid that were made by the environment (and not $\mathcal{F}_{\mathsf{NC}}$). This enables extraction when **Verify** is invoked for adversarially-generated values. We emphasize that $\mathsf{Hist}_{\mathsf{GRO}}$ does *not* include any queries made or programmed in the **Commit** phase, including those made or programmed by $\mathsf{SCode.Com}$ and $\mathsf{SCode.Equiv}$, to preserve hiding and binding.

$\mathsf{Program}$ **subroutine ($\mathcal{F}_{\mathsf{NC}}$ version).**

- $\mathsf{Program}(\mathsf{Hist}_{\mathsf{GRO}}, \Phi_{\mathcal{F}}, \mathsf{sid}, \mathsf{ActiveAlg}, x, y)$: # Run only if $(x, \cdot) \notin \mathsf{Hist}_{\mathsf{GRO}}$ of $\mathcal{F}$.
  1. Parse the inputs so that:
     (a) the following are honestly derived from the state of $\mathcal{F}$: $\mathsf{Hist}_{\mathsf{GRO}}$ is a list of GRO query-answer pairs, $\Phi_{\mathcal{F}}$ is the query-checking predicate for $\mathcal{F}$, sid is the calling party's session ID, $\mathsf{ActiveAlg}$ is the calling party/algorithm invoking $\mathsf{Program}$; and
     (b) the following may be chosen by $\mathsf{ActiveAlg}$: x is a GRO query in $\mathrm{Dom}(\mathcal{F}_{\mathsf{GRO}})$, and y is a GRO answer in $\mathrm{Cod}(\mathcal{F}_{\mathsf{GRO}})$.
  2. If $(x, \cdot) \notin \mathsf{Hist}_{\mathsf{GRO}}$: # The evaluation of x is undefined in $\mathcal{F}_{\mathsf{GRO}}$.
     (a) If $\Phi_{\mathcal{F}}(\mathsf{sid}, \mathsf{ActiveAlg}, x, y) = 1$: # $\Phi_{\mathcal{F}}$ is a predicate check.
        i. If sid is the local session ID of $\mathcal{F}$:
           A. Send subroutine input $(\mathtt{Program}, x, y)$ to $\mathcal{F}_{\mathsf{GRO}}$.
           B. Receive subroutine output $(\mathtt{EvalOutput}, y)$ from $\mathcal{F}_{\mathsf{GRO}}$.
     (b) Else, output $(\mathtt{EvalOutput}, \perp)$ to $\mathsf{ActiveAlg}$. # Error.
  3. Else (if there exists an entry $(x, y') \in \mathsf{Hist}_{\mathsf{GRO}}$), send $(\mathtt{EvalOutput}, y')$ to $\mathsf{ActiveAlg}$.

Fig. 4. The $\mathsf{Program}$ subroutine, which handles requests by simulator code to program $\mathcal{F}_{\mathsf{GRO}}$.

[3] We give an example that breaks binding for our Π_{NC} (Fig. 6) via programming. Suppose $\mathsf{SCode.Extr}(\mathsf{sid}, \mathsf{cm}, Q)$ is specified so that if it accepts, it additionally programs a collision in $\mathcal{F}_{\mathsf{GRO}}$, i.e. a query-answer pair $((\mathsf{sid}, m', \mathsf{dcm}'), \mathsf{cm})$ such that $m' \neq \overline{m}$ and dcm' is known to $\mathcal{E}$. This breaks binding.

The predicate $\Phi_{\mathcal{F}_{\mathsf{NC}}}$

- $\Phi_{\mathcal{F}_{\mathsf{NC}}}(\mathsf{sid}, \mathsf{ActiveAlg}, x, y) \rightarrow \{0,1\}$:
  1. Parse sid as the session ID of the calling party, ActiveAlg as a calling algorithm, x as a query point (sid', x') in $\mathrm{Dom}(\mathcal{F}_{\mathsf{GRO}})$, and y as a query answer in $\mathrm{Cod}(\mathcal{F}_{\mathsf{GRO}})$.
  2. If $\mathsf{sid} \neq \mathsf{sid}'$, output 0. # Disallow cross-domain programming.
  3. If $\mathsf{ActiveAlg} = \mathsf{SCode.Com}$: # The caller is SCode.Com.
     (a) If the h_{dcm}-bit prefix of x' is in r_{dcm} and the query answer $y \in r_{\mathsf{cm}}$, output 1. # Ensure programmed $\mathcal{F}_{\mathsf{GRO}}$ query and answer have sufficient min-entropy.
     (b) Else, output 0.
  4. If $\mathsf{ActiveAlg} = \mathsf{SCode.Equiv}$: # The caller is SCode.Equiv.
     (a) If this execution of SCode.Equiv has already programmed $\mathcal{F}_{\mathsf{GRO}}$, output 0. # Each execution of SCode.Equiv programs only once.
     (b) If the h_{dcm}-bit prefix of x' is in r_{dcm}, and the query answer $y \in r_{\mathsf{cm}}$, output 1. # Ensure programmed $\mathcal{F}_{\mathsf{GRO}}$ query and answer have sufficient min-entropy.
     (c) Else, output 0.
  5. Else, output 0. # Allow no other SCode algorithms to program.

Fig. 5. The predicate $\Phi_{\mathcal{F}_{\mathsf{NC}}}$, which verifies properties of $\mathcal{F}_{\mathsf{GRO}}$ programming requests originating from $\mathcal{F}_{\mathsf{NC}}$.

4.2 Security Guarantees Provided by $\mathcal{F}_{\mathsf{NC}}$

We discuss the security properties provided by $\mathcal{F}_{\mathsf{NC}}$.

4.2.1 Completeness and Consistency Completeness is the property that if $\mathcal{F}_{\mathsf{NC}}$ is asked to verify a triple $(\mathsf{cm}, \mathsf{dcm}, m)$ that was generated by $\mathcal{F}_{\mathsf{NC}}$, $\mathcal{F}_{\mathsf{NC}}$ always accepts. This is ensured by Step II(c)i, since tuples generated by $\mathcal{F}_{\mathsf{NC}}$ are recorded in CState.

Consistency is the property that two requests to verify a tuple $(\mathsf{cm}, \mathsf{dcm}, m)$ is always answered the same way. If the adversary first invokes $\mathcal{F}_{\mathsf{NC}}$ with **Verify**, then attempts to commit with the same information. In the **Commit** subroutine, Step II(c)i of $\mathcal{F}_{\mathsf{NC}}$ ensures consistency. In the **Verify** subroutine, Step IVb ensures consistency, because it ensures that $\mathcal{F}_{\mathsf{NC}}$'s outputs are consistent with past outputs, via CState.

4.2.2 Hiding Hiding is the property that, as long as the decommitment information remains unknown, interacting with $\mathcal{F}_{\mathsf{NC}}$ should provide no information on the message. We begin by comparing the hiding guarantees provided by the usual (interactive) commitment functionality $\mathcal{F}_{\mathsf{Com}}$ of [CF01] and the guarantees provided by $\mathcal{F}_{\mathsf{NC}}$.

Comparing the Hiding Guarantees of $\mathcal{F}_{\mathsf{Com}}$ and $\mathcal{F}_{\mathsf{NC}}$. Recall that $\mathcal{F}_{\mathsf{Com}}$ (see Fig. 2 of [CF01]) models perfect hiding because it never issues a commitment string cm (or decommitment string dcm).

In comparison, since $\mathcal{F}_{\mathsf{NC}}$ is non-interactive, its **Commit** subroutine, on input a message m, outputs a specific commitment string cm and decommitment string dcm. This subtle difference *inherently* gives $\mathcal{F}_{\mathsf{NC}}$ a weaker hiding guarantee compared to $\mathcal{F}_{\mathsf{Com}}$; $\mathcal{F}_{\mathsf{NC}}$ has a hiding error equal to the likelihood of guessing the valid dcm with respect to cm and m. In contrast, $\mathcal{F}_{\mathsf{Com}}$ has absolute hiding because $\mathcal{F}_{\mathsf{Com}}$ never outputs the commitment string cm, so the adversary cannot attempt to guess the correct dcm.

However, we re-emphasize that the non-interactive formulation of $\mathcal{F}_{\mathsf{NC}}$ is necessary for a modular analysis of computations in which a commitment string is used as part of the computation, e.g. for nodes in the Merkle tree of the Kilian-Micali ZK-SNARK.

Hiding in $\mathcal{F}_{\mathsf{NC}}$. To quantify the security provided by $\mathcal{F}_{\mathsf{NC}}$, we explicitly parameterize $\mathcal{F}_{\mathsf{NC}}$ with the min-entropy of the decommitment string dcm, denoted h_{dcm}. $\mathcal{F}_{\mathsf{NC}}$ enforces this min-entropy condition of dcm in the following manner: $\mathcal{F}_{\mathsf{NC}}$ provides its random tape to the simulator code SCode and checks that the simulated dcm indeed corresponds to its random tape. To model hiding, our $\mathcal{F}_{\mathsf{NC}}$ needs the following two properties:

1. The commitment string cm is distributed independently from the committed message m. In other words, seeing cm does not leak information about the committed m.
2. Given a particular commitment string cm, the decommitment string dcm is hard for the adversary to guess. To illustrate the necessity of this property, suppose $\mathcal{E}$ can efficiently recover the decommitment string dcm. We want the adversary to be unable to verify guesses, even if it receives the message as side information. Then, $\mathcal{E}$ learns the committed m upon receiving $(\mathtt{VerStatus}, 1)$ from $\mathcal{F}_{\mathsf{NC}}$.

To achieve these properties, $\mathcal{F}_{\mathsf{NC}}$ receives a $(\mathtt{Commit}, m \in \Sigma)$ message and does:

- For Property 1: $\mathcal{F}_{\mathsf{NC}}$ invokes $\mathsf{SCode.Com}$, which samples a commitment cm *without* access to m.
- For Property 2: $\mathcal{F}_{\mathsf{NC}}$ invokes $\mathsf{SCode.Equiv}$, which outputs each particular decommitment string dcm with min-entropy at least h_{dcm}, relative to the message m and cm. Further, $\mathcal{F}_{\mathsf{NC}}$ enforces that $\mathsf{SCode.Equiv}$ is limited to programming at most a single location in $\mathcal{F}_{\mathsf{GRO}}$.

We formalize the hiding property of $\mathcal{F}_{\mathsf{NC}}$ as a distinguishing game between two interactions that the environment may have with $\mathcal{F}_{\mathsf{NC}}$: Interaction 1, in which the decommitment string dcm is generated but not disclosed, and Interaction 2, in which dcm is not generated at all. Intuitively, this game captures hiding since the environment can only distinguish if it knows dcm; verification using dcm passes in Interaction 1 but not in Interaction 2.

We first define the general notion of a ideal commitment mechanism, then define the hiding game for ideal commitment mechanisms:

Definition 2 (Ideal commitment mechanism C). *We say that an interactive Turing machine C is an ideal commitment mechanism in the presence of global functionalities $\mathcal{F}_{\mathsf{GRO}}$ and $\mathcal{F}_{\mathsf{lib}}$, if C has the following interfaces:*

1. *On input $(\mathtt{Commit}, m)$, generates a commitment string cm and decommitment string dcm, outputs $(\mathtt{Receipt}, \mathsf{cm}, \mathsf{dcm})$ where cm is a commitment string and dcm is a decommitment string.*
2. *On input $(\mathtt{Verify}, \mathsf{cm}, m, \mathsf{dcm})$, outputs $(\mathtt{VerStatus}, v)$ where v is a bit indicating whether cm is a valid commitment to the plaintext m with decommitment dcm.*

Game 1 (Hiding game for C in the presence of $\mathcal{F}_{\mathsf{GRO}}$). Let C be an ideal commitment mechanism (Definition 2) in the presence of $\mathcal{F}_{\mathsf{GRO}}$ and $\mathcal{F}_{\mathsf{lib}}$. Let Σ be the plaintext alphabet (such that $\perp \notin \Sigma$). The adversary $\mathcal{E}$ selects a message $m \in \Sigma$ and attempts to distinguish between the following interactions:

Interaction 1. (a) C is invoked with input $(\texttt{Commit}, m)$.
(b) Receive the output $(\texttt{Receipt}, \mathsf{cm}, \mathsf{dcm})$ from C, as usual.
(c) Output cm to $\mathcal{E}$. # Though dcm may be generated, $\mathcal{E}$ only sees cm.

Interaction 2. This is identical to Interaction 1, except that the committed plaintext is $m = \perp$.
(a) C is invoked with input $(\texttt{Commit}, \perp)$.
(b) Receive the output $(\texttt{Receipt}, \mathsf{cm}, \mathsf{dcm})$ from C.
(c) Output cm to $\mathcal{E}$. # Though dcm may be generated, $\mathcal{E}$ only sees cm.

Additionally, in both interactions, $\mathcal{E}$ may: (a) access the global functionalities $\mathcal{F}_{\mathsf{GRO}}$ and $\mathcal{F}_{\mathsf{lib}}$; and (b) invoke both the **Commit** and **Verify** interfaces of C.

$\mathcal{E}$ wins if it distinguishes between Interactions 1 and 2.

Observe that our $\mathcal{F}_{\mathsf{NC}}$ is an ideal commitment mechanism. We show that no adversary can win the above hiding game against our $\mathcal{F}_{\mathsf{NC}}$, except with negligible probability.

Theorem 2. *Let $h_{\mathsf{cm}}, h_{\mathsf{dcm}} \in \mathbb{N}$. Let $\mathcal{E}$ be an adversary with runtime t. Then, for $\mathcal{F}_{\mathsf{NC}}(h_{\mathsf{cm}}, h_{\mathsf{dcm}})$ running any simulator code* SCode *in the presence of $\mathcal{F}_{\mathsf{GRO}}$ and $\mathcal{F}_{\mathsf{lib}}$, $\mathcal{E}$ wins Game 1 with probability $t \cdot 2^{-h_{\mathsf{dcm}}}$.*

We give a complete proof of Theorem 2 in the full version of this paper [CC25].

4.2.3 Binding Binding is the property that, once a commitment string cm is associated with a message m, it is (computationally/statistically) hard to decommit cm to another message $m' \neq m$. As a consequence, it is hard to find two valid ways to decommit to cm.

With non-interactive commitments in the plain model (e.g. as defined in [CSW22]), one can typically associate a commitment string to a single message using an injective function. This way, one can recover the committed plaintext using a *deterministic* extraction algorithm. We call the point at which the injective function from commitment strings to messages is fixed the *binding point*.

Binding via extraction in [CSW22]**.** As a starting point, we review how binding works in the plain model (i.e. without random oracles), as is defined in [CSW22].

For commitments that are honestly-generated using $\mathcal{F}_{\mathsf{NC}}$, binding is enforced via $\mathcal{F}_{\mathsf{NC}}$'s internal records, specifically CState. For all other commitments, $\mathcal{F}_{\mathsf{NC}}$ runs the extraction algorithm. Explicitly, when $\mathcal{F}_{\mathsf{NC}}$ is invoked with message $(\texttt{Verify}, \overline{\mathsf{cm}}, \overline{m}, \overline{\mathsf{dcm}})$:

1. If there exists an entry $(\overline{\mathsf{cm}}, m, \cdot, \cdot, 1) \in \mathsf{CState}$ such that $\overline{m} \neq m$, reject. This ensures perfect binding.

2. If there does not exist $(\overline{\mathsf{cm}}, \cdot, \cdot, \cdot, \cdot) \in \mathsf{CState}$, i.e. $\overline{\mathsf{cm}}$ is adversarially-generated, $\mathcal{F}_{\mathsf{NC}}$ runs the extraction algorithm SCode.Extr to extract a message. Since SCode.Extr is deterministic and only receives $\overline{\mathsf{cm}}$ as input, there is only a single possible extracted message. (The $\mathcal{F}_{\mathsf{NC}}$ of this paper defines SCode.Extr to output both m and dcm. We note that having dcm as an additional output does not affect binding; we omit dcm for simplicity of ensuing exposition.)

In contrast, for $\mathcal{F}_{\mathsf{NC}}$ in the presence of $\mathcal{F}_{\mathsf{GRO}}$, fixing the SCode.Extr does not fully fix the injective function between commitments and message because SCode.Extr can depend on the function table of $\mathcal{F}_{\mathsf{GRO}}$, which may change over time due to programming and the fact that $\mathcal{F}_{\mathsf{NC}}$ observes the environment's oracle queries. Instead, commitment strings are bound to messages during the course of execution, at various binding points.

Towards a Binding Definition for $\mathcal{F}_{\mathsf{NC}}$ in the Presence of $\mathcal{F}_{\mathsf{GRO}}$. To allow extraction depending on the observed function table of $\mathcal{F}_{\mathsf{GRO}}$, SCode.Extr additionally receives $\mathsf{Hist}_{\mathsf{GRO}}$, i.e. the list of GRO queries made by $\mathcal{E}$ in the domain controlled by $\mathcal{F}_{\mathsf{NC}}$ (in which queries are prefixed by the session ID sid of $\mathcal{F}_{\mathsf{NC}}$).

Unfortunately, this presents an opportunity for $\mathcal{E}$ to give auxiliary information to the extractor after a commitment string cm is issued, via querying $\mathcal{F}_{\mathsf{GRO}}$ in the domain controlled by $\mathcal{F}_{\mathsf{NC}}$. Since $\mathsf{Hist}_{\mathsf{GRO}}$ is an input to SCode.Extr, it could affect the message output by $\mathsf{SCode.Extr}(\mathsf{cm}, \mathsf{Hist}_{\mathsf{GRO}})$, thus changing the message to which cm is bound.

Hence, for $\mathcal{F}_{\mathsf{NC}}$ to intuitively express a binding commitment, we must identify the *binding point* at which a commitment string is bound to a single message. (Different commitment strings can have different binding points.) Further, we desire that the message m to which a commitment string is bound to does not change after the binding point, despite the fact that $\mathcal{F}_{\mathsf{NC}}$ observes the oracle queries of $\mathcal{E}$; in particular, only m will be valid when $\mathcal{F}_{\mathsf{NC}}$ verifies using cm. We note that this binding property is weaker than the binding guarantee of $\mathcal{F}_{\mathsf{NC}}$ in the plain model, in the sense that the message cm is bound to is not fixed ahead of time, as in the case of $\mathcal{F}_{\mathsf{NC}}$ in the plain model.

To build towards a binding definition for $\mathcal{F}_{\mathsf{NC}}$, we first identify the *binding point(s) for* cm in the execution, i.e. when the commitment string cm is bound to a single m. For $\mathcal{F}_{\mathsf{NC}}$ in the presence of $\mathcal{F}_{\mathsf{GRO}}$, there are three possible binding points for cm: (1) cm is output by $\mathcal{F}_{\mathsf{NC}}$ after an honest invocation to the **Commit** subroutine with message m; or (2) cm is output by $\mathcal{F}_{\mathsf{GRO}}$ after it receives m as input; or (3) cm was neither generated by the **Commit** subroutine, nor is an output of $\mathcal{F}_{\mathsf{GRO}}$, so binding is guaranteed by the fact that extraction algorithm SCode.Extr is deterministic, as in [CSW22].

Then, we can intuitively capture binding for $\mathcal{F}_{\mathsf{NC}}$ as follows: if $\mathcal{F}_{\mathsf{NC}}$ accepts (i.e. outputs $(\mathtt{VerStatus}, 1)$) on input $(\mathtt{Verify}, \overline{\mathsf{cm}}, \overline{m}, \mathsf{dcm})$, then $\overline{\mathsf{cm}}$ was already "bound" to $\overline{m}$ at the binding point for $\overline{\mathsf{cm}}$ during the execution. In other words, once the binding point occurs, $\mathcal{E}$ cannot change the message output by the extractor.

We formalize the above intuition by defining the notion of an extractable ideal commitment mechanism, then argue that no adversary wins the binding game with respect to $\mathcal{F}_{\mathsf{NC}}$ with more than negligible probability.

Definition 3 (Extractable ideal commitment mechanism). *We say that an ideal commitment mechanism* C *(Definition 2) is* ϵ*-extractable if there is some extraction function*

Extr *from states of an execution to the plaintext space of* C*, such that any* $\mathcal{E}$ *wins the following game with probability at most* ϵ*:*

1. *Run* $\mathcal{E}$ *in a standard execution in the UC model with* C *(with session ID* sid*),* $\mathcal{F}_{\mathsf{GRO}}$*, and* $\mathcal{F}_{\mathsf{lib}}$ *until* $\mathcal{E}$ *receives an output* $(\mathtt{VerStatus}, 1)$ *in response to an input* $(\mathtt{Verify}, \overline{\mathsf{cm}}, \overline{m}, \overline{\mathsf{dcm}})$ *to* C.
2. *For* $\overline{\mathsf{cm}}$*, rewind the execution to the latest of the following* binding points*, if they exist:*
   Case 1. $\overline{\mathsf{cm}}$ *is output by* C *as a commitment. Then in this case, the binding point is the state* State *of the (entire) execution immediately before the subsequent activation of* $\mathcal{E}$.
   Case 2. The first time $\mathcal{F}_{\mathsf{GRO}}$ *outputs* $(\mathtt{EvalOutput}, \overline{\mathsf{cm}})$*, in response to an* $\mathtt{Eval}$ *or* $\mathtt{Program}$ *input in which* x *has the form* $(\mathsf{sid}, \cdot)$*. Then in this case, the binding point is the state* State *of the (entire) execution immediately before the subsequent activation of* $\mathcal{E}$.
   Case 3. $\overline{\mathsf{cm}}$ *is not output by neither* C *nor* $\mathcal{F}_{\mathsf{GRO}}$*. In this case, the binding point is the state* State *of the execution after the initialization of* C*, immediately before the next activation of* $\mathcal{E}$.
3. *Extract a message* $\widehat{m}$ *using the state* State *at the binding point:*
   (a) In Case 1, output the message $\widehat{m}$ *that* C *used to generate* $\overline{\mathsf{cm}}$.
   (b) In Case 2 (resp. Case 3, run $(\widehat{m}, \widehat{\mathsf{dcm}}) \leftarrow \mathsf{Extr}(\mathsf{sid}, \overline{\mathsf{cm}}, \mathsf{State})$.
4. $\mathcal{E}$ *wins if the extracted message* $\widehat{m} \neq \perp$ *and* $\widehat{m} \neq \overline{m}$.

Next, we show that our $\mathcal{F}_{\mathsf{NC}}$ is an extractable ideal commitment mechanism. We note that $\mathcal{F}_{\mathsf{NC}}$ has a parameter for the length or min-entropy of commitment strings: h_{cm}, which is required in the proof of binding for $\mathcal{F}_{\mathsf{NC}}$.

Theorem 3. *Let* $h_{\mathsf{cm}}, h_{\mathsf{dcm}} \in \mathbb{N}$*. Let* $\mathcal{E}$ *be an adversary with runtime* t*. For any (adversarially-chosen)* SCode*,* $\mathcal{E}$ *interacting with* $\mathcal{F}_{\mathsf{NC}}(h_{\mathsf{cm}}, h_{\mathsf{dcm}})$ *(defined in Figs. 2 and 3) in the presence of* $\mathcal{F}_{\mathsf{GRO}}$ *and* $\mathcal{F}_{\mathsf{lib}}$ *is an* $(2t^2 \cdot 2^{-h_{\mathsf{cm}}})$*-extractable ideal commitment mechanism (Definition 3) with respect to the extraction function* $\mathsf{SCode.Extr}$ *that is used to define* $\mathcal{F}_{\mathsf{NC}}(h_{\mathsf{cm}}, h_{\mathsf{dcm}})$.

We give a complete proof of Theorem 3 in the full version of this paper [CC25].

We discuss immediate response, correctness, and adaptive security in the full version of this paper [CC25].

To simplify the description of $\mathcal{F}_{\mathsf{NC}}$, we define the following errors, which SCode algorithms may commit:

Definition 4. *An algorithm* $\mathcal{A}$ *in* SCode *may commit the following errors:*

- $\mathsf{SCodeTimeError}$*:* $\mathcal{A}$ *outruns its time budget; and*
- $\mathsf{SCodeError}$*:* $\mathcal{A}$ *halts without output (i.e. outputs* $\perp$*) or commits* $\mathsf{SCodeTimeError}$.

Protocol Π_{NC}

- **Parameters:** the decommitment length $h_{\mathsf{dcm}} \in \mathbb{N}$, the $\mathcal{F}_{\mathsf{GRO}}$ output length $h_{\mathsf{cm}} \in \mathbb{N}$, and the message alphabet Σ.
- **Commit:** The committer C does:
  1. Receive input $(\mathtt{Commit}, m)$.
  2. If $m = \bot$, sample $\mathsf{cm} \leftarrow \{0,1\}^{h_{\mathsf{cm}}}$ and set $\mathsf{dcm} := \bot$.
  3. Else:
     (a) Sample $\mathsf{dcm} \leftarrow \{0,1\}^{h_{\mathsf{dcm}}}$.
     (b) Send subroutine input $(\mathtt{Eval}, (\mathsf{sid}, \mathsf{dcm}, m))$ to $\mathcal{F}_{\mathsf{GRO}}(h_{\mathsf{cm}})$, where sid is the session ID of Π_{NC}.
     (c) Receive subroutine output $(\mathtt{EvalOutput}, y)$ from $\mathcal{F}_{\mathsf{GRO}}(h_{\mathsf{cm}})$.
  4. Output $(\mathtt{Commit}, \mathsf{cm} := y, \mathsf{dcm})$.
- **Verify:** The receiver R verifies that the decommitment is valid, as follows:
  1. Receive input $(\mathtt{Verify}, \overline{\mathsf{cm}}, \overline{m}, \overline{\mathsf{dcm}})$.
  2. Send subroutine input $(\mathtt{Eval}, (\mathsf{sid}, \overline{\mathsf{dcm}}, \overline{m}))$ to $\mathcal{F}_{\mathsf{GRO}}(h_{\mathsf{cm}})$, where sid is the session ID of Π_{NC}.
  3. Receive subroutine output $(\mathtt{EvalOutput}, y)$ from $\mathcal{F}_{\mathsf{GRO}}(h_{\mathsf{cm}})$.
  4. If $\overline{\mathsf{cm}} = y$, output $(\mathtt{VerStatus}, 1)$. Else, output $(\mathtt{VerStatus}, 0)$.

Fig. 6. The commitment protocol, with global subroutine $\mathcal{F}_{\mathsf{GRO}}$.

5 Π_{NC}: The Non-interactive Commitment Scheme

We describe a commitment protocol Π_{NC} (see Fig. 6) and prove that Π_{NC} UC-realizes $\mathcal{F}_{\mathsf{NC}}$ (Theorem 4); the proof appears in the full version of this paper [CC25].

Theorem 4. *Let $\mathcal{F}_{\mathsf{GRO}}(h_{\mathsf{cm}})$ be an ideal global random oracle, with output length $h_{\mathsf{cm}} \in \mathbb{N}$. Let $h_{\mathsf{dcm}} \in \mathbb{N}$ be a parameter denoting decommitment length.*

Then, $\Pi_{\mathsf{NC}}(h_{\mathsf{dcm}}, h_{\mathsf{cm}})$ in Fig. 6 UC-realizes the ideal commitment functionality $\mathcal{F}_{\mathsf{NC}}(h_{\mathsf{cm}}, h_{\mathsf{dcm}})$ in the presence of $\mathcal{F}_{\mathsf{GRO}}(h_{\mathsf{cm}})$ and $\mathcal{F}_{\mathsf{lib}}$, even against adaptive corruptions. Specifically, an environment making at most t queries to $\mathcal{F}_{\mathsf{GRO}}$ has distinguishing advantage at most $t \cdot 2^{-h_{\mathsf{dcm}}} + (2t^2 + 3t) \cdot 2^{-h_{\mathsf{cm}}}$.

Furthermore, in Π_{NC}, commitments are always h_{cm}-bit strings.

6 $\mathcal{F}_{\mathsf{NVC}}$: Non-interactive Vector Commitment

We introduce the ideal functionality for a non-interactive ***vector*** commitment $\mathcal{F}_{\mathsf{NVC}}$, which has access to global subroutine $\mathcal{F}_{\mathsf{GRO}}$. Recall that a vector commitment [CF13] is a primitive that allows committing to a vector $\mathbf{m}$, then decommitting to positions in the vector at a later time. Vector commitments allow a committer to jointly and succinctly commit to a vector of plaintexts, and then individually open each element in the vector. They have the following security properties: (a) **position binding**, i.e. decommitting any position in $\mathbf{m}$ to two different values is hard; and (b) **hiding**, i.e. even when some positions of $\mathbf{m}$ are decommitted, the non-decommitted positions remain hidden.

We present the description of $\mathcal{F}_{\mathsf{NVC}}$ in Figs. 7 and 8. Below, we give an intuitive overview of how $\mathcal{F}_{\mathsf{NVC}}$ generalizes $\mathcal{F}_{\mathsf{NC}}$ to the vector setting. We make use of the following notation: given a vector $\mathbf{m} \in \Sigma^n$, we denote the i-th element of $\mathbf{m}$ as $\mathbf{m}[i]$.

At a high level, the interfaces of $\mathcal{F}_{\mathsf{NVC}}$ and $\mathcal{F}_{\mathsf{NC}}$ differ as follows.

- **Committing to a vector.** $\mathcal{F}_{\mathsf{NVC}}$ receives as input a vector of values $n \in \Sigma^n$. $\mathcal{F}_{\mathsf{NVC}}$ outputs a commitment string cm and a *vector* of decommitments $\mathbf{dcm}$. In particular, $\mathbf{dcm}[i]$ is the decommitment associated with $\mathbf{m}[i]$ for every $i \in [n]$.
- **Decommitting to (i.e. verifying) positions in m.** Each invocation of **Verify** in $\mathcal{F}_{\mathsf{NVC}}$ checks a decommitment to a single index $i \in [n]$ of the committed vector $\mathbf{m}$. Specifically, verification messages have the form $(\texttt{Verify}, \overline{\mathsf{cm}}, \overline{i}, \overline{m}, \overline{\mathsf{dcm}})$, in which (a) $\overline{\mathsf{cm}}$ is a commitment string; (b) i is the position of $\mathbf{m}$ that the caller wants to decommit; (c) $\overline{m}$ is the claimed value for $\mathbf{m}[i]$; and (d) $\overline{\mathsf{dcm}}$ is the claimed decommitment for $\overline{m}$. Further, in order to verify a set of indices $I \subseteq [n]$, the calling party must invoke $(\texttt{Verify}, \cdot)$ for every $i \in I$.

Operationally, like for $\mathcal{F}_{\mathsf{NC}}$, $\mathcal{F}_{\mathsf{NVC}}$ obtains a set of adversarially-generated algorithms SCode from $\mathcal{F}_{\mathsf{lib}}$. SCode for $\mathcal{F}_{\mathsf{NVC}}$ contains four algorithms:

- $\mathsf{Setup}(n, \mathsf{sid}_{\mathsf{VC}})$.
  On input a message length n and a session ID $\mathsf{sid}_{\mathsf{VC}}$, Setup may only take controls of sub-sessions of $\mathsf{sid}_{\mathsf{VC}}$ in $\mathcal{F}_{\mathsf{GRO}}$, as well as instantiate any subroutine machines which may interact with $\mathcal{F}_{\mathsf{GRO}}$ with their sub-session ID.[4]
- $\mathsf{Com}(n, \mathsf{sid}_{\mathsf{VC}}, r) \rightarrow (\mathsf{cm}, \mathsf{st})$.
  On input a message length n, a session ID $\mathsf{sid}_{\mathsf{VC}}$, and randomness r, outputs a commitment string cm and the internal state st of Com. Com may query or program $\mathcal{F}_{\mathsf{GRO}}$, as well as execute subroutine machines which may interact with $\mathcal{F}_{\mathsf{GRO}}$ with their sub-session ID, in ways allowed by $\mathcal{F}_{\mathsf{NVC}}$.
- $\mathsf{Equiv}(n, \mathsf{sid}_{\mathsf{VC}}, \mathsf{cm}, \mathsf{st}, (i, m), r) \rightarrow (\mathsf{dcm}, \mathsf{State})$.
  On input a message length n, a session ID $\mathsf{sid}_{\mathsf{VC}}$, a commitment string cm, an internal state st, an index-message value pair (i, m), and randomness r, outputs a decommitment dcm for the message value m at index i and an updated committer state State for index i, which is returned upon adaptive corruption. Equiv may query or program $\mathcal{F}_{\mathsf{GRO}}$, under the restrictions imposed by $\mathcal{F}_{\mathsf{NVC}}$. Equiv can also execute subroutine machines that interact with $\mathcal{F}_{\mathsf{GRO}}$ from their sub-session ID, in ways allowed by $\mathcal{F}_{\mathsf{NVC}}$.
- $\mathsf{Extr}(n, \mathsf{sid}_{\mathsf{VC}}, \mathsf{cm}, Q) \rightarrow (\mathbf{m}, \mathbf{dcm})$.
  On input a message length n, a session ID $\mathsf{sid}_{\mathsf{VC}}$, a commitment cm, a list of GRO query-answer pairs Q, deterministically outputs a message vector $\mathbf{m}$ and a decommitment vector $\mathbf{dcm}$. Note that Extr extracts an *entire* committed message vector $\mathbf{m}$ for a particular commitment cm. Extr may not query or program $\mathcal{F}_{\mathsf{GRO}}$, but it may call/invoke subroutine machines which may interact with $\mathcal{F}_{\mathsf{GRO}}$ with their sub-session ID, in ways allowed by $\mathcal{F}_{\mathsf{NVC}}$.

[4] We note that, in general, the ability to "spawn" subroutine machines can be given to the algorithms Setup and Com. However, Equiv should not have this ability; since Equiv knows the committed value $\mathbf{m}$, it could spawn subroutines in a manner that leaks information about $\mathbf{m}$.

Functionality $\mathcal{F}_{\mathsf{NVC}}$ (main)

I **Parameters:** An alphabet Σ, an input vector length n, a conditional min-entropy for commitments h_{cm}, and a conditional min-entropy for decommitments h_{dcm}.

II **Commit:** Receive input ($\mathtt{Commit}, \mathbf{m} \in (\Sigma \cup \{\perp\})^n$) from a party C.

(a) If this is not the first ($\mathtt{Commit}, \cdot$) input, output ($\mathtt{Error}$). # Fail-close clause.

(b) If this is the first activation, run the Initialization subroutine (Step V).

(c) Compute $(\mathsf{cm}, \mathsf{st}) \leftarrow \mathsf{SCode.Com}(n, \mathsf{sid}_{\mathsf{VC}}, r_{\mathsf{cm}})$.
SCode.Com may program $\mathcal{F}_{\mathsf{GRO}}$ by calling Program (Figure 10).

i. If $f_0(\mathsf{cm}) \notin r_{\mathsf{cm}}[0]$, $(\mathsf{cm}, \cdot, \cdot, \cdot, v) \in \mathsf{CState}$, or SCode.Com commits SCodeError (Definition 4): # Error. Outputs default values when consistency is violated. Note f_0 is some injective function.

A. Run the default committer code (Step VII) with message $\mathbf{m}$.

B. Output ($\mathtt{Receipt}, \mathsf{cm}, \mathbf{dcm}$) to C.

ii. Else, continue to next step.

(d) Compute $\mathbf{dcm}$ and $\mathbf{State}_{\mathsf{VC}}$. For all $i \in [n]$:

i. If $\mathbf{m}[i] = \perp$, set $\mathbf{dcm}[i] := \perp$ and $\mathbf{State}_{\mathsf{VC}}[i] := \perp$. # Don't run SCode.Equiv.

ii. Else, run $(\mathbf{dcm}[i], \mathbf{State}_{\mathsf{VC}}[i]) \leftarrow \mathsf{SCode.Equiv}(n, \mathsf{sid}_{\mathsf{VC}}, \mathsf{cm}, \mathsf{st}, (i, \mathbf{m}[i]), r_{\mathsf{dcm},i})$.
SCode.Equiv may program $\mathcal{F}_{\mathsf{GRO}}$ by calling Program (Figure 10).

A. If for any index $i \in [n]$, we have $f(\mathbf{dcm}[i]) \notin r_{\mathsf{dcm},i}$, SCode.Equiv commits an SCodeError (Definition 4), run the default committer code (Step VII) with message $\mathbf{m}$. # Error. Note f is some injective function.

B. Else, append $(\mathsf{cm}, i, \mathbf{m}[i], \mathbf{dcm}[i], \mathbf{State}_{\mathsf{VC}}[i], 1)$ to CState for all $i \in [n]$. # No errors.

(e) Output ($\mathtt{Receipt}, \mathsf{cm}, \mathbf{dcm}$) to C.

III **(Adaptive) Committer Corruption:** On input ($\mathtt{Corrupt}$) from the adversary $\mathcal{E}$.

(a) For every $i \in [n]$, if there exists $(\mathsf{cm}, i, m, \mathsf{dcm}, \mathsf{State}, 1) \in \mathsf{CState}$, append State to a vector $\mathbf{State}_{\mathsf{VC}}$.

(b) Output ($\mathtt{Corrupted}, \mathbf{State}_{\mathsf{VC}}$) to $\mathcal{E}$. # If a valid commitment was generated, output internal state.

IV **Verify:** Receive input ($\mathtt{Verify}, \overline{\mathsf{cm}}, \bar{i}, \overline{m}, \overline{\mathsf{dcm}}$) from a party R.

(a) If this is the first activation, run the Initialization subroutine (Step V).

(b) If $(\overline{\mathsf{cm}}, \bar{i}, \overline{m}, \overline{\mathsf{dcm}}, \cdot, v) \in \mathsf{CState}$, output ($\mathtt{VerStatus}, v$) to R (thereby ending the activation). # Enforces completeness and consistency.

(c) If $(\mathsf{cm} = \overline{\mathsf{cm}}, i = \bar{i}, m, \mathsf{dcm}, \cdot, 1) \in \mathsf{CState}$ for some $m \neq \overline{m}$, then output ($\mathtt{VerStatus}, 0$) to R. # Enforces position binding.

(d) If $(\mathsf{cm} = \overline{\mathsf{cm}}, i = \bar{i}, m = \overline{m}, \mathsf{dcm}, \cdot, 1) \in \mathsf{CState}$ for some $\mathsf{dcm} \neq \overline{\mathsf{dcm}}$, then output ($\mathtt{VerStatus}, 0$) to R. # Enforces non-malleability, only allows a single decommitment.

(e) If $(\cdot, \overline{\mathsf{cm}})$ was programmed by SCode.Com or SCode.Equiv, output ($\mathtt{VerStatus}, 0$) to R.

(f) Else: # For extractability and non-malleability.

i. Compute the set $Q \subseteq \mathsf{Hist}_{\mathsf{GRO}}$ such that Q contains all queries before (and including) the latest query-answer pair of the form $(\cdot, \overline{\mathsf{cm}})$.

ii. Compute $(\mathbf{m}', \mathbf{dcm}') \leftarrow \mathsf{SCode.Extr}(n, \mathsf{sid}_{\mathsf{VC}}, \overline{\mathsf{cm}}, Q)$. # Extract committed vector.

iii. If $\mathbf{m}'[\bar{i}] \neq \overline{m}$, $\mathbf{m}'[\bar{i}] = \perp$, or SCode.Extr commits SCodeTimeError (Definition 4), set $v := 0$. # Check extraction.

iv. Else: # $\mathbf{m}'[\bar{i}] = \overline{m}$.

A. Set $v = 1$.

B. If $(\overline{\mathsf{cm}}, \bar{i}, \overline{m}, \cdot, \cdot, 1) \notin \mathsf{CState}$, append $(\overline{\mathsf{cm}}, i, \mathbf{m}'[i], \mathbf{dcm}'[i], \perp, 1)$ to CState for all $i \in [n]$. # If $\overline{m}$ does not appear in CState, add the entire extracted vector to CState.

C. Else, check that for all $i \in [n]$, there exists an entry $(\overline{\mathsf{cm}}, i, m = \mathbf{m}'[i], \cdot, \cdot, 1) \in \mathsf{CState}$. If not, set $v = 0$. # If $\overline{m}$ already appears in CState, only accept if $\mathbf{m}'$ is consistent with CState.

v. Output ($\mathtt{VerStatus}, v$) to R.

Fig. 7. The ideal functionality for non-interactive vector commitment in the presence of $\mathcal{F}_{\mathsf{GRO}}$.

Functionality $\mathcal{F}_{\mathsf{NVC}}$ (subroutines)

V **Initialization:** In the first activation do: # First activation can be `Commit` or `Verify`.
(a) Set the following variables as empty (i.e. as $\perp$):
- CState: a list of tuples $(\mathsf{cm}, i, m, \mathsf{dcm}, \mathsf{State}, v)$, in which cm is a commitment string, $i \in [n]$ is an index, $m \in \Sigma$ is an element of the message vector, dcm is a decommitment for m, State is the committer state with respect to entry i, and $v \in \{0,1\}$ is a bit representing whether $(\mathsf{cm}, i, m, \mathsf{dcm})$ is valid.
- $\mathsf{Hist}_{\mathsf{GRO}}$: a list of tuples (x, y), in which x is a query point, and y is a query answer.
- ActiveAlg: records which algorithm is currently interacting with $\mathcal{F}_{\mathsf{GRO}}$.
- SubFuncs: a list of tuples (ssid, State), in which ssid is a session ID, and State is internal state associated with session ssid.

(b) Take control of session $\mathsf{sid}_{\mathsf{VC}}$ (where $\mathsf{sid}_{\mathsf{VC}}$ is the local session ID) in $\mathcal{F}_{\mathsf{GRO}}$ by sending (`Control`) to $\mathcal{F}_{\mathsf{GRO}}$, and receive a message m from $\mathcal{F}_{\mathsf{GRO}}$.# Enables observing and programming GRO.
   i. If $m = (\mathtt{Ok}, \mathsf{Hist})$ such that $\mathsf{Hist} \neq \perp$, output $\perp$. # Failure.

(c) Send (`CodeRequest`, $\mathcal{F}_{\mathsf{NVC}}$) to $\mathcal{F}_{\mathsf{lib}}$ and receive (`Answer`, LinkedRecords), where $\mathsf{LinkedRecords} = (\mathcal{F}_{\mathsf{NVC}}, \mathsf{SCode}, \cdot)$ and SCode is a tuple of algorithms $\{\mathsf{Setup}, \mathsf{Com}, \mathsf{Equiv}, \mathsf{Extr}\}$.

(d) Run SCode.Setup. If SCode.Setup invokes (Spawn, ssid), run Step VI. # Spawn gateway functionalities for simulating sub-functionalities.

(e) Let $r_{\mathsf{cm}} \leftarrow (\{0,1\}^{h_{\mathsf{cm}}})^{\lambda} \times (\{0,1\}^{h_{\mathsf{dcm}}})^{\lambda}$, $r_{\mathsf{dcm},1}, \ldots, r_{\mathsf{dcm},n} \leftarrow (\{0,1\}^{h_{\mathsf{dcm}}})^{\lambda}$, $\widehat{r_{\mathsf{cm}}} \leftarrow (\{0,1\}^{h_{\mathsf{cm}}})^{\lambda}$, $\widehat{r_{\mathsf{dcm}}} \leftarrow (\{0,1\}^{h_{\mathsf{dcm}}})^{\lambda}$ denote the random strings of $\mathcal{F}_{\mathsf{NVC}}$. # The random strings $r_{\mathsf{cm}}, r_{\mathsf{dcm},i}$ will be given to SCode.Com and SCode.Equiv, respectively. $\widehat{r_{\mathsf{cm}}}$ and $\widehat{r_{\mathsf{dcm}}}$ are for running default code.

VI **Initialize gateway functionality:** When (Spawn, ssid) is invoked:
(a) If the input ssid has the form $(\mathsf{sid}_{\mathsf{VC}}, \cdot)$ and there is no entry of the form $(\mathsf{ssid}, \cdot) \in$ SubFuncs: # Ensure ssid is a valid sub-session ID of $\mathsf{sid}_{\mathsf{VC}}$.
   i. Send (Spawn, ssid) to the gateway functionality GF (Figure 9), and receive a message m from GF.
      A. If $m = (\mathtt{Ok}, \mathsf{Hist})$ and $\mathsf{Hist} = \perp$, add $(\mathsf{ssid}, \mathsf{State} := \perp)$ to the list SubFuncs, where State is the state associated with ssid.
      B. Else, output $\perp$. # Failure.

VII **Default commit code:** # Generates strings in event of errors.
(a) Set $\mathsf{cm} := \widehat{r_{\mathsf{cm}}}[0]$.
(b) Compute $\mathbf{dcm}$ such that for all $i \in [n]$:

$$\mathbf{dcm}[i] := \begin{cases} \perp & \text{if } \mathbf{m}[i] = \perp \\ \widehat{r_{\mathsf{dcm}}} & \text{o.w.} \end{cases}.$$

VIII **External request to program the GRO:** Upon receiving (`ProgramReq`, P, x) from $\mathcal{F}_{\mathsf{GRO}}$: # This interface allows $\mathcal{F}_{\mathsf{NVC}}$ to observe oracle queries.
(a) Sample $y \leftarrow \{0,1\}^{h_{\mathsf{cm}}}$ and add $(x, y) \in \mathsf{Hist}_{\mathsf{GRO}}$.
(b) Send subroutine input (`Program`, x, y) to $\mathcal{F}_{\mathsf{GRO}}$.

Fig. 8. The ideal functionality for non-interactive vector commitment in the presence of $\mathcal{F}_{\mathsf{GRO}}$, specifically the subroutines for initialization, for default committer code and for the interactions between $\mathcal{F}_{\mathsf{NVC}}$ and the global subroutine $\mathcal{F}_{\mathsf{GRO}}$.

Gateway functionality GF

- **Spawn.** Upon the invocation of (Spawn, ssid) by a caller $\mathcal{F}$ with session ID sid:
  1. Take control of session ssid in $\mathcal{F}_{\mathsf{GRO}}$ by sending (`Control`) to $\mathcal{F}_{\mathsf{GRO}}$.
  2. Receive a message from $\mathcal{F}_{\mathsf{GRO}}$ and forward it to $\mathcal{F}_{\mathsf{NVC}}$.
- **Internal request to program the GRO:** Upon receiving (`Program`, x, y) from an ideal functionality $\mathcal{F}$:
  1. Send (`Program`, x, y) to $\mathcal{F}_{\mathsf{GRO}}$.
  2. Receive subroutine output (`EvalOutput`, y) from $\mathcal{F}_{\mathsf{GRO}}$.
  3. Forward (`EvalOutput`, y) to $\mathcal{F}$.
- **External request to program the GRO:** Upon receiving (`ProgramReq`, P, x) from $\mathcal{F}_{\mathsf{GRO}}$: # This interface allows $\mathcal{F}$ to observe oracle queries.
  1. Sample $y \leftarrow \{0,1\}^\lambda$ and add (x, y) to $\mathsf{Hist}_{\mathsf{GRO}}$.
  2. Send subroutine input (`Program`, x, y) to $\mathcal{F}_{\mathsf{GRO}}$.

Fig. 9. Code for gateway functionalities, which are used for simulating interactions between subfunctionalities of a caller $\mathcal{F}$ and $\mathcal{F}_{\mathsf{GRO}}$.

When simulating composed protocols, we note that SCode must emulate the behavior of any ideal subroutines. To do so operationally, the description of SCode of $\mathcal{F}_{\mathsf{NVC}}$ may contain pointers for the SCode of its subroutines. $\mathcal{F}_{\mathsf{lib}}$ handles this code linking, prior to sending the completed SCode to $\mathcal{F}_{\mathsf{NVC}}$. However, note that any linked code should not be trusted; the environment can adversarially choose and upload the code to $\mathcal{F}_{\mathsf{lib}}$. As a preview, we will make use of such code linking for simulating Π_{NVC}, i.e. a Merkle tree vector commitment, in which the nodes are implemented using $\mathcal{F}_{\mathsf{NC}}$ which, in turn, obtains its own simulator code from $\mathcal{F}_{\mathsf{lib}}$.

6.1 The Interface Between $\mathcal{F}_{\mathsf{NVC}}$ and $\mathcal{F}_{\mathsf{GRO}}$

Similarly to $\mathcal{F}_{\mathsf{NC}}$, $\mathcal{F}_{\mathsf{NVC}}$ handles internal requests by SCode algorithms to program $\mathcal{F}_{\mathsf{GRO}}$ using the Program subroutine (Fig. 10) and also enables observing queries to $\mathcal{F}_{\mathsf{GRO}}$ made by an external party (e.g. the environment) (see Step VIII of $\mathcal{F}_{\mathsf{NVC}}$). The Program subroutine of Fig. 10 generalizes that of Fig. 4 to handle programming requests for sub-sessions of $\mathcal{F}_{\mathsf{NVC}}$; we detail this below. We highlight differences from $\mathcal{F}_{\mathsf{NC}}$, particularly for handling internal programming requests.

Programming. Like for $\mathcal{F}_{\mathsf{NC}}$, the simulator algorithms (in SCode) may program $\mathcal{F}_{\mathsf{GRO}}$ by invoking the Program subroutine (Fig. 10), subject to the restrictions enforced by a predicate $\Phi_{\mathcal{F}_{\mathsf{NVC}}}$ (Fig. 11) which maintain the security guarantees of $\mathcal{F}_{\mathsf{NVC}}$. The discussion in Sect. 4.1 (regarding the interaction between $\mathcal{F}_{\mathsf{NC}}$ and $\mathcal{F}_{\mathsf{GRO}}$) applies, with the following additions:

- **Programming bound for SCode.Equiv.** Like for $\mathcal{F}_{\mathsf{NC}}$, SCode.Equiv many only program a single time, each time it is invoked by $\mathcal{F}_{\mathsf{NVC}}$. Unlike $\mathcal{F}_{\mathsf{NC}}$, $\mathcal{F}_{\mathsf{NVC}}$ invokes SCode.Equiv $n = |\mathbf{m}|$ times, i.e. once for each entry in the committed vector $\mathbf{m}$. Note that each invocation of SCode.Equiv only receives access to a single entry of $\mathbf{m}$, plus its index $i \in [n]$, so the result does not depend on other entries in $\mathbf{m}$. We note that any discussion about sub-sessions may also apply to $\mathcal{F}_{\mathsf{NC}}$ and $\mathcal{F}_{\mathsf{NIZK}}$ if it is UC-realized by a protocols that uses ideal components.

- **Simulating subroutines in a protocol that realizes $\mathcal{F}_{\mathsf{NVC}}$.** When simulating a protocol that realizes $\mathcal{F}_{\mathsf{NVC}}$, the simulator for $\mathcal{F}_{\mathsf{NVC}}$ must emulate the behavior of any ideal sub-components in the protocol. In particular, the simulator must emulate any interactions between such sub-components and $\mathcal{F}_{\mathsf{GRO}}$.
  To do so, $\mathcal{F}_{\mathsf{NVC}}$ would need to take control of the sids of these sub-components. However, $\mathcal{F}_{\mathsf{GRO}}$ (Fig. 1) only allows parties to take control of their own session ID; in particular, it is unclear how to allow the simulator to control its sub-session IDs in $\mathcal{F}_{\mathsf{GRO}}$, which is needed to emulate interactions between subroutines and $\mathcal{F}_{\mathsf{GRO}}$.
  To address this, we define the formalism of a *gateway* functionality, which acts as a channel for accessing $\mathcal{F}_{\mathsf{GRO}}$ from a sub-session of $\mathcal{F}_{\mathsf{NVC}}$. During its initial activation, $\mathcal{F}_{\mathsf{NVC}}$ first takes control of its own session ID sid in $\mathcal{F}_{\mathsf{GRO}}$. Subsequently, $\mathcal{F}_{\mathsf{NVC}}$ takes control of a sub-session ID ssid via "spawning" a gateway associated with ssid, which enables observing and programming $\mathcal{F}_{\mathsf{GRO}}$ from ssid. (Note that $\mathcal{F}_{\mathsf{NVC}}$ uses a separate gateway functionality per sub-session.) As such, it's possible to simulate the interactions between any subroutines and $\mathcal{F}_{\mathsf{GRO}}$.
  However, recall that programming requests to $\mathcal{F}_{\mathsf{GRO}}$, including those for sub-sessions of $\mathcal{F}_{\mathsf{NVC}}$, should not compromise the security of $\mathcal{F}_{\mathsf{NVC}}$. As such, any requests of the simulator code are subject to safety constraints. Like for programming requests from the session ID of $\mathcal{F}_{\mathsf{NVC}}$, all programming requests from sub-session IDs of $\mathcal{F}_{\mathsf{NVC}}$ are done by invoking $\mathsf{Program}$ (Fig. 11), subject to the restrictions of $\Phi_{\mathcal{F}_{\mathsf{NVC}}}$ (Fig. 11). If a programming request for a sub-session of $\mathcal{F}_{\mathsf{NVC}}$ passes the checks of $\Phi_{\mathcal{F}_{\mathsf{NVC}}}$, $\mathsf{Program}$ routes the programming request through the gateway functionality with the corresponding sub-session ID.
  We give code of the gateway functionality in Fig. 9. That is, anytime $\mathcal{F}_{\mathsf{NVC}}$ initializes a gateway functionality GF (with a sub-session ID of the form $\mathsf{ssid} = (\mathsf{sid}_{\mathsf{VC}}, \cdot)$), GF has the code given in Fig. 9.
  Further, since $\mathcal{F}_{\mathsf{NVC}}$ (and thus GF) is not a global functionality, GF must also be subroutine respecting, i.e. it only interacts with the main party that spawned it ($\mathcal{F}_{\mathsf{NVC}}$) and $\mathcal{F}_{\mathsf{GRO}}$ but *not* the environment. (See full version for a diagram illustrating the communication channels [CC25].)

6.2 Security Guarantees Provided by $\mathcal{F}_{\mathsf{NVC}}$

We discuss the hiding and binding properties provided by $\mathcal{F}_{\mathsf{NVC}}$ in in the full version of this paper [CC25]; one can view them as generalizations of the same properties for $\mathcal{F}_{\mathsf{NC}}$. We also discuss mechanisms for the enforcing min-entropy of $\mathbf{dcm}$ strings in $\mathcal{F}_{\mathsf{NVC}}$ in the full version.

The $\mathsf{Program}$ **subroutine ($\mathcal{F}_{\mathsf{NVC}}$ version, also good for $\mathcal{F}_{\mathsf{NIZK}}$).**

- $\mathsf{Program}(\mathsf{SubFuncs}, \mathsf{Hist}_{\mathsf{GRO}}, \Phi_{\mathcal{F}}, \mathsf{sid}, \mathsf{ActiveAlg}, x, y)$:
  1. Parse the inputs so that:
     (a) the following are honestly derived from the state of $\mathcal{F}$: $\mathsf{SubFuncs}$ as the list gateway functionalities, $\mathsf{Hist}_{\mathsf{GRO}}$ is the list of GRO query-answer pairs, $\Phi_{\mathcal{F}}$ is the query-checking predicate for $\mathcal{F}$, sid is the calling party's session ID; and
     (b) the following may be chosen by $\mathsf{ActiveAlg}$: x is a GRO query in $\mathrm{Dom}(\mathcal{F}_{\mathsf{GRO}})$, and y is a GRO answer in $\mathrm{Cod}(\mathcal{F}_{\mathsf{GRO}})$.
  2. If $(x, \cdot) \notin \mathsf{Hist}_{\mathsf{GRO}}$: # The evaluation of x is undefined in $\mathcal{F}_{\mathsf{GRO}}$.
     (a) If $\Phi_{\mathcal{F}}(\mathsf{sid}, \mathsf{ActiveAlg}, x, y) = 1$: # $\Phi_{\mathcal{F}}$ is a predicate check.
        i. If sid is the local session ID of $\mathcal{F}$:
           A. Send subroutine input $(\texttt{Program}, x, y)$ to $\mathcal{F}_{\mathsf{GRO}}$.
           B. Receive subroutine output $(\texttt{EvalOutput}, y)$ from $\mathcal{F}_{\mathsf{GRO}}$.
        ii. If there exists an entry $(\mathsf{sid}, \cdot, \cdot) \in \mathsf{SubFuncs}$:
           A. Invoke the gateway functionality GF with session ID sid (and party ID $\mathsf{pid} = \bot$) with input $(\texttt{Program}, x, y)$.
           B. Receive $(\texttt{EvalOutput}, y)$ from GF.
           C. Forward $(\texttt{EvalOutput}, y)$ to $\mathsf{ActiveAlg}$.
     (b) Else, output $(\texttt{EvalOutput}, \bot)$ to $\mathsf{ActiveAlg}$. # Error.
  3. Else (if there exists an entry $(x, y') \in \mathsf{Hist}_{\mathsf{GRO}}$), send $(\texttt{EvalOutput}, y')$ to $\mathsf{ActiveAlg}$.

Fig. 10. The $\mathsf{Program}$ subroutine, which handles $\mathcal{F}_{\mathsf{GRO}}$ programming requests originating from an ideal functionality or a subroutine.

The predicate $\Phi_{\mathcal{F}_{\mathsf{NVC}}}$

- $\Phi_{\mathcal{F}_{\mathsf{NVC}}}(\mathsf{sid}, \mathsf{ActiveAlg}, x, y) \rightarrow \{0, 1\}$:
  1. Parse sid as the session ID of the calling party, x as a query point (sid', x') in $\mathrm{Dom}(\mathcal{F}_{\mathsf{GRO}})$, and y as a query answer in $\mathrm{Cod}(\mathcal{F}_{\mathsf{GRO}})$.
  2. If $\mathsf{sid} \neq \mathsf{sid}'$, output 0. # Disallow cross-domain programming.
  3. If $\mathsf{ActiveAlg} = \mathsf{SCode.Com}$: # The caller is $\mathsf{SCode.Com}$.
     (a) Check that $f(x') \in r_{\mathsf{dcm}}$. # Programmed $\mathcal{F}_{\mathsf{GRO}}$ query-answer pairs have sufficient entropy, f is some injective function.
     (b) If Step 3a passes, output 1 to $\mathsf{ActiveAlg}$. Else, output 0 to $\mathsf{ActiveAlg}$.
  4. If $\mathsf{ActiveAlg} = \mathsf{SCode.Equiv}$: # The caller is $\mathsf{SCode.Equiv}$.
     (a) If this execution of $\mathsf{SCode.Equiv}$ has already programmed $\mathcal{F}_{\mathsf{GRO}}$, output 0.
     (b) Check that all of the following conditions hold:
        i. This execution of $\mathsf{SCode.Equiv}$ has not already programmed $\mathcal{F}_{\mathsf{GRO}}$.
        ii. $f(x') \in r_{\mathsf{dcm}}$. # Programmed $\mathcal{F}_{\mathsf{GRO}}$ query-answer pairs have sufficient entropy, f is some injective function.
     (c) If Step 4b passes, output 1 to $\mathsf{ActiveAlg}$. Else, output 0 to $\mathsf{ActiveAlg}$.
  5. Else, output 0 to $\mathsf{ActiveAlg}$. # No other SCode algorithms can program.

Fig. 11. The predicate $\Phi_{\mathcal{F}_{\mathsf{NVC}}}$, which verifies properties of $\mathcal{F}_{\mathsf{GRO}}$ programming requests originating from $\mathcal{F}_{\mathsf{NVC}}$.

Protocol Π_{NVC}

- **Commit:** The committer C does:
  1. Receive input $(\texttt{Commit}, \mathbf{m})$, in which $\mathbf{m} \in (\{0,1\}^e \cup \{\bot\})^n$.
  2. Compute the Merkle tree depth $\mathsf{d} := \log n$.
  3. For all $i \in [n]$: # Initial commitment of the input.
     (a) Set session ID $\mathsf{sid}_{\mathsf{NC}} := (\mathsf{sid}_{\mathsf{VC}}, (\mathsf{d}+1,\ i))$, in which $\mathsf{sid}_{\mathsf{VC}}$ is the session ID of Π_{NVC}.
     (b) Send input $(\texttt{Commit}, \mathbf{m}[i])$ to the $\mathcal{F}_{\mathsf{NC}}$ of session ID $\mathsf{sid}_{\mathsf{NC}}$.
     (c) Receive output $(\texttt{Receipt}, \mathsf{cm}_{(\mathsf{d}+1,i)}, \mathsf{dcm}_{(\mathsf{d}+1,i)})$ from $\mathcal{F}_{\mathsf{NC}}$.
     (d) Output $\mathsf{cm}_{(\mathsf{d}+1,i)}$ as the output wire value.
  4. For layers $\ell \le \mathsf{d}$ and for $\mathsf{pos} \in [2^{\ell-1}]$: # Compute the Merkle tree, from leaves to root.
     (a) Set the node's session ID $\mathsf{sid}_{\mathsf{NC}} := (\mathsf{sid}_{\mathsf{VC}}, (\ell,\ \mathsf{pos}))$.
     (b) Find the left and right input values: $x_{\mathsf{L}} := \mathsf{cm}_{(\ell+1,\, 2\cdot\mathsf{pos}-1)}$ and $x_{\mathsf{R}} := \mathsf{cm}_{(\ell+1,\, 2\cdot\mathsf{pos})}$.
     (c) Send input $(\texttt{Commit}, (x_{\mathsf{L}}, x_{\mathsf{R}}))$ to $\mathcal{F}_{\mathsf{NC}}$ of session ID $\mathsf{sid}_{\mathsf{NC}}$.
     (d) Receive output $(\texttt{Receipt}, \mathsf{cm}_{(\ell,\mathsf{pos})}, \mathsf{dcm}_{(\ell,\mathsf{pos})})$ from $\mathcal{F}_{\mathsf{NC}}$.
     (e) Output $\mathsf{cm}_{(\ell,\mathsf{pos})}$ as the output wire value.
  5. Set $\mathsf{rt} := \mathsf{cm}_{(1,1)}$. # Merkle tree root.
  6. For $i \in [n]$: # Compute Merkle tree authentication paths.
     (a) Compute the authentication path:
     $$\mathsf{ap}_i := \{((\mathsf{sid}_{\mathsf{VC}}, \mathsf{Out}), \mathsf{cm}_{\mathsf{L}}, \mathsf{cm}_{\mathsf{R}}, \mathsf{dcm}_{\mathsf{Out}}, \mathsf{cm}_{\mathsf{Out}})\}_{\mathsf{Out}\in\mathsf{A}}\ ,$$
     in which $\mathsf{L} = (\ell+1,\ 2\cdot\mathsf{pos}-1)$, $\mathsf{R} = (\ell+1,\ 2\cdot\mathsf{pos})$, $\mathsf{Out} = (\ell,\ \mathsf{pos})$, and A is the set of all nodes on the path from $\mathsf{cm}_{(\mathsf{d}+1,i)}$ to rt.
  7. Define $\mathbf{dcm}$ as the vector such that entry $i \in [n]$ is $\mathbf{dcm}[i] := \left(\mathsf{ap}_i, \mathsf{dcm}_{(\mathsf{d}+1,\ i)}\right)$, where $\mathsf{dcm}_{(\mathsf{d}+1,\ i)}$ is decommitment from the initial commitment of the input $\mathbf{m}[i]$. # Vector of decommitments.
  8. Output $(\texttt{Commit}, \mathsf{cm} := \mathsf{rt}, \mathbf{dcm})$.
- **Verify:** The receiver R does:
  1. Receive input $(\texttt{Verify}, \overline{\mathsf{cm}}, i, \overline{m}, \overline{\mathsf{dcm}})$.
  2. Parse $\overline{\mathsf{cm}} = \overline{\mathsf{rt}}$ as a Merkle tree root.
  3. Parse $\overline{\mathsf{dcm}}$ as $\left(\overline{\mathsf{ap}}_i, \overline{\mathsf{dcm}}_{(\mathsf{d}+1,\ i)}\right)$, where $\overline{\mathsf{ap}}_i$ is a claimed authentication path and $\overline{\mathsf{dcm}}_{(\mathsf{d}+1,\ i)}$ is a decommitment associated with an initial commitment to $\overline{m}$.
  4. Check the initial commitment:
     (a) Set session ID $\mathsf{sid}_{\mathsf{NC}} := (\mathsf{sid}_{\mathsf{VC}}, (\mathsf{d}+1,\ i))$, in which $\mathsf{sid}_{\mathsf{VC}}$ is the session ID of Π_{NVC}.
     (b) Find the commitment value cm^* associated with $\overline{m}$ in $\overline{\mathsf{ap}}_i$:
        i. Identify the entry $(\mathsf{sid}_{\mathsf{NC}}, \mathsf{cm}_{\mathsf{L}}, \mathsf{cm}_{\mathsf{R}}, \cdot, \cdot)$ in $\overline{\mathsf{ap}}_i$.
        ii. If $i \bmod 2 = 1$, set $\mathsf{cm}^* := \mathsf{cm}_{\mathsf{L}}$. Otherwise, set $\mathsf{cm}^* := \mathsf{cm}_{\mathsf{R}}$.
     (c) Send input $(\texttt{Verify}, \mathsf{cm}^*, (\mathsf{sid}_{\mathsf{NC}}, \overline{m}), \overline{\mathsf{dcm}}_{(\mathsf{d}+1,\ i)})$ to $\mathcal{F}_{\mathsf{NC}}$.
     (d) Receive output $(\texttt{VerStatus}, v)$ from $\mathcal{F}_{\mathsf{NC}}$; this check passes if $v = 1$.
  5. Check that $\overline{\mathsf{ap}}_i$ is a valid authentication path:
     (a) For all $(\mathsf{sid}_{\mathsf{NC}}, x_{\mathsf{L}}, x_{\mathsf{R}}, \mathsf{dcm}, \mathsf{cm}) \in \overline{\mathsf{ap}}_i$,
     # Each entry of $\overline{\mathsf{ap}}_i$ corresponds to a node in the authentication path.
        i. Send input $(\texttt{Verify}, \mathsf{cm}, (\mathsf{sid}_{\mathsf{NC}}, x_{\mathsf{L}}, x_{\mathsf{R}}), \mathsf{dcm})$ to $\mathcal{F}_{\mathsf{NC}}$.
        ii. Receive output $(\texttt{VerStatus}, v)$ from $\mathcal{F}_{\mathsf{NC}}$; this check passes if $v = 1$.
     (b) The entries in $\overline{\mathsf{ap}}_i$ correspond to a path from leaf i to $\overline{\mathsf{rt}}$.
     (c) The value $\overline{\mathsf{cm}}$ is the output of the root node in $\overline{\mathsf{ap}}_i$. Specifically, there exists an entry
     $((\mathsf{sid}_{\mathsf{VC}}, (1,\ 1)), x_{\mathsf{L}}, x_{\mathsf{R}}, \mathsf{dcm}, \overline{\mathsf{cm}}) \in \overline{\mathsf{ap}}_i$.
  6. If all checks pass, output $(\texttt{VerStatus}, 1)$. Else, output $(\texttt{VerStatus}, 0)$.

Fig. 12. The vector commitment scheme protocol, with global subroutine $\mathcal{F}_{\mathsf{GRO}}$.

7 Π_{NVC}: The Non-interactive Vector Commitment Scheme

We construct a non-interactive vector commitment scheme Π_{NVC} (Fig. 12), which is a reformulation of Merkle tree succinct commitments [Mer89] in which the internal nodes are computed using non-interactive commitments $\mathcal{F}_{\mathsf{NC}}$ (Fig. 2). Subsequently, we show that Π_{NVC} *perfectly* UC-realizes $\mathcal{F}_{\mathsf{NVC}}$ (Theorem 5); the proof appears in the full version of this paper [CC25].

Prior to describing Π_{NVC}, we first fix a method for indexing nodes in the Merkle tree and utilize these indices as session IDs to identify invocations of $\mathcal{F}_{\mathsf{NC}}$ in Π_{NVC}.

Node Indices are Session IDs. A node's index is a layer-position pair $(\ell,\ \mathsf{pos})$. The output node has depth $\ell = 1$, and the input layer has depth $\ell = \mathsf{d} := \log|\mathbf{m}|$. Within layer ℓ, nodes are assigned a position $\mathsf{pos} \in [2^{\ell-1}]$. Then, the session ID used to identify $\mathcal{F}_{\mathsf{NC}}$ (a.k.a. a node of the Merkle tree) is $\mathsf{sid} := (\mathsf{sid}_{\mathsf{VC}}, (\ell,\ \mathsf{pos}))$, in which $\mathsf{sid}_{\mathsf{VC}}$ is the session ID of the vector commitment scheme invoking $\mathcal{F}_{\mathsf{NC}}$.

Our construction additionally applies $\mathcal{F}_{\mathsf{NC}}$ to each entry of $\mathbf{m}$, a process we call the "initial commitment". We notate this as layer $\mathsf{d} + 1$ of the Merkle tree. This is done so that unopened entries of $\mathbf{m}$ are hidden.

We describe the vector commitment protocol Π_{NVC} in Fig. 12. See the full version of this paper [CC25] for a diagram of the construction. In Π_{NVC}, we denote $n := |\mathbf{m}|$, in which $\mathbf{m}$ is the committed vector. In this paper, we specifically consider $n = 2^{\mathsf{d}}$ for some $\mathsf{d} \in \mathbb{N}$. Note that it's straightforward to generalize to committing to any message of length $\leq n$, via padding.

Theorem 5. *Let $\mathcal{F}_{\mathsf{GRO}}(h_{\mathsf{cm}})$ be an ideal global random oracle, with output length $h_{\mathsf{cm}} \in \mathbb{N}$. Let $\mathcal{F}_{\mathsf{NC}}(\Sigma, h_{\mathsf{cm}}, h_{\mathsf{dcm}})$ (Fig. 2) be an ideal commitment in the presence of $\mathcal{F}_{\mathsf{GRO}}(h_{\mathsf{cm}})$ and $\mathcal{F}_{\mathsf{lib}}$, in which $h_{\mathsf{dcm}} \in \mathbb{N}$ and Σ is the plaintext alphabet. Let $n \in \mathbb{N}$ be a parameter denoting the length of the committed vector.*

Then, Π_{NVC} in Fig. 12 perfectly UC-realizes the ideal vector commitment functionality $\mathcal{F}_{\mathsf{NVC}}(\Sigma, n, h_{\mathsf{cm}}, h_{\mathsf{dcm}})$ in the presence of $\mathcal{F}_{\mathsf{GRO}}(h_{\mathsf{cm}})$ and $\mathcal{F}_{\mathsf{lib}}$ (described in Fig. 7), even against adaptive corruptions.

Also, commitments are h_{cm}-bit strings.

Acknowledgments. Megan Chen is supported by DARPA under Agreement No. HR00 112020023. We thank Lawrence Roy, Jack Doerner, Ran Cohen, Eysa Lee, Anna Lysyanskaya and Pratik Sarkar for illuminating discussions about UC non-interactive functionalities. We further thank Giacomo Fenzi and Alessandro Chiesa for helpful discussions about concrete security analyses of Kilian-Micali and applications for our abstractions.

A A Weakness in Earlier Formulations of the Global Random Oracle

This section demonstrates and discusses a weakness in existing formulations of the global random oracle, namely the programmable version of the global random oracle in [CDG+18] and other formulations that build on it, such as those of [LR22,CF24]. As explained in Sect. 3, this weakness serves as one of the motivations for our new formulation of $\mathcal{F}_{\mathsf{GRO}}$.

The programmable version of the global random oracle in [CDG+18] allows anyone (in particular, the adversary) to determine the output of the oracle at any point that was not yet queried. By itself, such modeling would render the oracle useless since its value can be adversarial at programmed locations. To circumvent this "model attack", [CDG+18] allows any party of a protocol with session ID sid to check whether any point of the form (sid, v) has been programmed. Formally, this check is done via the IsProgrammed interface of their global random oracle functionality. Crucially, however, *neither the environment nor the adversary have access to this capability.*

At first, this stipulation appears to resolve the issue elegantly: On the one hand, a party can tell if a point in its own "reserved input space" has been surreptitiously programmed. On the other hand, simulators (i.e. ideal-model adversaries) can still program points without the environment being aware whether programming took place. Finally, since in reality oracles are never "programmed", in the real model of execution all IsProgrammed queries will always be answered negatively, so they need not be made "in practice."

However, a closer look reveals that the above argument is overly optimistic. In particular, the IsProgammed instruction provides a mechanism for a protocol to learn, by inspecting the state of the global random oracle, whether a subroutine call to an ideal functionality is fulfilled by the ideal functionality itself or else by a protocol that realizes the functionality. This means that any security analysis of the calling protocols needs to consider the protocol's behavior in all such cases, thereby either rendering the random oracle significantly less useful, or else doing away with the benefits of secure composition.

Effectively, the IsProgammed instruction provides a "side channel" that bypasses the protections provided by the UC theorem.

To make this point more concrete, consider some ideal functionality (say, $\mathcal{F}_{\mathsf{NIZK}}$), and let ρ be a protocol that securely realizes $\mathcal{F}_{\mathsf{NIZK}}$ in the presence of the programmable random oracle of [CDG+18, LR22, CF24]. Let S_π denote the simulator used in the proof that π realizes $\mathcal{F}_{\mathsf{NIZK}}$. Now, proceed as follows.

First, add to S_π an instruction to program the oracle at some fixed input, say $x = (\mathsf{sid}_0, 0)$, to a random value. (The session id of π is in general different than sid_0; still, this operation is allowed in the model.) Observe that the modified S_π is still a valid simulator for π, since the environment cannot tell whether the input x was programmed.

Next, consider a protocol ρ with session id sid_0, that instructs party P to use $\mathcal{F}_{\mathsf{NIZK}}$ to generate a proof that $(\mathbb{x}, \mathbb{w}) \in \mathcal{R}$, where $\mathbb{w}$ is secret. In addition, protocol ρ instructs P to perform the following instruction, once $\mathcal{F}_{\mathsf{NIZK}}$ returns an output:

1. Check whether the point $x = (\mathsf{sid}_0, 0)$ was programmed, via sending the query $\mathsf{IsProgrammed}(x)$.
2. If the response is negative, expose $\mathbb{w}$ and halt.

Now, let $\mathcal{E}$ be an environment machine that does not program the oracle. Observe that: (a) when P uses π and runs with environment $\mathcal{E}$ the point x is not programmed, so the instruction to output all secret information is carried out. (b) However, when the composition operation is performed (i.e., π is replaced for $\mathcal{F}_{\mathsf{NIZK}}$ along with S_π and the system remains otherwise the same), the point $x = (\mathsf{sid}, 0)$ is programmed, and so the instruction to output $\mathbb{w}$ is not carried out.

Note that this change in the behavior of ρ does not violate the UC theorem, nor does it point to a flaw in the proof that π securely realizes $\mathcal{F}_{\mathsf{NIZK}}$. Rather, the $\mathsf{IsProgammed}$ operation provides ρ with a "legitimate API" that indicates whether or not $\mathcal{F}_{\mathsf{NIZK}}$ was replaced by π. This API allows the unsuspecting ρ to be adversely affected by the introduction of ρ to the system.[5]

A natural avenue to providing better separation between protocol instances with respect to the random oracle is to only allow the adversary (and simulator) to program points that are "within the domain reserved for the relevant protocol instance". However, it is not clear how to enforce such separation while still allowing the adversary (which is a global entity that can attack multiple protocol instances at the same time) to directly interact with $\mathcal{F}_{\mathsf{GRO}}$. The formalism in Sect. 3 provides a way to implementing this idea.

References

[BCG+14] Ben-Sasson, E., et al.: Zerocash: decentralized anonymous payments from bitcoin. In: SP 2014 (2014)

[BCH+20] Badertscher, C., Canetti, R., Hesse, J., Tackmann, B., Zikas, V.: Universal composition with global subroutines: capturing global setup within plain UC. In: TCC 2020 (2020)

[BCS16] Ben-Sasson, E., Chiesa, A., Spooner, N.: Interactive oracle proofs. In: Hirt, M., Smith, A. (eds.) TCC 2016. LNCS, vol. 9986, pp. 31–60. Springer, Heidelberg (2016). https://doi.org/10.1007/978-3-662-53644-5_2

[BDH+17] Broadnax, B., Döttling, N., Hartung, G., Müller-Quade, J., Nagel, M.: Concurrently composable security with shielded super-polynomial simulators. In: Coron, J.-S., Nielsen, J.B. (eds.) EUROCRYPT 2017. LNCS, vol. 10210, pp. 351–381. Springer, Cham (2017). https://doi.org/10.1007/978-3-319-56620-7_13

[BFG+22] Bienstock, A., Fairoze, J., Garg, S., Mukherjee, P., Raghuraman, S.: A more complete analysis of the signal double ratchet algorithm. In: CRYPTO 2022 (2022)

[BMNW25] Bünz, B., Mishra, P., Nguyen, W., Wang, W.: Accumulation without homomorphism. In: ITCS 2025 (2025)

[Can01] Canetti, R.: Universally composable security: a new paradigm for cryptographic protocols. In: FOCS 2001 (2001)

[Can04] Canetti, R.: Universally composable signature, certification, and authentication. In: CSFW 2004 (2004)

[Can20] Canetti, R.: Universally composable security. J. ACM (JACM) (2020)

[CC25] Canetti, R., Chen, M.: Universally Composable Succinct Vector Commitments and Applications. ePrint Report 2025/1103

[CDG+18] Camenisch, J., Drijvers, M., Gagliardoni, T., Lehmann, A., Neven, G.: The wonderful world of global random oracles. In: Nielsen, J.B., Rijmen, V. (eds.) EUROCRYPT 2018. LNCS, vol. 10820, pp. 280–312. Springer, Cham (2018). https://doi.org/10.1007/978-3-319-78381-9_11

[5] It might look surprising at first that ρ is affected by the act of replacing $\mathcal{F}_{\mathsf{NIZK}}$ with a protocol that UC-realizes it, and yet the UC theorem is not violated. The reason that this is the case is that UC with global functionalities allows a global functionality (such as $\mathcal{F}_{\mathsf{GRO}}$) to be affected by the act of replacing an ideal functionality (such as $\mathcal{F}_{\mathsf{NIZK}}$) by a protocol that realizes it [BCH+20]. This inevitable situation means that it is up to the global functionality whether to make this information available to the protocol that called the ideal functionality in the first place (such as ρ in the above example).

[CDL+24] Cohen, R., Doerner, J., Lee, E., Lysyanskaya, A., Roy, L.: An Unstoppable Ideal Functionality for Signatures and a Modular Analysis of the Dolev-Strong Broadcast. ePrint Report 2024/1807

[CF01] Canetti, R., Fischlin, M.: Universally composable commitments. In: Kilian, J. (ed.) CRYPTO 2001. LNCS, vol. 2139, pp. 19–40. Springer, Heidelberg (2001). https://doi.org/10.1007/3-540-44647-8_2

[CF13] Catalano, D., Fiore, D.: Vector commitments and their applications. In: PKC 2013 (2013)

[CF24] Chiesa, A., Fenzi, G.: zkSNARKs in the ROMwith unconditional UC-security. In: TCC 2024 (2024)

[CGH04] Canetti, R., Goldreich, O., Halevi, S.: The random oracle methodology, revisited. In: JACM (2004)

[CJS14] Canetti, R., Jain, A., Scafuro, A.: Practical UC security with a global random oracle. In: CCS 2014 (2014)

[CJSV22] Canetti, R., Jain, P., Swanberg, M., Varia, M.: Universally composable end-to- end secure messaging: a modular analysis. In: CRYPTO 2022 (2022)

[CK02] Canetti, R., Krawczyk, H.: Universally composable notions of key exchange and secure channels. In: Knudsen, L.R. (ed.) EUROCRYPT 2002. LNCS, vol. 2332, pp. 337–351. Springer, Heidelberg (2002). https://doi.org/10.1007/3-540-46035-7_22

[CKN03] Canetti, R., Krawczyk, H., Nielsen, J.B.: Relaxing chosen-ciphertext security. In: Boneh, D. (ed.) CRYPTO 2003. LNCS, vol. 2729, pp. 565–582. Springer, Heidelberg (2003). https://doi.org/10.1007/978-3-540-45146-4_33

[CLOS02] Canetti, R., Lindell, Y., Ostrovsky, R., Sahai, A.: Universally composable twoparty and multi-party secure computation. In: STOC 2002 (2002)

[CP18] Cohen, B., Pietrzak, K.: Simple proofs of sequential work. In: Nielsen, J.B., Rijmen, V. (eds.) EUROCRYPT 2018. LNCS, vol. 10821, pp. 451–467. Springer, Cham (2018). https://doi.org/10.1007/978-3-319-78375-8_15

[CSV16] Canetti, R., Shahaf, D., Vald, M.: Universally composable authentication and key-exchange with global PKI. In: Cheng, C.-M., Chung, K.-M., Persiano, G., Yang, B.-Y. (eds.) PKC 2016. LNCS, vol. 9615, pp. 265–296. Springer, Heidelberg (2016). https://doi.org/10.1007/978-3-662-49387-8_11

[CSW22] Canetti, R., Sarkar, P., Wang, X.: Triply adaptive UC NIZK. In: ASIACRYPT 2022 (2022)

[DFKP15] Dziembowski, S., Faust, S., Kolmogorov, V., Pietrzak, K.: Proofs of space. In: Gennaro, R., Robshaw, M. (eds.) CRYPTO 2015. LNCS, vol. 9216, pp. 585–605. Springer, Heidelberg (2015). https://doi.org/10.1007/978-3-662-48000-7_29

[DN03] Damgård, I., Nielsen, J.B.: Universally composable efficient multiparty computation from threshold homomorphic encryption. In: Boneh, D. (ed.) CRYPTO 2003. LNCS, vol. 2729, pp. 247–264. Springer, Heidelberg (2003). https://doi.org/10.1007/978-3-540-45146-4_15

[GKO+23] Ganesh, C., Kondi, Y., Orlandi, C., Pancholi, M., Takahashi, A., Tschudi, D.: Witness-succinct universally-composable SNARKs. In: EUROCRYPT 2023 (2023)

[GOS06] Groth, J., Ostrovsky, R., Sahai, A.: Perfect non-interactive zero knowledge for NP. In: Vaudenay, S. (ed.) EUROCRYPT 2006. LNCS, vol. 4004, pp. 339–358. Springer, Heidelberg (2006). https://doi.org/10.1007/11761679_21

[GOS12] Groth, J., Ostrovsky, R., Sahai, A.: New techniques for noninteractive zeroknowledge. J. ACM (JACM) (2012)

[IMS12] Ishai, Y., Mahmoody, M., Sahai, A.: On efficient zero-knowledge PCPs. In: Cramer, R. (ed.) TCC 2012. LNCS, vol. 7194, pp. 151–168. Springer, Heidelberg (2012). https://doi.org/10.1007/978-3-642-28914-9_9

[KLP05] Kalai, Y.T., Lindell, Y., Prabhakaran, M.: Concurrent general composition of secure protocols in the timing model. In: STOC 2005 (2005)

[KPT97] Kilian, J., Petrank, E., Tardos, G.: Probabilistically checkable proofs with zero knowledge. In: STOC 1997 (1997)

[LR22] Lysyanskaya, A., Rosenbloom, L.N.: Universally composable Σ-protocols in the global random-oracle model. In: TCC 2022 (2022)

[MBB+15] Melara, M.S., Blankstein, A., Bonneau, J., Felten, E.W., Freedman, M.J.: CONIKS: bringing key transparency to end users. In: USENIX Security 2015 (2015)

[Mer89] Merkle, R.C.: A certified digital signature. In: Brassard, G. (ed.) CRYPTO 1989. LNCS, vol. 435, pp. 218–238. Springer, New York (1990). https://doi.org/10.1007/0-387-34805-0_21

[Mic00] Micali, S.: Computationally sound proofs. SIAM J. Comput. (2000). Preliminary version appeared in FOCS '94

[MMV13] Mahmoody, M., Moran, T., Vadhan, S.P.: Publicly verifiable proofs of sequential work. In: ITCS 2013 (2013)

[MPR10] Maji, H.K., Prabhakaran, M., Rosulek, M.: A zero-one law for cryptographic complexity with respect to computational UC security. In: Rabin, T. (ed.) CRYPTO 2010. LNCS, vol. 6223, pp. 595–612. Springer, Heidelberg (2010). https://doi.org/10.1007/978-3-642-14623-7_32

[Pro17] Protocol Labs. Filecoin: A Decentralized Storage Network. Whitepaper. https://www.filecoin.io/filecoin.pdf

[PS04] Prabhakaran, M., Sahai, A.: New notions of security: achieving universal composability without trusted setup. In: STOC 2004 (2004)

An Unstoppable Ideal Functionality for Signatures and a Modular Analysis of the Dolev-Strong Broadcast

Ran Cohen[1], Jack Doerner[2(✉)], Eysa Lee[3], Anna Lysyanskaya[4], and Lawrence Roy[5]

[1] Efi Arazi School of Computer Science, Reichman University, Herzliya, Israel
cohenran@runi.ac.il
[2] University of Virginia, Charlottesville, USA
j@ckdoerner.net
[3] Barnard College, New York, USA
eylee@barnard.edu
[4] Brown University, Providence, USA
anna_lysyanskaya@brown.edu
[5] Aarhus University, Aarhus, Denmark

Abstract. Many foundational results in the literature of consensus follow the Dolev-Yao model (FOCS '81), which treats digital signatures as ideal objects with *perfect* correctness and unforgeability. However, no work has yet formalized an ideal signature scheme that is both suitable for this methodology and possible to instantiate, or a composition theorem that ensures security when instantiating it cryptographically.

The Universal Composition (UC) framework would ensure composition if we could specify an ideal functionality for signatures and prove it UC-realizable. Unfortunately, *all* signature functionalities heretofore proposed are problematic when used to construct higher-level protocols: either the functionality internally computes a computationally secure signature, and therefore higher-level protocols must rely upon computational assumptions, or else the functionality introduces a *new* attack surface that does not exist when the functionality is realized. As a consequence, no consensus protocol has ever been analyzed in a modular way using existing ideal signature functionalities.

We propose a new *unstoppable* ideal functionality for signatures that is UC-realized exactly by the set of standard EUF-CMA signature schemes that are *consistent* and work in *linear time* in the length of the message. No adversary can prevent honest parties from obtaining perfectly ideal signature services from our functionality. We showcase its usefulness by presenting the first modular analysis of the Dolev-Strong broadcast protocol (SICOMP '83). Our result can be interpreted as a step toward a sound realization of the Dolev-Yao methodology. We also generalize our result to the threshold setting.

The full version of this paper can be found at the *IACR Cryptology ePrint Archive*, report 2024/1807.

B. Applebaum and H. Lin (Eds.): TCC 2025, LNCS 16271, pp. 675–708, 2026.
https://doi.org/10.1007/978-3-032-12290-2_22

1 Introduction

Digital signatures are one of the most fundamental tools of modern cryptography. Using a digital signature scheme, Alice can send a message to Bob in a way that convinces him that Alice is indeed the sender. Bob can then transfer the signed message to Charlie, who will also be convinced that Alice is the source. Signatures were first introduced by Diffie and Hellman [DH76], constructed by Rivest, Shamir, and Adleman [RSA78], and formalized by Goldwasser, Micali, and Rivest [GMR88]. Today's standard security definition requires a signature scheme to satisfy two properties. The first, *correctness*, asserts that the scheme's verification algorithm accepts messages that are honestly signed using honestly generated keys.[1] The second, *existential unforgeability under chosen-message attacks* (EUF-CMA), asserts that a polynomial-time adversary that can obtain signatures on arbitrary messages of its choice (via a signing oracle) is able to forge a valid signature on a new message with at most negligible probability.

Digital signatures play a central role in many distributed consensus tasks such as *Byzantine agreement*, wherein n parties must agree on a single common value even when t of them collude and actively cheat, and such as *broadcast*, wherein the agreement is on the value of a designated, potentially cheating sender. The papers that originally introduced these problems [PSL80, LSP82] showed that no solution exists in the plain model (i.e., without setup assumptions) for $t \geq n/3$. However, given *digital signatures* and a *public-key infrastructure* (PKI, a setup phase in which parties reliably distribute their verification keys) a solution exists with optimal resilience against $t < n/2$ for Byzantine agreement, and $t < n$ corrupted participants for broadcast.

The solutions proposed by these early works [PSL80, LSP82] are exponential in the number of parties n, and thus only useful if n is logarithmic in the security parameter. The first *efficient* broadcast was introduced not long afterward by Dolev and Strong [DS83]; like its predecessors it assumes only the existence of digital signatures and a public-key infrastructure. Further breakthrough results followed. For example, a line of works has proven that broadcast can be achieved with expected-constant round complexity in the honest-majority [FG03, KK06] and even *dis*honest-majority [GKKO07, FN09, WXSD20] settings. It remains true that when security against any arbitrary set of colluding parties is required, the only known broadcast protocols are based on Dolev-Strong [DS83]. These results supply important building blocks and influential techniques for secure multiparty computation (MPC). A common design pattern in MPC research is to use an *ideal* broadcast channel, which is later replaced by an efficient broadcast protocol.

Dolev-Strong vs. The Modular Reductionist Paradigm. Existing proofs of Dolev-Strong [DS83] (and all other signature-based Byzantine agreement and broadcast protocols) treat digital signature schemes as *perfectly correct* and *perfectly unforgeable*, and do not present an explicit reduction from an adversary attacking the protocol to the security of the signature scheme. This stands in

[1] This might hold *always*, or it might hold with overwhelming probability.

sharp contrast with the standard practice in cryptography, and with the modular spirit with which proofs are often structured in the literature of MPC. While it is typical to construct high-level protocols from ideal building blocks, it only makes sense in the case when we can instantiate these building blocks with sub-protocols that *securely realize* them. The analysis of each sub-protocol is conducted by considering a single instance in a simplified setting, and a *composition theorem* is used to reach a conclusion about the security of high-level protocols when these sub-protocols are plugged in.[2] Such a theorem translates any attack on a *composed* protocol (that uses real sub-protocols) into either an attack on the corresponding *un*composed protocol (that uses ideal building blocks) or an attack on a single instance of the real sub-protocol in isolation, with only a negligible difference in adversarial advantage.

For example, the classic MPC protocol of Goldreich, Micali, and Wigderson (GMW) [GMW87] is simple to formulate given an ideal broadcast channel and trusted parties that ideally compute oblivious transfer (OT) and zero-knowledge proofs. These ideal entities are known more generally as *ideal functionalities.* If the broadcast channel is realized by the Dolev-Strong protocol [DS83], then proving security requires translating every attack on the (composed) GMW protocol into an attack on the underlying signature scheme. Since attacks on secure digital signatures succeed with at most negligible probability by definition, such a proof ensures that an attack on the composed protocol can also succeed with at most negligible probability, or else the security of the signature scheme is invalidated. This pattern of describing MPC protocols using an ideal broadcast functionality, to be realized modularly, is found throughout the modern MPC literature, yet, as we have mentioned, no formal means of invoking a reduction to the security of signatures when such a realization is performed has been supplied.

Prior Pathways Towards Closing the Gap. The most direct solution in the case of any *specific* broadcast protocol would be to write an explicit proof that the protocol realizes the broadcast functionality, with a reduction to the security properties of the underlying signature scheme. While this approach can be used for analyzing broadcast protocols, it has not been applied in the literature; further, we note that this solution has a number of downsides, which we discuss in Sect. 1.1. The alternative is to construct a notion of ideal signatures that is *realizable* by standard EUF-CMA signatures while also being *compatible* with existing broadcast protocol proofs and with whichever composition theorem the higher-level protocol requires.

Devising an ideal functionality that captures the security of digital signatures is a challenging task, and numerous attempts have been made, starting with the work of Canetti [Can01]. Such ideal functionalities must be realizable

[2] The nature of the required composition theorem depends upon the ways in which the sub-protocols are invoked; in general they may be invoked concurrently and by arbitrary sets of participants, but simpler theorems exist for restricted settings.

by all *reasonable* signatures[3] on the one hand, and support a modular analysis of cryptographic protocols on the other. As we argue in Sect. 1.2, *all* previous formulations of an ideal functionality for digital signatures either rely on computational assumptions in the ideal computation (which results in a cumbersome proof), or introduce a means for the adversary to *block* honest parties from issuing signatures when the functionality is used in a hybrid model; this denial-of-service attack translates into an attack on the security of higher-level protocols such as the Dolev-Strong protocol, as we show explicitly in the full version [CDL+24].

Our Main Contribution. The main contribution of this work is a new ideal functionality for signatures, which on the one hand is realized by all EUF-CMA signatures (that satisfy a few additional properties) and on the other hand can never be blocked, thus preventing denial-of-service attacks by an adversary when it is used by another protocol. Because this functionality *always* delivers a useable output, we call it *unstoppable.* We showcase the usefulness of our unstoppable functionality by providing the first modular analysis of Dolev-Strong broadcast [DS83]. We also generalize our result to the threshold setting.

1.1 Shortcoming of Directly Using EUF-CMA in Protocols

Before we describe prior ideal signature functionality formulations, we note that using the correctness and unforgeability properties of signature schemes directly in the analysis of high-level protocols such as the Dolev-Strong protocol carries several disadvantages:

- The property-based EUF-CMA signature definition [GMR88, Gol04, KL14], now considered to be standard, does not explicitly address several security considerations that are important in the MPC context, such as *adversarially malformed keys*, *adaptive corruptions*, and *concurrent instances.* Moreover, additional properties seem to be required for analyzing protocols like Dolev-Strong, as discussed below.
- The resulting security proofs must be *monolithic* and are likely to be more complex than modular ones: if protocol analysis is property-based, i.e., it directly uses specific properties of a signature scheme and shows that they are violated if the higher-level protocol fails, then the underlying protocol cannot necessarily be decomposed into a "signature module" and a "high-level module" that uses the signature.
- Many lower bounds on broadcast and Byzantine agreement protocols apply only to *deterministic* protocols: for example, bounds on round [DS83] and communication [DR82] complexity. A protocol that explicitly uses signatures *cannot* be deterministic, and must admit a negligible (yet positive) error probability. Thus most bounds and most protocols in the literature are incompatible with one another. In the full version [CDL+24], we present a contrived

[3] We leave the qualifier somewhat ambiguous for now; our own functionality is realized by the set of EUF-CMA signatures that satisfy a few natural additional properties, which we introduce in Sect. 1.3 and formalize in Sect. 2.

example demonstrating that lower bounds on deterministic protocols are *not* applicable to protocols that are deterministic except for the use of signatures.

We exemplify the subtlety of determining the exact set of properties that we require of a signature scheme by considering adversarially malformed keys. EUF-CMA signatures are generally allowed to have probabilistic verification algorithms (e.g., the signature scheme of Boneh and Franklin [BF01]). When the verification algorithm is used with an honestly generated public key, the correctness property ensures that an honestly generated signature (using the corresponding secret key) will be accepted, and the EUF-CMA property ensures that signatures generated without access to the secret key will be rejected. However, there are *no guarantees* for maliciously generated public keys and signatures: the verification algorithm might provide inconsistent results for the same message/signature pair, which can be disastrous. In the full version [CDL+24], we describe an explicit attack against the Dolev-Strong protocol [DS83] in the absence of guarantees about malicious keys and signatures.

This shortcoming was previously addressed by Canetti [Can04], who defined a notion of "weak consistency" which ensures that when the public key is honestly generated, the verification of the same message/signature pair will return the same value with all but negligible probability (as pointed out by Canetti, this form of consistency is implied by the non-repudiation requirement in [GMR88]). This notion was strengthened by Garay, Kiayias, and Zhou [GKZ10] to capture maliciously generated keys. Our signature functionality also guarantees this stronger form of consistency: when verification is performed on the same input repeatedly, it always returns the same output.

The *correctness* property is also subtle, when it allows for a negligible error probability. For example, the definition in [GKZ10] ensures correctness with all but negligible probability for messages chosen before the signing key is sampled. Under this definition, it may not be possible for a signer to sign their own public key. In contrast, we require correctness for messages generated adaptively by an adversary with knowledge of the public key and all previous signatures.

As of now, the only proof that we are aware of that explicitly reduces the security of *any* broadcast protocol to the EUF-CMA security of signatures is by Lindell, Lysyanskaya, and Rabin [LLR02], who proved security under sequential composition for a very simple broadcast protocol among three participants. Their proof establishes only a property-based notion of broadcast, rather than the realization of an ideal broadcast functionality under arbitrary composition that we seek. Nevertheless, it illustrates the tediousness of formalizing such arguments even when the protocol is much simpler than the Dolev-Strong protocol and the proof intuition is straightforward. In contrast, the modular approach that we take in Sect. 4 yields a simpler proof with a strong resemblance to the original (in the uninstatiable Dolev-Yao paradigm) proof of Dolev-Strong.

1.2 The Evolution of Ideal Signature Formulations

The Dolev-Yao Model. In the Dolev-Yao model [DY81], cryptographic primitives such as encryption and digital signatures are considered as abstract symbolic operations with perfect security. This methodology is common in the literature of broadcast and Byzantine agreement; it was used in the original broadcast papers of the 1980s [PSL80,LSP82,DLM82,DS83], and it has regained popularity in recent years [BKL19,WXSD20,FLL21,GGL22,LL22,GLW22,TLP22] [LN24,ELP24]. In all of these works, signatures are considered to be perfectly correct and perfectly unforgeable; this approach has recently been pushed even further with works assuming perfectly secure *threshold* signatures [FLL21] and perfectly secure *unique* threshold signatures [GGL22].

Use of the Dolev-Yao model in a security proof carries the hope (at least implicitly) that the proven protocol remains secure when the ideal signatures within it are replaced by EUF-CMA signatures. However, this hope faces two formal shortcomings: First, the model does not include a formal definition for ideal signatures (or ideal public keys), and second, if there were such a definition, then there would still be no composition theorem to ensure security is retained when the ideal signatures are instantiated cryptographically. These shortcomings lead to several drawbacks when the Dolev-Yao model is used in security proofs.

First, Dolev-Yao is not a sound methodology in the sense that it is possible to construct protocols that are secure in the Dolev-Yao model, but insecure when instantiated with cryptographic schemes (see discussions in [AR02,Pat05,MP06, CH11]). For example, because the Dolev-Yao model hides all computational complexity measures, the protocols of Pease, Shostak, and Lamport [PSL80, LSP82] (whose complexity is exponential in the number of parties) are perfectly secure in the Dolev-Yao model, but are insecure when EUF-CMA signatures are used and the number of parties is super-logarithmic. Even more subtle are *inductive arguments*, which require great care in the Dolev-Yao model, because the soundness of such arguments can fail if even a negligible security loss is introduced in each inductive step, see, e.g., [Lin17b, Sect. 4.1].

Second, it is not always clear how to translate an attack on a protocol in the Dolev-Yao model into an attack on the concrete signature scheme used to instantiate the model. This stands in sharp contrast to the standard security paradigm for MPC protocols, which demands the existence of an explicit reduction.

Third, as opposed to modern MPC security definitions, the Dolev-Yao model restricts the adversarial strategies that are formally captured by the security proof. For example, the adversary cannot base its attack on the content of public keys and signatures strings generated by honest parties. Similarly, as signatures are represented as bit-strings, an adversary has a positive probability of forging a signature if it deviates from the protocol specification in *any* way, even if it does not *intend* to forge. It is not even necessarily the case that the adversary can determine whether it has forged or not (e.g., if the verification key is not public). Thus, the assumption that an adversary *cannot* forge a signature implies that in many settings an adversary can only be sure that it will never forge a signature if it follows the protocol specification exactly (and potentially causes some parties to crash). The Dolev-Yao model guarantees little if any security against adversaries that deviate from the protocol arbitrarily.

Supplying a Composition Theorem. Canetti's Universal Composability (UC) framework [Can01] provides the composition theorem that the Dolev-Yao model lacks. Informally, it guarantees that if a cryptographic scheme *UC-realizes* an ideal signature functionality $\mathcal{F}_{\mathsf{sig}}$, then that scheme can be used to replace $\mathcal{F}_{\mathsf{sig}}$ in any protocol that uses $\mathcal{F}_{\mathsf{sig}}$ as a subroutine. So, if a protocol π is secure (or has some other useful property) in an idealized model that is enhanced with $\mathcal{F}_{\mathsf{sig}}$, then it remains secure (and retains its other properties) when $\mathcal{F}_{\mathsf{sig}}$ is replaced by the cryptographic scheme. This leaves open a critical question:

> What formulation of $\mathcal{F}_{\mathsf{sig}}$ is both *useful* for such an outer protocol π, and also UC-realizable by all EUF-CMA signatures?

The First Generation of $\mathcal{F}_{\mathsf{sig}}$. We identify three prior approaches to the design of signature functionalities, which are differentiated by the method that is used to generate the string representations of signatures and public keys. The oldest approach first appeared in the original version of the UC paper [Can01], and has also appeared in numerous follow-up works [Can04, CR03, BH04, GKZ10, CSV16, BCH+20]. In this approach, every key-generation or signing request causes the functionality to ask the *adversary* to provide a public key or signature string, respectively. The benefit of this formulation is that the ideal-model adversary is granted a great deal of power, and so the task of simulating real-world adversaries is relatively simple. However, the power given to the adversary is also the shortcoming of this formulation: it enables attacks on higher-level protocols that use this version of $\mathcal{F}_{\mathsf{sig}}$ as a subroutine, as we will now illustrate.

When a signing request is received, the functionality passes the activation token to the adversary in order allow it to compute a signature string. This implies that the adversary learns when each signing attempt occurs, and learns on which message a signature has been requested, even if the signer is *honest* (the adversary also sometimes learns when honest parties verify signatures). Moreover, the adversary can dynamically and *indefinitely* delay the response, effectively giving it the power to arbitrarily block honest parties from producing signatures. In ideal-model experiments, the adversary is a well-behaved simulator (which might run the real-world adversary internally, as a subroutine), but in real-world experiments involving protocols that invoke $\mathcal{F}_{\mathsf{sig}}$, the adversary is in general directly under the control of the environment, and this passing of the activation token enables attacks that would not exist if a concrete EUF-CMA signature scheme were used instead.

An astute reader might object that message delivery is also under environmental control in the standard UC model, and therefore progress and termination cannot be guaranteed for interactive protocols in any case. There is, however, a more subtle issue, which enables an adversarial denial-of-service attack to be performed via this formulation of $\mathcal{F}_{\mathsf{sig}}$ even if all messages are delivered and all signature strings are supplied in a timely fashion.

We observe first of all that first-generation $\mathcal{F}_{\mathsf{sig}}$ formulations guarantee unforgeability by forcing verification to fail for all signatures on a message that has never before been signed. Second, we observe that such functionalities guarantee consistency by forcing identical verification queries to always produce the same response. If the UC environment causes a verification request to be performed on a never-signed message and a particular signature string, then this signature string is marked by the functionality as *invalid* for the requested combination of public key and message. If the environment subsequently causes a signing request to be performed on the same message under the same public key, and causes the same signature string to be returned by the adversary, then the functionality is trapped: it must either violate consistency, or else fail to output a signature. In either case, the functionality's behavior diverges from that of any *local* signing algorithm, and generally the authors of prior works have preferred the second option: most first-generation $\mathcal{F}_{\mathsf{sig}}$ formulations specify that the functionality outputs an "error" if this sequence of events occurs.

In this paper, we show that these issues are critical and that in fact the Dolev-Strong protocol *is broken* when instantiated with a first-generation $\mathcal{F}_{\mathsf{sig}}$. Specifically, in the full version [CDL+24], we recall an example of a first-generation signature functionality, and show an attack on the Dolev-Strong protocol instantiated with this $\mathcal{F}_{\mathsf{sig}}$.

The Second Generation of $\mathcal{F}_{\mathsf{sig}}$. The second generation of signature functionalities [Can05,Pat05,KT08,CKKR19] differ from the first in exactly one significant way: rather than interactively querying the adversary in order to obtain public key and signature strings, second-generation functionalities compute these strings internally using algorithms that are supplied by the adversary beforehand. The activation token is never passed to the adversary during honest parties' interactions with the functionality. This eliminates attacks that spring from direct side-channel knowledge of the queries of uncorrupted parties or delayed adversarial responses, but because the string-generation functions are supplied by the adversary,[4] the adversary retains enough power that it can simulate any EUF-CMA signature scheme in the ideal-world experiment.

While this second generation eliminates many simple attacks, the adversary can still render the functionality useless if it fails to provide the string generation algorithms at all. Moreover, the second generation does not make progress toward eliminating the more subtle issue we have described, because the adversary can still supply *bad* algorithms that cause the functionality to emit errors instead of signatures. For example, if the adversary supplies a signature generation algorithm that produces strings that the adversary can predict with noticeable probability, then it can attempt verifications on those strings before they are issued, and force a consistency violation. This is exactly the attack we have described against first-generation functionalities. Because this attack can be performed selectively (e.g., consistency violations can be forced only for cer-

[4] The adversary, in some sense, uploads a *small piece of itself* to the functionality, which is well-behaved at least with respect to leakage and runtime.

tain combinations of message and public key), it also re-opens the door for a more limited form of honest-query leakage.

The Third Generation of $\mathcal{F}_{\mathsf{sig}}$. The third generation of signature functionalities sidestep challenges with adversarially supplied strings and algorithms by *fixing* the exact algorithms in the functionality itself. Examples of such functionalities exist for ECDSA [Lin17a, DKLs18, DKLS19, GS22, DKLS24], Schnorr [Lin24], and BBS+ [DKL+23] to name but a few.[5] Third-generation functionalities typically omit any additional checks to ensure that the hard-wired algorithms are well-behaved.

The primary caveat with this approach is that hard-wiring the algorithm into the functionality implies that any protocol that *uses* the functionality must make a computational assumption, which implies in turn that the proof of such a protocol cannot be significantly simpler in terms of the reductions required or assumptions employed than the proof of an equivalent protocol that invokes the same algorithms directly, without the functionality.

What We Want in Generation Four. We wish to formulate $\mathcal{F}_{\mathsf{sig}}$ such that it *always* provides perfect signature services to honest parties, regardless of the behavior of the adversary. In other words, a valid signature should always be produced when an honest party makes a signing query, and the adversary should never be able to violate consistency or otherwise render the functionality useless, even with negligible probability. We call such a functionality *unstoppable.* In addition, our functionality should be UC-realized by as many existing signature schemes as possible.

1.3 Our Contributions and Technical Overview

The primary contribution of this work is a new ideal functionality for signatures that is both *unstoppable* and equivalent to exactly the set of all *consistent*, *linear-time* EUF-CMA signatures (we discuss these properties below and formalize them in Sect. 2). No matter what the adversary does, it cannot prevent honest parties from obtaining perfectly ideal signature services from our functionality. Our second contribution is a showcase of the usefulness of this unstoppable functionality comprising the first modular analysis of the broadcast protocol of Dolev and Strong [DS83] in the UC framework. Additionally, we show that the Dolev-Strong protocol is broken when instantiated with the first- and second-generations of the ideal signature functionality.

An Unstoppable Signature Functionality. Our functionality must satisfy a set of seemingly conflicting requirements. The code of the functionality must be fixed, and yet it must be able to emit the signature strings of a large variety of

[5] We note that those functionalities were designed for threshold signature MPC protocols. Though the protocols themselves are multiparty, the functionalities they realize are the exact algorithms of the ECDSA, Schnorr, and BBS+ signature schemes. In the full version, we generalize our result by showing that such functionalities can be used to realize a threshold version of our own functionality.

signature schemes. We resolve this tension in the same way as second-generation functionalities do, by allowing the adversary to upload three algorithms—Gen, Sign, and Verify—that are used to sample public key and signature strings, and verify unsampled ones. However, there is no way for the functionality to test whether the uploaded algorithms are well behaved (this task might even be undecidable). Thus our decision to give the adversary freedom in choosing these algorithms is in tension with our requirement for unstoppability.

We resolve this new tension by imbuing our functionality with an alternate *random* mode: the functionality enters this mode if and only if it detects that the sampling algorithms provided to it have failed or misbehaved (or if they are not provided in a timely fashion), and in this mode the functionality is always guaranteed to provide *perfect* signature services. Although the two modes are easily distinguishable, random mode will be entered with at most negligible probability when the adversary supplies a truly EUF-CMA signature scheme. Our functionality becomes observably distinct from a second-generation one only when a non-EUF-CMA trio of algorithms is supplied.

Random-Mode Signing. We will first explain under what conditions the random mode is triggered, and then we will describe what happens when functionality switches to random mode.

The first time the functionality is activated in some particular session,[6] it immediately requests the algorithms (Gen, Sign, Verify) from the adversary. If the functionality's second activation in the same session is not accompanied by a response from the adversary (i.e., if the adversary does not respond immediately), then it falls into random mode. If the adversary responds immediately, then in doing so it activates the functionality for the second time in the same session, and the algorithms supplied by the adversary are stored. Thereafter, the functionality enters random mode if and only if the algorithms fail to terminate within a specified time bound (as discussed below) or it observes the outputs of (Gen, Sign, Verify) to violate a set of invariants that we construe to define useful and well-behaved signatures:

Remark 1.1. (Signature Functionality Invariants).

1. The functionality should never respond differently to two identical verification queries. Doing otherwise would violate consistency.
2. The functionality should never emit a signature σ on a message m if it previously returned False to a verification query on the same (m, σ) under the same public key. Doing otherwise would violate correctness or consistency.
3. The functionality should always respond True to a verification query on some message m and signature σ if (m, σ) were previously issued by the functionality under the queried public key.
4. The functionality should never respond True to a verification query on some message m if m was never signed under the queried public key. Doing otherwise would violate unforgeability.

[6] Sessions are distinguished as usual via a unique session identifier, denoted sid.

5. The functionality should never emit the same signature in response to signing queries on two different messages under the same public key.
6. The functionality should never emit the same public key twice in response to honest key-generation queries.

Once the functionality enters random mode for some session, it remains in random mode *permanently* with respect to that session. In random mode, the functionality does not use the algorithms provided by the adversary, but instead samples public keys and signatures at random (without replacement), and behaves in such a way as to maintain these invariants. As a consequence, it is possible to reason about the functionality's behavior via the invariants when writing security proofs for protocols that invoke it.

Since there is no a priori bound on the number of keys and signatures that must be generated, and we wish to handle adversaries that can make even an unbounded number of queries, the functionality expands the domain from which keys and signatures are issued, as necessary. Specifically, it maintains length parameters ℓ_{pk} and ℓ_{sig} for those domains, respectively. Both are initialized to 1. When all the keys in $\{0,1\}^{\ell_{\mathsf{pk}}}$ have been issued, the functionality increments ℓ_{pk}; similarly, ℓ_{sig} is incremented when all the signatures in $\{0,1\}^{\ell_{\mathsf{sig}}}$ are used.

Before it switches to random mode, the functionality may have already issued some keys and signatures using the adversarially-provided algorithms. These will continue to be accepted by the verification interface of the functionality (and excluded from the domains of keys and signatures that can be sampled) even after the functionality has switched to random mode.

How the Algorithms (Gen,Sign,Verify) are Encoded. Let us now explain how our functionality expects the algorithms $(\mathsf{Gen}, \mathsf{Sign}, \mathsf{Verify})$ to be encoded. In the literature of signature schemes, Gen is typically modeled as a probabilistic Turing machine: it receives a sole input the security parameter 1^κ in unary, and relies on its random tape to generate keys. The algorithms Sign and Verify can be either deterministic or probabilistic.

If the adversary furnishes the algorithms together with the security parameter, and the adversary is free to request signatures on messages of arbitrary length, then there is nothing to prevent the adversary from furnishing algorithms that do not halt within the runtime allotted to the functionality (or within polynomial time, or, indeed, at all). Thus we need an alternative encoding scheme. The most obvious alternative is to require $(\mathsf{Gen}, \mathsf{Sign}, \mathsf{Verify})$ to be encoded as circuits, which effectively hard-wires the security parameter, and ensures a fixed running time. However, if the signature algorithm is represented as a circuit, then the size of its input is bounded a priori; this is contrary to the typical notion of digital signatures, which accept messages of any length, and it is a significant restriction on the usefulness of the resulting functionality. Therefore, we choose a third approach: we encode all three algorithms as Turing machines and bound them to run in a specific number of steps. For Gen, this number of steps is a constant supplied by the adversary, and for Sign and Verify this number of steps is *linear* in the length of the message, with a coefficient and a constant term supplied by the adversary. The adversary effectively hard-wires the security parameter into this constant, and we attain the benefits of the circuit representation without restricting the message space.

It may seem arbitrary to require a signature scheme to have linear running time (in the message length), but there are three reasons for this particular choice. First, we do not know how to allow the adversary to encode an arbitrary fixed polynomial runtime, without permitting it to encode higher complexity classes. If the adversary were allowed to pick a value c and Sign were allowed $|m|^c$ steps, then the adversary could choose c in $\omega(1)$. Second, if the security parameter is fixed, then practical signature schemes only require linear time (in the message length), since they typically compress the message to a fixed size using a hash function that is linear time (again, in the message length). Third, given any signature scheme with polynomial-time Sign and Verify algorithms (in the message length), it is possible to construct another scheme with linear-time algorithms and linear-size signatures. Nonetheless, our functionality can easily be adjusted to support a signature scheme with running time that is polynomial in the message length, so long as the polynomial is fixed a priori. This can be done by making the polynomial a parameter of the functionality.

Equivalence to EUF-CMA. We prove that our functionality is *equivalent* to a game-based signature definition that comprises four properties. These properties are correctness, existential unforgeability under chosen-message attacks (EUF-CMA), consistency, and linear time. Of these four, only *linear time* is a modeling artifact (as discussed above). EUF-CMA is the usual game-based security definition for signatures. The remaining two properties, correctness and consistency, were discussed in Sect. 1.1 and deserve further explanation.

Most signature definitions (e.g., [Gol04, KL14]) require perfect correctness, which insists that honestly signed messages *always* verify successfully, and deterministic verification. However, we wish to capture everything that could possibly realize our functionality (and be useful as a signature scheme in the context of Dolev-Strong), and our proof of realization goes through even if both of these properties are violated with negligible probability. Therefore, in Sect. 2.1 we define a notion *consistent* verification, which insists that Verify always produces the same output when given the same input, except with negligible probability.[7] We also give a weaker correctness definition, which allows for a negligible error. Our weakened correctness definition is distinct from that of Garay et al. [GKZ10]. Though theirs also allows for negligible error, it is too weak to be useful, because they only require correctness for messages chosen before the signing key is sampled. Under this definition, it may not be possible for a signer to sign its own public key. On the other hand, our definition requires correctness for messages generated adaptively by an adversary with knowledge of the public key and all previous signatures.

[7] Our definition follows that of Garay, Kiayias, and Zhou [GKZ10], and applies to adversarially generated public keys. Garay et al. showed a simple separation from the weaker consistency property defined by Canetti [Can04], which only requires Verify to behave consistently for *honestly* generated public keys.

The equivalence theorem that we prove in Sect. 3 (Theorem 3.2) takes the following form: First, any signature scheme satisfying the four properties enumerated above UC-realizes our signature functionality when it is embedded in an obvious and trivial protocol.[8] This holds even against malicious adversaries who corrupt parties adaptively. Second, it is possible to extract a signature scheme satisfying our four properties from *any* protocol that realizes our signature functionality in the plain model.

A Modular Analysis of Dolev-Strong Broadcast. As a test case for the usefulness of our signature functionality, we provide a modular analysis of the Dolev-Strong broadcast protocol [DS83] in the UC framework. Together with the UC composition theorem, this result implies that for every MPC protocol in the broadcast model (e.g., the general purpose MPC protocol of [CLOS02] that is UC secure against adaptive corruption of any subset of parties), there exists a protocol which preserves the security guarantees, and uses only point-to-point communication in the *public-key infrastructure* (PKI) model, assuming the existence of EUF-CMA signatures that are linear-time, correct, and consistent.

The Dolev-Strong broadcast protocol assumes a synchronous, fully connected network of point-to-point channels among the participant, and a PKI functionality. It proceeds in a round-by-round manner for $t+1$ rounds, where t is a bound on the number of corrupted parties. Before the protocols begins, the parties use the PKI functionality to reliably distribute their public keys to one another. In the first round, the *sender* signs its message and transmits it to all other parties. Each party P_i maintains a set of values $\mathcal{V}_i$ that is initially empty. In each round ρ, when a party P_i receives a message of the form $(m, \sigma_{j_1}, \ldots, \sigma_{j_{\rho-1}})$ it verifies that it constitutes a *valid signature chain*. That is, it verifies:

- σ_{j_1} is a valid signature of the sender on the message m.
- All of the indices $j_1, \ldots, j_{\rho-1}$ are distinct.
- $i \notin \{j_1, \ldots, j_{\rho-1}\}$, i.e., P_i has not yet contributed to this chain.
- For every $k \in \{2, \ldots, \rho-1\}$, the signature σ_{j_k} is a valid signature by P_j on the message $(m, \sigma_{j_1}, \ldots, \sigma_{j_{k-1}})$.

If the signature chain is valid and $m \notin \mathcal{V}_i$, then P_i adds m to $\mathcal{V}_i$, signs the message $(m, \sigma_{j_1}, \ldots, \sigma_{j_{\rho-1}})$ to obtain a signature σ_i, and sends the message $(m, \sigma_{j_1}, \ldots, \sigma_{j_{\rho-1}}, \sigma_i)$ to all parties whose signatures do not appear in the chain. For efficiency reasons, no party need send more than two such chains in the protocol (two chains with different values of m constitute a proof that the sender has cheated). After round $t+1$, each P_i checks whether $|\mathcal{V}_i| = 1$; if so P_i outputs the value in $\mathcal{V}_i$, and otherwise P_i outputs $\bot$. This concludes the protocol.

It is straightforward to prove that the above protocol achieves a *property-based* definition of broadcast using "ideal signatures" as Dolev and Strong did. *Termination* is guaranteed within $t+1$ rounds. *Validity* (which means that if the sender is honest then all honest parties output its message) follows since every

[8] The protocol: parties run the signing algorithms whenever the environment instructs them to, and forward all outputs to the environment, except for secret keys.

honest party receives the signed message in round 1, and to force an honest party to output $\perp$ the adversary must forge the honest sender's signature. *Agreement* (which requires that all honest parties output the same value, even if the sender cheats) follows from two observations: (1) if an honest party receives a valid signature chain on some message in round $\rho \leq t$, then it is guaranteed that every other honest party will accept this message in round $\rho + 1$, and (2) if an honest party receives a valid signature chain on some message in round $t + 1$, then it is guaranteed that some honest party accepted this message in a prior round, which implies (via our first observation) that all honest parties accept this message in round $t + 1$ or earlier. These arguments hold perfectly, by the assumed ideal nature of the signature scheme.

Proving UC Security for Dolev-Strong is a Subtle Task. UC is inherently asynchronous, which implies that if we translate the Dolev-Strong protocol naïvely, it is not guaranteed to terminate. Katz et al. [KMTZ13] introduced a method to model synchrony within standard UC, which we adopt. We refer the reader the full version [CDL+24] for an overview of this model, and give here a short account of its relevant features. The method of Katz et al. augments the protocol with an ideal clock functionality to synchronize honest parties and with bounded-delay channels. Indistinguishability of the real and ideal worlds can only be proven if the *round structure* of the real and ideal computations is the same. Therefore, the ideal broadcast functionality must keep a local round counter that advances based on activations it gets from honest parties, in a way that mimics the round counter in the real protocol. Our formalism follows that of Cohen et al. [CCGZ16] in that it separates the ideal functionality into two components: a simple *canonical synchronous functionality* (CSF) that has an input round and an output round and contains the core of the functionality's code, and a protocol-dependent *round-extending wrapper* that is responsible for maintaining the logistics of the round counter, etc. This approach allows our proof to be adjusted to accommodate alternative broadcast protocols such as those of Katz and Koo [KK06] or Garay et al. [GKKO07] which have expected-constant round counts and probabilistic termination.

In the spirit of [CR03], we wish to capture multiple instances of broadcast that share a single PKI. Correspondingly, each session of our broadcast functionality comprises a single setup phase and multiple subsequent broadcast phases that are distinguished by unique sub-session IDs that specify the sender and a specific subset of recipients. Such unique IDs are known to be necessary in order to support composition [LLR02]. Our broadcast functionality is formally specified in Sect. 4.1.

In Sect. 4.2 we reformulate Dolev-Strong modularly, in the $(\mathcal{F}_{\mathsf{sig}}, \mathcal{F}_{\mathsf{pki}})$-hybrid model. Much like our ideal broadcast functionality, the protocol consists of multiple phases. In the setup phase, each party obtains a public key from the ideal signature functionality $\mathcal{F}_{\mathsf{sig}}$ and registers it with the other parties via the PKI functionality $\mathcal{F}_{\mathsf{pki}}$. In subsequent broadcast phases (which might be concurrent), the parties execute the Dolev-Strong protocol as described above, using $\mathcal{F}_{\mathsf{sig}}$ to furnish the signatures.

The simulator we devise for Dolev-Strong (in Sect. 4.3) is relatively straightforward, which we view as evidence that our signature and broadcast functionalities are well-formulated. Nevertheless, there are a few subtleties. The simulator cannot send a corrupted sender's input to the broadcast functionality in the first round, since the adversary might send a conflicting signed message later. Furthermore, the simulator cannot be sure that honest parties should output $\perp$ even if some honest party receives two conflicting signed messages at some point in the simulation, because this party might later be corrupted adaptively. As a result, the simulator must wait until the final round of the protocol to send its input to the broadcast functionality. We emphasize that such issues as these *do not* arise when proving that a protocol achieves a property-based notion of broadcast, but they are crucial in simulation-based proofs.

Finally, we do not bound the number of corruptions by t and the number of rounds by $t+1$ as the original proof of Dolev-Strong does. Instead, we run the protocol for as many rounds as there are parties, and consider a setting where any subset of parties might be adaptively corrupted (including, potentially, *all* of them). In the standalone setting under static corruptions, a completely corrupt protocol is a trivial case, but in the UC model under adaptive corruptions, this case is known to be extremely challenging. However, including it in our proof allows our UC version of Dolev-Strong to be used in the context of adaptively secure MPC protocols (e.g., [CLOS02]).

Generalizing to the Threshold Setting. In the full version [CDL+24], we prove that our result generalizes to the threshold setting. Specifically, we show that we can realize a threshold variant of $\mathcal{F}_{\mathsf{sig}}$ given a functionality that computes the functions of a consistent, linear-time EUF-CMA signature scheme in a threshold fashion; such functionalities have been proposed by many threshold signing works; e.g., [Lin17a, DKLs18, DKLS19, GS22, DKL+23, Lin24, DKLS24]. In other words, we propose the first threshold ideal signature with *truly* guaranteed output, and demonstrate that it can be realized.

Lower Bounds on Protocols Derived from Deterministic Broadcast. As mentioned in Sect. 1.1, round-complexity lower bounds for cryptographically secure broadcast can be subtle: in the full version [CDL+24], we illustrate that one cannot simply "separate" a cryptographically secure broadcast into a randomized signature module and a deterministic module that uses the signatures, and then apply existing lower bounds for *deterministic* broadcast. In our counterexample, the deterministic module uses signatures in a non-black-box manner.

In the full version [CDL+24], we show that our signature functionality enables us to bridge the gap and analyze a certain family of *randomized*, computationally secure broadcast protocols using existing bounds on deterministic broadcast. Specifically, we capture the family of all broadcast protocols that are derived from *perfectly secure* protocols that are deterministic other than the use of $\mathcal{F}_{\mathsf{sig}}$ (among such protocols is the Dolev-Strong protocol in the $(\mathcal{F}_{\mathsf{sig}}, \mathcal{F}_{\mathsf{pki}})$-hybrid model, as described in Sect. 4). Perfect security implies that these protocols remain secure for *any* choice of the random tape used by $\mathcal{F}_{\mathsf{sig}}$, and fixing such a tape makes them deterministic; thus we can apply existing lower bounds for deterministic broadcast [DS83] to show that security against t corrupt participants implies $t+1$ rounds. The composition theorem then allows us to conclude that any *randomized* broadcast that is derived from such a deterministic, perfectly secure broadcast protocol in the $(\mathcal{F}_{\mathsf{sig}}, \mathcal{F}_{\mathsf{pki}})$-hybrid model must use signatures in a *black-box* way, and must also obey this bound.

2 Preliminaries

Notation. We use $=$ to denote equality, $:=$ for right-to-left assignment, and $\leftarrow$ for sampling from a distribution (often defined by a probabilistic algorithm) or uniformly from a set. We use bracket notation to generate inclusive ranges, so $[n]$ denotes the integers from 1 to n and $[5,7] = \{5,6,7\}$. In general, single-letter variables are set in *italic* font, multi-letter variables and function names are set in sans-serif font, string literals are set in `slab − serif` font, and we use **bold** to denote vectors.

2.1 Digital Signature Schemes

Definition 2.1. (Digital Signature Scheme [GMR88,Gol04,KL14]). A *signature scheme* is a tuple of probabilistic polynomial-time (PPT) algorithms, $(\mathsf{Gen}, \mathsf{Sign}, \mathsf{Verify})$ such that:

1. Given a security parameter κ, the Gen algorithm outputs a public key/secret key pair: $(\mathsf{pk}, \mathsf{sk}) \leftarrow \mathsf{Gen}(1^\kappa)$.
2. Given a security parameter κ, a secret key sk, and a message m, the Sign algorithm outputs a signature σ: $\sigma \leftarrow \mathsf{Sign}(1^\kappa, \mathsf{sk}, m)$.
3. Given a security parameter κ, a message m, a signature σ, and a public key pk, the Verify algorithm outputs a bit b indicating whether the signature is valid or invalid: $b \leftarrow \mathsf{Verify}(1^\kappa, \mathsf{pk}, m, \sigma)$.

Digital Signatures are almost always required to fulfill the properties of *correctness* and *existential unforgeability* (EUF-CMA). In addition to these two, we add the properties of *consistency* and *linear-timeness.*

We begin with correctness. The standard form the correctness property (e.g., [Gol04,KL14]) insists that it be perfect, and a few works have used a relaxed definition that permits negligible correctness error (e.g., [Can04,GKZ10]). We also permit negligible error, but strengthen the property by allowing the adversary to see the public verification key and signatures on messages of its choice during its attempts to cause a correctness error.

Definition 2.2 (Correctness). A signature scheme $\Sigma = (\mathsf{Gen}, \mathsf{Sign}, \mathsf{Verify})$ is *correct* if for all PPT adversaries $\mathcal{G}$, the following experiment outputs 1 with probability negligible in κ.

1. Generate the keys $(\mathsf{pk}, \mathsf{sk}) \leftarrow \mathsf{Gen}(1^\kappa)$.

2. Give pk to the adversary $\mathcal{G}$, who generates a stream of messages to sign. For each message m, run $\sigma \leftarrow \mathsf{Sign}(1^\kappa, \mathsf{sk}, m)$ and $b \leftarrow \mathsf{Verify}(1^\kappa, \mathsf{pk}, m, \sigma)$. If $b = 0$, exit the experiment with output 1. If $b = 1$, return σ to $\mathcal{G}$.
3. When $\mathcal{G}$ finishes, output 0.

Definition 2.3 (EUF-CMA [KL14]). A signature scheme $\Sigma = (\mathsf{Gen}, \mathsf{Sign}, \mathsf{Verify})$ is *EUF-CMA* if for all PPT adversaries $\mathcal{G}$, the following experiment outputs 1 with probability negligible in κ.

1. Generate the keys $(\mathsf{pk}, \mathsf{sk}) \leftarrow \mathsf{Gen}(1^\kappa)$.
2. Adversary $\mathcal{G}$ is given pk and oracle access to $\mathsf{Sign}(1^\kappa, \mathsf{sk}, \cdot)$. The adversary then outputs (m, σ).
3. Let $\mathcal{Q}$ denote the set of messages whose signatures were requested from the signing oracle by $\mathcal{G}$ during its execution. The output of the experiment is 1 if $m \notin \mathcal{Q}$ and $\mathsf{Verify}(1^\kappa, pk, m, \sigma) = 1$.

Most prior signature functionalities require that Verify be deterministic, while we generalize the signature scheme to allow Verify to be probabilistic.[9] However, probabilistic verification brings with it the possibility of disagreement upon the validity of a signature, which can be fatal for consensus protocols such as Dolev-Strong. We therefore define a *consistency* property, which requires that on every input, Verify must either output 0 with all but negligible probability, or output 1 with all but negligible probability. That is, the probability that Verify returns different outputs when run twice on the same input must be negligible. A similar consistency requirement was previously defined by Garay, Kiayias, and Zhou [GKZ10], who also showed it to be stronger than Canetti's consistency property [Can04], which only holds for honestly generated public keys.

Definition 2.4 (Consistency). A signature scheme $\Sigma = (\mathsf{Gen}, \mathsf{Sign}, \mathsf{Verify})$ is *consistent* if for all PPT adversaries $\mathcal{G}$ the following experiment outputs 1 with probability negligible in κ.

1. The adversary samples an arbitrary public key, message, and signature: $(\mathsf{pk}, m, \sigma) \leftarrow \mathcal{G}(1^\kappa)$.
2. The experiment samples two independent appropriate-length random bit-strings, r_1 and r_2.
3. The experiment outputs 1 if $\mathsf{Verify}(1^\kappa, \mathsf{pk}, m, \sigma; r_1) \neq \mathsf{Verify}(1^\kappa, \mathsf{pk}, m, \sigma; r_2)$

Finally, we introduce a novel property, which insists on a stricter time bound on the signature algorithms than the typical simple "polynomial time" requirement. Specifically, while runtime may grow polynomially with the security parameter, we insist that it grows at most linearly with the message length. Looking ahead, this is necessary because the adversary will supply arbitrary signature algorithms to our functionality, and the functionality must run them

[9] This decision is partially motivated by the fact that we wish to prove that a signature scheme can always be extracted from any protocol that realizes our functionality, and we cannot rule out probabilistic verification in the extracted scheme.

within a similarly strict time bound that is enforced by the UC model. In other words, this property is essentially a modeling artifact. As pointed out in Sect. 1.3, we can replace the requirement of linear time with polynomial time, as long as the polynomial is fixed and known a priori; however, in this paper we consider linear time for simplicity.

Definition 2.5 (Linear Time). A signature scheme $\Sigma = (\mathsf{Gen}, \mathsf{Sign}, \mathsf{Verify})$ is *linear time* if there exists a polynomial $T(\kappa)$ such that $\mathsf{Sign}(1^\kappa, \mathsf{sk}, m)$ and $\mathsf{Verify}(1^\kappa, \mathsf{pk}, m, \sigma)$ always halt within $T(\kappa) \cdot (\ell + 1)$ steps, where ℓ is the total length of the input.

The Universal Composability Model. We direct the reader to Canetti for further details [Can20]. We note that because the adversary controls communication between honest parties, the adversary can prevent any protocol in the plain UC framework from terminating. In other words, UC does not capture the notion of *Guaranteed Output Delivery*, which is a key aspect of broadcast and Byzantine agreement without which both problems become very easy to solve. The plain UC model is inherently asynchronous and provides no means to guarantee synchronicity; however, several works have addressed these shortcomings without altering the basic framework, by building additional abstractions atop UC. In this work we use the framework from [KMTZ13].

3 An Unstoppable Signature Functionality

In this section, we present our signature functionality $\mathcal{F}_{\mathsf{sig}}$. Section 3.1 contains the formal specification, and Sect. 3.2 a proof of equivalence to consistent linear-time EUF-CMA signatures.

3.1 The Functionality

For an overview of our functionality and a discussion of our design choices (such as random mode and the length parameters ℓ_{pk} and ℓ_{sig}), we direct the reader to Sect. 1.3. We wish to make a few additional remarks.

On Necessity of Per-Party Initialization. In Sect. 1.3, we specified that the adversary supplies a trio of algorithms $(\mathsf{Gen}, \mathsf{Sign}, \mathsf{Verify})$ to the functionality, but we did not specify a mechanism by which it should do so. This is a non-trivial concern.

Proofs in the UC model require *balanced* environments, which ensure that at every point in an experiment, the adversary has been given more computational resources than the honest particiapants have been. This can be construed to imply that the adversary (i.e., simulator, in the ideal experiment) is always activated *first*. Nevertheless, there is no general guarantee that an adversary will activate our functionality to supply the algorithms before the signing parties activate it with signature requests.

If the functionality is first activated by an honest party that expects a *response*, and then activates the adversary to retrieve the algorithms, the adversary has an opportunity to pass activation to the environment (or some other party) instead of replying to the functionality, which denies a timely response to the requesting party. Worse, when activation passes back to the requesting party, there will be no response from the functionality on its subroutine-output tape, and it is not clear in general how the party will react to this situation (the UC framework does not specify, so far as we are aware); the experiment may even deadlock.

To resolve this difficulty, we specify that the functionality must be activated at least once *without* the expectation of a response before it can be accessed *with* the expectation of a response. If a response-expecting activation occurs before the adversary supplies the algorithms, then by definition they have not been delivered in a timely fashion, and the functionality switches into random mode. To facilitate this, we add to our functionality an *initialization* interface that produces no response; since we do not wish our functionality to imply communication between parties, we insist that each party invokes this interface independently before that party invokes any other interfaces. This mechanism is sufficient for our purposes even if the adversary (i.e., simulator, in the ideal experiment) is *not* guaranteed to be activated before the first signature request.

We note that if the adversary is assumed to always be activated first, Universal Composition with Global Subroutines (UCGS) [BCH+20] enables an alternative mechanism that allows us to eliminate the initialization interface. Specifically, we can employ the library functionality $\mathcal{F}_{\mathsf{lib}}$ that was introduced by Canetti et al. [CJSV22]. This global functionality obtains the signature algorithms from the adversary before the protocol begins, and when necessary, $\mathcal{F}_{\mathsf{sig}}$ obtains the algorithms from $\mathcal{F}_{\mathsf{lib}}$ *without* passing the activation to the adversary. If the adversary did not supply the algorithms to $\mathcal{F}_{\mathsf{lib}}$ by the time $\mathcal{F}_{\mathsf{sig}}$ requests them, $\mathcal{F}_{\mathsf{lib}}$ indicates as much to $\mathcal{F}_{\mathsf{sig}}$, which enters random mode.[10]

We note that the two approaches are incomparable as the former requires "extra" activations but does not rely on the global resource of $\mathcal{F}_{\mathsf{lib}}$. The latter approach is cleaner and more activation-efficient, but operates in the $\mathcal{F}_{\mathsf{lib}}$-hybrid model, where $\mathcal{F}_{\mathsf{lib}}$ is an ideal global subroutine.

On The Precise Syntax and Runtime Bounds of the (Gen,Sign,Verify) Algorithms. In Sect. 1.3, we argued that we do not know how to allow the adversary to encode an arbitrary fixed polynomial runtime, without permitting it to encode higher complexity classes. Nevertheless, we wish to allow the algorithms time polynomial in the security parameter κ. Fortunately, κ is fixed per session, unlike the message length. Thus we can insist that the adversary *hard-code* κ into the algorithms it supplies. We next interpret the combined length of the algorithms supplied as an upper bound on the number of computational steps they each require per bit of the message. This is equivalent to forcing the

[10] The authors thank Ran Canetti for suggesting the use of $\mathcal{F}_{\mathsf{lib}}$ to remove the initialization round.

adversary to supply an explicit upper bound in unary; the adversary can give its algorithms more time by padding their length with no-op instructions.

How to Think About Such a Complex Functionality? Our $\mathcal{F}_{\mathsf{sig}}$ is long and complex, in defiance of the typical aesthetic desiderata for ideal functionalities. Like many of our readers, we the authors find it easier to reason about functionalities that have succinct descriptions. As we discussed in Sect. 1.3, the complexity of our functionality arises because it must satisfy a conflicting set of requirements within the confines of the standard UC model; we know of no way to simplify it without a significant compromise. However, the aspects of our functionality's behavior that are relevant to the security proofs of protocols that invoke it *can* be described as a set of simple invariants. We have given these invariants in Remark 1.1, and we suggest that they be used to reason about our functionality in most cases.

Functionality 3.1. $\mathcal{F}_{\mathsf{sig}}$ (An Unstoppable Signature Functionality)

This functionality interacts with an ideal adversary $\mathcal{S}$ and a number of real parties (all of them denoted P) that is not a-priori known. For simplicity of description, we assume this functionality has *per-session* memory. That is, all stored and recalled values are associated with the particular session ID sid of the query that generated them. Note that P may refer to a different party in every interaction.

Initialization.

1. Ignore any message from any party P that contains some session ID sid until *after* party P sends $(\mathtt{init}, \mathsf{sid})$ to $\mathcal{F}_{\mathsf{sig}}$.
2. Upon receiving $(\mathtt{init}, \mathsf{sid})$ for the *first time* for some particular sid, send $(\mathtt{init}, \mathsf{sid})$ to $\mathcal{S}$ and wait.
3. Upon receiving any second message that contains the session ID sid after the first $(\mathtt{init}, \mathsf{sid})$ message (regardless of whether the same party transmitted the two messages):
   (a) If the message arrived from $\mathcal{S}$ and is of the form $(\mathtt{algs}, \mathsf{sid}, \Sigma)$ where $(\mathsf{Gen}, \mathsf{Sign}, \mathsf{Verify}) := \Sigma$ is the description of three probabilistic Turing machines, store $(\mathsf{Gen}, \mathsf{Sign}, \mathsf{Verify})$ and $s := |\Sigma|$ in memory and set the flag $\mathsf{rmode} := 0$.
   (b) Otherwise, set the flag $\mathsf{rmode} := 1$.

   Regardless, set the integers $\ell_{\mathsf{pk}} := 1$ and $\ell_{\mathsf{sig}} := 1$, and initialize the set of assigned public keys $\mathcal{K} := \emptyset$ and the set of assigned signatures $\mathcal{Q} := \emptyset$. If $\mathsf{rmode} = 1$, process the second message for sid using the interfaces below.

Key Generation.

4. Upon receiving $(\mathtt{keygen}, \mathsf{sid})$ from a party P,
   (a) If $\mathsf{rmode} = 0$, then sample a uniformly random bit-string r_k of appropriate length,[a] and compute $(\mathsf{sk}, \mathsf{pk}) := \mathsf{Gen}(r_k)$. If $\mathsf{pk} \in \mathcal{K}$ or

Gen does not terminate in s computational steps, then switch to random mode by setting $\mathsf{rmode} := 1$ and following the instruction below for the case that $\mathsf{rmode} = 1$.

(b) If $\mathsf{rmode} = 1$, then sample $\mathsf{pk} \leftarrow \{0,1\}^{\ell_{\mathsf{pk}}} \setminus \mathcal{K}$ uniformly and set $\mathsf{sk} := \bot$ and $r_k := \bot$.

Regardless, update $\mathcal{K} := \mathcal{K} \cup \{\mathsf{pk}\}$ in memory and increment ℓ_{pk} until $\{0,1\}^{\ell_{\mathsf{pk}}} \setminus \mathcal{K} \neq \emptyset$. Store $(\texttt{key}, \mathsf{sid}, P, \mathsf{pk}, \mathsf{sk}, r_k)$ in memory and send $(\texttt{public-key}, \mathsf{sid}, \mathsf{pk})$ to the caller P.

Signing.

5. Upon receiving $(\texttt{sign}, \mathsf{sid}, \mathsf{pk}, m)$ from a party P, update $\mathcal{K} := \mathcal{K} \cup \{\mathsf{pk}\}$, and increment ℓ_{pk} until $\{0,1\}^{\ell_{\mathsf{pk}}} \setminus \mathcal{K} \neq \emptyset$. Check if a record of the form $(\texttt{key}, \mathsf{sid}, P, \mathsf{pk}, \mathsf{sk}, r_k)$ exists in memory for any $\mathsf{sk} \in \{0,1\}^* \cup \{\bot\}$ and any r_k. If not, return $\bot$ to P. Otherwise:
   (a) If $\mathsf{rmode} = 0$, then sample a uniformly random bit-string r_σ of appropriate length,[a] compute $\sigma := \mathsf{Sign}(\mathsf{sk}, m; r_\sigma)$ and check the following conditions:
   - $(\texttt{sig}, \mathsf{sid}, \mathsf{pk}, m', \sigma, r_\sigma)$ exists in memory such that $m \neq m'$.
   - $(\texttt{bad-sig}, \mathsf{sid}, \mathsf{pk}, m, \sigma)$ exists in memory.
   - Sign does not terminate in $(|m| + 1) \cdot s$ computational steps.

   If any of the above conditions holds, then switch to random mode by setting $\mathsf{rmode} := 1$ and following the instruction below for the case that $\mathsf{rmode} = 1$.

   (b) If $\mathsf{rmode} = 1$, then sample $\sigma \leftarrow \{0,1\}^{\ell_{\mathsf{sig}}} \setminus \mathcal{Q}$ and set $r_\sigma := \bot$.

   Regardless, update $\mathcal{Q} := \mathcal{Q} \cup \{\sigma\}$ and increment ℓ_{sig} until $\{0,1\}^{\ell_{\mathsf{sig}}} \setminus \mathcal{Q} \neq \emptyset$. Store $(\texttt{sig}, \mathsf{sid}, \mathsf{pk}, m, \sigma, r_\sigma)$ in memory and return $(\texttt{signature}, \mathsf{sid}, \mathsf{pk}, m, \sigma)$ to the caller P.

Verification.

6. Upon receiving $(\texttt{verify}, \mathsf{sid}, \mathsf{pk}, m, \sigma)$ from some party P, update $\mathcal{K} := \mathcal{K} \cup \{\mathsf{pk}\}$, and increment ℓ_{pk} until $\{0,1\}^{\ell_{\mathsf{pk}}} \setminus \mathcal{K} \neq \emptyset$. Next, scan the memory for records of the form $(\texttt{sig}, \mathsf{sid}, \mathsf{pk}, m, \sigma, *)$ or $(\texttt{bad-sig}, \mathsf{sid}, \mathsf{pk}, m, \sigma)$, for any σ, and for a record of the form $(\texttt{key}, \mathsf{sid}, P', \mathsf{pk}, *, *)$ for any P'.[b]
   (a) If the sig record exists, then set $b := 1$.
   (b) If there is no sig record, but there is a key record and P' is an honest party, then set $b := 0$.
   (c) If there is no sig record, but the bad-sig record exists, then set $b := 0$.
   (d) If Steps 6a through 6c do not apply, and $\mathsf{rmode} = 1$, then set $b := 0$.
   (e) If Steps 6a through 6c do not apply, and $\mathsf{rmode} = 0$, then set $b \leftarrow \mathsf{Verify}(\mathsf{pk}, m, \sigma)$. If Verify does not produce output before $(|m|+1) \cdot s$ computational steps have elapsed, then terminate its execution, set $b := 0$, and switch to random mode by setting $\mathsf{rmode} := 1$ in memory.

   If, after evaluating the above conditions, $b = 0$ but the record $(\texttt{bad-sig}, \mathsf{sid}, \mathsf{pk}, m, \sigma)$ is not stored in memory, then store it.

   If, after evaluating the above conditions, $b = 1$ but no record of the form $(\texttt{sig}, \mathsf{sid}, \mathsf{pk}, m, \sigma, *)$ exists in memory, then store $(\texttt{sig}, \mathsf{sid}, \mathsf{pk}, m, \sigma, \bot)$.

Regardless, update $\mathcal{Q} := \mathcal{Q} \cup \{\sigma\}$ in memory and increment ℓ_{sig} until $\{0,1\}^{\ell_{\mathsf{sig}}} \setminus \mathcal{Q} \neq \emptyset$. Finally, return $(\texttt{verified}, \mathsf{sid}, \mathsf{pk}, m, \sigma, b)$ to P.

Corruption.

7. Upon receiving $(\texttt{corrupt}, \mathsf{sid}, P)$ from $\mathcal{S}$, search the memory for all records of the form $(\texttt{key}, \mathsf{sid}, P, \mathsf{pk}, \mathsf{sk}, r_k)$, and for each such record compute the set $\mathcal{C}_{\mathsf{pk}}$ of all (m, σ, r_σ) such that there exists a record of the form $(\texttt{sig}, \mathsf{sid}, \mathsf{pk}, m, \sigma, r_\sigma)$ in memory. Return $(\texttt{corrupt}, \mathsf{sid}, P, \mathcal{C})$ to $\mathcal{S}$, where $\mathcal{C}$ is a set containing $(\mathsf{pk}, \mathsf{sk}, r_k, \mathcal{C}_{\mathsf{pk}})$ for every $(\texttt{key}, \mathsf{sid}, P, \mathsf{pk}, \mathsf{sk}, r_k)$ that was found.

[a] We assume that the amount of randomness that Gen, Sign, and Verify need is part of their description.
[b] P' may or may not be the same as P.

3.2 Equivalence to Consistent Linear-Time EUF-CMA

We prove two main theorems about $\mathcal{F}_{\mathsf{sig}}$. First, in this section, we prove Theorem 3.2, which assumes the existence of a simple non-interactive protocol that calls three algorithms that have the syntax of a signature scheme, and shows that if the algorithms achieve the game-based security notion of signatures, then the protocol realizes our functionality, and vice versa. In the full version [CDL+24], we generalize the aforementioned equivalence beyond protocols that are explicitly structured like signatures by demonstrating that it is possible to *extract* a secure game-based signature from *any* protocol that realizes $\mathcal{F}_{\mathsf{sig}}$ in the plain model.

A Real-World Dummy Protocol. As in the prior works of Canetti [Can01, Can04], we specify a simple *dummy protocol* π_Σ that allows us to straightforwardly convert a signature scheme $\Sigma = (\mathsf{Gen}, \mathsf{Sign}, \mathsf{Verify})$ into a real-world UC experiment that is a syntactic match for $\mathcal{F}_{\mathsf{sig}}$.[11] Each party ignores all instructions from the environment in the session sid until after it receives $(\texttt{init}, \mathsf{sid})$. Thereafter, if a party receives $(\texttt{keygen}, \mathsf{sid})$, it runs $(\mathsf{sk}, \mathsf{pk}) \leftarrow \mathsf{Gen}(1^\kappa)$, stores sk, and outputs $(\texttt{public-key}, \mathsf{sid}, \mathsf{pk})$. When P subsequently receives $(\texttt{sign}, \mathsf{sid}, \mathsf{pk}, m)$, it computes $\sigma \leftarrow \mathsf{Sign}(1^\kappa, \mathsf{sk}, m)$ and outputs $(\texttt{signature}, \mathsf{sid}, \mathsf{pk}, m, \sigma)$. If any party receives $(\texttt{verify}, \mathsf{sid}, \mathsf{pk}, m, \sigma)$, it sets $b \leftarrow \mathsf{Verify}(1^\kappa, \mathsf{pk}, m, \sigma)$ and returns $(\texttt{verified}, \mathsf{sid}, \mathsf{pk}, m, \sigma, b)$ to the environment.

Theorem 3.2. Let Σ be a linear-time signature scheme (Definition 2.5). The following are equivalent:

(1) Σ is correct (Definition 2.2), EUF-CMA secure (Definition 2.3), and consistent (Definition 2.4).
(2) π_Σ UC-realizes $\mathcal{F}_{\mathsf{sig}}$ with security against a malicious adversary who statically corrupts any number of parties.

[11] This is a basic precondition for any proof that the former UC-realizes the latter.

(3) π_{Σ} UC-realizes $\mathcal{F}_{\mathsf{sig}}$ with security against a malicious adversary who adaptively corrupts any number of parties.

The aforementioned lemmas and their proofs are given in the full version [CDL+24].

4 A Modular Analysis of the Dolev-Strong Broadcast

In this section, we use the signature functionality from Sect. 3 to provide a modular analysis of the broadcast protocol of Dolev-Strong [DS83]. In Sect. 4.1 we present a synchronous broadcast functionality $\mathcal{F}_{\mathsf{bc}}$. Then, in Sect. 4.2, we present the protocol of Dolev and Strong in the $\mathcal{F}_{\mathsf{sig}}$-hybrid model, and in Sect. 4.3 we prove that the protocol UC-realizes $\mathcal{F}_{\mathsf{bc}}$.

4.1 The Broadcast Functionality

In a broadcast protocol, a designated sender distributes its message to all recipients in a way that ensures *agreement*, *validity*, and *termination*. We follow the approach of Cohen et al. [CCGZ16] and model broadcast as a *canonical synchronous functionality*, in which the function to compute simply copies the sender's input to the outputs of all receivers,[12] and the leakage function outputs the sender's input (i.e., the entire message). We formalize this behavior below, as Functionality 4.2.

With the goal of MPC protocols in mind, we wish to capture multiple instances of broadcast with a known set of parties using the same PKI. Therefore, we model broadcast as a reactive functionality in which the first phase is a registration phase where every party registers to the functionality. This phase corresponds to the offline phase of establishing the PKI in broadcast protocols; a party that does not register cannot participate in future broadcasts. For each party P_i, the functionality maintains a boolean flag active_i indicating whether P_i is registered.

After the registration phase, each reactively-invoked broadcast phase has a unique sub-session id ssid that specifies the sender P_s and the set of recipients $\mathcal{P} \subseteq \{P_1, \ldots, P_n\}$ (all of whom must be registered). In the input round, the sender sends its message (denoted m_{out}) and the others provide no input (formally, they send an empty string). We note that a *corrupted* party can provide its input multiple times during the input round, which implies that the adversary can adaptively corrupt an honest sender based upon the initial value of m_{out}, and then replace m_{out} with a different message. In the output round, each recipient will receive the most recent m_{out}.

Once a sender provides its input to some broadcast phase, the functionality sends leakage to the ideal-world adversary. We define this leakage to be the sender's entire input. This corresponds to the traditional, property-based notion of broadcast. We do not capture stronger security notions that naturally arise

[12] There is no need for the auxiliary input from the adversary.

in simulation-based definitions of broadcast [HZ10, GKKZ11, CGZ23]. For example, we do not attempt to guarantee *corruption fairness* [CGZ23], which insists that the adversary cannot adaptively corrupt the sender and then replace its message, based upon the initial message that it sent when it was honest. To model this stronger notion of broadcast, the leakage function must be adjusted such that it reveals only the length of the sender's message to the adversary, rather than its contents. Although corruption-unfair broadcast is weaker, it is still sufficient for many MPC protocols, e.g., [GMW87, CLOS02]; furthermore, it can be enhanced to achieve corruption-fairness using atomic multisend channels and equivocal commitments [GKKZ11], or using time-lock puzzles in the programmable random oracle model [CGZ23].

Functionality 4.2. $\mathcal{F}_{\mathsf{bc}}$ (The CSF for Broadcast)

This functionality interacts with an ideal adversary $\mathcal{S}$ and parties $P_1, \ldots, P_n$. It has some memory associated with each unique session (distinguished by session ID sid), and in that memory it keeps the boolean values $\mathsf{active}_1, \ldots, \mathsf{active}_n$, which assume the value 0 initially and indicate whether each respective P_i has registered. It also associates a value m_{out} with every *sub*session (distinguished by the subsession ID ssid), which assumes the value $\perp$ initially. This functionality achieves synchrony through the framework of Katz et al. [KMTZ13], i.e., it only proceeds from one round to the next when all honest parties have indicated that it should do so. An honest party can be adaptively corrupted at any point, after which, depending on when the party is corrupted, the ideal adversary may send messages on its behalf and potentially overwrite previously stored values. In every round, the functionality ignores all messages other than the ones we explicitly specify that it can receive.

Setup.
1. **Input Round:** Upon receiving $(\mathtt{init}, \mathsf{sid})$ from some party P_i, set $\mathsf{active}_i := 1$ and send $(\mathtt{init}, \mathsf{sid}, P_i)$ to $\mathcal{S}$.
2. **Output Round:** Upon receiving $(\mathtt{fetch\text{-}output}, \mathsf{sid})$ from some P_i, send $(\mathsf{output}, \mathsf{sid}, (\mathsf{active}_1, \ldots, \mathsf{active}_n))$ to P_i.

Broadcast.
3. **Input Round:** Upon receiving $(\mathtt{input}, \mathsf{sid}, \mathsf{ssid}, v)$ from some party P_s where ssid is of the form $\mathsf{ssid}' \| P_s \| \mathcal{P}$: if there exists a $P_j \in \mathcal{P} \cup \{P_s\}$ such that $\mathsf{active}_j = 0$, then ignore the message. Otherwise, set $m_{\mathsf{out}} := v$ and send $(\mathtt{input}, \mathsf{sid}, \mathsf{ssid}, v, P_i)$ to $\mathcal{S}$.
4. **Output Round:** Upon receiving $(\mathtt{fetch\text{-}output}, \mathsf{sid}, \mathsf{ssid})$ from some party P_i, send $(\mathsf{output}, \mathsf{sid}, \mathsf{ssid}, m_{\mathsf{out}})$ to P_i.

Next, we define the *strict-termination wrapper functionality* corresponding to the realization of $\mathcal{F}_{\mathsf{bc}}$ with the Dolev-Strong protocol [DS83]. Recall that the registration phase of $\mathcal{F}_{\mathsf{bc}}$ corresponds to the setup phase of establishing the PKI.

The Dolev-Strong protocol assumes that the PKI has already been established, i.e., it works in the $\mathcal{F}_{\mathsf{pki}}$-hybrid model, where $\mathcal{F}_{\mathsf{pki}}$ (provided in Sect. 4.2) is an ideal functionality that establishes a public-key infrastructure. Thus, we set the output round for the setup phase to 2 (one round for providing inputs to $\mathcal{F}_{\mathsf{pki}}$ and one round for receiving output). In every other phase, i.e., a broadcast phase for sub-session id of the form $\mathsf{ssid}'\|P_s\|\mathcal{P}$, the output round is specified to be $\rho_{\mathsf{term}} := |\mathcal{P}| + 1$. This ensures security in the presence of an adversary corrupting any subset of $\mathcal{P}$.

Functionality 4.3. $\mathcal{W}_{\mathsf{DS}}(\mathcal{F}_{\mathsf{bc}})$ (The Strict Wrapper for DS [CCGZ16])

The wrapper functionality $\mathcal{W}_{\mathsf{DS}}(\mathcal{F}_{\mathsf{bc}})$ interacts with an ideal adversary $\mathcal{S}$ and parties $P_1, \ldots, P_n$, and it runs a copy of $\mathcal{F}_{\mathsf{bc}}$ internally.

Setup.

1. In round $\rho = 1$: Forward $(\mathtt{init}, \mathsf{sid})$ messages from each party P_i to $\mathcal{F}_{\mathsf{bc}}$. In addition, forward all messages between the back-door tape of $\mathcal{F}_{\mathsf{bc}}$ and the adversary.
2. In round $\rho = 2$: Forward $(\mathtt{fetch\text{-}output}, \mathsf{sid})$ messages from each party P_i to $\mathcal{F}_{\mathsf{bc}}$ and the response $(\mathsf{output}, \mathsf{sid}, *)$ to P_i.

Broadcast.

3. Upon receiving the *first* message of the form $(\mathtt{input}, \mathsf{sid}, \mathsf{ssid}, *)$ for a fresh ssid, parse ssid as $\mathsf{ssid}'\|P_s\|\mathcal{P}$, set the output round $\rho_{\mathsf{term}} := |\mathcal{P}| + 1$, and send $(\mathsf{output\text{-}round}, \mathsf{sid}, \mathsf{ssid}, \rho_{\mathsf{term}})$ to the adversary. Continue processing this message using the rules enumerated below.
4. At all times, forward $(\mathtt{input}, \mathsf{sid}, \mathsf{ssid}, *)$ messages from corrupted parties to $\mathcal{F}_{\mathsf{bc}}$.
5. In round $\rho = 1$: Forward $(\mathtt{input}, \mathsf{sid}, \mathsf{ssid}, *)$ messages from each party $P_i \in \mathcal{P}$ to $\mathcal{F}_{\mathsf{bc}}$. In addition, forward all messages between the back-door tape of $\mathcal{F}_{\mathsf{bc}}$ and the adversary.
6. In rounds $\rho > 1$: Upon receiving a message $(\mathtt{fetch\text{-}output}, \mathsf{sid}, \mathsf{ssid})$ from some party $P_i \in \mathcal{P}$:
   - If $\rho = \rho_{\mathsf{term}}$, forward the message to $\mathcal{F}_{\mathsf{bc}}$, and the response $(\mathsf{output}, \mathsf{sid}, \mathsf{ssid}, *)$ to P_i.
   - Otherwise, send $(\mathtt{fetch\text{-}output}, \mathsf{sid}, \mathsf{ssid}, P_i)$ to the adversary.

4.2 The Dolev-Strong Broadcast Protocol

Signatures on their own are not sufficient to overcome the impossibility of broadcasts when $t \geq n/3$ [PSL80, FLM86]; as we have alluded previously, we also need a PKI functionality. Much like our broadcast functionality, our PKI functionality is a CSF.

Functionality 4.4. $\mathcal{F}_{\mathsf{pki}}$ (The PKI Functionality)

This functionality interacts with an ideal adversary $\mathcal{S}$ and parties $P_1, \ldots, P_n$. It has some memory associated with each unique session (distinguished by session ID sid), and in that memory it keeps the values $\mathsf{pk}_1, \ldots, \mathsf{pk}_n$, which are initialized to $\perp$ and store the values that each respective P_i has registered. This functionality achieves synchrony through the framework of Katz et al. [KMTZ13], i.e., it only proceeds from one round to the next when all honest parties have indicated that it should do so. An honest party can be adaptively corrupted at any point, and if this happens during the input round, the ideal adversary may send messages on its behalf and potentially overwrite previously stored values. In every round, the functionality ignores all messages other than the ones we explicitly specify that it can receive.

Registration.
1. **Input Round:** Upon receiving $(\mathtt{input}, \mathsf{sid}, m)$ from some party P_i, set $\mathsf{pk}_i := m$ and send $(\mathtt{input}, \mathsf{sid}, P_i, m)$ to $\mathcal{S}$.
2. **Output Round:** Upon receiving $(\mathtt{fetch\text{-}output}, \mathsf{sid})$ from some party P_i, send $(\mathsf{output}, \mathsf{sid}, (\mathsf{pk}_1, \ldots, \mathsf{pk}_n))$ to P_i.

Now we are finally ready to describe the Dolev-Strong protocol [DS83] in the $(\mathcal{F}_{\mathsf{sig}}, \mathcal{F}_{\mathsf{pki}})$-hybrid model. We refer the reader to Sect. 1.3 for a high-level overview of our design choices.

Protocol 4.5. π_{DS} (Dolev-Strong Broadcast)

This protocol is run among n parties $P_1, \ldots, P_n$ in the $(\mathcal{F}_{\mathsf{sig}}, \mathcal{F}_{\mathsf{pki}})$-hybrid model. During the protocol, all parties ignore messages that are not explicitly specified.

Setup. Upon receiving $(\mathtt{init}, \mathsf{sid})$ from the environment, party P_i proceeds as follows:
1. **Round 1**: P_i sends $(\mathtt{init}, \mathsf{sid})$ followed by $(\mathtt{keygen}, \mathsf{sid})$ to $\mathcal{F}_{\mathsf{sig}}$ and receives $(\mathtt{public\text{-}key}, \mathsf{sid}, \mathsf{pk}_i)$ in response. Then P_i sends $(\mathtt{input}, \mathsf{sid}, \mathsf{pk}_i)$ to $\mathcal{F}_{\mathsf{pki}}$.
2. **Round 2**: P_i sends $(\mathtt{fetch\text{-}output}, \mathsf{sid})$ to $\mathcal{F}_{\mathsf{pki}}$ and receives $(\mathsf{output}, \mathsf{sid}, (\mathsf{pk}_1, \ldots, \mathsf{pk}_n))$ in response. For every $j \in [n]$, P_i internally sets $\mathsf{active}_j := 0$ if $\mathsf{pk}_j = \perp$, and $\mathsf{active}_j := 1$ otherwise. P_i outputs $(\mathsf{output}, \mathsf{sid}, (\mathsf{active}_1, \ldots, \mathsf{active}_n))$ to $\mathcal{Z}$.

Broadcast. Upon receiving $(\mathtt{input}, \mathsf{sid}, \mathsf{ssid}, v)$ from the environment such that $\mathsf{ssid} = \mathsf{ssid}' \| P_s \| \mathcal{P}$, party P_i proceeds as follows:

3. **Round 1**:

(a) P_i verifies that $\mathcal{P} \subseteq \{P_1, \ldots, P_n\}$, that $P_i \in \mathcal{P}$, and that for every $P_j \in \mathcal{P}$, $\mathsf{active}_j = 1$. If these conditions hold, then P_i initializes a set $\mathcal{V}_i^1 := \emptyset$; otherwise, P_i ignores the environment's message. The sets $\mathcal{V}_i^\rho$ correspond to the possible eventual outputs of party P_i as of round ρ.

(b) If $P_i = P_s$, then P_i sets $m := v$, sends $(\mathtt{sign}, \mathsf{sid}, \mathsf{pk}_i, (\mathsf{sid}, \mathsf{ssid}, i, m))$ to $\mathcal{F}_{\mathsf{sig}}$, and receives $(\mathtt{signature}, \mathsf{sid}, \mathsf{pk}_i, (\mathsf{sid}, \mathsf{ssid}, i, m), \sigma_i)$ in response. Next, P_i sends $(\mathsf{sid}, \mathsf{ssid}, m, (i, \sigma_i))$ to all other parties in $\mathcal{P}$.

(c) If $P_i \neq P_s$, then it ignores v.[a]

4. **Round ρ, for $\rho \in \{2, \ldots, |\mathcal{P}|\}$:** P_i initializes $\mathcal{V}_i^\rho := \mathcal{V}_i^{\rho-1}$ and receives between 0 and $|\mathcal{P}| - 1$ messages of the form $(\mathsf{sid}, \mathsf{ssid}, \tilde{m}, (j_1, \sigma_{j_1}), \ldots, (j_{\rho-1}, \sigma_{j_{\rho-1}}))$.[b] It processes every such message as follows:
   (a) P_i ignores the message[c] if $\tilde{m} \in \mathcal{V}_i^\rho$, or if $|\mathcal{V}_i^\rho| > 1$, or if the indices $j_1, \ldots, j_{\rho-1}$ are not all distinct, or if $i \in \{j_1, \ldots, j_{\rho-1}\}$, or if $j_1 \neq s$, where P_s is the designated sender.
   (b) For $k \in [\rho]$, let $\mathring{m}_k := \tilde{m} \| j_1 \| \sigma_{j_1} \| \ldots \| j_{k-1} \| \sigma_{j_{k-1}}$. For $k \in [\rho - 1]$, P_i sends $(\mathtt{verify}, \mathsf{sid}, \mathsf{pk}_{j_k}, (\mathsf{sid}, \mathsf{ssid}, j_k, \mathring{m}_k), \sigma_{j_k})$ to $\mathcal{F}_{\mathsf{sig}}$ and receives $(\mathtt{verified}, \mathsf{sid}, \mathsf{pk}_{j_k}, (\mathsf{sid}, \mathsf{ssid}, j_k, \tilde{m}_k), \sigma_{j_k}, b_k)$ in response.
   (c) If $\bigwedge_{k \in [\rho-1]} b_k = 1$ (i.e., all signatures verified), then P_i:
      - Sends $(\mathtt{sign}, \mathsf{sid}, \mathsf{pk}_i, (\mathsf{sid}, \mathsf{ssid}, i, \mathring{m}_\rho))$ to $\mathcal{F}_{\mathsf{sig}}$ and receives $(\mathtt{signature}, \mathsf{sid}, \mathsf{pk}_i, (\mathsf{sid}, \mathsf{ssid}, i, \mathring{m}_\rho), \sigma_i)$ in response.
      - Sends $(\mathsf{sid}, \mathsf{ssid}, \tilde{m}, (j_1, \sigma_{j_1}), \ldots, (j_{\rho-1}, \sigma_{j_{\rho-1}}), (i, \sigma_i))$ to every party $P \in \mathcal{P} \setminus \{P_{j_1}, \ldots, P_{j_{\rho-1}}, P_i\}$.
      - Updates $\mathcal{V}_i^\rho := \mathcal{V}_i^\rho \cup \{\tilde{m}\}$.
5. **Round $|\mathcal{P}| + 1$:** If the sender P_s received $(\mathtt{input}, \mathsf{sid}, \mathsf{ssid}, m)$ in Round 1, then it outputs $(\mathsf{output}, \mathsf{sid}, \mathsf{ssid}, m)$ to $\mathcal{Z}$; otherwise, it outputs $(\mathsf{output}, \mathsf{sid}, \mathsf{ssid}, \perp)$.
   Every other party P_i checks whether $\mathcal{V}_i^{|\mathcal{P}|} = \{m_i\}$ for some m_i. If so (i.e., $|\mathcal{V}_i^{|\mathcal{P}|}| = 1$) then P_i outputs $(\mathsf{output}, \mathsf{sid}, \mathsf{ssid}, m_i)$ to $\mathcal{Z}$; otherwise, it outputs $(\mathsf{output}, \mathsf{sid}, \mathsf{ssid}, \perp)$.

[a] The non-sending party does not have a meaningful input in this phase.
[b] The values of $\tilde{m}$, j_*, and σ_{j_*} may differ in each message.
[c] That is, is performs no further steps related to the message.

4.3 A Modular Proof of Security for Dolev-Strong

Theorem 4.1. The protocol π_{DS} *perfectly* UC-realizes $\mathcal{W}_{\mathsf{DS}}(\mathcal{F}_{\mathsf{bc}})$ in the $(\mathcal{F}_{\mathsf{sig}}, \mathcal{F}_{\mathsf{pki}})$-hybrid model against a (possibly unbounded) malicious adversary that can adaptively corrupt any set of parties.

Proof. Let $\mathcal{A}$ be any computationally unbounded malicious adversary that can adaptively corrupt any set of participants in the protocol π_{DS}. We will construct an ideal-process adversary $\mathcal{S}_{\mathsf{DS}}$ that runs $\mathcal{A}$ as a black-box subroutine and interacts with the ideal functionality $\mathcal{W}_{\mathsf{DS}}(\mathcal{F}_{\mathsf{bc}})$. $\mathcal{S}_{\mathsf{DS}}$ is guaranteed to be PPT if $\mathcal{A}$ and $\mathcal{Z}$ are.[13] We will prove that for every computationally unbounded environment $\mathcal{Z}$,

$$\left\{\mathrm{REAL}_{\pi_{\mathsf{DS}},\mathcal{A},\mathcal{Z}}(\kappa, z)\right\}_{\kappa\in\mathbb{N},z\in\{0,1\}^*} \equiv \left\{\mathrm{IDEAL}_{\mathcal{W}_{\mathsf{DS}}(\mathcal{F}_{\mathsf{bc}}),\mathcal{S}^{\mathcal{A}}_{\mathsf{DS}},\mathcal{Z}}(\kappa, z)\right\}_{\kappa\in\mathbb{N},z\in\{0,1\}^*}.$$

In the ideal-world experiment, we denote the dummy parties as $\tilde{P}$. We begin by specifying the simulator.

Simulator 4.6. $\mathcal{S}_{\mathsf{DS}}$ (Simulator for Dolev-Strong Broadcast)

The simulator $\mathcal{S}_{\mathsf{DS}}$ emulates an instance of the π_{DS} protocol internally, including n virtual parties $P_1, \ldots, P_n$ and the functionalities $\mathcal{F}_{\mathsf{sig}}$ and $\mathcal{F}_{\mathsf{pki}}$, which all behave exactly according to their specifications unless otherwise stated. In addition, $\mathcal{S}_{\mathsf{DS}}$ uses $\mathcal{A}$ as a black-box subroutine and emulates for $\mathcal{A}$ communication with the various protocol entities in the virtual π_{DS} instance. In particular, the back-door `init` message by which $\mathcal{F}_{\mathsf{sig}}$ requests its algorithms is forwarded to $\mathcal{A}$, and if $\mathcal{A}$ does not immediately reply, then the emulated $\mathcal{F}_{\mathsf{sig}}$ goes into random mode as expected. All messages from $\mathcal{Z}$ to $\mathcal{S}_{\mathsf{DS}}$ are forwarded to $\mathcal{A}$, and all values written on $\mathcal{A}$'s output tape are forwarded to $\mathcal{Z}$ via $\mathcal{S}_{\mathsf{DS}}$'s output tape.

Corruption Requests. When the parties in π_{DS} behave honestly, they have no random choices, and therefore need no random tapes. Observe that whenever $\mathcal{W}_{\mathsf{DS}}(\mathcal{F}_{\mathsf{bc}})$ receives an input from an honest party, it forwards that input to $\mathcal{S}_{\mathsf{DS}}$. Consequently, the activation order and emulated input tapes of the virtual parties exactly match the equivalent tapes in the real world experiment. The functionalities are randomized, but are emulated using the same code they use in π_{DS}; together these facts imply that the communication and output tapes of the virtual parties are distributed identically to the tapes of the actual parties in the real world π_{DS} experiment. When $\mathcal{A}$ requests to corrupt some party P, $\mathcal{S}_{\mathsf{DS}}$ corrupts the corresponding dummy party $\tilde{P}$ in the ideal world experiment and transmits the internal state of the virtual P to $\mathcal{A}$. Additionally $\mathcal{S}_{\mathsf{DS}}$ emulates the adaptive corruption processes of $\mathcal{F}_{\mathsf{pki}}$ and $\mathcal{F}_{\mathsf{sig}}$ to $\mathcal{A}$, which is possible since $\mathcal{S}_{\mathsf{DS}}$ knows those functionalities' entire internal states. From that point onward, $\mathcal{S}_{\mathsf{DS}}$ ceases to emulate P, and expects $\mathcal{A}$ to receive and produce messages P's behalf.

Setup.

[13] It is essential that $\mathcal{S}_{\mathsf{DS}}$ be PPT in the presence of a PPT adversary and environment, in order to ensure that the UC composition theorem holds in computationally bounded contexts. However, an unbounded environment might send exponentially many messages or exponentially long messages to $\mathcal{S}_{\mathsf{DS}}$, which require superpolynomial time to ingest, even if they are ignored.

1. Upon receiving $(\texttt{init}, \mathsf{sid}, \tilde{P}_i)$ from $\mathcal{W}_{\mathsf{DS}}(\mathcal{F}_{\mathsf{bc}})$ on its back-door tape such that $\tilde{P}_i$ is honest, $\mathcal{S}_{\mathsf{DS}}$ places $(\texttt{init}, \mathsf{sid})$ on the input tape of virtual P_i and activates it, emulating the operation of the protocol that results.
2. When $\mathcal{A}$ transmits $(\texttt{input}, \mathsf{sid}, \mathsf{pk}_i)$ to $\mathcal{F}_{\mathsf{pki}}$ on behalf of a corrupted party P_i, $\mathcal{S}_{\mathsf{DS}}$ sends $(\texttt{init}, \mathsf{sid})$ to $\mathcal{W}_{\mathsf{DS}}(\mathcal{F}_{\mathsf{bc}})$ on behalf of $\tilde{P}_i$, in addition to emulating the protocol π_{DS} towards $\mathcal{A}$.
3. When $\mathcal{A}$ transmits $(\texttt{fetch-output}, \mathsf{sid})$ to $\mathcal{F}_{\mathsf{pki}}$ on behalf of a corrupted party P_i, $\mathcal{S}_{\mathsf{DS}}$ forwards this message to $\mathcal{W}_{\mathsf{DS}}(\mathcal{F}_{\mathsf{bc}})$ on behalf of $\tilde{P}_i$.
4. $\mathcal{S}_{\mathsf{DS}}$ releases the corrupted P_i's output $(\mathsf{output}, \mathsf{sid}, (\mathsf{pk}_1, \ldots, \mathsf{pk}_n))$ to $\mathcal{A}$ on behalf of $\mathcal{F}_{\mathsf{pki}}$ *only* when it receives $(\mathsf{output}, \mathsf{sid}, (\mathsf{active}_1, \ldots, \mathsf{active}_n))$ from $\mathcal{W}_{\mathsf{DS}}(\mathcal{F}_{\mathsf{bc}})$ on behalf of $\tilde{P}_i$.

Broadcast.

5. **Round 1:** Upon receiving $(\texttt{input}, \mathsf{sid}, \mathsf{ssid}, v, \tilde{P}_i)$ from $\mathcal{W}_{\mathsf{DS}}(\mathcal{F}_{\mathsf{bc}})$ on its back-door tape such that $\tilde{P}_i$ is honest, $\mathcal{S}_{\mathsf{DS}}$ places $(\texttt{input}, \mathsf{sid}, \mathsf{ssid}, v)$ on the input tape of virtual P_i and activates it, emulating the operation of the protocol that results.
6. **Round ρ, for $\rho \in \{2, \ldots, |\mathcal{P}|\}$:** The simulator does not communicate with $\mathcal{W}_{\mathsf{DS}}(\mathcal{F}_{\mathsf{bc}})$ in these rounds,[a] but continues to simulate the corresponding rounds of π_{DS} using the internally emulated honest parties and functionalities, which communicate with $\mathcal{A}$ (who acts on behalf of corrupt parties) and with one another.
7. **Round $|\mathcal{P}|$** : If the emulated sender P_s is corrupted by $\mathcal{A}$ before the end of round $|\mathcal{P}|$, and at least one party in $\mathcal{P}$ remains honest when round $|\mathcal{P}|$ ends, then $\mathcal{S}_{\mathsf{DS}}$ selects one honest party P_{i^*} arbitrarily among those that remain. If $\mathcal{V}_{i^*}^{|\mathcal{P}|} = \{\hat{m}\}$ for some message $\hat{m}$ (i.e., $|\mathcal{V}_{i^*}^{|\mathcal{P}|}| = 1$), then $\mathcal{S}_{\mathsf{DS}}$ sets $m' = \hat{m}$; otherwise it sets $m' = \perp$. Regardless, $\mathcal{S}_{\mathsf{DS}}$ sends $(\texttt{input}, \mathsf{sid}, \mathsf{ssid}, m')$ to $\mathcal{W}_{\mathsf{DS}}(\mathcal{F}_{\mathsf{bc}})$ on behalf of the corrupt sender $\tilde{P}_s$. If the emulated sender is not corrupt, or no parties in $\mathcal{P}$ remain honest, then $\mathcal{S}_{\mathsf{DS}}$ sends nothing to $\mathcal{W}_{\mathsf{DS}}(\mathcal{F}_{\mathsf{bc}})$.
8. **Round $|\mathcal{P}| + 1$:** $\mathcal{S}_{\mathsf{DS}}$ does not communicate with $\mathcal{W}_{\mathsf{DS}}(\mathcal{F}_{\mathsf{bc}})$ in this round, but continues to simulate the corresponding round of π_{DS} using the internally emulated honest parties and functionalities, which communicate with $\mathcal{A}$. Note that the emulated honest parties do not send any messages in this round (though they may be corrupted), and that any dummy party $\tilde{P}$ that remains honest at the end of the round receives its ideal-world output directly from $\mathcal{W}_{\mathsf{DS}}(\mathcal{F}_{\mathsf{bc}})$.

[a]Except as specified in Step 7.

Since $\mathcal{S}_{\mathsf{DS}}$ emulates π_{DS} internally by following the exact instructions of the honest parties, the joint view of $\mathcal{A}$ and $\mathcal{Z}$ must be distributed identically in the real and ideal worlds until the honest parties reveal their outputs to $\mathcal{Z}$ in round $|\mathcal{P}| + 1$. It is therefore sufficient to prove that the outputs they produce in the ideal world are identical to their outputs in the real world. We divide the remainder of the proof into two cases: the first applies to the event that the sender remains honest at least until the end of round $|\mathcal{P}|$, and the second to the complementary event that the sender is corrupted before the end of round $|\mathcal{P}|$. Our theorem follows from the conjunction of Lemmas 4.2 and 4.3, which assert that the distribution of honest party outputs is identical between the real and ideal worlds in these two respective cases.

Lemma 4.2. If the sender remains honest until the end of round $|\mathcal{P}|$, then the outputs of honest dummy parties in the ideal experiment involving $\mathcal{W}_{\mathsf{DS}}(\mathcal{F}_{\mathsf{bc}})$ and $\mathcal{S}^{\mathcal{A}}_{\mathsf{DS}}$ are distributed identically to the outputs of honest parties in the real experiment involving π_{DS} and $\mathcal{A}$.

Lemma 4.3. If the sender is corrupted before the end of round $|\mathcal{P}|$, then the outputs of honest dummy parties in the ideal experiment involving $\mathcal{W}_{\mathsf{DS}}(\mathcal{F}_{\mathsf{bc}})$ and $\mathcal{S}^{\mathcal{A}}_{\mathsf{DS}}$ are distributed identically to the outputs of honest parties in the real experiment involving π_{DS} and $\mathcal{A}$.

The proofs of the lemmas can be found in the full version of the paper [CDL+24].

Acknowledgments. The work of Ran Cohen was supported in part by NSF grant no. 2055568 and by ISF grant no. 1834/23. The work of Jack Doerner and Eysa Lee was done while at Brown University and supported by the Brown University Data Science Institute. Anna Lysyanskaya is supported by NSF Grants 2312241, 2154170, and 2247305. The work of Lawrence Roy was supported by the European Research Council (ERC) under the European Union's Horizon 2020 research and innovation programme under grant agreement number 803096 "SPEC"; the Danish Independent Research Council under Grant-ID DFF-0165-00107B "C3PO"; and the DARPA SIEVE program (contract HR001120C0085 "FROMAGER"). Any opinions, findings and conclusions or recommendations expressed in this material are those of the authors and do not necessarily reflect the views of the funding entities. Distribution Statement "A" (Approved for Public Release, Distribution Unlimited).

References

[AR02] Abadi, M., Rogaway, P.: Reconciling two views of cryptography (the computational soundness of formal encryption). J. Cryptol. **15**(2), 103–127 (2002)

[BCH+20] Badertscher, C., Canetti, R., Hesse, J., Tackmann, B., Zikas, V.: Universal composition with global subroutines: capturing global setup within plain UC. In: Pass, R., Pietrzak, K. (eds.) TCC 2020, Part III. LNCS, vol. 12552, pp. 1–30. Springer, Cham (2020). https://doi.org/10.1007/978-3-030-64381-2_1

[BF01] Boneh, D., Franklin, M.: Identity-based encryption from the weil pairing. In: Kilian, J. (ed.) CRYPTO 2001. LNCS, vol. 2139, pp. 213–229. Springer, Heidelberg (2001). https://doi.org/10.1007/3-540-44647-8_13

[BH04] Backes, M., Hofheinz, D.: How to break and repair a universally composable signature functionality. In: Zhang, K., Zheng, Y. (eds.) ISC 2004. LNCS, vol. 3225, pp. 61–72. Springer, Heidelberg (2004). https://doi.org/10.1007/978-3-540-30144-8_6

[BKL19] Blum, E., Katz, J., Loss, J.: Synchronous consensus with optimal asynchronous fallback guarantees. In: Hofheinz, D., Rosen, A. (eds.) TCC 2019, Part I. LNCS, vol. 11891, pp. 131–150. Springer, Cham (2019). https://doi.org/10.1007/978-3-030-36030-6_6

[Can01] Canetti, R.: Universally composable security: a new paradigm for cryptographic protocols. In: 42nd FOCS, pp. 136–145. IEEE Computer Society Press (2001)

[Can04] Canetti, R.: Universally composable signature, certification, and authentication. In: 17th IEEE Computer Security Foundations Workshop, (CSFW), pp. 219–233. IEEE Computer Society (2004)

[Can05] Canetti, R.: Universally composable security: A new paradigm for cryptographic protocols. Version of December 2005 (2005). https://eccc.weizmann.ac.il/eccc-reports/2001/TR01-016

[Can20] Canetti, R.: Universally composable security. J. ACM **67**(5), 28:1–28:94 (2020)

[CCGZ16] Cohen, R., Coretti, S., Garay, J., Zikas, V.: Probabilistic termination and composability of cryptographic protocols. In: Robshaw, M., Katz, J. (eds.) CRYPTO 2016, Part III. LNCS, vol. 9816, pp. 240–269. Springer, Heidelberg (2016). https://doi.org/10.1007/978-3-662-53015-3_9

[CDL+24] Cohen, R., Doerner, J., Lee, E., Lysyanskaya, A., Roy, L.: An unstoppable ideal functionality for signatures and a modular analysis of the dolev-strong broadcast. Cryptology ePrint Archive, Report 2024/1807 (2024)

[CGZ23] Cohen, R., Garay, J.A., Zikas, V.: Completeness theorems for adaptively secure broadcast. In: Handschuh, H., Lysyanskaya, A. (eds.) CRYPTO 2023, Part I. LNCS, vol. 14081, pp. 3–38. Springer, Heidelberg (2023). https://doi.org/10.1007/978-3-031-38557-5_1

[CH11] Canetti, R., Herzog, J.: Universally composable symbolic security analysis. J. Cryptol. **24**(1), 83–147 (2011)

[CJSV22] Canetti, R., Jain, P., Swanberg, M., Varia, M.: Universally composable end-to-end secure messaging. In: Dodis, Y., Shrimpton, T. (eds.) CRYPTO 2022, Part II. LNCS, vol. 13508, pp. 3–33. Springer, Heidelberg (2022). https://doi.org/10.1007/978-3-031-15979-4_1

[CKKR19] Camenisch, J., Krenn, S., Küsters, R., Rausch, D.: iUC: flexible universal composability made simple. In: Galbraith, S.D., Moriai, S. (eds.) ASIACRYPT 2019. LNCS, vol. 11923, pp. 191–221. Springer, Cham (2019). https://doi.org/10.1007/978-3-030-34618-8_7

[CLOS02] Canetti, R., Lindell, Y., Ostrovsky, R., Sahai, A.: Universally composable two-party and multi-party secure computation. In: 34th ACM STOC, pp. 494–503. ACM Press (2002)

[CR03] Canetti, R., Rabin, T.: Universal composition with joint state. In: Boneh, D. (ed.) CRYPTO 2003. LNCS, vol. 2729, pp. 265–281. Springer, Heidelberg (2003). https://doi.org/10.1007/978-3-540-45146-4_16

[CSV16] Canetti, R., Shahaf, D., Vald, M.: Universally composable authentication and key-exchange with global PKI. In: Cheng, C.-M., Chung, K.-M., Persiano, G., Yang, B.-Y. (eds.) PKC 2016, Part II. LNCS, vol. 9615, pp. 265–296. Springer, Heidelberg (2016). https://doi.org/10.1007/978-3-662-49387-8_11

[DH76] Diffie, W., Hellman, M.E.: New directions in cryptography. IEEE Trans. Inf. Theory **22**(6), 644–654 (1976)

[DKL+23] Doerner, J., Kondi, Y., Lee, E., Shelat, A., Tyner, L.: Threshold BBS+ signatures for distributed anonymous credential issuance. In: 2023 IEEE Symposium on Security and Privacy, pp. 773–789. IEEE Computer Society Press (2023)

[DKLs18] Doerner, J., Kondi, Y., Lee, E., Shelat, A.: Secure two-party threshold ECDSA from ECDSA assumptions. In: 2018 IEEE Symposium on Security and Privacy, pp. 980–997. IEEE Computer Society Press (2018)

[DKLS19] Doerner, J., Kondi, Y., Lee, E., Shelat, A.: Threshold ECDSA from ECDSA assumptions: the multiparty case. In: 2019 IEEE Symposium on Security and Privacy. IEEE Computer Society Press (2019)

[DKLS24] Doerner, J., Kondi, Y., Lee, E., Shelat, A.: Threshold ECDSA in three rounds. In: 2024 IEEE Symposium on Security and Privacy. IEEE Computer Society Press (2024)

[DLM82] DeMillo, R.A., Lynch, N.A., Merritt, M.: Cryptographic protocols. In: 14th ACM STOC, pp. 383–400. ACM Press (1982)

[DR82] Dolev, D., Reischuk, R.: Bounds on information exchange for byzantine agreement. In: Probert, R.L., Fischer, M.J., Santoro, N. (eds.) 1st ACM PODC, pp. 132–140. ACM (1982)

[DS83] Dolev, D., Strong, H.R.: Authenticated algorithms for Byzantine agreement. SIAM J. Comput. **12**(4), 656–666 (1983)

[DY81] Dolev, D., Yao, A.C.-C.: On the security of public key protocols (extended abstract). In: 22nd FOCS, pp. 350–357. IEEE Computer Society Press (1981)

[ELP24] Elsheimy, F., Loss, J., Papamanthou, C.: Early stopping byzantine agreement in $(1+\epsilon)\cdot f$ rounds. In: Chung, K.-M., Sasaki, Y. (eds.) ASIACRYPT 2024, Part VI. LNCS, vol. 15489, pp. 398–424. Springer, Cham (2024). https://doi.org/10.1007/978-981-96-0938-3_13

[FG03] Fitzi, M., Garay, J.A.: Efficient player-optimal protocols for strong and differential consensus. In: Borowsky, E., Rajsbaum, S. (eds.) 22nd ACM PODC, pp. 211–220. ACM (2003)

[FLL21] Fitzi, M., Liu-Zhang, C.-D., Loss, J.: A new way to achieve round-efficient byzantine agreement. In: Miller, A., Censor-Hillel, K., Korhonen, J.H. (eds.) 40th ACM PODC, pp. 355–362. ACM (2021)

[FLM86] Fischer, M.J., Lynch, N.A., Merritt, M.: Easy impossibility proofs for distributed consensus problems. Distrib. Comput. **1**(1), 26–39 (1986)

[FN09] Fitzi, M., Nielsen, J.B.: On the number of synchronous rounds sufficient for authenticated byzantine agreement. In: Keidar, I. (ed.) DISC 2009. LNCS, vol. 5805, pp. 449–463. Springer, Heidelberg (2009). https://doi.org/10.1007/978-3-642-04355-0_46

[GGL22] Ghinea, D., Goyal, V., Liu-Zhang, C.D.: Round-optimal byzantine agreement. In: Dunkelman, O., Dziembowski, S. (eds.) EUROCRYPT 2022. LNCS, vol. 13275, pp. 96–119. Springer, Cham (2022). https://doi.org/10.1007/978-3-031-06944-4_4

[GKKO07] Garay, J.A., Katz, J., Koo, C.-Y., Ostrovsky, R.: Round complexity of authenticated broadcast with a dishonest majority. In: 48th FOCS, pp. 658–668. IEEE Computer Society Press (2007)

[GKKZ11] Garay, J.A., Katz, J., Kumaresan, R., Zhou, H.-S.: Adaptively secure broadcast, revisited. In: Gavoille, C., Fraigniaud, P. (eds.) 30th ACM PODC, pp. 179–186. ACM (2011)

[GKZ10] Garay, J.A., Kiayias, A., Zhou, H.-S.: A framework for the sound specification of cryptographic tasks. In: Myers, A., Backes, M. (eds.) CSF 2010 Computer Security Foundations Symposium, pp. 277–289. IEEE Computer Society Press (2010)

[GLW22] Ghinea, D., Liu-Zhang, C.-D., Wattenhofer, R.: Optimal synchronous approximate agreement with asynchronous fallback. In: Milani, A., Woelfel, P. (eds.) 41st ACM PODC, pp. 70–80. ACM (2022)

[GMR88] Goldwasser, S., Micali, S., Rivest, R.L.: A digital signature scheme secure against adaptive chosen-message attacks. SIAM J. Comput. **17**(2), 281–308 (1988)

[GMW87] Goldreich, O., Micali, S., Wigderson, A.: How to play any mental game or A completeness theorem for protocols with honest majority. In: Aho, A. (ed.) 19th ACM STOC, pp. 218–229. ACM Press (1987)

[Gol04] Goldreich, O.: Foundations of Cryptography: Basic Applications, vol. 2. Cambridge University Press, Cambridge (2004)

[GS22] Groth, J., Shoup, V.: Design and analysis of a distributed ECDSA signing service. IACR Cryptol. ePrint Arch. (2022). https://eprint.iacr.org/2022/506

[HZ10] Hirt, M., Zikas, V.: Adaptively secure broadcast. In: Gilbert, H. (ed.) EUROCRYPT 2010. LNCS, vol. 6110, pp. 466–485. Springer, Heidelberg (2010). https://doi.org/10.1007/978-3-642-13190-5_24

[KK06] Katz, J., Koo, C.-Y.: On expected constant-round protocols for byzantine agreement. In: Dwork, C. (ed.) CRYPTO 2006. LNCS, vol. 4117, pp. 445–462. Springer, Heidelberg (2006). https://doi.org/10.1007/11818175_27

[KL14] Katz, J., Lindell, Y.: Introduction to Modern Cryptography, 2nd edn. CRC Press (2014)

[KMTZ13] Katz, J., Maurer, U., Tackmann, B., Zikas, V.: Universally composable synchronous computation. In: Sahai, A. (ed.) TCC 2013. LNCS, vol. 7785, pp. 477–498. Springer, Heidelberg (2013). https://doi.org/10.1007/978-3-642-36594-2_27

[KT08] Küsters, R., Tuengerthal, M.: Joint state theorems for public-key encryption and digital signature functionalities with local computation. In: Sabelfeld, A. (ed.) CSF 2008 Computer Security Foundations Symposium, pp. 270–284. IEEE Computer Society Press (2008)

[Lin17a] Lindell, Y.: Fast secure two-party ECDSA signing. In: Katz, J., Shacham, H. (eds.) CRYPTO 2017, Part II. LNCS, vol. 10402, pp. 613–644. Springer, Heidelberg (2017). https://doi.org/10.1007/978-3-319-63715-0_21

[Lin17b] Lindell, Y.: Lecture notes on foundations of cryptography (2017). https://yehudalindell.com/wp-content/uploads/2023/06/main-89-856.pdf. Section 4.1, On the danger of induction arguments

[Lin24] Lindell, Y.: Simple three-round multiparty Schnorr signing with full simulatability. Commun. Cryptol. **1**(1), 25 (2024)

[LL22] Lenzen, C., Loss, J.: Optimal clock synchronization with signatures. In: Milani, A., Woelfel, P. (eds.) 41st ACM PODC, pp. 440–449. ACM (2022)

[LLR02] Lindell, Y., Lysyanskaya, A., Rabin, T.: On the composition of authenticated byzantine agreement. In: 34th ACM STOC, pp. 514–523. ACM Press (2002)

[LN24] Loss, J., Nielsen, J.B.: Early stopping for any number of corruptions. In: Joye, M., Leander, G. (eds.) EUROCRYPT 2024. LNCS, vol. 14653, pp. 457–488. Springer, Cham (2024). https://doi.org/10.1007/978-3-031-58734-4_16

[LSP82] Lamport, L., Shostak, R.E., Pease, M.C.: The Byzantine generals problem. ACM Trans. Program. Lang. Syst. **4**(3), 382–401 (1982)

[MP06] Micciancio, D., Panjwani, S.: Corrupting one vs. corrupting many: the case of broadcast and multicast encryption. In: Bugliesi, M., Preneel, B., Sassone, V., Wegener, I. (eds.) ICALP 2006, Part II. LNCS, vol. 4052, pp. 70–82. Springer, Heidelberg (2006). https://doi.org/10.1007/11787006_7

[Pat05] Patil, A.: On symbolic analysis of cryptographic protocols. Ph.D. thesis, Massachusetts Institute of Technology (2005)

[PSL80] Pease, M.C., Shostak, R.E., Lamport, L.: Reaching agreement in the presence of faults. J. ACM **27**(2), 228–234 (1980)

[RSA78] Rivest, R.L., Shamir, A., Adleman, L.M.: A method for obtaining digital signatures and public-key cryptosystems. Commun. Assoc. Comput. Mach. **21**(2), 120–126 (1978)

[TLP22] Tsimos, G., Loss, J., Papamanthou, C.: Gossiping for communication-efficient broadcast. In: Dodis, Y., Shrimpton, T. (eds.) CRYPTO 2022, Part III. LNCS, vol. 13509, pp. 439–469. Springer, Heidelberg (2022). https://doi.org/10.1007/978-3-031-15982-4_15

[WXSD20] Wan, J., Xiao, H., Shi, E., Devadas, S.: Expected constant round byzantine broadcast under dishonest majority. In: Pass, R., Pietrzak, K. (eds.) TCC 2020, Part I. LNCS, vol. 12550, pp. 381–411. Springer, Heidelberg (2020). https://doi.org/10.1007/978-3-030-64375-1_14

Author Index

B. Applebaum and H. Lin (Eds.): TCC 2025, LNCS 16271, pp. 709–710, 2026.
https://doi.org/10.1007/978-3-032-12290-2

GPSR Compliance

The European Union's (EU) General Product Safety Regulation (GPSR) is a set of rules that requires consumer products to be safe and our obligations to ensure this.

If you have any concerns about our products, you can contact us on ProductSafety@springernature.com

In case Publisher is established outside the EU, the EU authorized representative is:

Springer Nature Customer Service Center GmbH
Europaplatz 3
69115 Heidelberg, Germany

Batch number: 10682580

Printed by Printforce, the Netherlands